WINDOWS NT SERVER 4

Professional Reference

Second Edition

Karanjit S. Siyan, Ph.D., et al.

New Riders Publishing, Indianapolis, IN

Windows NT Server 4 Professional Reference,
Second Edition

By Karanjit S. Siyan, Ph.D., et al.

Published by:
New Riders Publishing
201 West 103rd Street
Indianapolis, IN 46290 USA

Copyright © 1997 by New Riders Publishing

Printed in the United States of America 1 2 3 4 5 6 7 8 9 0

Library of Congress Cataloging-in-Publication Data

CIP data available upon request

ISBN: 1-56205-805-3

Warning and Disclaimer

This book is designed to provide information about **Windows NT Server 4**. Every effort has been made to make this book as complete and as accurate as possible, but no warranty or fitness is implied.

The information is provided on an "as is" basis. The author(s) and New Riders Publishing shall have neither liability nor responsibility to any person or entity with respect to any loss or damages arising from the information contained in this book or from the use of the discs or programs that may accompany it.

Associate Publisher	David Dwyer
Publishing Manager	Laurie Petrycki
Marketing Manager	Kourtnaye Sturgeon
Managing Editor	Sarah Kearns

Product Development Specialist
Sean Angus

Acquisitions Editor
Sean Angus

Development Editors
Laura Frey
Chris Zahn

Project Editor
Suzanne Snyder

Copy Editor
Cliff Shubs

Technical Editor
Brian Komar

Coordinator of Editorial Resources
Suzanne Snyder

Software Acquisitions and Development
Dustin Sullivan

Assistant Marketing Manager
Gretchen Schlesinger

Team Coordinator
Amy Lewis

Manufacturing Coordinator
Brook Farling

Book Designer
Glenn Larsen

Cover Designer
Dan Armstrong

Cover Production
Casey Price

Director of Production
Larry Klein

Production Team Supervisor
Laurie Casey

Graphics Image Specialists
Kevin Cliburn, Tammy Graham

Production Analysts
Dan Harris
Erich J. Richter

Production Team
Lori Cliburn, Kim Cofer, Laure Robinson, Christy Wagner

Indexer
Joe Long

About the Authors

Karanjit S. Siyan, Ph.D, is president of Kinetics Corporation. He has authored international seminars on Solaris & SunOS, TCP/IP networks, PC Network Integration, Windows NT, Novell networks, and Expert Systems using Fuzzy Logic. He teaches advanced technology seminars in the United States, Canada, Europe, and the Far East. Dr. Siyan has published articles in *Dr. Dobbs Journal*, The *C Users Journal*, and *Databased Advisor*. He is actively involved in Internet research. Dr. Siyan has been involved with Windows NT since 1992. He holds a Ph.D in Computer Science. Before working as an independent consultant, Dr. Siyan was a senior member of the technical staff at ROLM Corporation. As part of his consulting work, Dr. Siyan has written a number of custom compiler and operating system development tools. His interests include Unix-based, Windows NT-based, NetWare-based, and OS/2-based networks. He is a Microsoft Certified Professional for Windows NT, and holds an ECNE certification for Novell-based networks. Dr. Siyan has written numerous books. Karanjit Siyan is based in Montana where he lives with his wife, Dei. Dr. Siyan can be reached at his e-mail address of karanjit@siyan.com.

Joe Casad is a freelance writer and editor who specializes in programming and networking topics. He was the managing editor of the short-lived, but well-received, *Network Administrator Magazine*, a journal of practical solutions for networking professionals. Joe received a B.S. in Engineering from the University of Kansas in 1980 and, before becoming a full-time writer and editor, spent ten years in the computer-intensive areas of the structural engineering profession. He now lives in Lawrence, Kansas with his wife Barb Dinneen and a pair of pint-sized hackers named Xander and Mattie.

Joel Millecan has been involved in the growth of the computer industry since learning Basic Programming in 1971. He currently specializes in network and telecommunication systems, with a strong focus on Windows NT, Novell NetWare, and various Unix operating systems. Joel considers the task of keeping pace with the rapid growth of technology, both hardware and software, an enjoyable responsibility.

David Yarashus is a Senior Network Engineer with Sylvest Management Systems Corporation in Lanham, MD. He specializes in designing and troubleshooting large multiprotocol internetworks. His work has taken him around the country, where he has been involved with some of the largest networks in the world. His industry certifications include Master CNE, CNX, and MCSE.

Barrie Sosinsky is an author and consultant in the area of desktop computing technologies. His company, Killer Apps, based in Newton, MA, creates workgroup solutions for clients in the areas of database development, web site and network analysis and design, electronic print, and online help systems. They also provide technical documentation sources and create manuals and packaging for technical products. Barrie is the author/co-author of 30 computer books on various subjects. He lives with his wife Carol Westheimer and daughter Alexandria in an electronic cottage in Newton. In his spare time, Barrie wonders what happened to his spare time.

Paul Tso is an independent consultant specializing in Windows NT networking. He has implemented large-scale network security and Internet-related projects. He lectures in computer networking courses at New York University, Information Technology Institute. Paul has a B.A. in Computer Science from Hunter College, C.U.N.Y. He is a CNE and a MCSE. On his weekends, Paul serves as a 1st Lieutenant Signal Officer in the U.S. Army Reserves.

Jason Shoults is a network engineer. He has been working with computers and networks for the last five years. Jason spends most of his time working with Novell and Microsoft products.

Howard Hilliker, David Sardella, and Robert Oliver also contributed to this book.

Trademark Acknowledgments

Contents at a Glance

Part III: Appendixes

Table of Contents

Part I: Overview of Windows NT Server

6   Implementing Windows NT Server Domains   181

7   Managing Windows NT Server Domain Accounts   229

Part III: Appendixes

INTRODUCTION

This book is for system administrators who are responsible for installing and administrating networks based on Windows NT. The book covers introductory and administration topics needed for the successful installation of a Windows NT network. Additionally, the book covers advanced topics, domain administration, registry management, DHCP and WINS administration, network browsing, and TCP/IP administration.

How This Book Is Organized

Windows NT Server 4 Professional Reference, 2nd Edition is divided into three parts: Part I, "Overview of Windows NT Server," Part II, "Windows NT Server Administration," and Part III, "Appendixes." Each part contains in-depth information that an administrator who is using the Windows NT Server environment should have. Each chapter can be read as a stand-alone text, complementing and enhancing, but not depending on the other chapters in each section.

The Chapters

Part I: Overview of Windows NT Server

Chapter 1, "Understanding Network Operating Systems." This chapter discusses Network Operating Systems in general and describes Windows NT in relationship to the OSI model. It also discusses issues such as security, management, and interoperability.

Chapter 2, "Windows NT Server Architecture." Windows NT is made up of several modular components such as HAL, Windows NT Executive, and the user-mode subsystems. This chapter discusses the modular architecture of Windows NT Server, as well as its components.

Part II: Windows NT Server Administration

Chapter 3, "Installing Windows NT Server." This chapter discusses the requirements for installing Windows NT Server. It provides the necessary background for understanding the Windows NT installation procedure.

Chapter 4, "Advanced Windows NT Server Installation." Several case studies that show different Windows NT Server installation configuration scenarios are presented. This chapter discusses how to customize the Windows NT installation procedure.

Chapter 5, "Designing Windows NT Server Domains." This chapter discusses Windows NT domains in detail. It also covers the basic differences between using a workgroup model and using a domain model.

Chapter 6, "Implementing Windows NT Server Domains." This chapter discusses the practical system administration issues for implementing Windows NT domains and performing domain-related operations. The various tools needed to manage domains and trust relationships are discussed.

Chapter 7, "Managing Windows NT Server Domain Accounts." This chapter discusses the procedures for creating and managing domain user accounts. The concept of groups is discussed. You also learn how to configure domain users' properties.

Chapter 8, "Managing User Profiles, Logon Scripts, and Environment Variables." Windows NT provides several mechanisms to configure a user's environment. This chapter discusses how you can use a combination of the various methods to customize a user's operating environment.

Chapter 9, "Managing Network Files and File Security Systems." This chapter discusses how network files are shared on a Windows NT network. It also discusses how directory and file permissions can be used to secure access to data and how file-system security can be further enhanced by using auditing.

Chapter 10, "Managing Windows NT Registry." The Windows NT Registry is the configuration database for Windows NT computers. This chapter discusses the organization of the Windows NT Registry and the tools to examine and directly modify Windows NT parameters that cannot be modified in any other way. This second edition includes several new practical examples of a Windows NT Registry.

Chapter 11, "Supporting Windows NT Server Clients." Windows NT Server comes with support for a variety of network clients. This chapter discusses how to install and configure these clients.

Chapter 12, "Integrating Windows NT Server with a NetWare Network." Windows NT computers are expected to be installed in existing NetWare-based networks. This chapter discusses the software tools and products that can be used to integrate these different networking technologies.

Chapter 13, "Introduction to TCP/IP Protocol Architecture." This chapter explores the TCP/IP layering concepts in terms of the DoD model. It explains the different classes of IP addresses and tells you how IP networks can be divided into smaller networks called subnets.

Chapter 14, "Installing and Configuring the TCP/IP Protocol Stack." This chapter discusses installing and configuring the Windows NT TCP/IP transport protocol stack. It teaches you how to configure the TCP/IP stack to use name services, configure SNMP services, and use host files. It also discusses configuring and using FTP services on a Windows NT server, configuring TCP/IP print services, and using command-line TCP/IP tools that come with Windows NT Server.

Chapter 15, "Windows NT Server DHCP Configuration." The DHCP protocol allows dynamic configuration of the IP parameters of TCP/IP nodes from a central DHCP server. A Windows NT server can be configured to act as a DHCP server. This chapter discusses how to install, configure, and administer a Windows NT Server-based DHCP server.

Chapter 16, "TCP/IP Name Resolution Using WINS." When the Windows NT NetBIOS is run over TCP/IP, the NetBIOS computer names need to be resolved into their IP addresses. This chapter discusses how Windows NT Server can be used to perform name resolution, with an emphasis on installing and configuring WINS name resolution on a Windows NT network.

Chapter 17, "Windows NT Printing." This chapter discusses the Windows NT network print architecture. The procedures for installing and administering Windows NT print servers and Windows NT print clients are discussed.

Chapter 18, "Remote Access Services." The Windows NT Server can support up to 256 remote connections over different point-to-point or WAN technologies. This chapter discusses how to install and configure Remote Access Services for a Windows NT server. You also learn how to use Remote Access Services to access the Internet. Point-to-Point Tunneling Protocol coverage has been greatly expanded for this second edition.

Chapter 19, "Windows NT Network Browser." Windows NT provides the capability to build a dynamic list of other Windows NT computers on the network. These lists can then be used in Windows NT applications to browse the list of network resources on the network. This chapter discusses how the browsing lists are built and the impact browsing has on network performance.

Chapter 20, "Data Protection for Windows NT Servers." With this second edition you will learn the best practices of backup and restoration processes within Windows NT Server. This chapter discusses the different fault-tolerant capabilities in Windows NT servers. Topics discussed include how RAID is supported and how backup services can be performed; including coverage on a variety of NT supported backup media options.

Chapter 21, "Performance Optimization of Windows NT Server–Based Networks." Updated for the second editon this chapter discusses the different factors that affect the performance of Windows NT Server-based networks. The operation of the Performance Monitor tool is described. You learn how to use this tool to monitor Windows NT Server parameters in real-time as well as in a log-mode.

Chapter 22, "Network Monitor Performance Analysis." This chapter is new to the second edition and discusses strategies for analyzing network data frames. The operation of the Network Monitor tool is described. You will learn how to identify bad data frames at a very detailed level to troubleshoot faulty packets for transmission problems.

Chapter 23, "Migration from Windows NT 3.5x." Migrating from Windows NT 3.5x to 4 isn't all that difficult. This chapter discusses issues that concern the Windows NT migration and several new features of the operating system and gives the reader step-by-step instructions for the Windows NT upgrade.

Chapter 24, "Domain Name Service." This chapter teaches you how to configure an NT server as a DNS server and how to manage DNS after it's running. It also touches on some security issues.

Chapter 25, "COM and DCOM." This chapter examines component software from the perspective of the application user. It discusses the impact component software has on the activities of application users. This chapter focuses primarily on showing the reader how to use DCOM's configuration utility, DCOMCNFG. Additional coverage included in this second edition is a discussion of the COM architecture that will appeal more to the network engineer or programmer.

Chapter 26, "Internet Information Server 4.0." This chapter discusses the structure and function of IIS 4.0. In this chapter you will learn how IIS 4.0 is integrated into the operating system.

Part III: Appendixes

Appendix A, "Windows NT Server Protocols." This appendix describes the most common protocols associated with Windows NT Server-based networks. This chapter introduces you to the concept of the OSI model, and gives examples of Windows NT-related protocols at each of the OSI layers.

Appendix B, "Bridging and Routing." As your Windows NT network grows in size, the deployment of bridges and router devices become increasingly important to extend the range of the network. This appendix gives you the background to appreciate bridging and routing issues with Windows NT services such as replication and name resolution, discussed elsewhere in the book.

Appendix C, "WANs and MANs." As Windows NT networks span metropolitan and geographical areas, the use of ATM, FDDI, ISDN, SMDS, and X.25 become increasingly important. This appendix discusses these WAN and MAN technologies.

Appendix D, "Command Line Reference." This appendix is an easy-to-use reference of all the vital command line information. Listed when appropriate are a description, syntax, and arguments.

New Riders Publishing

The staff of New Riders Publishing is committed to bringing you the very best in computer reference material. Each New Riders book is the result of months of work by authors and staff who research and refine the information contained within its covers.

As part of this commitment to you, the NRP reader, New Riders invites your input. Please let us know if you enjoy this book, if you have trouble with the information and examples presented, or if you have a suggestion for the next edition.

Please note, though: New Riders staff cannot serve as a technical resource for Windows NT Server or for related questions about software- or hardware-related problems. Please refer to the documentation that accompanies Windows NT Server or to the applications' Help systems.

If you have a question or comment about any New Riders book, there are several ways to contact New Riders Publishing. We will respond to as many readers as we can. Your name, address, or phone number will never become part of a mailing list or be used for any purpose other than to help us continue to bring you the best books possible. You can write us at the following address:

New Riders Publishing
Attn: Publisher Assistant
201 W. 103rd Street
Indianapolis, IN 46290

If you prefer, you can fax New Riders Publishing at (317) 817-7448.

You can send electronic mail to New Riders at the following Internet address:

sangus@mcp.com

NRP is an imprint of Macmillan Computer Publishing. To obtain a catalog or information, or to purchase any Macmillan Computer Publishing book, call (800) 428-5331.

Thank you for selecting *Windows NT Server 4 Professional Reference, 2nd Edition*!

Overview of Windows NT Server

1

Understanding Network Operating Systems

Windows NT server is a network operating system (NOS) that also can be used as an application server. This chapter examines some of the capabilities of a NOS and its relationship to the OSI model. Issues such as security, management, and interoperability also are examined in this chapter.

Defining a Network Operating System

Before understanding what a network operating system is, you must understand what an operating system is. An *operating system* is a program that manages the resources of a single computer (see fig. 1.1). An operating system manages some of the following resources:

- The local file system

- The memory in a computer

- The loading and execution of application programs that run in the computer's memory

- The input and output to peripheral devices attached to a computer

- The CPU scheduling among application programs

Figure 1.1

Resources managed by an operating system.

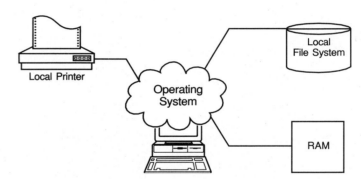

A network consists of resources (such as stations and printers) and communications devices (such as bridges, routers, and gateways). The job of a network operating system is similar to that of an operating system, except that it has to manage resources on a much larger scale. A *network operating system* is a program that manages resources across an entire network (see fig. 1.2). A network operating system manages some of the following resources:

- Remote file systems that are accessible by other workstations

- Memory on the computer on which a NOS runs

- Loading and execution of shared application programs

- Input and output to shared network devices

- CPU scheduling among NOS processes

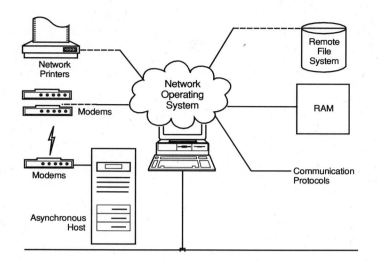

Figure 1.2
Resources managed by a network operation system.

Examining the Features of a Network Operating System

The NOS software can be distributed equally among all nodes, or a major portion of the NOS can reside in a central node. A NOS that is distributed equally among all nodes is called a *peer-to-peer NOS*. An example of this is Windows for Workgroups, or a peer-to-peer Windows NT Network. A NOS in which the major portion runs on a central node is a *centralized NOS*. The central node is called the *server*. Applications that make use of resources managed by the central node NOS are called *clients*. This architecture sometimes is referred to as the *client/server architecture*, even though the term client/server generally applies to client applications accessing server applications.

Because the client software runs on workstations, the workstations are sometimes referred to as *clients*. Only applications that make use of services, however, should be called *clients*. Applications and system software that provide services to other applications are called *servers*.

When a NOS runs on a user node (a workstation), it must communicate and interact with the native operating system on the user node. The native operating system that runs on the workstation is called a *workstation operating system* (WOS). Examples of a WOS are DOS, OS/2, Unix, Windows NT workstation, Windows 95, and Macintosh's System 7.

NOS and the OSI Model

Figure 1.3 shows the NOS in relationship to the OSI model. You can see in this figure that the NOS spans layers 3 through 7 of the OSI model. The NOS has three major aspects:

- Application layer protocols (APIs)

- Subnet protocols

- Network driver

Figure 1.3

The relationship between the NOS and OSI.

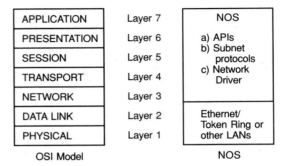

OSI Model		NOS
APPLICATION	Layer 7	NOS
PRESENTATION	Layer 6	a) APIs
SESSION	Layer 5	b) Subnet protocols
TRANSPORT	Layer 4	c) Network Driver
NETWORK	Layer 3	
DATA LINK	Layer 2	Ethernet/ Token Ring or other LANs
PHYSICAL	Layer 1	

The NOS communicates with the LAN hardware by means of a network driver. The network driver acts as a liaison between the network interface card (NIC) and the subnet protocols. The subnet protocols are communications protocols needed to send application and system messages across the network. The application layer protocols implement the NOS services and communicate with the subnet protocols. Each of these major aspects of a NOS is discussed in the next sections.

Network Drivers

A *network driver* is a program that spans portions of layers 2 and 3 of the OSI model. It provides an interface between the NIC and the upper-layer protocols.

The network driver masks the complexities of the way a NIC must be controlled for transmitting and receiving packets from upper layers. The network driver has an intimate understanding of the hardware operation of the NIC, such as the various control/status registers, dynamic memory access (DMA), and I/O ports. Vendors producing NICs according to LAN standards, such as the IEEE 802.5, implement the details of the NIC differently. This means that two IEEE 802.5 nodes might be able to communicate across a local area network (LAN) despite differences in implementation, such as use of IRQ lines, DMA, and I/O port mechanisms. Because the implementations are different, each NIC must have a different network driver, even though NICs can communicate with each other by using the same IEEE 802.5 protocol.

Network installers select the correct network driver for the card and integrate this network driver with the NOS. In the Windows NT Server and Workstation, this process is performed by a flexible dynamic binding mechanism when the OS is installed.

Windows NT comes with drivers for most popular cards. Drivers not included with the Windows NT Server distribution, must be obtained from the manufacturer of the card.

Often, you can find drivers and driver updates in Microsoft's CompuServe forums, web site, and FTP server. Usually, a NIC comes with a floppy disk (but not for long) that contains drivers for operating systems such as Windows NT, NetWare, LANMAN, VINES, and Unix. Many NIC vendors maintain their own bulletin boards, web sites, and FTP servers, where you can download network drivers. Some vendors supply drivers through the Windows NT CompuServe forum.

Windows NT network drivers are written to the NDIS 3.0 specification. NDIS-compliant drivers exist for most NICs, and enable protocol stacks such NetBEUI, SPX/IPX, TCP/IP, and DLC to be written to a common driver specification such as NDIS. A single NDIS driver therefore can support multiple protocol stacks. NDIS 3.0 drivers are not restricted to the 640 KB base memory that is typical in the DOS environment. Another improvement in NDIS 3.0 is the elimination of the Protocol Manager that was required in earlier NDIS versions to bind together the various protocol elements. Instead of using the Protocol Manager, Windows NT uses information in the *registry* (the internal database in Windows NT) and a software module called the *NDIS wrapper*, which surrounds the NDIS driver.

Subnet Protocols

Subnet protocols span layers 3 through 5 of the OSI model. These layers provide the network services that are essential for sending data across a LAN. The functions of layers 3 to 5 are discussed in Appendix A, "Windows NT Server Protocols."

Subnet protocols play an important role in the performance and functionality of a NOS. Fast subnet protocols result in a fast NOS. On the other hand, slow subnet protocols make for a sluggish NOS. Also, a subnet protocol that is fast on a LAN might be slow on a wide-area network (WAN).

The native subnet protocols used by Windows NT Server are NetBEUI for layers 3, 4, and 5 of the OSI model; IPX for layer 3; SPX for layer 4; IP for layer 3; and TCP and UDP for layer 5.

The original NetBIOS specification consisted of 17 commands for connection-oriented functions such as creation, maintenance, and deletion of network connections. The basic NetBIOS commands were extended and now are called the NetBIOS Extended User Interface (NetBEUI). In the late 1980s, a distinction between NetBIOS and NetBEUI was made. The NetBEUI protocol refers to the actual transport protocol, and the NetBIOS refers to the programming commands or the application programming interface (API). By separating the transport protocol from the API, it is possible to have the NetBIOS API be supported on other protocols besides NetBEUI. The NetBIOS API can be supported on IPX/SPX and TCP/IP, for example. This is important if NetBIOS-based applications are to function in an internetwork environment connected by routing devices. The NetBEUI protocol is not routable, whereas the IPX and the IP protocols are routable. Support for running NetBIOS on top of the TCP/IP stack is documented in RFC 1001 and RFC 1002. *RFCs* are *request for comments*, and are the documents that describe the standard and proposed protocols for the Internet.

The NetBEUI protocol is adequate for a single LAN solution without routers, consisting of a small number of workstations. In the first release of Windows NT (version 3.1), the NetBEUI protocol was the Windows NT native protocol stack. In a subsequent release (Windows NT 3.5), the IPX/SPX protocols were promoted to equal status with NetBEUI. Currently, in Windows NT Server and Workstation, when the Setup program asks you to select the protocol, both the NWLink (IPX/SPX) and TCP/IP choices are checked by default. You must explicitly enable the other protocol choices.

The Windows NT implementation of NetBEUI contains some extensions over the previous NetBEUI designed by Microsoft, IBM, and Intel Corp.; and it is referred to in the Windows NT documentation by NBF (NetBIOS Frame). NetBIOS had a limit of 254 communications sessions (connections) per node on the network, regardless of whether the node was a workstation or server. NBF removes the limit of 254 connections per computer, and permits each process in the Windows NT computer to communicate with up to 254 other nodes on the network. The actual limit is 254 computers per LANA (LAN Affinity) number per process. The protocol binding path to a network interface is identified by the LANA number.

The subnet protocols and their relationships to the OSI model are shown in figure 1.4.

Figure 1.4

The relationship between OSI and the Windows NT Server subnet protocols.

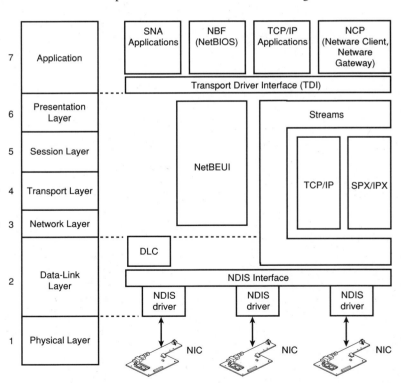

Windows NT Server support for TCP/IP protocols is important, because TCP/IP are the *de facto* transport and network layer transport protocols in a multivendor environment. Because Windows NT Server uses the TCP/IP protocols, it can be deployed in a multivendor network environment. TCP/IP is an industry standard protocol supported on Unix computers, mainframe computers, engineering workstations, and server platforms. The TCP/IP protocol also is used in the Internet—the largest computer network in the world. The TCP/IP protocol, therefore, enables Windows NT networks to be integrated with existing TCP/IP networks and the Internet. Applications such as FTP, TELNET, NFS, X-Windows, Gopher, and WWW (World Wide Web) can run on a Windows NT Server and be made to interoperate with their TCP/IP counterparts on other platforms such as Unix, VMS, NetWare, and MVS.

The IPX protocols were derived from Xerox's XNS (Xerox Network Standard) protocols. The relationship between XNS and IPX protocols is shown in table 1.1.

Table 1.1
XNS and IPX Protocols

XNS Protocol	NetWare Protocol
IDP (Internet Datagram Protocol)	IPX (Internet Packet Exchange)
PEP (Packet Exchange Protocol)	PXP (Packet Exchange Protocol)
SPP (Sequence Packet Protocol)	SPX (Sequence Packet Exchange)

Windows NT Server support for IPX is important, because many Windows NT Servers are expected to be deployed in NetWare-based networks. Many LAN vendors based their subnet protocols on XNS because these protocols had the reputation of working efficiently in a LAN environment. XNS protocols were not designed to be used for wide-area networks, which have larger time delays. Because, IPX, PXP, and SPX protocols were derived from XNS, they suffer from the same limitations as XNS protocols for WAN applications.

The IPX protocol provides the capability to send data across different interconnected LANs. IPX is a *datagram* (connectionless) service. SPX provides a *virtual circuit* (connections-oriented) service for those applications that need it.

The streams layer encapsulates the transport protocols such as TCP/IP and SPX/IPX (see fig. 1.4). The Streams specification was created by AT&T for its Unix System V operating system. Its primary purpose is to enable the encapsulation of the transport protocols within the operating system with a well-defined interface to both the applications at the top of the transport protocol stack (called the *stream head*) and the network drivers at the bottom of the protocol stack (called the *stream tail*). This specification enables transport protocol modules such as TCP/IP and SPX/IPX to be "pushed" and configured between the stream head and the stream tail. In Windows NT, the stream tail interfaces with the NDIS driver interface. Typically, a higher level interface such as the transport layer interface (TLI) is used by applications that will communicate using the transport protocols encapsulated by the Streams interface.

Inclusion of the Streams interface is primarily meant for developers to port other transport protocol stacks to Windows NT. In Windows NT, the streams interface is called Streams Environment. Windows NT is designed to use a new interface defined by Microsoft, called the *transport driver interface* (TDI), instead of the TLI interface used in the Unix System V operating system.

Windows NT computers can communicate with IBM mainframe computers across LANs using the Data Link Control (DLC) protocol. The DLC protocol device driver support comes with the Windows NT distribution. The inclusion of DLC within Windows NT is primarily for communication with IBM mainframes through an IBM 37×5 front-end processor (FEP), using an IBM 3270 terminal emulation program. However, the DLC protocol can be used by Windows NT to communicate with any device that supports DLC.

The Transport Driver Interface (TDI)

The NDIS interface provides a uniform interface to the network hardware and can be seen as providing an interface between the OSI network layer (layer 3) and the OSI data-link layer (layer 2). Microsoft created the transport driver interface, which is similar to the NDIS interface, that provides a uniform interface to the transport protocols (refer to figures 1.4 and 1.5). The TDI can be viewed as providing an interface between the OSI transport layer (layer 4) and the OSI session layer (layer 5).

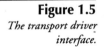

Figure 1.5

The transport driver interface.

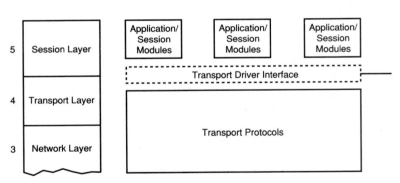

The TDI interface enables applications to be written to a common transport interface, regardless of the underlying transport protocol that is used for communication. The TDI interface is not a software module; instead, it is an interface specification to which the upper layer of the transport protocol and the lower layer of the application protocol are written.

Application Layer Protocols

Windows NT Server file- and print-sharing operations are performed by the Server Message Block (SMB) protocol. This protocol was developed by IBM for its IBM PC Network Program NOS, and was used in the LAN Manager NOS. Windows NT server uses version 3.0 of the SMB protocol.

The following are some of the functions that SMB provides:

- Opening files under different modes

- Providing shared universal naming convention (UNC) names for resources to be shared, such as server directories and print services

- Closing open files

- Reading data blocks from open files

- Writing data blocks to open files

- Getting a list of directory entries

- Manipulating the server database (registry)

- Providing high-level connection services

Windows NT Server supports the NetWare Core Protocol (NCP) client protocol that is used to access NetWare 3.*x* services. Client and Gateway Services for NetWare also supports NetWare 4.*x* Directory Services (NDS) and includes browsing of NDS resources, NDS authentication, and NDS printing. Third-party vendors, such as Beam & Whiteside and newer products from Microsoft, also implement the NCP server protocols so that a Windows NT Server can emulate NetWare 3.*x* file and print services. The NCP protocol is Novell's equivalent of the SMB protocol; it is used in Windows NT Server and performs functions that are equivalent to SMB.

Other application layer protocols that Windows NT Server supports are the Internet family of application protocols that use the TCP/IP protocols. These include application-level services such as FTP, TELNET, SNMP, NFS, X-Windows, Gopher, and WWW. These protocols and their configurations are examined in later chapters.

Multitasking versus Single Tasking

Operating systems like DOS are *single tasking*. This means that DOS can perform only one thing at a time. For the environment and applications for which DOS was conceived, this was not a problem. The operating system needed to manage only one user and one application at a time.

Some of the earlier NOSs, such as MS-NET from Microsoft and its derivatives, provided NOS services on top of DOS. A big performance penalty was paid by these earlier NOSs. Consider what would happen if several packet requests came to a server that was running MS-NET on top of DOS, for example. MS-NET would have to make use of DOS to provide access to the hard disks on the server. If a second packet request was allowed to be processed while the first one was in progress, the MS-NET server would crash. Why? Because DOS is nonreentrant.

Nonreentrant means that a piece of program code can be entered or executed only once at any given time. *Reentrant* code can be entered or executed by a number of processes at the same time. 3+SHARE from 3COM, an earlier NOS based on MS-NET, also was based on DOS. It avoided the DOS bottleneck by providing a reentrant piece of code that could access the server's resources. 3COM called this piece of reentrant code Concurrent I/O System (CIOSYS). Earlier MS-NET versions queued packet requests and allowed only one packet to be processed at a time.

Microsoft solved the MS-NET problem in LAN Manager because LANMAN runs on top of OS/2. OS/2 is a multitasking operating system and is reentrant; it can process several packet requests at a time.

The Windows NT Server is designed with built-in networking, and is a multitasking environmnt. Unlike the LAN Manager NOS, it does not run on top of another operating system such as OS/2. The operating system and the network operating system features are integrated into a single NOS called Windows NT Server.

Another important NOS, Virtual Network System (VINES) from Banyan, runs on top of a modified Unix System V. Unix is multitasking and reentrant, and it can process multiple packet requests.

A NOS must be multitasking and reentrant. If a NOS runs on top of another operating system, that operating system must, in turn, be multitasking and reentrant.

In a general-purpose operating system, issues of fairness are more important than throughput and efficiency. Consider a general-purpose, multitasking operating system (such as Windows NT) that is running several user applications. Although some applications (foreground tasks) might be more important than others (background tasks), it is important that no application is starved for CPU time. To achieve this goal, a process is given a certain amount of time, and then the CPU turns its attention to another process, regardless of what it is doing at the time. Although this procedure might be more democratic and fair, it has an adverse effect on the system throughput, especially when critical processes are interrupted.

The Windows NT Server and the Windows NT Workstation

The Windows NT products first were released in 1993 as a version 3.1 release. The products were named Windows NT 3.1 and Windows NT Advanced Server (NTAS). The Windows NT Advanced Server was earlier called LAN Manager for Windows NT. The Windows NT 3.1 product was meant to run at the workstation and could be used to form a peer-to-peer network and provide integration with Windows for Workgroups. The Windows NT Advanced Server 3.1 product was meant for centralized file, print, and application sharing.

Version 3.5 of the Windows NT Server products was released in 1994. The workstation product is called Windows NT Workstation; and the server product, previously called

Windows NT Advanced Server, is called Windows NT Server. The Windows NT Server is better suited for supporting centralized file, print, and application sharing. It can be used to implement the concept of a domain where several Windows NT Servers and Windows NT Workstations form a logical group, and you need to log on just once to access the resources in the domain. The Windows NT Workstation does not include support for domain user and group accounts. All user and goup accounts created for the Windows NT Workstation are local to that workstation and do not have a network-wide or global meaning.

The Windows NT Workstation can be used to build a small peer-to-peer network, or it can be used as a client to access the Windows NT Servers or other resources in a Windows NT domain.

Other NOS Choices

Several excellent NOS choices are available in the NOS marketplace, including NetWare 3.*x*, NetWare 4.*x*, VINES from Banyan, and IBM LAN Server from IBM. The history of these products is shown in figure 1.6.

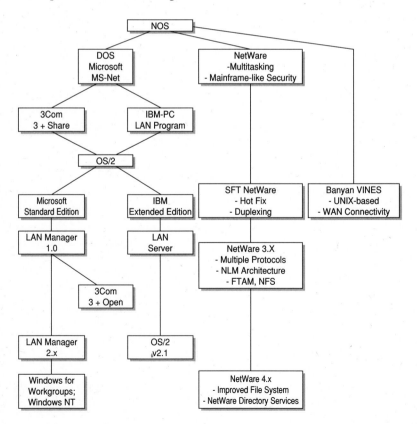

Figure 1.6

The history of network operating systems. (Graphic courtesy of Learning Group International)

LANMAN first was marketed through 3COM and other OEMs. For many years, the most advanced version of LANMAN was available from 3COM and was called 3+OPEN. Microsoft decided to market LANMAN through 3COM, because 3COM was then the well-known arch rival of Novell. 3COM added many improved features to LANMAN, such as sophisticated network administration, Demand Protocol Architecture (DPA), and Macintosh support. 3COM, however, quit the NOS business by early 1991. Many of the 3+OPEN features are integrated into LANMAN. LANMAN runs on the OS/2 platform. LANMAN also is available on Unix platforms through a port made by AT&T. Initially, Hewlett-Packard and AT&T worked on this port, but Hewlett-Packard eventually dropped out. Micro-Tempus has a LANMAN version for the IBM MVS mainframe platform. Many other licenses of LANMAN exist. Windows NT Server is the next step in the evolution of the LANMAN NOS.

IBM's first NOS offering was the IBM PC LAN Program (PCLP). PCLP was based on MS-NET and suffered from all the performance problems of running on DOS. PCLP still is available from IBM and is an example of a peer-to-peer NOS. When Microsoft released LANMAN as part of OS/2, IBM—through a license agreement with Microsoft—developed a NOS based on LANMAN. This NOS from IBM is the IBM LAN Server. It is based on OS/2 EE (Extended Edition). OS/2 EE has the additional components of a communications manager to interface with IBM SNA networks and a database manager that supports the IBM mainframe database (DB2).

VINES from Banyan is based on a modified Unix System V. It is a robust NOS with features comparable to NetWare and LANMAN. Because Unix comes with protocols like TCP/IP that work well with WANs, it is not surprising that VINES has very good support for wide-area networking. Banyan went one step further and designed a powerful distributed naming service that enables network resources to be accessed by a symbolic name, regardless of their locations anywhere on the network. This naming service is called *StreetTalk*, and is one of the reasons that VINES has enjoyed an edge in LAN/WAN integration.

Today, Windows NT Server's main competitor is NetWare. Novell has introduced a new version of NetWare called NetWare 4.*x* that includes support for X.500-like directory services and added features so that it can be used in an enterprise network.

One of the major drawbacks of NetWare is that writing application programs that run on the NetWare server itself (called NetWare loadable modules, or NLMs) is considered difficult by many developers. This is an advantage that Windows NT Server has over NetWare; it is easier to develop applications for a Windows NT Server than for a NetWare server.

Understanding Windows NT Server's NOS Security

Windows NT Server builds on the security features that were available in the LAN Manager NOS. The next few sections briefly examine some of the security features of Windows NT Server.

User Account Security

All Windows NT versions have a user name/password security feature. To use Windows NT, a user must have an account and a valid password on the system. In earlier versions of many NOSs, passwords were sent over the LAN in unencrypted form. When protocol analyzers became quite common, unencrypted passwords became an obvious security deficiency. *Protocol analyzers* examine packets on a LAN and easily see the password that is sent by a user workstation during the log-in sequence. For this reason, Windows NT encrypts the password at the station before sending it across the LAN.

Time Restrictions

By using the User Administration utilities, a Windows NT Server Administrator can impose time restrictions on when a user can log in. The time restrictions can be imposed in terms of one-hour intervals and can be set for any day.

The time-restriction feature is designed for network sites that have strict security measures in which access to the network needs to be denied to users (but also applies to Workstation logins).

Station Restrictions

Windows NT Server Administrators can use the User Administration tool to impose station restrictions on where a user can log in. The station restriction enables a user to log in from only stations that have a specified station address. Up to eight station addresses can be specified.

The station-restriction feature is designed for network sites that have strict security measures in which access to the network is possible through certain physical areas only. Station restrictions prevent users from wandering to other areas of the building and using workstations that do not belong to them.

Diskless Workstations

When LANs began to become popular and became a legitimate platform for running business applications in corporations, some MIS managers had misgivings about the LAN client/server technology. One reason for these misgivings was that user workstations had removable media, such as disks. It would be possible for an unscrupulous user to download sensitive information to a floppy disk or hard disk and walk away with the disk. With the traditional terminal/host architecture, the user can view this information on-screen but cannot walk away with a disk containing sensitive information.

One way to keep users from copying sensitive information onto floppy disks is to install diskless workstations. *Diskless workstations* do not have any storage media, such as floppy disk drives or hard disks. They boot their native operating system, such as DOS, from a copy of the operating system boot image that is stored on the server. The NIC cards on diskless workstations have a special boot programmable read-only memory (PROM) that enables the NIC to fetch the boot image from a public directory on the server.

Another advantage of diskless workstations is that they can be used to prevent the spread of viruses through the workstations, because it is not possible to install questionable software from the workstation.

Media Security

In many applications, LAN media security is a big concern. The LAN cabling should be installed so that it is not possible for an unauthorized user to access the LAN cables. Coaxial cables and twisted pair cables are easy to tap in order to read data. They also emit electromagnetic radiation. A determined person with sufficient resources can read LAN traffic through these emanations. Some military applications install LAN cabling in a metal conduit to prevent noise emanations and bury the cable in concrete to prevent physical access to the LAN cables.

The best LAN media for security purposes is fiber optic, because it is more difficult to tap. If a probe is inserted into the fiber-optic conductor, it can cause additional reflections and interference to the light signals and cause the fiber-optic link to crash.

Encryption

How do you secure data on the file server? One way is to make use of the security permissions provided by the NOS. The network Administrator with Supervisor or equivalent privileges, however, can read all files and directories on the server. This becomes a problem if you are dealing with sensitive information that you do not want other users, including the Supervisor, to see. One way of handling this is to encrypt databases and files that contain sensitive information. The file is decrypted when it is opened and encrypted when it is closed. As you can imagine, however, performance suffers because of the encryption and decryption operations.

A number of encryption programs are available. Some encryption programs are bundled with software tools, such as Borland's SideKick and Central Point's PC-TOOLS. Many use the Data Encryption Standard (DES) algorithms for encryption. Although many of these programs are DOS/Windows 3.1-based, they can run on Windows NT Server, because it supports virtual DOS machines (VDM) for running DOS and Windows applications.

Encryption also can be performed in hardware at the NIC level before transmitting packets across the LAN media. When encrypting LAN packets, only the data portion of the packet is encrypted. The network address and control fields in the packets usually are not encrypted, so that devices such as bridges and routers can interpret the network address and control fields.

Motorola's wireless LAN uses encryption to prevent users from tapping into the microwave frequency used for transmission. Wireless LANs have sophisticated encryption algorithms in which the seed used for encryption is changed randomly every two milliseconds. The *seed* is a number or code that is used as the key for the encryption algorithm.

Audits

LAN audits are very helpful for performing an analysis of the threats to which a NOS has been subjected.

A hostile user, for example, might try to guess passwords by repeatedly trying password combinations. In Windows NT Server, one way to prevent this threat is to lock out the user after a certain number of failed password attempts. Another way is to have an audit of all password attempts.

Windows NT Server enables you to set up audit policies so that you can track security-related events.

Managing Interoperability Issues in a NOS

As networks grow in size, one of the major problems a network Administrator faces is *interoperability.* When all the hardware and software components are from the same vendor, the system usually functions flawlessly. This is the reason why many users and corporations prefer a single vendor solution.

Many MIS departments are pure IBM, pure DEC, pure Microsoft, or pure Novell. Network applications and requirements have become so broad and diverse, however, that it is difficult for a single vendor to supply all possible needs. The larger vendors—such as IBM, DEC, and Hewlett-Packard—come very close to supplying these needs, but many of their solutions require the purchase of a proprietary platform. The vendor then can lock the user into a particular computing architecture, which makes it difficult to purchase equipment that is not from the same vendor.

Some end users are perfectly happy to be locked into a vendor's solution, because they do not have to deal with interoperability issues—the vendor does instead. Solutions from a single vendor, however, usually are not the most cost-effective. Competition and the free market system tend to drive down equipment prices and increase performance. Also, vendors have strengths in different areas. Many network managers exploit the strengths of various vendors, leading to multivendor networks.

One solution to the interoperability dilemma is the adoption of open systems in which vendors make products compliant to universally accepted standards. The development of the OSI model and standardization efforts of organizations—such as ISO, ANSI, IEEE, and ECMA—are steps in the right direction. Only time will tell the success of these efforts.

The following section discusses some of the more important aspects of interoperability as it relates to multivendor networks.

Defining Interoperability

Interoperability means that all the hardware and software components in a system cooperate at all levels. This is a broad, yet accurate, definition of interoperability and encompasses a wide range of issues. Although *interoperability* can be difficult to define, you begin to appreciate the *lack* of interoperability when your network stops working because of conflicting components.

As the following examples point out, interoperability usually is not discussed unless the hardware and software do not interoperate.

You can buy a telephone from a variety of sources and plug it into any telephone socket, for example. You do not have to be a technician or electrical engineer to perform this task. As long as that telephone jack is enabled by the telephone company, you can dial any telephone in the world. This is an example of interoperability at the highest level.

Another example is a Centronics parallel printer cable for IBM personal computers. You can buy it from any source, and it works just fine with any IBM PC clone. Likewise, all fax machines can "talk" to each other because they use the same Group 3 fax as the language used in sending facsimile data.

All these examples have one thing in common. They all conform to the same standard. In the case of telephones, the phone jacks and the signals used for communications comply to a standard. For the Centronics parallel printer cable, the cable connectors and the wiring conform to a standard. In the fax machine example, all fax machines use the same Group 3 fax code. When components operate as they should operate, interoperability usually is not a topic of discussion.

On the other hand, if you install a NetWare server on the same LAN as a VINES server and try to get the two servers to share data and applications, you begin to realize the importance of interoperability. Because NetWare and VINES use different architectures, they cannot communicate. This is an example of network software interoperability. Hardware interoperability issues also exist.

You cannot connect a Token Ring station directly to an Ethernet bus, for example, because each system uses different connectors and cables. Even if you manage to connect the Token Ring NIC to the Ethernet bus by a liberal use of a soldering iron and a wire cutter, the two stations will not be able to talk to each other. Ethernet uses a carrier-sense mechanism, and Token Ring uses token access. In other words, the two stations are incompatible at the physical and data-link layers of the OSI model.

On the other hand, you can connect a 10BASE5 Ethernet LAN and a 10BASE-T Ethernet LAN and expect them to interoperate. Both use different cable types; 10BASE5 uses coaxial cable and 10BASE-T uses unshielded twisted pair wiring. You can join these two LANs by a 10BASE-T transceiver, however, enabling the stations on the two LANs to communicate as if they were part of the same network. This is possible because both 10BASE5 and 10BASE-T use the same carrier-sense access mechanism. In this example, the two LANs are compatible at the data-link layer of the OSI model.

The OSI model is indispensable in analyzing problems concerning interoperability issues within networks. As you learned earlier in the chapter, interoperability problems stem from lack of standardization. If all networks followed the same standards, the term *interoperability* probably would not have been created by the networking industry. See Appendix A, "Windows NT Server Protocols," for a description of the OSI model.

Examining Interconnectivity versus Interoperability

Sometimes the term *interconnectivity* is confused with *interoperability*. You can put a Token Ring NIC in a Windows NT Server, an IBM LAN server, and a VINES server, for example; and then connect them to the same Token Ring LAN. The token in this Token Ring circulates through each of these servers. Data and control packets generated by each of these servers circulate to other servers. Compatibility exists at the data-link layer of the OSI model, because each of these servers uses the same token-access mechanism. These servers, however, cannot share and exchange applications and data. In this example, you have *interconnectivity* among these servers, but not *interoperability*. Figure 1.7 shows compatibility at the physical (layer 1) and data-link (layer 2) layers of the OSI model, but no compatibility at the upper layers.

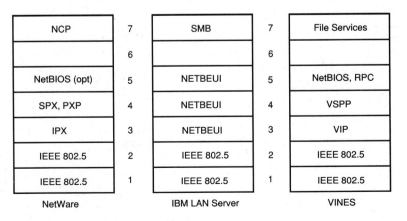

NCP	7	SMB	7	File Services
	6		6	
NetBIOS (opt)	5	NETBEUI	5	NetBIOS, RPC
SPX, PXP	4	NETBEUI	4	VSPP
IPX	3	NETBEUI	3	VIP
IEEE 802.5	2	IEEE 802.5	2	IEEE 802.5
IEEE 802.5	1	IEEE 802.5	1	IEEE 802.5
NetWare		IBM LAN Server		VINES

Figure 1.7

Notice the server compatibility at the physical and data-link layer only.

In figure 1.7, NetBEUI is the NetBIOS extended user interface, SMB is the file services protocol (server message block) used in Windows NT Server, VIP is VINES' Internet protocol, VSPP is VINES' sequenced packet protocol, and RPC is VINES' remote procedure call.

You can compare interconnectivity and interoperability to a room full of English-speaking and French-speaking people talking at the same time. Interconnectivity exists because each person can hear the utterances of each speaker. The English speakers, however, cannot understand the French speakers. Similarly, the French speakers cannot understand the English speakers. In other words, *interoperability among the people speaking in the room does not exist.*

Looking at the Different Levels of Interoperability

Interoperability should be considered in terms of the applications used by users. Can these applications run on different platforms? Can data files and information be exchanged between them? If a user can perform these general tasks, you will not hear much about interoperability problems.

In terms of the OSI model, interoperability exists when you have compatibility at the application layer (layer 7). How does layer 7 interoperability affect layers 1 through 6 of the OSI model? In the OSI model, a layer depends on the services provided by the layer below it. Layer 7 of the OSI model, therefore, uses the services provided by layer 6, which in turn uses the services provided by layer 5, and so on all the way down to layer 1. In order to have interoperability at layer 7 (the application layer), you must have interoperability at layers 1 through 6. The sole purpose of layers 1 through 6 is to provide interconnection between the application layers of two stations that are sharing information.

File-transfer protocols, such as Kermit, XMODEM, and File Transfer Protocol (FTP), are examples of interoperability. Kermit and XMODEM can be found on many different systems, and yet you can exchange files by using asynchronous dial-up lines (telephone lines) between these systems. FTP implementations exist on DOS machines, Windows NT, NetWare servers, and Unix machines. You can use FTP to transfer files between these systems.

In the preceding discussion, *interconnectivity* is compatibility at layers 1 through 6 of the OSI model. *True interoperability* is compatibility at layer 7 (the application layer) of the OSI model and the application software that makes use of it. True interoperability cannot exist without the interconnectivity support of layers 1 through 6 of the OSI model.

Examining Levels of Interoperability

The preceding section discussed interoperability issues at the different layers of the OSI model. The OSI model is used as a yardstick only because not many commercial implementations make use of ISO recommendations for the protocols at the OSI layers. Even among the OSI recommendations, several options are available from which to choose. Some of the layers have incompatible options. Two implementations, therefore, can claim to be OSI-compatible, but because they use incompatible options at some of the layers, no interoperability exists between them.

Interoperability at the Physical Layer

If stations are attached to the same physical media, such as coaxial cable, twisted pair cable, or fiber optic, they have interoperability at the physical media, or layer 1, of the OSI model. Examples of this are Ethernet stations that are connected by coaxial cable, or Token Ring stations connected by IBM Type 1 twisted pair wiring. Figure 1.8 shows the OSI model for two stations connected by the same media.

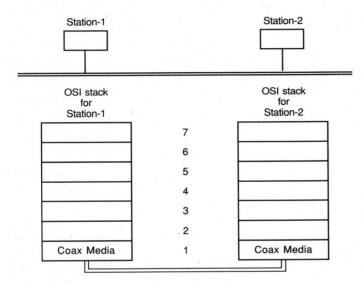

Figure 1.8

Interoperability at the physical layer with the same cable.

You also can have physical layer interoperability even when stations are connected by different media types. You can interconnect stations on a coaxial Ethernet LAN and on a 10BASE-T LAN, for example. Interoperability is established between the two LANs by a 10BASE-T transceiver that joins a 10BASE-T link to the transceiver cable and provides the signal conversion. Figure 1.9 shows the interoperability between these stations as it relates to the OSI model.

Interoperability at the Data-Link Layer

Figure 1.9 also shows interoperability at the data-link layer. Both stations use the same IEEE 802.3 mechanism for accessing the LAN, which ensures interoperability at the data-link layer.

You also can have interoperability for Ethernet and Token Ring LANs indirectly through a translating device, even though they use different data-link layer mechanisms. The translating device that provides interoperability between dissimilar data-link layers is called a *bridge*. The IBM 8209 bridge, for example, can be used to connect Ethernet and IBM Token Ring LANs. Figure 1.10 shows an example of a bridge.

Figure 1.9

Interoperability at the physical layer with coaxial and twisted pair cables.

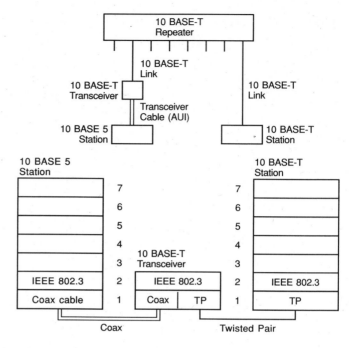

Figure 1.10

Interoperability at the data-link layer through a bridge.

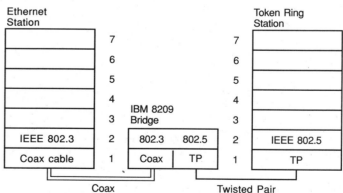

Interoperability at the Subnet Layers

Two Windows NT computers can communicate with each other because they use the same protocols at the subnet layers. *Subnet layers* are defined as layers 3 through 5 of the OSI model. Figure 1.11 shows two Windows NT stations that are interoperable at the subnet layer. In examining their OSI representations, you can see that the Windows NT computers use the same protocols at layers 3, 4, and 5. In this example, the stations are using the NetBIOS implementation to communicate. Two Windows NT computers can use just layer 3 (IPX) to communicate. Many applications that run on Windows NT computers use just the IPX layer for interoperation. An important point illustrated in figure 1.11 is that to have interoperability at the subnet layers, you must have interoperability at the physical and data-link layers (layers 1 and 2).

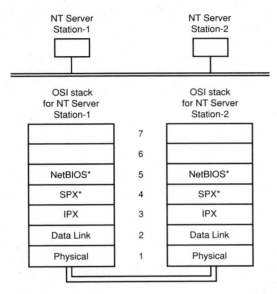

Figure 1.11

Interoperability at subnet layers for Windows NT computers.

* The NetBIOS and SPX layers are optional

Interoperability at the Application Layer

Earlier in this chapter, you saw that transferring files is an example of interoperability at the application layer. One area of great interest to many corporations is interoperability of different electronic mail systems. For PC-based networks, a variety of messaging standards exist, such as the Microsoft mail standard and Novell's Message Handling System (MHS).

Electronic mail messages can be represented by an international standard called X.400. X.400 is a general standard that enables text, binary, voice, and facsimile data to be sent in an electronic-mail message. All the major vendors in the United States, such as IBM and DEC, and the network industries in Europe and Japan support X.400. Many vendors use their own proprietary systems, but to interoperate with each other, vendors use X.400 gateways. X.400 gateways translate the proprietary message format into the X.400 format and vice versa. A related standard exists called the X.500, which handles network name services on a world-wide scale and is used with X.400.

Other interoperability issues at the application layer deal with application-level interoperability. The following section discusses how to run applications on both IBM PC and Macintosh computers. You also learn how to exchange application data files between the IBM and Macintosh.

Data Interoperability for DOS

Lotus 1-2-3 and Microsoft Excel spreadsheets can run on both the IBM PC and Macintosh platforms. These applications contain conversion routines to import and export spreadsheets between these two platforms. These conversion routines are necessary because the IBM PC and Mac operating systems use different file systems and methods to represent data. Data transparency does not exist between these systems. Excel and 1-2-3, for example, have built-in support for this conversion. Not all applications provide conversion routines, but third-party support tools that provide data conversion are available. Conversion between text files from IBM PC to Macintosh is easy. More complex file structures require special utilities. Some utilities (and their manufacturers) that you can use to convert more complex files between IBM PCs and the Macintosh follow:

- AutoImport (White Crane Software)

- Catapult (Tangent Group)

- DataLens Driver (Digital Networks)

- PC/SQL-Link Database Gateway (Micro Decisionware)

- Ally (Unisys)

Data Interoperability Provided by Windows NT Server

A network operating system such as Windows NT Server enables Macintosh, DOS, OS/2, and Unix workstations to store files on the server. Each of these workstations sees its own file system on the same Windows NT Server. Macintosh users see folders and icons that represent files, and DOS users see file names (consisting of an eight-character file name and a three-character extension) on the server. Windows NT Server supports this file transparency by using a general representation for files on the server.

Data Interoperability under Microsoft Windows and OS/2

Applications running in the Microsoft Windows or OS/2 environment can export and import data between applications. The most primitive mechanisms for doing this are the cut-and-paste operations that can copy application data into a temporary buffer. This data then can be imported into other applications that are running under Windows or OS/2. A much more powerful mechanism for providing data exchange is *dynamic data exchange* (DDE). DDE enables you to set up an interprocess communications link between two applications operating in a Windows or OS/2 environment. When data changes are made in one application, the changes are sent automatically to the linked application.

The problem with DDE is that it works with only true Windows or OS/2 Presentation Manager applications. Also, DDE does not provide data transparency. The applications linked by DDE need to understand each other's message format. DDE is concerned only with getting the message across. In this sense, DDE is similar to the transport and session layer protocols in the OSI model.

Data Interoperability Using Object Linking and Embedding

To better support data transparency, vendors such as Microsoft have developed *object linking and embedding* (OLE). OLE provides a way to share data between different applications. OLE introduces the notion of *data ownership*. The application that first creates the data owns the data. This association between an application and its data exists even when the data is exported to other applications.

If you have OLE-aware versions of AutoCAD and PageMaker, for example, you can create an illustration under AutoCAD and then export it to PageMaker. Because the illustration was created in AutoCAD, an ownership association exists between AutoCAD and the illustration and is retained even though the drawing now is in a PageMaker document. You can modify the illustration by using PageMaker, but each time you do this, AutoCAD is invoked to change the illustration. Pointers associated with the illustration notify the OLE-aware application as to what you are trying to accomplish and transparently take care of the operation by invoking the owner of the imported data. Although the illustration appears in the PageMaker document, it physically belongs to AutoCAD.

OLE manages data by treating it as an object. An *object* is a specific instance of a user-defined data class and consists of the data representation and the programs required to manipulate it (see fig. 1.12). To manipulate and link (import) an object to other applications, the object is placed in a *container*. The container has simple controls for the object. In most situations, these controls are all that you need to manipulate the object. If greater control is desired, OLE can be used to call the owner of the application directly.

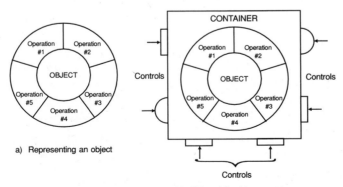

Figure 1.12
Data object definitions.

a) Representing an object

b) Object defined in a container

Configuring the Windows NT Server

As you install the Windows NT Server, you need to make a number of choices. Depending on the choices selected, appropriate software modules are loaded onto the Windows NT Server machine from the distribution media. You can add other network software components later by selecting the network option from the Windows NT Server Control Panel or by running the Windows NT Setup program.

Windows NT Server installation issues are discussed in Chapter 3, "Installing Windows NT Server," and Chapter 4, "Advanced Windows NT Server Installation."

Setting Up Nondedicated and Dedicated Servers

The choice of running the Windows NT Server in a dedicated or nondedicated manner can affect the performance of the server as viewed by clients. The Windows NT Server is a general-purpose operating system with certain optimizations made for file services. These optimizations enable the Windows NT Server to provide file and print services and also application services. If the Windows NT Server is being used primarily as a file and print server, it is best not to run other resource-intensive applications on the server, because this will impact the performance of file and print services. The exception to this is if you are running Windows NT Server software on a multiprocessor computer that has sufficient computing resources to adequately handle multiple services.

Similarly, if the Windows NT Server is to be used primarily as an application server such as a database server, it is best not to use the server for critical file and print services, unless you have adequate computing resources on the server machine.

Examining Peer-to-Peer Network Operating Systems

Peer-to-peer NOS offers an attractive, low-cost alternative to the more expensive centralized servers. For small networks, a peer-to-peer NOS can be adequate for most networking needs. This section briefly examines peer-to-peer network operating systems.

A peer-to-peer NOS—such as Windows for Workgroups, Windows NT Workstation computers, and NetWare Lite—enables an IBM PC-compatible computer to become a server. The PC computer can be a server, a workstation, or both.

Many small businesses are intimidated by the complexity involved in setting up a NOS such as Windows NT Server, NetWare, IBM LAN Server, LANMAN, or VINES. All they want to do is share files, printers, and a few applications. Many such organizations already have stand-alone PCs. All they really need is networking hardware and a simple and inexpensive NOS. The easiest small-business solution is a peer-to-peer NOS, also called an *entry-level NOS.*

Advantages of a Peer-to-Peer NOS

A peer-to-peer NOS has several advantages over the central-server approach:

■ Peer-to-peer NOSs are less expensive and easier to install and administer for a small number of users, compared to most central-server NOSs such as Windows NT Server, NetWare, LANMAN, IBM LAN Server, and VINES.

■ Any PC-compatible machine (usually with a hard disk) can be converted into a server for a peer-to-peer NOS. This is useful for quick sharing of files between users. In dedicated mode, servers on central-server NOSs cannot be used as DOS stations. Even in nondedicated mode, central-server NOSs might have limitations regarding the amount of memory available for applications, and you might not be able to use special memory-management drivers, such as expanded and extended memory-management drivers.

■ You do not need to dedicate a special machine as a server on peer-to-peer NOSs. This results in reduced costs for LANs.

Limitations of a Peer-to-Peer NOS

Compared to the central-server approach to LANs, the peer-to-peer NOS does have disadvantages. For a larger number of nodes (more than 25 or 50), the peer-to-peer NOS might quickly become unmanageable. Because users can set their workstation as a server, they can spend an inordinate amount of work time playing with and administering their server. Network administration can become an absorbing and interesting task. Consider an organization of 50 users of a peer-to-peer LAN who spend several hours a day putting special files, such as games, on their server and administering and fine-tuning their server. You can imagine what would happen to the productivity of the organization. For a large number of servers and nodes, central control still is one of the most effective ways of administering the network.

In stark contrast to this model of centralized control is the network administration on Internet, which can best be described as near anarchy! Luckily, there is no shortage of Internet experts and hackers (in the good sense of the word) who fix problems as they arise.

Because a PC is used as a server, the performance of peer-to-peer NOSs is limited by the file-system performance of the operating system running on the IBM PC. A DOS-based server, for example, can support fewer nodes more effectively than can a central server. This might not be a big disadvantage because peer-to-peer, NOS-based LANs generally have fewer nodes to support. Another disadvantage of peer-to-peer networks is that backing up the separate workstations is more difficult and time-consuming.

Another disadvantage of peer-to-peer NOSs is that organizations tend to grow, and when companies grow, networks must grow. When the number of nodes becomes very large, the networks might become difficult to manage. Also, for a larger number of nodes, the peer-to-peer LANs might become more expensive.

Examining Multipurpose NOSs

The earliest NOSs that were introduced in the networking industry were disk servers. *Disk server technology* provided remote disks to users on a LAN, but the users could not share files easily. Disk server technology was replaced by *file server technology,* in which files could be shared among users. File server technology gave LAN users a remote file system that could be accessed by the workstation operating system (WOS) commands and software interfaces. Generally speaking, file server technology gave birth to the client/server model for PC networks.

Depending on the application that is run on a server, the file server can be treated as a special application server. A server that has gateway software to networks, such as IBM's SNA network, can be called a *gateway server*. A server that supports a pool of modems that can be used to dial out or dial in is called an asynchronous communications server. A file server can be treated as a general-purpose computing platform and not just a provider of file services.

Servers are multifaceted and can provide a number of dedicated services.

Conclusion

In this chapter, you learned about some of the capabilities of network operating systems and the types of services they provide. You learned how to analyze a NOS in relationship to the OSI model and how the NOS functions map to the OSI model.

You also learned about the different types of interoperability and interconnectivity issues in a network environment. A brief review of the network protocol architecture for Windows NT Server was also presented in this chapter.

Windows NT Server Architecture

The Windows NT architecture is a vast improvement over Microsoft's operating systems, such as DOS and Windows 3.x, and even the Windows 95 architecture. The Windows NT operating system is a preemptive multitasking, multithreading operating system with security and networking provided as a core service.

Windows NT attempts to provide multiple personalities, known as environmental subsystems, which enable older applications, such as DOS, Windows 3.x, and OS/2 1.x character-mode applications, to run on a Windows NT computer. Windows NT's modular architecture and its use of a Hardware Abstraction Layer has allowed Microsoft to port the operating system to the Intel and many other RISC (Reduced Informaiton Set Computer) platforms.

This chapter introduces you to the Windows NT architecture, as well as its components.

Overview of Windows NT Server Architecture

In the early days of computing, operating systems were built using a monolithic model in which there was no clear division of the different components of the operating system. The operating system was one large software component. As operating systems became more sophisticated, the operating system designers quickly learned that monolithic software systems are difficult to change and a modular approach to building operating systems resulted in systems that were easier to change.

Windows NT was designed using a modular approach. The different modules (also called components) of Windows NT are shown in figure 2.1. The same basic architecture describes both the Windows NT Workstation and the Windows NT Server. Windows NT Server is optimized for server performance and provides support for the Windows NT domain architecture, as well as for server-specific tools and applications that are not available on Windows NT Workstation.

Figure 2.1

The Windows NT Architecture.

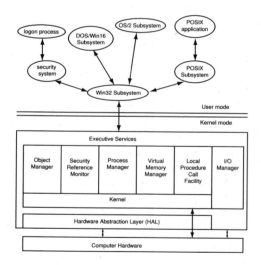

The Windows NT operating system components can run in two modes: user and kernel (refer to figure 2.1). When an operating system component runs in the *kernel* mode, it has access to the full range of machine instructions for that processor and can generally access all resources on the computer system. In Windows NT, the Executive Services, the Kernel, and the HAL run in the kernel mode. The Win32 subsystem and other environmental subsystems, such as DOS/Win16, OS/2, and POSIX subsystems run in the user mode. By placing these subsystems in the user mode, the Windows NT designers can modify them more easily without changing components that are designed to run in the kernel mode.

The Hardware Abstraction Layer (HAL) virtualizes the computer hardware so that the kernel can be written to the hardware virtual interface, instead of to the actual machine hardware. For the most part, the kernel uses the HAL to access computer resources. This means that the kernel and all the other components that depend on the kernel can be easily ported by Microsoft to other hardware platforms. A small portion of the kernel, as well as the I/O Manager, accesses the computer hardware directly without involving HAL.

The Kernel layer (refer to figure 2.1) provides the basic operating system functions used by other executive components. The Kernel component is relatively small and provides core operating system functions. The Kernel is primarily responsible for thread scheduling, hardware exception handling, and multiprocessor synchronization.

The Executive components are kernel-mode operating system components that implement services such as managing objects (object manager), security (security reference monitor), process management (process manager), memory management (virtual memory manager), local procedure call facility, and I/O Management (I/O Manager).

The subsystems, also called *environmental subsystems*, are user-mode servers that create and support an operating system environment, such as for DOS/Win16 applications, the OS/2 subsystem, the POSIX subsystem, and a security subsystem.

Windows NT Server Components

The previous section presented an overview of Windows NT's architectural components. The sections that follow discuss the components and the layers in additional detail.

The Hardware Abstraction Layer (HAL)

The Hardware Abstraction Layer software component interfaces directly with the computer hardware and provides the Windows NT kernel layer a machine-independent interface (see fig. 2.2). This machine-independent interface allows the kernel to be written in a machine-independent manner, which promotes the portability of the operating system. The HAL routines can be called by the base operating system and from device drivers.

For computer hardware that uses Symmetric Multi-Processing (SMP), HAL provides a number of virtual processors that can be used by the operating system kernel.

HAL can be used to provide a single device driver interface for the same device on different hardware platforms. Because HAL provides a virtual layer to the computer hardware, the same operating system image can support a large number of variations for a computer based on a specific processor.

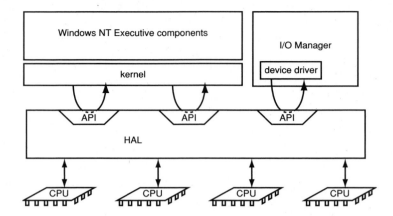

Figure 2.2
The HAL interface.

Kernel Component

The Kernel component is responsible for scheduling tasks for the computer hardware. If the computer hardware consists of multiple processors, the kernel uses the virtual processor's interface provided by the HAL to synchronize activity amongst the processors.

The unit of activity that the Kernel schedules is called a thread. The *thread* is the smallest atomic unit that can be scheduled, and it consists of a sequence of instructions executed by a processor within the context of a process. A process can have multiple threads, and must have at least one thread.

The Kernel dispatches threads on the next available processor. Each thread has a priority associated with it. There are 32 priority levels, divided into a *real-time* class that has priority levels from 16 to 31, and a *variable* (also called dynamic) class that has priority levels from 0 to 15. Higher priority level numbers imply higher priorities for the thread. Threads that have a higher priority level are executed first and can preempt lower priority level threads.

The Kernel is *nonpageable*, which means that the pages (fixed units of 4 KB memory) that belong to the Kernel component are not paged out (not saved temporarily to the page file PAGEFILE.SYS). The software code within the Kernel itself is not preemptive (cannot be interrupted), but the software outside the Kernel component, such as that used in the Windows NT Executive, is preemptive.

The Kernel can run simultaneously on all processors in a computer with multiprocessing hardware, and synchronize access to its critical regions in memory. The policy decisions about how resources are used are removed from the Kernel component and implemented by the Windows NT Executive components. This keeps the Kernel simple, and unchangeable if the operating system policy decisions are changed in future releases of the operating system. The Kernel does, however, make certain policy decisions about when to remove a process from memory.

The Kernel manages two classes of objects: dispatcher objects and control objects. *Dispatcher* objects are used for synchronization and dispatching operations and include objects such as events, semaphores, mutants, mutexes, timers, and threads (see table 2.1). *Control* objects are used for controlling the Kernel operation and do not have an effect on dispatching functions. Kernel control objects include interrupts, processes, profiles, and asynchronous procedure calls (see table 2.2).

Table 2.1
Dispatcher Objects

Object	Description
Event	Used to record the occurrence of an event and associated action that needs to be performed.
Semaphore	Used to control access to a resource. A number associated with a semaphore controls how many simultaneous accesses to the resource are allowed. When a thread accesses the resource, the semaphore number is decremented, and when it becomes zero, no other threads are permitted to access the resource. As threads release the resource, they increment the semaphore number. If the semaphore number is set to 1, only one thread at a time may access the resource.
Mutants	Used for controlling mutual exclusive access to a resource. Mutants can be used in the user mode, as well as the kernel mode, but they are typically designed for use in the user mode.
Mutex	Like mutants, mutexes also are used for controlling mutual exclusive access to a resource. Mutexes, however, can only be used by kernel mode components and are not available in the user mode.
Timer	Used to trigger events and actions at specific times. Timer objects record the passage of time.
Thread	The entity that executes the program code and is dispatched by the kernel to run on any available processor. Threads are owned by a process object and are used to provide concurrent execution behavior for a program.

Table 2.2
Object Controls

Object	Description
Interrupt	Associates an interrupt source with an interrupt service routine through an Interrupt Dispatch Table (IDT). The IDT contains the address of the interrupt service routines and is indexed by the interrupt number.
Process	Provides a virtual address space and environment under which the threads run. A process object must be initialized before any of its thread objects can run.
Profile	Used to record how much time is spent by threads in a block of user or system program code.
Asynchronous procedure call	Used to break into the execution of a specified thread and cause a procedure to be called.

Windows NT Executive Components

Windows NT Executive consists of the following components:

- Object Manager

- Security Reference Monitor

- Process Manager

- Virtual Memory Manager

- Local Procedure Call

- I/O Manager

The following sections discuss the Windows NT Executive components.

Object Manager

All operating system resources are implemented as objects. An object is an abstract representation of a resource. It describes the internal states and parameters of the resource and a set of *methods* (also called *actions* or *procedures*) that can be used to access and control the object. A file object will, for example, have the name of a file, status information on the file, and a list of methods, such as create, open, close, and delete, that describe the operations that can be performed on the file object (see fig. 2.3).

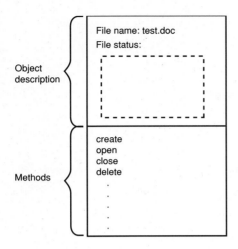

Object description
{
File name: test.doc
File status:

Methods
{
create
open
close
delete

Figure 2.3
The File object.

By treating all resources as objects, Windows NT can implement uniform methods for the following:

■ Creating the object

■ Protecting the object

■ Monitor who is using the object (object clients)

■ Monitor what resources are used by an object

The Object Manager provides a hierarchical naming system for all objects within the system. The object name, therefore, exists as part of a global name space and is used for keeping track of the creation and the use of the object. The following are some examples of the type of Windows NT objects:

■ Directory objects

■ File objects

■ Object type objects

■ Process objects

■ Thread objects

■ Section and segment objects (describes memory)

■ Port objects

■ Semaphore and event objects

■ Symbolic link objects

Security Reference Monitor (SRM)

The Security Reference Monitor is used to implement security in the Windows NT system. Requests for creating an object or accessing an object must pass through the SRM. The SRM determines if access to a resource is allowed. The SRM works with the user-mode security subsystem. The user-mode security subsystem is used for authenticating user logons to the Windows NT system.

All Windows NT objects have a security descriptor, called the Access Control List (ACL), associated with it (see fig. 2.4). The Access Control List consists of individual elements called the Access Control Entry (ACE). Each ACE contains a Security ID (SID) of a user or group. A SID is an internal number used with a Windows NT computer to describe a user and a group uniquely amongst Windows NT computers. In addition to the SID, the ACE contains a list of actions permitted or denied to a user or a group.

Figure 2.4

The Access Control List.

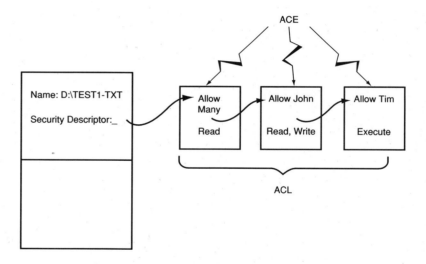

When a user logs on to the Windows NT computer after successful authentication, a Security Access Token (SAT) is created for the user. The SAT contains the SID of the user and the SIDs of all the groups the user belongs to (see fig. 2.5). The SAT then acts as a "passcard" for that user session and is used to verify all user actions.

When the logged-on user accesses an object, the Security Reference Monitor checks the object's security descriptor to see if a SID listed in the SAT matches an ACE entry (see fig. 2.6). If there is a match, the security permissions listed in the matching ACE apply to that user.

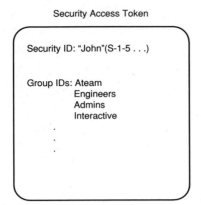

Security Access Token

Figure 2.5
A Security Access Token.

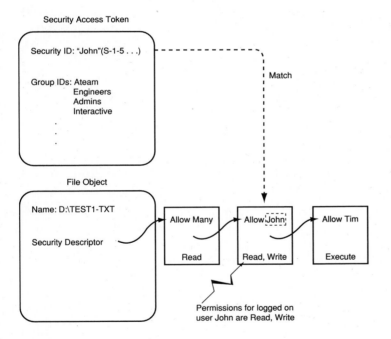

Figure 2.6
Checking an object's permission for a user.

Process Manager

The Process Manager is responsible for process objects and thread objects. A *process* consists of a virtual address space, a set of resources owned by the process, and a set of threads within the process. The thread is the schedulable entity that has its own set of registers, kernel stack, and environment block.

One of the responsibilities of the Process Manager component is to manage the creation and deletion of process objects. It implements APIs that are used for the creation of threads within a process. The policy and rules regarding threads and processes are implemented by the environmental subsystem and not by the Process Manager. The Process Manager does not, for example, enforce a parent/child relationship for a process, but an environmental subsystem, such as POSIX, does.

Virtual Memory Manager (VMM)

The Virtual Memory Manager implements the virtual memory capability within the operating system. Virtual memory enables an operating system to allocate more memory to processes than there is in the physical computer. Each process is allocated a virtual address space, which appears to be 4 GB in size. The first 2 GB of this virtual address space is reserved for the user program, and the remaining 2 GB is reserved for system storage.

The VMM maps the virtual address space to physical pages in the computer's memory (see fig. 2.7). A page is a contiguous memory unit that is 4 KB in size. If additional pages are needed, and all the pages in physical memory are used up, the oldest pages, called the least recently used (LRU) pages, are swapped to disk.

Figure 2.7
The Virtual Memory Manager.

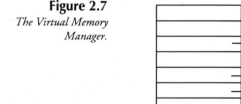

Physical Memory

4 KB

Swap in

LRU algorithm used to determine pages to swap-out

Virtual Address Space

Virtual Memory Manager

disk

Local Procedure Call (LPC)

An environmental subsystem acts as a server, and the applications that use it are the clients of that server. To provide the communication between the clients and servers in the Windows NT computer, the Windows NT Executive implements a message passing facility called the Local Procedure Call.

LPC works in a manner similar to the operation of the Remote Procedure Call (RPC) facility that is used between clients and servers separated by a network. The Windows NT LPC facility is optimized for clients and server processes within the same Windows NT computer (see fig. 2.8).

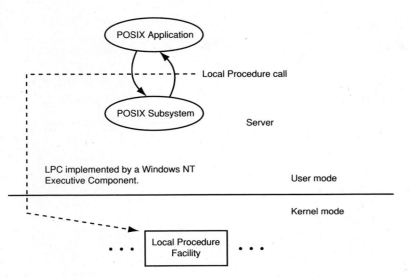

Figure 2.8
The Local Procedure Call.

I/O Manager

The I/O Manager is responsible for all input/output functions within the Windows NT operating system. The I/O Manager communicates with drivers for various devices. To communicate with disk storage devices, for example, the I/O Manager uses the file system drivers.

The I/O Manager uses a layered architecture for drivers. Each driver component in the layer performs a well defined function (see fig. 2.9). This layered approach enables a driver component to be easily replaced without affecting the rest of the driver components.

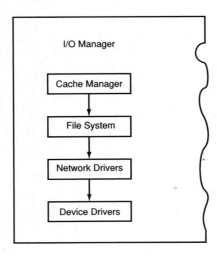

Figure 2.9
The I/O Manager Layered Device Drivers.

Environmental Subsystems

Windows NT was intended to run applications from different operating system architectures. One of the goals of the designers was to allow Windows NT to run existing applications from MS-DOS, OS/2 1.*x*, and Windows 3.*x* environments. In addition, Windows NT supports newer applications written for the Win32 subsystem and the POSIX subsystem.

The Windows NT Executive manages processes and memory. By default, when you run Windows 3.*x* applications, the applications run as tasks within a single process. Each process is protected. The Executive ensures that each process runs in its own memory area, and keeps processes from interfering with one another. If an application fails, the failure does not affect the rest of the OS.

The Win32 Subsystem

The newer 32-bit Windows NT APIs are implemented by the Win32 subsystem. The Win32 manages keyboard and mouse inputs and display outputs for all subsystems. In fact, other subsystems, such as DOS/Win16, POSIX, and OS/2, are all clients of the Win32 subsystem because they make use of Win32 API calls to implement their functionality.

The Win32 subsystem uses a desynchronized input model for Win32 applications and a synchronized model for Windows 3.*x* applications (see fig. 2.10). The use of these models is consistent with the expected behavior of the Win32 and Windows 3.*x* applications.

Figure 2.10

Synchronized and desynchronized model support in the Win32 subsystem.

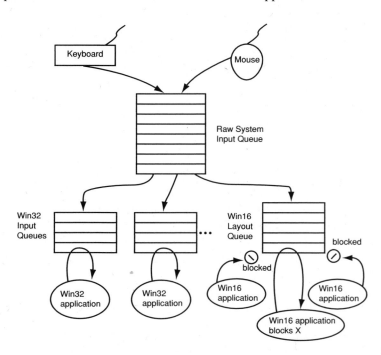

In the desynchronized model used in the Win32 subsystem, all messages from input devices, such as a keyboard and a mouse, are stored in a single raw system input queue. The Win32 subsystem transfers the message from this system input queue to the appropriate Win32 application queue. If an application stops retrieving its messages, other messages in other application queues are not affected.

In the synchronized model used in the Win16-based applications, all applications use a single queue. Because of the synchronized nature of the model, however, the messages are always retrieved in the order in which they are received by the queue. If a Win16 application ceases to retrieve its messages, all other Win16 applications are blocked.

MS-DOS Environment

MS-DOS applications are run in the context of a Virtual DOS Machine (VDM). The VDM is a Win32 application that emulates a complete virtual $x86$ (386 or higher) computer running MS-DOS. Apart from the physical resources that the Win32 VDM applications consumes, there is no limit to the number of VDMs that can run. After a VDM is created, the VDM is not destroyed, even if the MS-DOS application exits. When an MS-DOS application is run, an unused VDM is used if one is available. If all the VDMs are in use, a new VDM is created.

Because the VDM emulates a $x86$ processor in the Virtual-86 mode, most instructions in the MS-DOS application can be directly executed within the VDM. Instructions that involve I/O are emulated because direct execution of I/O instructions would bypass the device drivers used in the I/O Manager.

On a RISC processor there is no hardware support for executing $x86$ instructions directly; therefore, the $x86$ instructions are emulated. On an $x86$-based Windows NT computer, character-based applications can run in a window or full screen, but graphical applications can run only in full-screen. If an application that runs in a window changes the video mode, it is automatically switched to full-screen. On RISC-based Windows NT computers, character-based and graphical applications run only in a window.

The virtual computer environment created by a VDM has the following features:

- Execution of $x86$ instructions provided by the Instruction Execution Unit (IEU)

- ROM BIOS services provided by the MS-DOS emulation mode

- MS-DOS Interrupt 21 services provided in the MS-DOS emulation mode

- Virtual hardware support for screen and keyboard provided by Virtual Device Drivers (VDDs)

Figure 2.11 illustrates the environment created by the VDM.

Figure 2.11
MS-DOS VDM.

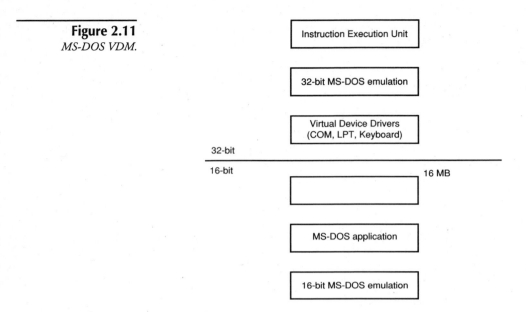

Windows 16-Bit Environment

Because existing Windows 3.*x* applications run on top of DOS, Windows NT uses a single multithreaded VDM to run 16-bit applications. Within the VDM, WIN16 applications use non-preemptive multitasking to emulate the behavior of Windows 3.*x* on DOS. The Win16 VDM, however, is itself preemptively multitasked with respect to other Win32 processes running in the system.

The Win16 VDM provides stubs for the Windows 3.*x* kernel, Graphical Device Interface (GDI) DLLs, and translation of Windows 3.*x* APIs and messages (see fig. 2.12). Win16 support on the Win32 subsystem is also known as Windows on Windows (WOW).

OS/2 Subsystem

The OS/2 subsystem supports OS/2 1.*x* character-based applications on *x*86. The OS/2 subsystem does not support the OS/2 Presentation Manager GUI or the Warp versions of OS/2. The OS/2 subsystem is not supported on RISC platforms, but OS/2 real-mode applications can run on a Windows NT computer in the MS-DOS environment.

Portable Operating System Interface for Computing Environments (POSIX) Subsystem

The Windows NT POSIX subsystem was designed to be compliant with POSIX.1 applications. POSIX is a set of standards developed by the Institute of Electrical and Electronic

Engineers (IEEE). POSIX.1 is just one of these standards and is also known by the designation IEEE Standard 1003.1-1990.

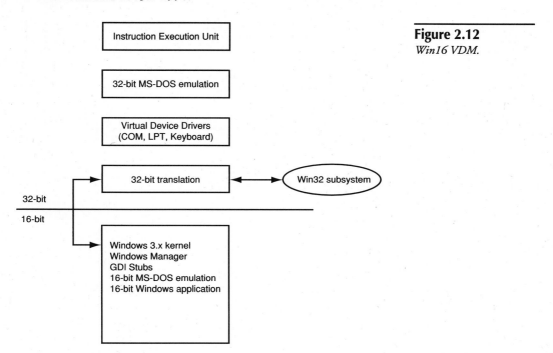

Figure 2.12
Win16 VDM.

The POSIX.1 specification deals with C-language API calls between an application and the operating system. The APIs are based on the Unix system calls. POSIX.1 does not deal with security or networking issues. Many real-world applications use non-POSIX APIs for security and networking. This makes POSIX.1 applications only partially portable to an operating system such as Windows NT.

POSIX.1 requires support for case-sensitive file names and file name aliasing (hard links). The NTFS file system supports these POSIX requirements.

Conclusion

Windows NT operating is a preemptive multitasking operating system with security and networking built in to the operating system. Windows NT uses layering and a client/server model to build its environmental subsystems.

The environmental subsystems provide support for applications, such as DOS, Windows 3.*x*, and OS/2 1.*x* character-mode applications, to run on a Windows NT computer. The POSIX environmental subsystem provides support for applications that are compliant with POSIX.1.

Windows NT Server Administration

3

Installing Windows NT Server

In this chapter, you examine installation issues for the Windows NT Server. Before you learn about Windows NT Server installation issues, however, you need to examine some background material to help you better understand the installation process.

Windows NT Server is designed to run on IBM PC ATs that have an Intel 80486 microprocessor or higher (Intel 80486, Pentium, or Pentium Pro) and other RISC processors such as the MIPS, Power PC, and Alpha. On the Intel architecture, Windows NT runs in the protected mode *of the Intel chip. In this area, the entire address space of the Intel 80486 architecture is available. The Intel 80486 processor has 32 address lines, creating an address space (RAM size) of 2 to the 32nd power, or 4 GB. This address space enables the Windows NT Server operating system to implement many of its performance-improvement features directly in RAM.*

Most server machines do not have 4 GB of physical memory. In this case, Windows NT Server uses virtual memory to temporarily "swap" sections of memory in chunks of 4 KB onto the server hard disk. The Windows NT Server keeps track of the sections of memory that have been swapped out. If the Windows NT Server operating system or an application running on it needs the memory data/program code that has been swapped out, the operating system brings the data back into physical memory. This enables the applications to run on Windows NT servers that have limited physical memory. Ideally, the server's physical memory should be large enough to run the operating system and the server applications so that swapping to disk is eliminated or kept at a minimum. This minimizes the server-swapping overhead.

Planning a Windows NT Server Installation

During the installation of Windows NT Server, you are asked to make a number of selections. Making the proper selection requires knowledge of Windows NT Server concepts. The sections that follow discuss the concepts needed for installing Windows NT Server.

Windows NT Server Requirements

Figure 3.1 shows the hardware and software components that you should understand in order to understand Windows NT Server. Table 3.1 summarizes the hardware system requirements.

Figure 3.1

Windows NT Server hardware components.

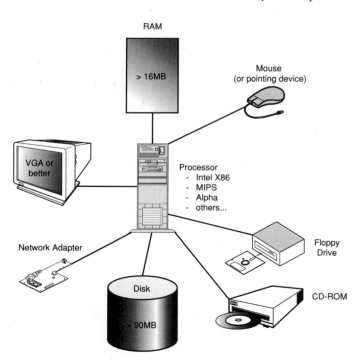

Table 3.1
Hardware Requirements for Windows NT Server

Component	Requirement
Processor	Intel 486, Pentium, Pentium Pro, or supported RISC-based system (example: MIPS R4x00, DEC's Alpha AXP). Windows NT supports up to 4 processors in a Symmetrical Multi-Processing (SMP) mode. Support for additional processors is available from OEMs (Original Equipment Manufacturers).
Display device	VGA or higher resolution.
Hard disk	Minimum 110 MB free disk space during installation for Intel-based systems. Minimum 110 MB free disk space for RISC-based systems.
Floppy disks	For Intel-based systems, a 3 $1/2$-inch, high density drive or a 5 $1/4$-inch, high density drive. These are needed to start the installation by booting from a Setup disk.
CD-ROM	CD-ROM drive or access to a CD-ROM over a computer network.
Network adapters	One or more network adapters. Strictly speaking, network adapters are optional, but without the network adapter, networking features are disabled and cannot be configured.
Memory	16 MB recommended minimum for both Intel- and RISC-based systems. The more the better. Windows NT Server uses virtual memory when more memory is needed to run applications than is physically available. Excessive use of virtual memory can adversely impact server performance.
Pointing device	A mouse or other pointing device, although optional, is highly recommended. Windows NT Server tools are GUI-based, and a mouse is helpful for using these tools.

Windows NT Server supports more than 2,350 Intel-based single processor systems. The Hardware Compatibility List document that ships with Windows NT Server contains a list of systems for which Windows NT Server is tested. You can access the most recent list of Windows NT Server-compatible systems at Microsoft's Web site, or via various newsgroups.

Windows NT Server SCSI Support

Windows NT Server supports the SCSI interface devices such as CD-ROMs, tape drives, and hard drives, as well as numerous non-SCSI devices. For uniformity of hardware access to these peripheral devices, it is recommended that you use a server that has a supported SCSI adapter. This will simplify the installation and hardware maintenance of the system.

SCSI devices from most major manufacturers such as CD-Technology, Chinon, COMPAQ, Digital Equipment Corporation, Hitachi, IBM, NEC, Panasonic, Pioneer, Sony, Texel, Toshiba, and Adaptec are supported. The SCSI (Small Computer Systems Interface) was developed by Adaptec and became an ANSI standard in 1982. It provides a logical bus interface based on the block multiplexor channel of IBM mainframe. Up to eight SCSI devices can be daisy-chained on a common bus (see fig. 3.2). Each SCSI device (including the SCSI controller) has a unique ID (identifier). The SCSI controller's ID is usually set to 7 on Intel-based machines, and the bootable SCSI hard drive is set to a SCSI ID of 0. The SCSI bus can operate at data rates from 7.5 Mbps to 80 Mbps and has increasingly become a popular device interface for large storage disks for workstations and servers.

Figure 3.2
An example of SCSI devices daisy-chained together.

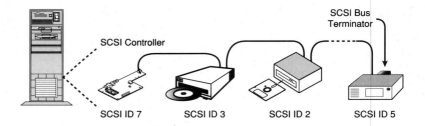

Another advantage of using the SCSI interface is that you can use it to support SCSI tape drives, which are important for backup operations for the Windows NT Server.

Another type of storage media that can be supported using the SCSI interface is removable media, such as cartridge or floptical drives.

Windows NT Server also supports SCSI scanners for the Intel platforms only. The devices that are supported include the HP ScanJet models IIC, IICx, and IIp.

For higher performance and reliability, Windows NT Server supports RAID SCSI disk drives.

Windows NT Server IDE Support

For Intel-based systems, standard PC disk drives are supported. Standard PC disk drives were developed by Shugart (now Seagate) Technologies and support a maximum of two drives per controller. The typical data rate for these drives is 4 Mbps, and 5 Mbps with extended BIOS (EIDE). Many current high performance EIDE drives support data rates of 20–32 Mbps.

Most standard PC drives now support the IDE (Integrated Device Electronics) interface developed by Conner Corp. in 1988. The IDE interface uses the same device interface as the Shugart drive but integrates device adapter electronics on the motherboard and the hard disk.

This results in improved performance compared to the standard PC disk drives (also called ISA/EISA disk drives).

Windows NT Server ESDI Support

Another type of disk drive that is supported by Windows NT Server is ESDI (Enhanced Small Devices Interface). ESDI was introduced by Maxtor Corp. in 1983. The ESDI interface was conceived for the minicomputer environment and supports data rates in the range of 10 Mbps to 24 Mbps.

The ESDI interface has an improved clock mechanism and track buffering compared to the standard PC disk drives. ESDI drives typically are found on older, Intel-based systems. In modern systems, most ESDI drives have been replaced by SCSI drives.

Windows NT Server Non-SCSI, CD-ROM Drives

Although a SCSI interface is recommended for high performance Windows NT Server systems, there are a large number of computers that use proprietary interfaces for CD-ROMs.

Windows NT Server Support for Display Chip Set

Windows NT Server supports most video adapter types that are at least VGA quality or better. Although there are many different video adapter types, they use some popular chip sets. If your video adapter type is not listed in the Windows NT Server installation disks, you can use table 3.2 to select the appropriate driver using the Display option in the Windows NT Server Control Panel.

Table 3.2
Display Chip Set and Display Driver

Chip Set	Compatible NT Driver
ATI 8514 Ultra	8514A
ATI MACH 8, 32, 64	ATI
Cirrus Logic 5422, 5424, 5426, 5428, 5434	CIRRUS
Compaq AVGA	AVGA
Compaq Qvision 1024, 1280	QV
Compaq Qvision 2000	MGA
Headlands Video 7	V7VRAM

continues

Table 3.2, Continued
Display Chip Set and Display Driver

Chip Set	Compatible NT Driver
IBM 8514/a	8514A
IBM XGA	XGA
Matrox MGA (ATLAS)	MGA
NCR77C22, NCR77C22E, NCR BLT 32	NCR77C22
S3 911, 911a, 924, 801, 805, 928, 864, 964	S3
Trident 9000, 8900c	TRIDENT
Tseng Labs ET4000, ET4000-W32i, pET4000-W32	ET4000
Western Digital WD90C30, WD90C31, WD90C33	WDVGA
Witek P9000	WITEKP9

Windows NT Server Support for Network Adapters

Windows NT Server supports most network adapters from vendors such as 3COM, AMD, Andrew, Cabletron, Cisco, Cogent, COMPAQ, COPS, Crescendo, DayStar, DCA, DEC, Hewlett-Packard, IBM, ICL, Intel, National Semiconductor, Intel, Madge, NCR, Network Peripherals, Novell/Eagle Technologies, Olicom, Proteon, Standard Microsystems, Thomas Conrad, Ungermann-Bass, and Xircom.

Most of the card types are Ethernet and Token Ring (most of these cards are Ethernet). There also is support for some FDDI and ARCnet network adapters.

For Computer laptop and notebook owners, the Xircom CreditCard Adapter (PCMCIA) and the Xircom Pocket Ethernet Adapters II and III are supported.

Windows NT Server Support for Multimedia Audio Adapters

Windows NT Server supports multimedia audio adapters for Intel, MIPS, and Alpha platforms.

Windows NT Server Software Distribution

The Windows NT Server distribution is available on floppy disks (3 ½-inch, high density) for Intel platforms and only on CD-ROM for RISC platforms. The CD-ROM distribution also is available for Intel platforms. The preferred installation method is through CD-ROM or by using preconfigured distribution files stored on a network server. If the CD-ROM method is used on the Intel platform, you also must use the three Setup disks that come with the Windows NT Server distribution unless you use the /B switch with WINNT (or WINNT32) to avoid using the Setup disks. The first Setup disk is bootable and is used to start the Windows NT Server installation.

Understanding Windows NT Server Installation

The following sections explain the necessary concepts for understanding the Windows NT Server installation.

These steps also are summarized for your reference:

1. Boot with Windows NT Server Setup disk, or use the WINNT /B command from the I386 (for Intel-based computers) directory on the CD-ROM distribution. If you are upgrading a previous version of NT 3.5x, run the WINNT32 command, and select your installation options.

2. Select the source media type. For Intel platforms, you can select the floppy distribution installation or the CD-ROM installation. If Setup recognizes a CD-ROM drive, it suggests that you use the CD-ROM method.

3. Verify and, if necessary, change the software and hardware components recognized by Setup.

4. Select the partition on which Windows NT Server is to be installed. You must decide between the file system types such as FAT and NTFS.

5. (Optional) Format the selected partition.

6. Select the default directory in which the Windows NT Server files will be installed.

7. Enter your name and organization.

8. Select the Licensing Mode. Choices are Per Server, and Per Seat.

9. Enter a unique computer name.

10. Decide on the security role of the server computer. Choices are Primary Domain Controller (PDC), Backup Domain Controller (BDC), and Stand-Alone Server.

11. Enter the password for the Administrator Account.

12. Select the option to create an emergency repair disk.

13. Select Components to install. Choices are Accessibility Options, Accessories, Communications, Games, Microsoft Exchange, and Multimedia.

14. Decide how the computer should participate on the network. Choices are Wired to the Network, and Remote Access to the Network.

15. (Optional) Select Install Microsoft Internet Information Server.

16. Decide on the method of detection of network adapters: autodetect or manual. Some network adapters—such as the Xircom CreditCard and the Xircom Pocket Ethernet adapter—only can be selected manually.

17. Select the network protocols to be used with the NIC. The choices are TCP/IP Protocol, NWLink IPX/SPX Compatible Transport, and NetBEUI Protocol.

18. Select Network Services. Choices are Microsoft Internet Information Server, RPC Configuration, NetBIOS Interface, Workstation, Server. By default, all of these options are selected.

19. Enter NIC parameters such as IRQ (interrupt request) number, IO port address, memory base address, DMA line, and so on.

20. If the NWLink IPX/SPX or TCP/IP Transport protocol was selected, you must configure them.

21. If you selected the server computer as a primary domain controller, you must enter the Computer Name, and the name of the domain that the PDC will manage.

22. If you chose to install the Internet Information Server, you will need to select and configure its component options.

23. Select Date/Time Properties. Set date, time, and time-zone information.

24. Select the Display Properties settings.

25. Create the Emergency Repair Disk.

Windows NT Server Installation Concepts

During the Windows NT Server installation, you are asked to make decisions involving the following:

- Determining type of file system: FAT or NTFS

- Determining security role of computer: primary, secondary domain controller, or stand-alone server

- Selecting a computer name

- Selecting the language (locale) settings

- NIC parameters: IRQ, DMA, IO Port, and Base Address

- Choice of protocol stacks: SPX/IPX, NetBEUI, or TCP/IP

- Time-zone information

These topics are discussed next.

Selecting the Type of File System for Windows NT Server

Windows NT Server can be installed on a partition formatted with FAT (File Allocation Table), or NTFS (NT File System). While installing the NT Server, you can install on an existing file system or a new file system. You can format a partition with FAT or NTFS.

The FAT File System

The FAT file system is the standard file system used for DOS/Windows computers. The *File Allocation Table* is a table of links that contain information on the data blocks that make up a file. All the files on a FAT partition share the same table of links, as illustrated in figure 3.3. The data blocks usually are allocated in clusters of four 512-byte units; therefore, each allocation unit is typically 2 KB.

The directory contains entries for file names and their attributes, such as file size, attribute byte (8 bits of information—archive file, system file, hidden file, read only), modification time (16 bits), modification date (16 bits), and starting allocation unit. The *starting allocation unit* is a pointer to an entry in the File Allocation Table.

In figure 3.3, for file example1.txt, the directory entry points to the first allocation unit in block 0002. Block 0002 in the FAT contains the entry 0009, which is a link to block 0009. Block 0009 contains the hexadecimal pattern FFFF. This bit pattern indicates that this is the end of the block chain. This means that allocation units 0002 and 0009 belong to the file example1.txt. Similarly, the file example2.txt's allocation chain is 0001, 0003, 0004, and 0007; and file example3.txt's allocation chain is 0008, 0005, and 0006.

As files are deleted and created, the FAT file system gets fragmented and the FAT chain must point to the correct allocation units for the file. The FAT file system is a simple file system originally designed for small disk and simple file system structures. In fact, the FAT file system was designed with the first version of DOS 1.0 that did not support subdirectories. Over the years, the FAT file system has been improved to accommodate larger disks. Beginning with DOS 4.0, the 12-bit FAT entries were increased to 16-bit entries to allow for partitions that were larger than 32 MB.

Figure 3.3
A File Allocation Table.

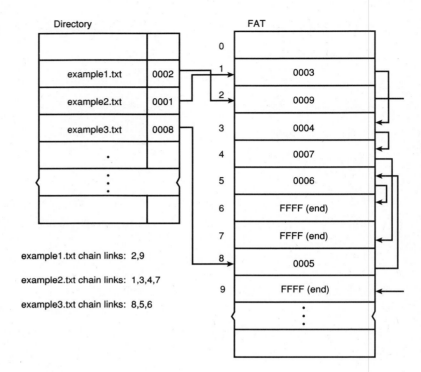

Figure 3.4 shows the FAT file system organization. The FAT is duplicated to provide a rudimentary level of fault tolerance. The root directory has a fixed size, and this limits the number of files that can be placed in the root directory. Subdirectories are special files that have 32-byte entries for each file in that directory. On a large disk, with heavy file use, the FAT file system can get fragmented and the performance is slower as the FAT table increases in size. Also, as the length of a FAT chain increases, the operating system has to traverse many entries in the FAT chain to access a random block of data in a file. Another limitation of the FAT is that it has the 8.3 (eight-character file name and three-character extension) naming convention, and lacks recoverability and security features.

You use FAT with Windows NT in order to have a compatible file system with DOS. However, you should be aware that disk-compression software such as DoubleSpace or Stacker is not compatible with Windows NT. If a disk has been compressed using these tools, the files cannot be accessed from Windows NT.

The NTFS File System

NTFS is the preferred file system for Windows NT. It includes a number of performance-enhancing, file-security, and recoverability features that make Windows NT Server a good server platform. NTFS can be used to assign permissions to files and directories on a user or group basis. This feature enables files and directories to be shared or kept private, and it provides the flexibility of implementing virtually any security policy.

In NTFS, files are treated as objects that have user- and system-defined attributes. These attributes are stored in the file itself. The file system information (metadata)—such as file name, file size, data, security descriptor, and so on—is part of the file, for example. Each attribute is defined by an attribute code and an optional attribute name.

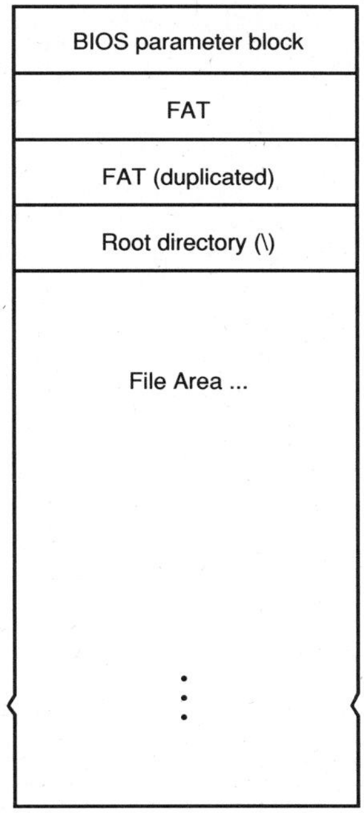

Figure 3.4
FAT disk partition organization.

Each NTFS volume has a Master File Table (MFT). An *MFT* is a special file that has information on files on the volume (see fig. 3.5). The first record is the MFT descriptor record, which describes the Master File Table itself. The second record is a duplicate of the first record, and is the MFT mirror record. The MFT mirror record provides redundancy of the MFT description in case the primary MFT record is corrupted. The locations of the data segments of the MFT record and its mirror are recorded in the boot sector. The boot sector is duplicated, and the duplicate is kept in the logical center of the volume.

The third record in the MFT is the Log File record, which is used for file recovery. After the first 16 records, follow the records that describe files and directories. If a file or directory is sufficiently small (approximately 1,500 bytes or less), it can be placed entirely in the MFT table. This is illustrated in figure 3.5 by the small file record and the small directory record, which do not have any extents. If a file or directory is large and cannot be placed entirely in the MFT table, extents are used for the additional data. Extents are external clusters in the volume, with pointers to it kept in the MFT table.

For small files, data access is rapid because a single lookup in the MFT retrieves all information on the file. Compare this to a FAT system where the FAT table would have to be accessed, and then the allocation chain for the file would have to be retrieved as separate disk-access operations. Directories are represented in a manner similar to ordinary files, except that the directory contains indices to file information. Although small directories are contained entirely in the MFT table, larger directories are organized as B-trees that are contained in extents. All information on a file, including its data, is called the *attributes* of a file. When a file or directory's attributes are contained entirely in the MFT, they are called *resident* attributes. The attributes of a file (such as data) that are kept in extents are called *nonresident* attributes. Table 3.3 shows the attributes that have been defined for NTFS.

Figure 3.5

The master file table (MFT).

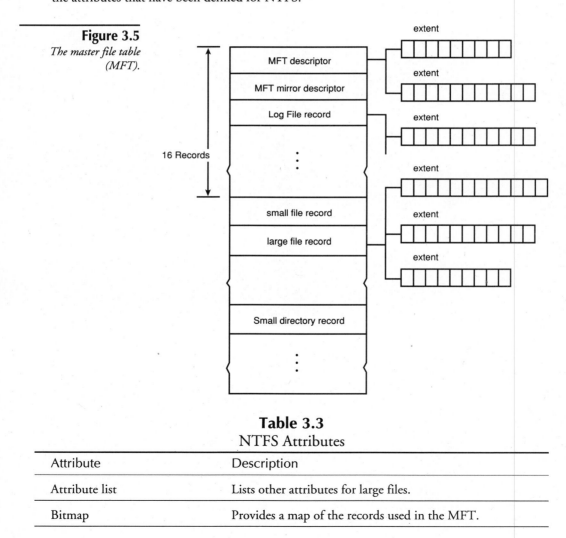

Table 3.3
NTFS Attributes

Attribute	Description
Attribute list	Lists other attributes for large files.
Bitmap	Provides a map of the records used in the MFT.

Attribute	Description
Data	Contains the file's data. A file has one unnamed data attribute. Optionally, you can give a file additional name data attributes by using a special syntax.
Extended attribute information	Used by file servers that are linked to OS/2 systems. Not used in Windows NT.
Extended attributes	Used by file servers that are linked to OS/2 systems. Not used in Windows NT.
File name	A file can have multiple file-name attributes such as short file names and long file names. Short file names are DOS-compatible, case-insensitive names for files that follow the 8.3 rule. Long file names can contain up to 255 unicode characters. The use of short file names also permits the NTFS file system to be accessed from DOS stations across a network. Additional names for POSIX compliance, such as hard and symbolic links, are considered as file-name attributes.
Index allocation	Used to implement index (?) directories.
Index root	Used to implement index (?) for the root.
Security descriptor	Shows security-related information such as permissions and ownership.
Standard attributes	Refers to time stamps, link counts (for POSIX file system support), file size, and so on.
Volume information	Attribute used for the volume system file. It contains a version number, volume name, and other volume-related information.

NTFS uses special system files that are hidden from view on the NTFS volume. These system files are used to store the volume's metadata and are created when the volume is formatted. Table 3.4 shows some of the system files.

Table 3.4
NTFS System Files

System File Name	Description
$.	Root file name index. This is the root directory.
$AttrDef	Attribute definition. Contains attribute names, numbers, and descriptions.

continues

Table 3.4, Continued
NTFS System Files

System File Name	Description
$BadClus	Bad cluster file. A table containing location of all the bad clusters in the volume.
$Bitmap	Cluster bitmap. This is a map of the allocation units that are in use for the volume.
$Boot	Boot file. This contains the bootstrap program for a bootable volume.
$LogFile	Log file. Used to record transaction steps that are used for recoverability purposes.
$Mft	Master file table (MFT). Lists the contents of an NTFS volume in which the file resides.
$MftMirr	A mirror of the critical parts of the MFT for redundancy purposes.
$Volume	Contains volume-related information such as volume name and version.

You can format any hard disk partition as a FAT or NTFS volume. You cannot format a floppy disk as an NTFS volume, however. The file system type can be established during installation. You also can use the FORMAT utility to specify the file system type option, or you can use the CONVERT utility to convert from FAT to NTFS. The use of these utilities is discussed next.

You must be a member of the Administrators group (the Windows NT group that lists all Administrator users) to format a hard drive. The syntax of the FORMAT command follows:

```
format drive: [/fs:fst] [/v[:label]] [/a:usize] [/q] [/f:size] [/t:tracks
➥/n:sectors] [/1] [/4] [/8]
```

Explanations of this syntax follow:

- **drive:** specifies the drive to be formatted. If the switches are not specified, FORMAT uses the drive type to determine the default format for the disk.

- **/fs:fst** specifies a value of FAT or NTFS for the corresponding file system type. Floppy disks can be formatted with a FAT file system only.

- **/v:label** specifies the volume label.

- **/a:usize** specifies the allocation unit size to use on NTFS disks. If the unit size is not specified, it is chosen based on disk size. The default is 512 bytes if the disk is less than 512 MB; 1,024 bytes if the disk is between 512 MB and 1 GB; 2,048 bytes if the disk is between 1 GB and 2 GB; and 4,096 bytes if the disk is more than 2 GB. A unit size of 512 bytes creates 512 bytes per cluster and 1,024 bytes per file record; a unit size of 1,024 bytes creates 1,024 bytes per cluster and 1,024 bytes per file record; a unit size of 2,048 bytes creates 2,048 bytes per cluster and 2,048 bytes per file record; and a unit size of 4,096 bytes creates 4,096 bytes per cluster and 4,096 bytes per file record.

■ **/q** deletes the file table and the root directory of a formatted disk, but does not scan the disk for bad areas. This is a quick format that should be used to format only previously formatted disks that you know are in good condition.

■ **/f:size** specifies the size of the floppy disk to format. The floppy disk sizes are listed in table 3.5.

Table 3.5
Floppy Disk /F Value

Parameter Value for /F	Floppy Disk Type
160 KB	160 KB, single-sided, double-density, 5 $\frac{1}{4}$-inch disk
180 KB	180 KB, single-sided, double-density, 5 $\frac{1}{4}$-inch disk
320 KB	320 KB, double-sided, double-density, 5 $\frac{1}{4}$-inch disk
360 KB	360 KB, double-sided, double-density, 5 $\frac{1}{4}$-inch disk
720 KB	720 KB, double-sided, double-density, 3 $\frac{1}{4}$-inch disk
1200 KB or 1.2 MB	1.2 MB, double-sided, quadruple-density, 5 $\frac{1}{4}$-inch disk
1440 KB or 1.44 MB	1.44 MB, double-sided, quadruple-density, 3 $\frac{1}{2}$-inch disk
2880 KB or 2.88 MB	2.88 MB, double-sided, 3 $\frac{1}{2}$-inch disk
20.8 MB	20.8 MB, 3 $\frac{1}{2}$-inch floptical disk

■ **/t:tracks** specifies the number of tracks on the disk. If you use the /t switch, you also must use the /n switch for sector size. The /t and /n switches provide an alternative method of specifying the size of the disk to be formatted. You cannot use the /f switch with the /t switch.

■ **/n:sectors** specifies the number of sectors per track. If you use the /n switch, you also must use the /t switch for number of tracks. The /n and /t switches provide an alternative method of specifying the size of the disk to be formatted. You cannot use the /f switch with the /n switch.

■ **/1** formats a single side of a floppy disk.

■ **/4** formats a 5 ¹/₄-inch, 360 KB, double-sided, double-density floppy disk on a 1.2 MB disk drive. When combined with the /1 switch, this switch formats a 5 ¹/₄-inch, 180 KB, single-sided floppy disk.

■ **/8** formats a 5 ¹/₄-inch disk with eight sectors per track. This switch formats a floppy disk to be compatible with MS-DOS versions prior to 2.0.

The CONVERT utility can be used to convert FAT volume to NTFS. You cannot convert the current drive, because the current drive is in use and cannot be locked. If CONVERT cannot lock the drive, it offers to convert it the next time the computer reboots. The syntax of the CONVERT command follows:

```
convert [drive:] /fs:ntfs [/v] [/nametable:filename]
```

Explanations of this syntax follow:

■ **drive:** specifies the drive that is to be converted to NTFS.

■ **/fs:ntfs** specifies to convert the volume to NTFS.

■ **/v** specifies verbose mode, in which details of the conversion process are displayed during conversion.

■ **/nametable:filename** creates a name-translation table in the root directory of the converted volume using the specified file name. You can use this switch if you encounter difficulty converting files with unusual file names.

You cannot convert from NTFS to FAT without backing up files, reformatting the partition, and restoring the backed up files. You will lose any security-related permissions associated with the directories and files.

Comparing the FAT and NTFS

Table 3.6 compares the features of FAT and NTFS.

Table 3.6
Comparison of FAT, HPFS, NTFS

Feature	FAT	NTFS
File name	8 plus 3 (8.3) character limit. Only single period allowed	255, 16-bit unicode characters with multiple periods allowed
Maximum path length	64	No limit

Feature	FAT	NTFS
File size	2^{32} bytes	2^{64} bytes
Partition	2^{32} bytes	2^{64} bytes
Directories	Unsorted	B-tree
Attribute	Few bit flags	All information, including data, is treated as attributes
Built-in security NTFS directory/file permissions	No	Yes
Design approach	Simple	Fast access with recoverability and security

You should select the NTFS partition instead of FAT except in the following situations:

■ Choose the FAT partition if you want the partition to be accessible from DOS, OS/2, and NTFS. In this situation, you have multiple operating systems installed on your computer.

■ If you are installing on an existing partition, choose the default option to keep the current files intact. After the installation is successful, you can convert to other partition types.

Tables 3.7 and 3.8 point out the relative advantages of each partition type.

Table 3.7
Advantages and Disadvantage of NTFS

Advantages	Disadvantages
Supports files and directories with up to 255 extended attributes.	NTFS is recognizable only by Windows NT. If you have multiple character names and operating systems installed on your computer,

continues

Table 3.7, Continued
Advantages and Disadvantage of NTFS

Advantages	Disadvantages
	the other systems cannot recognize the operating NTFS.
Automatically generates short DOS-compatible file names. Built-in reliability, because of log of activities kept in the log file. The log file can be used to restore files in the event of disk problems. Built-in security that enables you to specify permission on directories and files. DOS and OS/2 programs that run under the Windows NT DOS and OS/2 subsystems can access the NTFS volume.	

Table 3.8
Advantages and Disadvantage of FAT

Advantages	Disadvantages
Enables files to be accessed by DOS/Windows 3.1, OS/2, and Windows NT.	Less robust than Windows NT.
Most widely used file system for PCs.	Cannot support long file names.
	No built-in security for directories and files.

Selecting the Security Role of the NT Server Computer

A Windows NT Server computer can be set up as a primary or backup domain controller for a Windows NT domain, or as an ordinary server computer. During installation, you must select the security role served by the Windows NT computer.

A Windows NT *domain* is a group of servers that share a user accounts database and have a common security policy (see fig. 3.6). Because the user accounts database is shared in the domain, it is only necessary to define a user account for the entire domain rather than to define user accounts for each Windows NT Server. This greatly simplifies user account administration.

A server can belong to only one domain. One of the servers in the domain acts as the main or primary domain controller (PDC); the other servers act as backup domain controllers (BDCs). If the server belongs to a domain, it can either be a primary domain controller or a backup domain controller. There can be only one PDC per domain. Any one of the other servers that act as BDCs can be promoted to PDC in case of failure of the primary domain controller. This promotion is not done automatically; it is performed as a result of explicit actions taken by the network administrator. Both primary and backup domain controllers can authenticate network logons.

The PDC maintains the centralized security database of the domain. This security database is replicated to other BDCs on a periodic basis.

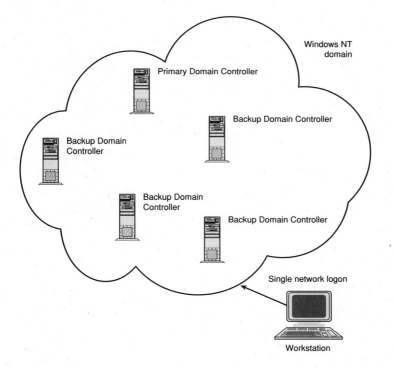

Figure 3.6
The Windows NT domain.

If your Windows NT Server is the first computer on the network, and you intend to use domains on your network, you must designate this server as a PDC. If your Windows NT server is not the first server in the domain, you must have at least a PDC connected to the network. You can designate the Windows NT Server as a BDC, in which case you must know the administrator password for the domain in order to join the domain. Knowledge of the password for the Administrator domain account is necessary; otherwise, anyone can install a Windows NT Server and have it join the domain. This can lead to chaos on real-life networks.

Selecting a Computer Name

As part of the Windows NT Server installation, you must specify a name that identifies your computer to the network. This must be a name that cannot exceed 15 characters and must be unique on the network. This name is used by NetBIOS, and the 15-character limitation is a NetBIOS limitation.

If you select a duplicate computer name, you can change it from the Network applet in the Windows NT Server Control Panel (see figs. 3.7 and 3.8).

Figure 3.7

The Network applet in the Control Panel.

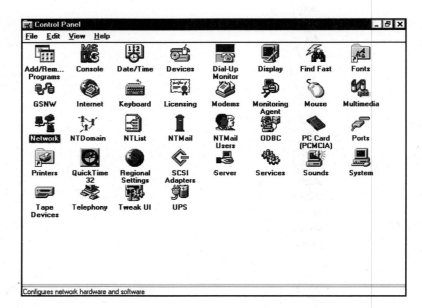

Table 3.9 shows the list of characters that should not be used for computer names. Using these characters can cause unexpected results when trying to access your computer over the network. In addition, you should not use spaces in computer names for servers to be used as domain controllers if you plan on using log-in scripts.

Table 3.9
Characters to Avoid for Computer Names

Character	Key Combination Used to Produce the Character
Bullet	Alt+0149
Currency sign	Alt+0164
Broken vertical bar	Alt+0166

Character	Key Combination Used to Produce the Character
Section sign	Alt+0167
Paragraph sign (MS Word)	Alt+0182

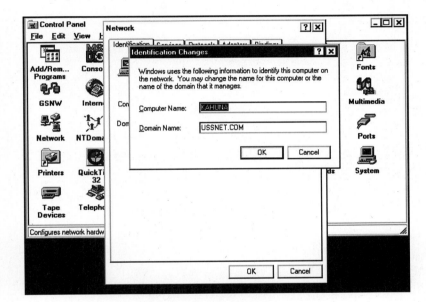

Figure 3.8

The Identification Changes dialog box.

Selecting the Language Settings

During installation, you must select the Time and Date, Time Zone or locale to be used on the Windows NT Server computer. This choice determines how the Windows NT Server formats date, timestamp, and currency information. You can change the language after setup is complete by running the Regional Settings applet from the Control Panel (see figs. 3.9 and 3.10).

You also can selectively change the date, time, currency, and number format regardless of the locale settings used.

Selecting NIC Parameters

Windows NT Server supports built-in networking. During installation, it tries to recognize any network boards on the server computer. Alternatively, you can manually select the network board type installed in the computer.

Figure 3.9

The Regional Settings icon in the Control Panel.

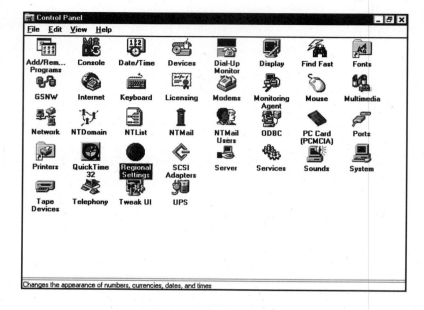

Figure 3.10

The Regional Settings dialog box for changing locale settings.

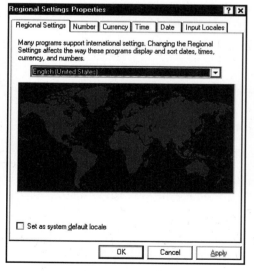

The network interface cards (NICs), are characterized by parameter settings such as IRQ number, I/O port address, DMA channel, and memory base address. On computers with an ISA bus, you must select these settings to avoid conflicts with other peripheral cards and devices that you are using in the computer.

The NIC parameters can be set manually by jumper settings or through software. The software usually is shipped by the vendor with the NIC. Most configuration software for NICs is DOS- or Windows-based.

A model for a network adapter is shown in figure 3.11. Data encapsulated in packets is transferred between the network and the CPU through the computer bus and the NIC. To encode signals suitably for transmission, the NIC provides a transmitter/receiver function. After the packet signal is received from the network, it is encoded as a bit pattern and stored in the NIC's data buffers. The adapter logic implements the media-access method used by the network (CSMA/CD for Ethernet, and token passing for Token Ring). The adapter logic also controls the transfer of network data by way of the computer's bus.

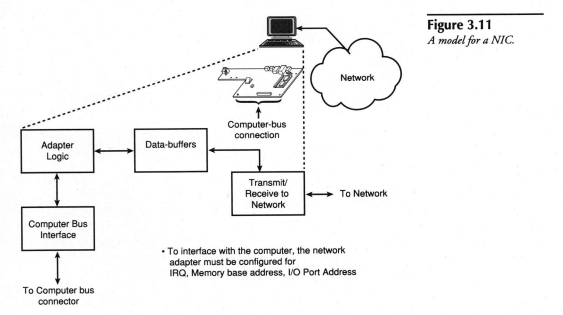

Figure 3.11
A model for a NIC.

When a packet arrives from the network, the computer is informed about this event through one of the interrupt lines (see fig. 3.12). On Intel processors, the IRQ line on which the interrupt is seen is used to index the interrupt vector table stored in lower memory. The interrupt vector table contains a pointer (address) of the interrupt service routines used to handle the packet.

For the Intel-based computers, there are 16 interrupt lines. Some of these interrupt lines are dedicated for standard peripheral devices. Table 3.10 shows standard IRQ assignments for some common devices. You must select an IRQ for the NIC that does not conflict with any existing device IRQs.

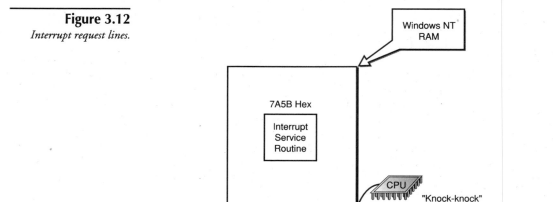

Figure 3.12

Interrupt request lines.

In the early PC/XT computers, there was only one interrupt controller chip: the Intel 8259 chip (see fig. 3.13). The 8259 chip supports only interrupt channels (usually numbered 0 through 7). The interrupt channel 0 was hard-wired to the system timer (triggers 18.2 times a second) on the motherboard, and the interrupt channel 1 was hard-wired to the Intel 8042 keyboard controller. Lower channel interrupt numbers have a higher priority than higher channel numbers. This ensures that the system timer has the highest priority and the keyboard the next highest. The PC/XT was designed for interactive use, so it made sense to give the keyboard a higher interrupt priority than most other devices.

When IBM designed the PC/AT, it realized that the eight interrupt channels were not enough, and decided to add another Intel 8259 chip controller to increase the number of interrupt levels to 16. In order to achieve this goal and to maintain compatibility with the PC/XT, IBM design engineers used the unused interrupt channel 2 of the first Intel 8259 controller chip, and connected it to the second Intel 8259 controller chip. The second Intel 8259 controller chip's interrupt channels were numbered 8 through 15, and IRQ 2 on the first Intel 8259 controller chip was connected to IRQ 9 on the second Intel 8259 controller chip. This means that whenever IRQs 8 through 15 on the second Intel 8259 controller chip are triggered, IRQ 9 is triggered. Because IRQ 9 on the second Intel 8259 controller chip is connected to IRQ 2 on the first second Intel 8259 controller chip, IRQ 2 is triggered. The implication of this is that IRQ 8 through 15 has higher priority than IRQ 3 through 7. IRQ 2 therefore acts as a "gateway" to IRQ 8 through 15. For some NICs that are installed with a setting of IRQ 2, you might have to tell the Windows NT Setup program that it is installed at IRQ 9 in order for the Setup program to recognize the NIC.

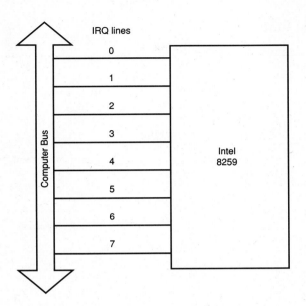

Figure 3.13
A single Intel 8259 interrupt controller for the PC/XT.

In table 3.10, you can see that COM2 is assigned an IRQ of 3, and COM 1 is assigned an IRQ of 4. In the initial PC systems, it was expected that the modem would be connected to COM2, and a parallel printer to COM1. The system was designed to give the modem a higher priority than the printer.

Table 3.10
IRQ Settings

IRQ	Device Used	Comments
0	Time	Hard-wired in the motherboard
1	Keyboard	Hard-wired in the motherboard
2	Cascaded to 8 through 16 IRQs	
3	COM2/COM4	
4	COM1/COM3	
5	LPT2	Not typically used; available for NICs
6	Floppy controller	
7	LPT1	
8	Real-time clock	Hard-wired in motherboard

continues

Table 3.10, Continued
IRQ Settings

IRQ	Device Used	Comments
9	—	IRQ 2 on first 8259 controller tied to second 8259 controller at IRQ 9
10	—	Can be used for NICs
11	—	Can be used for NICs unless used by some SCSI adapters
12	—	PS/2, in-port mouse
13	Math coprocessor	Used to signal detected errors in math co-processor
14	Hard drive	
15	Secondary disk controller	

When a packet arrives from the network, it must be transferred to the system memory used by the CPU. One way of accomplishing this is to map the data buffers on the NIC into the system memory map (see fig. 3.14). This method enables the CPU to access the packet in the data buffers directly. The start of the system memory to which the data buffers are mapped is called the *memory base address*. This is a parameter on the NIC that must be set to values between A0000 (hexadecimal) to FFFFF (hexadecimal), which also are called the *upper memory area*. Table 3.11 shows the memory base addresses used by common devices for the PC. You must ensure that the NIC's memory base address and range does not conflict with that of any device in the server computer.

Table 3.11
Memory Base Addresses of Common PC Devices

Memory Range	Device
B0000–B1000	Monochrome Adapter
B8000–C0000	Color Graphics Adapter
A0000–C0000	Enhanced Graphics Adapter
D0000–E0000	Expanded Memory
F4000–FFFFF	XT BIOS

Memory Range	Device
E0000–FFFFF	IBM AT BIOS
F0000–FFFFF	Clone AT BIOS

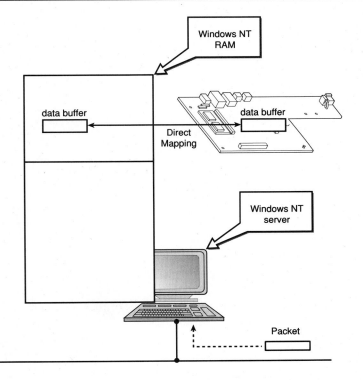

Figure 3.14
The memory base address.

The interrupt service routines (part of the network driver software) often need to find out the status of the NIC after issuing a command to the NIC (see fig. 3.15). This is done using I/O port addresses. The I/O port address for the Intel-based machines is independent of system memory and is 1,024 bytes. Some common I/O port addresses for devices are shown in table 3.12. You must ensure that the I/O address range of devices does not overlap.

Table 3.12
I/O Port Addresses of Common PC Devices

I/O Address	Device
278	LPT2
2F8	COM2

continues

Table 3.12, Continued
I/O Port Addresses of Common PC Devices

I/O Address	Device
300	—
378	LPT1
3BC	—
3F8	COM1

Figure 3.15
I/O port address.

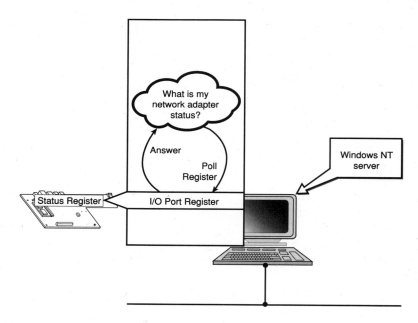

Selecting the Protocol Stack

Windows NT Server supports the following transport protocol choices:

- NWLink IPX/SPX Compatible Transport

- TCP/IP Protocol

- NetBEUI Protocol

- NWLink NetBIOS

- DLC Protocol

■ Point-to-Point Tunneling Protocol (PPTP)

■ Streams Environment

These transport protocol choices and their relationships with the OSI model are illustrated in figure 3.16.

The NWLink IPX/SPX Compatible Transport is Microsoft's implementation of Novell's IPX/SPX transport protocol stack. This choice is selected by default, because IPX/SPX is implemented at many sites. IPX supports routing and NetWare client/server applications. If you are running applications that make use of IPX/SPX sockets, you must select the NWLink IPX/SPX protocol.

The TCP/IP Protocol is Microsoft's implementation of the industry standard TCP/IP protocols. If your Windows NT Server needs to connect to the Internet or communicate with other Unix hosts or a host that uses TCP/IP protocols, you should select this option. Like IPX, the IP (Internet Protocol) protocol is routable. Select this option during installation if you are already familiar with TCP/IP network administration basics and have information such as the IP address, subnet mask, and DNS server address available at the time of installation. You always can install and configure the TCP/IP protocol as a separate step after the Windows NT Server installation. This option is selected by default.

The NetBEUI (Network BIOS Extended User Interface) transport is a native protocol used in Windows NT, LAN Manager, and IBM's LAN Server networks. NetBEUI is meant for small departmental-sized networks. According to Microsoft, NetBEUI is suitable for up to 200 clients. NetBEUI has some undesirable characteristics such as the fact that it is not routable because it does not have an explicit network layer (layer 3 of the OSI model). Its other shortcoming is that it tends to use frequent broadcasts, which can add to the network traffic for large networks. Its advantage is its simplicity, because it does not require any explicit network configuration. NetBEUI also is installed automatically if you install the Remote Access Server (RAS). If your Windows NT Server communicates with other computers such as Windows for Workgroups, or LAN Manager networks that use NetBEUI protocols, you must select NetBEUI as one of the protocols.

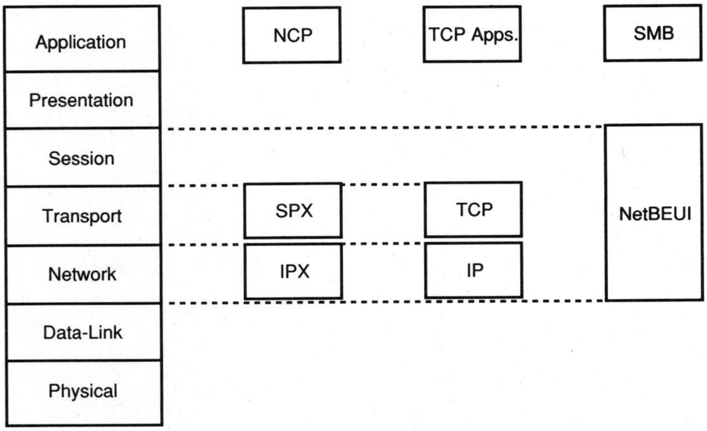

Figure 3.16
Windows NT Server transport protocol choices.

Installing Windows NT Server

This section describes the Windows NT Server installation procedure in detail and discusses the different ways of safely shutting down the Windows NT Server. You also will learn how to use the debug version of the hardware detection program, NTDETECT.COM.

Performing a Windows NT Server Installation

This section gives you a tour of a Windows NT Server installation. You can use the following checklist of information to perform your own Windows NT Server installation.

Windows NT Server Installation Checklist

1. Your computer name: _____

2. Your printer name: _____

3. Your printer model: _____

4. Network Adapter Card: SMC [WD] EtherCard 8013WB

   IRQ Level: _____

   Memory Base Address: _____

   IO Port Address: _____

5. Domain name: _____

6. Administrator Account Setup: _____

   Username: _____

   Password: _____

7. Time zone: _____

   [ ] Automatically switch to daylight savings time

   [ ] Standard time only

   [ ] Daylight savings time only

Additionally, you need the following disks:

   [ ] Windows NT Setup disks

   [ ] Windows NT CD-ROM distribution disk

   [ ] A writable floppy disk, labeled "Emergency Repair Disk," which will be created as part of the installation.

To install Windows NT Server, follow these steps:

1. Insert the NT Setup disk into drive A.

2. Insert the Windows NT CD-ROM into the CD-ROM drive.

3. Turn on the power (reboot) for your computer.

   The Setup program reads the Hardware Abstraction layer module (hardware-specific module for the hardware platform) and the Windows NT configuration data.

   The Windows NT Setup screen appears. You are prompted to insert Setup Disk #2.

4. Insert Setup Disk #2 and press Enter.

   The Setup program reads the locale-specific data, the keyboard drivers, and the FAT system files. You also see information on the number of processors recognized by Windows NT Server.

5. You can press F1 to learn more about the setup program. To continue with the installation, press Enter. To repair a damaged Windows NT Server installation, press the "R" key; you must have previously created an Emergency Repair Disk during the installation to use this option.

   If you need to stop the installation at this point, press the F3 key.

6. You see a message about the Windows NT Server setup. Setup automatically detects floppy-disk controllers and ESDI/IDE hard disks without user intervention. On occasion, detection of other hardware devices such as SCSI adapters and CD-ROM devices can cause the computer to become unstable. This happens because the Setup program probes the hardware by polling and writing to port addresses where it expects devices to be. Setup can become confused or make wrong decisions on devices if the different devices have similar characteristics. If this occurs, you can bypass Setup's mass storage device detection by pressing S and manually selecting the SCSI adapters, CD-ROM devices, and special disk controllers.

   If you want Setup to automatically detect mass storage devices, press Enter.

   Setup loads the different SCSI device drivers, and displays the SCSI hardware interfaces that it discovers.

7. Enter the third Setup disk when you are prompted to do so.

   You will see a list of mass storage devices that Setup has recognized.

   If Setup doesn't find the mass storage interface, you can press S to enter additional drivers.

8. Press Enter to continue.

Setup loads the NT File System (NTFS).

If one or more of your hard disks have more than 1,024 cylinders, NT displays a message informing you of this fact. MS-DOS normally is limited to 1,024 cylinders per hard disk. Some disk controllers use sector-translation modes to accommodate larger disks. In the sector translation mode, the number of cylinders does not exceed 1,024, but the number of heads and sectors are assigned "fictitious" or logical values to access all the disk space for DOS. If the disk size appears too small when Setup later displays this information, you should exit Setup and check your CMOS drive type settings. If you receive this message, press Enter to continue.

9. If NT detects that you have a CD-ROM drive, you see a message that it has detected a CD-ROM. To use the CD-ROM for installation, press Enter. To install Windows NT Server from 3 ½-inch disks, press A.

   If you are installing from CD-ROM, the CD-ROM file system is now loaded.

10. Setup displays the Windows NT Licensing Agreement. After you have read, and agree to the license agreement, press F8 to continue.

11. Setup will search for previous versions of Windows NT. If a previous version of NT is found, you will be able to press Enter to upgrade the existing NT installation. Press N to install a fresh copy of NT.

12. The Windows NT Server setup displays a list of hardware and software components. Ensure that the list matches your expectations of the hardware components. If your mouse is not plugged in, you see the message No Mouse or Other Pointing Device for the pointing device.

13. Change the settings, if necessary, to match your hardware configuration.

13. Highlight "The Above List Matches My Computer" and press Enter.

14. The partitions on your disk are displayed.

   To delete an existing partition, highlight it and press D. Then confirm your choice by pressing L.

   To create a partition in the unpartitioned space, press C. You see a form displaying the following information:

   ```
   The minimum size of the new partition: _____

   The maximum size of the new partition: _____

   Create partition of size (in MB): _____
   ```

15. The Setup program displays the minimum and maximum sizes of the partition. You must select the partition size to create.

16. If you have multiple partitions, such as a DOS partition and an NT partition, you see a list of partitions. Highlight the partition in which to install the Windows NT server.

    You are given a choice of formatting the selected file system to FAT or NTFS.

    Selecting the FAT files system has the advantage of it being used under MS-DOS, Windows NT, and OS/2. The disadvantage, however, is that it does not have the security, performance, and fault-tolerant features of Windows NT. Also, using the FAT file system limits you to the eight-character file names and three-character extensions.

    If you want to implement a locally secure file system and use NTFS's high-performance capabilities, you should select the NTFS file system. If you select the FAT file system, the files on the server can be compromised by booting the NT server with a DOS disk and accessing the files on the NT server's FAT file system.

    If you select the FAT file system, it is still possible to secure the files against network access, but not against local access.

    The Setup program displays a message saying that the partition is being formatted. You see a completion status bar on the percentage of the partition that has been formatted.

17. You see a screen informing you about the location where you want the files to be installed. The default location is \WINNT. If you want to install the Windows NT Server in a directory other than the default directory, you can edit this value.

18. Press Enter to continue.

19. In addition to performing a basic examination, Setup can perform an exhaustive, and potentially time consuming, secondary examination of some drives. To allow Setup to perform this secondary examination, press Enter. To skip the secondary examination, press Esc. It is recommended that you perform the secondary examination of the hard disk, unless you are installing a test server and are short on time.

    You see a status indicator showing the percentage of files being copied.

    Occasionally, problems with CD-ROM drives, SCSI adapters, hard disks, or system board incompatibilities result in a failure to copy critical files properly. The Setup program displays a message that the checksums on the files do not match. You must fix the hardware problem before you can install Windows NT Server successfully. Sometimes using different types of RAM chips and incompatibilities between the RAM devices can cause strange errors during installation when files are being copied from the CD-ROM. If SIMMs are being used, ensure that they are of the same type and from the same manufacturer.

20. After all the files are copied, the Setup program asks you to remove any Setup disks from the floppy drive. After you remove the floppy disk, press Enter to restart the computer.

    The Windows NT Server machine reboots.

21. After the computer restarts, you will see the Welcome to the Windows NT Setup Wizard screen. There are three parts to the Setup Wizard. The Setup Wizard parts are as follows:

    ■ Gathering information about your computer

    ■ Installing Windows NT Networking

    ■ Finishing Setup

    The Setup Wizard will guide you through the remainder of the setup process. Click on Next to continue and gather information about your computer.

22. You see a form asking you to enter your name and organization. Press Tab to go between fields or use the mouse to go to the next field (click on the next field). Click on Next to continue.

23. Enter your 10 digit "CD Key," located on the back of your CD case. Click on Next to continue.

24. You see the Licensing Modes screen asking you to choose "Per Server" or "Per Seat" licensing. If you choose "Per Server" licensing, you must specify the number of concurrent connections for which you're licensed. Each concurrent connection requires a separate CLIENT ACCESS LICENSE. If you choose "Per Seat" licensing, you can use the License Manager, located in the Administrative Tools folder, to record the number of CLIENT ACCESS LICENSES purchased. Click on Next to continue.

25. Enter a unique computer name (limited to 15 characters) for your server computer in your domain. Verify that you entered your computer name correctly and click on the Next button.

26. You see a form asking you to identify the Windows NT Server Type. You can select the Windows NT Server to act as a primary domain controller, backup domain controller, or as a stand-alone server computer. The domain controller is used to manage the domain's security policy and master database. If you do not want your server to manage the security policy and the master database for the domain, you should select the Windows NT Server as a stand-alone server computer.

    You can change this security role only be reinstalling the Windows NT Server.

27. You see the Administrator Account password screen. You must enter a password, which will be used by the Administrator account. The password can be 14 digits or less, and is case-sensitive. Re-enter the password in the Confirm Password field. Click on Next to continue.

28. Setup can create an emergency disk that contains information on repairing your Windows NT Server in case of file system or other damage. You see a prompt asking you whether

you want to create this emergency disk. You generally should answer Yes, unless you already have created such an emergency disk from a previous installation that used the same Setup configuration information. Click on Next to continue.

Note You can create (or update) the emergency disk after the installation by running the program RDISK.EXE, which is installed in the Windows NT Server SYSTEM32 directory.

29. Windows NT Setup displays a list of the following optional components groups that can be installed. These optional components groups follow:

   ■ **Accessibility Options.** Includes options to change keyboard, mouse, sound, and display for people with mobility, hearing, and visual impairments.

   ■ **Accessories.** Includes Windows NT accessories and enhancements.

   ■ **Communications.** Includes accessories to help you connect to other computers and online services.

   ■ **Games.** Includes Solitair, Pinball, Minesweeper, and Freecell.

   ■ **Multimedia.** Includes programs for video, animation, and for playing sound on CD-ROMs and sound cards.

   ■ **Windows Messaging.** Includes Electronic Mail and messaging utilities.

   The tasks that are to be performed have a "check" in the check box beside them. If you want to selectively install individual components or files within a component group, highlight the component group and click on the Details button. Figure 3.17 shows optional NT components.

The components with the amount of disk space follow:

Group Components	Bytes Used
Accessibility Options	0.1 MB
Accessories	7.1 MB
Communications	0.7 MB
Games	2.8 MB
Multimedia	6.6 MB
Windows Messaging	4.6 MB
Total	**21.5 MB**

Figure 3.17
*Optional Windows NT
components.*

30. After you make your component selections, click on the Next button.

31. The Setup Wizard is now ready to install Windows NT Networking. Click on Next to proceed.

32. Setup needs to know how your computer will participate on the network. The options are as follows:

    ■ **Wired to the network.** Your computer is connected to the network by an ISDN or Network adapter.

    ■ **Remote access to the network.** Your computer uses a modem to remotely connect to the network.

    You can choose to check both options.

33. During the installation process, Setup can detect network adapters installed in the Windows NT Server machine. You can select the Start Search button to have Windows NT automatically detect your network adapter. If you do not want to auto-detect the network adapter, but select the network adapter manually, you should select the "Select from list" button.

    If you select the auto-detection feature, Setup probes the server hardware for a network adapter and stops at the first one it identifies. You can accept the identified network adapter or select "Find Next," which causes Setup to look for additional network adapters.

If you click on the "Select from list" button, Setup displays the Network Adapter Setup dialog box.

34. The Setup program lists the network adapters it has detected. Select the Next button.

35. Setup needs to know if you want to install the Internet Information Server (IIS). The IIS includes a Web server, FTP server, and Gopher server. Click on Next to continue.

36. After the NIC drivers are selected, you must select the network protocols. Your choices follow:

   ■ **TCP/IP Transport.** This is Microsoft's implementation of the industry standard TCP/IP protocols. If your Windows NT Server needs to connect to the Internet or communicate with other Unix hosts or a host that uses TCP/IP protocols, you should select this option. Like IPX, the IP (Internet Protocol) protocol is routable. Select this option during installation if you already are familiar with TCP/IP network administration basics and have information such as the IP address, subnet mask, and DNS server address available at the time of installation. You can always install and configure the TCP/IP protocol as a separate step after the Windows NT Server installation. This option is selected by default.

   ■ **NWLink IPX/SPX Compatible Transport.** Select this protocol if you have applications that need this protocol, or if you are installing Windows NT in a NetWare-based network.

   ■ **NetBEUI Transport.** NetBEUI (Network BIOS Extended User Interface) is a native protocol used in Windows NT, LAN Manager, and IBM's LAN Server networks. It is meant for small departmental-sized networks. According to Microsoft, NetBEUI is suitable for up to 200 clients. NetBEUI has some undesirable characteristics, such as the fact that it is not routable because it does not have an explicit network layer (layer 3 of the OSI model). Its other shortcoming is that it tends to use frequent broadcasts, which can add to the network traffic for large networks. Its advantage is its simplicity, because it does not require any explicit network configuration. NetBEUI also is installed automatically if you install the Remote Access Server (RAS). If your Windows NT Server communicates with other computers such as Windows for Workgroups, or LAN Manager networks that use NetBEUI protocols, you must select NetBEUI as one of the protocols.

37. After you select the network protocols, select the Next button.

38. Setup displays a list of services to be installed. To add additional services, click on the Select from list button, and select the services.

   The following is a list of additional services:

   ■ DHCP Relay Agent

   ■ Gateway (and Client) Services for NetWare

- Microsoft DHCP Server

- Microsoft DNS Server

- Microsoft TCP/IP Printing

- Network Monitor Agent

- Network Monitor Tools and Agent

- Remoteboot Service

- RIP for Internet Protocol

- RIP for NwLink IPX/SPX compatible transport

- RPC support for Banyan

- SAP Agent

- Services for Macintosh

- Simple TCP/IP Services

- Windows Internet Name Service

Services can be added or removed later, by using the Network Applet, located in the Control Panel. Click on Next to continue.

39. Setup is now ready to install the previously selected network components. Click on Next to continue.

40. A dialog box appears that has filled in the NIC parameters that the Setup program recognizes. Verify that the NIC parameters shown match the actual hardware settings on the NIC. Click on the Continue button.

41. A dialog box appears that asks you if there is a DHCP server on the network.

   Network components will be copied to the server, and you will be asked to configure the selected network components, as the setup process proceeds.

42. If you selected the NWLink IPX/SPX protocol stack, you see the NWLink IPX/SPX Protocol Configuration dialog box.

   For Ethernet and Token Ring network adapters, you can select Auto Frame Type Detection to automatically detect the frame type for your network. You should select the auto-frame detection method if you are not sure of the frame type used for your network. If you know the different frame types that are used for your network, you can select the Manual Frame Type selection to add additional frame types.

If you are on a network that uses NetWare 3.11 or earlier servers, you can use Ethernet 802.2 frame types. For networks that use NetWare 3.12 (or higher) and NetWare 4.*x*, you can use Ethernet 802.2 frame types. For networks that use a mix of NetWare 3.11 (or earlier), NetWare 3.12 (or higher) and NetWare 4.*x*, you should specify both Ethernet 802.2 and Ethernet 802.3 frame types. If you have Macintosh stations on the network, you should add the Ethernet SNAP frame type. If you need to communicate with other TCP/IP-based workstations and servers that use the Ethernet II frame type (such as Unix workstations and NetWare TCP/IP platforms), you should add the Ethernet II frame types.

If asked, you also can select the IPX network number. This is an eight-digit hexadecimal number assigned to the cable segment.

43. For a Token Ring adapter, select the 802.5 frame type.

44. If you selected TCP/IP Protocol, you will see the TCP/IP Properties sheets. You must specify an IP Address, Subnet Mask, and Default Gateway. You also can configure DNS, WINS Address, DHCP Relay, and Routing.

    Click on the OK button to continue.

45. Setup presents you the option to disable or enable network bindings, or to arrange the order in which your computer will find information on the network. Click on Next to continue.

46. Setup is now ready to start the network, and complete the networking installation. Click on Next.

47. If you had requested that Setup create a Primary Domain Controller, you are asked to supply a Computer Name and a Domain Name. Click on Next to continue.

48. The Setup Wizard is ready to finish the installation process, and configure any remaining network related components. Click on Finish to complete the setup procedure.

49. If you has previously chosen to install the Internet Information Server, you are presented with the IIS installation options. Select the desired components and then select the installation directory. Click on OK to continue.

    Select the IIS component publishing directory locations. Click on OK to continue.

    Setup will copy and install the selected IIS components.

    Optionally, you can install ODBC drivers. Select an ODBC driver from the list and click on the Advanced button to configure advanced ODBC installation options. Click on OK after you finish.

50. Setup displays the Date/Time Properties screen. Windows NT Server-based networks can be enterprise-wide, with servers located in in different time zones. To support such enterprise networks, you must specify the time zone for the Windows NT Server. You specify the time zone as the number of hours offset from GMT. Windows NT Server has built-in knowledge of whether daylight savings apply to a particular time zone. The time zone for the state of Indiana in the United States, for example, is listed separately from Eastern Time (U.S. and Canada) because there is no daylight savings time in that state. If the time zone were set to Eastern Time (U.S. and Canada), daylight savings time would be observed.

You always can change the time zone setting after installation by activating the Date/Time Applet from the Windows NT Server Control Panel (see figs. 3.18 and 3.19). You can use the dialog box in figure 3.19 to set the date and time for the Windows NT Server computer.

You must select the date, time, and time-zone information. You also can check the box for automatically adjusting the daylight savings time. Make appropriate changes for your locale, then click on the Close button to continue.

Figure 3.18

The Date/Time applet.

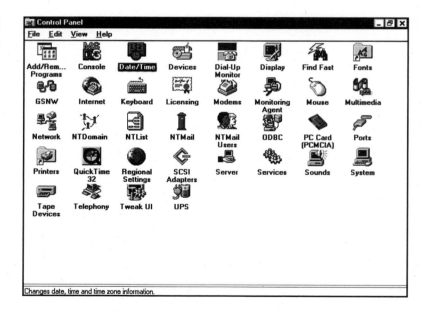

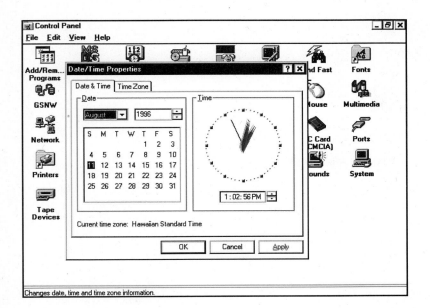

Figure 3.19
*The Date/Time Properties
dialog box.*

51. The Setup program displays the video adapter type that it found on your server computer. Select OK and use the controls to select the size and number of colors for your display (see fig. 3.20). You then can use the Test button to examine these settings.

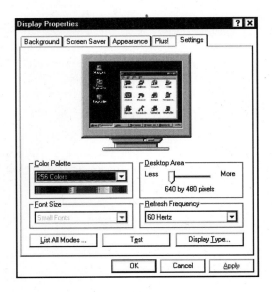

Figure 3.20
Using the Display settings.

The Display settings include information on the following:

- Color palette

- Font size

- Desktop area (in pixels)

- Refresh frequency

You can list the other resolution modes or change the display type.

52. After you select OK, your graphics adapter is reset and a test bitmap is displayed for five seconds. You then must answer whether the test bitmap displayed successfully.

    Click on the Ok button to save your configuration and continue.

53. Setup will copy any remaining files, set security on the system files, and save the configuration.

54. Setup is ready to create an "Emergency Repair Disk." Insert your ERD into the floppy drive and click on the OK button to continue. Setup usually formats the floppy disk and then copies the necessary files.

55. After the ERD has been created, remove all disks from floppy drives and remove compact discs from all CD-ROM drives. Click on the Restart Computer button to finish the setup installation process, then restart the computer.

56. The NTDETECT program probes the hardware, and the OS Loader loads Windows NT Server. During the installation, the type of system on the hard disk is FAT. After Windows NT boots from the hard disk, it converts the FAT file system to an NT file system because you have selected NTFS as your choice. After converting to NTFS, Windows NT reboots itself. The conversion is done only once at the time of installation.

57. After a few automatic reboots, you should see the Windows NT Server logo and log-on screen. Press Ctrl+Alt+Del to initiate the server login. Log in using the Administrator user name and the password that you set during installation for this account on the NT domain that you selected or created.

Shutting Down and Logging Out of a Windows NT Server

You can shut down or log out of a Windows NT Server by using any of the following methods:

Method 1

1. Click on the Start button on the Taskbar.

2. Click on Shut Down. You are then presented with three options, as follows:

   ■ Shut Down the computer?

   ■ Restart the computer?

   ■ Close all programs and log on as a different user?

   If you select the Shut down the computer? option, applications are terminated and unsaved data in memory is flushed to disk. If you select the Restart the computer? option, Windows NT shuts down and restarts the computer as if you had just turned on the power to the computer (cold boot for Intel platforms). If you select the Close all programs and log on as a different user? option, applications are terminated, unsaved data in memory is flushed to disk, and you see the Begin Logon dialog box.

Method 2

1. Press the Ctrl+Alt+Del.

   You see a screen that has a Logoff and Shut Down buttons, as well as Lock Workstation, Change Password, Task Manager, and Cancel (see fig. 3.21).

2. Click on the Logoff button or the Shut Down button. If you choose to log off or shut down, your applications are terminated and unsaved data in memory is flushed to disk. If you select the Shut Down option, you see another dialog box that contains a Shutdown and **R**estart option. When you choose the Shutdown and **R**estart option, Windows NT Server restarts the computer as if you had just turned on the power to the computer (cold boot for Intel platforms).

   If you choose the **L**ogoff option, you are asked to confirm your choice of ending the Windows NT session.

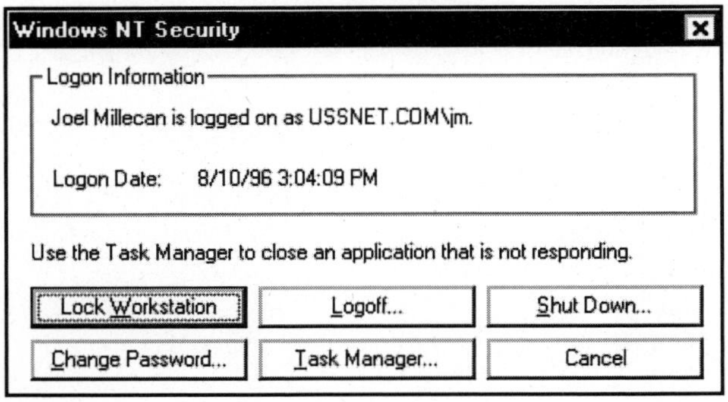

Figure 3.21
Using the Windows NT Security dialog box.

Conclusion

In this chapter, you learned about the installation issues for the Windows NT Server. A guided tour of the Windows NT Server was provided. Many of the installation concepts needed to understand the Windows NT Server installation were discussed prior to showing you the installation procedure.

The installation procedures discussed in this chapter should suffice for the majority of installation situations. The next chapter discusses variations to the standard installation procedure.

Advanced Windows NT Server Installation

*I*n this chapter, you will learn about upgrading
Windows NT Server from previous versions of the
operating system and migrating existing Windows 3.x
applications settings to Windows NT Server. You will
learn how to install Windows NT Server using an
unsupported CD-ROM or from a network. This
chapter also discusses installing Windows NT Server
on RISC-based platforms and customizing Windows
NT Server installation. Customizing Windows NT
Server installation is particularly important when
many server installations are to be performed and the
servers are to have similar installation settings.

Installing Windows NT Server on a Windows 3.x Partition

It is possible to use the Windows NT Server to run local applications and treat the server as a nondedicated server. For performance reasons, it is best to dedicate the Windows NT Server as a network server and not use it as a workstation. There are situations, however, where it is convenient to run local applications on the Windows NT Server.

During Windows NT installation, the Setup program checks whether a previous version of Windows has been installed on the computer. If a previous version exists, for example, you can install Windows NT in the same directory as Windows 3.x. Windows NT setup partially configures its environment based on the existing environment. This enables Windows NT to support all the features of previously installed Windows 3.x–based applications.

Windows 3.x stores configuration information in the System.ini and Win.ini system files. Windows NT stores configuration information in the Registry. These system files are present in Windows NT, and can be used by Windows 3.x–based applications.

If you choose to install Windows NT in the same directory as Windows 3.x, Windows NT migrates the Windows 3.x program groups and places the program groups on the Start menu.

Looking at Incompatibilities between Windows 3.x Applications Running on an NT Server

Windows 3.x programs that directly manipulate the DOS file system, the serial ports, and so on, might not function properly in NT. These include programs that undelete files or perform system diagnostics, or communications programs (such as faxes) that access the serial ports directly.

Updating Windows Fonts

NT Setup might not recognize your old Windows fonts properly. To remedy this problem, perform the following actions:

1. Open the Control Panel.

2. Activate the Fonts applet (see fig 4.1).

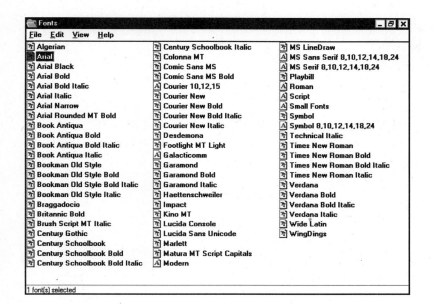

Figure 4.1
The Fonts dialog box, activated by selecting the Fonts applet from the Control Panel.

3. Choose File, Install New Font. The Add Fonts dialog box appears (see fig. 4.2).

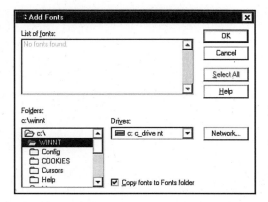

Figure 4.2
The Add Fonts dialog box.

4. Disable the Copy fonts to Fonts folder check box so that you avoid having two copies of the fonts.

    Select the Windows 3.x WINDOWS\SYSTEM directory and click OK. A list of the fonts found in that directory appears.

5. Select all the fonts by clicking the font at the top of the list, and then Shift-clicking the font at the bottom of the list. Click the OK button.

You might see a message telling you that a font already is installed, and asking you whether you want to remove this font and reinstall. This message appears for fonts already recognized by the system. Click OK each time this message appears.

6. After you finish adding fonts, close the font applet and the Control Panel.

Configuring Windows Applications on Windows NT Server

For the most part, you might not be interested in running Windows applications on the Windows NT Server—especially if you are interested in treating the server as a dedicated server. For small networks, it may be convenient to run a Windows application directly on the server occasionally. You also might be interested in running third-party applications written for Windows that convert the machine into an applications server. Examples of such Windows applications are FTP, NFS, and Internet servers. Ideally speaking, you should run the NT versions of these applications on the Windows NT Server, but you might not always have this choice because NT versions of these applications might not be available.

If you experience problems running the Windows applications on the Windows NT Server, you should check to see whether the applications' directories are on the search path. You can modify the search path from the System settings applet in the Control group. Follow this procedure to modify the search path:

1. Open the Control Panel from the Administrative Tools Folder.

2. Activate the System applet. The System Properties dialog box appears (see fig. 4.3).

Figure 4.3

The Systems Properties dialog box.

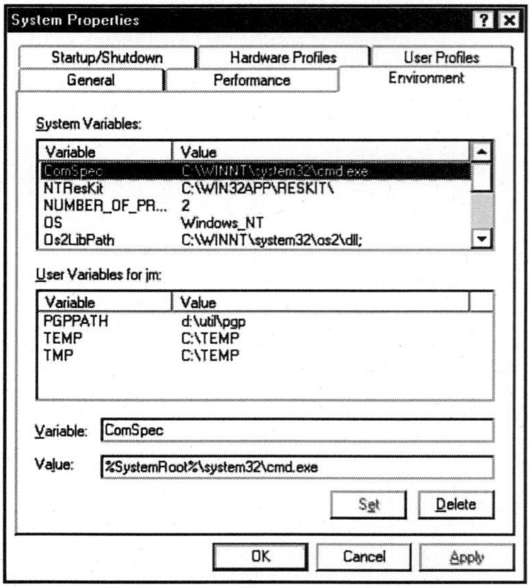

3. Select the Environment tab. The path variable can be changed in the **S**ystem Variables box or the **U**ser Variables for <username> box. Changes made to the system environment variables will apply to the entire Windows NT Server. The default system path is set to the following:

`%SystemRoot%\System32;%SystemRoot%`

The variable `%SystemRoot%` is set in the NT registry (the internal database for NT) to the directory in which the Windows NT Server is installed. Typically, this directory is C:\WINNT.

Changes made to the user environment variables affect only the user who is logged on to the system. The user path environment settings are appended to the system settings. You must decide whether you want the changes to the path statement to apply to the entire system or only to the user logging on.

Highlight the path variable to change. The variable and its current value are listed in the **V**ariable and Va**l**ue boxes at the bottom of the Environment settings dialog box (see fig. 4.4).

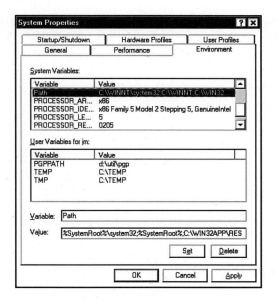

Figure 4.4

The setting for the Path variable.

4. Change the Va**l**ue field for the Path variable to add the Windows applications' directories.

5. Click the S**e**t button. You will see the modified Path variable listed in the **S**ystem or **U**ser Variables box. Click OK.

6. You must at least log off and log on again to register the changes to the system or user variables.

Another reason you might not be able to get your Windows applications to work properly is if they are unable to find their INI files. You might have to copy the applications' INI files in the %SystemRoot% directory. Usually, this is the \WINNT directory. After copying these files, you should change any relevant parameters in the INI file to run on the NT server.

If the Windows applications still do not work, you might have to reinstall the applications again on the NT machine.

To summarize, you can use the following approaches to get your Windows applications to run on NT:

- Ensure that the applications' directories are on the search path.

- Copy the Windows applications' INI files to the %SystemRoot% directory.

- If the first and second approaches fail, reinstall the Windows applications from scratch from the NT operating system.

Installing Windows NT Server from the Network

If you are installing a number of Windows NT Servers, you can keep a master copy of the Windows NT Server CD-ROM distribution on a network server and use this as the source for installing other NT servers (see fig. 4.5).

To perform this procedure, follow these steps:

1. Copy the Windows NT Server CD-ROM to a directory on a network server. You can use any server in which the file system can be accessed as a network drive, but you must ensure that you have read and write permissions to the network directory in order for the copy to succeed. Your choices include an NT server, NetWare server, VINES server, or NFS (Network File System) server. On MS-NET–based operating systems, you must share the source directory by creating a share name.

   You can copy the image by using the DOS or NT XCOPY command. You also can share the CD-ROM drive attached to a network server, but the installation will be slower than copying it to a network directory.

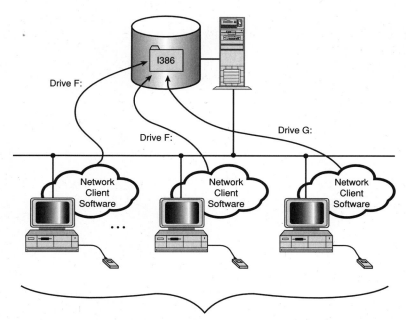

Figure 4.5
Installing Windows NT Server from a network.

Computers to be installed with Windows NT operating system

2. Boot the server machine on which Windows NT Server is to be installed. Use the MS-DOS disk that has the network client software to connect with the network server that has the distribution image.

   Alternatively, if you have Windows for Workgroups, Windows 95, or Windows NT Workstation software installed on the server machine, use the network client software to access the server.

3. Activate the network client software. The procedure depends on the network client software you are using.

4. Assign a drive letter, such as drive G, to the network directory on which the CD-ROM image was installed. Examples of commands to do this follow.

   If you are using MS-LAN Manager client software, use this syntax:

   ```
   NET USE G: = \\Server\Share name
   ```

   If you are using NetWare client software, use this syntax:

   ```
   MAP ROOT G: = Server\Volume:DirectoryName
   ```

   Make sure that the users who will be accessing this directory for installation have read permissions to the network drive.

5. Change to the drive assigned in step 4.

6. If you are accessing the network drive from MS-DOS network client software, run the program WINNT, which is found on the network drive. For Intel platforms, this is in the \I386 subdirectory. From a DOS prompt, type the following:

winnt

or

winnt /b

If you are accessing the network drive from NT Workstation software, run the WINNT32 program, which is found on the network drive (in the \I386 subdirectory). You can type the following command from the NT command prompt:

winnt32

or

winnt32 /b

Alternatively, you can run the WINNT32 program from the Windows NT Explorer or the Start Menu's Run option.

If you run the WINNT program without any options, you are prompted to create three new Setup disks. However, if you use the /b option, you can eliminate the creation of the Setup disks and perform the Setup disks without the installation procedure.

7. When asked to confirm the Windows NT Server source directory, enter the path where the Windows NT Server source files are stored.

8. If you did not use the /b option, you are prompted to insert the Setup disks. Format three high-density floppy disks and label them as follows:

   ■ Windows NT Server Setup Boot Disk

   ■ Windows NT Server Setup Disk #2

   ■ Windows NT Server Setup Disk #3

Insert these disks in the order in which you are prompted. The correct order follows:

   1. Windows NT Server Setup Disk #3

   2. Windows NT Server Setup Disk #2

   3. Windows NT Server Setup Boot Disk

The WINNT (or WINNT32) program writes to these disks. If files are missing or were not copied correctly to the source directory on the server, the WINNT (or WINNT32) program informs you of this.

The copy process also copies a minimum redirector needed for connecting to the network server.

9. After the files are copied, the system reboots. Follow the instructions on-screen to complete the installation. The installation procedure from this point on is the same as that discussed in the preceding chapter.

Installing Windows NT Server from an Unsupported CD-ROM

The Windows NT Server Setup program recognizes SCSI CD-ROM devices and a few non-SCSI CD-ROMs. If you have a CD-ROM that Windows NT Server does not recognize during Setup, you can boot the server with MS-DOS and use MS-DOS drivers to access the CD-ROM. You can proceed with the install using the procedure outlined in this section. This procedure, for the most part, is similar to the procedure outlined in the preceding section for network drives.

1. Boot the server machine with a floppy containing MS-DOS and CD-ROM drivers for the floppy. Use the MSCDEX command to assign a drive letter to the CD-ROM. Insert the Windows NT Server distribution CD-ROM into the drive.

2. Format three high-density floppy disks and label them as follows:

   ▪ Windows NT Server Setup Boot Disk

   ▪ Windows NT Server Setup Disk #2

   ▪ Windows NT Server Setup Disk #3

3. Make the CD-ROM drive your current drive.

4. Run the WINNT program found on the network drive. For Intel platforms, this is in the \I386 subdirectory. From a DOS prompt, type **winnt**.

5. When asked to confirm the Windows NT Server source directory, enter the path to where the Windows NT Server source files are stored. This should be the CD-ROM drive path.

6. You are prompted to insert the Setup disks. Insert these disks in the order in which you are prompted. The correct order follows:

   1. Windows NT Server Setup Disk #3

   2. Windows NT Server Setup Disk #2

   3. Windows NT Server Setup Boot Disk

   The WINNT (or WINNT32) program writes to these disks. If files are missing or were not copied correctly to the source directory on the server, the WINNT (or WINNT32) program informs you of this.

7. Follow the instructions on-screen to complete the installation.

Both the WINNT.EXE and WINNT32.EXE programs have several options that can assist the installation process. In the section "Installing Windows NT Server from the Network," earlier in this chapter, you learned how to use the /b option to perform a Windows NT installation without the Setup disks. You can learn about the other options by running the following commands:

winnt /?

or

winnt32 /?

The following listing shows the Help options for WINNT. These options are the same for the WINNT32 program. WINNT32 runs on an NT computer, and WINNT runs on a DOS computer:

```
WINNT [/S[:]sourcepath] [/T[:]tempdrive] [/I[:]inffile]
[/OX] [/X | [/F] [/C]] [/B] [/U:answer_file] [/udf:id,[udf file]]
/S[:]sourcepath
Specifies the source location of Windows NT files.
Must be a full path of the form x:\[path] or
\\server\share[\path].
The default is the current directory.
/T[:]tempdrive
Specifies a drive to contain temporary setup files.
If not specified, Setup attempts to locate a drive for you.
/I[:]inffile
Specifies the file name (no path) of the Setup information file.
The default is DOSNET.INF.
/OX     Create boot floppies for CD-ROM or floppy-based installation.
/X      Do not create the Setup boot floppies.
/F      Do not verify files as they are copied to the Setup boot floppies.
/C      Skip free-space check on the Setup boot floppies you provide.
/B      Floppyless operation.
/U      Unattended operation and optional script file (requires /s).
/UDF    Specifies the identifier that is to be used by the Setup program to apply
sections of the UDF_file in place of the same section in the answer file.
```

```
/R      Specifies optional directory to be installed.
/RX     Specifies optional directory to be copied.
/E      Specifies command to be executed at the end of GUI setup.
```

If you need to create Setup disks, you can do so by using the following command:

`winnt /ox`

To install without using Setup disks, use the following command:

`winnt /b`

Upgrading from Earlier Windows NT Server Versions

To upgrade an older version of the NT Server, you can boot the server with the Windows NT Server Setup disk. The Setup program detects any version of the Windows NT Server already installed on your computer and gives you a choice of upgrading the operating system.

If your NT Server is part of a Windows NT domain, you first should upgrade the computer acting as the primary domain controller (PDC) before upgrading any NT Servers acting as the backup domain controller (BDC). If you upgrade a BDC first, the security information on the BDC server is overwritten by the replicated information from the older PDC. Figure 4.6 illustrates this problem.

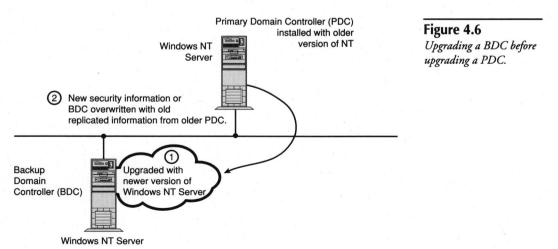

Figure 4.6

Upgrading a BDC before upgrading a PDC.

Windows NT Server versions come with a WINNT32.EXE program. The WINNT.EXE program can be run under DOS, and the WINNT32.EXE program can run on an NT server. You can use these programs to upgrade from source files in a network directory or on a CD-ROM.

If you are upgrading from a network directory, you must have at least 124 MB of free space locally to create local files for the upgrade process. If you do not have sufficient free space, the upgrade program warns you of this. If you run the upgrade from a CD-ROM, you need about 10 MB of free space.

When you upgrade your Windows NT Server version, the following information on the server is not modified:

- Local security accounts (users and groups)

- Custom program groups, desktop settings, and preferences set through the Control Panel

- Preference settings for Accessories and Administrative tools

- Network Adapter settings, protocols, and service configurations

- Settings for RAS (Remote Access Server) and Macintosh services

- Custom settings made by the Registry Editor

The upgrade process copies new versions of existing files required by the system and changes system settings and program groups for the new Windows NT Server version. As part of the upgrade, you must provide the following:

- Location of directory on which to install the Windows NT Server

- If the TCP/IP protocol already is installed in the existing Windows NT Server, you are asked to provide new information for the TCP/IP parameters

- An emergency repair disk for saving repair information

Although the upgrade process is safe, you must back up critical files as a precaution before performing the upgrade to protect yourself from unforeseen events.

Upgrading the Windows NT Server Using the WINNT32 Program

This section presents an outline of the procedure for upgrading an earlier version of Windows NT Server using the WINNT32 program. For Intel platforms, the WINNT32 program is in the \I386 directory on the Windows NT Server software distribution on the CD-ROM, or on the network drive. Follow these steps:

1. Boot up the server with the previous version of the Windows NT Server.

2. Connect to the network drive containing the master files of the new Windows NT Server. Alternatively, you can access the CD-ROM containing the Windows NT Server software.

3. From the Windows Explorer, locate the WINNT32.EXE program in the master source files. This should be in the \I386 subdirectory for Intel platforms.

4. Run the WINNT32.EXE program.

   Use WINNT32 /B if you do not want to use Setup disks.

   Use WINNT32 if you do want to use Setup disks.

5. In the Upgrade/Installation dialog box that appears, enter the directory that contains the master files for the new Windows NT Server (see fig. 4.7).

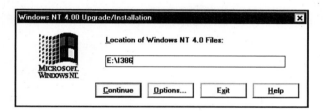

Figure 4.7
Using the Upgrade/ Installation dialog box with the WINNT32 program.

6. Select Continue and follow the instructions on-screen to complete the upgrade.

Upgrading a Windows NT Server from a Windows NT Workstation

You can upgrade a Windows NT Workstation computer to a Windows NT Server with the limitation that you cannot use the Windows NT Server as a domain controller in a Windows NT Server domain. If you want the Windows NT Server to act as a domain controller, you must reinstall the Windows NT Workstation computer from scratch.

When a Windows NT Workstation is upgraded to a Windows NT Server, an updated version of the User Manager is installed. You must delete your old user profile from the computer before the updated User Manager appears in the Administrative Tools folder. User Profiles are deleted by using the Control Panel's System Applet and choosing the User Profiles Tab. After deleting your user profile, you must log in again; this creates a new profile containing the updated User Manager. If you replace the NT Workstation with a new Windows NT Server installation, the Setup program installs User Manager for domains.

Reinstalling Windows NT Server

On occasion, you might have to reinstall the Windows NT Server. Before reinstalling the Windows NT Server, you should try other means, such as using the Emergency Repair disk that you created as part of the installation. If this fails to correct the problem, you might have to reinstall the Windows NT Server.

Reinstalling Windows NT Server is identical to a first-time Windows NT Server installation, unless you are reinstalling a computer that belongs to a domain or you are reinstalling a domain controller. In this case, you must take additional steps. These two situations are discussed next.

Reinstalling Windows NT Server on a Computer that Belongs to a Domain

If you are reinstalling Windows NT Server on a computer that belongs to a domain but is not a domain controller, you must log in as a domain administrator, delete the computer account for the computer, and create a new account. The computer account has an associated password that is used when you log in to the domain from the computer.

This computer password is a password that you, as a user or administrator, never see. The password is used by the primary domain controller to authenticate that a computer is what it says it is. This feature prevents an unauthorized computer from pretending to be a computer with a legitimate name and the right to access the domain resources. If a computer named NTS1 is off-line, for example, another computer can pretend to be NTS1 and can be used to access the domain resources.

The password is changed periodically by the domain controller for security reasons, and this information is synchronized to the computer. If you do not delete the computer account and create a new one, passwords on the reinstalled Windows NT Server computer and domain controller will not match, and you will be prevented from logging into the domain from the computer. You will get a message informing you that there is no domain controller available to validate your login.

To reinstall the server, you must therefore perform the following steps:

1. Remove the computer on which you will be reinstalling the Windows NT Server from the network. You can do this by shutting down the computer.

2. Log onto the domain as an administrator user and run Server Manager, which is located in the Administrative Tools folder. From the Server Manager, delete the computer name from the domain by following these steps:

    Activate the Server Manager.

Highlight the computer to be deleted from the domain.

Press Del or choose **C**omputer, **R**emove from Domain.

3. Connect the computer that you will be reinstalling to the network. Reinstall the Windows NT Server on this computer. Make sure that you specify that you are replacing the Windows NT Server software and not upgrading it.

4. During the installation, you will see a message asking whether you want to create a new computer account in the domain. A computer account must be provided for you in the domain or you must provide a password and account name that has membership in the domain's Administrators group to create a computer account.

Reinstalling Windows NT Server on a Domain Controller

If the Windows NT Server computer is a domain controller, you must perform the following steps to ensure the integrity of the user accounts database:

1. If the Windows NT Server is a primary domain controller, you must temporarily promote another backup domain controller to be the PDC. When you promote another BDC to a PDC, the original PDC automatically is demoted to a BDC. You can use the Server Manager in the Administrative Tools group to perform this task. To promote another BDC to be the PDC, follow these steps:

Activate the Server Manager.

Highlight computer to be promoted as the primary domain controller.

Choose the **C**omputer, Promote to Primary Domain **C**ontroller.

2. Reinstall Windows NT Server on the original PDC. Make this computer a BDC.

3. Wait for a few minutes for the security accounts database from the temporary PDC to be transferred to the BDC.

4. Promote the BDC to a PDC. Again, you can use the Server Manager to perform this function.

If you only have one domain controller—the PDC—on the network, you will not be able to perform the previously outlined procedure. You still can perform the reinstallation, however, taking into account the issues that are discussed next.

When you reinstall the PDC, even though you give it the same domain name, the Windows NT clients on your network will not recognize it. This is because NT uses internal identification numbers called *security identifiers* (SIDs) for computer names. When you reinstall the PDC, it has a different SID that the Windows NT clients do not know about. As a result, your Windows NT clients will not be able to log on to the domain.

You can use the following workaround:

1. Remove the Windows NT clients from the domain.

2. Make the Windows NT clients part of a fictitious or existing workgroup name.

3. Reinstall the Windows NT Server, if you have not already reinstalled it.

4. Make your Windows NT clients part of the domain.

Installing Windows NT Server on RISC-Based Computers

If you are installing Windows NT Server on an ARC-compliant RISC-based computer, you must be familiar with the manufacturer's instructions for starting programs from CD-ROM or disk. Different RISC platforms might have different procedures for starting the Setup program.

If you have an earlier version of Windows NT Server installed on your RISC machine, you can use the WINNT32.EXE program to upgrade to a newer version of Windows NT Server.

Before commencing the Windows NT Server installation on a RISC-based computer, you must have at least a 2-MB FAT system partition that will contain the hardware-specific files needed to load Windows NT Server.

The following steps for installing Windows NT Server are typical of many RISC-based computer installations:

1. Insert the Windows NT Server CD-ROM into its drive and restart the computer.

2. After the menu on the ARC screen is displayed, select Run A Program.

3. At the prompt, enter the following:

    ```
    cd:\system\setupldr
    ```

    Replace system with MIPS, ALPHA, or whatever, to identify the type of RISC platform. On some systems, you might have to replace cd: with the full device name. Refer to your RISC computer manual for more details.

4. Follow the instructions on-screen for the Windows NT Server installation.

The system partition contains the hidden files OSLOADER.EXE and HAL.DLL in the subdirectory \OS\WINNT. It is a good idea to install the rest of the NT files on a separate partition formatted to NTFS to make use of the file system security features.

Troubleshooting Windows NT Installations

This section offers some troubleshooting tips that you can use if you encounter problems during Windows NT Server installation, because as sometimes happens, the best laid plans can go awry. If this happens to your Windows NT installation, the following can be of help.

Creating and Updating the Emergency Repair Disk

You should create the emergency repair disk as part of the Windows NT Server installation. You can use the emergency disk for troubleshooting purposes. You need to boot the server with the Setup disks, and then wait for the word R=Repair to appear in the status line. Press R and follow the instructions on-screen for using the emergency disk.

If you neglected to perform this step, you always can create the emergency disk by running the program RDISK.EXE, which can be found in the %SystemRoot%\System32 directory. You also can use the RDISK program to update an existing emergency disk with new configuration information on the server. When you run the RDISK program, you will see a dialog box similar to the one shown in figure 4.8. You can use the Repair Disk Utility dialog box to create a new emergency repair disk or to update an existing disk.

Figure 4.8

The Repair Disk Utility dialog box.

The emergency repair disk contains registry configuration information on the system, security, SAM (Security Accounts Manager), and the software configurations. It also contains copies of the AUTOEXEC.NT and CONFIG.NT, which are kept in the %SystemRoot%\System32 directory. The AUTOEXEC.NT and CONFIG.NT files are used to initialize the DOS subsystem. A sample of the directory listing of the emergency disk follows:

```
Volume in drive A has no label.
Volume Serial Number is 1003-EA33
Directory of A:\
08/08/96  07:46p              112,838 system._
08/08/96  07:47p              395,964 software._
08/08/96  07:48p                7,798 security._
08/08/96  07:48p                7,940 sam._
08/08/96  07:48p               20,192 default._
08/08/96  07:48p               19,068 ntuser.da_
07/22/96  05:31p                  536 autoexec.nt
07/22/96  05:29p                2,586 config.nt
8 File(s)         566,922 bytes
830,976 bytes free
```

The registry database files (also called *hives*) are system._, software._, security._, and default._. The sam._ file contains the Security Accounts Manager database.

Note During an RDISK update, the Default, SAM, and security files are not updated; they remain as they were on original installation. To update the SAM files, run RDISK with the /S option.

If your floppy drive is 2.88 MB, you might have difficulty due to driver incompatibilities creating an emergency disk if you supply a disk formatted with 2.88 MB. In this case, supply a disk formatted with 1.44 MB.

Note Examples of cases when you should update the Emergency Repair Disk include the creation of new partitions using Disk Administrator (volume sets, mirror sets, Striped Sets, and so on), the conversion of FAT to NTFS, and the installation of new services.

Creating an NT Boot Disk

An NT boot disk can be useful in troubleshooting if the NT boot loader and system files such as BOOT.INI and NTDETECT.COM are corrupted.

Unlike DOS, whose system files can be placed in a single boot disk, the Windows NT Server cannot be placed in a single, high-density boot disk. It is convenient to have a single boot disk, however, that contains the minimum operating system files to jump-start the Windows NT Server if some critical files are missing or damaged on the Windows NT Server. You first should try to use the emergency disk, but this might not be able to repair the damage. Also, remember that each emergency disk is specific to the Windows NT machine.

To create a minimum NT boot disk, you can perform the following steps:

1. Format a floppy by using the Windows NT Explorer. You can do this by performing the following steps:

   ■ Start Explorer. Click on the Start button, Programs, Windows NT Explorer.

   ■ Select the floppy drive you want to format. Right-click on the selected floppy drive.

   ■ From the popup menu, select **F**ormat.

   ■ Choose the required parameters, and press the Start button.

   Alternatively, you can type the following from the NT command prompt:

   FORMAT A:

You might be tempted to think that you can format the floppy disk under MS-DOS because the FAT file system is used when a floppy disk is formatted under NT. However, this would not work because when a floppy disk is formatted under DOS, the bootstrap program installed in the first sector of the disk looks for IO.SYS and MSDOS.SYS (IBMBIO.SYS and IBMDOS.SYS for IBM's PC-DOS), in that order. When a floppy disk is formatted under NT, an NT-specific bootstrap program installed in the first sector of the disk looks for the NTLDR program. The NTLDR program is essential for the Windows NT boot process.

2. Copy boot files from the Windows NT Server root directory to the boot floppy. For an Intel-based system, you should copy the following files:

   ■ NTLDR

   ■ NTDETECT.COM

   ■ BOOT.INI

   ■ NTBOOTDD.SYS (if using a non-BIOS-enabled SCSI controller)

   These are system and hidden files. To view them using Explorer, follow these steps:

   ■ Choose **V**iew from the Explorer menu.

   ■ Choose **O**ptions.

   ■ Enable the Show all files Option Button.

3. Boot the Windows NT Server with the minimum NT boot disk and verify that you can boot the NT server machine.

Copying a Missing File from the Windows NT Distribution

If a few critical files on the Windows NT computer are corrupt, you can copy them from the Windows NT distribution. Many of the files in the Windows NT distribution are in the compressed format. To uncompress these files, use the EXPAND utility that is located in the \WINNT\SYSTEM32 directory. The following is the syntax for using the EXPAND utility:

```
EXPAND [-r] Source Destination
EXPAND -r Source [Destination]
-r              Rename expanded files.
Source          Source file specification. Wildcards may be used.
Destination Destination file | path specification. Destination may be a directory.
If Source is multiple files and -r is not specified,
Destination must be a directory.
```

> **Warning** If you have applied service packs, hot fixes, or updated drivers prior to the corruption, you will need to reapply them after recovering the original files from the distribution files.

Customizing the Windows NT Server Installation

If you are performing a larger number of Windows NT Server installations, it often is helpful to be able to customize the Windows NT Server Setup program to meet the needs of the organization. You can add files and applications to Windows NT Server as part of the installation, for example, or remove certain unused features such as POSIX and OS/2 support to save on server disk space.

Using Control Files

The Windows NT Server Setup program uses information in setup information files (SIF extension) and information files (INF extension) to control the behavior of the Setup program. You can customize these files and create an answer file that can be used for an unattended setup. Using an unattended setup means that you do not have to interactively answer questions during the installation because the answers are supplied from a special file called the *unattended answer file*. This method enables you to set up an unattended setup for computers that have a similar hardware configuration.

The key files used by Setup are described in table 4.1.

Table 4.1
Key Files Used in Windows NT Setup

File Name	Description
TXTSETUP.SIF	Controls the text-mode portion of the core Windows NT components.
DOSNET.INF	Contains the list of files copied to a local drive when you install using WINNT or WINNT32.
IPINFO.INF	Controls the default gateway IP address, adapter IP addresses, and subnet mask IP addresses.
LAYOUT.INF	Controls the text and graphical mode installation of Windows NT components.

The following sections describe in more detail how these files are used during Setup, as well as their format.

Using TXTSETUP.SIF

When you start the Windows NT installation, you are prompted for information such as where you want to install the operating system and the file system type to be used. This stage of the installation is done in text mode because the graphics components have yet to be installed. The minimum set of files is copied during the text mode. These files include drivers for the mouse, keyboard, disk controllers, video, and the hardware-abstraction layer DLL (HAL.DLL) for the computer.

The TXTSETUP.SIF file specifies which files are copied during Setup, and all the changes to be made to the registry during the installation and upgrade. This file is contained in the first Setup disk, so any changes to be made must be made to a copy of this disk or its copy in the distribution directory.

Using LAYOUT.INF

After the minimum set of files has been copied in text mode, Setup starts the computer in the graphical mode and installs the key components such as the Taskbar, Explorer, Windows NT subsystems (MSDOS, WIN16, OS/2, and POSIX), fonts, and compatibility files for MS-DOS. Only the key components are installed in this phase; the optional components are installed later. This phase of the installation is controlled by the LAYOUT.INF file.

After installing the key components, the LAYOUT.INF file initiates other parts of the Setup that install the optional components.

The LAYOUT.INF file also controls the installation of the optional components, such as games, screen savers, wallpapers, and README files.

To change the key components to install, you must modify the LAYOUT.INF file.

Using DOSNET.INF

The DOSNET.INF files are used only if you use the WINNT or WINNT32 programs to initiate the Windows NT installation. These programs copy files from the distribution directory to the target computer into a temporary directory called WIN_NT.~LS. The temporary directory is used to copy files for the rest of the installation. At the end of the installation, the temporary directory and its contents are deleted. The DOSNET.INF specifies which files are to be copied to the temporary directory.

The DOSNET.INF also contains the information that is needed to create the boot floppy disks used for installing Windows NT on Intel-based computers.

If you need to change the files that are copied to the target computer, you must modify the DOSNET.INF file.

The DOSNET.INF files and the other key files—TXTSETUP.SIF, and LAYOUT.INF—are interdependent. When making a change to the DOSETUP.INF file, make the corresponding changes to the TXTSETUP.SIF, and LAYOUT.INF files. If you make a change to the TXTSETUP.SIF, or LAYOUT.INF file, you must make a corresponding change to the DOSNET.INF file.

In order to customize the Setup, you need to modify the key Setup files. In order to modify these files, you need to understand their format. The next few sections discuss the format of the key files.

Looking at the LAYOUT.INF File Format

The LAYOUT.INF file is a text file that contains sections with section titles in brackets (see Appendixes B and C). Sections contain variable definitions used within the INF file, lists of files, and scripting-language statements that control the installation steps. For most customization tasks, the scripting language is not needed.

The files in the LAYOUT.INF file are listed in the following format:

filename_on_source = diskid,subdir,size,checksum,spare,spare

extra fields are nt-specific

If you examine Appendix B, you will see a section called [Files-i386-nt-system-drivers]. A portion of this section is reproduced here so that you can see an example of this syntax:

```
afd.sys      = 1,,62976,,,,,4,1,0
cdrom.sys    = 1,,22528,,,,_3,4,0,0
diskdump.sys = 1,,13824,,,,,4,0,0
diskperf.sys = 1,,5120,,,,,4,1,0
kbdclass.sys = 1,,9728,,,,_2,4,1
```

Lines that begin with a semicolon (;) signify a comment in the TXTSETUP.SIF and LAYOUT.INF files and are not processed.

Looking at the DOSNET.INF File Format

The DOSNET.INF lists the files using the following syntax:

`d1, filename`

In this syntax, d1 is not a disk number. It is a variable defined in the [Directories] section of the file and indicates where the files exist relative to the directory in which DOSNET.INF is located in the distribution directory. The following is the [Directories] section defining the d1 variable.

```
[Directories]
# Specification of the source directory structure. All directories
# are relative to the directory where DOSNET.INF was found on the
# remote source or the temp directory on the local source.
# Loading and trailing backslashes are ignored — to specify the root,
# leave the directory field blank or use \.
d1 = \
```

The DOSNET.INF file does not contain a scripting language. Also, the [Source Media Descriptions] section is absent because files are copied to a temporary directory and then are copied during installation.

Lines that begin with a pound sign (#) signify a comment in the DOSNET.INF files and are not processed. This is different from the semicolon (;) convention used in the TXTSETUP.SIF, and LAYOUT.INF files. Do not confuse these two conventions; otherwise, you will get unexpected results.

Looking at the TXTSETUP.SIF File Format

The TXTSETUP.SIF file is the most likely file you will need to customize the setup. It contains numerous sections, the most important of which are described in the following sections.

The [Files.DeleteOnUpgrade] Section

This section lists the files that might be installed in a previous version of Windows NT; these files need to be deleted when you upgrade to the most recent version. A partial example from this section follows:

```
; Upgrade File Sections
; =====================
 [Files.DeleteOnUpgrade]
; file , dir
ami4448.sys   , 4
cdfs_rec.sys  , 4
fat_rec.sys   , 4
hpfs_rec.sys  , 4
ntfs_rec.sys  , 4
lmuicmn0.dll  , 2
lmuicmn1.dll  , 2
.:
:
```

The following syntax is used for this section:

filename, dirnumber

The *dirnumber* is defined in the [WinntDirectories] section:

```
[WinntDirectories]
1  = \
2  = system32
3  = system32\config
4  = system32\drivers
5  = system
6  = system32\os2
:
:
```

The directories in the [WinntDirectories] section are subdirectories of the Windows NT root directory (usually, \WINNT).

The [Files.BackupOnUpgrade] Section

This section lists the files that might be installed in a previous version of Windows NT; these files must be backed up when you upgrade to the most recent version. An example from this section follows:

```
[Files.BackupOnUpgrade]
; file , dir , newname
perfc009.dat  , 2 , perfc009.bak
perfh009.dat  , 2 , perfh009.bak
```

The following syntax is used for this section:

```
filename, dirnumber, backupname
```

The *dirnumber* is defined in the [WinntDirectories] section defined earlier, and the *backupname* is the backed up name of this file.

The [Files.BackupOnOverwrite] Section

This section lists the files that might be installed in a previous version of Windows NT; these files must be backed up before they are overwritten when you upgrade to the most recent version. An example from this section follows:

```
[Files.BackupOnOverwrite]
; file , dir , newname
perfc009.dat  , 2 , perfc009.bak
perfh009.dat  , 2 , perfh009.bak
system        , 3 , system.bak
software      , 3 , software.bak
default       , 3 , default.bak
sam           , 3 , sam.bak
security      , 3 , security.bak
```

The following syntax is used for this section:

```
filename, dirnumber, backupname
```

The *dirnumber* is defined in the [WinntDirectories] section defined earlier, and the *backupname* is the backed-up name of this file before the file is overwritten.

The [Files.UpgradeWin31] Section

This section lists the files that might be installed in an existing version of Windows 3.x or Windows 3.x for Workgroups, which also are used by Windows NT. The files listed in this section are not to be replaced with the Windows NT files by the same file name. An example from this section follows:

```
[Files.UpgradeWin31]
; file , dir
write.exe       , 1
notepad.exe     , 1
taskman.exe     , 1
winhelp.exe     , 1
COMMDLG.DLL     , 5
MMSYSTEM.DLL    , 5
OLECLI.DLL      , 5
OLESVR.DLL      , 5
SHELL.DLL       , 5
VER.DLL         , 5
MMTASK.TSK      , 5
MCIWAVE.DRV     , 5
MCISEQ.DRV      , 5
MCIAVI.DRV      , 5
MSVIDEO.DLL     , 5
AVIFILE.DLL     , 5
```

The following syntax is used for this section:

```
filename, dirnumber
```

The *dirnumber* is defined in the [WinntDirectories] section defined earlier.

The [SetupData] Section

This section lists required resources, available disk space, and debugging options. An example of this section follows:

```
[SetupData]
SetupSourcePath = \
MajorVersion = 4
MinorVersion = 0
DefaultPath=\WINNT
OsLoadOptions = "/nodebug"
ProductType = 1
```

```
LoadIdentifier  = %srv_id%
BaseVideoLoadId = %srv_id_vga%
RequiredMemory = 12058624
FreeSysPartDiskSpace = 750
UpgradeFreeSysPartDiskSpace = 750
FreeDiskSpace = 131872
UpgradeFreeDiskSpace = 48368
```

The parameters that might need to be changed are described in table 4.2. The values that you specify in DefaultPath, LoadIdentifier, BaseVideoLoadId, and OsLoadOptions also end up in the BOOT.INI file on the boot partition of the Windows NT computer. The following is a sample BOOT.INI file from the author's notebook that he used as a Windows NT Server and a Windows NT Workstation:

```
[boot loader]
timeout=30
default=multi(0)disk(0)rdisk(0)partition(1)\WINNT
 [operating systems]
multi(0)disk(0)rdisk(0)partition(1)\WINNT="Windows NT Server Version 4.00"
multi(0)disk(0)rdisk(0)partition(1)\WINNT="Windows NT Server Version 4.00 [VGA
➥mode]" /basevideo
multi(0)disk(0)rdisk(0)partition(1)\WINNTW="Windows NT Workstation Version 4.00"
multi(0)disk(0)rdisk(0)partition(1)\WINNTW="Windows NT Workstation Version 4.00
➥[VGA mode]" /basevideo
C:\="MS-DOS"
```

Table 4.2
Important [SetupData] Parameters in TXTSETUP.SIF

Parameter	Description
FreeDiskSpace	Specifies the amount of free space needed for a new Windows NT installation. If you add or remove files from the standard installation, adjust this size accordingly. The size is in terms of KB.
UpgradeFreeDiskSpace	Specifies the amount of free space needed for an upgrade from an earlier version of Windows NT installation. If you add or remove files from the standard installation, adjust this size accordingly. The size is in terms of KB.
DefaultPath	Specifies the system root directory in which Windows NT is installed. If you have a custom installation that you want to install in another directory, change this value to the new directory.
LoadIdentifier	Specifies the text that appears during Setup to identify the system that is installed. This text also is placed in the BOOT.INI file on the boot partition to identify the Windows NT configuration that is loaded.

Parameter	Description
BaseVideoLoadId	Specifies the text that appears when the installation is using the /BASEVIDEO option. This text also is placed in the BOOT.INI file on the boot partition to identify the Base Video Windows NT configuration.
OsLoadOptions	Specifies the debugging options. Option values are in quotation marks and can be /NODEBUG, /DEBUG, /DEBUGPORT=COMx, /BAUD RATE=n, and /NoSerialMice. These option values apply to only the text mode portion of the installation. To have one or more of these options apply in the graphical mode, add the following line in the [SetupData] section: `OsLoadOptionsVar= /option [/option...]` /NODEBUG specifies that no debugging information is collected or transmitted during the installation. This is the default value. /DEBUG enables debugging, with the last COM port used for communicating debugging information, unless another COM port is specified using the /DEBUGPORT=COMx option. The /BAUDRATE=n option sets the baud rate (bits per second) on the COM port for remote debugging. The default baud rate is 19200. The /NoSerialMice option disables serial mice detection on certain ports and excludes ports used by the Uninterrupted Power Supply (UPS) system. The detection probe signal can cause certain UPS devices to power down, and then turn off the system, effectively halting the installation. You also can add this option in the BOOT.INI file for the reasons just described. If the /NoSerialMice option is specified by itself, mouse detection is disabled on all serial ports. To disable mouse detection on a single COM port, use /NoSerialMice= COMx. To disable mouse detection on multiple COM ports, use /NoSerialMice=COMx,COMy,...

The [SourceDisksFiles] Section

The [SourceDisksFiles] section lists all the files for the installation. This is a critical section for customization, because this controls which files are copied during the installation. A sample [Files] section follows. You can use this section as a documentation of all the Windows NT installation files:

```
[SourceDisksFiles]
at.exe        = 1,,,,,,,,2,1,0
att.ht        = 1,,,,,,,,2,3,3
atapi.sys     = 1,,,,,,,_3,4,0,0
atdisk.sys    = 1,,,,,,,_3,4,0,0
atkctrs.dll   = 1,,,,,,,,2,1
atsvc.exe     = 1,,,,,,,,2,1,0
attrib.exe    = 1,,,,,,,,2,1,0
audiocdc.hlp  = 1,,,,,,,,2,0,0
autochk.exe   = 1,,,,,,,_x,2,0,0
autoconv.exe  = 1,,,,,,,,2,1,0
autoexec.nt   = 1,,,,,,,,2,2
autolfn.exe   = 1,,,,,,,,2,0,0
avicap.dll    = 1,,,,,,,,2,0,0
avicap32.dll  = 1,,,,,,,,2,0,0
avifil32.dll  = 1,,,,,,,,2,0,0
avifile.dll   = 1,,,,,,,,2,0,0
bachsb~1.rmi  = 1,,,,,,,,2,3,3
backgrnd.gif  = 1,,,,,,,,2,3,3
backup.cnt    = 1,,,,,,,,2,0,0
backup.exe    = 1,,,,,,,,2,1,0
backup.hlp    = 1,,,,,,,,2,0,0
banana.ani    = 1,,,,,,,,2,3,3
barber.ani    = 1,,,,,,,,2,3,3
basesrv.dll   = 1,,,,,,,,2,0,0
beep.sys      = 1,,,,,,,,4,0,0
beetho~2.rmi  = 1,,,,,,,,2,3,3
bhctrl.cpl    = 1,,,,,,,,2,1
bhmon.dll     = 1,,,,,,,,2,1
bhnetb.dll    = 1,,,,,,,,2,1
```

The following is the syntax of each line in the [SourceDisksFiles] section:

```
filename_on_source = diskid,subdir,upgradecode,newinstallcode,spare,spare,
newfilename

extra fields are nt-specific
```

The *diskid* is used when a floppy disk installation is used.

The *subdir* is the directory to which files will be copied. Codes defined in the [WinntDirectories] section (discussed previously) of the TXTSETUP.SIF file are used to identify the destination directory.

The *upgradecode* is a single digit that is used if this is an upgrade from an earlier version. It specifies whether the file is copied during the text-mode portion. These codes are described in table 4.3.

The *newinstallcode* is a single digit that is used if this is a fresh installation. It specifies whether the file is copied during the text-mode portion. The same codes are used as for upgrading Windows NT and are described in table 4.3. The *newinstallcode* is optional; if not included, the file is not copied (code = 3).

The *newfilename* is the name the file will be renamed to if it is copied.

As an example, consider the following line from the [SourceDisksFiles] section shown earlier:

```
autochk.exe = 1,,,,,,,_x,2,0,0
```

The interpretation of this line follows: The file AUTOCHK.EXE can be found on the CD-ROM or disk with diskid d2 defined in the [Media] section. It also is found in Setup Disk 2 (_2), also defined in the [Media] section. The file is to be installed in directory 2, which is defined in the [WinntDirectories] section. If you look up the [WinntDirectories] section, directory 2 is the System32 subdirectory in the Windows NT root directory. The upgrade code and new installation code is 0, which means that this file always must be copied to the installation directory, whether this an upgrade from an earlier version of Windows NT or a fresh installation.

Table 4.3
Codes in the [Files] Section of TXTSETUP.SIF for File Copy Status

Code	Copy Action
0	Always copies the file
1	Copies the file only if it exists in the installation directory
2	Does not copy the file if it exists in the installation directory
3	Does not copy the file

Preparing to Customize Windows NT Setup

Before you make changes to the key Setup files, you must copy the files to an existing network server so that you can customize the distribution. The network server can be another Windows NT computer (workstation or server) that shares the distribution directory, a NetWare server, a Unix server, a VINES server, and so on. The only requirement is that you have the appropriate network client software running at the computer to be installed to access the distribution directory.

To set up a distribution directory on a Windows NT server, follow these steps:

1. Create a share directory on the network server. For example, you can use the following commands if the shared directory is on drive D of the server:

   ```
   md d:\i386
   ```

   ```
   net share winnt_dist=d:\i386
   ```

2. Copy the CD-ROM distribution to the shared subdirectory on the network server. If the CD-ROM is on a Windows NT client, and the network server name is NTUS, you can use the following commands:

```
net use f: \\NTUS\WINNT_DIST

xcopy e:\i386 f: /s /e /v
```

3. Make a custom distribution by modifying the files in the distribution directory.

4. Make the share directory read-only for installation clients.

5. Start the installation using the WINNT or WINNT32 programs as described earlier in this chapter.

Examining Case Studies in Windows NT Customization

The following sections discuss case studies in customizing Windows NT Setup. Make your customization changes carefully. A simple syntax error can cause an incorrect installation that can be difficult to troubleshoot.

Case Study 1: Excluding Files from Windows NT Installation

You can reduce the amount of disk space by eliminating unneeded components. You might want to exclude the games files, Windows NT Help files, or other infrequently used programs, for example. Use the steps as a guideline to exclude a file. In this example, the game FREECELL is excluded from the Windows NT installation:

1. Locate the file to be excluded in the [Files] section of DOSNET.INF and comment it out by using the pound (#) character in column 1:

```
 [Files]
d1,FRAMEBUF.DLL
#d1,FREECELL.EXE
#d1,FREECELL.HLP
d1,FS_REC.SYS
```

2. If the file is listed in LAYOUT.INF, comment it out using semicolons (;). In the case of FREECELL, it is not included in the LAYOUT.INF file.

3. If the file is listed in TXTSETUP.SIF, comment it out using semicolons (;). In the case of TXTSETUP.SIF, it is included in the [Files] section.

```
[SourceDisksFiles]
;freecell.exe = 1,,,,,,,,2,3,3
;freecell.hlp = 1,,,,,,,,2,3,3
```

You might find that the NT command FINDSTR can be useful for searching for a string in a file, so you can determine whether one of the key Setup files contains a reference to a file name. The syntax for using this command is included here for your reference and use:

```
FINDSTR [/B] [/E] [/L] [/R] [/S] [/I] [/X] [/V] [/N] [/M] [/O]
➡[/F:file][/C:string] [/G:file] [strings] [[drive:][path]filename[ ...]]
```

/B	Matches pattern if at the beginning of a line.
/E	Matches pattern if at the end of a line.
/L	Uses search strings literally.
/R	Uses search strings as regular expressions.
/S	Searches for matching files in the current directory and all subdirectories.
/I	Specifies that the search is not to be case-sensitive.
/X	Prints lines that match exactly.
/V	Prints only lines that do not contain a match.
/N	Prints the line number before each line that matches.
/M	Prints only the file name if a file contains a match.
/O	Prints character offset before each matching line.
/F:file	Reads file list from the specified file (/ stands for console).
/C:string	Uses specified string as a literal search string.
/G:file	Gets search strings from the specified file (/ stands for console).

strings   Text to be searched for.

[*drive:*][*path*]*filename*   Specifies a file or files to search.

Use spaces to separate multiple search strings unless the argument is prefixed with /C. For example, 'FINDSTR "hello there" x.y' searches for "hello" or "there" in file x.y. On the other hand, 'FINDSTR /C:"hello there" x.y' searches for "hello there" in file x.y.

Case Study 2: Excluding the OS/2 Subsystem

The Windows NT OS/2 subsystem supports only character-based OS/2 1.*x* applications. It does not support any Presentation Manager–based GUI applications. If you do not need the OS/2 subsystem, you can use the following steps as a guideline to exclude the subsystem from the installation:

1. In the DOSNET.INF file, comment out the OS/2 files:

   ```
   [Files]
   ...
   #d1,DOSCALLS.DLL
   #d1,NETAPI.OS2
   #d1,OS2.EXE
   #d1,OS2SRV.EXE
   #d1,OS2SS.EXE
   ```

2. In the LAYOUT.INF file, comment out the OS/2 files:

   ```
   ;doscalls.dll = 1,,12800,,,,,8,0,0
   ;netapi.os2  = 1,,248320,,,,,8,0,0,netapi.dll
   netapi.dll   = 1,,108544,,,,,2,1,0
   ;os2.exe     = 1,,443904,,,,,2,1,0
   ;os2srv.exe  = 1,,131072,,,,,2,1,0
   ;os2ss.exe   = 1,,9216,,,,,2,1,0
   ```

3. In the TXTSETUP.SIF file, comment out the OS/2 files:

   ```
   [SourceDisksFiles.x86]
   ;doscalls.dll = 1,,,,,,,8,0,0
   ;os2.exe     = 1,,,,,,,2,1,0
   ;netapi.os2  = 1,,,,,,,8,0,0,netapi.dll
   ;os2srv.exe  = 1,,,,,,,2,1,0
   ;os2ss.exe   = 1,,,,,,,2,1,0
   ```

4. If you are upgrading from an earlier version of Windows NT, list the OS/2 file names in the [Files.DeleteOnUpgrade] section of the TXTSETUP.SIF file. The line uses the following syntax:

   ```
   filename, dircode
   ```

   The *dircode* is assigned in the [WinntDirectories] section of the TXTSETUP.SIF file.

Case Study 3: Excluding the POSIX Subsystem

The Windows NT POSIX subsystem supports POSIX 1.0 APIs. If your Windows NT system does not need to support POSIX applications, you can use the following steps as a guideline to exclude them from the installation:

1. In the DOSNET.INF file, comment out the POSIX files:

```
[Files]
#d1,PAX.EXE
#d1,POSIX.EXE
#d1,PSXDLL.DLL
#d1,PSXSS.EXE
```

2. In the LAYOUT.INF file, comment out following the POSIX files:

```
[SourceDisksFiles]
;pax.exe      = 1,,54272,,,,,2,1,0
;posix.exe    = 1,,68608,,,,,2,1,0
;psxdll.dll   = 1,,36864,,,,,2,1,0
;psxss.exe    = 1,,94208,,,,,2,1,0
```

3. In the TXTSETUP.SIF file, comment out the POSIX files:

```
[SourceDisksFiles]
...
;pax.exe      = 1,,,,,,,2,1,0
;posix.exe    = 1,,,,,,,2,1,0
;psxss.exe    = 1,,,,,,,2,1,0
;psxdll.dll   = 1,,,,,,,2,1,0
```

4. If you are upgrading from an earlier version of Windows NT, list the POSIX file names in the [Files.DeleteOnUpgrade] section of the TXTSETUP.SIF file. The line uses the following syntax:

```
filename, dircode
```

The *dircode* is assigned in the [WinntDirectories] section of the TXTSETUP.SIF file.

Case Study 4: Excluding the WIN16 and MSDOS Subsystem

If you do not plan to run DOS or Windows 16-bit applications on the Windows NT system, you can exclude them from the installation by commenting out all references to MS-DOS and WIN16 files in the TXTSETUP.SIF, LAYOUT.INF, and DOSNET.INF files. If you are upgrading from an earlier version of Windows NT, list these file names in the [Files.DeleteOnUpgrade] section of the TXTSETUP.SIF file. The line uses the following syntax:

```
filename, dircode
```

The *dircode* is assigned in the [WinntDirectories] section of the TXTSETUP.SIF file.

Case Study 5: Updating the Registry during Setup

The Registry is an internal database in Windows NT that holds system- and application-specific settings. The Registry is organized as four separate trees (also called *hives*) where the leaf-nodes in the tree have a key, a type of key, and a value for the key.

Many system parameters are set by using predefined keys. You can edit the registry using the REGEDT32.EXE tool, which can be found in the SYSTEM32 subdirectory. You will learn more about the Registry in Chapter 11, "Supporting Windows NT Server Clients." You should attempt the procedure in this section only after you have read Chapter 12, "Integrating Windows NT Server with a NetWare Network," and are comfortable with changing the Registry.

You always can use REGEDT32 on each installation and interactively modify the Registry. The advantage of using the REGEDT32 procedure in this section is for doing a large number of custom installations that need a modified registry.

Three template hives are provided in the installation files that are copied in their entirety to the registry on a fresh installation. During an upgrade of an earlier Windows NT installation, only portions of the hives are copied. The template hives in the Setup procedure are System, Software, and Default.

You can edit the [KeysToAdd] section of the TXTSETUP.SIF file to create new keys, or you can add or change values under the keys. The [Values.section] in the TXTSETUP.SIF file contains the values for the keys listed in the [KeysToAdd] section.

A sample of the [KeysToAdd] section follows:

```
[KeysToAdd]
Software,    "Microsoft\Windows NT\CurrentVersion\Winlogon",Values.Winlogon
Software,    "Microsoft\Windows NT\CurrentVersion\WOW\Compatibility",
➡Values.WOW.Compatibility
Software,    "Microsoft\Windows NT\CurrentVersion\WOW\WowFax\SupportedFaxDrivers"
Software,    "Microsoft\Windows NT\CurrentVersion\MCI32", Values.MCI32
Software,    "Microsoft\Windows NT\CurrentVersion\MCI", Values.MCI
Software,    "Microsoft\Windows NT\CurrentVersion\Drivers32", Values.Drivers32
Software,"Microsoft\WindowsNT\CurrentVersion\IniFileMapping\system.ini\boot",
➡Values.IniFileMapping.SystemIni.Boot Software,
"Microsoft\Windows NT\CurrentVersion\IniFileMapping\win.ini",
➡Values.IniFileMapping.WinIni
Software,    "Microsoft\Windows NT\CurrentVersion\IniFileMapping\win.ini\windows",
```

Each line in the [KeysToAdd] section has the following syntax:

```
hivename,   key  [;Values.section]
```

The *hivename* is the name of the template hive. The key is the key in the hive that is to be copied. The Values.*section* refers to the section that defines the value for the key. If the Values.*section* is not specified, the Setup program looks for this information in the template hive—all values under the key as specified in the hive are copied.

Consider the following example from the [KeysToAdd] section:

```
Software,    "Microsoft\Windows NT\CurrentVersion\Winlogon", Values.Winlogon
```

This line means that the value for the key "Microsoft\Windows NT\Current Version\ Winlogon" is specified in the [Values.Winlogon] section.

An example of the [Values.Winlogon] section follows:

```
 [Values.Winlogon]
System
Shell
AutoRestartShell
VmApplet
```

The following is the general syntax of the [Values.section]:

```
name [,type, value]
```

The *name* is the name of the key that is added. If only name is specified, the entire key and its subkeys are copied. If a key by that name exists, it is overwritten. The *type* is the type of value such as REG_SZ, REG_BINARY, REG_EXPAND_SZ, REG_MULTI_SZ, REG_DWORD, and REG_BINARY_DWORD. *Value* is any value you specify. Key types that have a _SZ suffix are strings, and their corresponding values must be in quotation marks.

Case Study 6: Adding a File to the Installation

If you need to add a nonstandard file to the Windows NT installation, add the file name to the appropriate sections of the TXTSETUP.SIF and DOSNET.INF files.

Suppose that you need to add a file KALPA.DAT that provides on-line help for the organization Astro Universal, Inc. in a special directory called ASTRO. You then should add KALPA.DAT to the distribution and make the following changes:

■ In the TXTSETUP.SIF file, define the new directory ASTRO in the [WinntDirectories] section:

```
[WinntDirectories]
1  = "\"
2  = system32
3  = system32\config
4  = system32\drivers
5  = system
6  = system32\os2
7  = system32\ras
8  = system32\os2\dll
9  = system32\spool
10 = system32\spool\drivers
11 = system32\spool\drivers\w32x86\2
12 = system32\spool\prtprocs
13 = system32\spool\prtprocs\w32x86
```

```
14 = system32\wins
15 = system32\dhcp
16 = repair
17 = system32\drivers\etc
18 = system32\spool\drivers\w32x86
19 = system32\viewers
20 = inf
21 = Help
22 = Fonts
23 = Config
24 = Profiles
25 = Cursors
26 = Media
27 = ASTRO
```

By defining a new directory, in the [WinntDirectories], the Setup program creates the subdirectory for you.

■ In the [Files] section of TXTSETUP.SIF, specify that the file is to be copied during an upgrade or a new installation:

```
[Files]
KALPA.DAT  = 1,,,,,,,27,0,0
```

The syntax of the [Files] sections of the TXTSETUP.SIF is discussed earlier in this chapter.

■ If the user runs the installation using the WINNT or WINNT32 programs, you also should modify the DOSNET.INF file. In the [Files] section of the DOSNET.INF file, make the following change:

```
[Files]
 ...
d1, KALPA.DAT
```

Performing an Unattended Installation

The Windows NT Server 4 contains a tool called Windows NT Setup Manager (SETUPMGR.EXE) located in the following directory on the distribution CD: \support\deptools. Setup Manager can be used to create an *answer file*, which contains the answers to the Setup prompts and can be used to perform an unattended installation. You perform an unattended installation by using one of the following commands:

```
winnt /u:answerfile
```

```
winnt32 /u:answerfile
```

answerfile is the name of the answer file created by the SETUPMGR.EXE program. When the /u switch is used, it enables the /b switch. The /b switch is used for installation without Setup disks.

You can use SETUPMGR.EXE to create a new answer file, or to edit an existing answer file. The answer file can be used as a template for a group of computers that have a similar configuration.

To create a new answer file, follow these steps:

1. Using the Windows Explorer, change the current folder to the Support\Deptools*platform* folder on the Windows NT Server CD.

2. Run SETUPMGR.EXE.

   The Windows NT Setup Manager screen appears as shown in figure 4.9.

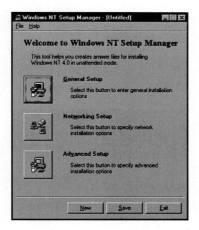

Figure 4.9
The Windows NT Setup Manager screen.

3. Enter values for each field corresponding to the response you would be making in an interactive answer session. The Windows NT Setup Manager dialog box enables you to enter the following installation information. If any of the fields are left blank, you are prompted for the value. Table 4.4 shows all the fields for each option in the Windows NT Setup Manager.

4. Click on the **S**ave button from the Windows NT Setup Manager screen, and specify the name of the unattended answer file.

Table 4.4
Fields and Installation Information

Field	Installation Information
General Setup: User Information	
Username	Owner of computer.
Organization	Name of organization to which Windows NT OS is installed.
Computer Name	If upgrading, leave this field blank.
Computer Role	Can be Workstation in Workgroup, Workstation in Domain, Server in Domain, Backup Domain Controller, or Primary Domain Controller.
Product ID	Number on Windows NT distribution.
General Setup: General	
	Confirm Hardware During Setup.
Upgrade Options	Options include: Prompt user for Windows NT installation to upgrade; Upgrade the current single Windows NT Installation; Upgrade the first Windows NT installation found; and Upgrade Existing Windows 3.1 or Windows for workgroup.
Run a program with Setup	By providing the full path name and any parameters needed in association with an executable, you can force the setup script to run additional applications during the installation process.
General Setup: Computer Role	
Computer Role	Options include: Workstation in Workgroup; Workstation in Domain; Server in a workgroup; Server in Domain; Backup Domain Controller; or Primary Domain Controller.
Workgroup / Domain Name	Specify applicable workgroup or domain name as determined by the computer role and associated workgroup or domain.
Create computer account	By supplying a Computer account name and password, you can automatically add the new computer to a domain.

Field	Installation Information
	General Setup: Install Directory
Installation Path	Options include: Can be Use Default directory; System Path or Prompt User During Setup for System Path installation directory; or Specify installation directory for a custom path.
	General Setup: Display Settings
Configure the graphics device at logon	Unless you know the display specifics of the computer you are affecting, it is advisable to use this option.
Settings	Permits you to specify display configuration details including: Bits per pixel; Horizontal resolution; Vertical resolution; refresh rate; or Flags.
	General Setup: Time Zone
Time Zone	Can be Prompt User During Setup or anyset to any of the Windows NT recognized time zones.
	General Setup: License Mode
Per Server	Used to indicate the maximum number of concurrent connections permitted to access the server using the Per Server licensing mode.
Per Seat	Select if the server is going to utilize the Per Seat licensing mode.
	Networking Setup: General
Manual Network Installation	Check this option if you want to perform a manual network installation during the installation process.
Unattended Network	This option permits three choices: Installation Automatically detect and install first adapter; Specify adapter(s) to be detected; and Specify adapter(s) to be installed.
	Networking Setup: Adapters
Adapter Section Name	Used to specify the header name in the setup script for adapter detection.

continues

Table 4.4, Continued
Fields and Installation Information

Field	Installation Information
Detect Count	Used to specify the number of network adapters detected during the installation process.
List of adapters	Provides the means of specifying network adapters to be setup during the installation process using the Add, Remove, and Parameters buttons.
Networking Setup: Protocols	
Protocol Section Name	Used to specify the header name in the setup script for networking protocols.
List of Protocols	Provides the means of specifying networking protocols to be setup during the installation process using the Add, Remove, and Parameters buttons.
Networking Setup: Services	
Service Section Name	Used to specify the header name in the setup script for services.
List of Services	Provides the means of specifying services to be setup during the installation process using the Add, Remove, and Parameters buttons.
Networking Setup: Internet	
Parameter Section Name	Used to specify the header name in the setup script for Internet parameters.
Installation Directory	Used to specify the installation path used for Internet services.
FTP Service Root	Used in conjunction with the Installation Directory path, to specify the full installation path used for the FTP service.
Gopher Service Root	Used in conjunction with the Installation Directory path, to specify the full installation path used for the Gopher service.
WWW Service Root	Used in conjunction with the Installation Directory path, to specify the full installation path used for the WWW service.

Field	Installation Information
Options	Options included are Internet Service Manager, HTMLA, and WWW.
Guest Account Name	Used to specify a quest account name.
Guest Account Password	Used to specify a password in conjunction with the Guest Account Name field.

Networking Setup: Modem

Port Number	Used to specify the communication port used by the modem.
Modem Description	General description of modem.
Manufacturer	Used to indicate the modems manufacturer, eg. Hayes.
Provider	Used to specify a provider
List of Modems to be installed	List box containing all currently selected modems to be installed.

Advanced Setup: General

Install a new HAL	Provides you with the ability to indicate a unique Hardware Abstraction Layer driver, including OEM variants.
Specify keyboard layout	Used to specify a unique keyboard layout such as US-International.

Advanced Setup: Reboot

Used to force a reboot	Can be set up for two situations: After Text Mode or After GUI Mode.
Skip Welcome wizard page	Check this box if you do not want the Welcome wizard page to initiate.
Skip Administrator Password wizard page	Check this box if you do not want the Administrators Password page to initiate. This will set the initial Administrator password to a null password.

continues

Table 4.4, Continued
Fields and Installation Information

Field	Installation Information
Advanced Setup: File System	
File System	Used to specify one of two file system options: Use current files system, or Convert to NTFS.
Extend OEM partition	If the computers hard disk exceeds two Gigs in size, select this option.
Advanced Setup: Mass Storage	
Mass Storage Driver Description	Using the Add and Remove buttons, you may optionally choose mass storage device drivers, or by checking the OEM box, you can choose OEM solution mass storage drivers.
List of Driver Descriptions	Indicates the currently selected mass storage device drivers to be installed.
Advanced Setup: Display	
Display Driver Description	Using the Add and Remove buttons, you may optionally choose display device drivers, or by checking the OEM box, you can choose OEM solution display device drivers.
List of Driver Descriptions	Indicates the currently selected display device drivers to be installed.
Advanced Setup: Keyboard	
Keyboard Driver Description	Using the Add and Remove buttons, you may optionally choose keyboard device drivers, or by checking the OEM box, you can choose OEM solution keyboard device drivers.
List of Driver Descriptions	Indicates the currently selected keyboard device drivers to be installed.
Advanced Setup: Printing Device	
Printing Device Driver Description	Using the Add and Remove buttons, you may optionally choose printing device drivers, or by checking the OEM box, you can choose OEM solution printing device drivers.

Field	Installation Information
List of Driver Descriptions	Indicates the currently selected printing device drivers to be installed.

Advanced Setup: Boot Files	
Boot File Name	Using the Add and Remove buttons, you may optionally choose boot files to be added during the installation process.
List of Boot File Names	Indicates the currently selected boot files to be installed.

Advanced Setup: Advertisement	
Banner text Logo graphics files Background graphics file	The Advertisement settings are used to customize the background used during the GUI portion of the setup process. It includes these three fields.

Note The License mode panel is only accessible if the computer role is that of a server.

The Modem panel is only accessible if Remote Access Service has been specified in the Services section.

If you leave the fields blank, the Unattended Answer File Information dialog box appears. Click on OK to continue or choose Cancel to go back and add values to the blank fields.

The unattended answer file is a text file that is organized by sections. The following is a sample unattended answer file, which also can be edited using a text editor:

```
[Unattended]
OemPreinstall = no
ConfirmHardware = no
NtUpgrade = no
Win31Upgrade = no
TargetPath = WINNT
OverwriteOemFilesOnUpgrade = no
[UserData]
FullName = "Your User Name"
OrgName = "Your Organization Name"
ComputerName = COMPUTER_NAME
[GuiUnattended]
TimeZone = "(GMT-08:00) Pacific Time (US & Canada); Tijuana"
[Display]
ConfigureAtLogon = 0
BitsPerPel = 16
XResolution = 640
YResolution = 480
```

```
VRefresh = 70
AutoConfirm = 1
[Network]
Attend = yes
DetectAdapters = ""
InstallProtocols = ProtocolsSection
JoinDomain = Domain_To_Join
[ProtocolsSection]
TC = TCParameters
 [TCParameters]
DHCP = yes
```

Using SYSDIFF.EXE with NT Installations

The Sysdiff tool is used to pre-install applications as part of an automated NT setup process, including applications that don't utilize scripted installations. Sysdiff is included only with the Windows NT Server Resource kit (not the NT Workstation Resource kit).

Sysdiff, in essence, takes a "snapshot" of an NT computer after a standard installation process as a source of reference. After which, you install any desired applications on the NT computer and compare the dissimilarities between the original "snapshot" information, and the alterations imposed by the installation of the additional applications. The dissimilarities are stored in a readable format in a difference file, or system difference packages (SYSDIFF.INF). The difference file can be applied to new NT installations, as part of an unattended setup process by including it in the distribution share, or it can be manually incorporated any time after the installation process has completed.

The following prerequisites must be met before using Sysdiff:

- Windows NT needs to be installed into identical directory structures on both the original and receiving systems.

- Both machines must be able to access one another via a network connection.

- Sysdiff requires that a properly configured sysdiff.inf file is in place.

- Both the original and receiving computers need to have the same hardware platforms.

- A shared distribution directory needs to be created, wherein the difference file created by the Sysdiff tool can be accessed by the receiving computer.

After you have determined that you meet the necessary prerequisites, use the following steps to use the Sysdiff tool:

1. Install Windows NT Workstation or NT server onto the reference computer.

2. Run the command sysdiff /snap on the reference computer.

3. Install any additionally desired applications onto the reference computer.

4. Run the command `sysdiff /diff` on the reference computer to facilitate the creation of the difference file.

5. If installing the difference file after NT installation, use the command `sysdiff /apply`.

6. If installing the difference file to the installation source, use the command `sysdiff /inf`.

Utilizing UDF Files

NT 4 supports unattended setup using Uniqueness Database Files (UDF). UDFs provide an easily managed ASCII text file used for deploying Windows NT 4 on a large scale. UDFs are used to merge or replace specific sections of the answer file in conjunction with the GUI stage of the setup process. UDFs are able to indicate specific per-computer parameters.

UDFs are formatted in two parameters:

■ **UniqueIDs.** Indicates the sections within the answer file that are going to be merged or replaced, and the UniqueID.

■ **UniqueID.** Indicates the data that will be merged or replaced in the answer file.

To utilize a UDF file during NT installation, use the following command-line switches with WINNT.EXE:

```
/u:answer_file
    /s:NT_Source
    /t:temp_drive
    /UDF:UniqueID,local_name_of_udf
```

Conclusion

In this chapter, you learned about upgrading Windows NT Server from previous versions of the operating system and migrating existing Windows 3.x application settings to Windows NT Server. You learned how to install Windows NT Server using an unsupported CD-ROM or by installing it from a network. You also learned how to customize a Windows NT installation. Customizing a Windows NT Server installation is particularly important if a large number of server installations are to be performed and the servers are to have similar installation settings.

Designing Windows NT Server Domains

*W*hen you design large networks using Windows NT
Servers, there are many advantages of designing the
networks using NT domains. This chapter explores the
Windows NT domain concept and how you can use it
to build enterprise-wide networks. You also will learn
about the basic differences between using a workgroup
model and using a domain model.

Using a Workgroup versus Using a Domain Model

In Windows NT networks, you can use either of the following models:

- Workgroup model

- Domain model

Before discussing domains, it is helpful to consider the differences between these models.

Understanding the Workgroup Model

Workgroups can be used for building small networks that have a peer-to-peer orientation. There is no requirement for a central server in a peer-to-peer network. Any workstation can act as a server and provide services that can be used by any workstation acting as a client. Although this arrangement might seem desirable at first, as the network grows, the flexibility can pose severe difficulties in managing the network. Workstations can be turned off at the end of the day, for example, and if there are critical services running on the network that are used by other workstations, these services are not available. Also, if a workstation crashes because of a user running faulty programs on it, the services running on the workstation temporarily are unavailable until the workstation and its services are activated.

A *workgroup* is a collection of Windows-based computers (Windows 3.x, Windows 95, and Windows NT, for example) that are grouped together for organizational or usage purposes. You can see this grouping from within File Manager when you try to assign a network drive to a network resource. Figure 5.1 shows the computers that belong to the Workgroup LGROUP. A screen similar to the one shown in figure 5.1 appears if you are using the Workgroup model on the network. You can take the following actions to view this screen:

- Run the Explorer.

- Choose **T**ools, Map **N**etwork Drive.

In figure 5.1, some of the computers are part of the workgroup GENERAL.COM. Workgroups are useful for browsing purposes. When you select the Workgroup name in figure 5.1, you can see all computers belonging to the group; this is called *browsing*. The computer on which this operation is being performed sends out query packets to find out which computers belong to the selected group. Workgroups can be used to represent resources belonging to a department or project in an organization.

Each computer in a workgroup maintains its own security policy and security accounts manager (SAM) database. On an NT computer belonging to a workgroup, you must log on with a user account defined on that computer. The SAM database on the NT computer includes the definitions of users and group accounts for that computer. That is, the user and group accounts in the workgroup have a significance that is local to the computer only. A user account named Mary on a Windows NT computer that is part of a workgroup will exist only on the computer on which it is defined, for example. If the computer on which Mary's user account is defined is down, the user Mary cannot log on to the network (see fig. 5.2). If there is another computer on which Mary is defined, it could be for another user named Mary, and this user account could have an entirely different password (see fig. 5.3).

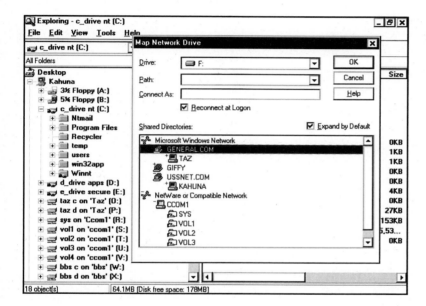

Figure 5.1

Browsing workgroups.

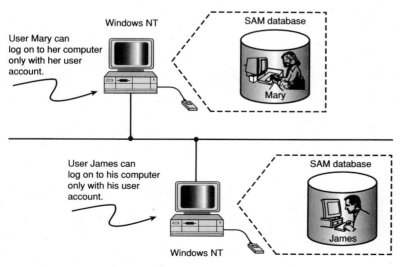

Figure 5.2

The local nature of user accounts in workgroups.

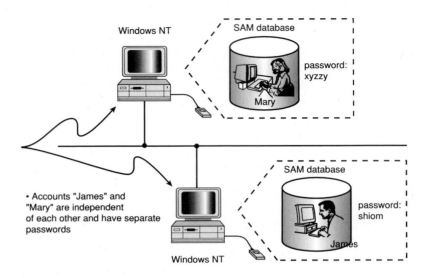

Figure 5.3

Passwords for the same user name account in a workgroup.

Because the security account database is local to each NT computer, administering the workgroup involves administering each security account database on each computer separately. This is similar to administering a stand-alone workstation. Any administration task that you perform on the computer affects that computer only. You might think of a stand-alone computer as a workgroup consisting of one computer only.

Understanding Local Login in an NT Workgroup

When a user logs into a Windows NT workstation belonging to a workgroup, the From box in the Welcome dialog box (which appears when the Windows NT workstation is started) lists only the computer name of the workstation. You cannot specify another value in the From box, such as another workgroup name or a domain name (unless your NT computer has been made part of the domain).

Figure 5.4 shows the NT components that are responsible for authenticating a user account on a local computer. The Security Policy database implements the security policy for that Windows NT computer, and the Security Accounts database contains the user account name, password, and other information. When a user logs in with the correct user name and password, the Local Security Authority (LSA) in Windows NT authenticates the user to the system and creates a security access token.

The security access token contains a Security Identifier (SID), which identifies the user logged in, and a list of SIDs for the groups of which the user is a member (see fig. 5.5). All user accounts and group accounts are represented internally within NT by a SID, which is a unique internal number that is a combination of the user/group name, computer name, and computer clock time. By using this specific combination, NT is able to ensure that a SID is unique in time and space. A user account for the user Mary created on separate NT computers on a network will be different if the computer names or times of creation are different, for example. It also means that if the user account Mary is deleted and re-created, the new SID for the user Mary will be different from the old SID, and any file and security permissions that were based on the old SID value for the user no longer are valid.

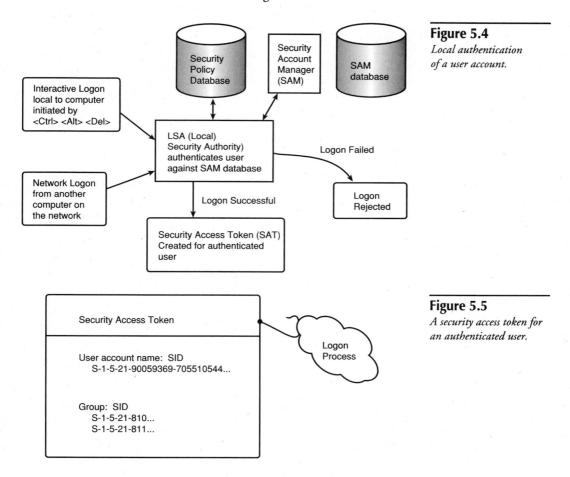

Figure 5.4

Local authentication of a user account.

Figure 5.5

A security access token for an authenticated user.

The security access token created for the logged-in user is attached to all processes that are started for the user. When the process tries to access a local or network resource, the security reference monitor (SRM), a component of the Windows NT Executive, with NT, checks to see whether any of the SIDs in the security access token attached to the process match a list called the *access-control list* (ACL) attached to that process. Each element of the ACL is called an *access-control entry* (ACE), and contains a SID describing a user or a group, as well as the permissions that are allowed for the resource.

Understanding the Domain Model

For larger networks, a certain amount of centralization in network-management functions is essential. The decentralized nature of the workgroup is not easily manageable on large networks. Indeed, decentralization often makes small networks unmanageable.

In large networks, the flexibility and power of the domain model provide centralized administration, which allows changes to the network account information to be made at a single location. The *domain* is a collection of computers that share a common security policy and user account database. The user accounts and security policy can be viewed as belonging to a common, centralized database. This means that accounts administration can be centralized, and this is considerably easier to manage than individually managing user accounts on each computer. You can use the domain model to build a uniform network policy across physical, divisional, and corporate boundaries.

Figure 5.6 illustrates that when a user account is added to the domain, its scope is the entire domain. This means that a user can log into the domain from any computer that belongs to the domain, rather than being required to log into a specific Windows NT Server. Additionally, the user accounts must be added just once to the domain. Figure 5.7 shows the addition of user accounts for a workgroup when you want the user to log into any computer in the workgroup. Notice that the user accounts have to be added separately for each computer in the workgroup.

Figure 5.6

A single addition of a user account for a domain.

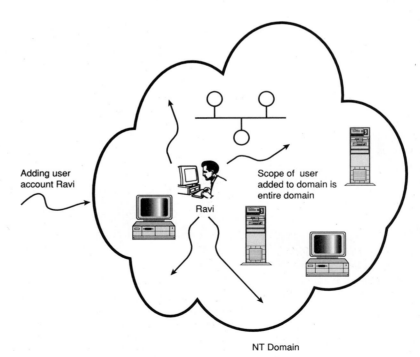

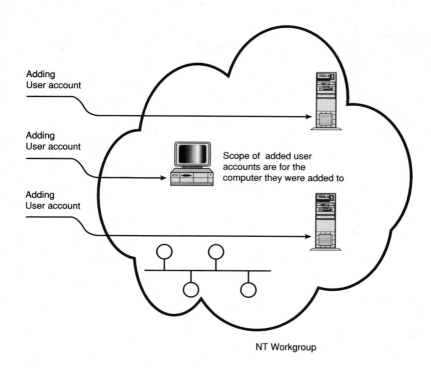

Figure 5.7
*Multiple additions of a
user's account in a
workgroup.*

To build domain-based networks, you need one or more Windows NT Server computers. Note that it is possible to integrate earlier LAN Manager-based domain networks into NT domains with some restrictions. An NT computer can belong to a workgroup or a domain, but not to both simultaneously.

Although DOS/Windows and LAN Manager workstations can log into a domain from any computer, an NT computer first must be authenticated to the domain. In other words, you cannot install a Windows NT Server or workstation and log in as a user account in the domain without the domain being informed of the NT computer's existence (see fig. 5.8). The NT computer must be authenticated to the domain before it can join the domain. This method prevents security breaches in which any NT computer (server or workstation) could be installed and used to log into the domain without proper authentication of the computer.

Authentication across a Network for an NT Workgroup

When you build a Windows NT Workgroup network, you can log into any NT computer from any other NT computer (see fig. 5.9). You can even log into other computers in other workgroups (see fig. 5.10). Figure 5.10 illustrates that there are no restrictions to logging in based on workgroup names, and a security policy within the operating system that prevents users from logging into different workgroups cannot be enforced. As you will see later in this chapter, this is another difference between workgroups and domains. By using domains, you can enforce a security policy within the operating system that can restrict users to log into specific domains.

Figure 5.8

Authenticating an NT computer to a domain.

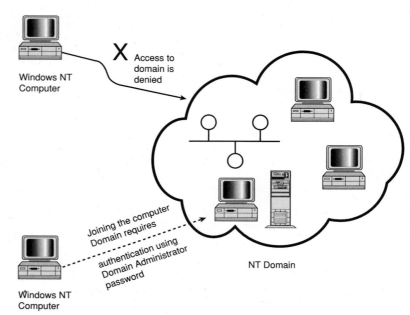

Figure 5.9

Logging into another NT computer within the same workgroup.

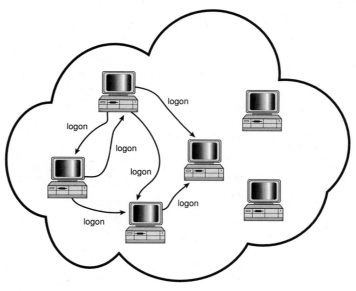

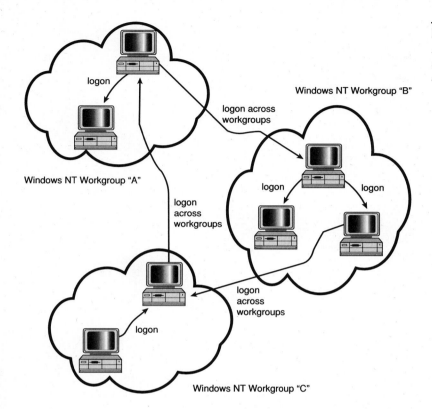

Figure 5.10

Logging in to another NT computer within a different workgroup.

Figure 5.11 shows two NT computers in a Windows NT workgroup. The computers are labeled WS1 and WS2. A user named Lolix logs into WS1. User Lolix first must be authenticated by the Local Security Authority (LSA) running on WS1. This LSA checks the supplied user name and password for Lolix against the local Security Accounts Manager (SAM) database kept in WS1. If the user Lolix succeeds in logging in, the user then can log in through the network to WS2. The network login for user Lolix is validated against WS2's SAM database. The user Lolix on WS1 must have a valid user account on WS2 and must supply the correct password for this user account in order to log in to WS2 successfully.

Because there is no automatic synchronization of passwords or any other user account properties on NT computers in a workgroup, it is convenient to keep the same user account name and password on the computers in a Windows NT workgroup. It is not essential for user Lolix to log into WS2 as user Lolix, however; this user can log in as another valid user name on WS2 if the password for that user is known (see fig. 5.12).

Figure 5.11

*Network login in a
workgroup.*

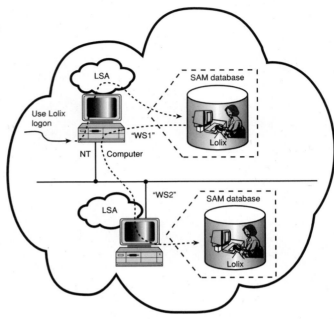

Windows NT Workgroup

Figure 5.12

*Network login for
workgroups with different
local and network user
accounts.*

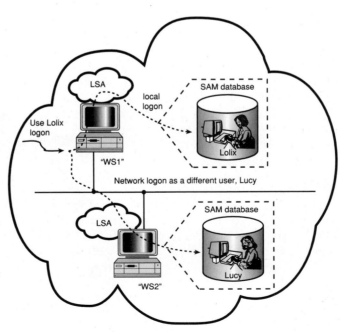

Windows NT Workgroup

If an invalid user account is supplied when logging into WS2, the user is logged in as a guest user on WS2 (see fig. 5.13). By default, the guest is created when Windows NT workstations are installed. If access to the guest account is not secured properly, this could result in a security breach.

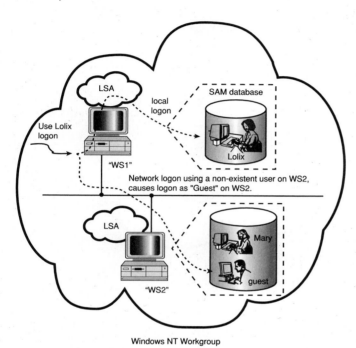

Figure 5.13
Default access by means of a guest account.

Windows NT Workgroup

Authentication across a Network for an NT Domain

When you build a Windows NT domain network, you can log into the domain from any NT computer in the same domain (see fig. 5.14). If your computer is in a different domain, you still can access a resource in another domain if your domain has been given access through a trust relationship (see fig. 5.15). In Windows NT domains, a *trust relationship* can be created between two domains to allow users in one domain to access resources in other domains.

When you log into a domain, you are authenticated against the domain security accounts manager database. This authentication is performed by one of the domain controllers in the domain.

Figure 5.14

Logging in from a computer in the same domain.

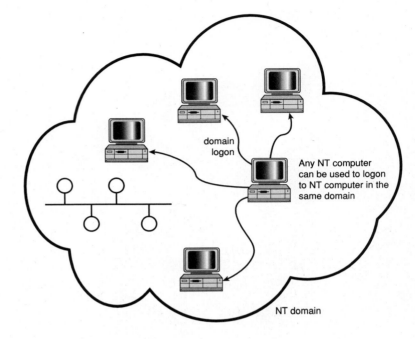

Figure 5.15

Logging in from a computer in another domain.

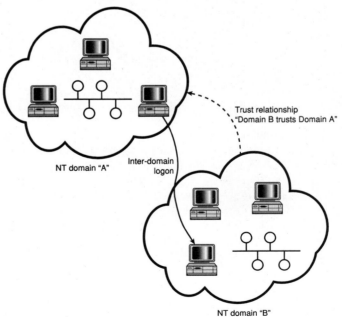

Deciding When to Use Workgroups

You can use NT workgroups when you want a low-cost connectivity solution. You can establish an NT workgroup using the Windows NT Workstation product instead of the more expensive Windows NT Server product.

If you establish a Windows NT workgroup, however, global security is difficult to implement because there is no concept of a global user account for the workgroup. You will have to create the same user accounts on each Windows NT workstation if you want transparent network logins to the Windows NT computers in the workgroup. Also, because there is no automatic password synchronization, if you want to maintain the same passwords, you have to maintain the passwords manually. If you want to perform backups, you have to back up each computer separately, because there is no centralized backup in Windows NT workgroups, unless you keep all the important files that need to be backed up on a single Windows NT workstation.

You can designate one of the Windows NT workstations as a central machine that can share its resources. Microsoft calls this a *client/server* configuration for Windows NT workstations. You can use the single central NT workstation as a single source for backup. The maximum number of simultaneous user connections to a single Windows NT workstation is limited to 10. The maximum number of simultaneous user connections to a single Windows NT server is controlled by the licenses granted to that server.

Deciding When to Use Domains

You can use domains when you want centralized administration. You must have a minimum of one Windows NT Server in order to build an NT domain. The centralized domain SAM database enables you to implement centralized security and to maintain user profiles for the domain users. You have the flexibility of implementing a variety of domain-configuration options to suit your organization's network security policy needs. The remote administration tools can be run from Windows NT workstations or from Windows 3.*x*/Windows 95 clients.

Because you are using at least one Windows NT Server to build an NT domain, you have the following benefits that are features of the Windows NT Server:

■ Disk fault tolerance by implementing RAID levels 1 through 5.

■ Remote Access Services (RAS) that allow up to 256 network-type connections over dial-up modem links.

■ Migration tool for NetWare that allows user accounts on a NetWare server to be migrated to a Windows NT Server.

■ A gateway service for NetWare servers that allows bindery-based access to NetWare servers using only a single licensed connection to the NetWare server.

- Services for the Macintosh such as File/Print services.

- The Windows NT Server can act as a remote boot server.

- Support for Windows Internet Name Service (WINS) based on the Internet DNS (Domain Name Service) protocol specification.

- Domain Name Service (DNS) that includes a graphical administration utility, and integration with WINS services for dynamic updates of host names and addresses. The WINS/DNS integration allows a user to use DNS "compound" names to access a network resource. For example, when using the Windows NT Explorer, you can access a share by using a DNS name such as \\server.yourcompany.com\data.

- Support for the Dynamic Host Configuration Protocol (DHCP) that can simplify IP address parameter settings on NT computers that are configured to use TCP/IP.

- Client support for DOS, OS/2, and Windows for Workgroups.

- Directory replication that allows both import and export. The Windows NT Workstation enables you to import directories, but not to export directories for replication. *Replication* enables the contents of a directory, designated as an *export directory*, to be copied to other directories (also called *import directories*) on computers on the network.

Designing a Domain

This section discusses the design and architecture of domains, and how they can be used to solve common security problems in an enterprise network. The tools and procedures for implementing domains are discussed in Chapter 6, "Implementing Windows NT Server Domains."

Domain Controllers

The SAM database for domains is maintained on servers that are designated as domain controllers. A domain can have two types of domain controllers: a primary domain controller (PDC) and a backup domain controller (BDC), which also is called a secondary domain controller (SDC). The PDC holds a master copy of the SAM database, and the BDC holds a backup copy of this database.

A domain can have only one primary domain controller (see fig. 5.16). All other domain controllers are designated as backup domain controllers (see fig. 5.17). The purpose of backup domain controllers is to avoid a single point of failure of the domain SAM database. If the PDC fails, you can designate another BDC as a PDC. This is called *promoting* a BDC to a PDC. You can use this process to replace a failed PDC, and you accomplish this by using the Server Manager tool.

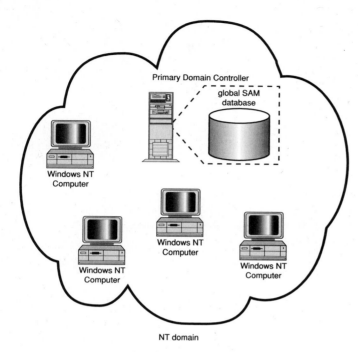

Figure 5.16
A domain with a single PDC.

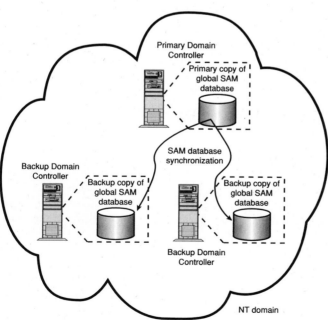

Figure 5.17
A domain with multiple BDCs.

A limitation of the NT domain architecture is that changes to the SAM databases can only be made to the PDC. The BDCs can be used for authentication, because they have a copy of the global SAM database kept at the PDC. The BDCs cannot be used for making changes to the global SAM database, however. For a large enterprise network that has a domain that includes NT servers in separate geographical regions, changes to the SAM database must be sent to the single PDC across potentially slow WAN links.

If you promote a BDC to a PDC while the PDC for the domain is online, then the PDC automatically is demoted to a BDC (see fig. 5.18). Although the Server Manager tool has a Promote to Primary Domain Controller option, it does not have an option for demoting a primary domain controller. This implies that you cannot explicitly demote a PDC to a BDC. The only way to demote a PDC is through a promotion operation such as making another BDC a PDC. This method has the advantage of ensuring that there is at least one PDC in the domain. You cannot inadvertently demote the only PDC for a domain to a BDC, because the demotion is performed indirectly by making another BDC a PDC.

Figure 5.18

Promoting a backup domain controller.

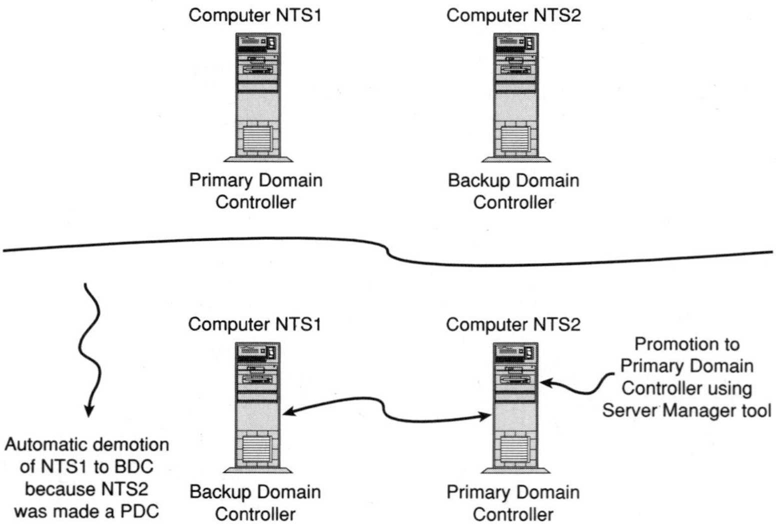

All changes made to the domain SAM database are replicated to the BDCs at periodic intervals (see fig. 5.19). This ensures that the BDCs are kept up to date with the SAM database on the PDC.

The BDCs provide read-only access to the SAM database. Updates are performed at the PDC and then replicated for backup purposes to the BDC. The BDCs can be used for satisfying domain log-in validation requests and account-query requests (see fig 5.20). The users that are not members of a domain are denied access to resources in a domain unless a trust relationship exists.

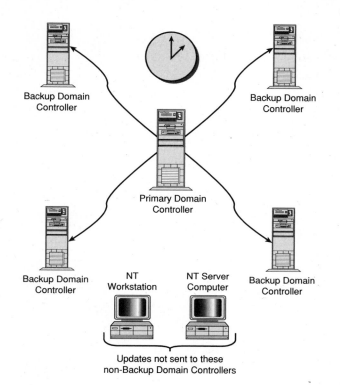

Figure 5.19
Synchronizing the domain database.

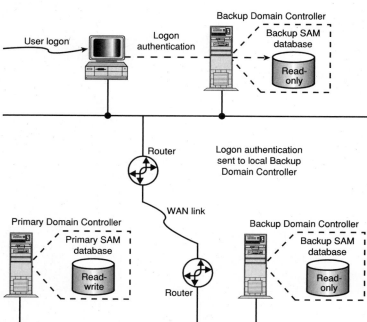

Figure 5.20
A read-only SAM database on a backup domain controller.

Domain Clients

For an NT domain, the PDC must be a Windows NT Server computer, but the clients of that domain can be any of the following computers:

- Windows NT workstations

- Windows 3.1

- Windows 3.11 (Windows for Workgroups)

- Windows 95

- OS/2 workstations

- Workgroup add-on for MS-DOS

- MS-DOS client

All these clients can access the servers on the domain (see fig. 5.21). The levels of network security depend on the client.

Figure 5.21
Windows NT domain clients.

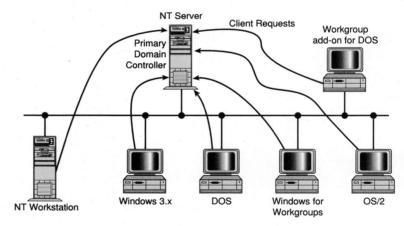

Accessing Domains

In order to access a domain, you must be a user in a domain or given a trust relationship. This section explores the types of trust relationships that are possible.

It is possible to have multiple domains on a corporate network. A Windows NT computer is a member of only one domain at a time. That is, a Windows NT computer cannot be a member of more than one domain at a time. The Windows NT computer is placed in the domain in which the resources it offers are most likely to be used by that computer. There are occasions, however, when you might need access to resources in other domains. You can use a trust relationship between domains to permit users in one domain to access resources in another domain.

Figure 5.22 shows that the trust relationship exists between the *trusting* domain and the *trusted* domain. The trust arrow in figure 5.22 is drawn from the trusting domain to the trusted domain. The trusting domain honors access from all domain user and group accounts from the trusted domain, as long as such access has been explicitly given. In other words, just because a trust relationship exists, it does not imply that any user or group in the trusted domain can access resources in the trusting domain. In addition to the trust relationship, an explicit administrative action needs to be performed to give domain user and group accounts explicit access to resources. By providing a trust relationship, it is possible for users to access resources in a domain that is different from the domain in which the user and group accounts are located.

The usage relationship and the trust relationship are shown in figure 5.22. Note that the usage arrow is in the opposite direction of the trust arrow. The usage arrow should help you conceptualize who is allowed access to a foreign domain.

Figure 5.22

A usage relationship versus a trust relationship.

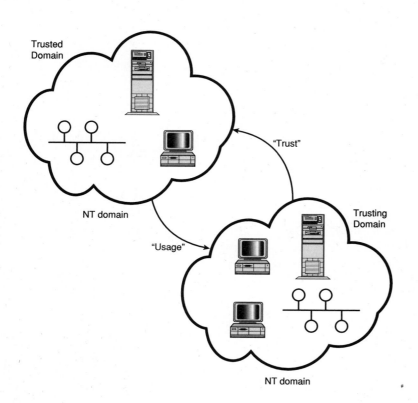

Trusted Domain

"Trust"

NT domain

Trusting Domain

"Usage"

NT domain

In order to facilitate the assignment of permissions to user accounts in a trusted domain, Windows NT provides a convenient capability that allows local groups in a trusting domain to contain domain accounts in the trusted domain. Then, the local group that contains the global accounts in another domain can be given permissions to a resource.

Trusts can be used to simplify administration of multiple domains. Without trusts, each domain exists as a separate administrative unit that has its own separate SAM database that must be managed separately. This means that if you have three domains, there will be three separate SAM databases per domain, which must be managed separately. If you use trust relationships between domains, you can manage the three separate domain databases as a single administrative unit. Trust relationships can be established only between Windows NT domains.

Using trust relationships gives you the following benefits:

- You can use a single user account to access resources across multiple domains.

- You can administer multiple domains from a central location. This is important in a complex network consisting of multiple domains. You can design a network with all user accounts in one domain, for example, and then use trust relationships to give users in the domain access to resources in other domains. This arrangement enables the network Administrator to manage the multidomain network using a single domain.

- You can access a resource in a domain, even if you do not have a user account defined in the domain that contains the resource.

Looking at the Types of Trust Relationships

Between any two NT domains, you can establish two types of trust relationships:

- One-way trust relationships

- Two-way (bidirectional) trust relationships

In one-way trust relationships, only one domain trusts another. Users in the trusted domain can access resources in the trusting domain (see fig. 5.23).

In a two-way trust relationship, each domain is the trusting domain and the trusted domain (see fig. 5.24). Because of the bidirectional trust relationship, user accounts in any domain can access resources in the other domain.

In figures 5.23 and 5.24, the arrow points to the domain containing the users you can trust. This is the domain that contains the user accounts—also called the *account domain*. The arrow originates from the trusting domain. This is the domain containing the resources that are to be accessed—also called the *resource domain*. To summarize, the trust arrow points from the resource domain to the account domain.

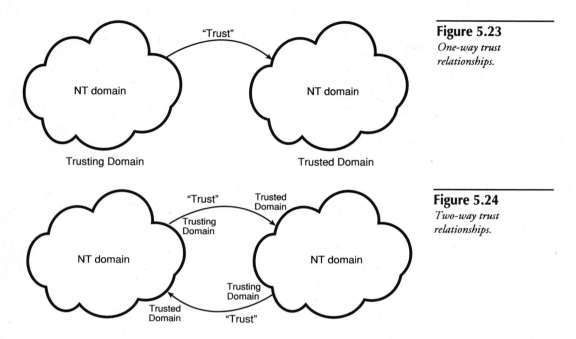

Figure 5.23
One-way trust relationships.

Figure 5.24
Two-way trust relationships.

Domain trust relationships are not *transitive.* This means that if domain A trusts domain B, and domain B trusts domain C, you cannot assume that domain A trusts domain C (see fig 5.25).

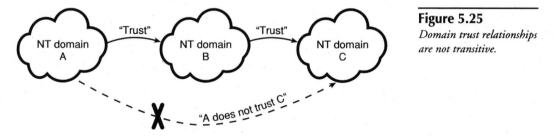

Figure 5.25
Domain trust relationships are not transitive.

As part of the process of designing domains, you must determine which domain will hold the user accounts (account domain), and which domain will hold the resources (resource domain). Next, you must determine what types of permissions should be assigned to users in other domains. The permissions that you assign depend on the network security policy you are implementing.

The trust relationship is initiated from either the account domain or the resource domain by using the Policies menu in the User Manager for Domains. To complete the trust relationship, both domains must establish the trust connection.

Using Pass-Through Validation

With the trust relationship established, the trusting server will pass a log-in request for validation to a trusted server if the trusting server is not able to validate the user locally. This method enables a user who has an account defined in one domain to access resources in another domain where they do not have a user account defined.

Pass-through validation is used in Windows NT domains when a user account must be validated but the local computer cannot validate the account because it is in another domain. The user account and password information supplied by the user are passed to the Windows NT Server that has the user account information to validate the user. The user information then is returned to the computer requesting the validation.

Figure 5.26 illustrates pass-through validation for a Windows NT domain-based network. In figure 5.26, user Amy is defined in domain A, and a trust relationship exists from domain B to domain A. Assume that user Amy enters an area of the network that has only computers for domain B. Amy would like to log into the network from a computer in domain B. This should be possible, because domain user account Amy is in a trusted domain (domain A). The problem is that validation occurs in a trusting domain (domain B), which does not have the SAM database that holds the user account definition. Consequently, the validation request must be sent to the server in domain A, which has the SAM database that holds the user account definition for user Amy.

The steps Amy takes follow:

1. Amy logs into a computer in domain B.

2. Amy cannot be validated by a computer in domain B because Amy's SAM information is in domain A.

3. Amy's validation request is sent as a pass-through to domain A.

4. Amy's log-in validation attempt is authenticated by a Windows NT Server computer in domain A.

5. Results of Amy's log-in validation request are sent back to domain B. If the validation request is successful, Amy will have access to resources in domain A and domain B.

Pass-through validation occurs during initial login from a trusting domain computer to a trusted domain, and when accessing resources in a trusting domain. Pass-through validations can occur only between trusted domains. In addition, pass-through validations are not transitive. This means that if domain A trusts domain B, and domain B trusts C, pass-through validations can occur from domain A to domain B, and from domain B to domain C, but not from domain A to domain C.

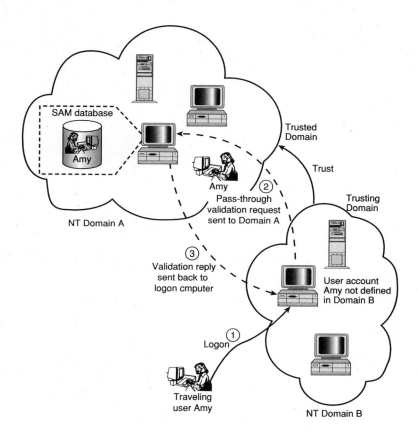

Figure 5.26
Pass-through validation.

Using Domain Models

When the network has a few domains, it is fairly easy to determine how to establish trust relationships. As the network grows, so can the number of domains. If you do not have a strategy for establishing trust relationships, you could end up with a network that has complicated trust relationships between the domains. As a result, domain administration could become complex and difficult.

To avoid the complicated domain designs, Microsoft recommends the following conceptual domain models:

- Single domain model

- Master domain model

- Multiple master domain model

- Complete trust model

These models are discussed in the following sections.

The Single Domain Model

If you have few users and computers on your network, you can place them in a single domain. This type of model is referred to as the *single domain model*; there are no trust relationships because you have only a single domain (see fig. 5.27). The single domain contains the SAM database for the entire network, and network administration can be performed from a central location.

Figure 5.27
The single domain model.

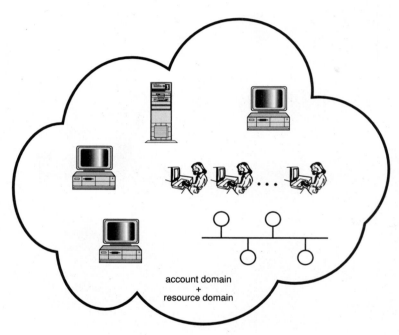

account domain
+
resource domain

All inclusive NT Domain

Domain user accounts and domain group accounts can be set up, and permissions to resources can be assigned on an individual user or group account basis. Domain user accounts and domain group accounts have a scope that includes all the computers in the domain. If several domain groups (also called *global groups*) are to be given access to resources on a single NT computer, you can define a local group on the NT computer and place the domain groups as members of the local group.

Table 5.1 lists the advantages and disadvantages of a single domain model.

Table 5.1
Advantages and Disadvantages of a Single Domain Model

Advantages	Disadvantages
Good model for networks with small number of computers	Has poor performance as the number of users and groups increases
No need to manage trust relationships	As network size increases, browsing becomes slow
Single centralized management of user/group accounts and network	No natural grouping of users' resources into departments
Local group needs to be defined only once	No natural grouping of resources by department

The Master Domain Model

The master domain model can be used for organizations that want to organize their networks into multiple resource domains but still have the benefits of centralized administration. By splitting the network resources into multiple domains, you have the benefit of organizing a large number of resources into manageable units. A master domain is used to provide centralized administration.

Figure 5.28 shows an example of the master domain model. In the master domain model, several resource domains trust a single master domain. The trust is a one-way trust relationship from the resource domain to the master domain. The master domain is the account domain that holds the domain accounts for the network that can be used to access resources in any domain. Because the accounts are in a single domain, they can be managed from a central location.

As long as the users log in from a computer in the master domain, they can be authenticated directly from the master domain. If they log in from one of the resource domains, pass-through validation is used to authenticate the user accounts that reside in the master domain. Because all resource domains trust the master domain, users in the master domain can access resources in any domain. For this reason, the master domain can be used for defining the accounts for the MIS department of an organization. This enables the MIS department to manage the network from a central location. Users with accounts in the trusting domains (resource domains) will not be able to access resources in other domains.

If a local resource on any computer is to be accessed by a number of users, you can use global and local groups in the following manner:

Figure 5.28
The master domain model.

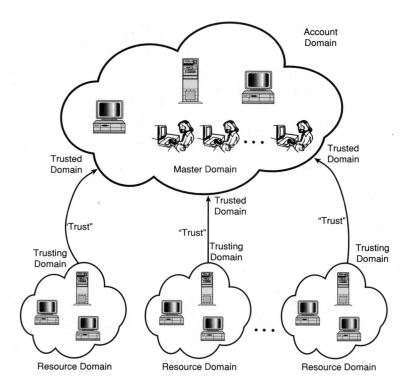

1. Create a local group on the computer that has the resources that need to be accessed by other users.

2. Create global groups to describe different categories of domain users. Place domain users in their appropriate global groups.

3. Place the global groups in the local group.

4. Give the local group permissions to the local resource.

With the previously described method of using local and global groups, as new domain users are added to their respective global groups, they automatically are assigned permissions because the global group is placed in the local group. The Administrator has to manage a fewer number of groups.

The master domain model can be used for the following situations:

■ There are less than 40,000 user groups and machine accounts.

■ The organization has a number of departments—each of which wants its own separate resource management.

■ The networks in the organization are to be managed by a central MIS department.

Table 5.2 lists the advantages and disadvantages of a master domain model.

Table 5.2
Advantages and Disadvantages of a Master Domain Model

Advantages	Disadvantages
Good choice for medium-sized companies that have fewer than 10,000 users and groups.	Has poor performance as the number of computers, users, and groups increases.
Global groups are defined once in the master domain.	Local groups are defined in the domain where they are used.
Provides for centralized management of domains.	
In addition to centralized department, each domain can have its administrators that manage the resources in that domain.	

If there are *n* resource domains in a master domain model, there are a total of *n* one-way trust relationships to maintain. The number of trust relationships is shown in figure 5.29.

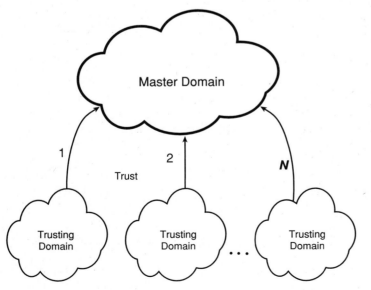

Figure 5.29
Number of trust relationships in a master domain model.

Number of one-way trust relationships = *N*

The Multiple Master Domain Model

The multiple master domain model can be used for organizations that have multiple divisions, and each division has multiple departments. In many such networks, there are separate MIS departments for each division that wants central management of the networks in the division. You can assign a master domain for each division and divide the departments in each division into separate resource domains. You can establish a trust relationship from the department domain to the division's master (MIS) domain. By splitting the network resources into multiple domains, you have the advantage of organizing a large number of resources into manageable units. The master domain for each division is used to provide centralized administration.

Figure 5.30 shows an example of the multiple master domain model. In the master domain model, several resource domains trust master domains. As seen in figure 5.30, there is a one-way trust relationship from the resource domain to the master domain. The master domain is the account domain and holds the domain accounts for the division. Because the accounts are in a single domain, they can be managed from a central location in the division. Note that in figure 5.30, it is possible for a single resource domain to trust more than one master domain. This is useful for modeling departments that are shared among several divisions. Between the master domains, there can be an optional two-way trust relationship that permits the domain users in master domains to access resources in other master domains.

Figure 5.30

A multiple master domain model.

Number of two-way trust relationships between master domains $= \dfrac{M\,(M-1)}{2}$

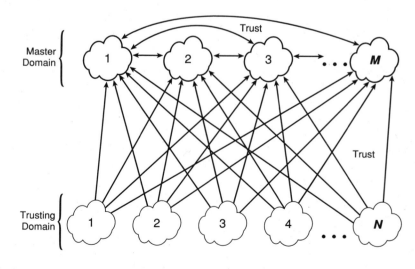

Number of one-way trust relationships to master domains $= M * N$

The Admin users for a domain log in from a computer in a master domain. If they have to log in from a trusting domain, they can use pass-through validation to authenticate their user accounts. Because a resource domain trusts at least one of the master domains, users in the trusted master domains (Admin users) can access resources in the resource domain. The master domains can be used for defining the accounts for the MIS departments of the divisions in an organization. This method enables the MIS divisions to manage the networks in each division. Users with accounts in the trusting domains (resource domain) will not be able to access resources in other master domains, and this is usually a requirement for an organization's network security policy.

The multiple master domain model is an extension of the master domain model. The major difference is that the multiple master domain model has multiple masters, and the master domain model has a single master.

Table 5.3 lists the advantages and disadvantages of a multiple master domain model.

Table 5.3
Advantages and Disadvantages of a Multiple Master Domain Model

Advantages	Disadvantages
Good choice for large-sized companies that have more than 15,000 users and groups.	Has poor performance as the number of master domains increases and there are substantial resources sharing network traffic.
Has good scalability as additional networks are added.	MIS domain accounts are not located in one domain.
Divisions of an organization can have their own administrative domains that can manage resources in the department.	Have to manage multiple trust relationships.

If there are n resource domains in a master domain model, and m master domains with trust relationships from each of the resource domains to each of the master domains, the formulas for the number of trust relationships would follow:

- ▪ Total one-way trust relationships to maintain = $m \times n$

- ▪ Total two-way trust relationships between master domains = $m \times (m - 1)/2$

The number of trust relationships is shown in figure 5.31.

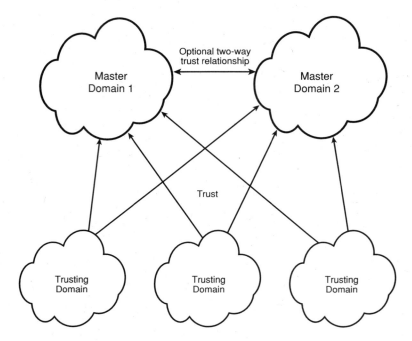

The Complete Trust Model

The master domain and multiple master domain models are suited for large companies that have a structured network administration scheme consisting of centralized MIS departments. The trust relationships between the domains in the master domain and multiple master domain models are well defined. In both the master domain models, for example, a one-way trust relationship exists from the resource domains to the central MIS domains.

If network growth in an organization is not well-planned, it is difficult to maintain well-defined trust relationships between the different domains. Consider the situation where there are no centralized MIS departments. In this case, there are MIS personnel in each domain who need access to resources in other domains. To give the MIS domain users unrestricted access to other domains, you must establish two-way trust relationships between all domains. The resulting model, called the *complete trust model,* is illustrated in figure 5.32. In this figure, a two-way trust relationship exists between all domains. There are no central domains designated as master domains, and there are no pure resource domains. Every domain has some user accounts and resources. That is, every domain is both an accounts domain and a resource domain. Pass-through validation is used when logging in as a user in a domain that does not hold the domain user account.

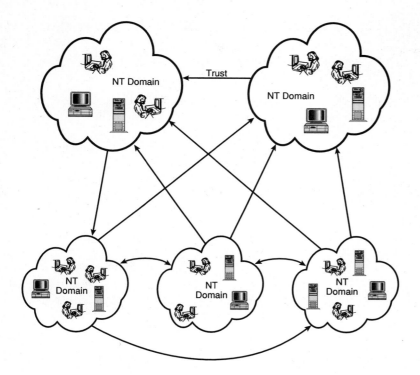

Figure 5.32
A complete trust model.

If you do not control the growth of your networks carefully, the master domain and multiple master domain models can mutate to a complete trust model. If there are *n* domains in a complete trust model, there is a total of $(n-1)\times n/2$ two-way trust relationships, and a total of $(n-1)\times n$ trust relationships to maintain. For a network consisting of 10 domains, the number of two-way trust relationships is $(10-1)\times10/2=45$, which consists of $2\times45=90$ one-way trust relationships.

In some instances, a complete trust model is suited for organizations in which the structure cannot support a centralized administration model. If the number of user accounts in an organization is relatively small, you might be better off by placing all the users in a single domain—that is, by using the single domain model. Remember that in a single domain model, you do not have to manage trust relationships; in a complete trust model, you do have to manage trust relationships. If an organization has decentralized departments that do their own network design and maintenance, single domain models might be unattractive for political reasons—especially when each department wants to maintain a distinct network individuality, and they all need access to each other. For this reason, you might have to resort to using a complete trust model.

The complete trust model assumes a high degree of confidence that the two-way trust relationships will not be abused. Because there is potential for misuse of the two-way trust relationships, you must take special care to avoid giving inadvertent permissions to local groups that contain domain users and global groups. If the Administrators of the domains are not alert, they can give excessive permissions to users in other domains. Administrators of each domain must ensure that they do not place inappropriate domain users and global groups in local groups, for example.

Consider the example in figure 5.33, which shows two of the domains in a complete trust model network. In domain B, a local group (*locgroupB*) is given permissions to the \CRITICAL directory on the NT computer. If the Administrator inadvertently (or by design to circumvent security) assigns user Amy and Mary in domain A as members of the local group *locgroupB*, these users will be given access to the \CRITICAL directory on the computer in domain B. In a complete trust model, domain administrators are forced to rely on other domain administrators to exercise security policies.

Figure 5.33

The dangers of inappropriate membership to local groups in a complete trust model.

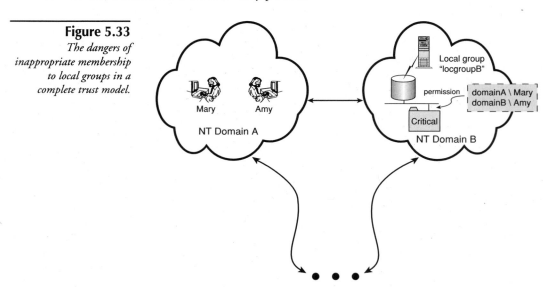

Table 5.4 lists the advantages and disadvantages of a complete trust model. Because of the potential for misuse of trust relationships and the difficulty of managing a large number of trust relationships, you should avoid using the complete trust model.

Table 5.4
Advantages and Disadvantages of a Complete Trust Domain Model

Advantages	Disadvantages
Suitable for companies that cannot support a centralized administrative model.	Does not have the benefit of centralized administration. Not suitable for most organizations that have a central MIS department.

Advantages	Disadvantages
Has good scalability as additional networks are added. Theoretically, there can be an unlimited number of domains; therefore, the number of users on the network also should theoretically be unlimited.	It is difficult to manage the very large number of trust relationships in this model.
Complete freedom for each domain to have its own domain administrative staff.	You must rely on Administrators of each domain to not put inappropriate users and global groups in local groups.

Looking at the Drawbacks of Domain Models

The domain model has a number of architectural flaws. These are listed in this section for the serious NT network designer, so that he or she can better understand NT-based networks. Needless to say, these flaws are not mentioned in any of the official NT documentation. These domain limitations are discussed for the sake of completeness and technical accuracy, and not in the spirit of belittling the NT product:

1. NT domains are flat in the sense that there is no way of expressing hierarchical relationships or grouping of resources in a single domain. Users can use trusts to express relationships between domains, but these are usage relationships and are not suited for organizing the network based on a geographical, resource ownership, logical, or organizational chart basis.

2. The single master domain model, according to Microsoft, is suitable for fewer than 40,000 users and groups. As the number of users and groups increases, so does the number of trust relationships and the cost of managing the trust relationships. In other words, the cost of network management can rise unexpectedly as the network size increases.

3. Users must be vigilant about the misuse of trust relationships—particularly two-way trust relationships. See "The Complete Trust Model," earlier in this chapter, for a discussion of this issue.

4. If you are not careful about assigning trust relationships, any of the domain models can degenerate to a complete trust model.

5. The backup domain controllers have a read-only copy of the master SAM database, and these cannot be used to perform network administration, if the PDC is not available.

6. NT domains are really workgroups with a single network login for the user. Here, the use of the word *workgroups* is in its more widely used meaning in the industry—as collections of users and computers working toward common goals. Workgroups, in this sense, could be departments or an entire small organization.

7. Without proper planning, users could end up with a complete trust model, with all its attendant problems. Because setting up and installing an NT network is relatively simple from a procedural point of view, there is a real danger that network installers might install a network that works well for the short term, rather than designing and installing a network for the long term that scales properly as the network grows, and as political turf wars over who trusts whom occur.

8. Windows NT replicates the accounts database to backup domain controllers in case of a primary domain controller failure. However, there is no replication of critical user account properties, such as profiles and log-in scripts. These properties are not part of the accounts database and are maintained as separate, external files. To replicate these properties, you need to configure the replication of these files as a separate step. The replication procedure is involved, and many network Administrators are unable to make it work the first time they try it. These files are part of the accounts database, and they contain explicit references to the computer names on which they are stored. If the computer on which the profile or log-in script is stored is not available, you cannot access the profile and log-in script files. You have to switch manually to a backup computer that has a copy of the profile and log-in script files. These problems can be solved by making the profile and log-in script a part of the accounts database that is replicated, but this cannot be done in Windows NT.

Many of these problems can be solved using a model based on directory services rather than a domain-based model. Examples of directory-based models are the CCITT/ITU X.500 directory services and the Distributed Computing Environment (DCE) directory services models. Discussion of these alternative models is beyond the scope of this book. Microsoft will introduce a directory-services model when it completes its project code named *Cairo*, which might address these shortcomings.

Synchronizing Domain Databases

The domain database on the primary domain controller is the master database for the domain. The backup domain controllers keep copies of the master domain database. Whenever changes are made to the master domain database (such as changes in user and group accounts), the changed database is copied to the backup domain controllers by a process called *replication*. The replication process ensures that the databases on the BDCs are synchronized to the database on the PDC. You can achieve domain synchronization by using one of these two methods:

■ Synchronize the BDC's account database to the PDC (this is called the *pull operation*).

■ Copy the domain database from the PDC to all BDCs (this is called the *push operation*).

In Windows NT domains, any domain controller (primary or backup) can validate logins to the domain. If the BDC is used for log-in validation but has not been synchronized to the PDC, domain logins will not work as expected. You can have problems with password mismatches, or unexpected results when attempts are made to access resources. In this case, you should ensure that the domain databases are synchronized, and log out and log in again to generate a new user access token based on the synchronized database.

Case Studies in Designing NT Domains

This section presents scenarios that show you how to use domain models. Before deciding on a domain model you should consider the following factors:

■ The number of users/groups in an organization

■ The growth factor of the networks

■ The number of departments

■ Political and administrative factors that will be affected if network administration will be centralized, decentralized, and so on.

Designing Domains: Case Study 1

A start-up organization, OMNICOM, has 100 employees; each employee needs an account on a Windows NT network. OMNICOM needs file-, print-, and applications-sharing capabilities. Not all the employees are expected to be online, and a single Windows NT Server should be adequate for providing the services. For load balancing and redundancy purposes, a second NT Server is added to the network. What type of domain model is adequate that will meet these requirements?

Solution

The number of user accounts is 100. There will be some additional group accounts for administration, but the total number of group accounts usually will be smaller than 100. Because this is a start-up company, there probably are no entrenched administrative schemes, and you can place all the 100 plus accounts in a single domain. You must select an appropriate name that defines the OMNICOM domain. The name can be any unique domain name that suitably reflects the organization. The single domain solution is illustrated in figure 5.34.

Figure 5.34

A single domain solution.

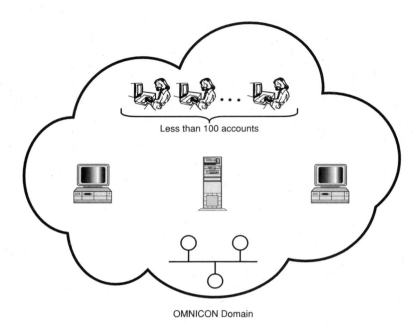

Less than 100 accounts

OMNICON Domain

Designing Domains: Case Study 2

An organization—MINDSHARE, Inc.—has four major departments: Corporate, Accounting, Manufacturing, and Engineering. The total number of employees in each department is less than 700. Each department has its own regional NT servers that serve the department and provides file-, print-, and applications-sharing capabilities. The number of servers in each department follows:

Department	Number of NT Servers
Corporate	3
Accounting	2
Manufacturing	4
Engineering	4

There is a central MIS department that manages the interdepartmental network. What type of domain model is adequate that will meet these requirements?

Solution

The maximum number of user accounts is 700 for each department. There will be some additional group accounts for administration, but the total number of group accounts usually will be quite small. Each department can be placed in its own NT domain. Because there is a central MIS department, this situation can be modeled as a master domain with a trust relationship from the departmental domain to the MIS domain. The MIS network Administrator accounts should be defined in the MIS domain. The trust relationships will permit these MIS accounts to access and manage the resources in the individual departments. The solution is illustrated in figure 5.35 and represents the single master domain model.

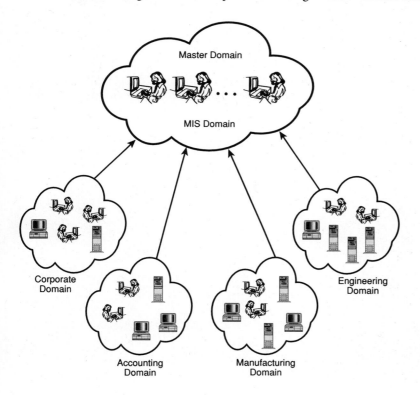

Figure 5.35

The single master domain solution.

Designing Domains: Case Study 3

An organization—Atlantis Explorers, Inc.—is a conglomerate of several separate companies named Allied Instruments, Oceandepth, and AtlaMining. Each company has its own departments and MIS organizations. The MIS departments of the different companies share information related to the management of their individual companies. The total number of employees in each department of each company is less than 9,000. Each organization has its own regional NT servers that serve the departments in that organization and provide file-, print-, and applications-sharing services. What type of domain model is adequate that will meet these requirements?

Solution

The maximum number of user accounts is 9,000 for each department of an organization. There will be some additional group accounts for administration, but the total number of group accounts usually will be quite small. Within an organization's network, each department can be placed in its own NT domain. The departments within each organization can be managed from a central location by the MIS department of that organization. For each organization, this situation can be modeled as a master MIS domain with a trust relationship from the departmental domain to the MIS domain. The MIS network Administrator accounts should be defined in the MIS domain. These trust relationships will permit these MIS accounts to access and manage the resources in the individual departments. Because the MIS departments need to share network administration-related information, trust relationships are set up between the MIS domains. The solution is illustrated in figure 5.36 and represents the multiple master domain model.

Figure 5.36

The multiple master domain solution.

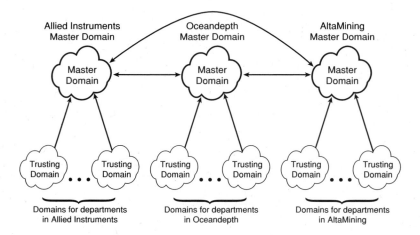

Conclusion

In this chapter, you learned about the basic differences between using a workgroup model versus using a domain model. When you design large networks using Windows NT Servers, there are many advantages of designing the networks using NT domains. There are at least four domain models: the single model, the master domain model, the multiple master domain model, and the complete trust domain model. You also learned about the advantages and disadvantages of using the different domain models to build enterprise-wide networks, using examples of case studies.

Implementing Windows NT Server Domains

*I*n the preceding chapter, you learned about Windows NT domains and how to design the NT domain model. In this chapter, you will learn how to implement domains and perform domain operations. These operations include selecting domains, establishing primary domain controllers (PDCs) and backup domain controllers (BDCs), synchronizing domains for administration, promoting to a PDC, establishing trusts between domains, and adding/removing workstations from domains. In addition to these domain operations, you will learn to configure replication services for domains.

The Server Manager is the primary tool used to perform domain administration. Some operations, such as establishing trust relations, are performed by the User Manager for Domains tool. Both these tools can be found in the Administrative Tools folder in the Windows NT Server.

Domain Operations

This section discusses the operations that can be performed on domains. These operations include the following:

- Creating domains

- Changing domain names

- Joining a domain

- Removing a computer from a domain

- Synchronizing a domain

- Administering domains and domain members using the Server Manager

- Promoting a backup domain controller to a primary domain controller

- Establishing a trust relationship

You can access the server management menu by using the Server Manager tool in the Administrative Tools folder or the Server applet in the Control Panel. You can perform administration on the following types of domains:

- Windows NT Server domains

- Windows NT Server and LAN Manager 2.*x* domains

- LAN Manager 2.*x* domains

After you have designed domains, as discussed in the preceding chapter, you must build the domain. This involves creating a domain and then joining other NT computers to the domain. Occasionally, as a network Administrator, you might be called upon to change domain names or remove NT computers from a domain. These and other maintenance tasks associated with domains are discussed next.

Creating a Domain

The first step in setting up a Windows NT network using domains is defining the domain. The domain is created when the Windows NT Server is installed as a primary domain controller, at which time the domain exists on the network.

When you set up the Windows NT Server as a primary domain controller, you are prompted for a domain name. The domain name you enter at this prompt is used by all NT computers (both BDC and server computers) to join the domain.

For details on installing the primary domain controller, see Chapter 3, "Installing Windows NT Server."

Changing the Domain Name

Domain names on the network must be unique. After you select the domain name, there usually is no need to change the domain name, unless you have conflicts with a previously selected domain name on the network. Another possible source of conflict in domain names can be when two previously physically separate networks are to be connected, and these separate networks have selected the same domain name.

You must change the domain name for a domain on the PDC if you discover conflicts in domain names on the network. However, you also have to change the domain name for all backup domain controllers in the domain. For this reason, it is best to decide on a domain name that will not have to be changed frequently. If you decide to change the domain name, use the following steps:

1. Log on locally to the server as an Administrator user.

2. Start the Control Panel folder, from Settings, on the Taskbar.

3. Double-click on the Network icon. Figure 6.1 shows a sample Network dialog box. In this example, the Computer Name is set to NTBAY and the Domain name is set to BAYDOM. Below the values of Computer Name and Domain, you see the **C**hange button. You use the **C**hange button to change the computer name and the domain name.

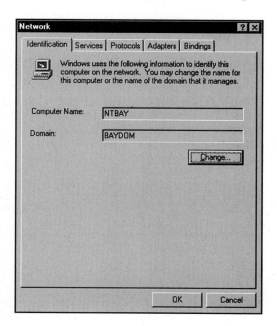

Figure 6.1

A Network dialog box.

4. Click on the **C**hange button with the computer name selected. The Identification Changes dialog box opens (see fig. 6.2).

Figure 6.2

The Identification Changes dialog box.

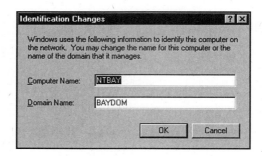

5. In the **C**omputer Name field, enter the new domain name and choose OK.

6. Go to each of the computer name controllers and change the computer name to the new name using steps 1 through 5.

Joining a Domain

In order to join the domain, your NT computer (NT Server, NT workstation) must be authenticated to the primary domain controller. Every NT computer on the network domain must have a unique computer name. This computer name is used to create a computer account on the domain controller. This computer account for joining the domain can be created by any of the following methods:

■ **During installation.** When an NT workstation or NT Server is installed, you must select the security role of the NT computer. You have a choice of making the NT workstation a part of a workgroup or a domain. For NT servers, you can set up a domain controller (primary or secondary) or a simple NT Server computer. If you select the option to join the domain, you can create a computer account for your computer name and be authenticated to the domain controller, and thereby join the domain. In order to join the domain, you must enter a domain administrator name and the corresponding password. This prevents non-domain administrators from joining an NT computer to a domain. The details of NT Server installation are covered in Chapter 3, "Installing Windows NT Server."

■ **Using the Server Manager tool.** You can use the Server Manager tool to add an NT computer to a domain. This procedure is described later in this chapter.

■ **Using the Network icon in the Control Panel.** This procedure also is described later in this chapter.

Joining the Domain Using the Server Manager Tool

You must run the Server Manager tool for the domain to which you want to add additional NT computers.

The following is an outline of the steps to add an NT computer to the domain:

1. Log on to the server as an Administrator user.

2. Start the User Manager from the Administrative Tools folder. Figure 6.3 shows a sample Server Manager screen. This figure shows that the Server Manager is running on a domain controller for the domain BAYDOM. The primary domain controller for this domain is listed as NTBAY. Other NT workstations already joined to the domain are LTREE2, LTREE4, LTREE6, LTREE8, LTREE10, and LTREE12. In the Server Manager screen, if the computer icon next to a computer name has a blue screen, the computer is accessible from the PDC; if the computer is not accessible (because the network link or computer is down), you see a gray screen on the computer icon.

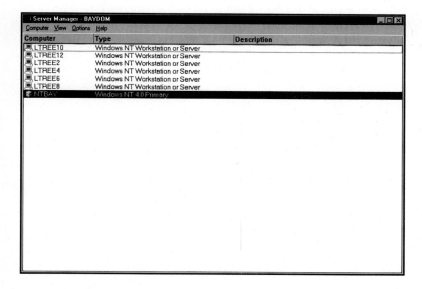

Figure 6.3

A Server Manager screen.

3. Choose **C**omputer, **A**dd to Domain.

The Add Computer To Domain dialog box appears (see fig. 6.4). You must identify the type of the computer to add to the domain. Your choices are a Windows NT **W**orkstation or Server, or a Windows NT **B**ackup Domain Controller.

In the Computer **N**ame field, enter a computer name (up to 15 characters) by which the network can know the computer. This name cannot be the same as any other computer name or domain name on the network. The name that you enter is stored and displayed in uppercase letters.

Figure 6.4

The Add Computer To Domain dialog box.

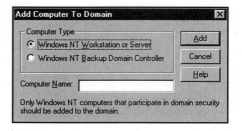

4. After you enter the computer name, choose the **A**dd button to add the new computer name to the domain. Figure 6.5 shows that the Windows NT Workstation named NTWS2 has been added to the domain BAYDOM.

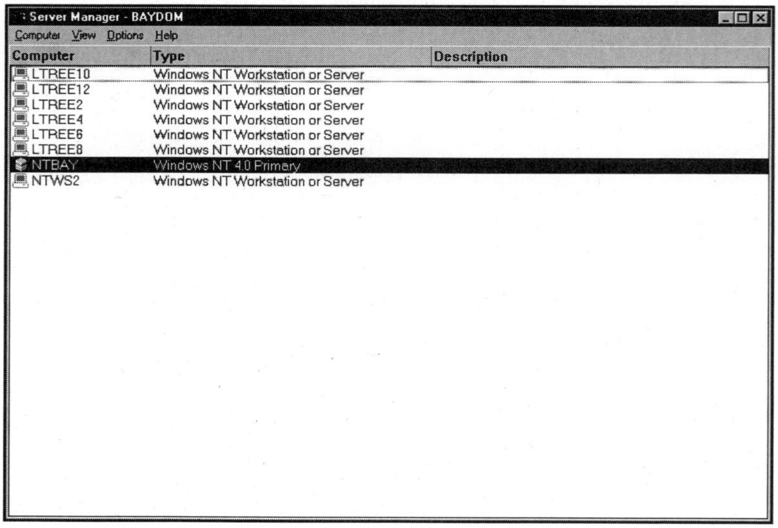

Figure 6.5

Adding the Windows NT Workstation NTWS2.

5. You next must add the NT computer to the domain from Control Panel, as described in the next section. Because a computer account for the NT computer already has been created in the domain, however, the NT computer can join the domain without having to specify an Administrator user password. That is, you can skip step 6 in the next section, "Joining the Domain Using the Control Panel."

The advantage of creating a computer account using the Server Manager tool is to preauthenticate the computer name to the domain. Any person knowledgeable enough to install and configure the NT computer can use the steps in the next section (minus step 6) to join the computer to the domain, without having to know a domain Administrator password. This is an advantage when the NT computer installation is carried out by non-domain administrator users. A window of time exists between creating the computer account and adding the computer to the domain from the Control Panel, however, during which someone who knows the pre-authenticated computer name can join the domain.

Joining the Domain Using the Control Panel

Perform the following steps to join an NT computer to the domain from the Control Panel.

1. Log on locally to the Windows NT computer that is to be added to a domain as an Administrator user.

2. Start the Control Panel folder from Settings, on the Taskbar.

3. Double-click on the Network icon.

4. Click on the **C**hange button next to the workgroup name. The Identification Changes dialog box appears (see fig. 6.6).

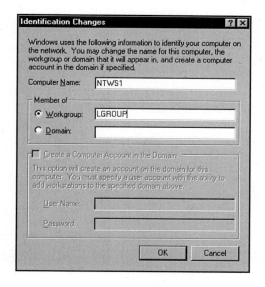

Figure 6.6

An Identification Changes dialog box.

5. Choose the **D**omain button. Replace the domain value that is highlighted with the domain that you want the NT computer to join.

6. If the computer account has not been created, check the box for **C**reate a Computer Account in the Domain.

   In the **U**ser Name and **P**assword fields, enter the user name and password of an Administrator user for the domain.

7. Choose OK.

8. If you have joined the domain successfully, a message welcoming you to the domain appears. If you cannot reach the domain controller or you have specified an incorrect administrator or password, you receive an error message that you cannot join the domain.

Removing an NT Computer from a Domain

On occasion, you might need to remove an NT computer from a domain. You can have a number of reasons for doing this. A common reason is that you need to reuse the NT computer for other purposes—possibly due to network reorganization. You can remove an NT computer using the Server Manager tool or the Control Panel of the NT computer that you want to remove from the domain.

Removing an NT Computer from a Domain Using Server Manager

You must run the Server Manager tool for the domain to which you want to remove additional NT computers.

The following is an outline of the steps to add an NT computer to the domain:

1. Log on to the server as an Administrator user.

2. Start the User Manager from the Administrative Tools group. Figure 6.7 shows a sample Server Manager screen. The Server Manager is running on a domain controller for the domain BAYDOM. The primary domain controller for this domain is listed as NTBAY. Other NT workstations already joined to the domain are LTREE2, LTREE4, LTREE6, LTREE8, LTREE10, LTREE12, NTWS1, REMNT, and XTEST.

3. Highlight the computer to be removed from the domain.

Figure 6.7

A Server Manager screen listing computers for the domain BAYDOM.

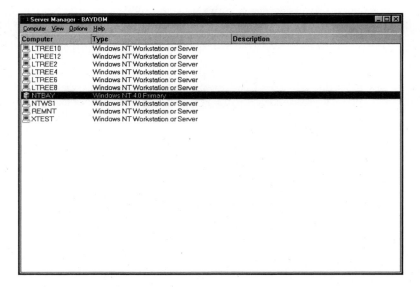

Choose **C**omputer, **R**emove from Domain, or press Del with the computer highlighted.

A message informs you of the consequences of your actions, that is, that the computer to be deleted will be incapable of authenticating domain logons until it is added to another domain (see fig. 6.8).

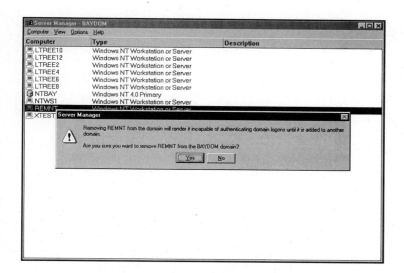

Figure 6.8

A message warning you of the consequences of deleting a computer from a domain.

Choose **Y**es if you want to remove the computer from the domain.

4. An updated list of domain members with the removed computer name missing from the list appears. Figure 6.9 shows the new list for domain BAYDOM. If you compare this figure to figure 6.7, you can see that the Windows NT computer REMNT has been removed from the domain BAYDOM.

Removing an NT Computer from a Domain Using the Control Panel

Perform the following steps to remove an NT computer from a domain using the Control Panel.

1. Log on locally to the Windows NT computer to be removed from a domain as an Administrator user.

2. Start the Control Panel folder from Settings, on the Taskbar.

3. Double-click on the Network icon. Figure 6.10 shows a sample Network Settings dialog box for a Windows NT workstation to be removed from an NT domain. In this figure, the Computer Name is set to XTEST, and this computer is a member of the domain BAYDOM.

Figure 6.9

The new list for domain BAYDOM.

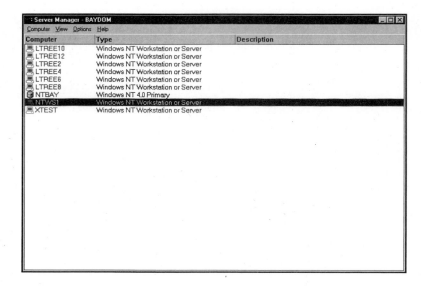

Figure 6.10

A Network dialog box for a Windows NT workstation.

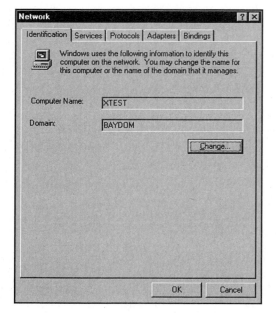

4. Click on the **C**hange button while you have the domain name selected. The Identification Changes dialog box appears.

5. Choose the **W**orkgroup button. Replace the workgroup name value that is highlighted with an existing or new workgroup name.

6. Choose OK.

7. If you have joined the workgroup successfully, a message appears welcoming you to the workgroup. Because you have joined a workgroup, you have removed yourself from the domain.

Synchronizing a Domain

You can synchronize an entire domain from the Server Manager tool. Normally, synchronization takes place automatically in the background, and you should not have to perform a manual synchronization operation. The synchronization interval for Windows NT domains is five minutes. This means that the accounts database in BDCs will be out of date by no more than five minutes. If a change has been made to the master copy of the domain SAM database on the PDC, but this change has not been replicated yet to other BDCs in the domain, then the accounts databases are out of synchronization. Symptoms of these out-of-synchronization situations are the failure of users to log into the domain because of nonexistent user accounts or changed user account properties. Under these circumstances, you can force a synchronization of the entire domain from the PDC.

It is important to note that although Windows NT Workstations in the network do not participate in accounts database synchronization, they do cache information on the most recently logged-on users. Therefore, if no server (PDC or BDC) is available to authenticate the user, the Windows NT Workstation can identify the user based on information stored in the last logon.

The following is an outline of how the synchronization can be performed:

1. Log on to the server as an Administrator user.

2. Start the Server Manager from the Administrative Tools folder. In the Server Manager screen, highlight the primary domain controller for the domain. You can identify the PDC from the Type column. It is listed as a Windows NT 4.XX Primary.

3. Choose **C**omputer, **S**ynchronize Entire Domain.

   A message from the server manager appears, informing you that the resynchronization of the domain may take a few minutes. You are asked whether you want to perform this operation (see fig. 6.11).

   Choose **Y**es. Another message appears, informing you that the PDC has asked all BDCs to start resynchronizing their user account databases (see fig. 6.12). However, you are not informed when resynchronization is complete. You must check the Event Log on the BDCs and the PDC to determine whether the synchronization was successful.

   Choose OK.

Figure 6.11

The resynchronize domain message.

Figure 6.12

A message telling you about synchronization completion.

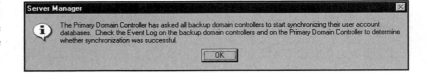

Administering Domains Using the Server Manager

You can perform administration of domains and domain members using the Server Manager. After a domain is established and its domain members are defined, you can (for the most part) manage the domain members using the Server Manager tool. The following sections outline some of the other domain administration operations that can be performed.

Selecting a Domain

When you start the Server Manager, it lists the domain members of the domain to which you are logged on. You can select other domains to administer by performing the following steps:

1. Log on to the server as an Administrator user.

2. Start the Server Manager from the Administrative Tools folder.

3. If you want to select another domain to administer, choose **C**omputer, **S**elect Domain.

   A list of domains available on the network appears (see fig. 6.13).

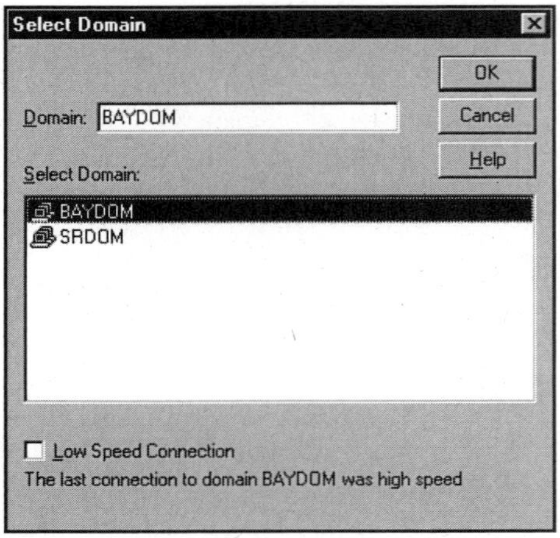

Figure 6.13

A list of domains available for selection.

4. Highlight the domain you want to administer, and choose OK.

The primary domain controller of the domain that you select must be available. If the PDC is not available, the system informs you that you still can perform some limited domain administration (see fig. 6.14).

Figure 6.14

A message informing you that you still can perform limited domain operations.

Examining Domain Member Properties

You can examine the properties of any domain member displayed in the Server Manager screen by performing the following steps:

1. Log on to the server as an Administrator user.

2. Start the Server Manager from the Administrative Tools folder.

3. Highlight a domain member and choose **P**roperties from the **C**omputer menu.

    Alternatively, you can highlight a computer and double-click.

4. If the domain member is accessible, you see the Properties screen for the domain member. Figure 6.15 shows the properties for the domain member NTBAY. There are three sessions to the domain member NTBAY, and there are zero file locks, open files, and open named pipes.

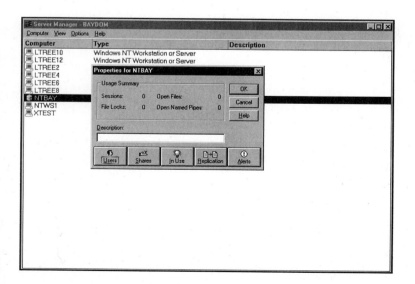

Figure 6.15

Properties for the domain member NTBAY.

Table 6.1 describes the fields in the domain member Properties dialog box.

Table 6.1
Domain Member Properties

Field	Description
Sessions	The number of users remotely connected to the domain member.
Open Files	The number of files open by remote computers.
File Locks	The number of file locks open on the domain member.
Open Named Pipes	The number of named pipes open on the domain computer. Named pipes are resources used for interprocess communications between computers.

Managing User Connections to Domain Members

You can use the Server Manager to manage the user connections to a domain member and, if necessary, to disconnect the user sessions.

1. Use the preceding section, "Examining Domain Member Properties," to see the property screen for the domain member (refer to figure 6.15).

2. Choose the Users button in figure 6.15. All users connected over the network to the domain member, and the resources that are opened by any of those users appear, as shown in figure 6.16. From figure 6.16, you can determine the following information:

   ■ The number of users connected to the domain member

   ■ The share names (resources) in use on the domain member

   ■ The duration of the connection and how much of this duration is idle time

   ■ Whether the user is logged in as a Guest user

   Table 6.2 describes the meanings of the fields in figure 6.18. You can use the information on the screen to determine the level of shared resource usage on any domain computer. To see the resources used by any of the connected users, highlight the user and a list of resources (if any) appears on the bottom half of the screen.

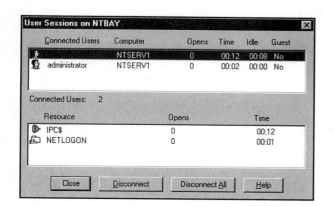

Figure 6.16

*User sessions on domain
member NTBAY.*

On occasion, you might want to disconnect the users from a domain computer. The
reasons for doing this can be any of the following:

■ To balance the load on the NT computer

■ To shut down the NT computer

■ To stop a server service

Before disconnecting a user, the user should stop using the service. You can alert the users
by sending them a warning message. In order to send a message from an NT computer,
the Messenger service must be running. You can check the status of the service by
running the Services applet from the Control Panel folder and verifying that the Messenger service is started on the computer to be used for sending the messages.

On the Windows NT 4 release, it still is possible for users to reconnect by accessing the
shared service, even after you have disconnected the users explicitly.

Table 6.2
User Connection Properties

Field	Displays
Connected Users	User name of a remotely connected user.
Computer	Name of the computer on which the user is logged on.
Opens	Number of resources opened on the domain member by the remotely connected user.
Time	Time elapsed since the user connection was established.
Idle	Time elapsed since the user last initiated an action; it is not the total idle time for the user session.

continues

Table 6.2, Continued

User Connection Properties

Field	Displays
Guest	A value of Yes or No. A value of Yes indicates that the user is logged on as a Guest user, and a value of No indicates that the use is not connected as a Guest user. In a Windows NT network, you can connect to any Windows NT Workstation or Windows NT Server as a Guest user if you do not have an account on the remote NT computer and the Guest account has not been disabled. By default, the Guest account is enabled on a Windows NT Workstation and disabled on a Windows NT Server. If the Guest account has excessive privileges, the automatic logon as a Guest user can result in a serious security breach.
Resource	Name of the shared resource to which the user is connected. The shared resources can be a shared directory, print queue, or a named pipe. Each of the shared resource has its own characteristic icon for easier identification.
Opens	Number of opens against the listed shared resource. This is the second Opens field that is on the bottom half of the screen.
Time	Time elapsed since the resource was last opened. This is the second Times field open on the bottom half of the screen.

3. To disconnect a particular user session, highlight the user session and choose the **D**isconnect button. To disconnect all user sessions, choose the Disconnect **A**ll button. As a safety precaution, you are prompted to confirm the deletion of a user session (see fig. 6.17).

Figure 6.17

Confirming the deletion of a user session.

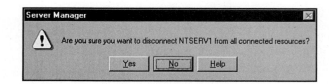

Managing Shares on Domain Members

You can use the Server Manager to manage the shares on a domain member by following these steps:

1. Use the previous section, "Examining Domain Member Properties," to see the property screen for the domain member (refer to figure 6.15).

2. Choose the **S**hares button, as shown in figure 6.15. All the shares on the domain member, the number of users using the shared resources, and the local name of the resource being shared appear, as shown in figure 6.18.

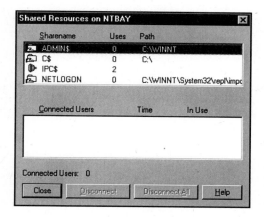

Figure 6.18

Sharenames on domain member NTBAY.

Figure 6.18 shows you the following information:

- The number of users connected to the shared resource on the domain member

- The share names (resources) on the domain member

- The local path name of the shared directory

Table 6.3 shows the meaning of the fields in figure 6.18. Using these fields, you can determine that the administrative share REPL$ has a local path name of D:\EXPORTS on the domain member, and this resource is being accessed by the user account RepAccount for the last four minutes, and the resource currently is not in use.

Table 6.3
Shared Resources Properties

Field	Displays
Sharename	Name of a shared resource such as directory, printer queue, or a named pipe. Names that have a $ character on the end such as A$, B$, C$, IPC$, and ADMIN$ are administrative shares accessible to users that are Administrators (members of the Administrators group). The administrative shares are not visible using the browse functions on a client. Table 6.4 shows typical administrative shares and their meanings.

continues

Table 6.3, Continued
Shared Resources Properties

Field	Displays
Uses	Number of connections to the shared resource. You can use this to determine and monitor the more heavily used resources on domain members.
Path	Local name of the shared resource. For directories, this is the full path name of the local directory on the NT computer that is shared.
Connected Users	Name of the connected user for the shared resource highlighted at the top half of the screen.
Time	Elapsed time since the user first connected to the selected resource.
In Use	Indicates whether the user currently is accessing the resource. This field has a value of No or Yes.

Table 6.4
Common Administrative Shares

Share Name	Meaning
driveletter$	The root device letter of a storage device that can be accessed remotely by members of the Administrators, Server Operators, and Backup Operators groups.
Admin$	The directory under which the Windows NT Server or Windows NT Workstation is installed. It is the directory used to perform remote administration.
IPC$	Interprocess communications resource used to share the named pipes interface needed by communications programs running on different computers.
NETLOGON	Logon server share set by default to %SystemRoot%\System32\Repl\Import. This is used by the NETLOGON service for processing domain requests and exists on Windows NT Servers.
PRINT$	Used to support shared printers.
REPL$	Export directory used for replication. By default it is set to %SystemRoot%\System32\Repl\Export.

Managing In Use (Open) Resources on Domain Members

You can use the Server Manager to manage the use of open resources on a domain member. Follow these steps:

1. Use the previous section, "Examining Domain Member Properties," to see the property screen for the domain member (refer to figure 6.15).

2. Choose the **I**n Use button, as shown in figure 6.15. All the open resources on the domain member, the user who has opened the resources, the type of operation on the resource, the number of locks, and the path of the open resource are shown. Figure 6.19 shows that two resources are open, for example. The resources are opened by the Admin user for Read and Execute. The path of the resources is D:\WINNT, and there are no locks on these resources.

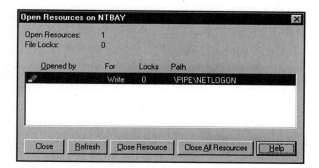

Figure 6.19

In use (open) resources on domain member NTBAY.

Table 6.5 shows the meanings of the fields in figure 6.19.

Table 6.5
In Use Resource Properties

Field	Displays
Open Resources	Total number of open resources such as files, printers, or named. pipes on the domain member.
File Locks	Total number of file locks on the open resources.
Opened by	Name of the users who have opened the resource.
For	Permissions granted when the resource was opened.
Locks	Number of locks on the resource.
Path	Local path to the open resource.

3. You can close the use of a specific resource by highlighting it and choosing **C**lose Re-source. To close all resources, you can choose Close **A**ll Resources. If you try to close a resource that is in use, you are prompted to confirm your choice (see fig. 6.20), because this operation can result in loss of data for the user who has opened the resource. In general, you should send a message to the users before you close resources they are accessing. In order to send a message, you must have the Messenger service running on the computer used to send the message.

Figure 6.20

Confirming your choice to close an open resource on a domain member.

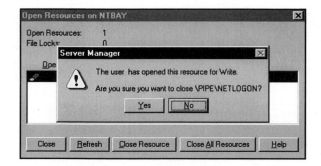

Managing Alerts to Domain Members

You can use the Server Manager to manage the alerts sent to domain members. Follow these steps:

1. Use the previous section, "Examining Domain Member Properties," to see the property screen for the domain member (refer to figure 6.15).

2. Choose the **A**lerts button, as shown in figure 6.15. You can use this screen to build a list of NT computers that are to receive administrative alerts. Figure 6.21 shows a **N**ew Computer or Username field, for example. You can use this field to add the name of a computer and user to receive administrative alert messages.

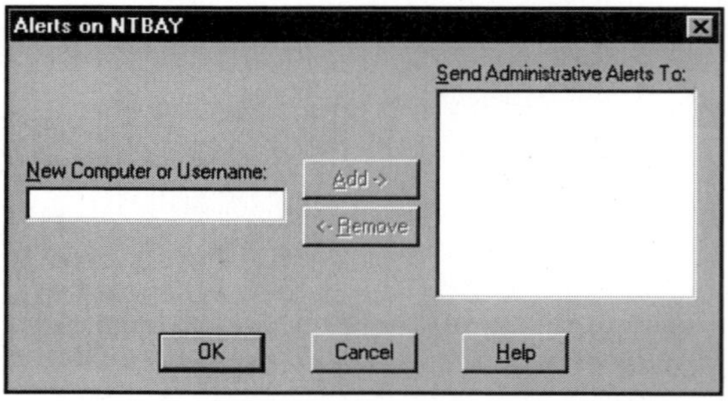

Figure 6.21

Building a list of computers to send administrative alerts.

3. After you enter a name, choose the **A**dd button to add this name to the list of computers/ users to which you want to send administrative alerts. Figure 6.22 shows that computers NWS1 and NWS2 have been added to the list, and a new computer name NTWS3 is being added to the list. As you add computer names to the list, no automatic validation of computer names is performed. You will not be able to send alerts to invalid computer names, of course.

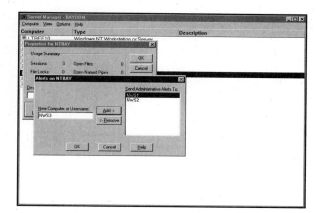

Figure 6.22

Adding names to an administrative alert list.

Promoting a Backup Domain Controller to a Primary Domain Controller

Only the primary domain controller (PDC) of a domain can be used for domain administration. The backup domain controller (BDC) has a read-only copy of the PDC's accounts database, but because this is a read-only copy, it cannot be used for domain administration. The read-only copy of the accounts database can be used for domain user logon, however, and this enables the BDCs to be used for domain user logins.

If the PDC for a domain is down, general domain administration cannot be performed, unless another computer is made the PDC. When you convert another BDC to a PDC for a domain, the existing PDC, if it is up, automatically is downgraded to a BDC. Converting a BDC to a PDC is called *promoting to a primary domain controller*. Whether you can convert an NT Server into a primary domain controller depends on the security role of the NT Server.

During the Windows NT Server installation, you must select the security role of the server computer. The following security roles for the Windows NT Server are defined:

■ Primary domain controller/backup domain controller

■ Server computer

Only Windows NT Servers that were installed with the primary domain controller/backup domain controller security role can act as domain controllers. A computer installed in the security role of a Server computer has to be reinstalled as a PDC/BDC before it can be used as a domain controller.

You can promote a BDC to a PDC by using the Server Manager tool. The following is an outline of the procedure used to promote a BDC to a PDC:

1. Log on to the server as an Administrator user.

2. Start the Server Manager from the Administrative Tools folder. From the Server Manager screen, highlight a backup domain controller that is to be promoted to a primary domain controller for the domain. You can identify the BDC from the Type column. It is listed with the description of Windows NT 4.XX Backup.

3. Choose Promote to Primary Domain **C**ontroller from the **C**omputer menu.

As you view the computers in the domain, you see that the original PDC has been demoted to a BDC, and the selected BDC has been promoted to a PDC.

Establishing Trust Relationships between Domains

As discussed in the previous chapter, domains act as separate networks with their own user accounts databases. If you want user accounts in one domain to access resources in another domain, you must set up a trust relationship between the domains. There are two types of trust relationships for NT domains:

■ One-way trust relationships

■ Two-way (bidirectional) trust relationships

Trust relationships are established using the User Manager for Domains tool in the Administrative Tools group.

Figure 6.23 shows the information needed to establish a trust relationship. This figure shows that domain_A is to be set up to trust domain_B. To identify a trust relationship, you first must identify a list of all domains that can trust a certain domain. In the example in figure 6.23, you must identify the domains that can trust domain_B—such as domain_A. With each domain that is identified, you must set up a password to validate this trust relationship. The use of a password is optional and is used only initially to set up the trust relationship. After the trust relationship is set up, the password is not used for any data flow between the domains. Next, the Administrator of the trusting domain, domain_A, specifies the name of domain_B as the trusted domain. When the name for domain_B is entered, the Administrator must specify the password established in the trusted domain for this trust relationship. If the password is correct, a trust relationship is established from domain_A to domain_B, enabling users in domain B to access resources in domain A.

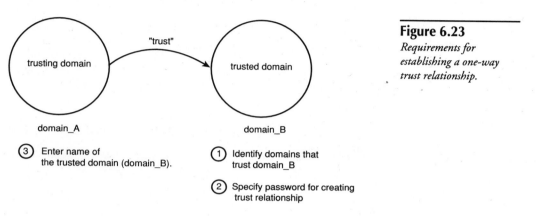

Figure 6.23

Requirements for establishing a one-way trust relationship.

The list of domains permitted to trust a domain and the associated passwords prevent unauthorized domains from setting up a trust relationship. Figure 6.23 shows that, because domain_B is a trusted domain, a user in domain_B can access information in the trusting domain. If the trusting domain is unauthorized, illegal information transfers can occur between the domains. A rouge network administrator, for example, can use the network to transfer sensitive information from domain_B to a directory on a computer in the unauthorized domain. In order to access a directory in the unauthorized domain, the rouge network administrator in domain_B needs directory permissions to appropriate directories in both domains. This directory permission can be granted for a directory in the unauthorized domain if the rogue administrator has cohorts in the unauthorized domain.

To summarize, trust relationships have to be acknowledged by both domains: the trusting and the trusted domains. The administrator of the trusted domain initiates the trust by entering the names of the trusting domains and specifying a password. The administrator in the trusting domain (resource domain) completes the trust establishment by entering the name of the trusted domain and the appropriate password.

How is the password used to set up a domain communicated between the administrators for the two domains involved in the trust relationships? Currently, no automated method of communicating this password exists, so you must resort to other secure techniques to send this password. An example of such a secure technique is encryption such as public/private key encryption methods. Examples of such methods are the RSA public key encryption and the PGP (Pretty Good Privacy) encryption tools. If the administrators of both domains are the same, there is no need to communicate the password. In most cases, however, administrators must communicate the password.

Setting Up a One-Way Trust Relationship

Consider an example in which domain_A is the resource domain (trusting domain), and domain_B is the administration domain (trusted domain). The following is a guideline on setting up a trust relationship from domain_A to domain_B:

1. Log in as Administrator domain user for domain_B. Domain_B is the trusted domain, so you must identify the domains that are permitted to trust domain_B.

2. Start the User Manager for Domains for accounts in domain_B (see fig. 6.24). If you are logged in as an Administrator user for domain_B, when you start the User Manager for Domains, you can manage the accounts on domain_B.

Figure 6.24

The User Manager for Domains for accounts in domain_B.

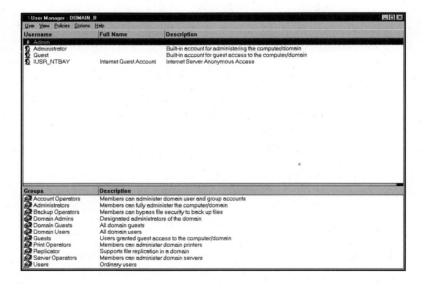

3. Choose **P**olicies, **T**rust Relationships.

The Trust Relationships dialog box appears (see fig. 6.25).

The Trust Relationships dialog box is the main user interface for specifying the trust relationships. Table 6.6 explains the fields in figure 6.25. You use the **A**dd and **R**emove buttons adjacent to the **T**rusted Domains and Tru**s**ting Domains boxes to add or remove domain names in their respective boxes.

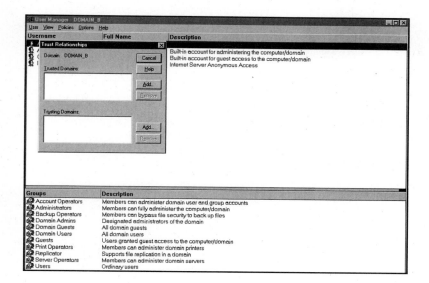

Figure 6.25
The Trust Relationships dialog box.

Table 6.6
Trust Relationship Dialog Box Fields

Field	Description
Domain	Displays the domain name of the domain being administered.
Trusted Domains	This is a box to which you can add the names of the domains that the domain being administered trusts.
Tr**u**sting Domains	This is a box to which you can add the names of the domains allowed to trust the domain being administered. Only Windows NT domains are permitted to trust another domain.

4. You must identify the domains that can trust the domain being administered. Choose the **A**dd button next to the Tr**u**sting Domains box. The Add Trusting Domain dialog box appears (see fig. 6.26). In this dialog box, use the **T**rusting Domain field to enter the name of the domain that trusts the domain being administered. Use the Initial **P**assword and the **C**onfirm Password fields to specify the password to be used in the establishment of the trust relationship.

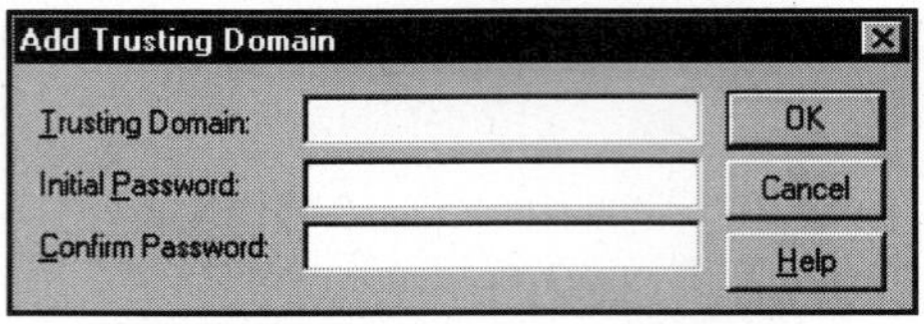

Figure 6.26

*The Add Trusting
Domain dialog box.*

Figure 6.27 shows the Trust Relationships dialog box with domain_A listed in the
Trusting Domains box. Because domain_ A is listed in the Trusting Domains box,
domain_A is trusting domain_B.

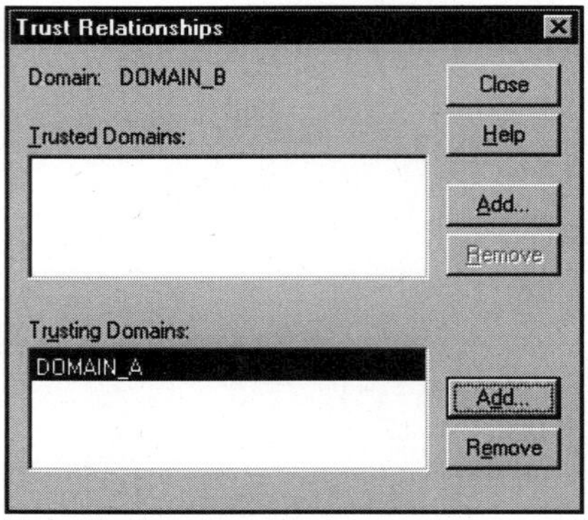

Figure 6.27

*Domain A is permitted to
trust domain B.*

5. Next, you must administer the trusting domains—domain_A, in this case—and make the
trusted domains known to the trusting domain.

You can log on as a domain Administrator to domain_A and perform the next step.

Alternatively, you can select domain_A while using the User Manager for Domains utility
and administering domain_B, the trusted domain. This approach is more convenient if
you are the domain administrator for both domains, because you do not have to log on
separately in domain_A. Perform the following steps to select a different domain from the
User Manager for Domains utility.

- Access the **U**ser menu from the User Manager for Domains utility.

- Choose the option **S**elect Domain.

- When you see the Select Domain dialog box (see fig. 6.28), select the trusting
  domain (domain A) to be administered.

6. From the User Manager for domain_A, choose **P**olicies, **T**rust Relationships.

7. The Trust Relationships dialog box for the trusting domain, domain_A, appears (see fig. 6.29).

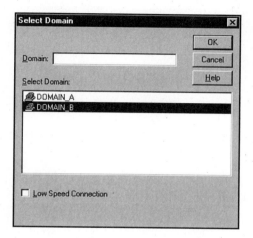

Figure 6.28

The Select Domain dialog box.

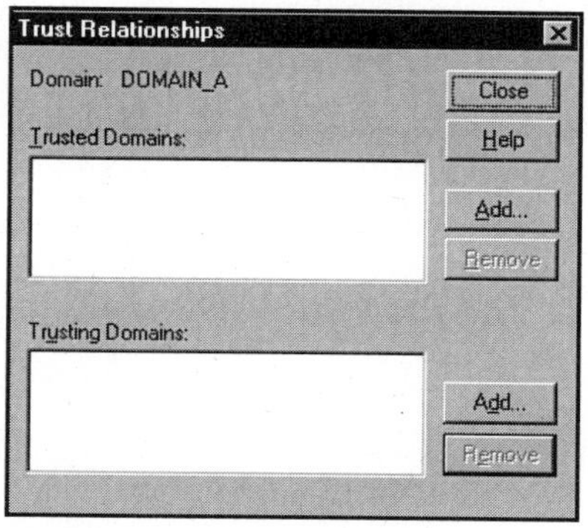

Figure 6.29

The Trust Relationships dialog box for the trusting domain.

8. Choose the **A**dd button next to the **T**rusted Domains list. The Add Trusted Domain dialog box appears (see fig. 6.30).

9. Enter the name of the trusted domains and the password specified in step 4. If you entered the trusted domain name and password correctly, the message shown in figure 6.31 appears. If you entered the incorrect domain name, the message shown in figure 6.32 appears, telling you that User Manager for Domains was unable to find the domain controller for this domain. If you entered an incorrect password, User Manager for Domains informs you that the password is incorrect.

Figure 6.30

The Add Trusted Domain dialog box.

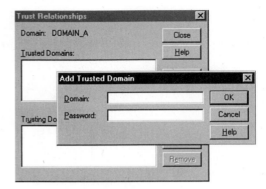

Figure 6.31

The Trust relationship with domain_name *successfully established message.*

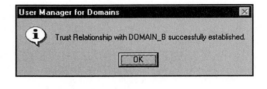

Figure 6.32

The Trust relationship failed message.

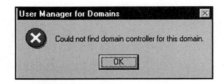

Figure 6.33 shows that domain_B was added to the list of trusted domains.

10. Repeat steps 5 to 9 for any other trusted domains.

Figure 6.33

Domains trusted by domain_A.

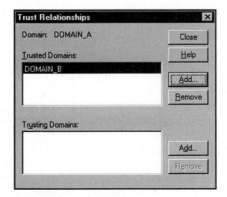

Setting Up a Two-Way Trust Relationship

In a one-way trust relationship, only one domain trusts another domain, and not vice versa. In a two-way trust relationship, both domains trust each other, thereby permitting each domain to have accounts that can access resources in the other domain. A two-way trust relationship enables users to log on from either domain to the domain that has their account. Domain user accounts and groups can be granted permissions to use the resource in either domain.

The procedure for setting up a two-way trust relationship is based on the procedure for setting up a one-way trust relationship. To set up a two-way trust relationship, you perform the procedure for one-way trust relationship twice.

Removing a Trust Relationship

To remove a trust relationship, you must remove the trust relationships from both sides. The recommended order for removing a trust relationship follows:

1. Users in the trusted domain should stop using the resources in the trusting domain.

2. The trusted domain should remove the trusting domain from its Permitted to Trust this Domain list box. You can find this dialog box by choosing the **T**rust Relationships option from the **P**olicies menu of the User Manager for Domains.

3. The trusting domain should remove the trusted domains from its **T**rusted Domains list box.

Experimenting with the Order of Setting Up Trust Relationships

In the procedures that have been outlined for establishing a trust relationship, the trusted domain has to identify the trusting domain first. This is the recommended order described in the Microsoft documentation. The question often asked by network administrators learning to set up trust relationships is "What happens if the trusting domain identifies the trusted domains first?"

The following experiment describes the effects of setting up a trust relationship in the reverse order when trying to set up a relationship from domain_A to domain_B.

1. Log in as domain Administrator to domain_A, the trusting domain.

2. Run User Manager for Domains and choose **P**olicies, **T**rust Relationships.

3. Choose the **A**dd button next to the **T**rusted Domains list box.

   Add the trusted domain, domain_B, and specify a password. Figure 6.34 shows that although domain_B is added as a trusted domain, a message appears informing you that the trust relationship cannot be verified at this time.

4. Log in as Administrator for domain_B.

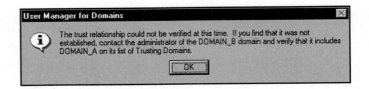

Figure 6.34

Attempting to set up a trust relationship without identifying the trusting domain.

5. Run User Manager for Domains for the trusted domain, domain_B, and choose **P**olicies, **T**rust Relationships.

6. Choose the **A**dd button next to the Tr**u**sting Domains list box.

   Enter the domain name for the trusting domain—domain_A. You are asked to specify a password. Enter any bogus password. The trust relationship now is established!

From these steps, you can see that the trust relationships can be established even if you establish the trust in the reverse order from what is described in the Microsoft documentation. What is surprising is that the trust relationship is established with bogus passwords in step 6 of this procedure. As long as the domain administrators know the names of the domains involved in the trust relationship, they can set up a trust relationship without exchanging passwords; therefore, no proper method exists for authenticating the establishment of domain trust relationships using passwords.

Troubleshooting Domain Trust Relationships

The following is a list of issues and solutions to consider when you are having problems in establishing trust relationships.

- **Cannot establish a trust relationship.** Verify that PDCs of the domains are up and reachable through the network. Verify that the correct passwords were supplied.

- **Trust relationship is broken.** You can verify this by examining the **T**rust Relationships option on the **P**olicies menu in User Manager for Domains. Symptoms of this are that trusted accounts and resources in the resource domain are not available for use.

- **Cannot verify the trust.** The trusted domain must permit the trusting domain to establish the trust before the trusting domain can establish the trust.

- **Cannot reestablish a broken trust.** Break the trust from both domains, and then reestablish the trust as if it were a new trust relationship.

- **Cannot use trusted accounts.** A common mistake is to establish the trust in the wrong direction. Break the existing trust and create it in the correct direction.

- **Cannot administer another domain.** Verify that the trusted domain global group Domain Admins is added to the local group Administrators.

Replication in Domains

Replication is a feature of Windows NT domains that enables identical directory structures and files to be maintained on multiple servers and workstations. Replication simplifies the tasks of maintaining identical sets of data because only a single master copy of the data needs to be maintained. All other computers synchronize their copy of the data to this master copy.

Replication can be used for load balancing, by keeping a copy of the master data on several NT servers. An example is clients that need to access data for lookup purposes on a central NT server. As the number of clients increases, so does the work load on the NT server. One way of distributing the load is to replicate copies of the master database on other NT servers. This allows several NT servers to handle the client requests and distribute the workload.

Figure 6.35 introduces the vocabulary used to describe the replication operation. The computer that has a master copy of the data is called the *export server.* The computers that receive a copy of the master data set, or the computers that synchronize their copies of the data set with the master, are called *import servers.*

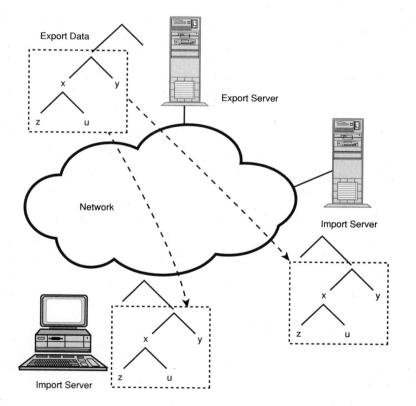

Figure 6.35

The replication operation.

The export server must be a Windows NT Server. The Windows NT Server contains the files and directories to be replicated to the import servers. The import servers can be any of the following:

- Windows NT Server

- Windows NT Workstation

- LAN Manager Server

On LAN Manager Server computers, the import directories and files must match the file-naming convention of the export computers. If the import directory is HPFS, you must ensure that the directory-naming conventions for exported and imported directories on the export and import computers match.

To use replication, you must have at least one Windows NT Server.

The data that is replicated can be system-related data such as logon scripts for users or application-specific data such as a database of employee records, word processing templates, phone lists for vendors, and so on.

Log-on scripts for users are maintained in files on NT computers and are not part of the domain accounts databases (SAM database) automatically replicated. Therefore, if you want changes in log-on scripts on the PDC to be copied to the BDCs, you must set up replication between the PDC and its BDCs for log-on scripts.

From a purely technical point of view, separating the log-on script replication from the replication of the user accounts information is a weakness in the Windows NT architecture. In the author's opinion, log-on scripts are a very important part of the user account property, and should be handled as part of the account's synchronization. This has been done successfully in other competing network architectures.

When you set up replication, you can specify whether the entire subtree under a specified directory should be replicated, or only specific files in the subtree. Locks can be applied to specific directories in the export and import trees to prevent them from being exported or imported.

The default export directory is %SystemRoot%\System32\Repl\Export, and the default import directory for import computers is %SystemRoot%\System32\Repl\Import.

The default log-on script directory on the PDC is %SystemRoot%\System32\Repl\Export\Scripts, and the default log-on script directory on import computers is %SystemRoot%\System32\Repl\Import\Scripts. By keeping the log-on script directory (Scripts) as a subdirectory of the default export and default import directory, log-on script replication is enabled if the default export/import directories are used when replication is enabled. Figure 6.36 shows the default export and import directories for replication.

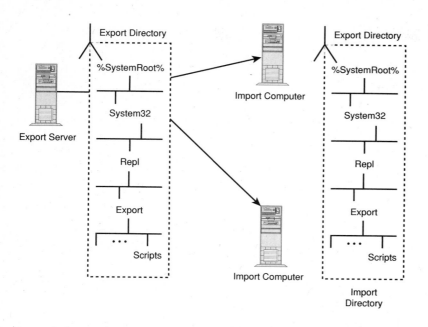

Figure 6.36
Default export/import directories for replication.

Only one directory tree can be exported from each export server. If you want to export multiple directories, you should have the directories as part of the same export directory tree structure. The default location for log-in scripts therefore is a subtree of the default export directory tree.

You can configure replication so that changes in the directory tree are propagated to other import computers immediately or after a two-minute stabilization period.

It is possible to use replication for backing up critical data directory structures on a server. However, you should not use this method as a replacement for normal backup procedures or as a solution to providing near-line backup of user information. In a 1992 TechEd conference paper titled *Enterprise Connectivity in a Multivendor Environment*, a case history is described where one organization attempted to replicate user directory information every six minutes. They found that even on a 100 Mbps FDDI backbone, this saturated the FDDI backbone. You can use the replication for critical data that changes infrequently, provided that the sizes of the files replicated do not adversely affect normal network traffic.

You can set up replication of directories to individual computers in a domain or to an entire domain. By default, the export servers export to the local domain, and the import client computers import from the local domain.

Exporting to an entire domain gives the entire domain access to the replicated directory (see fig. 6.37). Importing to a domain is often more convenient than exporting to individual computers in a domain. You also can replicate data to individual computers in a domain (see fig. 6.38).

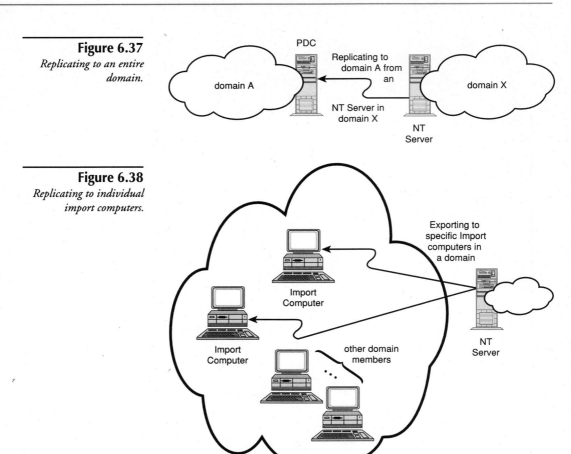

Figure 6.37

Replicating to an entire domain.

Figure 6.38

Replicating to individual import computers.

If you are exporting to a domain separated by a wide area network (WAN) bridge from the export server, the replication might not work because broadcast mechanisms are used to initiate the replication of data, and if the bridges are configured to block broadcast packets to minimize broadcast storms, the replication operation will not work (see fig. 6.39).

When exporting data to import computers separated from the export server across WAN bridges, it is preferable to specify the import computers by name (see fig. 6.40). Similarly, when importing from another domain across a WAN bridge, it is preferable to specify the export server by name rather than specifying the export domain name (see fig. 6.41). Use of explicit names avoids the use of broadcast query packets to discover explicit names of the computers involved in the replication operation.

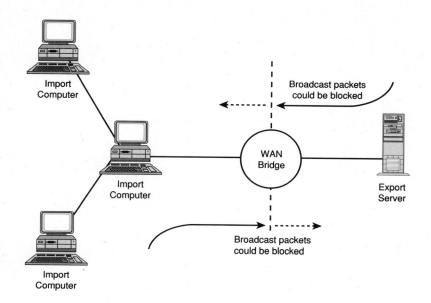

Figure 6.39

Replication across a WAN bridge.

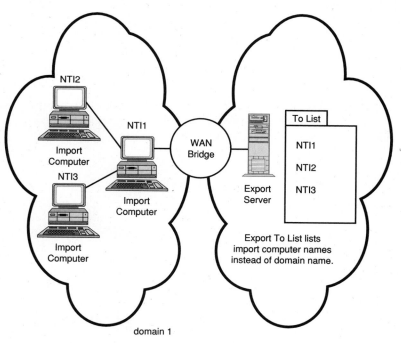

Figure 6.40

Exporting data to import computers across a WAN bridge.

Figure 6.41

Importing data from an export server across a WAN bridge.

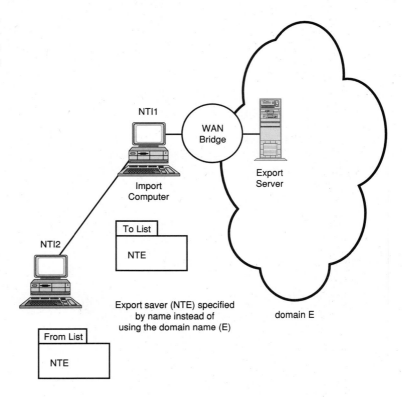

When exporting data across domains, you must ensure that appropriate trust relationships exist between the domains to permit data flow between domains. The previous section in this chapter discusses implementing trust relationships between domains.

Configuring Replication

Before you can configure replication, you must create a special user account under which the Directory Replicator service will run. You can use any user name except the name *Replicator*, because this is the name of a built-in domain group. Additionally, this special account must have the following properties:

■ The password account never expires. This is set by setting the Password Never Expires option and clearing the User Must Change Password At Next Logon option.

■ The account must be accessible 24 hours a day, seven days a week.

■ The account must be a member of the following domain groups: Backup Operators, Domain Users, and Replicator.

You must set up the same user name and password for the replicator account on both export and import computers.

Next, you must configure the Replicator Service to start automatically and log on under the Directory Replicator user account on the export server. This step can be performed by using the Server Manager.

Next, you must configure the export server and import servers. The following sections contain a more detailed outline on configuring the following steps for replication:

1. Setting up the replicator account.

2. Configuring the export server.

3. Configuring the import computer.

Setting Up the Replicator Account

The following is an outline for setting up the replicator account.

1. Log on to the domain of the export server using a domain Administrator.

2. Start the User Manager for Domains.

3. Choose Users, New User.

The New User Property dialog box appears (see fig. 6.42).

4. Enter the following property values:

Property	Value
Username	ReplicatorAccount (or any other name)
Full Name	Replicator Account (optional)
Description	Replicator account for replication purposes (optional)
Password	Suitable password
Confirm Password	Same password as in Password field
User Must Change Password at Next Logon	*Clear this check box*
Password Never Expires	*Check this box*

Figure 6.42

The New User dialog box.

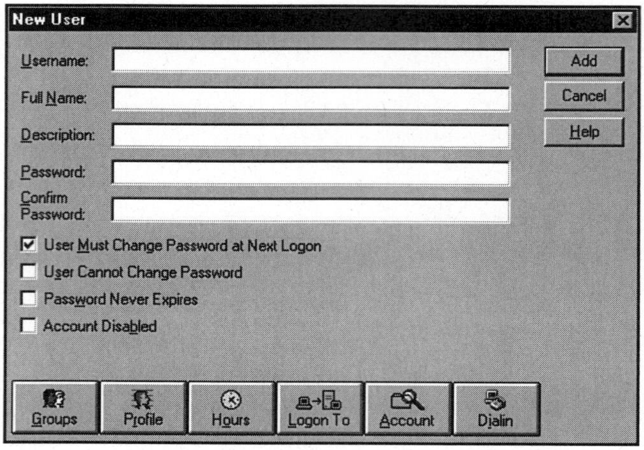

5. Choose the **G**roups button. A screen similar to figure 6.43 appears.

   Notice that the new account is already a member of the Domain Users group. To make the account a member of the Backup Operators and Replicator local group, select those accounts from the **N**ot member of list box, and choose the **A**dd button.

Figure 6.43

The Group Memberships dialog box.

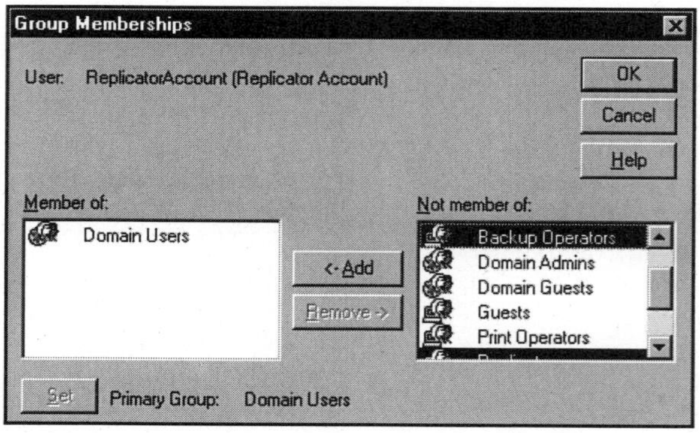

You can select multiple group names by holding down Ctrl while selecting the group name.

Figure 6.44 shows the desired group memberships of the replicator account.

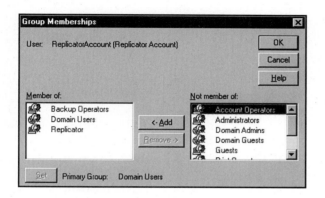

Figure 6.44

Desired group memberships for the replicator account.

6. Choose OK to save and exit group membership changes.

7. Choose the **A**dd button from the New User dialog box to create the replicator account.

8. Choose Close.

9. Select Services from the Control Panel folder. Alternatively, select the Services option from the Computer menu of the Server Manager after highlighting the export server. The Server Manager is in the Administrative Tools folder.

Figure 6.45 shows the services on the export server NTSB in domain B.

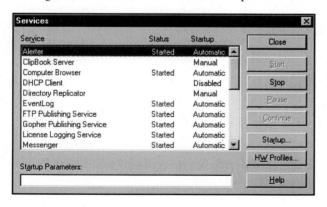

Figure 6.45

Services on the export server.

10. Highlight the Directory Replicator service and choose the Startup button. The Service dialog box for the Directory Replicator service appears (see fig. 6.46).

Figure 6.46

The Service dialog box for the Directory Replicator service.

11. Set the Startup Type to **A**utomatic.

12. Select the browse button to the right of the **T**his Account field. The Add User dialog box appears (see fig. 6.47). Highlight the Replicator account that you just created, choose the **A**dd button, and then choose OK.

Figure 6.47

The Add User dialog box for selecting the replicator account.

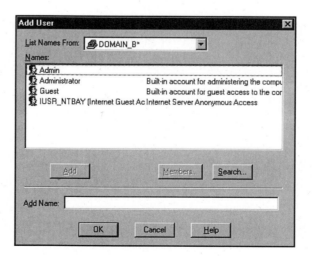

The replicator account name appears in the **T**his Account field.

13. Enter the password information for the replicator account in the **P**assword and the **C**onfirm Password fields.

14. Choose OK to save the startup information on the Directory Replicator service. A message informs you that the selected replicator account has been granted the Log On As A Service right (see fig. 6.48). If the account was not added to the Replicator group, it is added automatically to the Replicator local group.

Figure 6.48

A message informing you of the Log On As Service right given to the replicator account.

15. Start the Directory Replicator service by restarting the export server, or choosing the Start button from the Services screen.

16. Set up a domain user replicator account on import computers with the same user name and password, using the procedure outlined in steps 1 to 14.

Configuring the Export Server

On the export server (implemented on a Windows NT Server), you can perform the following:

- Identify the export directory tree that will export the data.

- Specify domain names or computer names to which to export data.

Replication is set up from the Directory Replication dialog box. You can access this dialog box doing either of the following:

- Select the Server icon in the Control Panel.

- Start Server Manager from the Administrative Tools folder. Then double-click on the export server (or select Properties from the **C**omputer menu).

The following is an outline of the rest of the procedure for configuring the export server:

1. From the Server Properties dialog box, choose the **R**eplication button. Figure 6.49 shows the Directory Replication dialog box for the export server.

2. Choose the **E**xport Directories radio button. The default path of %SystemRoot%\ System32\Repl\Export is listed. If you plan to use a non-default path for importing the data, you need to change the **F**rom Path field.

Figure 6.49

The Directory Replication dialog box.

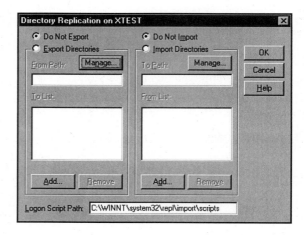

The **T**o List box is used to list the computers and domains to export the directory to. By default, this list is empty, which indicates that the export server exports to the local domain. If you add any entries in the **T**o List box, the local domain no longer is exported to. You can add the names of computers and domains to which the directory data will be exported. If you need to additionally include the local domain along with lists of computers and other domains, you must enter the local domain name explicitly.

3. Choose the **A**dd button under the **T**o List box to add a list of domain or import computers. The Select Domain dialog box appears, which lists the domains (see fig. 6.50). Double-clicking on a domain name lists the computers in that domain. You can select any combination of domain names and computer names to export the data to.

Figure 6.50

The Select Domain dialog box.

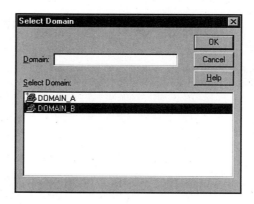

4. If you need to export selective subdirectories in the export path, you must choose the **M**anage button next to the **F**rom Path field. Figure 6.51 shows the Manage Exported Directories dialog box. This screen shows that the APP_DATA and the SCRIPTS The

directory under the export directory have been added to the list of subdirectories to be managed. You can add a directory to the managed list by choosing the **A**dd button, and you can remove a directory by choosing the **R**emove button.

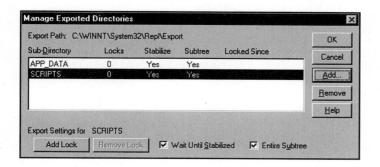

Figure 6.51

The Manage Exported Directories dialog box.

The Export Path is a display-only field and lists the path to the directory from which subdirectories and files are exported.

The Sub-**D**irectory column indicates the list of subdirectories exported from the computer. The subdirectories under the Export path are added automatically to this list, if the subdirectories were created prior to the start of the Directory Replication service on the export server. You can add additional subdirectories by choosing the **A**dd button.

The Locks column indicates the number of locks applied to the subdirectory. A lock prevents a subdirectory export, and you can have more than one lock placed on a subdirectory. A subdirectory is exported only if there are no locks placed on it; that is, the number of locks must be zero. You can add locks by choosing the Add Lock button, and you can remove locks by choosing the Remove Lock button. You can add locks to temporarily prevent subdirectories from being replicated.

If the Stabilize column value is set to Yes, it indicates that files and subdirectories in that subdirectory must be stable for at least two minutes before replication can occur. A value of No indicates that changed data will be replicated as soon as it is changed. The default value is No. You can change the setting by using the Wait Until **S**tabilized check box.

If the Subtree column value is set to Yes, it indicates that the entire subdirectory will be exported. A value of No indicates that only the first-level subdirectory will be exported. The default value is Yes. You can change the setting by using the Entire S**ub**tree check box.

The Locked Since field indicates the date and time since the oldest lock was placed on this directory.

5. Save any changes you made by choosing the OK button.

Configuring the Import Computer

On the import computer (implemented on a Windows NT Server, Windows NT Workstation, or LAN Manager server) you can perform the following tasks:

■ Identify the imported directory tree that will receive the replicated data.

■ Specify domain names or computer names from which the data will be imported.

Replication is set up from the Directory Replication dialog box. You can access this dialog box using one of the following procedures:

■ Select the Server icon in the Control Panel.

■ Start Server Manager from the Administrative Tools folder. Double-click on the export server (or choose **C**omputer, Properties).

The following is an outline of the rest of the procedure to configure the import computer:

1. From the Server Properties dialog box, choose the **R**eplication button. The Directory Replication dialog box on the import computer appears.

2. Select the **I**mport Directories radio button. The default path of %SystemRoot%\System32\Repl\Import is listed. If you plan on using a non-default path for exporting the data, you need to change the To **P**ath field.

   The Fr**o**m List box is used to list the computers and domains from which to import the replicated data. By default, this list is empty, indicating that the import computers import only from the local domain. If you add any entries in the Fr**o**m List box, the local domain no longer is imported from. You can add the names of computers and domains from which the directory data will be imported. If you need to additionally include the local domain along with lists of computers and other domains, you must enter the local domain name explicitly.

3. Choose the A**d**d button under the Fr**o**m List box to add a list of domains or import computers. The Select Domain dialog box appears, which lists the domains. Double-clicking on a domain name lists the computers in that domain. You can select any combination of domain names and computer names to export the data to.

4. If you need to import selective subdirectories in the export path, you must choose the **M**anage button next to the To **P**ath field. Figure 6.52 shows the Manage Imported Directories screen. This screen shows that the APP_DATA and the SCRIPTS directory under the import directory have been added to the list of subdirectories to be managed. You can add a directory to the managed list by choosing the **A**dd button, and you can remove a directory by choosing the **R**emove button.

Figure 6.52

The Managed Imported Directories screen.

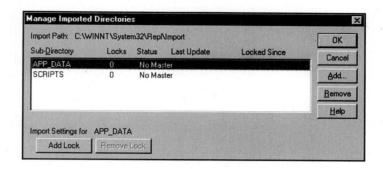

The Import Path field is a display-only field and lists the path to the directory from which subdirectories and files are imported.

The Sub-**D**irectory column indicates the list of subdirectories imported into the computer. The subdirectories under the Import Path field are added automatically to this list, if the subdirectories were created prior to the start of the Directory Replication service on the import computer. You can add additional subdirectories by choosing the **A**dd button.

The Locks column indicates the number of locks applied to the subdirectory. A lock prevents a subdirectory import, and you can have more than one lock placed on a subdirectory. A subdirectory is imported only if there are no locks placed on it; that is, the number of locks must be zero. You can add locks by choosing the Add Lock button, and you can remove locks by choosing the Remove Lock button.

The Status column indicates the status of the replication. The word OK indicates that the subdirectory is receiving regular updates from the export server, and the imported data is identical to the exported data. The words No Sync indicate that the subdirectory has received updates but the import data is not synchronized to the master data. This could occur because of communications failure, open files on export or import computers, export or import server malfunction, or not having enough access permissions at the export or import computers. The words No Master indicate that the import computer is not receiving updates. This can be because the export server is not running or has stopped sending updates. A blank entry in the Status column indicates that the replication has never occurred to that subdirectory. This can occur due to improper configuration of replication at the export or import computers.

The Last Update column indicates the date and time that the last update was made to the file in the import subdirectory or in its subtree.

The Locked Since field indicates the date and time the oldest lock was placed in the subdirectory.

Permissions Required for Replication

The Replicator group is assigned Change permissions to the export and import directory. If you change these permissions or do not assign appropriate permissions to the Replicator group for the export/import directory, the files might not be copied properly to the import computers. You also might see an access denied error in the event log.

You will learn more about directory permissions and the event log in later chapters in this book.

Troubleshooting Replication Services

Setting up replication services involves a number of configuration steps that have to be performed at the export and import computers. The following is a troubleshooting checklist you can use if replication services are not working as expected:

- Has the Directory Replicator service been started on export and import computers?

- Is there a network path between the export and import computers?

- Are the export and import computers able to talk to each other? Try sending messages or using the Browser in File Manager to see whether the export/import computers are visible on the network.

- Have you set up the replication account correctly and assigned this account as a member of the User Domains, Backup Operators, and the Replicator groups?

- If the export and import servers are in the same domain, the replication account and password must be the same on the export and import computers?

- Are there appropriate trust relationships between domains?

- Are files kept opened in the export or import directories? This can cause sharing violation errors in the event log.

- Are the clocks on the export and import servers approximately synchronized?

- Windows NT does not support HPFS extended attributes (EAs) written to noncontiguous parts of the disk, whereas OS/2's HPFS implementation does. You might have problems with extended attributes replicated from an HPFS volume on a Windows NT Server.

■ If you are importing to a LAN Manager server, ensure that no other user is using the replicator account. Replicator service will be suspended temporarily if another user is logged on with the replication account.

■ Does the Replicator group have Change permission to the export/import directories?

■ Is there a bridge between the export and import computers? If so, the replication should be configured to export directly to the import computers.

Conclusion

In this chapter, you learned how to implement domains and perform domain operations. The domain operations discussed included selecting domains, establishing primary domain controllers (PDCs) and backup domain controllers (BDCs), synchronizing domains, promoting to a PDC, establishing trusts between domains, and adding/removing workstations from domains.

In addition, you learned to configure replication services for domains.

7

Managing Windows NT Server Domain Accounts

In this chapter, you will learn how to set up domain user accounts and domain group accounts. You will learn how local groups and global groups can be used to simplify administration within domains, and the different capabilities and rights that can be set for the different users and groups.

The user and group accounts for Windows NT domains are called domain accounts because they have a scope of existence that extends throughout the domain. The domain accounts are in contrast to accounts defined on a Windows NT Workstation with a scope local to the Windows NT Workstation only. These local accounts are necessary when the Windows NT Workstation is not connected to a network and a logon is required to access the resources on the Windows NT Workstation.

Using Administrative Wizards

In NT 4, Microsoft has introduced wizards that can help simplify network administration tasks for the beginner. By prompting the user with a series of questions, the wizard can execute a complicated task based on answers the user provides. As you become more experienced with NT Server, the administrative utilities may prove to be quicker to use than wizards. Microsoft has provided eight wizards with NT 4:

- Add **U**ser Accounts

- **G**roup Management

- Managing **F**ile and Folder Access

- Add **P**rinter

- Add/**R**emove Programs

- Install New **M**odem

- **N**etwork Client Administrator

- **L**icense Compliance

To execute Administrative Wizards, click on the Start button, then choose Programs, Administrative Tools, and Administrative Wizards. Figure 7.1 shows the Administrative Wizards screen.

Figure 7.1

The Administrative Wizards screen.

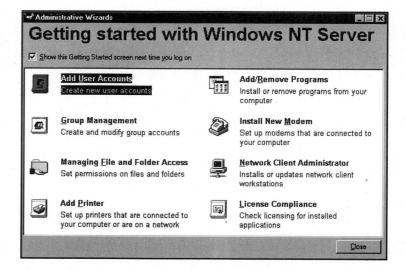

Understanding Users and Groups Accounts

When a Windows NT Server is installed, certain users and groups are created by the system to simplify administration. This section discusses the capabilities of these predefined users and groups.

To examine the accounts for a domain, run the User Manager for Domains. This application is in the Administrative Tools folder. Figure 7.2 shows a screen for the User Manager for Domains.

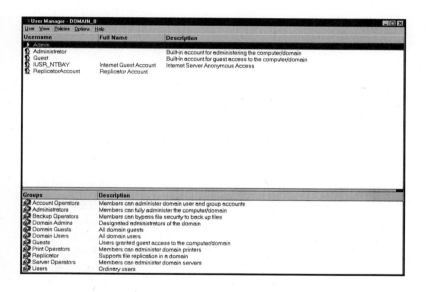

Figure 7.2

A User Manager for Domains screen.

The top half of the screen lists the user accounts, and the bottom half of the screen lists the group accounts.

Examining Built-In Domain User Accounts

The Administrator and Guest built-in domain user accounts are created by default during a Windows NT Server installation.

The Administrator domain user account is the primary account used for Windows NT Server administration. It is possible to create additional domain user accounts with the same privilege as the Administrator domain user account. The Administrator domain account is special because it cannot be deleted. The Administrator account can be renamed, however. Renaming the user account does not alter the Security Identifier (SID) used by the operating system to internally describe the user account. Therefore, the rights, capabilities, and permissions given to the Administrator account are not affected. You might want to rename the Administrator account so that hackers will have to overcome another hurdle in order to break into the system.

The Administrator account gives you the following capabilities:

- Creating and managing user accounts
- Creating and managing global groups
- Creating and managing local groups
- Assigning user rights
- Locking the server
- Formatting the server's hard disks
- Creating common groups
- Keeping local profiles
- Sharing and stop sharing directories
- Sharing and stop sharing printers

The Guest account has a limited set of privileges and is meant for occasional use. The Guest logon can grant automatic access to share names on the server if no password is set for the Guest account. Figure 7.2 shows how a Windows NT computer can access the share name on a server. In this figure, an incorrect user name or password is specified when making a connection using a network drive letter. If the logon under the specified user name is not successful, a Windows NT Server or a Windows NT Workstation attempts the logon using the built-in Guest account. If no password is set for Guest, the connection to the share name is automatic.

Figure 7.3

Network logon as Guest.

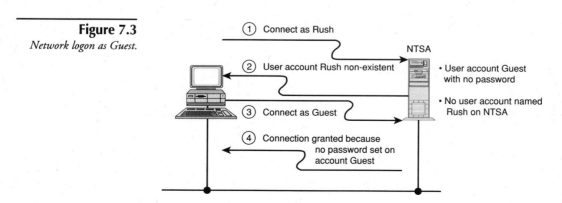

For the sake of completeness, the procedure for making a connection using a network drive letter is described here briefly for those who want to experiment with the automatic logon as Guest.

As an Administrator, you must exercise caution in assigning permissions to the Guest account. For security reasons, the domain Guest account is disabled by default on a Windows NT Server. It is enabled by default on Windows NT Workstations.

Figure 7.4 shows the user properties of the built-in Guest account on a newly installed Windows NT Server. Notice that the check box for Account Disabled is checked, thus disabling the Guest account. If you need to enable the Guest account, clear this check box and save the changes to the Guest account by choosing the OK button. By default, there is no password for the Guest account.

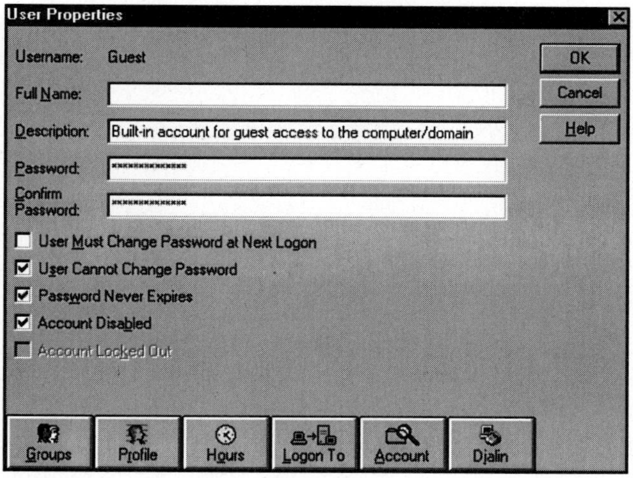

Figure 7.4

The User Properties dialog box for a Guest account on a newly installed Windows NT Server.

Understanding Group Accounts

Group accounts are used to simplify administration. A group account can be granted permissions to access a resource. By making user accounts members of the group accounts, you automatically assign to the user accounts the same permissions given to the group accounts.

You can log on using user accounts, but you cannot log on using group accounts. Group accounts exist only for the convenience of assigning the same permissions to a large number of users. This method is easier than assigning to each individual user the same permission. If a user leaves a department, you can remove the user as a member of the group accounts for that department. All the privileges needed by that user for his or her old department then are revoked for that user. You do not have to remove the user from the access control list (ACL) for each resource. If the same user joins another department, you can assign the user's account as a member of the groups that will grant to the user the needed permissions to accomplish the new job.

The advantages of using groups follow:

- Permissions can be granted to all members of a group.

- Permissions can be revoked from all members of a group.

- If a user is no longer a part of the group, he or she can be removed from the group; this automatically revokes permissions for that user.

- When new users join a department, they can be made members of groups that give them the needed permissions.

Understanding Global Groups versus Local Groups

Two types of groups exist for Windows NT Server: global groups and local groups.

Global groups are also called *domain groups.* The members of global groups are domain users. This is in contrast to local users who have a scope limited to the computer on which they are defined and cannot be members of the global group.

Global groups are a domain-level mechanism for gathering domain-level users. The scope of a global group is the entire domain on which users are defined, and is visible from any Windows NT computer that is in the domain. Permissions can be granted to a global group for a resource on any Windows NT Server or a Windows NT Workstation in the domain. The global group accounts are maintained on the primary domain controller for the domain and replicated to backup domain controllers for that domain.

Global groups are created using User Manager for Domains. Figure 7.5 illustrates the nature of global groups.

Global groups have the following characteristics:

- Members of a global group must be domain user accounts of the domain in which the group was created. This implies that the members of global groups cannot be domain user accounts of another domain.

- Global groups can be assigned permissions to any resource in the domain in which they are defined.

■ Global groups can be assigned permissions to resources in a domain that is different from the domain in which they are defined, as long as there are appropriate trust relationships between the domains.

■ Members of a global group can use resources in any domain in which the global group has permissions.

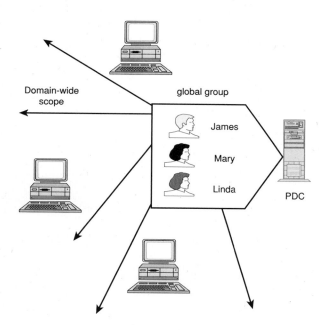

Figure 7.5
Global groups.

Local groups, on the other hand, can be assigned permissions for a resource on the Windows NT computer on which they are defined. On a stand-alone computer not connected to the network, local groups can be used to assign permissions for a group of local users who are members.

If a Windows NT computer is part of a domain, then for the sake of convenience in assigning permissions, a local group can contain domain user accounts and global groups in the domain where the Windows NT computer is a member, or users from a trusted domain.

Domain users can be assigned access to resources on any Windows NT computer in the domain. If a group of local users and domain users is to be assigned the same permission to a local resource on the Windows NT computer, it stands to reason that domain users should be members of a local group. If this were not possible, separate permission assignments would have to be made to each of the domain users.

Figure 7.6 illustrates the situation where separate permissions are made to domain users. Notice that the local user Tom and the domain users duser1 to duser10 are given the same permission of reading (Read) the directory C:\APPS\DATA on the Windows NT Work station in domain A. Eleven separate permissions have to be assigned to the directory C:\APPS\DATA—one permission for the local user Tom, and 10 permissions for the domain users duser1 to duser10. This is a lot of administrative overhead for the Administrator, especially because the same permission is set 11 times.

Figure 7.6

Assigning permissions to a local resource for local and domain users.

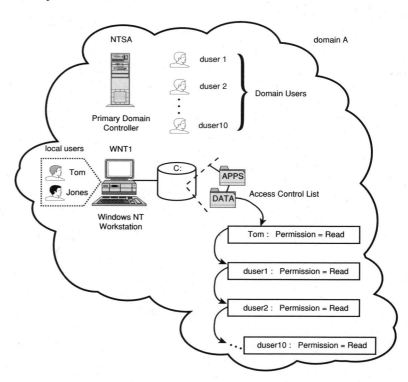

Figure 7.7 shows how the assignment of permissions in figure 7.6 can be simplified by using a local group that contains the domain users. In figure 7.7, a local group called APPSGROUP has been defined that contains the following:

■ Local user Tom

■ Each of the domain users duser1 to duser10

The Read permission is assigned to the local group APPSGROUP. All members of the group (local user Tom and the 10 domain users) inherit the Read permission to the directory. There is only one permission assigned to the C:\APPS\DATA directory in figure 7.6, versus 11 separate permissions in figure 7.5. Clearly, figure 7.6 has less administrative overhead because a local group containing domain Administrators is used.

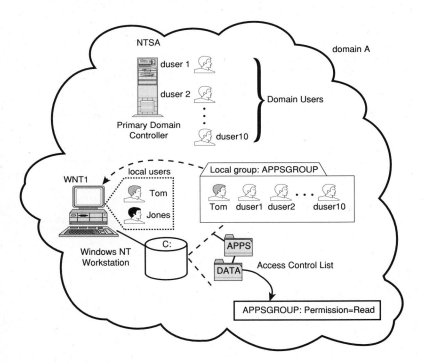

Figure 7.7

Assigning permissions to a local resource using local groups containing domain users.

Extending the example in figures 7.6 and 7.7, consider the following situation: There are several domain users already organized into domain groups, and all of these domain groups need Read directory access to the local resource C:\APPS\DATA on a Windows NT Workstation. Figure 7.8 shows the assignment of permissions for the 10 global groups and the local user Tom to C:\APPS\DATA. Again, 11 separate permissions have to be set, which results in a large administrative overhead. To solve this problem, Windows NT allows local groups to contain global groups. Figure 7.9 shows a local group called APPSGROUP that contains the local user Tom and the 10 global groups. As before, this local group then is assigned Read permission to C:\APPS\DATA. All members of the group inherit the Read permission to the directory. There is only one permission assigned to the C:\APPS\DATA directory in figure 7.9, versus 11 separate permissions in figure 7.8. Clearly, figure 7.9 has less administrative overhead because a local group containing global groups is used.

Figure 7.8

Assigning permissions to a local resource for local and global groups.

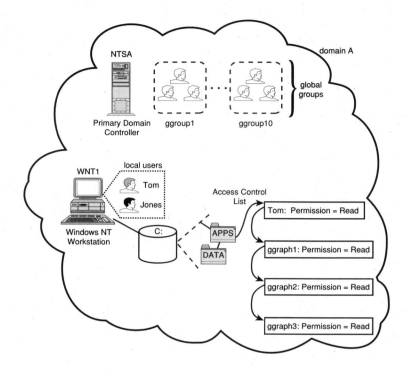

Figure 7.9

Assigning permissions to a local resource using local groups containing global groups.

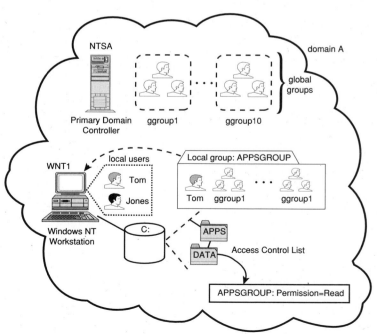

Figure 7.10 and table 7.1 summarize the rules for global groups.

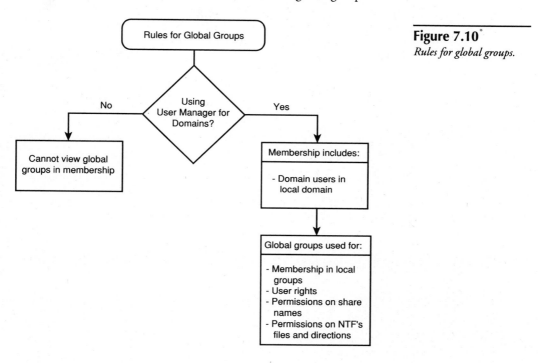

Figure 7.10
Rules for global groups.

Table 7.1
Global Group Properties

Property	Items
Can contain	Global users
Cannot contain	Local groups, local users, global groups, accounts from other domains
Scope	Local domain, all trusted domains

Certain global groups such as Administrators, Server Operators, Account Operators, Print Operators, Domain Users, and Guests are built into Windows NT Server. You can create additional global groups using User Manager for Domains. You can place only domain user accounts in global groups. You cannot place other global groups within a global group. In other words, nesting of global groups is not permitted. Additionally, global groups cannot contain local groups or local users, even though local groups can contain global groups and domain users.

Consider what would happen if a global group contained a local group or local user account: Because a global group can be assigned permissions to any domain resource, it would be possible for a local user account that is a member of the global group to inherit permissions applied to the global group (see fig. 7.11). However, such a possibility would violate the definition of locality of a local user account, which states that local user accounts can be assigned permissions only on the computers on which they are defined. In other words, local user accounts have a scope that is limited to the computers on which they exist.

Figure 7.11

Problems that would occur if a global group contained local user accounts.

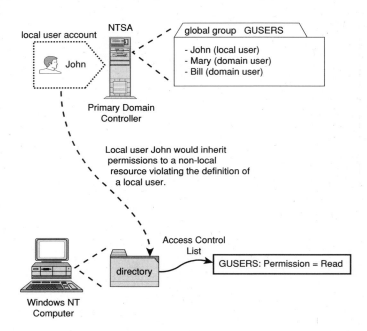

Within the domains in which they are defined, global groups are listed in the Windows NT utilities without the domain prefix. Outside the domains in which they are defined, global groups are listed in the Windows NT utilities with the domain prefix for the domain in which the global groups are defined. This method enables the system Administrator to determine whether he or she is dealing with a global group for the domain or a trusted domain.

You can distinguish the local from the global groups in the Windows NT utilities by looking at the icon next to the group name. Local groups icons have a picture of a computer, indicating that the scope of the local group is the computer, or PDC or BDC if account is in a domain; global group icons have a picture of the world. Figure 7.12 shows several groups for a PDC in domain DOMAIN_B. By observing the icons next to the group names, you can conclude that Account Operators, Administrators, Backup Operators, Guests, and Print Operators are local groups. Similarly, the world icon next to the group names Domain Admins, Domain Guests, and Domain Users in figure 7.11 indicates global groups.

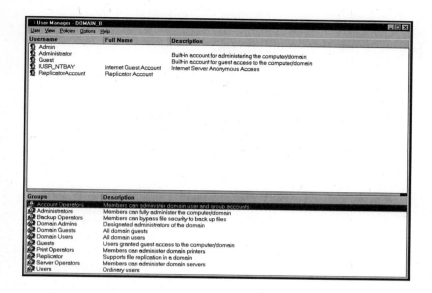

Figure 7.12
Icons for local and global groups.

Figure 7.13 and table 7.2 summarize the rules for local groups. If the computer in which the local group is defined is part of a domain, the local group can contain (in addition to local user accounts) domain user accounts from the domain in which it is located or from any trusted domain, and global groups from the domain in which it is located or from any trusted domain.

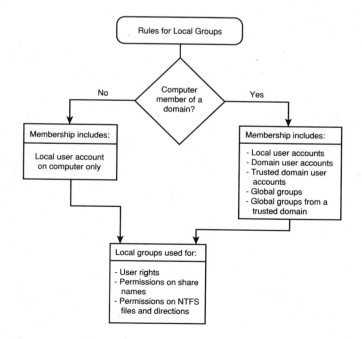

Figure 7.13
Rules for local groups.

Table 7.2
Local Group Properties

Property	Items
Can Contain	Local users, global groups, domain user accounts for trusted domains, global groups from trusted domains
Cannot contain	Other local groups
Scope	Local computer for resources to which permissions can be set

Local groups are very useful in a multi-domain network for grouping global groups from different domains into one manageable unit and assigning to this local group the permission for the local resource. Because of membership in the local group, the global groups inherit the permission. The alternative to this is to assign permissions to each global group separately.

A local group cannot contain other local groups. In other words, nesting of local groups with other local groups is not permitted.

Understanding Workstation Local Groups versus Domain Local Groups

Two types of local groups exist: workstation local groups and domain local groups.

A domain-based network consists of both Windows NT Workstations and Windows NT Servers. It therefore is important to understand the differences in the two types of local groups.

Workstation Local Groups

Workstation local groups exist on the Windows NT Workstation on which they are created. They are contained in the SAM database that resides on that Windows NT Workstation.

A local user created using the User Manager tool (which is different from the User Manager for Domains tool for Windows NT Server) for the Windows NT Workstation can have membership in the workstation local group only. A local group in a workstation can be used only on the computer on which it is created (see fig. 7.14) and not on any other Windows NT computer. This rule implies that a local user in a local group in a workstation does not inherit any access to resources on other Windows NT computers.

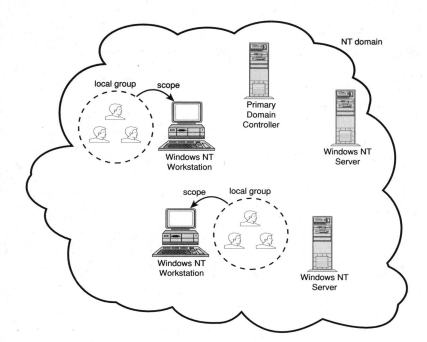

Figure 7.14
Using a local group.

Workstation local groups can contain the following:

■ Local user accounts from the workstation on which they are defined.

■ Domain user accounts and global groups from the domain in which they are defined.

■ Domain user accounts and global groups from other trusted domains.

Domain Local Groups

Although workstation local groups function at the Windows NT Workstation level, domain local groups function on Windows NT Servers at the domain level. A workstation local group is created using User Manager for Workstations, which runs on Windows NT Workstations, and a domain local group is created using User Manager for Domains.

Domain local groups can exist only on Windows NT Servers on which they are created. Thus, domain local groups can be used to access resources on Windows NT Server computers in the domain (see fig. 7.15) and not on Windows NT Workstation computers in the domain. Domain local groups can not be assigned permissions on non-domain controllers, even servers.

Figure 7.15
Using domain local groups.

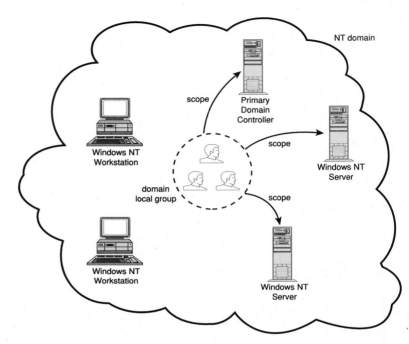

A domain local group can contain domain user accounts from the domain in which the Windows NT Server computer is defined, and from any domain trusted by this domain. You can grant permissions only to resources on the Windows NT Server computers in the domain, however.

Using Built-In Group Accounts and Implicit Groups

The Windows NT domain controllers have the following built-in domain local groups:

- Administrators
- Backup Operators
- Account Operators
- Guests
- Print Operators
- Replicator
- Server Operators
- Users

In addition to the built-in domain local groups, Windows NT domain controllers have the following global (domain) groups:

- Domain Admins
- Domain Guests
- Domain Users

Windows NT Workstations and Windows NT Server computers with a non-domain controller security role have the following built-in groups:

- Administrators
- Backup Operators
- Power Users
- Guests
- Replicator
- Users

Additional implicit groups exist for all Windows NT computers (domain controllers, ordinary servers that are not domain controllers, and Windows NT Workstations) that do not have an explicit membership. The membership of such groups is implied by the manner in which a user accesses a network resource, and it cannot be set explicitly. These groups are not displayed in the User Manager. They are displayed when setting permissions using the File Manager. The following implicit groups are defined:

- **INTERACTIVE.** Any user that is logged in locally.
- **NETWORK.** Anyone logged in through the network.
- **EVERYONE.** All interactive and network users. Everyone = INTERACTIVE + NETWORK.
- **SYSTEM.** The Windows NT operating system.
- **CREATOR OWNER.** Anyone who creates an object. This is used to automatically grant permissions to creators for files, directories, and print jobs.

Of chief importance here is the Everyone group, which includes all interactive users (users logged in locally) and users logged in from the network. The SYSTEM and CREATOR OWNER groups are used for assigning file and directory permissions, and are discussed in Chapter 9, "Managing Network Files and File Security Systems."

Understanding User Rights, Capabilities, and Permissions

Most user accounts created on a Windows NT network are members of one or more built-in groups. Being a member of a built-in group gives the user implied rights and capabilities to perform various administrative tasks. Being a member of the Backup Operators group, for example, gives the user the right to back up and restore files to that station even though the user might not have explicit permissions to read or write to the directories and files on the file system. If a user account is a member of more than one group, the user has the combined rights and capabilities of all the groups of which that user is a member.

In Windows NT, the following terms have specific meanings:

- **Permissions.** The access control lists (ACLs) associated with a resource. These are descriptions of rules and operations that can be performed on a resource. Permissions can be granted to users and groups. In the case of directories and file resources, permissions enable the user to read, write, delete, and change files and directories. Permissions regulate the types of operations that can be performed on the associated object. Permissions are set using the File Manager in Windows NT. You will learn more about permissions in the next chapter. Permissions are called *rights* on many other non-Microsoft operating systems. However, *user rights* has a very specific meaning in Windows NT.

- **User rights.** Configurable powers granted to a built-in group by the Windows NT operating system. A user right is an authorization for a user to perform administrative tasks on the system, such as shutting down the Windows NT computer, logging in locally, and so on. User Rights are configurable by the Administrator through the User Manager tool. User rights can override the permission settings. If you have the user right to back up and restore files on a Windows NT computer, for example, you can do so regardless of the permissions that you have to the Windows NT computer's file system. Windows NT comes with a set of default rights for various built-in groups.

- **Built-in capabilities.** Refer to inherent powers given to built-in groups. Unlike user rights, which can be changed by the Administrator user, capabilities cannot be changed.

Tables 7.3 and 7.4 show the user rights and capabilities for Windows NT Servers acting as domain controllers. An X in a row and a column indicates the presence of a right or capability; a blank entry indicates an absence of that right or capability.

Table 7.4 shows the following:

- Account operators can modify only the accounts they create. They cannot modify accounts for Administrators, Domain Admins, Server Operators, Account Operators, Print Operators, or Backup Operators groups.

- Members of the Users group can create local groups on a server, and can use User Manager for Domains to create local groups in the domain from another computer in the domain.

■ Even though the Everyone group has the capability to lock the server, only those users who can log on locally to the server can actually lock the server.

Table 7.3
User Rights for Windows NT Servers Acting as Domain Controllers

User Rights	Administrators	Server Operators	Account Operators	Print Operators	Backup Operators	Everyone	Users	Guests
Log on locally	X	X	X	X	X			
Network access to this computer	X					X		
Take ownership of files	X							
Manage auditing and security log	X							
Change the system time	X	X						
Shut down the system	X	X	X	X	X			
Force shutdown from a remote system	X	X						
Back up files and directories	X	X			X			
Restore files and directories	X	X			X			
Load and unload device drivers	X							
Add workstations to domain	X							

Table 7.4
Built-In Capabilities for Windows NT Servers Acting as Domain Controllers

Built-In Capabilities	Administrators	Server Operators	Account Operators	Print Operators	Backup Operators	Everyone	Users	Guests
Create and manage user accounts	X		X					
Create and manage global groups	X		X					
Create and manage local groups	X		X					
Assign user rights	X							
Manage auditing of system events	X							
Lock the server	X	X				X		
Override lock of server	X	X						
Format server's hard drive	X	X						
Create common program groups	X	X						
Keep local profile	X	X	X	X	X			
Share and stop sharing directories	X							
Share and stop sharing printers	X	X		X				

Tables 7.5 and 7.6 show the user rights and capabilities for Windows NT Workstations and Windows NT Servers that are not acting as domain controllers.

Tables 7.5 and 7.6 show the following:

■ Even though the Guests group does not have the user right to shut down the system, it still can do so because group Everyone has this right.

■ Power users can modify and delete only accounts that they have created.

■ Power users can create local groups. A power user can add and remove users from only the local groups they have created and the Power Users, Guests, and Users local groups. Power users cannot modify accounts for Administrators or Backup Operators groups.

■ Members of the Users group can create local groups, but they can modify only the local groups they have created.

Table 7.5
User Rights for Windows NT Workstations and Servers Not Acting as Domain Controllers

User Rights	Administrators	Power Users	Users	Guests	Everyone	Backup Operators
Log on locally	X	X	X	X	X	X
Network access to this computer	X	X			X	
Take ownership of files	X					
Manage auditing and security log		X				
Change system time	X	X				
Shut down system	X	X	X		X	X
Force shutdown from remote system	X	X				

continues

Table 7.5
User Rights for Windows NT Workstations and Servers
Not Acting as Domain Controllers

User Rights	Admin- istrators	Power Users	Users	Guests	Every- one	Backup Operators
Back up files and directories	X				X	
Restore files and directories	X				X	
Load and unload device drivers		X				

Table 7.6
Built-In Capabilities for Windows NT Workstations and Servers
Not Acting as Domain Controllers

User Rights	Admin- istrators	Power Users	Users	Guests	Every- one	Backup Operators
Create and manage user accounts	X	X				
Create and manage local groups	X	X	X			
Assign user rights	X					
Manage auditing of system events		X				
Lock computer	X	X			X	

User Rights	Admin-istrators	Power Users	Users	Guests	Every-one	Backup Operators
Override lock on computer	X					
Format computer's hard drive	X					
Create common program groups	X	X				
Keep local profile	X	X	X			X
Share and stop sharing directories	X	X				
Share and stop sharing printers	X	X				

The built-in groups and their rights and capabilities are discussed in greater detail in the following sections.

Administrators Group

User accounts in the local domain Administrators group on a Windows NT PDC or BDC Server have control over the entire domain. These administrative accounts have control over the entire domain and can perform almost any administrative function on domain member computers. These administrative accounts can create, delete, and manage local groups, global groups, and domain user accounts; assign user rights; manage shares on directories and printer resources; install operating system programs and files on remote workstations; grant resource permissions and user rights to users; lock the server; override the lock on the server; create common program groups; and format server disks.

The Administrator domain user and the Domain Admins global group are members of the Administrators local group for the domain (see fig. 7.16). This membership empowers domain Administrators to perform all administrative functions on a domain.

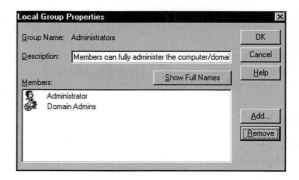

Figure 7.16

Default members of the Administrators domain local group.

The Administrators workstation local group on a Windows NT Workstation gives its members complete control over the workstation in which that group is defined. The default members of the Administrators workstation local group are the local Administrator user account for that workstation and the Domain Admins global group.

Backup Operators

Users who are assigned members of the backup operators local domain group can log on locally to the Windows NT Server and back up or restore files and directories. They can perform the backup tasks even if they do not have read/write permissions to the directories and files that are backed up.

Backup operators can shut down the system and keep a local profile of their desktop settings. By default, there are no predefined members of the backup operators domain local group.

Users who are assigned members can log on locally to the Windows NT Workstation and back up or restore files and directories. The Backup Operators workstation local group is similar to its domain local group, except that it applies to the workstation only.

Account Operators

Account Operators exist only on a Windows NT Server acting as a domain controller.

Users who are assigned members of the domain local group Account Operators can manage the server's domain user and group accounts. An account operator can create, delete, and manage almost all user accounts and group accounts, except those created by members of the Administrators group. Additionally, account operators cannot modify the Administrators,

Server Operators, Account Operators, Print Operators, and Backup Operators local groups. Account operators do not have the capability to assign user rights.

By default, there are no predefined members of the Account Operators group.

Guests

Users are assigned members of the Guests local group have a limited set of privileges.

The Guests local group exists for Windows NT Workstations and Windows NT Servers. On a Windows NT Server domain controller, the Guests group has the same rights as the domain local group Users; that is, members of these groups only have rights to access the server over the network and cannot log in locally.

By default, members of the domain local group Guests are the global group Domain Guests (see fig. 7.17).

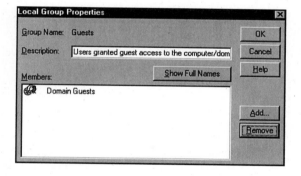

Figure 7.17

Default members of the Guests domain local group.

The workstation local group Guests has fewer rights than the workstation local group Users. The local Users group on the Windows NT Workstation can keep a local profile; lock the workstation; and create, delete, and modify local groups on the workstation—the workstation local group Guests can do none of these tasks.

By default, members of the workstation local group Guests are the global group Domain Guests and the local user Guest (see fig. 7.18).

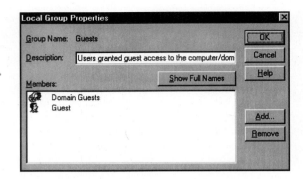

Figure 7.18

Default members of the Guests workstation local group.

Print Operators

Print Operators exist only on a Windows NT Server acting as a domain controller.

Users who are assigned members of the domain local group Print Operators can share printers, stop sharing printers, and manage printers running on a Windows NT Server. The members can log on locally at servers and shut them down.

If you want the print operators to additionally manage printers on Windows NT Servers that are not domain controllers, you can perform the following steps:

1. Create a global group—Pops, for example. Make the global group Pops a member of the domain's Print Operators local group.

2. Add the domain user account of each printer operator to the global group Pops.

3. On each non-domain controller Windows NT Server that manages printers, make the Pops global group a member of that server's Power Users local group.

By default, there are no predefined members of the Print Operators group.

Replicator

The Replicator group exists on all Windows NT computers (servers and workstations).

This account is used with directory replication service. By default, there are no predefined members of the Replicator group. For additional details on directory replication, see Chapter 6, "Implementing Windows NT Server Domains."

Server Operators

The Server Operators exist only on a Windows NT Server acting as a domain controller. The primary purpose of this group is to give its members the capability to keep the servers running.

Users who are assigned members of the domain local group Server Operators have many of the same powers as Administrators, but they cannot manage security on the server. Server operators can share and stop sharing of printers and directories and format the server's disks. They can log on at servers, back up and restore files, and shut down the server. Unfortunately, Server Operators cannot start and stop services, nor can they be assigned permission to do so.

By default, there are no predefined members of the Server Operators group.

Users

The Users group exists on all Windows NT computers (servers and workstations). Members of this group are typical network users who need to get their job done.

On a Windows NT Server acting as a domain controller, members of Users cannot log on locally by default. Members of Users can access the server through the network, however, because group Everyone is allowed to log on from the network.

On a Windows NT Workstation, members of the Users group can perform the following tasks:

- Log on to the workstation and use it to access the network.

- Lock and shut down the station.

- Keep a local profile at the workstation.

- Create and delete local groups at the workstation and manage local groups they have created.

On a Windows NT Server acting as a domain controller, the global group Domain Users and the local Administrator are predefined members of the local Users group. On Windows NT Workstations and Windows NT Servers that are not domain controllers, there are no predefined members of the local Users group.

Power Users

The Power Users group exists on Windows NT Workstations and Windows NT Servers that are not acting as domain controllers.

Power Users can do all the tasks that members of the Users group can do. In addition, Power Users can manage the user accounts they have created; put any user account on the computer in the Power Users, Users, and Guests built-in groups; and share and stop sharing directories and printers at the computer.

Because Power Users exist on workstations and not in domains, Microsoft recommends the following strategy for domain users: Make the domain user account a member of the Power Users group in its Windows NT Workstation. This gives the domain user more control over his or her workstation, such as being able to share directories and printers with other users. If you want the domain user to have less control, you can make him or her a member of the workstation's Users local group instead of the Power Users local group.

Domain Admins

The Domain Admins global group is a member of the Administrators local group for the domain, and also a member of the Administrators local group for each Windows NT Workstation in the domain. The Domain Admins global group contains the Administrator user of the domain by default.

To give other domain users administrative capabilities, add them to the Domain Admins group.

Domain Users

When a new domain user is created, it is made a member of the Domain Users group. Initially, the Domain Users group contains the Administrator account.

Domain Users can be managed by Administrators and Account Operators.

Domain Guests

The Domain Guests group initially contains the domain Guest account. The Domain Guests can be managed by Administrators and Account Operators.

Default Memberships for Built-In Groups

Throughout the discussion on built-in groups, the predefined members of these groups were discussed. Tables 7.7, 7.8, and 7.9 summarize the memberships of these groups for ease of reference.

Table 7.8 shows the following:

- If a Windows NT Workstation is added to a domain, the domain's Domain Admins group is added automatically to the workstation's Administrators local group.

- If a Windows NT Workstation is installed as part of a workgroup instead of a domain, the initial user account created is added to the local Administrators group.

Table 7.7
Membership Properties of Built-In Groups for Windows NT Servers
Acting as Domain Controllers

Group	Predefined Members	Who Can Modify?
Administrators	Domain Admins (global group) Administrator (user account)	Administrators
Users	Domain Users (global group) Administrator (user account)	Administrators, Account Operators
Guest	Domain Guests (global group) Guest (user account)	Administrators, Account Operators
Server Operators	None	Administrators
Print Operators	None	Administrators
Backup Operators	None	Administrators
Account Operators	None	Administrators
Replicator	None	Administrators, Account Operators, Server Operators

Table 7.8

Membership Properties of Built-In Groups for Windows NT Workstations and Servers Not Acting as Domain Controllers

Group	Predefined Members	Who Can Modify?
Administrators	Administrator (user account)	Administrators
Users	User account specified during installation of a Windows NT Work-station when work-station not added to a domain	Administrators, Power Users
Guest	Guest (user account)	Administrators, Power Users
Backup Operators	None	Administrators
Replicator	None	Administrators

Table 7.9

Membership Properties for Built-In Global (Domain) Groups

Group	Predefined Members	Who Can Modify?
Domain Admins	Administrator	Administrators
Domain Users	Administrator	Administrators, Account Operators
Domain Guests	Guest	Administrators, Account Operators

Setting Up Built-In User Accounts

All Windows NT computers (servers and workstations) have built-in Administrator and Guest user accounts.

On a Windows NT Workstation, these accounts are local user accounts. In a domain, these accounts are domain user accounts and have a domain-wide scope.

These user accounts cannot be deleted, but they can be renamed. Additionally, the Guest account can be disabled, but the Administrator user account cannot be disabled. This ensures that the Administrator cannot be locked out of the system.

On a Windows NT Workstation, the Guest user account initially is enabled with a null password. In a Windows NT domain, the domain Guest account is disabled initially and has a null password.

Setting Up a Domain User Account

The previous sections discussed the different types of built-in accounts in Windows NT. You can create additional accounts in a domain using the User Manager for Domains in the Administrative Tools program group.

The following sections discuss the domain user account properties and creation of user accounts.

Understanding Domain User Accounts

A user account is information a Windows NT station maintains about a user. The user account information is kept in the SAM database. For domains, the SAM database is kept on the primary domain controller Windows NT Servers and replicated to backup domain controllers. For workgroups, the SAM is kept local to each Windows NT Workstation.

User accounts are described in terms of properties. When you create a new user account, you must, at the very minimum, specify its user name. The user name is used to log into the domain as the user account. The user name often is referred to as the logon name, and can have up to 20 characters. The following characters in user names are illegal:

    / \ [ ] : ; | = , + * ? < >

A user name is used for the convenience of a user only. Internally, Windows NT uses a unique internal identifier called the SID (Security Identifier) that identifies the user account. When you rename a user name, you only change the user name property of the user account, and not its SID. The SID is used in the access control list (permissions list) to describe the operations permissible by the user on a Windows NT resource. Changing the user name therefore has no affect on internal security data structures such as access control lists.

When you delete a user account, however, the SID is lost. As mentioned in Chapter 10, the SID is a unique identifier based on the computer name, time of creation, and user name. Even if the user account is re-created with the same user name, it will have a different SID. Deleting a user account, therefore, means that the old SID values of the user account are no longer meaningful in access control lists, and the old permissions are lost.

You should use a uniform and consistent method for assigning user names for the user accounts. Some of the conventions for creating user names follow:

- **User's first name.** The user's first name works well in small LANs in which everyone is on a first-name basis. Examples of user names for accounts are MARY, JOHN, DAVID, and so on. If more than one user has the same first name, there is a name-collision problem, so use another naming scheme.

- **User's last name.** The user's last name is common in more formal organizations. If more than one user has the same last name, there is a name-collision problem again, and another naming scheme can be used.

- **User's first name and last-name initial.** Although the first name and last-name initial usually works (preventing most name collisions) it is not foolproof. If more than one user has the same first name and last initial, use another naming scheme.

- **User's first-name initial and last name.** The user's first-name initial and last name also works well to avoid most name collisions.

- **User's first-name initial, middle-name initial, and last name.** The user's first-name initial, middle-name initial, and last name also work well to avoid most name collisions. This method is helpful particularly if several users have the same first-name initial and last name, because the middle initial can be used to make the names unique per domain.

- **User's initials.** Although making the user's initials the user name seldom is done, this scheme can be used in organizations in which people usually are identified by their initials. To avoid name collisions, the initials of first, middle, and last names can be used. Examples of such user names are KSS, DGS, JFK, and so on. Unless these names are easily recognizable, they should be avoided. (Some users might not like to be referred to by their initials.)

- **Hash codes.** If confidentiality of a user name is important, unique *hash codes* can be used for user names. Examples of hash code user names are 2342K, 2550_1634, and so on.

User names can contain up to 20 characters, but limiting them to no more than eight characters is preferable if DOS clients are to be used. It is common practice to make the home directory name the same as the user name, for the sake of convenience. Because directory names under DOS cannot contain more than eight characters, the user name also should contain eight or fewer characters if the home directory will have the same name as the user name and is to be accessible from DOS clients.

The user name must be unique per domain. If the user name is local to the computer, such as a local user name in a Windows NT Workstation or a non-domain controller Windows NT Server, then the name must be unique within that workstation. On some Windows NT Server tools, such as in the File Manager and User Manager for Domains, the user names can be preceded with a domain name. This happens when you view user accounts in domains other than the current domain for which you are using the tool.

User names are only one of the properties of a user account. Table 7.10 lists the other properties of a user account. In table 7.10, do not select Yes for the Change Password at Next Logon and User Cannot Change Password options, because this will prevent the user from logging in.

Table 7.10
Domain User Account Properties

Property	Description
Username	This is the unique user name the user types on the Windows NT logon screen. User names are not case-sensitive, but the case used to create the user name is displayed by the Windows NT tools.
Password	The user's secret password. A password cannot be read even by a system Administrator. System Administrator can change a password, however. Passwords are encrypted using a one-way encoding. Only the encrypted form is stored and used for authentication. Passwords can contain up to 14 characters and are case-sensitive.
Full **N**ame	This is the user's full name. It is used for descriptive and documentation purposes only.
User **M**ust Change Password at Next Logon	When set to Yes, this forces users to change the password the next time they log on. The default value is Yes. This is useful for setting temporary passwords.
U**s**er Cannot Change Password	When set to Yes, the user cannot change their passwords. Default values is No for newly created accounts. The built-in Guest user has a default value of Yes, which prevents the Guest user from changing the Guest account's password. Set the value to Yes for shared accounts.

continues

Table 7.10, Continued
Domain User Account Properties

Property	Description
Password Never Expires	When set to Yes, the password never expires. The default value is No for newly created accounts. The built-in Guest user has a default value of Yes. Set the value to Yes for non-critical shared accounts. Accounts such as the Replicator account under which the replicator services are run should have this property set to Yes. Otherwise, the services can be prevented from running when the password expires.
Account Disabled	When set to Yes, the account is disabled and cannot be used for logging in. A disabled account still exists in the accounts data-base; it just cannot be used for logging in. The default value is No for newly created accounts. You can use this to disable user accounts to be used as templates to build other user accounts. The built-in Administrator account cannot be disabled. The built-in Guest user account has a default value of Yes on Windows NT Servers, which disables the Guest account (for Windows NT Workstations, the default value is No).
Account Locked Out	This is a status property, and is grayed out for most accounts. An account can become locked because of too many incorrect pass-word attempts. In this case, this field is available for clearing by Administrator users.
Home Directory	A private directory for the user on the server where the user has all permissions.
Logon Script	A batch file, command file, or an executable program that runs when the user logs in.
Profile	A file containing a description of the user's desktop environ-ment, such as program groups, screen colors and savers, and network connections. These settings determine which aspects of the user's environment a user can change.
Account Type	The account type can be global or local. Most accounts you create will be global. A local user account can be used in the following situations: allowing Windows NT users access to a LAN Manager server, allowing users of other non-Windows NT systems to access a Windows NT server, or allowing access to users whose home directories are in untrusted domains or domains not running Windows NT Server.

Property	Description
Logon Hours	The hours of the day during which the user is allowed to log in. The granularity is one hour. The logon hours affect the time the users can log in and access the servers. Whether users are forced to log in at the expiration of their log-in hour depends on the setting in the domain's security policy.
Dialin	When the Grant **d**ialin permission to user box is checked, the user is allowed to dial in to the Remote Access Server for the domain. The administrator can also specify the call back method (no call back, user-defined call back or predefined call back) for the user.
Logon Workstations	This lists the computer names of the stations from which the user is allowed to log on. By default, there are no restrictions placed on which computer station a user can log in from.
Expiration date	A future date when the account is to be disabled.
Groups	A list of groups of which the user is a member.

Before you set up a user account, you must plan your account setup. You can use the following user information sheet to plan user accounts.

User Account Information Sheet

1. User name _____

2. Initial Password (optional) _____

3. Full Name _____

4. Change Password at Next Logon   [] Yes   [] No

5. User Cannot Change Password   [] Yes   [] No

6. Password Never Expires   [] Yes   [] No

7. Account Disabled   [] Yes   [] No

8. Home Directory _____

9. Logon Script _____

10. Profile _____

11. Account Type   [] Global   [] Local

12. Logon Hours _____

    _____

    _____

13. Logon Workstations

    _____

    _____

    _____

    _____

14. Expiration Date _____

15. Groups _____

    _____

    _____

    _____

    _____

16. Dialin Grant RAS permission   [ ] Yes [ ] No

        Call Back Method

                [ ] No Call Back

                [ ] User-Defined Call Back

                [ ] Administrator-Defined Call Back

Creating Domain User Accounts

The following is a guided tour in creating a domain user account. Before attempting to create a user account, fill out the User Account Information sheet, which describes the information that you need in creating the user account. To create a domain user account, follow these steps:

1. Log in as an Administrator user in a domain.

2. Start the User Manager for Domains from the Administrative Tools group. The main screen in the User Manager for Domains shows the domain user accounts (in the top half

of the screen) and group accounts (in the bottom half of the screen). In figure 7.19, the domain user accounts Administrator and Guest are built-in accounts. The account ReplicatorAccount was created for replication purposes.

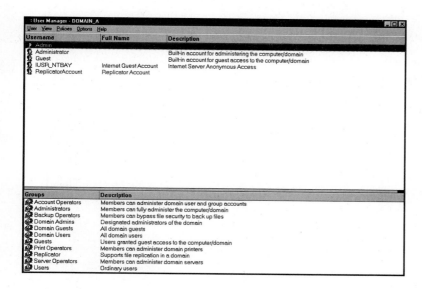

Figure 7.19
The main screen for the User Manager for Domains.

3. To create a new user account in the domain, choose **U**ser, New **U**ser.

    The New User dialog box appears (see fig. 7.20). The fields in this dialog box are described in table 7.10.

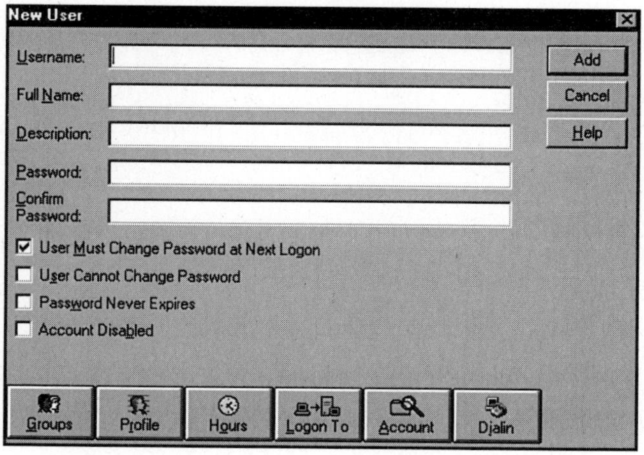

Figure 7.20
The New User dialog box.

4. Enter the information for the new user from your User Account Information sheet.

5. If you are done customizing the user account, choose Add. You see the new user account. To change additional properties such as groups, home directories, logon hours, and so on, double-click on the user account to see the properties of the user account and continue further customization of the user account.

   If you want to continue customizing the user account, proceed with the next step.

6. To change the group membership of the user, choose the **G**roups button at the bottom of the screen.

   The Group Memberships dialog box appears (see fig. 7.21). The **M**ember of list box shows the current groups the user is a member of, and the **N**ot member of list box shows the groups the user is not currently a member of, but could be made a member of.

   Notice that the newly created domain user is already a member of the Domain Users group.

Figure 7.21

The Group Memberships dialog box.

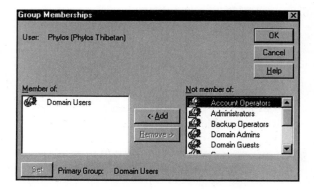

7. To add the newly created user to additional groups, select the group name in the **N**ot member of list box and choose the **A**dd button. To remove the user from a group, select the group name from the **M**ember of list box and choose the **R**emove button.

   The primary group setting for a user is displayed next to the **S**et button. The primary group is used when a user logs in using Windows NT Services for Macintosh or runs POSIX applications. Only global groups can be set as a primary group.

You cannot remove a user from its primary group. For example, in figure 7.21, the user Phylos is a member of the primary group Domain Users. If you attempt to remove the user from the Domain User group, you see the message shown in figure 7.22.

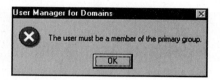

Figure 7.22

Attempting to remove a user from its primary group.

To change the user account's primary group, select a global group from the **M**ember of box and select the **S**et button.

Figure 7.23 shows that the user Phylos is made a member of the Domain Admins global group, and that the primary group for Phylos is set to Domain Admins.

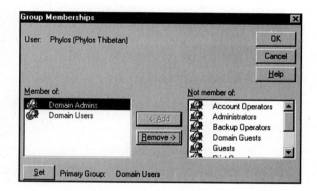

Figure 7.23

Changing the primary group for a user.

After you make your selections, select the OK button to save the group membership changes.

8. To change the logon hours for the user, select the H**o**urs button at the bottom of the New User screen (refer to figure 7.20).

The Logon Hours screen appears (see fig. 7.24), which is in the form of a weekly calendar. You can use this screen to restrict the days and hours during which a user can log into the domain. The default allows unrestricted access. This setting does not affect the user's capability to use his or her workstation; it only affects the capability to log into the domain. The logon hours indicate one-hour increments for the seven days of the week, starting from midnight to 11:59 a.m.

A filled box in the calendar indicates that the user is allowed to log on during that hour; an empty box indicates that logon is disallowed during that time.

To change the logon hours, highlight the hours in the weekly calendar and select the **A**llow button to allow access or the **D**isallow button to deny access. If a user is logged in when the logon hours are exceeded, the action taken depends on the setting of the option called Forcibly Disconnect Remote Users From Server When Logon Hours Expire in the Accounts Policy dialog box. If this option is set, logged-in users are disconnected. If this option is not set, logged-in users remain logged in but are denied new connections.

Figure 7.24
*The Logon Hours screen
for a domain user.*

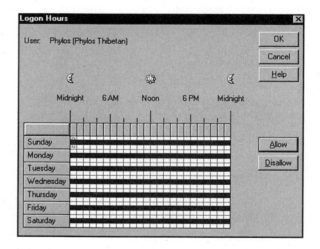

9. To change the logon workstations for the user, click on the **L**ogon To button at the bottom of the New User screen.

    The Logon Workstations dialog box appears (see fig. 7.25). You can use this screen to restrict the workstations a user can log onto the domain. The default allows unrestricted access from any workstation. This is indicated by the option User May Log On To **A**ll

Workstations. You optionally can specify up to eight workstations the user can log in from by selecting the User May Log On To **T**hese Workstations option.

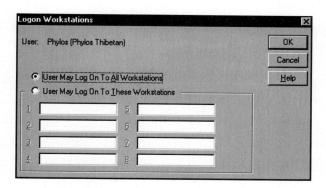

Figure 7.25

The Logon Workstations dialog box.

You can use the boxes numbered 1 to 8 to specify the Windows NT computer names of the workstations from which the user is restricted to log on.

Choose OK to return to the main screen.

10. To set the Account information for the user, choose the **A**ccount button at the bottom of the New User screen.

The Account Information dialog box appears (see fig. 7.26). You can use this screen to set an account expiration date and the account type.

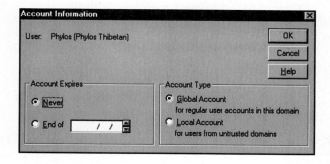

Figure 7.26

The Account Information dialog box.

The default is that the account never expires. If you want to set up a temporary account that expires after a future date, you can set the date in the **E**nd of field. The user account is disabled at the end of the day set in the **E**nd of field.

If a user is logged in when the user's account expires, the user remains logged in, but cannot establish new network connections. After logging off, the user cannot log in because the account is disabled.

The account type can be a **G**lobal Account or a **L**ocal Account. The default account type for a newly created user is global, and this is the normal account in the user's home domain.

The local account is provided for a user in this domain whose global account is not in a trusted domain. Remember that only Windows NT domains can be trusted. If the user is in a non-trusted Windows NT domain, a LAN Manager domain, or another type of domain or network that needs access to this domain, you should define the account type to be a local account.

Local accounts cannot be used to log on interactively to the Windows NT Server. They can be used to access the Windows NT computers across the network, and can be granted resource permissions and user rights. Local accounts created in a domain cannot be used in a trusting domain and are not visible in the Add Users and Add Groups dialog boxes in the trusting domains.

Click on OK in the Account Information dialog box to return to the main screen.

Windows NT 4 can now set user's Remote Access Service (RAS) permissions with User Manager (you also can use the RAS Admin tool to assign RAS permissions). See Chapter 18, "Remote Access Services," for more information on configuring and administering Remote Access Service. To enable RAS permission for the user, click on the D**i**alin button to open the Dialin Information dialog box (see fig. 7.27), then enable the Grant **d**ialin permission to user check box, select a call back method, and click on OK.

11. To set the user's environment profile, select the P**r**ofile button at the bottom of the New User screen.

    The User Environment Profile dialog box opens (see fig. 7.28). You can use this screen to set the user's profile or the user's home directory.

    The user profile consists of the name of the **U**ser Profile Path and the **L**ogon Script Name.

    The user profile path is the name of file on the server that contains the user's profile. Recall that the user's profile contains the user's desktop environment settings. Users can have a personal user profile (a file with a USER extension) or a mandatory user profile (a file with a MAN extension). Personal user profiles are configurable by the user, whereas mandatory user profiles are not configurable. The user's profile is created using the User Profile Editor.

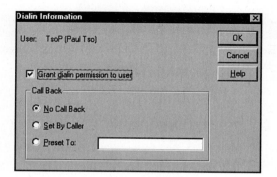

Figure 7.27
*The Dialin Information
dialog box.*

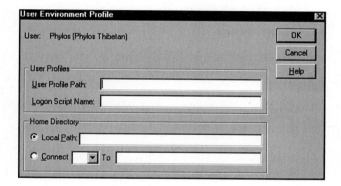

Figure 7.28
*The User Environment
Profile dialog box.*

The logon script name is another, more conventional way, to modify the user's environment. The logon script is the name of the batch file containing operating system specific commands that customizes the user's environment. If you do not specify a path with the logon script, it is created in the %SystemRoot%\System32\Repl\Import\Scripts directory at the workstation by default.

If you want the profile and logon script files to be replicated, you should create these in an exported path on the primary domain controller of the domain. The backup domain controllers should keep these files in the import path for replication.

User profile and logon scripts are discussed in the next chapter.

You can use the User Environment Profile screen to set the user's home directory. The user's home directory could be a local path on the workstation or a network path on the server. When setting a network path for the home directory, you need to assign a drive letter for the home directory.

When specifying the network path, you use the UNC (Universal Naming Convention) name for a network path. The UNC name contains the computer name, the share name on the computer, and all subdirectories under the shared directory. The general syntax for the UNC is:

\\computername\sharename\share_subdirectories\filename

For example, the network path to a home directory on a server named NTUS that has a share name of HOME could be the following:

\\NTUS\HOME\%USERNAME%

Windows NT substitutes the logon name of the user for %USERNAME%. If the logon name is David, the user's home directory will be \\NTUS\HOME\DAVID. The subdirectory DAVID would be under the shared directory on the server NTUS.

Windows NT will not create a complete subdirectory path for you if one does not exist. You have to create the subdirectory DAVID under the sharename \\NTUS\HOME in a separate step.

You can use the File Manager for creating share names.

The following is an example of using the network path for user profiles kept on a server named NTUS that has a share name of PROFILE:

\\NTUS\PROFILES\%USERNAME%.USER

For user name David, the profile path would evaluate to:

\\NTUS\PROFILES\DAVID.USR

Similarly, an example of using the network path for user logon scripts kept on a server named NTUS that has a share name of SCRIPTS follows:

\\NTUS\SCRIPTS\%USERNAME%.SCR

It is not necessary for the share names of PROFILES and SCRIPTS to refer to directories in different directory-tree branches. If the profiles and logon scripts are to be replicated, you should keep them in the same export tree. Using the example of the default export path on a Windows NT Server, this would be the %SystemRoot%\System32\Repl\Export directory. The share names PROFILES and SCRIPTS could have the following correspondence to the actual directories used on the Windows NT Server:

Share name	Directory on server
PROFILES	D:\WINNT35\System32\Repl\Export\ProfDir
SCRIPTS	D:\WINNT35\System32\Repl\Export\Scripts

12. Select OK in the main screen for User Manager for Domains, and you will see the newly created domain user account. Figure 7.29 shows the newly created user account for user Phylos. The full name and description of the account is displayed in the main screen.

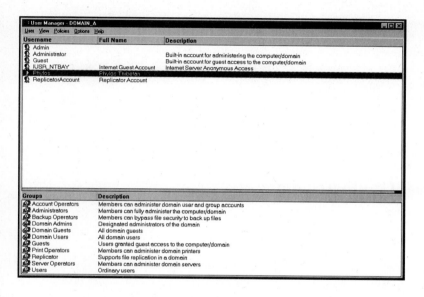

Figure 7.29
A newly created domain user account.

If you have a need for group accounts other than the built-in group accounts, you can create additional group accounts in a domain using the User Manager for Domains tool. Note that although user accounts can be renamed or disabled, groups cannot be renamed or disabled. You can delete a group that is created but you cannot delete the built-in system groups such as Administrators, Print Operators, Server Operators, and so on.

The following sections discuss the creation of group accounts.

Using Group Account Names

A group account is a convenient way of grouping users for simplifying administration. The earlier sections in this chapter went into detail on the different types of group accounts: global group (also called domain group) accounts, domain local group accounts, and workstation local group accounts. You might want to review the earlier sections on the distinctions between these group accounts.

Sometimes you may need to create additional group accounts in which you want to group users by a department or the use of an application.

Group names are not case-sensitive and can contain up to 20 characters. The following characters in group names are illegal:

/ \ [ ] : ; | = , + * ? < >

You can create group names based on job function or application usage.

You can create groups based on job functions, such as the Sales department, Engineering department, and so on. In this case, you can expect that users in these departments will have common needs for resource permissions and user rights. You therefore can create group names such as SALES, ENGINEERS, and so on that denote the job function.

You can create groups based on application usage for users who need to use specific applications on the server that need resource permissions or user rights. You can create a group for each of these applications and assign users who need to use these applications to their corresponding groups.

The following section discusses the creation of group accounts.

Creating Global Group Accounts

To create a global group account, follow these steps:

1. Log in as an Administrator user in a domain.

2. Start the User Manager for Domains from the Administrative tools folder. The User Manager for Domains main screen shows the group accounts (refer to figure 7.19).

3. To create a new global group account in the domain, choose User, New Global Group.

   The New Global Group dialog box appears (see fig. 7.30).

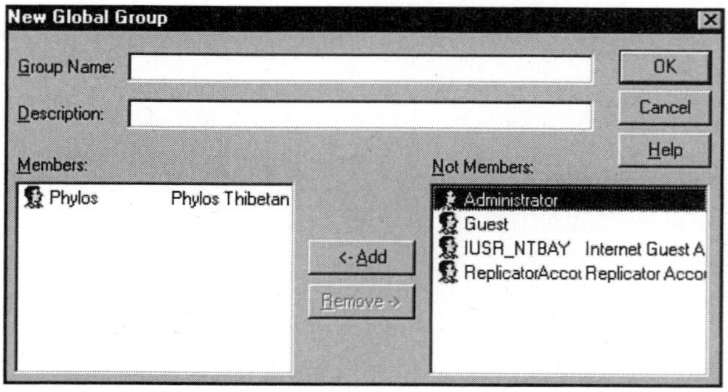

Figure 7.30
The New Global Group dialog box.

4. In the New Global Group dialog box, use the **G**roup Name and **D**escription fields to enter the group name and descriptions.

   You can select only domain users to be members of groups. The current domain users are listed in the **M**embers list box. If any domain users are highlighted in the User Managers for Domain window, they appear as initial members of the new global group.

   Domain users that can be added as members are displayed in the **N**ot Members list box. To add domain users as a members, select them from the **N**ot Members list box and choose the **A**dd button. Similarly, to remove domain users as members, select them from the **M**embers list box and choose the **R**emove button.

5. After making the member selections, select OK to save your changes.

Creating Domain Local Group Accounts

To create a local group account, follow these steps:

1. Log in as an Administrator user in a domain.

2. Start the User Manager for Domains from the Administrative Tools folder. The User Manager for Domains main screen shows the group accounts (refer to figure 7.19).

3. To create a new local group account in the domain, choose New **L**ocal Group from the **U**ser menu.

   The New Local Group dialog box appears (see fig. 7.31).

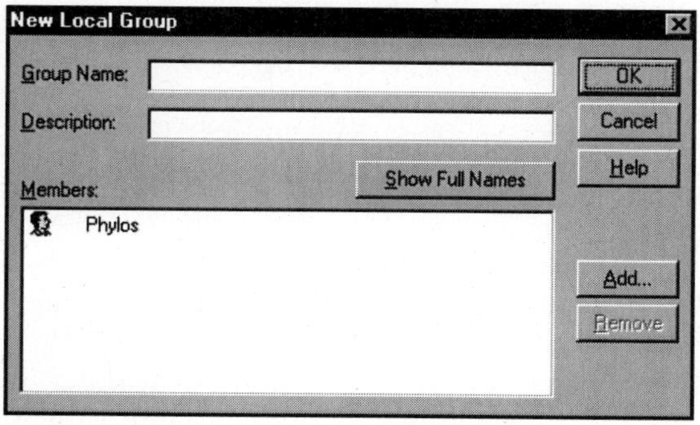

Figure 7.31

The New Local Group dialog box.

4. In the New Local Group dialog box, use the **G**roup Name and **D**escription fields to enter the local group name and descriptions. You can click on the **S**how Full Names button to display the full names of group members in the **M**embers list box.

The current members of the local group are listed in the **M**embers list box. If any users are highlighted in the User Managers for Domain window before you create the new local group, they appear as initial members of the new local group.

5. To add members, you can select the **A**dd button. This displays the list of accounts in the current domain that can be added as members (see fig. 7.32). Remember that local groups can contain local users, domain users, and global groups from the current domain and trusting domains. To see names from other domains, click on the arrow beside the **L**ist Names From field to access the drop-down list. A list containing the local domain name, trusted domains, and computer names appears.

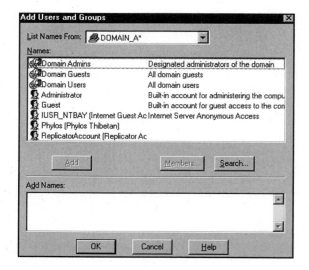

Figure 7.32

The Add Users and Groups dialog box.

If an asterisk follows a domain or computer name, the local groups of that domain or computer can be listed. The absence of an asterisk means that the local group cannot be listed.

The **N**ames list box shows the user accounts of the selected domain or computer. If a domain is selected, the list of global groups for that domain also are listed.

The names to be added as members of the local group are selected in the **N**ames list box.

When you select the **A**dd button, these names are added to the **A**dd Names list. You also can list members of a group in the **N**ames list by selecting the **M**embers button. Figure 7.33 shows a listing of the members of the Domain Admins global group for the KINETD domain obtained by clicking on the **M**embers button.

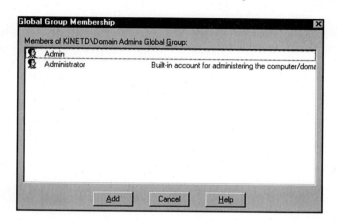

Figure 7.33

The Global Group Membership dialog box.

6. After adding names to the **A**dd Names list, click on the OK button to save changes. Figure 7.34 shows the newly added members of the new local group. Notice that group members in another domain, such as KINETD, are preceded with the name of the domain.

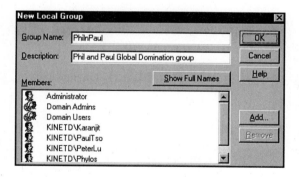

Figure 7.34

Newly added members of the local group.

7. Choose OK in the New Local Group dialog box to create the local group.

Using User and Group Templates

While creating a new user or group account, you can copy an existing user or group. The existing accounts used for creation of new accounts are called *template accounts*.

If you copy an existing user account, you copy the user's properties. If you use the %USERNAME% in the path for the user's home directory, log-in script path, or profile path, then these properties also will be meaningful for the new user. Even if you use the user's name in the home directory of the user template, the User Manager tool will substitute the user name of the new user. If the user template account is David, with a home directory of D:\USERS\DAVID, when you use David as a template account to create a new user account, Tom, the home directory of Tom will be D:\USERS\TOM. If you examine the home directory for Tom during account creation, you see the home directory listed as D:\USERS\%USERNAME%.

The following user properties are copied directly from an existing user account:

- Description
- Group account memberships
- Profile settings
- User Cannot Change Password
- Password Never Expires
- Logon Hours
- Account Type

After copying an existing user account, the following properties are cleared in the new user account:

- User name
- Full name
- User Must Change Password at Next Logon
- Account Disabled

If you copy an existing group, you copy the existing group members of that group.

Creating a User from a User Template

It is best to use the user template for account-creation purposes only. You can ensure that user templates are used only for this purpose by disabling the account. The following is an outline of the procedure for creating a user account from a template account:

1. Run User Manager for Domains while logged in as an Administrator user.

2. Highlight the user account to copy (template account) and press F8. Alternatively, choose **U**ser, **C**opy.

   A copy of the Template User dialog box appears.

3. Examine the properties of the new user account, and change it as needed. You will notice that most properties of the user template account, such as group memberships, logon hours, profile, account type, and so on are preserved.

Select the **A**dd button to save your changes for the new account.

Creating a Group from a Group Template

The following is an outline of the procedure for creating a group account from a template account:

1. Run User Manager for Domains while logged in as an Administrator user.

2. Highlight the group account (local or global group) to copy (template account), and press F8. Alternatively, choose **C**opy from the **U**ser menu.

   The dialog box for the new group account appears.

3. Examine the properties of the new group account and change them as needed. You will notice that the new group account has initial members that are the same as the template account.

4. Select OK to save your changes.

Managing the Accounts Policy

Windows NT Server allows the implementation of an account policy for all users in the accounts database. You can use the accounts policy to implement the following:

- Password restrictions for user accounts
- Account lockout policy

■ Capability to forcibly disconnect users from the server when logon hours expire.

■ Users must log in before they can change passwords.

The following is an outline on how to manage the accounts policy:

1. Run User Manager for Domains while logged in as an Administrator user.

2. Choose **A**ccount from the **P**olicies menu.

   The Accounts Policy screen appears.

3. After making the accounts policy changes, select OK to save your changes.

The settings in the Accounts Policy screen follow:

■ **Maximum Password Age.** The number of days before the system requires the user to change the password. Can be set so that the password never expires, or so that it expires within 1 to 999 days.

■ **Password Uniqueness.** Controls the number of new passwords that must be assigned before an old password can be used. Can be set so that the system does not keep a history of the previous passwords, which allows a user to enter the same password even when the system forces the user to change the password. If you want to prevent users from using older passwords when the system requires them to change the passwords, you should set the system to remember passwords. You can set the password uniqueness to remember from 1 to 24 older passwords. Note that some of the Windows NT documentation erroneously states that it can remember udialog boxp to eight passwords only.

■ **Minimum Password Age.** The amount of time a password must be used before the user can change it. Can be set to allow immediate changes to the password, or to allow changes from 1 to 999 days. The setting of this value can interact with the Password Uniqueness value. Do not allow users to change passwords immediately if you want the system to remember older passwords.

■ **Minimum Password Length.** Controls the minimum number of characters that can be used for the password. You can set the minimum number of characters from 1 to 14. Alternatively, you can permit the user to enter a blank password.

■ **No Account Lockout.** If you enable this option, user accounts are never locked out, no matter how many incorrect password attempts are made. The only reason to enable this option is when security is not of concern or if too many administrative problems are created by users constantly forgetting their passwords.

■ **Account Lockout.** When this option is enabled, users are subject to lockout if too many incorrect password attempts are made with no more than the specified amount of time between two logon attempts. The Lockout After option specifies the minimum number of password attempts the user can make before the account is locked out.

The number can range from 1 to 999 days. The Reset Count After option specifies the maximum number of minutes (from 1 to 99,999) between successive logon attempts before lockout can occur. Lockout Duration controls the amount of time an account will be locked until an Administrator unlocks the account. Lockout Duration can be set to forever, or from 1 to 99,999 minutes. Note that as a safety measure, the Administrator account created during Windows NT installation cannot be locked out. This allows the Administrator user to unlock locked-out accounts.

- **Forcibly Disconnect Remote Users from Server when Logon Hours Expire.** If this Option is enabled, users are forcibly disconnected when logon hours expire. If the option is disabled, users are not disconnected when log-in hours expire, but they cannot make any new connections. This option interacts with the log-in hours for the user.

  Users **M**ust Log On in Order To Change Password. If this option is enabled, users must log in to change their passwords. If their passwords expire, users will not be able to change their passwords, but must have the Administrator change it for them. If the option is cleared, users will be able to change their passwords without informing the Administrator.

Managing the User Rights Policy

The User Rights policy controls the actions users and groups can perform. A default set of user rights is defined for the built-in user and group accounts. User rights apply to the whole computer or domain and are different from permissions that represent usage policies (Read, Write, Delete, and so on) for a resource such as a file or a directory.

In general, you should not have a need to change the user policy for built-in groups, because these have been defined carefully by Windows NT designers for typical needs of the built-in users and groups. You do, however, have the capability to modify the rights for built-in accounts. You should change user rights after careful consideration of the effects this will have on the system. If you change the user rights, document your changes because the Windows NT system will not behave in a manner that is common to most Windows NT systems. Inappropriate changes will have a detrimental effect on the operation of the system.

For the most part, you can give a user the capability to perform an action by making the user a member of the appropriate built-in local group (Administrators, Print Operators, Backup Operators, and so on).

If you want to change the User Rights policy for several users, it is better to assign a group to the user right, and then assign users to this group. This is better than changing the user rights for each user account separately.

On Windows NT domain controllers, user rights are granted at the domain level. This means that if a group has a user right in a domain, its members have that right on all PDCs and

BDCs for that domain. On Windows NT Workstations, the user rights have a scope for that computer only.

The current version of Windows NT makes a distinction between the User Rights and the Advanced User Rights policy; these distinctions are listed in tables 7.11 and 7.12. The Advanced User Rights are designed for programmers and advanced users.

Table 7.11
User Rights

Right	Description	Granted Domains	Granted to Servers and Workstations
Manage auditing and security log	Specifies which types of access are to be audited.	Administrators of file and object security	Administrators
Backup of files and directories	Enables users without permissions to an NTFS volume to perform backup and restore operations.	Administrators, Server Operators, Backup Operators	Administrators, Backup Operators
Restore files and directories	Enables users without permissions to an NTFS volume to perform a restore to the volume.	Administrators, Server Operators, Backup Operators	Administrators, Backup Operators
Log on locally using keyboard and mouse	Enables users to log on interactively.	Administrators, Server Operators, Backup Operators Account Operators Print Operators	Administrators, Backup Operators, Power Users, Users, Guests
Change system time	Enables the changing of the NT computer time.	Windows Administrators, Server Operators, Backup Operators	Administrators, Backup Operators

Right	Description	Granted Domains	Granted to Servers and Workstations
Access this computer from the network	Log in or connect the computer through the network.	Administrators, Everyone	Administrators, Everyone, Power Users
Shut down the system on the computer	Capability to use the shutdown option.	Administrators, Server Operators, Backup Operators, Account Operators, Print Windows NT Operators	Administrators, Backup Operators Power Users, Users, Guests
Add workstations to a domain	Allows a user who is not a member of the Windows NT Administrators group to add new computers to the domain.	None. This is a built-in capability for Administrators and Server Operators, regardless of the assignment of this user right.	Not applicable
Take ownership of files and other objects	Enables a user to take ownership of files and directories.	Administrators	Administrators
Force shutdown from a remote system	Gives users right to shut down a remote system.	Administrators, Server Operators	Administrators, Power Users
Load and change device drivers	Enables users to unload device drivers.	Administrators	Administrators

Table 7.12
Advanced User Rights

Right	Description	Granted to Domains	Granted to Servers and Workstations
Act as part of the operating system	The user can perform operations as a secure, trusted part of the Windows NT operating system. Some Windows NT subsystems are granted this right.	None	None
Bypass traverse checking	The user can traverse directory trees. Deny access to users using POSIX applications.	Everyone	Everyone
Create a pagefile	The user can create a pagefile. Security is determined by users' access to the registry key \CurrentControlSet \Control\Session.	Administrators	Administrators
Create a token object	Used to create the user token on login. Only the LSA (Local Security Authority) can do this.	None	None

Right	Description	Granted Domains	Granted to Servers and Workstations
Create permanent shared objects	Required to create special permanent resources representing such devices as (\\Device) used internally in Windows NT.	None	None
Debug Programs	Enables user to debug low-level objects such as threads.	Administrators	Administrators
Generate security audits	Required for generating security audit log.	None	None
Increase quotas	Required for increasing object quotas.	Administrators (NT 3.51 and above), None (NT 3.5 and below)	Administrators, None (NT 3.5 and below)
Increase	Used for boosting scheduling priority of a process.	Administrators	Administrators, Power Users
Load and unload device drivers	Enables users to load and unload Windows NT device drivers.	Administrators	Administrators

continues

Table 7.12, Continued
Advanced User Rights

Right	Description	Granted to Domains	Granted to Servers and Workstations
Lock pages in memory	Enables user to lock pages in memory so they cannot be paged out to the PAGEFILE.SYS file. Locking pages reduces the amount of memory available to other applications and can lead to thrashing. This right is useful for dedicated real-time systems that do not want the critical applications pages to be paged out.	None	None
Log in as a batch job	The user can log in using a batch queue facility.	None	None
Log in as a service	The user can log in as a service that usually runs in the background. This option can be enabled for a service through	None	None

Right	Description	Granted to Domains	Granted to Servers and Workstations
	the Services icon in the Control Panel or through the Server Manager tool.		
Modify firmware environment variables	Enables user to modify system environment variables.	Administrators	Administrators
Profile single process	Enables user to use profiling capabilities on a process for measuring system performance.	Administrators	Administrators, Power Users
Profile system performance	Enables user to use profiling capabilities to measuring system performance.	Administrators	Administrators
Replace a process level token	Required to modify a process's security access token. This typically is used only by the system, as its misuse could cause security breaches.	None	None

The following is an outline of how to modify the User Rights policy:

1. Log in to an NT domain as Administrator and run the User Manager for Domains.

2. Choose **U**ser Rights from the **P**olicy menu.

   The User Rights Policy screen appears.

   The Righ**t** list box shows the user rights granted to users and groups listed in the **G**rant To box. The currently selected right is displayed in the Righ**t** field. If the **S**how Advanced User Rights check box is set, the advanced user rights listed in table 7.12 are displayed with the basic user rights listed in table 7.11. If the **S**how Advanced User Rights check box is cleared, only the basic user rights listed in table 7.11 can be managed.

3. To add users/groups to the **G**rant To list, select the **A**dd button; to remove users/groups from this list, select the **R**emove button. Clicking on the **A**dd button brings up the Add Users and Groups dialog box. The list initially shows groups for the selected domain. To see the lists of users along with the lists of groups, select the Show **U**sers button.

When you are done making changes, select the OK button to save your changes.

Removing Network Access Rights from Guest Accounts

A network Guest log onto a domain can occur when a user from an untrusted domain attempts to access the server over the network. Users on an MS-DOS computer are treated as being from an untrusted domain. Instead of completely rejecting this logon request, the server approves this request as a Guest logon, provided the Guest account is enabled and the Guest password is not set. The Guest user has the rights, permissions, and group memberships assigned to the Guest account on the computer, even if the logged in user did not specify Guest as the logon name.

By default, the Guest account on a Windows NT Server is disabled. Therefore, if you do not want to permit local or network logon through the Guest account, you do not need to do any additional configuration.

If you want to enable local Guest logon or network Guest logon, use the User Manager for Domains to enable the Guest account. If you want to enable local Guest logon but disable network Guest logon, enable the Guest login and revoke the Access This Computer From Network user right. If you want to enable network Guest logon but disable local Guest logon you should enable the Guest login, but revoke the Log On Locally user right.

Examining Strategies for Using Groups

As part of setting up the network, the network Administrator should identify the network tasks and responsibilities of the users in the domain. The Administrator should consider local groups for assigning the necessary permissions and rights. Local groups give its members the permissions and rights within the scope of its accounts database. If the local group is on a workstation, the permissions and rights are confined to resources on that workstation. If the local group is in a domain, the scope of this local group is the entire domain. This is the reason why the built-in domain local groups are used for giving users the capability to perform tasks in the entire domain.

You can make a domain user an Administrator for a domain by placing the user directly in the domain local Administrators group or in the global Domain Admins group. Although both methods work, it is better to place the domain user in the Domain Admins group. This allows the Domain Admins global group to represent all the Administrators in the domain. The Domain Admins global group then can be placed in the local group of another computer or domain, thereby granting to all Administrators in Domain Admins the capability to perform administrative tasks for the computer or domain. By default, when a Windows NT computer joins a domain, the Domain Admins global group for the domain is placed in the local Administrators group for that computer. This enables the domain Administrators to manage the computers in the domain.

When you create a domain user, it automatically is placed in the built-in Domain Users global group. The Domain Users global group is a member of the Local Users group for the domain and also a member of all Windows NT Workstations placed in that domain.

Every domain also has a Domain Guests global group initially placed in the domain's local group, Guests. The Domain Guests global group contains the Guest domain user account.

As you can see in the previous examples, global groups can be used effectively for exporting the group of users as a single unit to other Windows NT Workstations and domains by placing them in local groups. The users in the global group then inherit the permissions and rights assigned to the local group.

The Domain Admins, Domain Users, and Domain Guests are the only built-in global groups for a domain. You can create other global groups and use the same strategy described earlier for assigning rights to users by placing the global group in a local group. As an example, if you want to create domain-level back operator accounts, you can create a global group called BackupOps and place in it all the domain users that need to perform backup/restore tasks. You then can place the global group BackupOps in the local Backup Operators group for all the Windows NT computers that need to be backed up.

Table 7.13 summarizes the strategies for using local and global groups.

Table 7.13
Strategy for Using Local and Global Groups

Goal	Type of Group To Be Used	Method of Implementation
To group domain users into a single unit for use on other computers and domains	Global	Put the domain users in the global group, and the global group into a local group. Give appropriate permissions and rights to local groups.
Users need permissions and rights in a single domain	Local	Place users or global groups in the local group, and then assign appropriate permissions and rights to local group.
To contain other groups	Local	Only the local group can contain other global groups. You cannot have a group that can contain other local groups.
To include users from multiple domains	Local	Create a local group for the domain in which it is used. Remember that a local group can be used used only in the domain in which it is created. Assign users and global groups to the local group and grant appropriate permissions and rights to the local group. If the local group needs to be assigned permissions in multiple domains, you will have to manually create a local group in every domain.
Domain users need permissions on Windows NT Workstations	Global	Create a global group for the domain users. You can assign a global group permission to the Windows NT Workstation or make the global group a member of the workstation's local group. You cannot, however, grant permissions for a Windows NT Workstation to a domain's local group.

Conclusion

In this chapter, you learned how to set up domain user accounts and domain group accounts. You learned about the different types of user and group accounts possible with domains and stand-alone Windows NT computers. You learned how local groups and global groups can be used to simplify administration within domains, and the strategies for using these groups. For each of the group accounts, this chapter gave you a detailed understanding of the different capabilities and rights for the groups.

User Manager for Domains is the principal tool for managing the user and group accounts in a domain. You learned how to create user and group accounts, and how to set their properties. Although the logon script and profile paths are set during the user account creation, they are not part of the accounts database. Replication for these critical properties must be handled separately from the automatic replication of user account information to the backup domain controllers. The next chapter discusses the profile and logon script settings for user accounts in a domain.

8

Managing User Profiles, Logon Scripts, and Environment Variables

The preceding chapter discussed the creation of user domain accounts. One of the properties of the user domain account is the Profile settings. Under profile settings, the following properties can be set:

- Profile path
- Logon script file
- Home directory

This chapter discusses the user environment settings that can be controlled by user profiles and logon scripts. In addition, this chapter also explains the ways in which environment variables can be configured for a user session.

Components of a User Environment

On a Windows NT domain-based network, a user's environment settings have several components. These user environment settings include the following:

- User's network connections

- Available Windows NT program groups

- Available applications

- Windows NT desktop appearance

- Execution of Windows NT commands automatically during logon

- Environment variables specifying the search path, directory for temporary files, and so on.

On operating systems such as Unix, NetWare, DOS clients, and VMS, the traditional method of setting the user environment during logon is through logon scripts. Logon scripts can also be used with Windows NT networks. The logon script is the name of a file that is executed whenever a user logs on to the domain from any type of workstation (DOS, Windows NT Workstation, and so forth) on the network. The logon script is a batch file or an executable program. Logon script files are commonly implemented as batch files because they are easy to modify and set up by network administrators.

If the client is a Windows NT computer, there is much more to a user's environment setting than can be controlled by Windows NT commands in a logon script file. Because Windows NT is designed to be used predominantly through its graphical user interface, setting the user environment includes considerations such as the desktop's appearance and the program groups that are displayed. To solve this problem, Windows NT designers have created the concept of a profile for a user's Windows NT desktop that serves as a snapshot of the user's desktop appearance, program groups, program items in program groups, printer connections, network connections, screen colors, and so on. Additionally, the administrator can restrict the users' capability to change their profile settings. For this reason, Microsoft considers profiles as a more powerful method of controlling the users' settings.

Understanding Profiles

User profiles contain each user's settings of the Windows NT environment, such as the contents of the program groups, screen colors, and network and printer connections. These profiles are useful only to Windows NT clients; they have no effect on DOS workstations, Windows 3.1, or WFWG. Profiles can be used on Windows 95 machines, but they must be enabled first in order to be used on that type of client. The types of settings that are saved in a user's profile are described in table 8.1.

Table 8.1
User Profile Settings

Item	Description of Parameters Saved
Windows NT Explorer	All user-definable settings for the Windows NT Explorer.
Taskbar	All personally defined program groups and program items, their properties, and the Taskbar settings.
Printers Settings	All network printer connections.
Control Panel	All user-definable settings for Mouse, Color, Keyboard, International, Desktop Cursor, and Sound options. In the system option, entries in the User Environment Variables box are saved. Other control panel options do not contain user-specific settings.
Accessories	All user-specific application settings that affect the Windows NT environment. Also settings for the following: Calculator, Clock, Notepad, Paint, HyperTerminal, and other applets found in the Accessories program group on the Programs submenu of the Start menu.
Third-party Windows NT applications	Applications for Windows NT can be written so that they keep track of their application settings on a per-user basis. If this information exists, it can be saved in the user profile.
Command prompt	All user-definable settings for the command prompt, including fonts, windows position, colors, settings for screen size buffer, and so on.
Online Help bookmarks	Bookmarks placed in the Windows NT help system.

Six types of profiles are available:

- Local

- Server-based

- System default

- Default User

- All Users

- User (user name)

These profiles are discussed in the sections that follow.

Understanding Local Profiles

Local profiles are applicable to Windows NT Workstations and non-domain controller Windows NT Servers. If the Windows NT Workstation or server is a member of the domain, you can log on to the domain, or to the computer only. When logging on to the domain, you use the domain accounts in the Windows NT logon screen, and choose the name of the domain in the **F**rom box. When you log on to the Windows NT Workstation only, you choose the computer name of the workstation in the **F**rom box. The discussion on local profiles in this section applies to logging on to the Windows NT Workstation and not logging on to the domain.

When a user logs on to a Windows NT Workstation and then logs off after making changes, Windows NT saves any changed user-specific settings in a local profile. The exceptions to this rule are users who do not have the capability to save local profiles. Table 7.5, in Chapter 7, discusses the built-in capabilities of Windows NT Workstation and Server. One of these capabilities described in table 7.5 is the Keep local profile. Notice that the members of the Administrators, Power Users, Users, and Backup Operators have the built-in capability to keep a local profile, but members of Guest and the implicit group Everyone do not have this capability. On a Windows NT Workstation, the profile settings include all the items described in table 8.1.

Local profiles are created automatically by Windows NT Workstations; no additional work is required of administrators. When a user logs in again to the Windows NT Workstation, Windows NT determines whether a local profile already exists for the user.

If this is the first logon, a default profile is used by creating a copy of the Default User profile stored on each computer running Windows NT Workstation and Windows NT Server. That default file is a cached copy of the NTuser.DAT file that is part of the Default User configuration settings of the Windows NT Registry. Every user profile loads the common program groups that is stored in the All Users folder.

In subsequent logons to the workstation, Windows NT loads the last profile saved for that user.

On a workstation, each user's profile is kept in a separate folder. If the workstation is used by several users, Windows NT preserves the individual settings and preferences for each user (see fig. 8.1) in a set of folders contained in the Profiles folder of the system root folder, which by default is C:\WINNT. The local profile that is saved on a Windows NT Workstation, however, is local to that computer; if the user were to log on from a different workstation, a separate local profile would be created.

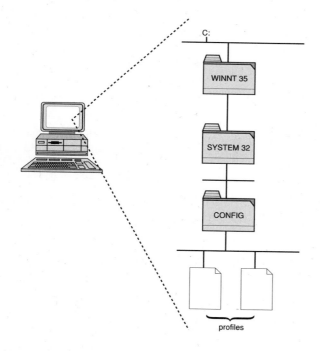

Figure 8.1

Local profiles on a stand-alone Windows NT Workstation are stored in folders within the C:\WINNT\Profiles folder.

The following is a list of common user profile folders and their contents:

- **Application Data.** Any application specific data is stored here. Some applications store preferences and data files in this manner.

- **Desktop.** Files and shortcuts to files that appear on the Desktop are stored in here.

- **Favorites.** The shortcuts to program items and to favorite locations, local, on your network, or on the Internet are stored in this folder.

- **NetHood.** Network Neighborhood items are stored in this folder.

- **Personal.** Your personal program items are stored in this folder.

- **PrintHood.** This folder contains a shortcut to the printer folder items.

- **Recent.** Recently used items that appear on the Documents menu of the Start menu are stored in this folder.

- **SendTo.** The SendTo folder stores shortcuts to document items.

- **Start Menu.** All shortcuts to program items are stored here.

- **Templates.** All shortcuts to template items are stored in this folder.

You do not see the NetHood, PrintHood, Recent, or Template folders, as they are hidden. To enable viewing hidden files and folders in the Windows Explorer, select the Options command on the View menu, and click on the Show All Files radio button.

The settings contained in the All Users folder is used to establish the program groups for all your users profiles. You will find Desktop and Start menu settings in the All Users folder.

Windows NT supports common program groups (shown as Application XXX (Common) on the Start menu's Program submenu) and personal program groups. Only an administrator can create common program groups. Personal program groups belong to the user who creates them.

Understanding Server-Based Profiles

If you use a Windows NT computer to log on to a domain, you can keep profiles that are specific to that domain user. These profiles, which are saved on the Windows NT Servers, are called *server-based profiles*. Following are the advantages of server-based profiles:

- Domain users have individual profiles that are located centrally on the domain servers. The domain user's profile is loaded when a user logs on from any Windows NT Workstation to the domain.

- You can configure the profile to restrict a user's access to his workstation, which then prevents the user from changing his workstation's configuration.

- If users are sharing the same profile, you can give these users access to an application simply by editing the common profile.

The first two benefits can be provided by what are called *personal profiles*. The third benefit, which involves a shared user profile, is provided by a *mandatory profile*. As the name suggests, personal server-based profiles are specific to a user. A user can change his personal profile, and these changes are uploaded to the server when the user logs off (see fig. 8.2). Mandatory profiles, on the other hand, cannot be permanently changed by the users. Users of mandatory profiles can change their settings after they are logged on. When they log off, however, these changes are not uploaded to their profile stored on the server (see fig. 8.3). When the user logs on again with a mandatory profile, the profile's original settings are loaded for the user. Any change made in the profile in the preceding session is lost because it was never saved.

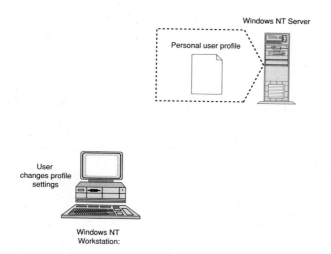

Figure 8.2

Personal user profile.

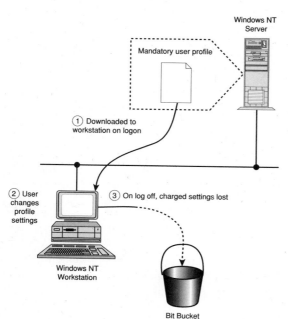

Figure 8.3

Mandatory user profile.

A user can have only one profile—a personal profile or a mandatory profile. The location of the profile file is stored in the user's account information using the User Manager for Domains. The procedure for setting the profile path is discussed in Chapter 7. Personal profile files must have an extension of .USR, and mandatory profile files must have an extension of .MAN.

Benefit of Using Server-Based Personal Profiles

Personal user profiles enable a user to store his desktop and connection preferences in a domain server. Any changes the user makes to his personal profile are saved in the user's personal profile settings at the server, and these settings are available from any workstation from which the user chooses to log on to the domain. You can choose to create a different profile on every computer you log in on, or you can create a server-based user profile called a "roaming" profile that is the same on every computer you log on at.

Figure 8.4 shows that the user Dave logs on to the domain from several workstations and receives the user profile on each of the different workstations. Moreover, any changes made to the user's personal profile are available on other workstations.

Figure 8.4

Advantage of personal profiles when logging on from different workstations.

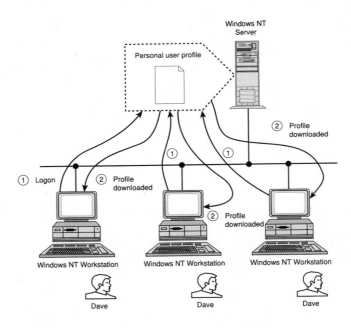

If the user's computer is changed or upgraded, no additional desktop configuration changes need to be carried out on the upgraded computer, because the user's profile will be downloaded from the server when the user logs on to a domain (see fig. 8.5).

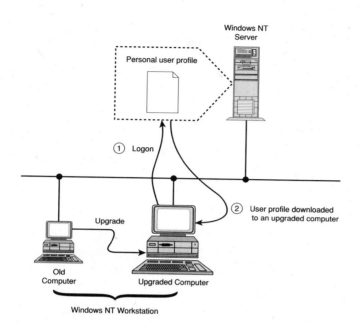

Figure 8.5

Advantage of personal profile in upgrading to a new computer.

Microsoft recommends that the user's personal profile file should have the same name as the user's logon name with a .USR extension. The advantage of this method is that when you create a new user account by copying an existing user account, the new user has his user name set as his profile name automatically. For example, if an existing user, David, has a profile file name of DAVID.USR, and you create a new account with a user name of Samuel, then when David's account is copied, the new account has its profile file name set to SAMUEL.USR.

Benefit of Using Server-Based Mandatory Profiles

Because personal profiles are not shared by users, it would not be practical to give access to new applications by editing the user's personal profile, because you would have to change each user's profile individually. In this case, you can use server-based mandatory profiles.

Mandatory profiles enable the administrator to store a user's desktop and connection preferences in a domain server so that these settings are downloaded every time the user logs on to the domain. The user cannot save any changes he makes to his mandatory profiles because changes are not saved when he logs off.

Mandatory profiles are useful in restricting the user's capability to perform certain tasks. And they are helpful in enforcing a common usage policy for an organization. A single mandatory profile is commonly assigned to several users. This setup enables the environment for several users to be updated with a single change to the mandatory profile. For example, you might want to add a new program item for a new application stored on the server for several users. You can carry out this task by making a change to the mandatory profile of those users.

Understanding Default Profiles

A user profile determines the desktop appearance and available desktop options. Not every user is assigned a profile file, and Windows NT computers can be running even when no user is logged in. In these cases, Windows NT uses a *user default profile* and a *system default profile*. You can modify the default profiles with the User Profile Editor.

User Default Profile

The user default profile is loaded when a user logs on and no specific profile is available for that user. Here are the situations in which this can occur:

- When this is the first time the user has logged on.

- When a profile has not been assigned for the user account.

- When a user logs on to the Guest account.

- When the network path for the user's assigned profile is unavailable. This situation could occur if the server is down.

Any changes a non-guest user makes to his profile is not made to the user default profile but is maintained separately for that user. When the user logs off, the per-user changes are stored to a locally cached file. When a user logs on again, Windows NT loads the saved copy of the locally cached profile from the most recent logon, rather than the user default profile.

For guest users, no locally cached profile is maintained. A guest user therefore always loads the default user profile.

The user profile stored in the Windows NT Registry as part of the HKEY_CURRENT_USER subtree. The NTuser.dat file is the stored cached copy of the user profile on the local computer. Among the settings stored in the registry database are: your computer's configuration, hardware and software settings, and other information. These settings restore the work environment for the user who logs on to the computer. You can view the HKEY_CURRENT _USER subtree in the Registry Editor.

You can customize the domain-wide default user profile for every NT Workstation and NT Server on the domain by changing the default user profile and copying it to the Primary Domain Controller.

To change the default user profile system-wide:

1. Log on to a Windows NT Workstation or NT Server and create a custom user profile.

2. Log off.

3. Log back on to the computer with the Administrator account.

4. Open the User Profile tab of the System control panel.

5. Click on the custom profile, then click on the Copy **T**o button.

6. Copy the user profile to the primary domain controller's Netlogon folder in the system root folder (for example, \\PDC Servername\Netlogon\Default User).

Windows NT Server creates the Default User (Network) folder on every computer when it starts up. If you want to create a custom default user profile on a computer in the domain, create a custom user profile and then copy it to the Default User folder on that computer.

When you log on to different computers, you may be working with different types of hardware that have different abilities. For example, one computer might be able to display a monitor in 1024×768 pixels, while another might not. Since the user profile sets up a desktop and is dependent upon screen resolution for the location of items, user profiles need to be configured to deal with this situation. In order to circumvent these difficulties, create or modify a user profile for a user on the same type of computer that the user will use. Pay particular attention to display characteristics, as this is the area that gives the most difficulty. Also, if you are creating a mandatory profile that several users will use, then make sure that you assign that profile to a group of users only if they have common video display characteristics on their computers.

Windows 95 User Profiles

Windows 95 also can work with user profiles, although they are not enabled under a normal installation. You enable the Windows 95 user profiles capability in the Passwords control panel. Windows 95 profiles operate similarly to Windows NT Workstation and NT Server. Roaming user profiles can be used on a Windows 95 computer in a Windows NT Server-based network if Client for Microsoft Networks is selected in the Passwords control panel as the primary network logon client. In a NetWare environment you should select the Client for NetWare Networks as the primary network login client for the Windows 95 client. Unlike Windows NT, when you use a mandatory user profile with a Windows 95 client, a different mandatory user profile must be created for each user.

There are some significant differences between Windows 95 user profiles and Windows NT user profiles. For one, you can't create a Windows 95 client from a computer running NT Workstation or NT Server. For another, there are differences in the names of the user profiles files in the Windows 95 registry. The files you see in the Windows 95 registry are named User.DAT, User.da0, and User.MAN.

Other Windows 95 differences are:

- It does not store common groups.

- It does not copy desktop items (other than shortcut (INK) or program information files (PIF)).

- Windows 95 doesn't support a centrally stored Default User profile.

- Windows 95 clients can use NT Server roaming user profiles. Roaming user profiles must be located in the user's home directory.

- Mandatory user profiles on NT Server or NT Workstation can only be used on Windows 95 when that profile is a custom user profile.

System Default Profile

The system default profile is used when no user is logged on to the Windows NT computer. The Welcome dialog box prompts the user to press Ctrl+Alt+Del to log on. The system default profile controls the screen savers, the wallpaper that is displayed when no one is logged on.

Settings for the system default profile appear in the Windows NT Registry in the .DEFAULT key of the HKEY_USERS tree.

Local Caching of Roaming User Profiles

If the user's Windows NT Workstation is not part of a domain, the locally cached file is the only profile for that user. If the user's Windows NT Workstation is part of a domain, the user can have an additional server-based profile. If the user has a server-based personal profile, a locally cached version of this profile is saved at the workstation (see fig. 8.6). This locally cached version is used when the server containing the user's profile is unavailable (see fig 8.7).

Figure 8.6

Local caching of personal profiles.

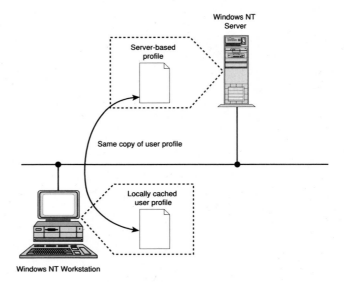

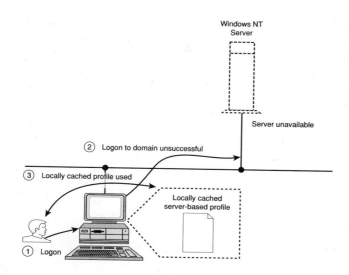

Figure 8.7

Use of local cached file when personal profile is unavailable.

If the user has a personal profile, the per-user settings are saved in the locally cached profile and the personal user profile on the server when the user logs off (see fig. 8.8). This process ensures that the locally cached profile is identical to the updated personal profile stored on the server.

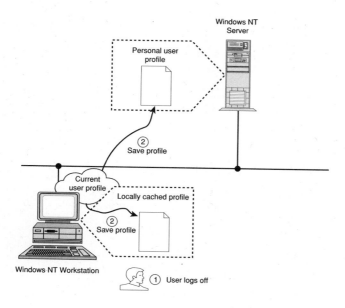

Figure 8.8

Saving of user settings for personal profile.

If the user has a mandatory profile, and the mandatory profile enables the user to make changes to the profile, the per-user changes are not saved in the mandatory profile on the server when the user logs off because the user cannot change his mandatory profile. Changes to the mandatory profile, however, are saved to the locally cached version of the mandatory profile at the workstation (see fig. 8.9). This means that if the user logs on and the computer on which the mandatory profile is kept is unavailable, the user receives the locally cached profile that has the changes made during the user's last session (see fig. 8.10).

Figure 8.9

Saving of user settings to local cache for mandatory profiles.

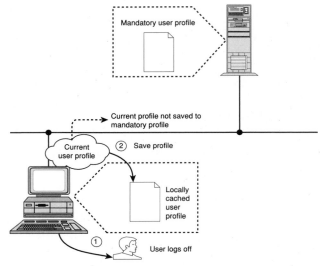

Figure 8.10

Receiving changes from local cached profile for mandatory profiles.

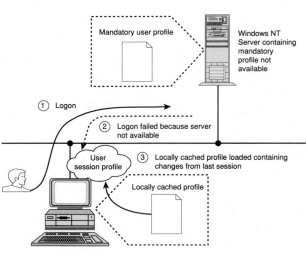

If the user has a personal profile and the user logs on, and both the personal profile and the locally cached profile are unavailable, the user default profile is loaded for the user (see fig. 8.11). If, however, the user has a mandatory profile and the user logs on, and both the mandatory profile and the locally cached profile are unavailable, the logon attempt is denied (see fig. 8.12).

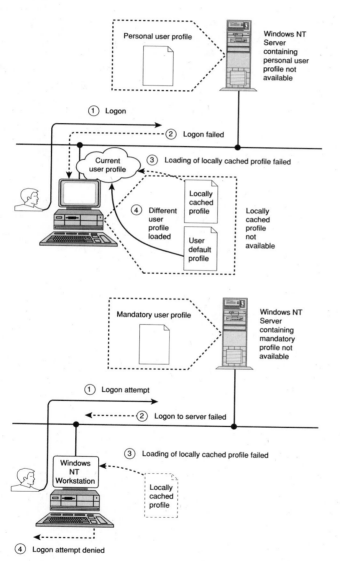

Figure 8.11

Both personal profile and local cache profile are unavailable.

Figure 8.12

Both mandatory profile and local cache profile are unavailable.

Profiles Differences between Windows 3.5*x* and Windows NT 4

In Windows NT Server 3.5*x*, there was a single user profile file. In version 4.0 a folder contains the user profile and a directory of links to the various items that reconstruct the user's environment based on that profile, items such as desktop items. Roaming user profiles in Windows NT 3.5*x* remains in the same server location in Windows 4.0, but the user profile is updated to a new format. In order to preserve backwards compatibility (for computers on the network using the older operating system), Windows NT 4 maintains both operating system versions of the user profile. In Window NT 3.5*x* you have a roaming/personal user profile file with the name username.USR. This is now replaced by the file name NTuser.DAT, and the roaming file name username.PDS (PDS = profile directory structure. For 3.5*x* mandatory files of the type username.MAN, these have been replaced with the mandatory file name username.PDM (PDM = profile directory mandatory) and the file name NTuser.MAN.

When a user who was on Windows 3.5*x* using a roaming user profile logs on to a Windows NT 4 computer, the user profile folder is created on the NT Server. The folder takes the user name for that user. For the siyan.USR file in 3.5*x*, the siyan.PDS folder is created. The appropriate folders and files are added to siyan.PDS to create the NT 4 user profile. Windows NT automatically looks for a Windows NT 4 user profile, even if the path specifies a Windows 3.5*x* profile.

In the instance where a mandatory profile is undergoing the upgrade, the upgrade must be done manually.

To upgrade a manual user profile from Windows 3.5*x* to Windows 4.0:

1. Log on to a computer and create a user profile with the desired settings for your mandatory user profile.

2. Log off.

3. Log back on as an Administrator.

4. Open the User Profile tab of the System Control Panel.

5. Copy the new user profile to the user profile path location.

   The location should be the profile folder with the same name as your 3.5*x* user profile, but with the .PDM extension (for example, \\servername\profilename.PDM).

6. In the Windows NT Explorer, find the new user profile folder and rename the NTuser.DAT file to NTuser.MAN.

The above procedure leaves the profilename.MAN file in the same location and makes it possible for you to log on to a Windows 3.5*x* machine on the network and have the correct mandatory user profile load.

Slow Connection Logons

Many network domains allow for Remote Access Service (RAS) connections. Most often these connections are dial-up modem connections, and are slow. For users on a slow link, you can use a local user profile instead of downloading the roaming user profile from your server. This option can greatly speed up your login time. When you choose to use a local user profile, a dialog box will appear asking you which profile you want to use.

For a user logged in on a slow connection, you can change your user profile type from roaming to local, and from local to roaming by opening the System Control Panel and selecting the user profile from the list in the User Profile tab (see the next section for more details). The profile you select will remain in effect until you go back to the User Profile tab and select another. For a local user account, the cached copy of your roaming user profile is used during a logon. Change you make to your environment are stored in the local user profile on your remote computer.

Managing Profiles

You use the User Manager for Domains to create new user profiles or modify existing ones. Changes you make to a profile are always saved to a file with a personal profile (.DAT) or mandatory profile (.MAN) extension. You can assign a profile to a user or group, or you can save it as a user default or system default profile.

The User Manager for Domains is located in the Administrative Tools group. You must be a member of the Administrators local group or the Domain Admins global group to use the User Profile Editor.

When you edit the user profile, the changes you make affect the account you are logged in as. You therefore should consider using a special administrator account for making just profile changes. In this way, you avoid making changes to your regular administrator account. You can use the User Manager for Domains to create such a profile administrator account (see Chapter 7, "Managing Windows NT Server Domain Accounts," for additional details).

A user profile can either be a local profile or a roaming profile. In the former case, your profile can be different on each of the workstations that you log on to. When a user has a user account on a local workstation as well as a domain user account (or more than one domain account), the local user profile can be different for each account, because each account has a different user profile with changes saved to it. A user's local user profile on a computer is saved to the user profile folder in the Ntuser.DAT file. Changes made to that profile are stored in a transaction log file called NTuser.LOG. The purpose of the log file is to allow Windows NT to restore a user profile should there be a system error or a shutdown occur and changes not be saved to the NTuser.DAT file. This system is a new fault tolerance feature built into Windows NT 4.

A roaming profile allows you to have the same server-based profile used on any workstation you log in at. A roaming profile works using the system that was described in the section "Local Caching of Roaming User Profiles," earlier in the chapter, which was the supported system in Windows NT 3.51 Server. When you log on and have a roaming profile assigned to you, the local profile and server profile are compared and the most recent copy is used. The other copy is updated, as necessary. This provides a centralized domain login model. In most instances, administrators prefer to assign central domain logins with roaming user profiles over multiple user accounts with local user profiles.

Creating a New User Profile

You create a local user profile by default. If a user logs on to a computer and there is no preconfigured roaming user profile assigned, a new user profile folder is created for that user. The contents of the Default User settings are copied to that person's new profile folder, as well as the common program groups settings from the All Users folder. From these two sources the user's desktop settings are comprised. As the new user makes changes to their environment, those changes are saved to the new user's profile folder when the user logs off of the system. The Default User profile on the server is left unchanged for future new users.

Roaming profiles are created in any of the following ways:

- Enter a profile path into each user account to automatically create an empty user profile folder for that user on the server, then allow the user to create their own profile.

- Enter a profile path into each user account, and then copy an existing user profile into that user's profile path.

- Enter a user profile path into each user account, then copy an existing user profile into that user account. Then rename the Ntuser.dat file to Ntuser.man in the user profile path.

The first two procedures create personal profiles, while the latter procedure creates a mandatory user profile.

Following is an outline for creating a new user profile:

1. Log in as an administrator. Use a special profile administrator account to avoid making changes to your personal desktop appearance, as discussed in the preceding section.

2. Configure the desktop appearance to be exactly as you want it for the user profile. See table 8.1 to view the changes that can be made to the desktop appearance.

3. Start the User Manager for Domains from the Administrative Tools group.

4. Select the New User command from the User menu. The New User dialog box shown in figure 8.13 appears.

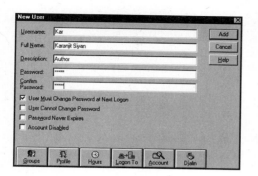

Figure 8.13

The New User dialog box.

5. Fill in the **U**sername, Full **N**ame, **D**escription, **P**assword, and **C**onfirm Password (same password again) text boxes, then click on the P**r**ofile button. The User Environment Profile dialog box appears (see fig. 8.14).

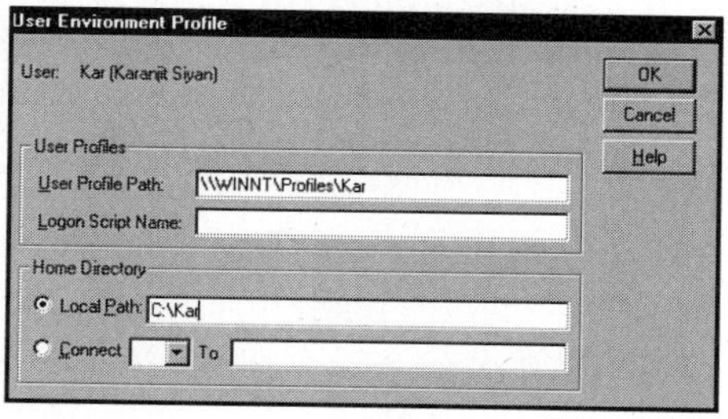

Figure 8.14

The User Environment Profile dialog box.

6. Enter the **U**ser Profile Path (the location and name of the Profile folder for that user), the **L**ogon Script Name (if there is one), and the path to the home directory (optional); then click on the OK button.

   If you leave the **U**ser Profile Path empty, then the account is a local user account and does not provide a central login profile.

7. Click on the Add button to add the user and their profile to your list of users.

8. Continue to add users, or close the User Manager for Domains to add the users and their profiles to your system.

The full path should be in the form: \\server\share\profilename. Share creates a Profile folder if one does not exist, and shares the folder with Everyone (a user group). The path location can be any server, not only a domain controller (although that is the most common choice). Profilename is the user name for the user account. When the user logs in, Windows NT Server opens the user's account, and then searches for the path to use that user profile.

The mandatory user profile operates just like the roaming user profile, but cannot be changed. Any changes made during a session are discarded when the user logs off. When a user with a mandatory profile logs on again, the same mandatory user profile is loaded again.

To create a mandatory user profile, open the Windows NT Explorer, locate the NTuser.DAT file, and change the file extension to NTuser.MAN.

A mandatory user profile is a read-only file. That same file can be used for any number of users you choose.

A mandatory user profile can store environmental settings for a group of users. A new feature in Windows NT 4 Server lets you control user choices, allowed applications, command selections, and other work style or security aspects of a user's work session through the use of system policys in the System Policy Editor. This subject is described in the section "System Policy Editor," later in this chapter.

Modifying a User Environment

If you need to modify the entire user environment of an existing user profile, you must log on with that profile setting, change it, and then save the profile. The reason for logging on with the existing profile settings is that it is the only way to change the desktop appearance. You cannot change the desktop appearance from the User Profile Editor. After you are logged on with an existing profile, the procedure for making changes is the same as that discussed in the previous section on creating a new user profile.

Following is a summary of the steps to follow to modify an existing profile:

1. Assign the existing profile file to the administrator account for changing profiles. You do this by using the User Manager for Domains and selecting the Profile button from the main screen.

2. Log on as the administrative account used for changing profiles.

3. Modify the Windows NT computer environment to meet the user's needs.

4. Open the User Environment Profile Editor and edit options as needed. This procedure was described in detail in the preceding section.

5. Save your profile changes.

Copying a User Profile

If you want to assign the same personal user profile to each user, you cannot share a common profile file as you can in the case of mandatory profiles, because each user's changes to the profile overwrites other users' profile settings. If the personal profile files are to be the same for the different users, you need to make a copy of the profile file. Simply making a file copy is not sufficient; you will also have to change the file permissions to the profile file so that users can access it.

To create a preconfigured roaming user profile, you would go through the above procedure and then open the User Profiles tab of the System Properties control panel (see fig. 8.15). From there you can copy a preconfigured user profile to the server.

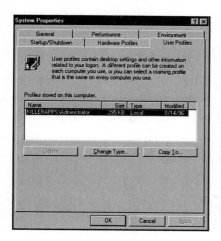

Figure 8.15

The User Profiles tab of the System Properties control panel.

When you click on the Copy **T**o button and locate the selected user profile, the location must be the same path as specified in that user's account in the User Manager for Domains. Figure 8.16 shows the Copy To dialog box with the new user's profile location filled in. The Permitted to use box indicates who has permissions to use the user profile. You can specify another user by clicking on the **C**hange button and adding that user or group to the permissions list for that particular user profile.

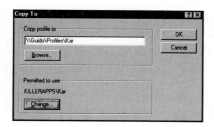

Figure 8.16

The Copy To dialog box.

When a user logs on, they will be given the preconfigured user profile on the server in place of the Default Profile. From there on in, the user profile is used in place of the default (standard) roaming user profile. Changes made in a session are saved to the user profile locally when they log off their computer.

You must use this method to copy a user profile. You cannot create a copy from within the Windows NT Explorer.

When a roaming user profile path is assigned to a group and when a group member ends his session, his user profile overwrites the common user profile. For this reason, Microsoft recommends that you use mandatory user profiles (see the following sections) instead of assigning a single roaming user profile to a group of users.

Deleting a User Profile

You can delete a roaming or mandatory user profile when that user is no longer required on the system. This is done from within the User Profiles tab of the System Properties control panel.

To delete a user profile:

1. Select the Control Panels command on the Settings submenu of the Start menu.

2. Double-click on the System control panel.

3. Select the user name whose policy you want to delete.

4. Click on the **D**elete button.

5. Click on the OK button.

The preceding steps remove the user profile, but do not delete the user's account. To do that, you need to delete it from the User Manager for Domains program.

Considerations for Setting Profiles

When setting up profiles, you should consider the following issues to avoid problems in profile settings:

■ When setting up profiles, you should position and lay out the desktop appearance using the same video display that will be used by the users to whom the profile is assigned. For example, if you lay out the desktop appearance on an SVGA display and the users use a VGA display, the window boundaries will be off the screen.

■ When setting up program paths, ensure that all Windows NT computers that will be used with the profile have a consistent path. If the applications are on a shared directory on a server, the path will be common regardless of the workstation used to access the application. If the application is installed at each workstation, ensure that you are using the same location to install the application. If you cannot take this action, ensure that the PATH environment variable on each workstation includes the location of the application, and do not specify the full path name for the program item.

■ Windows NT 3.5 (and higher) profiles do not work from Windows NT 3.1 computers. This is not a problem because most sites have upgraded from Windows NT 3.1 because of inherent problems with that release.

Understanding How Profiles Are Loaded and Saved

The previous sections described the way in which profiles are loaded and saved. Whether a profile is saved depends on considerations such as these:

- Are you logging to the domain or the Windows NT computer?

- Is this the first logon?

- Is this a user profile, or a mandatory profile?

- Is there a default profile?

System Policy

Windows NT 4 institutes a new and powerful system for controlling user work environments and the actions that users are allowed to take called system policies. You can control access to options in Control Panels, the nature of the desktop and network settings as part of a system policy setting. A system policy is a set of settings stored in the Windows NT Registry, which complements the user profiles that you have learned about. You change system policies using the System Policy Editor. System policies are seen to be a much more powerful method for enforcing restrictions that the mandatory user profiles that Windows NT 3.5x allowed.

As you have seen, the desktop, logon, and network connections you specify as part of a user profile are stored in the computer's Registry database. When you create system policy settings for a user, those settings overwrite the settings in the current user settings stored in the Registry. You can also create system policy settings for particular computers, and those will overwrite the current local machine settings stored in the Registry, as well. So system policy settings not only let you control the actions that are allowed as part of the user profiles you've created, but they also manage the actions allowed on individual computers. System Policy settings are optional, but are a more powerful method for allowing or denying access to users and machines than user profiles for mandatory behaviors.

The System Policy Editor

To open the System Policy Editor:

1. Select the System Policy Editor command from the Administrative Tools submenu of the Start menu.

Figure 8.17
The System Policy Editor.

The System Policy Editor is shown in figure 8.17.

2. Choose **F**ile, New Policy to view the Default User and Default Computer policy settings.

In the System Policy Editor you can:

■ Create system policies for a computer or user in an entire domain

■ Create custom settings for specific users, groups, or machine accounts

■ Create the download policy for any or all users

Notice that the System Policy Editor displays two icons for Default Computer and Default User. Clicking on these icons opens dialog boxes that contain the specific settings that apply to these policy profiles. You see a graphic representation of the Registry tree, replete with major categories, subcategories, and their settings. Figures 8.18 and 8.19 show you the major categories for the Default User Properties and Default Computer Properties, respectively.

Figure 8.18
The Default User Properties dialog box.

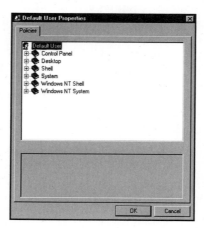

The Default User contains the following categories:

- **Control Panel.** This category restricts what can be done in the Display control panel.

- **Desktop.** Here you set the wallpaper and color scheme on the desktop.

- **Shell.** You can disable the Run, Find, or ShutDown commands here. Also, you can customize folders and specify program items, desktop icons, startup items, Network Neighborhood items, and Start menu items.

- **System.** This disables the Window NT Registry Editor (Regedt32.EXE) and the Windows 95 Registry Editor (Regedit.EXE), or creates a list of allowed applications for the Default User.

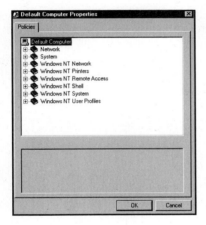

Figure 8.19
The Default Computer Properties dialog box.

The Default User contains the following categories:

- **Network.** Here you can remote update computers using system policy instead of settings found in. Enter a path to a different policy file if you want to manually update the policy file instead of having the server automatically apply the NTconfig.POL file in the Netlogon folder of the Primary Domain Controller.

- **System.** This controls the contents of the Run and Run once settings that determine which applications run when you boot your computer. The default SNMP (Simple Network Management Protocol) can also be changed in the System category.

- **Windows NT System.** There are three subcategories in this category: system security, logon security, and FTP logon policies.

- **System Security.** Has settings that affect the logon policy. Among the things you can do with system security is enable and disable automatic logon, have a message display at startup, or disable the startup screen and have the login dialog box display without users pressing the Ctrl+Alt+Delete keystroke.

- ■ **Login Security.** Enables or disables the Shut Down button in the Welcome dialog box.

- ■ **FTP Logon Policies.** Any computer with FTP Server Services: Either the Internet Information Server, Peer Web Services (on NT 4 Workstation), or another third-party product can be configured for allowing and logging anonymous logons, a timeout setting, and a home directory.

- ■ **Windows NT Printers.** You use these settings to disable the print spooler browse process, change print job priorities, and set an error beep.

- ■ **Windows NT Remote Access.** This category lets you set a maximum number of unsuccessful login attempts, a call back time interval, and a time limit for inactivity after which the caller is disconnected.

You can change settings in the System Policy Editor by clicking on the plus sign next to a category to look at subcategories (if there are subcategories), and then opening the subcategories to look at individual items. Figure 8.20 shows the result of clicking on the Wallpaper setting that enables a text box containing the wallpaper that will load as system policy. A tile check box can be clicked if you want that bitmap file to be tiled, as most small wallpaper files are. This is the typical manner in which system policy settings are made.

Figure 8.20

Setting wallpaper as system policy.

Settings in the System Profile Editor can refer to any of the following:

- ■ **Disabled.** The command will appear dim in the menu.

- ■ **Removed.** The command is not found in the menu.

- ■ **Hidden.** These items are not seen by the user.

As with all Windows check boxes, they have three states: on, off, and dimmed. A dimmed setting is used in this context to indicate that the previous setting in the Registry is used for this feature.

To save the changes in system policy to the registry:

1. Choose the Open Registry command in the System Policy Editor's File menu.

2. In response to the Do you want to save changes to (Untitled)? message box that appears (see fig. 8.21), click on the Yes button to save the changes.

Figure 8.21

The Do you want to save changes to (Untitled)? *message box.*

This saves a single change, or any changes in your session.

3. In the Save As dialog box, name the system policy default file to which to save all policies (for example, MyPolicy.POL). If you locate that file in the Default folder on the server (as shown in fig. 8.22), those policies are applied domain-wide.

Figure 8.22

The Save As dialog box where you save a policy file.

To make changes to a remote computer, use the Connect command on the System Policy Editor and locate that computer and its registry. In general, system policy is enforced throughout a domain. Individual policy settings on client machines are not usually enforced.

Customizing System Policy

You use the System Policy to create and modify policy settings. To work with user policy settings, you change the Default User settings in the System Policy Editor. To work with machine settings where logon and network connections can be altered, you modify the Default Computer settings. Settings you create in the System Policy Editor are stored in a file called NTConfig.POL. If you want your settings to apply universally, store this file in the Netlogon folder in your root directory of the primary domain controller (for example, \\PDCservername\Netlogon). During logon, Windows looks for this file in the PDC and if it finds the file, copies its settings into the local computer's Registry. The HKEY_CURRENT_ USER and HKEY_LOCAL_MACHINE keys in the Registry will be overwritten. Therefore, the settings for the NTConfig.POL and NTuser.DAT profile settings merge to control user behavior. Any settings for the Default Computer that are in addition to settings found in the user profile are written to the HKEY_LOCAL_MACHINE key of the Registry as well.

Normally, system policy is applied automatically from the PDC, regardless of who logs on to the system and from what computer. If you want to control this behavior and manually apply system policy, specify a path other than the Netlogon folder on the root of the PDC in the System Policy Editor. You must do this for each individual computer.

System Policy settings can be applied to users, groups, and specific computers as the need arises. When you create a user, group, or machine account in a domain, those entities can have individual entries in the NTConfig.POL file other than their default settings applied. When a user logs on to a domain, the user's user and group policy settings are applied to their Registry settings. The computer that the user has logged on to also is updated with the machine policy settings from the NTConfig.POL.

Since these policy settings are stored in the primary domain controller, there currently is no way to enforce policy settings across domains should a user log in at a machine in another domain.

There is a precedence for the manner in which profiles are applied to a user. A user profile is used in preference to a user profile for a group. If there is no specific user profile for a user, a group profile that the user belongs to will be used. If no profile can be assigned, then the Default User profile is applied.

When there is no computer profile for a computer, the Default Computer profile is applied. When there are two or more group profiles that are applicable to a user, the precedence order in the Group Priority dialog box is applied and the group with the highest precedence is used.

In order to speed up the creation and assignment of system policy to groups of users and machines, you can create system policy templates and apply them to Windows NT Server, Windows NT Workstation, and Windows 95 clients. When the System Policy Editor starts up for the first time, it creates the following files:

■ **WINNT.ADM.** This file contains settings applicable to the Windows NT operating system and to its Registry. These settings do not apply to Windows 95 machines.

- **WINDOWS.ADM.** This contains policy settings for Windows 95 Registries. A different file is required because of the differences between Windows NT and Windows 95 Registry structures. These settings do not apply to Windows NT machines.

- **COMMON.ADM.** Policy settings that are common to both Registry types are stored in this file.

Logon Scripts

Logon scripts are batch files or executable program files that are run automatically when the user logs on. Using a logon script is optional. If the workstation that is used for logging on is a Windows NT Workstation, the user's environment can be set entirely using profile files. If the workstation that is used to log on is a non-Windows NT Workstation, such as a DOS/Windows workstation, the logon scripts are needed to establish predefined network connections and execute other commands to set up the user environment.

When to Use a Logon Script

In general, logon scripts are used to provide users with network connections and start applications automatically when a user logs on.

Even though user profiles in Windows NT can do everything that logon scripts can, you might want to use logon scripts for the following reasons:

- You have non-Windows NT Workstations, such as MS-DOS workstations and LAN Manager clients, on the network.

- You want to manage only the network connections rather than the entire user environment.

- You do not have any interest in managing the desktop appearance and environment; your only interest is in managing available network connections and starting applications automatically.

- You want to share logon scripts with several users to create and maintain common network connections for the users.

- Logon scripts are easier to maintain using a simple text editor.

- You are integrating your network with a LAN Manager network that already uses logon scripts.

Table 8.4 shows a comparison between user profiles and logon scripts.

Table 8.4

User Profiles versus Logon Scripts

User Profiles	Logon Scripts
Available only on Windows NT computers.	Available to all network clients that perform logon validation. Can be used in conjunction with LAN Manager clients.
Can control the entire desktop environment, including desktop appearance and usage, network connections, and startup applications.	Can control network connections and startup applications. Cannot be used for controlling desktop appearance and usage.
A special tool, the User Profile Editor, is needed in order to manage profiles.	Any standard text editor can be used to manage logon scripts.
Several different profile types are available: local, personal, mandatory, and default. Although they offer different levels of control, they have subtle interactions with each other.	You can use a batch file or an executable program. Usually only the batch file is used.

Using a Logon Script

Logon scripts can be assigned to one or more user accounts or to group accounts using the User Manager for Domains. In the User Environment Profile for the user, type the file name on the server that contains the logon script in the **L**ogon Script Name field. If you specify only the logon script name, a default path prefix of %SystemRoot%\System32\Repl\Import\Scripts is used. You can specify a location under the default path by specifying the relative path name of the logon script file. You can specify an alternative path by including the full path name. You might want to configure Directory Replication to ensure that you receive up-to-date replicated copies of the logon script to your workstation.

The logon script is always downloaded from the server that authenticates the user's logon. For domain user accounts used to log on to a domain, the authenticating server must be a domain controller—either a primary domain controller or a backup domain controller. Because logon scripts are not automatically synchronized between primary and domain controllers, you should activate the Replicator service to synchronize logon scripts. Replicator service enables you to maintain identical copies of the directory tree on multiple computers. This topic is discussed in Chapter 6, "Implementing Windows NT Server Domains."

If you are using replication, you should maintain the master copy of the logon script on the export server so that logon script changes can be automatically copied to the import computers. One of the domain controllers should be set up as an export server, and the other domain controllers can act as import computers.

The logon script is typically a batch file with a .BAT or .CMD extension. If the .BAT file extension is used, the DOS-emulated command processor is used. For batch files with a .CMD extension, the NT command processor is used.

The commands that are used in the batch files are any Windows NT commands. For modifying the network connections and network environment, the Windows NT NET commands are used. The Windows NT NET commands are preceded by the keyword NET, followed by a command and other parameters:

`NET` *command parameters*

A very useful and frequently used NET command that is used in logon scripts is the NET USE command. This is the syntax of the NET USE command:

```
NET USE [devicename ¦ *] [\\computername\sharename[\volume] [password ¦ *]]
        [/USER:[domainname\]username]
        [[/DELETE] ¦ [/PERSISTENT:{YES ¦ NO}]]
NET USE [devicename ¦ *] [password ¦ *]] [/HOME]
NET USE [[/PERSISTENT:{YES ¦ NO}]
```

NET USE connects a computer to a shared resource or disconnects a computer from a shared resource. When used without options, it lists the computer's connections. The following list explains the parameters for the NET USE command.

devicename assigns a name to connect to the resource or specifies the device to be disconnected. There are two kinds of device names: disk drives (D: through Z:) and printers (LPT1: through LPT3:). Type an asterisk rather than a specific device name to assign the next available device name.

\\computername is the name of the computer controlling the shared resource. If *computername* contains blank characters, enclose the double backslash (\\) and the computer name in quotation marks (" "). The computer name can be from 1 to 15 characters long.

\sharename is the network name of the shared resource.

\volume specifies a NetWare volume on the server. You must have Client Services for NetWare (Windows NT Workstations) or Gateway Service for NetWare (Windows NT Server) installed and running to connect to NetWare servers.

password is the password needed to access the shared resource.

* produces a prompt for the password. The password is not displayed when you enter it at the password prompt.

/USER specifies a different user name with which the connection is made.

domainname specifies another domain. If the domain is omitted, the current logged on domain is used.

username specifies the user name with which to log on.

/HOME connects a user to his home directory.

/DELETE cancels a network connection and removes the connection from the list of persistent connections.

/PERSISTENT controls the use of persistent network connections. The default is the setting used last.

YES saves connections as they are made and restores them at the next logon.

NO does not save the connection being made or subsequent connections; existing connections are restored at the next logon. Use the /DELETE switch to remove persistent connections.

For example, you could use the NET USE commands in a logon script in the following manner to establish network connections:

```
NET USE F: /D
NET USE G: /D
NET USE F: \\NTUS\APPS
NET USE G: \\NTUS\PROGS
NET USE *  \\NTSCS\DATA
NET USE
VirCheck
```

The first two of these NET USE commands are used to delete any existing connections on drives F: and G:. The third NET USE command assigns drive letter F: to the shared resources APPS on computer NTUS. The fourth NET USE command similarly assigns drive letter G: to the shared resources PROGS on computer NTUS. The fifth command assigns the next available drive letter (*) to the share name DATA on computer NTSCS. The last NET USE command displays the current device usage. The last command is VirCheck, which is the name of a custom virus checking program that is started in the background.

The logon script also can include environment variables. Environment variables are set using the SET command. For example, to set the environment variable AUTHOR to a string Karanjit in the logon script, you would use the following statement:

```
SET AUTHOR=Karanjit
```

Environment variables set in the logon script are set during the execution of the logon script. After the logon script finishes executing, the environment is returned to the settings in the CONFIG.SYS and AUTOEXEC.BAT files.

You can use the special logon script variables listed in table 8.5.

Table 8.5
Windows NT Logon Script Variables

Variable	Description
%HOMEDRIVE%	The workstation's drive letter on which the home directory can be found
%HOMEPATH%	The full path name of the home directory, not including the drive letter
%HOMESHARE%	The share name containing the user's home directory
%OS%	The operating system running at the user's workstation
%PROCESSOR_ARCHITECTURE%	The processor type (80386, 80486, Alpha, MIPS, and so on) running at the user's workstation
%PROCESSOR_LEVEL%	The processor level of a user's workstation.
%USERDOMAIN%	The name of the domain containing the user's account
%USERNAME%	The logon name for the user that is logged on

Setting Home Directories

The home directory is the private directory for the user. The home directory is the user's default directory when a user opens the NT command prompt, or saves a file using the Save As dialog box in applications. Home directories are generally assigned individually to each user. Home directories also can be shared by several users. If the users have permissions to create files only in their home directories, the administrator has the assurance that by backing up the users' home directories, all the users' data on the server is backed up.

If a home directory has not been assigned, the default home directory is \USERS\DEFAULT on the drive where Windows NT is installed. The home directory is set using the User Manager for Domains in the User Environment Profile dialog box (refer to figure 8.18). The home directory can be set to a local directory on the user's workstation or a network path. If you are administering a domain and you set the home directory to a local path, you must manually create the home directory. If you specify a network path for the home directory, in most cases User Manager for Domains automatically creates the home directory for you. If it cannot, it informs you that you need to create the home directory manually.

The users need appropriate file permissions to their home directories. If the User Manger for Domains is used to create a home directory, it assigns the permissions automatically. When a new home directory is created while a single account is being administered, the user account is given Full Control permission to the home directory. If several accounts are being administered and a new home directory is created, the group Everyone is given Full Control permission to the home directory. If the home directory already exists, User Manager for Domains does not change directory permissions to the home directory. You must use File Manager to change permissions.

When specifying the home directory (or personal profile path), you can use the logon script variable %USERNAME%, for the last subdirectory in the path. The Windows NT system automatically substitutes the user name when it sees the %USERNAME% logon script variable.

Setting User Environment Variables

Environment variables are text strings that evaluate to a specific value. The operating system and application programs can read and set the values of the environment variables to control the behavior of the system and applications.

Windows NT has two types of environment variables:

> System environment variables

> User environment variables

The system environment variables are set for all users logging on to the system. The user environment variables are set on a per-user basis.

If a conflict exists between the different types of environment variables and the environment variable is not the PATH environment variable, Windows NT resolves the conflict in the following manner:

1. System environment variables are set first.

2. User environment variables are set next.

3. Variables defined in the AUTOEXEC.BAT file are set last.

If the environment variable is set as a system and also as a user environment variable, the setting of the user environment variable overrides the setting of the system environment variable. Variables in AUTOEXEC.BAT do not override the settings for system and user environment variables. If a variable in the AUTOEXEC.BAT file has a duplicate name, the value in the AUTOEXEC.BAT file is discarded.

Consider the following settings:

System:

```
SET APPL=\System\Appl
```

User:

```
SET APPL=\User\Appl
```

AUTOEXEC.BAT:

```
SET APPL=AUTOEXEC
```

When the user logs on, the environment variable APPL will be set to the user environment variable setting of \User\Appl. The setting in the AUTOEXEC.BAT file is ignored.

The PATH environment variable is processed differently than other variables. The directories specified in the PATH user environment variable are appended to the PATH specified in the system environment variable. If the PATH environment variable is also specified in the AUTOEXEC.BAT file, it is appended to the PATH environment variable last.

You also can prevent the AUTOEXEC.BAT file from being parsed by the system by modifying the Windows NT Registry. The Registry is the internal database for system-related settings. It is discussed in Chapter 10, "Managing Windows NT Registry."

User environment variables can be saved in user profiles. Table 8.6 shows the default system and user environment variables. You can change the system and user environment variables by using the System icon in the Windows NT control panel. To change the system or user environment variable, click on the variable in the system or user box and use the **V**ariable and **V**alue fields and the **S**et and **D**elete buttons to alter the value.

Table 8.6
Default Environment Variables

Variable	Type	Description
ComSpec	System	Specifies the location where the NT command interpreter, CMD.EXE, is kept.
OS2LibPath	System	Specifies the location where programs that run under the OS/2 subsystem should search for OS/2 DLL files.
Path	System	Specifies the directories that are searched for executable program files.
windir	System	Specifies the directory where Windows NT Server and Windows NT Workstation files are installed.
tmp	User	Specifies the default directory where an application can place temporary files.
temp	User	Specifies the default directory where an application can place temporary files. Both tmp and temp are needed because some applications use tmp whereas others use temp.

Conclusion

This chapter discussed the way in which user environment variable settings can be modified. You can control the user environment settings using a user profile, a logon script, security policies, a home directory, and environment variable settings. This chapter provided you with practical guidelines on setting and managing each type of environment setting.

Using user profiles is the preferred method of controlling a user environment if a Windows NT computer is used as a workstation. Mandatory settings can be imposed either through mandatory profiles, or by using a feature new to Windows NT 4, system policies. To provide support for other non-Windows NT computer clients, you can use logon scripts.

Managing Network Files and File Security Systems

his chapter discusses the ways in which network files are shared in a Windows NT network. A shared directory can be accessed simultaneously by more than one user. Ensuring that the users are given appropriate access to the shared directory is therefore important. Access to the shared directory is controlled by directory and file permissions. This chapter discusses the ways in which directory and file permissions can be used to secure access to data, and the ways in which file-system security can be further enhanced by using auditing.

Managing Network Files

The different types of file systems (NTFS, FAT) used on the Windows NT Server were introduced in Chapter 3, "Installing Windows NT Server." If you want to control access to files and directories with permission settings (ACL settings), you can do so only on an NTFS file system. In Windows NT, permission settings can be set for both directories and files. Windows NT, however, uses the term *file permissions* to discuss permission settings for both directories and files.

If you have installed a Windows NT Server with a FAT file system, and you then decide to use file permissions to control access to the files, you must convert the FAT volume to an NTFS volume.

Converting to an NTFS Volume

You can use the CONVERT command to convert a FAT volume to an NTFS volume. Following is the syntax of this command:

```
CONVERT drive: /FS:NTFS [/V] [/NAMETABLE:filename]
```

drive specifies the drive to convert to NTFS. Note that you cannot convert the current drive.

/FS:NTFS specifies to convert the volume to NTFS.

/V specifies that CONVERT should be run in verbose mode.

/NAMETABLE:filename specifies that CONVERT should construct a name-translation table and store it in the specified file in the root directory of the volume to be converted. The conversion takes place the next time the system is restarted.

The conversion is uni-directional. That is, you can convert from a FAT to an NTFS volume. You cannot, however, convert an NTFS volume to a FAT volume.

Converting a FAT Volume to an NTFS Volume

To convert a FAT volume to an NTFS volume, you must be logged on to the Windows NT computer as an administrator user. If you need to convert an existing drive C: that has been formatted to FAT, to NTFS, use the following command:

```
CONVERT D: /FS:NTFS
```

If CONVERT can't gain exclusive access to the drive, a message box informs you of the fact and asks whether you want to schedule the conversion the next time the system restarts. If you see this message, answer with a Y (yes) and restart the system.

Name Space Support for File Systems

As explained in Chapter 3, "Installing Windows NT Server," all files within NTFS, including the data associated with files, are viewed as a set of attributes. The main attributes of an NTFS file are these:

- **Standard Information.** File attributes (read-only, archive, system, hidden, compression—for NT 3.51 or higher); time stamps (creation date and last modified date); and hard link count (number of directory entries that point to the file—used for POSIX support).

- **Attribute List.** List of attributes that make up the file; file reference of the Master File Table (MFT) record in which the attribute is located. This attribute is used when a file requires more than one MFT record.

- **File Name.** The name of the file in Unicode characters.

- **Security Descriptor.** The owner of the file, and the ACL that defines who can access this file and the ways in which they can access it.

- **Data.** The data attribute, which is the contents of the file. Normal files have one unnamed data attribute, which is the contents of the file. A file can have multiple data attributes—multiple data contents or data streams.

Windows NT files can have names up to 255 characters long, and file sizes can be up to 16 exabytes (2 to the power of 64) long. The large size results from the fact that a double word, which is 64 bits long, is used for offsets within a file. The relationships of megabytes, gigabytes, terabytes, petabytes, and exabytes are shown here:

1024 = 1 KB (kilobyte)

1024 KB = 1 MB (megabyte)

1024 MB = 1 GB (gigabyte)

1024 GB = 1 TB (terabyte)

1024 TB = 1 PB (petabyte)

1024 PB = 1 EB (exabyte)

File names can consist of any characters except those that are used as wild-card characters (? and *), delimiters (\, /, :, and ;), redirection symbols (< and >), and piping between processes (|). You can have multiple periods and spaces in file names. If spaces are used, you must place the file name in quotation marks ("").

The next few sections discuss file name compatibility issues for NTFS and FAT file systems.

DOS-Style File Name Support under NTFS

To support access to the long file names from MS-DOS clients on a network, the NTFS long file names are converted to DOS-style file names that conform to the 8.3 file-naming rules (see fig. 9.1). The short file name (SFN) is created automatically for every long file name (LFN) that is created in NTFS. Because MS-DOS clients do not understand long file names, they use the short file name associated with the file. The short file name can be considered to be an alias to the file. When you use the DIR command to see a listing of the files, you see only the long file names. To see the short file names as well, use the /X option with the DIR command:

```
DIR /X
```

Figure 9.1

Access to long file names from MS-DOS clients.

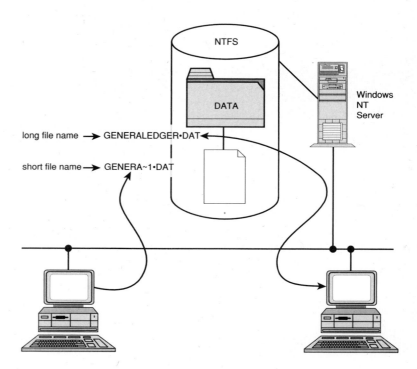

Following are the rules used by Windows NT to create a short file name from a long file name:

1. Spaces are removed from the long file name.

   If the long file name is TH^IS.IS A [LONG].FILE.DATA, it becomes TH^IS.ISA[LONG].FILE.DATA.

2. Characters that are not permissible in MS-DOS style names are replaced with an underscore (_).

The file name TH^IS.ISA[LONG].FILE.DATA becomes TH_IS.ISA_LONG_.FILE.DATA.

3. All periods except the last are removed.

The file name TH_IS.ISA_LONG_.FILE.DATA becomes TH_ISISA_LONG_FILE.DATA.

4. The name is truncated usually to the first six remaining characters, and ~n is appended. For the first short name that results, the value of n is 1. If more short names that use the same first six characters are created, the value of n is incremented to maintain uniqueness. If n is 10 to 99, only the first five characters of the file name are used; if n is 100 to 999, only the first four characters are used; and so on.

The file name TH_ISISA_LONG_FILE.DATA becomes TH_ISI~1.DATA.

5. The extension, which is the characters following the last period (if any), is truncated to the first three characters.

The file name TH_ISI~1.DATA becomes TH_ISI~1.DAT.

6. After the value of n reaches 4, future conversions maintain uniqueness by taking the first two characters of the long file name plus a four-letter hash string based on the long file name:

First six characters = First two characters of LFN + Four characters of hash string

Because the hash string usually turns out differently each time, the value of n remains at 5, unless it needs to maintain uniqueness in the file name.

To verify the rule given in step 6, conduct the following experiment on the NTFS:

1. Create a temp file called x with a few characters in a newly created temporary directory. You want to do this in a temporary directory so that you can delete the contents more easily after this experiment.

2. From the NT command prompt, execute the following COPY statements:

```
copy x THIS IS A LONG FILE 1"
copy x THIS IS A LONG FILE 2"
copy x THIS IS A LONG FILE 3"
copy x THIS IS A LONG FILE 4"
copy x THIS IS A LONG FILE 5"
copy x THIS IS A LONG FILE 6"
copy x THIS IS A LONG FILE 7"
copy x THIS IS A LONG FILE 8"
copy x THIS IS A LONG FILE 9"
```

3. Issue the DIR /X command to see the LFN and the SFN names. You should see a listing similar to this:

```
> DIR /X

Volume in drive C has no label.
Volume Serial Number is D0BD-BDC1
Directory of C:\users\default\test
06/13/95  05:43p       <DIR>                            .
06/13/95  05:43p       <DIR>                            ..
06/13/95  05:42p              14 THISIS~1     THIS IS A LONG FILE NAME 1
06/13/95  05:42p              14 THISIS~2     THIS IS A LONG FILE NAME 2
06/13/95  05:42p              14 THISIS~3     THIS IS A LONG FILE NAME 3
06/13/95  05:42p              14 THISIS~4     THIS IS A LONG FILE NAME 4
06/13/95  05:42p              14 TH0983~5     THIS IS A LONG FILE NAME 5
06/13/95  05:42p              14 TH1983~5     THIS IS A LONG FILE NAME 6
06/13/95  05:42p              14 TH2983~5     THIS IS A LONG FILE NAME 7
06/13/95  05:42p              14 TH3983~5     THIS IS A LONG FILE NAME 8
06/13/95  05:42p              14 TH4983~5     THIS IS A LONG FILE NAME 9
06/13/95  05:42p              14              x
     ...
```

4. Notice that after n becomes 4, the value remains at 5, because the four-character hash string makes the name unique.

5. Delete the temp directory that you created for this experiment.

You also can see the long file names and short file names by using the Explorer. You can reference the file by either its short file name or its long file name. For example, if you delete the file by using the short file name, the file is deleted, the same as if you had deleted it by using its long file name.

Long File Name Support under FAT

Windows NT has created extensions to the DOS FAT file system that allow for the creation of long file names on a FAT volume. When you create the long file name, a short file name is automatically generated for compatibility with MS-DOS clients. The short file name is generated by using the algorithm described in the preceding section.

When a long file name is created on FAT, its name must be accommodated in the existing directory structure. This is done by taking up one additional FAT directory entry for every 13 characters in the long file name. A 24-character file name takes up three directory entries—two directory entries for the long file name, plus one directory entry for the short file name. Similarly, a 38-character file name takes up four directory entries—three directory entries for the long file name, plus one directory entry for the short file name.

Each long-file-name entry on a FAT volume has the following attributes:

- **Volume.** This is a special attribute that is normally used to designate the entry as a volume name, rather than a file or directory. This attribute is always set for a long file name.

- **Read-only.** This attribute enables the file to be only read and not written to.

- **System.** This attribute indicates that the file is a system file.

- **Hidden.** If this attribute is set, the file does not show up in normal directory listings.

Normal MS-DOS files cannot have all four attributes. Files that have Read-only, System, Hidden attributes cannot have the Volume attribute. Likewise, files that have the Volume attribute cannot have the Read-only, System, Hidden attributes. The special combination of all four attributes is used by Windows NT to treat the directory entry as belonging to a long file name. This special attribute combination is not understood, however, by most MS-DOS disk utilities. If these utilities are run on a FAT volume that uses long file names, they generate error messages. The worst-case situation would be if these utilities attempted to correct the illegal use of all four attributes by removing the Volume attribute. This action would destroy the long-file-name entries. Microsoft's SCANDISK, DEFRAG, and CHKDSK do not harm these long-file-name entries. (Did you ever wonder how the developers of these tools had inside knowledge to be compatible with long-file-name support for FAT?)

Because the FAT root directory entry usually has a 512-entry limit, use of long file names can quickly use up the limited directory entries. By default, long-file-name support is enabled on FAT volumes. If you want to preserve true DOS compatibility, and avoid the risk of a user running third-party diagnostic tools that might destroy the long-file-name entries, you can disable the long-file-name support for FAT partitions by changing the appropriate entry in the Registry (see Chapter 10, "Managing Windows NT Registry").

Copying Long-File-Name Files

The Windows NT XCOPY and COPY commands use long file names when copying files. If a long file name is copied from an NTFS volume to a FAT volume that has long-file-name support turned off via the Registry (see fig. 9.2), the following error message is displayed:

```
The file name, directory name, or volume label syntax is incorrect.
```

If you must copy a long file name from an NTFS volume to a FAT volume that has long-file-name support turned off, use the /N switch to specify that the copy command should use the short file name when making the copy (see fig. 9.3).

Note that although COPY and XCOPY have the same names as their DOS counterparts, these are NT commands. The syntaxes for these commands are shown next.

Figure 9.2

Copying from NTFS to FAT with long file name support turned off.

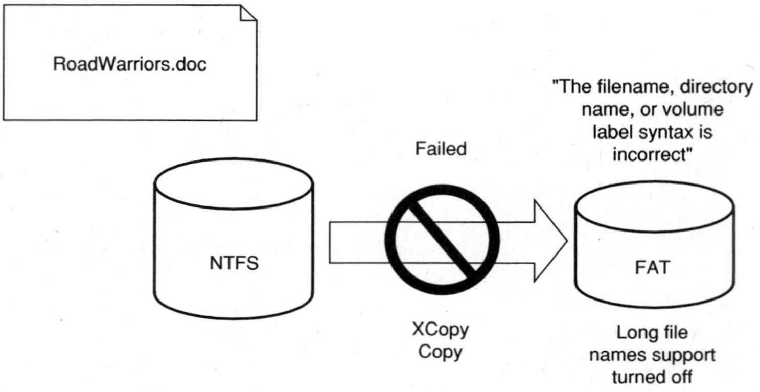

Figure 9.3

Use of /N switch in copying files.

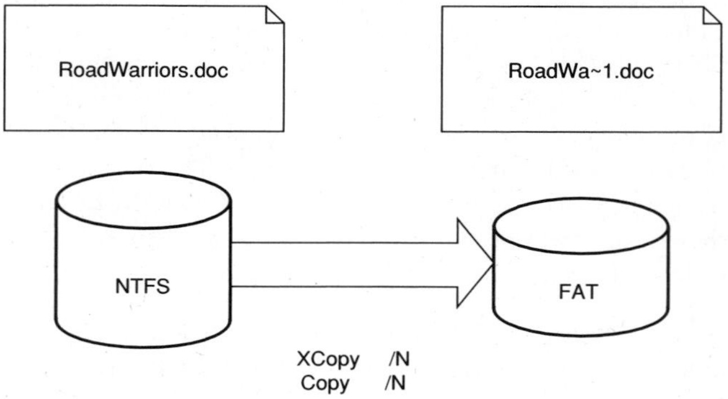

To copy one or more files to another location, use the following syntax:

```
COPY [/A ¦ /B] source [/A ¦ /B] [+ source [/A ¦ /B] [+ ...]] [destination [/A ¦ /
B]] [/V] [/N]
```

source specifies the file or files to be copied.

/A indicates an ASCII text file.

/B indicates a binary file.

destination specifies the directory and/or file name for the new files.

/V verifies that new files are written correctly.

/N uses short file name, if available, when copying a file with a non-8.3 name.

To append files, specify a single file for *destination* but multiple files for *source* (using wildcards or the *file1+file2+file3* format).

To copy files and directory trees, use the following syntax:

```
XCOPY source [destination] [/A ¦ /M] [/D[:date]] [/P] [/S [/E]] [/V] [/W]
                          [/C] [/I] [/Q] [/F] [/L] [/H] [/R] [/T] [/U]
                          [/K] [/N] [/Z]
```

source specifies the files to copy.

destination specifies the location or name of new files, or both.

/A copies files with the archive attribute set; doesn't change the attribute.

/M copies files with the archive attribute set, and turns off the archive attribute.

/D:date copies files changed on or after the specified date. If no date is given, copies only those files whose source time is newer than the destination time.

/P prompts you before creating each destination file.

/S copies directories and subdirectories except empty ones.

/E copies directories and subdirectories, including empty ones. Same as /S /E. Can be used to modify /T.

/V verifies each new file.

/W prompts you to press a key before copying.

/C continues copying even if errors occur.

/I if destination does not exist and more than one file is being copied, assumes that the destination must be a directory.

/Q does not display file names while copying.

/F displays full source and destination file names while copying.

/L displays files that would be copied.

/H copies hidden and system files also.

/R overwrites read-only files.

/T creates directory structure but does not copy files. Does not include empty directories or subdirectories. /T /E includes empty directories and subdirectories.

/U updates the files that already exist in the destination.

/K copies attributes. Normal Xcopy will reset read-only attributes.

/N copies using the generated short names.

/Z copies networked files in restartable mode.

Understanding Case-Sensitivity in File Names

Because Windows NT supports the POSIX subsystem, and POSIX requires case-sensitive file names, NTFS supports case-sensitive file names. This means that in NTFS, you can create file names that are the same name except in the case of the letters.

The MS-DOS, WIN16, OS/2, and WIN32 subsystems do not support case-sensitive names, which means that they cannot distinguish between file names that are different only in case.

Consider a POSIX application that creates the following file names in the same directory:

MyFile.Txt   MYFILE.TXT   myfile.txt

NTFS allows the creation of these files in the same directory for the POSIX application. When these files are accessed by using the Explorer or NT commands, however, the file names will create problems. For example, if you try to copy these files to another directory with the following command, all three files are copied on top of each other:

```
COPY MyFile.Txt
```

The target file has the contents of the last file copied.

If you use Windows NT Notepad, all three files are displayed in the Open Files dialog box, but regardless of which file you select, the file with all lowercase letters, myfile.txt, is opened. In the title bar, the all-uppercase version, MYFILE.TXT, is displayed.

Understanding File Objects in Windows NT

Internally, Windows NT treats all system resources, including files, as *objects*. Object creation and deletion are handled through the Object Manager executive component. This component, which is part of the Windows NT kernel, is responsible for managing object naming, object creation, and object deletion.

Figure 9.4 shows an example of creation of a file and the different NT components that are involved in the implementation of this operation. When an application issues a call to the Windows NT system services to create a file, that call is transferred to the I/O Manager component of the system executive. The I/O manager implements the file system by using a layered hierarchy of drivers. The I/O manager issues a request for creating the file-system object to the Object Manager.

All requests for services to the Object Manager are intercepted by the Security Reference Monitor kernel module. The Security Reference Monitor authenticates the create file request based on the user's Security Access Token (SAT) and the Access Control List (permissions list) of the directory in which the file is to be created. The user's Security Access Token contains the security ID (SID) of the user and the Security IDs of all groups the user is a member of. The Access Control List for a directory contains a list of users and group SIDs, and the operations (create, delete, and so on) they can perform.

File-System Security and Object Manager

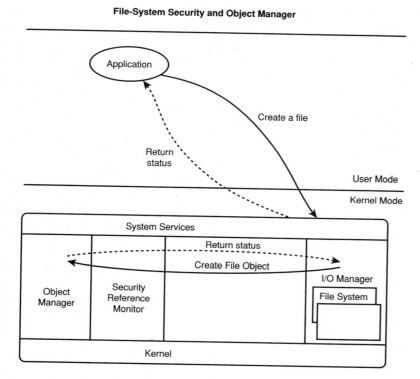

Figure 9.4

File-system security and the Object Manager.

If the Security Reference Monitor denies the create file object request, the request never reaches the Object Manager; instead, the Security Reference Monitor informs the requesting I/O Manager that permission for the requested operation was denied. If the create file object request is validated by the Security Reference Monitor, it is forwarded to the Object Manager. The Object Manager creates the file and sends a status code, representing the success or failure of the operation to the I/O Manager.

Notice that the Object Manager and Security Reference Monitor are central to the management of all objects in Windows NT. This approach has the advantage that all requests on objects are authenticated by a central facility—the Security Reference Monitor. Use of a central facility makes it easier to ensure security within the operating system.

File Objects

The use of objects is central to the design of Windows NT. An object is a way of modeling physical concepts and physical entities. Operating-system resources such as files, processes, memory, communication ports, and printer devices are treated uniformly. The uniform representation enables all objects to be protected the same way—in the case of Windows NT, by the use of the Security Reference Monitor. Objects also provide a convenient paradigm for the operating system to track its resources as objects.

A file object represents the concept of file as whole in manner that enables actions to be performed on the file without full knowledge of the file implementation details. Figure 9.5 shows a file object that lists the actions that can be performed on it, such as create, open, and close. These operations can be performed without knowing such implementation details as the file structure and the security control representation on the file object.

Figure 9.5

A file object.

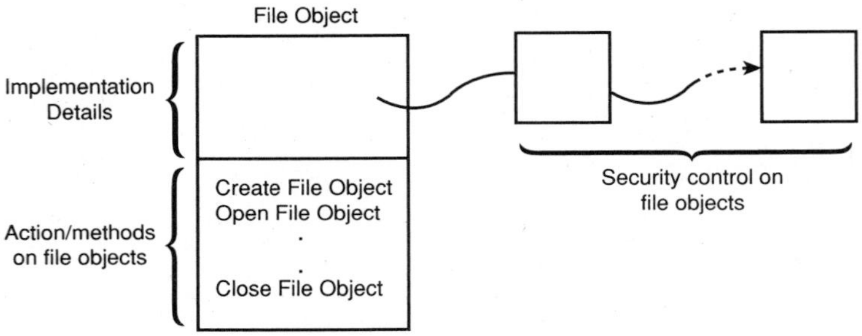

Object Names and Object Domains

All objects in the Windows NT operating system have an internal name. These objects could be files, processes, semaphores, or events. To keep track of the wide variety of objects in Windows NT, a naming scheme was devised to distinguish one object from another. The Windows NT objects are organized in an object name hierarchy (see fig. 9.6).

The object directories shown in figure 9.10 should not be confused with file-system directories. The naming scheme used for the object names is global to a single computer, and it closely matches the hierarchical file naming used by MS-DOS and POSIX file systems.

In the object naming scheme, the *root* is represented as an MS-DOS style backslash (\). Intermediate nodes that represent object directories can contain other objects or object directories. The *leaf nodes* represent individual objects. A complete object name consists of a backslash (\) followed by any object directories, separated by a backslash, down to the leaf node name.

For example, Event1 would be named by using a hierarchical naming scheme that begins with the root (\) and lists the object directories and finally the event object:

\ObjectDirectory3\ObjectDirectory4\Event1

The path of a file name such as C:\Apps\Spread\123.exe is actually under an object directory. Figure 9.7 shows that the hard disk resource is represented by the object name of\Device\ HardDisk0. The object name space provides an umbrella under which self-contained sets of objects called *object domains* exist. The object domains enable the object name space to be extended. The I/O Manager acts as a secondary object manager to the NT Executive Object Manager and is responsible for the object domain consisting of disk files and directories.

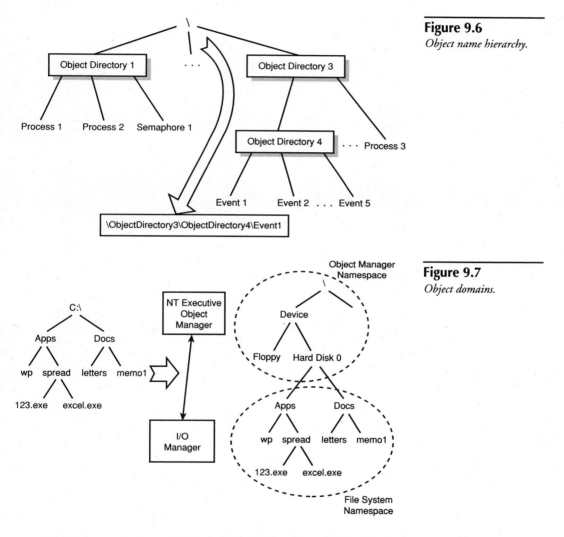

Figure 9.6
Object name hierarchy.

Figure 9.7
Object domains.

The object name space of \Device\HardDisk0 is handled by the object manager, but the naming of the contents of the hard disk—the file-system name space—is handled by the I/O manager.

Symbolic Links and Drive Letters

Windows NT uses drive letters such as A:, B:, and C: to represent hard disks and partition resources. These objects are actually implemented by symbolic links to the physical device to which the drive letter refers. A special type of object called the symbolic link object is implemented by the NT Object Manager to refer to an object by another name. The alternative name is called a *symbolic link* or an *alias*. Figure 9.8 shows examples of symbolic link objects in a POSIX directory file system. The symbolic links cl and ingres are alias names to the directories \MoreApps\vendor\ms and \MoreApps\vendor\tools\clink.

Figure 9.8

Example of symbolic links.

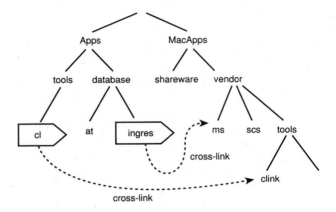

The symbolic link objects in the object manager space are similar in concept to the POSIX-style symbolic links. Figure 9.9 shows that the drive letter C: is under \Devices and is a symbolic link to \Device\HardDisk0. When Windows NT utilities refer to a file name such as C:\Spread\123.exe, the Object Manager replaces the drive letter with its actual value of \Device\HardDisk0. This translation is shown here:

C:\Spread\123.exe ———> \Device\HardDisk0\Spread\123.exe

If the drive letter refers to network drives such as F: and G:, these too are symbolic links. The difference is that the file names are handled by the network client software, also called the *network redirector*.

Figure 9.9

Internal resolution of file names.

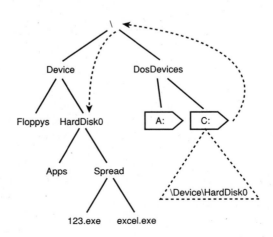

Using Share Names on a Windows NT Network

In the Windows NT architecture, resources that are available for sharing on an NT computer are given a name called a *share name*. A share name is a 12-character name assigned to the shared resource. Figure 9.10 shows that the resource C:\VENDOR\PROBS on Windows NT computer NTS1 is given a share name of Vprob, and the resource D:\DATA on Windows NT computer NTS2 is given a share name of DATA. The share names are independent of the names of the resources that are shared. In Figure 9.10, the share name Vprob is different from the name of the directory PROBS that is shared, and the share name DATA is the same as the name of the directory DATA being shared.

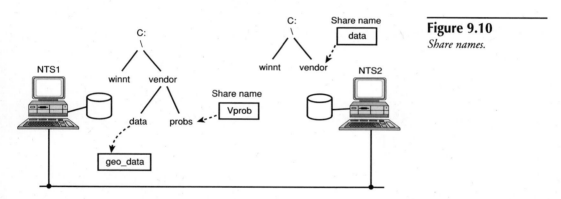

Figure 9.10

Share names.

A shared directory on a Windows NT Workstation can be shared simultaneously by no more than 10 users. No such limits are in place for shared resources on a Windows NT Server, except the legal license limits.

The same resource can have different share names. This feature is particularly useful if you want a different set of permissions to be placed on each separate share name for different classes of users. Figure 9.11 shows that two share names are assigned to the directory C:\TEST. The share name RTEST has Read permission to the directory only, whereas the share name WTEST has both Read and Write permissions. You will learn more about file permissions in this chapter.

The share name must be unique to a computer. Two computers can have the same share name, because the share name is used in conjunction with the computer name, which must be unique on a Windows NT network.

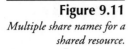

Figure 9.11

Multiple share names for a shared resource.

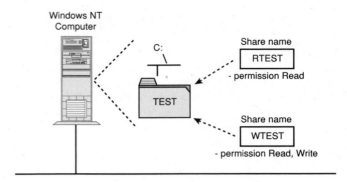

Creating and Deleting a Share Name

Share names are created by using either of the following methods:

- The NET SHARE command

- The Explorer

Using the NET SHARE Command to Create and Delete Share Names

The NET SHARE command makes a server's resources available to network users. At the time of sharing a resource, the share name is specified. The NET SHARE command has the following syntax:

```
NET SHARE sharename
         sharename=drive:path [/USERS:number ¦ /UNLIMITED]
                             [/REMARK:"text"]
         sharename [/USERS:number ¦ /UNLIMITED]
                   [/REMARK:"text"]
         {sharename ¦ devicename ¦ drive:path} /DELETE
```

sharename is the network name of the shared resource. Type NET SHARE with a share name only to display information about that share.

drive:path specifies the absolute path of the directory to be shared.

/USERS:number sets the maximum number of users who can simultaneously access the shared resource.

/UNLIMITED specifies that an unlimited number of users can simultaneously access the shared resource.

/REMARK:"text" adds a descriptive comment about the resource. Enclose the text in quotation marks.

devicename is one or more printers (LPT1: through LPT9:) shared by *sharename*.

/DELETE stops sharing the resource.

For example, if you want to share a directory named C:\PUBS\NTSPR on a Windows NT computer, and create a share name for it called NTSPR, you can use the following command:

```
NET SHARE NTSPR = C:\NTSPR
```

To delete the share name from the computer, you can delete it by using this command:

```
NET SHARE NTSPR /DELETE
```

You should ensure that no one else is using the share name before deleting it.

If you use NET SHARE without the share name and any options, information about all resources being shared on the computer is listed. Following is an example of output from this NET SHARE command:

```
> NET SHARE
Share name    Resource                        Remark
- - - - - - - - - - - - - - - - - - - - - - - - - - - - - - - - - - - - - - -
ADMIN$        C:\WINNT                        Remote Admin
C$            C:\                             Default share
IPC$                                          Remote IPC
HJPRO         C:\HJPRO                        Hijaak Pro
NETLOGON      C:\WINNT\SYSTEM32\REPL\IMP...   Logon server share
NTSPR         C:\PUBS\NTSPR
TEMP          C:\TEMP
The command completed successfully.
```

Notice that for each share name, Windows NT reports the device name or path name and a descriptive comment associated with it.

Using the Explorer to Create and Delete Share Names

You can use the Explorer to create and delete share names. The procedure for creating a share name is described here:

1. Start the Explorer by right-clicking on Start.

2. Highlight a directory you want to share.

3. Right-click and select the Sharing tab.

Figure 9.12

The Explorer toolbar.

If this is the first time you are sharing a directory, you see what's shown in figure 9.13. If a share for this directory already exists, you see what's shown in figure 9.14. The fields in the share dialog boxes are described in table 9.1.

Figure 9.13

The New Share dialog box.

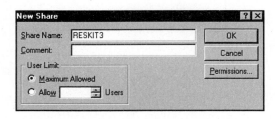

Figure 9.14

The Sharing tab.

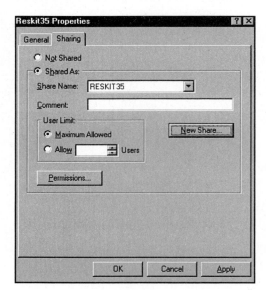

Table 9.1
Share Options

Option	Description
Share Name	The name that describes the shared resource on the network. After a share name is assigned, you cannot change its name directly—you can delete the share name and create a new name. A directory also can have multiple share names, each with different property settings. Names ending with a $ are administrative shares used by the Administrator user, and their listing is suppressed when commands and tools are being used to view share names on a computer.

Option	Description
Comment	Descriptive text that appears when you view the shared resource.
User Limit	A value used to control the number of simultaneous user sessions. You can select the **M**aximum Allowed or else Allo**w** a specific number of users. The limit is 10 for workstations and there is virtually no limit for the Windows NT Server. The real limit is determined by the legal licenses you have to the Windows NT Server. The actual hard limit is 4,294,967,294.
Permissions button	A button used to set the permissions on the directory.
New Share button	A button that appears only if the selected directory is already shared. You can use this to assign a new share name.

4. Make appropriate changes, and select OK. If a share name already exists for the directory, you must select the **N**ew Share button and assign the new share name. You will see the symbol of a hand under the share directory as a visual cue that the directory is shared.

To delete a share name, perform the following steps:

1. Start the Explorer.

2. Highlight a directory to be shared.

3. Right-click and select the Sharing tab.

4. Enable the N**o**t Shared radio button

Viewing Share Names

How does one find out which share names are in use on a specific computer? This question is of practical importance because you need to know the share name of a resource to use it. You can view the share names by using either of the following methods:

■ The NET VIEW command

■ The Network Neighborhood

Using the NET VIEW Command to Look Up Share Names

The NET VIEW command displays a list of resources being shared on a specific computer. The NET VIEW command has the following syntax:

```
NET VIEW [\\computername ¦ /DOMAIN[:domainname]]
```

```
NET VIEW /NETWORK:NW [\\computername]
```

computername is a computer whose shared resources you want to view.

/DOMAIN:*domainname* specifies the domain for which you want to view the available computers. If *domainname* is omitted, displays all domains in the local area network.

/NETWORK:NW displays all available servers on a NetWare network. If a *computername* is specified, the resources available on that computer in the NetWare network are displayed.

Following are some examples uses of the NET VIEW command:

```
> NET VIEW \\NTUS
Shared resources at \\NTUS
Share name   Type          Used as   Comment
- - - - - - - - - - - - - - - - - - - - - - - - - - - - - - - - - - - - - - - - - - - - - -
HJPRO        Disk                    Hijaak Pro
NETLOGON     Disk                    Logon server share
NTSPR        Disk          F:
TEMP         Disk
The command completed successfully.
```

The display lists the share name, the type of resources and whether the resource is being used as a device name (drive F: in the preceding display output) on the local computer, and a description of the shared resource (if available).

When NET VIEW is used without options, the display lists the computers in the current domain or network, as shown next:

```
> NET VIEW
Server Name          Remark
- - - - - - - - - - - - - - - - - - - - - - - - - - - - - - - - - - - - - - - - - - - - - -
\\NTSA
\\NTSB
The command completed successfully.
```

The preceding command shows that the computers NTSA and NTSB are in the current domain.

To see a list of domain names on the network, use the /DOMAIN option without specifying the domain name:

```
> NET VIEW /DOMAIN
Domain
- - - - - - - - - - - - - - - - - - - - - - - - - - - - - - - - - - - - - - - - - - - - - -
DOMAIN_A
KINETD
The command completed successfully.
```

The preceding command shows that the domains DOMAIN_A and KINETD are on the network.

To see a list of NetWare servers on the network, use the /NETWORK:NW option:

```
> NET VIEW /NETWORK:NW
Resources on NetWare Network
- - - - - - - - - - - - - - - - - - - - - - - - - - - - - - - - - - - - - - - - - - - - - - - - - - - - - - - - - - -
\\NW4KS
\\POSEID
\\S386
\\SCSRV
The command completed successfully.
```

The preceding command shows that the NetWare servers NW4KS, POSEID, S386, and SCSRV are on the network. For this command to work, you must install a NetWare client or Gateway Service for NetWare (for Windows NT Servers) on the NT computer that is used to execute the preceding command.

To see a list of shared resources on a specific NetWare server on the network, use the NetWare server name with the /NETWORK:NW option:

```
> NET VIEW \\NW4KS /NETWORK:NW
Shared resources at \\nw4ks
- - - - - - - - - - - - - - - - - - - - - - - - - - - - - - - - - - - - - - - - - - - - - - - - - - - - - - - - - - -
Print        \\NW4KS\Q_MAC
Print        \\NW4KS\QLINK1
Disk         \\NW4KS\SYS
Disk         \\NW4KS\VOL1
The command completed successfully.
```

The preceding command shows that the NetWare server NW4KS is sharing two network printer queues (\\NW4KS\Q_MAC and \\NW4KS\QLINK1) and two disk resources (\\NW4KS\SYS and \\NW4KS\VOL1). The disk resources are the NetWare volume names on the server. For this command to work, you must install a NetWare client or Gateway Services for NetWare (for Windows NT Servers) on the NT computer that is used to execute the preceding command.

Using the Network Neighborhood to Look Up Share Names

The Network Neighborhood is available through the Explorer and can be used to look up share names on the computer.

To view network shares, perform the following steps:

1. Start the Explorer.

2. Click on Network Neighborhood, Entire Network, Microsoft Windows Network.

3. Select the Domain and then double-click on the computer you want view shares from. Figure 9.15 shows the share names for computer M020ras1. The names Corpacct and Coslannt are Windows NT domain names.

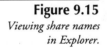

Figure 9.15

Viewing share names in Explorer.

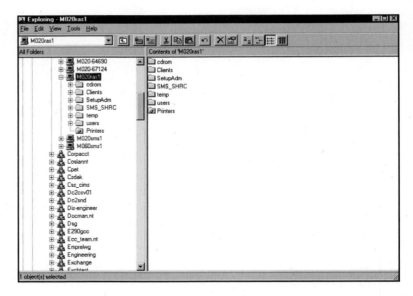

Using Share Names

After you determine the share name of a resource you want to use, you need to set up your local computer to access the shared resource. In Windows NT, you can use the share names by using any of the following methods:

- The NET USE command

- Direct use of UNC names

- The Explorer

Using the NET USE Command to Use Share Names

The NET USE command uses the Uniform Naming Convention (UNC) to access shared resources. The UNC is a computer name that has the format shown in figure 9.16. The UNC name begins with a special delimiter, \\, which indicates the start of the UNC name. This is followed by the computer name, which is an attribute of all Windows NT Workstations and Servers, and which is set during installation. The computer name is followed by the \ delimiter and the share name. If subdirectories are to be referenced under the shared directory, these are listed next.

Figure 9.17 shows the NET USE command that is used to access a shared resource. The NET USE command uses the network redirector on the NT computer to establish a connection to use the shared resource. The network redirector enables an unused drive, such as drive E: in figure 9.17, to be assigned for accessing a shared resource. The details of the network redirector mechanism are shown in figure 9.18. This figure shows that the network redirector mechanism is actually part of the I/O Manager module in Windows NT.

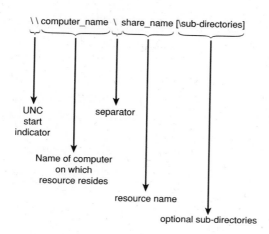

Figure 9.16

Uniform Naming Convention.

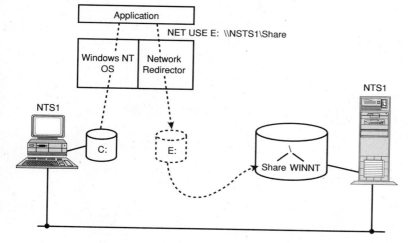

Figure 9.17

Operation of the NET USE command.

The Transport Driver Interface (TDI) is used on both computers to communicate with the transport protocols that are implemented by the network transport drivers. The different types of protocols can be installed and configured by using the networks icon in the Control Panel.

For the NET USE mechanism to work, the requesting computer must be running the Workstation service, and the computer sharing resources must be running the Server service (see fig. 9.18). Despite their names, these services run on every Windows NT computer—workstations and servers—because every Windows NT computer can act as a server and a workstation in a peer-to-peer network. Normally, the Workstation and Server services are started automatically, but if during the computer boot process NTDETECT.COM detects that the computer is not connected to the network, the Workstation and Server services will not be started. You must manually start these services by highlighting them and selecting the Start button (see fig. 9.19).

Figure 9.18

The Network Redirector Mechanism.

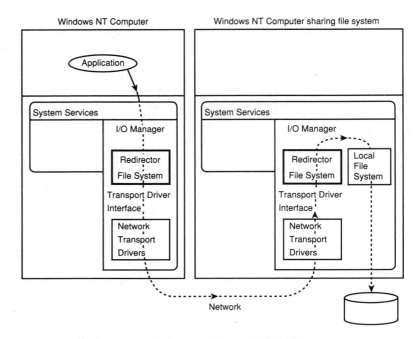

Figure 9.19

Services running on a Windows NT computer.

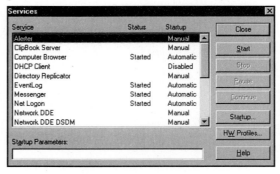

Following is the syntax for the NET USE command:

```
NET USE [devicename ¦ *] [\\computername\sharename[\volume] [password ¦ *]]
        [/USER:[domainname\]username]
        [[/DELETE] ¦ [/PERSISTENT:{YES ¦ NO}]]
NET USE [[devicename ¦ *] [password ¦ *]] [/HOME]
NET USE [/PERSISTENT:{YES ¦ NO}]
```

NET USE connects a computer to a shared resource or disconnects a computer from a shared resource. When used without options, it lists the computer's connections.

devicename assigns a name to connect to the resource or specifies the device to be disconnected. There are two kinds of device names: disk drives (D: through Z:) and printers (LPT1: through LPT3:). Type an asterisk rather than a specific device name to assign the next available device name.

\\computername is the name of the computer controlling the shared resource. If the computer name contains blank characters, enclose the double backslash (\\) and the computer name in quotation marks (""). The computer name can be from 1 to 15 characters long.

\sharename is the network name of the shared resource.

\volume specifies a NetWare volume on the server. You must have Client Services for NetWare (Windows NT Workstations) or Gateway Service for NetWare (Windows NT Server) installed and running to connect to NetWare servers.

password is the password needed to access the shared resource.

* produces a prompt for the password. The password is not displayed when you enter it at the password prompt.

/USER specifies that the connection is made with a different user name.

domainname specifies another domain. If *domainname* is omitted, the current logged-on domain is used.

username specifies the user name with which to log on.

/HOME connects a user to his home directory.

/DELETE cancels a network connection and removes the connection from the list of persistent connections.

/PERSISTENT controls the use of persistent network connections. The default is the setting used last.

YES saves connections as they are made, and restores them at next logon.

NO does not save the connection being made or subsequent connections; existing connections will be restored at next logon. Use the /DELETE switch to remove persistent connections.

Some examples of using the NET USE commands are shown next.

To assign drive letter Z: to the share name KALPA on server NTKS, use the following command:

```
NET USE Z: \\NTKS\KALPA
```

Notice that the \\NTKS\KALPA is the UNC for the share name KALPA.

To delete the preceding network drive assignment, use the following command:

```
NET USE Z: /D
```

To see a list of current devices used for redirection, use the NET USE command without any options:

```
> NET USE
New connections will be remembered.
Status          Local    Remote                    Network
-------------------------------------------------------------------------
                E:       \\NW4KS\SYS               NetWare Network
Disconnected F:          \\NTSA\i386               Microsoft Windows Network
OK              G:       \\NTSB\RESKIT35           Microsoft Windows Network
The command completed successfully.
```

In the preceding command, the message New connections will be remembered indicates that persistent connection was used last, and this will be used by default in subsequent NET USE commands. The Status column indicates the current status of the redirected device. A blank entry means that the status could not be determined. The Remote column shows the UNC for the shared resource. The Network column indicates the type of network in use.

Using UNC Names Directly to Use Shared Directories

The NET USE command assigns a driver letter or local device name that is set aside for using the share resource. This technique works on both DOS and Windows NT. If you are using a Windows NT Workstation, you can access a shared resource directly by using the UNC names, as shown in the following examples.

To see a directory listing under the share name KALPA on the NTKS computer, use the following command:

```
DIR \\NTKS\KALPA
```

To copy the file \\NTSA\I386\NTDETECT.COM to a local directory, use the following command:

```
COPY \\NTSA\I386\NTDETECT.COM
```

Following is an example that copies a file from the NTSA computer to the NTSB computer:

```
COPY \\NTSA\KALPA\MOON.DAT \\NTSB\DEVELOP\KALPA\SATELLITE.DAT
```

Using Explorer to Use Shared Directories

The Explorer can be used to connect network drives to share names on a computer on the network.

To use the Explorer for assigning network drives, perform the following steps:

1. Start the Explorer.

2. Select the Domain and Computer that contains the share that you want to map.

3. You can double-click on the computer names to look up the share names for that computer (see fig. 9.20). Right-click on the share that you want to map (see fig. 9.22)

   Alternatively, select the connect network drive icon from the toolbar. The different icons for the Explorer toolbar are identified in figure 9.12.

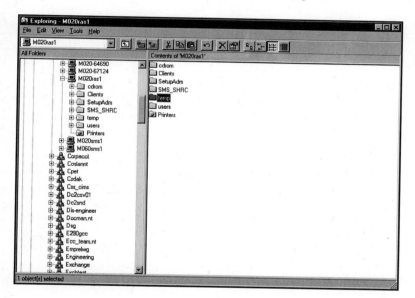

Figure 9.20

Assigning network drives in Explorer.

4. Choose **M**ap Network Drive. Figure 9.21 shows the Map Network Drive dialog box. In the **D**rive field, select a network drive you want to use for the shared directory. The next available drive is displayed by default.

   In the **P**ath field, you can type the UNC name of the shared resource.

   If you want to use your current logon user name and password to access the remote shared directory, leave the field **C**onnect As blank. If you want to log on as another user name, type the name in the **C**onnect As field; you also will be prompted for the password. If the remote computer can't authenticate your connection, but the Guest account on the remote computer is enabled (assuming its password isn't set), you are logged on as Guest.

Figure 9.21

The Map Network Drive dialog box.

Figure 9.22

Selecting the share name.

Enable the check box for **R**econnect at Logon if you want persistent connections. Persistent connections are those that are restored when you log on; they are saved in the user's profile.

5. Choose OK to establish the connection.

   You should notice a new drive icon in the Explorer.

To use the Explorer to disconnect a network drive, perform the following steps:

1. Start the Explorer.

2. Right-click on the share you want to disconnect, then select Disconnect.

   Alternatively, select the disconnect network drive icon from the toolbar. The different icons for the Explorer toolbar are identified in figure 9.12.

   You should see the Disconnect Network Drive dialog box (see fig. 9.23). Highlight the drives to disconnect, and choose OK.

Figure 9.23

The Disconnect Network Drive dialog box.

Implementing File-System Security Using File Permissions

When a directory is shared, by default, excessive permissions are assigned to the shared directory. For example, anyone accessing the shared directory from the network has full access to the directory. Although this approach simplifies peer-to-peer networking in the sense that no advanced knowledge is required to set up a share that any network user can access, it creates potential security hazards in large and more security-conscious organizations. To implement the security policies of your organization, you might need to restrict the default permissions assigned to shared resources or local files within a Windows NT computer.

Implementing an effective security policy using file permissions requires knowledge of the ways in which Windows NT implements file-system security. These concepts are covered next.

Understanding the Data Structures Used to Implement File Permissions

As discussed earlier, resources are represented in Windows NT by objects that are typically assigned names. All named objects in Windows NT can be secured. Typically, file-system security is implemented by Discretionary Access Control (DACL) mechanisms. Fundamental to DACL is the notion of ownership of resources. Windows NT resources, such as files, have an *owner*. The owner is a user or group that can gain complete control of the resource. DACL enables owners of a resource to specify who can access a resource and the extent of operations that can be performed.

The owners and users or groups that are assigned permissions to an object are identified by their Security Identifiers (SIDs). Security Identifiers were first discussed in Chapter 5, "Designing Windows NT Server Domains," and are discussed in greater detail in this section. The extent of operations that can be performed is specified through Access Control Lists (ACLs), also called *permissions lists*.

Understanding the Security Descriptor

The security information for an object is encoded in a special data structure called the Security Descriptor (SD). Figure 9.24 symbolically represents the Security Descriptor for a file object.

From this figure you can notice that the Security Descriptor for an object contains the following components:

■ **Owner Security Id.** This is the SID of the owner. The owner of an object can be a user or group. The owner of an object can gain complete control of an object and assign permissions to the object.

■ **Group Security Id.** This is a primary group associated with the object. It is optional. It is not used by Windows NT file-system security. The group security ID is included to simplify the implementation of a POSIX-compliant file system on top of NTFS. It can also be used for organizational purposes.

■ **Discretionary Access Control List.** This is the DACL for an object. It identifies the users and group SIDs that are to be granted or denied access for the object.

■ **System ACL.** This is what controls the auditing message that the system will generate.

Figure 9.24

Security Descriptor for a file object.

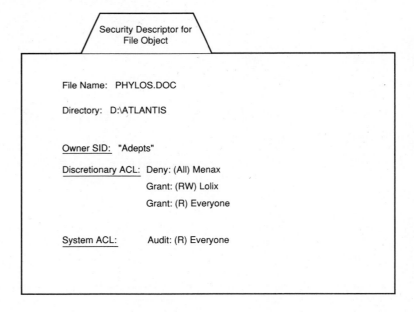

The Security Descriptor for an object is represented by Windows NT using two methods: the *absolute* method and the *self-referential* method.

In the absolute method (see fig. 9.25), the Security Descriptor components are pointers to the actual components that contain the information. This method enables each component to be allocated separately. This is a more flexible method of representation of the Security Descriptor in the Windows NT computer memory.

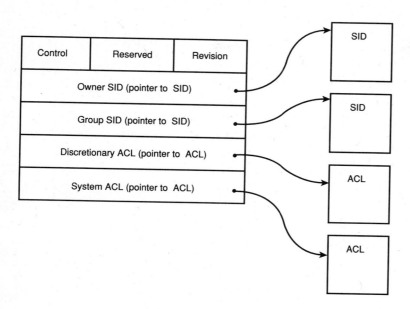

Figure 9.25

Absolute method of representing Security Descriptors.

In the self-referential or relative method (see fig. 9.26), the Security Descriptor components are contained in the body of the Security Descriptor data structure. The Security Descriptor is allocated as a contiguous block. The components are accessed by using offsets from the beginning of the data structure rather than using pointers. This relative method is suited for storing the Security Descriptor on secondary media—for example, when security information for a file is being backed up on tape. This is also a preferable method during transmittal of Security Descriptors outside the boundary of a Windows NT computer's memory, where absolute pointers to other blocks of memory would become invalid.

Understanding Security Identifiers (SIDs)

Security Identifiers are used to uniquely identify a user or group. SID values are created by using a hashing algorithm based on three 32-bit numbers generated from the following information:

- The computer name

- The system time on the computer

- The user-mode execution time of the current thread used to create the SID

This algorithm guarantees for all practical purposes that the SID is a statistically unique number and SID values will never be reused on a network. The SID value is represented using the following format:

$S\text{-}1\text{-}X\text{-}Y1\text{-}Y2\text{-}...Yn$

Figure 9.26

Relative method of representing Security Descriptors.

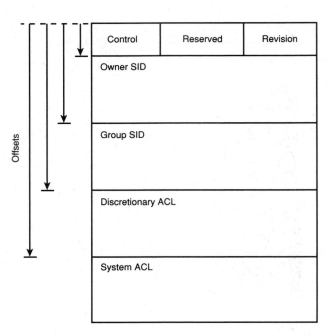

The S-1 indicates that this is a revision 1 SID. A revision 2 SID will therefore have a prefix of S-2. The *X* is a number representing the identifier authority. The *Y1-Y2-...Yn* represents the subauthority values. The authority and subauthority values are assigned by the internal components of Windows NT that need to manage the object. Figure 9.27 shows a graphical representation of a SID.

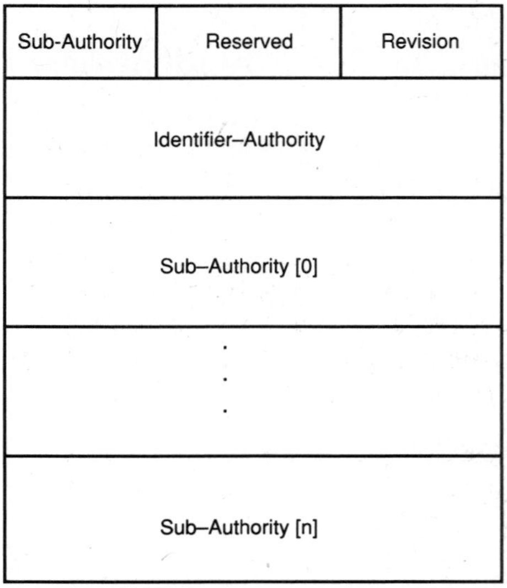

Figure 9.27

The SID data structure.

Sub-Authority	Reserved	Revision
Identifier–Authority		
Sub–Authority [0]		
. . .		
Sub–Authority [n]		

Certain SIDs, such as the Administrator user SID, are preset to well-known values across all Windows NT systems. Users with well-known SIDs cannot be deleted, thus ensuring that their SID values are the same across all systems.

Understanding Access Control Lists

An Access Control List is a list of users and groups with their individual permissions. Each user or group is represented as a separate entry in the ACL and is called the Access Control Element (ACE). All objects that are protected by Windows NT security have ACLs. Figure 9.28 shows a graphical representation of the ACL. The ACL is shown to have an array of ACE elements. The ACL Size field describes the size of the ACL structure. This field is needed because each ACE data structure is of variable length. The ACE Count field contains the number of ACE elements. The ACL is pointed to by Discretionary Access Control List and System Access Control List components within the Security Descriptor.

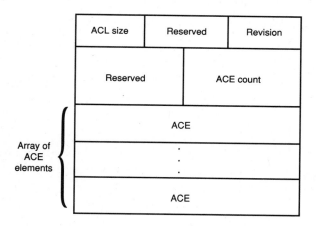

Figure 9.28
The ACL data structure.

Access Control Elements

The ACL consists of a list of Access Control Elements. Each ACE specifies the access or auditing permissions for that object—represented by the Security Descriptor—to a user or group. Three types of ACE are defined:

- **AccessAllowed.** This type is used for Discretionary Access Control to represent the permissions that are explicitly granted for that object to a user or group. Users and groups are represented by their SID values.

- **AccessDenied.** This type is used for Discretionary Access Control to represent the permissions that are explicitly denied for that object to a user of group. Users and groups are represented by their SID values.

- **SystemAudit.** This type is used for System Security to keep a log of security events such as recording who accesses which files. It is also used to generate and log audit security messages. Users and groups are represented by their SID values.

An important distinction needs to be made between a DACL that is empty and a DACL that is not assigned (see fig. 9.29). An empty DACL means that no access permissions are deliberately given to that object, and all users are denied permissions. The owner of the object still has the ability to change the DACL and give explicit permissions. A DACL that is not assigned means that no protection is assigned for that object, so any access request to that object is granted.

Figure 9.29

Empty DACL versus Unassigned DACL.

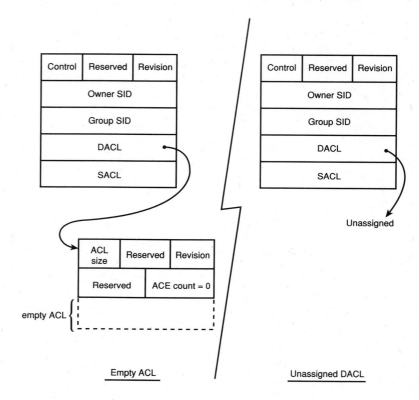

A graphical representation of the data structure for an ACE is shown in figure 9.30. The ACE Size is the size of the overall ACE structure. The ACE Flags are the actual permissions. The ACE Type values are the AccessAllowed, AccessDenied, or SystemAudit values described earlier in this section. The SID value is for the user or group that is to be denied access, and is variable in length. The Access Mask is described in the next section.

Figure 9.30

ACE data structure.

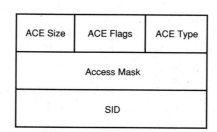

Understanding Access Masks

Each ACE has an Access Mask (refer to figure 9.30) that defines all possible actions for a particular object type. The actual permissions that are assigned are selected from the possible permissions described in the Access Mask. The list of possible permissions depends on the type of object. The different possible permissions can be categorized into three groups:

- Specific types

- Standard types

- Generic types

Specific types contain the Access Mask information that is specific to the object associated with the mask. Whenever an object type is defined, its specific type must be defined as well. Each object type can have up to 16 specific types. Windows NT files have the following specific access types:

- **FILE_READ_DATA.** Implies permission to read data for the file.

- **FILE_WRITE_DATA.** Implies permission to write data for the file.

- **FILE_APPEND_DATA.** Implies permission to append data to a file.

- **FILE_READ_EA.** Implies permission to read extended-attribute information.

- **FILE_WRITE_EA.** Implies permission to write extended-attribute information.

- **FILE_EXECUTE.** Implies execute permissions for a file.

- **FILE_READ_ATTRIBUTES.** Implies permission to read the standard attributes of a file.

- **FILE_WRITE_ATTRIBUTES.** Implies permission to write to the standard attributes of a file.

Unlike specific types, *standard types* apply to all objects. Standard types imply the following actions:

- **SYNCHRONIZE.** This is used to synchronize access and enable a process to wait for an object in the signaled state.

- **WRITE_OWNER.** This is used to grant or deny write access to the Owner SID for an object.

- **WRITE_DACL.** This is used to grant or deny write access to the DACL of an object.

- **READ_CONTROL.** This is used to grant or deny read access to the Security Descriptor for an object. If read access has been granted to the SD for an object, it is called the STANDARD_RIGHTS_READ. If write access has been granted to the SD for an object, it is called the STANDARD_RIGHTS_WRITE.

■ **DELETE.** This is used to grant or deny delete access to the object.

The last type, *generic types*, is created by mapping from specific types and standard type to a generic type. Files have the following generic types defined:

■ FILE_GENERIC_READ

■ FILE_GENRIC_WRITE

■ FILE_GENERIC_EXECUTE

These generic types are listed in the Windows NT Explorer as the special permissions Read (R), Write (W), and Execute (X). Table 9.2 shows the mappings from the file-specific and standard types to the file-generic types.

Table 9.2
File Generic Type Mappings

Generic Type	Mapped From
FILE_GENERIC_READ	STANDARD_RIGHTS_READ
	FILE_READ_DATA
	FILE_READ_ATTRIBUTES
	FILE_READ_EA
	SYNCHRONIZE
FILE_GENERIC_WRITE	STANDARD_RIGHTS_WRITE
	FILE_WRITE_DATA
	FILE_WRITE_ATTRIBUTES
	FILE_WRITE_EA
	FILE_APPEND_DATA
	SYNCHRONIZE
FILE_GENERIC_EXECUTE	STANDARD_RIGHTS_EXECUTE
	FILE_READ_ATTRIBUTES
	FILE_EXECUTE
	SYNCHRONIZE

Specific and standard types appear in the security log, which can be seen by using the Event Viewer tool. Generic types are not shown in the security log; instead, their corresponding specific and standard types are listed.

Standard and Special Permissions for Files and Directories

You can set security for local access to files and directories on an NTFS volume, but you cannot set security for local access to a FAT volume. Security settings are usually implemented by using the Windows NT Explorer. If you attempt to set security for local access to a FAT, you will not be able to because the security setting options will be disabled.

The only way in which you can set security for files or directories on a FAT volume is if these are used as shared directories and have been assigned a share name. In other words, you can set permissions on a share name, regardless of whether the file resource is on a FAT or NTFS volume.

Windows NT provides two ways of assigning file and directory permissions:

- Special permissions

- Standard permissions

Special Permissions

The special permissions were used by the predecessors of the Windows NT Server, such as the LAN Manager for OS/2. They are used when you need finer levels of control in assigning permissions. The special permissions (also called individual permissions) and the symbols used to describe them are shown here:

- R—special permission read

- W—special permission write

- X—special permission execute

- D—special permission delete

- P—special change permission

- O—special take-ownership permission

Special permissions behave differently for files and directories. This is to be expected because files and directories are different types of objects. Tables 9.3 and 9.4 show the special permissions and their associated actions on files and directories.

Table 9.3
Special Permissions for Files

Operation	R	W	X	D	P	O
Display the file's owner and permissions	X	X	X			
Display the file's data	X					
Display the file's attributes	X		X			
Change the file's attributes		X				
Change data and append data to a file	X	X				
Run the file if it is a program			X			
Delete the file				X		
Change the file's permission					X	
Take ownership of the file						X

Table 9.4
Special Permissions for Directories

Operation	R	W	X	D	P	O
Display file names in directories	X					
Display the directory's attributes	X		X			
Add files and subdirectories		X				
Change the directory's attributes		X				
Go to the directory's subdirectories			X			

Operation	R	W	X	D	P	O
Display directory's owner and permissions	X	X	X			
Delete the directory				X		
Change the directory's permission					X	
Take ownership of the directory						X

Standard Permissions

Although it is possible to use the special permissions for controlling access to files and directories, a simpler way is to use the standard permissions. Standard permissions are called standard because they are the standard or normal way in which permissions are assigned in Windows NT. Standard permissions are predefined combinations of special permissions. The rationale for doing this is that there are some combinations of special permissions you almost always want to assign for operations such as read or write.

Some of the standard permissions for files are different from those for directories. The following standard permissions have been assigned for files. The special permissions used to implement the standard permissions are shown next to the file standard permission:

- **Read (RX)**—Users can read the file and run it if it is an application.

- **Change (RWXD)**—Users can read, modify, or delete the file.

- **Full Control (RWXDPO)**—Users can read, modify, delete, set permissions for, and take ownership of a file.

- **No Access ()**—Users cannot access the file, even if the user is a member of a group that has been granted access.

For directories, the standard permissions are also defined. As before, the special permissions used to implement the standard directory permissions are shown next to the standard permissions. Two sets of special permissions are shown in the following format:

(directory permissions)(inherited permissions for files in directory)

The first set of permissions is for the directory itself, and the second set is for files that are in the directory (but not for files in subdirectories). For example, a directory permission described as (RWX)(RX) means that the (RWX) permissions are for the directory, and the (RX) permissions are for files in the directory.

The following standard permissions are defined for directories:

- ■ **List (RX)(Not Specified)**—Users can list only the files and subdirectories that are within this directory. Additionally, users who have this permission can change to the directory. Users cannot, however, access any new files in this directory that were created after the permission was set.

- ■ **Read (RX)(RX)**—Users can read the contents of files in this directory and run applications in the directory.

- ■ **Add (WX) (Not specified)**—Users can add files to the directory, but cannot read the contents of the files or change them.

- ■ **Add & Read (RWX)(RX)**—Users can add files to the directory and read files in the directory, but cannot change them.

- ■ **Change (RWXD)(RWXD)**—Users can add files, read files, and change the contents of the file in the directory.

- ■ **Full Control (RWXDPO)(RWXDPO)**—Users can add files, read and change files, change permissions for the directory, and take ownership of the directory and its files.

- ■ **No Access ()()**—Users cannot access the directory or files in the directory, even if the user is a member of a group that has been granted access.

A word of caution in understanding Windows NT directory permissions inheritance is warranted here. *Directory permissions inheritance* means that the directory permissions can be applied to files and subdirectories in the directory by the selection of appropriate options such as replacing permissions on existing files or subdirectories. Another form of inheritance is the fact that newly created files in a directory have the permissions set as indicated by the directory's file permission settings (the second group of parentheses). The inherited permissions actually replace the permission settings on files and subdirectories—they are not *calculated* inherited permissions, as is true in other network operating systems such as NetWare.

Table 9.5 and 9.6 describe the operations that can be performed with the standard permissions for files and directories.

Table 9.5
Standard Permissions for Files

Operation	No Access	Read	Change	Full Control
Display the file's owner and permissions		X	X	X
Display the file's data		X	X	X
Display the file's attributes	X	X	X	

Operation	No Access	Read	Change	Full Control
Change the file's attributes			X	X
Change data and append data to a file			X	X
Run the file if it is a program		X	X	X
Delete the file			X	X
Change the file's permission				X
Take ownership of the file				X

Table 9.6
Standard Permissions for Directories

Operation	No Access	List	Read	Add	Add & Read	Change	Full Control
Display file names in directories		X	X		X	X	X
Display the directory's attributes	X	X	X	X	X	X	
Go to the directory's sub-directories	X	X	X	X	X	X	
Change the directory's attributes				X	X	X	X
Add files and subdirectories				X	X	X	X
Display directory owner and permissions	X	X	X	X	X	X	X
Delete the directory						X	X
Change the directory's permission					X		X
Take ownership of the directory							X

When you set permissions for a directory, there is an implied permission for the files in the directory. The permissions for files in a directory are described in table 9.7.

Table 9.7
Standard Permissions for Files in Directories

Operation	No Access	List	Read	Add	Add & Read	Change	Full Control
Display the file's owner and permissions						X	X
Display the file's data			X		X	X	X
View filenames and subdirectory names	X	X			X	X	X
Display the file's attributes						X	X
Run the file if it is a program			X		X	X	X
Change the file's attributes						X	X
Add files and subdirectories				X	X	X	X
Change data and append data to a file						X	X
Delete the file						X	X
Change the file's permission							X
Take ownership of the file							X

Working with File Permissions

You should keep in mind the following points when working with file and directory permissions:

■ You can prevent a user from accessing a permission by simply not granting permission to that user. This means that you do not have to assign the No Access permission to every user or group that should not have access to a file or directory.

■ Permissions are cumulative. This means that if the user Bob is granted Read standard permission to the C:\APPS directory (see fig. 9.31), and the group World of which Bob is a member is granted Change standard permission to the same directory, the cumulative permissions for Bob are as shown here:

Read + Change = Change

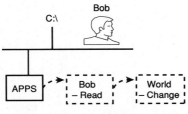

Figure 9.31
Example of cumulative permissions.

The exception to cumulative permissions is No Access permission. No Access permission to a file or directory overrides other permissions to the file or directory. In figure 9.32, Bob has No Access standard permission to C:\DATA. Even though Bob is a member of the World group that has Change standard permission, Bob has no access to the directory. In this example, the following statement is true:

No Access + Change = No Access

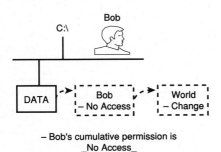

Figure 9.32
The No Access permission.

The No Access permission can be useful in making a special exception for a member of a group. Suppose that in the example shown in figure 9.32, all members of the group World are to be given Change permission to C:\APPS, and then it becomes necessary temporarily to deny Bob access to C:\APPS. If you remove Bob from the World group, that might deny Bob permissions to other resources that list the group World in the permissions list (DACL). A better way is to assign to Bob the No Access standard permission to C:\APPS, as shown in figure 9.32. This denies Bob access to C:\APPS while granting him access to other resources through the group World.

■ By default, new files and subdirectories inherit permissions from the parent directory in which they are created. Consider the situation in figure 9.33. Initially, the directory C:\PROJ has a permission list that includes the following:

C:\PROJ

Mary : Read permission

Dei : Change permission

Figure 9.33

Example of initial permission to a directory.

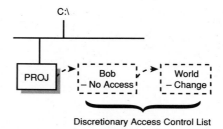

In figure 9.34, a new subdirectory and a new file are created. The new subdirectory and file inherit the permissions list for the parent directory C:\PROJ. The DACL of the new directory and file is shown here:

C:\PROJ\NewDir

Mary : Read permission

Dei : Change permission

C:\PROJ\NewFile

Mary : Read permission

Dei : Change permission

Figure 9.34

Inheritance of permissions for new directories.

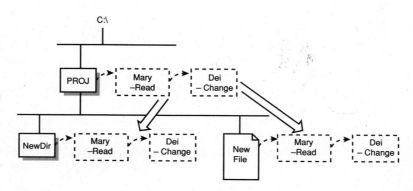

- When you use Explorer to change the permissions for an existing directory, you can select the following options:

  - Replace permissions on subdirectories

  - Replace permissions on existing files

The default is to *not* replace permissions on existing subdirectories, but to replace permissions on existing files in directories.

If you do not want the default behavior of setting permissions on older files and directories, enable or disable these options accordingly.

Figures 9.35 and 9.36 show the default behavior for changing permissions on a directory. In figure 9.35, the directory C:\EXP and its contents all have a permission list in which user John is assigned the Change standard permission. The permission for C:\EXP is changed by adding user Rick and giving this user the Full Control standard permission to C:\EXP. Figure 9.36 shows that if you select the default options, the permission on the old subdirectory is not changed, but the permission on the file OldFile is changed to the new permission settings for the directory.

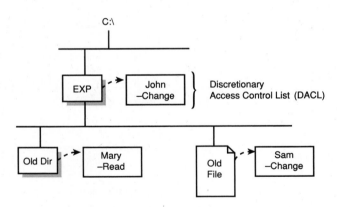

Figure 9.35

Example of initial permission to a directory.

- The user who creates a file or directory becomes the owner of the file or directory. The owner can always control access to a file by changing permission settings on the file.

Granting Permissions

Permissions to directories and groups can be granted on a user or group basis. The following users and groups can be used on the Windows NT Server for assigning file and directory permissions:

- Domain users in the domain containing the server

- Domain users in a trusted domain

■ Local groups in the domain containing the server

■ Global groups in the domain containing the server

■ Global groups in a trusted domain

■ Special identities: Everyone, INTERACTIVE, NETWORK, SYSTEM, and CREATOR OWNER

Permissions can be granted to built-in users and groups as well as any new users and groups you create.

Figure 9.36

Default permission changes to existing files and subdirectories.

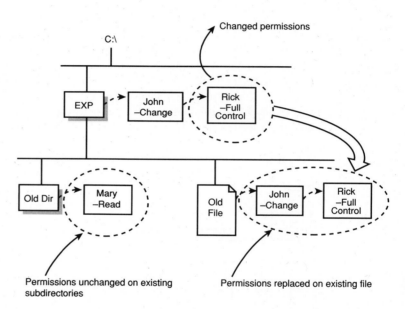

The implicit group Everyone includes all current and future users who are interactively logged on to the Windows NT computer or logged on to the computer from across the network. The group Everyone includes the groups INTERACTIVE and NETWORK:

> Everyone = INTERACTIVE + NETWORK

The implicit group INTERACTIVE includes all current and future users who are interactively logged on to the Windows NT computer. It does not include users who are logged on from the network.

The implicit group NETWORK includes all current and future users who are logged on to the Windows NT computer from the network. It does not include users who are logged on interactively.

The identity SYSTEM represents the Windows NT operating system running on the local computer. SYSTEM is automatically granted permissions to some system directories when Windows NT is installed. You should not change the SYSTEM privileges; otherwise, some system services will not work. Normally, you will not need to grant SYSTEM permissions to files and directories, unless a system service needs special access permissions.

Whereas all the entities, users, and groups considered so far can be granted permissions to files and directories, the CREATOR OWNER can be granted permissions to a directory only. A CREATOR OWNER represents users who subsequently create files and directories in the current directory. If you give to a CREATOR OWNER permissions to a directory, any users who subsequently create a file or directory will inherit these permissions.

Consider the example in figure 9.37, which shows that the directory D:\EXP has the following permissions list:

D:\EXP

CREATOR OWNER: Change (RWXD)(RWXD)

The user Phylos creates a file called D:\EXP\TESTP.DAT, and the user Amzimee creates a file called D:\EXP\TESTA.DAT. Each of these users is given the (RWXD) permissions to the individual files they create. They do not, however, have access to each other's files.

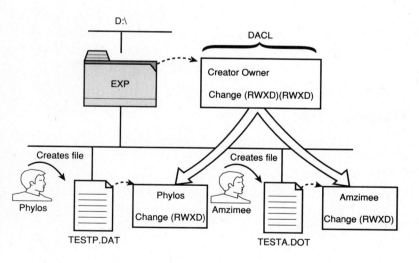

Figure 9.37

Example 1: CREATOR OWNER permissions.

Consider what would happen if the D:\EXP had the following permissions:

D:\EXP

CREATOR OWNER: Change (RWXD)(RWXD)

Everyone:Read (RX)(RX)

If the same new files as in the example shown previously are created by users Zalim and Anzimee, these new files inherit permissions from the directory. Figure 9.38 shows the permissions list for the newly created files. The users Phylos and Amzimee can change their individual files. In addition, they can read each other's files because Everyone has Read (RX) permission to the files.

Figure 9.38

Example 2: CREATOR OWNER permissions.

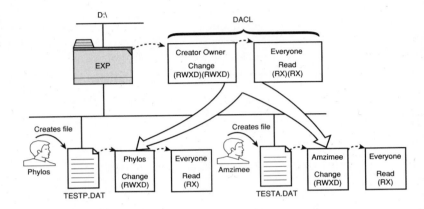

Setting Directory and File Permissions

The previous sections have given you a sufficient background to understand the ways in which directory and file permissions are set. This section explains the procedure for setting directory permissions on directories and files. The preferred method of setting permissions on directories and files is to use the Explorer. A later section shows a command-line method of setting permissions.

Setting Permissions on a Directory

Following is an outline of the procedure for setting directory permissions:

1. Log on as an Administrator user.

2. Start the Explorer.

3. Highlight the directory for which permissions are to be set.

4. Right-click, then choose Properties and select the Security tab. Click on the Permissions button.

   Alternatively, select the Properties icon from the toolbar.

5. You should see the Directory Permissions dialog box (see fig. 9.39).

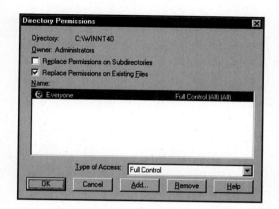

Figure 9.39

The Directory Permissions dialog box.

The Directory field displays the directory for which permissions are listed. You cannot change this field from the Directory Permissions dialog box. You must select the directory from the Explorer before activating the Directory Permissions dialog box.

The Owner field displays the user of group that is the owner of a directory. You cannot change this field from the Directory Permissions dialog box. You can change the owner by clicking on the Owners button under the Properties menu.

The Replace Permissions on Subdirectories check box enables you to specify whether the permissions listed in the Name box should be applied to all subdirectories. This option includes the entire directory tree under the selected directory. By default, this option is not set. If you set this option, you are prompted to confirm whether you want to set the permissions for all subdirectories.

The Replace Permissions on Existing Files check box enables you to specify whether the permissions listed in the Name list box should be applied to all existing files in the subdirectory. By default, this option is set, which means that the permission set for the directory is also set for files in the directory. If this is not the desired effect, you should clear this option.

The Name list box displays the current users and groups that are assigned permissions to the directory, and the type of permissions that are assigned. The Names list in figure 9.46 includes the default names and permissions that are set for a newly created directory. Notice that the group Everyone has Change (RWXD)(RWXD) permissions. This default permission is quite excessive because any user logged on from the network has Change standard permissions to the directory. As a practical matter, you should monitor closely the permissions set for newly created directories and adjust them according to your security policy. Note that, by default, the CREATOR OWNER has Full Control (All)(All) permissions to a newly created directory. This permission automatically assigns to users the Full Control to directories and files they create within a new directory. See the preceding section for a discussion on CREATOR OWNER.

The **T**ype of Access box lists the permissions that can be set for a selected user or group in the Names box. You use this list box to change the permissions for a selected user or group. You can select the following values from this list box:

- No Access

- List

- Add

- Add & Read

- Change

- Full Control

- Special Directory Access

- Special File Access

All except for the last two values are standard permissions for a directory. The Special Directory Access option enables you to select the individual permissions. Figure 9.40 shows the Special Directory Access screen when this option is selected. Note that you can select Full Control (All) permissions or any combination of the special permissions (R, W, X, D, P, and O). After you make your selections, choose OK to save your changes.

Figure 9.40

The Special Directory Access options.

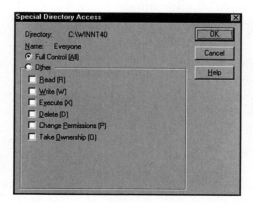

The Special File Access is used to control the inherited permissions that apply for files in the directory. These permissions will be applied to the directory's files only if the Replace Permissions on Existing **F**iles option is set. Special file permissions for a directory appear in the second set of parentheses in the **N**ame box. Figure 9.41 shows the special file permissions dialog box when the Special File Access option is selected. Note that your choices are Access Not **S**pecified, Full Control (**A**ll), or any combination of the special permissions (R, W, X, D, P, and O). If you select Access Not **S**pecified, there will be no inheritance of permissions to the files in the directory. After you make your selections, choose OK to save your changes.

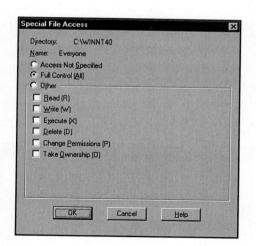

Figure 9.41

The Special File Access dialog box.

If you select special permissions for a directory, they are listed as special permissions (see fig. 9.42) in the **N**ame box. In figure 9.42, the local domain group Administrators is assigned the Special Access (RW)(All).

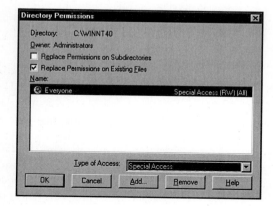

Figure 9.42

Assignment of special directory permissions.

Choose OK in the Directory Permissions dialog box to save any changes you have made (refer to figure 9.39).

6. To remove a user or group from the **N**ame list box in figure 9.39, select their names, and then click on the **R**emove button.

7. To add another name to the **N**ame box in figure 9.39, click on the **A**dd button. Figure 9.43 shows the Add Users and Groups dialog box that appears when you click on the **A**dd button.

The **N**ames list box displays the list of accounts in the current domain that can be assigned rights. The current domain is displayed in the **L**ist Names From drop-down list box. The domain name ITPNT in figure 9.43 has an asterisk symbol next to it. An asterisk next to a domain or computer name indicates that the local groups of that domain or computer can be listed. The absence of an asterisk means that the local group cannot be listed. Remember that local groups can contain local users, as well as domain users and global groups from the current domain and trusting domains. An examination of the **N**ames box in figure 9.43 shows that the groups Account Operators, Administrators, and Backup Operators are local groups for the selected domain.

Figure 9.43

The Add Users and Groups dialog box.

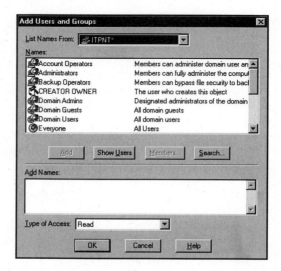

To list names from other domains, select the **L**ist Names From box, which displays a list that includes the local domain name, trusted domains, and computer names.

The **N**ames list shows the accounts of the selected domain or computer. If a domain is selected, the list of global groups for that domain are also listed. The initial display of accounts includes only group names. If you want to assign permissions to user accounts, you must select the Show **U**sers button, which also shows the user accounts in the domain that can be assigned permissions to the directory. Only group names are initially displayed to encourage you to think in terms of granting permissions to groups. You must perform an extra step to list user accounts that can be granted permissions.

You select the accounts to be granted permissions from the **N**ames list box. If you then select the **A**dd button, these account names are added to the A**d**d Names list. You also can list members of a group in the **N**ames list by selecting the **M**embers button. Figure 9.44 shows a listing of the members of the local group Administrators for the ITPNT domain obtained by using the **M**embers button. You can select any of the members of the group and select the Add button. The selected accounts are added to the A**d**d Names list.

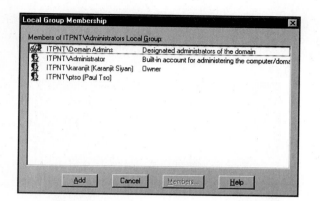

Figure 9.44

Listing group membership for permission assignment.

You can search for accounts in other domains by selecting the **S**earch button (see fig. 9.43). The Find Account dialog box in figure 9.45 can be used to locate a user account or group in a specific domain or all domains. The search results can then be added to the list of group members.

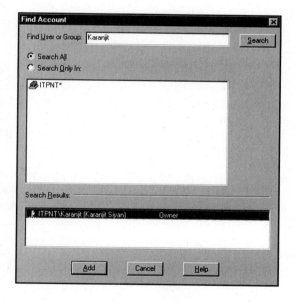

Figure 9.45

The Find Account dialog box.

8. After adding names to the A**dd** Names list, select the appropriate standard permission from the **T**ype of Access list. You can select only the standard permission at this point. If you want to select special permissions, you must modify the **T**ype of Access field in the Directory Permissions dialog box.

9. Choose OK to save your changes. Figure 9.46 shows the new accounts that are given permissions to the directory. In this example, the local groups Account Operators and

Backup Operators, and the domain user Karanjit, are given the standard Add and Read permissions to the directory. If you selected accounts that are in another domain, they are preceded with the name of the domain.

Figure 9.46

Newly added accounts that are given the Add & Read permissions.

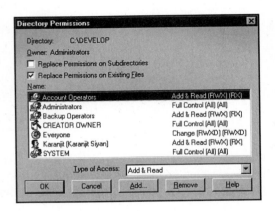

10. Choose OK in the Directory Permissions dialog box to save your changes.

Setting Permissions on Share Names

Permissions can be set on share names to control a network user's access to the shared directory. The share name can be a directory on the NTFS or FAT file system. Setting permissions on share names is the only way you can assign permissions for a FAT directory. By default, only the Administrators and Server Operators groups can change permissions on shares. On Windows NT Workstations and Windows NT Servers not acting as domain-controllers, the Power Users group can be used to change share permissions.

You can share directory resources with several share names and assign different permissions for each share. In figure 9.47, the shared directory D:\DEVELOP has two share names. The share name GRAPHDEV is assigned a permission list that consists of the group Developers that has the standard permission of Change (RWXD)(RWXD). The share name DOCS has a permission list that consists of the group Documentors that has the standard permission of Read (RX)(RX). This approach is useful if you want different groups of users to have different access permissions to the shared directory.

Permissions that are set for shared directories are effective only when the shared directory is accessed from a network and the shared permissions apply to all files and subdirectories within the shared directory. If you log on locally (interactively), the shared permissions do not apply to you—only the NTFS file and directory permissions are applicable. You must therefore ensure that the directory of file permissions can prevent local users undue permissions, or prevent local logon for these users. In the Windows NT Server, if the Account Type is set to a local account type, the users cannot log on locally and must log on from the network. For additional details on local account types, see Chapter 7, "Managing Windows NT Server Domain Accounts."

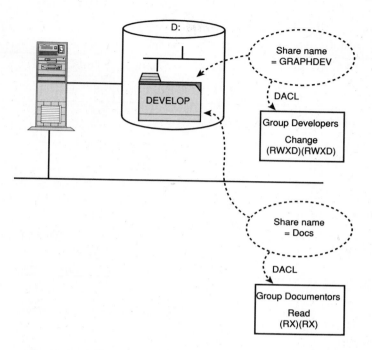

Figure 9.47
Multiple share names with different permissions.

The shared permissions operate in conjunction with the permissions set for the directory in an NTFS volume. The effective permissions are those that are more restrictive. If a user has Read permissions on the share name, and List permission to the directory, the user's access is restricted to List. That is, the user can perform a directory listing but cannot read the files in the directory.

Table 9.8 shows the permissions that can be granted to shared directories and the operations that users can perform for each permission.

Table 9.8
Share Permissions for Directories

Operation	No Access	Read	Change	Full Control
Display subdirectory names and file names		X	X	X
Display the data and attributes of a file		X	X	X
Run program files		X	X	X
Go to the directory's subdirectory		X	X	X

continues

Table 9.8, Continued
Share Permissions for Directories

Operation	No Access	Read	Change	Full Control
Create subdirectories and add files			X	X
Change data in files and append to files			X	X
Change file attributes			X	X
Delete subdirectories and files			X	X
Change permissions for NTFS files and directories				X
Take ownership of NTFS files and directories				X

Following is an outline of the procedure for setting directory permissions on share names:

1. Log on as an Administrator user.

2. Start the Explorer.

3. Highlight the shared directory for which permissions are to be set. If the directory already has been assigned a share name, you will see the symbol of a hand underneath the directory.

4. Right-click and choose Properties, then select the Share tab.

   Alternatively, select the Properties icon from the toolbar.

5. If this is a new share, you see the dialog box shown in figure 9.48. If a share name for the directory already exists, you should see the dialog box like in figure 9.49 which has a **New** Share button that you can use to create a new share name for the shared directory resource.

6. For the share name that is displayed, you can select the **P**ermissions button. You should see the Access Through Share Permissions dialog box (see fig. 9.50). The default permission is that group Everyone has the Full Control standard permission. This permission gives all users unrestricted access to the share name. If this is not what you want, you should change this permission.

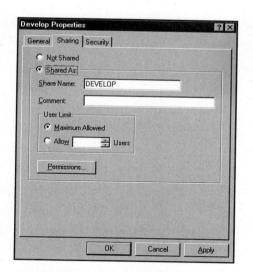

Figure 9.48
The Develop Properties Sharing tab.

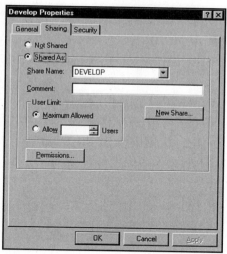

Figure 9.49
The Develop Properties Sharing tab when a share name for the directory already exists.

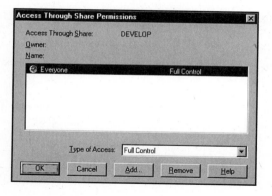

Figure 9.50
The Access Through Share Permissions dialog box.

The **N**ame box lists the accounts that have permissions to the share name. The **T**ype of Access field is used to change permissions. You can change the share permissions to any of the following types:

- No Access

- Read

- Change

- Full Control

7. To remove a name from the **N**ame box, highlight the name and choose the **R**emove button.

8. To add a name to the account box, choose the **A**dd button. Figure 9.51 shows the Add Users and Groups dialog box.

Figure 9.51

The Add Users and Groups dialog box for share names.

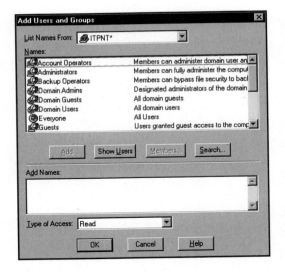

You select the accounts to be granted permissions from the **N**ames list box. If you then select the **A**dd button, these account names are added to the A**d**d Names list. You also can list members of a group in the **N**ames list by selecting the **M**embers button. You can select any of the members of the group and select the **A**dd button. The selected accounts are added to the A**d**d Names list.

You can search for accounts in other domains by selecting the **S**earch button. The Find Account dialog box is similar to that for assigning permissions to directories (refer to figure 9.45), and it can be used to locate a user account or group in a specific domain or all domains. The search results can then be added to the list of group members.

9. After adding names to the A**d**d Names list, select the appropriate standard permission from the **T**ype of Access list. You can select only the No Access, Read, Change, and Full Control standard permissions.

Select OK to save changes.

10. Select OK in the Access Through Share Permissions dialog box to assign the permissions.

Setting Permissions on a File

Following is an outline of the procedure for setting file permissions:

1. Log on as an Administrator user.

2. Start the Explorer.

3. Highlight the file for which permissions are to be set.

4. Right-click and select Properties. Then select the Security tab and the Permissions button.

   Alternatively, select the Properties icon from the toolbar.

5. You should see the File Permissions dialog box (see fig. 9.52).

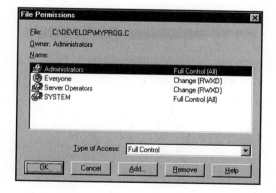

Figure 9.52

The File Permissions dialog box.

The **F**ile field displays the name of the file for which permissions are listed. You cannot change this field from the File Permissions dialog box. You must select the file from the Explorer before activating the File Permissions dialog box.

The **O**wner field displays the user or group that is the owner of the file. You cannot change this field from the File Permissions dialog box. You can change the owner by selecting the **O**wner option under the **S**ecurity menu.

The **N**ame list box displays the current users and groups that are assigned permissions to the directory, and the type of permissions that are assigned. For a newly created file, the file permissions are inherited from the directory's file permissions settings (the second group of parentheses).

The **T**ype of Access lists the permissions that can be set for a selected user or group in the **N**ame box. You use this list box to change the permissions for a selected user or group. You can choose the following values from this list box:

- No Access

- Read

- Change

- Full Control

- Special Access

All except for the last option are standard permissions for a file. The Special Access option enables you to select the individual permissions. Figure 9.53 shows the Special Access screen when this option is selected. Note that you can select Full Control (**A**ll) permissions or any combination of the special permissions (R, W, X, D, P, and O). After you make your selections, choose OK to save your changes.

Figure 9.53

The Special Access screen for setting file permissions.

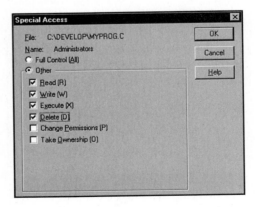

If you select special permissions for a file, they are listed as special permissions in the **N**ame list box (see fig. 9.54). In figure 9.54, the group Everyone is assigned the Special Access (RW).

Select OK on the screens to save any changes you have made.

6. To remove a user or group from the **N**ame box in figure 9.52, select their names and then choose the **R**emove button.

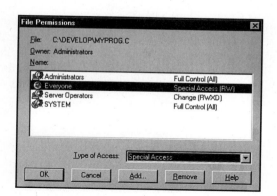

Figure 9.54
Assignment of special file permissions.

7. To add another name to the **N**ame box in figure 9.52, choose the **A**dd button. You see an Add Users and Groups dialog box similar to that for adding permissions to accounts for directories (see fig. 9.55). The only difference is that the **T**ype of Access field is restricted to the file permission settings of No Access, Read, Change, and Full Control.

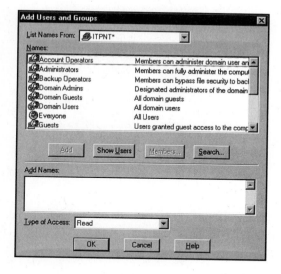

Figure 9.55
The Add Users and Groups dialog box for setting file permissions.

8. Choose OK on the screens to save your changes.

Permission Settings for Copying and Moving Files

When you copy a file, the target file that is created inherits the permission settings for the directory in which it is created. This is because copying a file involves creating a file in the target directory. The user who copies the file becomes the new owner of the copied file. If the user is a member of the Administrators group, the Administrators group becomes the owner. Thus, all administrators are able to manage the file. To move a file, you need permission to create the file in the target directory.

Figure 9.56 shows the permissions for the source file C:\TEST\file1.c to be copied to the target directory C:\DEVELOP. Figure 9.57 shows the directory permissions for the target directory. Figure 9.58 shows the permissions for the copied file C:\TEST\file1.c. Comparing these figures, you note that the copied file inherits the permission settings for the target directory C:\DEVELOP. In this case, the user who performed the copy was a member of the Administrators group, and therefore the owner of the copied file is also a member of Administrators.

Figure 9.56

Permission settings for the source file.

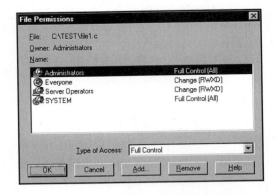

Figure 9.57

Permission settings for the target directory.

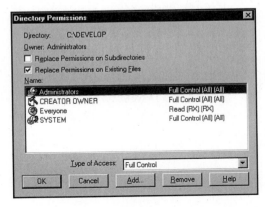

Figure 9.58

Permission settings for the copied file.

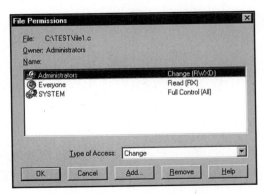

When you move a file to another directory, the original permissions for that file are preserved. To move a file, however, you need permission to create the file in the target directory, and permission to delete the field from the original directory. Figure 9.59 shows the permissions for the C:\TEXT\file1.c that was moved to the directory C:\DEVELOP. The permissions for this file and directory are the same as shown in figures 9.56 and 9.57. Notice that the file permissions of file1.c in the directory it was moved to are unchanged.

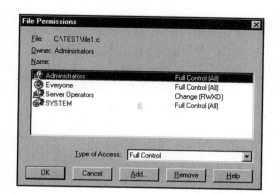

Figure 9.59

Permission settings for the moved file.

The Hidden File Delete Child Permissions

In Windows NT, the Full Control directory permission includes a hidden permission called the File Delete Child (FDC) permission. This permission allows users to delete a file in a directory regardless of the permission or attribute settings for the files. Thus, users with Full Control to a directory can delete files in that directory regardless of the permission attribute settings for the files.

The File Delete Child was created by the designers of Windows NT for POSIX compliance. The POSIX file system is based on the Unix file system. In Unix, a directory or file can have the read(r), write(w), and execute(x) permissions for the owner user, a primary group, and all others. In Unix, if a user has a write(w) permission to a directory, that user can delete files in that directory, because the write permission is treated as the permission to modify the directory entries for a file.

The Windows NT File Delete Child hidden permission was designed to implement the Unix write(w) permission for a directory. In Windows NT, only the standard Full Control directory permission has the File Delete Child permission; the Windows NT Write(W) permission does not have the File Delete Child permission.

File Attributes

Windows NT supports the following DOS attributes for files and directories:

- **Hidden.** The file is not visible in normal directory listings.

- **System.** Operating system files are flagged with this attribute.

- **Archive.** Files that have been modified and not backed up are flagged with this attribute, so backup utilities can back up files that have this attribute set.

- **Read only.** Files with this attribute cannot be deleted or modified.

From the preceding section, you know that the Full Control to a directory implies a File Delete Child permission.

Starting with Windows NT 3.51, a new attribute called the Compressed attribute has been added. Figure 9.60 shows the attributes for a file that can be set by using the Windows NT Explorer. To change a file's attributes, perform the following steps:

1. Highlight the file or directory from the Explorer.

2. Right-click and select the General tab.

3. Next, check or uncheck the boxes corresponding to the file attributes that you want to change.

Figure 9.60

File attributes.

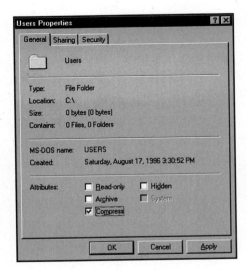

If you flag a file as being compressed by using the screen in figure 9.60, Windows NT immediately compresses the file. If you flag a directory as being compressed, Windows NT asks whether you want to compress all files in the directory. If you respond with a Yes, all files in the directory are compressed, and the compressed attribute is set for the directory and the files in the directory. If you respond with a No, the existing files in the directory are not compressed, but the directory's compressed attribute is set. Any files subsequently copied to a directory that has a compressed attribute set are immediately compressed.

When a program accesses a compressed file, Windows NT dynamically uncompresses the file's contents and returns these contents to the program. When the program closes the compressed file, the new contents of the file are compressed, as long as the file has the compressed attribute set.

Taking Ownership

The ownership permission(P) gives a user the capability to change the permission settings for a file or directory. The owner can even remove himself from the permissions list for a file or directory, in which case the owner cannot access the file or directory. The owner, however, always has the capability to change the permission settings for a file and gain access to the file or directory.

The Administrator user can take ownership of any file or directory. Ownership is always transferred by an explicit take-ownership operation. You cannot transfer ownership by *giving* it to another user or group; you can only take ownership. To take ownership, you must have one of the following items:

■ Full Access permissions

■ Special Access permissions that include the ownership(O).

■ Membership in the Administrators group

The act of taking ownership of a file or directory can be audited even for an Administrator user. This situation deters Administrator users from abusing their privileges.

To take ownership of a file or directory, you perform the following actions:

1. Highlight files or directories from the Explorer.

2. Right-click and select Properties. Click on the Security tab and click on the Ownership button.

   You see the Owner dialog box (see fig. 9.61). This dialog box shows the current owner. To take ownership, select the **T**ake Ownership button.

Figure 9.61

Owner dialog box.

3. If you are taking ownership of a directory that has files and subdirectories, you are given the option of taking ownership of these items also (see fig. 9.62).

Figure 9.62

Option of taking ownership of fields and subdirectories in the selected directory.

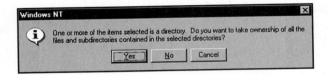

When taking ownership of files and directories in a domain-based network, you might occasionally have to wait for the ownership changes to be synchronized in the domain's security databases on all servers in the domain. During this synchronization period, you might not have access to the file or directory.

Default Permissions for the Windows NT Server

When you use the Explorer to examine the permissions for system directories, you will notice that certain permissions have already been set. This is because during Windows NT Server installation, default permissions are set on some system directories. Tables 9.9 through 9.15 show the default directory permission settings for the Windows NT Server users and groups. Notice that the Administrators have Full Control on almost all directories, except in the USERS directory, which typically contains the home directories for users. Also, by default, the SYSTEM entity, which is the Windows NT Authority, has Full Control to all directories.

Table 9.11 shows that Everyone has Change permissions to the root (\). This means that new directories and files created under the root inherit the Change directory permissions for group Everyone. This might be excessive permissions for group Everyone, and you should modify the default permissions accordingly.

Table 9.14 shows that the NETWORK users have No Access permissions to \SYSTEM32\ REPL\IMPORT. This prevents users logged on over the network from being able to see files in the import directory. Recall that the import directory can contain critical information such as logon scripts and profiles. Even though NETWORK has No Access permissions to \SYSTEM32\REPL\IMPORT, members of the Administrators and Server Operators groups, and interactive users in the Everyone group can access this directory due to the special way in which Windows NT sets up the initial permissions.

Table 9.9

Administrators Group: Default Directory Permissions on Windows NT Server

Directory	Permissions
\	Full Control
\SYSTEM32	Full Control
\SYSTEM32\CONFIG	Full Control
\SYSTEM32\DRIVERS	Full Control
\SYSTEM32\SPOOL	Full Control
\SYSTEM32\REPL	Full Control
\SYSTEM32\REPL\IMPORT	Full Control
\SYSTEM32\REPL\EXPORT	Full Control
\USERS	RWXD
\USERS\DEFAULT	RWX
\WIN32APP	Full Control
\TEMP	Full Control

Table 9.10

Server Operators Group: Default Directory Permissions on Windows NT Server

Directory	Permissions
\	Change
\SYSTEM32	Change
\SYSTEM32\CONFIG	None
\SYSTEM32\DRIVERS	Full Control
\SYSTEM32\SPOOL	Full Control
\SYSTEM32\REPL	Full Control
\SYSTEM32\REPL\IMPORT	Change

continues

Table 9.10, Continued

Server Operators Group: Default Directory Permissions on Windows NT Server

Directory	Permissions
\SYSTEM32\REPL\EXPORT	Change
\USERS	None
\USERS\DEFAULT	None
\WIN32APP	Full Control
\TEMP	Change

Table 9.11

Everyone Group: Default Directory Permissions on Windows NT Server

Directory	Permissions
\	Change
\SYSTEM32	Change
\SYSTEM32\CONFIG	List
\SYSTEM32\DRIVERS	Read
\SYSTEM32\SPOOL	Read
\SYSTEM32\REPL	Read
\SYSTEM32\REPL\IMPORT	Read
\SYSTEM32\REPL\EXPORT	None
\USERS	List
\USERS\DEFAULT	RWX
\WIN32APP	Read
\TEMP	Change

Table 9.12

CREATOR OWNER: Default Directory Permissions on Windows NT Server

Directory	Permissions
\	Full Control
\SYSTEM32	Full Control
\SYSTEM32\CONFIG	Full Control
\SYSTEM32\DRIVERS	Full Control
\SYSTEM32\SPOOL	Full Control
\SYSTEM32\REPL	Full Control
\SYSTEM32\REPL\IMPORT	Full Control
\SYSTEM32\REPL\EXPORT	Full Control
\USERS	None
\USERS\DEFAULT	Full Control
\WIN32APP	Full Control
\TEMP	Full Control

Table 9.13

Replicator: Default Directory Permissions on Windows NT Server

Directory	Permissions
\	None
\SYSTEM32	None
\SYSTEM32\CONFIG	None
\SYSTEM32\DRIVERS	None
\SYSTEM32\SPOOL	None
\SYSTEM32\REPL	None

continues

Table 9.13, Continued

Replicator: Default Directory Permissions on Windows NT Server

Directory	Permissions
\SYSTEM32\REPL\IMPORT	Change
\SYSTEM32\REPL\EXPORT	Read
\USERS	None
\USERS\DEFAULT	None
\WIN32APP	None
\TEMP	None

Table 9.14

NETWORK: Default Directory Permissions on Windows NT Server

Directory	Permissions
\	None
\SYSTEM32	None
\SYSTEM32\CONFIG	None
\SYSTEM32\DRIVERS	None
\SYSTEM32\SPOOL	None
\SYSTEM32\REPL	None
\SYSTEM32\REPL\IMPORT	No Access
\SYSTEM32\REPL\EXPORT	None
\USERS	None
\USERS\DEFAULT	None
\WIN32APP	None
\TEMP	None

Table 9.15

Windows NT Authority/SYSTEM:

Default Directory Permissions on Windows NT Server

Directory	Permissions
\	Full Control
\SYSTEM32	Full Control
\SYSTEM32\CONFIG	Full Control
\SYSTEM32\DRIVERS	Full Control
\SYSTEM32\SPOOL	Full Control
\SYSTEM32\REPL	Full Control
\SYSTEM32\REPL\IMPORT	Full Control
\SYSTEM32\REPL\EXPORT	Full Control
\USERS	Full Control
\USERS\DEFAULT	Full Control
\WIN32APP	Full Control
\TEMP	Full Control

Using the Command-Line CACLS Tool to Assign File Permissions

Commonly, file-permission–administration tasks are performed by using the Explorer. Occasionally, it is useful to be able to perform these tasks from the command line. The CACLS.EXE program is a command-line tool that can be used to modify the Discretionary ACLs of files and directories. You can use the CACLS (Change ACLs) tool in batch files to automate the assignment of permissions for users and groups.

Following is the syntax for using CACLS:

```
CACLS filename [/T] [/E] [/C] [/G user:perm] [/R user [...]]
               [/P user:perm [...]] [/D user [...]]
```

filename displays ACLs.

/T changes ACLs of specified files in the current directory and all subdirectories.

/E edits ACL instead of replacing it.

/C continues on access denied errors.

/G *user:perm* grants specified user's access rights. *perm* can be R Read, C Change (write), or F Full control.

/R *user* revokes specified user's access rights.

/P *user:perm* replaces specified user's access rights. *perm* can be N No Access, R Read, C Change (write), or F Full control.

/D *user* denies specified user access.

Wild cards can be used to specify more than one file in a command, and you can specify more than one user in a command.

Following are some examples of using the CACLS command.

To examine the permissions for the directory C:\TEMP, use the following command:

```
> CACLS C:\TEMP
C:\TEMP BUILTIN\Administrators:(OI)(CI)F
        Everyone:(OI)(CI)C
        CREATOR OWNER:(OI)(CI)F
        BUILTIN\Server Operators:(OI)(CI)C
        NT AUTHORITY\SYSTEM:(OI)(CI)F
```

The symbol F is for Full Control, and C is for Change. These symbols apply to the (OI) for directories, and (CI) for files in directories.

To examine the permissions for the file C:\TEMP\DATA.1, use the following command:

```
> CACLS C:\USERS\DEFAULT\3.TXT
C:\USERS\DEFAULT\3.TXT BUILTIN\Administrators:F
                       NT AUTHORITY\SYSTEM:F
```

This listing shows that Administrators and SYSTEM have Full Control to the file.

To examine the permissions for all files in C:\USERS\DEFAULT, use the following command:

```
> CACLS C:\USERS\DEFAULT\*
C:\USERS\DEFAULT\2.txt BUILTIN\Administrators:F
                       NT AUTHORITY\SYSTEM:F
C:\USERS\DEFAULT\3.TXT BUILTIN\Administrators:F
                       NT AUTHORITY\SYSTEM:F
```

```
C:\USERS\DEFAULT\basic.TRM BUILTIN\Administrators:F
                          NT AUTHORITY\SYSTEM:F
C:\USERS\DEFAULT\PROBREP.TXT BUILTIN\Administrators:F
                          NT AUTHORITY\SYSTEM:F
C:\USERS\DEFAULT\SETUP.TXT BUILTIN\Administrators:F
                          NT AUTHORITY\SYSTEM:F
C:\USERS\DEFAULT\test Everyone:(special access:)
                          READ_CONTROL
                          SYNCHRONIZE
                          FILE_GENERIC_READ
                          FILE_GENERIC_WRITE
                          FILE_GENERIC_EXECUTE
                          FILE_READ_DATA
                          FILE_WRITE_DATA
                          FILE_APPEND_DATA
                          FILE_READ_EA
                          FILE_WRITE_EA
                          FILE_EXECUTE
                          FILE_READ_ATTRIBUTES
                          FILE_WRITE_ATTRIBUTES

                Everyone:(CI)(IO)(special access:)
                          READ_CONTROL
                          SYNCHRONIZE
                          FILE_GENERIC_READ
                          FILE_GENERIC_WRITE
                          FILE_GENERIC_EXECUTE
                          FILE_READ_DATA
                          FILE_WRITE_DATA
                          FILE_APPEND_DATA
                          FILE_READ_EA
                          FILE_WRITE_EA
                          FILE_EXECUTE
                          FILE_READ_ATTRIBUTES
                          FILE_WRITE_ATTRIBUTES

                BUILTIN\Administrators:F
                CREATOR OWNER:(OI)(CI)(IO)F
                NT AUTHORITY\SYSTEM:F
                NT AUTHORITY\SYSTEM:(OI)(CI)(IO)F
C:\USERS\DEFAULT\utiliz.pmc BUILTIN\Administrators:F
                          NT AUTHORITY\SYSTEM:F
C:\USERS\DEFAULT\x BUILTIN\Administrators:F
                   NT AUTHORITY\SYSTEM:F
```

Notice that permissions for all files are displayed. Because the subdirectory TEST has special permissions, the specific, standard, and generic access types are displayed. Access types are discussed in the section "Understanding the Data Structures Used to Implement File Permissions," earlier in this chapter.

To add Change permission for user Karanjit to file C:\USERS\DATA\3.TXT, use the following command:

```
> CACLS C:\USERS\DEFAULT\3.TXT /E /P Karanjit:C
processed file: C:\USERS\DEFAULT\3.TXT
```

To verify the results of the preceding command, use this command:

```
> CACLS C:\USERS\DEFAULT\3.TXT
C:\USERS\DEFAULT\3.TXT BUILTIN\Administrators:F
                       NT AUTHORITY\SYSTEM:F
                       KINETD\Karanjit:C
```

Notice that the user Karanjit is added to the permissions list. The name KINETD preceding Karanjit specifies the domain name of the domain user account.

To revoke the user Karanjit from the permissions list, use this command:

```
> CACLS C:\USERS\DEFAULT\3.TXT /E /R Karanjit
Are you sure (Y/N)?Y
processed file: C:\USERS\DEFAULT\3.TXT
```

To replace existing permissions and deny a specific right to a group ggroup1 for C:\USERS\DEFAULT\3.TXT and verify your results, use the following command:

```
> CACLS C:\USERS\DEFAULT\3.TXT /D ggroup1
Are you sure (Y/N)?Y
processed file: C:\USERS\DEFAULT\3.TXT
> CACLS C:\USERS\DEFAULT\3.TXT
C:\USERS\DEFAULT\3.TXT KINETD\ggroup1:N
```

Notice that because the /E (edit rather than replace) option was not specified, the prior permissions are replaced with new permissions. The group ggroup1 has No Access permissions set.

Enhancing File-System Security through Auditing

Windows NT includes an auditing mechanism that can be used to audit successful and unsuccessful attempts for operations on files and directories. This mechanism enables you to track the usage of files and directories. The log of audited events can be viewed in the Security log of the Event Viewer program.

Enabling Auditing

The first step in configuring auditing is to enable it. Auditing is enabled by using the User Manager for Domains in the Administrative Tools group (for Windows NT Workstations, the User Manager tool is used).

Following is an outline of the steps for enabling auditing:

1. Log on as an Administrator user.

2. Start User Manager for Domains from the Administrative Tools folder.

3. Select **P**olicies, Au**d**it.

   You should see the Audit Policy screen (see fig. 9.63).

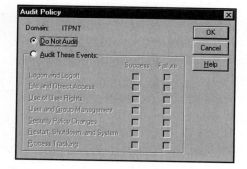

Figure 9.63
The Audit Policy screen.

   If the **D**o Not Audit option is selected, auditing is disabled. To enable auditing, select **A**udit These Events.

4. Check the appropriate box in the Success and Failure columns. You can audit the success or failure of the following events:

   ■ **Logon and Logoff.** User's logon or network connections by remote users.

   ■ **File and Object Access.** Access to files and directories. Sending print jobs.

   ■ **Use of User Rights.** A user's exercise of user rights, except those related to logon and logoff.

   ■ **User and Group Management.** Changes to user and group accounts such as creation, deletion, and renaming. Changes to passwords.

   ■ **Security Policy Changes.** Changes to User Rights, Audit, or Trust Relationships policy.

■ **Restart, Shutdown, and System.** Logs restart or shutdown of a system. Changes that affect the system security and security log on the system.

■ **Process Tracking.** Tracks program start, some forms of handle duplication, indirect object accesses, and program exit.

To audit file and directory usage, select the option to enable **F**ile and Object Access.

Choose OK to save your changes.

You should judiciously select the types of events to audit, because auditing can generate a large number of events, and if the auditing log is voluminous, system administrators tend not to pay as much attention to it.

Auditing Files and Directories

After auditing has been enabled for files and object access as outlined in the preceding section, you can specify the types of file and directory access that can be audited by using the Explorer.

You can audit a directory or a specific file in a directory. Auditing on a directory enables the same events on any *new* files or directories created in the directory. When setting auditing on a directory, you can optionally replace auditing on any existing files in the directory.

Tables 9.16 and 9.17 show which events you need to audit for specific activities for directories and files.

Table 9.16
Auditing Activities in a Directory

Activity	Read	Write	Execute	Delete	Change Permission	Take Ownership
Display file names	X					
Display attributes	X		X			
Change attributes		X				
Create subdirectories and files			X			
Go to the directory's subdirectories			X			
Display owner and permissions	X	X	X			

Activity	Read	Write	Execute	Delete	Change Permission	Take Ownership
Delete the directory				X		
Change directory's permissions					X	
Change directory's ownership						X

Table 9.17
Auditing Activities on a File

Activity	Read	Write	Execute	Delete	Change Permission	Take Ownership
Display file's data	X					
Display attributes	X		X			
Display owner and permissions	X	X	X			
Change data		X				
Change attributes		X				
Run the file if it is a program			X			
Delete the file				X		
Change file's permissions						X
Change file's ownership						X

Following is an outline of the procedure for setting up auditing on a directory or a file.

1. Log on as an Administrator user.

2. Start the Explorer.

3. Highlight a directory or a file.

4. Right-click then select the Security tab and click on the Auditing button.

If you select a directory for auditing, you see the Directory Auditing screen (see fig. 9.64).

If you select a file for auditing, you see the File Auditing screen (see fig. 9.65).

Figure 9.64

The Directory Auditing screen.

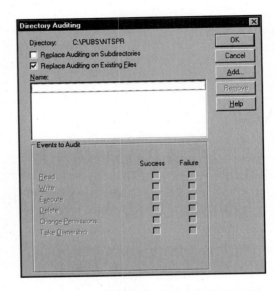

Figure 9.65

The File Auditing screen.

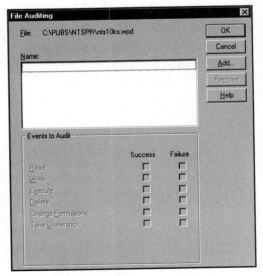

5. If you select auditing on a directory, you see two additional options to control the ways in which auditing applies to files and subdirectories (see fig. 9.64).

If the Replace Auditing in Subdirectories option is selected, the auditing changes you make will apply to all subdirectories. By default, this option is cleared, so you must explicitly set this option if you want the auditing changes to apply to subdirectories as well.

If the Replace Auditing on Existing Files is selected, the auditing changes you make will apply to all files in the directory. By default, this option is set, so the auditing changes apply to the directory and its files only.

Set these two options depending on whether you want to audit files or subdirectories, or only the selected directory.

6. To add users or groups to be audited, select the Add button. Figure 9.66 shows the Add Users and Groups screen for auditing.

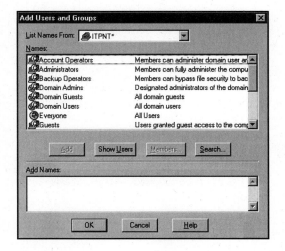

Figure 9.66

The Add Users and Groups screen for auditing.

This Names box displays the list of accounts in the current domain that can be assigned rights. The current domain is displayed in the List Names From field. The domain name ITPNT in figure 9.66 has an asterisk symbol next to it. An asterisk next to a domain or computer name indicates that the local groups of that domain or computer can be listed. The absence of an asterisk means that the local group cannot be listed. Remember that local groups can contain local users, as well as domain users and global groups from the current domain and trusting domains.

To list names from other domains, select the field List Names From. This field displays a list containing the local domain name, trusted domains, and computer names.

The Names list box shows the accounts of the selected domain or computer. If a domain is selected, the list of global groups for that domain are also listed. The initial display of accounts includes only group names. If you want to assign permissions to user accounts, you must select the Show Users button, which also shows the user accounts in the domain that can be audited. Only group names are initially displayed to encourage you to think in terms of auditing groups rather than individual users. You must perform an extra step to list user accounts that can be audited.

You select the accounts to be audited from the Names list box. If you then select the Add button, these account names are added to the Add Names list. You also can list members of a group in the Names list by choosing the Members button. You can select any of the members of the group and select the Add button to add the members to the Add Names list.

You can search for accounts in other domains by choosing the Search button. The Find Account dialog box that appears can be used to locate a user account or group in a specific domain or all domains. The search results can then be added to the list of group members.

Choose OK on the Add Users and Groups screen to add them to the Directory or File Auditing screen.

7. For each of the users and groups added to the Directory or File Auditing screen, select the events to be audited. The events to audit are maintained on a per-user or per-group basis. Figure 9.67 shows an example of the auditing events set for the selected user Karanjit. You could set auditing events for other users also.

8. Choose OK to save your audit settings.

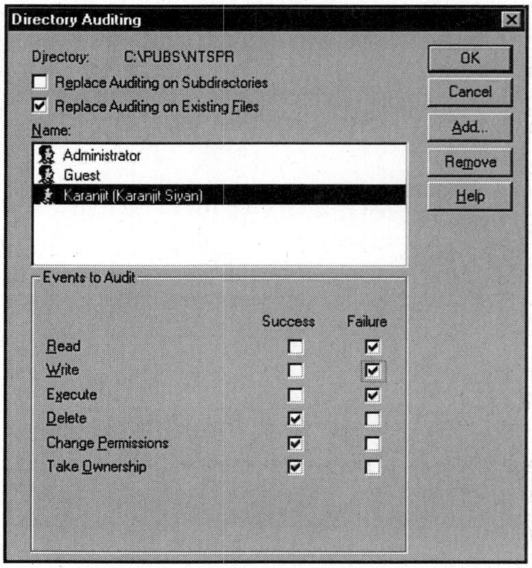

Figure 9.67

An auditing events for a selected user.

Viewing Audit Logs

You view the security log or any of the audit logs, such as system logs and application logs, by using the Event Viewer tool in the Administrative Tools group.

Following is an outline for viewing the security log:

1. Log on as an Administrator user.

2. Start the Event Viewer program from the Administrative Tools folder.

   If this is the first time you are using the Event Viewer, you should see the System Log (see fig. 9.68). The system log is very useful for monitoring and troubleshooting system-related events.

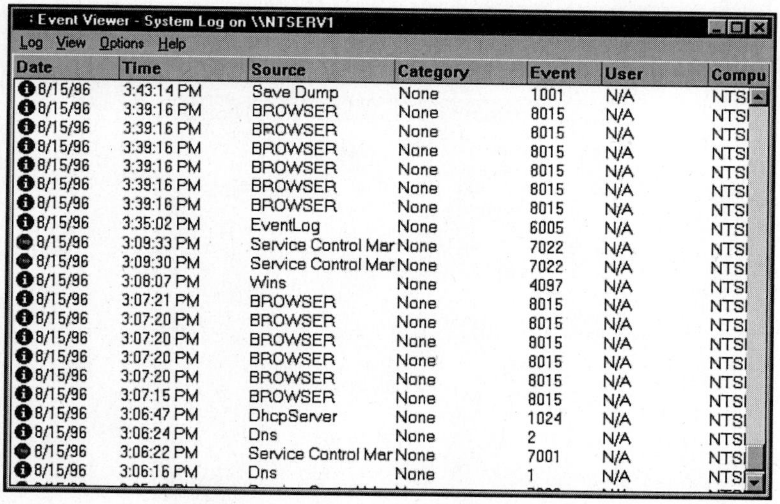
Event Viewer - System Log on \\NTSERV1
Log View Options Help
Date Time Source Category Event User Compu
8/15/96 3:43:14 PM Save Dump None 1001 N/A NTSI
8/15/96 3:39:16 PM BROWSER None 8015 N/A NTSI
8/15/96 3:39:16 PM BROWSER None 8015 N/A NTSI
8/15/96 3:39:16 PM BROWSER None 8015 N/A NTSI
8/15/96 3:39:16 PM BROWSER None 8015 N/A NTSI
8/15/96 3:39:16 PM BROWSER None 8015 N/A NTSI
8/15/96 3:39:16 PM BROWSER None 8015 N/A NTSI
8/15/96 3:35:02 PM EventLog None 6005 N/A NTSI
8/15/96 3:09:33 PM Service Control Mar None 7022 N/A NTSI
8/15/96 3:09:30 PM Service Control Mar None 7022 N/A NTSI
8/15/96 3:08:07 PM Wins None 4097 N/A NTSI
8/15/96 3:07:21 PM BROWSER None 8015 N/A NTSI
8/15/96 3:07:20 PM BROWSER None 8015 N/A NTSI
8/15/96 3:07:20 PM BROWSER None 8015 N/A NTSI
8/15/96 3:07:20 PM BROWSER None 8015 N/A NTSI
8/15/96 3:07:20 PM BROWSER None 8015 N/A NTSI
8/15/96 3:07:15 PM BROWSER None 8015 N/A NTSI
8/15/96 3:06:47 PM DhcpServer None 1024 N/A NTSI
8/15/96 3:06:24 PM Dns None 2 N/A NTSI
8/15/96 3:06:22 PM Service Control Mar None 7001 N/A NTSI
8/15/96 3:06:16 PM Dns None 1 N/A NTSI

Figure 9.68
A sample system log.

   Log events for system, security, and application logs are by default displayed with the newest events first. To change the default order, choose **V**iew, **O**ldest First.

3. To view the Security Log, choose **L**og, **S**ecurity Log.

   Figure 9.69 shows a sample security log. To view details of a particular event, highlight the event and press Enter, or double-click on the event. Figure 9.70 shows the details of a particular security event. This event shows that the access to the file C:\PUBS\NTSPR\NTSPROUT.WPD was successful.

   You can use the Previous button and Next button to move through the event log and examine other security-related events.

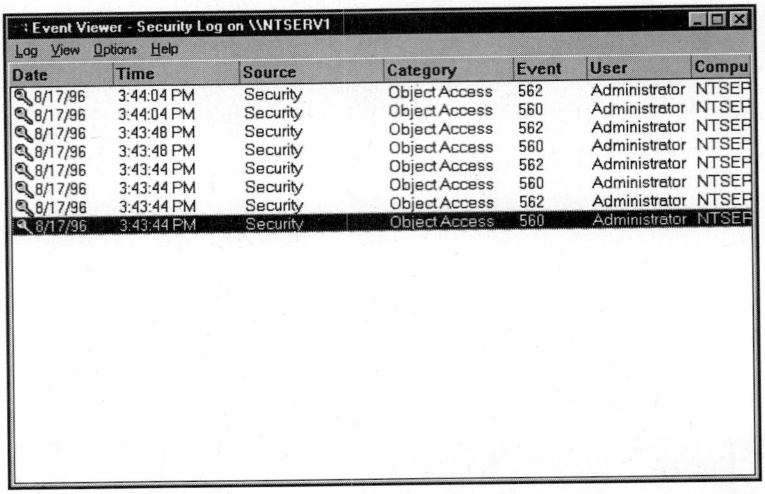

Figure 9.69

A sample security log.

Figure 9.70

A sample security event.

Conclusion

Because Windows NT has networking services built into the operating system, sharing of network files is important to understand. Windows NT file-system security permissions can be set only on NTFS files. This chapter discussed the ways in which existing FAT partition can be converted to NTFS.

Windows NT file and directory permission settings can be set by using the Explorer or the CACLS command-line tool. Both methods were discussed in this chapter. Windows NT file-system security can be further enhanced by using auditing. This chapter discussed the procedures for enabling and configuring auditing on a Windows NT Server.

Managing Windows NT Registry

The Windows NT Registry is an internal database that contains Windows NT configuration information. The Registry is meant as a replacement for the configuration files in the Windows 3.x environment. When Windows NT applications install and system programs run, they modify the Registry when changing configuration information.

The Registry is not a tool for the end user; it is a system administrator's tool for making changes that cannot be made through the system tool programs or application programs. You must exercise extreme caution when modifying the Registry; you could irrevocably alter the behavior of the Windows NT system for the worse.

Examining the Windows NT Registry

The Windows NT Registry is a structured database organized as hierarchical trees. Information is stored in a hierarchical tree to facilitate ease of browsing and maintenance of the databases. You can use the Registry in the following ways:

- To provide startup information during system boot

- To store general system configuration data

- To manage device driver configuration parameters

- To store new configuration data for added applications and system tools

- To assist system administrators in modifying Windows NT system configuration

The Registry is meant as a replacement for the INI files used in the Windows 3.x environment. The INI files have section headings for the grouping of parameters, whereas the Registry has keys that act as containers for parameters. The Registry keys can contain subkeys, in a manner similar to the way directories can contain subdirectories. This structure permits a finer level of organizational control than is possible with INI files, which do not support nested section headings. To maintain backward compatibility with 16-bit Windows applications and related setup programs, the INI files will continue to be supported in Windows NT.

The Registry Database

Figure 10.1 shows a more detailed view of the different Windows NT components that use the Registry.

The *Setup* component is the Windows NT Setup program used to install NT or Setup programs for other applications (see fig. 10.1). The Setup programs add configuration information for the loading of software modules onto the Windows NT system. As a new SCSI adapter is added, for example, the adapter configuration information is stored in the Registry.

The *Recognizer* component is the NTDETECT.COM program that runs when the Windows NT system is started (see fig. 10.1). NTDETECT.COM probes the system hardware and recognizes attached peripheral devices such as keyboard, display adapter, pointing device, network adapters, and so on, and stores this information in the Registry. This information is used in subsequent phases of the system boot to initialize the device drivers for the recognized devices. If a device is not recognized on an Intel-based system by the hardware recognizer, the corresponding device driver will not be initialized. If the device happens to be the network adapter, the network adapter device driver will not be activated. As a result, the network protocols and the services that depend on them will be disabled.

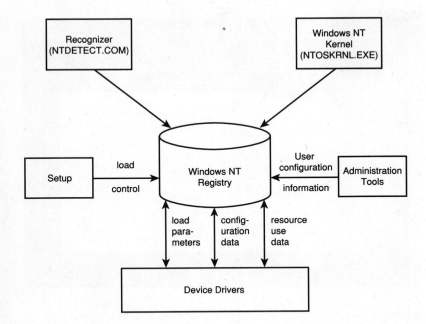

Figure 10.1
Components that use the Windows NT Registry.

The *Windows NT kernel* component is implemented by the NTOSKRNL.EXE program, and it retrieves from the Registry the order in which to load the device drivers and the hardware parameters for the device drivers. The NTOSKRNL.EXE passes information on the operating system version and name to the Registry.

The *device drivers* send and receive configuration information from the Registry, such as the parameters needed to load the device drivers and configuration information on the device drivers. The device drivers register information with the Registry about the hardware resources it uses, such as interrupt lines, DMA channel, I/O port addresses, and memory base addresses. The Registry adds this information to its database to avoid conflicts over hardware resources.

The *Administrative tools* are programs, such as User Manager for Domains, which store information on user accounts and settings in the Registry. Windows NT comes with a diagnostic program called WINMSD.EXE that can view information stored in the Registry for diagnostic and troubleshooting purposes.

The Registry Editor Tool

The Registry can be viewed by running the program REGEDT32.EXE, found in the %SystemRoot%\System32 directory. If a program item for this program does not exist on your system, you might want to define one in the Administrative Tools group. Figure 10.2 shows the subtrees of which Windows NT is aware.

Figure 10.2
*The Windows NT Registry
Editor.*

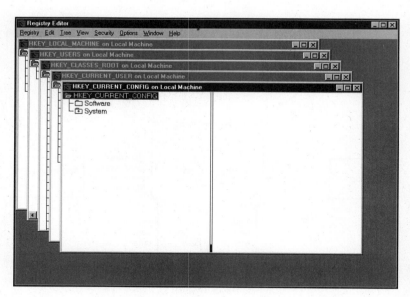

REGEDT32.EXE is being introduced early in the chapter in case you have access to a Windows NT Server computer and would like to browse its structure. Browsing the Registry with the Registry Editor is similar to browsing any hierarchical data structure, such as the file system, in a Windows environment.

If you are browsing the Registry Editor and want to prevent inadvertent changes to the Registry, you can place the Registry Editor in Read-Only mode by choosing **O**ptions, **R**ead-Only Mode.

To find a particular key in the Registry, follow these steps:

1. Choose **V**iew, **F**ind Key to open the Find Key dialog box.

2. In the Fi**nd** What field, enter the name of the key.

3. Enable or disable the following options:

    ■ Match **W**hole Word Only

    ■ Match **C**ase

4. Select the direction of search: **U**p or **D**own.

5. Click on the **F**ind Next button.

Note Windows NT 4 ships with two Registry editors: REGEDIT32.EXE and REGEDIT.EXE (same version packaged with Windows 95). Many functions can be accomplished with either version of the tool; however, the REGEDIT32.EXE variant is the tool that should be used in conjunction with NT because REGEDIT.EXE does not support certain data types, including:

- REG_MULTI_SZ

- REG_EXPAND SZ

The Windows 95 variant also lacks some of the printing and security features incorporated in the NT version.

For common functions, the REGEDIT.EXE version supplies a few advantages over REGEDIT32.EXE that you may want to take advantage of, including:

- Windows 95 GUI support

- Enhanced find features

The Structure of the Registry

The Registry consists of four hierarchical subtrees local to each Windows NT computer. The subtrees contain information on the computer and user accounts defined on the Windows NT computer. The five subtrees in the Windows NT Registry are

- HKEY_LOCAL_MACHINE

- HKEY_CLASSES_ROOT

- HKEY_CURRENT_USER

- HKEY_USERS

- HKEY_CURRENT_CONFIG

The intermediate nodes in the tree are called *keys* and are used for organizational purposes (see fig. 10.3). The leaf nodes in the tree contain data items called *value entries*. An individual key can contain value entries and *subkeys*. The Registry keys are analogous to directories in a file system, and the value entries are analogous to files.

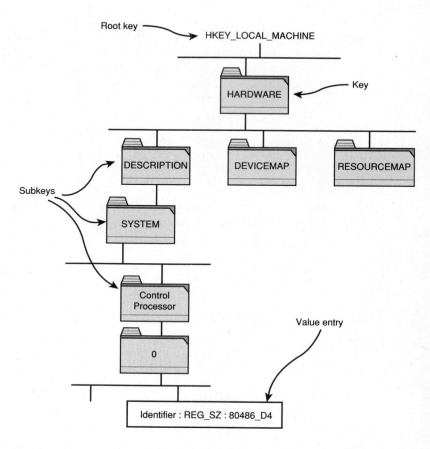

Figure 10.3
Keys, subkeys, and value entries.

The root keys of the Registry subtrees begin with an "HKEY_" prefix to indicate that these are *handle* keys that can be used within programs to identify that subtree. The previously listed subtrees all have this prefix.

Value entries consist of a *value name*, *value type*, and the actual *value*. Figure 10.4 shows the breakdown of the Identifier value entry shown in figure 10.3.

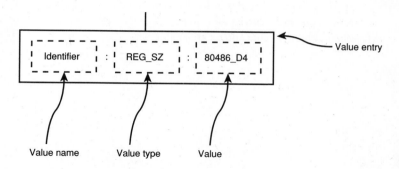

Figure 10.4
A Registry value entry.

Figure 10.5 shows other examples of value entries in the HKEY_LOCAL_MACHINE\
SYSTEM\CurrentControlSet\Services\Atdisk key. The value entries for this key have the
REG_SZ and REG_DWORD value types. Other types of value entries in the Registry are
REG_BINARY, REG_EXPAND_SZ, REG_MULTI_SZ, and REG_FULL_RESOURCE_
DESCRIPTOR.

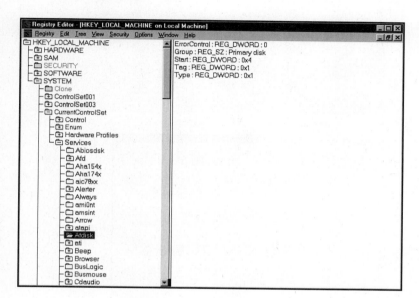

Figure 10.5

*An example of value
entries.*

Value types begin with a "REG_" prefix. The suffix "_SZ" indicates a string terminated with a
zero—this is common format used in the C language for describing strings. A value entry is
limited to a storage size of 1 MB, which is sufficient for most applications. If an application
needs more space, it can split the data into several value entries. The values from 0 to
7FFFFFFF (hexadecimal) are reserved for system use. Values from 80000000 to FFFFFFFF are
reserved for use by applications.

Table 10.1 describes the data types for value entries. You can double-click on a value entry
from the Registry Editor to invoke an editor for that data type. This editor then can be used to
edit the value field. Figure 10.6 shows the Binary Editor that is invoked when you double-click
on a value entry of REG_BINARY type. Figure 10.7 shows the Resources screen when you
double-click on the configuration data of the REG_FULL_RESOURCE_DESCRIPTOR type
for a disk controller.

Figure 10.6

The Binary Editor.

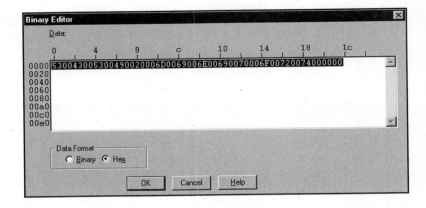

Figure 10.7

*A Resources screen for
REG_FULL_RESOURCE_
DESCRIPTOR for a disk
controller.*

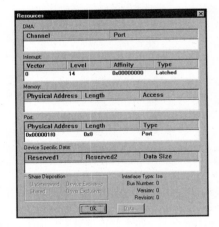

Table 10.1
Data Types for Value Entries in the Registry

Data Type	Description
REG_SZ	A sequence of characters forming a string value. An example of this data type is the computer name: ComputerName : REG_SZ : NTUS. Many Registry values that are more easily changeable by the system Administrator are of this type.
REG_DWORD	A numeric value that is 4 bytes long (double word). Device parameters, service values, and numeric configuration values such as interrupt levels are expressed as this data type. The Registry Editor can display this value in decimal, hexadecimal, or binary format. An example of this data type of memory address for a network adapter is

Data Type	Description
	MemoryAddress : REG_DWORD : 0xd0000. The "0x" prefix indicates that the value is expressed as a hexadecimal number. This is a common way of displaying the values of the REG_DWORD data type.
REG_MULTI_SZ	Contains multiple string values in a human-readable text. The string values are separated by null (ASCII 0), a common convention used in the C programming language. An example of this is the value that describes the dependencies for the CD-ROM file system: DependOnGroup : REG_MULTI_SZ : SCSI CDROM Class.
REG_EXPAND_SZ	An expandable data string that contains a variable to be replaced when the value is accessed by an application. A value that references the system variable %SystemRoot%, for example, would be of REG_EXPAND_SZ data type. The %SystemRoot% refers to the directory in which the Windows NT system is installed. When an application accesses a value that contains the system variable %SystemRoot%, it replaces this variable by the actual directory location where Windows NT was installed. An example of this is the image path of the network adapter driver, which contains a reference to the %SystemRoot%: ImagePath : REG_EXPAND_SZ: %SystemRoot%\System32\drivers\CENDIS3.sys.
REG_BINARY	The raw binary data format. Hardware configuration information is stored in this format. The Registry Editor also can display this data in hexadecimal format. Unless you have documentation on the meaning of the individual bits, it is risky to modify this information. You can use the Windows NT Diagnostic program (WINMSD.EXE) to view hardware-specific information stored in the REG_BINARY format. An example of this is the component information for a peripheral device: Component Information : REG_BINARY : 64 00 00 00 ...
REG_FULL_RESOURCE DESCRIPTOR	Used to hold configuration data for hardware devices. It represents a record of information that has field names describing the individual components of this record. An example of this is the configuration data for a hard disk controller: Configuration Data : REG_FULL_RESOURCE_ DESCRIPTOR : ...

The HKEY_LOCAL_MACHINE Subtree

The HKEY_LOCAL_MACHINE contains information on the local computer hardware, software, security accounts database, and system configuration information. Examples of hardware information are bus type, adapter cards, system memory, device drivers, startup order of device drivers, services to load, application-specific data, and so on. The information in the HKEY_LOCAL_MACHINE remains the same, regardless of the user who is logged in. Most system information is stored in HKEY_LOCAL_MACHINE. The HKEY_LOCAL_MACHINE tree has five subkeys. These are the Hardware, SAM (Security Accounts Manager), Security, Software, and System. These subkeys are described in table 10.2.

Table 10.2
Hives under HKEY_LOCAL_MACHINE

Subtree Key Name	Description
HARDWARE	The physical configuration of the computer: How the hardware uses device drivers, kernel-mode drivers, device maps, and resource maps. The data in this subtree is volatile, which means that it is re-created on system startup. The Windows NT Diagnostic program (WINMSD.EXE) uses the information in this subtree and displays it in an easier-to-understand format. Most of the data in this subtree is in binary format, which makes it difficult to decode. The subtree contains the following major subkeys: DESCRIPTION key, DEVICEMAP key, and RESOURCEMAP key. The DESCRIPTION key contains the information on the hardware that was recognized by NTDETECT.COM and the Windows NT Executive. The DEVICEMAP key contains information used by device driver classes in a special format. The RESOURCEMAP maps device drivers to the hardware resources they use.
SAM	Contains the user and group accounts information for the domain (for Windows NT Server) or local computer (for Windows NT Workstations). This information is managed by the User Manager for Domains and the list of users and groups displayed in File Manager. This subtree is mapped to the key HKEY_LOCAL_MACHINE\SECURITY\SAM, which means that changes made in any of these subkeys automatically appear in the other subkeys.
	In the case of a domain controller, the SAM also contains all of the workstation accounts, and the domain trust accounts for trusting domains. These are stored in the key

Subtree Key Name	Description
	HKEY_LOCAL_MACHINE\SAM\SAM\ DOMAINS\ACCOUNT\USERS\NAMES and can be viewed by starting the Registry Editor using the AT command so that it runs at the security level of the SYSTEM account: AT TIME /interactive REGEDT32.exe
SECURITY	Contains information on the security policy and user rights. This information is used by the Windows NT security subsystem.
SOFTWARE	Contains information on the software installed on the computer and miscellaneous configuration data.
SYSTEM	Controls the system boot, loading of device drivers, startup of Windows NT services, and various other operating system behavior.

The Security, SAM, Software, and System are called *hives* and have corresponding files located for them in the %SystemRoot%\System32\Config directory. Figure 10.8 shows the hive file names for a Windows NT Server computer. The main hive files in the HKEY_LOCAL_MACHINE subtree are highlighted. The SYSTEM.ALT and LOG files are backup hives and log files. Table 10.3 shows the standard hive files on a Windows NT computer.

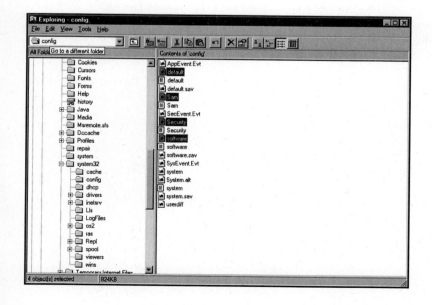

Figure 10.8

Hive files on a Windows NT Server.

Table 10.3
Standard Hives

Hive Name	Associated Files
HKEY_LOCAL_MACHINE\SAM	SAM, SAM.LOG
HKEY_LOCAL_MACHINE\SECURITY	SECURITY, SECURITY.LOG
HKEY_LOCAL_MACHINE\SOFTWARE	SOFTWARE, SOFTWARE.LOG
HKEY_LOCAL_MACHINE\SYSTEM	SYSTEM, SYSTEM.ALT
HKEY_CURRENT_USER	USER###, USER###.LOG, ADMIN###, ADMIN###.LOG
HKEY_USERS\DEFAULT	DEFAULT, DEFAULT.LOG

The HKEY_CLASSES_ROOT Key

The HKEY_CLASSES_ROOT key contains information on file associations and OLE. A file association associates an extension with a specific application. Double-clicking on a file that has an extension with an association described in the HKEY_CLASSES_ROOT invokes the corresponding application.

The HKEY_CLASSES_ROOT is an alias to the HKEY_LOCAL_MACHINE\ SOFTWARE\Classes key. These two keys contain the same information (see fig. 10.9). Changes made to any one of these subtrees are visible in the other subtrees. The aliases simply provide access to the subtree and assist in the conceptual understanding of how the trees are organized.

Figure 10.10 shows that the BMP key has a value entry of type REG_SZ that has a value of Paint Picture.

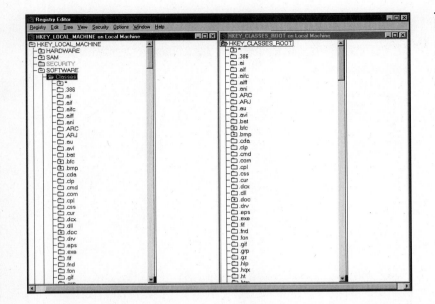

Figure 10.9
*The HKEY_
CLASSES_ROOT and the
HKEY_LOCAL_
MACHINE\SOFTWARE
Classes.*

Figure 10.10
Association for a BMP file.

The HKEY_CURRENT_USER Key

The HKEY_CURRENT_USER contains user profile information for the currently logged-in user. User profile contains information such as the desktop configuration and appearance, network connections, environment settings, and so on. User profiles are discussed in detail in Chapter 8, "Managing User Profiles, Logon Scripts, and Environment Variables."

Figure 10.11 shows an example HKEY_CURRENT_USER and its main subkeys.

Figure 10.11

The HKEY_CURRENT_USER subtree.

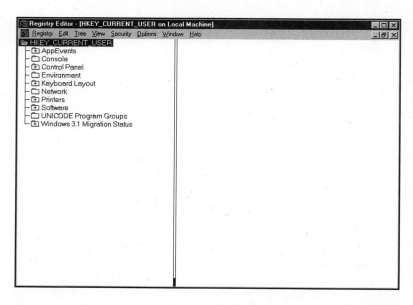

The *Console key* contains subkeys that define the console appearance, such as cursor size, fonts used, screen size, window colors, and so on. When you modify the Windows NT command-prompt settings, the Command Prompt subkey is created, which holds configuration information for the command-prompt window (see fig. 10.12).

Figure 10.12

The HKEY_CURRENT_USER\Console subkey.

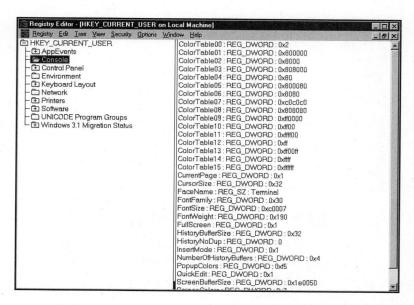

The *Control Panel key* contains subkeys that describe configuration information for applications in the Control Panel program group. This includes information such as color schemes, cursor settings, screen savers, international settings, mouse settings, and so on. Figure 10.13 shows the subkeys under the Control Panel key and the value entries under the Colors subkey. The value entries are all of REG_SZ type and contain the RGB (Red Green Blue) color codings for the desktop elements.

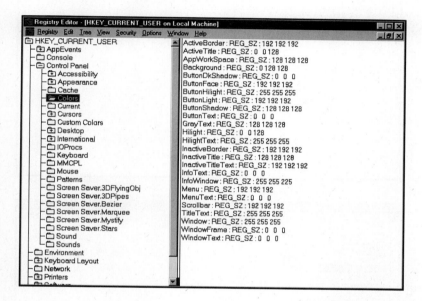

Figure 10.13

The HKEY_CURRENT_ USER\Control Panel subkey.

The *Environment key* contains the Environment variable settings for the user. Figure 10.14 shows the Environment variables TEMP and TMP defined for the current user. Although you can modify Environment variables and create new Environment variables using the Registry Editor, it is best to make changes using the System icon in the Control Panel program group.

The *Keyboard Layout key* describes the current active keyboard layout, such as the US, UK, and other country keyboards (see fig. 10.15). The changes to the keyboard layout should be made using the International icon in the Control Panel.

Figure 10.14

The HKEY_CURRENT_ USER\Environment subkey.

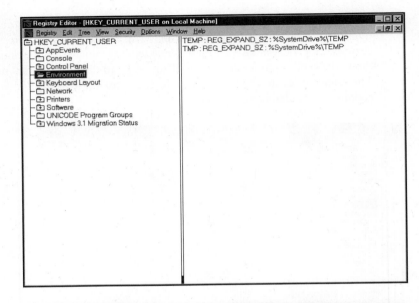

Figure 10.15

The HKEY_CURRENT_ USER\Keyboard Layout subkey.

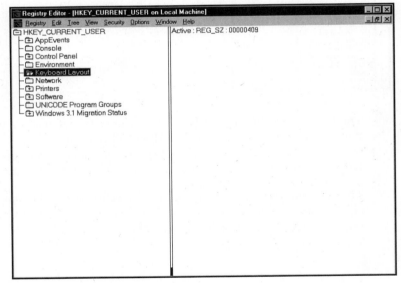

The *Network key* exists only if you have installed the networking components on the Windows NT system. This key contains information on the network usage for the current user. Figure 10.16 shows two subkeys: E and G. The E subkey is the network drive E for the network, and its value is shown by the value entry ProviderName (NetWare Network); the G subkey is for the network drive G, which is connected to the Microsoft Network. Under the E subkey, you can see the RemotePath value entry that shows the network path, \\NW4KS\SYS, to which drive E is mapped.

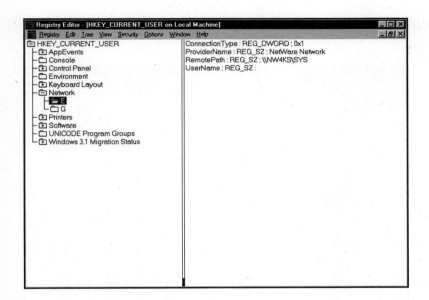

Figure 10.16

The HKEY_CURRENT_USER\Network subkey.

The *Printers key* describes the printers installed for the current user (see fig. 10.17). The settings should be changed using the Print Manager. Any printer connection information is stored in the Connections subkey.

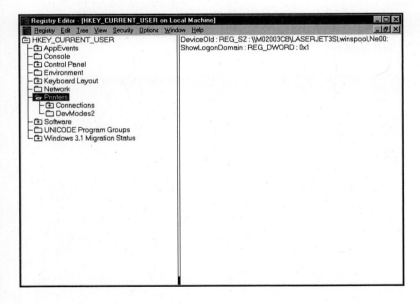

Figure 10.17

The HKEY_CURRENT_USER\Printers subkey.

The *Software key* contains subkeys for the current user's configuration settings for applications used by the user. Figure 10.18 shows the subkeys for Microsoft applications, such as the File Manager that comes with Windows NT. The appearance of the File Manager when it is started is saved in the File Manager subkey. The information in the Software key has the same structure as the information in the HKEY_LOCAL_MACHINE\SOFTWARE key.

Figure 10.18

*The HKEY_CURRENT_*
USER\Software subkey.

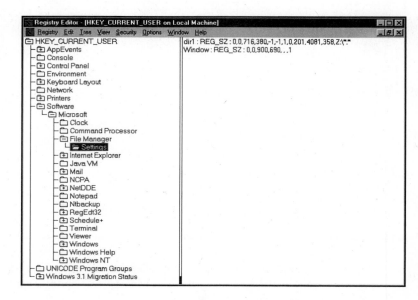

The *UNICODE Program Groups key* contains subkeys for the program groups for the current user (see fig. 10.19). The configuration information for the program groups should be modified using the Program Manager. Common program group definitions are stored in the HKEY_LOCAL_MACHINE\SOFTWARE\Program Groups key.

Figure 10.19

*The HKEY_CURRENT_*
USER\UNICODE
Program Groups subkey.

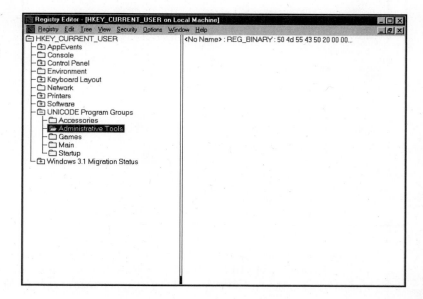

The *Windows 3.1 Migration Status key* contains information on the Windows 3.1 Groups and INI files that have been migrated to a Windows NT computer. The information on Groups and INI files is contained in the subkeys Groups and IniFiles (see fig. 10.20).

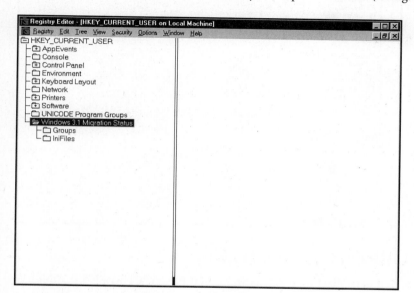

Figure 10.20

The HKEY_CURRENT_USER\Windows 3.1 Migration Status subkey.

The HKEY_CURRENT_USER is mapped to the HKEY_USERS\SID, where SID is the security ID for the currently logged-in user. The Windows NT Logon builds the user's personal profile environment based on information it finds in HKEY_USERS\SID. If no such information can be found, it uses the information in the HKEY_USERS\.DEFAULT key.

The HKEY_USERS Key

The HKEY_USERS subtree contains the actively loaded profiles for all users. The HKEY_USERS has at least two subkeys: the .DEFAULT subkey and the SID subkey for the currently logged-in user. The .DEFAULT subkey is used to create the user profile for a user who logs in without a personal profile. The .DEFAULT subkey is also used for the desktop settings when the system is locked or when no user is currently logged in.

Figure 10.21 shows the two subkeys under HKEY_USERS. Notice that the default subkey contains information on the Console, Control Panel, Environment, Keyboard Layout, Software, and UNICODE Program Groups settings. These subkeys were described in the preceding section.

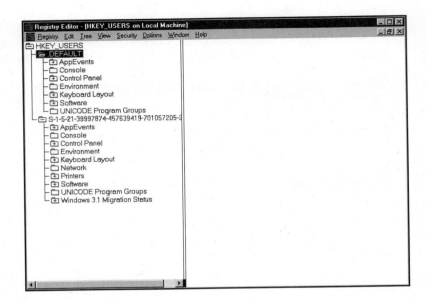

Figure 10.21

The HKEY_USERS subtree.

The HKEY_CURRENT_CONFIG Key

This key is a new addition to the Registry in Windows NT 4.0. HKEY_CURRENT_CONFIG contains hardware profile information from the local machine that is needed at system bootup.

The Registry Control Sets

In Windows NT, all startup configuration information is stored in the ControlSet subkeys under the HKEY_LOCAL_MACHINE\SYSTEM key. Because the ControlSet subkey is essential for the Windows NT startup, backup copies of the control sets are kept in the HKEY_LOCAL_MACHINE\SYSTEM key under the names ControlSet001, ControlSet002, and ControlSet003 (see fig. 10.22). The current ControlSet key is under the name CurrentControlSet; this is an alias for one of the other control sets.

Although up to four control sets are maintained, the two most important control sets Windows NT keeps track of are the CurrentControlSet and a LastKnownGood (LKG) control set that was known to start the system correctly. During Windows NT system bootup, you can revert to the LastKnownGood control set by pressing the spacebar.

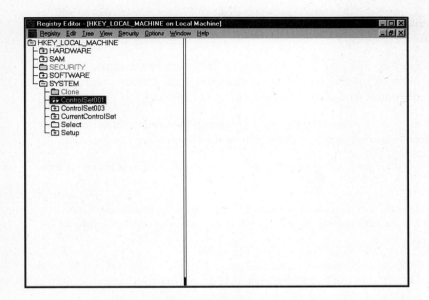

Figure 10.22
Multiple control sets in the Registry.

The Select subkey describes the different control sets (see fig. 10.23). This subkey contains the following value entries:

- Current

- Default

- LastKnownGood

- Failed

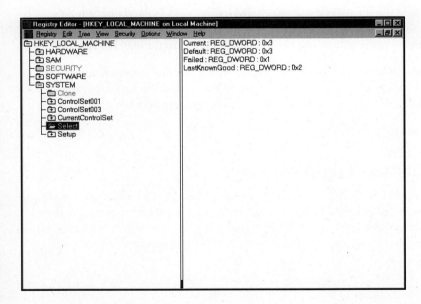

Figure 10.23
The Select subkey.

Each of these value entries is of type REG_DWORD, and the corresponding numeric value describes the control set number.

The Current value entry describes the current control set. In the example in figure 10.23, this is the control set number 0x3, or the control set ControlSet003. The CurrentControlSet key is a symbolic link to the control set described by the value entry Current.

The Default value entry specifies the number of the control set the system will use on its next startup unless an error is encountered or the user uses the LastKnownGood control set.

The LastKnownGood value entry specifies the number of a control set that is known to have worked.

The Failed value entry specifies the control set that was replaced if the LastKnownGood control set was used to start the system. You can use this entry to discover the identity of the offending control set.

Each time the system starts, the control set actually used to start the system is stored under the HKEY_LOCAL_MACHINE\SYSTEM\Clone subkey. If the startup is good, the LastKnownGood control set is discarded and the Clone subtree is copied to the LastKnownGood control set. A startup is good if there were no severe or critical errors on startup and the user has successfully authenticated to an account database.

If you need to make changes to the control set, make the changes to the CurrentControlSet.

Looking at Practical Uses of the Registry

Ordinarily, you should use the normal system-administration tools to configure Windows NT. Not all configuration tasks can be accomplished using the normal system-administration tools, however, so it is helpful to know how you can configure the system through the Registry.

This section describes how you can use the Registry for some practical configuration tasks. Note that you must be logged on as an Administrator to manipulate the Registry entries. To start the Registry Editor, enter the following command line into the Run box:

```
\%systemroot%\system32\regedit32.exe
```

Creating a Custom Login Message

When you log on to a Windows NT computer by pressing Ctrl+Alt+Del, you see the Welcome dialog box that asks you to enter a user name, domain name (or computer name), and password. You can design a custom message to be displayed when the user logs in. Such a message could warn users against unauthorized logins and display other appropriate legal warning messages.

To create a custom log-in message, follow these steps:

1. Select the following key:

   HKEY_LOCAL_MACHINE\SOFTWARE\Microsoft\Windows
   NT\CurrentVersion\Winlogon

   Figure 10.24 shows the value entries in the Winlogon subkey.

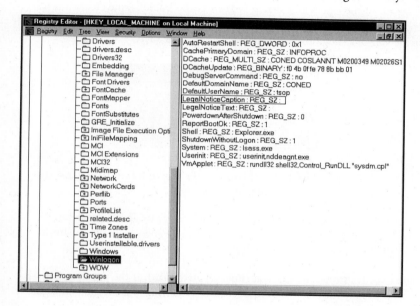

Figure 10.24

Value entries in the Winlogon screen.

2. Double-click on the value entry for LegalNoticeCaption (data type REG_SZ). In the String Editor dialog box, add an appropriate legal caption.

3. Double-click on the value entry for LegalNoticeText (data type REG_SZ). In the String Editor dialog box, add appropriate legal text.

4. Log off and log on again to test your message.

Notice that the user must acknowledge the message by clicking on the OK button.

Enabling Automatic Logon to a Windows NT Computer

On some computers dedicated for a special function such as print server or application server, you might want to bypass the Logon dialog box and automatically log on a user to the Windows NT computer.

To create an automatic logon to the computer, follow these steps:

1. Select the following key:

   HKEY_LOCAL_MACHINE\SOFTWARE\Microsoft\Windows NT\
   CurrentVersion\Winlogon

2. Add a value entry named AutoAdminLogon of type REG_SZ by choosing Add Value from the Edit menu. In the Add Value dialog box, enter the Value Name of AutoAdminLogon. In the Data Type field, select REG_SZ (see fig. 10.25). Then click on OK. In the String Editor dialog box that appears, enter a value of 1.

Figure 10.25

The Add Value dialog box.

3. Double-click on the value entry DefaultUserName. In the String Editor dialog box that appears, enter the name of the user to log on automatically.

4. Add a value entry named DefaultPassword of type REG_SZ by using the procedure outlined in step 4. Set the value of the DefaultPassword value entry to the password for the user name in the DefaultUserName value entry.

   Note that the password is stored in clear text (unencrypted form). If the log-in account is privileged, which is usually the case, you must set security permissions on the Winlogon subkey to prevent unauthorized users from reading the value of the DefaultPassword.

5. If you have an option to log on to the local computer or domain, you must ensure that the DefaultDomainName value entry under the WinLogon subkey is set correctly. If you have Windows NT Workstation in a domain or a Windows NT Server that is not a domain controller in a domain, you can log on locally to the computer or log on to the domain.

   Double-click on the DefaultDomainName value entry. In the String Editor dialog box, enter the computer name to log on or the domain name.

   Figure 10.26 shows the value entries used for automatic logon.

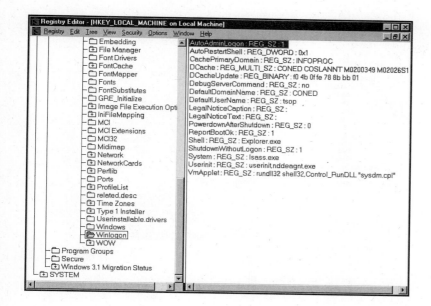

Figure 10.26
Automatic log-in value entries.

6. After double-checking all the changes you have made, log out. If you have made the changes correctly, you will be logged in automatically as the default user.

   To bypass the automatic logon, hold down the Shift key during logon until the Welcome Logon dialog box appears.

   To disable the automatic Logon, set the AutoAdminLogon value entry to 0.

Changing the Logon Screen

Before logging in to a Windows NT computer, you see the Microsoft Windows NT logo screen. The default Windows NT screen logos are kept in the WINNT.BMP file for Windows NT Workstations and the LANMANNT.BMP file for Windows NT Servers. You might want to stamp your own corporate identity to the Logon screen by creating your own bitmap file (BMP extension).

To create a custom log-in screen, follow these steps:

1. Select the following key:

   HKEY_USERS\.DEFAULT\Control Panel\Desktop

2. Double-click on the value entry Wallpaper (see fig. 10.27). In the String Editor dialog box that appears, enter the name of your bitmap file. If you do not have a bitmap file yet, try another bitmap file, such as the BALL.BMP file included in the Windows NT installation.

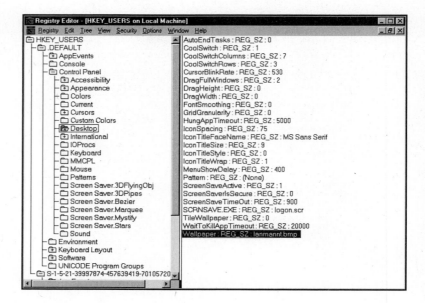

3. If you want to tile the bitmap that you have selected for the Windows NT Logon, double-click on the value entry TileWallpaper. In the String Editor dialog box that appears, enter a value of 1.

4. Log out and verify that your changes have been made.

Shutting Down without Logon

By default, on Windows NT Workstations, the Windows NT Logon dialog box shows a Shutdown button that can be used to shut down the workstation without logging into the workstation. On Windows NT Servers, there is no corresponding Shutdown button on the Logon screen by default. Because a Windows NT Server usually is shared by a number of users, it should not be shut down very easily—hence, the absence of the Shutdown button. Of course, somebody could bypass all these checks by turning off the power to a running Windows NT Server.

You might find it useful to enable or disable the Shutdown button on the Logon screen. In a small organization, for example, you might have to guide an end-user to shut down the Windows NT Server over the phone if you are away from the network site. You would like the user to shut down the server without giving him or her a privileged account password. If the Logon screen has a Shutdown button, the user can gracefully shut down the system by clicking on this button.

To enable (or disable) the Shutdown button, follow these steps:

1. Select the following key:

   HKEY_LOCAL_MACHINE\SOFTWARE\Microsoft\Windows NT\
   CurrentVersion\Winlogon

2. Double-click on the value entry ShutdownWithoutLogon (see fig. 10.28). In the String Editor dialog box that appears, enter a value of 1 for enabling the Shutdown button on the Logon screen. To disable the Shutdown button on the Logon screen, enter a value of 0.

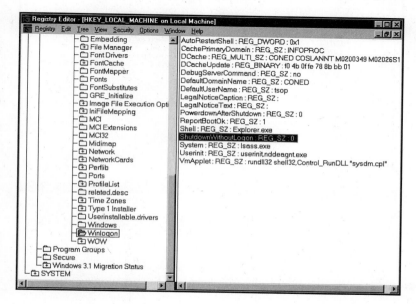

Figure 10.28

The ShutdownWithout-Logon value entry.

3. Log out and verify that your changes have been made.

Enabling the Shutdown and Power Off Option

The BIOS on some Windows NT computers supports a software shutdown. For such computers, Windows NT can be configured to support a software shutdown. When this option is enabled, you see the following new option in the Shutdown Computer dialog box:

   Shutdown and **P**ower Off

To enable (or disable) the Shutdown and **P**ower Off option, follow these steps:

1. Select the following key:

   HKEY_LOCAL_MACHINE\SOFTWARE\Microsoft\Windows NT\
   CurrentVersion\Winlogon

2. Double-click on the value entry PowerdownAfterShutdown (see fig. 10.29). In the String Editor dialog box that appears, enter a value of 1 to enable this option or a value of 0 to disable this option.

Figure 10.29

The PowerdownAfter Shutdown value entry.

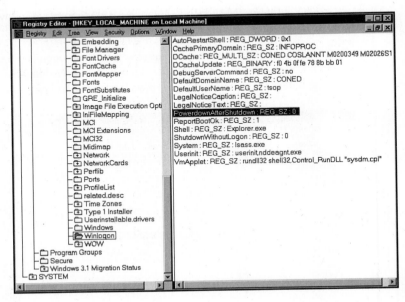

3. Shut down your Windows NT computer and verify the behavior of the Shutdown and **P**ower Off option.

If your Windows NT computer's BIOS does not support software shutdown, selecting the Shutdown and **P**ower Off option is the same as the Shutdown and Restart option.

Displaying the Last Logged-in User

By default, in the Username field of the Windows NT Logon dialog box, the name of the last user that logged in is shown.

To enable (or disable) the Shutdown button, follow these steps:

1. Select the following key:

   HKEY_LOCAL_MACHINE\SOFTWARE\Microsoft\Windows NT\
   CurrentVersion\Winlogon

2. If the DontDisplayLastUserName value entry does not exist, create this value entry of data type REG_SZ. Use the steps outlined in the earlier section for enabling automatic login to a Windows NT computer to create this value entry.

3. Set the value of DontDisplayLastUserName to 1 if you do not want the last login name to be displayed (see fig. 10.30). Set the value to 0 if you want the last login name to be displayed.

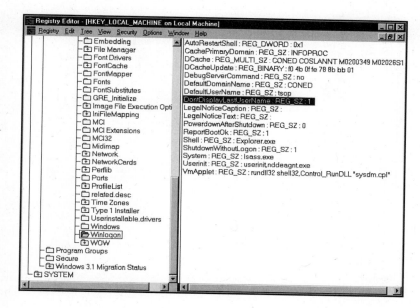

Figure 10.30
DontDisplayLastUserName value entry set disables the display of the last login user name.

4. Log out and log in again to verify that your changes have been made.

Parsing of the AUTOEXEC.BAT File

By default, Windows NT parses the AUTOEXEC.BAT file in the boot partition, if it exists, and sets the Environment variables. If the PATH Environment variable is specified in the AUTOEXEC.BAT file, its value is appended to the default system path every time the Windows NT computer is started.

If you do not want the AUTOEXEC.BAT file to be scanned for the setting of Environment variables, you can disable the parsing of the AUTOEXEC.BAT file.

To disable the parsing of the AUTOEXEC.BAT file, follow these steps:

1. Select the following key:

   HKEY_LOCAL_MACHINE\SOFTWARE\Microsoft\Windows NT\CurrentVersion\Winlogon

2. If the ParseAutoexec value entry does not exist, create this value entry of data type REG_SZ. Use the steps outlined in the earlier section on enabling automatic Logon to a Windows NT computer to create this value entry.

3. Set the value of ParseAutoexec to 0 if you do not want the system to process the AUTOEXEC.BAT file (see fig. 10.31). Set the value to 0 if you want the system to parse the AUTOEXEC.BAT file.

Figure 10.31

The ParseAutoexec value entry set to disable parsing of the AUTOEXEC.BAT file.

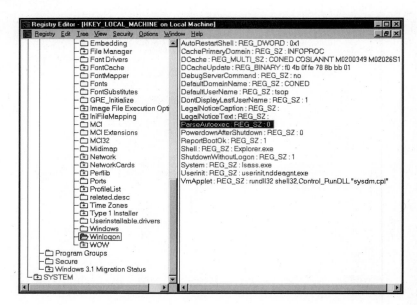

4. Restart the Windows NT computer and examine the Environment variable settings to verify that they are set as expected.

Examining Long File Name Support for FAT

By default, long file name support is enabled for FAT volumes on a Windows NT system. Windows NT uses additional directory entries to implement the long file name support. These additional directory entries use up the limited number of directory entries in the root directory on the FAT volume. Third-party diagnostic tools might not work with the extended directory entries, primarily because these directory entries are flagged with the Volume attribute. Normally, only one directory entry is flagged as a Volume entry on a FAT partition. Third-party tools might attempt to correct the extended directory entries by deleting them. You therefore might want to disable the long file name support for FAT volumes.

To disable long file name support on FAT volumes, follow these steps:

1. Select the following key:

   HKEY_LOCAL_MACHINE\SYSTEM\CurrentControlSet\Control\FileSystem

2. Set the value of Win31FileSystem to 1 if you want to disable long file name support on FAT volumes (see fig. 10.32). Set the value to 0 if you want to enable long file name support for FAT volumes.

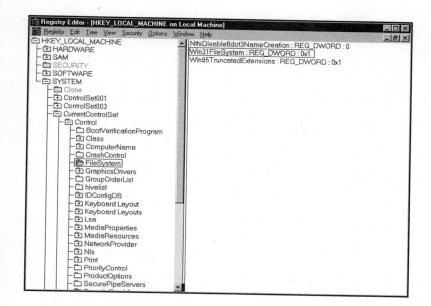

Figure 10.32
The Win31FileSystem value entry set to disable long file name support for FAT.

3. Verify that the creation of long file names behaves as expected.

You cannot enable or disable long file name support on a partition-by-partition basis. The changes that you specify apply to all FAT volumes on the Windows NT system.

Examining Short File Name Support for NTFS

By default, short file name support is enabled on NTFS volumes on a Windows NT system. Short file name support creates file names that obey DOS file-naming conventions. The purpose of this feature is to support DOS clients that need to access the NTFS volumes (for example, DOS workstations accessing an NTFS volume on a Windows NT computer over the network). If you do not expect to support DOS clients, you can disable the generation of short file names.

To disable short file name support on NTFS volumes, follow these steps:

1. Select the following key:

   HKEY_LOCAL_MACHINE\SYSTEM\CurrentControlSet\Control\FileSystem

2. Set the value of NtfsDisable8Dot3NameCreation to 1 if you want to disable short file name support on NTFS volumes (see fig. 10.33). Set the value to 0 if you want to enable short file name support for NTFS volumes.

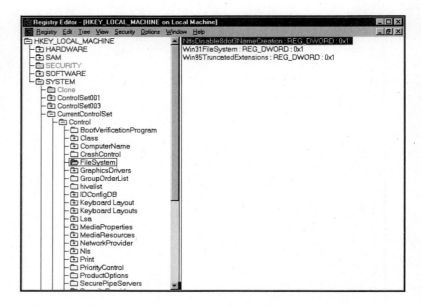

3. Verify that the creation of short file names behaves as expected.

You cannot enable or disable short file name support on an NTFS partition-by-partition basis. The changes that you specify apply to all NTFS volumes on the Windows NT system.

Distinguishing between User Profiles

It is useful to sometimes distinguish between the user profiles cached on the local Windows NT computer. You might want to do this for the purpose of system maintenance, such as backing up a particular user profile.

To determine a user's profile file, follow these steps:

1. Log on as the user to the Windows NT computer to discover the user's SID. If you do not have access to the user account, you might have the user perform the following operations to discover the SID value:

    ■ Open the HKEY_USERS subtree.

    ■ You should see two keys: the .DEFAULT key and the user's SID key (beginning with S-).

    ■ Record the user's SID: _____

2. Open the HKEY_LOCAL_MACHINE subtree.

3. Select the following key:

   HKEY_LOCAL_MACHINE\SOFTWARE\Microsoft\Windows NT\CurrentVersion\
   ProfileList

4. Select the SID key for the user you recorded in step 1.

   Figure 10.34 shows the SID keys under the ProfileList key.

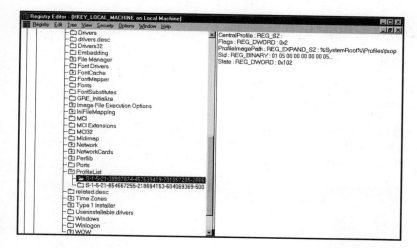

Figure 10.34
SID keys under the ProfileList key.

5. Double-click on the value entry ProfileImagePath to see the profile path for the user (see fig. 10.35).

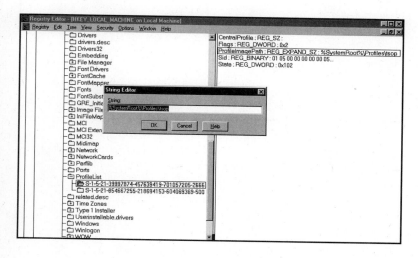

Figure 10.35
Locating the profile path for a user.

Determining the Device Using the Unlisted Serial Port

When connecting devices to serial ports, it is useful to determine what device is using an unlisted serial port.

To determine the device using an unlisted serial port, follow these steps:

1. Select the following key:

   HKEY_LOCAL_MACHINE\HARDWARE\DESCRIPTION\System\
   MultifunctionAdapter\0\SerialController

   For an EISA computer, select the following key:

   HKEY_LOCAL_MACHINE\HARDWARE\DESCRIPTION\System\
   EisaAdapter\0\SerialController

2. You should see the subkeys for each serial port on the system. Key 0 is for the COM1 port, key 1 is for the COM2 port, and so on. Figure 10.36 shows that there are two keys, 0 and 1, and hence two serial ports on the Windows NT computer.

Figure 10.36

Serial port keys in the Registry.

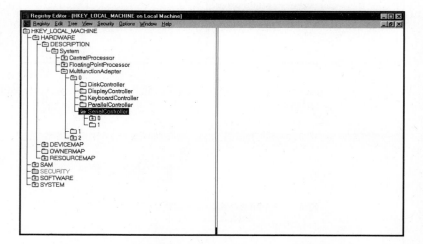

3. If a mouse is using a serial port, the serial port key will have a PointerPeripheral subkey. Figure 10.37 shows that key 0 (COM1 port) has the PointerPeripheral subkey.

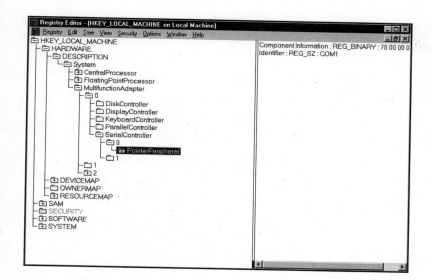

Figure 10.37
The PointerPeripheral subkey, indicating the presence of a mouse on the serial port.

If you do not see the PointerPeripheral key when you know that a pointer device such as a mouse is connected to the serial port, it indicates that another device is using the same serial port or the same interrupt number.

4. You can see information on the device connected to the serial port by examining the subkeys under the PointerPeripheral subkey. Figure 10.38 shows that the entry Identifier has a value of MICROSOFT SERIAL MOUSE for the pointing device connected to COM1.

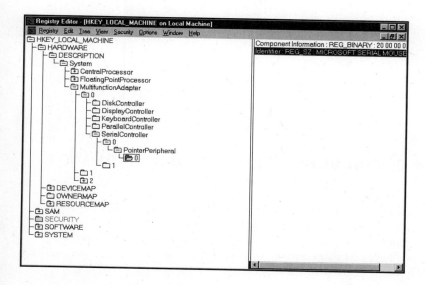

Figure 10.38
The identifier for the pointing device.

Double-clicking on the value entry Configuration Data shows additional configuration information on the pointing device (see fig. 10.40). This configuration information also is reported by the Windows NT Diagnostic program (WINMSD.EXE). Figure 10.40 shows the same serial port information displayed by the Windows NT Diagnostic programs. Aside from the differences in format, the information is the same.

Figure 10.39

Configuration data on the pointing device.

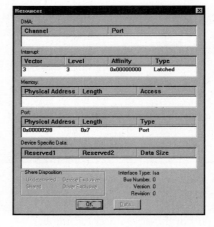

Figure 10.40

Serial device information shown by the Windows NT Diagnostic program.

Changing the Maximum Packet Size for a Network Adapter

On Token Ring networks, you might need to adjust the maximum packet size when sending data across bridges that might not be able to handle the maximum packet size of a Token Ring network. The maximum packet size for a Token Ring network actually is determined by the Token Holding Time (THT) for that network. You can change the maximum packet size used by the Windows NT computer by using the Registry.

To adjust the maximum packet size, follow these steps:

1. Select the following key:

   HKEY_LOCAL_MACHINE\SYSTEM\CurrentControlSet\Services\
   adaptername\ Parameters

   For the adaptername, select the name of the network adapter.

2. If the MaximumPacketSize value entry does not exist, create this value entry of data type REG_DWORD. Use the steps outlined in the previous section on enabling automatic Logon to a Windows NT computer to create this value entry.

3. Set the value of MaximumPacketSize to an appropriate number.

This method might not always work because it relies on the vendor of the network adapter writing the driver software to examine the value entry for MaximumPacketSize. If the driver software does not examine this value entry, setting its value will have no effect.

Disabling the CD-ROM AutoPlay Feature

Windows NT version 4 includes an AutoPlay feature for CD-ROMs. The AutoPlay feature automatically starts executables as specified by the CD's AUTORUN.INF file. This can be a real nuisance, or even an integrity issue on a server if the AutoPlay feature launches the application's setup program or other undesirable executable when a CD is inserted.

Note   You can manually stop the AutoPlay feature by holding down the Shift key while inserting a CD.

To disable the CD-ROM AutoPlay feature, follow these steps:

1. Select the following key:

   HKEY_LOCAL_MACHINE\SYSTEM\CurrentControlSet\Services\Cdrom

2. Double-click on the value entry for Autorun (data type REG_DWROD) and change the value from a 1 to a 0.

3. Log out and verify that your changes have been made.

Enabling HPFS Support Under NT 4

Although not supported by Microsoft under NT version 4, you may have a unique situation in which you need to support a High Performance File Systems (HPFS). Before attempting this, it is important to be aware that there may be some problematic issues involved when using this procedure with IIS, or FTP or with service packs added. Unless you need to support HPFS for a legitimate reason, such as restoring old data from a backup, there is no reason why you should not be utilizing NTFS.

To permit HPFS access, follow these steps:

1. You will have to copy the pinball.sys file from NT 3.51 to NT 4's %SYSTEMROOT%\System32\drivers directory. This can be from either an existing NT 3.51 system or from NT 3.51's distribution CD.

2. Select the following key:

   HKEY_LOCAL_MACHINE\SYSTEM\CurrentControlSet\Services\

3. From the menu, choose Edit and the Add Key command.

4. You should now have a dialog box entitled Add Key displayed. In the Key Name field, enter **Pinball**. Leave the Class field blank and click the OK button.

5. Scroll down the key listings and locate the newly created Pinball entry. With the Pinball key highlighted, choose Edit and Add Value from the menu.

6. You should now see the dialog box entitled Add Value. In the Value Name field, add the following entry with exactly the same capitalization and spelling: **ErrorControl**. In the Data Type scroll list, locate and select the REG_DWORD value and click the OK button.

7. Now the editor box should be displayed. Enter the value **1** in the Data field and click OK.

8. You need to add three more values to the Pinball key. With the Pinball key still highlighted, again choose Edit and Add Value from the menu.

9. You should now have a dialog box entitled Add Value displayed. In the Value Name field, add the following entry with exactly the same capitalization and spelling: **Group**. In the Data Type scroll list, locate and select the REG_SZ value and click the OK button.

10. Now the editor box should be displayed. Enter the value **Boot file system** in the Data field and click OK.

11. With the Pinball key still highlighted, again choose Edit and Add Value from the menu.

12. You should now have a dialog box entitled Add Value displayed. In the Value Name field, add the following entry with exactly the same capitalization and spelling: **Start**. In the Data Type scroll list, locate and select the REG_DWORD value and click the OK button.

13. Now the editor box should be displayed. Enter the value **1** in the Data field and click OK.

14. With the Pinball key still highlighted, again choose Edit and Add Value from the menu.

15. You should now see the Add Value dialog box displayed. In the Value Name field, add the following entry with exactly the same capitalization and spelling: **Type**. In the Data Type scroll list, locate and select the REG_DWORD value and click the OK button.

16. Now the editor box should be displayed. Enter the value **2** in the Data field and click OK.

17. You must now reboot the machine for this change to take effect.

Overcoming a User Application Error

Under some circumstances, you may find that a deleted application may leave some remnants of itself behind. If after removing an application, the NT machine displays an error message when a user logs on stating that it is unable to locate the deleted program, you may be able to overcome this problem by conducting the following steps to the system Registry:

1. Select the following key:

   HKEY_CURRENT_USER\Software\Microsoft\WindowsNT\CurrentVersion\Windows

2. Find the two values: Load and Run.

3. Examine the Load and Run values for entries that identify the names of the culprit applications. If either of these values contain the name of the deleted application then highlight the affected value, either Load or Run, choose Edit and String from the menu and remove the text in the field, and choose OK.

Restricting Access to NT's Registry from a Remote Computer

By default, the Registry Editor supports remote access to the Windows NT Registry by members of the Administrators group on NT 4, and by any user on NT 3.51. On Windows NT 3.51 with Service Pack 4 applied, or NT version 4 you can optionally restrict remote Registry access.

Note Use some precaution when restricting remote Registry access. There are some services that need access to the Registry as part of their normal functionality.

To specify restrictions for remote Registry access, follow these steps:

1. Select the following key:

   HKEY_LOCAL_MACHINE\SYSTEM\CurrentControlSet\Control\
   SecurePipeServers\winreg

2. With winreg highlighted, click Security and Permissions from the menu. Now simply Add or Remove users or groups that you want to grant access to the Registry to and specify their Type of access (see fig. 10.41).

Figure 10.41

Granting Users and Groups permissions for remote Registry access.

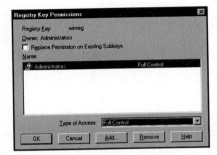

The optional subkey: HKEY_LOCAL_MACHINE\SYSTEM\CurrentControlSet\Control\ SecurePipeServers\winreg AllowedPaths specifies paths into the Registry that are allowed access by everyone, regardless of the security on the winreg registry key.

Interrupt Sharing Under NT

If resources are scarce, it may be desirable to share interrupts. In order to achieve this under NT 3.51 or 4, it is necessary to modify the Registry.

Note   To take advantage of sharing interrupts, it is necessary that the hardware is capable of sharing interrupts as well. Serial cards, for example, are available that have this capability.

To enable interrupt sharing, follow these steps:

1. Select the following key:

2. HKEY_LOCAL_MACHINE\SYSTEM\CurrentControlSet\Services\Serial

3. Double-click on the value entry for SermitShare and change the value from a 0 to a 1.

4. Reboot the machine for the changes to take effect.

Performing Registry Operations

Besides browsing the Registry and modifying the values, you can perform a number of useful operations on the Registry, such as the following:

■ Controlling Registry size

■ Managing Registry from the network

■ Loading and unloading hives

■ Backing up the Registry

■ Securing the Registry

These operations are discussed in the following sections.

Controlling Registry Size

Because Registry value entries can have values up to 1 MB, the Registry can become very large, but you can control the overall size of the Registry. The Registry size limit is set to a default value that is 25 percent of the value of the paged pool (32 MB). The default Registry size therefore is 8 MB, which is sufficient for about 5,000 user accounts.

The two parameters that affect the Registry size are the HKEY_LOCAL_MACHINE\ SYSTEM\CurrentControlSet\Control\RegistrySizeLimit, which is the maximum Registry size, and the HKEY_LOCAL_MACHINE\SYSTEM\CurrentControlSet\Control\Session Manager\Memory Management\PagedPoolSize. Figures 10.42 and 10.43 show sample values for these parameters using the Registry Editor.

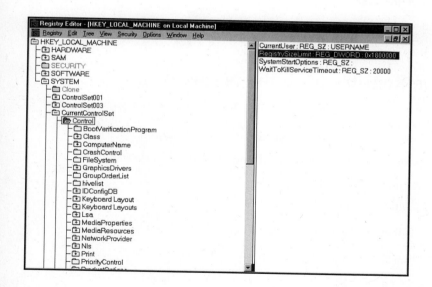

Figure 10.42

The RegistrySizeLimit parameter.

Figure 10.43

The PagedPoolSize parameter.

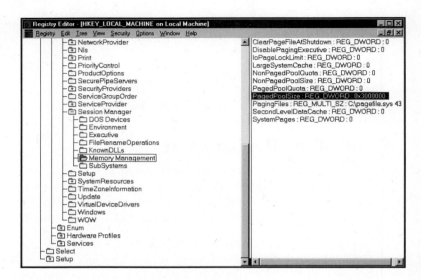

The Windows NT system ensures that the RegistrySizeLimit is between 4 MB and 80 percent of the the size of the PagedPoolSize. The maximum value of the PagedPoolSize is 128 MB. This limits the RegistrySizeLimit to about 102 MB, which can support a maximum of 80,000 users.

RegistrySizeLimit quota checking is not enforced until the first successful system boot. This ensures that wrong values of the RegistrySizeLimit will not prevent system boot.

Managing the Registry from the Network

The Windows NT Registry is local to each computer. You can manage the Registry by logging in locally to the Windows NT computer. The Registry Editor, however, has an option to manage the Registry of remote Windows NT computers over the network.

To manage the Registry of another computer on the network, follow these steps:

1. Log on as an Administrator user.

2. Run the Registry Editor (REGEDT32.EXE).

3. Choose **S**elect Computer from the Registry menu.

   The Select Computer dialog box appears (see fig. 10.44).

4. From the **S**elect Computer list box, select a remote computer to manage.

   If this is the first time you are remotely managing the Registry of the Windows NT computer, you see a message informing you that AutoRefresh is disabled (see fig. 10.45). Choose OK to acknowledge the message.

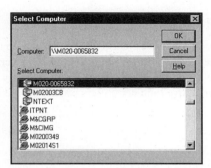

Figure 10.44

The Select Computer dialog box for remote management of the Registry.

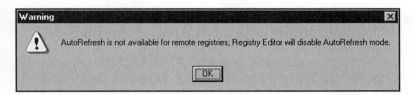

Figure 10.45

Confirming an AutoRefresh operation with a remote Registry.

Two new windows appear for the HKEY_LOCAL_MACHINE and HKEY_USERS subtrees on the remote Windows NT computer. Figure 10.46 shows these subtrees for the remote computer NTUS. The subtree HKEY_CLASSES_ROOT is not shown because it is a symbolic link to the HKEY_LOCAL_MACHINE\SOFTWARE\Classes. The HKEY_CURRENT_USER is meaningful for a locally logged-in user.

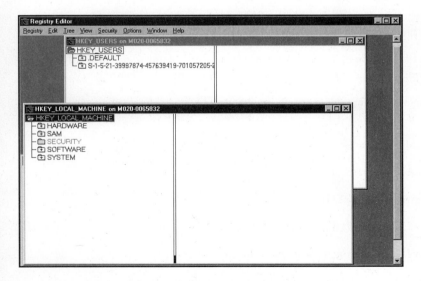

Figure 10.46

Registry windows for the remote computer.

5. You now can browse and manage the remote Registry using the same method for managing the local Registry.

Loading and Unloading Hives

When a Windows NT computer starts, it loads the Registry with the contents of the hive files kept on the computer. You can use the Registry Editor to view and manage entries in the Registry. You can load and unload the hives as a separate step. This capability is useful if you want to view or repair certain entries in a hive for a computer that is not configured correctly or cannot connect to the network.

The load and unload hive options affect only the HKEY_LOCAL_MACHINE and HKEY_USERS subtrees. You must have restore and backup privileges to load and unload hives. If you are logged in as an Administrator user, you have these privileges.

The Load Hive option is available only when HKEY_LOCAL_MACHINE or HKEY_USERS is selected in the Registry Editor. The Unload Hive option is available only when a subkey of these subtrees is selected.

To load a hive, follow these steps:

1. Log on as an Administrator user.

2. Run the Registry Editor (REGEDT32.EXE).

3. Select the HKEY_LOCAL_MACHINE or HKEY_USERS root key.

4. Choose **R**egistry, **L**oad Hive to open the Load Hive dialog box.

5. Select the file name that contains the hive file you want to load. The hive file can be one of the default hives or a file created by the Save Key command.

6. In the second Load Hive dialog box that appears, select the name under which the key should be loaded. You can specify any name except the name of an existing key.

You can view and edit the data under the new key name. The loaded hive remains loaded until it is unloaded.

To unload a hive, follow these steps:

1. Log on as an Administrator user.

2. Run the Registry Editor (REGEDT32.EXE).

3. Open the HKEY_LOCAL_MACHINE or HKEY_USERS subtree.

4. Select the key that represents the hive you want to unload.

5. Choose **U**nload Hive from the **R**egistry menu. Follow the instructions on-screen to complete the operation.

If you try to unload a key that is not a hive, you are prevented from doing so because the Unload Hive option is disabled. To save a key that is not a hive, use the Save Key option.

Unloading a selected key means that the key is no longer available to the system or for editing. Therefore, you cannot unload a hive that contains an open key or a hive that was loaded by the system.

Saving and Restoring Keys

You can save the information in a key and all its subkeys in a hive file. This hive file then can be used with the Restore and Load Key options.

You can use the Save Key option to save portions of the Registry in a file on a disk. To use the Save Key option, you must have backup privileges. You have these privileges if you are logged in as an Administrator user.

You cannot use the Save Key option to save volatile keys, such as the HKEY_LOCAL_MACHINE\HARDWARE key, which is destroyed when the system is shut down. If you need to view the hardware hive, you can save it as a text file using the Save Subtree As option.

To save a key in a hive file, follow these steps:

1. Log on as an administrator user.

2. Run the Registry Editor (REGEDT32.EXE).

3. Select the key that you want to save in a hive file.

4. Choose Save Key from the Registry menu. The Save Key dialog box appears.

5. Specify the name of the hive file to save to and choose OK.

The hive file is saved in a binary format. You can use the Load Hive option to load a hive saved by using the Save Key option. You also can use the Restore option to restore the saved keys as part of the system configuration. If you want to restore the keys temporarily to the system so that the keys disappear when the system is restarted, you can use the Restore Volatile option.

To use the Restore or Restore Volatile options, you must have Restore privileges. You have these privileges if you are logged in as an Administrator user.

To restore a key from a hive file, follow these steps:

1. Log on as an administrator user.

2. Run the Registry Editor (REGEDT32.EXE).

3. Select the key where you want to restore the hive file.

4. Choose Restore from the **R**egistry menu. Alternatively, choose Restore Volatile from the **R**egistry menu. The Restore Key dialog box appears.

5. Specify the name of the hive file to restore from, and then click on OK.

You cannot restore to a key if the key or its subkeys have opened handles. Because Windows NT always has opened handles to the SAM and SECURITY subtrees, you cannot restore these subtrees. The Restore option typically is used for the restoration of user profiles on a damaged system.

Viewing and Printing Registry Data

You can save the key as a text file for later examination and troubleshooting. You also can print data on a key and its subkeys from the Registry Editor.

To save a Registry key as a text file, follow these steps:

1. Log on as an administrator user.

2. Run the Registry Editor (REGEDT32.EXE).

3. Select the key to be saved as a text file.

4. Choose Save Subtree **A**s from the **R**egistry menu. The Save As dialog box appears.

5. Specify the name of the text file to save to and click on OK.

An example of the saved text file for a network adapter setting found in the HKEY_LOCAL_MACHINE\SYSTEM\CurrentControlSet\Services\ adaptername key is shown follows:

```
Key Name:          SYSTEM\CurrentControlSet\Services\SMCISA1
Class Name:        GenericClass
Last Write Time:   6/3/95 — 10:49 AM
Value 0
Name:              ErrorControl
Type:              REG_DWORD
Data:              0×1

Value 1
Name:              Start
Type:              REG_DWORD
Data:              0×3

Value 2
Name:              Type
Type:              REG_DWORD
Data:              0×4
```

```
Key Name:            SYSTEM\CurrentControlSet\Services\SMCISA1\Linkage
Class Name:          GenericClass
Last Write Time:     6/3/95 — 10:49 AM

Key Name:            SYSTEM\CurrentControlSet\Services\SMCISA1\Linkage\Disabled
Class Name:          GenericClass
Last Write Time:     6/3/95 — 10:49 AM

Key Name:            SYSTEM\CurrentControlSet\Services\SMCISA1\Parameters
Class Name:          GenericClass
Last Write Time:     6/3/95 — 10:49 AM
Value 0
Name:                BusNumber
Type:                REG_DWORD
Data:                0

Value 1
Name:                BusType
Type:                REG_DWORD
Data:                0×1

Value 2
Name:                InterruptNumber
Type:                REG_DWORD
Data:                0×3

Value 3
Name:                IOBaseAddress
Type:                REG_DWORD
Data:                0×280

Value 4
Name:                MediaType
Type:                REG_DWORD
Data:                0×1

Value 5
Name:                MemoryMappedBaseAddress
Type:                REG_DWORD
Data:                0×d0000
```

You can use this text file as documentation on the network adapter settings.

To create a printout of the Registry keys, follow these steps:

1. Log on as an administrator user.

2. Run the Registry Editor (REGEDT32.EXE).

3. Select the key to be saved as a text file.

4. Choose **P**rint Subtree from the **R**egistry menu.

Backing Up the Registry

You cannot use the Registry Editor to fully restore hives because parts of the Registry are in use, and the active parts can be replaced only by a Replace Key operation, which is not available through the Registry.

If your Windows NT system is damaged, you can use the Emergency Repair Disk that was created during the installation or by running the RDISK.EXE program. The Emergency Repair Disk contains the hive files at the time the disk was created. If you want a complete backup of the Registry, you must use special programs to perform backup and restore operations because parts of the Registry, such as the SAM and security information, always are in use.

The Windows NT Resource Kit (sold separately by Microsoft) contains tools to back up and restore the Registry on a Windows NT computer. These tools are the Registry Backup (REGBACK.EXE) and Registry Restore (REGREST.EXE) programs.

REGBACK allows you to back up pieces of the Registry (hives) even when the system has them open. You can back up the Registry on a floppy or on the hard disk. The Registry backup will fail if the hives cannot fit on the target device. If you need to back up on a floppy disk, and the hives do not fit on a single floppy disk, you first can back up the Registry to the hard drive and then use the BACKUP.EXE program to back up the files to multiple floppy disks.

The REGBACK.EXE program does not copy the hive files in %SystemRoot%\System32\Config directory because these do not reflect the most recent changes to the Registry. The files in the Config directory are inactive hive files, which are used to initialize the Registry on system startup.

The general syntax for using REGBACK follows:

```
REGBACK     targetdirectory
```

The targetdirectory is the directory location where the backed up hive files are to be stored. The first form of the REGBACK command backs up all the Registry hives. The command returns a non-zero error level code if the backup fails. You can test for this error level code in a batch file.

To back up the Registry in the target directory D:\RBACK, use the following command:

```
> REGBACK D:\RBACK
```

You then see the following messages:

```
saving SECURITY to D:\RBACK\SECURITY
saving SOFTWARE to D:\RBACK\software
saving SYSTEM to D:\RBACK\system
saving .DEFAULT to D:\RBACK\default
saving SAM to D:\RBACK\SAM
S—1—5—21—72291732—1469457266—160764864—500 to D:\RBACK\Admin000
```

You then can back up the files SECURITY, software, system, default, and user information file (Admin000, in the previous example) to a backup device such as a tape or floppies.

REGBACK does not override existing backed-up hive files, and it reports an error when an attempt is made to do so. If an attempt is made to again execute the command

```
> REGBACK D:\RBACK
```

for example, and the hive files have not been removed from the D:\RBACK directory, you see the following messages:

```
saving SECURITY to D:\RBACK\SECURITY
Save failed
hivebranch='machine', hive='SECURITY', result='0×000000b7'
file='D:\RBACK\SECURITY'
```

You can use the REGREST program to restore the Registry that was backed up using the REGBACK program. The restoration process renames the files and restores the hive when the system restarts. The backup files have to be on the same volume as the currently loaded hives. If the currently loaded hive files are in the D:\WINNT\System32\Config directory, for example, the backup files also must be on drive D. During the restoration of the hives, the backup files are destroyed, so you should save them in a separate location. The hives that are replaced during the restoration are saved in a directory specified with the REGREST command.

The general syntax to use for the REGREST program follows:

```
REGREST      backupdir oldhivedir
```

The backupdir is a directory that contains the files produced by REGBACK. The files in backupdir are deleted at the end of the restoration process. At the end of the restoration, the oldhivedir contains the hive files for the hive that was replaced. At the end of the Registry restoration, you must restart the system to make your change effective.

In the following example, D:\RBACK contains the hive files produced using REGBACK, and D:\SAVEHIVE is an empty directory to contain the hive that is replaced at the end of the restoration:

```
> REGREST D:\RBACK D:\SAVEHIVE
```

This command then displays the following messages:

```
replacing SECURITY with D:\RBACK\SECURITY
replacing SOFTWARE with D:\RBACK\software
replacing SYSTEM with D:\RBACK\system
replacing .DEFAULT with D:\RBACK\default
replacing SAM with D:\RBACK\SAM
replacing S—1—5—21—72291732—1469457266—160764864—500 with D:\RBACK\Admin000
```

You must reboot in order for changes to take effect. Use the following command:

```
> DIR D:\SAVEHIVE
```

You then see the following messages:

```
Volume in drive D has no label.
Volume Serial Number is 58C4—92A8
Directory of D:\SAVEHIVE
06/20/95  12:14p        <DIR>          .
06/20/95  12:14p        <DIR>          ..
06/20/95  11:01a              105,648 Admin000
06/20/95  10:03a              110,592 default
06/20/95  10:06a               16,384 SAM
06/20/95  10:03a               28,672 SECURITY
06/20/95  10:07a              376,832 software
06/20/95  12:02p              622,592 system
 8 File(s)      1,310,720 bytes
```

Securing the Registry

As long as the Windows NT system root (D:\WINNT) is installed on an NTFS volume, you can set access control lists on the different parts of the Registry to control users' access to the Registry. If the Windows NT system root is not installed on an NTFS volume, you cannot enforce permissions security on the Registry, and a user could tamper with the Registry by performing operations such as removing hives for user profiles that are not currently loaded.

You can use file-permission settings to control user access to the REGEDT32.EXE program and the Registry files on the Windows NT computer. Additionally, you might want to audit access to this file.

If you want additional protection for the Registry, you can set access control lists for the Registry keys and audit Registry activities.

Setting Permissions on Registry Keys

Windows NT defines permissions that can be set for users and groups for accessing the Registry keys. The standard permissions list for Registry keys is defined in table 10.4. The main standard permissions are Read and Full Control. You can specify Special Access permissions. These are similar to the individual permissions for file system security. Table 10.5 defines the special permissions for controlling access to Registry keys.

Table 10.4
Permissions for Registry Keys

Permission	Description
Read	Enables users in the ACL to read the key's contents but prevents changes from being saved.
Full Control	Enables users in the ACL to access, edit, or take ownership of a key.
Special Access	Enables you to specify a custom combination of access permissions for users.

Table 10.5
Special Permissions for Registry Keys

Permission	Description
Query Value	Permission to read a value entry from a Registry key.
Set Value	Permission to set (modify) a value entry in a Registry key.
Create Subkey	Permission to create a subkey under a Registry key.
Enumerate Subkey	Permission to identify (list) the subkeys of a Registry key.
Notify	Permission to open a key with Notify access.
Create Link	Permission to create a symbolic link from a Registry key.
Delete	Permission to delete a key.
Write DAC	Capability to modify the permissions list for a Registry key.
Write Owner	Capability to take ownership of a key.
Read Control	Permission to read the security information on the key.

To set permissions on a Registry key, follow these steps:

1. Log on as an Administrator user.

2. Run the Registry Editor.

3. Select the key for which permissions are to be set.

4. Choose **P**ermissions from the **S**ecurity menu.

   The Registry Key Permissions dialog box appears (see fig. 10.47).

Figure 10.47

The Registry Key Permissions dialog box.

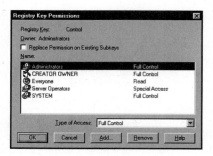

You can use the Replace Permission on Existing Subkeys option to set the assigned permissions for all subkeys in the subtree, with the selected key as the root.

The **N**ame list shows the list of users and groups to which permissions can be assigned. You can use the **A**dd and **R**emove buttons to change the **N**ame list. For each highlighted user in the **N**ame list, the permission in the **T**ype of Access field can be assigned. These permissions are the Read, Full Control, and Special Access permissions defined in table 10.4.

5. To add additional users or groups, click on the **A**dd button. The Add Users and Groups dialog box appears (see fig. 10.48).

Figure 10.48

The Add Users and Groups dialog box.

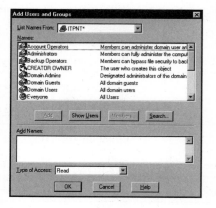

The **N**ames list box displays the list of accounts in the current domain that can be assigned rights. The current domain is displayed in the **L**ist Names From field. The domain name ITPNT in figure 10.48 is followed by an asterisk symbol. An asterisk following a domain or computer name indicates that the local groups of that domain or computer can be listed. The absence of an asterisk means that the local group cannot be listed. Remember that local groups can contain local users, as well as domain users and global groups from the current domain and trusted domains.

To list names from other domains, select the **L**ist Names From field. This displays a list that contains the local domain name, trusted domains, and computer names.

The **N**ames list shows the accounts of the selected domain or computer. If a domain is selected, the list of global groups for that domain will also be listed. The initial display of accounts only includes group names. If you want to assign permissions to user accounts, you must click on the Show **U**sers button, which also shows the user accounts in the domain that can be assigned permissions to the directory. Initially, only group names are displayed to encourage you to think in terms of granting permissions to groups. You must perform an extra step to list user accounts that can be granted permissions.

You select the accounts to be granted permissions from the **N**ames list box. If you then click on the **A**dd button, these account names are added to the A**d**d Names list. You also can list members of a group in the **N**ames list by clicking on the **M**embers button and selecting individual member accounts to be added to the A**d**d Names list.

You can search for accounts in other domains by clicking on the **S**earch button. You can use the Find Account dialog box to locate a user account or group in a specific domain or all domains. The search results then can be added to the list of group members.

After adding names to the A**d**d Names list, select the appropriate standard permission from the **T**ype of Access list. You can select only Read and Full Control at this point. If you want to select special permissions, you must modify the **T**ype of Access field in the Registry Key Permissions dialog box.

Click on the OK button to save your changes.

6. If you need to assign a user or group account the Special permission, highlight the user or group account in the Registry Key Permissions dialog box, and select Special Permission from the **T**ype of Access field. Figure 10.49 shows the Special Access dialog box that appears.

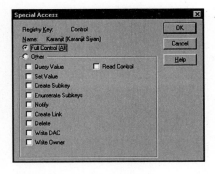

Figure 10.49
The Special Access dialog box.

Select the special permissions from the Special Access dialog box, and click on OK to save your changes.

7. Click on OK in the Registry Key Permissions dialog box to save your changes.

Taking Ownership of a Key

Normally, only the administrator user should have ownership of keys. You can take back ownership by following these steps:

1. Log on as an Administrator user.

2. Run the Registry Editor.

3. Select the key for which permissions are to be set.

4. Choose **O**wner from the **S**ecurity menu. The Owner dialog box appears.

5. Click on the **T**ake Ownership button.

Auditing Registry Access

Before you can set up auditing for a Registry key, you should turn on auditing using the User Manager for Domains. The procedure for performing this was outlined in Chapter 9, "Managing Network Files and File Security Systems." From the Policies menu in the User Manager for Domains, you should, at a minimum, check the Failure option for File and Object Access. If you check the Success option, it can cause a large number of audit events to be generated.

Next, you should set auditing on keys using the Registry Editor. This procedure follows:

1. Log on as an Administrator user.

2. Run the Registry Editor.

3. Select the key to be audited.

4. Choose **A**uditing from the **S**ecurity menu.

    The Registry Key Auditing dialog box appears (see fig. 10.50).

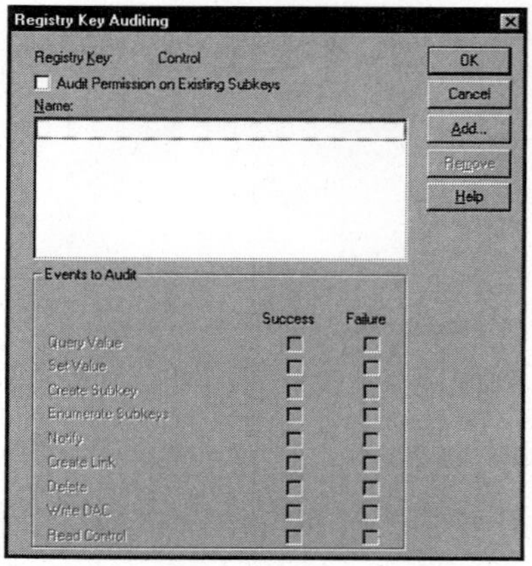

Figure 10.50

The Registry Key Auditing dialog box.

If the Audit Permission on Existing Subkeys option is selected, the auditing changes you make will apply to all keys in the subtree. By default, this option is not set, so the auditing changes apply to selected keys only.

To add users or groups to be audited, click on the **A**dd button. Figure 10.51 shows the Add Users and Groups screen for auditing.

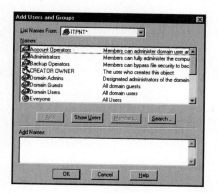

Figure 10.51

The Add Users and Groups dialog box for auditing Registry keys.

The **N**ames box displays the list of accounts in the current domain that can be assigned rights. The current domain is displayed in the **L**ist Names From field. An asterisk following a domain or computer name indicates that the local groups of that domain or computer can be listed. The absence of an asterisk means that the local group cannot be listed. Remember that local groups can contain local users, as well as domain users and global groups from the current domain and trusted domains.

To list names from other domains, select the **L**ist Names From field. This displays a list containing the local domain name, trusted domains, and computer names.

The **N**ames list shows the accounts of the selected domain or computer. If a domain is selected, the list of global groups for that domain also is listed. The initial display of accounts only includes group names. If you want to assign permissions to user accounts, you must click on the Show **U**sers button, which also shows the user accounts in the domain that can be audited. Initially, only group names are displayed to encourage you to think in terms of auditing groups rather than individual users.

You select the accounts to be audited from the **N**ames list box. If you then click on the **A**dd button, these account names are added to the A**d**d Names list. You also can list members of a group in the **N**ames list by clicking on the **M**embers button. You can select any of the members of the group and click on the A**d**d button to add the members to the A**d**d Names list.

You can search for accounts in other domains by clicking on the **S**earch button. The Find Account dialog box appears. You can use this box to locate a user account or group in a specific domain or all domains. The search results then can be added to the list of group members.

Click on the OK button in the Add Users and Groups screen to add the users and groups to the Directory or File Auditing screen. You are returned to the Registry Key Auditing screen.

5. For each of the users and groups added to the Registry Key Auditing screen, select the events to be audited. The events to audit are maintained on a per-user or per-group basis.

6. Click on the OK button to save your audit settings.

Examining the Windows NT Registry and Boot Sequence

The Windows NT boot process is controlled by information in the Registry. Understanding how the boot sequence is controlled by the Registry can help you troubleshoot problems in Windows NT, such as Windows NT not starting correctly.

On RISC-based computers, the Boot Loader menu and functionality of the NTLDR (on Intel computers) is not needed because this functionality is built into the computer's firmware. The initial stages of the boot sequence are controlled by the OSLOADER.EXE program on RISC-based systems. The NTDETECT.COM program used on Intel computers is not needed because this information is collected as a standard part of the POST (Power On Self-Test) process on RISC computers, and then reported to the OSLOADER.EXE program. The OSLOADER.EXE program eventually transfers control to the NTOSKRNL.EXE program. After this point, the boot sequence on Intel and RISC-based computers is the same.

After control is transferred to NTOSKRNL.EXE, the following initialization sequence takes place:

1. Kernel Load

2. Kernel Initialization

3. Services Load

4. Windows 32 Subsystem Start

The Kernel Load Phase

The Kernel Load phase commences when control is transferred to the NTOSKRNL.EXE program. The Hardware Abstraction Layer (HAL) component that hides platform-specific dependencies is loaded next. This is followed by the loading of the system hive component of the Registry.

The system hive contains information on the drivers and services that should be loaded. The drivers and services are loaded in the order specified in the value entry LIST under the HKEY_LOCAL_MACHINE\SYSTEM\CurrentControlSet\ServiceGroupOrder (see fig. 10.52). This portion of the load sequence can be identified by the appearance of the dots (...) that show the load progress. The drivers are loaded but not initialized in this phase. You can see the drivers that are loaded if you add the /SOS switch to the BOOT.INI. You see the following messages:

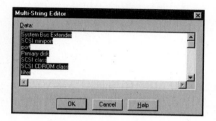

Figure 10.52

Loading the order of drivers and services.

```
[boot loader]
timeout=30
default=multi(0)disk(0)rdisk(0)partition(1)\WINNT
 [operating systems]
multi(0)disk(0)rdisk(0)partition(1)\WINNT="Windows NT Server Version 4.0" /SOS
multi(0)disk(0)rdisk(0)partition(1)\WINNT="Windows NT Server Version 4.0 [VGA
➡mode]" /basevideo /SOS
C:\="MS-DOS"
```

The Kernel Initialization Phase

When the Windows NT computer screen turns blue during the startup process, the Kernel Initialization phase begins. In this phase, the drivers that were loaded in the previous phase—the Kernel Load phase—are initialized. Drivers contain initialization routines that are invoked. These initialization routines initialize the hardware device that they control.

In this phase, the system hive is scanned again to determine high-level drivers that need to be loaded and initialized after the kernel initializes. The HARDWARE key in HKEY_LOCAL_MACHINE is initialized with the list of hardware components detected using NTDETECT.COM (or the POST on RISC computers). The Registry's CurrentControlSet is saved, and the Clone control set is created and initialized. The Clone control set is saved to the LastKnownGood control set only after a successful user Logon, which takes place after all the startup phases are completed.

If the driver failed to initialize, the action that is taken depends on the setting of the ErrorControl value entry in the HKEY_LOCAL_MACHINE\SYSTEM\CurrentControlSet\Services\DriverName key. The values for ErrorControl are explained in table 10.6. Figure 10.53 shows an example value entry (value 1), which indicates that if an error was encountered in initializing the Adaptec disk controller driver, treat it as a normal error.

Figure 10.53
*An ErrorControl value
entry.*

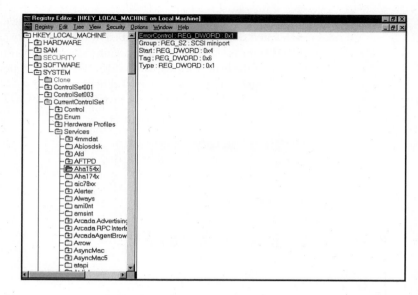

Figure 10.53
An ErrorControl value entry.

Table 10.6
ErrorControl Values

Value	Meaning
0×3	A critical error. The system will be restarted using the LastKnownGood state. If the system already is using the LastKnownGood state, the boot fails and an error message appears.
0×2	A severe error. The system will be restarted using the LastKnownGood state. If the system already is using the LastKnownGood state, the error is ignored and the boot sequence continues.
0×1	A normal error. The boot sequence displays the error, but otherwise ignores it.
0×0	The error is ignored. The boot sequence continues and the error is not displayed.

If you want to change when a driver or service is started, you can change the Start value entry under the HKEY_LOCAL_MACHINE\SYSTEM\CurrentControlSet\Services\DriverName key. The Start value entries are described in table 10.7. Figure 10.53 shows that the Start value entry for the Adaptec disk driver is 0, which means that it must be loaded by the boot loader.

> **Note** Be cautious when manipulating start value entries. Changing the start values is not recommended because dependent drivers and services may not have been started yet, and this could have catastrophic effects on the system.

Table 10.7
Start Values

Value	Start Type	Meaning
0×0	Boot	Loaded by the boot loader
0×1	System	Loaded at kernel initialization
0×2	Auto load	Loaded or started automatically at startup
0×3	Load on demand	Available, but started only by the user
0×4	Disabled	Not to be started under any conditions

The Services Load Phase

The Services Load phase starts the Session Manager program (SMSS.EXE). The Session Manager runs the programs listed in the BootExecute value entry under the HKEY_LOCAL_MACHINE\SYSTEM\CurrentControlSet\Control\Session Manager key. Figure 10.54 shows the default entry for the BootExecute key, which is the AUTOCHK program. The program AUTOCHK.EXE is a boot-time version of the CHKDSK.EXE program and checks each partition and displays its results during system startup in messages similar to the following:

```
The type of the file system is XXXX.
The volume is clean.
```

Because the BootExecute value entry is of type REG_MULTI_SZ, you can add multiple commands. If you add the /p option to the AUTOCHK program, it marks all bad areas on the disk in special files and performs this check every time the system restarts. You can use the following value for BootExecute, for example, to check bad areas of the disk:

```
autochk autochk /p *
```

To force a check on drive C, you add the following for BootExecute:

```
autochk autochk /p \DosDevices\C:
```

Figure 10.54

The BootExecute value entry key.

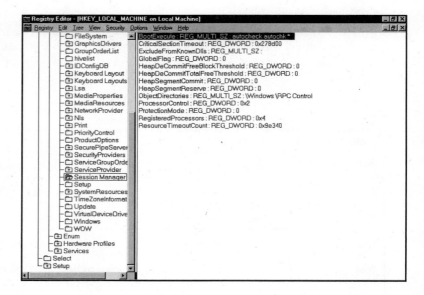

If a drive X has been set to be converted to NTFS during the next system boot, you see the following value added for BootExecute:

```
autochk autoconv \DosDevices\x: /FS:ntfs
```

After the drives are checked, Session Manager establishes the page files used for virtual memory under HKEY_LOCAL_MACHINE\SYSTEM\CurrentControlSet\Control\Session Manager\Memory Management. Figure 10.55 shows sample values for the parameters for the paged file. Notice that the PagingFiles value entry shows the name of the file to be C:\pagefile.sys with an initial size of 24 MB.

Next, the Session Manager loads the required subsystems listed under HKEY_LOCAL_MACHINE\SYSTEM\CurrentControlSet\Control\Session Manager\SubSystems. Figure 10.56 shows the required subsystems to be Debug and Windows (Win32 subsystem).

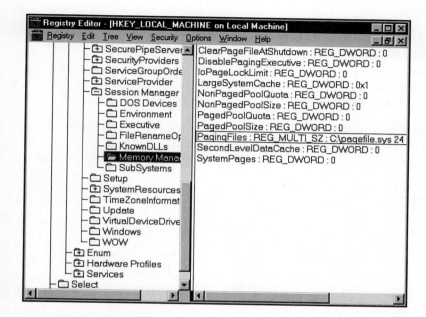

Figure 10.55
The PagingFile parameters in the Registry.

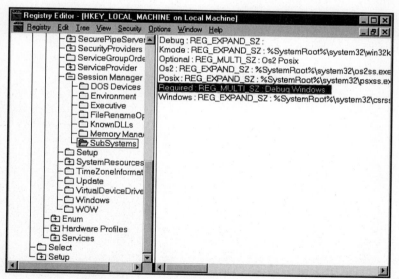

Figure 10.56
Required subsystem information in the Registry.

The Windows Subsystem Start Phase

The Session Manager starts the Win32 subsystem, as explained in the preceding section. When the Win32 subsystem starts, it starts the WINLOGON.EXE program, which displays the Ctrl+Alt+Del Logon box for initiating the log-in sequence. The WINLOGON.EXE also starts the Local Security Authority subsystem (LSASS.EXE) needed for authenticating user logins.

After the WINLOGON.EXE is started, the Win32 subsystem starts the Security Controller (SCREG.EXE) program, which makes a final pass through the Registry and starts any services that are marked for starting automatically. Examples of these auto-start services are the Workstation and Server services, which must be running for Windows NT computers on a network. Services that are started might depend on other services. These dependencies are specified in the DependOnGroup and DependOnServices entries.

The startup sequence is not considered good until a user logs in. If a Logon is successful, the Clone control set is copied to the LastKnownGood control set.

Conclusion

This chapter discussed the structure of the Windows NT Registry, the internal database that contains configuration information on every Windows NT computer. The Registry is a centralized database meant as a replacement for the configuration files in the Windows 3.x environment. The Windows NT Registry structure is hierarchical, and the information contained in it affects most aspects of the Windows NT computer system.

The Registry is not normally a tool for the end-user. It is used by the system administrator tool for making changes that cannot be made through the normal system tool programs or application programs. This chapter discussed how you can use the Registry to perform some practical system administration tasks, and how you can protect the Registry against unauthorized changes.

Supporting Windows NT Server Clients

*T*he Windows NT Server supports a number of different client computers, such as MS-DOS, Windows 3.x, Windows 95, Windows NT, OS/2, and Macintosh clients. This chapter discusses the network client architecture, protocols, and APIs used to access Windows NT Server resources.

You will learn about the Network Client Administrator tool and how you can use this tool to install and configure different client environments to access a Windows NT Server.

Examining the Architecture of Network Clients

In order to support a large number of different clients, the networking software supplied by Microsoft for clients to communicate with a server follows a general networking model. The network client architecture consists of a number of components that can be understood best in terms of the OSI model. The OSI model was discussed in Appendix A, "Windows NT Server Protocols." If you are unfamiliar with this model, you might want to review the discussion presented in that chapter.

Looking at Windows NT Clients and the OSI Model

Figure 11.1 shows a networking model for Windows NT clients. The following are the network components on the client:

- Network adapters

- Network drivers

- Client network protocol stacks

- Network APIs

- The Redirector

Figure 11.1

Network client architecture.

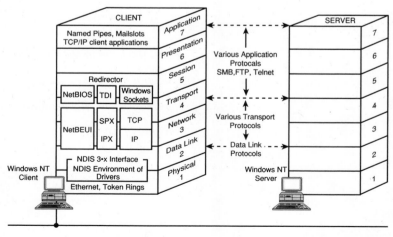

NetBEUI = NetBIOS Extended User Interface
NetBIOS = Network Basic Input Output System
TCP/IP = Transmission Control Protocol/Internet Protocol
TDI = Transport Driver Interface

NDIS = Network Driver Interface Specifications
SMB = Server Message Block
FTP = File Transfer Protocol

The network adapters can be considered as part of layers 1 and 2 of the OSI model, and are the physical aspects of the network on the client workstation.

Network Drivers

The network drivers provided by Microsoft are written using the NDIS interface (Network Driver Interface Specification) and enable multiple protocol stacks to communicate with a single or multiple network adapters inside the workstation. The NDIS drivers for most popular cards are bundled with the Windows NT distribution software. You can think of the NDIS drivers as the interface between layers 2 and 3 of the OSI model. Actual NDIS driver implementations can implement portions of layers 2 and 3 of the OSI model in order to provide this interface. Figure 11.2 shows the NDIS interface; the NDIS driver has a wrapper DLL around it that implements the NDIS interface. Multiple protocols—such as NetBEUI, TCP/IP with Streams, and IPX/SPX—communicate with the NDIS interface. In Windows NT clients, NDIS version 3 is used, which supports the use of 32-bit access and multiple processors.

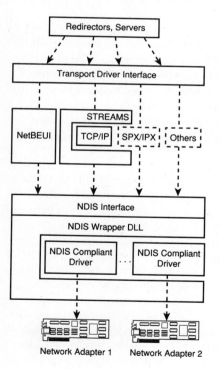

Network Adapter 1   Network Adapter 2

- NDIS shields details of physical networks from transport protocols

- NDIS allows multiple protocol stacks to share a network adapter

- NDIS allows a protocol stack to use multiple network adapters

- NDIS 3•x has been updated to use 32-bit addresses and multiprocessors

Figure 11.2
The NDIS interface.

Client Network Protocol Stacks

The network protocol stacks comprise layers 3, 4, and, optionally, layer 5 of the OSI model. At the Windows NT Server, you can select from the following communication protocols:

- NetBEUI

- IPX/SPX (called NWLink IPX Compatible Protocol in Windows NT)

- TCP/IP

A server and the clients that access it must use the same protocols. If you need to support Macintosh workstations that use the AppleTalk protocol, you must install Services for Macintosh at the Windows NT Server. This option implements the AppleTalk protocol stack on the server, enabling AppleTalk clients (Macintosh workstations) to communicate with the Windows NT Server.

Network APIs

If the client is using the NetBEUI protocol, the *Network Basic Input/Output System* (NetBIOS) interface is available to client applications. NetBIOS is a Session level interface used to communicate with other NetBIOS-compliant protocol stacks. Microsoft's implementation of NetBIOS often is called *NetBIOS Frame* (NBF). NetBIOS was developed by Sytek (now part of Hughes LAN Systems) for the IBM Broadband PC Network (PCN). It originally was implemented on a ROM (read only memory) chip; hence the name *NetBIOS* to compare it with the BIOS found on Intel computers. Later versions of NetBIOS were implemented by several vendors as device drivers and TSRs for DOS.

The network Redirector component of the network client software uses the NetBIOS interface to communicate with other computers running the same interface. The NetBIOS interface establishes logical names for computers on the network, and establishes virtual circuits between two logical names to ensure that data is transferred reliably between the logical names. NetBIOS names consist of 1 to 15 characters; this is the reason that computer names for Windows NT have a 1 to 15 character length limitation.

The *Windows sockets interface*, also called *WINSOCK*, is an implementation of the popular BSD sockets programming interface for TCP/IP networks. The sockets interface was developed for BSD Unix, but has been adopted widely on other Unix and non-Unix platforms. The WINSOCK interface is used by client applications to communicate with the TCP/IP protocol stack. Version 2 of the WINSOCK interface can be used with TCP/IP, IPX, DecNET, and OSI protocols. The advantage of using the WINSOCK interface is that it is familiar to programmers with a background in Unix. It enables Unix applications to be ported to the Windows environment more easily.

Both NetBIOS and WINSOCK are implemented as DLLs in a Windows environment.

The *Transport Driver Interface* (TDI) is used in Windows NT clients (and servers) to provide a uniform interface to the various transport protocols that can exist in the Windows NT environment. The TDI provides a common interface to the network components at the Session layer of the OSI model. The TDI interface enables virtual circuits to be established with applications on other computers using the same interface.

The Named Pipes and Mailslot Application Programming Interfaces (APIs) are modeled using file system operations such as Open, Read, and Write. However, the operations are not performed on actual files. Instead, they are translated as commands to the network transport protocols to communicate with other applications using the same APIs on remote computers on the network.

On Windows NT, the Named Pipes APIs are based on OS/2 APIs but have additional asynchronous support and increased security. The Mailslot APIs on Windows NT are a subset of the Mailslot APIs in OS/2. Mailslots are categorized as *first-class* mailslots, which provide connections-oriented communications, and *second-class* mailslots, which provide connectionless communications useful for messaging and broadcasting applications. In Windows NT, only second-class mailslots are used. Because second-class mailslots are connectionless, messages delivered using this API are not guaranteed to be delivered. Second-class mailslot messages are used by clients to identify other computers and services, and to send notification messages.

Windows NT clients have an added feature for named pipes called *impersonation*. Impersonation enables a server servicing a request to change its security ID (SID) to match the requesting client's SID. Impersonation ensures that, even though the server has the authority to execute a client's request because the request is carried out by impersonating the client's SID, it is permitted to execute only if the client has the authority to execute the request.

Remote access to named pipes and mailslots is provided through the Redirector component.

The Redirector

The *Redirector* is the component that enables a client computer to gain access to resources on another computer as if the remote resources were local to the client computer. The Redirector component communicates with other computers using the protocol stack to which it is bound through the TDI.

Figure 11.3 shows the Redirector's use of the Server Message Block (SMB) protocol in a Windows NT client. The Redirector is implemented as a file system driver and is represented by the object name \Device\Redirector. Requests by a client for a file on a remote computer are sent to the I/O Manager. The I/O Manager calls a driver entry point for the Redirector. The Dispatch routines within the Redirector translate the I/O request to SMB protocol requests. The SMB protocol can translate I/O requests into requests for services on the remote computer.

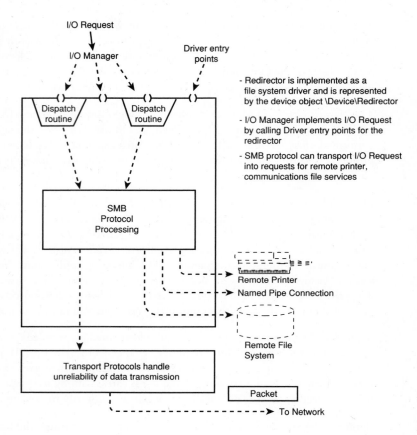

Figure 11.3
The Redirector and the SMB protocol.

Understanding the Interaction between a Client and a Windows NT Server

Figures 11.4 and 11.5 show the client-side and server-side view as requests are sent from the client to the computer. In this example, the client is shown issuing a request for a file resource on the server.

Client-side view of network operation (see fig. 11.4):

1. An application issues a request for a file service on the Windows NT Server.

2. In a Windows NT client, the I/O Manager creates an I/O request packet and passes it to the file system driver—in this case, the Redirector. In non-Windows NT clients, the request is sent directly to the Redirector component of the network client software.

3. The Redirector forwards the request for network processing to the network transport drivers.

4. The network transport drivers forward the request to the NDIS drivers.

5. NDIS drivers issue commands to transmit a packet containing the original request to the physical network.

Server-side view of network operation (see fig. 11.5):

6. The NDIS drivers on the server receive the packet from the network adapter. Data-link headers are stripped.

7. The network transport drivers receive the packet from the NDIS drivers. Network and Transport layer headers are stripped.

8. The request is received by the server module.

9. The server module decides if the request can be satisfied by the local file system. If the request needs to be sent to a gateway service, then the request is sent to that service. An example of a gateway service is Gateway Service for NetWare.

10. The local file system issues a command to the local disk drive on the server.

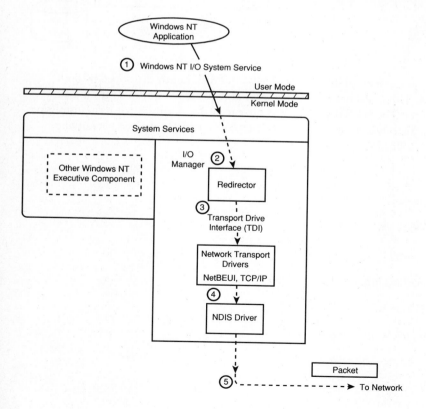

Figure 11.4

The client-side view of network I/O.

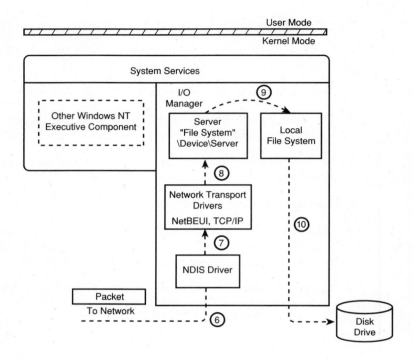

Figure 11.5

The server-side view of network I/O.

The SMB protocol was developed by IBM originally, and then jointly developed by both Microsoft and IBM. The actual network requests are encoded as Network Control Block (NCB) data structures. The NCB data structures are encoded in SMB format for transmission across the network. SMB is used in many of the Microsoft- and IBM-derived networking software such as the following:

- MS-Net

- IBM PC Network

- IBM LAN Server

- MS LAN Manager

- LAN Manager for Unix

- DEC PATHWORKS

- MS Windows for Workgroups

- Ungermann-Bass Net/1

SMB messages can be categorized into four types:

- **Session Control.** Commands that establish or destroy Redirector connections with a remote network resource such as a directory or printer.

- **File.** Used to access and manipulate file system resources on the remote computer.

- **Printer.** Used by the Redirector to send print data to a remote printer or queue, and to obtain the status of remote print devices.

- **Message.** Used by applications and system components to send unicast or broadcast messages.

Understanding How Network Drives Are Redirected to the Redirector

DOS, Windows, and Windows NT clients that need to access a directory on the Windows NT Server can do so using unused drive letters such as F, G, and so on. These drive letters are called *network drives*. The client operating system translates these network drive letter references to the Redirector. Figure 11.6 shows how this is accomplished for Windows NT clients. The drive letters such as A, B, ... F are implemented as symbolic links. The drive letter A is a symbolic link to \Device\Floppy0. The drive letter F is a symbolic link to the \Device\Redirector. A reference to the drive letter F therefore would be translated to the \Device\Redirector, which has information on what remote directory the drive letter F is assigned to.

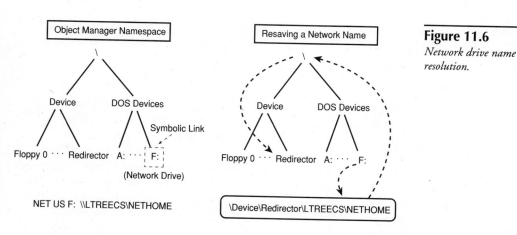

Figure 11.6

Network drive name resolution.

Understanding the Provider Component

To support connection with other network architectures such as NetWare and VINES, Windows NT network architecture uses the concept of a provider. Figure 11.7 shows the

Provider layer, called the *Multiple Provider Router* (MPR), which provides a common interface to access different network resources. In the example in figure 11.7, the MPR can use the Windows NT Redirector, the NetWare Redirector, or some other Redirector. The MPR can be accessed by applications through the *WNet APIs*, which are network system calls used by applications for accessing network resources. Because of the MPR, the WNet APIs can work with a variety of network architectures. The WNet API is part of the Win32 subsystem APIs and can be used to connect to multiple networks, browse computers in a workgroup or domain, and transfer data. The Windows NT File Manager is an example of an application that uses WNet API calls for managing network connections and for network browsing.

Figure 11.7

Provider architecture.

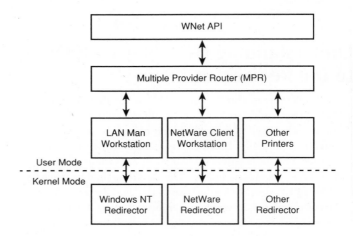

The WNet API is one of two methods used by applications for accessing network resources. The other method is the Uniform Naming Convention (UNC), which enables access to a network resource on a computer using the sharename defined for the resource:

```
\\server\sharename\subdir1\subdir2\...\filename
```

To support UNC names, a Multiple UNC Provider (MUP) component is provided that translates requests involving UNC names received from the I/O Manager to one of the registered UNC providers. During its initialization, Workstation services register with the MUP. MUP maintains a cache of UNC names that it has seen and resolved to a UNC provider for 15 minutes. If MUP has not seen the UNC name for the past 15 minutes, it sends the UNC name to each UNC provider in turn, and when a provider indicates that it can access the UNC resource, the MUP sends the remainder of the command to that provider. MUP tries each UNC provider (Redirector) in the order of the MUPs' registered priorities; the highest priority Redirector is tried first. MUP remembers the UNC name unless there has been no activity for 15 minutes.

Using Windows NT Server Clients

The following client software is included with Windows NT Server distribution software:

- MS Network Client for MS-DOS

- MS LAN Manager for MS-DOS

- MS LAN Manager for OS/2

- Windows for Workgroups

The Windows for Workgroups software is provided for convenience in installing the software from across the network. Before installing this software, you should ensure that you have a valid software license.

In addition to the previously mentioned client software, the Windows NT Server CD-ROM contains connectivity tools such as Remote Access Server for MS-DOS and MS TCP/IP 32-bit for Windows for Workgroups 3.11.

Figure 11.8 illustrates the different clients included for Windows NT Server.

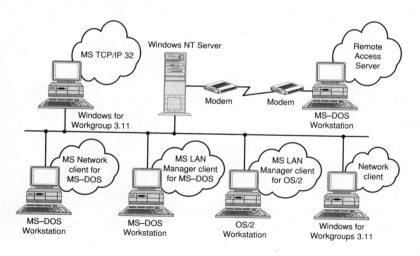

Figure 11.8

Clients for Windows NT Server.

Using the Network Client Administrator Tool

The network client software for different platforms is included in the Windows NT Server CD-ROM distribution. Before you can install the network client software, you need to generate the appropriate boot disks and set up the client software on the Windows NT Server for downloading and installation. The main tool used to accomplish these tasks is the Network Client Administrator tool. This tool enables you to quickly install the software clients on the Windows NT Server CD-ROM distribution. Using the Network Client Administrator, you can accomplish the following tasks:

- Create floppy disk sets for installing the network client software.

- Create a shared directory on a Windows NT server that can be used for installing Windows NT clients, Windows 3.x clients, and Windows NT Server tools.

- Create a network installation start-up disk that can be used to automate the installation of the network client for DOS or Windows for Workgroups on a workstation connected to the network.

You can use any of the following methods to access the client installation files and create a network client installation startup disk or disk set:

- Share the CLIENTS directory on the Windows NT Server and access this shared directory from workstations connected to the network.

- Share the CLIENTS directory on the CD-ROM device attached to a Windows NT computer that contains the CD-ROM distribution for Windows NT Server, and access this share from workstations.

- Copy network client installation files locally to a hard disk and access the installation files locally.

You use the Network Client Administrator tool to create a shared directory on the Windows NT Server. This shared directory then contains the client software that can be used for installing the network client software on the workstations.

If you intend to create floppy disks for the network client software installation, you should have a sufficient number of blank floppy disks. You can use table 11.1 as a guide for the number of disks that you need. To avoid disk incompatibility problems, ensure that the disks are formatted using the operating system that is on the computer on which the client software is to be installed. This means that if you are installing the client software on an OS/2 computer, you should format the disk with the OS/2 version running on the computer.

Table 11.1
Number of Floppy Disks Needed for Installation Files

Software	Installation Disk Set	Network Installation Startup Disk
MS Network Client for MS-DOS and Windows	2	1

Software	Installation Disk Set	Network Installation Startup Disk
MS LAN Manager Client for MS-DOS	4	
MS LAN Manager	4	
Client for OS/2		
MS TCP/IP 32-bit for Windows for Workgroups	1	
RAS for MS-DOS	1	

Creating the Share Name for the Client Installation Files

When you installed the Windows NT Server, a folder called Administrative Tools should have been created. Ensure that this folder exists on the Windows NT Server and that you have a CD-ROM device attached to the Windows NT Server that contains the Windows NT Server CD-ROM distribution disk.

To run the Network Client Administrator tool, follow these steps:

1. Log on as an Administrator user to the Windows NT Server and open the Administrative Tools (Common) Folder.

2. Start the Network Client Administrator tool.

   The Network Client Administrator dialog box appears (see fig. 11.9).

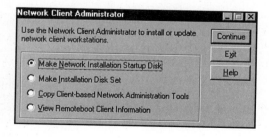

Figure 11.9

The Network Client Administrator dialog box.

You must select the appropriate option for creating the client installation files. You can use the options to create a network installation start-up disk, make an installation disk set, copy client network administration tools for Windows NT and OS/2, and view remoteboot client information.

If you are creating network installation disks or installation disk sets, you need to create the share name only once. If you decide to copy the files to the Windows NT Server for creating disk sets, you only need to copy it once by selecting either of the following options:

■ Make **N**etwork Installation Startup Disk

■ Make **I**nstallation Disk Set

3. If you select the Make **N**etwork Installation Startup Disk or Make **I**nstallation Disk Set option, the Share Network Client Installation Files dialog box appears (see fig. 11.10). You use this dialog box to indicate whether you want to share the network client installation files that are on the Windows NT CD-ROM, to copy the files to a new shared directory and then share the files, or to specify the share name of the directory to which files have been copied previously.

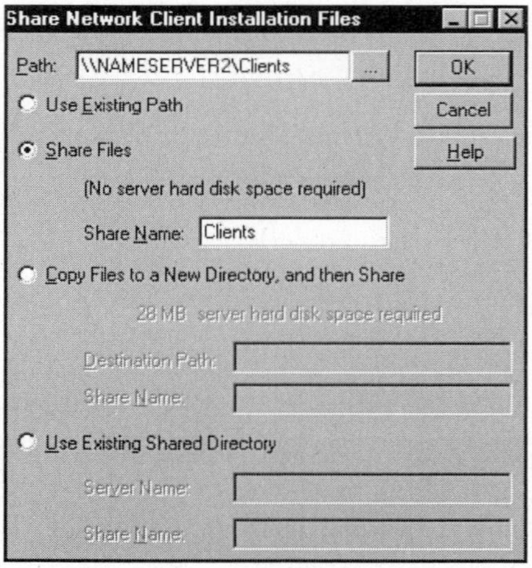

Figure 11.10

The Share Network Client Installation Files dialog box.

The **P**ath field indicates where the installation files are located. If this is the first time you have selected this Network Client Administrator option, the field should be set to the CD-ROM path.

If you previously installed the network client on a different path, select the Use **E**xisting Path option.

To share the files contained on the CD-ROM, select **S**hare Files and type the share name in the adjacent Share **N**ame field. The default name for the CD-ROM share is Clients.

To copy the CD-ROM installation files to a directory and then share the directory, select the Copy Files to a New Directory, and then Share option. This is the preferred option if you plan on installing client software for a large number of clients. If you select this option, you should enter information in the Destination Path field for the location of the files to be copied. Additionally, you should specify the share name in the Share Name field.

You need approximately 28 MB of disk space on the server if you select the Copy Files to a New Directory, and then Share option.

If you want to use installation files that have been copied, select the Use Existing Shared Directory option. If you select this option, you should specify the server and share name in the Server Name and Share Name fields.

After making your selections, select the OK button.

The menus that appear next depend on which option you selected in the Network Client Administrator dialog box, and are described in the following sections.

If you select the View Remoteboot Client Information option, you are told to refer to the Windows NT Server Installation Guide manual shipped with Windows NT Server.

Creating the Network Installation Startup Disk

To create an installation startup disk for automating the installation of client software for the MS Network client for MS-DOS or a Windows for Workgroups client, select the Make Network Installation Startup Disk in the Network Client Administrator dialog box. The installation disk you create with this option starts the client computer, connects to the computer containing the installation files, and initiates the client installation. This disk should be a bootable system disk formatted on the client workstation.

To make a network installation startup disk, follow these steps:

1. After starting Network Client Administrator, select the Make Network Installation Startup Disk option in the Network Client Administrator dialog box. Select Continue, and the Share Network Client Installation Files dialog box appears.

2. Specify the shared directory or path containing the client installation files and select OK. The Target Workstation Configuration dialog box appears (see fig. 11.11).

3. Select the floppy drive type in the Floppy Drive section. Your choices are Drive A: is 3.5" and Drive A: is 5.25".

   In the Network Client box, select the workstation software for which you are creating the installation disk. Your choices are Windows for Workgroups and Network Client for MS-DOS and Windows.

In the Network **A**dapter Card field, select the network adapter driver.

Select OK. The Network Startup Disk Configuration dialog box appears (see fig. 11.12).

Figure 11.11

*The Target Workstation
Configuration dialog box
for the network startup
disk.*

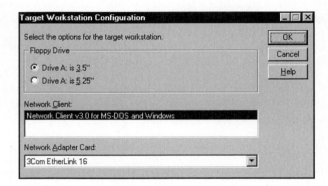

4. In the **C**omputer Name field, enter the computer name for the workstation client on the network. This is a 1- to 15-character unique computer name on the network.

   In the **U**ser Name field, enter the name that identifies the user to the network. This is a user account in the domain or computer that has at least Read privileges to the shared directory on the server.

   In the **D**omain field, enter the domain name or computer name of the Windows NT Server that contains the installation files.

   From the **N**etwork Protocol drop-down list, select the network protocol to be used to establish the network connection to the server for client installation. Your choices are NetBEUI, NWLink, or TCP/IP. The network installation disk can use a different protocol than the one used by the installed client software. You must ensure, however, that the server is configured to use the protocol that you select.

   If you select the NWLink client, the default frame type selected is 802.2 for Ethernet adapters. This frame type is saved in the \NET\PROTOCOL.INI file on the network installation startup disk. If you need to use a different frame type, such as 802.3 or Ethernet_II, you need to manually change the PROTOCOL.INI file.

   If you select the TCP/IP protocol, the network installation startup disk is by default configured as a DHCP (Dynamic Host Configurable Protocol) client. The DHCP client obtains its IP address configuration from a DHCP server. If a DHCP server is not set up, you must provide an IP address, subnet mask, and, optionally, a gateway IP address that can be used on the network. You can enter IP address information only if the Enable **A**utomatic DHCP Configuration check box is not enabled. You should be familiar with the contents of Chapter 18 on TCP/IP fundamentals for Windows NT Server before setting IP address configuration information. It is important that you do not select an IP address already in use, and that you select an IP address that belongs to the IP subnet to which the workstation connects.

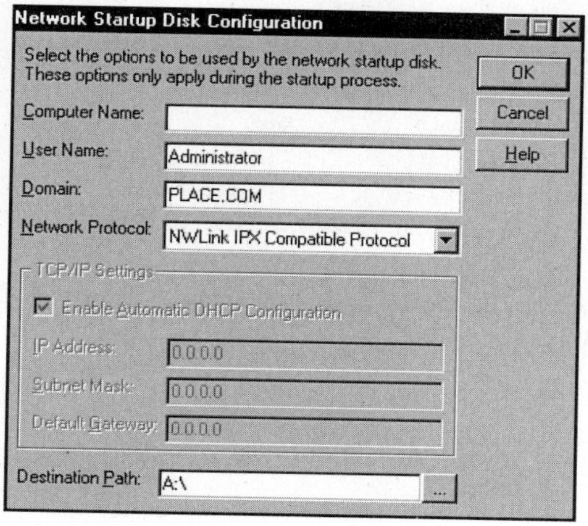

Figure 11.12

The Network Startup Disk Configuration dialog box.

In the Destination **P**ath field, select the location where startup files are to be copied. This is usually the floppy drive A. If you do not have a bootable system floppy disk properly formatted for the workstation, you can specify a destination path that is a directory. The Network Client Administrator will copy the network startup files to this directory. You can copy these files to the system disk later.

Select OK.

If you selected a destination path that is a directory, you see a message that the destination drive you selected does not match the drive type in the target workstation. Select OK to acknowledge this message.

The Confirm Network Disk Configuration information box summarizing your selections appears (see fig. 11.13). Confirm your selections by selecting OK.

If you selected a destination path that is a directory, you see another message that the target disk is not a system disk. Select OK to acknowledge this message.

5. After the files have been copied successfully, you see a message informing you of this fact. Select OK to continue.

6. Exit the Network Client Administrator if you have no other client Administrator tasks to perform.

Figure 11.13
*The Confirm Network
Disk Configuration
dialog box.*

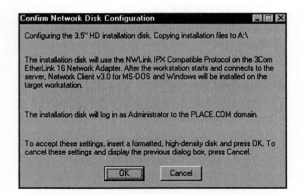

A directory listing of the files created on the startup disk for Network Client for MS-DOS and Windows is shown next for your reference.

```
Directory of A:\net

08/05/96  06:08p      <DIR>          .
08/05/96  06:08p      <DIR>          ..
08/05/96  06:08p              380 system.ini
08/05/96  06:08p              443 protocol.ini
05/07/96  01:30a            4,644 ifshlp.sys
05/07/96  01:30a            4,468 ndishlp.sys
05/07/96  01:30a          450,342 net.exe
05/07/96  01:30a           76,234 net.msg
05/07/96  01:30a          123,066 neth.msg
05/07/96  01:30a            1,531 setup.inf
05/07/96  01:30a            1,477 wcsetup.inf
05/07/96  01:30a              840 wfwsys.cfg
05/07/96  01:30a              622 shares.pwl
05/07/96  01:30a           29,136 himem.sys
05/07/96  01:30a          120,926 emm386.exe
05/07/96  01:30a           27,670 nwlink.exe
05/07/96  01:30a            9,792 elnk16.dos
05/07/96  01:30a           21,940 protman.dos
05/07/96  01:30a           13,782 protman.exe
             19 File(s)       887,293 bytes
```

The CONFIG.SYS file installs the helper for the installable file system (IFSHLP.SYS) and sets the LASTDRIVE to Z. Sample contents of the CONFIG.SYS file follow:

```
files=30
device=a:\net\ifshlp.sys
lastdrive=z
```

The AUTOEXEC.BAT file initializes the network interface, loads the communications protocols, starts the network client software, connects a drive to the Windows NT Server share directory, and runs the setup program. The following are sample contents of the AUTOEXEC.BAT file:

```
path=a:\net
a:\net\net initialize
a:\net\nwlink
a:\net\net start
net use z: \\NTSB\Clients
echo Running Setup...
z:\msclient\netsetup\setup.exe /$
```

The NET INITIALIZE command initializes the network interface. The NWLink command loads the IPX protocol stack. NET START starts the network client. The command NET USE Z: \\NTSB\Clients connects to the shared directory on the Windows NT Server named NTSB, which has the client installation files. If you need to connect to a different Windows NT Server, change the computer name in the NET USE command. The Z:\MSCLIENT\ NETSETUP\SETUP.EXE command starts the network installation. The /$ option indicates that the setup is for the network client for MS-DOS. A /# option is used for the network installation of Windows for Workgroups.

When the initial NET INITIALIZE command is executed, the information in the PROTOCOL.INI file is read and processed. The following are samples of content from the PROTOCOL.INI file in the NET subdirectory:

```
[network.setup]
version=0x3110
netcard=ms$elnk16,1,MS$ELNK16,1
transport=ms$ndishlp,MS$NDISHLP
transport=ms$nwlink,MS$NWLINK
lana0=ms$elnk16,1,ms$nwlink
lana1=ms$elnk16,1,ms$ndishlp

[ms$elnk16]
drivername=ELNK16$
; iobase=0x300

[protman]
drivername=PROTMAN$
PRIORITY=MS$NDISHLP

[MS$NDISHLP]
drivername=ndishlp$
BINDINGS=ms$elnk16

[ms$nwlink]
drivername=nwlink$
FRAME=Ethernet_802.2
BINDINGS=ms$elnk16
LANABASE=0
```

The [network.setup] section identifies the network elements, such as version number of client software, network adapter, and transport protocols. The [ms$elnk16]section contains the name of the driver. The [protman] section contains the name of the protocol manager device driver used for managing NDIS driver bindings. The [MS$NDISHLP] section contains the driver name for NDIS Help messages. The [ms$nwlink] section contains the driver name for the IPX protocol, frame type, bindings, and LAN affinity (controls affinity of the protocol to a particular network interface). If you need to select a different frame type, you should edit the FRAME= entry in the [ms$nwlink] section.

The network adapter drivers are configured with default settings. If the network adapter does not use the default settings, you must edit the parameters in the configuration files to use the network adapter settings.

Creating an Installation Disk Set

If you want to create an installation disk set for installing the client software for the MS Network client for MS-DOS, LAN Manager for MS-DOS client, LAN Manager for OS/2 client, RAS for MS-DOS, or TCP/IP for Windows for Workgroups, select the Make **I**nstallation Disk Set option in the Network Client Administrator dialog box.

The installation disk set you create with this option can be used to manually install the software on each client computer. The RAS for MS-DOS and TCP/IP for Windows for Workgroups can be installed over the network by creating a connection to the client share directory on the Windows NT Server.

To make client disk sets, follow these steps:

1. After starting Network Client Administrator, select the Make **I**nstallation Disk Set option in the Network Client Administrator dialog box. Select Continue; the Share Network Client Installation Files dialog box appears.

2. Specify the shared directory or path containing the client installation files and select OK. The Make Installation Disk Set dialog box appears (see fig. 11.14).

Figure 11.14

The Make Installation Disk Set dialog box.

3. In the **N**etwork Client or Service box, select the workstation software for which you are creating the installation disk.

In the **D**estination Drive box, specify the drive on which to place the disks. You can check the **F**ormat Disks option if you want the system to format the disk for you.

Select OK.

4. You are prompted to enter appropriately labeled disks. If you selected the **F**ormat Disks option, the Network Client Administrator quick-formats the disk. You next see a status of the files that are copied.

5. Follow the instructions on-screen to create the remaining disks in the disk set.

A directory listing of the files created on the disks for Network Client for MS-DOS and Windows follows for your reference:

```
Network Client for MS-DOS and Windows Disk 1 of 2:
Directory of A:\
05/07/96  01:30a                 6,347 am2100.do_
05/07/96  01:30a                    88 comdev.in_
05/07/96  01:30a                11,004 depca.do_
05/07/96  01:30a                 4,656 e20nd.do_
05/07/96  01:30a                 5,229 e21nd.do_
05/07/96  01:30a                 5,349 elnk.do_
05/07/96  01:30a                 7,318 elnk16.do_
05/07/96  01:30a                 9,606 elnk3.do_
05/07/96  01:30a                 8,172 elnkii.do_
05/07/96  01:30a                 7,454 elnkmc.do_
05/07/96  01:30a                10,308 elnkpl.do_
05/07/96  01:30a                 7,221 exp16.do_
05/07/96  01:30a                16,378 expand.exe
05/07/96  01:30a                 5,276 i82593.do_
05/07/96  01:30a                 7,107 ibmtok.do_
05/07/96  01:30a                 3,780 ifshlp.sy_
05/07/96  01:30a                   589 lm21drv.up_
05/07/96  01:30a                24,436 msdlc.ex_
05/07/96  01:30a                12,375 ndis39xr.do_
05/07/96  01:30a                 3,264 ndishlp.sy_
05/07/96  01:30a                 9,669 ne1000.do_
05/07/96  01:30a                 9,918 ne2000.do_
05/07/96  01:30a               272,977 net.ex_
05/07/96  01:30a                37,657 net.ms_
05/07/96  01:30a                 8,513 netbind.com
05/07/96  01:30a                51,567 neth.ms_
05/07/96  01:30a                 6,300 ni6510.do_
05/07/96  01:30a                27,670 nwlink.exe
05/07/96  01:30a                   688 oemdlc.inf
05/07/96  01:30a                   294 oemodi.in_
05/07/96  01:30a                   579 oemras.in_
05/07/96  01:30a                 1,673 oemtcpip.inf
```

```
05/07/96   01:30a                    35,187  olitok.do_
05/07/96   01:30a                    26,306  pe2ndis.do_
05/07/96   01:30a                    18,041  pendis.do_
05/07/96   01:30a                    13,718  pro4.do_
05/07/96   01:30a                    30,224  prorapm.dw_
05/07/96   01:30a                     9,230  protman.do_
05/07/96   01:30a                     6,035  protman.ex_
05/07/96   01:30a                     1,094  rascopy.ba_
05/07/96   01:30a                    18,194  readme.txt
05/07/96   01:30a                   286,032  setup.exe
05/07/96   01:30a                    11,706  smcmac.do_
05/07/96   01:30a                    12,273  smc_arc.do_
05/07/96   01:30a                    30,176  strn.do_
05/07/96   01:30a                     6,659  tlnk.do_
05/07/96   01:30a                    37,231  wcnet.inf
05/07/96   01:30a                     1,477  wcsetup.inf
05/07/96   01:30a                       177  wcsys.ini
05/07/96   01:30a                        84  workgrp.sy_
                    50 File(s)    1,127,306  bytes


Network Client for MS-DOS and Windows Disk 2 of 2:
Directory of A:\
05/07/96   01:30a                    14,032  addname.ex_
05/07/96   01:30a                    17,336  dnr.ex_
05/07/96   01:30a                     1,407  emsbfr.ex_
05/07/96   01:30a                       715  hosts
05/07/96   01:30a                     8,509  ipconfig.ex_
05/07/96   01:30a                       817  lmhosts
05/07/96   01:30a                     1,764  nemm.do_
05/07/96   01:30a                     8,513  netbind.com
05/07/96   01:30a                       395  networks
05/07/96   01:30a                    12,434  nmtsr.ex_
05/07/96   01:30a                    47,277  ping.ex_
05/07/96   01:30a                       795  protocol
05/07/96   01:30a                     5,973  services
05/07/96   01:30a                    27,497  sockets.ex_
05/07/96   01:30a                     2,810  tcpdrv.do_
05/07/96   01:30a                    48,433  tcptsr.ex_
05/07/96   01:30a                       233  tcputils.ini
05/07/96   01:30a                    23,561  tinyrfc.ex_
05/07/96   01:30a                     2,353  umb.co_
05/07/96   01:30a                     9,524  vbapi.386
05/07/96   01:30a                     9,535  vsockets.386
05/07/96   01:30a                    25,236  winsock.dl_
05/07/96   01:30a                    16,122  win_sock.dl_
05/07/96   01:30a                     3,271  wsahdapp.ex_
05/07/96   01:30a                    15,862  wsockets.dl_
                    25 File(s)      304,404  bytes
```

The installation is started by running the SETUP.EXE program found on the first disk. Many of the files in this listing are in compressed format. The files include drivers for some of the popular network adapters; support for Windows; and support for the NetBEUI, NWLink, and TCP/IP protocols at the workstation.

Using the Copy Client-Based Network Administration Tools

If you need to run network administration tools for Windows NT from a Windows NT or Windows 95 workstation, you should select the **C**opy Client-based Network Administration Tools option in the Network Client Administrator dialog box.

You can run tools such as User Manager for Domains on Windows 95 or Windows NT Workstation.

To copy client-based server tools to the Windows NT Server, follow these steps

1. After starting Network Client Administrator, select the **C**opy Client-based Network Administration Tools option in the Network Client Administrator dialog box. Select Continue. The Share Client-based Administration Tools dialog box appears (see fig. 11.15). You use this dialog box to indicate whether you want to share the server tools' installation files that are on the Windows NT CD-ROM, to copy the files to a new shared directory and then share the files, or to specify the share name of directory to which files have been copied.

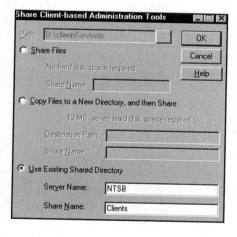

Figure 11.15

The Share Client-based Administration Tools dialog box.

The **P**ath field indicates where the installation files are located. If this is the first time you have selected this Network Client Administrator option, this field is set to the CD-ROM path.

2. To share the files contained on the CD-ROM, select **S**hare Files and type the share name in the Share **N**ame field. The default name for the CD-ROM share is Clients.

3. To copy the CD-ROM installation files to a directory and then share the directory, select the **C**opy Files to a New Directory, and then Share option. This is the preferred option if you plan on installing client software for a large number of clients. If you select this

option, you should enter information in the **D**estination Path field for the location of the files to be copied. Additionally, you should specify the share name in the Share **N**ame field.

You need approximately 13 MB of additional disk space on the server to copy the server tools if you select the **S**hare Files option.

4. If you want to use installation files that have been copied previously, select the **U**se Existing Shared Directory option. If you select this option, you should specify the server and share name in the Ser**v**er Name and Share **N**ame fields.

Figure 11.15 shows that, by default, the **U**se Existing Shared Directory radio button is enabled, and the Ser**v**er Name and Share **N**ame fields under this option have default values. These defaults appear because the client software for generating network startup disks and disk sets was copied in a previous step. You must select the **C**opy Files to a New Directory, and then Share option if you plan on copying server tools installation files to the Windows NT Server.

When you select the **C**opy Files to a New Directory, and then Share option, the **D**estination Path and Share **N**ame fields are filled with the default values of C:\clients\srvtools and SetupAdm. You can keep the default values or change them. If drive C on the Windows NT Server is a FAT partition with limited space, you should change the **D**estination Path to specify another drive.

After making your selections, choose the OK button.

A status of the copied files appears.

Copying the Client Distribution Files to the Windows NT Server

When you select the Make **N**etwork Installation Startup Disk or Make **I**nstallation Disk Set options in the Network Client Administrator dialog box and copy the installation client software on the Windows NT Server, the directory structure of the copied files is shown in figure 11.16.

Each subdirectory under the clients directory contains the installation files and disk software for a particular client or service. You can browse the clients directory to better understand how the installation files are organized.

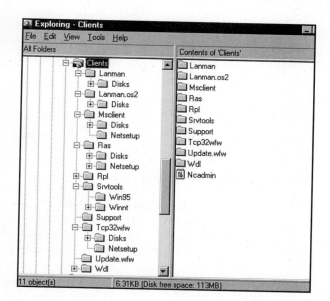

Figure 11.16

Client directory setup on Windows NT Server for making disk sets.

Installing the Network Client Software and Services

After you set up the share name for the network installation client software on the Windows NT Server, and after you create the network startup disks or client installation disk sets as described in the previous sections, you can proceed with installing the client software.

The sections that follow discuss typical tasks that you perform for installing and verifying the operation of MS-DOS and Windows network client software.

Installing a Network Client for MS-DOS and Windows

You should have created the installation disk set for the network client for MS-DOS and Windows, as described in the section "Creating an Installation Disk Set," earlier in this chapter.

The MS-DOS workstation should meet the following minimum configuration requirements:

■ Processor should be Intel 8088 or higher

■ RAM in workstation should be at least 640 KB

■ At least 1 MB of free space on hard disk

■ A network adapter for which network driver support exists

■ MS-DOS 3.3 or later

■ Optionally, MS Windows running at the workstation

In order to run Network Client Setup, you must have 429 KB of available conventional memory.

To install the network client for MS-DOS and Windows, follow these steps:

1. Boot up the MS-DOS workstation and examine the CONFIG.SYS and AUTOEXEC.BAT files on the workstation. Remove from these files any references to network driver client software for other network architectures, such as NetWare, VINES, and so on. Remove any components that could occupy additional RAM and conflict with the installation.

   Reboot the workstation if you made changes to the CONFIG.SYS and AUTOEXEC.BAT files.

2. Insert the first disk in the MS Network Client for MS-DOS and Windows disk set that you created into a floppy drive and issue the following command:

   A:\SETUP

   The Setup for Microsoft Network Client screen appears (see fig. 11.17).

Figure 11.17

The Setup for Microsoft Network Client screen.

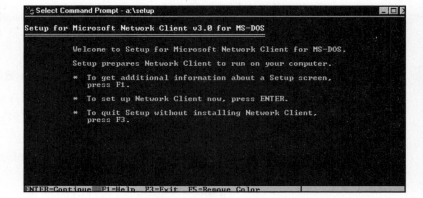

3. Press Enter to continue.

   A screen appears, prompting you for the location for placing the network client software (see fig. 11.18).

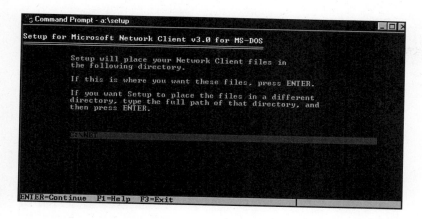

Figure 11.18
Specifying the location for MS-DOS/Windows client software.

4. Enter a location path or accept the default, and press Enter.

The next screen asks you to select a network card from the list provided (see fig. 11.19).

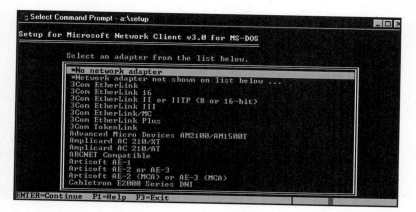

Figure 11.19
Network Card selection.

A Set Network Buffers information box shows the default setting which optimizes network performance by using Network Buffers. This takes more memory, and you can choose not to use this option.

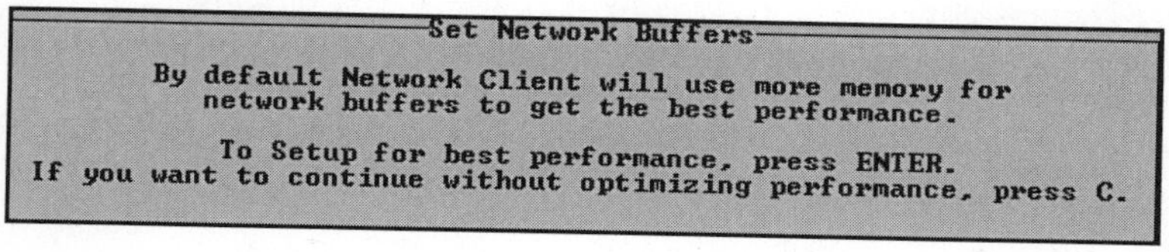

Figure 11.20
Network buffers.

A screen appears, prompting you to enter the user name (see fig. 11.21). The user name you select should be the workstation user's logon name to the workgroup or domain.

Figure 11.21

*Specifying the user name
for MS-DOS/Windows
client software.*

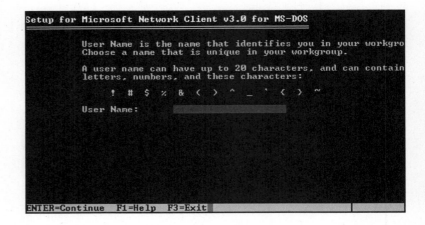

5. Enter a user name and press Enter.

    A screen for changing names, setup options, and network configuration appears (see
    fig. 11.22).

Figure 11.22

*The Changing Options
screen for MS-DOS/
Windows client software.*

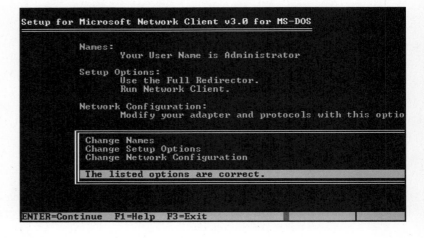

6. Select the Change Names option.

    A screen for changing user name, computer name, workgroup name, and domain names
    appears (see fig. 11.23). The default computer name is assumed to be the same as the user
    name. If this is not true, change the computer name.

    Change the Workgroup or Domain Name to which the workstation belongs.

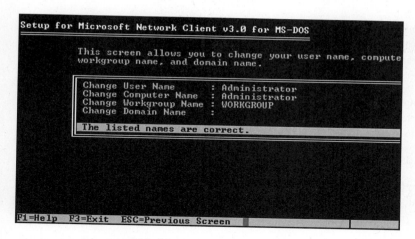

Figure 11.23

The Names Change screen for MS-DOS/Windows client software.

7. Select the The Listed Names Are Correct option. The Changing Options screen appears again.

8. Select the Change Setup Option.

   The screen for changing the Redirector, startup, logon, and net pop-up options appears (see fig. 11.24).

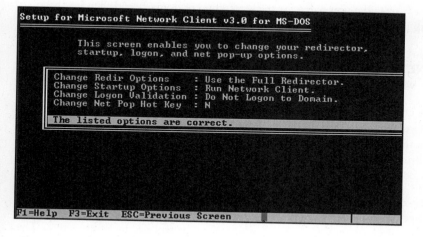

Figure 11.24

The Setup Options screen for MS-DOS/Windows client software.

You can set the Redirector to be a Full Redirector or a Basic Redirector. The Full Redirector gives you access to all network client features, such as logging into Windows NT and LAN Manager domains and using advanced network options, such as named pipes. You should select this option unless you have memory-constraint problems or do not need the advanced options, in which case you should select Basic Redirector. The Basic Redirector uses less memory and disk space than the Full Redirector, but does not encrypt passwords. It provides workgroup functions, such as connecting to share directories and printers.

If you are using Remote Access Services or MS Windows, or you are logging into a domain, you should select Full Redirector and start it with the following command before starting Windows:

```
net start full
```

The Windows for Workgroups and Windows NT Workstations have their own built-in network client, and you should not use the MS-DOS network client on these workstations.

The Startup options (refer to figure 11.24) can be set up to automatically run networking functions when the workstation is booted. You can select from the following Startup options:

- **Run Network Client.** Starts the network client that prompts you for your logon user name for the workgroup or domain.

- **Run Network Client and Load Pop-Up.** Starts the network client that prompts you for your logon user name for the workgroup or domain, and then loads the pop-up interface into memory.

- **Do Not Run Network Client.** The network client will not be started. You must type **NET LOGON** at the command prompt to start the network client, which then prompts you to log on.

The Change Logon Validation option can be set to log on to a domain or to not log on to a domain. If you plan on using the workstation in a Microsoft workgroup network, you should select the Do Not Logon to Domain option. If you plan on using the workstation for logging into a Windows NT or LAN Manager domain, select the Logon To Domain option. The domain name is set in the Change Names.

After the pop-up interface is loaded, you can display it by pressing Ctrl+Alt+N. If you need to change the pop-up key, set the new key in the Change Net Pop Hot Key field. The pop-up key is of the form Ctrl+Alt+X, where X can be replaced by letters A to Z. The letter N is the default.

9. After making changes to the Setup Options screen, select the The listed options are correct option. You then return to the Changing Options screen.

10. Select the Change Network Configuration option.

The screen for installing network adapters and protocol drivers appears (see fig. 11.25). Use the Tab key to move between boxes, and change the network configuration for your network adapter and protocols.

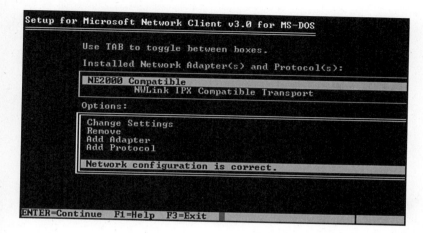

```
Setup for Microsoft Network Client v3.0 for MS-DOS

    Use TAB to toggle between boxes.
    Installed Network Adapter(s) and Protocol(s):

    NE2000 Compatible
            NWLink IPX Compatible Transport
    Options:

    Change Settings
    Remove
    Add Adapter
    Add Protocol
    Network configuration is correct.



ENTER=Continue  F1=Help  F3=Exit
```

Figure 11.25

Changing the network adapter and protocol drivers screen for MS-DOS/Windows client software.

Figure 11.26 shows a sample configuration that has the SMC EtherCard PLUS adapter drivers and the NWLink IPX, NetBEUI, and TCP/IP protocols selected. Remember that if you select multiple protocols, they will take up more memory, and this could prevent some applications from running.

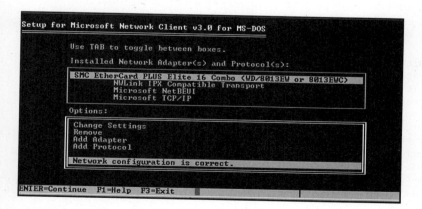

```
Setup for Microsoft Network Client v3.0 for MS-DOS

    Use TAB to toggle between boxes.
    Installed Network Adapter(s) and Protocol(s):

    SMC EtherCard PLUS Elite 16 Combo (WD/8013EW or 8013EWC)
            NWLink IPX Compatible Transport
            Microsoft NetBEUI
            Microsoft TCP/IP
    Options:

    Change Settings
    Remove
    Add Adapter
    Add Protocol
    Network configuration is correct.


ENTER=Continue  F1=Help  F3=Exit
```

Figure 11.26

The network adapter and protocol drivers screen for MS-DOS/Windows client software.

11. After making the changes, select the option `Network Configuration is correct`. You are returned to the Changing Options screen.

Select the option `The listed options are correct` from the Changing Options screen.

The Setup program configures your network drivers and copies the software to the workstation. At the completion of the installation, you see the completion screen informing you of the changes that have been made (see fig. 11.27).

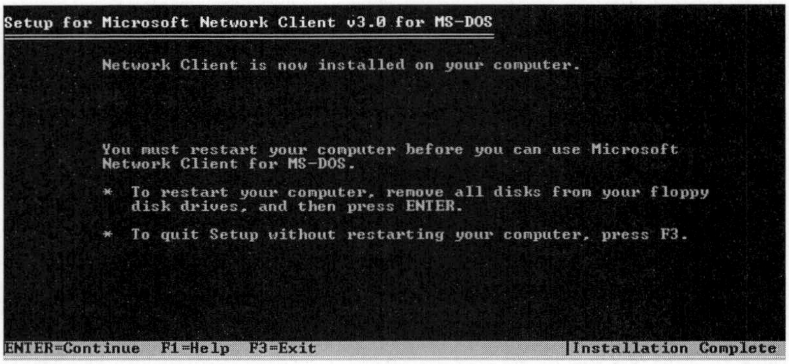

Figure 11.27

The completion screen for MS-DOS/Windows client software.

12. Remove the disks and press Enter to reboot the workstation. Alternatively, you can press F3 to exit without rebooting the workstation.

Verifying Network Client for MS-DOS and Windows

If you selected the drivers and other configuration options correctly, you will see messages indicating that the driver initialized properly. The following is an example working session for logging on to the domain. In this example, the built-in Administrator account was changed to Admin, so the user Admin was typed in order to log on to the domain:

```
The command completed successfully.
Standard Microsystems EtherCard Plus MAC Module v1.19
Microsoft(R) NWLINK Version 1.0
Copyright(c) Microsoft 1994. All Rights Reserved.
Type your name, or press ENTER if it is ADMINISTRATOR: Admin
Type your password:********
There is no password-list file for ADMIN.
Do you want to create one? (Y/N) [N]: Y
Please confirm your password so that a password list can be created: ********
Please enter your password for the domain KINETD:********
The command completed successfully.
```

The password list file is used for workgroup connections. It is stored in the C:\NET directory and referenced in the SYSTEM.INI file in the [Password Lists] section. If you create this password file once, you will not be prompted for it when the workstation boots the next time.

If you have installed the pop-up interface, press Ctrl+Alt+N to verify the pop-up program interface (see fig. 11.28). You can use this interface to create or delete network drive connections to shared directory and print resources.

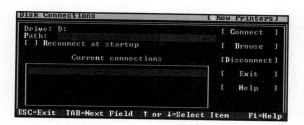

Figure 11.28
The pop-up interface for MS-DOS Client.

If you need to unload the pop-up interface, use the following command:

```
NET STOP POPUP
```

To restart the pop-up interface, use the following command:

```
NET START POPUP
```

The NET.EXE program that implements the NET commands is copied to the C:\NET directory during installation. You can use the NET /? command to see the list of NET commands and learn how to obtain help on them. Table 11.2 shows the NET commands available from an MS-DOS client. You can use this table to test the network client. In table 11.2, you can see that using the NET CONFIG command displays information about the workgroup settings. An example of the type of information shown by this command follows:

```
> NET CONFIG
Computer name               \\WKS1
User name                   ADMIN
Software version            3.11
Redirector version          2.51
Workstation root directory  C:\NET
Workgroup                   WORKGROUP
The command completed successfully.
```

The NET CONFIG command displays version numbers of the network client software, the computer name, and the logged-on user name.

Table 11.2
NET Commands on an MS-DOS Client

Command	Description
NET	Loads the pop-up interface into memory and displays it on your screen.
NET CONFIG	Displays information about your workgroup settings.
NET DIAG	Runs the Microsoft Network Diagnostics program to display diagnostic information about your network.

continues

Table 11.2, Continued
NET Commands on an MS-DOS Client

Command	Description
NET HELP	Provides information about commands and error messages.
NET INIT	Loads protocol and network-adapter drivers without binding them to Protocol Manager.
NET LOGOFF	Breaks the connection between your computer and the shared resources to which it is connected.
NET LOGON	Identifies you as a member of a workgroup and reestablishes your persistent connections.
NET PASSWORD	Changes your logon password.
NET PRINT	Displays information about print queues and controls print jobs.
NET START	Starts services or loads the pop-up interface.
NET STOP	Stops services or unloads the pop-up interface.
NET TIME	Displays the time on, or synchronizes your computer's clock with, the clock on a Microsoft Windows for Workgroups, Windows NT, or LAN Manager time server.
NET USE	Connects to or disconnects from a shared resource or displays information about connections.
NET VER	Displays the type and version number of the workgroup Redirector you are using.
NET VIEW	Displays a list of computers that share resources or a list of shared resources on a specific computer.

The Full Redirector configuration consumes a substantial amount of memory. Use the DOS MEM /C command to see how memory is used by the network client. The following example shows a sample of the memory usage of the network DOS client. The memory used by the network client components is in italics. In a practical configuration, you will find it necessary to use memory-optimization techniques. In the configuration example shown here, no attempt was made to load DOS HIGH or to use any other memory-optimization technique:

```
> MEM /C
Modules using memory below 1 MB:
  Name              Total       =    Conventional   +   Upper Memory
- - - - - - - - - - - - - - - - - - - - - - - - - - - - - - - - - - - - - - - -
  MSDOS          65,357  (64K)      65,357   (64K)         0   (0K)
  HIMEM           3,792   (4K)       3,792    (4K)         0   (0K)
  IFSHLP          3,968   (4K)       3,968    (4K)         0   (0K)
  COMMAND         6,272   (6K)       6,272    (6K)         0   (0K)
  SMARTDRV       29,024  (28K)      29,024   (28K)         0   (0K)
  PROTMAN           400   (0K)         400    (0K)         0   (0K)
  ELNK3           8,416   (8K)       8,416    (8K)         0   (0K)
  NDISHLP         1,440   (1K)       1,440    (1K)         0   (0K)
  NWLINK         10,144  (10K)      10,144   (10K)         0   (0K)
  PROTMAN         2,560   (3K)       2,560    (3K)         0   (0K)
  REDIR         102,256 (100K)     102,256  (100K)         0   (0K)
  NETPOP         34,832  (34K)      34,832   (34K)         0   (0K)
  Free          385,696 (377K)     385,696  (377K)         0   (0K)

Memory Summary:

  Type of Memory         Total   =     Used    +     Free
  - - - - - - - - - -     - - - - -     - - - - -     - - - - - -
  Conventional          654,336       268,640       385,696
  Upper                       0             0             0
  Reserved                    0             0             0
  Extended (XMS)     15,728,640     2,229,248    13,499,392
  - - - - - - - - - - -   - - - - - - - - - -   - - - - - - - - - - -   - - - - - - - - - -
  Total memory       16,382,976     2,497,888    13,885,088

  Total under 1 MB      654,336       268,640       385,696

  Largest executable program size        250,464   (245K)
  Largest free upper memory block              0     (0K)
```

The high memory area is available. The memory configuration example shows that 102 KB of RAM is used by the Full Redirector.

To configure Windows on the MS-DOS workstation to run with the MS-DOS network client, perform the following steps:

1. Start Windows and run Windows Setup from the Main program group.

2. Choose **C**hange System Settings from the **Op**tions menu.

3. In the Network Settings dialog box, select Microsoft Network (or 100% compatible).

4. Save your changes. If you are asked to insert Windows Setup disks, do so, or specify the directory containing the Microsoft Network device driver.

Updating the MS-DOS Network Client Configuration

If you need to update the MS-DOS Network Client configuration, you can manually edit the network configuration files or run the SETUP.EXE program in the installed directory (usually, C:\NET) on the workstation. Figure 11.29 shows the SETUP.EXE screen for making configuration changes.

Figure 11.29

SETUP for making MS-DOS network client configuration changes.

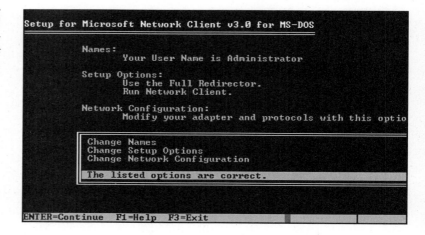

If you do not have enough memory to run SETUP.EXE, unload the network Redirector, if it is running, by using the following command:

```
NET STOP RDR
```

Use the SETUP screen to examine the network client configuration settings, make any desired changes, and save your settings. The procedure for making changes is similar to the steps you take when you use SETUP to create the installation disks.

Examining the Configuration Files for the Network Client

After you install the network client software, you can study the changes made to the workstation configuration files to better understand how the network client operates.

The CONFIG.SYS file should have the following lines added to it for supporting the network client:

```
device=C:\NET\ifshlp.sys
LASTDRIVE=Z
```

These lines load the installable file system helper, and set the last drive in the MS-DOS drive configuration table to Z.

The AUTOEXEC.BAT should have the following lines added to it in order to run the network client:

```
C:\NET\net initialize
C:\NET\nwlink
C:\NET\net start
```

The NET INITIALIZE command loads protocol and network-adapter drivers without binding them to Protocol Manager. If you install the MS-DLC protocol, you must edit the AUTOEXEC.BAT file to add "/dynamic" to the NET INITIALIZE line. The line should be as follows:

```
net initialize /dynamic
```

If the NETBIND command does not exist, add it to the line after all lines in AUTOEXEC.BAT that load network drivers. The line should be as follows:

```
netbind
```

The NWLINK loads the NWLink protocol stack if you selected the IPX protocol during the client installation. Note that the NWLINK only supports the IPX protocol; it does not support the SPX protocol.

The NET START command loads the Redirector in the configuration that was specified when the network client software was installed. The default Redirector to use is specified in the preferredredir statement in the [networks] section of the SYSTEM.INI file.

If you want to start the Redirector in a different mode, you can specify additional options to the NET START command. The general syntax of the NET START command and the options you can use follow:

```
NET START [POPUP ¦ BASIC ¦ FULL ¦ WORKSTATION ¦ NETBIND ¦ NETBEUI]
          [/LIST] [/YES] [/VERBOSE]
   POPUP         Loads the pop-up interface into memory.
                 Use this option if the pop-up interface
                 is not automatically loaded each time you
                 start your computer.
   BASIC         Starts the basic redirector.
   FULL          Starts the full redirector.
   WORKSTATION   Starts the default redirector.
   NETBIND       Binds protocols and network-adapter drivers.
   NETBEUI       Starts the NetBIOS interface.
   /LIST         Displays a list of the services that are
                 running.
   /YES          Carries out the NET START command without
                 first prompting you to provide information or
                 confirm actions.
   /VERBOSE      Displays information about device drivers and
                 services as they are loaded.
```

If you decide that you need to load the basic Redirector instead of the full Redirector, for example, you can use the following command in the AUTOEXEC.BAT file:

```
NET START BASIC
```

A SYSTEM.INI file is installed in the C:\NET directory. This file is used by the network client at startup. If you are using Windows on your workstation, add the statements in this file to your Windows SYSTEM.INI file also. The following is an example of the SYSTEM.INI file:

```
[network]
sizworkbuf=1498
filesharing=no
printsharing=no
autologon=yes
computername=WKS1
lanroot=C:\NET
username=ADMINISTRATOR
workgroup=WORKGROUP
reconnect=yes
dospophotkey=N
lmlogon=1
logondomain=KINETD
preferredredir=full
autostart=full,popup
maxconnections=8
[network drivers]
netcard=smcmac.dos
transport=ndishlp.sys
devdir=C:\NET
LoadRMDrivers=yes
[Password Lists]
*Shares=C:\NET\Shares.PWL
ADMINISTRATOR=C:\NET\ADMINIST.PWL
ADMIN=C:\NET\ADMIN.PWL
```

The [network] section contains the network parameter settings. These parameter settings are described in table 11.3. The [network drivers] section defines the location and names of network drivers. The [Password Lists] section defines the passwords used for a Windows for Workgroups network.

Table 11.3
Parameters in the [network] Section of the SYSTEM.INI File

Parameter	Description
filesharing	Used if the workstation can act as a server. Does not apply to Network Client.
printsharing	Used if the workstation can act as a server. Does not apply to Network Client.

Parameter	Description
autologon	Determines whether Network Client automatically prompts you for logon when it starts.
computername	The name of your computer.
lanroot	The directory in which you installed Network Client.
username	The username used by default at logon.
workgroup	The workgroup name. Note that this might be different from the logon domain setting.
reconnect	Determines whether Network Client restores previous connections when it starts.
dospophotkey	Determines the key you press (with Ctrl+Alt) to start the pop-up interface. The default is N, meaning that you press Ctrl+Alt+N.
lmlogon	Determines whether Network Client prompts you for a domain logon when you log on. Set this to 1 if you need to log onto a Windows NT Server or LAN Manager domain.
logondomain	The name of the Windows NT Server or LAN Manager domain.
preferredredir	The Redirector that starts by default when you type the NET START command.
autostart	If you choose a network adapter during setup and specify the startup option Run Network Client Logon, autostart determines which Redirector you are using. If you select No Network Adapter from the adapter list, or Do Not Run Network Client from the startup options, autostart has no value, but the NET START command still appears in your AUTOEXEC.BAT file.
maxconnections	Used if the workstation can act as a server. Does not apply to Network Client.

The PROTOCOL.INI file in the C:\NET directory of the Network Client software contains the network setup, protocol settings, and the Protocol Manager settings. A sample PROTOCOL.INI file for an MS-DOS network client for the SMC network adapter and the NWLink protocol follow for your reference:

```
[network.setup]
version=0x3110
netcard=ms$w13ew,1,MS$W13EW,1
transport=ms$nwlink,MS$NWLINK
transport=ms$ndishlp,MS$NDISHLP
lana0=ms$w13ew,1,ms$nwlink
lana1=ms$w13ew,1,ms$ndishlp
[MS$NWLINK]
FRAME=ETHERNET_802.2
IOADDRESS=0x3000
SLOT=3
DriverName=nwlink$
BINDINGS=MS$W13EW
[MS$W13EW]
DriverName=SMCMAC$
[protman]
DriverName=PROTMAN$
PRIORITY=MS$NDISHLP
[MS$NDISHLP]
DriverName=ndishlp$
BINDINGS=MS$W13EW
```

Installing MS Network Client for MS-DOS Using Network Startup

To install an MS Network client for MS-DOS using the network setup disk, you first should have created the network setup disk using the steps outlined in the section "Creating the Network Installation Startup Disk."

Next, you should boot the MS-DOS workstation with the network setup disk. You see messages similar to the following:

```
A>a:net\net initialize
Standard Microsystems EtherCard Plus MAC Module v1.19
The command completed successfully.
A>a:\net\nwlink
Microsoft(R) NWLINK Version 1.0
Copyright(c) Microsoft 1994. All Rights Reserved.
A>a:\net\net start
Type your name, or press ENTER if it is ADMINISTRATOR:
Type your password:********
There is no password-list file for ADMINISTRATOR.
Do you want to create one? (Y/N) [N]: Y
Please confirm your password so that a password list can be created: ********
The command completed successfully.
A>net use z: \\NTSA\Clients
The command completed successfully.
A> echo Running Setup
Running Setup
A>z:\msclient\netsetup\setup.exe /$
    :
    :
```

The last command initiates the installation process and copies the file to the workstation. If the network installation fails at any point, use this listing as a guide for what you should expect to see. If the installation process fails after the network adapter driver is loaded, for example, it could be because you are using a wrong network adapter driver or network adapter parameters. If the network installation fails after the SETUP.EXE command is executed, ensure that you have sufficient rights to access the SETUP.EXE file on the Windows NT Server. You might want to manually execute the network startup and SETUP.EXE commands to see whether you have access to the clients shared directory on the Windows NT Server.

Installing LAN Manager for MS-DOS–Enhanced Clients

If you are integrating the Windows NT server into existing LAN Manager clients, you can install the LAN Manager for MS-DOS–enhanced clients on MS-DOS workstations.

You should have created the installation disk sets for the LAN Manager for DOS clients using the procedure in the section "Creating an Installation Disk Set," earlier in this chapter.

The MS-DOS workstation should meet the following minimum configuration requirements:

- Processor should be Intel 8088 or higher

- RAM in workstation should be at least 640 KB

- At least 4 MB of free space on hard disk

- A network adapter for the network driver support that exists

- MS-DOS 3.3 or later

- Optionally, MS Windows running at the workstation

To install the LAN Manager for an MS-DOS–enhanced client, follow these steps:

1. Boot up the MS-DOS workstation and examine the CONFIG.SYS and AUTOEXEC.BAT files on the workstation. Remove from these files any references to network driver client software for other network architectures, such as NetWare, VINES, and so on. Remove any components that could occupy additional RAM and conflict with the installation.

   Reboot the workstation if you made changes to the CONFIG.SYS and AUTOEXEC.BAT files.

2. Place the first disk in the MS Network Client for MS-DOS and Windows disk set that you created into a floppy drive and run the following command:

   `A:\SETUP`

The Microsoft LAN Manager Setup screen appears (see fig. 11.30).

Figure 11.30

The Microsoft LAN Manager Setup screen.

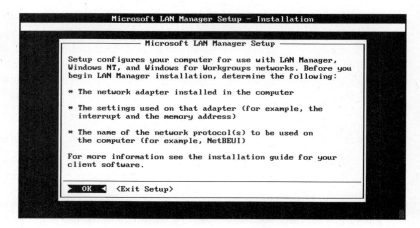

3. Select OK to continue.

   A screen appears, telling you how to use the mouse and keyboard in the setup (see fig. 11.31).

Figure 11.31

Information on the keyboard and the mouse in the setup program.

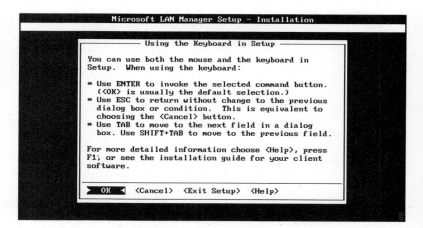

4. Select OK to continue.

   The Install LAN Manager screen appears, telling you about the location of installation files and the target directory (see fig. 11.32). Make any necessary changes.

Figure 11.32
Selecting the location of files.

5. Select OK to continue.

   The Install LAN Manager screen on selecting an enhanced or basic installation appears (see fig. 11.33).

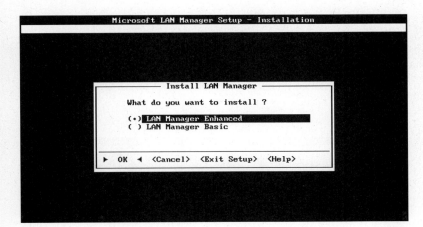

Figure 11.33
Selecting basic or enhanced clients.

The enhanced client gives you access to all network client features, such as connecting to LAN directories and printers, sending and receiving messages, and using services such as named pipes. You should select the Enhanced Client option unless you have memory-constraint problems or you do not need the more advanced options, in which case you should select the Basic Client option. The basic client uses less memory and disk space than the enhanced client. It provides workgroup functions, such as connecting to share directories and printers. You can issue network commands only from the command line.

6. Select the client type, and then select OK to continue.

You should see the status of files being copied.

When prompted for other disks, such as driver disks, insert them into the floppy drive.

7. At the end of the file copy, the Network Adapter Drivers screen appears (see fig. 11.34).

Figure 11.34

The Network Adapter Drivers screen.

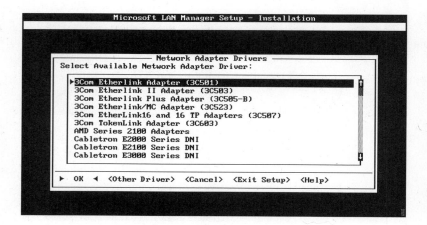

Select the appropriate network driver. If you cannot find a compatible driver in the list, select the <Other **D**river> option to add other drivers.

8. After selecting the network adapter driver, select OK to continue. A list of protocol choices appears (see fig. 11.35).

Figure 11.35

LAN Manager protocol choices.

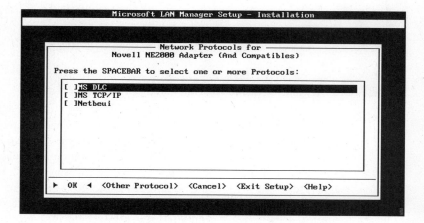

Select the protocol you want to use. To install another protocol, select the <Other **P**rotocol> option to add other protocols.

9. Select OK to continue. The Workstation Configuration screen appears, which lists the network adapters and protocols you have selected (see fig. 11.36).

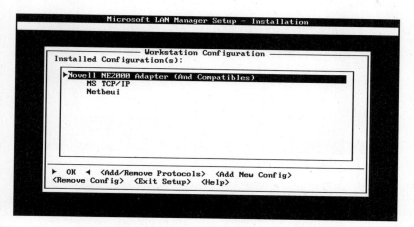

Figure 11.36

The Workstation Configuration screen.

10. Make any necessary network adapter and protocol changes and select OK to continue. If you chose to install TCP/IP then the TCP/IP Settings screen appears (see fig. 11.37).

Type the IP address, Subnet Mask, and default gateway or let the DHCP server do this for you.

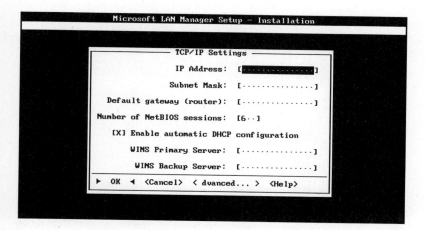

Figure 11.37

The TCP/IP Settings screen.

The Workstation Settings form appears next (see fig. 11.38).

Enter the computer name, user name, and workstation name.

In Other Domains to Monitor, enter the names of other domains in which this workstation can participate. This enables the NET VIEW command to list the servers in the specified domains. Other Domains to Monitor can be used only with enhanced client services.

The Messaging Services option enables workstations to send and receive messages. The default is Yes.

11. After changing the workstation settings, select OK to continue. The Support for the Windows Environment dialog box appears (see fig. 11.39).

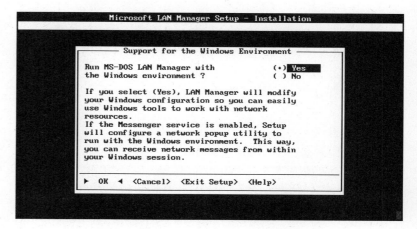

Choose Yes if you have Windows installed and need to use network services from Windows.

12. If you selected Yes for installing Windows-related files, the Windows directory screen appears. Enter the name of the Windows directory at the workstation and select OK.

To run LAN Manager with Windows, the setup program needs to modify certain configurations in Windows. The Windows directory screen appears asking for the Windows path and directory (see fig. 11.40)

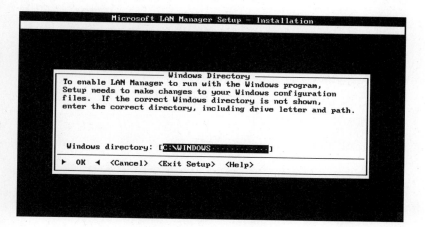

Figure 11.40
The Windows Directory screen.

13. If you selected the Messaging Services, you are given a choice of when to run the messaging services (see fig. 11.41).

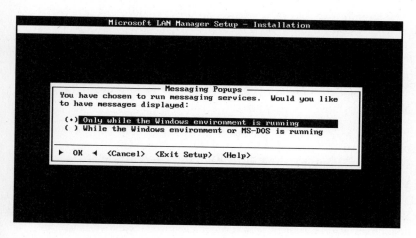

Figure 11.41
The Messaging Popups screen.

14. After making your messaging selections, select OK to continue. The Memory Management screen appears if setup detects extended memory (see fig. 11.42), and you are asked whether you want setup to maximize application memory. The default choice is Yes, and you usually should allow setup to optimize memory usage.

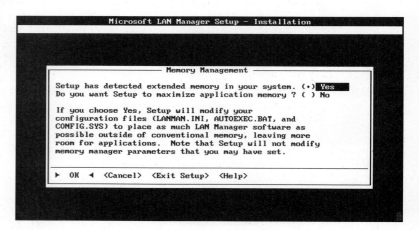

Figure 11.42

The Memory Management screen.

15. Select OK to continue. The Configuration Complete screen appears.

    Select <**R**eview> to review your configuration settings. This displays all the configuration screens one by one.

    Select <**S**ave> to save your configuration changes.

16. Follow the instructions on-screen to insert the driver disks.

17. At the completion of the installation, you see the Installation Complete screen.

18. Follow the instructions on-screen to exit Setup, or reboot your computer.

The installation procedure adds lines similar to the following in the CONFIG.SYS file:

```
DEVICE=C:\LANMAN.DOS\DRIVERS\DOSUTILS\EMM386.EXE NoEMS
LASTDRIVE=Z
DOS=HIGH,UMB
DEVICE=C:\LANMAN.DOS\DRIVERS\PROTMAN\PROTMAN.DOS /i:C:\LANMAN.DOS
DEVICE=C:\LANMAN.DOS\DRIVERS\ETHERNET\SMCETH\SMCMAC.DOS
```

The first DEVICE statement loads the memory manager driver. The LASTDRIVE statement sets the size of the DOS drive table to handle drive letters up to Z. The DOS=HIGH,UMB statement loads DOS high and in the upper memory blocks. The second DEVICE statement loads the NDIS protocol manager. The last DEVICE statement loads the network adapter driver.

You will find lines similar to the following added in the AUTOEXEC.BAT file by the installation procedure:

```
SET  PATH=C:\LANMAN.DOS\NETPROG;%PATH%
NET  START WORKSTATION
LOAD NETBEUI
```

The PATH statement adds the LAN Manager program directory to the PATH statement. The NET START statement starts the workstation client service. The last command loads the NETBEUI protocol.

The PROTOCOL.INI file in the C:\LANMAN.DOS directory contains protocol configuration information for the LAN Manager client for MS-DOS. A sample PROTOCOL.INI for the LAN Manager client follows:

```
[PROTMAN]
  DRIVERNAME = PROTMAN$
  DYNAMIC = YES
  PRIORITY = NETBEUI
[NETBEUI_XIF]
  Drivername = netbeui$
  SESSIONS = 6
  NCBS = 12
  BINDINGS = "SMCETH_NIF"
  LANABASE = 0
[SMCETH_NIF]
    drivername = SMCMAC$
;    enable these setting if card does not support soft setup
;    irq = 3
;    ramaddress = 0xd000
;    iobase = 0x280

    receivebufsize = 1024
```

The [PROTMAN] section contains parameters for the protocol manager, such as the protocol manager driver name and the priority of binding to a specific protocol.

The [NETBEUI_XIF] section contains the interface parameters for the NETBEUI protocol, such as the NetBEUI protocol driver name, number of sessions supported, number of network control blocks, the network adapter to which NetBEUI is to be bound, and LAN affinity information.

The [SMCETH_NIF] section is the name specified in the BINDINGS parameter in the [NETBEUI_XIF] section and contains network adapter driver settings. This includes the name of the network adapter driver and its receive buffer size. If the card does not support software settings, you must specify the network adapter parameters explicitly.

The LANMAN.INI file in the C:\LANMAN.DOS directory contains the LAN Manager client configuration information. A sample LANMAN.INI for the LAN Manager client follows:

```
;*********************************************************************;
;**               Microsoft LAN Manager                          **;
;**           Copyright(c) Microsoft Corp., 1993                  **;
;*********************************************************************;
[networks]
  netservices = chknet, minses
[workstation]
  wrkservices = encrypt,messenger,minipop
  computername = WKS1
  domain = domain_A
  othdomains = KINETD
  numdgrambuf = 4
  lanroot = C:\LANMAN.DOS
[netshell]
  username = Administrator
[version]
  lan_manager = 2.2c.0
[messenger]
[services]
  chknet       = netprog\chknet.exe
  minses       = netprog\minses.exe /n
  workstation     = netprog\netwksta.exe
  messenger     = services\msrv.exe
  netpopup      = services\netpopup.exe
  encrypt       = services\encrypt.exe
  minipop       = services\minipop.exe
```

The [networks] section describes the network services that are started. The [workstation] section describes the parameter settings, such as computer name, domain names, other domain names, and number of datagram (packet) buffers at the workstation. The [netshell] section specifies the default user name for the workstation. The [version] section displays the LAN Manager client version. The [messenger] section contains parameters for the messenger service. The [services] section contains the relative path name to the LANROOT parameter where the program files for the LAN Manager services reside.

You can use any of the NET commands described in table 11.2 to test the operation of the network client.

For example, you can use the NET CONFIG command to verify your LAN Manager client configuration:

```
> NET CONFIG Workstation
Computer name                 \\WKS1
User name                     ADMINISTRATOR
Software version              3.11
Redirector version            2.20
Workstation root directory    C:\LANMAN.DOS

Workstation Domain            Domain_A
Logon Domain                  Domain_A
Other Domains                 The command completed successfully.
```

If you installed the Windows components during the LAN Manager client installation, you can start Windows to verify the client installation. You should see the WinPopup icon that you can use for sending messages if you enabled messenger services. Figure 11.43 shows an example use of the WinPopup application.

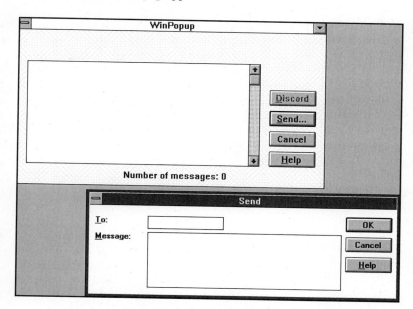

Figure 11.43
The LAN Manager client WinPopup interface.

Installing Client-Based Server Administration Tools

In addition to performing Windows NT Server administration by logging on locally to a Windows NT Server, you can perform Windows NT Server or domain administration from a Windows 95 or Windows NT workstation. The following 32-bit Windows tools are supported:

- **User Manager for Domains.** Used for administering domain accounts.

- **User Profile Editor.** Used for administering server-based user profiles.

- **Event Viewer.** Used for viewing the Windows NT Server event log.

- **Server Manager.** Used to manage Windows NT Server resources.

- **Remoteboot Manager.** Used for administering remoteboot clients.

- **Remote Access Administrator.** Used for administering remote access services.

- **DHCP Manager.** Used for DHCP administration.

- **WINS Manager.** Used for WINS server administration.

Setting Up Server Tools on a Windows NT Workstation Client

One of the most common tools used by a Windows NT Server Administrator is the User Manager for Domains. This tool and other server-based tools are not included with Windows NT Workstation. If you plan on using a Windows NT Workstation for performing server and domain administration, you should install the Windows NT Server tools on Windows NT Workstation clients.

To install the Windows NT Server tools on Windows NT Workstation clients, follow these steps:

1. Install the client-based tools on a Windows NT Server, as outlined in the previous section, "Using the Copy Client-Based Network Administration Tools," earlier in this chapter.

2. Logon as an Administrator user to a Windows NT Workstation.

3. Use File Manager to set up a connection to the \clients\srvtools directory on the Windows NT Server. The default share name for this directory is SetupAdm. Alternatively, you can use the following command:

   ```
   NET USE X: \\servername\SetupAdm
   ```

   Substitute an unused drive letter for *X* and the server computer name for *servername*.

4. Locate the file SETUP.BAT in the \clients\srvtools\winnt directory.

5. Run the SETUP.BAT file from the directory in which it is installed.

   Figure 11.44 shows the results of executing the SETUP.BAT file.

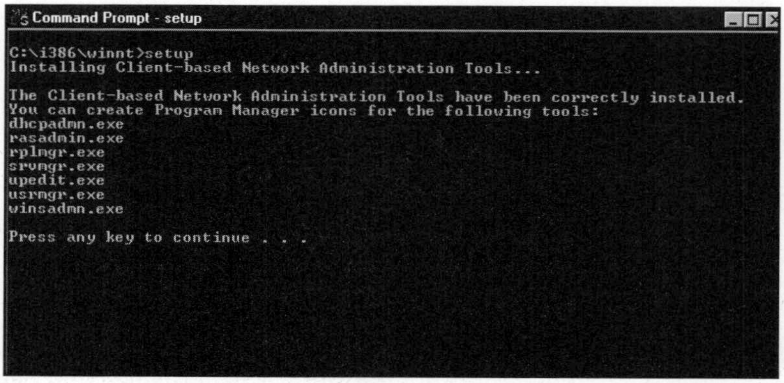

Figure 11.44

Installing client-based server tools by running SETUP.BAT.

```
Command Prompt - setup

C:\i386\winnt>setup
Installing Client-based Network Administration Tools...

The Client-based Network Administration Tools have been correctly installed.
You can create Program Manager icons for the following tools:
dhcpadmn.exe
rasadmin.exe
rplmgr.exe
srvmgr.exe
upedit.exe
usrmgr.exe
winsadmn.exe

Press any key to continue . . .
```

6. When the client-based server tools are installed at the Windows NT Workstation, a program folder and program items are not created automatically. You must create these as a separate step.

Table 11.4 shows the file names of the server-based tools that are copied to the %SystemRoot%\System32 directory. You need these program file names for creating the program items.

Figure 11.45 shows a program group for server tools created on Windows NT Workstation. The Event Viewer program at the Windows NT Server and the Windows NT Workstation is the same.

Figure 11.45
The Windows NT Server Tools group on a Windows NT Workstation.

Table 11.4
File Names for Server-Based Tools

File Name	Server Tool
dhcpadm.exe	DHCP Manager
rasadmin.exe	Remote Access Server Administrator
rplmgr.exe	Remoteboot Manager
srvmgr.exe	Server Manager
upedit.exe	User Profile Editor
usrmgr.exe	User Manager for Domains
winsadmn.exe	WINS Manager

Setting Up Server Tools in Windows 95

You can install the server tools for NT on your Windows 95 workstation. You need about 2.5 MB of disk space to install them.

1. Double-click the Add/Remove icon in the Control Panel. Choose the Windows Setup tab.

2. Click the Have Disk button. You can specify a local directory or a share on the network. It is important that the directory you specify contains the Srvtools.inf file.

3. Choose OK.

4. Check the Windows NT Server Tools box.

5. Choose Install, then OK.

6. You will need to edit the AUTOEXEC.BAT to include the Server Tools directory in the path. The default installation copies them to C:\srvtools.

7. Restart the computer.

   You must be logged on to the network before you can use the NT Server Tools.

   The installation automatically generates the NT Server Tools icons in the NT Server Tools program folder.

Installing Network Client Support for Windows 95 Clients

MS Windows 95 clients have a built-in Client for Microsoft Networks configuration. This client can be used to make connections to any Windows NT Server because the client uses network protocol and Redirector software that is compatible with the Windows NT Server.

During Windows 95 installation, if the installation procedure can recognize a network adapter, it automatically installs the Client for Microsoft Networks. Figure 11.46 shows the network configuration on a Windows 95 workstation connected to a network. The list of components installed includes the Client for Microsoft Networks and the NetBEUI protocol used by this client. Figure 11.46 also shows that the Client for Microsoft Networks configuration is set to be the primary client used at the workstation.

You can use the Windows 95 workstation to connect to network drives on any Windows NT Server and Windows NT Workstation.

To establish a connection with a Windows NT Server, follow these steps:

1. Right-click the My Computer icon.

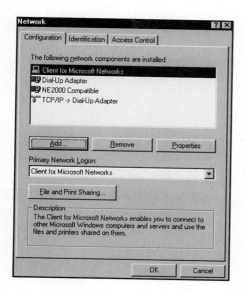

Figure 11.46
The Windows 95 Network Configuration tab.

2. Select Map **N**etwork Drive.

   The Map Network Drive dialog box appears (see fig. 11.47).

Figure 11.47
The Windows 95 Map Network Drive dialog box.

3. Select the drive to use for mapping from the **D**rive field, and specify the UNC name of the path in the **P**ath field.

4. Figure 11.48 shows an example of drive G mapped to share name SetupAdm on a Windows NT Server named Nameserver1.

5. If you try to connect to an administrative share, you are prompted for a valid password. Figure 11.49 shows an attempt to connect to the Administrator share Admin$ on the Windows NT Server Nameserver1. Notice that you are required to specify a password.

6. To disconnect from a network drive, right-click the computer name and select the **D**isconnect Network Drive option. The Disconnect Network Drive dialog box appears (see fig. 11.50). Use this dialog box to select the network drive to disconnect.

Figure 11.48

Mapping to a share name on a Windows NT Server.

Figure 11.49

Connecting to an Administrator share on a Windows NT Server.

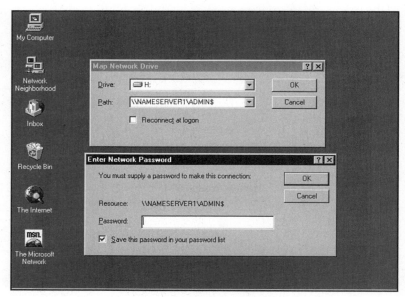

Figure 11.50

The Disconnect Network Drive dialog box in Windows 95.

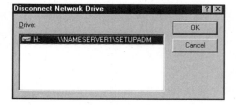

Supporting Macintosh Clients

Macintosh clients have built-in network client software that enables them to talk to other AppleShare servers. The Macintosh clients communicate with AppleShare servers using the AppleTalk protocols (see fig. 11.51). The AppleTalk protocols are a suite of protocols built into every Macintosh computer. AppleTalk protocols are discussed in Appendix A. The network adapters used on a Macintosh network can be LocalTalk, a proprietary networking technology; or a standards-based technology such as Ethernet, Token Ring, FDDI. These are called EtherTalk, TokenTalk, and FDDITalk, respectively.

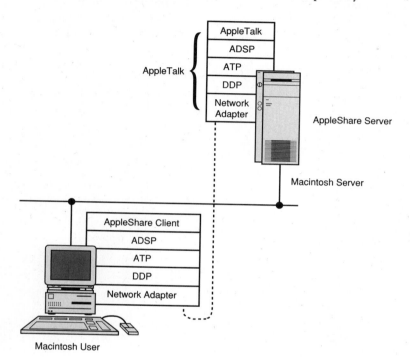

Figure 11.51

Macintosh clients and AppleShare servers.

Windows NT Server can support Macintosh clients by emulating an AppleShare server. Emulation of the AppleShare server is implemented by supporting the AppleTalk protocols on the Windows NT server (see fig. 11.52). This emulation is implemented by Services for Macintosh in Windows NT. Windows NT Server includes a special network client for Macintosh computers. This client can be downloaded by logging on as a Guest user to the Windows NT Server using the AppleTalk protocols.

The Services for Macintosh provide you with the following benefits:

- **File sharing.** For AppleShare clients, and between Macintosh clients and non-Macintosh clients.

- **Print sharing.** Enables PCs and Macintosh computers to share printers.

- **Simplified administration.** You can use a common server—the Windows NT Server—as an NT server and an AppleShare server.

- **AppleTalk routing support.** The Windows NT server with multiple network adapters can be used to provide routing at the Datagram Delivery Protocol (DDP) layer for AppleTalk computers. This enables the Windows NT Server to act as a router to join different AppleTalk network segments.

Figure 11.52
Windows NT Server support for AppleTalk clients.

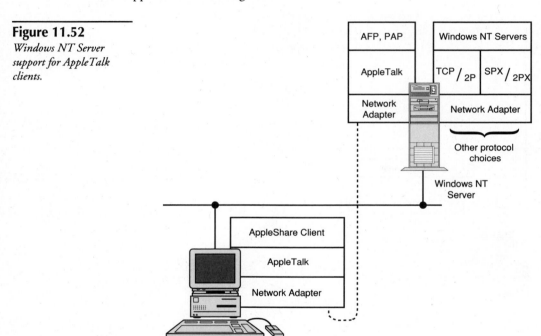

There are three steps involved in setting up services for the Macintosh:

1. Installing Services for Macintosh on the Windows NT Server.

2. Configuring Macintosh Accessible volumes.

3. Setting authentication services for Macintosh Client.

Installing Services for Macintosh on Windows NT Server

To set up Services for Macintosh, follow these steps:

1. Log on as an Administrator to the Windows NT Server.

2. Open the Control Panel.

3. Double-click the Network icon.

   The Network dialog box appears (see fig. 11.53).

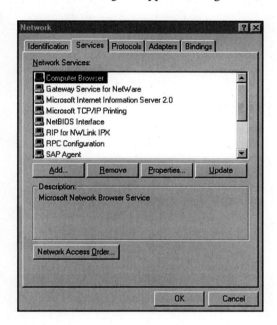

Figure 11.53
The Network Services tab.

4. Choose the **A**dd button.

   The Select Network Service dialog box appears (see fig. 11.54).

5. Select Services for Macintosh from the list.

6. Select the OK button. The Windows NT Setup dialog box appears.

7. Enter the path name of the Windows NT Server distribution files, then select Continue.

8. If you have not set up NTFS, an information dialog box appears, reminding you to do so. You don't have to do it before you add the Macintosh Service (see fig 11.55). Setup copies the necessary files and configures the Registry.

9. Select the **P**roperties button.

   The Macintosh AppleTalk Protocol Properties dialog box appears (see fig. 11.56).

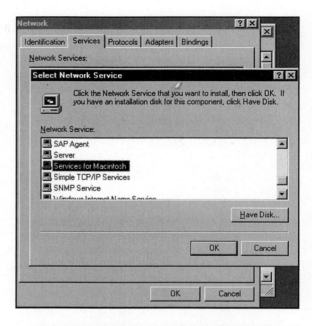

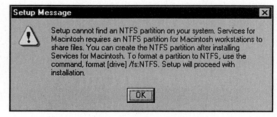

10. Select the network adapter information from the Default **A**dapter drop-down list and select the zone name of the AppleTalk network from the Default **Z**one drop-down list.

Zones are similar to the workgroup concepts in Windows NT networks. Although Microsoft documentation says that zones are similar to domains, zones are closer in concept to workgroups. Zones are used primarily to simplify browsing operations, which is typically the reason for using Windows NT workgroups. There is no concept of a zone user account or logging on to the zone. You can assign multiple zone names to a physical network segment.

A *physical network segment* is a network that does not contain routers. If routers exist on the physical network segment, they represent the boundary of the physical network segment.

For simpler networks, a single zone name is associated with a physical network segment. If you have multiple zone names for a physical network segment, select a default zone name for the segment.

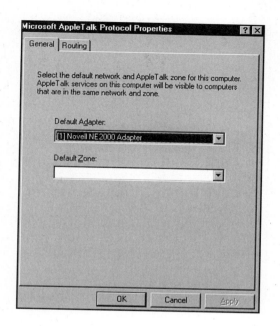

Figure 11.56

The Microsoft AppleTalk Protocol Properties dialog box.

If there are no AppleTalk routers or AppleShare servers on the network, and this is the first Windows NT Server on which you are configuring Services for Macintosh, no zone names are defined. In this case, you should select the Routing tab and set the Enable **R**outing option to set the Windows NT Server as an AppleTalk router. Normally, an AppleTalk router has multiple network adapters. However, you can have a computer act as a *seed* for information on zones and network numbers associated for the physical network attached to a Windows NT Server's network interface. A *seed router* is a supplier or source of information on the network numbers and zone names associated with the network.

11. Select the Routing tab (see fig. 11.57) and enable the Ena**b**le Routing check box.

Enable the **U**se this router to seed the network check box option so you can enter values for other fields.

In the Network Range section, enter a range of unique network numbers associated with the network segment. Network numbers are used by AppleTalk routers to identify a physical network segment. AppleTalk Phase I protocols supported only 254 nodes per network. When the currently used AppleTalk Phase II was introduced, the 254-node limitation per network segment was removed by allowing additional network numbers to be associated with a physical network segment. Windows NT 4.0 only supports the AppleTalk phase II protocols.

If you have only one network number assigned to the network segment, enter the same number in the Fr**o**m and **T**o fields.

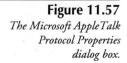

Figure 11.57

The Microsoft AppleTalk Protocol Properties dialog box.

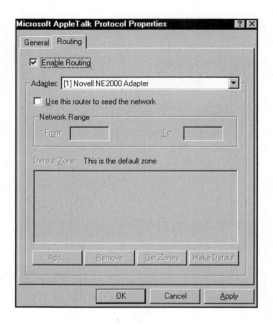

In the **Z**one section, enter zone names for the network attached to the Windows NT Server network interface. The previously added zone names appear in the list box. Use the list to specify the default zone. The first zone name you enter becomes the default zone name.

Figure 11.58 shows some sample settings for the AppleTalk Protocol Properties dialog box.

Select OK to return to the AppleTalk Protocol Properties screen. Notice that you now can set the **Z**one field using the new zones you have added.

12. Select OK. A message should appear, telling you that AppleTalk Protocol was configured successfully.

13. Select OK. You are returned to the Network Settings Change dialog box.

14. Select Yes.

15. Restart the Windows NT Server so that your changes will take effect.

After the Services for Macintosh are installed and the Windows NT Server restarts, you need to configure the volumes on the Windows NT Server that will be accessible to Macintosh clients.

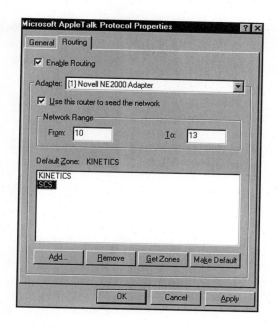

Figure 11.58

Sample settings for a Microsoft AppleTalk Protocol Properties dialog box.

To configure Macintosh-accessible volumes, follow these steps:

1. Log on as an Administrator to the Windows NT Server.

2. Open the Control Panel.

   An icon for MacFile appears as a result of successfully installing Services for Macintosh (see fig. 11.59).

3. Double-click the MacFile icon.

   The MacFile Properties dialog box appears (see fig. 11.60).

4. Select the MacFile **A**ttributes button.

   The MacFile Attributes dialog box appears (see fig. 11.61).

   Type text in the **L**ogon Message box to change the welcome log-on message.

   Select the options in the Security box to change the logon options. After installing the Microsoft authentication files on the Macintosh clients, you can select the **R**equire Microsoft Authentication option.

   Select the options in the Sessions box to allow unlimited sessions (default) or a limited number of sessions to the Windows NT Server. You might want to limit the number of sessions to limit the level of activity of Macintosh clients.

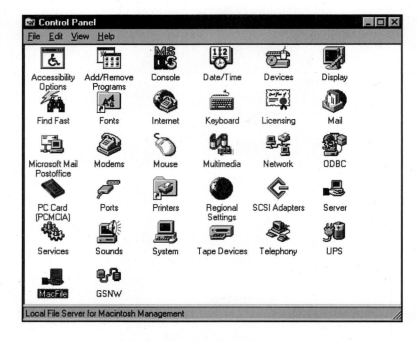

5. Open the File Manager and verify that you have the Microsoft UAM folder in the Ntfs partition (see fig. 11.62). This directory was created as a result of installing Services for Macintosh. This directory contains the authentication files for Macintosh clients, so they can log on using Microsoft's logon authentication, which provides encrypted passwords. These passwords are difficult to decrypt even if they are captured by protocol analyzer devices. By default, the AppleShare servers implemented for Macintosh support only clear text (unencrypted) passwords.

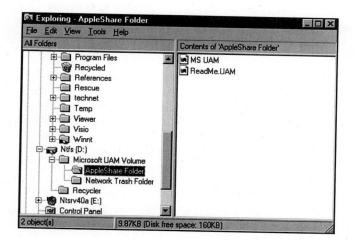

Figure 11.62

The Microsoft UAM folder viewed from the File Manager.

Setting Authentication Services for Macintosh Clients

You can set up authentication services for AppleShare by downloading the authentication files from the Windows NT Server. Microsoft's authentication services are an extension of AppleShare services and provide a more secure logon to a Windows NT Server emulating an AppleShare server. As you learned earlier, this emulation is provided by Services for Macintosh installed on the Windows NT Server. Microsoft authentication encrypts passwords and stores them on the Windows NT Server.

By using the Microsoft authentication on a Macintosh client, users can specify the domain they can log on to and change their passwords.

To install the configuration files, follow these steps:

1. Select Chooser from the Macintosh Apple menu. The Chooser dialog box appears.

2. Select the AppleShare icon.

   Also select the zone in which the client resides from the AppleTalk Zones list. A client can only reside in a single zone even if other zones overlap with it on the cable segment.

3. From the list of servers displayed for the zone, select the Windows NT Server acting as an AppleShare server and then select OK. The Sign-In dialog box appears.

4. Select the Guest or Registered User option. Then select OK. The Server dialog box appears.

5. Select the Microsoft UAM Volume option. Then select OK.

6. Close the Chooser dialog box. An icon for the Microsoft UAM volume appears on the Microsoft desktop.

7. Open the Microsoft UAM volume. The Microsoft UAM Volume window and the AppleShare folder inside the window appear.

8. Drag the AppleShare folder to the System folder.

   If you already have an AppleShare Folder inside the System folder, you are asked if you want to overwrite it. If this is another valid folder, such as a NetWare UAM folder used by Macintosh clients to access a NetWare server, you should not overwrite it. You can drop the Microsoft UAM folder inside the existing AppleShare folder inside the System folder.

9. Restart the Macintosh workstation.

10. When you log on next, select the Windows NT Server as you did earlier. This time, you see a Sign-on dialog box asking you to select the logon method.

    If the Macintosh workstation is running System 7.1 or later, and the Cleartext and Guest options are disabled at the AppleShare server, you see only the choice for the Microsoft authentication logon method. In earlier systems, you would see both choices: the Cleartext and the Microsoft authentication logon, regardless of the fact that the Cleartext and Guest options are disabled at the AppleShare server.

11. Select Registered User and Microsoft Authentication.

    Enter your user name and password, and select OK. A list of Macintosh-accessible volumes appears.

12. Select a volume to access its contents.

If a volume icon is grayed out, you might not have the correct privileges to access it, or you already might be logged on to that volume.

Managing Macintosh Users, Volumes, and Files on Windows NT Server

You can use the MacFile icon in the Control Panel to manage Macintosh client users who have made connections to the Windows NT Server.

To manage the user connection properties, follow these steps:

1. Logon as an Administrator user to the Windows NT Server.

2. Double-click the MacFile icon in the Control Panel.

   The MacFile Properties dialog box appears. This properties box displays the active AppleTalk sessions, number of open file forks, and file locks.

3. Select the Users button.

   The Macintosh Users dialog box appears (see fig. 11.63). You can use this screen to disconnect specific user connections or to send messages to the Macintosh users.

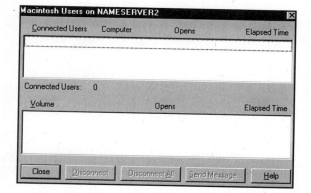

Figure 11.63

The Macintosh Users dialog box for Windows NT Server.

   Select Close to return to the MacFile Properties dialog box.

4. Select the Volumes button.

   The Macintosh-Accessible Volumes dialog box appears (see fig. 11.64). You can use this screen to monitor Macintosh users connected to a specific volume, the amount of time they have been connected, and whether the volume is being used. You also can disconnect specific user connections.

   Select Close to return to the MacFile Properties dialog box.

5. Select the Files button.

   The Files Opened by Macintosh Users dialog box appears (see fig. 11.65). You can use this dialog box to monitor the files opened by Macintosh users, the permissions they have to a specific file, the number of locks for a specific file, and the directory path to the file. You also can close a fork opened by the Macintosh users.

Figure 11.64

The Macintosh-Accessible Volumes dialog box for Windows NT Server.

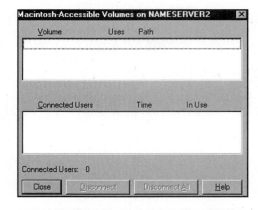

Figure 11.65

Files Opened by Macintosh Users screen on Windows NT Server.

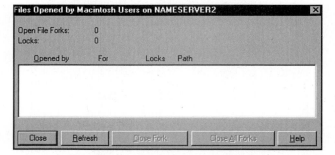

Select Close to return to the MacFile Properties dialog box.

6. Select Close to exit the MacFile Properties dialog box.

Conclusion

The Windows NT Server supports a number of different client computers, including MS-DOS, Windows 3.*x*, Windows NT, OS/2, and Macintosh clients. This chapter discussed the network client architecture, protocols, and APIs used to access Windows NT Server resources.

This chapter also discussed the different options available in the Network Client Administrator tool for setting up installation files for network clients. You also learned how to configure different types of network clients to access a Windows NT network.

Integrating Windows NT Server with a NetWare Network

Windows NT Server provides a number of capabilities that enable the integration of Windows NT Server in a NetWare network. One of these capabilities is the Gateway Services for NetWare that runs on Windows NT servers and enables Microsoft network clients to access NetWare servers. The Gateway Services for NetWare enables a single connection to the NetWare server to be shared by an unlimited number of clients. If only a single Windows NT computer (workstation or server) needs access to NetWare servers, you can install Microsoft's Client Service for NetWare or Novell's NetWare Client for Windows NT. Given an option, you should use Novell's client because it can work with all versions of NetWare, and you can expect Novell to better understand access to NetWare servers.

If you decide to convert NetWare servers to Windows NT Servers, you can use NWCONV, a Migration Tool that is installed on Windows NT Servers. You can use this Migration Tool to transfer NetWare user and group account information to equivalent Windows NT Server user and group accounts.

Gateway Service for NetWare

The Gateway Service for NetWare is a software service that runs on Windows NT Server and provides the Microsoft networking client with access to NetWare servers file and print resources. Figure 12.1 shows a possible configuration using the Gateway Service for NetWare. Microsoft network clients can use the Gateway Service for accessing file and print services on the NetWare server.

Figure 12.1

Use of the Gateway Service for NetWare.

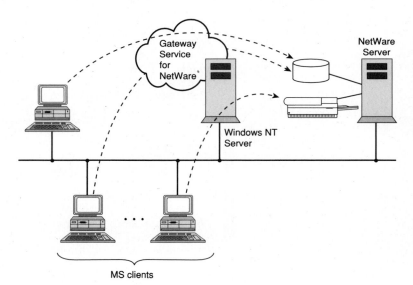

Windows NT Server and Microsoft clients use the SMB protocol at the application layer of the OSI model. Microsoft clients translate their requests for network services to SMB requests. Windows NT Servers receive these SMB requests, execute the requested action and send back replies using the SMB protocol. The transport protocol used for the transmission of SMB requests can be NetBEUI, TCP/IP, IPX, or another protocol (DEC supplies the DecNET protocol as one of the choices).

NetWare servers and clients, however, use the IPX/SPX transport protocols and the NCP protocols. Other protocol choices, such as TCP/IP, are possible on NetWare servers and clients, but the native protocol used is IPX and NCP. Although Windows NT Server and Microsoft clients can use the IPX protocol, they do not natively support NCP used by NetWare.

The Gateway Service for NetWare receives the SMB requests and translates these into equivalent NCP requests to the NetWare server (see fig. 12.2). The requests are processed by the NetWare server and the replies sent back to the Gateway Service for NetWare running on the Windows NT Server. The Gateway Service for NetWare translates the replies back to SMB replies. As far as the Microsoft clients are concerned, the NetWare server resources appear to be on the Windows NT Server. The NetWare resources are available without requiring any change to the Microsoft clients. Because the access to NetWare services occurs through a gateway, the performance is worse than when using direct access to NetWare servers.

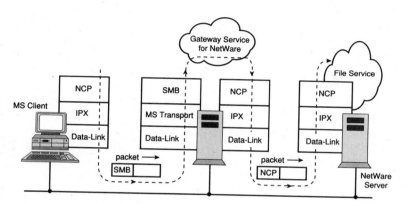

Figure 12.2

Protocol translation between SMB and NCP.

Salability of the Gateway Service for NetWare Solution

The gateway solution to NetWare servers is adequate for a small network with occasional NetWare access. The MS clients share a single network connection to the NetWare server and take up only a single user license on the NetWare server. Legal issues aside, the moral issue remains: The original intent of the NetWare server license is circumvented. You therefore are making use of multiple user sessions to the NetWare server without paying for them.

If the NetWare servers are accessed frequently, you can install the Client Services for NetWare on Windows NT workstations (see fig. 12.3).

NetWare 4 servers keep user account and other configuration information on the network in a global database called the NetWare Directory Services (NDS). NDS is based on CCITT/ITU's X.500 standards and provides a distributed database with hierarchical organizational and naming capabilities.

NetWare 4 servers provide a backwards compatibility to earlier NetWare clients and servers by emulating NetWare 3 servers to these older clients. This emulation capability is called *bindery emulation.* If the NetWare 4 server is configured in the bindery emulation mode, you can use the Microsoft client (Client Services for NetWare) to access the NetWare 4 servers. You can access only those resources on the NetWare 4 servers that are available to bindery-based clients.

Figure 12.3
Client Services for NetWare.

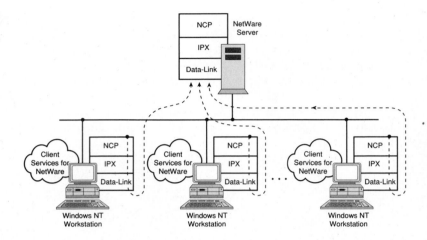

To ensure that the NetWare 4 server is configured for bindery emulation, the NetWare server must have the following statement placed in its AUTOEXEC.NCF file:

```
SET BINDERY CONTEXT=container1;container2;...;containerN
```

As many as 16 containers can be specified. Containers are used for organizing the global database, and can contain network objects and other containers. Network objects contain description and configuration information on network resources. Figure 12.4 shows an example of NetWare 4 servers being accessed by Windows NT workstations running Microsoft's Client Services for NetWare. All network objects including user accounts, group accounts, NetWare volumes, and so on that can be emulated as equivalent bindery objects are accessible by Windows NT workstations.

Novell supplies a separate client for Windows NT workstations—the NetWare Services for Windows NT—that is NetWare-Directory-Services-compliant and can be used to access NDS resources on a NetWare 4 network. NetWare Services for Windows NT is available from Novell at `www.novell.com` and through Novell's NetWire forum on CompuServe.

Installing Gateway Services for NetWare

Before you install Microsoft's Gateway (and Client) services for NetWare, you should remove any existing redirectors such as the NetWare Services for Windows NT from Novell. These redirectors conflict with the redirector capability provided by Gateway Services for NetWare.

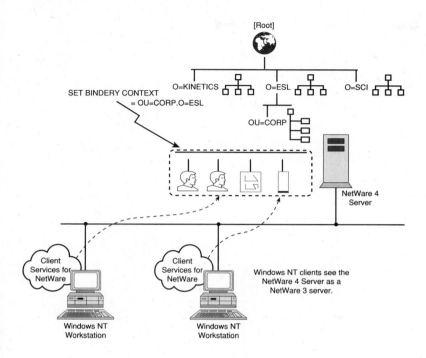

Figure 12.4

Access of NetWare 4 servers in the bindery emulation mode.

If you have these redirectors installed, you can use the following list as a guideline for removing these redirectors:

1. Log on as an administrator user.

2. Double-click on the Network icon in the Control Panel.

3. In the Network dialog box, select the Services tab and highlight the network redirector to remove.

4. Choose the **R**emove button.

5. Confirm your choice to remove the redirector.

6. Select Close from the Network dialog box.

7. Choose **Y**es to restart the Windows NT computer to make your changes effective.

Gateway Services for NetWare makes use of the NWLink (IPX/SPX) transport protocol. If this protocol is not installed, it is automatically installed as part of the installation procedure for Gateway Services for NetWare. Use the following as a guideline to install and configure Gateway Services for NetWare:

1. Log on as an administrator user.

2. Open the Control Panel and select the Network icon. You should see the Network dialog box (see fig. 12.5).

Figure 12.5

The Network dialog box.

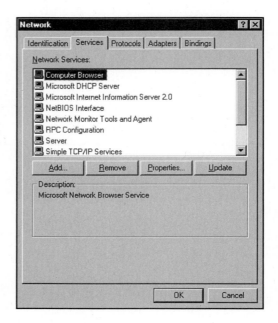

3. Select the Services tab and choose the **A**dd button. You should see the Select Network Service dialog box (see fig. 12.6).

Figure 12.6

The Select Network Service dialog box.

4. Select the Gateway (and Client) Services for NetWare and then choose the OK button.

You should see a dialog box prompting you for the path of the distribution files. If you have a CD-ROM on the Windows NT Server, the path to the CD-ROM distribution files is listed by default.

5. Choose the Continue button. You should see the Installing NWLink IPX protocol and related components information box and a status of the copy operation as files are copied.

   At the return of the Network Services screen, choose the Close button. The Network Settings Change information box will ask if you want to restart the computer for the settings to take effect. Select **Y**es.

6. If you have not installed the NWLink protocol prior to installing Gateway Services for NetWare, you see the Gateway Service for NetWare dialog box (see fig. 12.7) after you log on. Use this dialog box to indicate your preferred NetWare server if you are using NetWare 3.*x* or bindery emulation. Otherwise, select Default Tree and type in the tree and context information. If you set the name of valid NetWare server, the Gateway Services for NetWare tries to log on using the user name and password specified when you logged on to the Windows NT Server. If such a username does not exist on the NetWare server, the logon fails.

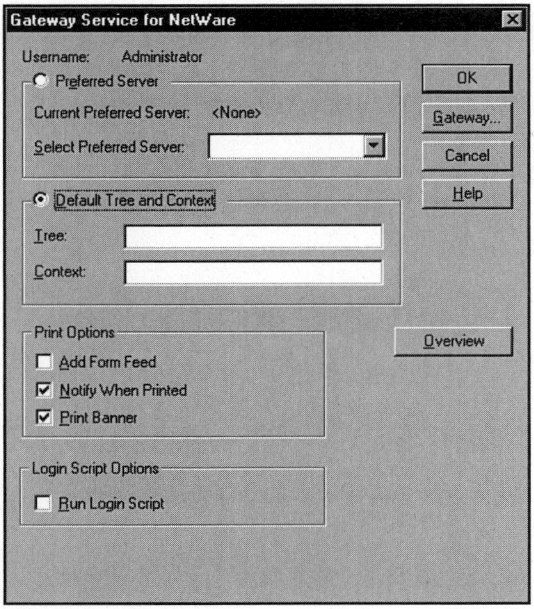

Figure 12.7

The Gateway Service for NetWare dialog box.

7. When the system reboots a new icon labeled GSNW (Gateway Service for NetWare) is added to the Control Panel (see fig. 12.8).

Figure 12.8
The new GSNW icon.

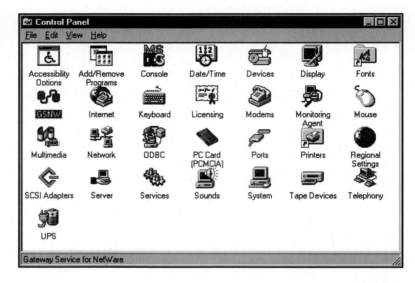

If you are logging on as Administrator on the Windows NT Server, you should know that, by default, no user accounts are named Administrator on the NetWare server. On a NetWare 3.*x* server, the administrator account is SUPERVISOR, and on a NetWare 4 server, the administrator account is Admin. If bindery emulation is set on the NetWare 4 server, a virtual SUPERVISOR account exists on the NetWare 4 server. If you are setting up gateway services to a NetWare 4 network, you might consider renaming the Windows NT Server administrator account to the shortened name Admin. This is easier to type and matches the Admin named account on the NetWare 4 server.

By default, the NetWare network is added as the first network provider to be searched by the MUP when resolving UNC names. The MUP was discussed in Chapter 11, "Supporting Windows NT Server Clients."

Configuring Gateway Services for NetWare

Before configuring the Gateway Services for NetWare, you must create the following accounts:

- A User account on the NetWare server with adequate rights to the NetWare file system directories to which users on the Microsoft network need access.

- A Group account named NTGATEWAY on the NetWare server with adequate rights to the resources you want to access.

  The user account you created on the NetWare server needs to be a member of the NTGATEWAY group.

The NetWare user account is used by the Gateway Service for NetWare to create a connection with the NetWare server. This connection appears on the Windows NT Server as a redirected drive. Windows NT Server can share the redirected drive as if it were a resource on the Windows NT Server. For example, you could create a network connection on drive N: to the NetWare directory that has the UNC name of \\NW3S\SYS\APPS. You could then share the drive N: as if it were a local drive on the Windows NT Server. If the share name is NWAPPS and the Windows NT Server computer name is NTSA, Microsoft clients can access this resource using the UNC name of \\NTSA\NWAPPS (see fig. 12.9). The shared resource can be on the Windows NT Server or the NetWare server this fact is completely transparent to the Microsoft clients.

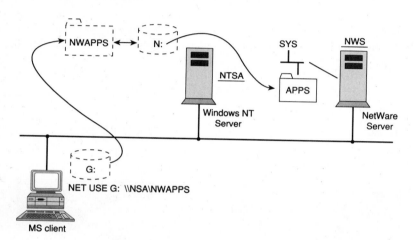

Figure 12.9

The use of Windows NT Server shared name to access NetWare resources.

The user connection to the NetWare server used for the Gateway Services for NetWare is global to all users on the Windows NT Server. The gateway user connection still exists when a user logs off from the Windows NT Server. The user connection for the gateway connection is disconnected only if the Windows NT server or NetWare server is shut down, or the Windows NT server administrator disables the Gateway Services. Note that all clients accessing NetWare files through the gateway service have the same rights on the NetWare server. You can create different shares to control users effective rights on the NetWare server.

Because the user account and the NTGATEWAY group account are on the NetWare server, the NetWare administrator has total control over the rights allowed through the Gateway Service for NetWare. You must coordinate with the NetWare administrator to assign the rights needed by Microsoft clients.

The following sections describe the steps for configuring the Gateway Services for NetWare:

- Configure NetWare servers with gateway accounts

- Enable the Gateway Services for NetWare

- Set permissions on the gateway share

Configuring NetWare 3.x Servers with Gateway Accounts

You must create a user account and make this user a member of a specially created group called NTGATEWAY that is used for Gateway Services for NetWare.

On a NetWare 3.x server, you can use the NetWare system administrator tool called SYSCON for creating user and group accounts. On a NetWare 4 server, you can use the system administration tools NETADMIN in DOS, or NetWare Administrator (NWADMN) in Windows. You can have your NetWare administrator assist you in setting up these accounts. In case you are both the Windows NT Server and NetWare administrator, the following procedures can be used as a guideline in setting up user accounts. For additional details, consult the Novell documentation or the latest edition of *NetWare: The Professional Reference* from New Riders.

The following is an outline of the procedure for creating user and group accounts on a NetWare 3.x server.

1. Log on to the NetWare server as a SUPERVISOR or supervisor-equivalent user.

2. Run SYSCON. You should see the main screen for SYSCON (see fig. 12.10).

Figure 12.10
The SYSCON main screen.

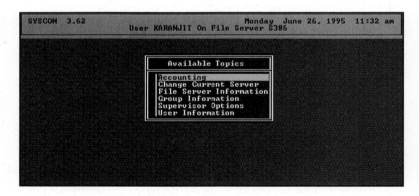

3. Select User Information. You should see the list of currently defined users (see fig. 12.11).

4. Press Ins to add a new user.

   You are prompted to enter a user name. Enter a suitable user name that is to be used by the Gateway Service for NetWare, such as the user name NTGWUSER, and press Enter.

   You are asked to enter a path to the user's home directory (see fig. 12.12). Accept the default home directory or specify another path. If the directory does not exist, select Yes to verify creation of the home directory.

   You see the new user name appear in the Users List (see fig. 12.13).

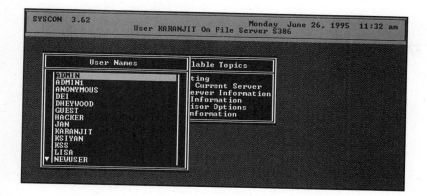

Figure 12.11

A list of currently defined users on a NetWare server.

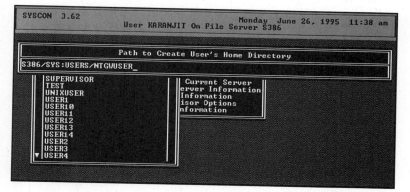

Figure 12.12

Creating a user's home directory.

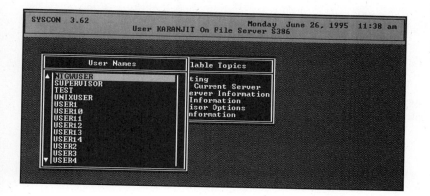

Figure 12.13

The newly created NT gateway user.

5. Select the new user name. You see a list of administrative tasks that you can perform on the new user (see 12.14).

6. Select Change Password from figure 12.14 to set the user's password.

Figure 12.14

A list of administrative tasks on the new user.

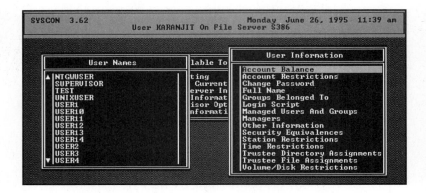

7. Select Account Restrictions from figure 12.14 to verify that no logon restrictions exist and that the account is enabled by default (see fig. 12.15).

Figure 12.15

Account Restrictions.

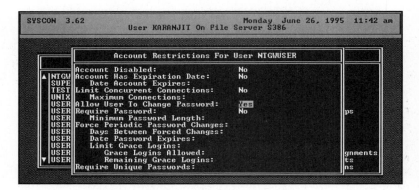

As a precaution, you might want to set the Allow User To Change Password to No in figure 12.15.

8. Select Time Restrictions from figure 12.14 to ensure that no default time restrictions exist for the NT gateway user (see fig. 12.16). You should see an asterisk for each 30-minute interval of the days to which the user can log on.

9. Select Trustee Directory Assignments from figure 12.14 to assign rights to the NT user account to the NetWare file system (see fig. 12.17).

To add a directory for which the NT gateway user is a trustee, press Ins, and enter the name of the directory. Figure 12.18 shows that the directory SYS:DATA has been added to the Trustee Directory Assignments and the NT gateway user has the R (Read) and F (File scan) rights to this directory.

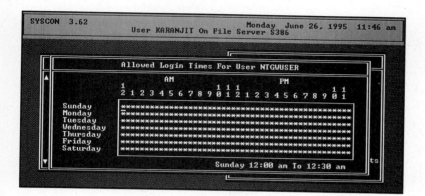

Figure 12.16

Time Restrictions for the gateway user.

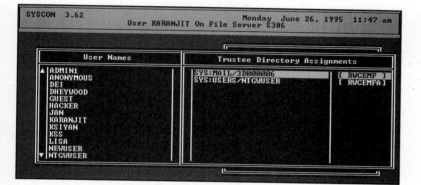

Figure 12.17

Trustee Directory Assignments for a user.

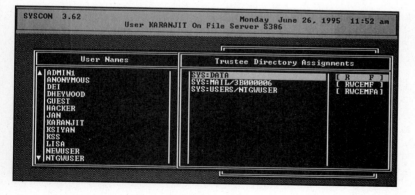

Figure 12.18

New directory added to the Trustee Directory Assignments.

To change these default rights, select the directory name in the Trustee Directory Assignments list. You should see a list of the current rights that are granted (see fig. 12.19). To add a new right to this list, press Ins. You should see a list of trustees not granted (see fig. 12.20). Use the F5 key to mark the additional rights to be granted, and press Enter. You see the new rights added to the Trustee Rights Granted list.

Figure 12.19
Trustee Rights Granted.

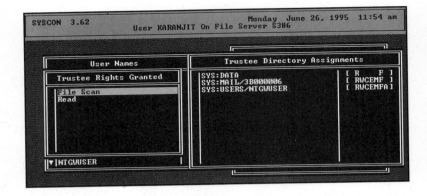

Figure 12.20
Trustee Rights Not Granted.

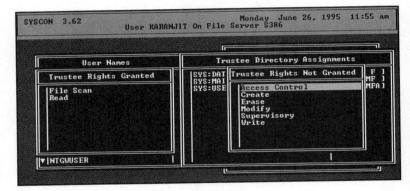

10. Press the Esc key a few times until you are back to the SYSCON main screen (refer to figure 12.10).

Next, you can create the NTGATEWAY group account.

11. Select Group Information.

You should see the Groups currently defined on the server (see fig. 12.21).

Figure 12.21
Groups currently defined on the NetWare server.

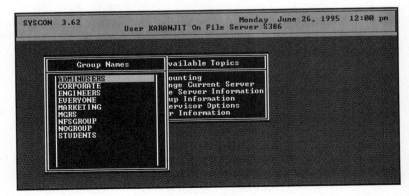

12. Press the Ins key to add a new group name.

    Enter the group name NTGATEWAY and press Enter.

    You should see the newly created group NTGATEWAY (see fig. 12.22).

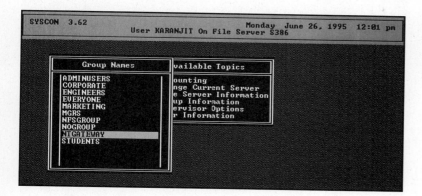

Figure 12.22
*Newly created
NTGATEWAY group
account.*

13. Select the newly created NTGATEWAY account. You see the Group Information task
    list for the new group account (see fig. 12.23).

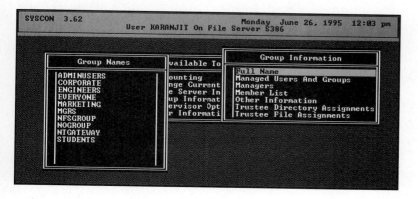

Figure 12.23
*The Group Information
list.*

14. Select Member List. You see a list of members for this account. Because this is a newly
    created group, the member list is empty.

15. Press Ins. You see the Not Group Members list (see fig. 12.24).

16. Highlight the NT user that you just created and press Enter to add this user as member of
    the NTGATEWAY group (see fig. 12.25).

Figure 12.24

The Not Group Members list.

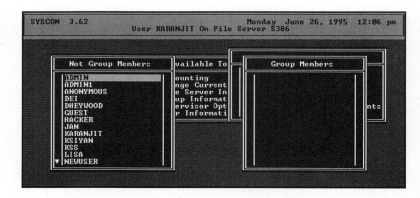

Figure 12.25

Adding the NT user as a member of NTGATEWAY group.

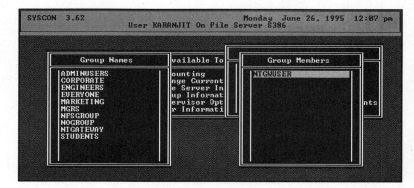

17. Press Esc to return to the Group Information list.

18. Select Trustee Directory Assignments to add to the group rights to NetWare directories. The procedure for adding directories to the Trustee Directory Assignments list is the same as that discussed in step 9. Use this as a guideline to adding to the trustee assignments for the NTGATEWAY group.

19. Press Alt+F10 to exit SYSCON.

Configuring NetWare 4.x Servers with Gateway Accounts Using NWAdmin

The procedure described in the preceding steps is for a NetWare 3.x server. On a NetWare 4 server, you may want to create the user and group objects in the container that is part of the bindery context. If, for example, the SET BINDERY CONTEXT command on a NetWare 4 server is the following, then you can create the user and group objects in any of the containers O=ESL or OU=CORP.O=ESL (see fig. 12.26).

```
SET BINDERY CONTEXT = O=ESL;OU=CORP.O=ESL
```

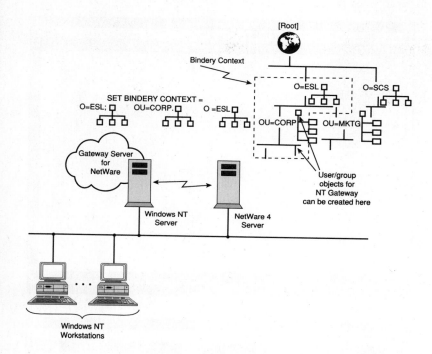

Figure 12.26

NT gateway user, group accounts, and the NDS tree.

The following procedure outlines the configuration steps on a NetWare 4 server for creating the necessary accounts for the Gateway Services for NetWare.

1. Log on as the Admin user to the NetWare 4 server network.

2. Start the NetWare 4 Administrator tool from a Windows or OS/2 workstation. Installing and using the NetWare Administrator on the NT computer is covered under "NetWare Client for Windows NT," later in this chapter.

   The NetWare Administrator main window appears (see fig. 12.27). To see the entire tree, select **V**iew, Set C**o**ntext, and enter the name [Root] in the **N**ew Context field.

3. Navigate the NDS tree and locate the container that is in the server's bindery context in which you are going to create the NT gateway accounts. Figure 12.28 shows that the CORP container under ESL has been selected for creating the user and group accounts.

4. Right-click on the selected container and select **C**reate. You should see the New Object dialog box (see fig. 12.29).

5. Select the user object from the list of **C**lass of New Object and select OK.

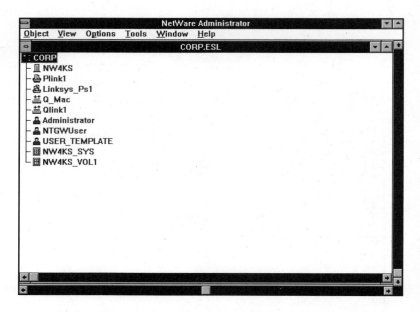

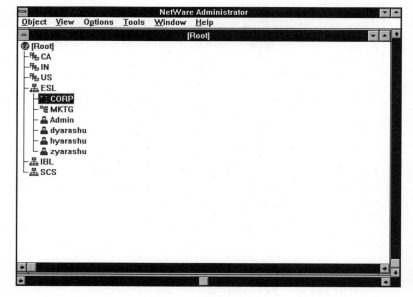

6. The Create User dialog box appears (see fig. 12.30). Enter the Login **N**ame for the NT
   user account to be used by the Gateway Service for NetWare. This can be a user name
   such as NTGWUser. Enter the **L**ast Name; the actual value of this field is not important.
   It is, however, required for complying with the X.500 standard. Enable the **D**efine
   Additional Properties check box.

Figure 12.29

The New Object dialog box.

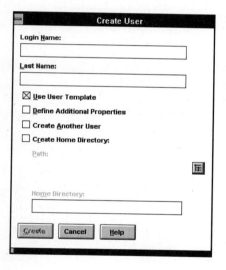

Figure 12.30

The Create User dialog box.

7. Select the **C**reate button. You should see the user NTGWUser's property dialog box that defines the user's properties (see fig. 12.31).

8. Select the Password Restrictions page button. The Password Restriction dialog box appears (see fig. 12.32).

9. Select the C**h**ange Password button and specify the NTGWUser's password.

   Select Cancel to exit the dialog box.

10. Right-click on the selected container, and select **C**reate.

11. Select the Group object from the **C**lass of New object, and choose OK. The Create Group dialog box appears (see fig. 12.33).

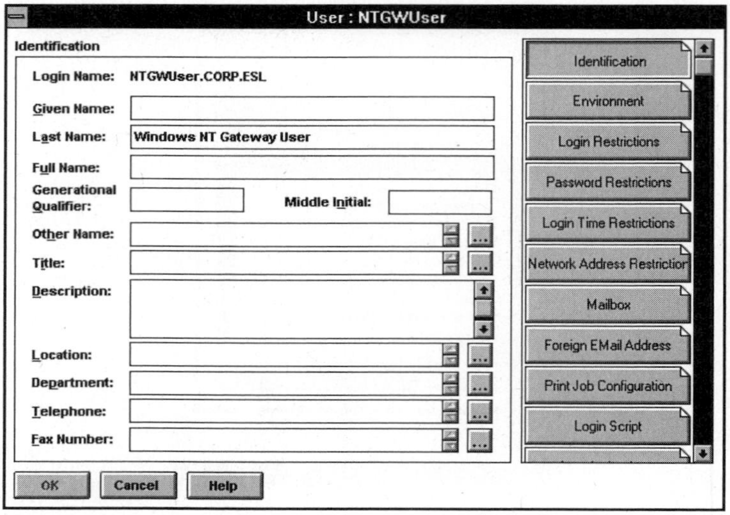

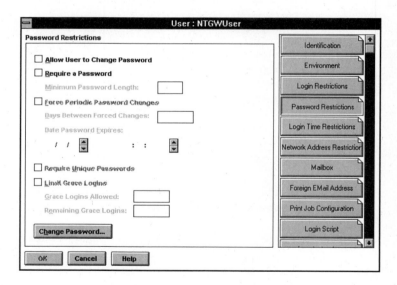

Figure 12.31
The User NTGWUser's property dialog box.

Figure 12.32
The Password Restrictions dialog box.

12. In the Group **N**ame field, enter **NTGateway**.

13. Check the **D**efine Additional Properties box, then choose the **C**reate button.

    You should see the group object properties dialog box (see fig. 12.34).

14. Choose the Members page button. The Group Members properties appear. Because this is a new group, no members are defined for the group.

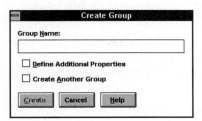

Figure 12.33
*The Create Group
dialog box.*

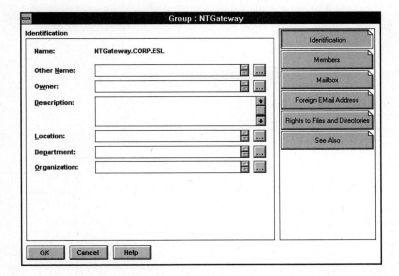

Figure 12.34
*The group object's
properties dialog box.*

15. Choose **A**dd. The Select Object dialog box appears (see fig. 12.35).

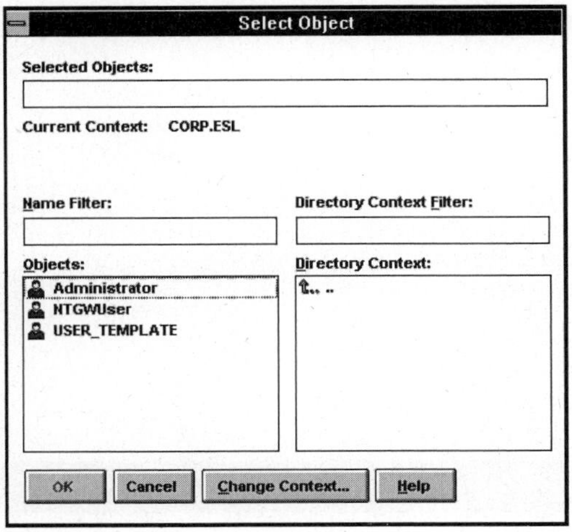

Figure 12.35
*The Select Object
dialog box.*

16. Select the NTGWUser from the **O**bjects: list box, and choose OK.

The NT gateway user is now a member of the NTGateway group object (see fig. 12.36).

Figure 12.36

The added member of NTGATEWAY group object.

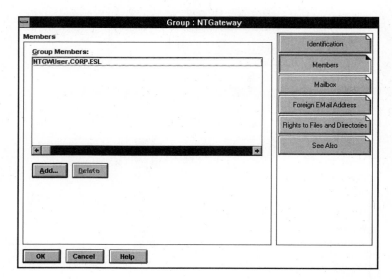

17. Select OK. You can see the newly created user objects in the selected container. Figure 12.37 highlights the NT gateway accounts just created.

Figure 12.37

The NT gateway accounts on a NetWare 4 server.

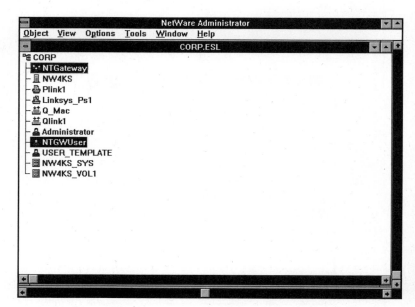

18. Assign file system rights to the NetWare file system for the user and group accounts you have created.

    To assign these rights, double-click on the volume object that causes the volume's contents to be displayed (see fig. 12.38).

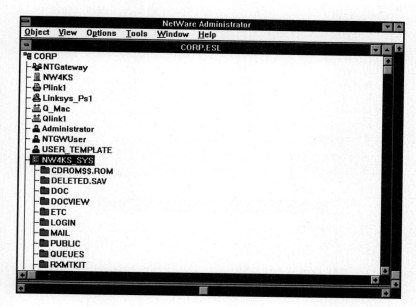

Figure 12.38

The directories under the volume object.

19. Highlight the directory to which you want to assign rights, then right-click and select Details. Next, select the Trustees of this Directory page button.

    If you want to assign rights to the root of the selected volume, right-click on the volume object and select Details. Next, select Trustees of the Root Directory.

    Figure 12.39 shows the dialog box for setting trustee rights.

20. Choose **A**dd Trustee.

    The Select Object dialog box appears (see fig. 12.40).

    Normally, you use the Directory Context **F**ilter in the Select Object dialog box to find the trustees for whom rights are to be assigned to the directory. In this case, because the volume object and the NT gateway accounts are in the same context, these accounts are listed in the **O**bjects list box.

21. Select the NT user and group gateway accounts in the **O**bjects list box and click on OK. Figure 12.41 shows that the NT gateway accounts are added as trustees to the directory. Use the Access **R**ights and **I**nheritance Filter boxes to assign appropriate rights to the NT user and group gateway accounts.

Figure 12.39

The trustees of the directory dialog box.

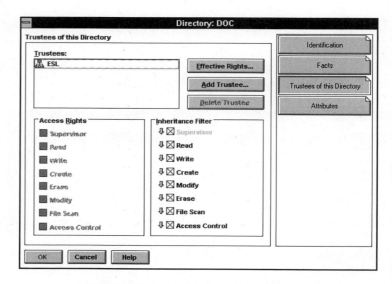

Figure 12.40

The Select Object dialog box.

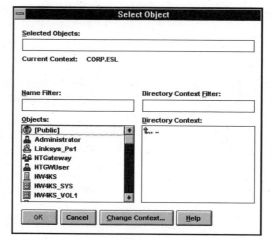

22. Select OK and exit the NetWare Administrator tool.

Configuring the Gateway Services for NetWare

After you have created the user and NTGATEWAY group account on the NetWare server, you can use this information to enable the Gateway Services for NetWare on the Windows NT Server. The following is an outline of the procedure for enabling the gateway:

1. Log on as administrator to the Windows NT Server on which you have installed Gateway (and Client) Services for NetWare.

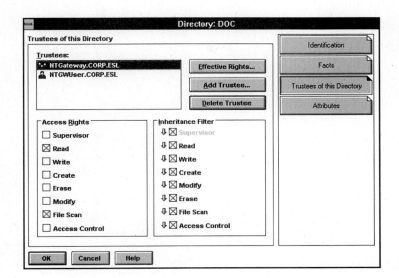

Figure 12.41

The NT user account trustees.

2. Double-click on the GSNW icon in the Control Panel.

   The Gateway Service for NetWare dialog box appears (see fig. 12.42).

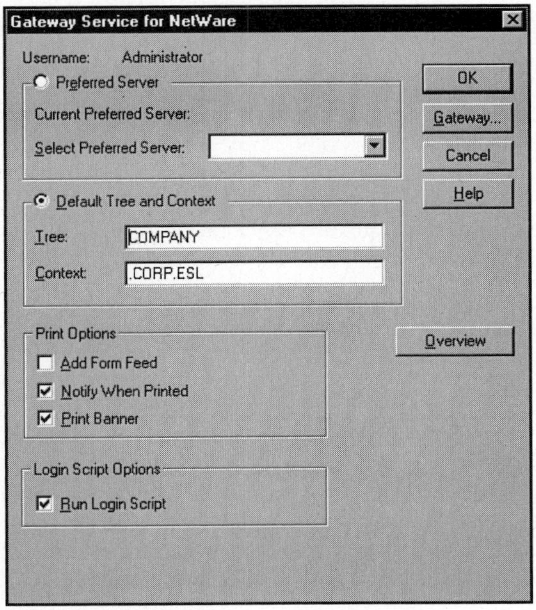

Figure 12.42

The Gateway Service for NetWare dialog box.

3. Choose **G**ateway and the Configure Gateway dialog box appears (see fig. 12.43).

Figure 12.43

The Configure Gateway dialog box.

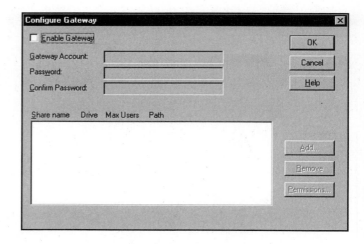

4. Check the **E**nable Gateway box to enable the Gateway Service.

5. In the **G**ateway Account field (refer to figure 12.43), enter the NetWare user name that you created in the previous section. In the Pass**w**ord and **C**onfirm Password fields, enter the NetWare user account and password.

6. Select the **A**dd button to create a NetWare share to be used by Microsoft networking clients. You should see the New Share dialog box for creating the NetWare share (see fig. 12.44).

   In the **S**hare Name field enter the name of the NetWare directory that is known to Microsoft clients. If you want the share name to be visible to MS-DOS clients, limit the length to eight characters.

   In the **N**etwork Path field enter the NetWare directory name using the UNC name. If, for example, the NetWare directory is SYS:ATLA on a server named POSEID, then the UNC name is \\POSEID\SYS\ATLA. Similarly, if the NetWare directory is the root of the SYS: volume on the NetWare server NW4KS, the UNC name is \\NW4KS\SYS.

   In the **C**omment field enter some descriptive text about the share name. This comment is visible to MS clients that examine shares on the Windows NT Server.

   In the **U**se Drive field select a drive letter on the Windows NT Server to be assigned to the NetWare directory. This drive letter is used as long as the Gateway Service for NetWare is running. By default, the first drive assigned is Z for the first share name.

   In the User Limit box, you can control the number of users who share the NetWare connection, or specify an unlimited number of users. For load balancing purposes, you may want to control the number of users using a particular share name.

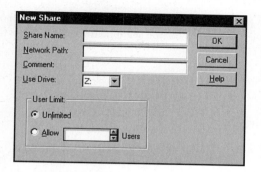

Figure 12.44
*The New Share dialog box
for Gateway Service for
NetWare.*

7. Choose OK to save your changes.

    You return to the Configure Gateway screen. Figure 12.45 shows an example of the share name NW4KSYS on path \\NW4KS\SYS assigned to drive N: with an unlimited number of users.

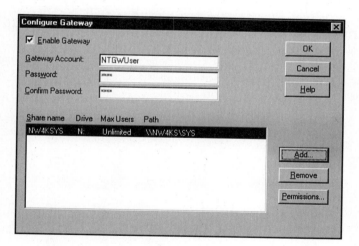

Figure 12.45
*A NetWare share name
assigned to Gateway
Service for NetWare.*

8. Select OK to exit the Configure Gateway dialog box.

9. Select OK to exit the Gateway Service for NetWare dialog box.

    Your changes will take effect next time you log on.

Setting Permissions on the Gateway Share

After the share name for accessing the NetWare directory is created, you can set access permissions on it, in the same manner as you would on a share name for a resource on a Windows NT computer. In Chapter 9, "Managing Network Files and File Security Systems," you learned that you can set access permissions for a share name using the NT Explorer. You can use the same method for setting permissions for the share name to a NetWare resource, except that you use the Configure Gateway Service.

The following is an outline of the procedure for setting access permissions using the Gateway Service:

1. Log on as administrator to the Windows NT Server.

2. Double-click on the GSNW icon in the control panel.

3. When the Gateway Service for NetWare dialog box appears (refer to figure 12.42), choose the **G**ateway button.

4. In the Configure Gateway dialog box that appears (refer to figure 12.45), highlight the NetWare share name and choose the **P**ermissions button. If this button is grayed-out, ensure that the Gateway Service is enabled and running.

You should see the current permission settings for the share name. By default, the Windows NT group Everyone has Full Control over the share name (see fig. 12.46). This is the default permission that is set for all new shares in Windows NT. You might want to restrict the share permissions in a secure environment. You can set the permissions to No Access, Read, Change and Full Control. The method for changing access permissions is described in detail in Chapter 9, "Managing Network Files and File Security Systems."

Figure 12.46

The Access Through Share Permissions dialog box.

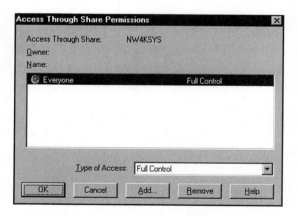

The share-level permissions that you set for a share name apply to all MS clients who access that share. If you need to have separate permissions set for different MS clients, you must create separate share names and set permissions on each share name.

The trustee rights settings on the NetWare directory on NetWare server, override any share level permissions that you set. For example, if the NetWare directory rights are set to allow Read (R) and File Scan (F) rights, and you set the share name to have Change permissions, the

MS client is not able to modify, create or delete files on the NetWare server, even though they are allowed these Change permissions through the Change share permissions. Figure 12.47 graphically illustrates the order in which the permissions are applied.

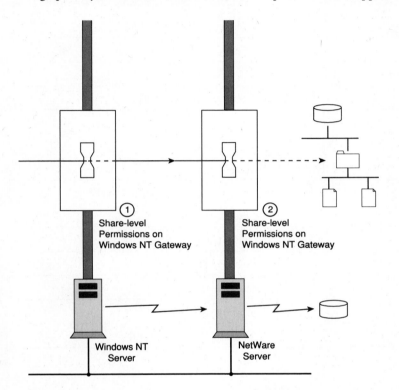

Figure 12.47
Order of permissions for a Gateway Service for NetWare.

Tables 12.1 and 12.2 show the NetWare rights equivalents to the Windows NT file permissions for directories and files. Table 12.3 shows the NetWare file attributes and the corresponding Windows NT file attributes.

Table 12.1
Directory Rights Equivalence

NetWare Directory Rights	Windows NT Directory Permissions
Supervisor (S)	Full Control (All) (All)
Read (R)	Read (RX)(RX)
Write (W)	Change (RWXD)(RWXD)
Create (C)	Add (WX)(not specified)

continues

Table 12.1, Continued
Directory Rights Equivalence

NetWare Directory Rights	Windows NT Directory Permissions
Erase (E)	Change (RWXD)(RWXD)
Modify (M)	Change (RWXD)(RWXD)
File Scan (F)	List (RX)(not specified)
Access Control (A)	Change Permissions (P)

Table 12.2
File Rights Equivalence

NetWare File Rights	Windows NT File Permissions
Supervisor (S)	Full Control (All)
Read (R)	Read (RX)
Write (W)	Change (RWXD)
Erase (E)	Change (RWXD)
Modify (M)	Change (RWXD)
Access Control (A)	Change Permissions (P)

Table 12.3
File Attributes Equivalence

NetWare File Attributes	Windows File Attributes
Delete Inhibit (d)	Read Only (R)
Copy Inhibit (Ci)	None
Rename Inhibit (R)	Read Only (R)
Archive (A)	Archive (A)
System (Sy)	System (S)
Hidden (H)	Hidden (H)
Immediate Compress (Ic) for NetWare 4	Compression (c) for Windows NT 3.51 and higher

NetWare File Attributes	Windows File Attributes
Read Write (Rw)	None
Don't Compress (Dc)	None
Shareable (Sh)	None
Transactional (T)	None
Indexed (I)	None
Migrate (M) for NetWare 4	None
Don't Migrate (Dm) for NetWare 4	None

Connecting to a NetWare Volume or Directory

When you log on to a Windows NT Server that is configured as a Gateway Service for NetWare, the logon process automatically attempts to log you on to a NetWare server using the user name that you use to log on to the Windows NT Server (see fig. 12.48). If your user name and passwords are different on the Windows NT Server and the NetWare server, you are prompted for a user name or password. It is more convenient to users for logon and authentication purposes that the user name and password are the same on the Windows NT Server and the NetWare server. If this is so, you are not prompted for a user name and password to connect to the NetWare server.

A part of the Gateway Service for NetWare is a NetWare client service that is available to any user logging on to the Windows NT Server (see fig. 12.48). The network connections that are established with this client connection cannot be shared by other MS clients. This network connection is for the convenience of the logged on user to the Windows NT Server, who is typically a network administrator. In order to share a connection to the NetWare server, you must configure the Gateway Service for NetWare as described in the previous section. Other MS clients share the network connection to the NetWare server using the share name assigned for this purpose.

Changing Passwords for Logon Accounts

To simplify logging on to the NetWare server when a user logs on to the Windows NT Server, you should keep the same username and passwords on the Windows NT Server and NetWare server. To change the user name and password on a Windows NT Server, use the User Manager for Domains. On NetWare 3.*x* servers, you can use the SETPASS command or the

SYSCON tool. To provide transparent access to several NetWare 3.*x* servers, you need to change the password of the user account on all NetWare servers. Because NetWare 4 user accounts are global to the network, you need to change the user password only once in the global database. You can use either NETADMIN or NWADMN to change your NetWare 4 user password.

Figure 12.48

Client portion of Gateway Service for NetWare.

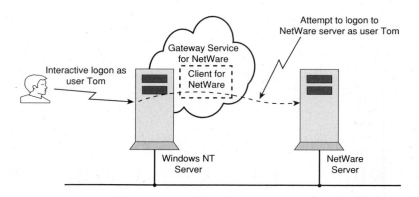

You can run the SETPASS utility from the SYS:PUBLIC directory of a NetWare server or from the NT command prompt. For example, if drive N: is mapped to the SYS: volume on a NetWare server, NWS, you can use the following from an NT command prompt:

```
N:> cd public
N:\public> setpass NWS
```

The previous example illustrates that some NetWare tools can run from an NT command prompt.

Configuring the Preferred Server for the Logged on User

To configure the preferred connection for the logged on user, you must log on as the user, and use the following procedure:

1. Double-click on the GSNW icon in the control panel.

   The Gateway Service for NetWare dialog box appears (see fig. 12.49).

2. From the **S**elect Preferred Server, select the NetWare server that is the preferred server. If <None> is specified, the client connects to the first server who responds to a Get Nearest Server request from the client.

If the preferred server option is set, the next time you log on, the Gateway Service for NetWare connects to the NetWare server you specified as the preferred server.

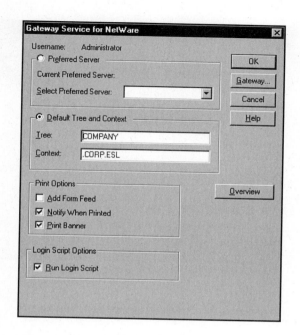

Figure 12.49

The Gateway Service for NetWare dialog box.

Note that the preferred server only affects the account that you log on as when setting the preferred server option. If another user logs on, he or she can have a different server name as the preferred server.

Connecting to a NetWare Directory Using the File Manager

If the Gateway Service for NetWare is installed and configured, you can use any Microsoft network client to access the NetWare directory that is shared on the Windows acting as the gateway.

The following is an outline of the procedure to connect to a NetWare share:

1. Create a share name for the NetWare directory on the Windows NT Server using the procedure outlined in previous sections.

2. Start the NT Explorer.

3. Choose **T**ools, **M**ap Network Drive (see fig. 12.50).

4. You should see the Map Network Drive dialog box. Double-click on the Windows NT Server running the Gateway Service for NetWare. You should see the share names on the Windows NT Server. One of these share names is the NetWare server share name.

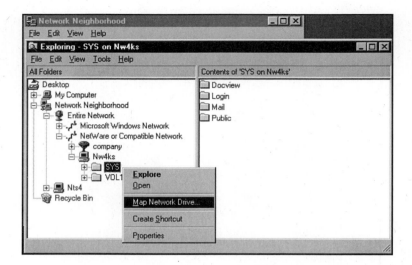

Figure 12.50

*Choose the Map Network
Drive option to open a
dialog box that contains
the NetWare server share
name.*

5. Select the gateway share name, or type the network path in the **P**ath box.

6. Select the drive letter to assign for accessing the gateway share name in the **D**rive field.

7. Network drive connections can be made persistent which means that an attempt is made to create the connection every time you log on. If you are using the File Manager and want to make the network connections persistent, ensure that the option Restore At Logon is set.

8. Choose OK to connect the network drive.

Connecting to a NetWare Directory from the Command Prompt

Occasionally, you might find it more convenient to connect to the NetWare directory from the command prompt. The NET VIEW command can be used to view the NetWare servers on the network from a Windows NT Server configured with Gateway Service for NetWare, or a Windows NT Workstation that has the Client Service for NetWare installed. To display a list of NetWare servers, use the following command:

```
> NET VIEW /NETWORK:NW
Resources on NetWare Network
- - - - - - - - - - - - - - - - - - - - - - - - - - - - - - - - - - - - - - - - - - -
\\NW4KS
\\POSEID
\\S386
\\SCSRV
The command completed successfully.
```

The previous command shows the NetWare servers NW4KS, POSEID, S386, and SCSRV are on the network. For this command to work, you must install a NetWare client for NetWare (for Windows NT Servers) on the NT computer that is used to execute the previous command.

To see a list of shared resources on a specific NetWare server on the network, use the NetWare server name with the /NETWORK:NW option:

```
> NET VIEW  /NETWORK:NW \\NW4KS
Shared resources at \\nw4ks
-------------------------------------------------------------------
Print          \\NW4KS\Q_MAC
Print          \\NW4KS\QLINK1
Disk           \\NW4KS\SYS
Disk           \\NW4KS\VOL1
The command completed successfully.
```

The previous command shows the NetWare server NW4KS is sharing two network printer queues (\\NW4KS\Q_MAC and \\NW4KS\QLINK1) and two disk resources (\\NW4KS\SYS and \\NW4KS\VOL1). The disk resources are the NetWare volume names on the server. In order for this command to work, you must install a NetWare client for NetWare (for Windows NT Servers) on the NT computer that is used to execute the previous command.

To connect a drive to a gateway share name, use the following syntax:

```
NET USE X: \\gatewayserver\netware_share
```

Replace drive *X:* with an unused drive letter. The *gatewayserver* is the computer name of the Windows NT Server on which the Gateway Service for NetWare is configured. The *netware_share* is the share name on the gateway server assigned to the NetWare directory. To create a network drive F: on a Microsoft client that is assigned to the NetWare share name NWSYS on the Windows NT Server NTSA, use the following command:

```
NET USE F: \\NTSA\NWSYS
```

To assign the next available drive to the NetWare share name, replace the drive letter with the asterisk symbol (*). For example, you could use the following:

```
NET USE * \\NTSA\NWSYS
```

If you receive a message that the password is invalid, it means that the user name and password you specified when logging on to the Windows NT client could not be validated on the preferred NetWare server. You could connect under another valid user name and password by using the following syntax for the NET USE command:

```
NET USE X: \\gatewayserver\netware_share /user:username password
```

Replace the *username* and *password* with a valid user and password combination on the NetWare server. Specifying the password on the command line itself is a security risk. You can replace the password with an asterisk (*) if you want to be prompted for the password. The password you type at the prompt is not displayed on the screen.

You can use the NET USE command to examine the status of all network drive connections.

Network drive connections can be made persistent which means that an attempt is made to create the connection every time you log on. To make the network connection persistent, using the NET USE command, ensure that you use the /persistent:yes option. For example, the following connection to the share name NWSYS on the Windows NT Server NTSA is persistent:

```
NET USE F: \\NTSA\NWSYS /persistent:yes
```

Using NetWare Print Resources

You can use the Gateway Service for NetWare to access two types of resources on NetWare servers: file resources and network printer resources. When you enable the gateway, you enable both file and print gateway functions. No separate step for enabling print gateway functions exists. After the Gateway Service for NetWare is enabled, the NetWare print queues appear on the Windows NT Server as shared printers. Your next step for configuring the gateway is to configure the NetWare print gateway using the Print Manager. Using the Print Manager, you define a share name for the print device on the NetWare network. The print share name can then be used by Microsoft clients to connect to the NetWare printers.

Configuring the NetWare Print Gateway

The following is an outline of the procedure for configuring the NetWare print gateway:

1. Log on to the Windows NT Server as an Administrator user.

2. Double-click on the Printer icon in the Control Panel. Select the Add Printer icon. You should see the Add Printer Wizard main window (see fig. 12.51).

Figure 12.51

The Add Printer Wizard window.

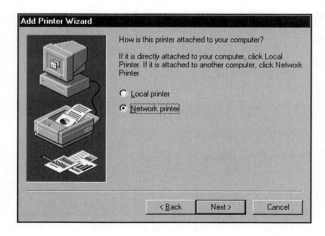

3. Select **N**etwork Printer and then the Next button. You should see the Connect to Printer dialog box (see fig. 12.52).

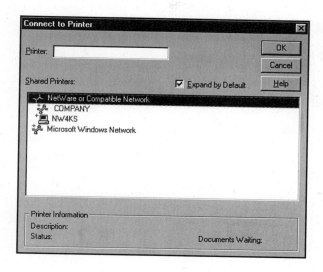

Figure 12.52

The Connect to Printer dialog box.

Click on the NetWare Server icon to expand the network and select the NetWare print queues. Figure 12.53 shows that the NetWare print queue QLINK1 on NetWare server NW4KS has been selected.

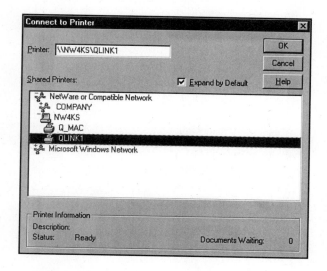

Figure 12.53

Selecting a NetWare print queue.

4. Select OK on the screen in figure 12.53.

5. An information box will ask if you want to install the print drivers on your local machine. Choose OK.

The Add Printer Wizard dialog box appears (see fig. 12.54). Select the appropriate print driver and choose OK. Enter the path where the driver can be found and choose the Continue button. If you are prompted for Printer Setup information such as amount of RAM on printer, enter the information for the printer you have selected.

Figure 12.54

The Add Printer Wizard dialog box for a NetWare printer.

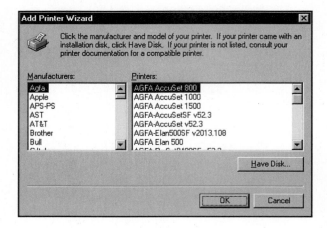

6. The Printer Properties dialog box appears (see fig. 12.55).

Figure 12.55

The Printer Properties dialog box.

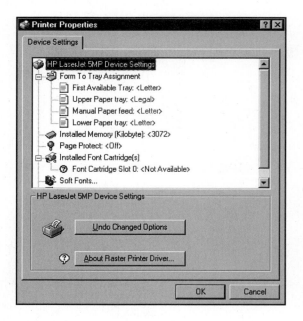

7. The Add Printer Wizard screen will return. Click on the OK button.

The Printers window will now display an icon for the newly created printer. Click on this icon to display the configuration window for the printer (see fig. 12.56).

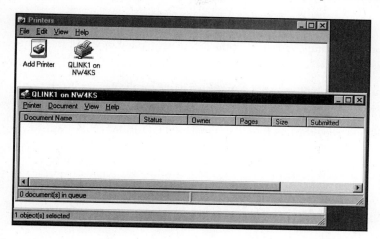

Figure 12.56
The configuration window for the newly created printer.

8. Choose **P**rinter, **S**haring to make this printer a shared device. The Print Manager creates a DOS-compatible share name in the Sh**a**re Name field. You can accept this default value or enter a different share name. If you have DOS clients that need to access the share name, restrict the share name to eight characters or less.

9. By choosing Properties from the Printer menu, you can configure General information, Ports, Scheduling, Sharing, Security, and Device Settings.

10. After configuring the Printer Properties, choose OK.

Because you have created a share name for the printer, MS clients on the network can use it.

Connecting to a NetWare Printer Using Print Manager

Once you have created a share name for the NetWare printer, a Microsoft client can connect to it using the Print Manager.

The following is an outline of the procedure for connecting to the NetWare print queue on the Windows NT Server running Gateway Service for NetWare. The procedure is similar to the first part of configuring the print gateway described in the previous section, so only the barest outline without any screen captures is presented.

1. Log on to the Windows NT client as a user. This need not be the administrator account.

2. Double-click on the Printers icon in the Control Panel.

3. Select the Add Printer icon and choose Network Printer from the Add Printer Wizard.

4. Browse the NetWare network in the Shared Printers box to select the share name corresponding to the NetWare print queue.

5. Select Next.

6. The Printer Wizard will prompt you to select the manufacturer and model of the printer. Select them and click on Next.

7. The Printer Wizard will prompt you with a suggested name for the printer. Accept or change it and click on Finish.

8. Windows NT will now copy the files from the installation CD-ROM or the path you specify.

9. You should now see the new printer icon in the Printers window.

Connecting to a NetWare Printer Using Command-Line Tools

You can connect to a NetWare printer using the NET USE command. The following is the syntax for connection to the shared printer.

```
NET USE lptx \\gatewayserver\printshare
```

For example, to connect local printer LPT1 to the share name QLINK1 on the Windows NT Server NTSA, use the following command:

```
NET USE LPT1 \\NTSA\QLINK1
```

The effect of this command is to redirect print jobs sent to the port LPT1 to the print queue QLINK1 on the NTSA server. Because QLINK1 is a share name for a NetWare print queue, this print job is further redirected to the NetWare print device (see fig. 12.57).

Configuring Print Options

The print options are set for the user logging on to the Windows NT Server acting as a Gateway Service for NetWare and also for the Microsoft clients using the Gateway Service using the same interface. Setting these print options affects all gateway users and all NetWare print queues being used on the Windows NT gateway server.

1. Log on as an administrator user.

2. Double-click on the GSNW icon. The Gateway Service for NetWare dialog box appears (see fig. 12.58).

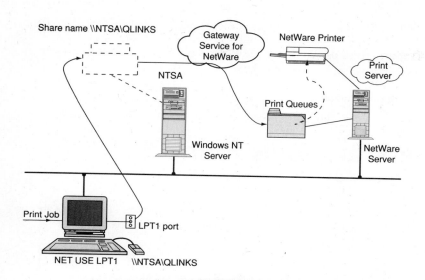

Share name \\NTSA\QLINKS

Figure 12.58
The Gateway Service for NetWare dialog box.

3. In the Print Options section, you can specify any of the following options:

   ■ **Add Form Feed.** The form feed character is added to the end of the job causing the printer to eject a page. Not set by default.

- ■ <u>N</u>otify When Printed. Notify the user at the completion of a job. Set by default.

- ■ <u>P</u>rint Banner. Print a banner that acts as a page separator on the NetWare print device preceding a print job. Set by default.

4. Modify the print options and select OK.

Running NetWare Tools from Windows NT

Many of the NetWare 3.*x* tools can be run from the NT Command prompt. These tools are designed to run on DOS workstations. When they run at the Windows NT command prompt, they run under NT's DOS subsystem.

NetWare Tools Supported by Windows NT

Table 12.4 lists the NetWare 3.*x* utilities that are supported by Windows NT. Some of these utilities require the SYS$MSG.DAT file or the $RUN.OVL file (for NetWare 3.11). These files are found in the SYS:PUBLIC directory on the NetWare 3.*x* server. If you run the NetWare 3.*x* utilities outside the SYS:PUBLIC directory, you may see error messages that indicate these files are missing.

Figure 12.59 shows the SYSCON utility being run from an NT command prompt. To run SYSCON and other utilities that require access to the NetWare bindery, you must be logged on to the NetWare server. In order to log on to the NetWare server from a Windows NT computer, you must be running Client Service for NetWare on a Windows NT Workstation or the Gateway Service for NetWare on Windows NT Server.

Table 12.4
NetWare 3.*x* Utilities Supported by Windows NT

Supported NetWare Utility	Description
chkvol	Checks NetWare volume and reports information on volume
colorpal	Changes the color palette of the graphical tools
dspace	Sets disk space quota
flag	Changes file attributes
flagdir	Changes directory attributes
fconsole	File server console

Supported NetWare Utility	Description
filer	File Manager tool
grant	Assigns rights
listdir	Lists directories
map	Performs drive mapping
ncopy	Network copy of files
ndir	Network directory listing
pconsole	Printer console utility
psc	Print Server Control
pstat	Printer status
rconsole	Remote console
remove	Removes users/groups as trustees of directories and files
revoke	Revokes rights for directories and files from users/groups
rights	Assigns rights
security	Checks security of server
send	Send messages
session	Session manager tool
setpass	Set password for logged on user on server
settts	Sets the logical and physical transaction tracking record lock thresholds
slist	Displays list of servers on network
syscon	General purpose System Console tool used for administrator functions
tlist	Displays list of trustees for a directory/file
userlist	Displays list of active users and their connection information
volinfo	Utility that dynamically displays information on volume usage and number of directory entries per volume
whoami	Displays information on currently logged on user

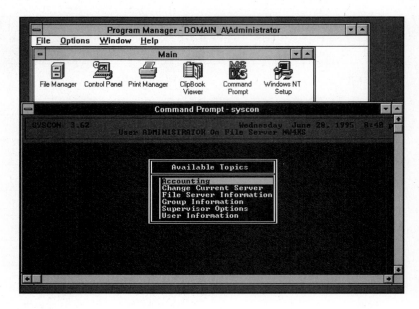

Figure 12.59
The SYSCON utility run from an NT command prompt.

The Windows NT NET USE command can be used for performing the functions of the NetWare MAP and CAPTURE commands. The NET VIEW command can be used to perform the functions of the SLIST command.

Special Considerations for Running NetWare-Aware Applications

NetWare applications designed to run for Windows 3.1 make use of special DLLs and drivers. If you install these applications on a Windows NT computer, these applications look for the special files. Windows NT, by default, does not come with these special DLL and drivers. In order to run these applications, you must therefore install these files on the Windows NT computer. In many cases, you can use the Windows 3.1 files, and in some cases you must obtain a version of these files from Novell.

The files needed by Windows 3.1 applications are:

- **NWIPXSPX.DLL.** This file must be found on the PATH statement on the Windows NT computer. Copy this file to the *SystemRoot*\System32 directory which is normally on the search path. For RISC platforms, you must obtain this file from Novell. For RISC platforms, you should also have a copy of the TBMI2.COM file in the *SystemRoot*\System32 directory. In the AUTOEXEC.NT file on the RISC computer, you must insert the following line immediately after the line that refers to VWIPXSPX:

```
lh winnt\system32\tbmi2.com
```

- **NETWARE.DRV, NWNETAPI.DLL, NWCALLS.DLL.** NetWare applications may require the NETWARE.DRV and the NWNETAPI.DLL or the more recent NWCALLS.DLL to support the network APIs. When you install the Gateway Service for NetWare, the NETWARE.DRV file is installed in *SystemRoot*\System32. If your application needs the NWNETAPI.DLL or NWCALLS.DLL, these files must be on the search path. Copy these files in the *SystemRoot*\System32 directory, which usually is on the search path.

- **BREQUEST.EXE.** This is the Btrieve requester used by MS-DOS or Windows 3.1 applications. Load the BREQUEST.EXE in the AUTOEXEC.NT file specifying the path to this file:

```
LH D:\BTRIEVE\BREQUEST.EXE
```

Gupta SQL Base for NetWare systems and Lotus Notes are examples of applications that depend on the NWIPXSPX.DLL, NETWARE.DRV, and NWNETAPI.DLL files.

Configuring IPX-Related Services and Tools

Besides the Client Service for NetWare and the Gateway Service for NetWare, other MS-DOS applications ported to the Windows NT environment can make use of the IPX/SPX protocol implemented by NWLink. The IPX protocol is datagram-based. It can be used for general purpose delivery, and network applications that need broadcast capability. The IPX protocol does not provide a guarantee for delivery of messages. If you need guaranteed delivery, the applications must use SPX which builds a virtual circuit on top of the IPX protocol.

Some applications make use of the NetBIOS API. Microsoft's NWLink supports a NetBIOS component that interfaces with the NWLink transport protocols. The NWLink NetBIOS includes Microsoft's extensions to the Novell's NetBIOS implementation for DOS/Windows platforms.

Configuring the NWLink IPX/SPX Compatible Transport Protocol

The default settings for NWLink should be optimal for most network environments, and you should not have to change the NWLink parameter settings. If you need to change the NWLink parameters, such as bind the NWLink protocol to a different network adapter, you can use the following as an outline for configuring NWLink:

1. Log on as an administrator user to the Windows NT computer.

2. Double-click on the Network icon in the Control Panel.

3. From the Network dialog box, select the Protocols tab (see fig. 12.60). Highlight the NWLink IPX/SPX Compatible Transport and click on the <u>P</u>roperties button.

Figure 12.60

The selection of IPX/SPX protocols for configuration.

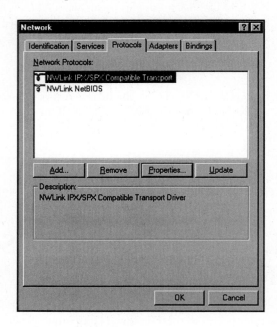

4. Choose the Configure button. The NWLink IPX/SPX Protocol Configuration dialog box appears (see fig. 12.61).

   In the Ada<u>p</u>ter field, select the name of the network adapter to which you want to bind the NWLink transport protocol.

   You can specify the frame format of the data-link layer packets by selecting the A<u>u</u>to Frame Type Detection or <u>M</u>anual Frame Type Detection options. By default, NWLink automatically detects the frame type of the packets.

   Choose OK when finished making changes.

5. Choose Close in the Network Protocols dialog box.

6. At the Network Settings Change information box, select <u>Y</u>es to restart the computer for the changes to take effect.

Configuring IPX/SPX Routing on a Token Ring Network

Each computer on a Token Ring Network uses a source routing table that is maintained on the computer. The source routing table is used for finding the optimal path on Token Ring networks connected using interconnection devices such as bridges and routers.

When an NT computer on a Token Ring network receives a broadcast packet, multicast packet, or a packet whose MAC address is not in its source routing table, by default, the computer forwards the packet as a Single Route Broadcast (SRB) frame. If you need to modify this default behavior, or clear the source routing table, you can do so using the IPXROUTE utility.

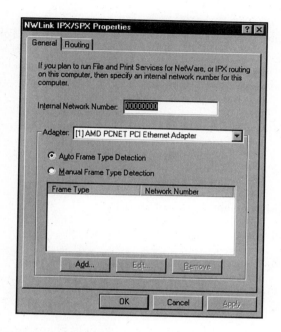

Figure 12.61
The NWLink IPX/SPX Properties dialog box.

Microsoft's IPXROUTE utility is based on Novell's ROUTE utility that is available for DOS and OS/2 clients. In fact, even some of the options in IPXROUTE are the same as those for ROUTE.EXE. IPXROUTE has been extended so that it can now manipulate the network layer IPX routing table.

To see the current settings for IPX/SPX packets, just type the command IPXROUTE without any options:

```
> IPXROUTE
NWLink Routing and Source Routing Control Program v2.00
DEFault Node    (Unknown) Addresses are sent using SINGLE ROUTE BROADCAST
Broadcast (FFFF FFFF FFFF) Addresses are sent using SINGLE ROUTE BROADCAST
Multicast (C000 xxxx xxxx) Addresses are sent using SINGLE ROUTE BROADCAST
```

The previous command shows that unknown addresses and broadcast and multicast addresses are sent in the SRB mode. To see the information on IPX bindings, specify the CONFIG option:

```
> IPXROUTE CONFIG
NWLink Routing and Source Routing Control Program v2.00
net 1: network number 000e8022, frame type 802.2, device CENDIS31 (0080c7d66f0f)
```

This command shows that the IPX network number of the network is E8022, the frame type is 802.2 and the driver name is CRNDIS31. The node address of the Windows NT computer is 0080C7D66F0F.

Though the IPXROUTE command is designed for Windows NT computers on a Token Ring network, the commands listed previously also work on other networks such as Ethernet and FDDI networks. You therefore are able to use the IPXROUTE CONFIG command to discover the network number, frame type, driver name and MAC address of a Windows NT computer on a network.

The general syntax of the IPXROUTE command is shown next:

IPXROUTE

IPXROUTE CONFIG

IPXROUTE board=n [clear] [def] [gbr] [mbr] remove=xxxxx

board=n specifies the board number whose parameters are to be changed.

clear clears the source routing table.

def forwards packets as All Routes Broadcast (ARB) frames if the MAC address cannot be found in the source routing table. Default is SRB.

gbr forwards general broadcast packets (destination address of FFFFFFFFFFFF) as All Routes Broadcast (ARB) frames.

mbr forwards multicast broadcast packets (destination address of C000xxxxxxxx) as All Routes Broadcast (ARB) frames.

remove=xxxxx removes specified address from the source routing table.

The IPXROUTE changes the parameters only for the current Windows NT session. When you log off or reboot, the current settings are lost. You can place the IPXROUTE command in the logon script or set the parameters in the Registry to make the changes permanent.

Managing NWLink Parameter Using the Registry

Whenever possible, you should change NWLink parameters using the Control Panel. If you need more direct control over the NWLink parameters, however, or you need to change parameters that cannot be changed using normal administrator tools, you can change the parameter settings in the Registry.

You should exercise extreme caution when changing Registry values. Incorrect values can permanently disable your Windows NT computer or make the Windows NT computer operation inefficient.

Not all parameters listed in this section may exist in the Registry. If a parameter value does not exist, the default value listed in this section applies. If you need to change the default value, you must create a value entry under the specified Registry key. The procedure for creating value entries and modifying the Registry by using the Registry Editor is discussed in detail in Chapter 10, "Managing Windows NT Registry."

The Registry Editor is started by running the REGEDT32.EXE program. If you have created an icon for this program, you can double-click on the icon. You can start the Registry Editor from the command prompt using either of the following:

REGEDT32

START REGEDT32

The last command returns control to the command prompt after starting the Registry Editor.

To change the NWLink parameters, activate the HKEY_LOCAL_MACHINE window. Figures 12.62 and 12.63 show the IPX and SPX parameters under their respective keys. The IPX parameters can be controlled using the value entries under the key HKEY_LOCAL_MACHINE\SYSTEM\CurrentControlSet\Services\NWLnkIPX\Parameters. The SPX parameters can be controlled using the value entries under the key HKEY_LOCAL_MACHINE\SYSTEM\CurrentControlSet\Services\NWLnkSPX\Parameters. Tables 12.5 and 12.6 describe the IPX and SPX Registry value entries.

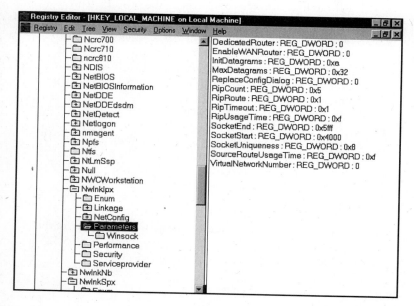

Figure 12.62

NWLink IPX parameters in the Registry.

Figure 12.63

NWLink SPX parameters in the Registry.

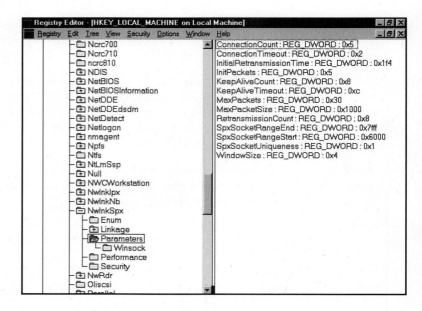

Table 12.5
IPX Registry Value Entries

Parameter	Description
RipAgeTime	The IPX protocol uses the Routing Information Protocol (RIP) to find routes to computers on the network. This parameter informs RIP how long to wait before requesting an update for a route entry in the RIP routing table. The RIP timer for a route entry is reset when a new updated is received. The type of this parameter is REG_DWORD. It can range from 1 to 65,535 minutes and has a default value of 5 minutes.
RipCount	If RIP is unable to find a route on the network, it retries to find the route. This parameter controls how many times RIP retries to find the route before giving up. The type of this parameter is REG_DWORD. It can range from 1 to 65,535 and has a default value of 5.
RipTimeout	This controls the time-out period for not receiving a reply for a RIP request to find a route on the network. The type of this parameter is REG_DWORD. It can range from 1 to 65,535 half-seconds and has a default value of 1 half-second.

Parameter	Description
RipUsageTime	IPX builds a cache of the RIP routing table. If an update for a route entry is not received for a period of time, that entry is deleted from the cache. This parameter controls the maximum age of a route entry before deleting the route entry. An update to a route entry resets the timer. The type of this parameter is REG_DWORD. It can range from 1 to 65,535 minutes and has a default value of 15 minutes.
SourceRouteUsageTime	This parameter controls the maximum age of an unused entry in the source routing cache of a Windows NT computer on a Token Ring network. The entry is deleted after this inter-val. The type of this parameter is REG_DWORD. It can range from 1 to 65,535 minutes and has a default value of 15 minutes.
InitDatagrams	This parameter controls the number of datagram buffers initially allocated for IPX. The type of this parameter is REG_DWORD. It can range from 1 to 65,535 and has a default value of 10.
MaxDatagrams	This parameter controls the number of maximum datagram buffers allocated for IPX. The type of this parameter is REG_DWORD. It can range from 1 to 65,535 and has a default value of 50.
SocketStart	This parameter specifies the start of the range of socket numbers that are dynamically allocated. The type of this parameter is REG_DWORD. It can range from 0 to 65,535 and has a default value of 0x4000.
SocketEnd	This parameter specifies the end of the range of socket numbers that are dynamically allocated. The type of this parameter is REG_DWORD. It can range from 1 to 65,535 and has a default value of 0x8000.
SocketUniqueness	This parameter specifies the number of sockets starting with SocketStart that are set aside when assigning socket numbers. If the SocketUniqueness is set to 8 and the Socket Start is 0x4000, then sockets 0x4000 to 0x4007 are set aside. The type of this parameter is REG_DWORD. It can range from 1 to 65,535 and has a default value of 8.

continues

Table 12.5, Continued
IPX Registry Value Entries

Parameter	Description
VirtualNetworkNumber	This is the IPX internal network number for the Windows NT computer. The type of this parameter is REG_DWORD. It can range from 0 to 4,394,967,295 and has a default value of 0.
RipTableSize	This controls the number of buckets used in the RIP hash table. The hash table is used for quickly finding RIP entries. Increase this value only if you expect the RIP table to be very large. The type of this parameter is REG_DWORD. It can range from 1 to 65,535 and has a default value of 7.
DedicatedRoute	When set to 1, the computer is used as a dedicated router and does not have services running on it. The type of the parameter is REG_DWORD, and is treated as a Boolean with value of 0 or 1. Default value is 0.
EthernetPadToEven	When set to 1, Ethernet frames that are sent should be padded to even length to accommodate other computers that can receive only even-length frames. The type of the parameter is REG_DWORD, and is treated as a Boolean with a value of 0 or 1. Default value is 1.
SingleNetworkActive	When set to 1, only the LAN or WAN link can be active on the computer. This is used in the Gateway Service for NetWare to correctly locate the NetWare servers on the WAN when dialing in. The type of the parameter is REG_DWORD, and is treated as a Boolean with a value of 0 or 1. Default value is 0.
DisableDialoutSAP	When set to 1, SAP announcements and responses are not sent on dial-out WAN links. This prevents SAP traffic from saturating the WAN link. The type of the parameter is REG_DWORD, and is treated as a Boolean with a value of 0 or 1. Default value is 0.
DisableDialinNetbios	When set to 1, NetBIOS packets of type 20 are not sent on dial-in lines. This prevents unneeded NetBIOS traffic from saturating a dial-in WAN link. Set this to 0 only if a NetBIOS application on the local computer needs to connect to a remote computer over a dial-in WAN link. The type of the parameter is REG_DWORD, and is treated as a Boolean with a value of 0 or 1. Default value is 1.

Table 12.6
SPX Registry Value Entries

Parameter	Description
ConnectionCount	This controls the number of times connection attempts (connection probes) are made to connect to a remote node if no response is received in the time specified by the ConnectionTime parameter. The type of this parameter is REG_DWORD. It can range from 1 to 65,535 and has a default value of 10.
ConnectionTimeout	This controls the time between connection requests to connect to a remote node. The type of this parameter is REG_DWORD. It can range from 1 to 65,535 half-seconds and has a default value of 2 half-seconds (1 second).
KeepAliveCount	When there is no activity on an SPX virtual circuit, a keep-alive packet is sent to verify if the connection is still valid. The keep-alive packet verifies whether the remote node is reachable and active. This parameter controls the number of times the keep-alive packet should be sent if there is no response. The type of this parameter is REG_DWORD. It can range from 1 to 65,535 and has a default value of 8.
KeepAliveTimeout	When there is no activity on an SPX virtual circuit, a keep-alive packet is sent to verify if the connection is still valid. The keep-alive packet verifies if the remote node is reachable and active. This parameter controls the time that the node should wait before sending a probe to the remote node to verify that the SPX virtual circuit is still valid. The type of this parameter is REG_DWORD. It can range from 1 to 65,535 half-seconds and has a default value of 12 half-seconds (6 seconds).
WindowSize	SPX uses an Allocation Field (see Chapter 2), to tell the remote node how many receive packet buffers it has. The value in the Allocation field is called the window size because it controls how many packets the remote can send before the buffers overflow. This parameter specifies the initial value to place in the Allocation Field. The type of this parameter is REG_DWORD. It can range from 1 to 10 SPX packets and has a default value of 4.

continues

Table 12.6, Continued
SPX Registry Value Entries

Parameter	Description
InitPackets	This parameter specifies the initial number of packet buffers SPX allocates. The type of this parameter is REG_DWORD. It can range from 1 to 65,535 and has a default value of 5.
MaxPackets	This parameter specifies the maximum number of packet buffers SPX allocates. The type of this parameter is REG_DWORD. It can range from 1 to 65,535 and has a default value of 30.
InitialRetransmissionTime	SPX dynamically adjusts the retransmission time interval used to resend a packet that has not been acknowledged. This parameter specifies the initial retransmission interval value. The type of this parameter is REG_DWORD. It can range from 1 to 65,535 milliseconds and has a default value of 500 milliseconds.
SpxSocketStart	This parameter specifies the start of the range of SPX socket numbers that are dynamically allocated. The type of this parameter is REG_DWORD. It can range from 0 to 65,535 and has a default value of 0x4000.
SpxSocketEnd	This parameter specifies the end of the range of SPX socket numbers that are dynamically allocated. The type of this parameter is REG_DWORD. It can range from 1 to 65,535 and has a default value of 0x7FFF.
SpxSocketUniqueness	This parameter specifies the number of SPX sockets starting with SocketStart that are set aside when assigning socket numbers. If the SpxSocketUniqueness is set to 8, and the SpxSocketStart is 0x4000, then sockets 0x4000 to 0x4007 are set aside. The type of this parameter is REG_DWORD. It can range from 1 to 65,535 and has a default value of 8.
MaxPacketSize	This parameter is used to support SPX II that uses this parameter value to negotiate the maximum packet size the remote node can support. The type of this parameter is REG_DWORD. It can range from 1 to 65,535 bytes and has a default value of 4,096 bytes.
RetransmissionCount	This parameter controls the number of times a packet can be retransmitted while waiting for an acknowledgment for the packet. The type of this parameter is REG_DWORD. It can range from 1 to 65,535 and has a default value of 8.

The NetBIOS parameter settings can be controlled through the Registry. These parameters can be found under the HKEY_LOCAL_MACHINE\SYSTEM\CurrentControlSet\Services\ NWLnkNB\Parameters (see fig. 12.64). Table 12.7 describes these parameters. Some of these parameters are Microsoft extensions to the NetBIOS parameters found on traditional NetBIOS implementations such as the NetBIOS stack in NetWare. Microsoft claims that applications using the NetBIOS extensions have significant performance gains over the standard NetBIOS implementation. Very few applications in the NetWare environment now use NetBIOS. Using IPX/SPX directly is preferable because it gives better performance and avoids the limitations of NetBIOS, such as excessive broadcast traffic. NWLink is able to detect automatically if the remote node supports Microsoft extensions; if it does not, NWLink uses the standard NetBIOS only.

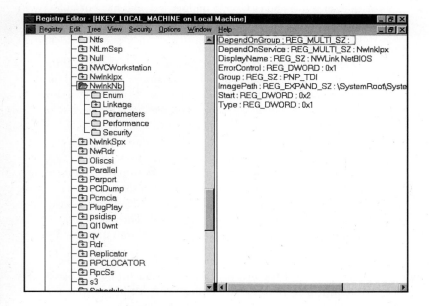

Figure 12.64

NetBIOS parameters for IPX.

The following parameters in table 12.7 relate to Microsoft extensions:

Extensions

AckDelayTime

AckWindow

AckWindowThreshold

EnablePiggyBackAck

RcvWindowMax

Table 12.7
NWLink NetBIOS Registry Parameters

Parameter	Description
Extensions	When set to 1, it specifies whether the NWLink NetBIOS extensions are to be used. The type of this parameter is REG_DWORD. It is treated as a Boolean type with a value of 1 or 0 (default is 1).
AckDelayTime	This parameter controls the value of the delayed acknowledgment timer. The type of this parameter is REG_DWORD. It can range from 50 to 65,535 milliseconds and has a default value of 250 milliseconds.
AckWindow	This parameter controls the number of frames to receive before sending an acknowledgment. A value of 0 turns off the sending of acknowledgments. This parameter can be used for flow control. If the sender and receiver are separated by a slow link (WAN or satellite link) or a link that has considerable time delay, you can set this parameter to a larger value. If little delay occurs on the link, and both sender and receiver are matched in terms of speed of sending and receiving packets, you can set this parameter to 0 to turn off sending of acknowledgments to sender. The setting of the parameter AckWindowThreshold can also be used to determine whether the AckWindows parameter value is used. The type of this parameter is REG_DWORD. It can range from 0 to 65,535 frames and has a default value of 2.
AckWindowThreshold	This parameter specifies the threshold value for the estimated round-trip delay that defines when the AckWindow parameter value is ignored. If the round trip delay is less than the value in the AckWindowThreshold, the acknowledgments are not sent; that is, the value in AckWindow is ignored. If the round-trip delay is greater than the threshold value, the value in AckWindow is used. If the value of the AckWindow Threshold is set to 0, the value in AckWindow is used; that is, the threshold setting in AckWindowThreshold is ignored. The type of this parameter is REG_DWORD. It can range from 0 to 65,535 milliseconds and has a default value of 500 milliseconds.

Parameter	Description
EnablePiggyBackAck	When set to 1, acknowledgments can be sent if the data response is returned by the receiver to the sender. This parameter is called piggy-back acknowledgments, because the acknowledgment gets a piggy-back ride on the data frame. This is more efficient than sending a separate acknowledgment frame. Piggy-back acknowledgments typically are sent when the receiver has detected the end of a NetBIOS message. If the traffic is one-way (simplex) with no expected response from the receiver, set this parameter to 0. If the EnablePiggyBackAck is set to 1 (piggy-back acknowledgments enabled), but no reverse traffic from receiver to sender exists, the setting in AckDelayTimer parameter is used to determine when to send a separate acknowledgment packet. The piggy-back acknowledgment is temporarily disabled until the receiver begins to send data, at which time piggy-back acknowledgment support is enabled. The type of this parameter is REG_DWORD. It is treated as a Boolean type with a value of 1 or 0. The default value is 1.
RcvWindowMax	This specifies the number of frames the receiver can receive at one time. This parameter is exchanged during session negotiation so that the sender knows the upper boundary on the number of frames to be sent at any one time. This parameter is affected by the settings of the AckWindow and the AckWindowThreshold parameters. The type of this parameter is REG_DWORD. It can range from 1 to 49,152 frames and has a default value of 4 frames.
Internet	When set to 1, this parameter specifies when to change the packet type from 0x04 to 0x14 (Novell WAN Broadcast). The type of this parameter is REG_DWORD. It is used as a Boolean type with a value of 1 or 0. The default value is 1.
BroadcastCount	This parameter specifies the number of times to send a broadcast. If the Internet parameter is set to 1, the value is doubled. The type of this parameter is REG_DWORD. It can range from 1 to 65,535 and has a default value of 3.
BroadcastTimeout	This parameter controls the time between Find-Name requests. The type of this parameter is REG_DWORD. It can range from 1 to 65,535 half-seconds and has a default value of 1 half-second.

continues

Table 12.7, Continued
NWLink NetBIOS Registry Parameters

Parameter	Description
ConnectionCount	This parameter specifies the number of times a connection request is to be attempted before declaring that the connection could not be established. If the Internet parameter is set to 1, this parameter value is doubled. The type of this parameter is REG_DWORD. It can range from 1 to 65,535 and has a default value of 5.
ConnectionTimeout	This parameter specifies the time between connection attempts when initiating a connection. The type of this parameter is REG_DWORD. It can range from 1 to 65,535 half-seconds and has a default value of 2 half-seconds (1 second).
InitialRetransmissionTime	Like SPX, NetBIOS dynamically adjusts the retransmission time interval used to resend a packet that has not been acknowledged. This parameter specifies the initial retransmission interval value. The type of this parameter is REG_DWORD. It can range from 1 to 65,535 milliseconds and has a default value of 500 milliseconds.
KeepAliveCount	When there is no activity on a NetBIOS connection, a keep-alive packet is sent to verify if the connection is still valid. The keep-alive packet verifies whether the remote node is reachable and active. This parameter controls the number of times the keep-alive packet should be sent if no response occurs. The type of this parameter is REG_DWORD. It can range from 1 to 65,535 and has a default value of 8.
KeepAliveTimeout	When no activity occurs on a NetBIOS connection, a keep-alive packet is sent to verify whether the connection is still valid. The keep-alive packet verifies whether the remote node is reachable and active. This parameter controls the time that the node should wait before sending a probe to the remote node to verify that the NetBIOS connection is still valid. The type of this parameter is REG_DWORD. It can range from 1 to 65,535 half-seconds and has a default value of 60 half-seconds (30 seconds).
RetransmitMax	This controls the maximum number of times a sender should retransmit before assuming that there is a problem with the connection. The type of this parameter is REG_DWORD. It can range from 1 to 65,535 and has a default value of 8.

Under the HKEY_LOCAL_MACHINE\SYSTEM\CurrentControlSet\Services\NWLnkIPX\ NetConfig*adapter_name* key, you find parameters for each binding of the NWLink transport protocol to a network adapter (see fig. 12.65). Table 12.8 describes the adapter-binding parameters that can be used to configure the adapter bindings. The source routing parameters are for Token Ring network adapters.

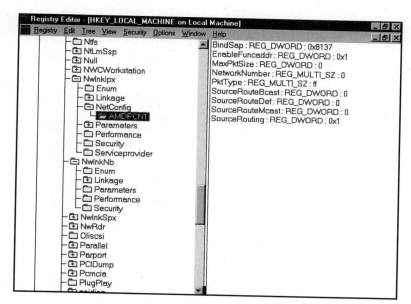

Figure 12.65

Network Adapter parameters.

Table 12.8
NWLink Parameters for Network Adapter

Parameter	Description
BindSap	This parameter specifies the Ethertype value for Ethernet_II frame. The Ethernet type is a 2-byte field that is part of an Ethernet_II frame, and is used to specify the type of data in the Ethernet frame. The Ethernet type field is defined for most well-known protocols and is documented in the RFC (Request for Comment) titled Assigned Numbers available on the Internet. The type of this parameter is REG_ DWORD. It can range from 1,501 to 65,535 and has a default value of 8137 (hex) for IPX packets.

continues

Table 12.8, Continued
NWLink Parameters for Network Adapter

Parameter	Description
EnableFuncaddr	When set to 1, this enables the use of the IPX functional address C00000800000 (hex) for Token Ring adapters. When set to 0, IPX functional address is disabled. It is up to an application to make use of the IPX functional address. The type of the parameter is REG_DWORD and is treated as a Boolean with a value of 0 or 1. The default value is 1.
MaxPktSize	Specifies maximum frame size for the network adapter. If set to 0, NWLink gets this information from the network adapter driver. The type of this parameter is REG_DWORD. It can range from 0 to 65,535 and has a default value of 0, which means that parameter value is read from the network adapter driver.
NetworkNumber	This is the network number of the network segment the adapter is connected to. IPX network numbers are 4 bytes (8 hex digits) long. If this parameter is set to 0, NWLink determines the network number from an IPX router on the network. In a NetWare-based network, all NetWare servers act as IPX routers. If you set a non-zero value, it must be compatible with the network number set for other IPX nodes such as NetWare servers that are on the same physical cable segment. You can set the network number from the Network icon in the Control Panel. The type of this parameter is REG_MULTI_SZ. It can be an 8-digit hexadecimal number and has a default value of 0.
PktType	NWLink can run on a variety of different physical networks such as Ethernet, Token Ring, FDDI, ArcNET, etc. This parameter specifies the frame type to use. The following frame types are used: Ethernet_II(0), Ethernet_802.3(1), 802.2(2), SNAP(3), ArcNET(4), Auto-detect (FF). The numbers in parenthesis in the previously mentioned frame types are the values of the PktType that denote the frame type. Ethernet can have a PktType with values of 0 through 3. Token Ring and FDDI can have values 2 or 3. For ArcNET, you select a value of 4. If you have a Token Ring or FDDI network adapter, a value of 0 or 1 works the same as a value of 2. The type of this parameter is REG_MULTI_SZ. It can have a value of 0 to 4, and has a default value of 1 (802.3 frame).

Parameter	Description
SourceRouteBcast	This parameter specifies the source route to be used for broadcast MAC packets which have a destination address of FFFFFFFFFFFF. When set to 0, the packet is transmitted to the Single Route Broadcast(0xC2, 0x70). When set to a no-zero value, the packet is transmitted to the All Routes Broadcast(0x82, 0x70). The type of the parameter is REG_DWORD and is treated as a Boolean. The default value is 0.
SourceRouteDef	This parameter specifies the source route to be used for a packet with a destination address that is not in the source routing table. If the destination address is in the source routing table, the route in the table is used. When set to 0, the packet is transmitted to the Single Route Broadcast(0xC2, 0x70). When set to non-zero value, the packet is transmitted to the All Routes Broadcast(0x82, 0x70). The type of the parameter is REG_DWORD and is treated as a Boolean. The default value is 0.
SourceRouteMcast	This parameter specifies the source route to be used for a packet with a multicast destination address (C000xxxxxxxx). When set to 0, the packet is transmitted to the Single Route Broadcast(0xC2, 0x70). When set to non-zero value, the packet is transmitted to the All Routes Broadcast(0x82, 0x70). The type of the parameter is REG_DWORD and is treated as a Boolean. The default value is 0.
SourceRouting	This parameter specifies whether source routing is to be used. The parameter is valid only for Token Ring networks. If you do not have source routing bridges, you can disable this parameter and all the source routing logic. A value of 1 enables source routing, and a value of 0 disables source routing. The type of the parameter is REG_DWORD and is treated as a Boolean. The default value is 0.

continues

Table 12.8, Continued
NWLink Parameters for Network Adapter

Parameter	Description
DefaultAutoDetect	This specifies the frame type to be used if NWLink cannot detect any servers or network traffic on startup. If a new packet is subsequently detected, the default initial value for the frame type is overridden by the detected frame type. The following frame types are used: Ethernet_II(0), Ethernet_802.3(1), 802.2(2), SNAP(3), ArcNET(4). The numbers in parenthesis in the previously mentioned frame types are the values of the default frame type. The type of the parameter is REG_DWORD and can have a value from 0 to 4. The default value is 2, which means that the default frame type is 802.2.
EnableWanRouter	When set to 1, the RIP router is enabled for the specified network adapter interface. The type of the parameter is REG_DWORD and is Boolean. The default value is 1.

Migrating Tools for NetWare in Windows NT Server

Windows NT Server comes with a migration tool for NetWare called NWCONV that can be used to copy NetWare account information into equivalent accounts on a Windows NT Server. Because the two systems are quite different, no exact translation of NetWare to Windows NT Server accounts exists. Regardless of the claims made by any documentation, the author's experience shows that some manual configuration is still required. In some cases where there is considerable manual configuration after running the migration tool, it may be better to build the Windows NT Server user accounts from scratch without using the migration tool.

Figure 12.66 shows how the migration procedure works for transferring NetWare account information to a Windows NT Server in a single NT domain. First users and group accounts are transferred to the Windows NT Server acting as the domain controller. If backup domain controllers exist, the transferred user account information is automatically replicated to the backup domain controllers. Next, the directories and files on the NetWare server are transferred to a selected Windows NT Server.

Figure 12.67 shows how the migration procedure can be used for transferring NetWare account information to a Windows NT Server that is part of a master domain model. First user and group accounts are transferred to the master domain. If backup domain controllers exist, the transferred user and account information is automatically replicated to the backup domain controllers in the master domain. Next, the directories and files on the NetWare server are transferred to a selected Windows NT Server in a resource or trusting domain.

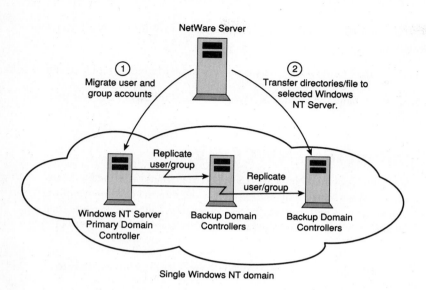

Figure 12.66
Migrating to a single NT domain network.

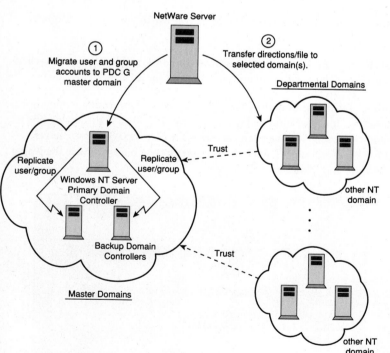

Figure 12.67
Migrating to a master domain network.

The migrating tool can be run on the Windows NT Server to which you are migrating or another Windows NT Server. The target Windows NT Server (the server to migrate to), must have the following:

■ NTFS installed for converting NetWare file system security to Windows NT file system security information.

■ NWLink installed on the Windows NT Server on which the Migration tool is to run.

■ Installed Gateway and Client Services for NetWare on the Windows NT Server that runs the Migration tool.

Using the Migration Tool, NWCONV

Before running the Migration Tool on a NetWare 3.x server, you should run the NetWare utility BINDFIX on the NetWare server. This utility verifies the internal consistency of the bindery on the NetWare server and performs any necessary repairs. You should ensure that a network path (LAN, WAN, or whatever) exists between the NetWare and Windows NT Servers.

The following is an outline of a procedure to migrate NetWare 3.x or 4.x information to a Windows NT Server:

1. Log on as an administrator to the Windows NT Server on which you run the Migration tool.

2. Run the NWCONV program. You can run this from the command line, or double-click on the NWCONV icon if you have a program item created for it.

3. If this is the first time you are running the Migration Tool since performing a migration, you see the Select Servers for Migration dialog box (see fig. 12.68). Use this dialog box to select the source and target servers. The source server is the NetWare 3.x or 4.x server, and the target server is a Windows NT Server. Select the Browse buttons to see the dialog box for adding NetWare and Windows NT Servers.

Figure 12.68

The Select Servers For Migration dialog box.

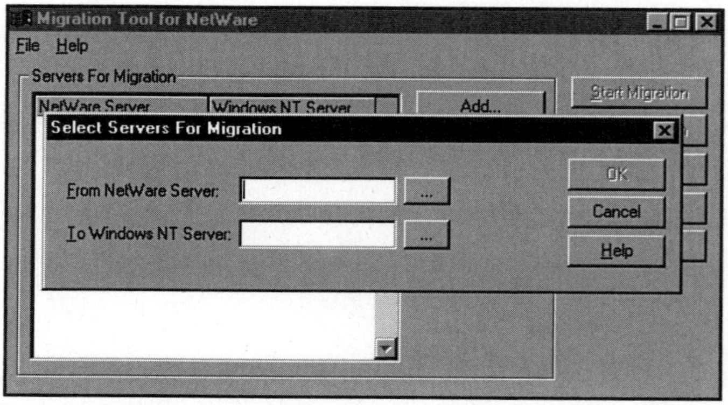

4. After you have selected the source and target servers, you see the main screen for Migration Tool for NetWare screen (see fig. 12.69).

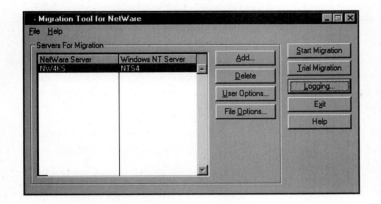

Figure 12.69
The Migration Tool for NetWare dialog box.

Use the **A**dd button to add additional source and target servers. To delete a source/target server combination, highlight it and press the **D**elete button. You can select more than one NetWare server to migrate or more than one Windows NT Server to accept accounts and data. You can, for example, decide to copy user accounts on a single NetWare server to multiple Windows NT Servers in different domains or combine user accounts from several NetWare servers to a single Windows NT Server.

To select a NetWare server to migrate, you must be logged on as a supervisor-equivalent user to the NetWare server. When you log on locally to the Windows NT Server that has a Gateway Service for NetWare running, it automatically attempts to log you on to the NetWare server using the user account/password combination you use to log on locally to the Windows NT Server. To transfer data to a Windows NT Server, you must be logged on as a member of the Administrators group.

You can set the migration options individually for each pair of servers. The migration options set for the current pair of servers apply to the next pair that you add.

5. Select the **U**ser Options button to configure how accounts are transferred (see fig. 12.70).

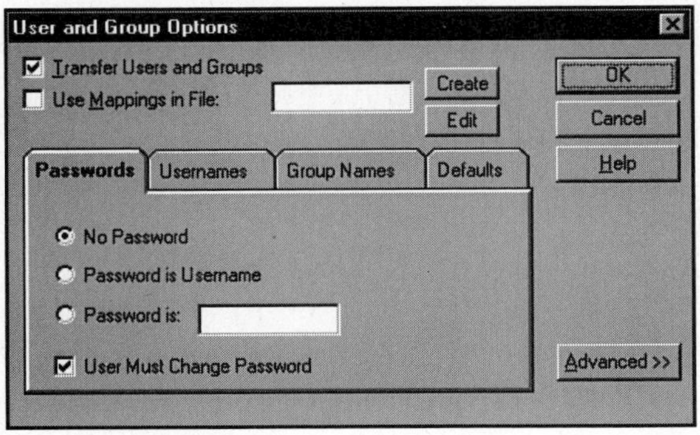

Figure 12.70
The User and Group Options dialog box.

By default, the **T**ransfer Users and Groups option is enabled, which means that the user and group accounts on the NetWare server are transferred to the Windows NT Server.

The Use **M**appings in File option enables you to specify the user and group accounts that are transferred in a text file. This option gives you more flexibility as it enables you to edit this text file. In order to use this option, you must have first created the mapping file. This process is described in the next section.

You can select how passwords, user names, group names, and certain other default options are affected during the migration procedure by selecting the appropriate index tab.

6. Select the Password Tab to see the password options. The Password Tab is displayed by default when you first open the User and Group Options dialog box (refer to figure 12.70).

   For user accounts that are transferred to the Windows NT Server, you can set passwords to any of the following: No Password, Password is Username, or Password is:, where you select a specific password for all users. By default, the User Must Change Password option is checked, meaning users who log on to the Windows NT Server after the migration are forced to change their passwords.

   If you want to specify an individual password for each transferred user account, you can create a mapping file, and edit it to specify the individual passwords. You must then set the Use **M**appings in File option and specify the mapping file name in figure 12.70.

   For security reasons, NetWare user account passwords are not preserved because no APIs exist for obtaining a password for an account or transferring passwords.

7. Select the Usernames tab to see how duplicate user name conflicts are resolved (see fig. 12.71). Duplicate names conflicts result when the NetWare user account name already exists on the Windows NT Server or domain.

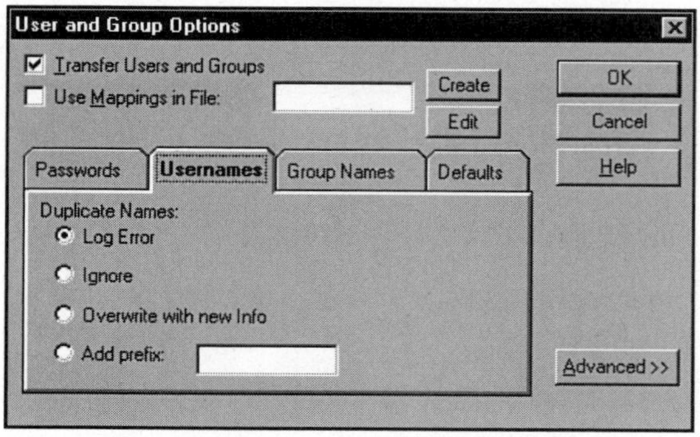

Figure 12.71

The Usernames tab in the User and Group Options dialog box.

If the Log Error option (default) is selected, conflicting usernames are not transferred to the Windows NT Server, but are written to the ERROR.LOG file. You can inspect this error log file to manually resolve the user name conflicts. If you are transferring user accounts from several NetWare servers that have duplicate names, you might want to select this option.

If the Ignore option is selected, it means that conflicting usernames are not transferred to the Windows NT Server, but also *not* written to the error log file; that is, they are ignored.

If the Overwrite With New Info is selected, it means that on conflicting usernames, the existing account on the Windows NT Server is written with the new information. Such conflicts are also written to the ERROR.LOG file. You can inspect this error log file to manually resolve the user name conflicts.

If the Add Prefix is selected, it means that on conflicting usernames, the new account is created by adding the specified prefix to the username created on the Windows NT Server. Username conflicts also are written to the ERROR.LOG file. You can inspect this error log file to manually resolve the user name conflicts. You must keep the prefix short enough so that the overall user name does not exceed the Windows NT Server limit of 20 characters. Usernames can contain upper and lower case characters except the following:

\ / : [ ] ; l = + , ? * < >

8. Select the Group Names tab to see how duplicate group name conflicts are resolved (see fig. 12.72). Duplicate names conflicts result when the NetWare group account name already exists on the Windows NT Server or domain.

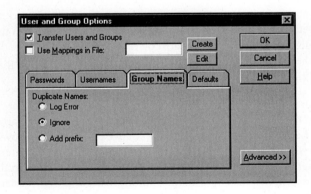

Figure 12.72
The Group Names tab in the User and Group Options dialog box.

If the Log Error option is selected, it means that conflicting groupnames are not transferred to the Windows NT Server, but are written to the ERROR.LOG file. You can inspect this error log file to manually resolve the group name conflicts. If you are transferring group accounts from several NetWare servers that have duplicate names, you may want to select this option.

If the Ignore option (default) is selected, it means that conflicting usernames are not transferred to the Windows NT Server, but also *not* written to the error log file; that is, they are ignored.

If the Add Prefix is selected, it means that on conflicting groupnames the new group account is created by adding the specified prefix to the group name created on the Windows NT Server. Groupname conflicts also are written to the ERROR.LOG file. You can inspect this error log file to manually resolve the group name conflicts. You must keep the prefix short enough so that the overall groupname does not exceed the Windows NT Server limit of 20 characters. Groupnames can contain upper and lower case characters, except for the following: \ /   : [ ] ; | = + , ? * < >

9. Select the Defaults tab to see how account restrictions are transferred (see fig. 12.73).

Figure 12.73

The Defaults tab in the User and Group Options dialog box.

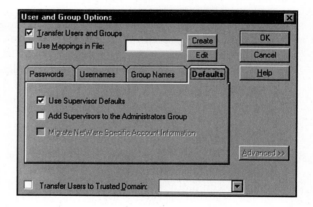

If the Use Supervisor Defaults option is set, NetWare default account restrictions that are set are transferred to individual user accounts created on the Windows NT Server. If this option is cleared, then the equivalent current Windows NT account policy settings are used. By default, this option is set.

If the Add Supervisors to Administrators Group option is set, NetWare supervisor-equivalent user accounts that are transferred are added to the Administrators group on the Windows NT Server. These users then have full administrative powers on Windows NT server. If the Add Supervisors to Administrators Group option is cleared, NetWare supervisor-equivalent user accounts are not added to the Administrators group on the Windows NT Server. You can manually give administrator privileges to the transferred NetWare user accounts using the User Manager for Domains. By default, this option is cleared.

10. To transfer NetWare accounts to a Windows NT network organized using the master domain, you can transfer NetWare accounts to the domain controller for the master domain by selecting the Advanced button in figure 12.70. You should see a new option to Transfer Users to Trusted **D**omains. Select the Master Domain from the list next to this option name.

11. Select the File Options button to control the files that are copied from the NetWare server to the Windows NT Server (see fig. 12.74). By default, all server files are copied to the Windows NT Server except the following:

- Hidden files

- System files

- \SYSTEM, \MAIL, \LOGIN, and \ETC directory contents

When determining where to transfer the files, the Migration Tool looks for a share name on the Windows NT Server that matches the volume name of the NetWare server. If such a share name does not exist, the Migration Tool creates the share name and locates it on the NTFS volume. If space is insufficient to copy the files on an NTFS volume, it looks for space on FAT volumes.

To disable a specific file transfer, highlight the source/target pair and clear the option Transfer Files. To add a volume to be transferred, select the **A**dd button; to remove a volume select the **D**elete button.

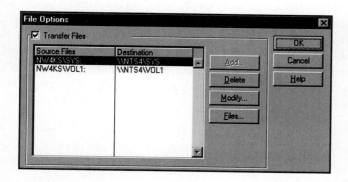

Figure 12.74

File Options for the Migration Tool.

12. Suppose that you want to selectively transfer only certain files on a NetWare volume. In that case, you can select the File's button in figure 12.74. You see the Files To Transfer Dialog box (see fig. 12.75). The directory structure of the volume is displayed in the left pane, and the files in the directory are shown in the right pane. Next to the directory and file names are check boxes that indicate whether the directory or file is to be transferred. If the check box is marked, the corresponding file or directory is transferred; if it is cleared, the file or directory is not transferred.

Figure 12.75

The Files To Transfer dialog box.

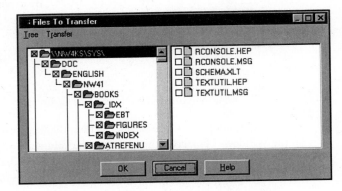

13. To select system files for transfer, select the Transfer, System Files from the Files To Transfer dialog box. To select hidden files for transfer, select Transfer, Hidden Files from the Files To Transfer dialog box.

14. To specify a different destination directory on the Windows NT Server where files are to be transferred, select the Modify button on the File Options screen (refer to figure 12.74). The Modify Destination dialog box appears (see fig. 12.76). To transfer to a different destination, choose the New Share button and specify the new share name and the UNC path to the Windows NT Server directory. To change the path of new share, select the Properties button. To transfer files to a subdirectory under the shared directory, enter the subdi-rectory name in the Subdirectory field.

After you have configured your selections, you can run a trial migration to see how the users, groups and files are transferred. The trial migration generates three log files: LOGFILE.LOG, SUMMARY.LOG and ERROR.LOG. The LOGFILE.LOG contains information on users, groups and files including information that currently exists on the NetWare server.

Figure 12.76
The Modify Destination dialog box.

15. To make a trial run, select the Trial Migration button from the Migration Tool for NetWare screen (refer to figure 12.69). You should see the Verifying Information dialog box that shows the status of information being verified. At the end, you see a Transfer Completed screen (refer to figure 12.77). Select the View Log Files button to examine the log files. You see a window for each log file. Figures 12.78, 12.79 and 12.80 show sample log files produced by a trial migration run. Some of the errors in the ERROR.LOG file are caused by duplicate usernames and the fact that the NetWare BINDFIX utility was not run prior to the trial migration run. Other errors are features of the Migration Tool itself.

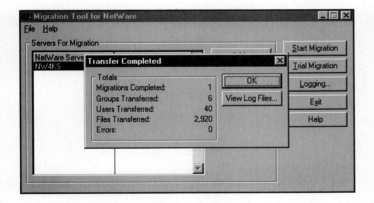

Figure 12.77
The Transfer Completed screen.

16. After correcting the problems, if any, reported in the trial run, you can perform the actual migration. You do this by selecting the Start Migration button from the Migration Tool for NetWare screen (refer to figure 12.69). You should see the same Verifying Information dialog box that you saw during the trial migration. This dialog box shows the status of information being verified. You should then see the Converting Dialog box that shows the status of the migration. At the end, you see a Transfer Completed screen (refer to figure 12.77). Choose the View Log Files button to examine the log files.

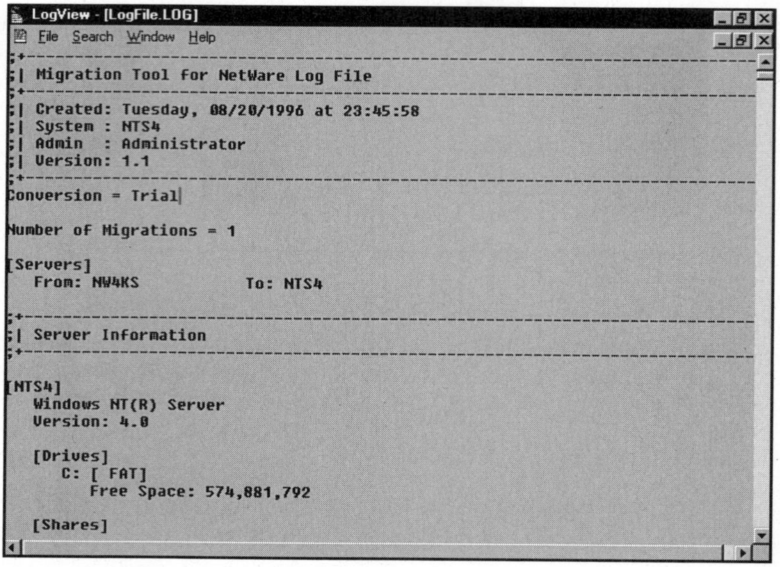

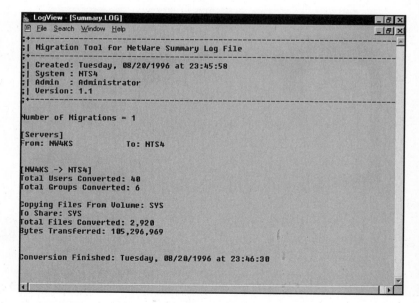

Figure 12.78
A sample LogFile.LOG for a trial migration run.

Figure 12.79
A sample Summary.LOG for a trial migration run.

17. Choose the Exit button to exit from the Migration Tool.

18. Use the User Manager for Domains to examine the properties of the accounts that were transferred. You should also examine the permission settings on the files to see whether they are transferred as expected to the Windows NT Server.

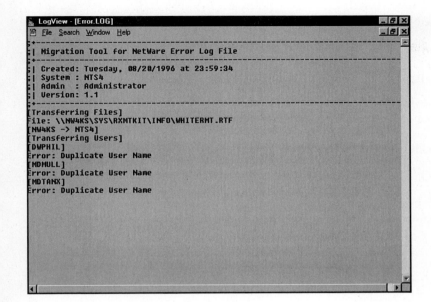

Figure 12.80

A sample Error.LOG for a trial migration run.

Creating a User Mapping File

You can use the User and Group Options dialog box to create a mapping file that specifies how account information is transferred from the NetWare server to the Windows NT Server.

To create the initial mapping files, use the following as a guideline:

1. Run the Migration Tool, NWCONV.

2. In the Servers for Migration List, select the NetWare server whose accounts you want to map.

3. Select the User Options button.

4. Set the Use Mappings In File option in the User and Group Options dialog box and enter the name of file in which the account mappings are created.

5. Optionally, set any account transfer options as described in the previous section.

6. Select OK.

The Migration Tool creates the specified text file that contains the user and group account information that are transferred. You are prompted concerning whether you want to edit this file. Answer Yes.

Figure 12.81 shows the edit screen that appears. You can edit the user and password information in this file. The mapping file contains sections for each user and group name in the following form:

NetWareUserName, NewName = Windows NT name, Password = *newpassword*

Consider the following entry in the mapping file for NetWare user Bill:

BILL, BILL, password

The previous entries mean that the new account on the Windows NT Server is BILL with no passwords set. If you edit the mapping file to make the following changes, the NetWare user account BILL is transferred as Windows NT Server user account BILLG with an initial password set to 'saddle':

BILL, BILLG, saddle

When assigning passwords, remember that Windows NT passwords are limited to 14 characters and are case-sensitive.

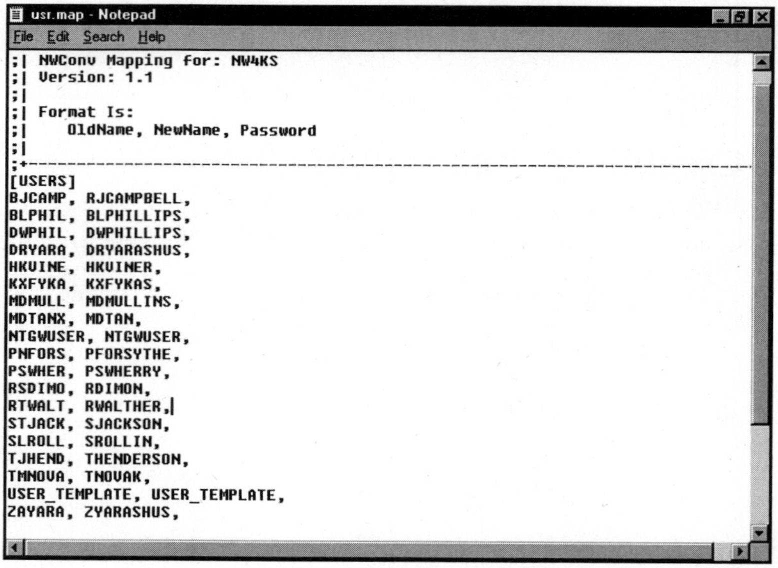

Figure 12.81
The User Mapping file.

```
; | NWConv Mapping for: NW4KS
; | Version: 1.1
; |
; | Format Is:
; |    OldName, NewName, Password
; |
;+------------------------------------------------
[USERS]
BJCAMP, RJCAMPBELL,
BLPHIL, BLPHILLIPS,
DWPHIL, DWPHILLIPS,
DRYARA, DRYARASHUS,
HKUINE, HKUINER,
KXFYKA, KXFYKAS,
MDMULL, MDMULLINS,
MDTANX, MDTAN,
NTGWUSER, NTGWUSER,
PNFORS, PFORSYTHE,
PSWHER, PSWHERRY,
RSDIMO, RDIMON,
RTWALT, RWALTHER,
STJACK, SJACKSON,
SLROLL, SROLLIN,
TJHEND, THENDERSON,
TMNOVA, TNOVAK,
USER_TEMPLATE, USER_TEMPLATE,
ZAYARA, ZYARASHUS,
```

Understanding Account Restriction Differences between NetWare and Windows NT Server

Many of the attributes of user accounts between NetWare 3.*x* and Windows NT Server are common. The accounts have a user name, password, group membership, and home directories, for example. One of the major differences between the NetWare and Windows NT server is the differences in account restrictions.

In NetWare 4.*x*, default account restrictions are set using the USER_Template in each context. In NetWare 3.*x,* default account restrictions are set using the Supervisor Options in the SYSCON tool. When a new NetWare account is created, the default account restrictions are copied to the individual account. You can individually customize the account restrictions per user account. In Windows NT, some account restrictions can be set individually per user basis, whereas other account restrictions must be set globally for all user accounts through the user account policy.

Table 12.9 summarizes the NetWare account restrictions, their Windows NT equivalents, and how these accounts are transferred.

Table 12.9
NetWare and Windows NT Account Restrictions

NetWare Account Restriction	Windows NT Account Restriction	How Account Is Transferred
Expiration date	Expiration date	Per individual user account
Account disabled	Account disabled	Per individual user account
Limit concurrent connections	None	Not transferred
Require password	Permit blank password	User policy for all accounts
Minimum password length	Minimum password length	User policy for all accounts
Force periodic password changes	Password never expires	Per individual user account
Days between forced changes	Maximum password age	User policy for all accounts
Grace logins	None	Not transferred
Allow user to change passwords	User cannot change passwords	Per individual user account
Require unique passwords	Password uniqueness	User policy for all accounts
Station restrictions	None	Not transferred
Time restrictions	Logon hours	Not transferred
Intruder Detection/ Lockout	Account Lockout	User policy for all accounts
User disk volume restriction	None	Not transferred

NetWare Client for Windows NT

Novell's NetWare client service for Windows NT supports NetWare Directory Services and can be used to access a NetWare 4 network. The NT client kit can be downloaded from the NetWare OS Files forum on CompuServe or Novell's Web Server with the URL address of http://www.novell.com. The client kit also includes a 32-bit version of the NetWare Administrator tool used to manage the NetWare Directory Services tree.

The NetWare Client for Windows NT supports 32-bit applications for Windows NT and 16-bit MS Windows applications that make calls to the 16-bit NWCALLS library.

The following is an outline of the procedure for installing and configuring the NetWare client.

1. After downloading the files, you will have the following files:

   - NT35B1.EXE

   - NT35B2.EXE

   - NWADM1.EXE

   - NWADM2.EXE

   - NTC#.EXE (required patches)

   Copy these to the same directory and run them. These program files are self-extracting and create disk images and an installation routine. Except for the LICENSE.TXT file, all the files are unique.

   Read the instructions in the files to generate the client disks.

2. To make the client disks run the following from the NTCLI directory:

   MAKEDISK

   You need two 3.5-inch, high-density, formatted floppy disks for the NT Client. Label them and insert them as prompted.

   To create the NetWare Administrator installation disks, run the following command:

   MAKEDISK ADMIN

   You need two 3.5-inch, high-density, formatted floppy disks for the NetWare Administrator. Label them and insert them as prompted.

   The patches will generally fit on one 3.5-inch high-density, formatted floppy disk. You will need the patch level 6 (NTC6.EXE) or higher.

3. If you have installed Microsoft's Gateway and Client for NetWare, use the Network icon in the control panel to remove it.

4. Log on as administrator user to the Windows NT workstations or server.

5. Double-click on the Network icon in the control panel.

6. Select the Services tab. Choose the **A**dd button in the Network dialog box.

7. In the Select Network Services dialog box select Gateway (and Client) Service for NetWare. Choose the **H**ave Disk button.

8. In the Insert Disk dialog box, select the floppy drive you are using for the installation of the client software.

9. Insert Disk 1 of the NetWare for Windows NT client and choose the OK button.

   If you have inserted the correct disk, you should see the Select OEM Options dialog box that lists the Novell NetWare Client Services (see fig. 12.82)

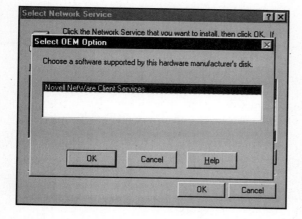

Figure 12.82
The Select OEM Option dialog box.

10. Choose the OK button in the Select OEM Options dialog box.

    You see a status of files being copied to the %SystemRoot%\System32 directory. The National Language Specific (NLS) files are copied to the NLS subdirectory under the System32 directory.

11. When prompted to insert the second NetWare client for Windows NT disk, do so and click on OK.

12. In the Network box, you see the following item added to the Network Services list:

```
Novell NetWare Client Services
```

In the Protocols tab under **N**etwork Protocols, you see the following item added:

```
Novell NetWare IPX/SPX Transport
```

The Novell NetWare IPX/SPX is separate from Microsoft's NWLink transport. NWLink is Microsoft's implementation of IPX/SPX and is not as efficient as Novell's implementation.

13. Choose the Close button in the Network dialog box. You should see the IPX Configuration dialog box.

    Select the frame type. In most cases, the default value of AUTO DETECT is adequate.

    If you select the **A**dvanced button in the IPX Configuration dialog box, you can set additional SPX parameters and Watchdog timeout timers (see fig. 12.83).

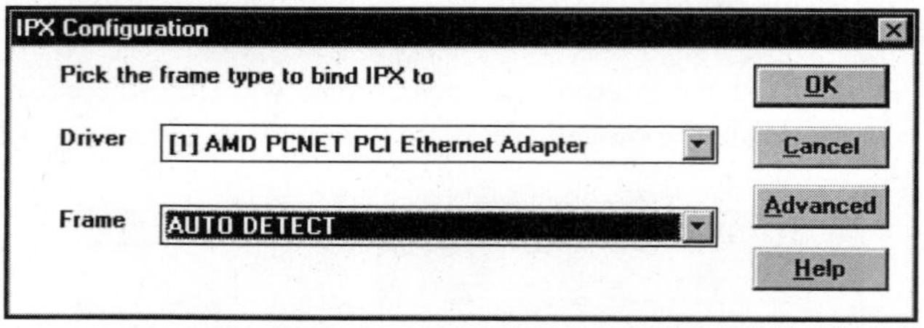

Figure 12.83
*The IPX Configuration
dialog box.*

After making your changes, choose OK on each of the screens.

14. When the Network Settings Change dialog box appears, select **N**o. It is important not to restart until you have installed the patches or your system will crash.

    Insert the floppy disk that contains the patches in the disk drive. From the Start Menu's **R**un command, type **A:\Update**. A DOS box appears, showing you the status of the changes being made. When the Update is complete, you are asked if you want to reboot the system. Remove the floppy disk from the disk drive and choose Y (Yes).

15. When you log on to the Windows NT computer, you see the NetWare Client Setup screen which asks you to enter the following information:

    Preferred Tree: The name of the NDS tree

    Name Context: The initial location in the NDS tree.

    Preferred Server: You specify this to log on to a specific NetWare server using bindery services.

    The NetWare Client for Windows NT uses the user account and password that you use to log on to the Windows NT computer to authenticate you to the NDS tree.

16. To verify that you can use the NetWare Directory Service, Click on the Network Neighborhood icon. Select Entire Network and choose **E**xplore from the **F**ile menu. Double-click the NetWare Services item. This will expand the NetWare components of the network underneath which you can see the NetWare Directory Services and the NetWare Servers (see fig. 12.84).

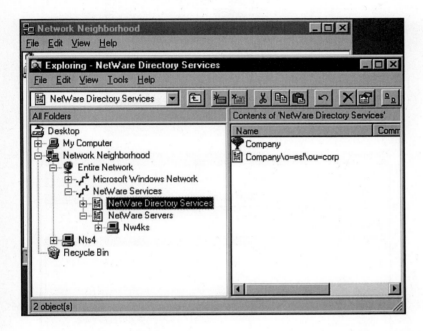

Figure 12.84

NetWare Directory Services in the Network Neighborhood screen

17. Additionally, you can verify that you can access the NetWare print resources from the Add Printer Wizard. Figure 12.85 shows an attempt to connect a network printer by selecting Network Printer and clicking on Browse. In this figure, the NDS print queue objects in the current context are displayed as shared printer objects that you can connect to.

18. As part of the installation for NetWare Client for Windows NT, a NetWare Start Menu folder is created that contains the DOS support and Getting Started icons. The DOS support icon starts a private DOS session that can be used for bindery-based API tools such as CAPTURE, FILER, MAP, and so on.

19. If you examine the Control Panel, you see a NetWare icon for configuring the NetWare client for Windows NT. Double-clicking on this icon enables you to configure the NetWare client. Figure 12.86 shows the connection information, print configuration options, available NetWare queue, broadcast message settings, and whether the first NetWare password used is stored in memory and used for subsequent NetWare server connections.

Figure 12.85

Connecting to NetWare Directory Services print queue objects.

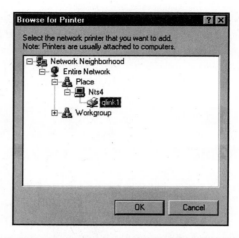

Figure 12.86

The NetWare Client control panel.

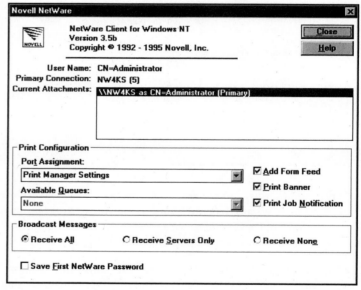

After the NetWare client for Windows NT is installed, you can install and run the NetWare Administrator tool. The NetWare Administrator tool is installed on the NetWare server in the SYS:PUBLIC\NT directory so that you have a shared location for this tool on the network. To install the NetWare Administrator tool, perform the following steps:

1. Load the INSTALL NLM on the NetWare 4 server:

   LOAD INSTALL

2. Select Product Options.

3. Select Install an unlisted product.

4. Insert the first disk for NetWare Administrator for Windows NT in the floppy drive. Specify the location of the floppy drive when prompted.

5. Select Enter to continue.

   You should see a display of the file group found on the NetWare Administrator install disks.

6. Select the file group and press F10. You should see the status of the files as they are copied. A subdirectory called NT is created under SYS:PUBLIC that contains NT specific DLLs and support files.

7. Follow instructions on the screen to add the remainder of the disks.

8. The NetWare Administrator program is implemented by the NWADMN32.EXE program which can be found in the SYS:PUBLIC\NT directory.

   Create a program item for the SYS:PUBLIC\NT\NWADMN32.EXE program. If you have a network drive mapping to the SYS: volume, you can use this drive mapping. Alternatively, you can use the UNC name of this program. For example, if the NetWare 4 server name is NW4KS, you could specify the following path:

   \\NW4KS\SYS\PUBLIC\NT\NWADMN32.EXE

9. Figure 12.87 shows the NetWare Administrator tool running on a Windows NT computer. The tool shows a graphical display of the NDS tree. Provided that you have sufficient rights, you can perform the NDS tree administration using the NetWare Administrator tool.

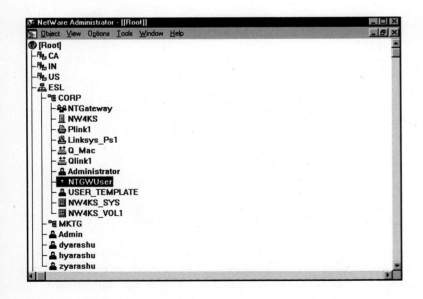

Figure 12.87

NetWare Administrator for Windows NT.

Directory Service Manager for NetWare

Microsoft has released a tool for administration of a mix of Windows NT and NetWare based networks. The tool is called Directory Service Manager for NetWare (DSMN). The name of the tool is misleading because it does not provide any integrated directory service for NetWare and it works only with NetWare 3.*x* and NetWare 4.*x* servers running in bindery emulation mode.

DSMN provides centralized management of NetWare networks using Windows NT management tools. This approach is more reasonable if your site contains a larger number of Windows NT servers than NetWare servers, because once DSMN is installed, you cannot use traditional tools on NetWare to manage NetWare servers. If you use NetWare tools to manage user accounts, synchronization with the user account database kept on the Windows NT Server is sacrificed. However, the NT DSMN does offer access for management via dialup or from an NT or Windows 95 workstation. Figure 12.88 illustrates the DSMN approach where the Windows NT Server contains the accounts database for NetWare servers. Modifications to the accounts are performed on the Windows NT Server and these modifications are sent back to the NetWare servers. If you use NetWare tools such as SYSCON or NETADMIN to modify the accounts database on NetWare servers, the central database on the Windows NT Server becomes out of date.

Figure 12.88

Directory Service Manager for NetWare.

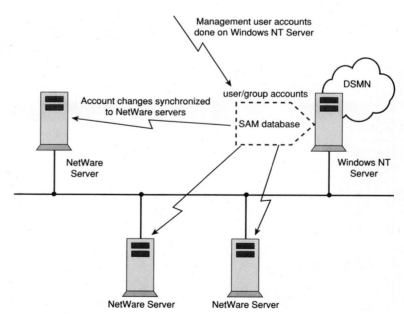

The Windows NT Server running the DSMN software must be a primary domain controller that has Gateway Service for NetWare installed and running. You can perform most NetWare account management functions, but you cannot use the DSMN tools to maintain the users logon scripts. The User Manager for Domains on the Windows NT Server has a new NetWare

Compatible Properties button. Also DSMN allows for a trial synchronization of the user accounts. If, however, you disable a NetWare user account on a NetWare server, you delete that user account permanently on the NetWare server.

The approach taken by DSMN is similar to that taken by Novell in the NetSync product that provides a centralized database of accounts on a NetWare 4 server to provide global accounts on all NetWare 3.x servers. The NetWare 3.x accounts become part of the NetWare Directory Services and the servers and accounts can be managed from a central database. The NetSync approach is illustrated in figure 12.89. If you compare figures 12.88 and 12.89 you notice that the major difference is that the central server is Windows NT Server in one case and a NetWare 4 server in the other. The NetSync approach is more suitable if you have predominantly NetWare servers and few Windows NT servers. If the NetSync approach is used, then, from a NetWare 3.x server's perspective, the NetWare 3.x servers are part of NetWare domain.

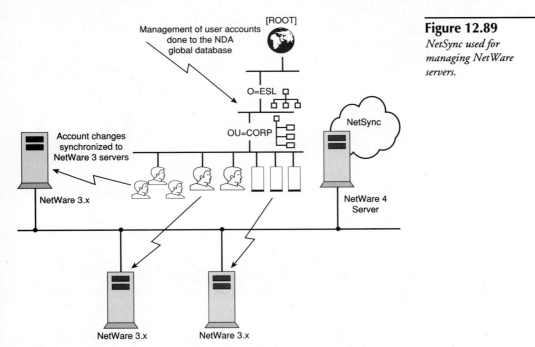

Figure 12.89

NetSync used for managing NetWare servers.

File and Print Services for NetWare

File and Print Services for NetWare (FPNW) is an add-on tool that can be installed on a Windows NT Server to make the Windows NT Server look like a NetWare compatible file and print server. FPSN does not emulate the behavior of a NetWare 4 server, so you do not have access to NetWare Directory Services.

Figure 12.90 shows the configuration in which FPSN can be used. The NetWare 3.*x* clients continue to access the Windows NT Server because they see a NetWare server instead of Windows NT Server. Microsoft clients can access the Windows NT Server using their client software.

The Windows NT Server can be used to run Windows NT applications, but cannot be used to run the installed base of NLMs.

Figure 12.90

File and Print Services for NetWare.

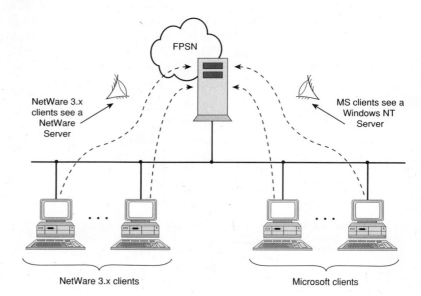

Conclusion

Windows NT Server comes with built-in capabilities that enable the integration of Windows NT Server in a NetWare network. The Gateway Services for NetWare that runs on Windows NT servers and enables Microsoft network clients to access NetWare servers enables a single connection to the NetWare server to be shared by an unlimited number of clients.

If only a single Windows NT computer needs access to NetWare servers, you can install Microsoft's Gateway and Client Service for NetWare or Novell's NetWare Client for Windows NT. If you decide to convert NetWare servers to Windows NT Server, you can use a Migration Tool called NWCONV that is installed on Windows NT Servers. You can use this Migration Tool to transfer NetWare user and group account information to equivalent Windows NT Server user and group accounts. Other tools that are available include the DSNW and the FPNW.

Introduction to TCP/IP Protocol Architecture

This chapter discusses TCP/IP applications and TCP/IP layering concepts. A familiarity with TCP/IP layering concepts is important because these concepts provide insight into the different protocol elements needed for TCP/IP applications in a Windows NT platform. This chapter discusses how the DoD networking model can be used to provide a conceptual understanding of the TCP/IP protocol stack.

It is also important to understand how IP addresses are specified for a network interface and how subnets are used on a TCP/IP network. The IP addressing parameters are important in installing and configuring TCP/IP in Windows NT.

Protocol Layering

A TCP/IP network, such as the one shown in figure 13.1, can be organized into the following major network elements:

- Physical connections

- Protocols

- Applications

The physical connections provide the medium over which the bits comprising the messages can be transmitted. The physical connections can be coaxial cable, twisted-pair wiring (shielded or unshielded), fiber-optic, telephone lines, leased lines, microwave links, infrared links, radio links, or satellite links. Many choices are available for the physical connections of a network. You must make your choice based on factors such as bandwidth of medium, ease of installation, maintenance, media cost, and end-equipment cost.

Figure 13.1

The elements of a TCP/IP network.

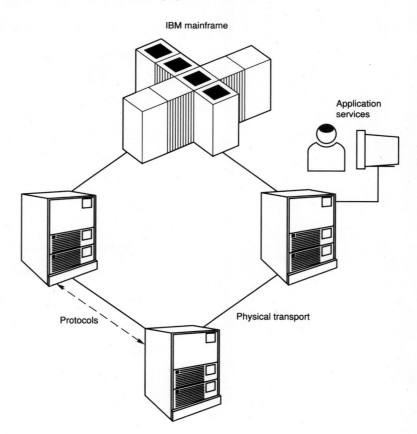

The physical connections represent the lowest level of logical functionality needed by the network. To operate the network, you need to have a standard set of rules and regulations that all devices must obey in order to communicate and work with each other. The rules and regulations by which devices on the network communicate are called protocols. A variety of such rules and regulations (protocols) exist, and these rules provide different types of functions for a network.

Network applications use the underlying network protocols to communicate with network applications running on other network devices. The network protocols, in turn, use the network's physical connections to transmit the data.

When you consider that network operation consists of physical connections, protocols, and applications, you can see that these network elements form a hierarchy: The applications are at the top and the physical connections are at the bottom. The protocols provide the bridge between the applications and the physical connections.

To understand the hierarchy between the network elements and the functions that they perform, you need a "yardstick" or model for defining these functions. One commonly accepted model is the OSI reference model. The OSI model is discussed in Appendix A, "Windows NT Server Protocols." Another model, the DoD, was designed particularly for describing TCP/IP protocols.

The DoD Model

The OSI model was created in 1979, although protocol-layering concepts existed long before they were formalized by the OSI model. An example of an earlier successful protocol that used protocol layering concepts is the TCP/IP protocol suite. Because of TCP/IP's historical ties with the Department of Defense, the TCP/IP protocol layering is called the DoD Model.

Figure 13.2 describes the DoD model, which consists of four layers. The bottom-most layer is the Network Access layer. The Network Access layer represents the physical connection components such as the cables, transceivers, network boards, link protocols, LAN access protocols (such as CSMA/CD for Ethernet and token access for Token Ring), token bus, and FDDI. The Network Access layer is used by the Internet layer.

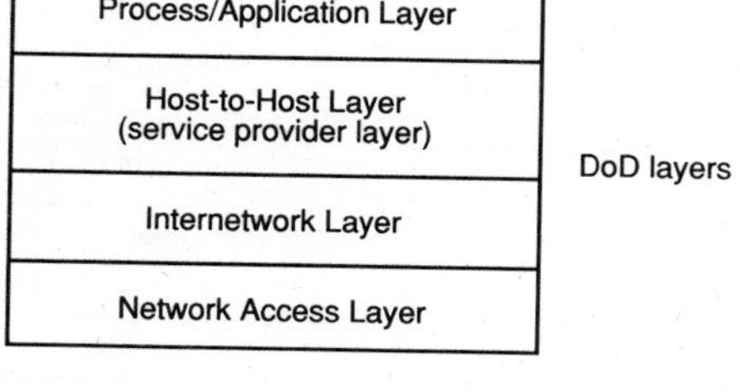

| Process/Application Layer |
| Host-to-Host Layer (service provider layer) |
| Internetwork Layer |
| Network Access Layer |

DoD layers

Figure 13.2
The DoD model.

The Internet layer is responsible for providing a logical address for the physical network interface. The DoD model's implementation of the Internet layer is the Internet Protocol (IP). This layer provides a mapping between the logical address and the physical address provided by the Network Access layer by using Address Resolution Protocol (ARP) and Reverse Address Resolution Protocol (RARP). Problems, diagnostic information, and unusual conditions associated with the IP protocol are reported by a separate protocol called the Internet Control Message Protocol (ICMP) that also operates at the Internet layer.

The Internet layer also is concerned with the routing of packets between hosts and networks. The Internet layer is common to the DoD upper layers. The upper layer that directly uses the Internet layer is the Host-to-Host layer.

The Host-to-Host protocol implements connections between two hosts across a network. The DoD model implements two Host-to-Host protocols: Transmission Control Protocol (TCP) and User Datagram Protocol (UDP). The TCP protocol is responsible for reliable, simultaneous, full-duplex connections. The term reliable means that TCP takes care of transmission errors by resending the portion of data that was in error. The Process/Application layers that use TCP do not have to be concerned with reliability of data transmission because this job is handled by TCP.

TCP also provides for simultaneous connections. Several TCP connections can be established at a host and data can be sent simultaneously, independent of data on other connections. TCP provides full-duplex connections, which means that data can be sent and received on a single connection. The UDP protocol is not as robust as TCP and can be used by applications that do not require the reliability of TCP at the Host-to-Host layer.

The Process/Application layer provides applications that use the Host-to-Host layer protocols (TCP and UDP). Examples of these applications are File Transfer Protocol (FTP), Terminal Emulation (TELNET), Electronic Mail (SMTP), and Simple Network Management Protocol (SNMP). The Process/Application layer represents the user's interface to the TCP/IP protocol stack.

If you compare the functionality of the DoD model with the OSI model, you can see that they are similar. Figure 13.3 shows these similarities.

Figure 13.3

OSI versus DoD model.

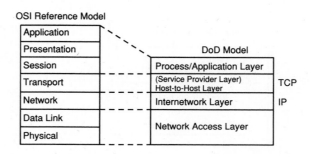

The Network Access layer of the DoD model corresponds to two layers of the OSI model, the physical layer and the data link layer.

The Internet layer of the DoD model corresponds to the network layer of the OSI model.

The Host-to-Host layer of the DoD model corresponds to the transport layer of the OSI model.

The Process/Application layer of the DoD model corresponds to three layers of the OSI model: session layer, presentation layer, and application layer.

Table 13.1 summarizes this information.

Table 13.1
DoD and OSI Comparison Summary

DoD Layer	OSI Layer Number	OSI Layer
Network Access	1	Physical
	2	Data link
Internet	3	Network
Host-to-Host	4	Transport
Process/Application	5	Session
	6	Presentation
	7	Application

Data-Flow across TCP/IP Networks

Figure 13.4 shows communication between two hosts using the DoD model. The data transmitted by a host is encapsulated by the header protocol of the Process/Application layer. The Application/Process layer data is, in turn, encapsulated by the Host-to-Host (TCP or UDP) layer. The Host-to-Host layer protocol is then encapsulated by the Internetwork layer (IP). Finally, the Internetwork layer protocol is encapsulated by the Network Access layer protocol.

When the encapsulated data is received by the remote host, it decapsulates the headers at each of the DoD model layers and sends the resulting data to the layer above it until the original data is recovered.

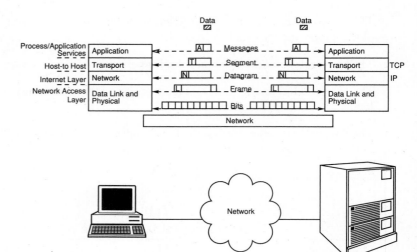

Figure 13.4
DoD Protocol layering and communications.

An important difference between the OSI and DoD models is the difference in terminology used to describe data at each layer. In the OSI model, the term Protocol Data Unit (PDU) was used to describe data at a layer. In the DoD model, the term *message* is used to describe data at the Process/Application layer. The term *segment* is used to describe data at the Host-to-Host layer. The term *datagram* is used to describe data at the Internetwork layer, and the term *frame* is used to describe data at the Network Access layer.

Understanding the TCP/IP Suite

The TCP/IP protocols and applications, often called the TCP/IP protocol suite, are defined by Request for Comments (RFCs) and Standard numbers. Table 13.2 shows the RFCs and the Standard numbers for the protocols used by the DoD model. Although all Internet standards have an RFC number, not all RFCs are part of the Internet Official Standards. Many RFCs are concerned with experimental and proposed standards; some are just tutorials. Vendors are required to comply with the list of official Internet standards. The RFC describing the list of Internet Official Protocol standards, at the time of writing this book, is RFC 1600. It is important to realize that table 13.2 contains only the more well-known standards.

Table 13.2
Standards Used in the DoD Model

Standard Name	Standard Number	RFC	DoD Model Layer
File Transfer Protocol (FTP)	9	959	Process/ Application

Standard Name	Standard Number	RFC	DoD Model Layer
Telnet Protocol (TELNET)	8	854, 855	Process/ Application
Trivial File Transfer Protocol (TFTP)	33	1350	Process/ Application
Simple Mail Transfer Protocol (SMTP)	10	821	Process/ Application
Simple Network Management (SNMP)	15	1157	Process/ Application Protocol
Domain Name System (DNS)	13	1034, 1035	Process/ Application
Mail Routing and the Domain System (DNS-MX)	14	974	Process/ Application
Transmission Control Protocol (TCP)	7	793	Host-to-Host
User Datagram Protocol (UDP)	6	768	Host-to-Host
Internet Protocol (IP)	5	791	Internet
IP Subnet Extension	5	950	Internet
IP Broadcast Datagrams	5	919	Internet
IP Broadcast Datagrams with Subnets	5	922	Internet
Internet Control Message Protocol	5	792	Internet

TCP/IP Implementation Hierarchy

The TCP/IP protocol suite has evolved to include a rich set of application services that can utilize a variety of physical networking technologies, such as WANs, LANs, radio, satellite links, and Integrated Services Digital Network (ISDN) lines.

Figure 13.5 shows a partial list of TCP/IP application services and a large variety of Network Access protocols that support TCP/IP. The application services are shown in relationship to the DoD model. An implementation may support only a few of the application services or other protocols, such as ARP, RARP, proxy ARP, and routing protocols. For example, the TCP/IP host in figure 13.5 supports only the TCP/IP application services FTP, TELNET, and SMTP.

Figure 13.5

TCP/IP implementation hierarchy.

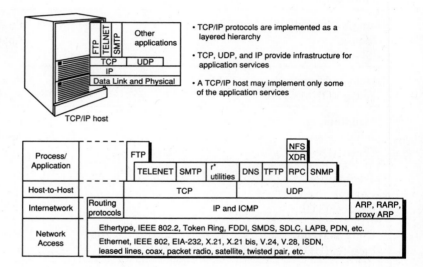

The application services in figure 13.5 are called "TCP/IP application services" because of their historical association with the TCP/IP protocol. There is nothing to prevent the application services described by the Process/Application layer from being built around a different transport or network layer protocol. SNMP, for example, is historically associated with TCP/IP but also can run on an IPX protocol stack (RFC 1420), AppleTalk protocol stack (RFC 1419), and the OSI protocol stack (RFC 1418). Similarly, services that are traditionally non-TCP/IP based, such as Server Message Block (SMB) and NetBIOS, which normally runs on a NetBEUI network protocol, and X.500, which uses the OSI protocols, can also run on TCP/IP. In Windows NT, NetBIOS can run on top of the TCP/IP stack as described by RFCs 1001 and 1002. The ISO Development Environment (ISODE) provides X.500 services over TCP/IP.

Protocol Multiplexing and Demultiplexing

Figure 13.6 shows TCP/IP communications between two hosts. Each host is running TCP/IP application services such as FTP, TELNET, Trivial File Transfer Protocol (TFTP), and SMTP.

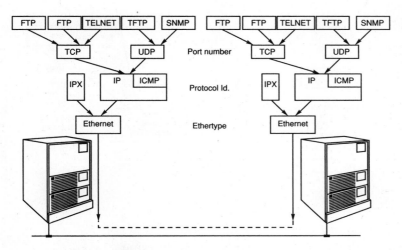

Figure 13.6

Protocol multiplexing and demultiplexing.

TFTP = Trivial File Transfer Protocol

Several sessions exist between the hosts that use FTP. You might wonder how networking software on each host distinguishes between multiple applications or protocols at a given layer.

For instance, the Ethernet in figure 13.6 supports IP and ICMP protocols and potentially other protocols such as IPX and AppleTalk's IDP. How does Ethernet determine whether a packet arriving from a network interface is destined for IP or ICMP? To make this distinction, Ethernet uses a 2-byte Ethertype field that is part of the Ethernet frame (see fig. 13.7). Table 13.3 shows some of the values of Ethertype fields used for network layer protocols. Using table 13.3, you can see that IPX has been assigned an Ethertype of 8137 and 8138.

◄─6 bytes─►	◄─6 bytes─►	◄─2 bytes─►	◄──── max of 1500 bytes ────►	◄─4 bytes─►
Destination Address	Source Address	Ethertype		CRC

Figure 13.7

2-byte Ethertype field used for protocol multiplexing/ demultiplexing.

The Ethertype field at the data link layer makes it possible to multiplex several network protocols at the sender and demultiplex them at the receiver (see fig. 13.8).

Figure 13.8
Multiplexing/ demultiplexing using the Ethertype field.

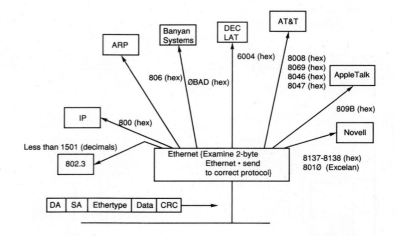

Table 13.3
Example Ethertype Value Used for
Data Link Layer Multiplexing/Demultiplexing

Ethertype Value (decimal)	Ethertype Value (hexadecimal)	Protocols or Organizations to which Ethertype Field is Assigned
0–1500	0–05DC	IEEE 802.3 length field
1536	0600	XEROX NS IDP
2048	0800	DoD IP
2049	0801	X.75 Internet
2050	0802	NBS Internet
2051	0803	ECMA Internet
2052	0804	Chaosnet
2053	0805	X.25 Level 3
2054	0806	ARP (Address Resolution Protocol)
2055	0807	XNS Compatibility
2076	081C	Symbolics Private

Ethertype Value (decimal)	Ethertype Value (hexadecimal)	Protocols or Organizations to which Ethertype Field is Assigned
2184–2186	0888–088A	Xyplex
2304	0900	Ungermann-Bass Net Debugger
2560	0A00	Xerox IEEE 802.3 PUP
2561	0A01	PUP Address Translation
2989	0BAD	Banyan Systems
4096	1000	Berkeley Trailer Negotiation
4097–4101	1001–100F	Berkeley Trailer encapsulation/IP
5632	1600	Valid Systems
16962	4242	PCS Basic Block Protocol
21000	5208	BBN Simnet
24576	6000	DEC Unassigned (Experimental)
24577	6001	DEC MOP Dump/Load
24578	6002	DEC MOP Remote Console
24579	6003	DEC DECNET Phase IV Route
24580	6004	DEC LAT
24581	6005	DEC Diagnostic Protocol
24582	6006	DEC Customer Protocol
24583	6007	DEC LAVC, SCA
24584–24585	6008–6009	DEC Unassigned
24586–24590	6010–6014	3COM Corporation
28672	7000	Ungermann-Bass download

continues

Table 13.3, Continued
Example Ethertype Value Used for
Data Link Layer Multiplexing/Demultiplexing

Ethertype Value (decimal)	Ethertype Value (hexadecimal)	Protocols or Organizations to which Ethertype Field is Assigned
28674	7002	Ungermann-Bass dia/loop
28704–28713	7020–7029	LRT
28720	7030	Proteon
28724	7034	Cabletron
32771	8003	Cronus VLN
32772	8004	Cronus Direct
32773	8005	HP Probe
32774	8006	Nestar
32776	8008	AT&T
32784	8010	Excelan (Novell)
32787	8013	SGI diagnostics
32788	8014	SGI network games
32789	8015	SGI reserved
32790	8016	SGI bounce server
32793	8019	Apollo Computers
32815	802E	Tymshare
32816	802F	Tigan, Inc.
32821	8035	Reverse ARP
32822	8036	Aeonic Systems
32824	8038	DEC LANBridge
32825–32828	8039–803C	DEC Unassigned
32829	803D	DEC Ethernet Encryption
32831	803F	DEC LAN Traffic Monitor

Ethertype Value (decimal)	Ethertype Value (hexadecimal)	Protocols or Organizations to which Ethertype Field is Assigned
32832–32834	8040–8042	DEC Unassigned
32836	8044	Planning Research Corp.
32838–32389	8046–8047	AT&T
32841	8049	ExperData
32859	805B	Stanford V Kernel exp.
32860	805C	Stanford V Kernel prod.
32864	805D	Evans & Sutherland
32866	8062	Counterpoint Computers
32869–32870	8065–8066	Univ. of Mass. at Amherst
32871	8067	Veeco Integrated Auto
32872	8068	General Dynamics
32873	8069	AT&T
32874	806A	Autophon
32876	806C	ComDesign
32877	806D	Computgraphic Corp.
32878–32887	806E–8077	Landmark Graphics Corp.
32890	807A	Matra
32891	807B	Dansk Data Elektronik
32892	807C	Merit Internodal
32893–32895	807D–807F	Vitalink Communications
32896	8080	Vitalink TransLAN III
32897–32899	8081–8083	Counterpoint Computers
32923	809B	AppleTalk
32924–32926	809C–809E	Datability

continues

Table 13.3, Continued
Example Ethertype Value Used for
Data Link Layer Multiplexing/Demultiplexing

Ethertype Value (decimal)	Ethertype Value (hexadecimal)	Protocols or Organizations to which Ethertype Field is Assigned
32927	809F	Spider Systems Limited
32931	80A3	Nixdorf Computers
32932–32947	80A4–80B3	Siemens Gammasonics, Inc.
32960–32963	80C0–80C3	DCA Data Exchange Cluster
32966	80C6	Pacer Software
32967	80C7	Applitek Corporation
32968–32972	80C8–80CC	Intergraph Corporation
32973–32975	80CD–80CE	Harris Corporation
32975–32978	80CF–80D2	Taylor Instruments
32979–32980	8CD3–80D4	Rosemount Corporation
32981	80D5	IBM SNA Service on Ethernet
32989	80DD	Varian Associates
32990–32991	80DE–80DF	Integrated Solution TRFS
32992–32995	80E0–80E3	Allen-Bradley
32996–33008	80E4–80F0	Datability
33010	80F2	Retix
33011	80F3	AppleTalk AARP (Kinetics)
33012–33013	80F4–80F5	Kinetics
33015	80F7	Apollo Computer
33023	80FF–8103	Wellfleet Communications
33031–33033	8107–8109	Symbolics Private
33072	8130	Waterloo Microsystems

Ethertype Value (decimal)	Ethertype Value (hexadecimal)	to which Ethertype Field is Assigned
33073	8131	VG Laboratory Systems
33079–33080	8137–8138	Novell, Inc.
33081	8139–813D	KTI
33100	814C	SNMP Research
36864	9000	Loopback
36865	9001	3COM(Bridge) XNS Sys. Mgmt.
36866	9002	3COM(Bridge) TCP Sys.
36867	9003	3COM(Bridge) loopdetect
65280	FF00	BBN VITAL-LanBridge cache

When the IP layer receives a packet from Ethernet, it has to distinguish between packets that need to be processed by the TCP and UDP protocol module. It makes this determination by examining an 8-bit Protocol Id field of the IP packet. Table 13.4 shows some common values for the Protocol Id field. These values can also be found in the *SystemRoot*\System32\drivers\ etc\protocol file on Windows NT computers and /etc/protocols file on Unix hosts.

Table 13.4
Example Protocol Id Values Used for
Network Layer Multiplexing/Demultiplexing

Protocol Id	Next Layer Protocol in IP Packet
0	Reserved
1	Internet Control Message Protocol (ICMP)
2	Internet Group Management Protocol (IGMP)
4	IP in IP encapsulation
5	Stream IP
6	Transmission Control Protocol (TCP)

continues

Table 13.4, Continued
Example Protocol Id Values Used for
Network Layer Multiplexing/Demultiplexing

Protocol Id	Next Layer Protocol in IP Packet
8	Exterior Gateway Protocol (EGP)
9	Any private interior gateway protocol (example: CISCO's IGP)
11	Network Voice Protocol (NVP-II)
12	Parc Universal Protocol (PUP)
16	Chaos protocol
17	User Datagram Protocol (UDP)
21	Packet Radio Measurement (PRM)
22	XEROX NS IDP (XNS-IDP)
29	ISO Transport Protocol Class 4 (ISO-TP4)
30	Bulk Transfer Protocol (NETBLT)
36	Express Transport Protocol (XTP)
37	Datagram Delivery Protocol (DDP)
75	Packet Video Protocol (PVP)
80	ISO Internet Protocol (ISO-IP)
83	VINES

When the TCP or UDP protocol modules receive a packet from the IP layer, they have to distinguish between packets that need to be processed by an application service such as FTP, TELNET, SMTP, and SNMP. The TCP and UDP protocol modules do this by examining the 16-bit port number field of their respective packets. Tables 13.5 and 13.6 show a few common values for port numbers for TCP and UDP. Because TCP and UDP protocol modules are distinct from each other, their port number address spaces are distinct. Also, notice that some TCP/IP applications are listed in both tables 13.5 and 13.6 with the same port number because these application services are available over both TCP and UDP. The port number values supported on a system can be found in the *SystemRoot*\System32\drivers\ etc\services file on Windows NT computers and /etc/services file on Unix hosts.

Table 13.5
Example Port Number Values Used for
TCP Multiplexing/Demultiplexing

TCP Port Number	Application Layer Service
0	Reserved
1	TCP Port Service Multiplexor
2	Management Utility
3	Compression Process
5	Remote Job Entry
7	Echo
9	Discard
11	Active Users (systat)
13	Daytime
17	Quote of the Day (QUOTD)
20	FTP data port
21	FTP control port
23	Telnet
25	SMTP
35	Any private printer server
37	Time
39	Resource Location Protocol
42	Host name server (nameserver)
43	Who Is (nickname)
49	Login Host Protocol (login)
52	XNS Time Protocol
53	Domain Name Server (domain)
54	XNS clearing house

continues

Table 13.5, Continued
Example Port Number Values Used for
TCP Multiplexing/Demultiplexing

TCP Port Number	Application Layer Service
66	Oracle SQL*NET (sql*net)
67	Bootstrap Protocol Server (bootps)
68	Bootstrap Protocol Client (bootpc)
70	Gopher protocol
79	Finger protocol
80	World Wide Web HTTP
88	Kerberos
94	Trivoli Object Dispatcher (objcall)
95	SUPDUP
102	ISO-TSAP
107	Remote Telnet Service (rtelnet)
108	SNA Gateway Access Server (snagas)
110	Post Office Protocol—Version 3 (POP3)
111	Sun Remote Procedure Call (sunrpc)
119	Network News Transfer Protocol (NNTP)
123	Network Time Protocol (NTP)
134	INGRES-NET Service
137	NETBIOS Naming Service (netbios-ns)
138	NETBIOS Datagram Service (netbios-dgm)
139	NETBIOS Session Service (netbios-ssn)
142	Britton-Lee IDM
191	Prospero
194	Internet Relay Chat Protocol (irc)

TCP Port Number	Application Layer Service
201	AppleTalk Routing Maintenance (at-rtmp)
202	AppleTalk Name Binding (at-nbp)
213	IPX
215	Insigniax (Soft PC)
217	dBASE Unix
372	Unix Listserv
519	unixtime
525	Time Server (timed)
533	For emergency broadcasts (netwall)
556	RFS server (remoterfs)
565	Who Am I (whoami)
749	Kerberos Administration (kerberos-adm)
767	Phone (phonebook)
1025	Network Blackjack (blackjack)
1352	Lotus Notes (lotusnote)
7000–7009	Used by Andrew File System (AFS)
17007	ISODE Directory User Agent (isode-dua)

Table 13.6
Example Port Number Values Used for
UDP Multiplexing/Demultiplexing

UDP Port Number	Application Layer Service
0	Reserved
2	Management Utility
3	Compression Process
5	Remote Job Entry

continues

Table 13.6, Continued
Example Port Number Values Used for UDP Multiplexing/Demultiplexing

UDP Port Number	Application Layer Service
7	Echo
9	Discard
11	Active Users (systat)
13	Daytime
17	Quote of the Day (QUOTD)
35	Any private printer server
37	Time
39	Resource Location Protocol
42	Host name server (nameserver)
43	Who Is (nickname)
49	Login Host Protocol (login)
52	XNS Time Protocol
53	Domain Name Server (domain)
54	XNS clearing house
66	Oracle SQL*NET (sql*net)
67	Bootstrap Protocol Server (bootps)
68	Bootstrap Protocol Client (bootpc)
69	Trivial Transfer Protocol (tftp)
70	Gopher protocol
79	Finger protocol
80	World Wide Web HTTP
88	Kerberos
94	Trivoli Object Dispatcher (objcall)
95	SUPDUP
102	ISO-TSAP

UDP Port Number	Application Layer Service
107	Remote Telnet Service (rtelnet)
108	SNA Gateway Access Server (snagas)
110	Post Office Protocol—Version 3 (POP3)
111	Sun Remote Procedure Call (sunrpc)
119	Network News Transfer Protocol (NNTP)
123	Network Time Protocol (NTP)
134	INGRES-NET Service
137	NETBIOS Naming Service (netbios-ns)
138	NETBIOS Datagram Service (netbios-dgm)
139	NETBIOS Session Service (netbios-ssn)
142	Britton-Lee IDM
161	SNMP
162	SNMP Traps
191	Prospero
194	Internet Relay Chat Protocol (irc)
201	AppleTalk Routing Maintenance (at-rtmp)
202	AppleTalk Name Binding (at-nbp)
213	IPX (Used for IP Tunneling)
215	Insignia (Soft PC)
217	dBASE Unix
372	Unix Listserv
513	Maintains database on who is logged on to machines on a local net and the load average of the machine (who)
519	unixtime
525	Time Server (timed)
533	For emergency broadcasts (netwall)

continues

Table 13.6, Continued
Example Port Number Values Used for
UDP Multiplexing/Demultiplexing

UDP Port Number	Application Layer Service
556	RFS server (remoterfs)
565	Who Am I (whoami)
749	Kerberos Administration (kerberos-adm)
767	Phone (phonebook)
1025	Network Blackjack (blackjack)
1352	Lotus Notes (lotusnote)
7000 to 7009	Used by Andrew File System (AFS)
17007	ISODE Directory User Agent (isode-dua)

TCP/IP Implementation and the Host Operating System

The performance of a TCP/IP implementation, its configuration, and its ease of maintenance depend on the operating system platform on which it runs. To show the interaction between the TCP/IP protocol and the application, vendors try to show the operating system as part of the OSI model. Unfortunately, the operating system does not fit neatly into the OSI model because the OSI model is designed for communication functions. The operating system has its own multiple-layer model. One such model is shown in figure 13.9.

Figure 13.9
Operating system layering.

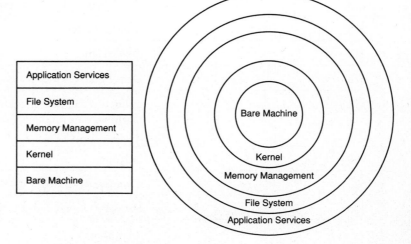

By comparing this figure with figure 13.2, you can see that these models are distinct. An operating system is a program that is a resource manager. The network communication system (modeled by the OSI model) is just one resource the operating system has to manage. In many operating systems, such as Windows NT, the network communication system is treated as part of the I/O Manager of the operating system.

Although the operating system is theoretically not necessary for running TCP/IP—the TCP/IP protocol could be embedded in ROM in an embedded application—most commercial implementations of TCP/IP interact with the operating system.

TCP/IP's interaction with the operating system can be classified in any of the following ways:

- As part of the operating system kernel

- As a device driver

- As an application process

In operating systems such as Unix, TCP/IP is implemented as part of the operating system kernel. This type of TCP/IP implementation tends to be fast because there is little overhead in accessing the OS kernel for communication functions.

Operating systems that have device driver implementations of TCP/IP include Windows NT, VMS, OS/2, MS Windows, and MS-DOS. In MS Windows, the VxD virtual device driver implements the TCP/IP stack as a 32-bit driver that uses extended memory and avoids the use of base memory of the Intel processor. (Base memory is memory below 640 KB.)

Operating systems that have application process implementations of TCP/IP are IBM's mainframe operating systems MVS and VM, MS Windows, and MS-DOS. Some MS Windows and MS-DOS TCP/IP implementations use terminate-and-stay-resident (TSR) programs and Dynamic Link Libraries (DLLs).

Unless the TSR can be loaded in upper memory by using DOS's LOAD HIGH command, the TSR resides in base memory where it must compete for memory with other applications.

If the TCP/IP stack is to be used only from within MS Windows, it can be implemented as a Dynamic Link Library. A standard interface, called the WinSock (Windows Socket) interface to this DLL, has been defined by vendors such as Microsoft, Novell, and FTP Software. Vendors that provide the WinSock DLL include Microsoft, Novell, Beam & Whiteside, FTP Software, and NetManage. Public domain versions of WinSock are also available (example: Trumpet WinSock).

TCP/IP Network Services

The TCP/IP network services consist of the following:

- Application services

- Host-to-Host services

- Internet services

- Network Access services

These services correspond to the layers of the DoD model.

This section examines some of the more important TCP/IP application services, including the following:

- FTP

- TFTP

- TELNET

- SMTP

- DNS

- Web clients

- HTTP

- Gopher

File Transfer Using FTP

The File Transfer Protocol (FTP) uses the TCP transport protocol to transfer files between two computers reliably. TCP is used as the transport protocol because of its guaranteed delivery of services.

FTP enables the user to access files and directories interactively on remote hosts and to perform directory operations, such as the following:

- List files in a remote or local directory

- Rename and delete files (if you have permission)

- Transfer files from remote host to local host (download)

- Transfer files from local host to remote host (upload)

Figure 13.10 shows a transfer of a file from the local host to the remote host. The FTP session to perform this transfer is outlined in this figure. The FTP session is initiated by the FTP client across a TCP/IP network. The computer the remote client logs on to is called the FTP host. The FTP host must have a software component called the FTP server that interacts with the file system of the host.

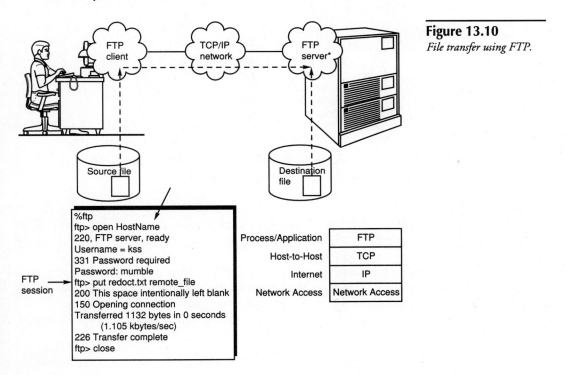

Figure 13.10
File transfer using FTP.

* FTP server is also called FTP daemon.

In general, to use FTP or any TCP/IP application service, you must have a client version of these applications. These client applications are available on Unix hosts and Windows NT computers configured for TCP/IP. For DOS clients, you must purchase a variety of separate products from different vendors.

To start an FTP session, you can use the following command:

```
ftp    [hostname]
```

The hostname is the symbolic name or IP address of the host to which you are logging on. If the hostname is left out, you can issue a number of FTP commands. If you type the help

command or ?, you can obtain help on the FTP commands. The list that follows outlines some
of the FTP commands available while you are logged on to the INTERNIC.NET host:

```
ftp> ?
Commands may be abbreviated.   Commands are:
!          cr          macdef    proxy       send
$          delete      mdelete   sendport    status
account    debug       mdir      put         struct
append     dir         mget      pwd         sunique
ascii      disconnect  mkdir     quit        tenex
bell       form        mls       quote       trace
binary     get         mode      recv        type
bye        glob        mput      remotehelp  user
case       hash        nmap      rename      verbose
cd         help        ntrans    reset       ?
cdup       lcd         open      rmdir
close      ls          prompt    runique
```

If you want to perform an FTP session to the host INTERNIC.NET, use the following
command:

```
ftp INTERNIC.NET
```

If you know the IP address of the host, you can use the following command:

```
ftp 137.65.4.1
```

Using host names that are resolved dynamically by DNS is strongly encouraged over using IP
addresses. Using host names allows you to continue using a system if its address changes, and it
also allows the administrator of the site you are accessing to perform load balancing by
returning the address of different systems with the same resources as those of the system whose
name you entered.

Please be aware that to connect to hosts outside your network environment, you need access to
these hosts through a TCP/IP internetwork. One way to access another host is through the
Internet.

You must specify a user name and a password to log on to an FTP host. The FTP server uses
the FTP host's underlying authentication mechanism to verify the privileges an FTP user
should have. If you have a user account, Bob, on the computer acting as the FTP host, you can
log on as user Bob, and use the same password that you would normally use to log on to that
computer's native operating system. Many FTP hosts provide anonymous logins. This means
that if you specify the user name as anonymous and the password as guest (some computers
expect an e-mail address containing the @ character), you can log on to the FTP host with a
limited set of privileges determined by the system administrator of the FTP host.

The following is a short, guided tour of an FTP session to the INTERNIC.NET host:

1. Type the ftp command and supply the name of the host:

```
% ftp internic.net
```

The % symbol in the preceding command is the default Unix prompt. internic.net is the host name and uses the Domain Name Syntax discussed later in this chapter.

2. If the host is reachable, a message similar to the following appears. Details of the sign-on messages may differ. The following is an example of the sign-on message for the INTERNIC.NET host. This Internet host is the one responsible for Internet Registration services.

```
Connected to internic.net.
220-*****Welcome to the InterNIC Registration Host  *****
     *****Login with username "anonymous" and password "guest"
     *****You may change directories to the following:
       policy          - Registration Policies
       templates       - Registration Templates
       netinfo         - NIC Information Files
       domain          - Root Domain Zone Files
220 And more!
Name (internic.net:karanjit):
```

As the message indicates, you can log on as the user anonymous with password guest.

3. Supply the user name and password:

```
Name (internic.net:karanjit): anonymous
331 Guest login ok, send "guest" as password.
Password:guest
230 Guest login ok, access restrictions apply.
ftp>
```

Some FTP servers request your e-mail address as a password. Although the validity of your e-mail address usually is not checked, you should comply with the FTP server's request. Some servers do check your address using a DNS reverse lookup and will not let you access their services unless the address you supply matches the one DNS identifies as assigned to the IP address of the system your traffic is originating from.

4. After you are logged on, you can use the ? or help command, as follows:

```
ftp>?
```

5. The command to see your current directory on the FTP host is pwd:

```
ftp> pwd
257 "/" is current directory.
```

The status of each FTP command is returned as a numeric code such as 257, and a text message accompanying it.

6. To see a list of files in the current directory, use the ls or dir command.

```
ftp> ls
200 PORT command successful.
150 Opening ASCII mode data connection for file list.
bin
usr
dev
etc.
pub
policy
templates
home
netinfo
domain
ls-ltR
netprog
archives
rfc
226 Transfer complete.
99 bytes received in 0.04 seconds (2.4 Kbytes/s)
```

This list includes only the file names and does not give information about the size of a file or whether it is a directory. To see this information, it is preferable to use the dir command.

```
ftp> dir
200 PORT command successful.
150 Opening ASCII mode data connection for /bin/ls.
total 22
drwxr-xr-x  2 root     1             512 Mar 22 21:40 archives
dr-xr-xr-x  2 root     1             512 Feb 25  1996 bin
drwxr-xr-x  2 root     1             512 Mar  9  1996 dev
drwxr-xr-x  2 root     1             512 Apr  1  1996 domain
dr-xr-xr-x  2 root     1             512 Feb 25  1996 etc
drwxr-xr-x  2 root     1             512 Mar  9  1996 home
-rw-r—r—   1 root     1            9035 May  4 19:12 ls-ltR
drwxr-xr-x  2 root     1            1024 Apr 14 14:57 netinfo
drwxr-xr-x  2 root     1             512 Apr  1  1996 netprog
drwxr-xr-x  2 root     1            1024 May  4 19:11 policy
drwxr-xr-x  4 root     1             512 Apr 20 15:01 pub
lrwxrwxrwx  1 root     1               6 Aug  9  1996 rfc -> _policy
drwxr-xr-x  2 root     1             512 May  3 19:54 _templates
drwxr-xr-x  3 root     1             512 Feb 25  1996 usr
226 Transfer complete.
875 bytes received in 0.25 seconds (3.4 Kbytes/s)
```

The information is reported in the Unix-style list format because you are logged on to a Unix system.

7. If you know that you are logged on to a Unix system acting as an FTP server, you can use the following useful trick:

If you use the ls command, the Unix ls command is executed. You can supply to the ls command any of the Unix options, such as the -lR option that gives a recursive long form list of files in subdirectories. You should realize that the -lR option is not a part of the standard FTP commands and only works for Unix FTP servers or those FTP servers that emulate this behavior. The following example shows the output of the ls -lR command. You can use this command to get a quick overview of the files available on the FTP host—but be careful, because you could generate a very long listing.

```
ftp> ls -lR
200 PORT command successful.
150 Opening ASCII mode data connection for /bin/ls.
total 22
drwxr-xr-x   2 root           512 Mar 22 21:40 archives
dr-xr-xr-x   2 root           512 Feb 25  1996 bin
drwxr-xr-x   2 root           512 Mar  9  1996 dev
drwxr-xr-x   2 root           512 Apr  1  1996 domain
dr-xr-xr-x   2 root           512 Feb 25  1996 etc
drwxr-xr-x   2 root           512 Mar  9  1996 home
-rw-r—r—    1 root          9035 May  4 19:12 ls-ltR
drwxr-xr-x   2 root          1024 Apr 14 14:57 netinfo
drwxr-xr-x   2 root           512 Apr  1  1996 netprog
drwxr-xr-x   2 root          1024 May  4 19:11 policy
drwxr-xr-x   4 root           512 Apr 20 15:01 pub
lrwxrwxrwx   1 root             6 Aug  9  1996 rfc -> policy
drwxr-xr-x   2 root           512 May  3 19:54 templates
drwxr-xr-x   3 root           512 Feb 25  1996 usr
:
   (and more output)
:
usr/lib:
total 576
-r-xr-xr-x   1 root         40960 Feb 25  1996 ld.so
-rwxr-xr-x   1 root        516096 Feb 25  1996 libc.so.1.8
-rwxr-xr-x   1 root         24576 Feb 25  1996 libdl.so.1.0
226 Transfer complete.
remote: -lR
9228 bytes received in 1.2 seconds (7.5 Kbytes/s)
```

8. To change your directory to a particular directory, such as rfc, use the cd command, as follows:

```
ftp> cd rfc
250 CWD command successful.
```

9. To see a list of the files in the /rfc directory, use ls or dir.

```
ftp> ls
200 PORT command successful.
150 Opening ASCII mode data connection for file list.
asn.index
domain.index
index
master.index
network.index
rfc1009.txt
rfc1011.txt
rfc1031.txt
:
   (and more output)
:
226 Transfer complete.
496 bytes received in 0.045 seconds (11 Kbytes/s)
```

10. If you try to get a file that does not exist, such as the file rfc1365.txt, FTP displays the following message:

```
ftp> get rfc1365.txt
200 PORT command successful.
550 rfc1365.txt: No such file or directory.
```

Remember that file names under Unix are case sensitive.

11. To copy a file from the FTP server to the local host, the FTP command is as follows:

```
get   remotefile   [localfile]
```

remotefile is the name of the file on the remote host, and localfile is the name of the file on the local machine. If localfile is not specified, the local file is given the same name as the remote file.

For text files, FTP performs the proper carriage return to carriage-return/linefeed conversions between different operating systems if the transfer mode is ASCII. To use the ASCII transfer mode, use the FTP command ascii. To transfer binary files, use the command image or binary to disable carriage-return/linefeed conversions.

The following shows the FTP get command:

```
ftp> get rfc1400.txt
200 PORT command successful.
150 Opening ASCII mode data connection for rfc1400.txt (13009 _bytes).
226 Transfer complete.
local: rfc1400.txt remote: rfc1400.txt
13404 bytes received in 0.78 seconds (17 Kbytes/s)
        12.    To close the current FTP connection, use the close command.
ftp> close
221 Goodbye.
ftp>
```

13. To exit FTP completely, use the bye command. This command also closes existing FTP connections before exiting FTP:

```
ftp> bye
%
```

Trivial File Transfer Protocol

The File Transfer Protocol uses TCP to achieve reliable communications across a network. If the network is inherently reliable (as is true on most LANs), or a simpler file transfer protocol is needed (as is often true in embedded systems), you can use the User Datagram Protocol (UDP) as the underlying transport (Host-to-Host) protocol. An example of a file transfer protocol that uses UDP is the Trivial File Transfer Protocol (TFTP).

Figure 13.11 shows a TFTP session used to transfer files between two hosts. TFTP can be used to transfer files between hosts without requiring user authentication. Files can be transferred by just specifying the file name. Because a user account and a password are not required for transferring files in TFTP, many system administrators disable TFTP on their systems, or restrict the types of files that can be transferred. Implementations can also deny access to a file unless every user on the host can access the file.

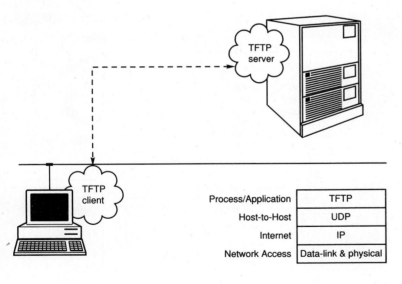

Figure 13.11
A TFTP session.

TFTP is used in conjunction with diskless workstations that need to download a boot image of the operating system from a server. The TFTP protocol is small enough to be efficiently implemented on a Boot ROM on the workstation's network board. Sun Unix workstations may be configured to use TFTP in conjunction with RARP or BOOTP. RARP and BOOTP can be used to obtain the IP address of the workstation. TFTP can then be used for downloading the operating system image. The TFTP protocol uses UDP as the Transport (Host-to-Host) layer protocol.

Windows NT computers configured with TCP/IP support the TFTP client, but not the TFTP server. The TFTP server is available on most Unix computers.

Terminal Emulation Using TELNET

The TELNET protocol is used for emulating a terminal connection to a remote host. It makes use of TCP as a transport protocol to transmit information from a user's keyboard to the remote host, and displays information from the remote host to the user workstation's display.

Figure 13.12 shows a TELNET session. To support a TELNET session, you must have a TELNET client component running at the user's workstation and a TELNET server running at the remote host. A TCP/IP session is set up between the TELNET client and the TELNET server. As the user types the keyboard commands, the characters are received by the TELNET server component and sent to the operating system on which the TELNET server runs. The characters appear as if they were typed in by a locally attached terminal.

Figure 13.12
TELNET session.

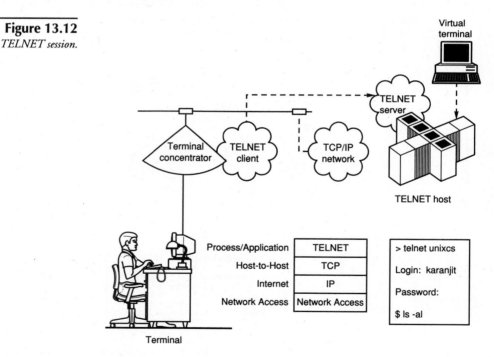

The results of the commands are sent by the TELNET server to the TELNET client. The TELNET client displays the results received from the TELNET server on the user workstation's display unit. To the person using the TELNET client, the response seems to be from a machine attached locally to the workstation.

After you are logged on, you can type any command that you are permitted on the remote operating system. To log on to a remote host, you must have an account on that machine.

TELNET can be an excellent troubleshooting tool. By specifying the TCP/IP destination port, you can connect with and interrogate other servers—like SMTP mailers. This sort of interactive testing—where you TELNET to the port a server uses when someone reports a problem with that particular service—can help you identify when a daemon has crashed but the system is still up (and responding to PING, for example).

The following is an example of a TELNET session to a Unix host:

```
% telnet world.std.com
Trying 192.74.137.5 ...
Connected to world.std.com.
Escape character is '^]'.
* To create an account on The World login as new, no password.
SunOS Unix (world)
login: karanjit
Password:password
Last login: Tue May 10 17:52:29 from karanjit-slip.cs
OS/MP 4.1C Export(STD/arlie)#15: Fri Mar 13 17:25:40 1996
        Welcome to the World!  A 6 CPU Solbourne 6E/900.
     Public Access Unix — Home of the Online Book Initiative
        Type 'help' for help! — Stuck?  Try 'help HINTS'.
     When you see MORE, hit the space bar for the next page.
           Use 'exit' or 'logout' to leave the system.
              Still Stuck?  Send mail to 'staff'.
You have mail.
Over disk quota on /home/ie, time limit has expired, remove 120K
TERM = (vt100)
Erase is Backspace
No new messages.
An authority is a person who can tell you more about something than you really
care to know.
from: postel@isi.edu [no subject]
% ls -alr
total 1011
-rw— — —  1 karanjit    21852   Apr 13 21:56 veronica
drwx— — —  2 karanjit      512   Dec 28  1996 temp
-rw— — —  1 karanjit     4780   Jun  4  1996 snapip.dmp
-rw— — —  1 karanjit     1319   Jul  9  1996 Index
-rw— — —  1 karanjit        8   Apr 13 20:43 .sh_history
-rw— — —  1 karanjit     7035   May 10 17:53 .pinerc
drwx— — —  2 karanjit      512   Apr 13 20:01 .nn
-rw— — —  1 karanjit   138402   Apr 13 20:01 .newsrc.bak
-rw-r—r—  1 karanjit   138102   Apr 13 20:01 .newsrc
-rw-r—r—  1 karanjit        4   Apr  7 12:55 .msgsrc
-rw— — —  1 karanjit       11   Dec 28  1996 .mh_profile
-rw-r—r—  1 karanjit      386   Dec 19  1996 .login
-rw— — —  1 karanjit        0   Apr  7 17:35 .gopherrc
-rw-r—r—  1 karanjit      538   Dec 19  1995 .emacs
```

```
drwx———   2 karanjit      512  Jan 22  1996 .elm
-rw-rw-r—  1 karanjit      799  Feb  1  1996 .cshrc
-rw———     1 karanjit        0  Dec 19  1995 .addressbook
drwxrwxr-x1911 root       61952  May 24 12:55 ..
drwx———   7 karanjit     1024  May 10 17:56 .
% ping ftp.microsoft.com
ftp.microsoft.com is alive
% logout
```

Mail Services Using SMTP

Mail services are one of the most widely used applications on the Internet. Several protocols for mail services are available, but the most widely used is Simple Mail Transfer Protocol (SMTP).

SMTP enables ASCII text messages to be sent to mail boxes on TCP/IP hosts configured with mail services. Figure 13.13 shows a mail session that uses SMTP. A user who wants to send mail interacts with the local mail system through the User Agent (UA component of the mail system). The mail is deposited in a local, outgoing mailbox. A sender-SMTP process periodically polls the outgoing box and, when it finds a mail message in the box, establishes a TCP connection with the destination host to which mail is to be sent. The Receiver-SMTP process at the destination host accepts the connection, and the mail message is sent on that connection. The Receiver-SMTP process deposits the mail message in the destination mailbox on the destination host. If no mailbox with the specified name exists on the destination host, a mail message is sent to the originator indicating that the mailbox does not exist.

Mail addresses used in SMTP follow the RFC 882 standard. The mail headers are often referred to as 882 headers. An example of an 882 address is as follows:

KSS@SHIVA.COM

The text string before the @ symbol specifies the mailbox name, and the text string after it specifies the host name. If the mailbox name contains special characters, such as the percent symbol (%), the mailbox name is given a special encoding so that it can be used by mail gateways. In the mail address of KSS@SHIVA.COM, the text string KSS is the name of the mailbox on host SHIVA.COM.

SMTP expects the destination host receiving the mail to be online. Otherwise, a TCP connection cannot be established with the destination host. For this reason, it is not practical to establish an SMTP session with a desktop machine because they are often turned off at the end of the day. In many network environments, SMTP mail is received by an SMTP host that is always active on the network. This SMTP host provides a mail drop service. Workstations interact with the SMTP host and retrieve messages using a client/server mail protocol, such as POP3 (Post Office Protocol, Version 3), described in RFC 1460.

If you want to send non-text messages using SMTP, you can encode the message as a text message by using the UUENCODE utility available on many systems. The receiver has to decode the encoded message using a utility called UUDECODE. Another way of sending non-text messages is to use the Multipurpose Internet Mail Extensions (MIME) protocol. MIME is described in RFCs 1521, 1522, 1563. MIME has become the preferred encoding because most mail systems handle encoding and decoding MIME attachments transparently.

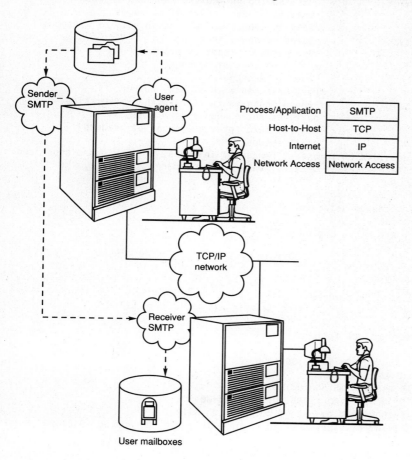

Figure 13.13

An SMTP session.

Process/Application	SMTP
Host-to-Host	TCP
Internet	IP
Network Access	Network Access

A sample mail session using the Unix mail program illustrates how the user can interact with the User Agent (UA).

```
% mail
Mail version SMI 4.0 Thu Jul 23 13:52:20 PDT 1996  Type ? for help.
"/usr/spool/mail/karanjit": 1 message
>   1 kss@RAMA.COM     Mon Apr 25 19:32 5148/153370
& ?
cd [directory]                  chdir to directory or home if none given
d [message list]                delete messages
e [message list]                edit messages
f [message list]                show from lines of messages
h                               print out active message headers
m [user list]                   mail to specific users
n                               goto and type next message
```

```
p [message list]               print messages
pre [message list]             make messages go back to system mailbox
q                              quit, saving unresolved messages in mbox
r [message list]               reply to sender (only) of messages
R [message list]               reply to sender and all recipients of messages
s [message list] file          append messages to file
t [message list]               type messages (same as print)
top [message list]             show top lines of messages
u [message list]               undelete messages
v [message list]               edit messages with display editor
w [message list] file          append messages to file, without from line
x                              quit, do not change system mailbox
z [-]                          display next [previous] page of headers
!                              shell escape
A [message list] consists of integers, ranges of integers, or user names separated
by spaces. If [message list] is omitted, Mail uses the current message.
& m karanjit@kscs.com
Subject: Mail demonstration message
This is a demonstration on using the
simple mail program interface.
When finished, you must type period (.)
:-)
.
EOT
& h
(Print out active message headers)
>   1 kss@RAMA.COM    Mon Apr 25 19:32 5148/153370
& p
(Print message. Message now follows)
Message  1:
From kss@RAMA.COM Mon Apr 25 19:32:35 1996
Return-Path: <kss@RAMA.COM>
Received: by world.std.com (5.65c/Spike-2.0)
        id AA01519; Mon, 25 Apr 1996 19:31:33 -0400
Received: from sita.RAMA.COM by relay1.UU.NET with SMTP
        (5.61/UUNET-internet-primary) id AAwnfh17101; Mon, 25 Apr 96 19:21:26 -0
400
Received: by sita.RAMA.COM (5.67/PERFORMIX-0.9/08-16-95)
        id AA03921; Mon, 25 Apr 96 16:21:21 -0700
Date: Mon, 25 Apr 94 16:21:21 -0700
From: kss@RAMA.COM (K S)
Message-Id: <9404252321.AA03921@learn1.Lrntree.COM>
To: karanjit@world.std.com
Status: RO
X-Status: D
#! /bin/sh
# This is a shell archive.  Remove anything before this line, then unpack
# it by saving it into a file and typing "sh file".  To overwrite existing
# files, type "sh file -c".  You can also feed this as standard input via
# unshar, or by typing "sh <file", e.g.. If this archive is complete, you
# will see the following message at the end:
#               "End of shell archive."
# Contents:  INSTALL Makefile Prospero RCS README acalloc.c archie.c
#   archie.man atalloc.c dirsend.c get_pauth.c get_vdir.c p_err_text.c
```

```
#    pauthent.h pcompat.h perrno.h pfs.h pmachine.h pprot.h ptalloc.c
#    regex.c stcopy.c support.c uw-copyright.h vl_comp.c vlalloc.c
# Wrapped by darwin@king.csri on Wed Jan  5 20:28:52 1996
PATH=/bin:/usr/bin:/usr/ucb ; export PATH
if test -f 'INSTALL' -a "${1}" != "-c" ; then
  echo shar: Will not clobber existing file \"'INSTALL'\"
else
echo shar: Extracting \"'INSTALL'\" \(1725 characters\)
sed "s/^X//" >'INSTALL' <<'END_OF_FILE'
X[Last changed: 07/31/91]
(Rest of message....)
& x
(Quit and do not change system mailbox)
%
```

Domain Name System (DNS)

The examples of sending e-mail messages discussed in the preceding section used a symbolic name for the host name on which the mailbox resided. In general, users can more easily remember symbolic names for names of hosts. The alternative is to remember the IP address of the host. The IP address of a host name is a 32-bit number, which most people find difficult to use and remember. The TCP/IP protocol software, on the other hand, uses the IP address. Any symbolic name used by the TCP/IP application service is translated to the equivalent 32-bit IP address. This translation is performed by the Domain Name System (DNS).

The DNS system essentially acts as a names database (also called a name server). When given a host name, DNS translates it to an IP address. DNS can also do reverse translations (also called pointer queries), which means that when given an IP address, DNS can return the host name registered for that IP address.

DNS is implemented as a distributed database for looking up name-to-IP address associations and IP address-to-name associations. Another way of performing the name lookup is to keep the name-to-IP address information in a static file. On Unix systems, this static file is the /etc/ hosts file. On Windows NT computer, this static file is kept in the *SystemRoot*\System32\ drivers\etc\hosts file. Windows NT computers also use the LMHOSTS and WINS files for NetBIOS over TCP/IP applications.

The following sample host file shows this organization:

```
# Local network host addresses
#
#ident "@(#)hosts  1.1 - 88/05/17"
#
127.0.0.1        local lb localhost loopback
144.19.74.1      sparc1 sp1
144.19.74.2      sparc2 sp2
144.19.74.3      sparc3 sp3
144.19.74.4      sparc4 sp4
144.19.74.5      sparc5 sp5
144.19.74.6      sparc6 sp6
```

```
144.19.74.7      sparc7 sp7
144.19.75.1      sparc8 sp8
144.19.75.2      sparc9 sp9
144.19.75.3      sparc10 sp10
144.19.75.4      sparc11 sp11
144.19.75.5      sparc12 sp12
144.19.75.6      sparc13 sp13
144.19.75.7      sparc14 sp14
144.19.74.101    cdos
144.19.74.102    server1 s386 nw
144.19.74.103    spws sparcsrv sps ss
144.19.74.201    sparcc1 spc1
144.19.74.202    sparcc2 spc2
```

The IP address 127.0.0.1 is a special address called the loopback address. Packets sent to this address never reach the network cable. The loopback address can be used for diagnostic purposes to verify that the internal code path through the TCP/IP protocols is working. The loopback address can also be used by client applications to communicate with software programs running on the same machine. In other words, the loopback address can be used for the local host.

The address 127.0.0.1 is used as the loopback address. It also can be used to address the local host.

Each <IP Address, Host name> pair is expressed on a single line using the style shown in the hosts file. The multiple host names for the host are alias names. The protocol software, if configured to perform name resolution using this static host file, looks up the information for resolving a name. Consider the following command:

```
telnet sp14
```

The protocol software uses the following entry in the host's file to resolve the name sp14:

```
144.19.75.7      sparc14 sp14
```

The name sp14 is an alias for the host name sparc14. The corresponding IP address is 144.19.75.7. The protocol software resolves the name sp14 to 144.19.75.7. The preceding command then becomes the following:

```
telnet 144.19.75.7
```

The static host file approach has several problems. As the number of hosts on a network becomes large, it is increasingly difficult to keep this file up-to-date. In addition, many organizations have more than one network administrator. It is difficult for these administrators to coordinate with each other every time host files need to be changed. Even keeping this information in a large central static file quickly becomes unmanageable as the number of entries in this file becomes large.

The DNS system was developed to overcome the problems of name resolution on a large IP network. It provides a distributed database of names and IP addresses. The names could be host names or names of mail exchanger hosts. This system also has provisions for keeping text descriptions of host names and for providing name resolution for other protocol families besides TCP/IP (such as Chaosnet and XNS). It is, however, used predominantly for resolving host names for the TCP/IP protocols.

Figure 13.14 shows DNS operation; a TELNET session is being initiated using the command telnet archie.ans.net.

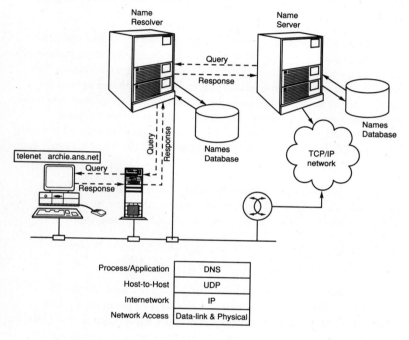

Figure 13.14

A DNS name resolution example.

A portion of this TELNET session is shown:

```
% telnet archie.ans.net
Trying 147.225.1.2...
Connected to nis.ans.net.
Escape character is '^]'.
AIX telnet (nis.ans.net)
IBM AIX Version 3 for RISC System/6000
(c)Copyrights by IBM and by others 1982, 1990.
login:
```

The immediate response from the telnet session is the following message:

```
Trying 147.225.1.2...
```

The TCP/IP software translated the host name archie.ans.net to the 32-bit IP address 147.225.1.2. The client resolver used DNS to perform this translation.

TCP/IP application software can be configured to use DNS to resolve names. When a TCP/IP application encounters a host name, it sends a query to a name resolver to translate the name to an IP address. On many Unix systems, the name resolver can be on the same workstation where the query was issued. If the name resolver cannot find the answer, it sends the query to a known name server. Typically, the name server exists on the workstation's network. If the name server cannot find the answer, the query can be sent to another name on the TCP/IP network.

The DNS system relies on a query/response-type behavior and uses the UDP protocol as a transport protocol for end station requests. The UDP protocol is more suited for applications that are query/response based because there is no overhead of maintaining a connection for transmitting data. The TCP protocol also can be used for query/response-based applications, but it requires an initial opening of a connection and a breakdown of the connection when the query/response is done. If only a single query/response or an occasional query/response transaction is expected (as is typical for end stations), the overhead of establishing and breaking a connection can be excessive. DNS servers, however, commonly use TCP when querying each other.

The most widely used implementation of DNS is the Berkeley Internet Name Domain (BIND) server, originally made available on BSD Unix, but now available on most Unix platforms. On Unix systems, it is often called the named (name daemon) program.

BIND implementations for DOS and OS/2 are available from FTP Software. A simple Windows front-end for BIND is available from Chameleon's NETMANAGE product.

Windows NT Server uses a NetBIOS Name Server called WINS for resolving NetBIOS names. Windows NT computers include a DNS client that can be used for querying DNS servers for resolving DNS names. Windows NT Server 4 includes a BIND-compatible DNS server implementation that has significant advantages in a Windows network environment because of its interface to WINS and its graphical administration tool.

Understanding Domain Names

The examples of the host names in the preceding section have periods in them. These types of names use a hierarchical naming convention.

In the hierarchical name scheme used in DNS, names are organized into a hierarchical tree. At the top of the tree is the root domain named by the period symbol (.). Because all names have this common root, the period is omitted when specifying the hierarchical name in most TCP/IP applications. Below the root domain are top-level domains (see fig. 13.15). These reflect how names are organized. Table 13.7 shows examples of top level domains.

The two-letter designations are assigned to a country as per the CCITT standards (now called ITU standards) and the ISO-3166 standard (except for Great Britain, which uses UK rather than the designated GB). These are the same country designations used for specifying country objects in NetWare Directory Services. Below the top-level domains are middle-level domains.

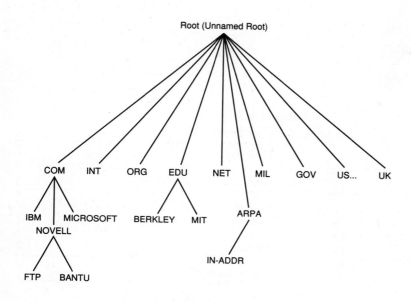

Figure 13.15
Hierarchical names in DNS.

There can be a number of middle-level names. Each name is separated from another by use of the period (which can never occur as part of the name of a domain). An example of a complete domain name is shown here:

`archie.ans.net`

A name cannot exceed 255 characters. In the name archie.ans.net, the name of the host is as follows:

`archie`

This domain is named:

`ans.net`

If another host, named sparky, were in the same domain, its fully qualified domain name (FQDN) would be the following:

`sparky.ans.net`

Many of the middle-level names refer to names of organizations. An organization is free to define subdomains within the organization. If it does this it should provide appropriate name services to resolve names in these subdomains. Consider, for example, the organization SCS that has been given the following domain name:

`SCS.COM`

If this organization has separate networks for its corporate, marketing, and research arms, it could define three separate subdomains named CORP, MKTG, RESCH, and provide a DNS server or a number of DNS servers to resolve names on its networks. The domains, in this case, would be the following:

- CORP.SCS.COM

- MKTG.SCS.COM

- RESCH.SCS.COM

Table 13.7
Examples of Some Top-Level Domains

Top-Level Domain	Description
COM	Commercial organization
EDU	Education institution. Universities, schools, and so on
MIL	Military
GOV	Government, U.S.A.
NET	Network provider
ORG	Organization
ARPA	ARPANET. Now historical. Still used for inverse address mapping
INT	International organization
US	U.S.A.
CA	Canada
UK	United Kingdom
DE	Germany
SE	Sweden
FR	France
IN	India
CN	China
JA	Japan

As local government agencies, schools, and community colleges join the Internet, the Domain Name organization under the U.S. domain has become more complex. The Internet Network Information Center (INTERNIC) has guidelines on the U.S. domain organization.

Membership in the U.S. domain is open to any computer in the United States. In the past, the computers registered in the U.S. domain were primarily owned by small companies or individuals with computers at home. The U.S. Domain has grown and currently registers hosts in federal and state government agencies, technical/vocational schools, K12 schools, community colleges, private schools, libraries, city and county government agencies, as well as in businesses and homes.

The U.S. Domain hierarchy is subdivided into states, and then locality (that is, city or county), and then organization or computer name and so on. The state codes are those assigned by the U.S. Postal Service. Within the state name, locality names such as cities, counties, or some other local names are used, but incorporated entities are not.

Registered names under locality can be of the following types:

- *hostname*.CI.*locality*.*state*.US (for city government agency)

- *hostname*.CO.*locality*.*state*.US (for county government agency)

- *hostname*.*locality*.*state*.US (for businesses)

The code of CI is used for a city government, and CO is used for a county government. Businesses are registered directly under the locality name.

If a county and a city have the same locality name, uniqueness still is maintained because of the use of the CO or CI keyword.

Cities can be designated by their full names (spelled out with hyphens replacing spaces, as in San-Francisco or New-York), or by a city code. The preference should be to use the full city name. If it is appropriate, you can also use the well-known city abbreviation known throughout a locality. It is very desirable, however, if all users in the same city use the same designator for the city. That is, any particular locality should have just one DNS name.

For example, the Fire Department of Park County in Montana (MT) could have the following DNS name:

```
Fire-Dept.CO.Park-County.MT.US.
```

The state code is the postal code—MT for Montana. The locality is the Park County. The keyword CO designates that this a reference to the county government. The Fire-Dept is the name of the department in the Park County government.

Besides CO and CI, other codes such as the ones listed here are used:

- **K12.** Used for public school districts

- **PVT.** Used in the place of a school district name to designate private schools

- **CC.** Used for state-wide or community colleges

- **TEC.** Used for technical and vocational schools and colleges

- **LIB.** Used with libraries for state, region, city, and county

- **STATE.** Used for state government agencies

- **GEN.** General independent entity that does not fit easily into any other structure listed. These could be state-wide associations, clubs, or domain parks

- **FED.** Used for agencies of the federal government

- **DNI.** Distributed National Institutes. This branch is to be used for organizations that span state, regional, and other organizational boundaries and that are national in scope

The general syntax of the domain names that use these codes are as follows:

- *school.district.*K12.*state.*US

- *school-name.*PVT.K12.*state.*US

- *school-name.*CC.*state.*US

- *school-name.*TEC.*state.*US

- *org-name.*STATE.*state.*US

- *org-name.*GEN.CA.US

- *org-name.*FED.US

- *org-name.*DNI.US

Figure 13.16 shows the second-level domains under U.S. Figure 13.17 shows third level domains under the example state of California. Figure 13.13 shows a view of state, regional, and general agencies. Figure 13.19 shows the locality domains for Los Angeles and Santa Monica.

Anyone requesting to register a host in the U.S. must fill a special U.S. Domain Template. Generally, having the Internet service provider that connects you to the Internet handle your domain name registration is the easiest and most efficient way to handle your name request. Domain names used to be free, but recently the InterNIC has started charging a yearly fee with the first two years paid in advance.

If you want to register a name in a delegated zone, you should register with the contact for that zone. You can obtain this information through anonymous FTP or by using whois. The file is in-notes/delegated-domains.txt from venera.isi.edu. You also can send an e-mail message to RFC-INFO@ISI.EDU and include the following as the only text in the message:

```
Help: us_domain_delegated_domains
```

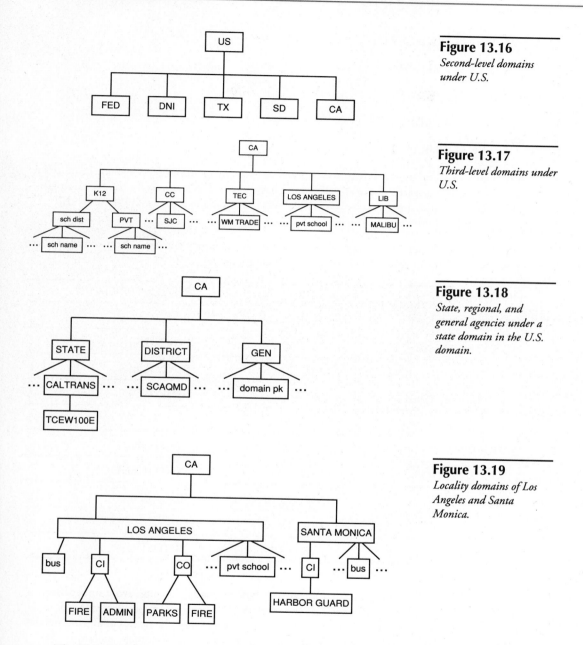

Figure 13.16
Second-level domains under U.S.

Figure 13.17
Third-level domains under U.S.

Figure 13.18
State, regional, and general agencies under a state domain in the U.S. domain.

Figure 13.19
Locality domains of Los Angeles and Santa Monica.

The U.S. domain is currently supported by the following seven name servers:

- VENERA.ISI.EDU

- NS.ISI.EDU

- RS.INTERNIC.NET

- NS.CSL.SRI.COM

- NS.UU.NET

- ADM.BRL.MIL

- EXCALIBUR.USC.EDU

Although a DNS server is not required for each domain, it is common to have one or more for each domain being served. Figure 13.15 would have several DNS servers for the root domain. These servers would know about names of the top-level domains such as COM, EDU, MIL, ORG, NET, and others.

A number of name servers manage the domain names at the root domain. These root domain servers, at the time of this writing, are shown in the following table:

HOSTNAME	NET ADDRESSES	SERVER PROGRAM
NS.INTERNIC.NET	198.41.0.4	BIND (Unix)
NS.NIC.DDN.MIL	192.112.36.4	BIND (Unix)
NS1.ISI.EDU	128.9.0.107	BIND (Unix)
AOS.ARL.ARMY.MIL	128.63.4.82	BIND (Unix)
	192.5.25.82	
C.NYSER.NET	192.33.4.12	BIND (Unix)
TERP.UMD.EDU	128.8.10.90	BIND (Unix)
NS.NASA.GOV	192.52.195.10	BIND (Unix)
	128.102.16.10	
NIC.NORDU.NET	192.36.148.17	BIND (Unix)

Several DNS servers can be used for a domain to perform load balancing, avoid unnecessary network traffic, and for reliability in case the primary DNS server is not available. In this setup, the COM domain has one or more DNS servers that know the names of all commercial organizations in the COM domain. Within the COM domain, a subdomain such as IBM.COM has its own DNS servers for that domain. Hosts within a domain query the local

DNS server for the domain to resolve names. For example, the host WORLD.STD.COM would query the DNS server for the domain STD.COM to find out the IP address of the host FTP.NOVELL.COM or the IP address of ATHENA.SCS.ORG. When this query is resolved, the results usually are cached locally for a configurable period of time.

The DNS servers for a domain need to resolve names of hosts in their domains. Secondary DNS servers in a domain must know the IP address of the primary server in the domain so that it can contact it and resolve a name query. A DNS server must also know the IP address of the parent DNS server.

DNS usually uses UDP as a transport protocol to send DNS queries and receive responses from DNS servers.

If you have an Internet connection and access to the whois client program, you can use this client utility to obtain information on a domain and the person(s) responsible for administering the domain.

The following are results of running the whois utility on some interesting domain names:

```
% whois microsoft.com
Microsoft Corporation (MICROSOFT-COM)
    3635 157th Avenue
    Building 11
    Redmond, WA 98052
    Domain Name: MICROSOFT.COM
    Administrative Contact:
        Kearns, Paul  (PK47)  postmaster@MICROSOFT.COM
        (206) 882-8080
    Technical Contact, Zone Contact:
        NorthWestNet Network Operations Center  (NWNET-NOC)  noc@nwnet.net
        (206) 685-4444
    Record last updated on 11-Apr-96.
    Domain servers in listed order:
    DNS1.NWNET.NET      192.220.250.1
    DNS2.NWNET.NET      192.220.251.1
    NS1.BARRNET.NET    131.119.245.5
% whois nic.ddn.mil
Government Systems, Inc. (DIIS)
    14200 Park Meadow Dr., Suite 200
    Chantilly, VA 22021
    Hostname: NIC.DDN.MIL
    Nicknames: DIIS.DDN.MIL
    Address: 192.112.36.5
    System: SUN running Unix
    Host Administrator:
        McCollum, Robert  (RM584)  bobm@NIC.DDN.MIL
        (703) 802-8476
    Domain Server DDN user assistance    (800) 365-3642 NIC@NIC.DDN.MIL
                                         (703) 802-4535
        Computer Operations    (703) 802-4535   ACTION@NIC.DDN.MIL
        WHOIS updates, user registration         REGISTRAR@NIC.DDN.MIL
```

```
        Host changes and updates          HOSTMASTER@NIC.DDN.MIL
        Suggestions                       SUGGESTIONS@NIC.DDN.MIL
     Record last updated on 17-Sep-95.
To see this host record with registered users, repeat the command with a star
('*') before the name; or, use '%' to show JUST the registered users.
The InterNIC Registration Services Host ONLY contains Internet Information (Net-
works, ASNs, Domains, and POCs).
Please use the whois server at nic.ddn.mil for MILNET Information.
% whois 130.57
```

(The preceding line is querying whois service for a domain name for IP net address of 130.57.0.0—class B address. You learn about class addresses later in this chapter.)

```
Novell, Inc. (NET-NOVELL-WEST)
    122 East 1700 South
    Provo, UT  84606
    Netname: NOVELL-WEST
    Netnumber: 130.57.0.0
    Coordinator:
       Richardson, Mark  (MR46)  mark_richardson@NOVELL.COM
       (801) 429-7974
    Domain System inverse mapping provided by:
    NS.NOVELL.COM                137.65.1.1, 137.65.4.1
    NEWSUN.NOVELL.COM            130.57.4.1
    Record last updated on 28-Sep-95.
% whois 1
```

(The preceding line is querying whois service for a domain name for IP net address of 1.0.0.0—class A address—actually the first class A address ever assigned! You learn about class addresses later in this chapter.)

```
BBN Communications Corporation (ASN-BBN)
    33 Moulton Street
    Cambridge, MA 02238
    Autonomous System Name: BBN-CORE-GATEWAYS
    Autonomous System Number: 1
    Coordinator:
       Brescia, Michael  (MB)  BRESCIA@BBN.COM
       (617) 873-3662
    Record last updated on 27-Jun-94.
The InterNIC Registration Services Host ONLY contains Internet Information (Net-
works, ASNs, Domains, and POCs). Please use the whois server at nic.ddn.mil for
MILNET Information.
```

Web Clients

The World Wide Web (WWW) is one of the main driving factors of the Internet's growth. The Web's easy-to-use client software combined with the vast amount of well-presented information have resulted in a huge demand for Internet Access.

The software you use to access the Web is called a web client, such as Internet Explorer, NetScape Navigator, and Mosaic. All of these web clients (and most others) support a variety of major protocols, several of which are not directly required to access the WWW. The only protocols needed to access the Web are TCP/IP and support for HTTP. Other protocols like gopher and ftp are supported in most web clients as a matter of convenience.

HTTP Web Clients

The *HyperText Transfer Protocol (HTTP)* defines a way of transferring hypertext data across TCP/IP networks. This hypertext data is organized into documents that are formatted using *HTML*, the HyperText Markup Language. Any HTML document can reference any other HTML document, which makes navigating through related documents easy, even for inexperienced computer users.

HTTP is a network protocol that web browsers like Internet Explorer or NetScape Navigator use to transfer text, graphics, and sounds to and from web sites. Web browsers have been the primary driving force behind the recent explosion of Internet growth because they make presenting information attractively easy.

The Web got started in 1990 as a way for physicists at CERN in Switzerland to share information within their research community. The original web software was written for NeXT workstations, but it was rapidly ported to other systems. CERN is still one of the best sources of web-related information.

The Internet has surged in popularity during the last few years because HTTP clients, better known as "web browsers," have become common. All the major online services now support some form of web access, and a whole new industry of Internet Service Providers (ISPs) has sprung up to meet the demand for easy, inexpensive Internet access.

HTTP is used to transfer the contents of web pages from HTTP servers (like Microsoft's Internet Information Server) to HTTP clients (like Internet Explorer or Navigator). These contents may be plain text, formatted text, binaries, graphics, sound, animations, or even Java-based applications.

HTTP works by opening a TCP/IP connection (usually on TCP port 80, the port assigned to HTTP by the Internet Assigned Numbers Authority) and transfers the data for each object on the web page being viewed. A single web page typically has quite a few objects on it—perhaps a background, the text for the page, a graphic for each different button you can select, and some other things to liven up the page (maybe some additional graphics or a Java applet that waves a flag or scrolls some text).

To access a web document, you first have to locate that document. Documents are identified using Uniform Resource Locators, or URLs. An URL consists of a protocol identifier and a location. To access the Microsoft home page on the Internet, you would enter `http://www.microsoft.com/` in the URL field of your browser. Web browsers are versatile, however, and you could use one to access the Internet's primary RFC archive by entering `ftp://ds.internic.net/`. To find information from gopher, you might enter `gopher://gopher.tc.umn.edu/` for your URL.

There are HTTP clients (web browsers) for all common Unix and desktop operating systems, as well as for some not-so-common operating systems.

Gopher Web Clients

Gopher is a text-based client/server information retreival tool. It uses a menu-driven interface to find and transfer any information that a gopher server has been configured to make available. This menu-driven interface is in many ways a logical precursor to the now more popular graphics-oriented World Wide Web (WWW). The major conceptual difference between them is that Gopher was designed to help people find things, while the typically-graphical Web was designed to let the information you find look nice as you browse it.

Windows NT does not come with a stand-alone gopher client, but all the major WWW clients also support accessing what is called *gopherspace*. To access a gopher server from a web browser, just enter gopher://*servername* in the URL field of your web browser where *servername* is the DNS name or IP address of the particular gopher server you want to access.

Tip	A great way to find which gopher servers have information you are interested in is to start out by querying the University of Minnesota's gopher server at gopher:// gopher.tc.umn.edu.

Gopher was invented at the University of Minnesota, where its goal was to help users find information. It grew from there, and today there are private individuals with their own gopher servers in their homes. Collectively, all of the gopher servers and the information they provide make up gopherspace.

Gopher usually uses TCP/IP connections on TCP port 70, the port assigned to it by the Internet Assigned Numbers Authority.

Using Network File System (NFS)

Network File System (NFS) is a file service protocol originally developed by SUN Microsystems and licensed to a large number of vendors. It enables a computer on which the NFS server software is running to export its file systems to other clients. Exporting a file system means that it is made available to clients on a variety of different operating system platforms as long as they are running the NFS client software.

Figure 13.20 shows that the NFS server is exporting the /usr/public directory. This exported directory can be accessed simultaneously by Unix NFS clients, Macintosh NFS clients, IBM PC DOS clients, and VAX/VMS NFS clients.

Each NFS client views the file system exported by the NFS server in the environment of the client's native file system. For example, a DOS NFS client accesses the exported file system through a network drive letter assignment; a Unix NFS client sees the exported file system linked to its local file system.

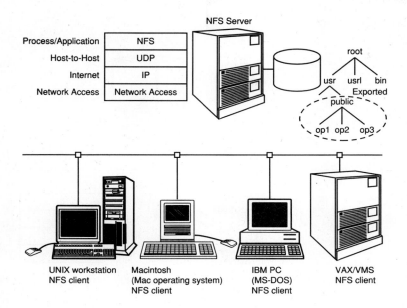

Figure 13.20
Using NFS.

*NFS uses the UDP transport protocol.

The NFS file system messages are sent using the UDP transport protocol. The NFS protocol uses UDP as its transport (Host-to-Host) protocol.

Simple Network Management Protocol (SNMP)

SNMP can be used to manage a TCP/IP network. The SNMP Manager is a special station on the network that can send management queries to other nodes being managed on the network. Figure 13.21 shows an example SNMP management scenario. The managed nodes on the networks can be bridges, routers, and hosts. Each node that is managed must run a special program called the SNMP agent. The SNMP agent accepts the queries sent by the SNMP Manager and sends back the requested information.

SNMP uses the UDP as a transport protocol to send and receive requests. The SNMP protocol uses UDP as its transport (Host-to-Host) protocol.

Protocol Summary for TCP/IP Applications

Table 13.8 shows a summary of the transport protocol usage of the TCP applications discussed in this section. All the applications in Table 13.8 use the IP protocol.

Figure 13.21
Use of SNMP.

Table 13.8
Transport Protocol Usage Summary

Process/Application Layer	Primary Transport Protocol
FTP	TCP
TELNET	TCP
SMTP	TCP
DNS	UDP
HTTP	TCP
Gopher	TCP
NFS	UDP
SNMP	UDP
TFTP	UDP

Host-to-Host and Internet Layer Protocols

The DoD model uses two protocols at the Host-to-Host layer: the TCP and UDP protocols. The DoD model uses the IP and ICMP protocols at the DoD Internet layer. For broadcast networks (Ethernet, Token Ring, FDDI, and others), additional protocols, such as the ARP and RARP, can be used to support the Internet layer. Highlights of the TCP, UDP, and IP protocols are examined in the following sections.

Transmission Control Protocol (TCP)

The Transmission Control Protocol (TCP) provides reliable, full-duplex connections between two hosts. The connections that TCP provides are analogous to telephone circuits and are called virtual circuits. Figure 13.22 shows a TCP connection between two hosts.

- Uses virtual circuits

    - Similar to telephone circuits
    - Open connection
    - Reliable data transfer

Figure 13.22

TCP connection used to transmit data.

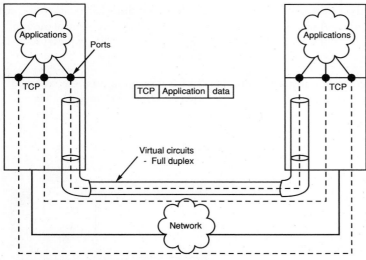

Virtual circuits are not suitable for packet broadcasts.

For TCP to be used for the transmission of data, a connection must be established between the two hosts. This is similar to the process of establishing a connection between two telephones. After the connection is established, port numbers that act as logical identifiers are used to identify the virtual circuit. On a TCP virtual circuit, data can be transmitted in either direction simultaneously. This is called full-duplex operation. The TCP connection is maintained for the duration of data transmission. If no more data transmission is expected on the TCP circuit, the connection can be closed. Closing a connection releases any operating system resources such as memory and state tables needed to keep the connection alive.

TCP has its own built-in mechanism for reliable data transmission. Message segments not received at the destination are automatically present at the expiration of a time-out interval.

The time-out interval is dynamic and takes into account factors such as changing delays caused by network congestion and alternate routes being used by underlying network services.

The TCP protocol provides reliable connections between hosts.

Although TCP is suited for applications that require reliable data transmission, it is not suited for applications that require broadcast traffic. To send a broadcast datagram to multiple destinations, TCP would have to establish a virtual circuit to each destination host and then send the datagram on each one of the virtual circuits. This is a time-consuming and resource-intensive process. For applications that depend on broadcasts, UDP is a more suitable transport layer protocol.

User Datagram Protocol (UDP)

UDP can send data without requiring that a data-circuit be established. Each data unit is sent with complete source and destination IP addresses and port numbers that identify the application-level processes involved in the data exchange. UDP is similar to ordinary postal services because complete addressing information is sent with each UDP message.

UDP is called a connectionless transport protocol because it does not use a pre-established connection to transmit data. Figure 13.23 shows the use of UDP to exchange data between two hosts.

Figure 13.23

UDP connection used to transmit data.

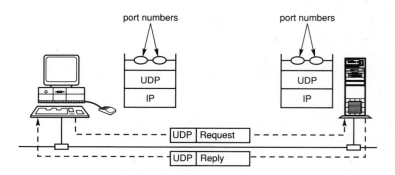

UDP has less overhead than TCP. UDP does not, however, guarantee that data arrives in the order in which it is sent; TCP guarantees that messages are assembled in the order in which they are sent. UDP includes an optional checksum that can be used to ensure data integrity of the message being sent. If additional reliability, such as data being received in the order in which it was sent (called sequenced delivery), is required, the application-level process/protocol has to provide for it.

A big advantage UDP has over TCP is that it is more suited for applications that require broadcast data. A single datagram can be broadcast on the network by specifying a broadcast address on the destination address.

UDP is popular in many LAN-based applications that are broadcast-based and do not require the complexity of TCP applications that use UDP are NFS, DNS, SNMP, and TFTP. The WINS server used for resolving NetBIOS names use UDP. UDP is also used by IP Tunneling which is used to transmit a non-TCP/IP application data over a TCP/IP network.

Internet Protocol (IP)

The Internet Protocol (IP) is used to encapsulate TCP and UDP message segments (see fig. 13.24). The IP provides a logical network address for the hardware network interface. This logical network address is a 32-bit address (called the IP address) and can be used to identify separate physical networks joined by interconnecting devices called routers. The logical IP address provided by the Internet Protocol identifies the destination network and the host address on the network to which the data is to be sent. It can, therefore, be used for routing a data unit, called a datagram, to its correct destination.

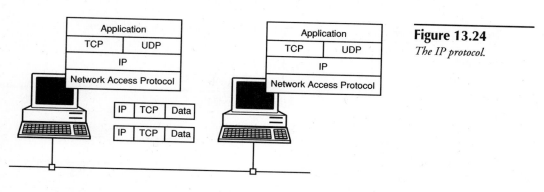

Figure 13.24

The IP protocol.

The IP protocol is a connectionless protocol: it does not require the establishment of a virtual circuit for sending a datagram.

Internet Control Message Protocol (ICMP)

The Internet Control Message Protocol (ICMP) is used to report problems encountered with the delivery of a datagram, such as an unreachable host or unavailable port. ICMP can also be used to send an echo request packet to a host to see if it is "alive." The host that receives an ICMP echo request sends back an ICMP reply packet if it is "alive" and still functioning. This is called the "PING" test.

ICMP also can be used by router devices to send an ICMP redirect message to other devices indicating that a better path has been found.

IP Protocol Elements

When two TCP/IP hosts are connected through a network, each protocol layer of the TCP/IP host communicates with the corresponding protocol layer of the other TCP/IP host. The DoD model discussed earlier in this chapter comprises four layers, the Process/Application layer, Host-to-Host layer, Internet Layer, and Network Access layer. As each of these protocol layers communicates with the peer layer of the remote TCP/IP host, it uses its own addressing.

The Process/Application layer uses host names. Because the Process/Application layer is seen directly by users, it makes sense for this layer to use host names, which are much easier to identify and remember. The Host-to-Host layer uses port numbers to describe the interface points to this layer. The port numbers can be seen as the addresses of the software processes that reside on the same TCP/IP host. The Internet layer uses IP addresses. An IP address is needed for each network interface in a TCP/IP host. TCP/IP hosts that have multiple network interfaces (such as hosts acting as routers) are called multi-homed hosts.

Table 13.10 summarizes the addressing method used in each of the DoD layers.

Table 13.10
Addressing Method in the DoD Model

DoD Layer	Addressing Method
Process/Application	Host name
Host-to-Host	Port number
Internet	IP address
Network Access	Hardware address (MAC address)

Process/Application Layer Addressing

Host names are used as addresses in the Process/Application layer. The host names are translated (mapped) to IP addresses by using either DNS or a host name file.

DNS was discussed earlier in this chapter in the section "Domain Name System (DNS)." For small networks, a static host table can be used to perform the mapping between host names and IP addresses in order to avoid the expense of configuring and maintaining a DNS server. Figure 13.25 shows the translation between host names and IP addresses using a host name file. The host name file is the /etc/hosts file on Unix servers. On NetWare servers, the host name file is implemented by SYS:ETC/HOSTS file.

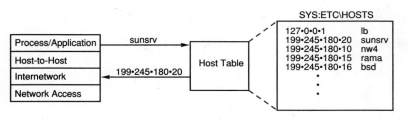

Figure 13.25

Host name translation using a host name file.

Internet Layer Addressing

The Internet Layer addresses are represented by 32-bit numbers called IP addresses. Each network interface in a node that supports an IP stack must have an IP address assigned to it. The IP address is a logical address independent of the underlying network hardware or network type.

IP Address Classes (Classes A, B, C, D, and E)

The IP address consists of two parts: a network ID netid and a host ID hostid, as shown in figure 13.26. The most significant bits are used to determine how many bits are used for netid and the hostid. Five address classes are currently defined: Classes A, B, C, D, and E. Of these, classes A, B, and C addresses are assignable. Class D is reserved for multicasting and is used by special protocols to transmit messages to a select group of nodes. Class E is reserved for future use.

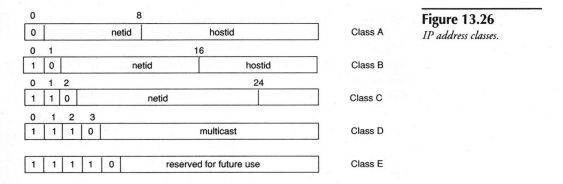

Figure 13.26

IP address classes.

The netid portion of the IP address identifies the network uniquely. Interconnected networks must have unique netids. If your network is going to be connected to other networks such as the Internet, you must apply to a central authority to obtain a netid (network number) not used by anyone else. The central Internet Address Network Authority (IANA) is as follows:

To connect to the MILNET:

> DDN Network Information Center
> 14200 Park Meadow Drive, Suite 200
> Chantilly, VA 22021, USA
> E-mail address: HOSTMASTER@NIC.DDN.MIL

To connect to the Internet:

> Network Solutions
> InterNIC Registration Services
> 505 Huntmar Park Drive
> Herndon, VA 22070
> E-mail address: HOSTMASTER@INTERNIC.NET

Older reference works on TCP/IP may list the Stanford Research Institute (SRI) as the IANA. This information no longer is true, but you still can obtain RFCs from SRI.

Reasons for Using Specific Address Classes

The different types of IP address classes are defined to address the needs of networks of different sizes. On request, the network registration authority assigns a network number (the netid field) to an organization. It is the sole responsibility of an organization that has been allocated a network number to assign the host numbers (the values for the hostid field).

The number of hosts that can be assigned for a given network number depends on the number of bits in the hostid field. The number of bits in the hostid field depends on the address class to which the network number belongs. A class A network number has the largest number of bits in the hostid field and, therefore, has the largest number of hosts. Similarly, a class C address has the smallest number of bits in the hostid field and therefore has the smallest number of hosts. Table 13.11 shows the number of networks and nodes possible with each address class.

Table 13.11
Reasons for Using Specific Address Class

Address Class	Number of Networks	Number of Nodes
A	127	16,777,214
B	16,383	65,534
C	2,097,151	254

A class A network is suitable for very large networks, but because their netid field (see fig. 13.26) is only 7 bits, there can be only 127 such networks. The original ARPANET is an example of a class A network. Class B networks are medium-size networks and are suited for medium-to-large organizations. Class C networks are suited for small organizations, in which each network can have no more than 254 nodes.

Dotted Decimal Notation

The 32-bit number is represented for convenience as four decimal numbers corresponding to the decimal value of the four bytes that make up the 32-bit IP address. The decimal numbers are separated by periods (.). This shorthand notation for IP addresses is called dotted decimal notation. The following shows an IP address in its binary form and in dotted decimal notation:

```
IP Address = 10010000 0001011 01001010 1001001

IP Address = 144.19.74.201
```

Figure 13.27 shows the relationship between the binary representation of the IP address and the dotted decimal notation. From this figure, you can see that the first group of 8 bits (10010000) that has a decimal value of 144 becomes the first decimal number of the dotted decimal IP address. Similarly, the second, third, and fourth groups of 8 bits are each represented by their decimal values in the dotted decimal notation.

- To make a 32-bit binary number more human-readable, dotted decimal notation is used

Figure 13.27

Dotted decimal notation.

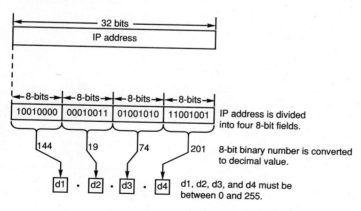

Example: Dotted decimal 144 • 19 • 74 • 201

Calculating an Address Class

Given an IP address in the dotted decimal notation form, it is important to know the address class to which it belongs. The IP address class determines the number of bits assigned to the hostid field. The size of the hostid field limits the number of hosts that can be on the network.

Another reason for knowing the address class is because it can be used to determine how to divide a network into smaller networks, called subnets.

One method of determining the IP address class is to convert the IP address into its binary form and to examine the first few most significant bits (bits on the left of the binary pattern for the IP address). The most significant bits of an IP address determine the IP address class. From figure 13.28, you can see that if the most significant bit of the IP address is a 0, the IP address is a class A address. If the first two most significant bits of the IP address are 10, the IP address is a class B address; and if the first three most significant bits of the IP address are 110, the IP address is a class C address. Table 13.12 summarizes these rules.

Figure 13.28
Determining IP address class.

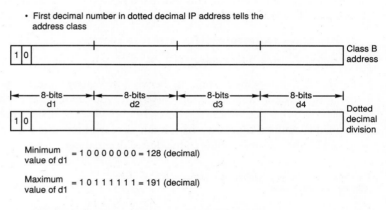

- First decimal number in dotted decimal IP address tells the address class

Minimum value of d1 = 1 0 0 0 0 0 0 0 = 128 (decimal)

Maximum value of d1 = 1 0 1 1 1 1 1 1 = 191 (decimal)

- Conclusion: For a class B address, the first decimal number must be between 128 and 191

Table 13.12
Determining IP Address Class from the Most Significant Bits of the IP Address

Most Significant Bits	IP Address Class
1	Class A
10	Class B
110	Class C
1110	Class D

Consider an IP address of 137.65.4.1. If you convert this IP address to its binary representation, you obtain the following 32-bit pattern:

    1001001 01000001 00000100 00000001

The most significant two bits of this bit pattern are 10. The IP address 137.65.4.1, therefore, is a class B address.

Consider another example in which the IP address is 199.245.180.10. If you convert this IP address to its binary representation, you obtain the following 32-bit pattern:

1100111 11110101 10110100 00001010

The most significant three bits of this bit pattern are 110. The IP address 199.245.180.10, therefore, is a class C address.

Although this technique works, it is a laborious way of determining the IP address class because it involves converting the IP address to a bit pattern. Fortunately, a simpler way is available. Consider the class B address shown in figure 2.39. For a class B address, the two most significant bits are 10. The minimum value of the first 8 bits occurs when the remaining 6 bits are 0; the maximum value occurs when the remaining 6 bits are 1.

The minimum value of the first 8 bits of a class B address, therefore, is 10000000 and the maximum value is 10111111. These minimum and maximum values correspond to a decimal value of 128 and 191. This means that if the first decimal number of an IP address in the dotted decimal notation is a number between 128 and 191 (inclusive), the IP address is a class B address. In the preceding example of an IP address of 137.65.4.1, the number 137 is between 128 and 191, and therefore 137.65.4.1 is a class B address.

Using the same reasoning, the minimum and maximum for the first decimal number of a class A and class C address in its dotted decimal notation form can be worked out as shown:

- Minimum value of first decimal for class A = 00000000 = 0

- Maximum value of first decimal for class A = 01111111 = 127

- Minimum value of first decimal for class C = 11000000 = 192

- Maximum value of first decimal for class C = 11011111 = 223

Table 13.13 shows the range of values for the first decimal number of an IP address in the dotted decimal notation. This table can be used to determine the IP address class by merely examining the first decimal number of an IP address.

Table 13.13
Determining IP Address Class from the First Decimal Number of an IP Address Expressed in Dotted Decimal Notation

IP Address Class	Minimum	Maximum
A	0	126
B	128	191
C	192	223

continues

Table 13.13, Continued
Determining IP Address Class from the First Decimal Number of an IP Address
Expressed in Dotted Decimal Notation

IP Address Class	Minimum	Maximum
D	224	239
E	240	247

Consider the following questions:

1. What is the IP address class for 40.12.33.1?

2. What is the IP address class for 191.122.65.234?

3. What is the IP address class for 204.17.206.10?

By examining table 13.13, the first decimal number of 40 in the IP address 40.12.33.1 indicates that it is a class A address. The first decimal number of 191 in the IP address 191.122.65.234 indicates that it is a class B address; and the first decimal number of 204 in the IP address 204.17.206.10 indicates that it is a class C address.

Software Loopback

If you examine table 13.13, you see that the number 127, which should be in the class A range of values, is missing. This number is reserved for the software loopback address. Any packet sent by a TCP/IP application to an IP address of 127.X.X.X, with X being any number from 0 to 255 results in the packet coming back to the application without reaching the network media. The packet is copied from transmit to receive buffer on the same computer. This is why the IP address 127.X.X.X is called a loopback address. The software loopback address can be used as a quick check to see that the TCP/IP software is properly configured.

Although any address of the type 127.X.X.X indicates a loopback address, Windows NT servers use the IP address 127.0.0.1; many Unix systems use a software loopback address of 127.1.

Special IP Addresses

A hostid value of 0 or all 1s is never assigned to an individual TCP/IP host. An IP address with a hostid value of 0 indicates the network itself. The IP address of 137.53.0.0, therefore, indicates the class B network 137.53.

If the hostid value contains all 1s in the bit pattern, it indicates a directed broadcast address. A directed broadcast address is seen by all nodes on that network. For the network number

137.53, therefore, the broadcast address is 137.153.255.255. The network number 137.53 is class B address and has 16 bits in the hostid field. If 1s are used for the 16 bits of the hostid, they correspond to a decimal value of 255.255.

Another type of broadcast, called the *local broadcast* or *limited broadcast,* is represented by the value of 255.255.255.255. This type of broadcast can be used in local area networks, where a broadcast never crosses a router boundary.

The broadcast address of 255.255.255.255 is used by the broadcast name resolution method, called b-node method, in Windows NT.

An important exception to all 1s in the hostid field used for broadcasts is TCP/IP software derived from 4.2 BSD Unix, which Unix used the convention of all 0s in the hostid field to indicate a broadcast address. At the time 4.2 BSD Unix was written, the RFCs were unclear about the convention used for broadcast addresses. This problem was resolved in later RFCs, which stated that all 1s in the hostid field should be used for broadcast addresses. 4.3 BSD Unix was modified to conform to the RFCs. Software derived from 4.2 BSD Unix, unless modified, still can use the all 0s broadcast convention. If hosts that use all 0s to broadcast are placed on the same physical network as hosts that use all 1s for broadcasts, the broadcast mechanism does not work as expected. A symptom of this is failure of TCP/IP applications on the specific network to work correctly.

An IP address of 0.0.0.0 is used to refer to the network itself. The Windows NT Dynamic Host Configurable Protocol (DHCP) clients on requesting IP parameter information from a DHCP server use a source address of 0.0.0.0.

The 0.0.0.0 address is also used in routing tables to indicate the network entry for the default router's (often called default gateway) IP address.

Subnet Masks

After an IP network number has been assigned for a network, it is up to the network administrator to assign values for the host number field.

Consider an IP network number of 149.108.0.0. Sixteen bits are assignable for this network number, and this gives a total of 2^{16} possible host number combinations. Two to the power of 16 is equal to 65536. Out of 65536 combinations, the pattern consisting of all 1s (broadcast) cannot be used. In addition, the pattern consisting of all 0s (the network itself) should not be used for host number assignments. So, from a total of 65536 host numbers, two host numbers cannot be used, resulting in a total number of 65534 hosts (see table 13.12).

Figure 13.29 shows the network number 149.108.0.0 (called Network 1) connected to the Internet using a router. All traffic for network number 149.108.0.0 is sent to the router for that network. It is possible to have 65534 hosts on the network. If the network is inside a building, probably fewer than 65534 hosts are on the same physical network in the building.

The network does have the capacity, however, to grow up to 65534 hosts, even though this may not be practical.

Figure 13.29

A class B network connected to the Internet.

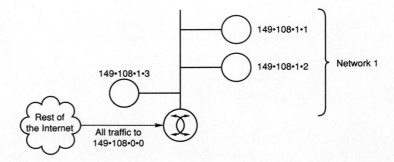

If the organization decides to build a second network, perhaps in a separate building, and to have this network also connected to the Internet, what network number should the organization use? If the network number of 149.108.0.0 also was used for the new second network, then the first and the second networks are the same because the IP router cannot distinguish between these by examining the netid field of the IP address for a host on these networks. A different network number assignment that belongs to class A, B, or C could be used, but this involves applying for a new network number assignment even though many hostid bit patterns on network 1 are not in use and may never be used. A better way would be to use some of the bits in the hostid field for distinguishing between the two networks and leave the rest for the host number assignments. This scheme is called subnetting, and the resulting networks are called subnets. The scheme for subnetting is documented in RFC 950.

Figure 13.30 shows that a second network (Network 2) can be connected to the first network and the rest of the Internet using the same router used in figure 13.29 if it has an extra, unused port. In figure 13.30, the first byte of the hostid field is used to distinguish between the two networks; the bits used to distinguish between the two networks are called subnet numbers. Network 1, therefore, has been given a subnet number value of 1 and network 2 a subnet number value of 2.

Subnetting is a scheme that enables you to break a network into smaller networks using the same network number assignment. The advantages of subnetting include the following:

■ Simplified administration

■ Restructuring of internal networks without affecting external networks

■ Improved security

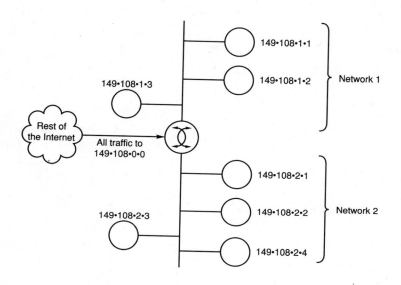

Figure 13.30
*A class B network
connected to the Internet
using subnets.*

Simplified administration results from the capability to use routers to partition networks using logical boundaries. This capability often allows smaller networks to be administered independently and more efficiently. The smaller networks may even be managed by their own independent network administration staff. This type of setup even avoids or eliminates certain types of political problems between department staffs that may want to have greater control over their network.

The use of subnets allows the network to be structured internally without the rest of the connected network being aware of changes in the internal network. In figure 13.30, the internal network has been divided into two subnets, but external traffic coming from the internal network still is sent to the network address 149.108.0.0. It is the responsibility of the router (refer to figure 13.30) that belongs to the organization to make a further distinction between IP addresses belonging to its subnets. An important benefit of the internal network being "invisible" to external networks is that an organization can achieve this internal restructuring without having to obtain an additional network number. With the internetwork running out of network numbers, this "invisibility" is a great advantage.

Because the structure of the internal subnetworks is not visible to external networks, use of subnets results in an indirect improvement in network security.

Figure 13.31 shows the relationship between the different fields of an IP address and subnetworks that have been discussed so far. If the subnets in figure 13.31 are to be connected, routers must be used between them. The routers, furthermore, must understand that subnetting is being used and know how many bits of the hostid field are being used for subnets.

Figure 13.31

Subnets and subnet numbers.

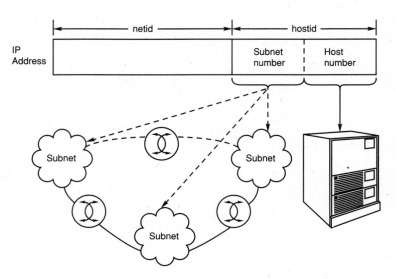

The router in the example of figure 13.30 must be made to understand that the hostid field of the IP address is to be treated specially—a part of it used for the subnet number and the remaining part for the host number. This information typically is represented to the router as the subnet mask.

The subnet mask is used by routers and hosts on a subnet to interpret the hostid field in such a way that they can determine how many bits are being used for subnetting. The subnet mask divides the hostid field into the subnet number and the host number. The subnet mask is a 32-bit number whose value is formed by using the following rules:

■ Ones (1s) in the subnet mask correspond to the position of the netid and subnet number in the IP address.

■ Zeros (0s) in the subnet mask correspond to the position of the host number in the IP address.

Figure 13.32 shows an application of the previously stated rules. This figure shows a class B network number used for subnetting. Eight bits of the hostid field are being used for the subnet number. The resulting subnet mask is also shown in figure 13.32. The subnet mask is a 32-bit pattern and is conventionally written in a dotted decimal notation form. Because a group of eight 1s corresponds to a decimal value of 255, the subnet mask of figure 13.32 can be written in the following manner:

255.255.255.0

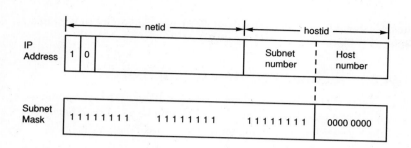

Figure 13.32
Subnet mask representation.

If a subnet mask value of 255.255.0.0 is used for a class B address, the indication is that no subnetting is being used. A class B address has 16 bits of netid field. This netid field is accounted for by the first two 255s (255.255) in the 255.255.0.0 subnet mask value. The remaining value of 0.0 must correspond to the host number. No 1s are in the subnet mask for the subnet number or field, and, therefore, no subnetting is being used.

If the same subnet mask value of 255.255.0.0 is used for a class A address, it indicates that subnetting is being used. A class A address has 8 bits of netid field. This netid field is accounted for by the first 255 in the 255.255.0.0 subnet mask value. The remaining 255 must correspond to the subnet number, which is 8 bits long.

If a subnet mask value of 255.255.255.0 is used for a class C address, this indicates that no subnetting is being used. A class C address has 24 bits of netid field. This netid field is accounted for by the first three 255s (255.255.255) in the 255.255.255.0 subnet mask value. The remaining value of 0 must correspond to the host number. No 1s are in the subnet mask for the subnet number field, and, therefore, no subnetting is being used.

If a subnet mask value of 255.255.0.0 is used for a class C address, this is an illegal value. A class C address has 24 bits of netid field, but the first two 255s in the 255.255.0.0 account for only 16 bits of the netid. At least another 255 are needed to cover the remaining 8 bits of netid.

The subnet mask value usually is required at the time you specify the IP address for a host or router. It can be expressed as the dotted decimal notation value, seen in earlier examples. An alternate form used by some TCP/IP software is a hexadecimal pattern or a dotted hexadecimal notation. A subnet mask of 255.255.255.0, therefore, can also be expressed in the following ways:

FFFFFF00   (hex pattern)

0xFF.0xFF.0xFF.0xFF.0x00   (a dotted hexadecimal notation)

The dotted hexadecimal notation is an alternative form that can be used on some TCP/IP hosts.

The subnet mask usually is stored in an internal database. For Unix systems, it can be stored in /etc/rc.local or /etc/netd.cf files.

Conversion between Decimal and Binary Numbers

As you work through the following examples of subnet masks and IP addresses, you come across situations in which you need to convert between decimal numbers and their binary values. This section is a short tutorial in performing these conversions.

First, examine the problem of converting a binary number to a decimal value. You later learn how to convert a decimal number to its binary form.

Consider an 8-bit binary pattern of 10101000 whose decimal value you need to find to solve an IP address problem. Please note that, because IP addresses are typically represented in a dotted decimal notation in which 8 bits of the IP address are converted to a decimal value, only 8-bit patterns are discussed in this section.

The binary number of 10101000 uses a base 2 system, just as a decimal number such as 143 use a base 10 system.

In a decimal number such as 143, the 1 represents the 100's position; the 4 represents the 10's position; and the 3 represent the 1's position. The digit 1 represents the 100's position because two digits are to the right of it. The two digits to the right of 1 correspond to a magnitude of 10 to the power of 2 (102), or 100. Similarly, the digit 4 in the number 143 represents the 10's position because one digit is to the right of it. The one digit to the right of 4, corresponds to magnitude of 10 to the power of 1, or 10. Finally, the digit 3 in the number 143 represents the 1's position because zero digits are to the right of it.

Now consider again the bit pattern of 10101000. The 1 in the left-most position of this bit pattern has seven bits to the right of it. This 1 must correspond to a magnitude of 2 to the power of 7, or 2^7. The value of 2^7 is 128. You can use table 2.15 to find the decimal value for the powers of 2 up to 7, or you can use a simple mathematics trick to find out the decimal value. 2 can be expressed as a product of 2^3, 2^3, and 2, as shown in the following:

$$2^7 = 2^3 \times 2^3 \times 2^1 = 8 \times 8 \times 2 = 128$$

In the preceding equation, the index 7 has been expressed as the sum of 3 + 3 + 1.

The next 1 in the bit pattern of 10101000 has five bits to the right of it. Its magnitude is 2^5 or 32 (see table 13.14). The remaining 1 in the bit pattern of 10101000, has three bits to the right of it. Its magnitude is 2^3 or 8. You could write the bit pattern of 10101000 in the following form:

$$10101000 = 1 \times 2^7 + 0 \times 2^6 + 1 \times 2^5 + 0 \times 2^4 + 1 \times 2^3 + 0 \times 2^2 + 0 \times 2 + 0 \times 1 = 128 + 32 + 8 = 168$$

Table 13.14
Powers of 2 Table

Power of 2	Decimal value
2^0	1
2^1	2
2^2	4
2^3	8
2^4	16
2^5	32
2^6	64
2^7	128

Now consider the problem of converting the number 145 to a binary 8-bit pattern. One way of performing this conversion is to use entries in table 2.15 and express 145 as the sum of powers of 2. This can be done as follows:

$145 = 128 + 16 + 1 = 2^7 + 2^4 + 2^0$

From the preceding discussion, 2^7 consists of a binary pattern of 1 with seven 0s after it. 2^4 consists of a binary pattern of 1 with four 0s after it. 2^0 consists of a binary pattern of 1 with no 0s after it.

$2^7 = 10000000$

$2^4 = 00010000$

$2^0 = 00000001$

Adding up these bit patterns yields the following answer:

$14 = 128 + 16 = 10000000 + 00010000 + 00000001 = 10010001$ (binary pattern)

You can use table 13.14 to convert base 10 numbers to binary patterns or use an alternate technique, which uses the following rules:

1. Divide the number by 2. Call the quotient (whole number) of the division Q, and the remainder R.

2. Place the remainder R in the binary pattern. The placement of the remainder (0 or a 1 because you are dividing by 2) starts with the right-most position and gradually works its way to the left.

3. Use the quotient Q as the number to divide in step 1. Repeat this process until the quotient becomes a zero.

Apply these rules to convert 145 to a binary pattern:

Round 1:

Divide 145 by 2.

Quotient is 72.

Remainder is 1.

Bit pattern is 1.

Round 2:

Divide 72 by 2.

Quotient is 36.

Remainder is 0.

Bit pattern is 01.

Round 3:

Divide 36 by 2.

Quotient is 18.

Remainder is 0.

Bit pattern is 001.

Round 4:

Divide 18 by 2.

Quotient is 9.

Remainder is 0.

Bit pattern is 0001.

Round 5:

Divide 9 by 2.

Quotient is 4.

Remainder is 1.

Bit pattern is 10001.

Round 6:

Divide 4 by 2.

Quotient is 2.

Remainder is 0.

Bit pattern is 010001.

Round 7:

Divide 2 by 2.

Quotient is 1.

Remainder is 0.

Bit pattern is 0010001.

Round 8:

Divide 1 by 2.

Quotient is 0   (stop the algorithm).

Remainder is 1.

Bit pattern is 10010001.

Because the quotient is a 0, you stop the conversion. The resulting bit pattern of 10010001 is the answer.

Subnet Example Scenario: Using Class B Address with Subnet Mask on a Byte Boundary

Given the following IP address and subnet mask values:

IP address = 128.12.34.71

Subnet Mask = 255.255.255.0

What is the value of the following:

Subnet number = ?

Host number = ?

Directed broadcast address = ?

Examine the subnet mask of 255.255.255.0. You can see that the division of 1s and 0s in the subnet mask fall on a byte boundary. The byte boundary simplifies the calculation.

The IP address 128.12.34.71 is a class B address because 128 is between 128 and 191 (see table 13.14). The first two 255s of the subnet mask of 255.255.255.0 correspond to the 16 bits of a class B netid. The remaining 255 must therefore correspond to the subnet number on the IP address. The subnet number, therefore, is 34. To express this in the dotted decimal notation, you type the following:

Subnet number = 0.0.34.0

The 0 in the subnet mask of 255.255.255.0 corresponds to the host number. The host number in the IP address must be 71. To express this in the dotted decimal notation, you type the following:

Host number = 0.0.0.71

The directed broadcast for the network must have all 1s in the host number field. The last byte of the subnet, therefore, must have all 1s. To express this in the dotted decimal notation, you type the following:

Directed broadcast address = 128.12.34.255

Subnet Example Scenario: Using Class C Address with Subnet Mask on a Non-Byte Boundary

Given the following IP address and subnet mask values:

IP address = 192.55.12.120

Subnet Mask = 255.255.255.240

What is the value of the following:

Subnet number = ?

Host number = ?

Directed broadcast address = ?

When you examine the subnet mask of 255.255.255.240, you can see that the division of 1s and 0s in the subnet mask is in the last byte on a bit boundary. The bit boundary complicates the calculation.

As an aid to computing the desired values, the bit patterns for the various values to be computed are shown in figure 13.33.

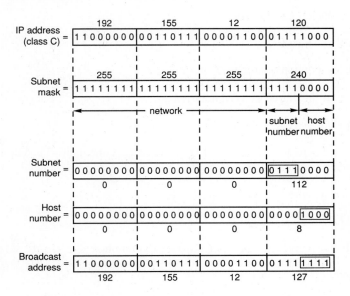

Figure 13.33
Subnet example solution.

The IP address 192.55.12.120 is a class C address because 192 is between 192 and 223 (see table 13.13). The first three 255s of the subnet mask of 255.255.255.240 correspond to the 24 bits of a class C netid. The remaining 240 must, therefore, correspond to the subnet number on the IP address. The decimal value 240 has a bit pattern of 1110000. The following is the subnet mask represented as a bit pattern:

    11111111 11111111 11111111 11110000

The last four 1s correspond to the subnet number field in the IP address. The following is the bit pattern representation of the IP address with the subnet field highlighted in bold:

    11000000 00110111 00001100 **0111**1000

The subnet number field bit pattern of 0111 has a decimal value of 7, but this value is part of the last 8-bit value of the IP address. The subnet number expressed as a bit pattern is:

    00000000 00000000 00000000 01110000

The subnet number expressed in the dotted decimal notation is:

    Subnet number =0.0.0.112

The 0s in the subnet mask of 255.255.255.240 correspond to the host number. The host number in the IP address is shown in bold in the IP address pattern:

11000000 00110111 00001100 0111**1000**

The host number expressed as a bit pattern is:

00000000 00000000 00000000 00001000

The host number expressed in the dotted decimal notation is:

Subnet number = 0.0.0.8

The directed broadcast for the network must have all 1s in the host number field. The last four bits of the subnet, therefore, must have all 1s.

The directed broadcast address expressed as a bit pattern is:

11000000 00110111 00001100 0111**1111**

The directed broadcast address expressed in the dotted decimal notation is:

Directed broadcast address = 192.55.12.127

Non-Byte Boundary Subnet Masks

In the preceding example, a subnet mask of 255.255.255.240 is used. The last decimal number 240 translated into a bit pattern of 11110000. In general, it is useful to know the bit pattern representations when a subnet number field of 1 to 7 bits is used. Table 13.15 shows the decimal subnet size and the decimal values in the subnet mask. The table assumes that the subnet number bits are all contiguous. This normally is true for most real-world networks.

The RFCs do not absolutely prohibit the subnet numbers from being non-contiguous—but they very strongly discourage it. That is, it is at least theoretically possible to have a subnet mask where the subnet number bits and host number bits may alternate! It is possible, for example, to have the following subnet mask for a class B address:

11111111 11111111 **10110101** 0000**1111**

or

255.255.171.15

In this subnet mask, nine subnet number bits (bold in the preceding bit pattern) exist, but they are interspersed with the host number bits.

Even though the RFCs allow such monstrosities for subnet masks, most TCP/IP software does not function with non-contiguous subnet number bits. No useful purpose is served in using such subnet masks, except to confound future network administrators.

Table 13.15
Subnet Size and Decimal Values

Subnet Size (bits)	Bit Pattern	Decimal Value
1	10000000	128
2	11000000	192
3	11100000	224
4	11110000	240
5	11111000	248
6	11111100	252
7	11111110	254

Case Studies about IP Address and Subnet Masks

This section provides the solutions to IP address and subnet mask case studies. The case studies are designed to test your understanding of IP address and subnet masks:

1. What is the network address of a TCP/IP host that has an IP address of 203.23.32.34?

   Answer: 203.23.32

   Reason: The address 203.23.32.34 is a class C address (see table 13.13). For a class C address, the first three bytes are the network address. The first three bytes of 203.23.32.34, therefore, are the network address.

2. What is the node (or host) address of a TCP/IP host that has an IP address of 182.23.32.34?
   Answer: 32.34

   Reason: The address 182.23.32.34 is a class B address (see table 13.13). For a class B address, the first two bytes are the network address, and the last two bytes are the host address. The last two bytes of 182.23.32.34 are, therefore, the node address.

3. What is the subnet mask for 184.231.138.239, if first ten bits of node address is used for subnetting?

   A. 255.255.192.0

   B. 255.255.224.0

   C. 255.255.255.224

   D. 255.255.255.192

Answer: Choice D (255.255.255.192)

Reason: The IP address 184.231.138.239 is a class B address. This means that the first two bytes of 184.231.138.192 are the network address. Its subnet mask must have two bytes of all 1s for the first two bytes of the network address. In addition, because the first 10 bits of the host address (also called node address) are used for subnetting, 10 bits of all 1s must follow the 1s corresponding to the network address field. The subnet mask is, therefore, the following:

11111111 11111111 **11111111 11**000000

The bits in bold in the subnet mask correspond to the subnet number. The dotted decimal value of this subnet mask is as follows:

255.255.255.192

4. Which of the following hosts must use a router to communicate with the host 129.23.144.10 if the subnet mask is 255.255.192.0?

   A. 129.23.191.21

   B. 129.23.127.222

   C. 129.23.130.33

   D. 129.23.148.127

Answer: Choice B (129.23.127.222)

Reason: The subnet mask of 255.255.192.0 translates to a bit pattern of:

11111111 11111111 **11**000000 00000000

The address 129.23.144.10 is a class B address (see table 13.13). The first two bytes of the class B address are the network address. In the subnet mask of 255.255.192.0, the first two bytes cover the network address of the class B address. The last two bytes, 192.0, describe the subnet mask. In the previously stated bit representation of the subnet mask, the subnet bits are shown in bold. The subnet mask 255.255.192.0 has two subnet bits.

The IP address of 123.23.144.10 has a host address (hostid) of 144.10. Because the subnet mask of 255.255.192.0 is used, the first two bits of this host address are the subnet number. If you convert 144.10 to a binary pattern, you have the following:

10010000 00001010

The subnet bits are the first two bits of 10. Hosts that have the bit pattern of 10 in these first two bits of the host address (subnet number) are on the same network and do not require a router to communicate with each other. A host that has a different subnet number (different value from 10 in the first two bits of host address) requires a router to communicate with host 123.23.144.10. The previously stated question becomes one of finding the first 2 bits of the host address for the following:

> 129.23.191.21

> 129.23.127.222

> 129.23.130.33

> 129.23.148.127

The host address of 129.23.191.21 is 191.21, which converts into the following:

- ■ The Bit pattern of 191.21 is 10111111 00010101.

- ■ Subnet bits are 10, which is the same as subnet bits for 123.23.144.10.

The host address of 129.23.127.222 is 127.222, which converts into the following:

- ■ The Bit pattern of 127.222 is 01111111 11011110.

- ■ Subnet bits are 01, different from subnet bits for 123.23.144.10.

The host address of 129.23.130.33 is 130.33, which converts into the following:

- ■ The Bit pattern of 130.33 is 10000010 00100001.

- ■ Subnet bits are 10, which is the same as subnet bits for 123.23.144.10.

The host address of 129.23.148.127 is 148.127, which converts into the following:

- ■ The Bit pattern of 148.127 is 10010100 01111111.

- ■ Subnet bits are 10, which is the same as subnet bits for 123.23.144.10.

The only host with a subnet number different from 123.23.144.10 is 129.23.127.222. The answer to the question, therefore, is the host 129.23.127.222.

You might have observed that only the bit pattern of the third byte was needed because the subnet number was in this byte.

5. Which IP address is located on the same subnet as 130.12.127.231 if the subnet mask is 255.255.192.0?

   A. 130.45.130.1

   B. 130.22.130.1

C. 130.12.64.23

D. 130.12.167.127

Answer: Choice C (130.12.64.23)

Reason: All choices have a class B address, but choice A and B can be eliminated because they have network addresses of 130.45 and 130.22, which are different from the network address of host 130.12.120.231. Because choice A and B have a different network address than 130.12, they cannot be on the same subnetwork.

Choice C and D are on the same class B network because they have the same network address of 130.12, but you are informed that subnetting is in use. These addresses, therefore, could be on different subnets. The subnet mask is 255.255.192.0. This subnet mask has a bit representation of:

11111111 11111111 **11**000000 00000000

The first two bytes of all 1s in the subnet mask correspond to the network address of the class B address. The 1s in the third byte correspond to the subnet number. Only the first two bits of the first byte host address (hostid) are used as a subnet number. Because of this, you need only examine the third byte of the IP address to answer the question.

The subnet number of IP address 130.12.127.231 is in the third byte. The third byte, which has a value of 127 has a bit pattern of:

01111111

The subnet number is the first two bits and has a value of 01.

The third byte of IP address 130.12.64.23 is 64. This byte has a bit pattern of:

01000000

The subnet number is the first two bits and has a value of 01.

The third byte of IP address 130.12.167.63 is 167. This byte has a bit pattern of:

10100111

The subnet number is the first two bits and has a value of 10.

Only the IP address 130.12.64.23 has the same subnet number as the IP address 130.12.127.231, and, therefore, the answer is 130.12.64.23.

Using Different Subnet Masks for a Network

In the examples covered so far, the same subnet mask was used for a given network. For a network address of 134.65.0.0, a class B address, the subnet mask could be 255.255.255.0, which means that eight bits of the host address field are used for subnetting. TCP/IP enables you to use different subnet masks for the same network address of 134.65.0.0. A subdivided network of the network 134.65.0.0, for example, could use a subnet mask of 255.255.255.192, whereas another uses a subnet mask of 255.255.255.0. When different subnet masks are used, restrictions apply on what combinations of host IP addresses and subnet masks can be used. Setting up such subnet masks requires advanced knowledge and skill in bit manipulation and is beyond the scope of this book.

The current RIP (Routing Information Protocol) algorithm used on many TCP/IP networks does not handle a mix of different subnet masks for the same network address. As a result of this RIP limitation, the network topology reported by RIP does not accurately reflect the network topology that you have set up.

Need for Address Resolution

The DNS is used to provide an association between symbolic names for host and the IP address. Knowing the symbolic name, a host can discover the corresponding IP address. To transmit a message to a host on a network with a broadcast capability, such as in Ethernet and token ring, the sender must know the hardware address of the destination host. The hardware address, also called the MAC—Media Access Control address, is needed in the MAC header of the packet used to send a message. The host software knows the IP address of the destination by using DNS or a table lookup. Figure 13.34 shows the problem of determining the hardware address of the destination host.

Determining MAC Address

One method of solving the problem of determining a remote host's MAC address is to use a table of IP address and MAC address associations similar to the hosts file table discussed earlier. The problem with this approach is that if a network board is replaced on a host, the MAC address probably changes, and this table must be updated. If the network board is changed by a technician, it is unlikely that he or she informs the administrator of this change immediately.

A more flexible scheme is needed to dynamically determine the MAC address knowing a host's IP address. This dynamic mechanism is implemented as a separate protocol called the Address Resolution Protocol.

Address Resolution Protocol (ARP)

Figure 13.35 shows how ARP works. In this figure, Host A wants to determine the hardware address of destination B before it sends a message.

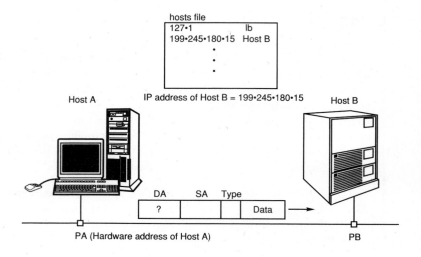

Figure 13.34
Need for address resolution.

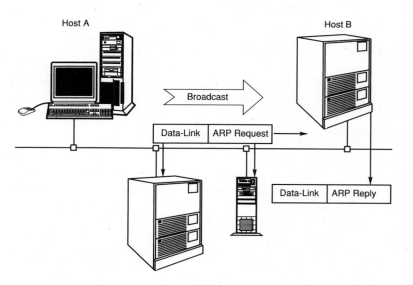

Figure 13.35
ARP Operation.

Host A sends a MAC broadcast frame called the ARP request frame on the network. The ARP request frame contains the sender Host A's IP and MAC address and the destination B's IP address. The ARP request frame contains a place-holder field for destination B's hardware address. All nodes on the physical network receive the broadcast ARP request frame. All other nodes that receive the broadcast frame compare its IP address to the IP address in the ARP request. Only the host that has the same IP address as the one requested in the ARP request frame responds.

If Host B exists on the network, it responds with its IP address encoded in an ARP reply frame. The Host A initializes its ARP cache table (kept in RAM) with the answer contained in the ARP reply. The ARP cache entries are timed out after a certain period, which can be configured in some TCP/IP implementations. The ARP typical cache time-out is 10 minutes. After an ARP cache entry has timed-out for a specific host, the ARP request frame is sent again to discover the host's hardware address.

Many TCP/IP implementations enable you to make manual entries in the ARP cache table. No need normally exists to make manual entries in the ARP table; the dynamic ARP operation determines the IP address and hardware associations. ARP entries made manually are not timed out and can be used to fix problems with incorrect entries in the ARP table because of duplicate IP address problems or malfunctioning software.

The assumption in the operation of the ARP protocol is that the underlying physical network supports a broadcast capability. This assumption proves true in LANs such as Ethernet, token ring, FDDI, and ARCnet.

Other related address resolution protocols, besides the ARP protocol, are RARP (Reverse Address Resolution Protocol) and Proxy ARP.

RARP is used to discover the IP address, when the hardware address is known, and can be used in diskless workstations. RARP is described in RFC 903.

Proxy ARP can be used in networks that use old TCP/IP software that does not understand subnetting. Proxy ARP is described in RFC 1027.

Conclusion

This chapter explored the TCP/IP layering concepts in terms of the DoD model. The DoD model is useful as an aid to understanding how TCP/IP components interact with each other. The different classes of IP address were explained, and you learned how IP networks can be divided into smaller networks called subnets. Most large networks use subnets, and it is important for administrators of these networks to understand when subnets are needed and how to use subnet masks to describe subnetting.

Installing and Configuring the TCP/IP Protocol Stack

The previous chapter introduced you to the theory of TCP/IP protocols and services as it applies to Windows NT Server. This chapter discusses the installation and configuration of the Windows NT TCP/IP transport protocol stack.

You also learn to configure the TCP/IP stack to make use of name services and configure SNMP services and host files. You learn to configure and use FTP services on a Windows NT Server, configure TCP/IP print services, and use the command line TCP/IQ2 tools that come with Windows NT Server.

The actual configuration of specialized servers, such as the DHCP and name servers, is discussed in later chapters.

Installing and Configuring TCP/IP Services

A Windows NT Server 4 installation automatically includes the TCP/IP protocol stack if you choose to install any network services. This section discusses the procedures for installing and configuring the Windows NT TCP/IP protocol stack. You will only have to install the TCP/IP protocol stack manually if you have previously removed it but now need to add support for TCP/IP services.

1. Log on to the Windows NT Server as an Administrator user.

2. Double-click the Network icon in the Control Panel. The Network dialog box appears (see fig. 14.1). Select the Protocols Tab.

Figure 14.1

The Network dialog box.

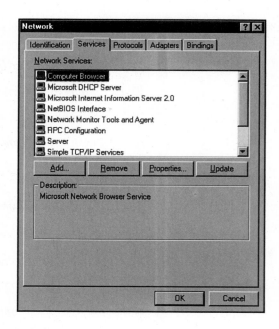

3. If you are reinstalling the TCP/IP protocol stack, click the **A**dd button. You should see a list of protocols you can add (see fig. 14.2).

4. Select TCP/IP Protocol and then choose OK.

    A Windows NT TCP/IP Installation Options dialog box appears and asks if you want to obtain an IP address from a DHCP server on your network or if you want to manually configure the IP address. If you choose **O**btain an IP Address from a DHCP Server, the

Windows NT TCP/IP stack requests its IP address from a DHCP server when it initializes. Make sure that all the other TCP/IP configuration entries are empty, otherwise they will override the parameters assigned by the DHCP server.

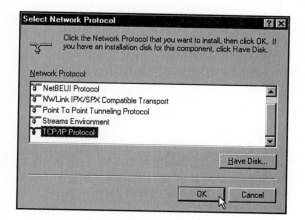

Figure 14.2

The Select Network Protocol list.

5. If you have a DHCP server on your network, choose **Y**es; otherwise, select **N**o.

   You see a dialog box prompting you for the path of the distribution files. If you have a CD-ROM on the Windows NT Server, the path contains the path to the CD-ROM distribution files. If the Windows NT Server distribution files are not in the path displayed, enter their drive and directory.

6. Choose Continue.

   You see a status of the copy operation as files are copied.

7. The Configuring Network status screen appears as the setup program performs binding analysis and configuration.

The TCP/IP protocol is now installed. Your next step is to configure the TCP/IP settings.

Configuring the IP Address Tab

If you're not using DHCP to assign a TCP/IP address to the Windows NT Server dynamically, the Microsoft TCP/IP Properties dialog box appears (see fig. 14.3). In this dialog box, you specify the **I**P Address, S**u**bnet Mask, and Default **G**ateway address of the network interface.

1. If a DHCP server already is on the network and you want to use it to configure the Windows NT computer, you should choose the **O**btain an IP address from a DHCP server option. A DHCP server contains TCP/IP configuration information for other TCP/IP hosts. When a TCP/IP host starts, it requests its configuration information from the DHCP server.

Figure 14.3

The Microsoft TCP/IP Properties dialog box.

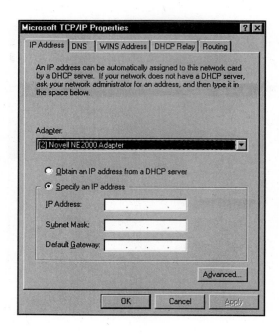

If you have enabled the **O**btain an IP address from a DHCP server radio button, the Windows NT computer will obtain the IP address and subnet mask values from the DHCP server. If you enter values for the IP address and subnet mask, the entered values override any information from the DHCP server. You might want to override the default DHCP configuration for troubleshooting purposes. The message shown in figure 14.4 warns you of the consequences of setting the IP address and subnet mask when DHCP is enabled.

Figure 14.4

The message informing you of consequences of setting IP address and subnet mask when DHCP is enabled.

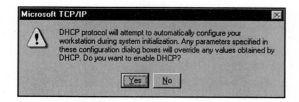

2. If no DHCP server is yet on the network, or if you are installing the Windows NT Server for use as a DHCP server, you must set the IP address and subnet mask manually. Enter the IP address and subnet mask for the Windows NT Server's network interface in figure 14.3.

3. If your network is connected to other TCP/IP networks or subnetworks, you must specify a value for the Default **G**ateway fields so that you can reach the other networks. TCP/IP recognizes whether the destination address is on another network and forwards the packet to the default gateway (or default router, correctly speaking).

4. If you have multiple network adapters, each must be configured individually. Specify the IP address configuration (IP address, subnet mask, default gateway, use of DHCP server) for each adapter bound to the TCP/IP protocol by selecting the network cards in the Ada**p**ter field one at a time.

   Each network adapter must have a unique IP address, even if the adapter is in the same Windows NT computer.

5. Click the A**d**vanced button if you want to configure multiple IP addresses for a single network adapter, multiple default gateways for a network adapter, security options, or the Point to Point Tunneling Protocol. Select the network adapter to configure from the Ada**p**ter field in the Advanced IP Addressing dialog box (see fig. 14.5). Note that the IP configuration settings in this dialog box apply only to the selected network adapter.

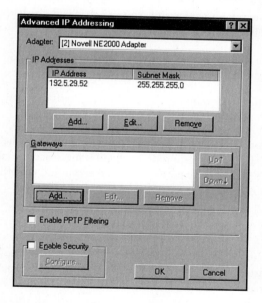

Figure 14.5

The Advanced IP Addressing dialog box.

6. You can enter multiple IP addresses and subnet masks for the selected adapter by entering the IP address and subnet mask values in the IP Address and Subnet Mask boxes and clicking the **A**dd button.

   Multiple IP addresses and subnet masks are particularly useful when you want a single physical system to look like several systems. The mail server might be x.1, for example, the DNS server x.2, the ftp server x.3, and so on. Also, multiple IP addresses and subnet masks can help during transition to a different IP network number assignment for the network. You also can use multiple IP addresses if your network consists of multiple logical IP networks. During the transition phase, it is useful to have both IP network numbers be applicable. You can specify up to five additional IP addresses and subnet masks for a selected network adapter through this dialog box. If you need more than six IP addresses for a single interface, you can add more addresses by editing the registry directly.

To remove an IP address and subnet mask combination, highlight it and choose the Remove button.

7. If you need to specify alternative default gateways, you can enter the IP addresses of the default gateways in the **G**ateways field and choose the corresponding A**dd** button.

   The default gateway field is the IP address of a router on the local network. When a packet is sent to an IP address that is not on the local network and not specified in the local routing table at the Windows NT computer, the default gateway is used. If you have specified multiple default gateways, they are tried in the order in which they are listed if an attempt to use a default gateway is unsuccessful. You can change the order in which the default gateways are tried by selecting a gateway's address and moving it by using the **U**p or D**o**wn buttons.

   To remove a gateway, highlight it and choose the Re**m**ove button.

8. You may enable PPTP filtering by checking the Enable PPTP **F**iltering option.

9. You can enable and configure security on each adapter. Check the E**n**able Security box and click the **C**onfigure button. The TCP/IP Security dialog box appears. The security options act as a type of filter. This may be appropriate if you want to accept only traffic for some well-defined services with specific port numbers. You can find the official port and protocol numbers in the Assigned Numbers RFC, RFC 1700.

Configuring the DNS Tab

If you want to use DNS for host name resolution on Windows networks, select the DNS tab from the Microsoft TCP/IP Properties dialog box. DNS is the most commonly used name resolution method on the Internet and other Unix-based networks. If you enable DNS name resolution, you must have a DNS server that the Windows NT computer can contact, or have the Windows NT computer configured as a DNS server. The Windows NT computer needs to know the IP address of the DNS server. The IP address of the DNS server is specified in the TCP/IP DNS tab. This section discusses the DNS client software.

When accessing other TCP/IP hosts on the network, you can use their IP addresses. Users typically find it easier to remember and use symbolic names for computers rather than IP addresses. This is why the computer names usually are used for Windows NT computers rather than just IP addresses. The Domain Name System (DNS) is used for naming TCP/IP nodes, such as Windows NT computers and Unix hosts. The naming scheme is hierarchical and consists of names such as wks1.kinetics.com or wks2.cello.org. DNS is the most widely used name service for Unix hosts and on the Internet. If you plan on using your Windows NT computer on a Unix network or the Internet, you should configure your Windows NT computer to use DNS. TCP/IP applications written to use the Windows Sockets API, such as Internet Explorer, FTP, and TELNET use DNS or the local HOSTS file to resolve symbolic names.

When the TCP/IP connectivity components are installed on a Windows NT computer, the DNS client software for resolving DNS names also is installed. The DNS client software is in addition to the dynamic name resolution used for resolving NetBIOS computer names through WINS servers and NetBIOS over TCP/IP. When you configure DNS on a Windows NT computer, it applies to all network adapters installed on a computer.

The following steps outline the procedure to follow to configure your Windows NT computer to use DNS client software:

1. The **H**ost Name field in the DNS tab in the Microsoft TCP/IP Properties dialog box is where you enter the TCP/IP host name of the computer (see fig. 14.6). You usually just use the same name as the computer name. If you want to use another TCP/IP host name, you can enter the name in the **H**ost Name field without affecting the computer name. The host name can be any combination of A to Z letters, 0 to 9 digits, and the hyphen (-), plus the period (.) character used as a separator.

    Host name to IP address mappings are stored on DNS servers. The Berkeley r* utilities, such as rcp, rsh, rexec, and so on, use the host names for authentication.

Note In host names, you cannot use some characters that you can use in Windows NT computer names, particularly the underscore. If you are connected to the Internet, you probably should use DNS-compatible names so that both naming systems can use the same names for the same computers.

2. You can enter an optional domain name in the D**o**main field (see fig. 14.6). If, for example, the host name is NTWS1 in the domain name KINETICS.COM, you should enter the name KINETICS.COM in the D**o**main field. A DNS domain differs from a Windows NT or LAN Manager domain. Windows NT domains and LAN Manager domains are proprietary in nature, whereas DNS domains are universal and also apply to non-Microsoft products.

Note The domain name is optional, because a small organization not connected to the Internet doesn't need to use hierarchical domain names. The domain name is combined with the host name to create a fully qualified domain name (FQDN) for the computer.

FQDN = host name + domain name

In the previous example, the FQDN for host NTWS1 is the following:

continues

FQDN = NTWS1 + KINETICS.COM = NTWS1.KINETICS.COM

When the Windows NT computer uses a DNS query to resolve a name that is a simple host name without the domain extension, the domain name specified in the Domain Name field is appended to the host name.

The domain name can be any combination of A to Z letters, 0 to 9 digits, and the hyphen (-), using the period (.) character as a separator.

Figure 14.6
The DNS tab.

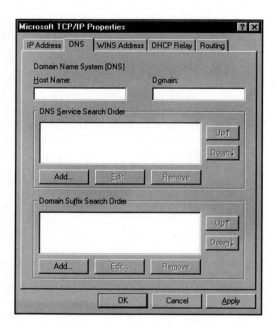

3. You can use the Domain Suffix Search Order box (refer to figure 14.6), to enter the IP address of the DNS servers that are used for domain name resolution. After you enter the IP address of the DNS server in the field, choose the Add button to move the IP address to the list of IP addresses for the DNS servers.

    You can specify up to three IP addresses for DNS servers. The DNS servers that you specify are queried in the order they are listed. You can change the order in which the DNS servers are searched by highlighting the IP address of a DNS server and using the Up and Down buttons to move it within the list.

    To remove a DNS server from the list, highlight its IP address and choose the Remove button.

4. In the Domain Suffix Search Order box (refer to figure 14.6), enter the domain suffixes that are appended to host names during domain name resolution.

You can add up to six domain suffixes. If you need to change the search order of the domain suffixes, highlight the domain name and use the up and down buttons to move the domain name.

To remove a domain name, highlight it in the Domain Suffix Search Order list and choose the Remove button.

Figure 14.7 shows a sample DNS configuration for the host NTKS. The local domain name is KINETICS.COM. The DNS servers are 199.245.180.10 and 199.245.180.16. First, the DNS server with IP address 199.245.180.10 is used to resolve a name. If this server can't resolve the name to its IP address, then the DNS server at 199.245.180.16 is used. The domain suffix search order is SCS.COM and LTREE.COM.

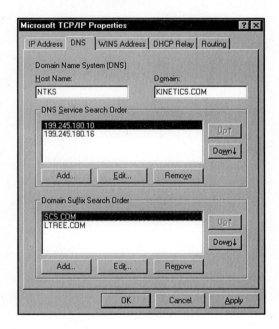

Figure 14.7
A sample DNS configuration.

5. Choose OK after you set the DNS configuration options.

Configuring the WINS Address Tab

If you have WINS (Windows Name Services) servers installed on the network, you can use WINS servers in combination with name query broadcasts to resolve computer names.

If you are not using the WINS server, the Windows NT computer uses name query broadcasts and the local LMHOSTS file to resolve computer names to IP addresses. Broadcast resolution is confined to the local network.

The name query broadcasts use the b-mode for NetBIOS over TCP/IP and are discussed in greater detail in Chapter 16, "TCP/IP Name Resolution Using WINS."

1. To specify that you are using WINS servers, enter the IP addresses of the primary and secondary WINS servers (see fig. 14.8). The secondary WINS server is used as a backup in case the primary WINS server cannot respond.

Figure 14.8

The WINS Address tab.

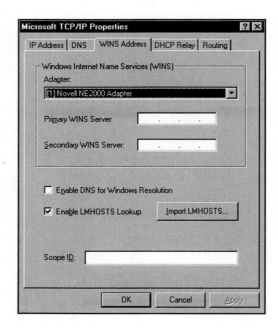

If a computer is configured to use DHCP, name resolution using WINS is automatically enabled and configured for that computer.

If the computer being configured is a WINS server, then the computer automatically uses WINS to resolve computer names, regardless of how you configure name resolution for the local computer.

2. You can enable the Enable DNS for Windows Resolution check box to do just what it sounds like.

3. You can use the local file LMHOSTS for resolving NetBIOS computer names on Windows networks. If you want to use the LMHOSTS file, enable the Enable LMHOSTS Lookup check box. You can import computer names and IP addresses from an existing LMHOSTS file by clicking the Import LMHOSTS button and specifying the directory path for the LMHOSTS file. You can use the Import LMHOSTS option when you have already created an LMHOSTS file for the computer names on your network and want to use the information in this file for all computers on the network.

By default, the LMHOSTS file is found in the \%*SystemRoot*%\SYSTEM32\DRIVERS\ ETC directory. If you are using a WINS server, the LMHOSTS file is consulted last after trying the WINS server. Using LMHOSTS files works well for Windows networks that have a small number of computers and for networks that do not experience many changes, but using LMHOSTS files is problematic for larger, more dynamic networks. Keeping all the different computers' LMHOSTS files in sync becomes highly difficult on a larger network, and creating situations in which two computers (even ones sitting next to each other) may have different views of the network becomes all too easy.

4. You use the Scope I**D** field to specify the computer's scope identifier on a network that uses NetBIOS over TCP/IP. You use scope IDs only for NetBIOS over TCP/IP. Computers using NetBIOS over TCP/IP to talk to each other must have the same scope ID. By default, this field is left blank. If this field is left blank, the computers have the same Scope ID by default. If you want to set up groups of Windows NT computers that can only communicate among themselves using NetBIOS over TCP/IP, then you can have different Scope IDs for different groups.

Configuring the DHCP Relay Tab

If you want to set up your Windows NT computer to relay BOOTP and DHCP messages to a server on a different network or subnet, you can enable this option from the DHCP Relay tab (see fig.14.9).

1. The seconds threshold is based on the number of seconds since the client was initialized. If the secs field in the DHCP request is larger than this setting, the DHCP relay agent cannot forward the packet. Set the **S**econds threshold. The default is 4 seconds, which works in most environments.

2. Set the Ma**x**imum hops. This is the total number of DHCP relay hops a DHCP request can cross. If the NT server receives a DHCP request packet that has reached the maximum number of hops, it cannot forward the request. You can use this setting to expire packets caught in a loop between two DHCP relays.

3. Type the IP addresses of the DHCP servers and choose the A**d**d button. You will need to configure a DHCP relay agent if you are using DHCP and not all the DHCP clients are on the same subnet as a DHCP server.

Configuring the Routing Tab

You can use a Windows NT Workstation or Windows NT Server as a simple IP router (see fig. 14.10). Such a router routes only between two IP subnetworks. The Windows NT IP router understands only static routes, unless you install the RIP for Internet protocol service.

Figure 14.9
The DHCP Relay tab.

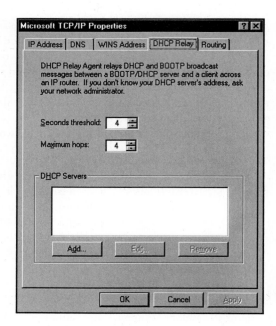

Figure 14.10
Windows NT as a simple IP router.

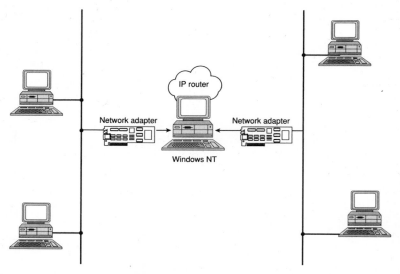

The E**n**able IP Routing option in the Routing tab enables the Windows NT computer to participate in routing on a network. This option does not turn the Windows NT Server into a general-
purpose dynamic router. It enables the Windows NT Server to perform static IP routing, but does
not enable any form of dynamic routing. In dynamic routing, routers exchange information about
the networks and routes they know about, but in static routing the routers are silent and know
only about the networks they have been connected to or otherwise configured to know about.

If your Windows NT Server has more than one network interface and you want the system to perform static routing, be sure to enable the E**n**able IP Routing option. If you have the Windows NT Server connected to multiple different networks but have chosen not to have the Windows NT Server route between them, be sure to disable this option. You might want to disable routing when connected to multiple networks if the Windows NT Server is performing an important function (such as a web server) and you do not want it to use CPU cycles to deal with other tasks that you already have other systems dedicated to performing.

The Enable IP Routing option is not available if your Windows NT Server has only one network adapter and one IP address. To configure the Windows NT computer as a simple IP router, you must have at least two network adapters, such as Ethernet, Token Ring, or FDDI adapters, installed in the Windows NT computer.

The SLIP/PPP connection does not count as a network interface for the purpose of enabling IP routing. If you need to enable IP routing with a SLIP/PPP connection, specify a second IP address for your network interface which then allows you to access the Enable IP Routing option.

1. To enable simple IP routing, check the E**n**able IP Routing check box in the Routing tab.

2. Choose OK after you set the TCP/IP properties.

3. When the Network Protocols dialog box reappears, choose Close.

4. When the Network Settings Change dialog box reappears, choose **Y**es to complete the TCP/IP configuration, to restart the computer so the changes can take effect.

SNMP Support for Windows NT

The Simple Network Management Protocol (SNMP) is a general purpose method of managing remote devices on the network. SNMP can be used to manage TCP/IP hosts and devices which have SNMP agents running in them. While SNMP has its origins on TCP/IP networks, it has been adapted for use over IPX, DecNET and OSI protocols.

An SNMP manager station is used to poll the SNMP agents to obtain information on the devices (see fig. 14.11). A value on a device that the SNMP agent can access or modify is described by an SNMP object. The SNMP manager also can modify the values of SNMP objects if such an operation is permitted by the SNMP agent. When an exceptional condition is detected by an SNMP agent in the device that it is monitoring, it sends a special alert message to the SNMP Manager called a trap message. The application layer protocol that is used for the transmission of management related information is the Simple Network Management Protocol itself.

The sets of SNMP objects comprise a logical database called the Management Information Base (MIB). The SNMP objects in the MIB are also sometimes called MIB objects. MIB objects are described using a special language that is a subset of the Abstract Syntax Notation, version 1 (ASN.1). MIB descriptions written using ASN.1 can be read by most commercial SNMP managers such as Hewlett Packard's OpenView. This enables SNMP manager devices to manage new devices.

Figure 14.11

SNMP management.

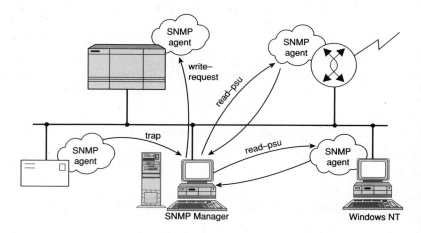

Windows NT computers include support for SNMP and define MIB objects for Windows NT, DHCP, and WINS servers. The following sections discuss installation and configuration of basic SNMP services.

Installing SNMP on Windows NT

You install the SNMP service by adding the SNMP Service option in the Windows NT Network Services dialog box.

The following is an outline of the procedure for installing SNMP on Windows NT if you have not installed it on the computer. To install SNMP, you must have the TCP/IP protocol installed.

1. Log on to the Windows NT Server as an administrator user.

2. Double-click the Network icon in the Control Panel.

3. Choose the Services tab from the Network dialog box.

4. Choose the **A**dd button.

5. Highlight the SNMP Service option and choose OK (see fig. 14.12).

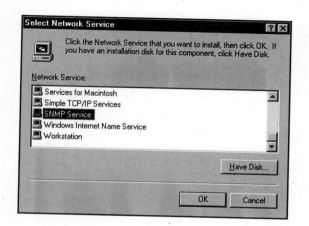

Figure 14.12
*The Select Network Service
list for installing SNMP.*

You should see a dialog box prompting you for the path of the distribution files. If you have a CD-ROM on the Windows NT Server, the path contains the path to the CD-ROM distribution files.

6. Ensure that you have the appropriate distribution media in the install device and choose Continue.

   You should see a status of the copy operation as files are copied.

7. At the end of the file copy, the SNMP Service Properties dialog box appears.

The following sections discuss configuring various SNMP properties.

Configuring the SNMP Agent

All SNMP devices have MIB values for information on the contact, location, and type of service. You can specify these values by configuring the SNMP agent running on the Windows NT computer.

The following is an outline of the procedure for configuring SNMP agents in Windows NT:

1. Log on to the Windows NT Server as an administrator user.

2. Double-click the Network icon in the Control Panel.

3. Go to the Services tab. Select SNMP Service in the Network Services list box, and then click on the **P**roperties button. The SNMP Service Configuration dialog box appears.

4. Choose the Agent tab in the SNMP Properties dialog box (see fig. 14.13).

Figure 14.13

The Agent tab.

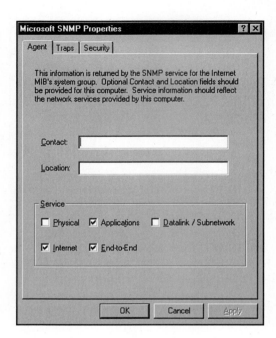

5. In the **C**ontact field, enter the name of the person or organization responsible for the Windows NT computer.

6. In the **L**ocation field, enter the location of the Windows NT computer.

7. In the **S**ervice box, select all options that apply to the Windows NT computer.

   ■ Choose the **P**hysical option if the Windows NT computer manages a physical device, such as a repeater.

   ■ Choose the Applica**t**ions option if the Windows NT computer runs TCP/IP applications, such as FTP. This option should be selected for all Windows NT computers.

   ■ Enable the **D**atalink/Subnetwork option if the Windows NT computer manages a datalink device, such as a bridge, or a TCP/IP subnetwork.

   ■ Select the **I**nternet option if the Windows NT computer acts as a router (also called IP gateway).

   ■ Check the **E**nd-to-End option if the Windows NT computer acts as a host (called end-system in the OSI model). This option should be selected for all Windows NT computers.

8. Choose OK. The SNMP Service Properties dialog box reappears.

9. You can choose OK again on successive screens to complete the SNMP service configuration, or go on to the next tab, Traps.

Configuring SNMP Traps

1. Log on to the Windows NT Server as an administrator user.

2. Double-click the Network icon in the Control Panel.

3. Go to the Services tab. Select SNMP Service in the Network Services list box, and then choose the **P**roperties button to open the SNMP Service Properties dialog box.

4. Select the SNMP Properties Traps tab, which identifies the communities and trap destinations.

   Community names are used for authentication purposes. An SNMP agent only responds to an SNMP command if the command includes a community name of which it is aware. In other words, the community name acts as a simple password scheme.

   When the Windows NT SNMP service receives a request for information that does not contain a valid community name and does not match an accepted host name for the service, the SNMP service sends an authentication-failure trap message to the trap destinations for the community name.

   To add community names that the Windows NT computer knows about, enter the community name in the C**o**mmunity Names field and choose the **A**dd button. When the Windows NT computer sends trap messages, it includes the community name in the SNMP packet when the trap is sent. To delete a community name, highlight it and choose the **R**emove button.

   You can use any alphanumeric characters for community names. Community names are case-sensitive. All hosts typically belong to the community name public, which is the standard name for the common community of all hosts.

5. In the **T**rap destination box, you enter the trap destinations for a selected community name that receives trap messages. Trap destinations are specified by listing the IP address of hosts (usually SNMP Managers) that receive the trap messages by the SNMP service running on the Windows NT computer.

   To enter trap destinations, highlight the community name to which you want the Windows NT computer to send traps. Next, enter the IP address or IPX address of the host in the IP Host/Address Or IPX Address field. Choose the **A**dd button to add to the list of trap destinations. To delete a trap destination from the list, highlight it and choose the **R**emove button.

Configuring SNMP Security

Windows NT SNMP Services enables you to specify the community names and hosts the Windows NT computer will accept requests from. You also can specify whether to send an authentication trap when the Windows NT computer receives an unauthorized community in an SNMP command.

The following is an outline of the procedure for configuring SNMP security on Windows NT:

1. Log on to the Windows NT Server as an administrator user.

2. Double-click the Network icon in the Control Panel.

3. Go to the Services tab. Select SNMP Service in the Network Services list box, and then choose the Properties button.

   The SNMP Service Properties dialog box appears.

4. Choose the Security tab in the Microsoft SNMP Properties dialog box (see fig. 14.14).

Figure 14.14

The Microsoft SNMP Properties Security tab.

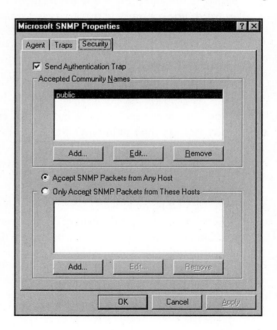

5. If you want to enable the sending of SNMP trap messages for unsuccessful authentications, set the Send Authentication Trap option (refer to figure 14.14); otherwise, clear the check box for this option. The default is to send authentication trap messages on unsuccessful authentication attempts.

6. In the Accepted Community **N**ames list, enter the community names from whom the Windows NT computer accepts requests. By default, requests that have the community name public are always accepted, which is why you see the community name public already listed in figure 14.14. To add additional community names, enter the community name in the Accepted Community **N**ames field, and click the Add button. To remove a community name from the Accepted Community **N**ames list, highlight it and choose the **R**emove button.

7. You can select an option to accept SNMP packets from any host or only from specified hosts.

   If the A**c**cept SNMP Packets from Any Host option is selected, SNMP packets are not rejected on the basis of their address. This option is selected by default.

   If the Only Acce**p**t SNMP Packets from These Hosts option is selected, SNMP packets are filtered based on their source address. Only those SNMP packets that are from the hosts listed are accepted; all other SNMP packets are rejected. In the Only Acce**p**t SNMP Packets from These Hosts box, enter the host name, IP or IPX address, of the hosts from which the Windows NT computer accepts SNMP requests. Next, choose the Add button to add to the list of accepted hosts. To delete an entry in the host list, highlight it and choose the Re**m**ove button.

8. Choose OK. The SNMP Service Configuration dialog box reappears.

9. Choose OK again on successive screens to complete the SNMP Service Configuration.

10. It is necessary to reboot the computer in order to make the changes effective.

Configuring the LMHOSTS File

On small Windows NT networks that use NetBIOS over TCP/IP, the name resolution for computer names typically is provided by the LMHOSTS file. If you have WINS servers on the networks, it is not necessary to use the LMHOSTS file, except as a backup. Use of the LMHOSTS file relies on broadcasts for name resolution, whereas WINS does not rely on broadcasts. Use of LMHOSTS, consequently, is adequate for small networks where broadcast network traffic usually is not a major concern. On larger networks, broadcast network traffic can consume a substantial amount of available network bandwidth and generally is avoided by the network designer.

Understanding the Syntax of the LMHOSTS File

The LMHOSTS file contains mappings between Windows NT NetBIOS computer names and their IP addresses. The file is located in the \%*SystemRoot*%\SYSTEM32\DRIVERS\ETC directory and is compatible with the LMHOSTS file syntax used in MS LAN Manger 2.*x*.

The following is a sample Windows NT LMHOSTS file that is installed on Windows NT computers:

```
# Copyright (c) 1993-1995 Microsoft Corp.
#
# This is a sample LMHOSTS file used by the Microsoft TCP/IP for Windows
# NT.
#
# This file contains the mappings of IP addresses to NT computernames
# (NetBIOS) names.  Each entry should be kept on an individual line.
# The IP address should be placed in the first column followed by the
# corresponding computername. The address and the computername
# should be separated by at least one space or tab. The "#" character
# is generally used to denote the start of a comment (see the exceptions
# below).
#
# This file is compatible with Microsoft LAN Manager 2.x TCP/IP lmhosts
# files and offers the following extensions:
#
#      #PRE
#      #DOM:<domain>
#      #INCLUDE <filename>
#      #BEGIN_ALTERNATE
#      #END_ALTERNATE
#      \0xnn (non-printing character support)
#
# Following any entry in the file with the characters "#PRE" will cause
# the entry to be preloaded into the name cache. By default, entries are
# not preloaded, but are parsed only after dynamic name resolution fails.
#
# Following an entry with the "#DOM:<domain>" tag will associate the
# entry with the domain specified by <domain>. This affects how the
# browser and logon services behave in TCP/IP environments. To preload
# the host name associated with #DOM entry, it is necessary to also add a
# #PRE to the line. The <domain> is always preloaded although it will not
# be shown when the name cache is viewed.
#
# Specifying "#INCLUDE <filename>" will force the RFC NetBIOS (NBT)
# software to seek the specified <filename> and parse it as if it were
# local. <filename> is generally a UNC-based name, allowing a
# centralized lmhosts file to be maintained on a server.
# It is ALWAYS necessary to provide a mapping for the IP address of the
# server prior to the #INCLUDE. This mapping must use the #PRE directive.
# In addition the share "public" in the example below must be in the
# LanManServer list of "NullSessionShares" in order for client machines to
# be able to read the lmhosts file successfully. This key is under \machine\
# system\currentcontrolset\services\lanmanserver\parameters\nullsessionshares
# in the registry. Simply add "public" to the list found there.
#
# The #BEGIN_ and #END_ALTERNATE keywords allow multiple #INCLUDE
# statements to be grouped together. Any single successful include
# will cause the group to succeed.
```

```
#
# Finally, non-printing characters can be embedded in mappings by
# first surrounding the NetBIOS name in quotations, then using the
# \0xnn notation to specify a hex value for a non-printing character.
#
# The following example illustrates all of these extensions:
#
# 102.54.94.97      rhino          #PRE #DOM:networking  #net group's DC
# 102.54.94.102     "appname  \0x14"                     #special app server
# 102.54.94.123     popular        #PRE                  #source server
# 102.54.94.117     localsrv       #PRE                  #needed for the include
#
# #BEGIN_ALTERNATE
# #INCLUDE \\localsrv\public\lmhosts
# #INCLUDE \\rhino\public\lmhosts
# #END_ALTERNATE
#
# In the above example, the "appname" server contains a special
# character in its name, the "popular" and "localsrv" server names are
# preloaded, and the "rhino" server name is specified so it can be used
# to later #INCLUDE a centrally maintained lmhosts file if the "localsrv"
# system is unavailable.
#
# Note that the whole file is parsed including comments on each lookup,
# so keeping the number of comments to a minimum will improve performance.
# Therefore it is not advisable to simply add lmhosts file entries onto the
# end of this file.
```

Comments are preceded with the # character. If the first several characters following # match any of the keywords explained in table 14.1, they are treated as commands to perform special processing. Because the keywords are preceded with the comment character, the contents of the files are compatible with the syntax used by the HOSTS file. The HOSTS file is used by Windows Socket applications and Unix applications.

Table 14.1
LMHOSTS Keywords

Keyword	Description
#PRE	This keyword is added after an entry in the LMHOSTS to preload the entry into the name cache. Entries that do not have a #PRE keyword are not preloaded into the name cache and are parsed only after WINS and name query broadcasts fail to resolve a name. You must preload entries that are added using the #INCLUDE statement. #PRE, therefore, must be appended for entries in the files referenced in #INCLUDE statements; otherwise, the entry is ignored.

continues

Table 14.1, Continued
LMHOSTS Keywords

Keyword	Description
#DOM: *domain_name*	This keyword is used to identify that the computer name is that of a domain controller (PDC or BDC). The *domain_name* is the name of the Windows NT domain that the computer is a domain controller of. The #DOM affects the behavior of the Browser and Logon services on a network consisting of network segments joined by routers.
#INCLUDE *filename*	The specified *filename* is processed for computer name mappings. The *filename* can use UNC names, which enables the mappings file to be on remote computers. If the computer referenced in the UNC name is outside the local broadcast region, you must include a mapping for the computer name in the LMHOSTS file so that it can be found. You can add the #PRE for the UNC computer name mapping to ensure that it is preloaded. Entries that appear in the INCLUDE file must be preloaded using the #PRE keyword, or they are ignored.
#BEGIN_ALTERNATE	Used to mark the beginning of a group of #INCLUDE statements. The name resolver attempts to use the #INCLUDE statements in the order in which they are listed. Any single successful attempt to use one of the #INCLUDE statements causes the group to succeed, in which case none of the other #INCLUDE statements in the group are processed. If none of the files in the #INCLUDE statement can be accessed, an event is added to the Event Log indicating that the block inclusion failed. You can examine this Event log using the Event Viewer program.
#END_ALTERNATE	This marks the end of the #INCLUDE block. Every #BEGIN_ ALTERNATIVE must have a corresponding #END_ ALTERNATIVE.
\0x*nn*	Escape code for including non-printable characters in NetBIOS names. The NetBIOS names that use this code must have double quotes around the names. Use this code only for special device names and custom applications. When using this notation, take into account the fact that the NetBIOS name in quotes is padded with spaces if it is less than 16 characters.

Understanding How the LMHOSTS File Is Processed

The LMHOSTS file is particularly useful if the network segment on which the Windows NT client resides does not have a WINS server. In this case, broadcast name resolution is used. Broadcast name resolution makes use of IP-level broadcast packets that are usually blocked by IP routers. The broadcast name resolution, therefore, never is transmitted beyond a router boundary. To solve this problem, Windows NT name resolution operates in the following manner when a WINS server is not specified:

1. Windows NT maintains a local cache of names that is initialized during system startup. The name cache is consulted first to see whether the name can be resolved.

2. If no matching entry is in the name cache, Windows NT uses broadcast to resolve names. The broadcast name resolution is called the b-node broadcast protocol and is documented in RFCs 1001 and 1002.

3. If the broadcast name resolution fails, the LMHOSTS file is parsed and any matching entry is used.

4. If no matching entry is in the LMHOSTS file, name resolution fails, and an error message is generated.

Figure 14.15 illustrates the name resolution for the LMHOSTS file. The name cache is initialized with entries that are marked with the #PRE keyword in the LMHOSTS file. For example, the LMHOSTS could contain the following entries, with only some of the entries marked with the #PRE keyword:

144.19.74.1	uziel	
144.19.74.2	zadkiel	#PRE
144.19.74.3	gabriel	
144.19.74.4	uriel	
144.19.74.5	michael	#PRE
144.19.74.6	chamuel	

In this LMHOSTS file, the mappings for host zadkiel and michael are preloaded into the name cache on system startup. If the Windows NT computer needs to resolve the names zadkiel and michael, no broadcast packets are generated, because the name cache provides the name resolution. If the Windows NT computer needs to resolve the names uziel, gabriel, uriel and chamuel, broadcast name resolution is used. If the broadcast name resolution is unsuccessful, the LMHOSTS file is parsed for these names. When a non-preloaded name is resolved by parsing the LMHOSTS file, it is cached for a period of time so that it can be reused.

The preload cache has a limit of 100 entries. If more than 100 entries are in the LMHOSTS file are marked with #PRE, only the first 100 entries are preloaded. Additional entries are not loaded in the name cache, but are resolved if the LMHOSTS file is parsed.

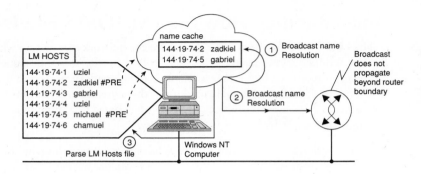

Figure 14.15

LMHOSTS name resolution.

If you have made changes to the LMHOSTS file in terms of the entries that are marked with the #PRE keyword, you can purge and reload the name cache by using the following command:

```
nbtstat -R
```

The advantage of using nbtstat is that you can preload the cache without restarting the Windows NT computer.

Strategy for Using Common LMHOSTS Files

The LMHOSTS file is kept on the local Windows NT computer in the \%*SystemRoot%*\ SYSTEM32\DRIVERS\ETC directory. The maintenance of this local LMHOSTS file on every computer can become a problem when frequent changes are made.

The use of the #INCLUDE statement can simplify the maintenance of the LMHOSTS file. You could keep the LMHOSTS file on a Windows NT server named NTKS and include the following reference to this file on other Windows NT computers:

```
#INCLUDE \\NTKS\ETC\LMHOSTS
```

In this example, the ETC is the shared name of the \%*SystemRoot%*\SYSTEM32\DRIVERS\ ETC directory on the NTKS computer. The advantage of this approach is that all the common names that need to be preloaded are kept in a common file. If the NTKS computer is not in the broadcast region, you must include a specific mapping for it. If the NTKS has an IP address of 134.21.22.13, for example, you could use the following entries in the LMHOSTS file:

```
134.21.22.13    NTK         #PRE
#INCLUDE        \\NTKS\ETC\LMHOSTS
```

To ensure that the common LMHOSTS file is always available, you can replicate this file to other Windows NT computers using the Windows NT replicator service. The common LMHOSTS file must be on Windows NT Server because only the Windows NT Server can act as an export server for replication.

If you have redundant servers, you need to specify that the LMHOSTS file can be found on any of the redundant servers. In this situation, using the #BEGIN_ALTERNATIVE and #END_ALTERNATIVE commands comes in handy. Recall from table 14.1, that these statements mark a block of #INCLUDE statements so that any one of the #INCLUDE statements can be used.

Consider the following example where an alternate list of LMHOSTS files are specified on Windows NT computers on network segment:

```
#BEGIN_ALTERNATIVE
#INCLUDE \\NTKS\ETC\LMHOSTS         # Main source of LMHOSTS file
#INCLUDE \\NTBC1\ETC\LMHOSTS        # Backup 1
#INCLUDE \\NTBC2\ETC\LMHOSTS        # Backup 2
#END_ALTERNATIVE
```

In this example, the LMHOSTS file on NTKS is assumed to be replicated to backup Windows NT computers NTBC1 and NTBC2. The shared name for the \%*SystemRoot*%\SYSTEM32\ DRIVERS\ETC directory is ETC on all the Windows NT computers. The block inclusion is successful if any of the files on the three Windows NT computers is available. If the file is not available because the Windows NT computers are down or in incorrect path is specified, an event is added to the Windows NT computer's event log.

Specifying Domain Controllers in the LMHOSTS File

The domain controllers contain the user account security database, and are frequently accessed by clients in a domain. Besides logon authentication, domain controllers are involved with activities such as user account database synchronization (also called domain *pulses*), password changes, master browser list synchronization, and other changes. On a large network, domain controllers for the domain may be on different network segments separated by routers from the Windows NT computer requesting access to the domain controller.

You can use the #DOM keyword for Windows NT domain controller computer names in the LMHOSTS file. Entries that are marked with the #DOM keyword are loaded in a special *internet group name cache* that is used to limit the distribution of requests for a local domain controller.

If the domain controller is on a local network segment, it can be reached by broadcast name resolution requests. If, however, the domain controller is beyond a router boundary, perhaps on a different subnet, the domain controller is not reachable by broadcast requests. By marking an entry in the LMHOSTS file with the #DOM keyword, Microsoft TCP/IP uses IP datagrams with a destination address of the domain controller. Because these IP datagrams are not broadcast datagrams, the local routers are able to route the request to the proper destination beyond the router boundary. Figure 14.16 shows that the entry for the domain controller NTS1 in the file LMHOSTS does not have the #DOM keyword, whereas the following entry for NTS2 specifies that it is a domain controller for the domain KINETD:

```
192.12.60.2    NTS2         #DOM:KINETD
```

In the example in figure 14.16, the broadcast name resolution request for NTS1 is blocked by the IP router, whereas the name resolution request for NTS2 is forwarded by the IP router because it is marked with the #DOM keyword.

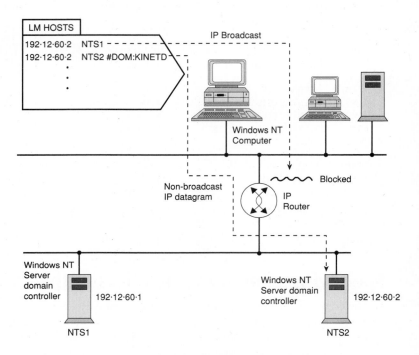

Figure 14.16

Use of the #DOM keyword in a LMHOSTS file.

If a name resolution request involves a domain controller name that is in the internet group name cache, the name is resolved first through a WINS server (if one exists), or a name broadcast. If this name resolution fails, the datagram request is sent to the domain controllers for the domain listed in the internet group name cache, and a local broadcast occurs.

Because domains can span multiple IP subnetworks, you can use the following as a guideline to ensure proper name resolution:

- All domain controller names referenced in Windows NT computer's local LMHOSTS files must have a #DOM keyword to ensure that domain controllers can be reached across IP routers.

- All domain controllers for a domain must have mappings in their LMHOSTS file for all other domain controllers so that if a BDC is promoted to a PDC, the names are properly resolved. These mappings also ensure that the domain controllers are able to communicate properly with each other.

■ If you want to browse another domain, you must make sure that the local LMHOSTS file has the IP address mapping for the PDC of that domain and also for the BDCs in case one of the BDCs is promoted to a PDC.

■ If a trust relationship exists between domains, ensure that the domain controllers in the trusting domains are listed in the LMHOSTS file.

Installing and Configuring FTP Server Service

Windows NT Servers and Workstations can be set up as FTP servers to enable files in the Windows NT computer to be accessed by FTP clients. The FTP clients can be other Windows NT computers, Unix computers, DOS/Windows computers, Macintosh computers, VMS computers, and so on.

The Windows NT FTP Server supports all the FTP client commands, is implemented as a multi-threaded Win32 application, and complies with RFCs 959 and 1123 that describe the FTP protocols and services.

FTP servers use the user accounts of the host operating system. In the case of Windows NT, the FTP user accounts are the ones created on the FTP computer and the FTP anonymous user account.

The FTP Server is a part of the Microsoft Internet Information Server (IIS). The following section includes some general installation and utilization information.

Installing and Configuring the FTP Server Service

You can choose to install the FTP Service and other Internet services when you do your original NT 4 installation. Select the Microsoft Internet Information Server box during installation. The FTP Server will automatically be installed as a part of IIS.

If you have already installed the NT Server without the Internet Information Server, you can add IIS now. The FTP Server service relies on the TCP/IP protocol, so you must install and configure the TCP/IP protocol before you can install FTP Server services.

The following is an outline for installing the FTP Server.

1. Log on as administrator user on the Windows NT computer (Windows NT Server or Workstation).

2. Double-click the Network icon in the Control Panel to display the Network dialog box.

3. Select the Services tab and choose the **A**dd button.

4. Select Microsoft Internet Information Server 2.0 from the list in the Add Network Services dialog box. Choose OK. Enter the path for the installation files when prompted.

   The Microsoft Internet Server Setup Welcome screen appears. Click OK.

   The next screen lets you choose the options available for the Internet Information Server (see fig. 14.17).

Figure 14.17

The Microsoft Internet Information Server 2.0 Setup dialog box.

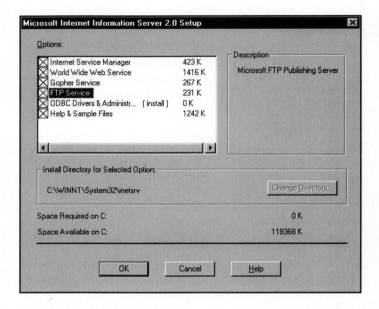

5. Check the FTP Service option and choose OK.

6. The Publishing directories screen appears next. Choose OK to accept the default directory or specify another directory.

7. You see the status of files being copied to the Windows NT computer.

   At the end of the file copy, you see the Services tab again. Select Close to exit the Network dialog box.

8. To configure the FTP Service, click the Microsoft Internet Server (Common) icon in the Programs folder and select Internet Service Manager. Double-click the server running the FTP service to bring up the FTP Service Properties dialog box appears (see fig. 14.18).

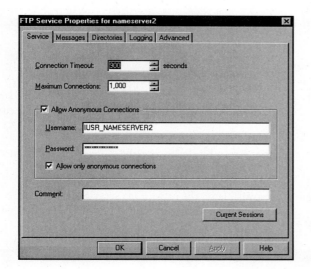

Figure 14.18

The FTP Service Properties dialog box.

9. Use the **M**aximum Connections field to specify the number of simultaneous FTP sessions to the FTP server. The default value is 20, and the maximum is 32,767. If a value of 0 is entered, it indicates that no maximum limits exist and it enables an unlimited number of user connections. Use this field to perform appropriate load balancing. Restricting the number of FTP connections to between 50 and 250 connections to avoid overwhelming a server is common practice.

10. Use the **C**onnection Timeout field to specify how long an FTP user can remain connected without generating any activity before being disconnected. The default value is 10 minutes and the maximum is 60 minutes. A value of 0 disables the idle timeout feature. The value is primarily used for security reasons to reduce the threat of unattended FTP sessions.

11. Enable the option All**o**w Anonymous Connections to allow users with the user account named anonymous or FTP to log on to the FTP server. A user is not required to enter a password while logging on as an anonymous user, even though the user is prompted for an e-mail address as a password. The user name anonymous is reserved on the Windows NT computer for anonymous logon. You cannot, therefore, use a Windows NT user account named anonymous.

    By default, anonymous connections are not allowed and, therefore, this option is not set.

12. Use the **U**sername field to specify the name of the Windows NT user account to be used for the user who logs on as anonymous. The access permissions for the anonymous FTP user are the same as that for the specified user. By default, the Guest system account is used for the anonymous user.

13. Use the **P**assword field to specify the password for the user account specified in the **U**sername field.

14. Enable the A**ll**ow only anonymous connections check box option if you want only anonymous user logons to ensure that Windows NT users do not log on with their Windows NT user name and passwords. Remember that FTP passwords are not encrypted and that if they are used on the network, passwords could be compromised. By default, this option is disabled.

    You can see the FTP User Sessions screen by clicking on the Cur**r**ent Sessions button (see fig. 14.19).

    Other configuration options are available on the other FTP Service Properties tabs.

15. Choose OK to save your FTP service settings.

Figure 14.19

The initial FTP User Sessions screen.

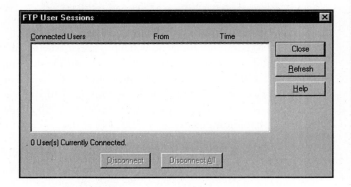

Managing FTP Services

After the FTP Server service is installed and configured, it is automatically started each time the server computer is started. To administer the FTP server, you must log on to the Windows NT computer as an administrator user.

You can use the NET STOP and NET START commands to stop and start the FTP Service. If you want to stop the FTP Services on the Windows NT computer, for example, you use the following command:

```
NET STOP FTPSVC
```

This command abruptly disconnects all FTP users from the FTP server. If you want to determine if any FTP users are connected, use the FTP Server icon in the Control Panel.

Instead of abruptly disconnecting users with the NET STOP command, you can temporarily pause FTP Services by using the following command:

```
NET PAUSE FTPSVC
```

Pausing the FTP Services prevents new users from connecting to the FTP Server, but does not disconnect currently logged on users. New users connecting to the FTP server receive the following message:

```
421-Service not available, closing control connection.
```

After users who are logged on are disconnected, you can stop the FTP service without causing users to lose their sessions.

You can use the Services icon in the Control Panel for starting, stopping, and pausing FTP Services as well as the Internet Service Manager.

You can use the Microsoft Internet Server Manager to manage existing user sessions. The FTP User Sessions dialog box displays the following information:

- Name of connected user

- IP address of connected computer

- Duration of connection

- For anonymous users, their passwords (usually e-mail accounts) are displayed.

- Anonymous users have a question mark (?) next to their icons, whereas users authenticated by Windows NT do not.

You can disconnect any single user or all users from the FTP User Sessions dialog box.

Advanced FTP Server Configuration

The configuration of the FTP server described so far is adequate for most FTP Server installations. This connection describes additional configuration that can be done on the FTP Server. These configuration options are built into the Microsoft Internet Service Manager for FTP Services. You can also do many of the advanced FTP Server configurations by making direct changes to the Registry. You must, therefore, be familiar with making changes to the Registry, as discussed in Chapter 10, "Managing Windows NT Registry."

All of the FTP Service parameters discussed in this section are found under the following Registry key:

```
HKEY_LOCAL_MACHINE\SYSTEM\CurrentControlSet\Services\MSFTPSRV\Parameters
```

Figure 14.20 shows the default entries under this Registry key. If a value entry does not exist, its default value is used. To change to a non-default value, you must create the value entry. The value entries, their data type, and values are discussed in this section.

Figure 14.20

*FTP Service parameters in
the Registry.*

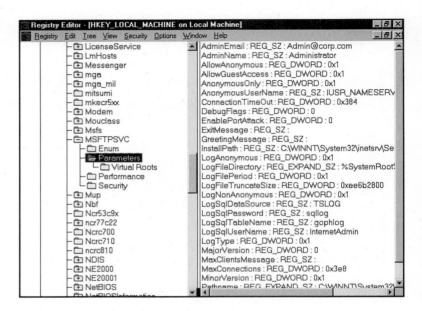

You can perform all FTP Server configuration by editing the Registry, or the following value entries can be set when configuring the FTP Server in the Network Settings dialog box:

- AllowAnonymous

- AllowNonAnonymous

- AnonymousUsername

- ConnectionTimeout

- HomeDirectory

- MaxConnections

The following value entries can be set by using the FTP Server icon in the Control Panel, and then by selecting the Security button:

- ReadAccessMask

- WriteAccessMask

Specifying Annotated Directory Descriptions

When a user changes to a directory on the FTP server, you can display for the user a text file named ~FTPSVC~.CKM, which contains a description of the directory. It also is a good idea to flag this file as hidden so that it does not show up in directory listings. You can use the File Manager for this purpose or use the following command:

```
ATTRIB +H ~FTPSVC~.CKM
```

On many FTP clients the directory descriptions can be toggled by using the FTP site specific CKM command:

```
QUOTE SITE CKM
```

The AnnotatedDirectories value entry defines the behavior of directory annotation for newly connected FTP users. The value entry is of data type REG_DWORD. It has a value of 0 or 1. A value of 1 means that the directory annotated file ~FTPSVC~.CKM is used to display directory description to the user. The default value is 0, which means that directory annotation is off.

Customizing Greeting and Exit Messages

When a user logs on to an FTP server, you can display a customized greeting message that informs the user of the usage policy on the server or some other site-specific information. The greeting message is not sent if the user logs on as anonymous and uses the minus character (-) before the user name.

The greeting message is stored in the GreetingMessage value entry. This value entry is of data type REG_MULTI_SZ. You can use any string characters. The default is no greeting messages.

When a user logs off, you can display a signoff message. The signoff message is specified in the value entry ExitMessage. This value entry is of data type REG_SZ, and has a default value of Goodbye.

Logging FTP Connections

As FTP users connect to the FTP Server, you can log the connections in the system event log by setting the value entries LogAnonymous and LogNonAnonymous.

The LogAnonymous value entry is of data type REG_DWORD and has a value of 0 or 1. If set to 1, anonymous user connections are logged in the system event log; otherwise, logging is disabled. The default value is 0, which means that logging is disabled.

The LogNonAnonymous value entry is similar to the LogAnonymous value entry, except that it applies to non-anonymous users such as Windows NT user accounts. The LogNonAnonymous value entry is of data type REG_DWORD and has a value of 0 or 1. If set to 1, non-anonymous user connections are logged in the system event log; otherwise, logging is disabled. The default value is 0, which means that logging is disabled.

The LogFileAccess value entry controls the logging of file access to the FTPSVC.LOG, which is kept in the *SystemRoot*\SYSTEM32 directory. The LogFileAccess is of data type

REG_DWORD and has a value of 0 or 1. If set to 1, file accesses are logged in the FTPSVC.LOG file; otherwise, logging is disabled. The default value is 0, which means that logging is disabled. The following is an example of the contents of the FTPSVC.LOG file:

```
************** FTP SERVER SERVICE STARTING Fri July 7 11:05:00 am 1995
132.12.23.13 kss opened d:\FTP\sample.txt Fri July 7 11:10:03 am 1995
132.12.23.12 kss appended d:\FTP\sample.txt Fri July 7 11:22:12 am 1995
132.12.23.12 kss created d:\FTP\readme.txt Fri July 7 11:55:32 am 1995
************** FTP SERVER SERVICE STOPPING Fri July 7 11:59:56 am 1995
```

From the previous sample log, you can see that the log file contains entries for the IP address of the connecting computer, the user name, the operation on the file (create, deleted, opened, appended), pathname of file, and date/timestamp information.

Configuring Display Format for Directory Listings

You can use the following FTP command to toggle the directory listing format between MS-DOS and Unix style formats:

```
QUOTE SITE DIRSTYLE
```

The directory listing format is important in those applications that depend on a particular directory listing format. Most of these are Unix-based applications.

The initial format of the directory listing is controlled by the MsdosDirOutput value entry. The MsdosDirOutput value entry is of data type REG_DWORD and has a value of 0 or 1. If set to 1, the directory listing looks like that for MS-DOS when the **DIR** command is used; otherwise, directory listings look like that for Unix when the **ls** command is used. The default value is 1, which means that directory listings look like that for MS-DOS. If the value is set to 1, backward slashes (\) are used in the **pwd** command, and if set to 0, forward slashes (/) are used in the **pwd** command.

Another parameter that affects directory listings is LowercaseFiles. The LowercaseFiles value entry is of data type REG_DWORD and has a value of 0 or 1. If set to 1, file names returned by the **list** and **nlst** commands are mapped to lowercase for noncase-preserving file systems, such as FAT. If set to 0, the mapping to lowercase names is not performed. This flag has no affect on HPFS and NTFS file names because these file systems are case-preserving.

Changing the Maximum Clients Message

If you have set limits to the number of maximum FTP user sessions, and this limit is exceeded, the new FTP users receive the following message:

```
Maximum clients reached, service unavailable.
```

If you want to change this default message you can change the MaxClientsMessage value entry. The MaxClientsMessage value entry is of data type REG_SZ and can be set to any string value.

Printing to Unix Printers Using TCP/IP

Windows NT supports printing to Unix printers on the network. The print jobs are sent using the TCP/IP protocol. Windows NT printing support for Unix printers conforms to RFC 1179.

To print to a Unix computer, only one Windows NT computer (workstation or server) needs to have the TCP/IP protocol installed and configured as well as the Microsoft TCP/IP Printing Service. This Windows NT computer, then acts as print gateway for other Microsoft clients (see fig. 14.21). The other Microsoft clients do not need TCP/IP installed on them to use the print gateway. Figure 14.21 shows that the computer named NTKS has TCP/IP print support and has defined the shared printers \\NTKS\Unix_PR1 and \\NTKS\Unix_PR2. These printers correspond to a directly connected Unix printer, and a printer attached to a Unix computer. Other Microsoft clients connect to the shared printers as if they were Microsoft print devices. A print job sent to the shared printer names \\NTKS\Unix_PR1 and \\NTKS\UNIS_PR2 is redirected by NTKS to the corresponding Unix printer.

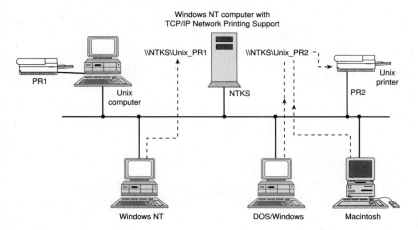

Figure 14.21

TCP/IP Printing using Windows NT.

Installing and Configuring TCP/IP Printing

The following is an outline for installing and configuring TCP/IP printing.

1. Log on as administrator user on the Windows NT computer (Windows NT Server or Workstation).

2. Double-click the Network icon in the Control Panel to display the Network dialog box.

3. Choose the Services tab in the Network dialog box.

4. Choose the **A**dd button. Select Microsoft TCP/IP Printing by highlighting it in the Select Network Service list box and then choosing OK.

5. When prompted, enter the path for the distribution files and choose Continue.

   You see the status of files being copied to the Windows NT computer.

6. When the Network Services dialog box reappears, choose Close.

7. The Network Settings Change dialog box prompts you to restart the computer to ensure that the changes take effect. Choose **Y**es.

   After the Windows NT computer restarts, you must create a TCP/IP printer so that Microsoft clients can use it as a print gateway to Unix computers. After the Windows NT computer restarts, proceed with the following steps to create the TCP/IP printer.

8. Double-click the Printers icon in the Control Panel, and click the Add Printer icon. The Add Printer Wizard will appear (see fig. 14.22). Select either local or network management of the printer, and then choose the **N**ext button.

Figure 14.22

The Add Printer Wizard.

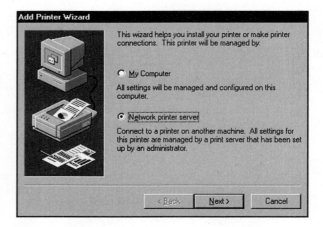

9. Click the Add Po**rt** button. The Printer Wizard displays a list of **A**vailable Printer Ports.

10. Choose LPR Port from the list and click OK (see fig. 14.23).

    You should see the Add LPR compatible printer dialog box (see fig. 14.24).

11. In the **N**ame or address of server providing lpd field, enter the DNS name or IP address of the Unix device (host or directly attached printer) on which the lpd service is running. The lpd service is the line printer daemon service which acts as a Unix print server.

12. In the Name of p**r**inter or print queue on that server field, enter the Unix printer name on that computer system.

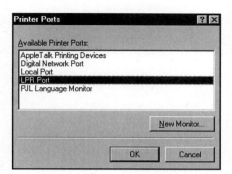

Figure 14.23

Printer ports.

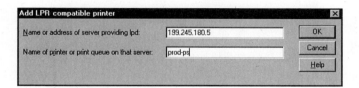

Figure 14.24

The Add LPR compatible printer dialog box.

Choose OK after filling in the Add LPR compatible printer dialog box.

13. Choose the Close button in the Printer Ports dialog box. Check the port box of the printer you want to configure and click the **N**ext button when the Add Printer Wizard reappears.

14. Select the manufacturer from the **M**anufacturers list and the printer from the **P**rinters list by highlighting the appropriate choices. Choose the **N**ext button after you finish.

15. The Add Printer Wizard now displays the **P**rinter name and asks if you want this to be the default printer. Select **Y**es or **N**o, then choose the **N**ext button.

16. The Add Printer Wizard now enables you to choose whether this printer will be shared on the network. Select **S**hared or N**ot** Shared. Type the share name in the Share Name field. By default, the share name is the same as the printer name that you entered earlier (see fig. 14.25). This printer name is seen by other Microsoft clients. Highlight which operating systems will be using the printer in the available list. Select the OK button.

17. Optionally, you can print a test page. This is recommended to verify your configuration is accurate. Select **Y**es or N**o**. Choose the Finish button.

18. You now are prompted to supply the directory for the Windows NT Printer files in the **C**opy files from box.

19. Choose OK to save your printer settings.

You should see the Printer Properties screen appear (see fig. 14.26). In the Device Settings tab you can make any changes such as selecting the form type, form source, and printer memory that are specific to the printer that you are using, and choose OK to save your changes.

Figure 14.25

Shared printer name setting.

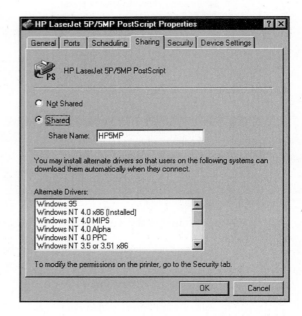

Figure 14.26

The Printer Properties dialog box for Unix printer, the Device Settings tab.

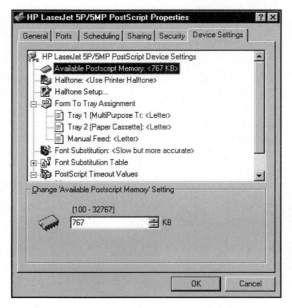

20. You should see an icon window for the new printer in the Printers window.

21. The TCP/IP printer is configured. You can close the Printers window.

Printing to a Windows NT Computer from a Unix Computer

The previous section outlined the configuration procedure for printing to a Unix printer from Microsoft clients. On a network consisting of a mix of Unix computers and Microsoft clients, you might need to print from a Unix client to a Windows NT printer.

To print from a Unix client to a Windows NT computer, you must have TCP/IP Print services running on the Windows NT computer. Unix print clients expect to communicate with a Unix line printer daemon (lpd). You can start the Windows NT Lpdsvc service, which emulates a Unix line printer daemon. Figure 14.27 shows how Unix clients can print to a Windows NT computer.

You can start, pause, continue, or stop the Windows NT lpdsvc by using the following NET commands:

- NET START LPDSVC

- NET PAUSE LPDSVC

- NET CONTINUE LPDSVC

- NET STOP LPDSVC

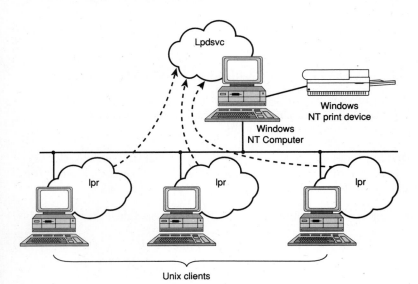

Figure 14.27

Printing from Unix clients to a Windows NT computer.

Alternatively, you can use the Services icon in the control panel to start, pause, continue, or stop the lpdsvc. The lpdsvc is called TCP/IP Print Server in the Services dialog box (see fig. 14.28). By default, this service is started manually. You can use the Startup button in the Services dialog box to automatically start this service when the Windows NT computer is started.

Figure 14.28

*The TCP/IP Print Server
in the Services dialog box.*

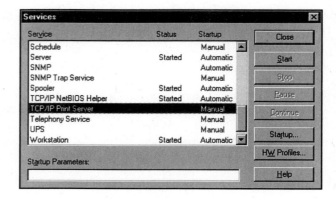

On the Unix printer, you must use the appropriate Unix command, usually lpr, to submit print jobs to the Windows NT computer. Consult your Unix documentation for the details of this command. The general syntax of the lpr command is as follows:

```
lpr -s NTHost -P NTPrinter filename
```

The *NTHost* is the DNS name of the Windows NT computer running the Lpdsvc. The *NTPrinter* is the name of the Windows NT printer created on the *NTHost*, and *filename* is the name of the Unix file to be printed.

Using TCP/IP Command-Line Tools

Windows NT comes with a number of TCP/IP command line tools. These command line tools are, for the most part, based on their Unix counterparts. If you have used these tools on Unix computers, you are already familiar with their function.

In addition to command line tools, Windows NT supports simple TCP/IP services such as echo, daytime, chargen and discard. These services are available on most Unix computers. You must, however, install them in Windows NT using the Simple TCP/IP Services option.

This section describes the installation of the Simple TCP/IP services, and then the basic command line tools.

Installing Simple TCP/IP Services

The following is an outline for installing and configuring Simple TCP/IP services.

1. Log on as administrator user on the Windows NT computer (Windows NT Server or Workstation).

2. Double-click the Network icon in the Control Panel to display the Network dialog box.

3. Select the Services tab. Choose the **A**dd button in the Network Services dialog box.

4. Select the Simple TCP/IP Services from the Select Network Service dialog box and then choose OK.

5. When prompted, enter the path for the distribution files and choose Continue.

6. You see the status of files being copied to the Windows NT computer.

7. When the Network Settings Change dialog box reappears, choose **Y**es to restart the computer so the changes can take effect.

TCP/IP Commands

Windows NT supports the following command line tools:

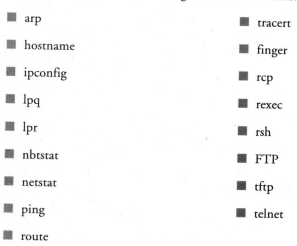

- arp
- hostname
- ipconfig
- lpq
- lpr
- nbtstat
- netstat
- ping
- route
- tracert
- finger
- rcp
- rexec
- rsh
- FTP
- tftp
- telnet

The FTP, ftpsvc, rexec, and telnet utilities require authentication, but the passwords are not encrypted before they are sent. Using these utilities, therefore, is a potential security risk. You should try to use different user accounts for these utilities so that the Windows NT user account passwords are not compromised.

Using the arp Command

The arp command can be used to display or edit the Address Resolution Protocol (ARP) cache maintained by the Windows NT computer. ARP is used for mapping IP addresses to the hardware address of the network interface. Most TCP/IP transmissions on a broadcast-media-based network such as a LAN, are preceded by an ARP request which is used to discover the hardware address of the destination node given to its IP address.

The following is the syntax for using the arp command:

```
arp -a [inet_addr] [-N [if_addr]]
arp -d in_addr [if_addr]
arp -s in_addr mac_addr [if_addr]
```

-a displays all entries when specified by itself. *inet_addr* is the IP address of the interface, and, if specified, only the IP and physical addresses for the specified computer are displayed.

-N displays or modifies the ARP entries for the network interface specified by the IP address *if_addr*. If not present, the first applicable interface is used.

-d is used to delete the entry specified by *inet_addr*.

-s is used to add an entry in the ARP cache table. The IP address *inet_addr* is associated with the physical address *mac_addr*. The MAC address is specified as 6 hexadecimal bytes separated by hyphens. The IP address is specified in the dotted decimal notation. The entry is marked as permanent and not timed-out.

The following is an example of using the arp command:

```
> arp -a
Interface: 199.245.180.13
Internet AddressPhysical AddressType
199.245.180.1000-00-c0-dd-14-5c dynamic
199.245.180.3100-00-c0-86-d9-8f dynamic
```

In the previous command the network interface 199.245.180.13 has mappings for two hosts with IP addresses of 199.245.180.10 and 199.245.180.31.

Using the hostname Command

The hostname command simply prints the host name of the computer of the TCP/IP protocol that is installed.

```
> hostname
ntks
```

Using the ipconfig Command

The ipconfig command is used to display current TCP/IP network configuration parameter values. The command can be used on systems running DHCP to determine the TCP/IP configuration values that have been configured by DHCP. The general syntax of the command is as follows:

```
ipconfig [/all | /renew [adapter] | /release [adapter]]
```

all shows all the parameters. If this switch is not used, only the IP address, subnet mask, and default gateway values for network adapters are displayed.

renew reloads DHCP configuration parameters for the specified *adapter*, and is used only on systems running the DHCP Client. To determine the value of the *adapter*, run the ipconfig command without any parameters.

release releases current DHCP configuration for the specified *adapter* on DHCP clients. To determine the value of the *adapter*, run the ipconfig command without any parameters.

The following are examples of using the ipconfig command:

```
> ipconfig
Windows NT IP Configuration
Ethernet adapter NE20001:
        IP Address. . . . . . . . . : 199.245.180.13
        Subnet Mask . . . . . . . . : 255.255.255.0
        Default Gateway . . . . . . : 199.245.180.10

> ipconfig /all
Windows NT IP Configuration
        Host Name . . . . . . . . . : ntks.kinetics.com
        DNS Servers . . . . . . . . : 199.245.180.10
        199.245.180.16
        Node Type . . . . . . . . . : Broadcast
        NetBIOS Scope ID. . . . . .:
        IP Routing Enabled. . . . . : No
        WINS Proxy Enabled. . . . . : No
        NetBIOS Resolution Uses DNS : No
Ethernet adapter NE20001:
        Description . . . . . . . . : Novell 2000 Adapter.
        Physical Address. . . . . . : 00-40-05-16-08-9B
        DHCP Enabled. . . . . . . . : No
        IP Address. . . . . . . . . : 199.245.180.13
        Subnet Mask . . . . . . . . : 255.255.255.0
        Default Gateway . . . . . . : 199.245.180.10
```

Using the lpq Command

The line printer queue (lpq) command is used to obtain the status of a print queue on a computer running the line printer daemon (lpd) server. The following is the general syntax for using this command:

```
lpq -S LPDserver -P Printer [-l]
```

-S *LPDserver* specifies the host running the print server daemon.

-P *Printer* specifies the name of the printer for the desired queue.

-l displays queue status in detail.

Using the lpr Command

The lpr command is used to send print jobs to a host running an LPD server. The following is the general syntax of this command:

```
lpr -S server -P printer [-C class] [-J jobname] filename
```

-S *server* is the name of the LPD host to which the printer is attached.

-P *printer* specifies the name of the printer to which the job is to be sent.

-C*class* specifies the content of the banner page for the class.

-J *jobname* specifies the name of this job.

Using the nbtstat Command

The nbtstat command displays protocol information of NetBIOS over TCP/IP. The following is the general syntax for using this command:

```
nbtstat [-a remotename] [-A IPaddress] [-c] [-n] [-R] [-r] [-S] [-s] [interval]
```

-a lists a remote computer's name table using its computer name, *remotename*.

-A lists a computer's name table using its *IP address*.

-c lists the contents of the NetBIOS name cache and the IP address mappings to the NetBIOS name.

-n lists the local NetBIOS names. Registered indicates that the name is registered by broadcast (Bnode) or WINS (other node types).

-R reloads the LMHOSTS file after purging all names from the NetBIOS name cache.

-r lists name resolution statistics for network name resolution. On a WINS server, this option displays the number of names resolved and registered via broadcast or via WINS.

-S displays client and server sessions, listing the remote hosts by IP address only.

-s displays client and server sessions, listing remote hosts by the name used in the HOSTS file.

interval redisplays statistics, in *interval* seconds. Without this parameter, statistics are displayed only once.

The following are examples of using the nbtstat command:

To display the remote computer NTWB's name table, use the following:

```
> nbtstat -a NTWB
 NetBIOS Remote Machine Name Table
 Name Type Status
------------------------------------------------
NTWB <00>UNIQUERegistered
DOMAIN_A <00>GROUP Registered
NTWB <03>UNIQUERegistered
NTWB <20>UNIQUERegistered
DOMAIN_A <1E>GROUP Registered
DOMAIN_A <1D>UNIQUERegistered
..__MSBROWSE__.<01>GROUP Registered
ADMINISTRATOR<03>UNIQUERegistered
MAC Address = 00-00-C0-86-D9-8F
```

The previous example shows that NetBIOS names are padded to 16 characters. The last byte of the name is displayed in its hexadecimal value. It is significant because the same name can be present several times on a computer. The type of a name can be UNIQUE or a GROUP name.

To display the name cache, use the following command:

```
> nbtstat -c
Node IpAddress: [199.245.180.13] Scope Id: []
NetBIOS Remote Cache Name Table
NameType Host AddressLife [sec]
------------------------------------------------
NTWB <00>UNIQUE199.245.180.3160
```

The previous example shows the name and IP address mapping and the remaining time (Life) in seconds that the name cache entry can live before it is purged.

Using the netstat Command

The netstat command displays protocol statistics and current TCP/IP connections. The following is the general syntax for using this command:

```
netstat [-a] [-e] [-n] [-s] [-p protocol] [-r] [interval]
```

-a displays all connections and listening ports.

-e displays Ethernet statistics. This option can be combined with the -s option to display per-protocol statistics.

-n displays addresses and port numbers in numerical form rather than symbolic form.

-r displays the IP routing table and active connections.

-s displays per-protocol statistics for TCP, UDP, ICMP, and IP. You can use -p option to specify a subset of the default protocols.

-p replaces *protocol* with the name of the protocol for which connection statistics are to be seen. You can combine this with the -s option to see active connections on the protocol.

interval redisplays statistics, in *interval* seconds. Without this parameter, statistics are displayed only once.

To see a list of all connections and listening ports, use the following:

```
> netstat -a
Active Connections
ProtoLocal AddressForeign AddressState
TCPntwb:1037NTKS:nbsession ESTABLISHED
TCPntwb:ftp NTKS:1082ESTABLISHED
UDPntwb:1025*:*
UDPntwb:nfs *:*
UDPntwb:echo*:*
UDPntwb:discard *:*
UDPntwb:daytime *:*
UDPntwb:qotd*:*
UDPntwb:chargen *:*
UDPntwb:603 *:*
UDPntwb:619 *:*
UDPntwb:portmap *:*
UDPntwb:snmp*:*
UDPntwb:nbname*:*
UDPntwb:nbdatagram*:*
```

In the previous command, the services under the UDP protocol are in listening state, waiting for connections. The two active connections are on TCP port 1037 for a NetBIOS session and port FTP (well-known port 21) on the computer NTWB. The state of these connections is ESTABLISHED, which means that the TCP connections are valid.

To see a list of per-protocol statistics for TCP, UDP, IP, and ICMP use the following command:

```
> netstat -s
IP Statistics
Packets Received = 1170
Received Header Errors = 0
Received Address Errors= 0
Datagrams Forwarded= 0
Unknown Protocols Received = 0
Received Packets Discarded = 0
Received Packets Delivered = 1170
Output Requests= 793
Routing Discards = 0
Discarded Output Packets = 0
Output Packet No Route = 0
Reassembly Required= 0
Reassembly Successful= 0
Reassembly Failures= 0
```

```
Datagrams Successfully Fragmented= 0
Datagrams Failing Fragmentation= 0
Fragments Created= 0
ICMP Statistics
ReceivedSent
Messages 7 7
Errors 0 0
Destination Unreachable 0 0
Time Exceeded 0 0
Parameter Problems 0 0
Source Quenchs 0 0
Redirects 0 0
Echos 4 3
Echo Replies 3 4
Timestamps 0 0
Timestamp Replies 0 0
Address Masks 0 0
Address Mask Replies0 0
TCP Statistics
Active Opens= 12
Passive Opens = 5
Failed Connection Attempts= 0
Reset Connections = 0
Current Connections = 1
Segments Received = 138
Segments Sent = 146
Segments Retransmitted= 1
UDP Statistics
Datagrams Received= 1025
No Ports= 0
Receive Errors= 0
Datagrams Sent= 639
```

The previous command shows the protocol statistics per protocol. It is useful for diagnostic purposes. Many of the values under ICMP relate to protocol problems. A high value for Destination Unreachable, Parameter Problems, Time Exceeded, and so on, can indicate problems with the network.

To see only protocol statistics for TCP and active connections for TCP, use the following command:

```
> netstat -s -p tcp
TCP Statistics
Active Opens= 12
Passive Opens = 5
Failed Connection Attempts= 0
Reset Connections = 0
Current Connections = 1
Segments Received = 138
Segments Sent = 146
Segments Retransmitted= 1
Active Connections
```

```
ProtoLocal AddressForeign AddressState
TCPntwb:ftp NTKS:1038ESTABLISHED
```

To see the contents of the local routing table, use the following command:

```
> netstat -r
Route Table
Active Routes:
Network Address      Netmask              Gateway              AddressInterface      Metric
```

Network Address	Netmask	Gateway	AddressInterface	Metric
0.0.0.0	0.0.0.0	199.245.180.10	199.245.180.31	1
127.0.0.0	255.0.0.0	127.0.0.1	127.0.0.1	1
199.245.180.0	255.255.255.0	199.245.180.31	199.245.180.31	1
199.245.180.31	255.255.255.255	127.0.0.1	127.0.0.1	1
199.245.180.255	255.255.255.255	199.245.180.31	199.242.180.31	1
224.0.0.0	224.0.0.0	199.245.180.31	199.245.180.31	1
255.255.255.255	255.255.255.255	199.245.180.31	199.245.180.31	1

```
Active Connections:
ProtoLocal AddressForeign AddressState
TCPntwb:ftp NTKS:1038ESTABLISHED
```

Using the ping Command

The ping command is used for diagnostic purposes to verify whether the host is reachable. The ping tool causes an ICMP echo-request datagram to be sent. The destination is required to send this packet back as an ICMP echo-reply packet. Ping stands for Packet InterNet Groper and is one of the most common tools used to diagnose TCP connections. The following shows the general syntax of this command in Windows NT:

```
ping [-t] [-a] [-n count] [-l length] [-f] [-i ttl] [-v tos] [-r count] [-s count]
Â[[-j host-list] | [-k host-list]][-w timeout] destination-list
```

-t specifies that the host must be pinged continuously.

-a is used to resolve addresses to hostnames.

-n sends ICMP ECHO packets a specified number of times. The default is 4.

-l sends ICMP ECHO packets padded to the specified length. The data that is sent consists of a repeated string of the letters 'a' to 'w' The default packet length is 64 bytes and the maximum is 8192. On an Ethernet network that has a maximum data size of 1,500 bytes, specifying a size larger than 1,500 causes the datagram to be fragmented.

-f sends a Do not Fragment flag in the IP datagram packet to ensure that the ICMP echo-request and echo-reply datagrams are not be fragmented by gateways on the route. If you specify a value in the -l option that forces fragmentation and also specify the -f option, the

ICMP echo-request is not sent. You receive a message that the packet needs to be fragmented, but DF is set. The DF stands for the Don't Fragment flag.

-I specifies the value of the Time To Live (TTL) field in the IP datagram. Values can range from 1 to 255. Illegal values will cause a Bad Option error message.

-v can be used to specify the value of the Type Of Service (TOS) field in the IP datagram.

-r records the route of the ICMP request and the ICMP reply packets in the Record Route field of the IP datagram. A minimum of 1 and a maximum of 9 hosts must be specified by the value of *count*.

-s specifies the timestamp for the number of hops specified by the value of *count*.

-j specifies loose source routing, where a list of hosts on the path are specified by host-list. Consecutive hosts may be separated by intermediate routers. The maximum number of hosts allowed by IP is 9.

-k specifies strict source routing, where a list of hosts on the path are specified by host-list. Consecutive hosts cannot be separated by intermediate routers. The maximum number of hosts allowed by IP is 9.

-w specifies a timeout interval in milliseconds.

destination-list specifies the remote hosts to ping.

To ping the host at IP address 199.245.180.13, five times, use the following:

```
> ping -n 5 199.245.180.13
Pinging 199.245.180.13 with 32 bytes of data:
Reply from 199.245.180.13: bytes=32 time=10ms TTL=32
Reply from 199.245.180.13: bytes=32 time<10ms TTL=32
Reply from 199.245.180.13: bytes=32 time<10ms TTL=32
Reply from 199.245.180.13: bytes=32 time<10ms TTL=32
Reply from 199.245.180.13: bytes=32 time<10ms TTL=32
```

Using the route Command

The route command is used to manually change the routing table at the host. You can use this to specify which local router to use to reach specific remote networks and hosts. The following is the general syntax for using the route command:

```
route [-f] [command [destination] [mask subnetmask]
[gateway]]
```

-f is the flush option, which clears the routing table. When used in conjunction with other commands, the table is cleared prior to running the command.

command specifies the print, add, delete, or change command. These commands are used to print, add, delete, or change route table entries.

destination specifies the destination of the route table entry.

subnetmask specifies a mask to be associated with this route entry. If not specified, the mask of 255.255.255.255 is used, identifying the entry as a route to a specific host.

gateway specifies the router to which the IP datagram is to be forwarded to reach the *destination.*

If symbolic names are used for *destination* or *gateway,* the names are resolved by searching the NETWORKS and HOSTS files, respectively.

The following are examples of the use of the route command on a Windows NT computer.

To add a route to reach the subnetwork 144.14.74.0 that has a subnet mask of 255.255.255.0 through the router at IP address 199.245.180.91, use the following command:

```
> route add 144.14.74.0 mask 255.255.255.0 199.245.180.91
```

To view a list of route table entries, use the following command:

```
> route print
Active Routes:
```

Network Address	Netmask	Gateway	AddressInterface	Metric
0.0.0.0	0.0.0.0	199.245.180.10	199.245.180.31	1
127.0.0.0	255.0.0.0	127.0.0.1	127.0.0.1	1
144.14.74.0	255.255.255.0	199.245.180.91	199.245.180.31	1
199.245.180.0	255.255.255.0	199.245.180.31	199.245.180.31	1
199.245.180.31	255.255.255.255	127.0.0.1	127.0.0.1	1
199.245.180.255	255.255.255.255	199.245.180.31	199.245.180.31	1
224.0.0.0	224.0.0.0	199.245.180.31	199.245.180.31	1
255.255.255.255	255.255.255.255	199.245.180.31	199.245.180.31	1

Notice that the route for the network 144.14.74.0 has been added to the host route table.

Using the tracert Command

The tracert command is used to discover the path taken to reach a destination. The tracert command works by sending ICMP echo packets with different Time To Live (TTL) values to the destination. IP routers on the network path are required to decrement the TTL on an IP datagram by at least 1 before forwarding it. When the TTL on the IP datagram reaches 0, the IP router sends back an ICMP message that TTL was exceeded and discards the datagram.

Tracert first sends an ICMP echo-request packet with a TTL of 1 and increments the TTL by 1 on each subsequent transmission until the target responds or the maximum TTL is reached. The routes are determined by examining the ICMP TTL messages sent back by intermediate routers. If the router does not send an ICMP message back on discarding IP datagrams that have a TTL value of 0, or the ICMP TTL exceeded message is lost, then that router is not seen by the tracert command.

```
tracert [-d] [-h maximumhops] [-j hostlist] [-w timeout]
destination
```

-d specifies not to resolve addresses to hostnames.

-h specifies the maximum number of hops to search for the destination.

-j specifies loose source routing, where a list of hosts on the path are specified by host-list. Consecutive hosts may be separated by intermediate routers. The maximum number of hosts allowed by IP is 9.

-w specifies a timeout interval in milliseconds.

destination specifies the destination for which the network path is to be discovered.

The finger Command

The finger command is used to display information about a user on a host running the finger service. Most Unix hosts have a finger service running. The following is the general syntax for using the finger command:

```
finger [-l] [user]@host [...]
```

-l displays user information in long list format.

user represents the name of the user you want to finger for information. If the user parameter is not entered, information about all users on the *host* is listed.

@host represents the host on which the user names are to be listed.

To find out information for User 2 on Unix host at IP address 199.245.180.15, use the following command:

```
> finger user2@199.245.180.15
[199.245.180.15]
Login: user2              Name: User 2
Directory: /usr/ltree/user2              Shell: /bin/csh
On since Mon Jul 10 11:09 (MDT) on ttyp0, idle 0:01, from 199.245.180.13
No Plan.
```

Notice that the finger command reveals the time the user has logged on and the host from which the user logged on. The user's home directory and shell also are displayed.

Using the rcp Command

The rcp command is part of the Berkeley r* utilities, and performs a remote copy between two TCP/IP hosts. The remote computer must be running the remote shell daemon (rshd). The rshd daemon is available on most Unix computers, but not on Windows NT computers. You can use the rcp command to copy files between two remote computers (called third-party transfer) as long as the remote computers are running rshd. The following is the syntax for using rcp.

```
rcp [-a |-b] [-h] [-r] source1 source2 ... sourceN destination
```

-a specifies that the ASCII transfer mode, which also is the default mode, is to be used. In the ASCII transfer mode, carriage return/linefeed characters are converted to carriage returns on outgoing files and linefeed characters to carriage return/linefeeds for incoming files.

-b specifies that the binary transfer mode, is to be used. In the binary transfer mode no carriage return/linefeed characters conversions are performed.

-h specifies that source files marked with the hidden attributes are to be transferred. If this option is not specified, hidden files are not found by the rcp command.

-r performs a recursive copy of the contents of all subdirectories from the source to the destination directories.

Both source and destination must be of the form [*host*[.*user*]:]*filename*. If the [*host*[.*user*]:] is not specified, the host is the local computer. If the *user* is not specified, the Windows NT username currently logged on is used. If a fully qualified domain name (FQDN) is used, then you must use the keyword user as part of the name. Consider the following source file syntax:

```
ucs.kinetics.com.user:karanjit
```

In this example, the keyword user is used to indicate that the name that follows the colon (:) character is the user karanjit.

Permissions for performing the rcp command are controlled by the .rhosts and hosts.equiv files on the remote system. These files contain the name of the host and, optionally, user on the host that can perform the command. Refer to the author's book *Internet Firewalls and Network Security* by New Riders Publishing on a discussion of the contents of these files and related security issues.

Using the rexec Command

The rexec is used to run commands on a remote computer that has the rexecd daemon running on it. You can run only command line commands with rexec; you cannot run interactive commands such as editors. The following is the general syntax for using this command:

```
rexec host [-l username] [-n] command
```

host specifies the remote compute on which to run *command*. The remote computer must be running rexecd.

-1 specifies the *username* under which the command is run on the remote host.

-n redirects the input of rexec to the NUL device.

The rexec command copies the standard input of the local computer (the computer on which the rexec command is run) to the standard input of the remote command, the standard output of the remote command to the standard output of the local computer, and the standard error of the remote command to the standard error of the local computer.

Example 1:

To append a remote file accts.text on computer ucs to a local file monthly.text, use the following:

```
rexec ucs cat accts.text">>" monthly.text
```

Example 2:

In the previous example, if the file is to be redirected to a remote file, use quotes "" around the redirection symbols:

```
rexec ucs cat accts.text""monthly.text
```

Using the rsh Command

The rsh command invokes the shell on a remote computer to execute the specified command. The remote computer must have the rshd daemon running on it. The command is similar to the rexec command, but is more specific to Unix systems and uses the same .rhosts and hosts.equiv files used by the rcp command for user validation.

The following is the general syntax for using the rsh command:

```
rsh host [-1 username] [-n] command
```

host specifies the remote compute on which to run *command*. The remote computer must be running rshd.

-1 specifies the *username* under which the command is run on the remote host.

-n redirects the input of rexec to the NUL device.

The rsh command copies the standard input of the local computer (the computer on which the rsh command is run) to the standard input of the remote command; the standard output of the remote command to the standard output of the local computer; and the standard error of the remote command to the standard error of the local computer.

Example 1:

To append a remote file accts.text on computer ucs to a local file monthly.text, use the following:

```
rsh ucs cat accts.text >> monthly.text
```

Example 2:

In the previous example, if the file is to be redirected to a remote file, use quotes "" around the redirection symbols:

```
rsh ucs cat accts.text">>"monthly.text
```

Using the ftp Command

The ftp command is used to start an interactive session to transfer files to and from a computer running the FTP Server. The following is the general syntax for using the ftp command:

```
ftp [-v] [-d] [-i] [-n] [-g] [-s: filename] [host]
```

-v suppresses display of responses from the remote FTP server.

-n suppresses auto-login upon initial connection.

-i disables interactive prompting during multiple file transfers, using the FTP commands mget and mput.

-d enables debugging and displays all the ftp commands between the FTP client and the FTP server.

-g disables file name globbing. *Globbing* is a term used to refer to the use of wildcard characters in local file and path names.

-s specifies that the *filename* is a text file that contains the commands that run when ftp starts.

host is the name or IP address of the remote host that is the FTP server.

Using the tftp Command

The tftp command implements the Trivial File Transfer Protocol (TFTP) to transfer files. This command is a command line tool, and does not require authentication. The remote computer must be running the tftpd daemon. The following is the general syntax for using this command:

```
tftp [-i] host [get ¦ put] source [destination]
```

-i specifies that the binary image transfer mode will be used. In this mode, no end-of-line (EOL) character translation is done. When the -i option is omitted, the ASCII file transfer mode (default mode) is used. The ASCII mode converts the EOL characters to a carriage return for Unix and a carriage return/line feed combination for MSDOS.

host specifies the local or remote host.

put specifies that the file *source* is transferred from the local host to remote destination.

get specifies that the file is transferred from the remote host to the *source* file on the local host.

If you use the character - for the local file, then the remote file is printed out on stdout of the local computer with the get option, and is read from stdin with the put option.

Using the telnet Command

The telnet command is a general-purpose client tool to establish remote connections. The telnetd daemon must be running on the remote computer. Windows NT does not support the telnetd daemon, so this command generally is only used with Unix, VMS, and MVS computers. The following is the general syntax of this command:

```
telnet host [port]
```

The *host* specifies the name or IP address of the remote computer. The *port* specifies the TCP port to which the remote computer connects. The default value for this port is specified in the \%*SystemRoot*%\system32\drivers\etc\services file. If no entry is in the services file, a default of 23 is used.

When a nondefault value is specified, you can use telnet to connect to special services running on the remote computer at the specified port.

Besides starting telnet from the command prompt, you also can start telnet by running it from the Telnet icon in the Accessories group.

Figure 14.29 shows the telnet session to a Router started with the following command:

```
telnet 199.245.180.1
```

You can configure the terminal emulation options by choosing **T**erminal, **P**references. You can use the **E**dit menu to select, copy, and paste text from the terminal session.

Though telnetd daemon is not supported on Windows NT computers, you can use telnet on a Windows NT computer to connect to another Windows NT computer that is running Simple TCP/IP services, such as daytime, echo, discard, chargen, and quote. You must specify the TCP port number for these services.

Figure 14.29

A Windows NT telnet session.

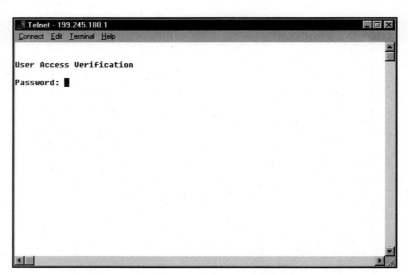

Removing TCP/IP Components

After you have installed TCP/IP on a Windows NT computer, its removal should probably never be necessary. If you have a major reorganization of your network, however, and are no longer using TCP/IP applications and services, you can remove TCP/IP from the Windows NT computer.

Use the following as a guideline for removing TCP/IP.

1. Log on to the Windows NT Server as an administrator user.

2. Double-click the Network icon in the Control Panel.

3. Select the Protocols tab and highlight the TCP/IP Protocol from the list box, then choose the **R**emove button.

    Windows NT warns you that the action permanently removes that component. Also, you cannot reinstall a component that has been removed until after you restart the computer.

4. After removing the component or service, choose Close. The Network Settings Change dialog box prompts you to restart the computer so the changes can take effect. Select **Y**es.

Conclusion

This chapter discussed how you install and configure basic TCP/IP services. The TCP/IP protocol is one of the built-in choices that comes with Windows NT. The configuration of TCP/IP is performed using the Network Settings icon in the Control Panel.

Using the Network Settings in the Control Panel, you can configure the TCP/IP stack parameters, such as IP addresses, subnet masks, default gateways, DHCP client, use of name services, SNMP services, and host files. Other TCP/IP issues discussed in this chapter are configuring and using FTP services on a Windows NT Server, configuring TCP/IP print services, and using the command line TCP/IP tools that come with Windows NT Server.

Windows NT Server DHCP Configuration

On large networks, configuring TCP/IP parameters for each workstation can be a difficult and time-consuming task, particularly when the TCP/IP parameters, such as IP addresses and subnet masks, need to be changed. The changes can occur because of a major restructuring of the network or because the network has many mobile users with portable computers that can be connected to any of the network segments. The network connections can be direct physical connections or wireless connections. Because the TCP/IP parameters for computers depend on the network segment they connect to, appropriate values must be set up whenever a computer is connected to a different network segment.

Understanding the consequences of TCP/IP parameter changes requires knowledgeable network administrators. For TCP/IP internetworks several auto-configuration protocols, such as Boot Protocol (BOOTP) and Dynamic Host Configuration Protocol (DHCP), have been developed by the Internet Engineering Task Force (IETF). A Windows NT Server can be configured as a DHCP server, which simplifies the configuration of TCP/IP devices (workstations, servers, routers, and so on.) on the network. This chapter discusses the DHCP protocol and how it can be configured on a Windows NT Server.

Understanding the DHCP Protocol

DHCP can be used for dynamic configuration of essential TCP/IP parameters for hosts (workstations and servers) on the network.

The DHCP protocol consists of two elements:

- A mechanism for allocating IP addresses and other TCP/IP parameters

- A protocol for negotiating and transmitting host specific information

The TCP/IP host requesting the TCP/IP configuration information is called the DHCP client, and the TCP/IP host that supplies this information is called a DHCP server. On a Windows NT network, the *DHCP clients* are Windows NT workstations or servers, but the *DHCP server* can only be a Windows NT Server.

Understanding IP Address Management

DHCP uses the following three methods for IP address allocation:

- Manual allocation

- Automatic allocation

- Dynamic allocation

In the *manual* allocation method, the DHCP client's IP address is set manually by the network administrator at the DHCP server, and DHCP is used to convey to the DHCP client the value of the manually configured IP address.

In the *automatic* allocation method, no manual assignments of the IP address needs to be made. The DHCP client is assigned an IP address when it first contacts the DHCP server. The IP address assigned using this method is permanently assigned to the DHCP client and is not reused by another DHCP client.

In the *dynamic* allocation method, DHCP assigns an IP address to a DHCP client on a temporary basis. The IP address is on loan or leased to the DHCP client for a specified duration. On the expiry of this lease, the IP address is revoked, and the DHCP client is required to surrender the IP address. If the DHCP client still needs an IP address to perform its functions, it can request another one.

The dynamic allocation method is the only one of the three methods that affords automatic reuse of an IP address. An IP address does not always have to be surrendered by the DHCP client on the expiry of the lease. If the DHCP client no longer needs an IP address, such as when the computer is being gracefully shut down, it can release the IP address to the DHCP server. The DHCP server then can reissue the same IP address to another DHCP client making a request for an IP address.

The dynamic allocation method is particularly useful for DHCP clients that need an IP address for temporary connection to a network. Consider, for example, a situation where there are 300 users with portable computers on a network, and a class C address has been assigned to a network. This enables the network to have 253 nodes on the network (255–2 special addresses = 253). Because computers connecting to a network using TCP/IP are required to have unique IP addresses, all of the 300 computers cannot be simultaneously connected to the network. If there are at most only 200 physical connections on the network, however, it is possible to use a class C address by reusing IP addresses that are not in use. Using DHCP's dynamic IP address allocation, IP address reuse is possible.

Dynamic IP address allocation is also a good choice for assigning IP addresses to new hosts that are being permanently connected, and where IP addresses are scarce. As old hosts are retired, their IP addresses can be immediately reused.

Regardless of which of the three IP address allocation methods is used, you can still configure IP parameters at a central DHCP server once, instead of repeating the TCP/IP configuration for each computer.

The DHCP IP Address Acquisition Process

Upon contacting a DHCP server, a DHCP client goes through several internal states, during which it negotiates the use of an IP address and the duration of the use. The operation of how a DHCP client acquires the IP address can best be explained in terms of a state transition diagram (also called a finite state machine). Figure 15.1 shows the state transition diagram that explains the interaction between the DHCP client and DHCP server.

Figure 15.1

The DHCP state transition diagram showing DHCP client/ server interaction.

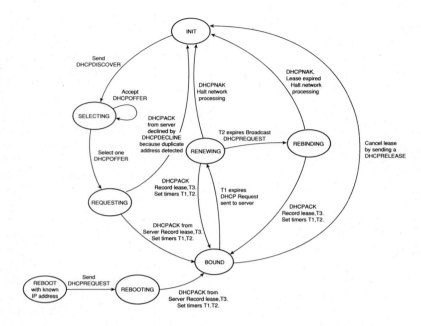

When the DHCP client is first started, it begins in the INIT (initialize) state. At this point, the DHCP client does not know its IP parameters, and so sends a DHCPDISCOVER broadcast. The DHCPDISCOVER is encapsulated in a UDP/IP packet. The destination UDP port number is set to 67 (decimal), the same as that for a BOOTP server. This similarity occurs because the DHCP protocol is an extension of the BOOTP protocol. A local IP broadcast address of 255.255.255.255 is used in the DHCPDISCOVER packet. If DHCP servers are not on the local network, the IP router must have DHCP-relay agent support to forward the DHCPDISCOVER request to other subnetworks. DHCP-relay agent support is discussed in RFC 1542.

Before sending the DHCPDISCOVER broadcast packet, the DHCP clients wait for a random time interval between 1 and 10 seconds. This is done to prevent DHCP clients from starting at the same time; simultaneous powerups are sometimes attempted after power failures.

After sending the DHCPDISCOVER broadcast, the DHCP client enters the SELECTING state. In this state, the DHCP client receives DHCPOFFER messages from the DHCP servers that have been configured to respond to the DHCP client. The time period over which the DHCP client waits to receive DHCPOFFER messages is implementation dependent. The DHCP client must select one DHCPOFFER response if it receives multiple DHCPOFFER responses. After selecting a DHCPOFFER message from a server, the DHCP client sends a DHCPREQUEST message to the selected DHCP server. The DHCP server responds with a DHCPACK.

The DHCP client may optionally perform a check on the IP address sent in the DHCPOFFER to verify if the address is not in use. On a broadcast network, the DHCP client can send an ARP request for the suggested IP address to see if there is an ARP response. An ARP response would imply that the suggested IP address is already in use, in which case the DHCPACK from the sever is ignored and a DHCPDECLINE is sent, and the DHCP client enters the INIT state and retries to get a valid IP address that is not in use. When the ARP request is broadcast on the local network, the client uses its own hardware address in the sender hardware address field of the ARP packet, but sets a value of 0 in the sender IP address field. A sender IP address of 0 is used, rather than the suggested IP address so as not to confuse ARP caches on other TCP/IP hosts in case the suggested IP address is already in use.

When the DHCPACK from the DHCP server is accepted, three timer values are set, and the DHCP client moves into the BOUND state. The first timer, T1, is the lease renewal timer; the second timer, T2, is the rebinding timer; and the third timer, T3, is the lease duration. The DHCPACK always returns the value of T3, the lease duration. The values of timers T1 and T2 can be configured at the DHCP server, but if they are not set, default values are used based on the duration of the lease. The following shows the default values used for T1 and T2.

T1 = renewal timer

T2 = rebinding timer

T3 = duration of lease

$T1 = 0.5 \times T3$

$T2 = 0.875 \times T3$

The actual times at which the timer values expire are computed by adding to the timer value the time at which the DHCPREQUEST that generated the DHCPACK response was sent. If the time at which the DHCP request was sent was T0, then the expiration values are computed as follows:

Expiration of $T1 = T0 + T1$

Expiration of $T2 = T0 + T2$

Expiration of $T3 = T0 + T3$

RFC 1541 recommends that a fuzz factor be added to timers T1 and T2 to prevent several DHCP clients from expiring their timers at the same time.

At the expiration of timer T1, the DHCP client moves from the BOUND state to the RENEWING state. In the RENEWING state, a new lease for the allocated IP address must be negotiated by the DHCP client from the DHCP server that originally allocated the IP address. If the original DHCP server does not renew the release, it sends a DHCPNAK message, and the DHCP client moves into the INIT state and tries to obtain a new IP address. If the original DHCP server sends a DHCPACK message, this message contains the new lease duration. The DHCP client sets its timer values and moves to the BOUND state.

If the T2 timer expires while waiting in the RENEWING state for a DHCPACK or DHCPNAK message from the original DHCP server, then the DHCP client moves from the RENEWING state to the REBINDING state. The original DHCP server may not respond because it or a network link is down. Note from the previous equations that T2 > T1, so the DHCP client waits for the original DHCP server for a duration of T2–T1 to renew the release.

At the expiration of timer T2, a broadcast DHCPREQUEST is sent over the network to contact any DHCP server to extend the lease, and the DHCP client is in the REBINDING state. A DHCPREQUEST broadcast is sent because the DHCP client assumes, after spending T2–T1 seconds in the RENEWING state, that the original DHCP server is not available, and the DHCP client tries to contact any DHCP server that is configured to respond to it. If a DHCP server responds with a DHCPACK message, the DHCP client renews its lease (T3), sets the T1 and T2 timers and moves back to the BOUND state. If no DHCP server is able to renew the release after expiration of timer T3, the lease expires and the DHCP client moves to the INIT state. Note that by this time, the DHCP client has tried to renew the lease, first with the original DHCP server and then with any DHCP server on the network.

When the lease expires (when timer T3 expires), the DHCP client must surrender the use of its IP address and halt network processing with that IP address.

The DHCP client does not always have to wait for the expiration of the lease (timer T3) to surrender the use of an IP address. It could voluntarily relinquish control of an IP address by canceling its lease. A user with a portable computer may, for example, connect to the network to perform a network activity. The DHCP server on the network might set the duration of the lease for one hour. Assume that the user finishes the network tasks in 30 minutes and now wants to disconnect from the network. After the user gracefully shuts down his or her computer, the DHCP client sends a DHCPRELEASE message to the DHCP server to cancel its lease. The IP address that is surrendered is now available for use by another DHCP client.

If DHCP clients are run on computers that have a disk, the IP address that is allocated can be stored on the computer's disk, and when the computer reboots, it can make a request for the same IP address. This was shown in figure 15.1 in the state labeled REBOOTING with known IP address.

DHCP Packet Format

The DHCP packet format is shown in figure 15.2. The DHCP messages use a fixed format for all the fields, except the options field that has a minimum size of 312 octets. Readers that are familiar with the BOOTP protocol will recognize, with the exception of the flags field and the options field, that the message formats for DHCP and BOOTP are identical. In fact, the DHCP server can be programmed to answer BOOTP requests.

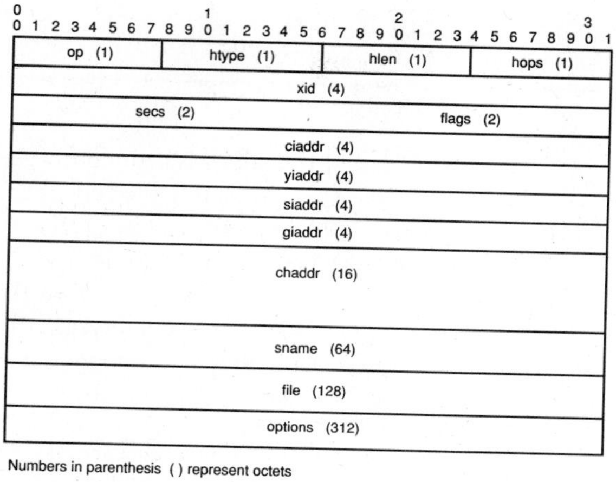

Figure 15.2
The DHCP packet format.

Table 15.1 gives an explanation of the fields used in the DHCP protocol. Only the left-most bit of the DHCP options field is used (see fig. 15.3). The other bits in the options field must be set to 0.

Table 15.1
DHCP Fields

Field	Octets	Description
op	1	Message operator code (message type). A value of 1 means it is a BOOTREQUEST message, and a value of 2 means it is a BOOTREPLY message.
htype	1	The hardware address type. The values are the same as that used for the ARP packet format. For example, a value of 1 is used for 10 Mbps Ethernet.
hlen	1	The hardware address length in octets. Ethernet and Token Ring hardware address length is 6 bytes.
hops	1	The DHCP client sets this to zero. This is used optionally by relay-agents running on routers when they forward DHCP messages. When a DHCP message traverses a router, the hop field is incremented by 1.

continues

Table 15.1, Continued
DHCP Fields

Field	Octets	Description
xid	4	A Transaction ID, which is a randomly generated number chosen by the DHCP client when it generates a DHCP message. The DHCP server uses the same Transaction ID in its DHCP messages to the client. The Transaction ID enables the DHCP clients and servers to associate DHCP messages with the corresponding responses.
secs	2	This field is filled by the DHCP client. It is the seconds elapsed since the client started trying to boot.
flags	2	The left-most bit is used to indicate if this is a broadcast message (bit value of 1). All other bits must remain zero.
ciaddr	4	The DHCP client's IP address. It is filled by the DHCP client in a DHCPREQUEST message to verify the use of previously allocated configuration parameters. If the client does not know its IP address, this field is set to 0.
yiaddr	4	This is the DHCP client's IP address returned by the DHCP server. This is the field that used to return the DHCP client's IP address.
siaddr	4	If the DHCP client wants to contact a specific DHCP server, it inserts the server's IP address in this field. The DHCP server's IP address might have been discovered in prior DHCPOFFER, DHCPACK messages returned by server. The value returned by the DHCP server may be the address of the next server to contact as part of the boot process. For example, this may be the address of a server that holds the operating system boot image.
giaddr	4	This is the IP address of the router that runs the relay agent.

Field	Octets	Description
chaddr	16	The DHCP client's hardware address. A value of 16 octets is used to allow different network hardware types. Ethernet and Token Ring use only 6 octets.
sname	64	This is an optional server host name if known by the DHCP client. It is a null terminated string.
file	128	This is the boot file name. It is a null-terminated string. If the DHCP client wants to boot with an image of the operating system downloaded from a network device it can specify a generic name such as unix for booting a Unix image in a DHCPDISCOVER. The DHCP server can hold more specific information about the exact operating system image needed for that workstation. This image name can be returned by a fully qualified directory-path name in the DHCPOFFER message from the DHCP server.
options	312	This is an optional parameters field.

Most of the DHCP messages sent by the DHCP server to the DHCP client are *unicast* messages (messages sent to single IP address). This occurs because the DHCP server learns about the DHCP client's hardware address in messages sent by the DHCP client to the server. The DHCP client can request that the DHCP server respond with a broadcast address by setting the left-most bit in the options field to 1. The DHCP client does this if it does not know its IP address, yet. The IP protocol module in DHCP client rejects a datagram it receives if the destination IP address in the datagram does not match the IP address of the DHCP client's network interface. If the IP address of the network interface is not known, the datagram is still rejected. The IP protocol module will, however, accept any IP broadcast datagram. Therefore, to ensure that the IP protocol module accepts the DHCP server reply when the IP address is not yet configured, the DHCP client requests that the DHCP server reply using broadcast messages instead of unicast messages.

The options field (see fig. 15.3) is variable in length, with the minimum size extended to 312 octets, so that the total minimum size of a DHCP message is 576 octets, which is the minimum IP datagram size a host must be prepared to accept. If a DHCP client needs to use larger messages, it can negotiate this using the "Maximum DHCP message size" option. Because the sname and file fields are quite large and might not always be used, DHCP options can be further extended into these fields by specifying the Option Overload option. If present, the usual meanings of the sname and file are ignored, and these fields are examined for options. Options are expressed using the T-L-V (Type, Length, Value) format. Figure 15.4 shows that in DHCP, the option consists of a 1-octet Type field, followed by a 1-octet Length field. The value of the Length field contains the size of the Value field. The different DHCP messages themselves are expressed using a special Type value of 53. The option values that describe the DHCP messages are shown in figure 15.5.

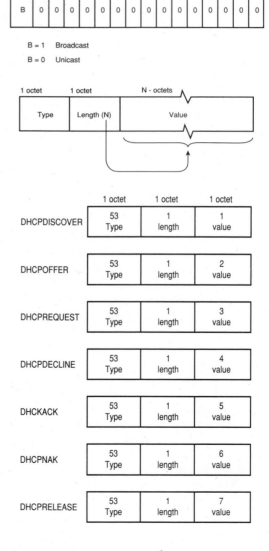

Figure 15.3
The DHCP options field.

B = 1   Broadcast
B = 0   Unicast

Figure 15.4
The Option format for DHCP messages.

Figure 15.5
The Option values for the DHCP messages.

DHCP on a Windows NT Server

Now that you understand how DHCP works, you can better understand the parameter choices involved in installing, configuring, and administering DHCP servers. The following sections describe the procedures for maintaining and administering DHCP servers.

Installing DHCP Server on a Windows NT Server

The DHCP server can only be installed on Windows NT Servers and not on Windows NT Workstations. Figure 15.6 shows a simple network configuration using Windows NT Server DHCP servers and Windows NT DHCP clients. Notice that if DHCP servers are separated by routers, the routers must be configured to forward BOOTP messages.

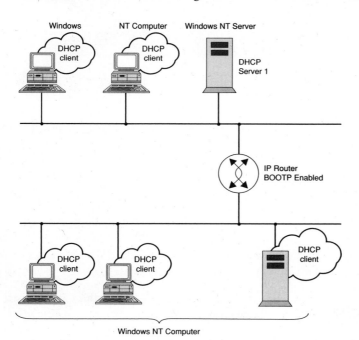

Figure 15.6

Use of DHCP Windows NT Servers.

The following is an outline of the procedure for installing a DHCP server on a Windows NT Server.

1. Log on to the Windows NT Server as an administrator user.

2. Double-click on the Network icon in the Control Panel.

   You should see the Network dialog box.

3. Select the Services tab and click on the **A**dd button.

4. You will see the list of possible services you can add in the Select Network Service dialog box (see fig. 15.7). Select Microsfot DHCP Server from the **N**etwork Service list.

Figure 15.7

The Select Network Service dialog box.

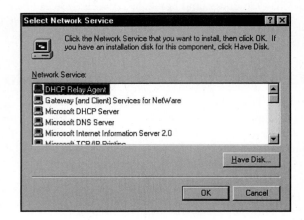

5. Click on the OK button.

    You should see a dialog box prompting you for the path of the distribution files. If you have a CD-ROM on the Windows NT Server, the path should contain the path to the CD-ROM distribution files.

6. Choose the Continue button.

    You should see a status of the copy operation as files are copied.

7. At the end of the file copy, you should see an information box reminding you that any adapters on this server that were using DHCP to obtain their IP addresses must now use static IP addresses. Choose OK. If any adapters were using dynamic IP addresses, a TCP/IP Property sheet appears for you to specify a permanent address.

8. Choose Close. The binding analysis completes the configuration. At this point, you are prompted to restart. Choose **Y**es so the changes can take effect before you continue.

9. Use the Services icon in the Control Panel to verify whether the DHCP Server Services is running. If the DHCP Server is not running, you can start it by using the Start button in the Services dialog box, or start it by using the following command:

```
NET START DHCPSERVER
```

Configuring the DHCP Server

After the DHCP Server is installed as described in the previous section, you must configure it using the DHCP Manager. A DHCP Manager icon is installed in the Network Administration Tools program group. You can also run the DHCP Manager by executing the following command:

```
start dhcpadmn
```

The following is an outline of the procedure for configuring a DHCP server:

1. Log on to the Windows NT Server as an administrator user.

2. Double-click on the DHCP Manager icon in the Network Administration Tools program group.

   If this is the first time you have started the DHCP Manager, you should see that the DHCP Manager shows the local computer (see fig. 15.8).

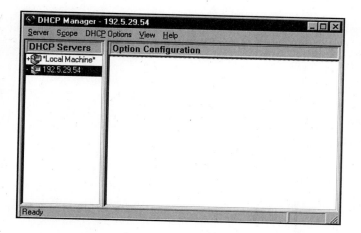

Figure 15.8

The screen you see the first time you use DHCP Manager.

Subsequent to the first startup, the DHCP Manager screen shows the DHCP servers to which the DHCP Manager is connected, and their scopes.

3. Connect the DHCP Manager to a DHCP Server by choosing **A**dd from the **S**erver menu.

   You should see the Add DHCP Server to Server List dialog box (see fig. 15.9).

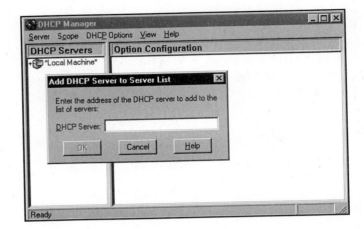

4. In the **D**HCP Server field, add the IP address of the DHCP Server you want to connect to. This should be the IP address of the DHCP Server you want to administer.

5. Choose OK after you finish making changes.

    You should be back to the DHCP Manager screen showing the DHCP servers that have been added to the DHCP Server List (see fig. 15.10).

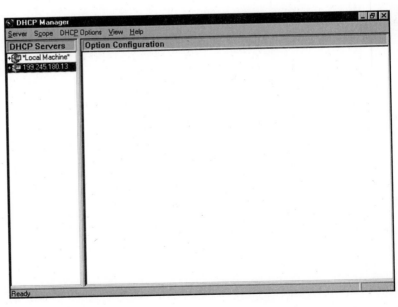

You must next define a DHCP scope. A DHCP *scope* is a grouping of DHCP client computers. You must create a DHCP scope for each IP subnetwork on your network. The DHCP scope defines parameters for that subnet, such as a subnet mask and lease duration values. The DHCP scope is identified by a DHCP scope name that is created at the time of defining the scope.

6. Highlight the Local Computer in the DHCP Manager screen and select Scope, Create to initiate creating a DHCP scope.

The Create Scope dialog box appears (see fig. 15.11).

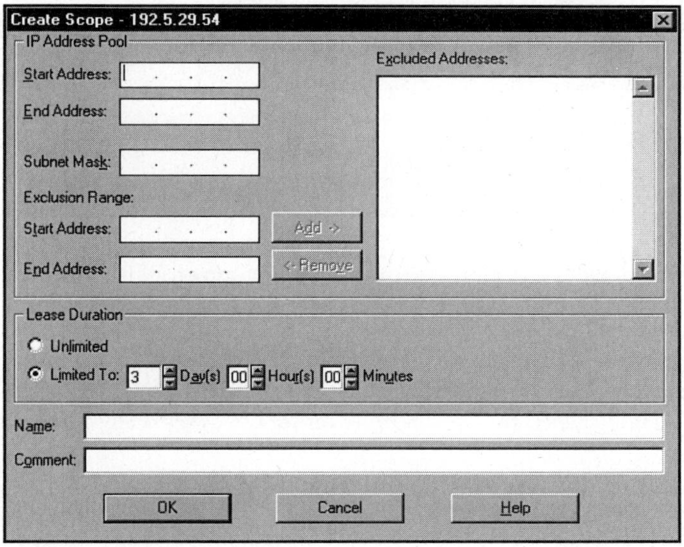

Figure 15.11

The Create Scope dialog box.

7. Use the Start Address and End Address fields to define the range of IP addresses that are available to the DHCP clients.

Figure 15.12 shows that the range of IP addresses is 199.245.180.1 to 199.245.180.254. In this example, 199.245.180.0 and 199.245.180.255 have been excluded because these IP addresses have special meanings on TCP/IP networks. Refer to Chapter 13 "Introduction to TCP/IP Protocol Architecture," for additional details on special IP addresses.

Figure 15.12

Example of an IP address pool defined on a DHCP server.

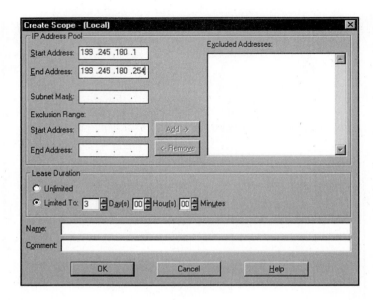

8. In the Subnet Mas**k** field, enter a valid subnet mask for the group of DHCP clients.

9. In the Exclusion Range group of fields, specify any IP addresses that are to be excluded from the IP address range pool that you specified in step 7. You might, for example, want to exclude IP addresses that are permanently assigned to certain TCP/IP hosts on the network or to non-DHCP clients, and are not to be part of the dynamically allocated IP address pool.

    To define an exclusion range, enter the start IP address in the **S**tart Address field and the end IP address in the **E**nd Address field, then choose the A**d**d button. The excluded addresses are listed in the E**x**cluded Addresses list box.

    To exclude a single IP address, enter the address in the **S**tart Address field and leave the **E**nd Address field blank. Next, choose the A**d**d button.

    Figure 15.13 shows a range of IP addresses that are excluded from the pool of IP addresses. IP addresses from 199.245.180.9 to 199.245.180.30, 199.245.180.102, 199.245.180.201, and 199.245.180.51 are excluded from the range of IP pool addresses 199.245.180.1 to 199.245.180.254.

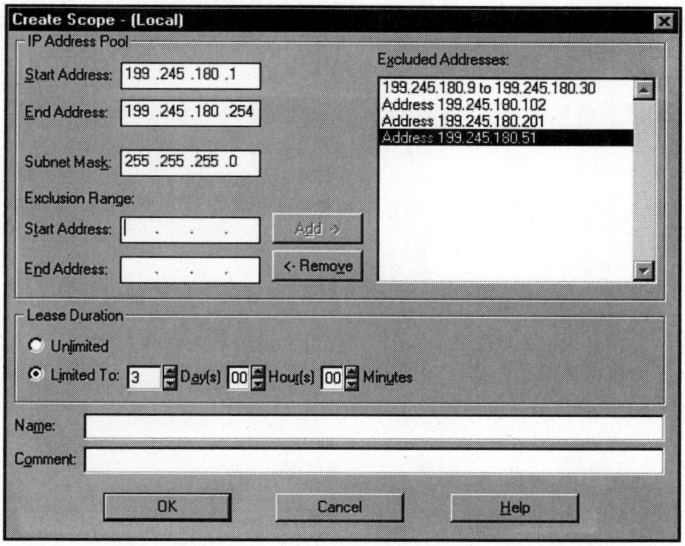

Figure 15.13

An example of excluded IP addresses on the DHCP server.

10. In the Lease Duration section (refer to figure 15.11), you can specify a permanent lease by selecting the Unlimited option, or you can specify a lease of a limited duration.

   If you specify a limited duration lease, you can specify the value in days, hours, and minutes.

   Note that default values of the renewal timer and rebinding timers are calculated by the DHCP client based on the duration of the lease specified in the Lease Duration box. For a discussion on the lease timers, refer to the section "The DHCP IP Address Acquisition Process," earlier in this chapter. The default lease duration is 3 days. Using the Limited To option, you can specify a maximum lease of 999 days, 23 hours, and 59 minutes.

11. In the Name field, specify the DHCP scope name, which is used to describe the subnet. It can contain alphanumeric characters and hyphens (-). Blank spaces, underscores (_), and unicode characters are not allowed.

12. In the Comment field, you have the option to enter a comment describing the DHCP scope you are creating.

Figure 15.14 shows a sample filled-out DHCP scope form. In the DHCP scope, the lease duration is set to 4 days.

Figure 15.14

A sample filled-out DHCP scope form.

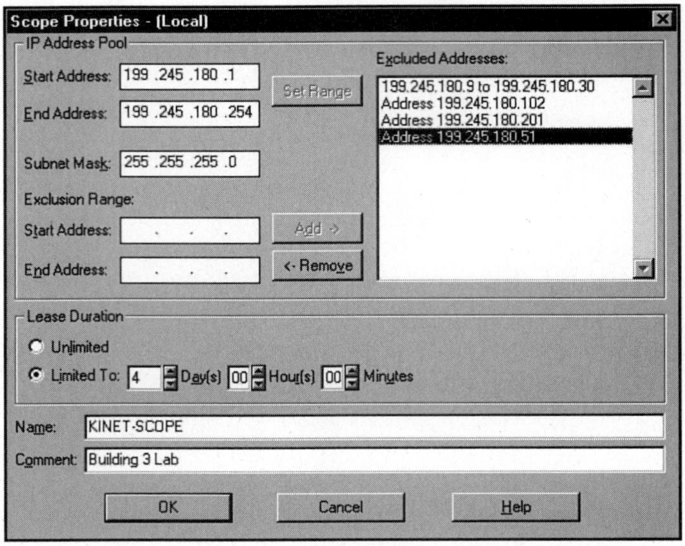

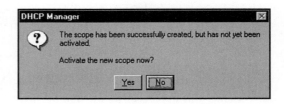

13. Choose OK to create the DHCP scope.

    You will see a message informing you that the scope has been created (see fig. 15.15).

Figure 15.15

The DHCP message about creating scope.

Unless you have already configured DHCP options described in a later step, do not activate the scope now. You can activate the scope after configuring the DHCP options.

Next, you must configure the DHCP options. The DHCP options enable you to configure special classes of devices, such as DNS servers, Routers, and so on. You can use the standard options defined in RFC 1542 or define new ones. Additionally, you can specify that the DHCP options are Global to all scopes or apply to a selected scope only. The DHCP options that you specify for a scope are included in the DHCPOFFER message sent by the DHCP Server to the DHCP Client. You can, therefore, use the DHCP options to configure a large number of TCP/IP parameters, such as those documented in RFC 1542.

Note that your configuration may not involve making any DHCP option changes. In this case, skip to step 19.

14. In the DHCP Manager screen, select the scope you want to configure and make the following selections:

    DHC**P** Options, Global for global settings for all scopes

    DHC**P** Options, Scope for settings per scope

15. Figure 15.16 shows the DHCP Options when the global option is selected, and figure 15.17 shows the settings when a specific scope is selected.

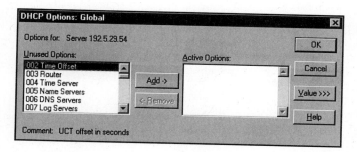

Figure 15.16
The Global dialog box.

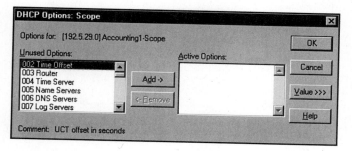

Figure 15.17
The Scope dialog box.

16. In the **U**nused Options list, select the name of the DHCP option you want to apply and choose the A**d**d button.

Figure 15.18 shows an example of some DHCP options that are selected. The active options that are displayed are the WINS/NBT Node Type and WINS/NBNS Servers. These options allow DHCP configured computers to find and use WINS servers automatically.

Figure 15.18

The active DHCP options for finding and using WINS servers automatically.

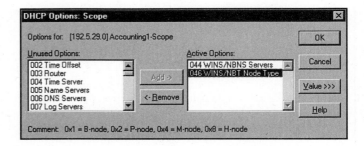

17. To define a value for a selected option, select the name of the option in the **A**ctive Options list, then choose the **V**alue button.

For example, the WINS/NBT Node Type is set to an h-node type using the **V**alue button in figure 15.19.

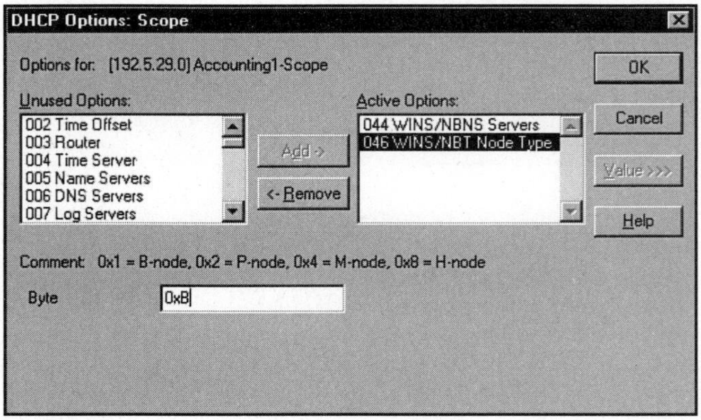

Figure 15.19

An example of using the Values button.

Certain value types require the use of special built-in editor tools. Specifying the IP address of the WINS/NBNS servers, for example, and selecting the Edit Array button starts the Array Editor which can be used to enter the IP addresses of the WINS servers (see fig. 15.20).

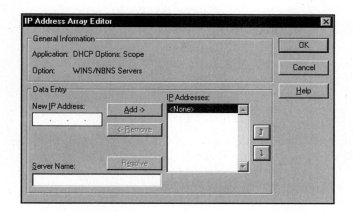

Figure 15.20
The IP Address Array Editor dialog box, for specifying IP addresses.

18. Choose OK to save DHCP configuration changes.

   You should be back to the DHCP Manager main screen. The new DHCP options that you select are displayed on the right side panel under Option Configuration. Figure 15.21 shows some sample DHCP options that were configured.

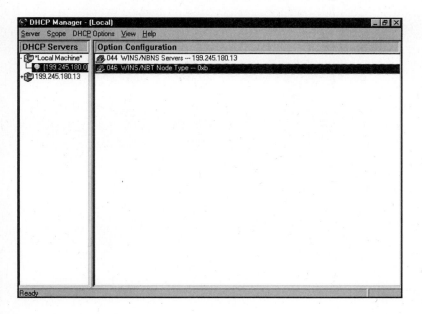

Figure 15.21
Sample DHCP Options defined for a scope in the DHCP Manager main screen.

19. To activate the scope, select S<u>c</u>ope, Activate.

    You will see the light bulb icon lighted up next to the scope that you have activated.

20. Exit the DHCP Manager.

Configuring the DHCP Client

After configuring the DHCP server, you can configure the Windows NT computers on the network with DHCP clients that will obtain the IP parameters from the DHCP server.

If you are installing the TCP/IP protocol for the first time on a Windows NT computer, enable the **O**btain an IP address from a DHCP server radio button option in the Microsoft TCP/IP Properties dialog box, IP Address tab, as shown in figure 15.22. Refer to Chapter 14, "Installing and Configuring the TCP/IP Protocol Stack," which covers installing the TCP/IP protocol.

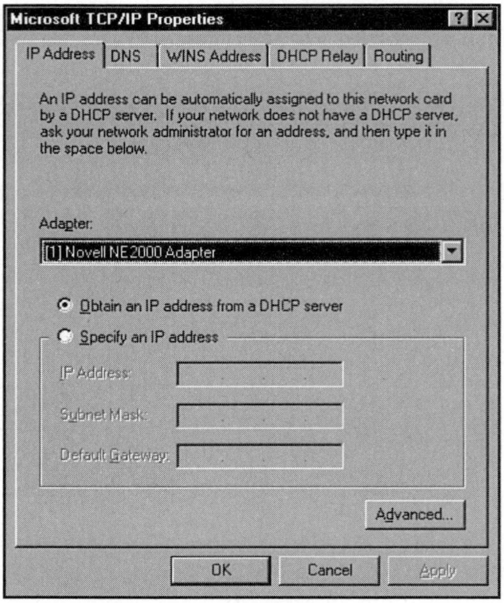

Figure 15.22

The IP Address tab in the TCP/IP Properties dialog box.

If the TCP/IP protocol is already installed on the Windows NT computer, you can enable the DHCP client by performing the following steps:

1. Log on as the administrator user to the Windows NT computer.

2. Start the Network icon from the Control Panel.

3. In the Network dialog box, choose the Protocols tab and select the TCP/IP protocol, then click on the **P**roperties button.

4. In the TCP/IP Properties dialog box that appears, check the **O**btain an IP address from a DHCP server radio button option.

5. Notice that the **I**P Address, S**u**bnet Mask, and Default **G**ateway fields in the dialog box shown in figure 15.22 are grayed out, and the manually configured values are no longer displayed. If you choose A**d**vanced, the Advanced IP Addressing dialog box indicates DHCP Enabled in the IP Addresses box. Select OK to return to the TCP/IP Properties IP Address tab.

6. Click on OK to return to the Protocols tab. Select OK again to close.

7. Select **Y**es to restart the computer for changes to take effect.

Administering Client Leases

The IP addresses assigned by a DHCP server have an expiration date. The lease must be negotiated by the DHCP client as described in the section "The DHCP IP Address Acquisition Process." You can monitor the lease duration and change settings for reserved IP addresses for DHCP clients. Reserving IP addresses for DHCP clients is discussed in the next section.

To manage client lease information, perform the following steps:

1. Log on to the Windows NT Server as an administrator user.

2. Start the DHCP Manager.

3. Highlight the DHCP scope in the main screen and select S**c**ope, Active Leases. The Active Leases dialog box appears (see fig. 15.23).

Figure 15.23

The Active Leases dialog box.

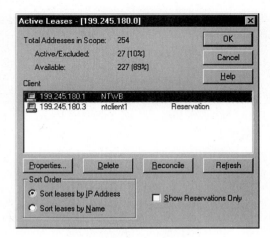

4. The Active Leases dialog box displays the number of Active/Excluded and Available leases in terms of number and percentages. The Client box displays the current leases. IP addresses that are reserved are marked with the text "Reservation." To see only the reserved IP addresses, enable the Show **R**eservations Only check box option.

5. To see details of a particular lease, highlight the lease description in the Clients box and choose the **P**roperties button. Alternatively, double-click on the lease description.

6. Figure 15.24 shows the detail properties of the client lease for IP address 199.245.180.3. The field names in this dialog box are grayed out, indicating that you can only view information and not change it. Notice that the lease expiration time is also listed in this dialog box.

Figure 15.24

Client lease information.

Client Properties	
IP Address:	199 .245 .180 .3
Unique Identifier:	00c086d08f
Client Name:	ntclient1
Client Comment:	NT Client 1 in Bldg 3
Lease Expires:	N/A

OK   Cancel   Help   Options...

7. Figure 15.25 shows the detail properties of the reserved IP address 199.245.180.3 (refer to figure 15.23). You can change the **U**nique Identifier, the Client **N**ame, and Client **C**omment fields. These fields are described in the next section "Reserving DHCP Client IP Addresses." Notice that the lease expiration time is not listed because the IP addresses are reserved and, as such, never expire.

8. To define the DHCP options for reserved IP addresses, choose the **O**ptions button (see fig. 15.25), which opens the DHCP Options: Reservation dialog box (see fig. 15.26).

   Use the Reservation dialog box to add and configure DHCP options for the device types listed in the **U**nused Options list.

   The procedure for selecting a device type to configure as a DHCP option is discussed in steps 16 to 18 in the section "Configuring the DHCP Server," earlier in this chapter.

   Select OK on successive screens to return to the main Active Leases screen.

9. To cancel a lease or an IP address reservation manually, highlight it and choose the **R**emove button in the **A**ctive Options screen. If you attempt to delete a lease, you are prompted to confirm the action. If you delete the lease, it has the same affect as the lease being expired. The DHCP client attempts to negotiate a fresh release.

   If you delete an IP address reservation, you must create a new reservation. This is described in the next section.

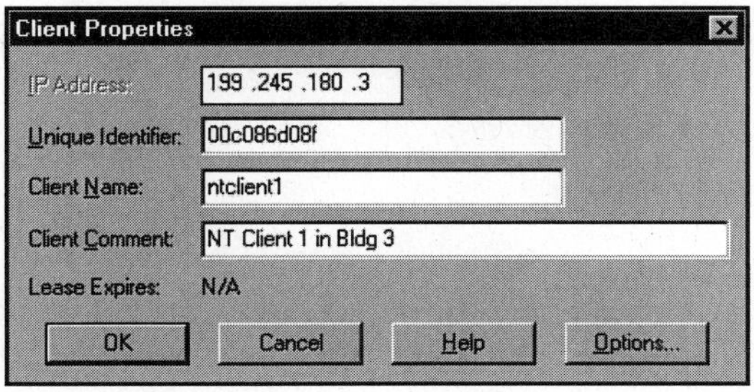

Figure 15.25

Reserved IP address information.

Figure 15.26

*The DHCP Options:
Reservation dialog box.*

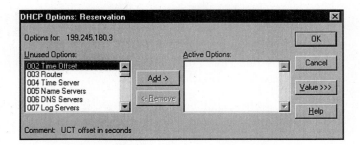

Reserving DHCP Client IP Addresses

Unless you have reserved an IP address for a DHCP client, an IP address is assigned dynamically by the DHCP server, when the DHCP client sends a request for its IP parameter initialization. This IP address is chosen from a pool of available IP addresses. On a network with many DHCP clients, the IP address assigned to the DHCP client on restarting is likely to be different. For most DHCP clients, having a different IP address each time is not a problem. For some Windows NT computers, however, it is important to reserve a specific IP address. You would, for example, need to reserve IP addresses in the following situations:

- Windows NT domain controllers that also use the LMHOSTS file that defines the IP addresses of the domain controllers for DNS Servers, SMTP, web servers, FTP servers, Gopher servers, and any servers that need to be identified in an external public DNS.

- Assignment by RAS servers to non-DHCP clients.

- Clients that have static IP address assignments.

DHCP servers do not communicate or synchronize information amongst themselves. If there are multiple DHCP servers in a DHCP scope, you must ensure that the IP addresses reserved for clients are identical on each DHCP server.

Note   IP addresses and static names specified in the WINS database take precedence over IP address assignments by a DHCP server. Such clients create IP address reservations using the IP address defined in the WINS database.

The following is the procedure for reserving an IP address for a client:

1. Log on to the Windows NT Server as an administrator user.

2. Start the DHCP Manager.

3. Highlight the DHCP scope in the main screen and select S**c**ope, Add Reservations.

    You will see the Add Reserved Clients dialog box (see fig. 15.27).

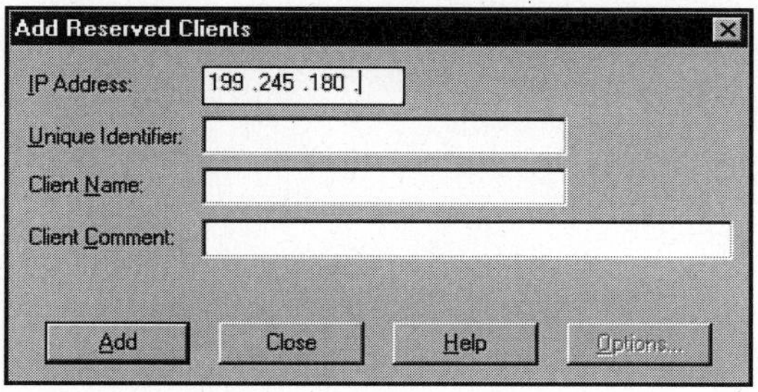

Figure 15.27

The Add Reserved Clients dialog box.

4. Enter the IP address that you want to reserve in the **I**P Address field (refer to figure 15.27).

5. Enter a value in the **U**nique Identifier field to specify the MAC address for the DHCP client. On a Windows NT computer, you can determine the MAC address by using the following commands:

    ```
    NET CONFIG WKSTA
    ```

    or

    ```
    NET CONFIG WORKSTATION
    ```

6. Enter the Windows NT computer name in the Client **N**ame field. This is used for identification purposes only and does not affect the actual client computer name that is used.

7. Optionally, you can enter a text description of the client in the Client **C**omment field.

   Figure 15.28 shows a completed sample Add Reserved Clients form. Notice that the MAC address is expresses as 12 hexadecimal digits for an Ethernet network interface.

Figure 15.28

A completed sample Add Reserved Clients form.

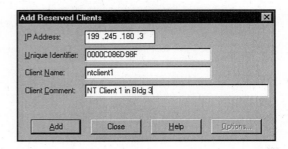

8. Choose the **A**dd button to add the reservation in the DHCP database.

9. Repeat steps 4 to 8 to add other client reservations.

10. After you finish adding client reservations, click on the Close button.

11. To enable the changes to take effect, restart the client computer for whom you have reserved IP addresses.

To change an existing IP address reservation, you must first delete the existing reservation, then add the new reservation. You can delete the existing reservation by selecting S**c**ope, Active Leases, then selecting the Properties button, followed by the Delete button. For details on managing active leases, refer to the previous section.

Advanced Registry Parameter Configuration for DHCP

The DHCP parameters for the DHCP server that can be configured using the Registry Editor are kept under the following key:

`HKEY_LOCAL_MACHINE\SYSTEM\CurrentControlSet\Services\DHCPServer\Parameters`

Figure 15.29 shows the DHCP parameters in the Registry.

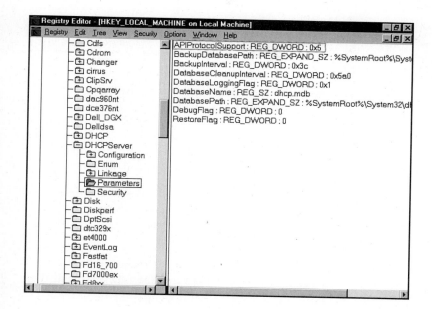

Figure 15.29

DHCP Server parameters in the Registry.

With the exception of the RestoreFlag value entry, changes made to the DHCP parameters require restarting the Windows NT computer before they take effect.

Table 15.2 describes the DHCP parameter value entries. To change the DHCP parameters in the Registry, use the Registry Editor as described in Chapter 10, "Managing Windows NT Registry."

Table 15.2
DHCP Server Value Entries in the Windows NT Registry

DHCP Value Entry	Description
APIProtocolSupport	Specifies the API protocol supported for the DHCP server. You can change this to ensure that computers running a supported protocol can access the DHCP server. The value entry has a data type of REG_DWORD of values 0x1, 0x2, 0x4, 0x5, 0x7, with a default of 0x1. The values have the following meanings: 0x1 = RPC over TCP/IP, 0x2 = RPC over named pipes, 0x4 = RPC over local procedure call (LPC) protocols, 0x5 = RPC over TCP/IP and RPC over LPC, 0x7 = RPC over TCP/IP, named pipes, and LPC (all three API protocols).

continues

Table 15.2, Continued
DHCP Server Value Entries in the Windows NT Registry

DHCP Value Entry	Description
BackupDatabasePath	Specifies the location of the backup data path where DHCP database files are backed up periodically. The value entry is of data type REG_EXPAND_SZ and has a default value of %SystemRoot%\system32\ dhcp\backup. You should not use a network path because DHCP cannot access a network path for backup and recovery.
BackupInterval	Specifies the interval in minutes for backing up the database. The value entry is of type REG_DWORD and has a default value of 15 minutes.
DatabaseCleanupInterval	Specifies the interval for removing expired client records in the DHCP database. The value entry is of type REG_DWORD and has a default value of 0x15180 (864,000 minutes = 24 hours).
DatabaseLoggingFlag	Specifies whether to record the database changes in the DHCP transaction log file J50.LOG. The J50.LOG and related files are used for database recovery after a crash. The value entry is of type REG_DWORD and can have a value of 0 or 1. The default is 1, which means that database logging is turned on. Turning on database logging has an effect on system performance but increases the fault tolerance of the database.
DatabaseName	Specifies the file used to store the DHCP database information. The value entry is of type REG_SZ and has a default name of dhcp.mdb.
DatabasePath	Specifies the directory path under which the database files are created and opened. The value entry is of type REG_SZ and has a default name of %SystemRoot%\ system32\dhcp.
RestoreFlag	Specifies whether to restore the database from the backup directory. The value entry is of type REG_ DWORD and has a value of 0 or 1. A value of 1 means restore, and a value of 0 means do not restore. The default value is 0. The flag is set to 0 automatically after a successful restore.

The Registry parameters for the DHCP client are kept under the following key on the client computer:

`HKEY_LOCAL_MACHINE\SYSTEM\CurrentControlSet\Services\DHCP\Parameter\option#`

The *option#* are the list of DHCP options that the client can request from the DHCP server. For each option, the following value entries are defined:

RegLocation

KeyType

Figure 15.30 shows the DHCP client parameters for DHCP option 44 (WINS/NBNS Servers). The value of the RegLocation parameter is shown in the String Editor dialog box because its full value is to large for the space in the right panel.

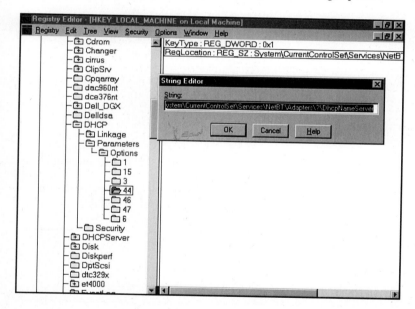

Figure 15.30
DHCP option 44 in the Registry Editor for a DHCP client.

RegLocation is of type REG_SZ and specifies the location in the Registry where the option value is written when it is obtained from the DHCP server. The ? character evaluates to the adapter name that the option value applies to.

The KeyType specifies the type of Registry key for the option. It is of type REG_DWORD and has a default value of 0x7.

SNMP Parameters for Managing DHCP

The DHCP parameters can be managed by an SNMP manager. The DHCP MIB parameters and DHCP Scope group are described in tables 15.3 and 15.4. The SNMP manager must have the capability to import these MIB objects that are specific to DHCP. The values shown in { } are the ASN.1 object IDs for the parameters. The labels, such as DhcpPar, DhcpScope, and so on, are ASN.1 macros that expand to an ASN.1 prefix value defined by Microsoft.

Table 15.3
Windows NT DHCP MIB Parameters

Parameter	Description
ParDhcpStartTime	The DHCP Server start time. {DhcpPar 1}
ParDhcpTotalNoOfDiscovers	The total number of the DHCPDISCOVER messages sent. {ParDhcp 2}
ParDhcpTotalNoOfRequests	The total number of DHCPREQUEST messages sent. {ParDhcp 3}
ParDhcpTotalNoOfReleases	The total number of DHCPRELEASE messages sent. {ParDhcp 4}
ParDhcpTotalNoOfOffers	The total number of DHCPOFFER messages sent. {ParDhcp 5}
ParDhcpTotalNoOfAcks	The total number of DHCPACK messages sent. {ParDhcp 6}
ParDhcpTotalNoOfNacks	The total number of DHCPNAK messages sent. {ParDhcp 7}
ParDhcpTotalNoOfDeclines	The total number of DHCPDECLINE messages sent. {ParDhcp 8}

Table 15.4
Windows NT DHCP Scope Group Parameters

Parameter	Description
ScopeTable	The list of subnets maintained by the DHCP server. {DhcpScope 1}
sScopeTableEntry	The row in the scope table corresponding to a subnet. {ScopeTableEntry 1}
SubnetAdd	The subnet address. {sScopeTableEntry 1}
NoAddInUse	The number of IP addresses in use. {sScopeTableEntry 2}

Parameter	Description
NoAddFree	The number of free IP addresses that are available. {sScopeTableEntry 2}
NoPendingOffers	The number of IP addresses that are offer state. {sScopeTableEntry 2}

Understanding the DHCP Database Files

The DHCP database files are kept by default in the \\%*SystemRoot%*\\System32\\dhcp directory. Figure 15.31 shows the contents of this directory.

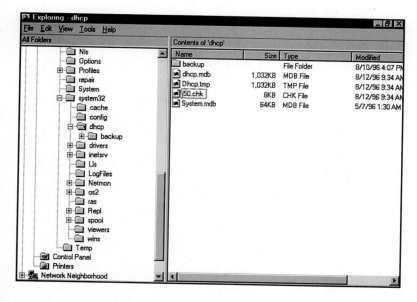

Figure 15.31
DHCP database files.

The DHCP.MDB is the main DHCP database file. The DHCP.TMP is a temporary file that DHCP uses. The J50.LOG and J50*.LOG are transaction log files used to recover from incomplete transactions in case of a system crash. The SYSTEM.MDB is the database schema file that contains information on the structure of the database.

The DHCP database and related Registry value entries are backed up at periodic intervals controlled by the Registry parameter HKEY_LOCAL_MACHINE\\SYSTEM\\CurrentControlSet\\Services\\DHCPServer\\Parameters\\BackupInterval which has a default value of 15 minutes. The backed up files are kept by default in the HKEY_LOCAL_MACHINE\\SYSTEM\\CurrentControlSet\\Services\\DHCPServer\\Parameters\\BackupDatabasePath. By default the backup database path is in the backup subdirectory under the *SystemRoot*\\System32\\dhcp directory.

Conclusion

DHCP solves the important problem of automatic configuration of IP parameters, such as IP addresses and subnet masks, for individual devices on the network. DHCP is a client/server protocol and defines two components, the DHCP client and the DHCP server. Although any Windows NT computer can be a DHCP client, only a Windows NT Server can be a DHCP server.

This chapter provided a comprehensive discussion of the operation of the DHCP protocol. The procedures necessary for the installation and configuration of a DHCP server were discussed. A step-by-step outline and explanation of setting up and administering DHCP servers was presented.

TCP/IP Name Resolution Using WINS

*W*indows NT computers require the use of a computer name to uniquely identify the computer on the network. If the TCP/IP protocol is used, a unique IP address per network interface must be assigned in the computer. While the TCP/IP protocol software uses IP addresses, users typically prefer using symbolic names, such as computer names to identify the computers on the network. On TCP/IP networks, the mechanism of resolving computer names to their IP addresses is called name resolution.

This chapter discusses the name resolution methods used in Windows NT networks in general, with a special emphasis on how you can install and configure WINS name resolution on a Windows NT network.

Overview of Windows NT Name Resolution Methods

Windows NT makes use of any of the following methods for name resolution:

- WINS

- Broadcast Name Resolution

- LMHOSTS file

- DNS

The WINS method uses Microsoft's name resolution server that runs on Windows NT Servers only. Windows NT computers on the network can send name resolution requests to the WINS server. The WINS server contains a dynamic database that is used to map computer names to IP addresses. The WINS name resolution method can be used in conjunction with the broadcast name resolution method. WINS makes use of NetBIOS over TCP/IP mode of operation. This mode of operation is defined in RFC 1001/1002 as a p-node.

The broadcast name resolution using NetBIOS over TCP/IP is another method that can be used in conjunction with WINS for resolving names. In the broadcast name resolution, computers use IP-level broadcasts to register their names. When a Windows NT computer starts up, it announces its name on the network. If a computer name already exists on the network, the computer with that name challenges attempts to register a duplicate name. The first computer on the network that registers its name, therefore, owns that name and must challenge attempts by other computers to use that name. The computer that owns the name responds to name queries for its registered name. This broadcast name resolution is defined in RFC 1001/1002 as b-node.

The LMHOSTS file on a Windows NT computer is used to specify NetBIOS computer name and IP address mappings. The syntax and semantics of this file are discussed in detail in Chapter 14, "Installing and Configuring the TCP/IP Protocol Stack." The LMHOSTS syntax is compatible with the syntax of the HOSTS file that is used by Windows Socket applications. LMHOSTS is popular for use in small networks for providing name resolution. It also can be used in remote subnets where a WINS server might not always be available.

The Domain Name System (DNS) is a distributed database of name services that provides a method of name lookup for computers connecting over a large network. Although WINS is specific to Microsoft Networks, DNS can be used on all computer types, including Windows NT network. DNS is a proven technology that is deployed and widely used on the Internet.

Windows NT Server 4 includes a new feature that provides DNS/WINS integration. This feature combines the universal reach of DNS and the convenience of WINS. DNS/WINS integration also provides WINS name resolution over the Internet. A DNS server on a Windows NT server can use WINS to resolve the host name of a Fully Qualified Domain Name (FQDN). This means that you can let WINS maintain a list of IP addresses dynamically. Your local DNS server will automatically refer to WINS for host name resolution. See Chapter 23, "Domain Name Service," for more on WINS/DNS integration.

Understanding NetBIOS over TCP/IP Name Resolution

NetBIOS over TCP/IP is described in RFCs 1001 and 1002. These RFCs describe NetBIOS-to-IP address name resolution methods. These methods describe how NetBIOS names are registered and resolved on the network. Name registration is the process used to define a unique name for each computer on the network. When a Windows NT computer starts, it attempts to register itself using the computer name that is stored in its Registry. Name resolution is the process of determining an IP address corresponding a specific computer name. To provide flexibility in the NetBIOS-to-IP address name resolution, the following methods are defined:

- **b-node.** Uses broadcasts to resolve names (also called the broadcast method)

- **p-node.** Uses point-to-point communications with a name server to resolve names (also called the name query method)

- **m-node.** Uses b-node first, and if it fails, then p-node

- **h-node.** Uses p-node first, and if it fails, then b-node

The method used by a computer to resolve a name also is called its *node type*. Computers that use the broadcast method exclusively are called b-node types, for example, and computers that use the name query method are called p-node types.

If DHCP is used to configure the IP parameters of a computer, their node types are defined by selecting the DHCP option 046 WINS/NBT Node Type for the DHCP scope on the DHCP server. For details on DHCP Configuration, refer to Chapter 15, "Windows NT Server DHCP Configuration."

If a Windows NT client is configured to use WINS servers for name resolution, the client uses NetBIOS over TCP/IP, p-node name queries to resolve computer names. If no WINS servers are on the network, NetBIOS over TCP/IP uses b-node broadcasts to resolve names.

Depending on how TCP/IP is configured on a Windows NT computer, the Windows NT computer also can use LMHOSTS files and DNS for name resolution. The NETBT.SYS module that implements NetBIOS over TCP/IP functionality supports name registration and resolution modes discussed in this chapter.

The different NetBIOS over TCP/IP methods of name resolution are discussed in further detail in the sections that follow.

Understanding the B-Node Method

The b-node mode method uses NetBIOS broadcast packets encapsulated in UDP/IP frames for name registration and resolution. Consider the example shown in figure 16.1. If the Windows NT computer NT1 wants to communicate with another Windows NT computer NT2, it uses an IP-level broadcast on the network with destination address of 255.255.255.255. It then waits a specified time for NT2 to respond. If NT2 does not respond, the name NT2 cannot be resolved and the name resolution software on NT1 returns an error message.

Figure 16.1

B-node name resolution.

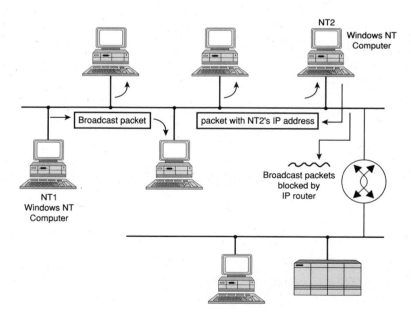

While the b-node name resolution is simple and requires minimal configuration, several disadvantages are evident with the b-node name resolution. Problems include the following:

■ The broadcast packets can consume substantial amounts of network bandwidth.

■ Routers usually are not configured to forward broadcast packets, meaning that b-node resolution fails for computers on network segments separated by routers.

Understanding the P-Node Method

The p-node method overcomes the limitation of the broadcast method by neither creating nor responding to broadcasts requests. Windows NT computers are required to register themselves with the WINS server. The WINS server is a NetBIOS Name Server (NBNS) with Microsoft-specific enhancements.

In order for Windows NT computers to register themselves with the WINS server, you must explicitly provide an IP address of the WINS server when configuring the Windows NT TCP/IP protocol. Because all computers that use WINS must register themselves with the WINS server, the WINS server acts as a central database of computer names and their IP address mappings. The WINS server also ensures that no duplicate computer names exist on the network.

Figure 16.2 shows how the Windows NT computer NT1 uses the p-node method for discovering computer NT2's IP address. The computer NT1 is configured with the IP address of a WINS server on the network. Computer NT1 queries the WINS name server NTS about NT2's IP address. The name server NTS replies with the IP address of NT2. Computer NT1 then uses the IP address of NT2 to communicate with it directly. Because the name queries are sent to the WINS server, and all request/response packets are unicast packets, no broadcast traffic is generated for name resolution. Unlike the broadcast packets, the unicast packets are not blocked by IP routers and, therefore, p-node name resolution can be used in network segments separated by routers.

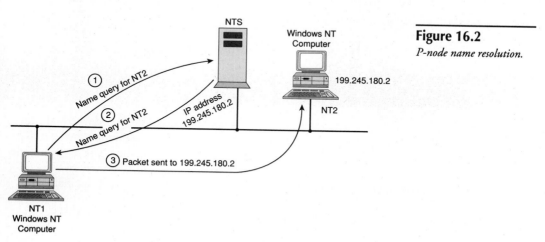

Figure 16.2

P-node name resolution.

While the p-node solves the broadcast and spanning across IP routers problem, it introduces the following concerns:

■ Computers on the network must be configured to know the address of the WINS server. If DHCP is used, this problem can be alleviated by defining the appropriate DHCP option for the WINS server's IP address.

■ The WINS server introduces a single point of failure problem. If the WINS server is down, or not accessible because of network faults, the computers that rely on the WINS server cannot resolve computer names.

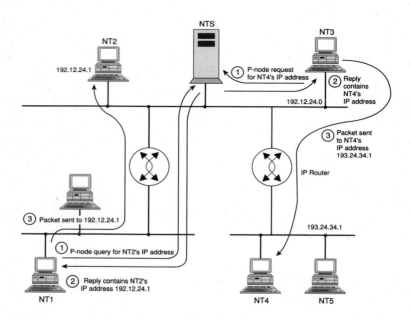

Figure 16.3

P-node name resolution across routers.

Understanding the M-Node Method

The m-node mode method is a combination of using the b-node and the p-node methods. In the m-node method, a computer first attempts registration and resolution using b-node. If b-node cannot resolve the computer name, it switches to the p-node method. Use of the b-node method generates broadcast traffic. This traffic, however, does not cross IP routers and is confined to the local network. For computers on the local network, the m-node method works the same as the b-node method (see fig. 16.4). If the computer is not found on the local network, the p-node, which crosses IP routers, is used to resolve the computer names (see fig. 16.5).

The advantage of the m-node method is that computers on the local network segment can be reached via the b-node even if the WINS server is down or unreachable. Because in most environments local computers are accessed more often than remote computers, most computer names are resolved using the b-node.

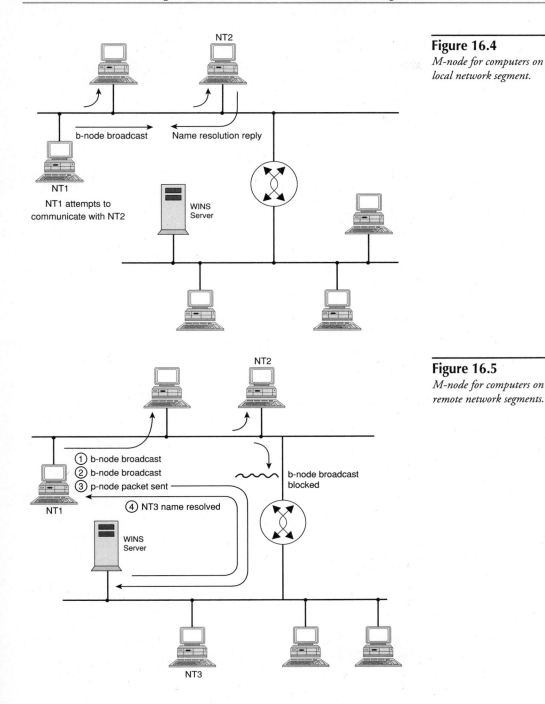

Figure 16.4
M-node for computers on local network segment.

Figure 16.5
M-node for computers on remote network segments.

Understanding the H-Node Method

The h-node method is also a combination of the b-node and the p-node methods. In the h-node method, a computer first attempts registration and resolution using p-node. If p-node cannot resolve the computer name because the WINS server is down or unreachable, it switches to the b-node method. Unlike the m-node or b-node method, use of the p-node method first does not generate any initial broadcast traffic. If the p-node method fails, then the node tries to use the b-node method to resolve names. Because the b-node broadcast requests do not cross IP routers, remote computer names cannot be resolved. Local computer names, however, always can be resolved.

Because the h-node method uses the p-node method first, it avoids broadcast requests if the WINS server is active and can be reached. If the WINS server is down or unreachable, h-node uses b-node local broadcasts but continues to poll the WINS server. As soon as the WINS server comes back online, the h-node computers switch back to using p-node.

Figure 16.6 shows the operation of the h-node when the WINS server can be reached. In figure 16.6 the use of broadcasts packets is completely avoided. Figure 16.7 shows the operation of the h-node when the WINS server cannot be reached. This figure shows that b-node broadcast packets are used as a last resort to resolve local computer names.

Figure 16.6

H-node operation when WINS server is reachable.

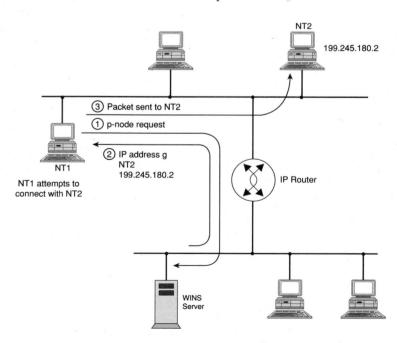

On a Windows network, the h-node can optionally be configured to use LMHOSTS after broadcast name resolution fails. Figure 16.8 shows the sequence of steps that will cause the LMHOSTS file to be used. In this figure both the p-node and the b-node methods fail, and the LMHOSTS file is used as a last resort. The h-node method is the default method used if TCP/IP is configured manually and WINS server addresses are specified.

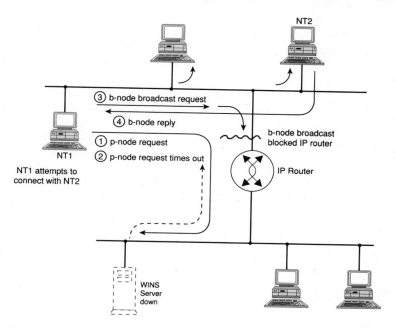

Figure 16.7

H-node operation when WINS server is not reachable.

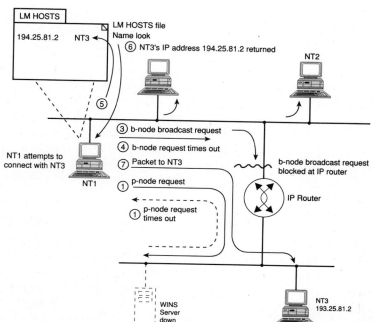

Figure 16.8

H-node operation with LMHOSTS file.

Combining B-Node with LMHOSTS Name Resolution

Except for the method described in figure 16.8, the b-node, m-node and h-node methods described in RFCs 1001 and 1002 do not use the LMHOSTS file. Microsoft has added extensions to the standard b-node method that can use the LMHOSTS file. In the Microsoft extensions, if b-node fails to resolve the name, the LMHOSTS file is used to resolve names. Because b-node broadcasts cannot cross router boundaries, you can use the LMHOSTS file to resolve names for remote computers. The remote computers could be important servers and hosts, such as primary domain controllers and backup domain controllers, for a Windows NT domain. Windows NT uses the Microsoft extensions only if the WINS server is not specified for the Windows NT computer. Windows 3.11 for Workgroups and MS LAN Manager always use the b-node method with Microsoft extensions.

The Windows Internet Name Service (WINS)

Microsoft's WINS server, which can be installed only on Windows NT Servers, is an implementation of the NetBIOS Name Server (NBNS) described in RFCs 1001 and 1002. The WINS server, however, adds extensions to the NBNS specification. One such extension is the interaction with DHCP. If DHCP is used to automatically generate IP addresses for Windows NT computers, the IP addresses assigned using DHCP are updated automatically in the WINS database.

Name Resolution with WINS Servers

WINS uses a client/server architecture that consists of the WINS server and a WINS client. All Windows NT computers that have TCP/IP installed can be enabled to use the WINS client by specifying the IP address of the WINS server in the WINS Address tab of the Microsoft TCP/IP Properties dialog (see fig. 16.9). To reach the Microsoft TCP/IP Properties dialog, select TCP/IP in the Protocols tab of the Control Panel Network application and click on the **P**roperties button. Figure 16.9 shows that a primary and secondary WINS server can be specified for a Windows NT network. As shown in figure 16.9, the WINS Address tab also lets you enable the WINS/DNS integration describe earlier in this chapter, as well LMHOSTS lookup for IP addresses.

Windows 3.11 or Windows computers that are WINS-client enabled can also use the WINS server. Non-Microsoft clients that do not have a WINS client but are b-node compatible, as described by RFCs 1001 and 1002, still can access WINS servers through proxies. WINS proxies are Windows NT computers that listen for b-node broadcasts. The proxies contact the WINS server and return the reply to the computer that originated the b-node name query. Figure 16.10 describes the behavior of WINS proxies. Proxies are used for forwarding name query packets and verifying that duplicate computer names do not exist. Proxies do not, however, register b-node computer names with the WINS database. The proxy does not maintain its own names database. It can, however, cache the results of the name resolution for a period of time. If possible, the proxy resolves the name by looking up its cache.

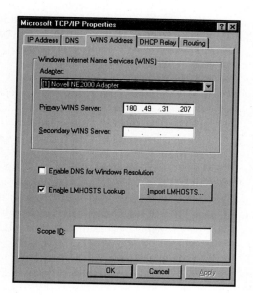

Figure 16.9

The WINS Address tab in the Microsoft TCP/IP Properties dialog box.

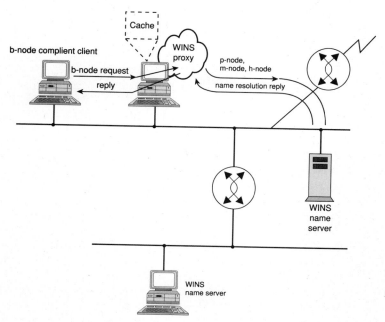

Figure 16.10

Use of a WINS proxy to contact a WINS server.

If a Windows NT network does not have a WINS server, then the administrator must ensure that the user's primary domain has a master browser on each network segment. This provision allows browsing on a network consisting of multiple network segments connected by routers. The master browser dynamically records a list of computer names on the network segment. The list of computer names is returned to a browser client, such as another Windows NT computer. The master browser can be any Windows NT workstation or server. The master browsers also need entries for the domain controllers on other network segments in their LMHOSTS file.

If a Windows NT network has WINS servers, browsing is provided transparently, even in situations where the domain spans router boundaries.

If a WINS server is not specified in the TCP/IP configuration for a Windows NT computer, the computer registers its name by broadcasting name registration request packets at IP address 255.255.255.255 on the local subnet using UDP datagrams. The registration requests are sent to UDP port 137 (well-known port for NetBIOS name service). To resolve a computer name, the non-WINS computer sends b-node broadcast name query request packets on the local network. If the computer is on a remote network the b-node method fails. If the b-node method fails, the computer attempts to resolve the name by consulting the LMHOSTS file. Figure 16.11 explains this behavior when WINS is not enabled.

Figure 16.11

Windows NT name resolution for non-WINS computers.

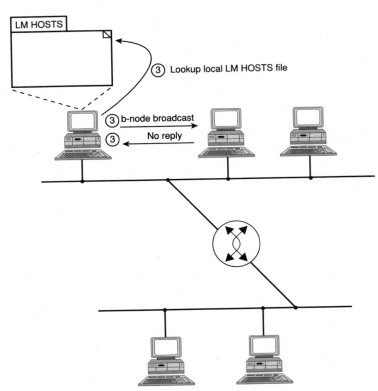

If a WINS server is specified in the TCP/IP configuration for a Windows NT computer, the computer first queries the WINS server. If the WINS server does not respond or is unable to resolve the name query, the name registration and query requests are broadcast via UDP datagrams in the h-node. The following steps describe the behavior in more detail:

1. A name query request is sent to the WINS server. If the request could originate from remote clients on another subnetwork, the request is forwaded by IP routers. The name query request is encapsulated in a UDP/IP datagram. If the WINS can resolve the name by consulting its database, the client attempts to establish a session to the IP address returned by WINS.

2. If the WINS is unable to resolve the name, and if the Windows NT computer client is configured as an h-node, the client sends a b-node broadcasts name query request packet.

3. If the b-node broadcasts name query finally fails, the Windows NT computer client checks the local LMHOSTS file.

Name Registration Using WINS

Name registration is used to ensure that the computer's name and IP address are unique for each device. Name registration involves the following processes:

- **Name Registration.** The computer claims its name and IP address mapping.

- **Name Release.** The computer relinquishes control over its computer name and IP address mapping.

- **Name Renewal.** The computer name undergoes a timed re-registration.

Name Registration

If a computer is configured to use a WINS server, its name registration request is sent directly to the WINS server. The WINS server examines the registration request and accepts or rejects it based on the information in its database. For instance, if the WINS database contains a different IP address for the computer name, the WINS server challenges the current computer name entry to determine whether that computer still claims the name. If current computer name entry is valid, the WINS server rejects the name registration attempt. If no challenge to the new registration request is made, the WINS server accepts the registration request and adds it to its local database. The new registration is time stamped, and an incremental unique version number and other information also are added. The version number is used to ensure that changes in a WINS database is propagated correctly to other WINS servers.

If a computer is not configured to use a WINS server, its name registration request is broadcast to the local network. The broadcast packet contains the computer name and IP address. If another computer has previously claimed that name, it challenges the name registration, assuming that the computer still is active on the network. The challenge is sent in the form of a negative name registration response, which contests the registration name request. After receiving a negative name registration response, a computer should report an error. In the case of Windows NT computer, this error also is recorded in the system event log, which can be viewed by the Event Viewer. If the registration attempt is not contested within a specific time period, the computer can use that name and IP address. Computers that have claimed a name must challenge duplicate name registration attempts and respond to name queries with the IP address of the computer.

Name Release

When the computer is shut down, it releases its computer name and IP address mapping. Again, two situations occur: one in which the Windows NT computer is configured with a WINS server, and another in which it is not.

If a computer is configured to use a WINS server and the computer is shut down gracefully, then it sends a release message to the WINS server as part of the shutdown process. After receiving the release message, the WINS server marks the computer name entry in its database as released. If the entry continues to remain released for a period of time, the WINS server marks the entry as being extinct. This time period is called the *Extinction Interval,* and can be configured for the WINS server. The version number for this entry is updated so that the database changes are propagated among the WINS servers.

Extinct entries are held in the database for a period of time, called the *Extinction Timeout,* that is sufficiently long enough for all changes to have been propagated before the entry is scavenged (deleted) from the database. The last time an entry is scavenged it is reported as a statistic parameter for a WINS server. The Extinct Timeout can be set for each WINS server.

If a WINS database entry is in the released state and a new registration request arrives that uses the same computer name, but a different IP address, then the WINS server registers the new computer name knowing that the old client has released that name because it is no longer being used.

If a computer is shut down abruptly, and another computer attempts to register the same computer name with a different IP address, the WINS server does not initially know of the shutdown and, therefore, seeks to verify whether the old registration still is valid by attempting to contact the old client. If the client still is shut down or has rebooted with a different IP address (in case of a DHCP client, for example), then the WINS server allows the new registration attempt to succeed.

If a computer is not configured to use a WINS server, and the computer is gracefully shut down, it sends a directed broadcast datagram on UDP port number 138 (a well-known NetBIOS datagram port) to the subnet to releases its name. Other Windows NT computers that have cached the computer name must delete the computer name from their cache. If, during this shutdown period, the computer receives name query or registration packets specifying its name, it ignores the packets, enabling other computers to claim the computer name and IP address mapping.

WINS Name Renewal

When a WINS server registers a computer name, it returns to the WINS client a renewal time for the computer name called the *Renewal Interval.* The client must re-register the computer name within the renewal time, or the WINS server will mark the name as released. A request to renew a computer name and IP address mapping is treated as a new name registration. The Renewal Interval can be configured for a WINS server. The client typically registers in half the value of the Renewal Timer.

By forcing computers to renew their registration, the WINS server ensures that its database does not contain old entries for computer names that were shut down abruptly.

The WINS server periodically verifies if old names are still active. The time interval for performing this check is called the *Verify Interval.*

Implementing WINS on a Windows NT Network

The previous section has exposed you to theory behind WINS servers. This section discusses how to implement a WINS server on a Windows NT network. The following sections discuss installing and configuring WINS servers, administering WINS servers, configuring replication partners, and managing static mappings.

Installing a WINS Server

The WINS Server can be installed as part of installing other TCP/IP and related components, or in a separate step. The following is the procedure for installing the Windows NT Server in a separate step.

1. Logon to the Windows NT Server as an administrator user.

2. Double-click on the Network icon in the Control Panel.

   You should see the Network dialog box.

3. Choose the Services tab.

4. Click on the Add button.

You should see the Select Network Service dialog (see fig. 16.12). Select Windows Internet Name Service and click on OK.

Figure 16.12

*The Select Network
Service dialog box.*

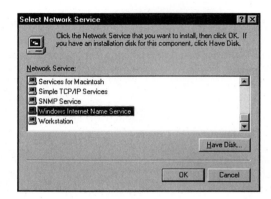

5. Choose OK to continue.

   You should see a dialog box prompting you for the path of the distribution files. If you have a CD-ROM on the Windows NT Server, the path contains the path to the CD-ROM distribution files.

6. Choose OK to continue.

   A status bar showing the status of the copy operation appears.

7. After the configuration and binding analysis completes, restart the Windows NT Server.

8. Use the Services icon in the Control Panel to verify if the WINS Server Services is running. If the WINS Server is not running, you can start it using the Start button in the Services dialog box, or start it using the NET START WINS command.

Using the WINS Manager

The WINS Server is managed by using the WINS Manager. The WINS Manager icon is created in the Administrative Tools program group. You can use the WINS Manager to view and configure parameters for any WINS server on the network. You can start the WINS Manager using the WINS Manger icon, or using the following command:

```
START WINSADMN [WINServerIPaddress]
```

To start WINS on the local server, use the following command:

```
START WINSADMN
```

To start WINS in the server at 199.245.180.14, use the following command:

```
START WINSADMN 199.245.180.14
```

The following is a guided tour for showing you the features of the WINS Manager tool.

1. Logon as administrator user. Select Programs in the Start menu and then choose Administrative Tools. Select WINS Manager.

2. If the WINS server is running on the local computer, you will see the WINS server statistics (see fig. 16.13).

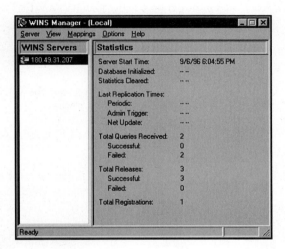

Figure 16.13
WINS Server Statistics.

The basic statistics that are displayed in figure 16.13 are explained next.

- **Server Start Time.** The time the WINS server service was started.

- **Database Initialized.** The time when this WINS database was first initialized.

- **Statistics Cleared.** The time when statistics for the WINS server was last cleared.

- **Last Replication Times.** The time when the WINS database was last replicated.

- **Periodic.** The last time the WINS database was replicated based on the replication interval specified in the Preferences dialog box.

- **Admin Trigger.** The last time the WINS database was replicated because the administrator chose the Replicate Now button in the Replication Partners dialog box.

- **Net Update.** The last time the WINS database was replicated as a result of a network request. A network request is a push notification message that requests propagation.

■ **Total Queries Received.** The number of name query request messages received by this WINS server. Successful indicates how many names were successfully resolved, and Failed indicates the number of names the WINS server could not resolve.

■ **Total Releases.** The number of messages received that indicate a NetBIOS application has shut itself down. Successful indicates how many names were successfully released, and Failed indicates how many names this WINS server could not release.

■ **Total Registrations.** The number of name registration messages received from WINS clients.

3. If the WINS server is not running on the WINS server, when you start the WINS Manager, the Add WINS Server dialog box will appear.

   In general, to add other WINS servers in the list displayed on the left panel so you can administer them, choose **S**erver, **A**dd WINS Server.

   You should see the Add WINS Server dialog box (see fig. 16.14). You can only enter a WINS server that is available on-line. Figure 16.15 shows the Validate WINS Server dialog box that appears if you are unable to validate a WINS server.

Figure 16.14
The Add WINS Server dialog box.

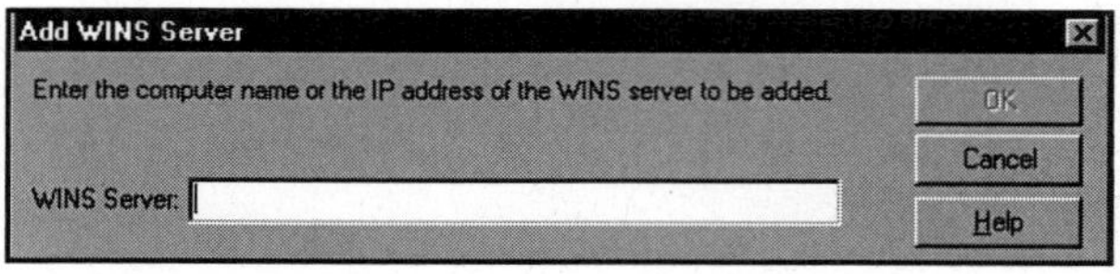

Figure 16.15
The Validate WINS Server dialog box.

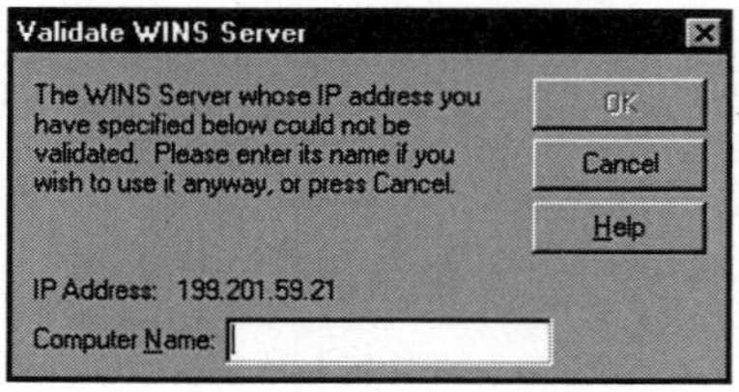

4. The statistics screen is not automatically refreshed (refer to figure 16.13). To refresh the statistics display, choose **V**iew, Refresh or press F5.

5. To clear the statistics counters, choose **V**iew, Clear Statistics.

6. To see detailed information about the current WINS server, choose **S**erver, Detailed Information. The Detailed Information screen appears (see fig. 16.16).

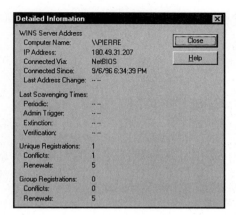

Figure 16.16
*Detailed Information on
WINS server.*

The meanings of the different detailed information parameters for WINS are explained next.

- **Last Address Change.** The time at which the last WINS database change was replicated.

- **Last Scavenging Times.** The last times that the database was cleaned for specific types of entries.

- **Periodic.** Indicates when the database was cleaned based on the renewal interval specified in the WINS Server Configuration dialog box.

- **Admin Trigger.** Indicates when the database was last cleaned because the administrator chose the Initiate Scavenging option.

- **Extinction.** Indicates when the database was last cleaned based on the Extinction interval specified in the WINS Server Configuration dialog box.

- **Verification.** Indicates when the database was last cleaned based on the Verify interval specified in the WINS Server Configuration dialog box.

- **Registrations.** The number of name registration requests that this WINS server has accepted.

- **Conflicts.** The number of conflicts encountered during registration of unique computer names registered at the WINS server.

- **Renewals.** The number of renewals received for unique computer names.

- **Group Registrations.** The number of registration requests for groups that have been accepted by this WINS server.

- **Conflicts.** The number of conflicts encountered during registration of group names.

- **Renewals.** The number of renewals received for group names.

Configuring WINS Servers

Each WINS server can be configured for renewal, verification, and extinction intervals. Because the WINS server database is crucial for name resolution and registration, WINS servers can be configured with other servers as replication partners. Within a WINS replication partnership you can have a *pull partner* that pulls or fetches the database entries from its replica partner (see fig. 16.17). A *push partner* is a WINS server that pushes or sends update notification messages to its partner that the WINS database has changed (see fig. 16.18). As part of configuring a WINS server, you can specify the push and pull parameters for replicated servers.

Figure 16.17

A pull partner for replicated WINS databases.

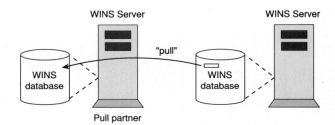

Figure 16.18

A push partner for replicated WINS databases.

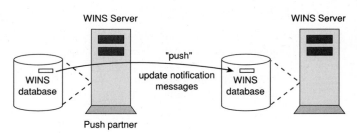

The following is an outline of a procedure for configuring WINS servers:

1. Log on as administrator to the WINS server.

2. Start the WINS Manager.

3. Choose **S**erver, **C**onfiguration.

   The WINS and Pull/Push Parameters appear in the WINS Server Configuration dialog box (see fig. 16.19).

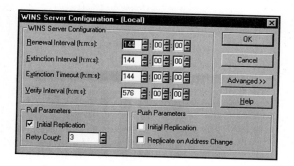

Figure 16.19
The initial WINS Server Configuration screen.

Use the screen in figure 16.19 to specify the renewal, extinction, and verify parameters in hours, minutes and seconds.

The **R**enewal Interval specifies that the client must re-register its name within this time period. The default setting us is 96 hours (4 days). WINS clients will typically re-register and renew in half this time interval, that is in 2 days.

The **E**xtinction Interval specifies the time interval between when an entry is marked as released and when it is marked as extinct. The default is 96 hours (4 days).

The E**x**tinction Timeout is the time interval between when an entry is marked extinct and when the entry is finally scavenged from the database. The default is the same as the renewal interval (96 hours or 4 days).

The **V**erify Interval is the time interval after which the WINS server must verify that old names it does not own are still active. The default is 576 hours (24 days).

You should adjust the values of the interval timers based on your network requirements. You should take into account how often computer names and IP addresses need to change and the amount of traffic generated by renewal, verification, and extinction intervals.

4. Check the **I**nitial Replication option in the Pull Parameters box, if you want the WINS server to pull replicas of new WINS database entries from its partners when the system is initialized, or when a replication-related parameter changes. In the Retry Cou**nt** specify how many attempts should be made if the pull operation does not succeed. Retries occur at the replication interval specified in the Preferences dialog box. If all the retries fail, WINS waits for a period of time controlled in the Preferences dialog box, before starting replication again.

5. Check Initi**a**l Replication option in the Push Parameters section, to send notification messages to the replica partners of the WINS database status when the system is initialized. To send notification messages about IP address changes to the replication partners, check the Rep**l**icate On Address Change option in the Push Parameters section.

6. To see the Advanced options, choose the Advanced button.

Additional options appear for the WINS Server Configuration dialog box (see fig. 16.20).

Figure 16.20

The WINS Server Configuration screen, with advanced options.

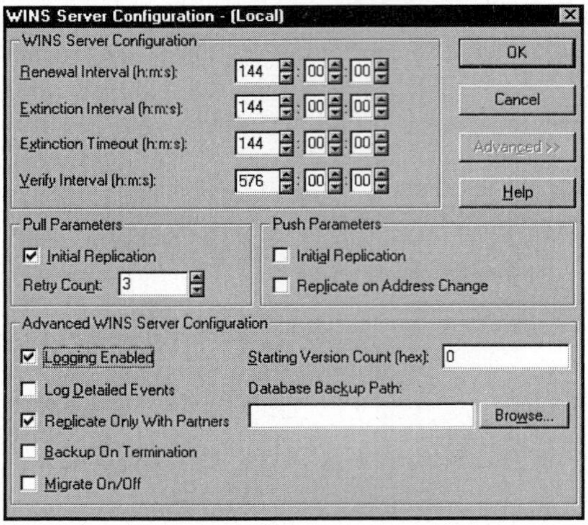

The advanced options are explained next:

The Logging Enabled option specifies whether logging of database changes to the transaction log file JET.LOG should be turned on. The transaction log file is used to recover from incomplete transactions in the database. This option is enabled by default.

The Log Detailed Events option specifies whether detailed information should be reported when events are logged. Logging detailed events consume considerable system resources and should be turned off if you are tuning for performance. This option is disabled by default.

The Replicate Only With Partners option specifies that replication will be performed only with WINS pull or push partners. If this option is not enabled, an administrator can ask a WINS server to pull or push from or to a non-listed WINS server partner. This option is enabled by default.

The Backup On Termination option specifies that the database will be backed up automatically when WINS Manager is closed. This option is disabled by default.

The Migrate On/Off option specifies that static unique and multihomed (multiple network board) records in the database are treated as dynamic and overwritten when they conflict with a new registration or replica. Check this option if you are upgrading a non-Windows NT systems to Windows NT. This option is disabled by default.

The **S**tarting Version Count option specifies the starting version ID number for the database. Normally, you will not need to change this value unless the database becomes corrupted and needs a new start. In this case, set this number to a number higher than that which appears as the version number counter for this WINS server on all the remote partners that have a replica of the WINS server's database records. The version number can be seen in the View Database dialog box in WINS Manager.

The Database Bac**k**up Path option specifies the directory where the WINS database backup files will be stored. WINS uses this directory to perform an automatic restoration of the database if the current database is found to be corrupted when WINS is started. You should not specify a network path for this field.

Configuring WINS Replication

WINS servers can be configured in partnership among themselves so that they can replicate their databases. This ensures that the names registered on WINS servers are replicated to all WINS replication partners on the network. Replication changes are performed within the Replication Interval specified in the Preferences dialog box.

Replication is not performed indiscriminately among WINS servers on the network. Rather, you must explicitly specify WINS servers that are in a replication partnership. In the example in figure 16.21, NTS2 and NTS5 have only one replication partner, NTS1. However, NTS1 has two replication partners; NTS2 and NTS5. NTS3 and NTS4 do not have any replication partners, and are therefore vulnerable to failure.

As explained earlier, a WINS server can be configured as a push or a pull partner, or both. The pull partner gets its information by requesting and obtaining information from its push partner. A push partner sends notification changes to its pull partner. Version numbers associated with the WINS database records are used to decide the latest version of the information in the records.

Replication is initiated, also called *triggered,* when a WINS server polls another WINS server to get a replica. The polling can occur during WINS system initialization, at a specific time, and then repeat at the Replication Interval for periodic replication. Replication can also be triggered when a WINS server reaches an Update Count threshold set by the administrator. The server then notifies its pull partners that it has reached its threshold, and the other servers can then decide to pull replicas.

The following is an outline of how to configure replication partners for WINS servers:

1. Logon to the WINS server as an administrator user.

2. Start the WINS Manager.

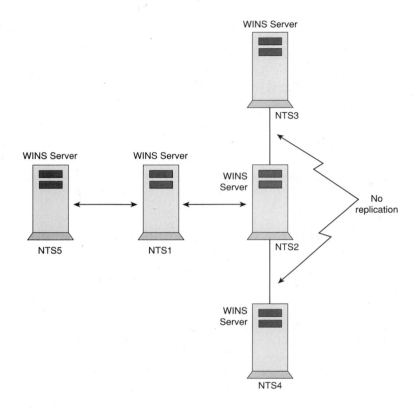

Figure 16.21
*A WINS server replication
example.*

3. Choose **S**erver, **R**eplication Partners.

   The Replication Partners dialog box appears (see fig. 16.22).

Figure 16.22
*The Replication Partners
dialog box.*

4. Choose the **A**dd button.

   The Add WINS Server dialog box appears (see fig. 16.23).

Figure 16.23
The Add WINS Server dialog box.

5. In the WINS Server field, enter the name or IP address of the WINS server that is a potential candidate to be added to the replicator list.

   Choose OK.

   If the WINS Server can be found, it will be added to the WINS Server list in the Replication Partners dialog box (see fig. 16.24).

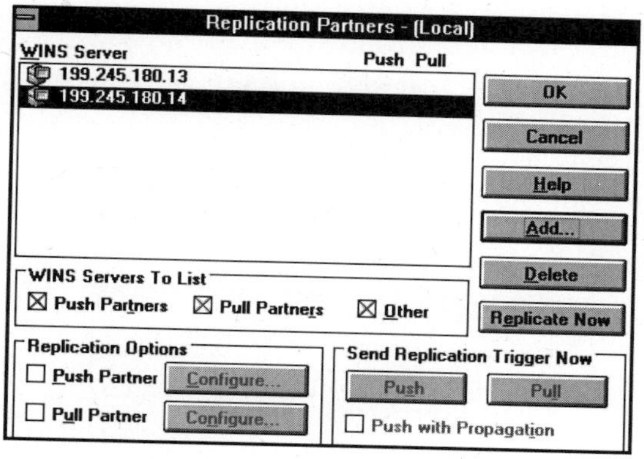

Figure 16.24
WINS Server added to server list.

6. If you want to control which WINS servers are displayed in the Replication Partners dialog box, check or clear the options in the WINS Servers To List box:

   To display push partners for the current WINS server, enable the Push Par**t**ners option.

   To display pull partners for the current WINS server, enable the Pull Partne**r**s option.

   To display WINS servers that are neither push partners, or pull partners enable the **O**ther option.

7. From the **W**INS Server list in the Replication Partners dialog box, select the WINS server to be made a push or pull partner of the current WINS server.

8. Check either the **P**ush Partner or P**u**ll Partner option, or both to specify the replication partnership with the current server, and choose the corresponding **C**onfigure button.

9. If the Pull Partner option is selected, you will see the Pull Partner Properties dialog box (see fig. 16.25).

Figure 16.25

The Pull Partner Properties dialog box.

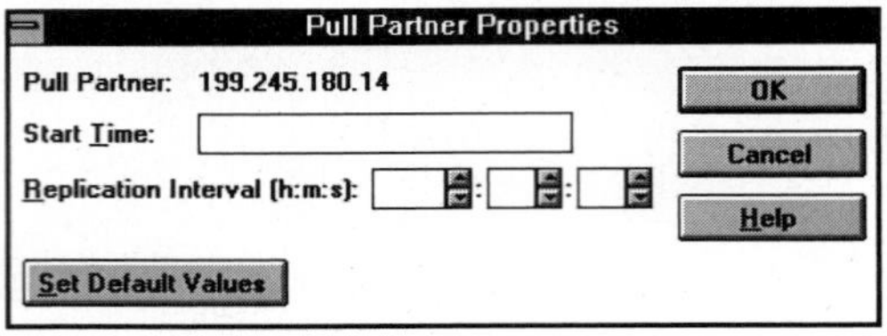

In the Start **T**ime field of the Pull Partner Properties dialog box, enter the time when replication should begin.

In the **R**eplication Interval field of the Pull Partner Properties dialog box, enter the Replication Interval value.

If you want to use the values specified in the Preferences dialog box, choose the **S**et Default Values button.

Choose OK in the Pull Partner Properties dialog box to return to the Replication Partners dialog box.

10. If the Push Partner option is selected, you will see the Push Partner Properties dialog box (see fig. 16.26).

Figure 16.26

The Push Partner Properties dialog box.

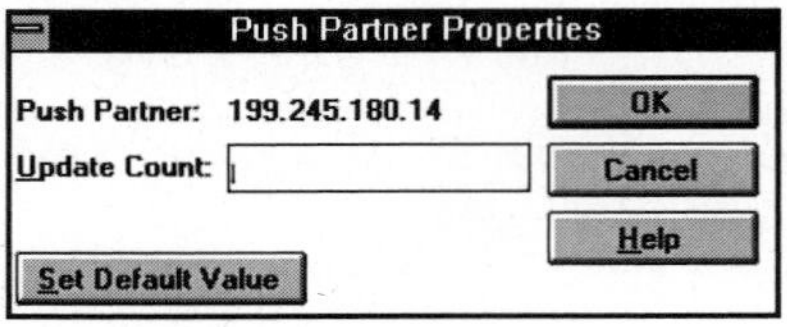

In the **U**pdate Count field of the Push Partner Properties dialog box, specify a number for the additions and updates that are made to records in the WINS database that will result in a notification message being sent to the WINS partner that the changes need replication. If the push server is also acting as a pull server, replications that have been pulled from the partners are not part of the update count. The minimum value for Update Count is 5.

If you want to use the values specifed in the Preferences dialog box, choose the **S**et Default Value button.

Choose OK in the Pull Partner Properties dialog box to return to the Replication Partners dialog box.

11. You can send replication triggers for the partners you add immediately from the Replication Partners dialog box. This option is useful if you have made substantial changes to the WINS database and want to replicate the database between the partners immediately, rather than waiting for the start time or replication interval.

   To send a replication trigger, select the WINS servers to which you want to send a replication trigger, and then choose the Push or Pull button, depending on whether you want to send the trigger to push partners or pull partners.

   If you want the selected WINS server to propagate the trigger to all its pull partners after it has pulled the latest information, set the Push With Propagation option. If the selected WINS server does not need to synchronize because it has the same or more up-to-date replicas than the source WINS server, it does not propagate the trigger to its pull partners.

   If Push With Propagation is not set, the selected WINS server will not propagate the trigger to its other partners.

12. If you need to start replication immediately, choose the Replicate Now button in the Replication Partners dialog box.

13. If you need to delete replication partners, select one or more servers in the WINS Server list in the Replication Partners dialog box, and then choose the **D**elete button, or press Del.

   WINS Manager will asks you to confirm the deletion if you have enabled Delete Confirmation in the Preference dialog box.

Configuring WINS Preferences

In the previous sections, the WINS Preference dialog box was mentioned several times. This dialog box enables you to configure several global options for WINS administration.

The following is an outline of configuring WINS preferences:

1. Start the WINS Manager while logged as an administrator user.

2. Choose **O**ptions, **P**references to open the Preferences dialog box (see fig. 16.27).

3. Choose the P**a**rtners button to see all of the available preferences (see fig. 16.28).

4. The Address Display section can be used to specify how you want address information to be displayed throughout WINS Manager. Your choices are computer name, IP address, computer name with IP address in parentheses, or IP address with computer name in parentheses. The kind of address display affects how a connection is made to the WINS server. For IP addresses the connection is made via TCP/IP. For computer names the connection is made via named pipes.

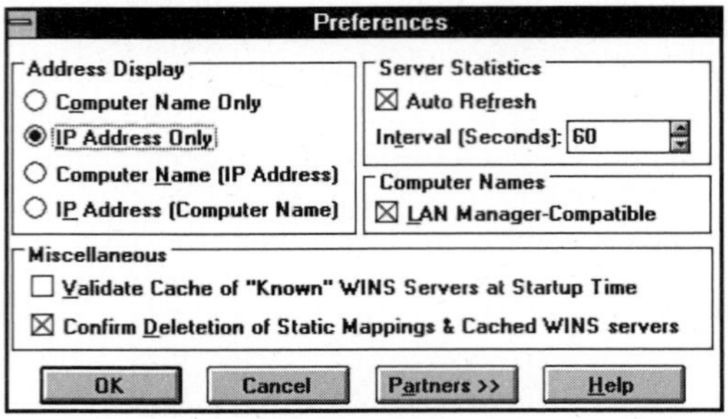

Figure 16.27

The Initial WINS Preferences dialog box.

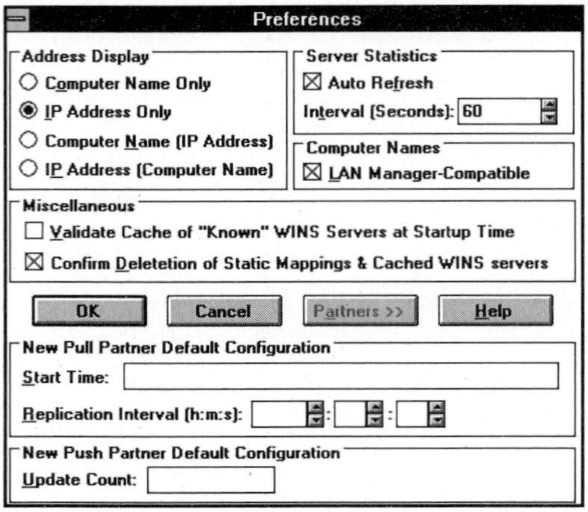

Figure 16.28

The WINS Preferences dialog box with all the available options.

5. Enable the Auto Refresh option if you want the statistics in the WINS Manager window to be refreshed automatically at intervals specified in the Interval (Seconds) field.

   The statistics display is also refreshed whenever an action is initiated while you are working in WINS Manager.

6. Enable the **L**AN Manager-Compatible option if you want computer names to obey the LAN Manager naming convention. LAN Manager computer names are limited to 15 characters, as opposed to 16-character NetBIOS names used by applications such as Lotus Notes. In LAN Manager names, the 16th byte is used to indicate the device type: server, workstation, messenger, and so on. When this option is enabled, WINS adds and imports static mappings with 0, 0x03, and 0x20 as the 16th byte.

   For Microsoft Windows Networks, you should follow the LAN Manager convention, and enable this option.

7. Enable the **V**alidate Cache Of "Known" WINS Servers at Startup Time option if you want the WINS server to query the list of servers each time the WINS server starts to find out if the servers in the list are available.

8. Enable the Confirm **D**eletion of Static Mappings & Cached WINS servers option, if you want a warning message to appear each time you delete a static mapping or the cached name of a WINS server.

9. In the **S**tart Time field enter the default value for the replication start time for new pull partners.

10. In the **R**eplication Interval field enter the time interval at which data replicas will be exchanged between the partners.

11. In the **U**pdate Count field, enter a number for the registrations and changes that will cause a replication trigger to be sent by this server when it is a push partner. The minimum value is 5.

12. After making the changes to the preference settings, choose OK to save your changes.

Creating Static Mappings

Not all TCP/IP hosts on your network may have a WINS client to register with a WINS server or obtain name resolution information from the WINS server. For these TCP/IP hosts, you can create a permanent computer name/IP address mapping in the WINS database. Static mappings are created manually by the administrator for non-WINS enabled computers and are not challenged or removed by the WINS protocols. The administrator can, of course, create, edit, import, or delete static mappings for any TCP/IP host.

If DHCP is also used on the network to assign IP addresses, a reserved IP address allocated by a DHCP server will override any WINS server settings. You should not assign static mappings to WINS-enabled computers.

The following is an outline of a procedure to view, add, and edit static mappings:

1. Start the WINS Manager while logged on as an Administrator user.

2. From **M**appings menu, choose **S**tatic Mappings.

   The Static Mappings dialog box appears (see fig. 16.29). If you have not assigned any static mappings, the Filter: None section will be empty.

3. To change the order in which the names are listed select either of the following options:

   Sort Static Mappings by **I**P Address

   Sort Static Mappings by Computer **N**ame

4. You can import static mappings by choosing the I**m**port Mappings button or add static mappings by choosing the **A**dd Mappings button.

Figure 16.29

The Static Mappings dialog box.

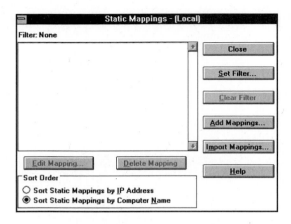

5. If you select the **A**dd Mappings button to add static mappings, you will see the Add Static Mappings dialog box (see fig. 16.30).

Figure 16.30

The Add Static Mappings dialog box.

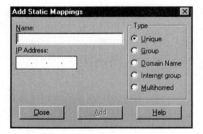

Note that changes you make to the static mappings are effective immediately—you cannot cancel changes because there is no Cancel button. To correct an error, you must manually delete the entry and then add it again.

6. In the **N**ame field of the Add Static Mappings dialog box, enter the computer name that will have a static mapping. Computer names are represented in their UNC notation with two back slashes (\\) preceding them. If you do not type the two backslashes, WINS Manager will add them for you.

7. In the **I**P Address section of the Add Static Mappings dialog box, enter the IP address for the computer.

8. In the Type section, select the type of the static mapping. The meanings of the different types are described next:

    ▪ **Unique** is for computer names that are unique in the database, with one address per name.

■ **Group** is used for computers on a subnet. It does not store addresses for individual members. A group can be defined for any subnet and can be registered with more than one WINS server. If the WINS server receives a name resolution query for the group name, it resolves it to the limited broadcast address 255.255.255.255. The WINS client will then use 255.255.255.255 as the destination address in the datagram sent to the group name. This will result in a local broadcast on the subnet. The group name is renewed when any member of the group renews the group name. The group's time stamp shows the last time for any change received for the group.

■ **Domain Name** is a group of up to 25 NetBIOS names that have 0x1C as the 16th byte. Each group member must renew its name individually. If you try to register more than 25 names, the WINS Manager overwrites a replica address in the group. If no replica address is present, WINS manager overwrites the oldest entry.

■ **Internet Group** is a group of up to 25 NetBIOS names and IP addresses. A character space (0x20) is appended to the group name. You can override the default 0x20 16th byte by placing a different character in brackets at the end of the Ineternet group name, however, you can't use the character 0x1C, which is reserved for domain name groups (see the preceding entry). Name registrations received for the Internet groups are stored with their actual IP address rather than the subnet broadcast address. In addition a time stamp and owner ID is stored with the actual IP address. The owner ID indicates the WINS server registering that address. If the Internet Group name has fewer than 25 members, dynamically registered names can be added to the Internet Group. If the Internet Group already has the maximum of 25 members, WINS looks for and removes a member registered by another WINS server (replica member) and adds the new member. If there are no replica members; that is, all the 25 members are owned by this WINS server, then, the oldest member is replaced by the new one. WINS gives members in an Internet Group name that registered with it precedence over remote members. This means that the Internet Group name always contains the geographically closest Windows NT Server computers. WINS resolves a query for the Internet Group name by returning the 24 closest Windows NT Server computers in the domain plus the domain controller. The Internet Group Name can also be used to discover a Windows NT Server in a domain when a Windows NT computer needs a server for pass-through validation. Note that the Internet Group Name list is static and does not accepts dynamic updates from WINS-enabled computers.

■ **Multihomed** is used for computers with multiple network cards or multiple IP addresses bound to NetBIOS over TCP/IP. A multihomed computer can register its IP addresses at different times by sending a special name registration packet. A multihomed group name can contain up to 25 IP addresses. New registration requests received for a multihomed group that already has reached its limit of 25 computers, will result in replica address being overwritten first, and if no replicas are present, then the oldest registered name is overwritten.

Note that when the Internet Group or Multihomed group is selected, additional controls are added to the Add Static Mappings dialog box to add multiple IP addresses.

Table 16.1 summarizes the different types of NetBIOS names that are distinguished by the 16th character. You can view the NetBIOS names registered on a computer by using the `nbtstat -n` command:

Table 16.1
NetBIOS Computer Names

Character ending a NetBIOS name	Description
0x1E	This is a group name. Browsers broadcast to this name and listen on it to elect a master browser. The broadcast is done on the local subnet using the limited broadcast address 255.255.255.255 and should not cross routers. WINS always returns the limited broadcast address 255.255.255.255 when resolving a group name.
0x1D	Clients resolve this name to access the master browser for server lists. There is one master browser per subnet.
0x1C	This refers to the Domain name group.
0x20	This refers to the Internet Group. Each member of the group must renew its name individually or be released. The Internet Group has a maximum of 25 names. WINS returns a positive response for a dynamic registration of a static Internet Group name, but the address is not added to the list. When a static Internet Group name is replicated which clashes with a dynamic Internet Group name on another WINS server, the members of the group are merged, and the Internet Group name is marked as static.

9. After adding a computer name and IP address and selecting the type in the Add Static Mappings dialog box, choose the **A**dd Mappings button, and repeat the previous steps for adding additional names.

10. Another method of adding static entries is to import them from the file containing the computer name/IP address mappings. The file that contains these mappings must have the format of the LMHOSTS file. The LMHOSTS file format was discussed in Chapter

14, "Installing and Configuring the TCP/IP Protocol Stack." However, group names and multihomed names can be added only by interactively entering them in the Add Static Mappings dialog box.

To import a file containing static mappings, choose the I**m**port Mappings button in the Static Mappings dialog box.

You should see the Select Static Mapping File dialog box (see fig. 16.31). Use this dialog box to select the mappings file, and select OK.

Figure 16.31

The Select Static Mapping File dialog box.

With the exception of the #DOM keyword used in the LMHOSTS file, all other keywords are ignored. If there is a #DOM entry in the file, an Internet Group name is created and the address is added to the group. Figure 16.32 shows the result of importing an LMHOSTS file.

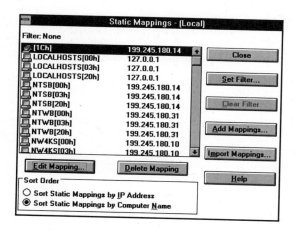

Figure 16.32

Static Mappings from importing an LMHOSTS file.

11. To edit a static mapping, select the mapping you want to change and choose the **E**dit Mapping button in the Static Mappings dialog box. Alternatively, double-click on the mapping entry in the list (see fig. 16.33).

Figure 16.33

The Edit Static Mapping dialog box.

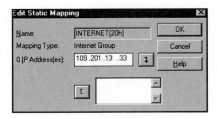

You can only change the IP address in the mapping. You can only view the Computer Name and Mapping Type values.

To change the Computer Name or Mapping Type, you must delete the entry and create a new mapping entry.

After making changes in the Edit Static Mapping dialog box, choose OK to save your changes.

12. To delete a mapping entry, select it in the Static Mappings dialog box, and choose the **D**elete Mapping button or press the Del key.

13. To limit the range of IP addresses or computer names displayed in the dialog boxes, choose the **S**et Filter button.

The Set Filter dialog box appears (see fig. 16.34).

Figure 16.34

The Set Filter dialog box.

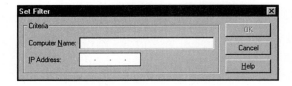

In the Computer **N**ame and **I**P Address fields, use an asterisk (*) for portions of computer names and IP addresses. For example, to only see computer names on subnet 144.19.74.0, use the notation, 144.19.74.*, and to see only computer names beginning with the letters 'KNT', use \\KNT*.

After defining the filter, choose OK.

To cancel a filter, choose the **C**lear Filter button in the Static Mappings dialog box.

Managing the WINS Database

The WINS database files are stored in the \systemroot\SYSTEM32\WINS directory. Table 16.2 describes the WINS database files.

Table 16.2
WINS Database Files

File Name	Description
WINS.MDB	This is the WINS database file.
SYSTEM.MDB	This file contains the structure (schema) for the WINS database.
JET.LOG	This file contains a log of all transactions performed on the WINS database. The file is used by WINS to recover from incomplete transactions.
WINSTMP.MDB	This is a temporary file that WINS creates. The file may remain in the WINS subdirectory after a system crash.

Scavenging the WINS Database

The WINS database should be periodically cleaned of old entries and backed up. The periodic cleaning up of the WINS database is called scavenging in the Microsoft literature. Scavenging is done automatically at times set by the Extinction Timeout interval defined in the WINS Server Configuration dialog box (see fig. 16.20).

You can also scavenge the WINS database manually. To scavenge a database, manually select Initiate Scavenging from the **M**appings menu.

You will see a message that the scavenging command has been queued. Table 16.3 explains the state of database information before and after scavenging.

Table 16.3
Scavenging Status

State Before Scavenging	State After Scavenging
Active names with Renewal interval expired	Marked released
Released names with Extinct interval expired	Marked extinct
Extinct names with Extinct timeout expired	Deleted
Replicas of extinct names with Extinct timeout expired	Deleted

continues

Table 16.3, Continued
Scavenging Status

State Before Scavenging	State After Scavenging
Replicas of active names with Verify interval expired	Revalidated
Replicas of extinct or deleted names	Deleted

Compacting the WINS Database

If the WINS server has been active for a long time, the database can grow in size. You can compact the database to improve the WINS performance. To compact the WINS database, perform the following steps:

1. Stop the WINS server so that you can compact the database files. You can perform this using the Services icon in the Control Panel, or using the command net stop wins.

2. Run the Jetpack.exe program (kept in the \systemroot\SYSTEM32 directory).

3. Restart the WINS service with the net start wins command.

Backing up the WINS Database

After the WINS database has been scavenged and compacted using the steps outlined in the previous section, you can backup the WINS database. The WINS Manager includes backup capabilities for the WINS database. You must specify a backup directory for the WINS database. The WINS server then performs complete database backups every 24 hours using the specified directory.

The following is an outline for configuring the WINS backup.

1. Start the WINS Manager while logged on as an administrator user.

2. Select **B**ackup Database from the **M**appings menu.

   The Select Backup Directory dialog box appears (see fig. 16.35). Use this dialog box to specify the location of the backup directory. For example this could be the WINS subdirectory.

3. After you select the backup directory and choose OK, WINS creates a backup subdirectory named wins_bak that contains the backed-up database files.

You should also periodically back up the WINS Registry entries for the WINS server. For details on backing up the Registry refer to Chapter 10, "Managing Windows NT Registry." A brief outline of the procedure is presented here for your convenience.

Figure 16.35
*The Select Backup
Directory dialog box.*

1. Run REGEDT32.EXE.

2. Select the following key:

   HKEY_LOCAL_MACHINE\SYSTEM\CurrentControlSet\Services\WINS

3. Select Save Key in the **R**egistry menu.

4. Specify the path where you backup the WINS Registry Key.

Viewing the WINS Database

You can view the current active and static mappings in the WINS database. The following is an outline of the procedure for viewing the WINS database:

1. Start the WINS Manager while logged on as an administrator user.

2. Select **M**appings, **S**how Database from the WINS Manager screen:

   The Show Database dialog box appears (see fig. 16.36).

3. Select the Sho**w** Only Mappings from Selected Owner radio button option to view the mappings in the database for a specific WINS server that you have selected from the Select **O**wner list box.

   Select Show A**l**l Mappings to see all mappings for all servers in the Select **O**wner list box.

4. Select a Sort Order option to sort by IP address, computer name, time stamp for the mapping, version ID, or type. The default is to sort by computer name.

5. To view only a range of mappings, choose the **S**et Filter button. To cancel a filter setting, choose the **C**lear Filter button.

6. Use the scroll bars in the Mappings box to view entries in the database. Then choose Close when you are finished viewing.

Figure 16.36

The Show Database dialog box.

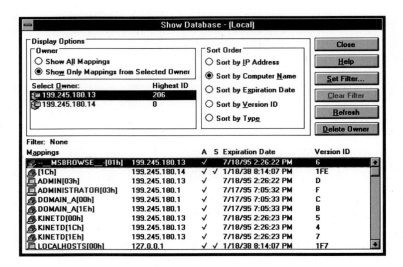

7. In the Mappings list (refer to figure 16.36), you see the following information for each record in the WINS database.

   The Computer name, which is the NetBIOS name for the computer.

   The IP address that is the assigned Internet Protocol address.

   The A or S indicators that indicate of the mapping is Active (dynamic) or Static.

   The Expiration Date that shows when the mapping is scheduled to expire.

   The Version ID, which is a unique hexadecimal number assigned by the WINS server during name registration. The Version ID is used by the server's pull partner to find new and changed records.

8. You can delete a record by highlighting it and choosing the Delete Owner button.

Advanced Registry Parameters for WINS

The WINS parameters for the WINS server that can be configured using the Registry Editor are kept under the following key:

HKEY_LOCAL_MACHINE\SYSTEM\CurrentControlSet\Services\WINS\Parameters

Figure 16.37 shows the WINS parameters in the Registry. If a parameter is not listed in the Registry, its default value is assumed.

The DbFileNm value entry is of data type REG_EXPAND_SZ, and has a default value of %SystemRoot%\system32\wins\wins.mdb. This value entry specifies the full path name for the WINS database file.

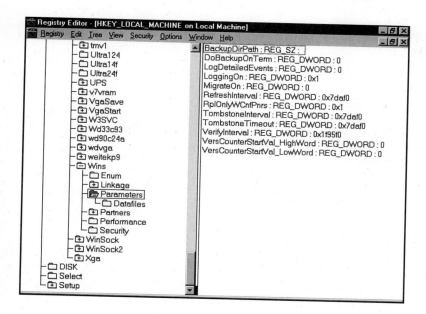

Figure 16.37
WINS Server parameters in the Registry.

The DoStaticDataInit value entry is of data type REG_DWORD and has a value of 0 or 1. The default value is 0, which means that the WINS server does not initialize its database. If this parameter is set to 1, the WINS server reads one or more files listed under the \Datafiles subkey to initialize its database. This initialization occurs when WINS is started or whenever a change is made to one or more values of the \Parameters or \Datafiles keys.

Table 16.4 lists the parameters most of which can be set from the WINS Server Configuration dialog box.

Table 16.4
Registry Parameters Set in the WINS Server Configuration

Registry Parameter	WINS Server Configuration Option
LogDetailedEvents	Log Detailed Events
LogFilePath	Not specified
LoggingOn	Logging Enabled
RefreshInterval	Renewal Interval
RplOnlyWCnfPnrs	Replicate Only With Partners
TombstoneInterval	Extinction Interval
TombstoneTimeout	Extinction Timeout
VerifyInterval	Verify Interval

The Wins\Partners Registry key has two subkeys, Pull and Push. Under these subkeys are the IP addresses of all push and pull partners of the WINS server.

A push partner's IP address, listed under the Partners\Pull subkey, has the MemberPrec value entry. The MemberPrec value entry is of data type REG_DWORD, has a value of 0 or 1, and specifies the order of precedence for this WINS partner. The default is 0, which indicates low precedence. A value of 1 indicates high precedence. Dynamically registered names have a high precedence. Set the value to 1 if the WINS server is serving a nearby location.

Under the Partners\Pull subkey are defined the InitTimeReplication and CommRetryCount value entries. These correspond to the Initial Replication option and the Retry Count field in the WINS Configuration dialog box.

Under the Partners\Pull*IpAddress* are defined the SpTime and TimeInterval value entries. These correspond to the Start Time for pull partners and Replication Interval in the WINS Preferences dialog box.

Under the Partners\Push subkey are defined the InitTimeReplication and RplOnAddressChg value entries. These correspond to the Initial Replication option and the Replicate on Address Change option in the WINS Configuration dialog box.

Under the Partners\Push*IpAddress* is defined the UpdateCount value entry. This corresponds to the Update Count field in the WINS Preferences dialog box.

SNMP Parameters for WINS

The WINS parameters can be managed by an SNMP manager. The WINS MIB parameters are described in tables 16.5 to 16.9. The parameters are grouped in separate tables by their SNMP group. Most of the management tasks for the WINS server can be performed by reading or writing to the SNMP MIB objects defined in these tables. Table 16.9 is particularly interesting, because it can be used to trigger management actions such as sending push notification messages, initiating scavenging of a WINS database, and so on.

The SNMP manager must have the ability to import these MIB objects that are specific WINS parameters. The values shown in { } are the ASN.1 object IDs for the parameters. The labels such as Par, Datafiles, Pull, and so on are ASN.1 macros that expand to an ASN.1 prefix value defined by Microsoft.

Table 16.5
Windows NT WINS MIB Parameters

Parameter	Description
ParWinsStartTime	WINS start time. {Par 1}
ParLastPScvTime	Most recent time stamp at which a planned scavenging took place. {Par 2}

Parameter	Description
ParLastATScvTime	Most recent time stamp at which scavenging took place as a result of administrative action. {Par 3}
ParLastTombScvTime	Most recent time stamp at which extinction scavenging took place. {Par 4}
ParLastVerifyScvTime	Most recent time stamp at which revalidation of old active replicas took place. {Par 5}
ParLastPRplTime	Most recent time stamp at which planned replication took place. {Par 6}
ParLastATRplTime	Most recent time stamp at which administrator-triggered replication took place. {Par 7}
ParLastNTRplTime	Most recent time stamp at which network-triggered replication occurred. Network-triggered replication occurs as a result of an update notification message from a Push partner. {Par 8}
ParLastACTRplTime	Most recent time stamp at which address change-triggered replication occurred. Address change-triggered replication occurs when the IP address changes because of a new registration. {Par 9}
ParLastInitDbTime	Most recent time stamp at which static entries in the local WINS database was generated by importing from data files. {Par 10}
ParLastCounterResetTime	Most recent time stamp at which the local counters were initialized to zero. {Par 11}
ParWinsTotalNoOfReg	Number of registrations received. {Par 12}
ParWinsTotalNoOfQueries	Number of queries received. {Par 13}
ParWinsTotalNoOfRel	Number of releases received. {Par 14}
ParWinsTotalNoOfSuccRel	Number of releases that succeeded. {Par 15}
ParWinsTotalNoOfFailRel	Number of releases that failed because the address of the requestor did not match the address of the name. {Par 16}

continues

Table 16.5, Continued
Windows NT WINS MIB Parameters

Parameter	Description
ParWinsTotalNoOfSuccQueries	Number of queries that succeeded. {Par 17}
ParWinsTotalNoOfFailQueries	Number of queries that failed. {Par 18}
ParRefreshInterval	Renewal interval in seconds. {Par 19}
ParTombstoneInterval	Indicates the Extinct interval in seconds. {Par 20}
ParTombstoneTimeout	Extinct timeout in seconds. {Par 16}
ParVerifyInterval	Verify interval in seconds. {Par 22}
ParVersCounterStartVal_LowWord	The value of low word of the version counter that WINS should start with. {Par 23}
ParVersCounterStartVal_HighWord	The value of the high word of the version counter that WINS should start with. {Par 24}
ParRplOnlyWCnfPnrs	Specifies if replication is allowed with nonconfigured partners. A non-zero value specifies that replication will be done only with partners listed in the Registry. {Par 25}
ParStaticDataInit	Specifies if static data should be read in at initialization and reconfiguration time. {Par 26}
ParLogFlag	Specifies whether logging should be done. {Par 27}
ParLogFileName	Specifies the path to the log file. {Par 28}
ParBackupDirPath	Specifies the path to the backup directory. {Par 29}
ParDoBackupOnTerm	Specifies if WINS should perform a database backup upon exit. {Par 30}
ParMigration	Specifies whether static records in the WINS database should be treated as dynamic records during conflict with new name registrations. Values can be 0 for NO or 1 for YES. {Par 31}

Table 16.6
Windows NT Datafiles Group MIB Parameters

Parameter	Description
DFDatafilesTable	The list of datafiles specified under the \Datafiles key in the Registry. The files are used for static initialization of the WINS database. {Datafiles 1}
dDFDatafileEntry	Data file name record. {DFDatafilesTable 1}
dFDatafileIndex	Index into the datafiles table. {dDFDatafileEntry 1}
dFDatafileName	Name of the datafile used for static initialization. {dDFDatafileEntry 2}

Table 16.7
Windows NT Pull Partner Group MIB Parameters

Parameter	Description
PullInitTime	Specifies if pull should be done at WINS start and at reconfiguration. Modifying pull or push group's MIB variable constitutes a reconfiguration. {Pull 1}
PullCommRetryCount	Specifies the retry count in case of communication failure during a pull replication. {Pull 2}
PullPnrTable	List of partners for performing a pull replication. {Pull 3}
pPullPnrEntry	The row corresponding to a partner. {PullPnrTable 1}
PullPnrAdd	The IP address of the remote WINS partner. {pPullPnrEntry 1}
PullPnrSpTime	The time at which pull replication should occur. {pPullPnrEntry 2}
PullPnrTimeInterval	The time interval for pull replication. {pPullPnrEntry 3}
PullPnrMemberPrec	The precedence to be given to members of the group pulled from the WINS. The precedence of locally registered members of a group is greater than that of any replicas. {pPullPnrEntry 4}
PullPnrNoOfSuccRpls	The number of times replication was successful with WINS after startup or reset of counters. {pPullPnrEntry 5}

continues

Table 16.7, Continued
Windows NT Pull Partner Group MIB Parameters

Parameter	Description
PullPnrNoOfCommFails	The number of times replication was unsuccessful with the WINS because of communication failure. {pPullPnrEntry 6}
PullPnrVersNoLowWord	The value of the low word for the highest version number found in records owned by this WINS. {pPullPnrEntry 7}
PullPnrVersNoHighWord	The value of the high word for the highest version number found in records owned by this WINS. {pPullPnrEntry 8}

Table 16.8
Windows NT Push Partner Group MIB Parameters

Parameter	Description
PushInitTime	Specifies if a push notification message should be sent at WINS startup. {Push 1}
PushRplOnAddChg	Specifies if a notification message should be sent when an address changes. {Push 2}
PushPnrTable	Specifies WINS partners with which push replication is to be initiated. {Push 3}
pPushPnrEntry	The row corresponding to the WINS partner. {PushPnrTable 1}
PushPnrAdd	IP address of the WINS partner. {pPushPnrEntry 1}
PushPnrUpdateCount	Number of updates that should trigger a push notification message. {pPushPnrEntry 2}

Table 16.9
Windows NT Command Group MIB Parameters

Parameter	Description
CmdPullTrigger	When set, it causes the WINS to pull replicas from the remote WINS server identified by the IP address. {Cmd 1}

Parameter	Description
CmdPushTrigger	When set, it causes WINS to send push notification message to the remote WINS server identified by the IP address. {Cmd 2}
CmdDeleteWins	When set, it causes all information pertaining to a WINS server to be deleted from the local WINS server. This command could be used hen the owner-address mapping table is nearing capacity. {Cmd 3}
CmdDoScavenging	When set, it causes WINS to initiate scavenging. {Cmd 4}
CmdDoStaticInit	When set, WINS will perform static initialization using the file specified as the value. When set to 0, WINS will perform static initialization using the files specified in the Registry. {Cmd 5}
CmdNoOfWrkThds	Reads the number of worker threads in WINS. {Cmd 6}
CmdPriorityClass	Reads the priority class of WINS. {Cmd 7}
CmdResetCounters	Resets the WINS counters. {Cmd 8}
CmdDeleteDbRecs	When set, it causes only the data records pertaining to a WINS server to be deleted from the local WINS server. {Cmd 9}
CmdDRPopulateTable	Gets records of a WINS server whose IP address is provided and uses it to generate the WINS database. {Cmd 10}
CmdDRDataRecordsTable	This is the table that stores the WINS data records. The records are sorted by computer name. The table is cached for a time period. To regenerate the table, set the CmdDRPopulateTable MIB variable. {Cmd 11}
CmdDRRecordEntry	This is the data record owned by the WINS server whose IP address was specified in the CmdDRPopulateTable command. {CmdDR Data RecordsTable 1}
CmdDRRecordName	Name in the record. {cCmdDRRecordEntry 1}

continues

Table 16.9, Continued
Windows NT Command Group MIB Parameters

Parameter	Description
CmdDRRecordAddress	The addresses of the mapping record. If the record is a multi homed record or an Internet group, the addresses are returned sequentially in pairs, where each pair consists of the address of the owner WINS server followed by the address of the computer or of the Internet group member. The records are always returned in network byte order. {cCmdDRRecordEntry 2}
CmdDRRecordType	The type of the record: unique, multi homed, group, Internet group. {cCmdDRRecordEntry 3}
CmdDRRecordPersistenceType	Specifies of the mapping record is static or dynamic. {cCmdDRRecordEntry 4}
CmdDRRecordState	Specifies the state of the record: active, released, or extinct. {cCmdDRRecordEntry 5}
CmdWinsVersNoLowWord	The value of the low word of the version number counter of the record. {Cmd 12}
CmdWinsVersNoHighWord	The value of the high word of the version number counter of the record. {Cmd 13}

Conclusion

Windows NT computer names need to be resolved to their equivalent IP address values if the TCP/IP protocol is used on Windows NT network. This chapter discusses the different name resolution methods for NetBIOS over TCP/IP. These methods include the b-node, p-node, m-node, and h-node name resolution methods. The operation of these name resolution methods was discussed in this chapter.

The WINS server can be used to simplify the management of Windows NT names on a large network consisting of subnets connected by IP routers. You learned how to install and configure a WINS server. Guideline procedures for performing typical maintenance tasks such as adding, deleting, importing, updating and backing up the information in the WINS databases were presented.

Windows NT Printing

Any printer connected to a Windows NT workstation or server can be accessed by remote network clients. The Windows NT computer providing access to the printer becomes a print server. This chapter discusses the different print configurations that can exist on a Windows NT computer.

In this chapter, you learn how to install, configure, administer, and modify printer properties on Windows NT computers. You also learn how to control access to Windows NT printers by setting permissions on them and auditing their use in a manner similar to that for files and directories in Windows NT.

Understanding Windows NT Printing Architecture

Any Windows NT computer can provide printing services to local users or other network users. To provide flexibility in setting up different printing configurations, Windows NT makes a distinction between the physical printer called the *printing device* and a logical representation of a printer called the *logical printer.*

The printing device is the electro-mechanical device used for printing that plugs into a serial or parallel port of a computer or attaches directly to the network.

The logical printer is a software interface created by using the Add Printer tool in the Printers folder of Windows NT. The logical printer is sometimes just called the printer. This might, at times, be confusing because the conventional use of the term printer is to refer to the physical printing device. The logical printer can be used to control the following aspects of a print job:

- Where the print job is sent: local printer port, remote print share, or file

- When the print job is sent

- The print job priority

Each logical printer uses its own printer drivers. This, for example, enables one logical printer to have drivers for an HP printer device and another to have drivers for a Panasonic print device.

Print Configurations

By separating the logical printer definition from the physical printer, Windows NT provides flexibility on how the printing devices are used. Figure 17.1 shows the simplest print configuration in which a single logical printer is assigned to a single printing device. Print jobs sent to the logical printer will be printed on the associated printing device.

Figure 17.1
Single logical printer to single printing device.

Print jobs   Logical Printer   Printing Device

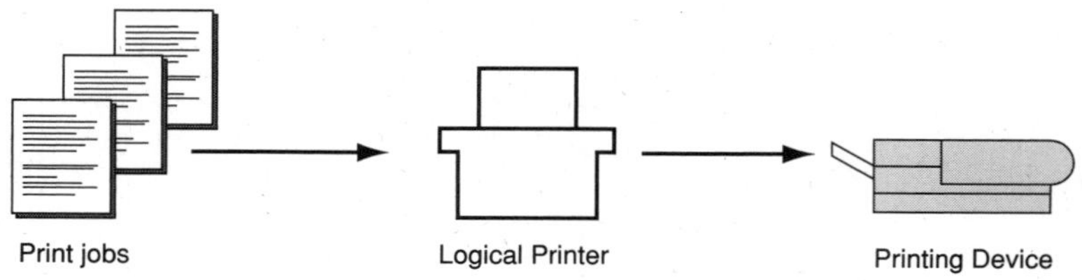

Figure 17.2 shows a print configuration in which multiple logical printers are assigned to a single printing device. Print jobs sent to any of the logical printers will be printed on the single associated printing device. Each logical printer might be defined differently. One logical printer, for example, can be configured to print separator pages at the same time another printer isn't so configured. In addition, one logical printer can be configured to hold print jobs and print them only during certain times of the day, such as at night, when little activity is expected.

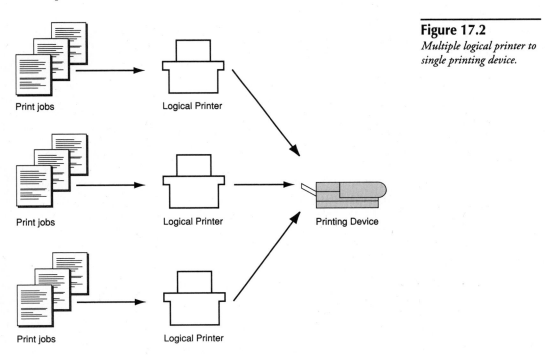

Figure 17.2
Multiple logical printer to single printing device.

Print jobs   Logical Printer

Print jobs   Logical Printer   Printing Device

Print jobs   Logical Printer

Figure 17.3 shows a print configuration in which a single logical printer is assigned multiple printing devices. Print jobs sent to the logical printer will be printed on any of the pooled printing devices. Because only a single logical printer is used, the print driver configured with it must work for all the printers in the pool. This means that the printers must be identical or must be configured to emulate the same type of print device. The pooled printer configuration can be use to spread the print load on several printing devices. This is useful if you have large amounts of printing activity and you want to increase the effective throughput of printing. Because the users see the logical printer and not the printing device, additional printing devices can be added to the printing pool without affecting the user configurations.

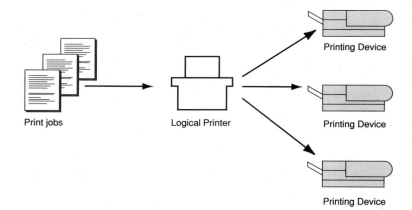

Figure 17.3

Single logical printer to multiple printing devices

Logical Printer versus Logical Print Queue

If you are accustomed to other print architectures such as OS/2 and NetWare 3.*x*, you should note that while Windows NT uses the concept of a logical printer, other NOSs use the concept of a print queue. Thus Windows NT users print jobs to a logical printer, whereas OS/2 and NetWare 3.*x* users print jobs to a print queue. NetWare 4.*x* enables you to print to a logical printer as well as a print queue. Figure 17.4 compares the logical printer and Print Queue approaches.

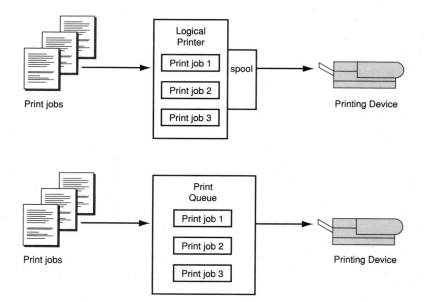

Figure 17.4

Logical Printer and Print Queue.

Windows NT Print Processing Model

Windows NT print processing consists of several components that interact with each other. Printing problems usually are associated with the failure of one or more of these components.

Figure 17.5 shows the printing events that occur when a print job is submitted. In this figure, the printing components are split in a client and server portion. For print jobs sent to a printer attached locally to the Windows NT computer, the client and server reside on the same machine. On larger networks that share printing devices, the client and server will be on different Windows NT computers connected through a network.

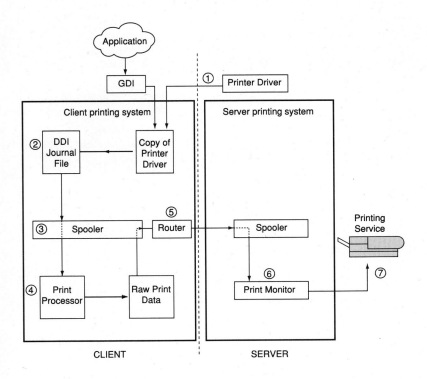

Figure 17.5

Printing Events for Windows NT printing.

The print job can be sent directly from an application, or to a logical port such as *server**sharedprinter*, which will redirect the print job to the remote shared printer.

The steps illustrated in figure 17.5 are explained in greater detail here:

1. The printer driver is loaded. If the server component is on the same computer as the client, the printer driver is loaded from the local hard drive. If the server component is on a different computer, the print driver is downloaded from the remote computer.

2. The application generates an output file using the Graphics Device Interface (GDI). The output file contains Device Driver Interface (DDI) calls to the printer driver that was loaded in step 1. The output file generated in this phase is called the DDI *journal file*.

3. The spooler component receives the journal file and passes it to the appropriate print processor.

4. The print processor processes the journal file and creates raw print data, which can be sent to a printing device.

5. If the client and server are on different computers, the spooler on the client computer takes the raw document and routes it to the spooler on the print server computer. The print server is the Windows NT computer with the physically attached printing device. The print job routing is performed by the Windows NT router component.

    If the router fails, the user will not see the print job or any error message.

Note   Windows NT 4.0 also supports EMF (enhanced metafile) spooling. Using EMF spooling, the client spooler sends an EMF across the network to the print server. The document is then rendered at the print server. Because the document is rendered at the print server rather than at the client machine, enhanced metafile spooling can reduce network traffic and improve printing speed.

6. The spooler on the print server passes the document to the print monitor. The print monitor sends the data to the appropriate print destination (LPT1:, COMx:, MAC address of network printer, and so on).

7. The print job is sent to the printing device. When the job completes, a message is sent to the user of the print job announcing the completion. The message is received as a pop-up message, assuming that the pop-up service is running on the print server, and the messenger service is running on the client computer.

The different print components are described in greater detail in the following sections.

The Printer Driver

Printer drivers are used to generate the data that eventually is translated to the print job. In Windows NT, every print driver is implemented as a Print Graphics Driver DLL, a Printer Interface Driver DLL, and a configuration file or mini-driver.

The Print Graphic Driver DLL consists of the image rendering and image management portion of the driver. This DLL provides the API calls used by the GDI.

The Print Interface Driver DLL consists of the user interface configuration and management portion of the driver. This user interface is used by the administrator to configure the printer using the Windows NT Add Printer application.

The configuration file or mini-driver contains printer configuration information such as paper trays, memory, and printer resolution. This is used by the print driver DLLs to determine printer specific information.

Windows NT comes with print graphics and print interface driver DLLs for a universal raster printer driver (RASDD.DLL, RASDDUI.DLL) and a universal PostScript printer driver (PSCRIPT.DLL, PSCRPTUI.DLL). This permits printer manufactures to supply only the configuration file or mini-driver. Some printer manufacturers, however, might supply their own print graphics and print interface driver DLLs.

Mini-drivers for raster printers are implemented as DLLs. Mini-drivers written for the Windows 3.1 universal driver (UNIDRV.DLL) can be ported to Windows NT with a few changes but must be recompiled for Windows NT.

Mini-drivers for PostScript printers are implemented as Adobe PostScript Printer Description (PPD) files. The PPD file is a text file that contains printer specific information. The PPD files usually are shipped by the printer vendor with the printer. Windows NT PostScript print drivers can directly interpret these PPD files.

The Print Spooler

The Print Spooler is the Windows NT Spooler service. The Spooler Service can be started, paused, or stopped by using the Services icon in the Control Panel, or by using the following NET commands:

- NET START SPOOLER

- NET PAUSE SPOOLER

- NET STOP SPOOLER

The Print Spooler can perform a certain amount of rendering on the print job submitted to it by an application. *Rendering* is the process of transforming the print data in a form that can be printed on a printer. The Print Spooler also transfers the raw print data received from the print router to the print monitor on the server. The spooler uses a directory on the print server to store the print jobs that are queued for printing. The following are some of the main tasks performed by the Print Spooler:

- Tracking ports associated with printers

- Tracking jobs to be sent to the appropriate printer

- Assigning priorities to print jobs

- Routing print jobs to correct ports

The default spool directory on the print server is the \ *SystemRoot*\System32\Spool directory. To change the default spool directory, double-click on the Printers icon in the Control Panel and select Server Properties from the File menu in the Printers folder. Choose the Advanced tab and enter the path to the new spool directory in the **S**pool Folder text box (see fig. 17.6). You also can specify an alternative default spool directory for all printers by creating a value entry DefaultSpoolDirectory of data type REG_SZ under the following Registry key:

```
HKEY_LOCAL_MACHINE\SYSTEM\CurrentControlSet\Control\Print\Printers
```

In the DefaultSpoolDirectory value entry, specify the path of the new spool directory.

Figure 17.6

The Print Server Properties Advanced tab.

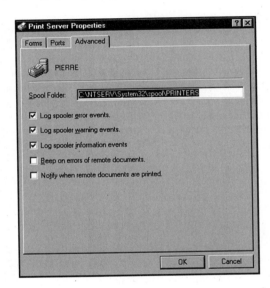

You might want to specify an alternative default spool path if the drive for the default path has limited storage for storing print jobs. The alternate default spool directory affects all printers on that Windows NT computer. To specify a different spool directory on a per printer basis, create the value entry SpoolDirectory of data type REG_SZ under the following Registry key:

```
HKEY_LOCAL_MACHINE\SYSTEM\CurrentControlSet\Control\Print\Printers\PrinterName
```

You must restart the Windows NT computer for these Registry changes to take effect.

The Print Processor

The Print Processor receives the print job from the spooler. The spooler can perform a limited amount of print job rendering by examining the data type of the print job, but the print processor completes the rendering. After rendering the print job, the print processor sends the job back to the spooler. The interactions between the print processor and the spooler are illustrated in figure 17.7.

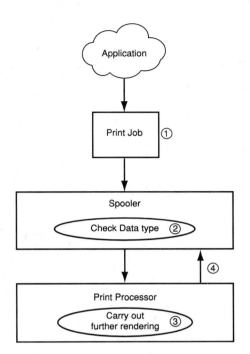

Figure 17.7

The print processor interactions with print spooler.

The Windows NT print processor is implemented by the WINPRINT.DLL. The print processor recognizes the following print job data types:

- **Windows NT journal files.** Contains DDI commands that describe the document. Journal files contain resolution and font information. Journal files need to be rendered using the GDI to the raw data format suitable for printing.

- **Raw data.** Refers to data that is ready for printing on a printer.

- **NT EMF (enhanced metafile format).** Reduces network traffic and improves printing speed (see note earlier in this chapter).

- **Text.** Consists of printable ASCII characters with a few control characters such as carriage returns, line feeds, form feeds, and so on. This type of data is ready for printing.

If the Print Processor DLL, WINPRINT.DLL, becomes corrupted or is unable to recognize the print job data type, the printer output usually is garbled. You can use the Emergency Disk to replace the print processor file.

The Print Router

The print router is responsible for the following tasks:

- Locating the requested printer

- Copying the print driver to the local computer

- Routing the print job from the client spooler to the print server spooler

Figure 17.8 illustrates the tasks performed by the print router.

Figure 17.8

The Print router.

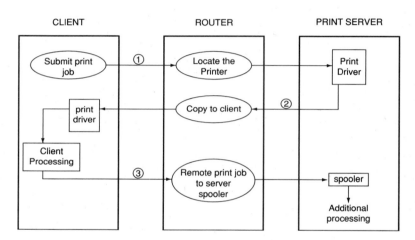

The Windows NT print router is implemented by WINSPOOL.DRV. This file is located in the *SystemRoot*\System32 directory.

Before copying the printer driver from the print server, the router compares the print driver copy, if one exists, to the client computer. The printer driver on the server is copied to the client computer only if it is a newer version. This approach is advantageous to the administrator who has to install the printer driver only once on the print server, because it lets you avoid manually installing it on all the clients. If the printer driver needs to be updated, you can update it on the print server only. Other clients, on discovering that the print server has a more recent version of the print driver, will download the new printer driver.

If the router file, WINSPOOL.DRV, is corrupted or missing, the printer driver is not copied to the client computer. You can use the Emergency Disk to replace the router file.

The Print Monitor

The print monitor is responsible for accessing a print port, printing to the print port, and releasing access to the print port. Other functions performed by the print monitor include:

- Handling error messages from printer.

- Sending end-of-job notification messages to the spooler after the job is printed so that the spooler can delete the print job stored in the print queue.

- Monitoring printer status. If printing errors are detected, the printer monitor notifies the spooler to resubmit the print job.

Examples of print monitors are the LOCALMON.DLL and HPMON.DLL. The LOCALMON.DLL manages the data stream to the COMx, LPT1, FILE: named pipes, and remote print share destinations. The HPMON.DLL handles output for the HP network interface printing devices. Both files are located in the *SystemRoot*\\System32 directory.

The Printers Folder

Use the Printers folder in Control Panel to create, secure, configure, and manage printers. You can also reach the Printers folder via the Settings command in the Start menu.

Creating a Printer Definition

After you physically connect the printing device to the network or a Windows NT computer, you can create a logical printer definition for it using the Add Printer application in the Printers folder.

The two methods for creating printer definitions are:

- Install a new printer

- Establish a connection to a printer server on another computer

The new printer can be either a printer attached locally to your computer or a printer connected directly to the network for which your computer will act as a print server. To install a new printer, you must be logged on as member of the Administrators, Print Operators, or Server Operators group. To establish a connection to a print server, you must have print privileges. The following sections discuss the two methods for creating printer definitions.

Installing a New Printer

To create a printer definition for a new printer, follow these steps:

1. Log on as a user who can create a printer.

2. Select Settings in the Start menu and choose the Printers option.

The Printers folder appears (see fig. 17.9). If you have created printer definitions before, you should see (along with the Add Printer icon) an icon for each printer definition. Figure 17.9 shows the icons for two printer definitions.

Figure 17.9

The Printers folder.

3. Double-click on the Add Printer icon.

    The first screen of the Add Printer Wizard appears (see fig. 17.10).

Figure 17.10

The Add Printer Wizard.

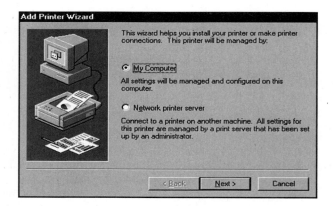

4. Enable the **M**y Computer radio button and then click on **N**ext. In the next screen (see fig. 17.11), choose the port (or ports) you want to use for the printer. If you choose more than one port, Windows NT prints to the first available port. If you have installed a printing device that is connected locally, you can select the appropriate LPT1: or COMx: port. Note that you also can choose to print to a file. If you choose the FILE: option, Windows NT prompts you for a file name each time you print.

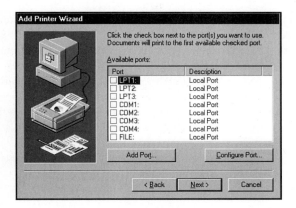

Figure 17.11
Choosing a printer port.

If you are installing a printer that is connected directly to the network, such as an HP network printer, a digital network printer, or a TCP/IP printer, click on the Add Por**t** button to invoke the Printer Ports dialog box, which lets you add a new Digital network port, local port, or PJL language monitor (see fig. 17.12). You can install a new print monitor by clicking on the **N**ew Monitor button in the Printer Ports dialog.

If you have installed the Data Link Control protocol, a Hewlett-Packard Network Port option appears in the Printer Ports dialog box.

If you have installed the Microsoft TCP/IP Printing service, an LPR Port option appears in the Printer Ports dialog. You use the LPR port choice to create a print gateway to a Unix printer. The procedure for installing a print gateway to a Unix printer was discussed in the Chapter 14, "Installing and Configuring the TCP/IP Protocol Stack."

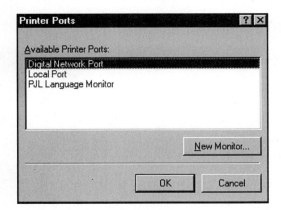

Figure 17.12
The Printer Ports dialog box.

5. After you select your port or ports, click on **N**ext. The next screen asks you to specify the printer manufacturer and model (see fig. 17.13). The purpose of this screen is to assign a printer driver that NT can use to communicate with the printer. If you don't see your printer on the list, click on the **H**ave Disk button to install a new driver. Or, if you don't see the name of your printer but do see the name of a printer that you think might be compatible with your printer, select that printer. You might have to consult your printer vendor or printer documentation if you aren't sure of what would be the correct selection. After you select a printer manufacturer and model, click on **N**ext.

Figure 17.13

Specifying the printer manufacturer and model.

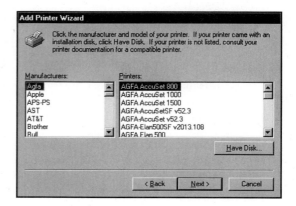

6. In the next screen (see fig 17.14), enter a name of up to 32 characters in the **P**rinter name field. The printer name identifies the printer icon. The printer name also appears on the title bar of the printer window. This screen also lets you choose whether the printer becomes the default printer for Windows applications. Choose the **Y**es or N**o** radio button and click on **N**ext.

Figure 17.14

Entering a printer name.

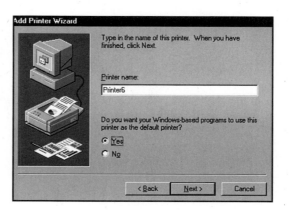

7. The next screen (see fig. 17.15) lets you choose whether to share the printer with other computers on the network. If you want to share the printer on the network, enable the **S**hared radio button option and specify a share name. (The share name defaults to the computer name specified in the preceding screen.) The box below the share name asks you to specify the operating systems of all computers that will be printing to the printer. The reason for this box is that NT must be prepared to download the appropriate printer driver to any client that submits a print job.

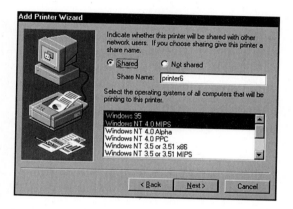

Figure 17.15

Entering network information.

8. In the final screen, the Add Printer Wizard asks you whether you would like to print a test page. The Wizard then installs the new printer. You may be prompted to insert the Windows NT Server CD-ROM if the printer requires some files that are not presently on your system.

After the wizard finishes the installation, the Printer Properties dialog box for the new printer appears. The section entitled "Printer Properties," later in this chapter, describes the Printer Properties dialog box, which you can use to provide additional configuration information or to change present configuration settings.

Defining a Connection to a Network Print Server

To define a connection to a printer elsewhere on the network, follow these steps:

1. Log on as a user with Print privileges.

2. Select Settings in the Start menu and choose the Printers option. The Printers folder appears (refer to figure 17.9). If you have created printer definitions before, you should see (along with the Add Printer icon) an icon for each printer definition. Figure 17.9 shows the icons for two printer definitions.

3. Double-click on the Add Printer icon. The first screen of the Add Printer Wizard appears (refer to figure 17.10).

4. Activate the Network printer server radio button option and click on **N**ext.

5. The Connect to Printer dialog appears (see fig. 17.16). The Connect to Printer dialog box shows a diagram of your network. Click on any computer in the diagram to display the shared printers attached to that computer. Select a shared printer and click on OK.

6. The final screen asks if you want your Windows-based applications to use this printer as the default printer.

Figure 17.16

The Connect to Printer dialog box.

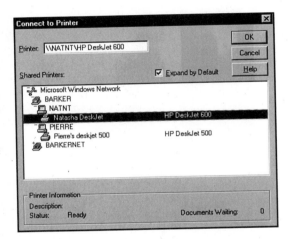

Changing Sharing Status

When you create a printer definition, you must decide whether to share the printer over the network. You may decide later to change that sharing status. The Sharing tab in the Printer Properties dialog box lets you share (or un-share) an existing printer.

See the section "The Printer Properties Sharing Tab," later in this chapter, for a description of how to change the sharing status of an existing printer.

Configuring a Printer's Properties

After you create the printer, you can change and configure the printer's properties. You'll find printer configuration information in the Printers folder's three dialog boxes, which you open as follows:

■ **Print Server Properties dialog box.** Choose **F**ile, Server Properties in the Printers folder.

■ **Default Document Properties dialog box.** Click on a printer icon and choose **F**ile, Document Defaults.

■ **Printer Properties dialog box.** Click on a printer icon and choose File, Properties.

The following sections discuss the various settings you can maintain from the three configuration dialog boxes of the Printers folder.

Print Server Properties

Choosing File, Server Properties in the Printers folder invokes the Print Server Properties dialog box (see fig. 17.17). The settings in the Print Server Properties dialog box are specific to your computer and not to a given printer.

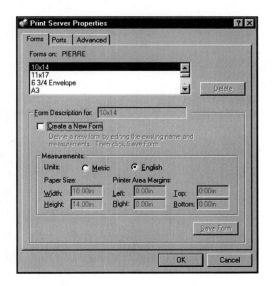

Figure 17.17

The Print Server Properties Forms tab.

> **Note** If you pull down the File menu *without* first selecting a Printer icon, you'll notice that the Server Properties command is the only available option (other than Close). You don't have to select a printer to access the Print Server Properties dialog box because the Print Server Properties dialog box applies to *your* computer. If you want to change the server properties of a remote computer, you must use Network Neighborhood.

The following three sections discuss the three tabs of the Print Server Properties dialog box.

The Print Server Properties Forms Tab

The Forms tab of the Printer Server Properties dialog box lets you define print forms that will be available to the print server. A *print form* is a description of a type of paper you will use for printing. The print form specifies the dimensions and the printer area margins of the paper.

The Forms tab contains descriptions of the forms available on the print server. In the Device Settings tab of the Printer Properties dialog box (discussed later in this chapter) you will map one or more of these descriptions to actual locations on actual printers.

Windows NT ships with several built-in print forms. Scroll through the box at the top of the Forms tab for a list of available print forms. To create a new form, enable the **C**reate a New Form check box, enter a name for the new form in the **F**orm Description for text box, and enter the dimensions of the new form in the Measurements section at the bottom of the tab. Click on the **S**ave Form button to add the new form to the forms list.

Print Server Properties Ports Tab

The Print Server Properties Ports tab (see fig. 17.18) contains a list of ports available to the print server. This tab is similar to the Printer Ports dialog box (described in the section "Installing a New Printer," earlier in this chapter) except that right now you're not actually specifying a port for a particular printer.

Figure 17.18

The Print Server Properties Ports tab.

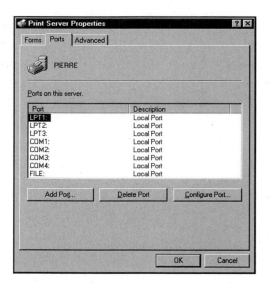

Print Server Properties Advanced Tab

You saw the Print Server Properties Advanced tab earlier in this chapter (refer to figure 17.6). Recall that this tab lets you set the default spool folder for the print server. As shown in fig. 17.6, the Advanced tab also lets you configure Windows NT to log certain spooler events, beep on remote document errors, and display a notification when a remote document is printed.

Document Defaults

If you select a printer icon and choose Document Defaults in the Printers folder File menu, you invoke the Default Document Properties dialog box. The Default Document Properties dialog box contains defaults for paper size, paper orientation, graphics resolution, and a variety of other settings. These default settings are specific to the printer you select in the Printers folder. You should set the document defaults to whatever you most commonly use. Most Windows applications include options to override the print job defaults on a per-print job basis.

The Default Document Properties Page Setup tab (see fig. 17.19) describes the paper size, paper source, and paper orientation (portrait or landscape). You also can toggle the default Color **A**ppearance from C**o**lor to **G**ray Scale.

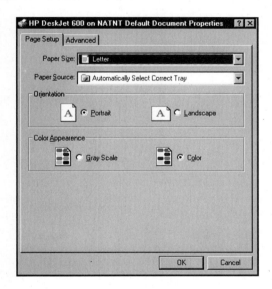

Figure 17.19

The Default Document Properties Page Setup tab.

The Default Document Properties Advanced tab (see fig. 17.20) tablulates your choices for paper, graphic, and document options. Select any setting (for instance, in figure 17.20, Graphic Resoultion is selected) and the available options appear in the box at the bottom of the tab. To change a setting, select a new option in the box and click on OK.

Figure 17.20
*The Default Document
Properties Advanced tab.*

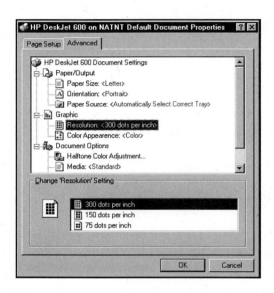

The Document Options settings in the Advanced tab includes some significant options (as follows):

- The Print Text as Graphics option disables device fonts and prevents the downloading of TrueType fonts. Use this option to avoid printing problems when the document has overlapping text and graphics.

- The Scan for Rules optimization speeds up print jobs that contain horizontal and vertical lines. (If your printer does not support this option, it simply doesn't appear in the Document Options list.) Disable the Scan for Rules option if your print jobs do not print properly when it is enabled.

To adjust the default printer settings for halftone colors, select Halftone Color Adjustment under Document Options and click on the Halftone Color Adjustment button that then appears at the bottom of the tab. You'll see the dialog box shown in figure 17.21.

Printer Properties

You can set and change printer configuration parameters in the Printer Properties dialog box (see fig. 17.22). To reach the Printer Properties dialog box, select a printer in the Printers folder and choose Properties in the File menu. Or, you can right-click on a printer and choose Properties from the resulting context menu. You must be a member of the Administrators, Server Operators, or Print Operators group before you can change the printer configuration.

Printer configuration information is stored by subject in the six tabs of the Printer Properties dialog box (see fig. 17.22). The six Printer Properties tabs are as follows:

- General

- Ports

- Scheduling

- Sharing

- Security

- Device Settings

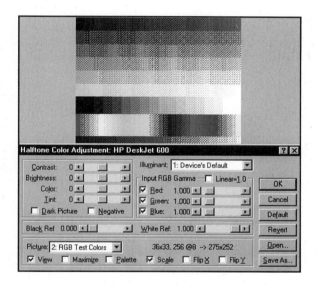

Figure 17.21
The Halftone Color Adjustment dialog box.

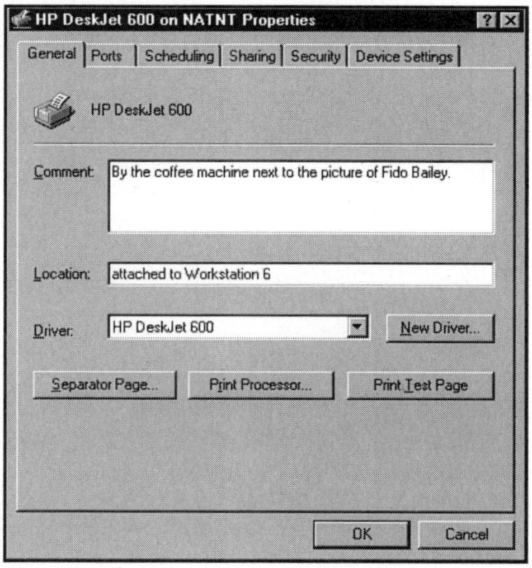

Figure 17.22
The Printer Properties General tab.

The following sections describe how to configure your printer using the tabs of the Printer Properties folder.

The Printer Properties General Tab

The Printer Properties General tab (refer to figure 17.22) lets you add an optional comment and an optional location description to help you identify the printer.

The **D**river drop-down list box lets you choose a different driver for the printer. Click on the drop-down arrow to display the drivers currently installed on your system. Or, click on the **N**ew Driver button if you need to install a new driver.

The Print **T**est Page button is a handy troubleshooting option. The P**r**int Processor button shows the print processor and the default datatype (see the section "The Print Processor," earlier in this chapter).

The **S**eparator Page button lets you designate a file that contains separator page information. The separator page is a banner page that prints before each print job. The separator page separates successive print jobs and identifies the owner of the print job. Windows NT includes three default separator page files that can be found in the *SystemRoot*\\System32 directory.

- **PSCRIPT.SEP.** Switches the printing mode to PostScript but does not print a separator page before each document.

- **SYSPRINT.SEP.** Switches the printing mode to PostScript and does print a separator page before each document prints.

- **PCL.SEP.** Switches the printing mode to PCL, and prints a separator page before each document. PCL typically is used for HP series printers.

Printers that are configured for auto-switching will switch printing modes automatically; you don't have to specify the PCL.SEP or PSCRIPT.SEP files.

You can edit the default separator files or create your own separator file using any text editor. You can use the special codes listed in table 17.1 for creating a separator file. A sample separator file using these codes is listed here:

```
@
@D
@T
@0
@L Print job for user
@N
@0
@E
```

An example of the separator page the above code would produce is as follows:

```
8/12/95 12:05:00 PM
Print job for user Anzimee
```

Unless you use the @*n* escape code to skip *n* lines, the output is placed on a single line. In the previous example, @0 causes the printing to continue on the next line.

If a separator file is not specified, a default separator that is equivalent to the following escape codes is used:

@N@I@D

The default separator doesn't actually exist as a physical file. The codes for the default separator translate to the user name, job number, and date.

Rather than select the separator page using the browse button, you can enter its full pathname. The separator page file information is stored in the Registry. You cannot use a separator file on a network drive.

Table 17.1
Escape Codes for Separator Pages

Escape Code	Description
@	Specifies for every separator page to begin with a single @.
@N	Prints user name of user submitting the print job.
@I	Prints the job number.
@D	Prints the date, using the format set by using the Regional Settings applet in the Control Panel.
@T	Prints the time, using the format set by using the Regional Settings applet in the Control Panel.
@n	Skips *n* lines. @0 skips to the next line.
@L	Prints characters that follow it to the next escape code as it encounters them.
@F*pathname*	Prints contents of file *pathname* without any processing.
@H*xx*	Sends a printer escape code sequence to the printing device. *xx* represents hexadecimal numbers. The printer codes are specific to a printing device.
@W*dd*	Sets the width of the separator page where *dd* is the width as a decimal number. The default width is 80 columns, and the maximum width is 256. Characters beyond the width specified are not printed.

continues

Table 17.1, Continued
Escape Codes for Separator Pages

Escape Code	Description
@U	Disables block printing.
@B@S	Prints single width block characters until @U is encountered.
@B@M	Prints double width block characters until @U is encountered.
@E	Ejects a page. This is usually placed at the end of a separator page to force printing on the next page.

The Printer Properties Ports Tab

The Printer Properties Ports tab (see fig. 17.23) resembles the Printer Ports dialog box you encounter when you install a new printer (see the section "Installing a New Printer," earlier in this chapter).

Figure 17.23

The Printer Properties Ports tab.

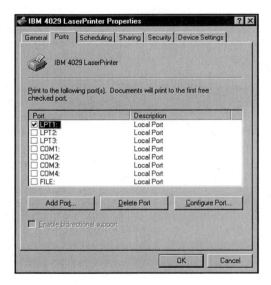

The Ports tab allows you to change the port assigned to the printer. Or, you can choose more than one port. Selecting more than one port allows you to create a printer pool. Windows NT can treat a pair of HP Deskjet 600 printers, for instance, as a single printer. You could connect the two Deskjets to separate ports under the same printer definition. If you select more than one port, a print job prints through the first free port of those selected.

The Add Por**t** button lets you add an additional port or print monitor. As discussed earlier in this chapter, the Add Por**t** button (which invokes the Printer Ports dialog box) is useful for installing a DLC or TCP/IP printing device attached directly to the network.

The **C**onfigure Port button lets you change the timeout settings for a parallel port. If you select a Com port, clicking on the **C**onfigure Port button invokes a dialog box similar to the Printer Ports dialog box in which you can set a number of parameters, including the baud rate, data bits, parity, and flow control.

The Printer Properties Scheduling Tab

The Printer Properties Scheduling tab (see fig. 17.24), lets you specify when the printer will be available, set a priority level for the printer, and specify certain other scheduling parameters.

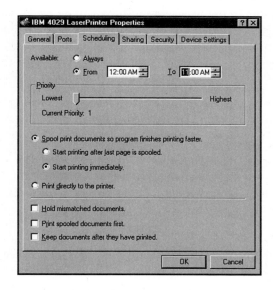

Figure 17.24

The Printer Properties Scheduling tab.

1. In the Available **F**rom and **T**o fields, set the time period that the printer is available for printing. The print server will queue the print jobs but print them only during the specified hours.

2. In the **P**riority section, you can specify the priority level for the printer, to anywhere from 1 to 99, with larger numbers representing higher priority levels. The default priority level is 1, the lowest priority. Print jobs at a higher priority level are printed before lower printer priority jobs. If you create several printers for a single printing device (see the following note), you can give each printer a different priority level.

Note A common practice is to create two or more printer definitions for the same printing device. One definition makes the printing device available at all times and one definition restricts the availability of the printing device to certain times. Print jobs sent to the restricted-time printer are held and then printed only during the available hours; print jobs sent to the unrestricted-time printer print anytime. Long print jobs that would otherwise tie up the printer during business hours could then be sent to the restricted-time printer and printed during off hours.

Using the same arrangement, you could provide a multiple-priority print queue system by creating several printer definitions with different priorities.

3. The other buttons and check boxes in the Schedule tab are as follows:

- **Spool print documents so the program finishes printing faster.** Under this option (the default), print jobs are spooled so the application can continue processing as soon as the print job is stored on disk. If the print jobs are not spooled, the application must wait for the printing device. If you select this option, you can choose whether to start printing immediately or wait until the last page is spooled.

- **Print directly to the printer.** This option is an alternative to spooling the print document. Windows NT bypasses the spooling mechanism and prints directly to the print device. The only reasons for enabling this option are if you have insufficient space on the disk or if you want to bypass the spooling system for troubleshooting purposes.

- **Hold mismatched documents.** Select this option if you want print jobs that don't match the current printer setting to be held in the queue. For example, under this option, if the print job specifies a legal size form and the letter size form currently is mounted on the printer, the print job is held in queue. You will have to mount the legal size form on the printer or disable the **H**old mismatched documents option if you want the job to print. By default, this option is not enabled.

- **Print spooled documents first.** Enable this option if you want the print jobs that have been completely spooled to start printing before print jobs that are still being spooled, regardless of the priority levels of the print jobs. This means that a low priority, completely spooled print job will be printed before a higher priority, partially spooled print job. If no print jobs have completed spooling, the larger spooling jobs print before the smaller spooling print jobs.

- **Keep documents after they have printed.** Enable this option if you want Windows NT to keep the print jobs after they print. By default, this option is disabled to prevent print job files from accumulating in the spool directory. This option lets you keep a copy of the raw document available for later printing. If you enable this option, you must remove the print job files manually.

The Printer Properties Sharing Tab

The Printer Properties Sharing tab (see fig. 17.25) lets you specify whether to share the printer on the network.

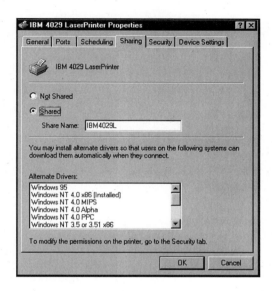

Figure 17.25
The Printer Properties Sharing tab.

To change the sharing status of your printer:

1. Select a printer in the Printers folder and choose Properties in the File menu. Select the Sharing tab in the Printer Properties dialog box.

2. Enable the **S**hared radio option button to share the printer. (Enable the N**o**t Shared option if you want to stop sharing the printer.)

3. Enter a share name for the printer. The share name defaults to the printer name. You can keep this default name or change it. If you want the share name to be accessible from MS-DOS computers, limit it to 12 characters.

4. In the Alternate Drivers list box, specify the operating systems and hardware platforms of all clients that will share the printer. You need to do this step because the printer driver is downloaded from the print server to the client computer, and each operating system or hardware platform has a different printer driver.

The Printer Properties Security Tab

The three buttons on the Printer Properties Security tab (see fig. 17.26) allow you to specify the permissions, the auditing, and the ownership of the printer. The following three sections discuss printer permissions, auditing, and ownership.

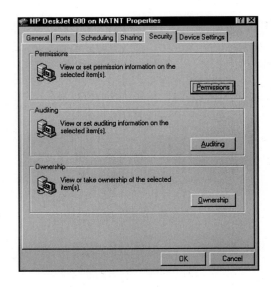

Figure 17.26

The Printer Properties Security tab.

Setting Printer Permissions

Windows NT enables you to set permissions for printers. These permissions control which users and groups can access the printer. Users and groups can have any of the following printer permissions:

- No Access

- Print

- Manage Documents

- Full Control

The actions that can be performed with each of these permissions are described in table 17.2.

Table 17.2
Printer Permissions

Task	No Access	Print	Manage Documents	Full Control
Print documents		X		X
Control settings for documents			X	X
Pause, resume, restart, delete print jobs			X	X
Change print job order				X
Pause, resume, purge printer				X
Change printer properties				X
Delete printer				X
Change printer permissions				X

Permissions are cumulative, except that as with file permissions, the No Access permission overrides other permission settings for the printer.

By default, if you have the Print permission, you also have the capability to control the printing of your print jobs. This is because as a CREATOR OWNER of the document, you can inherit the permissions granted to the CREATOR OWNER. You should, therefore, not modify the CREATOR OWNER's permissions or remove the CREATOR OWNER from the permissions list.

The following procedure describes how to set Printer permissions.

1. Select a printer icon in the Printers folder and choose Properties in the File menu. In the Security tab of the Printer Properties dialog box, click on the **P**ermissions button. The Printer Permissions dialog box appears (see fig. 17.27).

Figure 17.27

The Printer Permissions dialog box.

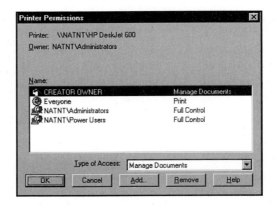

By default, the groups Administrators, Server Operators, and Print Operators have Full Control permissions over the printer. The group Everyone has Print permissions enables local and network users to send print jobs to the printer.

To remove a name from the permissions list, select it and choose the **R**emove button. To add a user or group to the permissions list, see steps 2 through 5. If you want to change the permissions for a user or group that already appears in the Printer Permissions list, skip to step 6.

To add a user or group to the permissions list:

2. Choose the **A**dd button in the Printer Permissions dialog box. The Add Users and Groups dialog box (see fig. 17.28) appears.

3. The **N**ames list in the Add Users and Groups dialog box shows the groups defined for your system. To include individual users in the **N**ames list, click on the Show **U**sers button.

   Select one or more names you want to add to the permissions list and click on the **A**dd button. The names appear in the A**d**d Names list.

4. Click on the arrow to the right of the **T**ype of Access drop-down list box and select the permissions you want to assign to the new users or groups.

5. Choose OK.

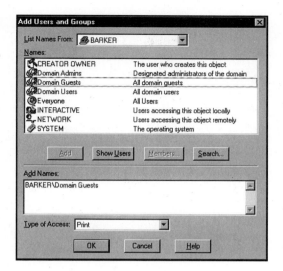

Figure 17.28

The Add Users and Groups dialog box.

To change the permissions for a user or group on the permissions list:

1. Select one or more names in the permissions list of the Printer Permissions dialog box.

2. Click on the arrow to the right of the **T**ype of Access drop-down list box and select the permissions you want to assign to the names in the list.

3. Click on OK.

Auditing Printer Usage

Windows NT enables you to audit how printers are used on the network. You must specify the following information for printer auditing:

- Users/groups to be audited

- Actions you want to audit for the selected users/groups

- Success or failure of action to be audited

Audited events are stored in the Audit Log, which you can view using the Event Viewer tool.

To set up auditing, follow these steps:

1. Select a printer icon in the Printers folder and choose Properties in the File menu. In the Security tab of the Printer Properties dialog box, click on the **A**uditing button. The Printer Auditing dialog box appears (see fig. 17.29).

Figure 17.29
*The Printer Auditing
dialog box.*

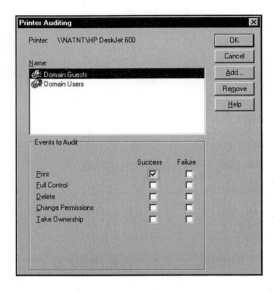

By default, the **N**ame list in the Printer Auditing dialog box is empty. The event boxes at the bottom of the Printer Auditing dialog box appear grayed out until you add some names to the auditing list. To add a user or group to the auditing list, click on the **A**dd button and see steps 2, 3, and 5 of the preceding section.

To remove a name from the auditing list, select it and choose the Re**m**ove button.

2. Select the users/groups you want to audit (refer to figure 17.29).

3. In the Event check boxes at the bottom of the Printer Auditing dialog box, check the Success or Failure boxes to audit the success or failure of any of the events in the list. You can check both success and failure for a given event if you want. Use table 17.3 as a guide for selecting the events to audit.

4. After you make your changes, choose OK.

Table 17.3
Events to Audit

Events	Print	Full Control	Delete	Change Ownership	Take Ownership
Print documents	X				
Change print job settings	X				

Events	Print	Full Control	Delete	Change Ownership	Take Ownership
Pausing, restarting, moving and deleting print jobs	X				
Sharing a printer	X				
Modifying printer properties	X				
Deleting a printer			X		
Changing				X	
Taking ownership					X

Taking Ownership of a Printer

If you have Full Control permissions for a printer, you can take ownership of the printer. A member of the Administrators group can always take ownership of a printer. An ownership can be taken, but it cannot be given back by a simple command. Another user must take owner-ship for the transfer of ownership to occur.

To take ownership, follow these steps:

1. Select a printer icon in the Printers folder and choose Properties in the File menu. In the Security tab of the Printer Properties dialog box, click on the **O**wnership button. The Owner dialog box appears on-screen (see fig. 17.30).

2. Choose the **T**ake Ownership button.

Figure 17.30

The Owner dialog box.

The Printer Properties Device Settings Tab

The Device Settings tab in the Printer Properties dialog box (see fig. 17.31) contains settings that describe certain properties of the printing device. The available options in the Device Settings tab vary depending on the options available on your printer.

Figure 17.31

The Printer Properties Device Settings tab.

The Device Settings tab is similar to the Advanced tab of the Default Document Properties dialog box, except you use it to assign settings to a particular printer rather than to specify defaults. Select a setting in the upper box and the available options appear in the lower box. In figure 17.31, Form To Tray Assignment/Auto: <Letter> is selected.

1. The Form To Tray Assignment setting lets you assign a print form (see the section "The Print Server Properties Forms Tab," earlier in the chapter) to a tray on an actual printer. The Form To Tray Assignment setting, in effect, tells Windows NT what kind of paper is in which tray of the printer.

2. The Font Cartridges setting (if available) specifies the fonts installed on the printer. Choose the Fonts button to add the fonts.

3. The Printer Memory box (if available), specifies the amount of memory installed on the printer. If your printer supports page protection, you can optionally enable it. Enabling this option instructs the printer to create the printed page in memory before printing it. This ensures that complex pages are printed properly. The page protect option is grayed out if it is not available.

4. Choose Halftone Setup and click on the Halftone button to adjust the printing of half-tone colors.

Administering a Remote Printer

To perform remote administration of a remote printer on the network, you must have Full Control privileges to the computer that is acting as the printer's print server.

Use Network Neighborhood to access the Printers folders of other computers on the network. Alternatively, if you have defined a connection to the printer in your own Printers folder (see the section in this chapter entitled "Defining a Connection to a Network Print Server"), you can access the Printer Properties dialog box (if you have the correct privileges) and the printer window from your own Printers folder.

Advanced Print Configuration Using the Registry

The Windows NT printer configuration parameters are stored in the following Registry locations:

- **HKEY_LOCAL_MACHINE\System\CurrentControlSet\Control\Print.** Contains system-wide printer configuration parameters

- **HKEY_CURRENT_USER\Printer.** Contains parameters for the currently logged on user, such as default printer and persistent connections.

- **HKEY_CURRENT_USER\Software\Microsoft\Windows NT\CurrentVersion\ PrinterPorts.** Contains printer port definitions for the currently logged-on user.

Most of the Windows NT Printer parameters can be set using the Printer Properties dialog in the Printers folder. The parameters in table 17.4 under the HKEY_LOCAL_ MACHINE\ System\CurrentControlSet\Control\Print key, however, can be set only by directly modifying the Windows NT Registry. If the value entry does not exist under the key, its default value is used. You use the Registry Editor to modify the Registry parameters. The Registry Editor is discussed in Chapter 10, "Managing Windows NT Registry."

Table 17.4
Windows NT Printer Value Entries That Can Be Set Only
in the Windows NT Registry

Parameter	Description
BeepEnabled	When remote print jobs encounter an error, you can enable beeping each time the print job is retried by setting this REG_DWORD value entry to 1. The default value is 0 (disable beeping).
DisableServerThread	The value entry is of type REG_DWORD and can have a value of 1 or 0. When set to 1, the printing browse thread is disabled. The printing browse thread is used to call other print servers and notify them that this printer exists. This causes additional network traffic.
EventLog	This is used to enable/disable event logging by the spooler. The value entry is of type REG_DWORD and is under the Print\Providers key. It has a default value of 0 which means event logging by the spooler is disabled.
FastPrintSlowDownThreshold	See the discussion on FastPrintThrottleTimeout. The default value is calculated by dividing the FastPrint WaitTimeout by FastPrintThrottleTimeout.
FastPrintThrottleTimeout	When printing jobs while they are being spooled, some printers will timeout if they do not receive data for a time interval that is about 15 seconds for PostScript printers. To prevent this, data sent to the printer is throttled back when the FastPrintSlowDownThreshold is reached, at which time 1 byte per FastPrintThrottleTimeout period is sent until the threshold is exceeded again. This value entry is of data type REG_DWORD and has a default value of 2,000 milliseconds (2 seconds).
FastPrintWaitTimeout	This parameter specifies how long the port thread will wait for a job that is printed while being spooled before pausing the print job and moving on to the next print job. The value entry is of data type REG_DWORD and has a default value of 240,000 milliseconds (4 minutes).
NetPopup	To enable net pop-up messages for remote print jobs, set this REG_DWORD value entry to 1 under the Print\ Providers key. The default value is 1.

Parameter	Description
NetPrinterDecayPeriod	This specifies the amount of time, the information on a network printer is cached. The cache is used by the browser to display a list of printers. The value entry is of type REG_DWORD and has a default value of 3,600,000 milliseconds (1 hour).
PortThreadPriority	This sets the priority level of the port threads. The default priority level is THREAD_PRIORITY_NORMAL. Other values are THREAD_PRIORITY_ABOVE_NORMAL and THREAD_PRIORITY_BELOW_NORMAL.
PriorityClass	This is used to control the priority class of the spooler. The value entry is of type REG_DWORD. If the value entry does not exist or is set to 0 the priority class is 7 for workstations and 9 for servers.
SchedulerThreadPriority	This sets the priority level of the scheduler threads used to assign print jobs to printer ports. The default priority level is THREAD_PRIORITY_NORMAL. Other values are THREAD_PRIORITY_ABOVE_NORMAL and THREAD_PRIORITY_BELOW_NORMAL.
ServerThreadTimeout	This specifies the amount of time the printing browse thread waits (sleeps) before calling other print servers to notify them that this printer exists. The value entry is of type REG_DWORD and has a default value of 600,000 milliseconds (10 minutes). If this value entry is set larger than the NetPrinterDecayPeriod, other servers will not display this printer.

Conclusion

This chapter discusses how you can configure a Windows NT Server as a print server. Windows NT provides flexibility in setting up different print configuration environments. You learned about the Windows NT network printing architecture and how to install, configure, administer, and modify printer definitions on a Windows NT computer.

You can control access to printers by setting printer permissions list and auditing printer usage. Although you can perform most administration tasks by using the Printers folder, you must use the Registry Editor directly for some tasks. This chapter discussed the printer configuration parameters you can modify only by using the Registry.

Remote Access Services

Windows NT Server and Workstation include a copy of Remote Access Services (RAS), which can be used to connect a Windows NT computer and other workstations to a Windows NT network from a remote location. This capability is particularly useful for mobile users who need to connect to their corporate network. LAN users commonly use RAS to dial out and access services on other networks. And recently, RAS has become popular with Internet service providers as a means of supporting PPP connections. This chapter discusses the features of the Windows NT Remote Access Services and provides procedures on how to install and configure these services. Also discussed are the IPX and IP routing capabilities of the RAS server.

Overview of Remote Access Services

Remote Access Services enables remote users to connect to a Windows NT computer using dial-up lines, a WAN link, or a protocol such as ISDN. Figure 18.1 illustrates how RAS can be used. The remote access clients can be Windows, Windows for Workgroups, Windows 95, MS-DOS, or LAN Manager RAS clients. Although a Windows NT Workstation can be used as a RAS server, the RAS server is typically a Windows NT Server that supports up to 256 remote RAS clients. If a Windows NT Workstation is used as a RAS server, it can support only one remote RAS client.

Figure 18.1

A Remote Access Services example.

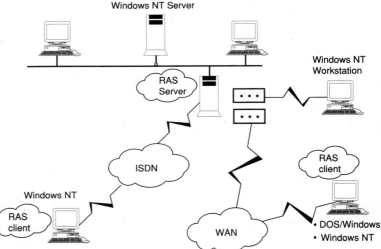

The RAS client and RAS server software is bundled with the Windows NT distribution software. It is not, however, automatically installed when you install the Windows NT operating system. You must install and configure the RAS software in a separate step. See the section "Installing RAS Server" later in this chapter.

To access a RAS server from DOS workstations, you must be running Microsoft Network Client for MS-DOS in the full redirector mode.

The Windows NT RAS client uses the authentication and security features of Windows NT to log on to the Windows NT network. The RAS client users log on to the network as if they were logging on through a LAN connection. For additional security, Windows NT clients can encrypt data using the RSA encryption.

The physical connections and the protocols between the RAS client and the RAS server are discussed in the following sections.

RAS Physical Connection Options

You can connect the RAS client to the RAS server over any of the following options:

■ Phone lines

■ ISDN

■ X.25

■ RS232C null-modem.

Each of these are discussed in the following sections.

Windows NT Server 4 also provides Multilink. Multilink, a new feature based on the IETF standard RFC 1717, lets you increase your bandwidth by combining different communication paths into a single connection. A multilink connection can include both analog modem paths and digital paths (such as ISDN).

Phone Lines

Phone lines are still the most ubiquitous means of creating a physical connection between the RAS client and the RAS server. Most phone lines are analog lines, and therefore a modem is required at the client and the server to convert the digital signals used by the RAS computers to analog signals used by the phone lines.

Windows NT provides compatibility with more than 200 different types of modems. To ensure compatibility between the modems for the RAS client and the server, your modems should comply with the same modem protocol standard or, even better, be of the same make and model. The two modem standards that are widely used are the V.32bis, which operates at 14.4 Kbps, and the V.34bis, which operates at 28.8 Kbps.

Microsoft publishes a hardware compatibility list that describes the modems that have been tested. If your modem is not supported, you can configure Windows NT to support your modem by editing the MODEMS.INF file. You can also choose a modem from the list that your unlisted modem can emulate or is compatible with. Details for configuring the MODEMS.INF file are described in Appendix E of the Microsoft manual titled *Microsoft Windows NT: Remote Access Service.*

ISDN

Many parts of the world support access to remote locations through Integrated Services Digital Network (ISDN). The ISDN line is installed at the customer premises, usually by the local phone company. You need an ISDN card in the Windows NT computer to connect to the ISDN line. Figure 18.2 shows an example of the range of services that can be connected with an ISDN network.

Figure 18.2

Example ISDN services.

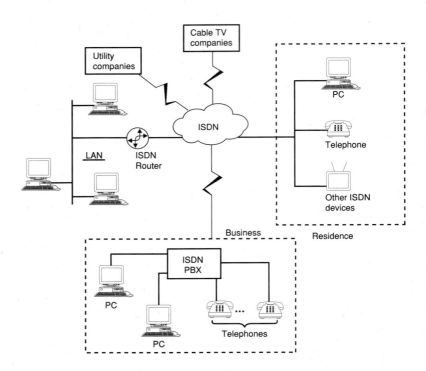

ISDN services have many classifications, two of which are the Basic Rate Interface (BRI) and the Primary Rate Interface (PRI). The BRI provides two digitized channels for user information at 64 Kbps and one Data channel for signal control purposes. The 64 Kbps channel is referred to as the B (Bearer) channel, and the data signaling channel is called the D channel. For this reason, the BRI is often said to provide 2B + D channels. For BRI, the D channel operates at 16 Kbps. The BRI is typically used to provide access to an ISDN central office for residential customers.

The PRI provides 23 B channels operating at 64 Kbps, and one D channel operating at 64 Kbps. The PRI provide 23B + D channels.

With BRI services you can transmit data up to 128 Kbps; and with PRI you can transmit up to 1.544 Mbps. These data rates are larger than those available through most modems and therefore are very attractive.

X.25

The X.25 protocols are used to implement a packet-switched network (PSN). The X.25 protocols describe the first three layers of the OSI model, although if some X.25 options are enabled, some functionality of layer 4 (transport layer) of the OSI model also is implemented.

RAS clients and servers interface with the X.25 network through a Packet Assembled Disassembler (PAD) device (see fig. 18.3). The PAD is provided by the X.25 provider (Sprintnet, Infonet, PSS, and so on). Some companies such as Hewlett-Packard, DEC, and IBM maintain their own private X.25 networks. The Windows NT computers must have an X.25 card installed.

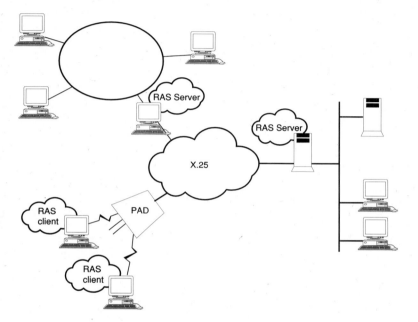

Figure 18.3

Using RAS with an X.25 network.

The connections to the PAD can be dial-up connections that are established for only the duration of the call. Dial-up connections are therefore suitable for occasional access to the remote computers. If you need permanent access to remote computers, it is preferable to have a direct X.25 connection. As you might expect, the direct connection is equivalent to the leased line connection and is therefore more expensive. X.25 PADs can provide both types of connections.

The RAS also supports X.25 smart cards. X.25 smart cards act as modem cards and have a PAD embedded in the card itself. The smart card appears to the Windows NT computer as several communication ports attached to the PADs. Figure 18.4 shows an example of RAS using X.25 smart cards. Table 18.1 shows the X.3 parameters that must be set for the PAD and the X.25 card interface for X.25 RAS connections to work properly.

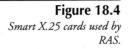

Figure 18.4

Smart X.25 cards used by RAS.

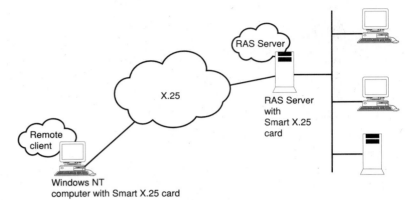

Table 18.1

X.3 Configuration Parameters for X.25 PADs Used with Windows NT RAS

Parameter Number	X.3 Parameter	Value
1	PAD Recall	0
2	Echo	0
3	Data Forward Char.	0
4	Idle Timer	1
5	Device Control	0
6	PAD Service Signals	1
7	Break Signal	0
8	Discard Output	0
9	Padding after CR	0
10	Line Folding	0
11	(Not set)	N/A
12	Flow Control	0
13	Linefeed Insertion	0
14	Passing after LF	0
15	Editing	0

Parameter Number	X.3 Parameter	Value
16	Character Delete	0
17	Line Delete	0
18	Line Display	0
19	Editing PAD Srv Signals	0
20	Echo Mask	0
21	Parity Treatment	0
22	Page Wait	0

RS-232C Null Modem

If a network attachment is not available between two computers, you can physically connect them by using an RS-232 null-modem cable.

The RS-232C null-modem cable provides a direct point-to-point attachment between the two computers through a specially prepared cable (see fig. 18.5). The null-modem cable connects to the serial ports of both computers. Physical modems are eliminated when this special cable is used, and hence the name null modem is used for the cable.

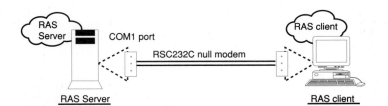

Figure 18.5

RAS connections using a null-modem cable.

Null-modem cables can be purchased or specially built. If you have to build null-modem cables for RAS connections, use tables 18.2 and 18.3 for building a 9-pin or 25-pin null-modem cable.

Table 18.2

9-pin Null-Modem Pin-Out Connections for RAS Connections

Called Host Pin	Calling Host Pin	Signal
3	2	Transmit data
2	3	Receive data
7	8	Request to Send
8	7	Clear to Send
6, 1	4	Data Set Ready and Carrier Detect
5	5	Signal Ground
4	6, 1	Data Terminal Ready

Table 18.3

25-pin Null-Modem Pin-Out Connections for RAS Connections

Called Host Pin	Calling Host Pin	Signal
3	2	Transmit data
2	3	Receive data
4	5	Request to Send
5	4	Clear to Send
6, 8	20	Data Set Ready and Carrier Detect
7	7	Signal Ground
20	6, 8	Data Terminal Ready

RAS Protocol Options

The protocols that are used over the physical connections outlined in the previous section are the Serial Line Interface Protocol (SLIP), Point-to-Point protocol (PPP), and the Microsoft RAS protocol.

Serial Line Interface Protocol

The Serial Line Interface Protocol (SLIP) is one of the simplest protocols used to connect two devices. The data octet stream is sent without any headers. Special octet values are used for control signals. An escape mechanism is used for control octets that might occur as part of the data stream. The SLIP protocol was developed by Rick Adamson for BSD-Unix, and came into widespread use before there was an RFC describing it. When the RFC 1055 was written describing the SLIP protocol, it was based on existing Unix implementations and was therefore called "A Nonstandard for Transmission of IP Datagrams for Low-Speed Serial Lines."

The original SLIP protocol did not support TCP/IP header compression. A later addition of the protocol called Compressed SLIP (CSLIP) has been implemented that provides for data compression. This protocol is described in RFC 1144 and is titled "Compressing TCP/IP Headers for Low-Speed Serial Links."

SLIP does not support protocol multiplexing and demultiplexing. This means that a SLIP connection cannot be used for transmitting different protocol traffic from multiple sessions between two computers.

SLIP is popularly used for dial-up connections to Internet hosts that provide SLIP connections. Figure 18.6 shows the TCP/IP connections over the SLIP protocol used by a RAS client.

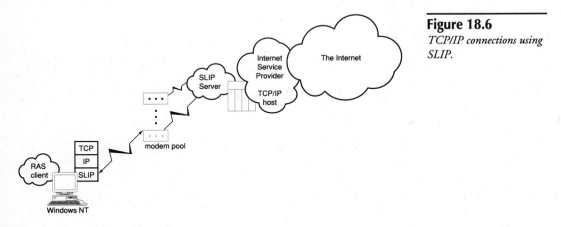

Figure 18.6
TCP/IP connections using SLIP.

Point-to-Point Protocol

The Point-to-Point protocol overcomes the limitations of SLIP. PPP can be used for protocol multiplexing and demultiplexing. Like SLIP, PPP is popularly used for dial-up connections to Internet hosts. PPP also is used to provide point-to-point connections between routers. Figure 18.7 illustrates the uses of PPP.

Figure 18.7
Uses of PPP.

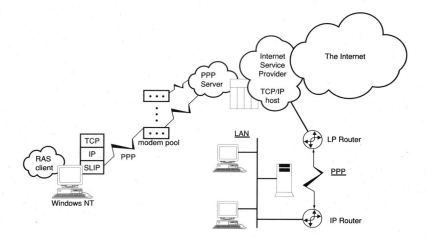

Unlike SLIP, PPP provides a framing protocol that is based upon the High Level Data Link Control (HDLC) protocol, and provides for compression and authentication. PPP is described by numerous RFCs, which indicates the importance of this protocol. These RFCs are listed as follows for your reference and further study:

- RFC 1598 PPP in X.25

- RFC 1570 PPP LCP Extensions (Updates RFC 1548)

- RFC 1552 The PPP Internetwork Packet Exchange Control Protocol (IPXCP)

- RFC 1549 PPP in HDLC Framing

- RFC 1548 The Point-to-Point Protocol (PPP)

- RFC 1547 Requirements for an Internet Standard Point-to-Point Protocol

- RFC 1378 The PPP AppleTalk Control Protocol (ATCP)

- RFC 1377 The PPP OSI Network Layer Control Protocol (OSINLCP)

- RFC 1376 The PPP DecNET Phase IV Control Protocol (DNCP)

- RFC 1334 PPP Authentication Protocols

- RFC 1333 PPP Link Quality Monitoring

- RFC 1332 The PPP Internet Protocol Control Protocol (IPCP)

Both SLIP and PPP are in widespread use. Over time, PPP is expected to become more widely used than SLIP.

MS RAS Protocol

The Microsoft RAS Protocol is a proprietary protocol that uses NetBIOS for RAS connections. Microsoft RAS requires RAS clients to use the NetBEUI protocol. The RAS server acts as a gateway for other protocols such as IPX and TCP/IP. Microsoft RAS is only supported on Windows 3.1 clients, Windows for Workgroups clients, MS-DOS clients, and LAN Manager clients.

Installing RAS Server

RAS server installation varies depending on the network protocols that you have installed. If you intend to use IPX or TCP/IP with RAS, you must install and configure these protocols before installing RAS.

Before installing RAS, ensure that you have the appropriate modem, multiport, X.25 smart card, or ISDN card connected to the RAS server.

Although the procedure in this section is described for setting up the RAS server, you can use this procedure as a guideline for configuring RAS clients as well. To install the RAS software, perform the following steps:

1. Log on as administrator user to the Windows NT server.

2. Start the Network option in the Control Panel. You should see the Network dialog box. In the Network dialog box, choose the Services tab (see fig. 18.8).

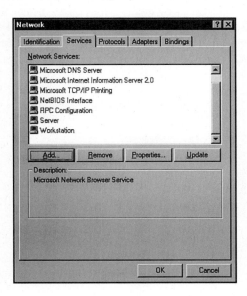

Figure 18.8

The Network Services tab.

3. In the Network Services tab, choose the **A**dd button to invoke the Select Network Service dialog box (see fig. 18.9).

Figure 18.9

*The Select Network Service
dialog box.*

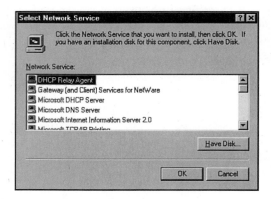

4. In the Select Network Service dialog box, select Remote Access Service and then choose the OK button.

5. Enter the path for the distribution files and choose the Continue button.

6. You should see a status of the files as they are copied to the server computer.

7. The Add RAS Device dialog box (see fig. 18.10) displays a list of RAS-capable devices on your system. Click on the arrow button to display the list. If a modem is installed on your system, it should appear in the list of RAS-capable devices. After you choose the device you want to use, click on OK. To install a new modem, click on the Install **M**odem button, which launches the Install New Modem wizard. To install an X.25 PAD, click on the Install X25 **P**ad button. Before you can install an X.25 PAD, the PAD device must be present on your system. Consult your X.25 provider if you want to configure Remote Access Service for X.25.

Figure 18.10

*The Add RAS Device
dialog box.*

8. The Remote Access Setup dialog box (see fig. 18.11) shows the device (or devices) to be included in your RAS configuration. To add a new device, click on the **A**dd button. (The **A**dd button sends you back to the Add RAS Device dialog box shown in figure 18.10, but now the devices you already selected for RAS don't appear in the list.)

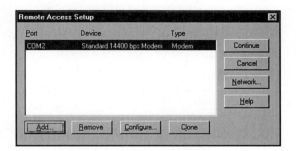

Figure 18.11
The Remote Access Setup dialog box.

9. In the Remote Access Setup dialog box, click on the **C**onfigure button to open the Configure Port Usage dialog box (see fig. 18.12). In the Configure Port Usage dialog box, select whether RAS will use the port for dial-out connections, dial-in connections, or both.

    Select the option Dial **o**ut only to set the computer up to be a RAS client only.

    Select the option **R**eceive calls only to set the computer up to be a RAS server only.

    Select the option **D**ial out and Receive calls to set the computer up as a RAS client or server. The computer cannot be a client and a server simultaneously, however.

After you choose a port usage option, click on OK.

10. If you want to copy a modem setup from one modem to another, choose the C**l**one button in the Remote Access Setup dialog box.

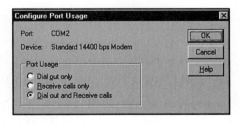

Figure 18.12
The Configure Port Usage dialog box.

11. To configure network settings such as network protocols and encryption options, select the device in the list of installed devices and then choose the **N**etwork button to open the Network Configuration dialog box (see fig. 18.13). The choices for the Network settings are discussed in the next section,"Configuring RAS to Use LAN Protocols."

Figure 18.13

The Network Configuration dialog box.

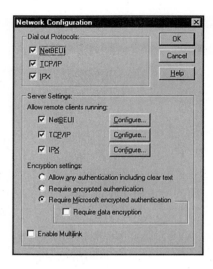

After you finish making changes to the Network Configuration dialog box, click on OK. After you finish making changes to the Remote Access Setup dialog box, click on the Continue button.

12. You will see the dialog boxes for the protocols to be used with RAS. Complete the steps listed in the next section, "Configuring RAS to Use LAN Protocols."

13. After you finish making changes to the Remote Access Setup dialog box, click on the Continue button. Setup completes the installation.

14. Restart the RAS computer to make the changes effective.

Configuring RAS to Use LAN Protocols

If the LAN protocols, such as NetBEUI, IPX, and TCP/IP, are installed at the LAN server, they are enabled for RAS use when the RAS server service is installed. If the network protocols are installed after RAS is installed, or if you want to change the RAS configuration for an already installed protocol, you must explicitly configure these protocols for RAS usage.

The following sections describe the procedure for configuring the LAN protocols.

Common Procedure for Configuring LAN Protocols

You can use the following common procedure for configuring all of the network protocols. The sections that follow this one discuss specific configuration issues for the NetBEUI, TCP/IP, and IPX protocols.

1. Log on as Administrator and start the Network option in the Control Panel.

2. From the Network dialog box, select the Services tab and choose Remote Access Service. Click on the **P**roperties button.

3. You should see the Remote Access Setup dialog box (refer to figure 18.11).

   Choose the **N**etwork button. You should see the Network Configuration dialog box (refer to figure 18.13).

4. In the Dial out Protocols section, select the protocols that you want the computer to use for dialing out. Your choices are **N**etBEUI, **T**CP/IP, and **I**PX. If you do not select a protocol in this box, you can't select that protocol when you configure the phone book for dialing out.

   You can select Dial out protocols only if you have configured a port; otherwise, the choices are grayed out.

5. In the Server Settings box (refer to figure 18.13), select the Encryption method to use. On a RAS client, you don't see the Server Settings box.

   Enable the Allow **a**ny authentication including clear text radio button option to support any authentication the RAS client uses. This option is useful if you have different types of RAS clients. This is the least secure of all the options, beacause it includes support for the Password Authentication Protocol (PAP). PAP uses plain-text password authentication and isn't an especially secure authentication protocol. PAP is useful if you have different types of RAS clients, and for supporting third-party clients that do work with PAP only.

   Other authentication protocols supported by the Require any authentication including clear text option are CHAP, MD5-CHAP, DES, and SPAP. Briefly, CHAP is the Challenge Handshake Authentication Protocol used by RAS clients for its speed, simplicity, and small code size. Microsoft's CHAP implementation is based on the Message Digest 5 (MD5) encryption. The DES is the Data Encryption Standard designed by the National Bureau of Standards (NBS). The SPAP is the Shiva Password Authentication Protocol (SPAP) implemented by the company Shiva, Inc. Use of SPAP provides compatibility with Shiva clients. Unlike PAP, SPAP does not send the clear-text password and is therefore more secure than PAP.

   Select the Require **e**ncrypted authentication option to support any authentication used by the RAS client except the Password Authentication Protocol (PAP).

   Select the Require **M**icrosoft encrypted authentication option to permit authentication using Microsoft's CHAP only.

   Select the Require **d**ata encryption option if all data sent on the RAS link is to be encrypted.

6. Enable the Enable Multilink check box to activate the Windows NT 4 Multilink option. Multilink lets you increase your remote-access bandwidth by using two or more communications links for a single connection.

7. In the Server Settings box (refer to figure 18.13), select the protocols for the computer to use for servicing calls received from remote clients. Your choices are Net**B**EUI, TC**P**/IP, and IP**X**. Select the Configure button next to each of these protocols to configure them. The steps for protocol configuration are described in the following sections, "Configuring a RAS Server to Use NetBEUI," "Configuring a RAS Server to Use TCP/IP," and "Configuring a RAS Server to Use IPX."

Configuring a RAS Server to Use NetBEUI

Because NetBEUI addressing is based on NetBIOS computer names, no additional addresses have to be configured. To configure the RAS server to use NetBEUI for network connections, use the following steps:

1. Log on as Administrator and start the Network option in the Control Panel.

2. From the Network dialog box, select the Services tab and choose Remote Access Service. Click on the **P**roperties button.

3. You should see the Remote Access Setup dialog box (refer to figure 18.11).

   Choose the **N**etwork button. You should see the Network Configuration dialog box (refer to figure 18.13).

4. In the Server Settings box, choose the **C**onfigure button next to the Net**B**EUI protocol. You should see the RAS Server NetBEUI configuration dialog box (see fig. 18.14).

Figure 18.14

The RAS Server NetBEUI Configuration dialog box.

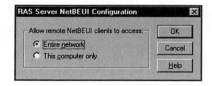

5. Select the Entire **n**etwork option if you want the RAS NetBEUI clients to access the entire network. This is the default choice.

6. Select This **c**omputer only if you want to the RAS NetBEUI clients to access this RAS computer only. You may want to select this option to limit access to the network.

7. Choose OK in successive dialog boxes after completing any additional configuration steps.

8. Restart the RAS computer for the changes to take effect.

When the RAS server is configured with NetBEUI, it also acts as a NetBIOS gateway between NetBEUI and other NetBIOS-compatible protocols on the gateway. The NetBIOS gateway allows NetBEUI clients access to the NetBIOS names of resources used on the network, even though the network may be configured to use NetBIOS over TCP/IP or IPX (see fig. 18.15).

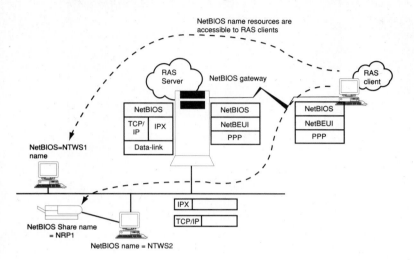

Figure 18.15

RAS server as a NetBIOS gateway.

Configuring a RAS Server to Use TCP/IP

If RAS clients need to run TCP/IP applications that use the Windows Sockets interface over TCP/IP, you must configure the RAS server to use TCP/IP. The RAS server computer must have TCP/IP installed and configured on it so that it can be a TCP/IP host on the LAN that it connects to. In addition, the RAS server must also be configured to supply IP addresses to RAS clients.

RAS clients that use TCP/IP require a unique IP address. If the client does not have an IP address already assigned to it when it connects with the RAS server, the RAS server assigns an IP address to the RAS client. You can also configure the RAS server to use DHCP to assign IP addressing information for remote clients. The IP addresses assigned by the RAS server to the RAS clients must be valid to access the local subnet to which the RAS server is connected.

To configure the RAS server to use TCP/IP for network connections, use the following steps:

1. Log on as administrator and start the Network option in the Control Panel.

2. From the Network dialog box, choose the Services tab and select Remote Access Service. Click on the **P**roperties button.

3. You should see the Remote Access Setup dialog box (refer to figure 18.11).

    Choose the **N**etwork button. You should see the Network Configuration dialog box (refer to figure 18.13).

4. In the Server Settings box, choose the Configure button next to the TCP/IP protocol.

You should see the RAS Server TCP/IP Configuration dialog box (see fig. 18.16).

Figure 18.16

*The RAS Server TCP/IP
Configuration dialog box.*

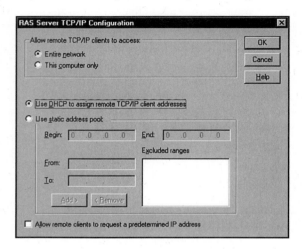

5. Select the Entire network option if you want the RAS TCP/IP clients to access the entire network. This is the default choice.

6. Select the This computer only option if you want to the RAS TCP/IP clients to access this RAS computer only. You may want to select this option to limit access to the network.

7. Enable the Use DHCP to assign remote TCP/IP client addresses option if you have configured a DHCP server (as illustrated in Chapter 15) that will be used for allocating IP addresses.

8. If you are not using a DHCP server, you can alternatively use the Remote TCP/IP client address pool box to configure the IP addresses to be allocated to RAS clients.

In the Begin and End fields, enter the range of IP addresses that will be used. The Begin field contains the first number in the range and the End field contains the last number in the range.

To specify a range of IP addresses to be excluded from the range specified in the Begin and End fields, you can enter the excluded range in the From and To fields, and then choose the Add button. The specified range will be listed in the Excluded ranges box. To delete an excluded range, select it in the Excluded ranges box and choose the Remove button.

9. If remote RAS clients are configured with an IP address, you can enable the Allow remote clients to request a predetermined IP address option. The predetermined IP address used by the client must be compatible with the subnet that the RAS server connects to, or this could cause IP routing to get confused on the network.

10. Choose OK in the RAS Server TCP/IP Configuration dialog box, and in successive dialog boxes after completing any additional configuration steps.

11. Restart the RAS computer for the changes to take effect.

Configuring a RAS Server to Use IPX

If RAS clients need access to NetWare servers on the network, you must configure the RAS server with IPX. To configure a RAS server to use IPX for network connections, use the following steps:

1. Log on as Administrator and start the Network option in the Control Panel.

2. From the Network dialog box, choose the Services tab and select Remote Access Service. Click on the Properties button.

3. You should see the Remote Access Setup dialog box (refer to figure 18.11).

   Choose the **N**etwork button. You should see the Network Configuration dialog box (refer to figure 18.13).

4. In the Server Settings box, choose the **C**onfigure button next to the IPX protocol.

   You should see the RAS Server IPX Configuration dialog box (see fig. 18.17).

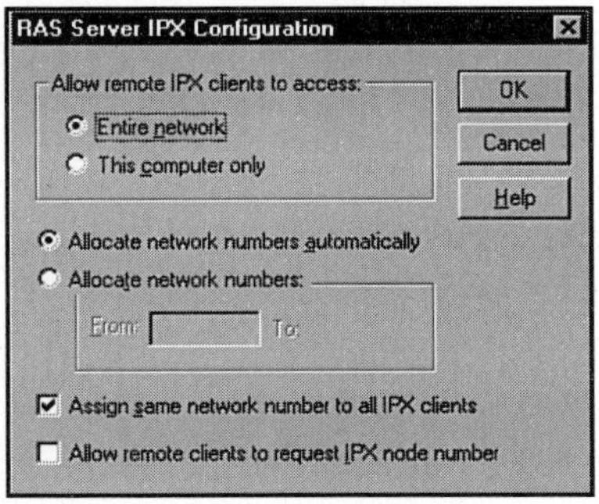

Figure 18.17

The RAS Server IPX Configuration dialog box.

5. Select the Entire **n**etwork option if you want the RAS IPX clients to access the entire network. This is the default choice.

6. Select the This **c**omputer only option if you want to the RAS IPX clients to access this RAS computer only. You may want to select this option to limit access to the network.

7. Select the Allocate network numbers **a**utomatically option if you want the RAS server software to obtain the network number by querying an IPX router using the RIP protocol. The IPX network number obtained is then assigned to the RAS client.

8. Select the Allocate network numbers option if you want the network numbers to be assigned from the specified range. RAS assigns one network number for each port starting from the value in the From field. It automatically fills in the ending network number in the To field. Select this option if you want to treat the RAS IPX clients as if they belong to different networks. The RAS server must perform IPX routing to reach other IPX networks.

9. Select the Assign same network number to all IPX clients option if you want to treat RAS IPX clients as belonging to the same IPX network. This option can be used in conjunction with automatic assignment of IPX network numbers or manual assignment of IPX network numbers.

10. Select (or deselect) Allow remote clients to request IPX node number.

11. Choose OK in successive dialog boxes after completing any additional configuration steps.

12. Restart the RAS computer for the changes to take effect.

Starting Remote Access Services

After restarting the Remote Access Server, you must verify whether the Remote Access Server Service is running. You can verify whether this service is running using the Services option in the Control Panel. If the Remote Access Server service is marked as a Manual start-up service, you have to start the RAS service manually, every time the RAS server is restarted.

To ensure that the RAS service starts automatically every time the RAS server is restarted, select Remote Access Server in the service list of the Control Panel Services application and click on the Startup button. In the Service dialog box, set the Startup Type to Automatic (see fig. 18.18).

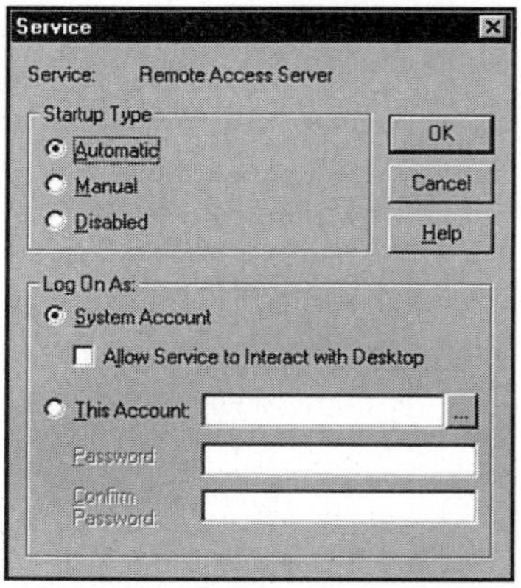

Figure 18.18

Enabling automatic start-up of RAS server.

Administering RAS

Use the following four programs to configure, control, monitor, and update Windows NT Remote Access Service.

■ Remote Access Admin (located in the Administrative Tools program group): Used to perform Remote Access Administration.

■ Dial-Up Monitor (located in Control Panel): Used to set dial-up preferences; view dial-up connections; and monitor transmit, receive, error, and carrier detect signals.

■ Dial-Up Networking (located in the Accessories program group): Used to add phone book entries to make RAS calls.

■ User Manager for Domains (located in the Administrative Tools program group): Used to configure which users have dial-in permissions and what level of call back security is configured for each dial-in user.

Using the Remote Access Admin

The following is a guided tour that explains the features and capabilities of the Remote Access Admin program.

1. Log on as an Administrator user to the RAS server.

2. Select Programs in the Start menu and choose Administrative Tools. Double-click on the Remote Access Admin icon.

   You should see the Remote Access Admin screen (see fig. 18.19).

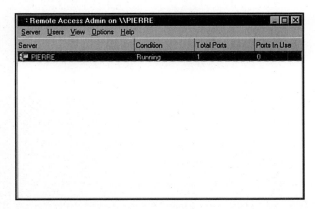

Figure 18.19

Remote Access Admin screen.

3. To manage other RAS servers on the network, choose **S**erver, Select **D**omain or Server.

   You should see the Select Domain dialog box, which you can use to browse and select other RAS servers (see fig. 18.20). Enable the **L**ow Speed Connection check box option if you want to avoid generating excessive traffic over a low-speed WAN link and prevent browsing for the selected domain. You can directly enter the name of the RAS server to administer by typing its UNC name (\\computername) in the **D**omain text box.

Figure 18.20

The Select Domain dialog box.

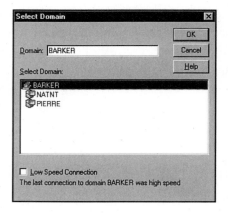

4. If the Remote Access Service is not started on the server, choose **S**erver, **S**tart Remote Access Service from the Remote Access Admin screen.

   Specify the name of the computer on which you want to start the Remote Access Service in the Start Remote Access Service dialog box that appears (see fig. 18.21) and choose OK. If you select a RAS server in the Select Domain dialog box (refer to figure 18.20), that server will appear in the Remote Access Admin screen and will become the default for the Start, Stop, and Pause options on the Server menu.

Figure 18.21

The Start Remote Access Service dialog box.

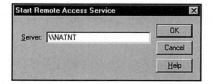

Note You can also start the Remote Access Service using the Services option in the Control Panel.

5. To examine the port status on the RAS server, double-click on the RAS server in the Remote Access Admin screen or choose **S**erver, **C**ommunication Ports.

You should see the Communication Ports dialog box (see fig. 18.22). If a port is in use, you will see the user name and the time the user started using it. You can send messages to any users using a port by choosing the Send **M**essage button or the Send To **A**ll button. You can disconnect a user's session by choosing the **D**isconnect User button.

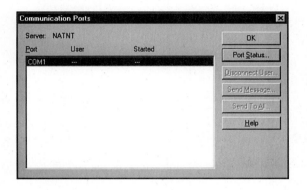

Figure 18.22
The Communication Ports dialog box.

6. To examine the Port Settings, choose the Port **S**tatus button in the Communication Ports dialog box.

   You should see the Port Status dialog box (see fig. 18.23). You can use the information in the dialog box for troubleshooting purposes if the hardware settings do not match the settings in the Port Status dialog box. To reset the statistics counters, choose the **R**eset button.

7. To see a list of active users, you would choose from the Remote Access Admin screen **U**sers, **A**ctive Users (refer to figure 18.19).

8. To set permissions for users, you would choose from the Remote Access Admin screen **U**sers, **P**ermissions (refer to figure 18.19). You should see the Remote Access Permissions dialog box (see fig. 18.24).

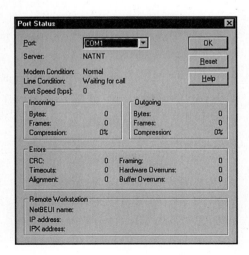

Figure 18.23
The Port Status dialog box.

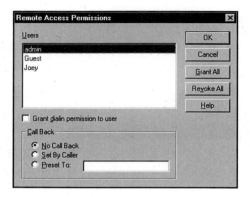

Figure 18.24

The Remote Access Permissions dialog box.

9. Use the Remote Access Permissions dialog box to grant or revoke privileges to users.

   Highlight the user name for whom the permissions are to be set, and check or clear the option Grant **d**ialin permission to user.

   To grant dial-in permissions to all users, choose the **G**rant All button.

   To revoke dial-in permissions from all users, choose the Re**v**oke All button.

Note   You also can set dial-in permissions using the User Manager for Domains tool. See Chapters 7 and 8.

You can set the call back options in the Remote Access Permissions dialog box. Call back refers to the feature in which the RAS server, on receiving a connection from a remote user, terminates it and calls the user back at a specified number. This reduces the risk of security attacks.

The default is **N**o Call Back, which disables the call back feature for the selected user. If the **S**et By Caller option is selected, it means that the server will prompt the user for a call back number. If the **P**reset To option is selected, the server will call the remote user at the fixed number specified in the field next to it.

10. After setting permissions in the Remote Access Permissions dialog box choose OK.

11. Exit the Remote Access Admin program.

Using the Dial-Up Networking Program

The following is a guided tour that explains the features and capabilities of the Dial-Up Networking program.

1. Log on to the RAS server.

2. Start the Dial-Up Networking program from the Accessories folder. If the phonebook is empty, you see a message informing you accordingly. Choose OK to add a phone entry.

   You should see the New Phonebook Entry Wizard screen (see fig. 18.25).

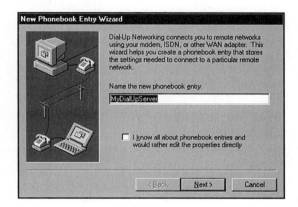

Figure 18.25
The New Phonebook Entry Wizard screen.

3. In the field labeled Name the new phonebook entry, type the name of the server, host, or organization that is to be called. This entry is used for ease of identification. Click on **N**ext.

4. In the next screen (see fig. 18.26), check any of the options that apply to your connection and click on **N**ext. If you are connecting to the Internet, see the section "Configuring Remote Access for Internet Use," later in this chapter.

   The third option, **T**he non-Windows NT server I am calling expects me to type login information after connecting, or to know TCP/IP addresses before dialing, alerts the New Phonebook Entry Wizard to prompt you for login and TCP/IP information later in the setup process.

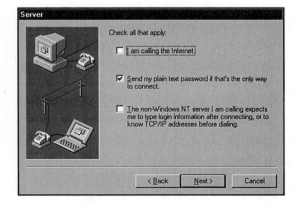

Figure 18.26
Add New Phonebook Wizard Server options.

5. In the next screen (see fig. 18.27) enter the phone number to call. Click on the **A**lternates button to enter additional phone numbers. If the first phone number does not succeed, the other phone numbers are tried in the order they are listed.

Enable the **U**se Telephony dialing properties check box if you want to use dialing properties defined in the Control Panel Telephony application.

Figure 18.27

Add New Phonebook Wizard Phone Number options.

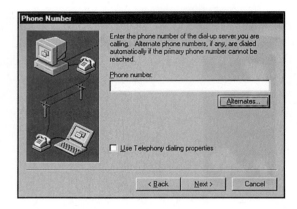

Click on **N**ext after you finish configuring phone number options.

6. If you checked the third box in step 4 (**T**he non-Windows NT server I am calling expects me to type login information after connecting, or to know TCP/IP addresses before dialing), you will see four more screens asking you about the serial line protocol, the login process, the IP address, and DNS and WINS server addresses. Skip to step 11 if you didn't check the box.

7. In the next screen, choose whether you would like to use **P**oint-to-Point Protocol (PPP) or **S**erial Line Internet Protocol (SLIP) for the Internet connection (see fig. 18.28). PPP, the default, is newer and more versatile. If you are not sure which protocol to use, start with PPP.

Choose **N**ext.

Figure 18.28

Choosing a serial line protocol.

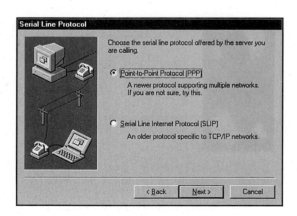

8. In the next screen (see fig. 18.29), configure the login option you want to use for the Internet connection. This screen appears if you checked the third box (**T**he non-Windows NT server I am calling expects...) back in step 4. Most Internet service providers require some kind of login process. If you select the Use a **t**erminal window radio button, a terminal window appears on-screen as soon as you establish a connection with the server, and you can enter your user name and password at the prompt in the terminal window. If you select the Automate with this **s**cript radio button, you can designate a login script that executes as you connect and automatically supplies the login information. The **E**dit scripts button invokes a text file, called Rasread.txt, that provides instructions on how to create your own login scripts.

Click on **N**ext.

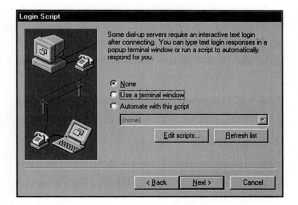

Figure 18.29
Dial-Up login script options.

In the next screen, enter your IP address if the remote server doesn't supply an IP address (see fig. 18.30). Check with your access provider before you enter an IP address here. Internet servers commonly are configured to assign IP addresses to connecting customers. If the server will supply your computer with an IP address, let the IP address default to 0.0.0.0. As the screen points out, don't choose the same address as your network adapter.

Click on **N**ext.

Figure 18.30

Entering your IP address.

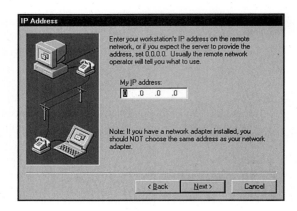

10. In the next screen, enter the IP addresses of a DNS server and/or a WINS server for the connection (see fig. 18.31). Consult with your access provider. If the server will provide you with DNS server and WINS server addresses, enter 0.0.0.0 for each of these fields.

11. In the next screen, click on Finish to complete the phonebook entry.

Figure 18.31

Entering your DNS and/or WINS server addresses.

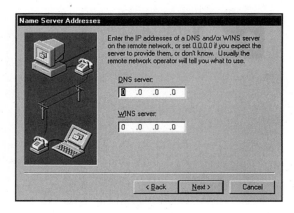

12. After you add your first entry, you see the Dial-Up Networking screen (see fig. 18.32). This is the screen that appears when you start the Dial-Up Networking application.

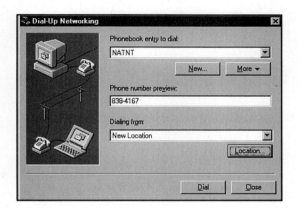

Figure 18.32
The Dial-Up Networking dialog box.

Click on the down arrow beside the Phonebook entry to dial drop-down list to display phonebook entries.

To add additional phone entries, choose the **N**ew button and follow the procedure for adding phone entries as outlined in the previous steps.

The Dialing fr**o**m drop-down list specifies a dialing location. The dialing location defines dialing properties you'll need to dial from a specific location. You can edit location information by clicking on the **L**ocation button, invoking the Location Settings dialog box. To add or remove a location, click on Location list in the Location Settings dialog box (see fig. 18.33). The Location Settings dialog box is designed to let you specify a dialing prefix and suffix. You also can use the Control Panel Telephony application to create and edit dialing locations. The Telephony application offers additional configuration options and a more comprehensive user interface.

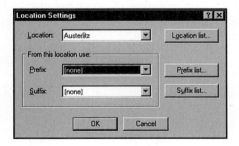

Figure 18.33
The Location Settings dialog box.

13. To dial using an entry, double-click on the entry in the entry list of the Dial-up Networking screen, or select the entry and then choose the **D**ial button (refer to figure 18.32).

    To hang up a connection, choose the **C**lose button.

14. For addtional options, click on the **M**ore button (see fig. 18.34).

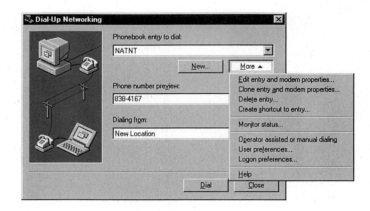

Choose the **E**dit entry and modem properties option to invoke the Edit Phonebook Entry dialog box (see fig. 18.35). The five tabs of the Edit Phonebook Entry dialog box provide configuration options for the phonebook entry, as follows:

■ The **Basic tab** defines basic characteristics of the entry, such as the entry name, phone number, and modem. You also can enable/disable Telephony dialing properties and enter an optional comment.

■ The **Server tab** enables and disables network protocols and software compression. The TCP/IP Settings button invokes the PPP TCP/IP Settings dialog box (see fig. 18.36).

■ The **Script tab** lets you define a script to run after dialing (see fig. 18.37). You can call for a terminal window to appear after dialing. Click on the **B**efore dialing button to run a script or pop-up a terminal window before dialing.

■ The **Security tab** lets you define authentication and encryption options for the connection. The options are similar to those provided in the Network Configuration dialog box (refer to figure 18.13).

■ The **X.25 tab** provides settings for an X.25 connection (see fig. 18.38).

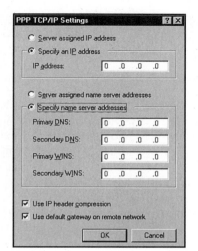

Figure 18.36
The PPP TCP/IP Settings dialog box.

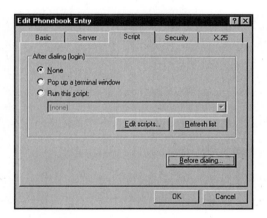

Figure 18.37
The Edit Phonebook Entry Script tab.

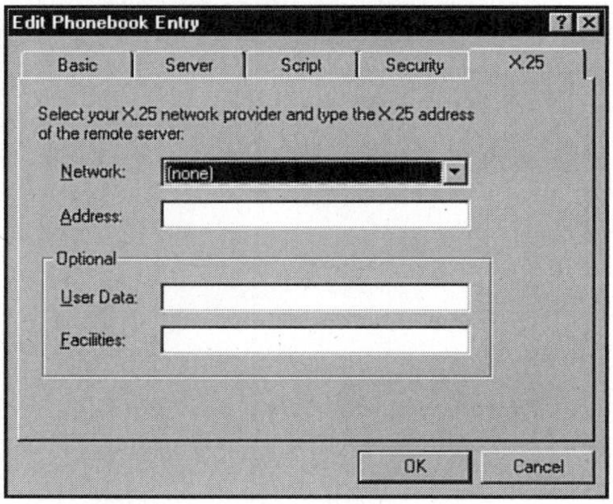

Figure 18.38
The Edit Phonebook Entry X.25 tab.

Select Clone entry and modem properties (refer to figure 18.34) if you want to copy a phonebook entry, make minor modifications to it, and save the copy as a new phonebook entry.

Select Monitor status (refer to figure 18.34) to access the Dial-Up Networking Monitor (described in the next section).

The User preferences and Logon preferences options in the **M**ore button menu (refer to figure 18.34) enable you to specify preferences for the remote access session. The subsequent User Preferences and Logon Preferences dialog boxes are markedly similar. The Logon Preferences dialog box controls preferences that take effect if you enable the Logon using Dial-Up Networking check box at the Windows NT Ctrl-Alt-Del Login prompt. The Logon Preferences option doesn't appear unless you are logged on as Administrator. The User Preferences dialog box enables you to control preferences that are specific to the current user. The Preferences dialog boxes each have four tabs, as follows:

- The **Dialing tab** specifies the number of redial attempts, the seconds between redial attempts, and the idle seconds before hanging up (see fig. 18.39). The User Preferences has an additional option called **E**nable auto-dial by location. Auto-dial is a Windows NT feature that will maintain an association between a Dial-Up Networking entry and a network address. In other words, if Windows NT encounters a reference to a file that can be accessed only through a dial-up connection (such as a shortcut to a file on another PC), NT will attempt to make the Dial-Up connection automatically. In figure 18.39, auto-dial is enabled at the Moscow and Paris locations and disabled at Austerlitz (the current location) and New Location.

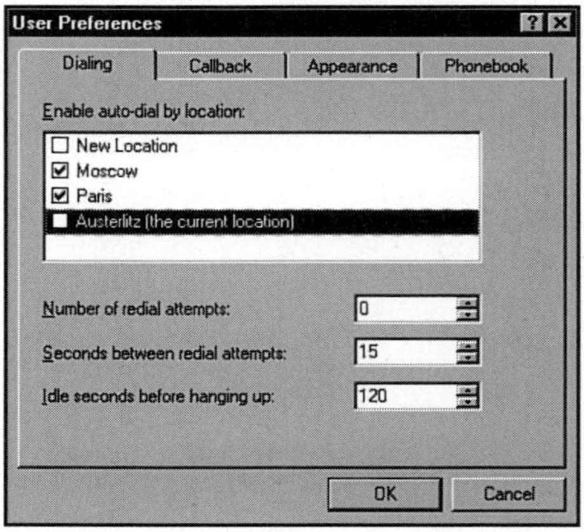

Figure 18.39

The User Preferences
Dialing tab.

Note   You can't use auto-dial unless the Remote Access Autodial Manager service is running. Check the service list in the Control Panel Services application and make sure Remote Access Autodial Manager is started.

■ The **Callback tab** defines Callback properties for the connection (see fig. 18.40). If Callback is enabled for your account, you can place a call to the server and the server will immediately call you back to make the connection. This reduces the phone charges for the remote client. The Callback tab specifies how your system should respond if the server offers the callback option.

■ The **Appearance tab** specifies a number of display preferences pertaining to the phonebook entry (see fig. 18.41). The Logon Preferences Appearance tab offers additional options for editing the phonebook and location during login.

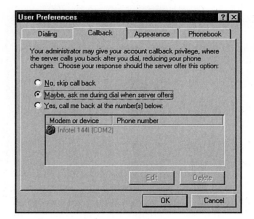

Figure 18.40

The User Preferences Callback tab.

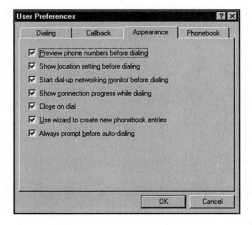

Figure 18.41

The User Preferences Appearance tab.

■ The **Phonebook tab** specifies the active phonebook (see fig. 18.42). Dial-Up networking entries are stored in a phonebook (actually, a *.pbk file). The default phonebook is the system phonebook, but you can create a personal phonebook of dial-up entries that are separate from the system-wide dial-up entries. The first time you select the My **p**ersonal phonebook radio button option in the User Preferences Phonebook tab, Windows NT creates a personal phonebook file using the first eight characters of your user name and the .pbk extension. If you select OK, your personal phonebook becomes the active phonebook. The name of the active phonebook (if it's different from the system phonebook) appears in the title bar of the main Dial-Up Networking screen. You also can select the This a**l**ternate phonebook radio button option in the Phonebook tab and click on the **B**rowse button to browse for a phonebook file. (The Logon Preferences Phonebook tab does not offer the personal phonebook option.)

Figure 18.42
The User Preferences
Phonebook tab.

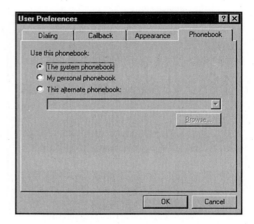

15. After you add to and change the phonebook entries, exit the Dial-Up Networking dialog box.

Configuring Remote Access for Internet Use

Before you can use RAS to make a connection to the Internet through an Internet Service Provider (ISP), you must create and configure a phonebook entry in the Dial-Up Networking program to call an Internet Access Provider.

The settings for your Dial-Up Networking Internet connection will depend on your service provider's configuration. Your access provider should supply you with the information you need to set up the connection. Your provider may not have a ready-made recipe for connecting to the server via Windows NT 4 Remote Access Service, and if not, you may need to customize your Internet setup based on your provider's exact configuration requirements. If you can't get direct information about Windows NT 4 setup from your service provider, you can glean most of the necessary settings from your provider's Windows NT 3.51 or Windows 95 setup instructions.

Before you set up a phonebook entry for Internet access, ask your service provider to supply you with answers to the following questions:

■ Does the server require login information after connecting?

■ Does the server assign an IP address, or should you predefine an IP address for your PC?

■ What are the IP addresses of DNS or WINS servers used by the Internet account?

■ What type(s) of password authentification does the Internet server support?

■ What type(s)of data compression does the Internet server support?

Creating a PPP/SLIP Phonebook Entry for Your ISP

The following is an outline of the procedure for creating a PPP/SLIP phonebook entry to connect to your Internet Service Provider:

1. Start the Dial-Up Networking program from the Accessories Program group.

2. Choose the New button and click on Next. (If this is your first phonebook entry, Setup skips this step and you begin with step 3.)

3. In the New Phonebook Entry Wizard screen (refer to figure 18.25), enter a name for the new phonebook entry and click on **N**ext.

4. Configure the next screen (refer to figure 18.26) as follows:

   Enable the **I** am calling the Internet check box.

   If you want to permit plain-text (unencrypted) passwords, enable the **S**end my plain text password if that's the only way to connect check box.

   If the Internet server is a non-Windows NT server that asks for login information after making the connection, or if you must predefine an IP address before dialing, enable the **T**he non-Windows NT server I am calling expects... check box (refer to figure 18.26).

   Click on **N**ext.

5. In the next screen, enter the phone number and any alternative phone numbers (refer to figure 18.27) and click on **N**ext. You also may enable **U**se Telephony dialing properties.

6. In the next screen, choose whether you would like to use **P**oint-to-Point Protocol (PPP) or **S**erial Line Internet Protocol (SLIP) for the Internet connection (refer to figure 18.28). PPP, the default, is newer and more versatile. If you are not sure which protocol to use, start with PPP.

   Choose **N**ext.

7. In the next screen (refer to figure 18.29), configure the login option you want to use for the Internet connection. This screen appears if you checked the third option (**T**he non-Windows NT server I am calling expects...) in step 4. Most Internet service providers require some kind of login process. If you select the **U**se a terminal window option, a terminal window appears as soon as you establish a connection with the server, and you can enter your user name and password at the prompt in the terminal window. If you select the Automate with this **s**cript option, you can designate a login script that executes as you connect and automatically supply the login information. Clicking on the **E**dit scripts button invokes a text file called Rasread.txt that provides instructions on how to create your own login scripts.

   Click on **N**ext.

8. In the next screen (refer to figure 18.30), enter your IP address if the remote server doesn't supply an IP address. Check with your service provider before you enter an IP address here. Internet servers are commonly configured to assign IP addresses to connecting customers. If the server will supply your computer with an IP address, let the IP address default to 0.0.0.0. As the screen points out (refer to figure 18.30) do not choose the same address as your network adapter.

   Click on **N**ext.

9. In the next screen (refer to figure 18.31), enter the IP addresses of a DNS server and/or a WINS server for the connection. Consult with your access provider. If the server provides you with DNS server and WINS server addresses, enter 0.0.0.0 for each of these fields.

   Click on **N**ext.

10. The next screen asks you to click on Finish to save the new entry. Click on Finish. The Dial-up Networking screen appears (refer to figure 18.32). To complete your PPP TCP/IP settings, click on the **M**ore button and choose **E**dit entry and modem properties.

11. In the Edit Phonebook Entry dialog box, choose the Server tab (see fig. 18.43).

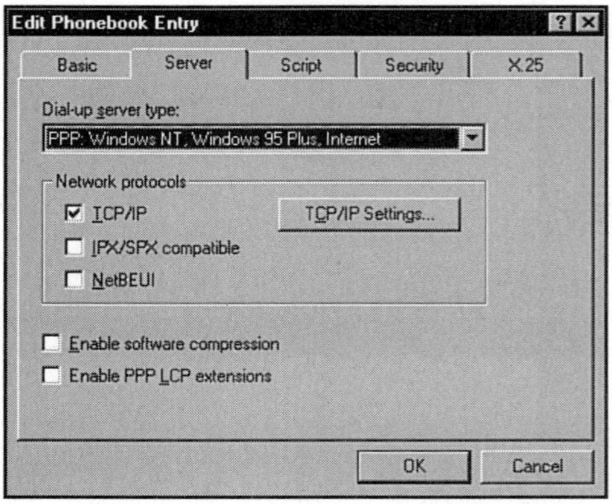

Figure 18.43

The Edit Phonebook Entry Server tab.

The Enable PPP <u>L</u>CP extensions check box enables newer PPP features specified in RFC 1570. If your Internet provider supports this option, check it. Clear this option if you can't establish a connection with the option enabled.

Enable the <u>E</u>nable software compression check box option if you want to use software compression. Software compression is an alternative to modem compression. According to Microsoft, software compression provides better throughput than modem compression.

12. Click on the T<u>C</u>P/IP Settings button to invoke the PPP TCP/IP Settings dialog box (refer to figure 18.36). Verify that the settings in this dialog box coincide with the setup instructions your Internet access provider gives you. The DNS, WINS, and IP address configuration should be as specified in steps 8 and 9.

    IP header compression is enabled by default. Disable this option if your provider doesn't support header compression.

    The Use default <u>g</u>ateway on remote network check box is enabled by default. Leave it that way unless your provider instructs you to do otherwise.

    Click on OK.

13. Click on the Edit Phonebook Entry Security tab (see fig. 18.44) and choose the authentication method specied by your Internet provider. Click on OK.

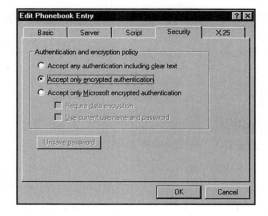

Figure 18.44
The Edit Phonebook Entry Security tab.

14. After you finish editing the Edit Phonebook Entry dialog box, click on OK.

Configuring RAS as a Router

A RAS server that is configured with IPX or IP can act as a static IPX or IP router. Static routers do not participate in dynamic routing update exchanges as normal routers do, and can route only between the networks they are connected to. The following sections discuss the RAS IPX and IP routers.

RAS IPX Router

The static routing capability enables RAS to forward IPX messages between RAS clients and IPX hosts on the network. Figure 18.45 shows the RAS IPX client running Client Services for NetWare to access NetWare server on the LAN. Because the RAS acts as an IPX router, the RAS NetWare client server can access NetWare servers on the network.

Figure 18.45

An IPX routing example using a RAS server.

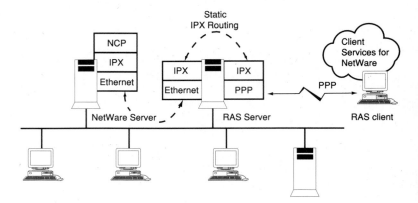

The IPX router component on a RAS server can forward NetBIOS broadcast requests to resolve NetBIOS resource names. If you need to prevent the RAS IPX router from forwarding broadcasts, you should modify the value entry NetBIOSRouting of data type REG_DWORD in the RAS server's Registry. This value entry is located under the following key:

```
HKEY_LOCAL_MACHINE\SYSTEM\CurrentControlSet\Services\NwlnkRip\Parameters
```

The NetBIOSRouting value entry can have the following values:

    0 = Do not forward broadcasts

    2 = Enable forwarding of NetBIOS packets from RAS clients to LAN (default)

    4 = Enable forwarding of NetBIOS packets from LAN to RAS clients

    6 = Enable two-way forwarding of NetBIOS packets between LAN and RAS clients

RAS TCP/IP Router

The static routing capability enables RAS to forward TCP/IP messages between RAS clients and TCP/IP hosts on the network. The IP routing is limited to the networks to which the RAS server directly connects.

Figure 18.46 shows an example of static IP routing in which the RAS TCP/IP client is running a Windows Sockets application such as an FTP client to access FTP servers on the network.

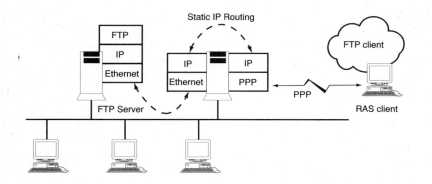

Figure 18.46
IP routing example using a RAS server.

The IP router component on a RAS server does not forward the b-node broadcast requests sent by the RAS clients to the address 255.255.255.255 (limited broadcast) by RAS clients.

Configuring RAS IP Router for Using the Internet

You could use the RAS IP router to provide routing between a simple LAN and the Internet over a dedicated PPP account provided by your Internet Access Provider.

Figure 18.47 illustrates a small LAN using the RAS server as an IP router. The default gateway IP address of the TCP/IP clients must be configured to the IP address of the RAS IP router.

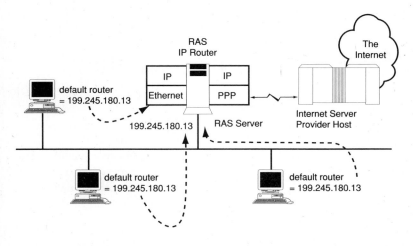

Figure 18.47
Small LAN connected to the Internet using a RAS IP router.

Additionally, you must configure two value entries in the RAS server's Registry. The first Registry value entry to configure is the DisableOtherSrcPackets. This value entry is of data type REG_DWORD and must be created under the following key:

```
HKEY_LOCAL_MACHINE\SYSTEM\CurrentControlSet\Services\RasArp\Parameters
```

If the value entry does not exist, its default value is 0, which means that the IP packets sent by the RAS server will have the IP address of the RAS server as the source address. For the RAS to be used as a router, packets originating from a TCP/IP node on the LAN must have their IP address in the IP header. Therefore, you must create the value entry DisableOtherSrcPackets and set its value to 1. If you are not familiar with creating value entries in the Registry, refer to Chapter 10, "Managing Windows NT Registry."

If the subnet that you have has the same network class as your Internet Access Provider, you must add the PriorityBasedOnSubNetwork value entry of data type REG_DWORD under the following key:

```
HKEY_LOCAL_MACHINE\SYSTEM\CurrentControlSet\Services\RasMan\PPP\IPCP
```

If the PriorityBasedOnSubNetwork value entry does not exist, it has a default value of 0. You must create the PriorityBasedOnSubNetwork value entry and set its value to 1.

Normally, if the RAS connection and the LAN adapter have the same network number in their IP address, and the Use Default Gateway On Remote Network option in the PPP TCP/IP Settings dialog box is checked (see fig. 18.36), all IP packets are sent to the RAS connection. This means that if the network adapter has an IP address of 132.156.190.12 and the RAS connection has an IP address of 132.156.195.2, RAS sends all packets destined for 132.156.*.* to the RAS connection because the network number 132.156.0.0 is the same for the RAS connection and the network adapter. If the PriorityBasedOnSubNetwork value entry is set to 1, RAS will send the 132.156.190.* packets to the network adapter and the 132.156.195.* packets to the RAS connection, assuming that a subnet of 255.255.255.0 is being used.

Overview of Point-to-Point Tunneling Protocol

The Point-to-Point Tunneling Protocol (PPTP) enables remote clients to connect to private servers over TCP/IP-based networks. PPTP provides a secure communications channel between PPTP clients and PPTP servers on both corporate and public networks, including the Internet and other public TCP/IP based networks. PPTP enables remote users to dial into local Internet Service Providers (ISPs) and connect via the Internet to a remote private server connected to the Internet.

Though run over TCP/IP networks, PPTP supports networking protocols, IP, IPX, and NetBEUI. Since PPTP encapsulates IP, IPX or NetBEUI protocols inside of IP packets, remote users can still access systems running these protocols or use applications that may be network protocol dependent.

Virtual Private Network

PPTP makes use of Virtual Private Networks, VPNs; a Virtual Private Network is a connection between two remote computers in different locations. The connection between these two computers, referred to as a *tunnel*, must maintain security and privacy and can take place over a public or private network using a PPTP device. Although VPN refers to a virtual connection between computers, Microsoft refers to the device used to create the virtual connection as a VPN. When you are installing or configuring PPTP on Windows NT or Windows 95, you will actually be configuring VPNs, which are PPTP devices.

Installing the Point-to-Point Tunneling Protocol

Installation of the Point-to-Point Tunneling Protocol is comprised of installing the PPTP network protocol and configuring Virtual Private Network devices. Setup and configuration is similar to those sections that have been covered in the Remote Access Services section of this chapter.

To install the PPTP software and configure the VPN devices, perform the following steps:

1. Log on as Administrator user to the Windows NT Server.

2. Start the Network option in the Control Panel. You should see the Network dialog box. In the Network dialog box, choose the Protocols tab (see fig. 18.48).

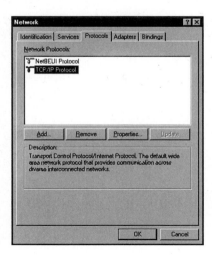

Figure 18.48

The Network Protocols tab.

3. In the Network Protocols tab, choose the **A**dd button to invoke the Select Network Protocol dialog box (see fig. 18.49).

Figure 18.49

The Select Network Protocol dialog box.

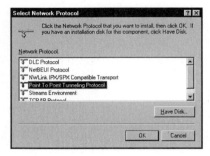

4. In the Select Network Protocol dialog box, select Point-to-Point Tunneling Protocol.

5. Enter the path for the distribution files and choose the Continue button.

6. You should see a status of the files as they are copied to the server computer. After the files are copied, the PPTP Configuration dialog box appears as shown in figure 18.50.

Figure 18.50

The PPTP Configuration dialog box.

7. Select the number of Virtual Private Networks by clicking on the down arrow. The number of Virtual Private Networks is the number of VPN connections you want your server to support simultaneously. Windows NT Server can support up to 256 Virtual Private Networks.

8. After setting the number of Virtual Private Networks, RAS Setup will be invoked so that a Virtual Private Network port can be configured. This is the same dialog box that is used to setup Remote Access Services on the server (see fig. 18.51).

Figure 18.51

The Remote Access Setup dialog box.

9. Add the VPN device by selecting **A**dd from the Remote Access Setup dialog box. The Add RAS device is displayed. Selecting the RAS-capable devices arrow displays all the virtual private network devices which can be set up as RAS-capable devices. Refer to figure 18.52.

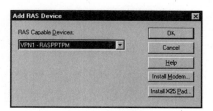

Figure 18.52
The Add RAS Device dialog box.

For each VPN device you want to set up, you will need to add the VPN device as a RAS-capable device. After adding your RAS capable devices, choose OK to exit from the Add RAS Device dialog box. After exiting from the Add RAS Device dialog box, the dialog box in figure 18.53 is displayed.

Figure 18.53
The Remote Access Setup dialog box.

10. For each Virtual Private Network, you will need to configure the Port Usage as you did in Remote Access Setup earlier in the chapter. For each port, you can select dial-out only, receive calls only, or dial-out and receive calls. By default, the dial-out only option is selected for NT Workstation and receive calls only is selected for NT Server. If this machine is a server and is expected only to receive calls, select the receive calls only option. If the server is to dial-out and receive calls, then select the dial-out and receive calls option.

11. Click on the **N**etwork button in the Remote Access Setup dialog box to configure the appropriate network protocols for use. This task is similar to setting up the Network Options covered previously in the chapter.

12. After completing the Network Setup, close the Network dialog box, shutdown the computer, and restart.

After the system restarts, you should be able to accept connections via the Virtual Private Network devices that you configured.

Configuring PPTP Filtering on the PPTP Server

The Enabling PPTP Filtering option is on the Advanced IP Addressing dialog box, which you can reach from Control Panel, Networks, Protocols, TCP/IP Properties, Advanced button. The Enabling PPTP Filtering option provides additional security by filtering all non-PPTP network packets from reaching your network. PPTP filtering should only be enabled on the network adapter that is connected to the Internet because if PPTP filtering is enabled on another adapter, even simple TCP/IP utilities, such as PING, will not work.

To enable PPTP filtering perform the following steps:

1. Log on as administrator user to the Windows NT Server.

2. Start the Network option in the Control Panel. You should see the Network dialog box. Choose the Protocols tab (refer to fig. 18.48).

3. In the Network Protocols dialog box, select TCP/IP Protocol. Click on the IP Address tab and select Advanced.

4. In the Advanced IP Addressing dialog box, select the adapter connected to the Internet. Then select the Enable PPTP Filtering option (see fig. 18.54).

Figure 18.54

The Advanced IP Addressing dialog box.

5. Click on OK and close the Advanced IP Addressing dialog box. Choose OK and close the Network dialog box.

6. Shutdown and restart the computer.

With the Enabling PPTP Filtering option configured, all non-PPTP network packets are kept from reaching your network.

Installing and Configuring PPTP Clients

Windows NT Server, Windows NT Workstation, and Windows 95 can be used as PPTP clients. Each of these clients uses a Virtual Private Networking device to connect to the PPTP server. The Setup for each is similar to the setup for the Dial-Up Networking Client. The following sections review the installation of PPTP clients on Windows NT Server, Windows NT Workstation, and Windows 95.

Installing PPTP on a Windows NT System

Installation of the Point-to-Point Tunneling Protocol is comprised of installing the PPTP network protocol and configuring Virtual Private Network devices. Setup and configuration are similar to those sections that have been covered in the Remote Access Services section of this chapter.

To install the PPTP software and configure the VPN devices, see the Installing the Point-to-Point Tunneling Protocol section earlier in this chapter.

Configuring Dial-Up Networking on a Windows NT System

The most common method of connecting to a private network using PPTP is through the Internet. In order to use this method, the PPTP client must have two entries configured in the phonebook; one for the Internet through the Internet Service Provider and one for the PPTP server that will be connected using the Internet connection. The steps to create phonebook entries, and setting up a connection to the Internet were covered earlier in the chapter.

To configure a phonebook entry for a PPTP connection perform the following steps:

1. Log on to the Windows NT system.

2. Start the Dial-Up Networking program from the Accessories folder. If the phonebook is empty, you see a message informing you accordingly. Choose OK to add a phonebook entry.

   You should see the New Phonebook Entry Wizard screen.

3. In the field labeled "Name the new phonebook entry," type the name of the server that is to be called. Click on Next.

4. In the next screen, check the option to Connect to the Internet.

5. In the next screen (see fig. 18.55) enter the TCP/IP address of the server to connect. For configuring and establishing a connection to the PPTP server, the address of the server is required, not the server's phone number

Figure 18.55

Add New Phonebook Wizard Phone Number options.

6. Click on Next after you finish configuring PPTP server's TCP/IP address.

After configuring your connection to the Internet Service Provider and your connection to the PPTP server, you are ready to connect to the PPTP server.

1. Using Dial-Up Networking, dial and connect to the Internet via your Internet Service Provider.

2. Using Dial-Up Networking, connect to the PPTP server across the Internet.

You should have two Dial-Up Networking dialog boxes for your connections.

Note   After the connection has been established to the PPTP server, you will no longer be able to gain access to the Internet. Internet access will only be possible during the PPTP session, if the remote network allows access to the Internet.

Note   A Windows NT Workstation is installed exactly as a Windows NT Server.

Installing PPTP on a Windows 95 System

Windows 95 also supports PPTP as a client. With the latest release of Dial-Up Networking, PPTP is an available option for Remote Access. You must download version 1.2 or greater of the Dial-Up Networking software for Windows 95 in order to install and configure PPTP.

Note   This section assumes that Dial-Up Networking version 1.2 or greater has already been installed on the Windows 95 system and that a connection has already been created for connecting to the Internet Service Provider.

To configure the VPN device and use PPTP on the Windows 95 system, perform the following steps:

1. From the Start menu, select Programs, select Accessories, and then click on Dial-Up Networking.

2. Click Make New Connection. The Make New Connection wizard appears.

3. Type the name of the server in the Type a name for the computer you are dialing box.

4. Select Microsoft VPN Adapter in the Select a modem box. Click on Next.

5. Type the name or IP address of the PPTP server in the Host Name or IP address box. Click Next and then Finish. An icon for connecting to the server is created in the Dial-Up Networking folder.

6. Double click the icon in the Dial-Up Networking folder to connect to your ISP.

7. Double click the PPTP Server Icon in the Dial-Up Networking folder to connect to the PPTP server. Enter the user name and password to connect to the remote server. You will now have two connections established, one to the ISP and one to the PPTP server.

Note   After the connection has been established to the PPTP server, you will no longer be able to gain access to the Internet. Internet access will only be possible during the PPTP session, if the remote network allows access to the Internet.

As with Remote Access for other communication devices, the Remote Access Admin Administrator tool is used to monitor connections. Please refer to the topic discussed earlier in the chapter for Remote Access Admin.

Conclusion

Remote Access Services can be used to convert a Windows NT computer into a general purpose communications server. The Remote Access Services can be used by mobile users to connect to a Windows NT network from a remote location and also to dial out of the network.

The Point-to-Point Tunneling Protocol allows remote clients to access Corporate networks using public data networks such as the Internet. PPTP supports the encapsulation of NetBEUI and IPX packets, and TCP/IP.

This chapter discussed the features and capabilities of the Windows NT Remote Access Services, as well as how to install and configure RAS. You can use the Remote Access Server as a simple IPX or IP router that directly connects two networks together. Dynamic IPX or IP routing is not supported by the RAS router. The RAS server can also be used as NetBIOS gateway to access NetBIOS-named resources on the network, if the NetBEUI protocol is enabled at the RAS server.

Windows NT Network Browser

The network browser is used within a Windows NT or a LAN Manager network to discover the network resources that are available for use on the network. Only resources with NetBIOS names can be discovered in this manner. The computers that have NetBIOS names for resources participate in the browsing protocols so that lists of resource names are maintained on browser servers. Any Windows NT computer can be a browser server. This chapter discusses browsing concepts as they apply to Windows NT, and how a computer becomes a master browser through an election process.

Understanding Browsing Concepts

Windows NT computers can use the browser to discover resources that are available online on the network. For example, when the users open Network Neighborhood (see fig. 19.1), they see a list of computers and printers on the network whose resources can be accessed.

Figure 19.1

Network Neighborhood displays computers and printers on the network.

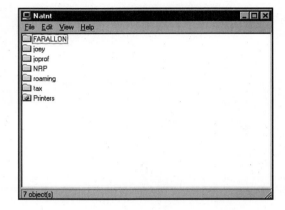

The list of resources displayed in figure 19.1 is built by browser servers. Windows NT networks can have the following types of browser servers:

- Master Browser

- Domain Master Browser

- Backup Browser

- Preferred Master Browser

Any Windows NT Workstation or Windows NT Server can be a browser server. To appreciate the role of a browser, consider a network such as a LAN Manager network that does not support the concept of a network browser (see fig. 19.2).

Figure 19.2

LAN Manager network without browsers.

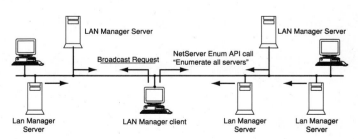

The LAN Manager client who wants to connect to a network server makes the NetServerEnum API call. This call results in the generation of broadcast datagrams sent to all class 2 mail slots on the network. All LAN Manager servers reply simultaneously, and the LAN Manager client must select which LAN Manager server to connect to. Because all LAN Manager servers reply at once, on a large network this can result in delayed responses.

In a Windows NT network, a Windows NT client wanting to find out what resources exist on the network makes an NetServerEnum2 API call to a master browser or a backup browser on the network (see fig. 19.3). The browser on the network responds with a list of computers that it knows about. In a Windows NT domain, the primary domain controller is the master browser. In a Windows NT workgroup network, the master browser is elected. If the master browser fails, other computers detect this and participate in an election to determine the new master browser.

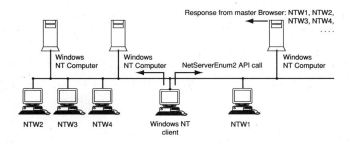

Figure 19.3

Use of browsers on a Windows NT network.

Understanding Browser Elections

In a Windows NT domain, every Windows NT Server computer is a browser. The Browser service is responsible for maintaining the browse list, making API calls for the browse list, and managing the browser roles. The browser service is implemented by the file SERVICES.EXE and the support file BROWSER.DLL, both located in the *SystemRoot*\System32 directory. The Registry parameters for the Browser service are under HKEY_LOCAL_ MACHINE\ SYSTEM\CurrentControlSet\Services\Browser.

The Windows NT Server that is the primary domain controller for the domain is the master browser for that domain. All other Windows NT Server computers (backup domain controllers or ordinary Windows NT Servers) in that domain are backup browsers. If there is more than one Windows NT Server active in the domain, no Windows NT Workstation will ever be a browser.

If the workgroup consists of Windows NT Workstation computers, there is always one master browser. If there are at least two Windows NT Workstations on the network, there is a backup browser in addition to the master browser. For every 32 Windows NT Workstations, there is an additional backup browser.

The master browser is determined by an election protocol. The same election protocol is used when a master browser fails and one of the backup browser must be elected as a master browser. A Windows NT computer can force an election by sending a special election datagram (see fig. 19.4). An election usually occurs under the following conditions:

- A client computer cannot locate a master browser.

- A backup browser tries to update (synchronize) itself with the browser list from the master browser but cannot find the master browser.

- A computer designated as the preferred master browser comes online.

- A primary domain controller comes on-line.

Figure 19.4

Initiating the browser election.

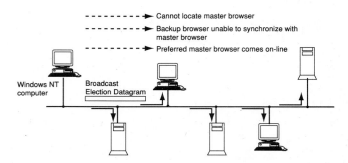

Browser election events are logged in the system event log and can be viewed using the Event Viewer.

The election datagram contains the sender's 16-bit election version and a 32-bit election criteria. The browser that receives the election datagram compares the election version in the election datagram with its own. If a browser that receives the election datagram has an election version that is higher than that of any other browser, it wins the election and becomes a master browser regardless of the election criteria (see fig. 19.5). If the election versions are identical, the election criteria is considered.

Figure 19.5

Winning browser election based on election version only.

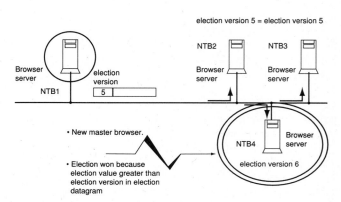

The 32-bit election criteria is expressed as a hexadecimal number for the purposes of determining how it is composed. The following rules determine how the election criteria is used:

- If the receiving browser has a higher election criteria than the browser that issued the election datagram, the receiving browser issues its own election datagram and joins the election that is in progress.

- If the receiving browser does not have a higher election criteria than the browser that issued the election datagram, the receiving browser attempts to determine the outcome of the election; that is, it attempts to determine the new master browser.

Figure 19.6 illustrates the application of these rules. In this figure, the Windows NT Server that has the highest election criteria value becomes the master browser.

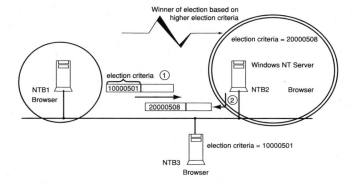

Figure 19.6

Winning browser election based on election criteria.

The election criteria value is determined by taking into account the following:

- The operating system type of the browser

- Protocol election version

- If browser is a Primary Domain Controller

- If browser is a WINS client

- If browser is preferred master browser

- If browser is a running master browser

- If browser maintains the server list

- If browser is a running backup browser

The election criteria value as a hexadecimal number is expressed as the following:

SSEEEEBB

The *SS* are two hexadecimal digit codes for the operating system type. These hexadecimal digits have the following values:

- Windows NT Server = 20

- Windows NT Workstation = 10

- Windows for Workgroups = 01

The *EEEE* are the four hexadecimal digits that represent the 16-bit election version.

The *BB* are two hexadecimal digit codes for the browser type. These hexadecimal digits have the following values:

- Primary Domain Controller = 80

- WINS client = 20

- Preferred master browser = 08

- Running master browser = 04

- MaintainServerList = Yes in the Registry = 02

- Running backup browser = 01

The components of the election criteria value are summarized in figure 19.7.

Figure 19.7

Components of the election criteria.

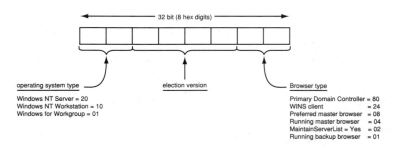

If two or more browsers have the same election version and the same election criteria values, the tie is broken by electing the browser that has been running for the longest time. If there is still a tie, the browser with the lexically lower name wins the election. Thus, a browser with the name ALPHA will win over a browser named GATED.

If the browser wins the election, it broadcasts up to four election datagrams to ensure that there are no other browsers that could possibly win the election (see fig. 19.8). During this time period, the browser is in the *running election* state. In this state, the election datagrams are sent at intervals determined by the type of the browser:

■ Master browser delay by 200 milliseconds

■ Backup browsers delay by 400 milliseconds

All other browsers delay by 800 milliseconds.

Thus, the less important the browser, the longer it has to wait.

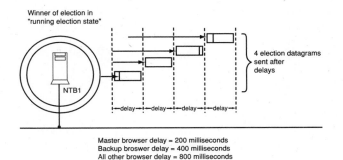

Figure 19.8

Election datagrams in the running election state.

If a running master browser receives an announcement from another computer that claims to be the master browser, it demotes itself to a backup browser and forces an election by sending the election datagram.

Understanding the Role of the Master Browser

The master browser maintains a *browse list*, which contains a list of all servers in the master browser's domain or workgroup and a list of all domains on the network. The term *server*, when discussing browsers, refers to any computer that uses NetBIOS names for its resources and is capable of sharing its resources on the network. This includes Windows NT Workstations and Windows NT Servers, Windows or Windows for Workgroup workstations, and DOS workstations. In a peer-to-peer network, any computer can act as a server.

Computers that provide services (servers) announce their presence on the network by broadcasting a server announcement to the domain or workgroup's master browser. On receiving this announcement, the master browser adds the server to its browse list.

On networks that use IPX or NetBEUI, the broadcast name queries can cross router boundaries, so a Windows NT domain can be supported by a single master browser (see fig. 19.9). On networks that use TCP/IP, the broadcast name query (sent to limited broadcast address of 255.255.255.255) does not cross router boundaries. In this case, the master browser also returns a list of backup browsers in the local subnet that can then be used by computers in that local subnet.

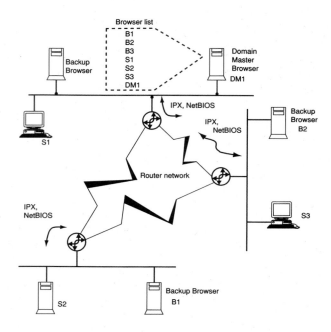

Figure 19.9
*Broadcasts in IPX and
NetBEUI permit single
master browser.*

A new master browser request can request other servers to register themselves by sending a
Request Announcement broadcast datagram. Computers that receive a *Request Announcement*
broadcast datagram respond at random times in the next 30 seconds. The random delay avoids
excessive network traffic and ensures that the master browser is not overloaded by too many
responses.

Domain Master Browser

The browser service running on a Primary Domain Controller for a domain is the domain
master browser. As explained in the section on "Understanding Browser Elections," earlier in
this chapter, the Primary Domain Controller has the highest election criteria value among all
other browser types.

On a domain running the TCP/IP protocol and consisting of several TCP/IP subnets connected by IP routers, each subnet has its own master browser (see fig. 19.10) and backup
browsers. There is still a single master browser for the entire domain called the *domain master
browser.*

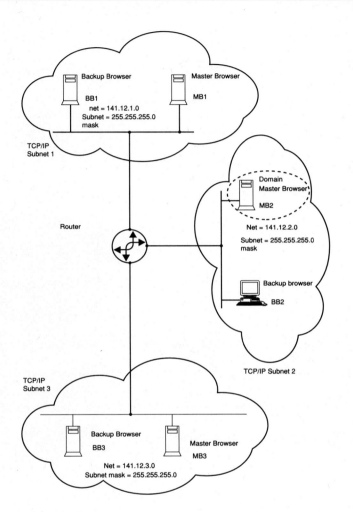

Figure 19.10
*Master browsers on
TCP/IP subnets.*

Each TCP/IP subnet must have a master browser because browser datagrams are not forwarded across router boundaries. The subnet master browsers send a directed datagram (nonbroadcast datagram) called the Master Browser Announcement datagram, which announces the existence of the master browser to the domain master browser (see fig. 19.11).

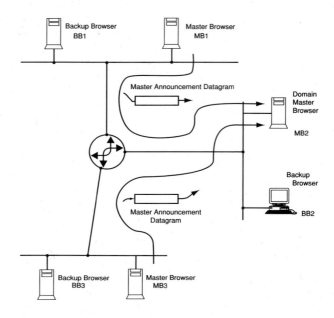

Figure 19.11

Master browsers on subnets announce to domain master browser.

The domain master browser then issues a NetServerEnum API call for each master browser on the subnet. The NetServerEnum API call to the master browser causes requests to be sent to the master browser to return a list of servers connected on the master browser's subnet. The domain master browser builds a master list of servers in the domain by merging the replies sent by the master browsers (see fig. 19.12).

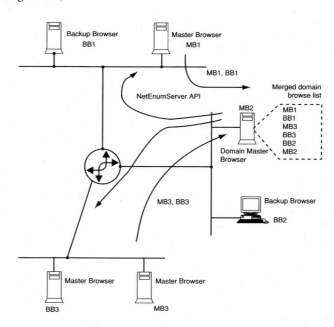

Figure 19.12

Building a master domain list at the domain master.

The master browsers on the subnet also issue the NetServerEnumAPI call to the domain master to obtain a master list of servers in the domain. This enables the master browsers to synchronize with the domain master browser (see fig. 19.13). Backup browsers in turn synchronize with their master browsers every 15 minutes. This master list is used in response to browse queries from clients on the subnet.

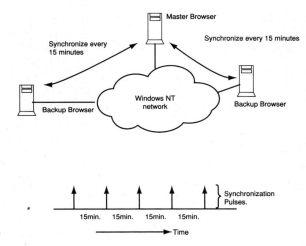

Figure 19.13

Synchronizing between browsers.

The MasterBrowseAnnoucement and the subsequent NetServerEnum API calls are repeated every 15 minutes. This ensures that a relatively updated master browser list for the domain is always available.

If the Windows NT clients on a TCP/IP network are not WINS clients, and use the LMHOSTS file for name resolution, then for browser services to work correctly, you must use the #DOM keyword in the LMHOSTS file to identify the domain controllers that are not on the local subnet. For details on how to configure the LMHOSTS file, see Chapter 14, "Installing and Configuring the TCP/IP Protocol Stack."

Understanding the Role of the Backup Browsers

As the name suggests, backup browsers are maintained to provide browser fault tolerance. If the master browser fails, one of the backup browsers becomes the master browser.

Backup browsers call their master browser every 15 minutes to obtain the most up-to-date copy of the browser list. If the backup browser is unable to find the master browser, it forces an election. The backup browser caches the browser list and returns the list when any of the browser clients issue a NetServerEnum API call to the backup browser.

Understanding the Role of Preferred Master Browsers

A Windows NT computer has the IsDomainMaster value entry of data type REG_SZ under the following Registry key:

```
HKEY_LOCAL_MACHINE\SYSTEM\CurrentControlSet\Services\Browser\Parameters
```

If the IsDomainMaster is set to TRUE, it makes the Windows NT computer a preferred master browser. A preferred master browser has been configured at an advantage to win in browser elections. This means that the preferred browser computer will be given a higher election criteria value during browser elections, and is therefore more likely to be selected as a master browser. Recall that the preferred master browser (see the earlier section, "Understanding Browser Elections") is assigned a hexadecimal code of 08, which is greater than the code values for the running master browser (code 04), the running backup browser (code 01), and the MaintainServerList=Yes computer (code 02). Only the Primary Domain Controller and the WINS servers have a higher election criteria value than the preferred master browser, all other conditions being the same.

The default value of the IsDomainMaster value entry is FALSE. That is, Windows NT computers are by default not configured as preferred browsers.

Potential Browsers

A *potential browser* is any computer that can be elected as browser. A potential browser can be any Windows NT Server domain controller, Windows NT Server nondomain controller, Windows NT Workstation, Windows NT Advanced Server, Windows for Workgroup workstation, or earlier Windows NT version.

Table 19.1 summarizes the operating system type and the potential browser role that it can assume.

Table 19.1
Potential Browsers

Operating System Type	Browser Role
Windows NT Server primary domain controller	Will be a Domain master browser
Windows NT Server backup domain controller	Will be a backup browser or domain master if PDC is down
Windows NT Server non-domain controller	Can be a master browser or backup browser
Windows NT Advanced Server	Will be a master or backup browser

Operating System Type	Browser Role
Windows for Workgroups workstation	Can be a master browser or backup browser
Earlier Windows NT workstation versions	Can be a master browser or backup browser

Whether a Windows NT computer becomes a browser is further controlled by the MaintainServerList value entry that is kept under the Registry key:

```
HKEY_LOCAL_MACHINE\SYSTEM\CurrentControlSet\Services\Browser\Parameters
```

The MaintainServerList value entry is of data type REG SZ and can have the values of No, Yes, and Auto. If the value entry is set to No, the Windows NT computer will never become a browser. You may want to set the value of MaintainServerList to No for a Windows NT computer that you know is turned off frequently or is unreliable.

If the MaintainServerList value is set to Yes, the Windows NT computer will become a browser. On startup, the Windows NT computer contacts the master browser to obtain the current browse list. If the master browser cannot be found, it forces an election, and can potentially become a master browser. For Windows NT Server computers, the default value of MaintainServerList is Yes.

If the MaintainServerList value is set to Auto, then the computer is a potential browser. Whether or not the Windows NT computer becomes a browser depends on the number of existing browsers. The master browser informs the Windows NT computer if it becomes a backup browser. For Windows NT Workstation computers, the default value of MaintainServerList is Auto.

If the value of MaintainServerList is Yes or Auto, the browser service will start automatically on that computer.

The browser service is called Computer Browser in the Services dialog box (started by running the Services option in the Control Panel). You can use the services dialog box to start, pause, or stop the Computer Browser service. You also can start, pause, continue, and stop this service using the following commands:

- NET START BROWSER

- NET PAUSE BROWSER

- NET CONTINUE BROWSER

- NET STOP BROWSER

These commands can be placed in batch files to automate the desired action.

Computer Announcements

When a computer is started, it broadcasts announcement datagrams to the workgroup or domain browser starting at one-minute intervals, and gradually increasing it till announcements are sent at 12-minute intervals. If the master browser does not see an announcement from the computer for three announcement intervals ($3 \times 12 = 36$ minutes), it will delete the computer from the browser list. For this reason, there could be a delay of up to 36 minutes before a computer that is offline is removed from the browser list.

Domain Announcements

When a browser is elected to a master browser, it broadcasts domain announcement datagrams every minute for the first five minutes. After the first five minutes, the domain announcements are broadcast every fifteen minutes. Domain announcement datagrams contain the following information:

- The name of the domain

- The name of the domain master browser

- The operating system type (Windows NT Server or Windows NT Workstation) of the domain browser

- Whether the master browser is a Primary Domain Controller

Master browsers in other domains also receive the domain announcement datagrams and add the domain name specified in the datagram to their browser list. If the master browsers in other domains do not see a domain announcement datagram for three domain announcement intervals ($3 \times 15 = 45$ minutes), they will delete the domain name from their browser lists. For this reason, there could be a delay of up to 45 minutes before a domain that is down is removed from the browser list.

When a potential browser first becomes a master browser for a domain, it can request other domains to announce themselves because its browser list is initially empty.

The domain master browser also adds the list of domains that have registered their NetBIOS domain names with the WINS server. On TCP/IP-based networks that have subnets, the WINS server has a list of all domain names.

How Clients Use Browsers

Browser clients are any computers on the network that need the browse list. This includes computers that use the NET VIEW command to see a list of resources or computers that access the network via Network Neighborhood.

Figure 19.14 illustrates the process of how clients use browsers.

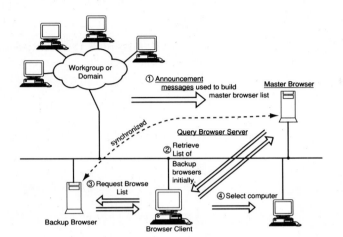

Figure 19.14
How clients use browsers.

To receive the browse list, the browser client issues a NetServerEnum API call to the browser service. If this is the first time the browser client has issued this API call—for example, when the user first starts using a network service—then the browser client sends a Query Browser Servers broadcast datagram. This datagram is processed by the master browser for that network (or subnet, in the case of TCP/IP networks). The master browser returns a list of backup browsers that are active in that workgroup, domain, or TCP/IP subnet. The browser client caches the names of three backup browsers from that list for future use. A backup browser is chosen randomly from the three browsers saved by the browser client.

If after three attempts, the master browser still cannot be found, the client forces an election of a master browser by issuing the election datagram.

Coping with Browser Failures

If nonbrowser computers fail to announce themselves for three announcement intervals (12 minutes each) to the master browser, the master browser will remove the computer from its browser list. The computer could fail to announce itself if the Server service fails, or if the computer is abruptly shut down. The master browser learns of the computer failure in 3×12 = 36 minutes. The backup browsers can take up to an additional 15 minutes to synchronize their lists to the master list, and therefore the total time for all systems to learn of the computer failure could be up to 36 + 15 = 51 minutes.

If a backup browser fails, it is also removed from the master browser list in the same amount of time as a nonbrowser; that is, 36 minutes. This is because the backup browsers announce themselves to the master browser in the same manner as nonbrowser computers. If the client is unable to obtain a browse list from a backup browser, it tries another backup browser from its cached list of backup browsers. Recall that when the client first starts, it obtains a list of up to three backup browsers from the master browser. If the client exhausts its known list of backup browsers, it attempts to obtain the browse list from the master browser. If the master browser is not available, the client forces an election.

If the master browser fails, a backup browser will detect the failure within 15 minutes—the time interval for backup browsers to synchronize with the master browser—and force an election.

If the browser is shut down gracefully (using the Shutdown option in Windows NT), it sends an announcement that causes the master browser to remove the browser from the browser list. If the browser that is shutting down is a master browser, it sends an election datagram.

Configuring Windows NT Browser Services for LAN Manager Interoperability

Because Windows NT and LAN Manager browsers work differently, you have to make special configuration choices to make LAN Manager and Windows NT computers interoperate. You need to configure Windows NT so that the Windows NT computers are visible from LAN Manager clients, and configure LAN Manager domains to be visible to Windows NT browsers. These issues are discussed in the sections that follow.

Making Windows NT Computers Visible to LAN Manager Clients

If you have LAN Manager clients and want Windows NT computers to be visible to them, you must configure Windows NT to announce itself to LAN Manager servers. You can do this directly through the Registry by changing the LMannouce value entry of data type REG_DWORD to 1. The LMannounce value entry can be found under the following key:

```
HKEY_LOCAL_MACHINE\SYSTEM\CurrentControlSet\Services\LanmanServer\Parameters
```

Alternatively, you can use the Network option in Control Panel to change this entry. Choose the Services tab in the Network dialog box and choose **S**erver. Then click on the **P**roperties button to invoke the Server Properties dialog box. Enable the Ma**k**e Browser Broadcasts to LAN Manager 2.x Clients check box (see fig. 19.15) and choose OK.

Making LAN Manager Domains Visible to Windows NT Browsers

You can configure Windows NT browsers so that LAN Manager domains are visible to them. You can do this directly through the Registry by adding the LAN Manager domains to the OtherDomains value entry of data type REG_MULTI_SZ. The OtherDomains value entry is created under the following key:

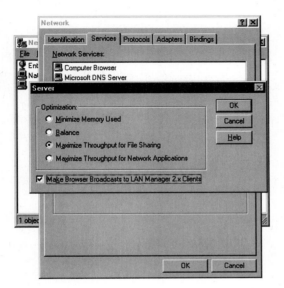

Figure 19.15
Making Windows NT servers visible to LAN Manager clients.

```
HKEY_LOCAL_MACHINE\SYSTEM\CurrentControlSet\Services\LanmanServer\Parameters
```

Alternatively, you can use the Network option in Control Panel to change this entry. Select Computer Browser in the Services tab and click on the **P**roperties button. In the Browser Configuration dialog box (see fig. 19.16), use the box on the left to enter a LAN Manager domain name and choose the **A**dd button to add it to the list on the right.

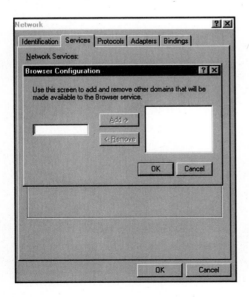

Figure 19.16
Adding LAN Manager domains to Windows NT browser.

Conclusion

In this chapter you learned how the network browser is used to discover the NetBIOS network resources that are available for use on the network. The different types of browsers and the protocol used to elect a master browser are discussed in detail. A master browser is needed because it provides the authoritative view of the network resources. The browsing protocols try to keep the browser list updated when computers are abruptly turned off. Some time may elapse, such as almost an hour, before all the systems learn of the most recent changes on the network.

This chapter also discussed how you can configure Windows NT browsers to integrate LAN Manager clients and domains in Windows NT networks.

Data Protection for Windows NT Servers

As businesses begin to depend on computers, protecting the data kept on them is vital to the successful operation of a company. If an organization's data is kept on a central computer, such as a Windows NT Server, which is shared by many users, keeping the server operational becomes even more critical.

This chapter explores the Windows NT Server mechanisms for ensuring data reliability. The RAID architecture and the way in which it can be implemented on Windows NT Server is discussed. Also discussed are Windows NT Backup services and uninterrupted power supply (UPS) services.

Overview of Data Protection Features in Windows NT

Windows NT Server provides software-based fault tolerance using the following methods:

- Disk mirroring

- Disk striping with parity

- Sector sparing

These methods are described in terms of RAID (Redundant Array of Inexpensive Disks) Levels. RAID levels 0 to 5 are defined and provide different levels of reliability, performance, and cost. Windows NT supports only RAID levels 0, 1, and 5.

Table 20.1 provides a brief summary of each of the RAID levels. Windows NT directly supports RAID fault tolerance only on Windows NT Servers. Windows NT RAID fault tolerance support is software-based. Many disk storage vendors provide hardware-based fault tolerance by providing RAID disk controllers and special disk arrays. The hardware-based RAID solutions also can be used with Windows NT Workstations and with any other supported operating system.

Table 20.1
RAID Level Support in Windows NT Server

RAID Level	Description
0	Disk striping
1	Disk mirroring
5	Block striping. Parity blocks distributed over multiple drives

Two other methods of increasing fault tolerance of the data and the entire Windows NT computer system are the following:

- Backup services

- UPS services

Backup services are integrated into Windows NT computers and when performed on a regular basis can help you recover lost data caused by disk or system failures.

The UPS service is driver-level support for external uninterrupted power supply (UPS) devices. UPS devices must be purchased separately; only their driver support comes with Windows NT.

Backup and UPS services are available both for Windows NT Servers and Windows NT Workstations.

Implementing RAID Fault Tolerance

The RAID concept was first proposed by David A. Patterson, Garth Gibson, and Randy Katz of the University of California, Berkeley (Report no. UCB/CSD 87/39, December 1987). The report, "A Case for Redundant Array of Inexpensive Disks or RAID," discusses the concept of using an array of disks to distribute data that can provide reliability and improve disk performance. Because disk performance continues to be a bottleneck on PC server-based solutions, interest in RAID technology is great.

Understanding RAID

The key concept behind RAID is a technique called striping. *Striping* enables data blocks to be interleaved across several drives that have the same performance and storage characteristics, instead of storing them on the same drive. Each drive operates independently of the others, which enables data to be transferred in parallel from each drive. If an array of n disks is operating in parallel, therefore, the data is transferred in $1/n$ the time, compared to data transferred using a single disk, which results in an n-fold improvement in disk transfer rate. Figure 20.1 shows data being read in a RAID subsystem using three drives. The numbers in the figure represent data blocks and show that they are interleaved across the three disks.

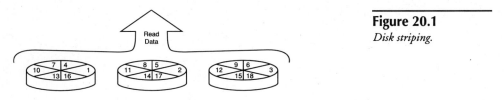

Figure 20.1

Disk striping.

Reliability in RAID is achieved by using one of the disks for storing a check byte. The check byte is constructed in such a way that, if one of the drives fails, the data in that drive can be reconstructed from the remaining data drives (including the check byte drive). A popular algorithm to construct the check byte is the exclusive OR (XOR) operation.

Figure 20.2 shows how the XOR checksum byte is used to reconstruct the data in a three-disk RAID drive. Two of the drives are used to hold the data. The third drive is the check drive. The first data drive in this example has a bit pattern of 11100011, and the second drive has the data pattern 11101101. The check byte using the XOR operation is 00001110 (see table 20.2). If drive 2 fails, its data can be recovered by an exclusive OR (XOR) operation of the bytes in the remaining drives.

> **Note**   XOR computes the exclusive OR of two operands. The result is a 1 if the corresponding bits of the operands are different; each bit is 0 if the corresponding bits are identical.

Figure 20.2

Reconstructing data for a failed drive.

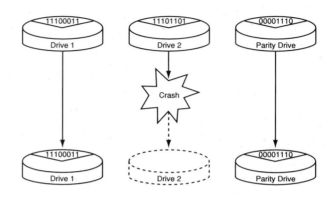

Table 20.2
Exclusive OR Operation for Computing Check Byte

Drive	Drive Status	Bit Pattern
Data drive 1	Running	11100011
Data drive 2	Running	11101101 XOR
Check Byte drive	Running	00001110

If data drive 2 fails, table 20.3 shows how data can be reconstructed.

Table 20.3
Recovering Data from a Failed Drive

Drive	Drive Status	Bit Pattern
Data drive 1	Running	11100011
Check Byte drive	Running	00001110 XOR
Data drive 2	Failed	11101101

The check byte is re-computed if a byte location is changed and if the changed check byte has to be written to the check disk. If the check byte is maintained on a single drive, it can result in a bottleneck that negates the speed improvements of the interleaved drives. For this reason, the check byte is distributed across the disks for improving performance.

The check byte disk represents a storage overhead, but for an *n*-array RAID system, it is $1/n$ of the total storage. For a value of *n* larger than 2, it represents a smaller overhead than a mirrored/duplexed system.

The following table is an example of the results of an XOR calculation. It describes how the missing information might be built during recovery.

XOR	0	1
0	0	1
1	1	0

RAID Levels

Disk arrays that use RAID technology are classified in terms of RAID levels 0 to 5.

RAID level 0 makes use only of the striping feature of RAID, but has no provision for redundancy. Striping improves the performance of the disk array, but because no check bytes are used, fault-tolerance is not improved compared to a single-disk system.

RAID level 1 provides disk mirroring along with striping. Every disk has a mirror that has an exact data copy of the primary disk. For best performance, the disks should be designed so that the reads and writes can be performed independently. This design results in speed improvements because the read request is completed by the first drive that returns the result. Microsoft's definition of RAID level 1 does not include the striping feature defined in Patterson, Gibson, and Katz's original paper on RAID. Microsoft defines RAID level 1 as consisting of disk mirroring (see fig. 20.3) or disk duplexing (see fig. 20.4).

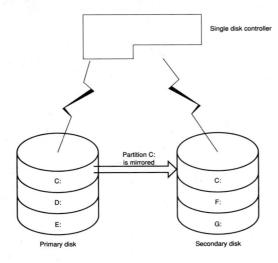

Single disk controller

Partition C:
is mirrored

C:
D:
E:

Primary disk

C:
F:
G:

Secondary disk

Figure 20.3
Disk mirroring.

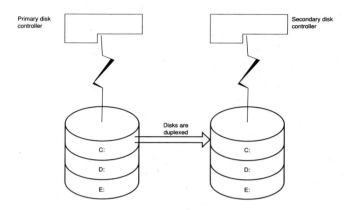

Figure 20.4

Disk duplexing.

Disk mirroring is one of the simplest strategies for protecting against a single-disk failure. It involves only the expense of an additional disk, and is, therefore, affordable for smaller networks. The problem with disk mirroring is that it does not protect against disk controller failures. Disk duplexing provides all of the advantages of disk mirroring. In addition, it protects against disk controller failures by having two disk controllers: a primary and a secondary disk controller. Disk duplexing involves the expense of a separate disk and a separate controller.

Note In case you're wondering about RAID Levels 2,3, and 4 (which aren't presently supported by Windows NT):

RAID level 2 has a provision for data recovery with one disk reserved for data recovery. The striping function is performed at the bit level, which means that the bits are scattered consecutively across the disks. The first bit, for example, is written on the first disk in the array, the second bit on the second disk, and so on. RAID 2 is not implemented commonly for microcomputers.

RAID level 3 provides striping at the byte level, with one disk reserved for the check byte. The check-byte disk is called the parity drive and, as already explained, can be used to recover information on the failed drive. It is common to design the spindle rotation of disks so that parallel reads can be done efficiently.

RAID level 4 provides striping at the block level. A block is the amount of data transferred in a single read/write operation. Like RAID level 3, a disk is reserved for a parity drive.

RAID level 5, like RAID level 4 (see Note), provides striping at the block level. Unlike RAID level 4, however, it spreads the error-correcting block data evenly across the disks, avoiding the bottleneck of writing error-correcting data to a single disk.

RAID disk drivers are available from the manufacturers of the drives for NetWare and other operating system platforms, such as OS/2, Unix, and Windows NT.

Regardless of whether you choose the disk mirroring/duplexing approach or the RAID approach, the disk subsystem should be fast and reliable. You can build server disk subsystems using IDE, ESDI, or SCSI. The best choice is SCSI because of its flexibility for both disk mirroring/duplexing approaches and RAID.

Sector Sparing

In addition to providing support for levels 0,1, and 5 of the RAID architecture, Windows NT also includes support for sector sparing. In sector sparing, all write operations are verified in the following manner:

1. When the file system is formatted, all sectors are verified. Bad sectors are detected and mapped-out, meaning that they are not used in the mapping of files to disk sectors. Spare sectors on the disk replace the mapped-out sectors.

2. When a write operation is performed, a check is made to see whether it is successful. If the sector that is written to is bad, it is mapped-out, and a spare sector on the disk is used instead.

Configuring Disk Mirroring

Disk mirroring and other disk administration tasks are performed by the Disk Administrator, which can be found in the Administrative tools group. You must have a minimum of two hard disks with sufficient space on each disk to create a mirrored set.

The following is an outline of the procedure for configuring disk mirroring:

1. Log on to the Windows NT Server as an Administrator.

2. Start the Disk Administrator.

3. If this is the first time you have run the Disk Administrator, then you receive a message. Acknowledge this message by choosing OK.

   You should see the Disk Administrator screen.

4. On the first disk, select the partition to be mirrored by clicking on the partition that is to be in the mirrored set.

5. Hold Ctrl and click on the partition on the second disk. The partition on the second disk must have an area that is greater than or equal to the first partition that was selected.

6. Choose **F**ault Tolerance, Establish **M**irror.

   You should see a message indicating that you are mirroring the partition. Acknowledge the message by selecting OK.

7. You should see that the mirrored partitions now have the same drive letter and are marked in purple (on a color monitor). Partitions marked with purple are mirrored.

8. Exit the Disk Administrator by choosing **P**artition, **E**xit.

9. You should see a confirmation message prompting you to save your changes before exiting.

   Choose Yes to keep the mirrored set.

10. A message prompting you to restart the computer appears. Choose Yes.

11. A message appears stating that you need to update your Emergency Repair Disk for the Windows NT computer. This message is sent because your disk configuration has changed. Choose OK.

    The addition of any new partitions can require changes to the boot.ini file, if Windows NT was installed to an extended partition. Any mirrored partitions or components in a stripe set will cause the logical drive to be renumbered for ARC name purposes. An additional dialog box may appear notifying that changes must be made to the boot.ini.

12. You should see another message indicating that you should restart the computer. Choose OK to initiate restart of the computer.

13. After the system restarts, log on as administrator and start the Disk Administrator.

    The text labels in the mirrored partition appear in red, indicating that the mirrored drives are being regenerated.

14. Select the mirror of the partition (the secondary partition). The status at the bottom of the screen shows INITIALIZING. When mirroring is complete, the status changes to HEALTHY.

15. Exit the Disk Administrator.

Configuring Disk Striping with Parity

To implement disk striping with parity, which is RAID level 5, you need a minimum of three hard disks. You can create a striped set with parity by selecting an area of free space on each of the disks. Disk Administrator creates a striped set with parity using equal-sized partitions that are a multiple of the smallest partition size. The minimum partition size is 5 MB although, for practical use, the value must be much higher.

The system and boot partitions cannot be part of the striped set. You can format the striped set as an NTFS or FAT partition.

Use the following outline to create a striped set with parity:

1. Log on as an Administrator user and start the Disk Administrator.

2. On the first disk, select an area of free space on the first disk.

3. Hold Ctrl and click free space on at least two other disks. You must have at least three disks for a striped set with parity.

4. Choose **F**ault Tolerance, Create Stripe Set With Parity.

   Disk Administrator displays the minimum and maximum sizes for your new striped set with parity. In the Create Stripe Set with Parity dialog box, enter a size that falls within the range of possible values and click on OK.

   Disk Administrator divides the total size by the number of disks and places equal-sized unformatted partitions on the disks in the set, then assigns a single drive letter for the entire set.

   You should see that the striped partitions now have the same drive letter and are marked in green (on a color monitor). Partitions marked with green are part of the striped set with parity.

5. Exit the Disk Administrator by choosing **P**artition, E**x**it.

6. A confirmation message appears, prompting you to save your changes before exiting. Choose Yes to save the striped set you have created.

   Choose Yes again.

7. A message appears, stating that you need to update your Emergency Repair Disk for the Windows NT computer. This update is needed because your disk configuration has changed. Choose OK.

8. Another message appears, indicating that you should restart the computer.

   Choose OK to initiate restart of the computer.

9. After the system restarts, logon as administrator and start the Disk Administrator.

10. Format the striped set as NTFS or FAT. You can format the striped set using the **F**ormat option in Disk Administrator's **T**ools menu, or you can use the FORMAT command.

11. Exit from the Disk Administrator.

Disk Striping without Parity

You also can use Disk Administrator to configure disk striping without parity. (See the description of RAID Level 0 earlier in this chapter.) Ordinary disk striping (without parity) can have certain performance benefits, but it doesn't provide fault tolerance so you cannot use it to protect your data. Note that in the following procedure, the Create Stripe Set option isn't even on the Fault Tolerance menu.

To create a stripe set:

1. Log on as an Administrator user and start the Disk Administrator.

2. On the first disk, select an area of free space on the first disk.

3. Hold Ctrl and select free space on at least one other disk. You must have at least two disks for a striped set with parity.

4. Choose **P**artitions, Create Stripe Set.

Disk Administrator displays the minimum and maximum sizes for your new striped set. In the Create Stripe Set dialog box, enter a size that falls within the range of possible values and click on OK. Disk Administrator divides the total size by the number of disks and places equal-sized unformatted partitions on the disks in the set. Disk Administrator then assigns a single drive letter for the entire set.

If you delete a striped set, you lose all the data in the set. If you want to preserve the data, perform a backup before you delete the striped set.

To delete a striped set:

1. Log on as an Administrator user and start Disk Administrator.

2. Select the striped set that you want to delete.

3. Choose **P**artitions, Delete.

4. In the Confirm message box, click on Yes.

Recovering from Partition Failures

When a member of a mirrored partition set fails, the I/O operations are directed to the remaining disk. The remaining disk provides fault tolerance. Similarly, if a single member of the striped set with parity fails, the I/O operations are redirected to the remaining members. The use of the parity block enables the recovery of the data on the failed drive.

If two disks fail simultaneously in the striped set, then the parity information is not sufficient to recover the data. In this case, you must resort to rebuilding the mirrored set with the last tape backup.

The following sections describe the procedures for breaking a mirrored set, fixing a mirrored set, and regenerating a striped set with parity.

Breaking a Mirrored Set

You must know how to break a mirrored set before you can fix a mirrored set. You also might want to break a mirrored set because your disk configuration no longer requires mirrored partitions. Breaking a mirrored set does not delete the data in the set, but Microsoft nevertheless recommends that you perform a backup before you break a mirrored set. Performing a backup protects you from unforeseen complications. A backup also enables you to delete the unmirrored partitions after you have broken the set.

Use the following as a guideline to break a mirrored set:

1. Log on as an Administrator user and start the Disk Administrator.

2. Select the mirrored set you want to break.

3. Choose <u>F</u>ault Tolerance, <u>B</u>reak Mirror.

4. You are asked to confirm the Break Mirror operation. Choose <u>Y</u>es.

   You can see that the mirrored partition receives the next available drive letter.

5. Choose <u>P</u>artition, C<u>o</u>mmit Changes Now from the Disk Administrator screen.

6. You should see a message prompting you to confirm your changes. Choose <u>Y</u>es.

7. A message appears, indicating that you need to update your Emergency Repair Disk for the Windows NT computer because your disk configuration has changed. Choose OK.

8. Exit from the Disk Administrator.

Fixing a Mirrored Set

You might have to fix a mirrored set if one of the members fails or you suspect that the two disks no longer are synchronized. The following is an outline of the procedure for fixing a mirrored set.

1. Log on as an Administrator user and start Disk Administrator.

2. Break the mirrored set (see the procedure in the preceding section, "Breaking a Mirrored Set").

3. Assign to the working member of the mirrored set the drive that was previously assigned to the complete mirrored set.

   The failed member of the mirrored set receives the next available drive letter.

4. Create a new mirrored set relationship with the working member of the previously failed mirrored set and another working disk with sufficient free space.

5. Restart the computer.

   The data from the working partition will be transferred to the new member of the mirrored set.

Regenerating a Striped Set with Parity

If a single member of a striped set with parity fails, the data in the failed member is recovered by using the parity block. Computing the values of the data block in the failed drive requires CPU cycles and, as a result, system performance is affected. You should, therefore, try to replace the failed member as soon as possible.

Use the following as a guideline to replace the failed member and regenerate the data on a new member:

1. Log on as Administrator and start Disk Administrator.

2. Select the striped set with parity.

3. Next, select free space on another hard disk that is the same size or larger than other members of the striped set. (If the failure resulted from a power or cabling failure of a single disk in the stripe set, you also can use the original partition on the failed disk after the disk is repaired.)

4. Choose **F**ault Tolerance, **R**egenerate.

5. Exit Disk Administrator and restart the Windows NT Server.

   When the Windows NT Server restarts, it regenerates the data in the failed member on the new member.

Implementing Backup Services

Using the mirrored set and RAID services provides fault tolerance and continued operation in case of a single disk failure in the mirrored set or the striped set with parity. If, however, more than one member of these sets fail, or if a system failure occurs on the Windows NT computer itself, data is lost. For this reason, you must implement a backup strategy.

A Windows NT computer comes with a tape backup program called NTBACKUP.EXE. To start the NTBACKUP.EXE, select Programs from the Start menu and choose Backup from the Administrative Tools program group. You can use this program or a third-party program (Arcada, Cheyenne, and so on) to implement backups on a Windows NT computer.

Comprehending Backup Strategies

Backup strategies are complex and need to be planned and implemented well. Backup strategies include not only the more obvious factors, such as which data needs to be backed up and how often, but should also include concepts such as hardware, proper documentation, tape storage, security, data verification, and disaster-recovery concepts. The next sections focus on these important issues.

Archiving and Storage Issues

A common poor practice is keeping backup tape sets in a drawer next to the server. In the case of a fire or a natural disaster, having the tapes in the same location as the data they protect won't help you very much. All the effort put into backups will have been wasted. Keep monthly, weekly, or daily backup copies (depending on your specific backup needs) at an off-site, safe location or in a water- and fireproof safe or vault. Keeping tapes at an alternative location ensures that you can restore the server in the case of a catastrophe.

As the world becomes less dependent on paper, archiving accurate records electronically becomes more critical. Maintaining historical data is vital to corporations and organizations. Such things as tax audits, legal actions, and statistical-analysis needs are a few examples.

Note Most magnetic-tape media are rated to retain data for only a few years. You should implement a plan to copy archived tapes before they lose their magnetic information.

Alternatively, you can use an optical solution. Optical solutions have an estimated shelf life of 20 years. Optical drives use a variety of methods including a laser to burn pits, a phase-change material in the disk's substrate, or the use of a thin layer of dye which the laser burns through. Each of these technologies alters the optical media to represent binary data instead of the less-reliable magnetic signatures used on tapes. Tape and optical solutions are detailed later in this chapter.

Disaster-Recovery Planning

Even the simplest networks should have a disaster-recovery plan. A disaster-recovery plan is a set of procedures to follow in the event of a natural or man-made catastrophe. Floods, fire, theft, and earthquakes can devastate any company or organization. Keep in mind also that one of the worst man-made disasters is when a user or administrator accidentally deletes essential files or entire directories. Having a plan in place, with a set of established and tested policies, can get the organization up and running on short notice.

Getting the network back up and online with current data in a timely manner is critical to most companies. Accomplishing this can be difficult if you have not implemented and tested a disaster-recovery plan. It may seem to be a simple matter of purchasing a new server (good luck on short notice), retrieving your off-site tapes, and restoring the server, but it is actually far more involved. Among the things that need to be included in the disaster-recovery plan are the following:

- **Spare or replacement servers.** It may be a good idea to maintain an off-site, standby server at either a manager's or administrator's home or at a branch office. Keep an off-site listing of sales-representative contacts from whom you can purchase replacement hardware.

- **Spare or replacement workstations and printers.** Replacing all the on-site workstations and printers can prove very difficult if the disaster's effects are widespread, such as in a hurricane. You will find that supplies may be diminished and that you may have to wait a few days to establish enough devices. Keep an off-site listing of sales-representative contacts from whom you can purchase replacement hardware.

- **A current, undamaged tape-backup set.** Perhaps the most critical aspect of disaster recovery is having a current, undamaged set of backup tapes. Keep backup tapes in an off-site vault or branch office and make sure you can get to those tapes quickly. Make sure you have more than one copy of your set of backup tapes in case one set is flawed.

- **Backup hardware and software.** Keep in mind that many backup solutions are proprietary and even different hardware and or software products from the same manufacturer may not be interchangeable. Make sure you keep a copy of your tape backup software at a couple of sites (including another city) and have the essential hardware easily available.

- **A Windows NT Server installation CD and application software.** Make sure that you can get your hands on a copy of the Windows NT installation CD and copies of all your application software. Also, keep a set of installation disks for the workstation environments you need to support.

- **A list of available relocation sites.** An important consideration that is often neglected is a new location. Should your office complex burn down, it is a good idea to have a set of backup locations in mind. Work with a local realtor who can maintain a listing of potential office spaces for you. If your company has branch offices, implement a plan of action to temporarily squeeze as much space as possible out of your other locations. Another alternative is to work on a reciprocal hardware and office space agreement with a company in another city since empty office space could be hard to obtain in a widespread disaster.

- **Personnel backups.** Make sure each person on the recovery team has a backup. Some disasters may mean that the primary person may not be able to get to the recovery site or that person may need to put the welfare of their family first.

- **Written procedures.** Make sure your written procedures are easy to follow and well documented with supplementary information as needed (configuration information, group and user permissions and so on). Test the readability and supplementary documentation of your procedures by having both primary and secondary members of your team perform a test recovery. Update and refine these procedures regularly.

As you can see, getting your server and network back online in a hurry can be a very involved process. You should have a plan of action in place no matter how small or large your network environment may be!

There are consultants and companies that specialize in disaster-recovery planning. In addition, many mainframe shops have disaster recovery plans in place and have been practicing them for years (they usually simulate a drill at least once a year). If you know someone at such a site you could pick up many hints and tips from them. If your network is large, it is well worth seeking advice from these professionals. They implement incredibly detailed plans, and often supply a number of alternative plans as well. Often, they can coordinate agreements between separate companies to serve as hot sites for one another.

Several book titles detail disaster-recovery planning polices and strategies. You may want to get your hands on such a book if you don't currently have a disaster-recovery plan.

Scheduling Regular Backups

Backing up network data is a very serious matter that should be fully understood by all personnel involved in its process. Make no mistake about it: Doing regular backups and verifications can really save you and your business. Backing up is perhaps the most monotonous task left to the administrator, but it is one of the most important. Network administrators have been fired, given raises, chastised, or given promotions based on their network backups. An example of the cost of not backing up the files every day might be if a sales document or contract worth hundreds of thousands of dollars accidentally is deleted by a temporary secretary. If you practice daily backups, you will be able to retrieve it from the previous day's backup.

Issues Regarding Backup Security

Tape backups often contain a copy of every bit of information on the network. This data can be a real security risk: If your environment has backups of sensitive data, you should keep tapes well logged and stored in a secure location such as a vault or lock box. Alternatively, many companies specialize in high-quality secure off-site storage.

Windows NT Server provides a special group called the Backup Operators group. This group is granted extended permissions that enable them to perform backup and restore procedures. Both administrators and backup operators, and Server Operators can conduct backup procedures. Make sure that users designated as backup operators are trustworthy, reliable individuals.

It is good practice to keep servers that perform backups in a locked room, especially if the backup procedure is automated. Dishonest individuals are apt to steal a tape from an unattended system. Such people may get hold of a backup operator's or administrator's account name and password, enabling them to retrieve critical information. Additionally, use a password-protected screen saver so that the server is protected from unauthorized access during periods when no one is attending it.

> **Warning** Tape cartridges fit easily into pockets, briefcases, purses, and lunch bags. Don't leave tapes sitting on desktops or in any other accessible location.

Microsoft Windows NT Backup provides the means to lock tapes in order to prevent them from being read by unauthorized users. The only users able to read a locked tape are members of the Administrators or Backup Operators group and the owner (creator) of the tape. Locking tapes is a good practice if the data is personal or sensitive or if it contains company secrets from an engineering or research and development division. If the tape is stolen or falls into the possession of non-authorized personnel, they will not be able to unlock it.

The Importance of Keeping Proper Backup Logs

Keeping accurate logs of your backups is very important. Such logs identify tapes and some-times confirm that backup jobs have been performed properly. Without tracking backups, there is no real way of knowing that a backup job has been performed or verified. Documenta-tion can assist you in tracking tape locations, including current sets, archived sets, and rotation sets. Documentation can also help you contact the responsible person if something goes wrong.

> **Note** If you maintain your backup tracking log electronically (as a spreadsheet or data-base) on the network, make sure that it is replicated or printed out on a regular basis. A log won't do you much good if the file has been erased or brought down along with the server, and you have a difficult time figuring out which tapes are current, which contain the data you're interested in, and so on.

Backup Hardware Options

In the ever-changing technical world, two real contenders for backup hardware exist. The first (and most popular) are tape backup devices, the second is optical hardware. Either solution is acceptable; but deciding which is appropriate for you is a matter of need, desire, and money. You should always purchase the best backup solution possible. A tape-drive unit and its associated tapes represent a few thousand dollars at most and could save a company or corpora-tion thousands or maybe millions of dollars. In some cases, the amount of data that needs to be archived can be the deciding factor in what technology to use. If, for example, it takes ten tapes and half a day to back up the data, then the need for a faster or bigger backup solution is mandated. Other factors to be considered include the following:

■ What hardware solution accommodates the data you need to back up?

■ How fast can that hardware solution back up that amount of data?

- How reliable is the hardware solution?

- Is the capacity of the device adequate to take you through substantial disk drive growth over the next three to five years?

Note Don't forget those historical archives! If you are considering a backup device upgrade, it is important to either keep the old unit in working condition or purchase a unit that can utilize the media and format of the old archived data.

Confirming Support with the Microsoft Windows Hardware Compatibility List

To avoid potential compatibility problems, use the NT hardware compatibility list (HCL) and introduce it to staff. For the latest HCL listing, check the Microsoft web page at `http://www.microsoft.com/ntserver/info/hwcompatability.htm`.

Speed and Capacity Considerations

In addition to having exceptional quality, it is imperative that a backup device is fast enough and can hold enough data to handle the backup demands of your network.

The speed of the backup device needs to be suitable for completing backup jobs within a given time period. Most administrators conduct their backup jobs in the late evening or early morning hours, backing up the previous day's data while the network is quiet and few files are open. Some backup units can back up huge amounts of data quickly, while other units may take hours. Make sure that the speed of the device you are evaluating can perform backups in a time sufficient to your needs.

Just as critical as speed is the storage capacity of the backup device. You want to use a backup device that can hold all the data in the backup procedure. Otherwise, you will have to use multiple tapes or optical disks; this requires that an individual be on hand to swap the media when prompted, imposes further security risks, and may add substantial time to the backup if the person forgets or misses a swapping queue.

Don't forget future network growth when calculating capacity. Remember that a large number of networks add substantial disk space every year: It's not unusual for sites to double current disk space annually. Try to plan at least three to five years into the future when making your backup capacity plans.

> **Note**   If your backup procedure dictates enormous amounts of data need backup, using multiple tapes or optical disks may be unavoidable. You may want to consider using an auto-feeding tape device or an optical-disk jukebox unit. These devices are covered later in this chapter in the "Optical Solution" section.

Tape Drives

Tape drives are by far the most common form of backup used on today's networks. Tape drives do have their problems, however, including tape breakage, stretching, and a relatively short magnetic shelf life. Because of the mechanical problems associated with tapes, a lot of large corporations use elaborate jukebox Write Once Read Many (WORM) optical drive solutions instead.

The variety of tape devices available is rather large. Tape devices have large ranges in speed, capacity, and cost. Carefully consider the model you choose. It needs to serve not only your current backup needs, but the expected backup needs of the future. The following sections detail some of the popular tape-device technologies.

DC-6000 QIC Tape Drives

The DC-6000 (DC means Data Cartridge) Quarter Inch Cartridge (QIC) format was developed by the 3M Corp. It contains 600 feet of one-quarter-inch-wide magnetic tape. These tapes are housed in large cartridges measuring four by six inches by just over one-half-inch thick. These cartridges range in capacity from .5 GB to over 2 GB. They are specifically designed to be very reliable, and they utilize a rubber drive belt to minimize the potential of the tape being stretched. They have a nonmagnetic, strong aluminum base and are designed to protect the tape from being touched, incorporating a protective door that remains closed unless the tape cartridge is inserted into the drive. The drawback of the DC-6000 series is that they are slow compared to digital audio tape (DAT) systems.

DC-2000 QIC Tape Drives

The DC-2000 was also developed by 3M. It was designed to lower the cost of the QIC backup cartridges. DC-2000 are commonly used for home- or workstation-level backups. These tapes are housed in a cartridge measuring two and a half by three inches by just over a half-inch thick. These cartridges have a wide range of capacities, ranging from 40 MB to over 2 GB. The tapes are sometimes portable between these various capacities, but not always! If you need tape portability between two or more machines, make sure that the backup devices can read each other's data. The drawbacks of the DC-2000 series is that they are slow and often require a long formatting process (unless you purchase preformatted tapes).

Among the more popular DC-2000 series QIC formats currently available are the following:

- **QIC 40.** 40 MB capacity utilizing uncompressed data.

- **QIC 80.** 80 MB capacity utilizing uncompressed data. However, DC2120 and DC2120XL can contain up to 120 or 250 MB of data.

- **QIC 3010.** 340 MB capacity utilizing uncompressed data, 700 MB with compression.

- **QIC Wide.** Currently, these proprietary drives can hold over 2 GB.

DAT Drives

DAT drives, or digital audio tape drives, use a technique called *helical-scan* recording that was copied from the videotape industry. This method writes data at an angle, which increases the data density of tapes. Under such a system, the recording head moves rapidly while the tape moves slowly. This provides for increased tape reliability and density. DAT drives come in two basic variations:

- **8mm Cartridges.** The 8mm format was created by Exabyte. The format is borrowed from the 8mm tape format developed by Sony Corp. You may be familiar with the Betamax video devices that Sony developed.

Note   The density requirements for 8mm tape backup drives are significantly higher than those used for video devices. 8mm data devices use the same cartridge design as their audio counterparts, but you shouldn't intermix the tapes—they are certified differently. Always use data-grade tape cartridges.

The 8mm DAT systems are available in capacities ranging from 1 to 5 GB (10 GB compressed). The 8mm devices remain proprietary technology and are manufactured only by their creator, Exabyte. This probably contributes to the fact that they are less popular than the 4mm DAT drives, which are manufactured by several vendors and are also an ideal candidate for network-backup usage.

- **4mm Cartridges.** The 4mm format is an offshoot of the DAT format invented by Sony. These devices support extremely high capacities, approaching 16 GB! These drives are also incredibly fast and can easily record over 30 MB per minute. This makes 4mm cartridges the best current all-around contender for network-backup solutions.

Auto-Loader Tape Systems

A rather nifty device is a tape auto-loader. These can hold a magazine of tapes and automatically swap tape cartridges as needed. Some auto-loaders hold up to a dozen or more tapes, and when combined with 4-GB or 16-GB DAT cartridges, you have a tremendous amount of capacity: up to 192 GB! If you are backing up a huge network, this may be an excellent solution.

> **Note** An alternate and common backup implementation on large networks is to segment or share the backup responsibilities among multiple servers and administrators, making each responsible for either a domain or specific portion of the network.

Optical Solutions

It is inevitable that optical solutions will eventually replace most tape-backup devices. However, the optical-technology arena is still in its infancy and remains open and nonstandardized. Optical solutions provide faster throughput, random access capabilities, and a longer shelf life, making them a much better all-around technology for network backups.

The two primary contenders for optical-backup technology are

■ **WORM (Write Once Read Many).** WORM drives are designed to archive large amounts of data. They use a laser to burn a pit in a plastic medium. These pits represent digital ones and zeros. The devices have a tremendous shelf life because they are not affected by electromagnetic field depletion, but they are not well-suited for daily backup activities unless you want to use 365 of them every year. Once WORM disks have been written to, they are not rewritable. A newer technology enables you to write several times by having several plastic layers, but they are still not practical for much other than archiving purposes.

■ **MOD (Magnetic Optical Drives).** Magnetic optical drives combine lasers and magnetic recording technology to hold high-density data. They use a laser to heat a magnetic substrate, forcing it to change its polarization. MODs are not as well-suited for the archiving role because they rely on magnetic signatures to store their data; they are a probable future replacement for most tape-backup systems and are currently in wide use. These devices can be implemented into a jukebox, a device that holds multiple MOD platters, switching them out as needed, much as an old musical jukebox does with LP records.

Optical platforms have been made popular by standard CD-ROM (compact disc-read only memory) devices. Of course, a CD-ROM is not a contender for backups because it can't perform writes.

Installing Backup Devices

The physical installation of backup hardware is usually detailed by the manufacturer. Most devices can be mounted in standard drive bays with a controller card and data and power cables in much the same fashion as typical floppy disk drives. Other, more elaborate solutions use an external cabinet to hold the tape-drive device. The common DC-2000 series often utilize existing floppy controller cards to control the device.

> **Note** These backup devices can cause problems if you try to access a floppy while performing a backup! Check the documentation that comes with the drive for more details regarding this issue. It's better to have your backup device on a separate controller anyway to avoid possible conflicts and provide redundancy.

More elaborate devices, such as jukeboxes or auto-loaders, may require professional installation and setup. These devices come with installation guides and user manuals, but they can still be intimidating.

After the physical installation has been completed, you will need to add the tape-device driver into Windows NT. This is done through the Windows NT Backup tool and is covered next.

Adding a SCSI and Tape Device

Before you can begin tape-backup operations, you must install the necessary drivers that are associated with the tape hardware device and its controller card. This is done differently among different versions of Windows NT Server.

Adding SCSI controller adapters and tape drive devices under Windows NT 4 is handled under two separate tools. The following two tools are located in the Control Panel:

- ■ **SCSI Adapters.** Used to manage and install SCSI adapter cards

- ■ **Tape Devices.** Used to manage and install tape drive devices

To install a SCSI adapter card under Windows NT 4, follow these steps:

1. Launch the SCSI adapter tool by double-clicking its icon, located in the Control Panel.

2. Choose the Drivers tab when the SCSI Adapters dialog box is displayed.

3. Click on the Add button. The Install Driver dialog box displays (see fig. 20.5). Select SCSI and other interface adapters by scrolling down the Manufacturers list box and choosing the desired SCSI Adapter in the right-hand portion of the dialog box.

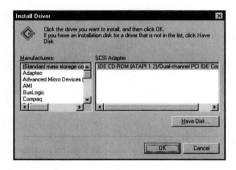

Figure 20.5

Select the applicable backup SCSI and other interface adapter hardware drivers from the Install Driver dialog box.

To install a tape device under Windows NT 4, follow these steps:

1. Launch the Tape Devices tool by double-clicking its icon, located in the Control Panel.

2. Choose the Drivers tab when the Tape Devices window is displayed.

3. Click on the Add button. This displays the Install Driver dialog box. Select tape devices by scrolling down the Manufacturers list box and choosing the desired Tape Device in the right-hand portion of the dialog box (see fig. 20.6).

Figure 20.6

Select the applicable tape backup hardware device drivers from the Install Driver dialog box.

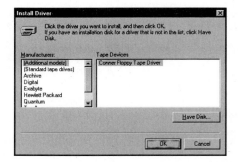

Planning a Backup Schedule

The backup schedule that you choose to implement needs to be well planned. Factors that affect a backup schedule plan include the following:

- How critical the network data or particular files or directories are.

- How frequently the data is modified.

- How often the network has low activity periods (nonbusiness hours, usually).

- Factors already discussed, such as the speed and capacity of the backup device.

These factors, and possibly others, need to be addressed before implementing your backup schedule. There are numerous types of backup strategies and techniques.

Microsoft Windows NT Server includes a full-featured backup tool called Backup, or more specifically, NTBACKUP.EXE. The following sections introduce you to the Backup tool and present an overview of the various backup schedules you can implement with it.

A key part of tape-backup scheduling is the tapes themselves. The tapes need to be rotated in a manner that best utilizes the tapes and retains the most amount of data for both in-house and off-site locations. The next section investigates tape rotation scheduling.

Planning a Tape-Rotation Schedule

An important consideration in backup scheduling is the tapes themselves. Rotating the tapes used for the backup process is a common practice because it is more economical than using a vast number of tapes and provides ready historical data for those times when a user deletes a file on Monday but doesn't realize it until Thursday. Many strategies for rotating tapes optimize their use, increase tape longevity, and ensure data integrity.

One of the strategies is to use ten tapes divided into two sets of five. This can be thought of as a biweekly, or odd-week, schedule, in which one set of tapes (even) is used one week, and the other set (odd) is used the following week. The Friday tape can be rotated off-site using as many tapes as you deem necessary depending on your archiving needs, as shown in figure 20.7.

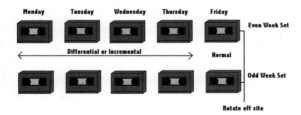

Figure 20.7

Common "10-tape" backup strategy.

More elaborate strategies provide more secure and historical archiving. Expanding on the previous concept by adding 12 monthly tapes or increasing the number of sets from two to ten provides for longer periods of time between backups on the tape sets.

Give some serious thought to what type of tape-rotation strategy best fits your network's needs. The more vital the information is, the more tape sets should be used.

Using the Backup Tool

The Backup tool is located in the Administrative Tools group or folder. It has changed little between Windows NT Server version 3.51 and 4. Upon launching the Backup tool, you are presented with the dialog box seen in figure 20.8.

Figure 20.8

The Windows NT Backup tool interface.

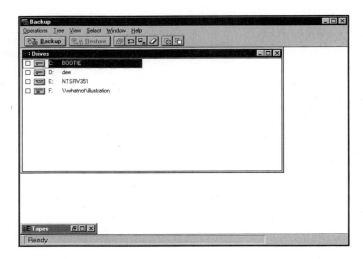

Note   You must be a member of the administrators group, the server operators group, or the Backup Operators group to use the Backup tool.

The Backup tool is a simple-to-use graphical application. It provides the ability to back up and restore the server by using a variety of options. The out-of-the-box Backup tool does lack some vital abilities however, including:

- **Selective file restoration.** Under full set backups, you must restore all files, rather than selectively choosing the desired files that are needed.

- **Lack of GUI scheduling service.** You must schedule backups using the command line. See section later in this chapter entitled "Automating Backups."

- **Lack of enterprise-wide backups.** Although the Backup tool incorporated into Windows NT Server can back up attached network drives, it does not provide the ability to conduct network or enterprise-wide backups. You will either have to backup servers and workstations separately and locally, or you will have to seek a third-party solution. However, a lot of network environments are centralized on a single Primary Domain Controller (PDC). In these situations, the Backup tool is capable of handling your needs.

- **Lack of support for backing up SQL datastores.** If your server runs SQL, you cannot utilize the included backup tool. Only third-party solutions offer the ability to back up critical SQL datastores.

If any of these features are required for your network environment, you will have to investigate a third-party backup software solution.

The following sections are an overview of the various functions, abilities, and options of the Backup tool.

Selecting a Backup Method

With the Windows NT Server Backup tool up and running, you need to specify which drives, directories, and files you want to backup. This is done in the Drives dialog box.

Simply select or deselect the directories and files by using the check boxes associated with them, as shown in figure 20.9.

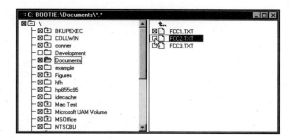

Figure 20.9

Selecting files to backup by selecting their associated check boxes.

After you are satisfied with the selection of files you want to back up, either click on the Backup button on the toolbar or choose the Backup option from the Operations menu. This presents you with the Backup Information dialog box (see fig. 20.10).

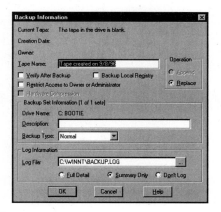

Figure 20.10

The Backup information dialog box provides a variety of backup options.

The Backup Information dialog box enables you to select a variety of backup options:

■ **Current Tape.** Displays the name of the tape that is currently installed into the tape backup device. If it is a blank tape, or if a tape is not present, you are told so.

■ **Creation Date.** Displays the creation date of the original backup set or the last date that it was replaced.

- **Owner.** Displays the name of the owner or creator of the first backup set on the tape.

- **Tape Name.** Use this field to enter a descriptive name for the tape cartridge. Can contain up to 32 characters.

- **Verify After Backup.** Verifies the data's accuracy after the backup procedure is completed. This should always be used in any environment.

- **Backup Local Registry.** Backs up the system registry. This is an important option to use since the registry changes often.

- **Operation.** Select the Append option if you want the backup procedure to add sets at the end of existing backup sets. Choose the Replace option if you want to overwrite the information on the tape.

- **Restrict Access to Owner or Administrator.** If this option is selected, only the creator of the backup set or a member of the Backup Operators or Administrators group can read, write, or erase the tape. This is a valuable option if the data is sensitive or confidential.

- **Hardware Compression.** Available only if the tape-backup device supports hardware-level compression. Do not choose this option if the tape will need to be read on another device that does not support the same type of compression.

- **Description.** Use this field to enter a description (up to 32 characters) of the backup set. If you are backing up more than one disk drive, you can use the scrollbar to enter a different description for each backup set.

- **Backup Type.** Use this drop-down list box to select the type of backup you want to conduct on the backup set. These options are detailed in the next section.

- **Log File.** A log of all backup operations. You may specify an alternate file name in this field. Also, you can specify the amount of detail you want to log by choosing either the Full Detail or Summary Only or skip it altogether by choosing the Don't Log option.

Selecting a Backup Type

The type of backup set that you create is dependent on your current backup-set needs. Following are the different types of available backups:

- **Normal.** A normal backup backs up all the files that have been selected without regarding the archive-bit status on the files. It then clears the archive bits of all the backed up files, indicating that all have been backed up.

Note The archive bit is a file attribute assigned by the operating system. It is used to distinguish files that have been archived or need to be archived.

- **Copy.** Like a normal backup, a copy backup backs up all the files that have been selected without regarding the archive-bit status on the files. However, it does not change the archive bit. This enables other backup methods to conduct themselves without being affected by the backup "copy" process.

- **Differential.** Differential backups are used to back up all files that have changed since the last backup procedure. In other words, they back up all selected files that have their archive bits set, indicating that they have been changed since they were last backed up. After the differential backup process has been completed, it does not change the archive bit on the files it backs up. Differential backups are used primarily to save time. A common backup strategy is to conduct normal (full) backups one or two days a week, usually on a weekend day and in the middle of the week, and then conduct differential backups on the remaining weekdays. In the event that you need to rebuild or restore your server, you only need to restore the weekend's normal backup and then a single differential backup on top of it. The archive bit is not changed, so a Wednesday differential backup would contain Monday's through Wednesday's changes.

- **Incremental.** Incremental backups are similar in concept to the differential backup method. Incremental backups back up only the selected files that have had their archive bit changed since the last backup process. The key difference is that an incremental backup clears the archive bit to indicate that the files have been backed up. Like differential backups, incremental backups are intended as a time-saving strategy. The key difference, however, is that if a server goes down on a Thursday, you have to restore the weekend's normal backup and then restore each consecutive incremental backup. The archive attribute is cleared during an incremental backup. An incremental backup saves even more time than a differential backup because it only backs up data that has changed since the last normal or incremental backup process, or a single day's worth of data under most circumstances.

Note Before you consider an incremental backup strategy (or even a differential strategy) remember that the whole purpose of backing up is so that information can be restored quickly and easily. It's more important that the restore process is easy than that the backup process is easy.

- **Daily.** A daily backup is a strategy that backs up data by investigating the selected file's date stamp. If the file has been modified on the same day that the daily backup process is being run, it will back it up without marking the files being marked as backed up. Daily backups are usually used in mission-critical environments, often running two or more times each day.

Whatever combination of backup types you conduct on your network, there is no way to ensure that all files can be safely archived; any new files, or files that have been modified from the last backup, will be at risk until they are backed up. You should complement your backups with other technologies such as fault-tolerant RAID storage subsystems, NTFS, and the directory-replication service.

Backup and File-System Security Settings

To perform a backup, the user must have the user right Backup Files and Directories. The Administrators, Backup Operators, and Server Operators groups are, by default, assigned this user right. If you do not have the Backup Files and Directories user right, you can back up only files for which you have permission.

Additionally, the following files are not backed up:

- Paging files. These are temporary files used to implement virtual memory.

- Registry files on remote computers.

- Exclusively locked files. Windows NT cannot back up files locked by application software. It does, however, support backup of local files that are locked by the Windows NT operating system.

If a file is open, Windows NT backs up the last saved version of this file.

When an NTFS file system is backed up, Windows NT preserves the file permissions, ownership, and audit flags for the files and directories. If the backed up files are restored on a new computer, they are restored without preserving security settings. If the files are restored without security permissions, they inherit the permissions of the directories in which they are placed. If the directory in which the files are placed does not have any permission settings, the previous permissions of the file are retained.

Backing Up the System Registry

Backing up the system registry is vital! The registry information is critical to the proper operation of the NT Server system. If the system becomes corrupted, having archived backups of it can be extremely beneficial.

Poor drivers and unsupported hardware are usually the culprits when it comes to Registry problems. Careless or uneducated network administrators have also been known to be at the root of Registry problems. Whatever the source, the Registry is vital to Windows NT operations and current backups of the Registry are very important.

Automating Backups

The Backup tool included with Windows NT Server does not directly support automated backups. However, it does support them indirectly by using command lines within a batch file in conjunction with the Windows NT scheduling service.

Note　Most third-party backup software solutions provide for more sophisticated automatic scheduling than the Windows NT AT command can provide.

The command-line method of backing up data can be used as a manual method or in conjunction with the Windows NT Server schedule service. To conduct backups from the command line, you must first become familiar with the command-line syntax for the backup service. The command to start a backup from the command prompt is NTBACKUP. The syntax for the command follows:

```
NTBACKUP operation path [/a][/b][/d "text"][/e][/hc:[ON¦OFF]][/l "filename"][/r]
[/t option][/TAPE:n][/v][/nopoll][/missingtape]
```

The parameters for the NTBACKUP command are as follows:

- **operation.** Indicates whether the operation is to be a backup or a tape eject.

- **path.** Used to indicate single or multiple directories to be backed up.

- **/a.** Append switch, causes backup sets to be added after the last backup set on the tape.

- **/b.** Indicates that the NT Server local registry is to be backed up.

- **/d "text".** Used to indicate a description of the backup set to be created.

- **/e.** Forces the backup log to store exceptions only.

- **/hc:[ON|OFF].** Used to indicate whether hardware device compression is to be used.

- **/l "filename".** Used to specify the file name of the backup log.

- **/r.** Used to restrict access to owner, Administrators, and Backup Operators.

- **/t.** Used to indicate the backup type. The options are /t normal, /t copy, /t incremental, /t differential, and /t daily.

- **/TAPE:n.** In platforms with multiple tape drive devices, used to indicate which drive to use, where n is a range from 0 to 9.

- **/v.** Forces backup verification process.

- **/nopoll.** Causes a tape to be erased. Do not use with any other parameters (requires user input).

- **/missingtape.** Used to specify that a tape is missing (not part of) a backup set, when the backup utilizes multiple tape backup (requires user input).

Now that you have an idea of what the various command-line options are for the NTBACKUP command, you need to be exposed to the AT command to automatically start a backup procedure.

Note You must have the schedule service running before you can utilize the AT command to automate your backups. You can start and setup the starting parameters for the schedule service from the Services tool in the Control Panel or by using the following command line:

```
net start schedule
```

The AT command is used in conjunction with the Windows NT Scheduling service to automate procedures and functions. Here is an overview of the AT command's syntax:

```
AT [\\computername][[id][/delete] ¦ [/delete [/yes]] time [/interactive]
[/every:date[,…] ¦ [/next:date[,…]] "command"
```

Here is the breakdown of the command parameters:

- ***computername.*** Indicates the UNC name of the Windows NT computer to execute the AT command upon.

- **id.** Indicates the identification number of the scheduled job. (The scheduling service assigns all jobs a sequential id number.)

- **id /delete.** Used to cancel a specific scheduled job, indicated by its ID number.

- **/delete.** Used to cancel all scheduled jobs, prompting confirmation for each.

- **/delete /yes.** Used to cancel all scheduled jobs without prompting confirmation for each.

- ***time.*** Used to indicate the time at which to perform the scheduled job. This is in a 24-hour military clock format.

- **/interactive.** Enables the user to interact with the scheduled job; otherwise, the backup is run in the background.

Note Do not use the /interactive switch if the backup is to be run automatically during non-business hours. If a user is not logged on to the system, the scheduled job will attempt to establish itself with a nonexistent desktop and will fail.

- **/every:*date.*** Indicates a repetitive job sequence using either Monday through Sunday or 1 through 31 format.

- **/next:*date.*** Indicates to repeat a job once on a specific date using Monday through Sunday or 1 through 31 format.

- ***command.*** Indicates the command to be executed: either a BAT, CMD, COM, or EXE file.

Now that you have a grasp of the details of the NTBACKUP and AT command-line operations, you should be able to construct an automated backup process utilizing batch files. Here is an example:

```
AT \\PHOENIX 01:30 /every:Tuesday,Wednesday,Thursday WKDAYBU.CMD
```

The contents of WKDAYBU.CMD are this:

```
NTBACKUP backup c:\nonsense /a /b /v /t differential
```

An alternative to the command-line format is available through Microsoft. The Microsoft Windows NT 4.0 Resource Kit contains a utility called the Command Scheduler (WINAT.EXE) that provides an easy-to-use graphical tool to conduct scheduled events and is perfect for conducting automatic backup procedures.

Verifying Backups

Always perform your tape backups with the data verification option marked whenever you can. Sometimes the additional time needed to conduct a verification comparison process is not available. In such cases, make it a point to verify your data at least once a week, perhaps on the weekend's normal (full) backup process.

Additionally, conduct an occasional test run. By restoring data once in a while to an alternate location, you can verify that the data is intact, and that the backup device is fully functional.

Maintaining Healthy Tapes

It is important to keep tapes in a dry, cool location away from sunlight and electromagnetic sources, such as speakers and telephones. To extend the life of tapes, you can also use the Retention Tape command from the Operations menu. This alleviates loose spots in the tape by winding the tape evenly, enabling it to conduct smoother operations during a backup and restore process. It is also important to regularly clean the tape drives read and write heads as recommended by the manufacturer.

> **Note** Most tape manufacturers specify how often the tape should be retensioned. The average is approximately once for every 20 uses. DAT tapes do not need to be retensioned, and the option is grayed out if you have such a device.

Restoration Procedures

To restore files onto the server, you need to select the files that you want to have restored. To select the desired files, follow these steps:

1. Insert the tape you want to conduct a restore action upon into the tape-drive device.

2. Open the Tapes dialog box by double-clicking the Tapes icon in the Backup tool.

3. The Backup tool reads the catalog from the tape and displays the available backup sets (see fig. 20.11).

Figure 20.11

Viewing backup sets.

4. Apply check marks next to the drives, folders, and files that you want to restore.

5. Either click the Restore button on the toolbar or choose the Restore option from the Operations menu. This opens the Restore Information dialog box from which you can choose several options (see fig. 20.12).

Figure 20.12

Specify restore configuration options within the Restore Information dialog box.

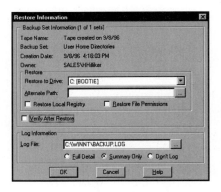

The Restore Information dialog box displays key information and provides the following options:

- **Tape Name.** Indicates the name of the tape currently conducting the restore action.

- **Backup Set.** Indicates the name assigned to the backup set.

- **Creation Date.** Indicates the date that the backup set was created.

- **Owner.** Indicates the name of the user who initially created the backup set.

- **Restore to Drive.** Indicates the drive and path location to which the restore action will write or overwrite. You may optionally indicate an alternative path to which to conduct the restore.

- ■ **Alternate Path.** If files are not restored to their original destination, use this field to indicate to where the files should be restored.

- ■ **Restore Local Registry.** Restores the system Registry as it was at the time of backup. This option is available only if the registry was backed up to the tape.

- ■ **Restore File Permissions.** Applies only to NTFS volumes to which you want to apply file permissions as they were at the time of the backup.

- ■ **Verify After Restore.** Verifies the data, after it is restored to the disk, to the original data on the tape.

- ■ **Log File.** Indicates message-logging options pertaining to the restoration process. It is identical in composition to the options available under the backup process, including Full Detail, Summary Only, and Don't Log.

After you are satisfied with your options, begin the restoration process by clicking on the OK button. A Restore Information dialog box provides status information and prompts you for the next tape cartridge if your backup set is spanned across two or more tape cartridges.

Server Restoration Actions

In the event of a total server failure, such as when the boot hard disk dies, you have to re-create the server. If you make certain modifications to your drive configuration you may also need your system backup tapes to recreate your system.

Follow these steps to perform a complete server restore:

1. Replace the physical boot drive.

2. Install Microsoft Windows NT Server, using the Repair option in conjunction with the Emergency Repair Disk. This should restore vital system Registry entries.

3. After the server is up and running, conduct a restore of the boot partition by using your last normal (full) backup along with any differential or incremental backup conducted.

4. Restart the server to apply any changes.

Implementing UPS Services

Windows NT comes with an UPS service, which interfaces with third-party UPS devices. The UPS service in the Windows NT computer and the UPS device communicate over a serial port.

The UPS service can be configured from the UPS option in the Control Panel.

The following is an outline of the way in which you can configure the UPS service:

1. Log on as an Administrator user.

2. Run the UPS option from the Control Panel.

   The UPS dialog box appears.

3. Enable the **U**ninterruptible Power Supply is installed on check box and select the serial port used for controlling the UPS device.

4. In the UPS Configuration area, specify the insterface voltages (positive or negative) of the following control signals used by the UPS device:

   > **P**ower failure signal

   > **L**ow battery signal at least two minutes before shutdown

   > **R**emote UPS Shutdown

   The Remote UPS shutdown signal is sent only if the system shutdown is initiated because of a power failure or a low battery signal.

5. If you want to execute a command file when the UPS service initiates a power shutdown, check the box for E**x**ecute Command File and specify the file name. The file can be a batch file (BAT, CMD extension) or an executable file (COM, EXE extension).

6. In the UPS Characteristics area, specify the timing parameters as follows:

   In the **E**xpected Battery Life field, specify the time in minutes that the UPS system can supply battery power. The value can range from 2 to 720 minutes and has a default value of 2 minutes.

   In the **B**attery recharge time per minute of run time box, specify the number of minutes the battery must be recharged for every minute of run time. The value can range from 1 to 250 minutes and has a default of 100 minutes.

7. In the UPS Service area, specify the following:

   In the **T**ime between power failure and initial warning message box, specify the time in seconds between when a power failure occurs and the first warning message is sent. The value can range from 0 to 200 seconds and has a default of 5 seconds.

   In the **D**elay between warning messages field, specify the time in seconds between messages sent to users. The messages warn the users about the power failure and advise them to stop using the computer.

8. After making the changes in the UPS dialog box, choose OK to save your configuration.

9. To ensure that the UPS service is always started when the system starts, start the Services option in the Control Panel. Select UPS in the service list and choose the Startup button. Be sure to set the Startup Type of the UPS service to **A**utomatic.

Besides using the Services option in the Control Panel to start, pause, and stop the UPS service, you also can use the following commands:

- NET START UPS

- NET STOP UPS

- NET PAUSE UPS

- NET CONTINUE UPS

If you discover that the UPS device is powered off when the Windows NT computer boots, it might be because of the probe sent by NTDETECT.COM, the hardware recognizer, to the serial port to recognize the hardware connected to the serial port. On some UPS devices, this probe is misinterpreted as a signal to turn the device off. To keep this mistake from occurring, use the /NoSerialMice switch in the BOOT.INI file to prevent NTDETECT.COM from sending the signal to the COM port in use by the UPS device. The following example is of a BOOT.INI file where the COM2 port is used by the UPS device. Notice that the /NoSerialMice switch is set to COM2 so that a probe signal is not sent to this port.

```
[boot loader]
timeout=30
default=scsi(0)disk(0)rdisk(0)partition(2)\WINNT
 [operating systems]
scsi(0)disk(0)rdisk(0)partition(2)\WINNT="Windows NT Server Version 4.00"
➥/NoSerialMice=COM2
scsi(0)disk(0)rdisk(0)partition(2)\WINNT="Windows NT Server Version 4.00
➥[VGA mode]"/basevideo /sos /NoSerialMice=COM2
C:\="MS-DOS"
```

Table 20.5 summarizes how the RS-232C modem control signals are used between the UPS and the serial port on the Windows NT computer.

Table 20.5
UPS Signals

RS-232C Signal	UPS Signal
Data Terminal Ready (DTR)	Remote UPS Shutdown
Clear To Send (CTS)	Power Failure Signal
Data Carrier Detected (DCD)	Low Battery Signal

Conclusion

This chapter explained the RAID architecture and different RAID levels. Windows NT Server supports RAID levels 0, 1, and 5. RAID level 5 is called Disk Striping with Parity in Windows NT Server.

The RAID support in Windows NT Server implements the RAID solution through special RAID drivers. The RAID drivers are supported in Windows NT Server, but not in Windows NT Workstation. Some vendors offer hardware-based solutions that implement different RAID levels. The hardware-based RAID solutions can be implemented on any Windows NT computer.

This chapter discussed Windows NT Backup services. Backup services are useful when multiple failures occur on the Windows NT computers. If two or more disk members of a striped set fail, for example, you lose access to the data on the disk. If files become corrupted because of disk, computer, or network failure, the Backup set can be used to go back to a previously consistent state.

To prevent a computer from being shut down as a result of a power failure, you can use a UPS device. Windows NT provides a UPS service that can communicate with and control the UPS device.

Performance Optimization of Windows NT Server–Based Networks

In this chapter, you learn about the factors affecting performance of Windows NT Server–based networks. These factors include hardware-related elements, such as bus speed, network topology, network cards, memory, and the operating system configuration.

Windows NT operating system can be monitored using the Performance Monitor tool. This chapter provides guidelines and procedures that you can use to monitor and optimize Windows NT Server performance.

Understanding the Factors Affecting Network Performance

Because the network is made up of hardware and software components, the factors that affect network performance are hardware- and software-related.

The following sections enable you to have better understanding of the hardware and software performance factors. A strong relationship exists between hardware and software factors, and both must be considered together in order to evaluate the performance of a network. This chapter first examines the hardware performance factors and then the software factors.

Hardware Components Affecting Server Performance

The following major hardware-related factors affect network performance:

- Disk subsystem: speed and storage capacity

- Network adapters: speed, bus width, and network access technology

- Server bus characteristics

- Symmetric multiprocessing

- Memory subsystem

The hardware-related factors are not confined to any single piece of equipment, such as the server machine. These factors also include the type of network adapters at the server and the workstation, and the network access speed and method (CSMA/CD, Token Access, and so on). One of the most important hardware elements is the server computer, its disk subsystem, and the type of network adapter inside the server. In Windows NT Server–based LANs, the server computer plays a central role; any improvements on the server hardware directly affect network performance.

Sometimes, replacing the server with a faster computer does not improve performance. Understanding this is important because the performance of the entire network is limited by its slowest component. If the physical layer is the slowest component of the network, for example, replacing the server machine or disk subsystem with a faster component does not improve performance in general.

Some of the tools described here can help you determine which component is the cause of the bottleneck. Generally, however, no cut-and-dried formulas for determining performance bottlenecks exist. Most experienced network managers use a combination of the following: a knowledge of their network, knowledge of underlying technology, and good common sense and intuition to detect and isolate performance-related problems. Some promising technology exists. Expert systems are being developed to solve these problems, but expert systems are only as good as the people programming them. They can help guide you to a solution to the problem, but cannot necessarily solve the problem for you.

Disk Subsystem

Because the server files are stored on the server disk, a fast disk subsystem results in faster file services and, from a user's perspective, a faster network. The disk subsystem in Windows NT is managed by the I/O Manager component in the kernel, and is responsible for receiving network requests and sending backup replies. The I/O Manager manages an internal cache that should be large enough to satisfy most network read-retrieval requests from cache. The disk subsystem should be fast enough to keep the I/O Manager cache full of needed data.

The data transfer rate between the CPU and the disk is determined by the disk, the disk controller, and the bus interfaces. The older PC AT disks that used MFM encoding are among the slowest hard disks. Today, most disks use a higher level of RLL encoding, enabling them to pack more data per sector, which means that the disk has to rotate smaller distances (requiring less time) to deliver the same amount of data. Data-transfer rates, therefore, are faster.

The types of disks that give the best performance in the marketplace today are disks based on Integrated Device Electronics (IDE), Enhanced Small Devices Interface (ESDI), and Small Computers Systems Interface SCSI), or RAID disk subsystems (discussed in Chapter 20, "Data Protection for Windows NT Servers").

The IDE disks replace the older, AT-style disks and provide a higher performance interface between the computer and the disk, enabling them to be faster than the AT-style disks. IDE implements most of its logic on the electronics on the drive itself. IDE, however, uses the computer's CPU to perform many of its tasks. It is limited to two drives per controller. Older IDE drives have a data transfer rate of 2 to 3 MB/sec, but more recent models acheive data transfer rates of 10 to 20 MB/sec. IDE drives have a maximum storage capacity of 528 MB, due to PC BIOS limits. Although some recent IDE drives perform close to SCSI speeds when one drive is used, IDE usually performs at less than SCSI speed when two drives are used because the device electronic controls must be shared by two drives.

The Enhanced IDE drive (EIDE) avoids some of IDE's limitations. EIDE drivers aren't limited by the 528 MB storage capacity, and the EIDE controller can support more than two devices.

The ESDI interface developed out of the I/O interface used in minicomputer environments and is faster than the IDE disks. The SCSI interface is the most versatile because it enables multiple devices to be connected to an external I/O bus. SCSI disk drives usually are external; they have their own power supply and, therefore, tend to be more reliable.

The disk manufacturers seem to have voted the SCSI interface the best technique for providing high-capacity, high-speed disks. The SCSI-II interface has some performance improvements over the older, SCSI-I interface. SCSI-III products are beginning to appear. The evolving SCSI-III standard has enormous potential—SCSI devices may eventually use a (optical) fiber channel to transfer data at up to 100 MB/sec—but SCSI-III is still new, and it may take some time for vendors to fully implement the advantages of SCSI-III. Watch for developments in SCSI-III. SCSI-III promises faster speeds, less noise, fewer termination problems, and greater cabling distances than are possible under SCSI-II.

SCSI devices can transfer at rates up to 40 MB/sec (320 Mbps), which well exceeds the speed of Ethernet (10 Mbps), Token Ring (16 Mbps), ARCnet PLUS (20 Mbps), and FDDI (100 Mbps). In actual practice, these devices achieve smaller data-transfer rates if used with the ISA-style bus because the ISA bus currently is limited to transfer rates of 4 Mbps to 8 Mbps.

SCSI-I uses an 8-bit bus. Seven devices per master device (the SCSI controller) can be daisy-chained on the SCSI bus. Only one command can be pending for a SCSI device.

SCSI-II supports the SCSI-I command set and uses parity checking on the bus to detect errors. It also supports a bus disconnect feature where a SCSI device releases the bus while performing a command. This feature makes the SCSI bus available for other devices. SCSI-II overcomes the SCSI-I limitation of one command per SCSI device. With SCSI-II, multiple commands can be issued to a SCSI-II–compatible device, which is kept in the Tag Command Queue (TCQ). Because the device holds commands in a queue, it can execute them in sequence as each command finishes and does not have to wait for the next command from the SCSI controller, as in the case of SCSI-I. This quick execution leads to a dramatic improvement in performance. Other performance-improvement features of SCSI-II are a bus clock speed double that of SCSI-I, and bus width of 16 bits, also double that of SCSI-I. The current classifications used in the industry for classifying SCSI features are shown in table 21.1.

Table 21.1
SCSI Classifications

Classification	Bus Width (bits)	Data Transfer Rate (MB/sec)	Command Queuing
SCSI-I	8	5	Single command only
SCSI-II	8, 16, 32	5, 10, 20	Supports Tag Command Queuing
Fast SCSI-II	8	10	Supports Tag Command Queuing
Fast and Wide SCSI-II	16	20	Supports Tag Command Queuing
Fast and 32-bit Wide SCSI-II	32 (most devices do not support 32 bits)	40	Supports Tag Command Queuing

Network Adapters

In a networking environment, the network adapters determine the data-transfer rate through the network media. Not all adapters for a network technology are created equal. Many manufacturers of Ethernet adapters exist, for example. They all comply with the Ethernet standard of 10 Mbps but have different effective data rates. Network adapters from 3COM are quite popular, but at least two types of adapters exist for IBM PCS: 3COM EtherLink and 3COM EtherLink Plus. The 3COM EtherLink Plus is a higher-performance card, and is, therefore, more expensive. It has more packet buffers and faster circuitry. Ideally, all stations on a network should have high-performance cards to obtain the maximum possible data-transfer rate. If cost is a major factor, at least the server computer and external routers should have a high-performance card. Using a high-performance network adapter for the server can dramatically improve the network performance.

The following factors affect the performance of a network adapter:

- Media access scheme

- Raw bit rate

- Onboard processor

- NIC-to-host transfer

The media access scheme refers to the arbitration mechanism, inherent in baseband LANs, that limits how the messages are placed on the media. Examples of this are CSMA/CD, used in Ethernet and IEEE 802.3, and Token Access, used in IBM Token Ring (IEEE 802.5). Token Access gives a deterministic performance even under heavy network loads, whereas CSMA/CD is susceptible to reduced throughput because of collisions under heavy loads. Under light loads, on the other hand, the CSMA/CD access method is simpler and faster than Token Access.

The raw bit rate is the maximum bit rate possible on a given medium. The effective bit rate (taking into account protocol, overhead, and queue and processing delays) is much lower. The raw bit rate represents an upper limit for the medium.

Effective use of an onboard processor can speed up a network adapter. If the firmware for the NIC is poorly written, however, it can have just the opposite effect as that seen in the earlier IBM PC Broadband LAN adapters. Some vendors implement upper-layer protocol processing on the NIC card itself for better overall throughput. An example of such a NIC is Federal Technologies' EXOS series board that has onboard TCP/IP processing.

Data arriving on the network adapter needs to be transferred into the host computer's memory. The NIC connection to the host channel can be implemented using shared memory, DMA, or I/O ports. NICs can use any of these methods or a combination of them. Observations have shown that shared memory is the fastest, followed by I/O ports and then DMA. Avoid NICs that use DMA exclusively for transferring data because they probably are slow. Some cards use a combination of shared memory and DMA, which gives them a certain level of parallelism that can improve their performance.

The data width of the bus interface has a dramatic effect on NIC-to-host transfer speeds. (See the following section for a discussion of server bus characteristics.) Current data widths are 8, 16, or 32 bits. The wider the data width, the faster the data transfer. A high transfer speed at the server can greatly enhance network performance because so much traffic is concentrated at the server interface.

Try to avoid mixing network adapters from different vendors on one LAN. Although all vendors claim to follow a standard, important implementation differences that can affect the performance of a network might exist between them. Some Ethernet vendors implement the random-time backoff algorithm differently, for example, so that in case of Ethernet bus contention and collision, they time out earlier than network adapters from other vendors. In practical terms, these network adapters access the LAN bus earlier than network adapters from other vendors. Another way to look at this is to see these network adapters as "poor citizens" on the network. One way to handle these network adapters is to isolate them in their separate LAN segment, where they have minimum impact on other stations on the network.

Another property of most PC LANs and LANs based on the IEEE standards is that the bigger they are (in geographical size), the smaller their network utilization is. This factor is often overlooked during the design of backbone LANs to span large distances. Network administrators are surprised by the drop in network utilization, and data throughput, as LAN size increases. The reason for this drop is technical and very interesting.

Network utilization is defined as the percentage of time spent in transferring data, not including the time spent in packet processing and transmission delays. One can estimate the maximum utilization achievable by assuming that under the best possible conditions, there is zero processing delay and queue delay; but the transmission delay cannot be avoided because of the finite propagation speed of the signal.

The data transmit time (Tx) is the time it takes to deliver data to the LAN media for a given transmission rate. The transmission delay (Td) is caused by the finite propagation speed of signals in the LAN media. Under the highest possible data-transfer rate, the messages are sent one after another with minimal delays. The message consists of a channel-use time of Tx and a propagation delay (non-use) time of Td. The actual utilization (U) is the fraction of useful time spent transmitting data. You can make this determination by using the following formula:

$$U = Tx / (Tx + Td) = 1 / (1 + Td/Tx)$$

$$U = 1 / (1 + a) \text{ (1) in which } a = Td/Tx$$

If the LAN data rate for transmitting a packet of size P bits is D bps, then

$$Tx = P/D \text{ seconds (2)}$$

If the propagation velocity of signal in media is V meters/sec and the size of the LAN is L meters, then

$$Td = L/V \text{ seconds (3)}$$

Studies show that the average packet size for most LAN applications is small (about 128 bytes). Using this, you can compute the network utilization of the 10BASE-T LAN.

In the 10BASE-T LAN of figure 21.1, the maximum length of the LAN is 200 meters, not including the backplane. The backplane CSMA/CD bus in the 10BASE-T concentrator has a length of about 0.5 meters. Using the formulas for 10BASE-T LAN, and assuming a signal propagation speed of 0.7 times speed of light in vacuum, you can make the following calculation:

P (Packet size) = 128 × 8 bits = 1024 bits
D (Data Transfer Rate) = 10 Mbps (fixed for Ethernet)
L (Length of LAN) = 200.5 meters
V (Signal Propagation speed) = 0.7 × speed of light in vacuum
$\qquad\qquad\qquad\qquad\qquad$ = 0.7 × 3 ×100,000,000
$\qquad\qquad\qquad\qquad\qquad$ = 2.1 × 100,000,000
Tx = P/D = 1024/10 Mbps = 102.4 microseconds
Td = L/V = 200.5 / (2.1 × 100,000,000) = 0.95 microseconds
a = Td/Tx = 0.95/102.4 = 0.0093
U (10BASE-T) = 1 / (1 + a) = 1 / (1 + 0.0093) = 99 percent

Figure 21.1 also shows a larger LAN, such as an IEEE 802.3 10BASE-5 LAN that has a maximum size of 2,800 meters. Repeating the calculations with the 10BASE-5 parameters gives the following result:

P (Packet size) = 128 × 8 bits = 1024 bits
D (Data Transfer Rate) = 10 Mbps (fixed for Ethernet)
L (Length of LAN) = 2800 meters
V (Signal Propagation speed) = 2.1 × 100,000,000 meters/sec
Tx = P/D = 1024/10 Mbps = 102.4 microseconds
Td = L/V = 2800/(2.1 × 100,000,000) = 13.3 microseconds
a = Td/Tx = 13.3/102.4 = 0.13
U (10BASE-5) = 1/(1 + a) = 1/(1 + 0.13) = 88.4 percent

A drop of about 10 percent in performance is noted between 200-Meter 10BASE-T network (99%) and 2800-Meter 10BASE-5 network (88.4%). These calculations do not include processing and queuing delays at the network adapters. Actual network utilization is much less if these additional delays are taken into account; nevertheless, it explains why connecting a 10BASE-T LAN to a 10BASE-5 by means of a repeater results in a drop in performance for the 10BASE-T stations. One solution to this problem is to connect the 10BASE-T LANs to the 10BASE-5 through bridges so that the CSMA/CD mechanism is partitioned into separate domains (see fig. 21.2).

Figure 21.1

A large 10 BASE-T LAN.

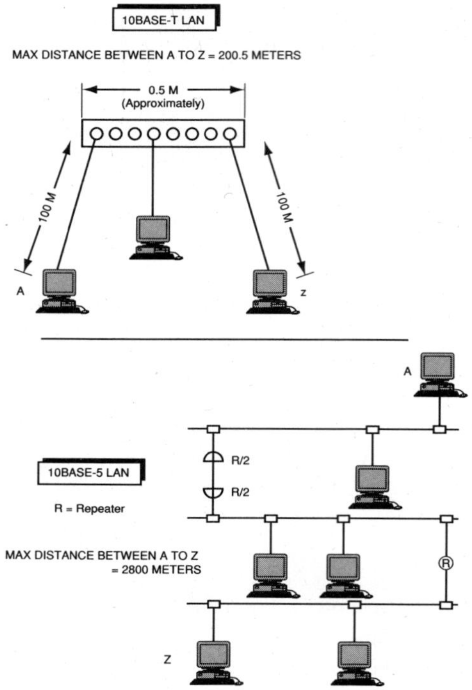

10BASE-T LAN

MAX DISTANCE BETWEEN A TO Z = 200.5 METERS

0.5 M
(Approximately)

100 M   100 M

A   Z

10BASE-5 LAN

R = Repeater

R/2
R/2

A

MAX DISTANCE BETWEEN A TO Z
= 2800 METERS

Z   (R)

Figure 21.2

*Partitioned CSMA/CD
networks.*

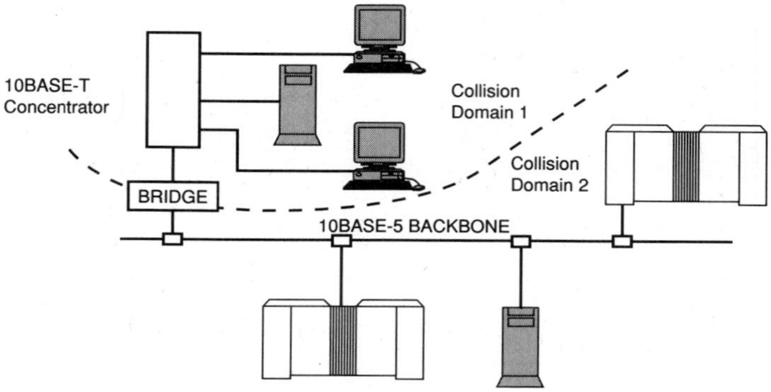

10BASE-T
Concentrator

BRIDGE

Collision
Domain 1

Collision
Domain 2

10BASE-5 BACKBONE

For faster network performance, you might want to consider EtherSwitches, Fast Ethernet, ATM, and Virtual LANs.

Server Bus Characteristics

The server bus reliability and performance has an effect on server performance. If you are using a high performance Fast and Wide SCSI-II interface with a slow ISA bus, for example, the ISA bus speed could be a bottleneck in I/O operations. The following are some of the parameters to consider in evaluating the server bus requirements:

- Data integrity

- Reliability

- Performance

- Compatibility with existing hardware and software

- Industry acceptance

- Flexible architecture that enables growth and increased functionality

Data integrity and reliability imply that the data should be transferred reliably over the server bus without errors. A bus should implement at least a parity scheme in order to detect single bit errors. Errors can be caused by faulty electronics, electrical interference, particle bombardments, and radiation from other devices. If such errors are detected, the receiving device on the server bus can request that the corrupt data be re-sent.

Performance can be increased by using a bus with a wide data path and by using bus mastering. *Bus mastering* is a technique that allows a device to gain control of the bus and transfer data, enabling the performance of I/O without processor intervention and overhead.

Common server buses on Intel-based servers are

- ISA

- EISA

- Micro Channel

- PCI

The Industry Standard Architecture (ISA) bus is used in old AT designs and has a data path width of 16 bits. It transfers data at 10 MB/sec and does not use bus mastering or bus parity.

The Extended Industry Standard Architecture (EISA) uses software configuration to automatically configure EISA boards and uses a 32-bit wide bus. It can be used to support the older ISA bus cards. It uses full bus mastering but does not have bus parity. It can transfer data up to 66 MB/sec.

The Micro Channel bus, developed by IBM, is a complete redesign of the bus and is not compatible with ISA or EISA cards. It is a 32-bit wide bus and has auto-configuration capability and full mastering and bus parity. It can transfer data between 10 MB/sec to 160 MB/sec. Besides IBM PCS, it is used in the RS/6,000 workstations, Communications Controllers (IBM 3172), and mainframes (IBM 9370).

The Peripheral Component Interconnect (PCI) is a redesign of the system bus by Intel. It is a 64-bit wide bus and has auto-configuration capability and full mastering and bus parity. It can transfer data between 132 MB/sec and 264 MB/sec. It can accommodate fast video transfers needed with client operating systems that have a graphical interface.

Symmetrical Multiprocessing

To increase the performance of Windows NT Server, you can consider installing it on a hardware platform that has multiple processors. Windows NT can utilize multiple processors by distributing tasks to any available processor. The CPU load, therefore, can be evenly spread across multiple processors. This approach is called Symmetrical Multiprocessing (SMP).

Another type of approach used to increase system performance is called Asymmetrical Multi-processing (AMP). This approach differs from SMP in one very important way: the processors are dedicated to performing specific tasks instead of spreading the workload evenly over the processors, as in SMP. An example of the AMP approach is a processor dedicated to executing user applications, another for managing I/O requests, and another for executing network requests.

Figure 21.3 contrasts the approaches taken by SMP and AMP. In SMP, the threads on the server can run on any available processor. The passage of the CPU through a sequence of instructions is called a *thread*; that is, a thread is a sequence of instructions that is executed. In Windows NT, a process must include at least one *thread of execution* (see fig. 21.4). A Windows NT process or task can have many threads that enable parallelism in computation.

Figure 21.3

SMP versus AMP.

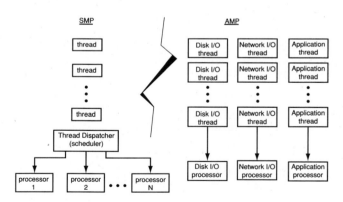

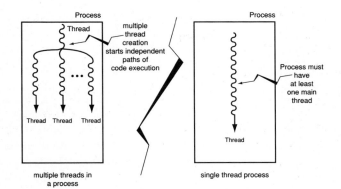

Figure 21.4
Defining threads.

A Windows NT thread is a unit of execution that can be *scheduled* independently on a processor. On a multiprocessor, machine threads within a process can run on different processors using SMP. An advantage of using threads is that threads within a process share the same address space. This makes all of the process' resources available to all threads within a process. Threads can share resources without requiring elaborate data-passing mechanisms. Threads have less overhead and are faster to create compared to processes. For this reason, threads often are called *lightweight processes.*

Examples of thread usage are Windows NT applications (Win32), such as a spreadsheet that can create a special thread to perform recalculations while another thread is ready to receive user input; or a word processor that uses a thread to periodically save a document that a user is editing; or a database server handling many requests for services on a network with a thread assigned for each request.

Note Windows NT supports SMP, but at the time of this writing, it does not support AMP.

Upgrading Windows NT Hardware Configuration

Now that you comprehend which subsystems affect NT performance, you can investigate how upgrading hardware affects NT Server. In the fast-paced microcomputer industry, new technologies are constantly extending the limits of computing power. State-of-the-art equipment often performs its first actions in networked environments. A server platform bought today is certain to be quickly outclassed.

Thankfully, most servers accommodate expansion and upgrades. High-end server platforms provide extra capacity for future memory and hard disk expansions. High-end servers also often provide the capability to replace or upgrade the CPU, either by using a Zero Insertion Force (ZIF) socket or a dedicated CPU complex on an expansion type card.

You should always plan for inevitable upgrades and expansions by acquiring a system that can serve the requirements of its environment well into the future.

Stepping Up Your RAID Level

A common way to increase the fault tolerance and performance characteristics of a Windows NT Server is by changing the current RAID level. As the size of your network grows and the number of users increases, hard disk drives can become extremely busy. Some of the RAID levels are poor performers when it comes to speed, thus upgrading to a more advanced disk array can overcome these bottlenecks. The following sections overview the methods used to upgrade your RAID specification.

Changing from Mirroring to Duplexing

If you're currently running RAID 1 (disk mirroring), you can inexpensively increase both speed and reliability by running disk duplexing (adding an additional controller card). The built-in Windows NT fault tolerance support for RAID level 1 can be utilized in either configuration.

An additional controller decreases the overhead of a single controller using a mirror solution. A second controller adds significant fault tolerance and reduces the risk of a bad controller corrupting both disks.

Note   If you need to purchase a second hard disk or hard disk set, be aware that mirrored or duplexed partitions need to be the same size. There is no need to purchase a 2.0 GB secondary disk drive if the first drive is only 1.6 GB. On the other hand, if the reverse is true, you will want to make sure that the second drive is big enough!

The cost of adding an additional controller is almost insignificant; you can still utilize the existing disk drives, and you only need to acquire another compatible controller card. This addition is possible with most current drive technologies. These include ESDI-, IDE-, and SCSI-controlled storage subsystems.

Utilizing RAID 0 and 5 for Performance Benefits

Currently, the two fastest RAID levels are 0 (disk striping) and 5 (disk striping with parity). If your storage subsystem is becoming a bottleneck, consider stepping up to either one of these RAID levels. Both of these RAID levels are supported "out-of-the-box" with Windows NT Server.

Your specific fault tolerance requirements determine which RAID level to properly implement. If you need disk redundancy, you need to use RAID 5, if not, use level 0.

Adding Drives to Disk Arrays

Many manufacturers have elaborate hard disk array storage subsystems available on the market. These devices can utilize 3 to 32 disk drives. By planning ahead, you can acquire a working system with a minimal number of disk drives but still have the ability to add drives as your network and data storage expand.

Note Adding working drives to an array is not as simple as it seems. You may need to re-create partitions in order to utilize additional drives. This is achieved by using either the Disk Administrator tool or the manufacturer's utilities.

If the partition that you want to expand is also your boot partition, it may be necessary to reinstall the network operating system. Be sure that you have three good backup sets before doing such a procedure.

Proprietary disk arrays are another important consideration. This type of disk array often utilizes synchronized hard drives. The timing between these drives is critical, and you must purchase certified drives for these particular systems.

Adding Memory

Microsoft Windows NT Server performs optimally with additional memory. Server memory resources can become greatly taxed as additional services, users, and applications are added to the system. A server can become burdened with RAS, Internet, and Macintosh services, to name a few of these demanding entities. Most memory bottleneck issues can be managed by utilizing the Performance Monitor tool.

Note Check with the manufacturer of the application or Windows NT service to see what kind of memory requirements they demand. This information is sometimes printed right on the box.

Adding additional memory to the server is quick and painless, and it can increase performance characteristics drastically.

Note Try to maintain consistency among the memory modules that you utilize in the server or workstation platform. Often, different manufacturers' memory architectures are not completely compatible, which can cause subtle problems. Also bear in mind the speed rating; you need to maintain consistency of the nanosecond rating on all your memory banks.

Upgrading the Server CPU

It is always advisable to run the fastest, state-of-the-art processor on your servers. Most modern, high-end servers provide simple CPU upgrade paths. These servers permit quick, reliable, snap-in type upgrades. However, older servers or inexpensive solutions often do not directly support processor upgrades. These systems are sometimes salvageable by third-party solutions such as the Intel Overdrive.

Upgrading a server's CPU from a 486DX2 66 MHz to a Pentium Pro 200 MHz is possible when using high-end servers. Such servers utilize a processor-complex expansion card that can be replaced with a higher-end CPU complex. Often these solutions are available in multiprocessor varieties as well.

If your processor utilization is high, you should consider a multiprocessor upgrade, which is a common solution for a multithreaded application server such as the Microsoft SQL Server. If your server does not support a multiprocessor upgrade option, you will probably have to retire it and replace it with a new unit.

The Windows NT Server 4 Resource Kit includes a uni-multiprocessor upgrade tool that can aide you in a multiprocessor upgrade.

Note   Upgrading to a multiprocessor solution will require you to reinstall Windows NT Server.

Upgrading the Server NIC

If your server is not utilizing a 32-bit bus-mastering network card, you may want to consider upgrading. Upgrading the server's NIC can drastically improve the network I/O characteristics on the network. The server is like the brain of a vast nervous system. Millions of bits of information flow to and from it constantly! It is foolish not to supply the central point of the network with the best interface possible.

Upgrading or Replacing the Server UPS

UPSs are devices that usually get replaced every several years. If your current UPS does not support full communication management capabilities, it is a good idea to upgrade to one that does. The benefits of an intelligent UPS add additional fault tolerance to the server.

Changing Domain Servers

It is inevitable that your powerful server will eventually become a dinosaur. When your server is ready to go out to pasture, replacing it with modern equipment can cause real headaches. A good strategy is to implement the new server as a BDC and eventually migrate everything to it. Then, when you are satisfied with its performance and correct behavior, take the original PDC off-line and promote the new BDC to the PDC role.

Windows NT–Specific Optimization Techniques

The previous section discussed general techniques that can be used to improve the performance of the computer hardware system. This section covers optimization and performance monitoring techniques specific to Windows NT.

Optimizing Virtual Memory Performance

Windows NT can address up to 4 GB of memory. Each process has its own view of the memory based on 32-bit addresses. The size of a process address space is 2 to the power of 32, or 4 gigabytes. The lower 2 GB are used for program storage, and the upper 2 GB are used by the operating system for system storage (see fig. 21.5). Most computer systems have far less physical memory than 4 gigabytes. It is possible, however, to run programs that are larger than the amount of physical memory available by using a mechanism called *virtual memory*.

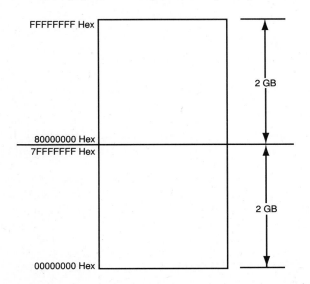

Figure 21.5

System storage.

When physical memory becomes full (overcommitted), the Virtual Memory Manager (VMM) transfers some of the memory contents to disk. If the memory contents transferred to disk are needed again, VMM brings them back into memory (see fig. 21.6). The transferring of memory contents to disk is called *swapping* to disk. In Windows NT, the VMM manages memory contents in blocks of 4 KB called *pages*. Memory is handled and transferred to disk in page sizes. To swap to disk is sometimes called *page-out* the memory, and to bring back the pages from disk to memory is called *page-in*. A certain amount of memory in the NT Address space layout is nonpaged. *Nonpaged* memory is used for critical system tables such as the page directory, which keeps track of pages in memory and whether they are in physical memory or disk.

Figure 21.6
Virtual Memory mechanism.

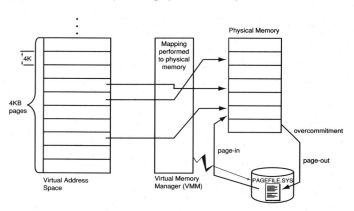

Use of fixed-size pages reduces the amount of unutilized fragmented system memory that would otherwise occur when the system has been used for some time. Minimizing fragmentation of memory is an automatic optimization in Windows NT and requires no additional configuration. The use of a fixed page size results in a small amount of wasted memory when the program or data size in memory is not an exact multiple of 4 KB. If, for example, a page stores only 1 byte of data, then 4,095 bytes of memory are wasted (1 page = 4,096 bytes). On the average, however, only 2 KB (2,048 bytes) of memory is wasted.

Usually, all of a program's pages do not need to be in memory because most programs exhibit a behavior called *locality of reference*, which means that the program spends most of its time in a small section of the address space. For this reason, it is not necessary to have the entire program in physical memory at any time. The set of pages that a program needs for its execution for a given duration of time (seconds or few minutes) is called the *working set*.

When a program references a page that is not in physical memory, it generates a page-fault that causes the VMM to bring the page from disk to physical memory. If physical memory is overcommitted, however, a physical page that has not been used for some time is paged out to a special file called PAGEFILE.SYS (refer to figure 21.6).

If the working set size of programs running at any one time exceeds the physical memory size, it leads to a condition called *disk thrashing*, which results in constant disk I/O activity due to swapping and page-faults. As part of implementing C2-level security in Windows NT, when a physical memory page is made free, its contents are zeroed so that when the memory pages are allocated to another process, the data that belonged to the older process is not available.

Windows NT enables you to control the location and size of the PAGEFILE.SYS. The PAGEFILE.SYS cannot be deleted while Windows NT is running. If the PAGEFILE.SYS is deleted when booting and running another operating system, a new page file is created automatically the next time you start Windows NT.

The actual virtual memory address space is limited by the amount of physical memory, and the maximum size to which the PAGEFILE.SYS can grow is given by the following equation:

Actual virtual address space = Physical Memory + Maximum PAGEFILE.SYS size

If, for instance, a Windows NT computer has 16 MB of physical memory and a maximum of 80 MB PAGEFILE.SYS, the actual virtual address space on that system cannot exceed 16 MB + 80 MB = 96 MB.

> **Note**   Overly active hard disks, or disk thrashing, is frequently misdiagnosed as a problem with the disk subsystem rather than a shortage of memory causing excessive paging.

You can change the PAGEFILE.SYS file by selecting the System icon in the Control Panel and then choosing the Performance tab. Click on the Change button in the Virtual Memory section of the Performance tab. The Virtual Memory dialog box appears (see fig. 21.7).

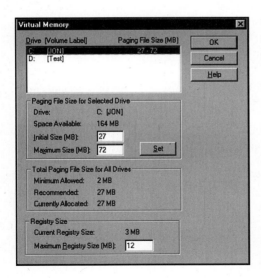

Figure 21.7
The Virtual Memory dialog box.

You can use the fields **I**nitial Size and Ma**x**imum Size in figure 21.7 to set the starting page file size and maximum page file size. The minimum size is 2 MB. The Virtual Memory dialog box also reports the currently allocated page file size. You should set the initial size to the recommended value, eliminating the time required by the system to set the page file size to the recommended value.

If your system has multiple drives, you can improve system performance by moving the page file off the drive that contains the system files because the system files are accessed frequently by Windows NT. If you have separate controllers for the system drive and the page file drive or a controller that can perform simultaneous read/write of the two drives, the system performance improves significantly, especially when a large amount of paging activity occurs.

You also can have a separate page file, PAGEFILE.SYS, for each logical drive. If the page files are on separate physical drives, then concurrent swapping can take place, resulting in better response times under heavy paging activity.

If striped sets with parity (also called RAID level 5—see Chapter 20) are being used, you improve not only fault tolerance but the speed of access to data and the page file on the striped set. This results in smaller delays for page-out and page-in operations.

Prioritizing Threads and Processes

In Windows NT, the scheduler is called the thread *dispatcher*, which uses a preemptive scheduling mechanism. The scheduling mechanism is preemptive in the sense that the dispatcher decides when to stop a thread on a processor and run another thread in its place. The criteria used by the dispatcher for scheduling a thread is based on the following:

■ Priority of thread

■ Expiration of time-quantum allocated to a thread

■ Processor affinity of thread: Processor affinity is the set of processors on which a thread can run.

A higher-priority thread is scheduled before a lower-priority thread. Additionally, a lower-priority thread is preempted if a higher-priority thread becomes ready to execute.

Windows NT supports 32 priority levels (see fig. 21.8) divided into the following two classes:

■ Real-time

■ Variable priority

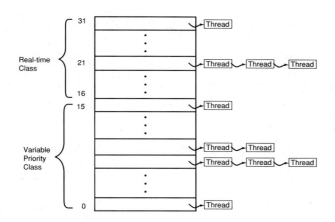

Figure 21.8

Priority levels in Windows NT.

The real-time class processes can run at priority levels from 16 to 31 and are used for time-critical tasks. These priority levels are available to the Windows NT operating system kernel processes but not to applications in general.

The variable priority class (also called the *dynamic* priority class) can run from priority levels 0 to 15 and is used by applications. A process generally starts with a base priority level, which is adjusted dynamically by the system by as much as 2 levels. A priority level of 8 is called the *normal priority level* because, by default, a process starts at a normal priority level. Within the variable priority class, user interactive threads run at high priority (11–15), I/O-bound threads run at intermediate priority (6–10), and compute-bound threads run at low priority (1–5).

Threads belonging to a process inherit the process's base priority level. Threads at the same priority level share the same priority thread by taking an equal time slice from a processor. If a higher-priority thread becomes available for running, it must be run immediately. The priority levels are adjusted by the Windows NT dispatcher for optimizing response time. Windows NT can dynamically adjust the priority of a thread under the following conditions:

- Threads waiting to receive a user input receive a priority boost of 2 when the user supplies the input, making the application appear more responsive to the user.

- Threads receive a priority boost after awakening from a voluntary wait, which should encourage programmers to write applications to use voluntary wait if the application design requires one.

- Priorities are lowered for compute-bound threads.

- I/O-bound threads generally get more frequent priority boosts.

- All threads receive priority boosts periodically, preventing low-priority threads from starving for too long, which also should encourage programmers to avoid using low-priority threads to lock shared resources that may be needed by higher priority threads.

You can use the START command to start applications at different priority levels. The syntax of this command is shown:

```
START ["title"] [/Dpath] [/I] [/MIN] [/MAX] [/SEPARATE ¦ /SHARED]
[/LOW ¦ /NORMAL ¦ /HIGH ¦ /REALTIME] [/WAIT] [/B] [command] [parameters]
```

"title" is the title to display in the window title bar.

path is the initial directory in which the program starts.

I is the new environment that will be the original environment passed to the CMD.EXE (Windows NT command processor) and not the current environment.

MIN starts the window minimized.

MAX starts the window maximized.

SEPARATE starts the 16-bit Windows program in separate memory space.

SHARED starts the 16-bit Windows program in shared memory space.

LOW starts the application in the IDLE priority class. Priority level value is 4.

NORMAL starts the application in the NORMAL priority class. Priority level value is 8.

HIGH starts the application in the HIGH priority class. Priority level value is 13.

REALTIME starts the application in the REALTIME priority class. Priority level value is 24.

WAIT starts the application and waits for it to terminate.

B starts application without creating a new window. The application is set to ignore ^C signals. Unless the application enables ^C processing, ^B (Break) is the only way to interrupt the application.

command is the name of the application to run. If command is an internal command or a batch file, then the command processor is run with the /K switch to cmd.exe. The /K switch causes the window to remain after the command finishes running. If it is not an internal command or batch file, then the program runs as either a windowed application or a console application.

parameters passes parameters to the command.

You can change the priority of a process using Task Manager. Microsoft, however, does not necessarily recommend using Task Manager to change a process priority. If you are going to use Task Manager to change the priority of a process, be prepared to answer Yes to the following message:

WARNING: Changing the priority class of this process may cause undesired results including system instability. Are you sure you want to change the priority class?

To change the priority of a process using Task Manager:

1. Right-click on an empty place in the taskbar to display Task Manager.

2. Select the Processes tab.

3. Right-click on a process and choose Set **P**riority from the context menu (see fig. 21.9).

4. Select a priority option: **R**ealtime, **H**igh, **N**ormal, or **L**ow. Windows NT displays the preceding warning message.

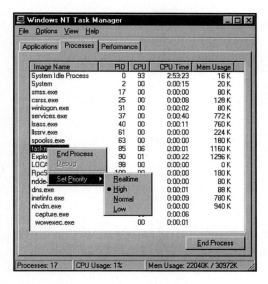

Figure 21.9

Changing priorities in Task Manager.

Applying Service Packs

Part of keeping your NT Server in optimal condition is keeping it current. Service packs are patches that add additional functionality, correct bugs and misbehaviors, and support the latest devices with additional drivers. Microsoft occasionally releases service packs for Windows NT Server. As of the writing of this edition, Windows NT Server version 3.51 is up to service pack 5 and Windows NT Server version 4 is up to service pack 3.

Note Windows NT Server patches and Service packs can be downloaded from Microsoft's web site:

```
ftp://ftp.microsoft.com/bussys/winnt/winnt-public/fixes/usa
```

The Windows NT diagnostic tool (in the Administrative Tools group or folder) can be used to display the current service pack level. Figure 21.10 displays the OS Version dialog box for a Windows NT Server 3.51 with service pack 4 applied. You can also view the service pack level by using the WINVER tool.

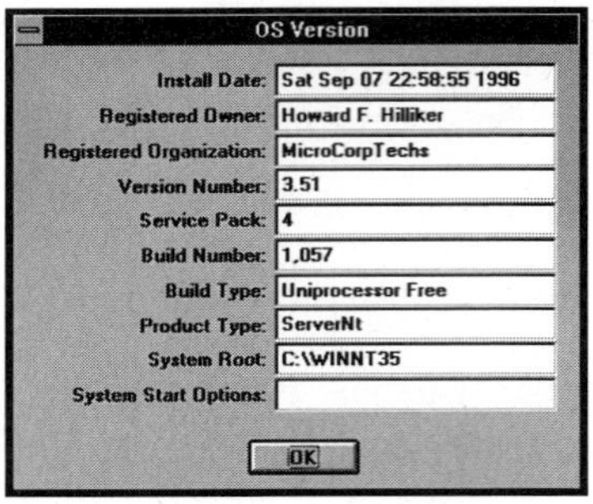

Figure 21.10
*You can verify service pack
level information using
the Windows NT
Diagnostic tool.*

Note Although Microsoft tests service packs thoroughly, you should apply them cautiously. When applying new, unproven software, you may suffer unnecessarily. So when a new service pack is released, wait a while until it has proven itself in the field before you use it on your own server. The accompanying service pack documentation specifies what issues it addresses; only apply service packs when they are urgently needed.

If services, protocols, or hardware are added to an existing NT system, the latest service pack must be reapplied.

Microsoft Windows NT Hot Fixes

Besides Service Packs, Microsoft also provides *hot fixes*, which provide solutions to specific new errors and bugs found before they are addressed by a Service Pack. In fact, some such hot fixes correct problems brought on by service packs themselves. Hot fixes often address critical issues and should be investigated often. Microsoft categorizes hot fixes as either pre-Service Pack or post-Service Pack files. As is the case for Service Packs, Microsoft does not recommend applying hot fixes unless they address a specific problem or issue that needs correcting. Also, if any protocols, services, or hardware are added to the NT computer, you must reapply the hot fix, as well. It is important to read any accompanying documentation associated with the hot fix before applying it. These hot fixes and associated documentation files are available for download from the following ftp site:

```
ftp://ftp.microsoft.com/bussys/winnt/winnt-public/fixes/usa
```

Maintaining the Latest Drivers

Many hardware manufacturers release updated or improved device drivers. Although some manufacturers will notify you when they have an update, most don't. Occasionally, check the World Wide Web site or Bulletin Board Service of the manufacturer to see if they have released a new device driver.

The installation instructions of new drivers is generally included with the update in a README.TXT or similar file.

Monitoring and Optimizing Windows NT Server Performance

Windows NT Server comes with a Performance Monitoring tool (PERFMON.EXE). Performance monitoring helps you analyze the system performance and identify bottlenecks. After you eliminate the performance bottlenecks, you have a better-optimized system.

A very important part of performance analysis is to establish a *baseline*, which is a measurement of the performance of a system under normal load and operational conditions. You use the baseline to compare the performance of the system when the system parameters are changed or under heavily loaded conditions.

By using the Performance Monitor tool, you can perform the following tasks:

- Monitor real-time performance

- Record a performance history

- Identify bottlenecks

- Identify resource usage trends

- Monitor remote computers

- Determine system capacity

- Monitor effects of system changes

- Send alerts when system parameters exceed threshold values

The Performance Monitor is started from the Administrator Tools group. Figure 21.11 shows the main Performance Monitor screen.

Note You also can use Task Manager to monitor system performance. The Task Manager's Processes tab displays the CPU time and Memory Usage of each currently running process. The Processes tab helps you identify processes that may be taxing the system. Tasks Manager's Performance tab tracks overall system performance, graphing CPU usage history and tracking parameters such as available memory and % CPU usage.

Figure 21.11

*The main Performance
Monitor screen.*

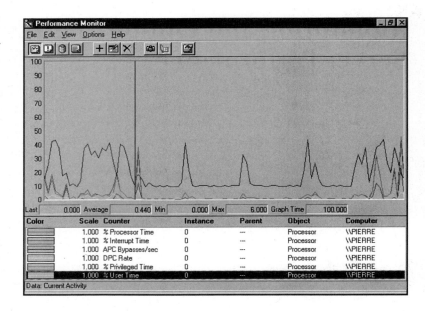

When you first start Performance Monitor, the graph appears empty. To begin monitoring
your system or network, choose **E**dit, Add to Chart, which opens the Add to Chart dialog box
(see fig. 21.12). Use the Add to Chart dialog box to select the parameters you want to monitor.

Figure 21.12

*Performance Monitor's
Add to Chart dialog box.*

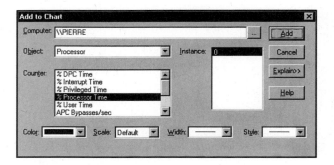

The **C**omputer field in the Add to Chart dialog box is used to specify the computer that you
want to monitor. By default, Performance Monitor monitors the local Windows NT computer.
If you want to monitor a remote computer, choose the browse button next to this field to invoke
the Select Computer dialog box, which you can use to select a computer on the network.

In Windows NT, all resources are described as *objects*. You use the O**b**ject list box in the Add to
Chart dialog box to select the Windows NT objects that can be monitored. For example, figure
21.11 shows that the Processor object is selected. For each selected object, the list of parameters

that can be monitored is displayed in the Counter list box. When you talk about a Windows NT parameter to be monitored, you qualify it with the name of the object. For example, some of the parameters that can be monitored in figure 21.11 are % Processor Time, % Interrupt Time, and so on. If you click on the **E**xplain button in the Add to Chart dialog box, you get an explanation of the parameter that you have highlighted in the Counter list. The **E**xplain button is a quick way to learn the meaning of an object parameter. Figure 21.13 shows the counter definition for the % DPC Time parameter when you enable the Explain option.

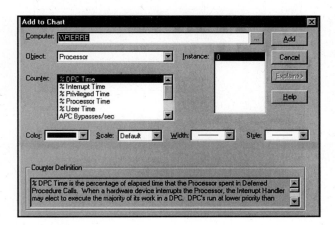

Figure 21.13

The Add to Chart dialog box with the Explain option enabled. Note the Counter Definition.

In the Colo**r**, **S**cale, **W**idth, and St**y**le fields of the Add to Chart dialog box, you can select values to control the appearance of the chart.

The **I**nstance field shows the occurrence of the activity that produces information about the selected parameter. If two processors exist, the processor object has two instances. In figures 21.12 and 21.13, the instance value is shown as 0 for the first processor.

After you select a parameter, choose the **A**dd button. You can continue adding parameters by selecting the object and its counter values. When you are finished making your selections, click on the Done button in the Add to Chart dialog box. The selected parameters are charted in real-time. Figure 21.14 shows a real-time charting of some of the processor object's parameters.

Figure 21.14

*Example real-time chart of
the Processor parameters.*

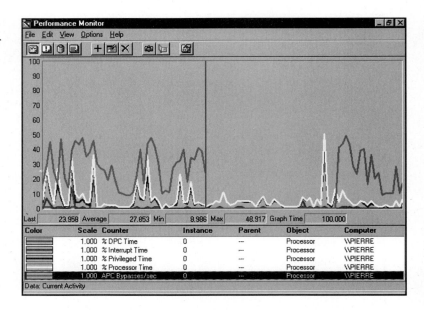

For each parameter, the real-time chart displays the Last, Average, Minimum, Maximum, and Graph Time values (refer to figure 21.14). The Last value is the value over the last second. The Average value is a running average. The Graph time is the time it takes to complete plotting a chart within the window. The Last, Average, Min, Max, and Graph Time values apply to the parameter that is selected in the parameter's list at the bottom of the main Performance Monitor window.

> **Tip** If you are monitoring several counters simultaneously, the Performance Monitors screen can become somewhat hectic and hard to read. To aide in the monitoring process, you can optionally highlight a single counter by using the Ctrl+H key combination with the desired counter selected in the listbox, located at the bottom of the Performance Monitor window.

Table 21.2 shows some of the standard object types that can be monitored using the Performance Monitor. If you have added protocol stacks (such as AppleTalk, TCP/IP, IPX, NetBEUI) and services (Services for Macintosh, WINS Server, DHCP Server), then objects for these protocols and services also can be monitored. An application may register and provide its own built-in objects and counters, which can be tracked.

Table 21.2
Windows NT Objects Monitored by Performance Monitor

Object	Usage
Browser	Use this object to monitor the browsing function on Windows NT computers, such as browser announcements, elections, requests, and so on.
Cache	Use this object to monitor the utilization of the disk cache.
LogicalDisk	Use this object to monitor a logical drive to which a letter (D:, E:, and so on) has been assigned.
Memory	Use this object to monitor memory usage and virtual memory operation in the system.
Objects	Use this object to keep track of objects in the system. Objects take up system resources, so you can use this object to identify unnecessary objects that take up additional system resources.
PagingFile	Use this object to monitor paging file activity, such as paging usage and page peak activities.
PhysicalDisk	Use this object to monitor separate physical disks that contain logical disks.
Process	Use this object to monitor processes within the system.
Processor	Use this object to monitor activity on each processor within the system.
Redirector	Use this object to monitor redirector services, such as connecting to a network resource.
Server	Use this object to monitor server processes on the system.
System	Use this object to monitor all the processors on the system as a group.
Threads	Use this object to monitor threads within the system.

> **Note** Some counters are maintained by the NT kernel and are turned off at system boot because they would hinder system performance. Both physical and logical disk performance counters are included in this grouping. To enable and disable monitoring of disk performance counters, use the following command line:
>
> ```
> DISKPERF [-Y[E] ¦ -N] [\\computername]
> ```
>
> DISKPERF -Y[E]   Instructs the system to start disk performance counters when it is restarted.
>
> E   Enables the disk performance counters used with measuring performance statistics of a physical drive in a striped disk set when the system is restarted.
>
> DISKPERF -Y   Without the E switch, this restores normal disk performance counters.
>
> DISKPERF -N   Disables disk performance counters when the system is restarted.
>
> \\computername   Indicates the name of the computer for which you want to set disk performance counter usage.

Windows NT Resource Kit Performance Monitoring Tools

The Windows NT Resource Kit, sold separately by Microsoft, contains performance-monitoring tools that can be used to augment the information in the Performance Monitor.

To install the Windows NT Resource Kit performance-monitoring tools, change to the directory containing the performance tools. If the CD-ROM drive is E: and the performance tools are in the PERFTOOL directory, type the following command to initiate the installation:

```
INSTALL E:\PERFTOOL
```

Follow the instructions on-screen to complete the installation.

Monitoring Disk Performance in Real-Time

To monitor disk performance, you must first enable the disk performance counters. Disk performance counters are disabled by Windows NT during system boot. This disabling is done by default because enabling disk performance counters decreases system performance by about 2 percent on Intel-based 486 Windows NT computers. To enable disk performance counters, execute the following command from the system prompt:

```
DISKPERF [-Y[E] ¦ -N] [\\computername]
```

Where:

> `DISKPERF -Y[E]`   Instructs the system to start disk performance counters when it is restarted.
>
> `E`   Enables the disk performance counters used with measuring performance statistics of a physical drive in a striped disk set when the system is restarted.
>
> `DISKPERF -Y`   Without the E switch, this restores normal disk performance counters.
>
> `DISKPERF -N`   Disables disk performance counters when the system is restarted.
>
> `\\computername`   Indicates the name of the computer for which you want to set disk performance counter usage.

You see a message that the disk performance counters are enabled when the system restarts. Restart the system and perform the steps outlined here:

1. Log on as an administrator user.

2. Start Performance Monitor.

3. Choose **E**dit, Add to Chart (or click on the plus sign button on the toolbar).

4. Select the Logical Disk object and the drive you want to monitor, and add the following counters:

    Logical Disk: Avg. Disk sec/transfer

    The *Avg. Disk sec/transfer* tells you the average time a disk takes to fulfill its request. A high value (greater than 0.3 seconds) indicates disk problems caused by retries or excessive fragmentation.

    Logical Disk: Disk Bytes/sec

    The *Disk Bytes/sec* indicates disk throughput. If this value is low (lower than 20 KB/sec), the disk is being accessed inefficiently.

    Logical Disk: Disk Queue Length

    The *Disk Queue Length* is the number of disk requests that are waiting in a queue to be processed. If this number is large, the disk controller/disk could be a bottleneck in system performance. You can determine the Average queue time by using the following formula:

    Avg. Queue Time = Disk Queue Length × Avg. Disk sec/transfer

5. When you have finished making your counter selections, choose Done.

You should see a real-time graph of the activity on the logical drive. If the Windows NT Server drives are actively being used—for example, by network clients—you see the graph of the counters indicating the level of the activity.

6. Exit the Performance Monitor after you finish making your observations.

7. To disable the Disk Performance counters, type the following command and restart the system:

```
diskperf -n
```

Monitoring Disk Performance Using a Log

A problem with monitoring disk performance or other system parameters in real-time is that you have to be present to monitor the activity. It is much more convenient to log the activity that you want to monitor and display the activity logs at your leisure.

The following procedures introduce you to the way in which logging can be performed for the parameters of any object you want to monitor. To make this example more concrete, the same LogicalDisk parameters that were monitored in the previous section are logged.

To monitor disk performance, you must first enable the disk performance counters. Execute the following command from the system prompt:

```
diskperf -y
```

You see a message that the disk performance counters are enabled when the system restarts. Restart the system, and perform the steps outlined next:

1. Log on as an Administrator user.

2. Start Performance Monitor.

3. Choose **O**ptions, Data **F**rom. The Data From dialog box appears (see fig. 21.15). Select **C**urrent Activity and choose OK.

Figure 21.15

The Data From dialog box.

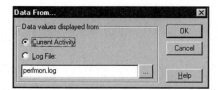

4. In the Performance Monitor, choose **V**iew, **L**og. The log screen appears. Because no objects are selected for logging, you do not see a list of objects that are being logged.

5. From the Log screen, choose **E**dit, **A**dd to Log. The Add To Log dialog box appears (see fig. 21.16).

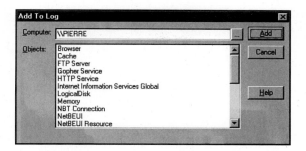

Figure 21.16
The Add To Log dialog box.

6. In the **O**bjects list, select the object from which counters will be logged and then choose OK. For monitoring the logical drive performance, select the LogicalDisk object. If you intend to monitor other objects, such as a protocol object (NetBEUI, IP, TCP, NWLINK IPX, AppleTalk, and so on) you also should add them to your log list.

   You can add multiple objects to the log by holding down the Ctrl key when you select the objects. After you finish adding objects to the log, choose the **A**dd button.

   Figure 21.17 shows examples of objects that have been added to the log.

7. Choose **O**ptions, **L**og. The Log Options dialog box appears (see fig. 21.18).

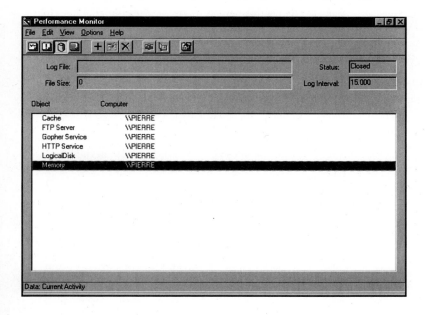

Figure 21.17
Example of objects added to the log.

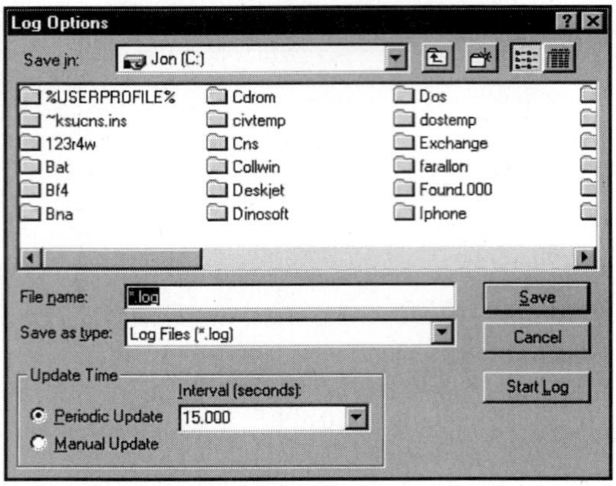

Figure 21.18

The Log Options dialog box.

8. In the Log Options dialog box, make the following changes:

   Enter the log file name in the File **n**ame box. Use the directories list box to navigate and set the directory.

   Enter the **P**eriodic Update **I**nterval value in the Update Time section. Counter values are sampled and logged at this interval. The default is 15 seconds and is designed for long term sampling. You might want to change this default to sample the counter values more frequently.

9. Choose the Start **L**og button to start logging.

   If you have selected an update interval of a few seconds, you can see that the size of the log file grows in the File Size field (refer to figure 21.17).

To stop the log and display data, perform the following:

1. From the Performance Monitor Log screen, choose **O**ptions, **L**og. Click on the Stop Log button.

2. Choose **V**iew, **C**hart. The screen looks similar to the main screen in Performance Monitor, except that you are in the log mode.

3. Choose **O**ptions, Data **F**rom.

4. In the Data From dialog box, click on the **L**og File button and use the browse button next to Log File to select the name of the log file that you created. Choose OK.

5. Choose the **A**dd button on the toolbar or choose **E**dit, **A**dd To Chart. The Add To Chart dialog box appears.

6. You can select only objects that you added to the log file from the Objects list.

7. Select the object and the counters (parameters) to monitor, and click on the **A**dd button. After you select the counters, choose the Done button.

8. If you selected the LogicalDisk object, add the following parameters:

   Logical Disk: Avg. Disk sec/transfer

   Logical Disk: Disk Bytes/sec

   Logical Disk: Disk Queue Length

Optimizing Server Settings

You can configure the Server service of a Windows NT Server for different optimization settings. Use the following as a guideline for changing the optimization settings:

1. Start the Network option in the Control Panel.

2. Click on the Services tab and select **S**erver from the Network Services list. Click on the **P**roperties button. The Server optimization dialog box appears (see fig. 21.19).

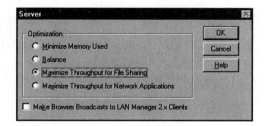

Figure 21.19

The Server optimization dialog box.

3. Choose the **M**inimize Memory Used option if you want the server to minimize its memory usage and to accept a low number of network connections (up to 10).

4. Choose the **B**alance option if you want the server to initially allocate memory for up to 64 network connections.

5. Choose the M**a**ximize Throughput for File Sharing option if you want the server to initially allocate memory for an unlimited number of connections (up to 71,000 network connections).

6. Choose the M**a**ximize Throughput for Network Applications option if you want the server to initially allocate memory for an unlimited number of connections but not set aside as much memory for cache.

Optimizing Application Tasking

By default, Windows NT Server is set up to primarily allocate resources for foreground applications. This is ideal for conducting a lot of administration on the server but impractical for systems that simultaneously run many background applications, such as on a SQL Server or NT Workstation. This default value can be modified.

To change the tasking option through Windows NT 4, follow these steps:

1. From the Control Panel, double-click on the System icon. This opens the System Properties dialog box (see fig. 21.20).

2. Choose the Performance tab.

Figure 21.20

Under Windows NT Server 4, use a slider tool to specify foreground versus background responsiveness.

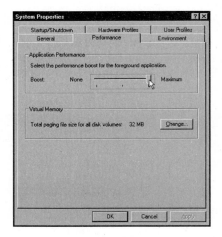

3. Slide the Application Performance sliding tool to the right for better foreground response. Move it to the left to have an equal balance of foreground and background applications.

Conclusion

In this chapter, you learned which hardware and software factors need to be taken into account in understanding performance of Windows NT Server–based networks. The Windows NT Server components that are critical to performance are the disk subsystem, network adapters and protocols, server bus characteristics, multiprocessing configuration, and operating system settings.

You can use the Performance Monitor tool to monitor the operating system settings and obtain insights into the potential cause of a performance bottleneck. The Performance Monitor tool provides a large number of objects with parameters (called *counters*) that can be monitored. You can monitor performance of local as well as remote computers in a real-time mode or log the parameter values for later display and analysis.

22

Network Monitor Performance Analysis

*I*n this chapter, you will learn about the Windows NT

Server Network Monitor tool. The Network Monitor

Tool is used to capture, filter, and analyze network

data packets, the very essence of computer networking.

By capturing these data frames and analyzing the

information, you can decipher and troubleshoot

potential network problems affecting overall network

performance.

Introduction to Network Monitor

The Windows NT Server Network Monitor tool provides you with the ability to monitor, filter, and analyze network data frames or packets transmitted and received by the local Windows NT machine. Each frame of data contains a header that encapsulates information including:

- Protocol type

- Source address

- Destination address

- Data

Note   The Network Monitor Tool packaged with WINDOWS NT Server 4 is a restricted version of the Network Monitor Tool, which is shipped with Microsoft's System Management Server. The full-featured version included in the BackOffice product can capture virtually all network frames, whereas the limited variant included with NT Server 4 can capture only local or broadcast type frames, which include the following frame types:

- Multicast frames

- Broadcast frames

- Frames transmitted by the Server

- Frames received by the Server

The Network Monitor Tool included with Windows NT Server 4 does not permit you to analyze data frames intended for other computers on the attached Windows NT Network.

When it comes to measuring network statistics, the Network Monitor tool takes over where Windows NT's Performance Monitor leaves off. Although the Performance Monitor provides you with the ability to measure the number of network frame errors, it does not provide you with the ability to analyze individual network data frames. The Network Monitor permits you to investigate intricate details of data frames, including certain types of errors, which may be affecting network traffic.

The Network Monitor includes individual modules for specific protocol frames called protocol *parsers*. There is a wealth of protocol parsers included with Network Monitor (over 60) to cover almost all of the protocols utilized in Windows NT network environments. The included protocol parsers are

AARP	LAP	SMT
ADSP	LCP	SNAP
AFP	LLC	SPX
ARP_RARP	MSRPC	TCP
ASP	NBFCP	TMAC
ATP	NBIPX	TOKENRING
BONE	NBP	UDP
BPDU	NetBIOS	XNS
BROWSER	NETLOGON	ZIP
CBCP	NFS	
CCP	NMPI	
DDP	NSP	
DHCP	NWDP	
DNS	OSPF	
ETHERNET	PAP	
FDDI	PPP	
ICMP	PPPCHAP	
IGMP	PPPPAP	
IP	RIP	
IPCP	RIPX	
IPX	SAP	
IPXCP	SMB	

The version of Network Monitor tool included with NT Server 4 utilizes NT 4's NDIS4, which captures network data with very little performance degradation in local mode. In contrast, the version of Network Monitor that ships with SMS works in promiscuous mode with the capability to monitor all network data frames.

Network Monitor Installation

The Network Monitor is an optional Windows NT tool included on the distribution CD-ROM. It is not installed during the setup process, and must be manually installed. Installing the tool copies the following items to your Windows NT machine:

- Network Monitor Tools. This option provides the Windows NT computer with the ability to analyze network frame data.

- Network Monitor Agent. This option provides the ability to have the Windows NT machine monitored by a remote Windows NT machine. The Network Monitor Agent is a proxy program that collects and forwards frame data to a specified computer (Windows NT Server running Network Monitor) for statistical analysis.

- Network Monitor Help file (Netmon.hlp)

- Network Monitor Help glossary file (Nmgloss.hlp)

If you do not currently have the Network Monitor Tool installed, you may want to install it before you dive much deeper into this chapter. To install the Network Monitor tool, follow these steps:

1. Double-click the Network icon located within the Control Panel.

2. Click the Services tab and then click Add.

3. Within the Network Services box, double-click Network Monitor Tools and Agent.

4. Supply the path for the Windows NT Server distribution CD or alternate source location and click OK.

5. Click the Close button on the Network dialog box after all the necessary files have been copied.

6. You will be prompted to restart your Windows NT machine so that the changes can take effect. Click the Yes button.

After completing the installation of the Network Monitor Tool, you should notice the following changes to your Windows NT machine:

- Monitoring Agent located in the Control Panel

- Network Monitor Tool located in the Administrative Tools

- Addition of Network Segment object in Performance Monitor

Note If you install the version of Network Monitor included with SMS, you will still need to install the Network Monitor Agent service in order to utilize the Network Monitor tool.

Network Monitor Security Configuration

By its very design, the Network Monitor Tool can be a potential security threat in that it can view virtually all network packets that are transmitted and received by the associated Windows NT Server. Any of these thousands of packets could possibly contain sensitive data that may be your responsibility to protect. The Network Monitor Tool provides two security features to help protect your Windows NT network against unauthorized usage of the Network Monitor Tool. These two security measures include:

- Password protection

- Network Monitor Tool detection

These two security measures are investigated in the following two sections.

Network Monitor Password Protection

The Network Monitor incorporates two types of password protection. One type restricts who can view captured data, and the second restricts who can capture data and view it. To restrict unauthorized users from using the Network Monitor, you can assign the following two distinct password types:

- **Display password.** Restricts users from opening and viewing previously saved frame data capture files.

- **Capture password.** Restricts users from capturing and displaying frame data on the local machine.

Note The capture password also affects access to the Network Monitor Agent from SMS.

The Network Monitor passwords are configured using the Monitoring Agent in the Control Panel. Once the initial Configure Network Monitoring Agent dialog box is displayed (see fig. 22.1), click on the Change Password button. The Network Monitoring Password Change dialog box is displayed (see fig 22.2).

Figure 22.1

The Configure Network Monitoring Agent dialog box.

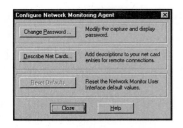

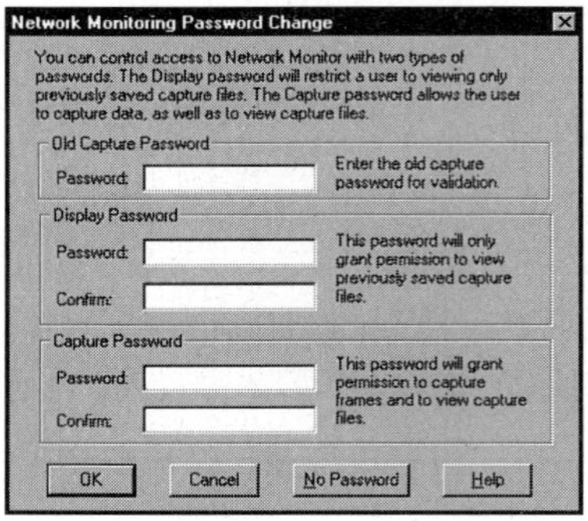

Figure 22.2

Assigning and changing Network Monitor Tool passwords.

You are presented with the following options from which to choose:

- **Old Capture Password.** This field is used to enter the current password to permit assignment of a new or replacement password in either the Display or Capture Password fields.

- **Display Password.** This field is used to assign and confirm Display Passwords.

- **Capture Password.** This field is used to assign and confirm Capture Passwords.

- **No Password.** Located at the bottom of the dialog box, this option is used to remove all passwords associated with the Network Monitor. Once selected, click the OK button to confirm.

Note   After Network Monitor installation, the default setting for the Network Monitor is no passwords. This permits any user running Network Monitor to capture and view frames. It is vital in a secure environment with sensitive data to assign passwords and change them on a regular basis as well.

Network Monitor Tool Detection

The Network Monitor Tool provides a method to detect other Network Monitor sessions running on the network (via SMS, or Windows NT Server's Network Monitor). This feature is a useful security asset because others utilizing the Network Monitor Tool have the potential to view your sensitive data frames, and you can monitor for others capturing and viewing such data.

To initiate Network Monitor detection, select the Identify Network Monitor Users option from the Tools menu of the Network Monitor Tool. If remote users are using the Network Monitor Tool, you will be able to view the following information regarding them:

- Their network card or MAC address

- Their computer name

- Their logged on user name

- Their version number of the Network Monitor Tool

- Their Network Monitor current status: running, capturing, or transmitting

As you can imagine, having this information could provide you with key security information for policing your Windows NT system against unwanted Network Monitor intrusions.

General Overview of the Network Monitor Tool

Upon launching the Network Monitor Tool, the initial screen displays a menu, toolbar, and four distinct sections, or panes, in the main area (see fig. 22.3). The important functionalities of the menu and the toolbar are covered at various points within this chapter.

Figure 22.3

The Network Monitor Tools initial screen.

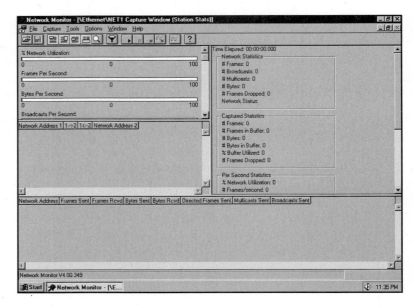

The four sections of the main window encapsulate the following information:

- **Horizontal Bar Graph pane.** Located in the upper left section of the main viewing area, the bar graph's function is to display real-time or dynamic network activity. The five graphs cover statistics, including:

  - % Network Utilization. Note that a line within this bar graph indicates the highest percentage found.

  - Frames Per Second. Number at right end of graph indicates highest computation found.

  - Bytes Per Second. Number at right end of graph indicates highest computation found.

  - Broadcasts Per Second. Number at right end of graph indicates highest computation found.

  - Multicasts Per Second. Number at right end of graph indicates highest computation found.

  The Horizontal bar graph pane can be turned on and off by clicking the Toggle Graph Pane button on the toolbar.

Note See the section "Monitoring Network Bandwidth and Capacity" later in this chapter for more information regarding how these network statistics can be utilized to analyze network issues.

■ **Session Statistics.** Located in the middle-left section of the main screen, this section displays dynamic data on sessions, which are currently active on the network. (This is restricted to the local machine with the version shipped with Windows NT Server.) The session statistics pane can be turned on and off by clicking the Toggle Total Session Pane button on the toolbar.

■ **Station Statistics.** Located in the upper-right pane of the main window, it displays cumulative data on network sessions pertaining to the local computer including:

  ■ Network address

  ■ Frames sent

  ■ Frames received

  ■ Bytes sent

  ■ Bytes received

  ■ Directed frames sent

  ■ Multicasts sent

  ■ Broadcasts sent

The station statistics pane can be turned on and off by clicking the Toggle Total Station Statistics Pane button on the toolbar.

■ **Total Statistics.** Located in the upper-right pane of the main window, it displays cumulative data on network statistics in the following five areas:

  ■ Network statistics

  ■ Captured statistics

  ■ Per second statistics

  ■ Network card (MAC) statistics

  ■ Network card (MAC) error statistics

The Total statistics pane can be turned on and off by clicking the Toggle Total Statistics Pane button on the toolbar.

Each of these individual panes can be given exclusive focus and zoomed upon by selecting the desired pane, and clicking on the Zoom Pane button on the toolbar.

Network Interface Card Description

The Monitoring Agent can be modified to give a comprehensive description of any associated network cards under its control. This proves useful under circumstances where one computer will monitor another. The Monitoring Agent provides an easily identifiable description of the computer's network interface card.

To describe a network interface card, look at figure 22.4 and follow these steps:

Figure 22.4

Network Interface Card description.

1. Launch the Monitoring Agent located in the Control Panel and click on the Describe Net Cards button.

2. When the Describe Net Cards dialog box is displayed, highlight the desired network adapter and click on Edit Description.

3. When the Change Net Card Description dialog box displays, simply enter a new logical and easy to understand description such as Server KEYSTONE1, NICA and click OK.

You can optionally repeat the last step for any additional network interface cards you wish to describe.

Capturing Network Frames

Capturing data frames is accomplished utilizing the Capture menu. The following data capture options are available from the Capture menu:

■ Start

■ Stop

■ Stop and View

■ Pause

■ Continue

These capture options can also be controlled using the VCR-style controls located on the toolbar.

While a network capture is taking place, all data frames that the Windows NT Server transmits and receives are stored in the server's memory buffer. The amount of frame data stored in the memory buffer is restricted by how much system memory is available. The default setting is a maximum amount of system memory minus 8 MB. This setting can be tuned at your discretion by using the Buffer Settings command from the Capture menu (see fig. 22.5). The capture buffer is stored in memory, not on the disk drive. It is possible for the Network Monitor to use virtual memory for a capture buffer, but this is not advisable because critical frames may be lost. Try to keep the size of the buffer optimal by not being too small, thus preventing swapping to virtual memory, and not too large so as to affect other Windows NT Server services, and so on. After the buffer is filled, old data is erased to make room for new data. If buffer size is critical for a capture session, you may want to stop as many applications as possible during the session to free up more buffer space.

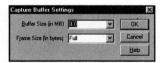

Figure 22.5

Setting the capture buffer size.

The second setting in the Capture Buffer Settings dialog box provides the means to designate Frame Size (in bytes). This can be useful if you only want to capture the header of the frames, rather than the default setting of Full, or the entire packet. The buffer size can be especially critical on huge or busy networks where the buffer could fill up extremely quickly by restricting the amount of data that is captured. The smallest size you can designate is 64 bytes.

Figure 22.6 displays the Network Monitor during an active data capture session. Note how dynamic data is automatically updated in the four different panes. Also take notice how the bar graphs maximum values peak.

Figure 22.6

An active Network Monitor capture session.

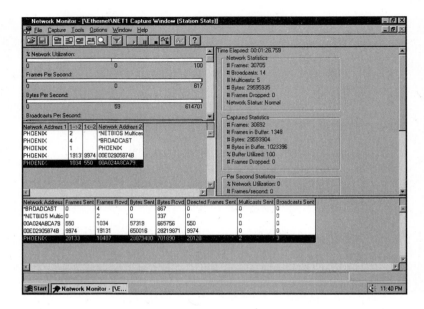

Saving Captured Data

After you have stopped capturing data, you can save it to a file archive for historical analysis purposes. This is accomplished simply by choosing File, Save As. The files are saved with an extension of CAP. For easier administration, it is recommended that you utilize a logical naming system when saving these archives. For instance, using the date in the name, such as 10NOV97.CAP, will help in determining the file's place in the historical record, rather than relying on the date stamp attribute, which can change. The default location for these archive files is

`\%SYSTEMROOT%\SYSTME32\NETMON\CAPTURES`

Creating an Address Database

By default, the Network Monitor utilizes physical network addresses (MAC) for identification purposes. However, the Network Monitor Tool incorporates a method by which Windows NT administrators can optionally identify computers by their more traditional NetBIOS names. To use NetBIOS names, the Network Monitor needs to build an address database.

Building the NetBIOS name database is accomplished by collecting captured data for an extensive time period. As frames are captured, computers are added to both the Session Statistics and the Station Statistics panes. After capturing the large volume of data, stop the capturing process and choose the Find All Names option from the Capture menu. An automatic process begins in which the capture memory buffer is queried, and any names found are added to the address database. The address database is saved in a file entitled DEFAULT.ADR.

Note Using the Find All Names option only adds entries for computers, which are active on the network during the capture session and have participated in NetBIOS traffic. Thus, any computers that are not powered up or are not generating any network traffic will not be included in the listing.

With the address database built, all future capture sessions will have computers identified by their NetBIOS name. In order to keep the address database current and to add any computers that were not active on the network during the capture session, you should occasionally run the Find All Names option after capturing frames.

At any time, you can investigate the current listing of NetBIOS names stored in the address database by choosing the Addresses option from the Capture menu. The listings displayed in the Address Database may have several entries with identical names because it stores entries for dissimilar protocols and network types. The Address Database dialog box provides you with the ability to add, edit, and delete individual entries. It will also load and save the database to a file with a default extension of ADR, as desired.

Choosing a Network to Monitor

The Network Monitor Tool is capable of monitoring only a single network. However, if the Network Monitor Tool is attached to two or more networks via multiple network adapter cards, you can still choose which network you want to monitor. To select which network to monitor, choose the Networks option in the Capture menu. The Select Capture Network dialog box displays from which you may select a network adapter and click on the Connect button.

If your system has enough system resources at its disposal, you could optionally run multiple instances of the Network Monitor Tool.

The network that the Network Monitor Tool will monitor is signified by the term CON-NECTED under the Connect State header (see fig. 22.7).

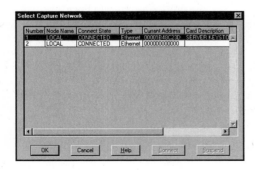

Figure 22.7

Choosing a network to monitor.

Dedicated Capture Mode

The dedicated capture mode option provides a method of capturing dynamic data without having to update all the dynamic data panes. Otherwise, a large amount of the computer's processing time is spent updating the various panes in the Network Monitor. Keep in mind that if the server's CPU is too busy, there is the potential for losing some frames.

To activate the dedicated capture mode, choose the Dedicated Capture Mode option from the Capture menu. With dedicated capture mode activated, the Dedicated Mode dialog box will display when capturing data. As you can see in figure 22.8, the dedicated capture mode only updates the Total Frames Captured counter as opposed to having to update all of the various dynamic fields and gauges it normally does.

Figure 22.8

*The Dedicated Capture
Mode dialog box.*

Capture Filters

Another method that economizes buffer space is the utilization of capture filters. On busy or large networks, the amount of frames involved can be enormous. Capture filters provide you with the means to focus on specific kinds of frames from a specified grouping of protocols and computers.

Performance statistics are not affected by any capture filter settings. Capture filters only specify what frames are stored in the capture buffer.

Filter Types

The filters included with the Network Monitor Tool provide different types of filtering capability. The Network Monitor provides three types of filters:

- SAP/ETYPE filters

- Address Filters

- Data Pattern Filters

To activate capture filters, choose the Filter option from the Capture menu or press F8 and follow any specific instructions in the following sections.

SAP/ETYPE Filters

The SAP (service access points) and ETYPE (EtherTypes) filters are associated with upper-layer protocols and identified by hexadecimal numbers. The default setting is to capture all protocol types. However, protocols can be filtered by entering the hexadecimal value for any SAPs and ETYPEs that you do not want captured.

To create a SAP/ETYPE capture filter, highlight the SAP/ETYPE= line located in the Capture Filter dialog box and choose Line in the Edit section. This will display the Capture Filter SAPs and ETYPEs dialog box (see fig. 22.9). The Network Monitor will only capture packets included in the Enabled Protocols list.

Note If you take a close look at the Capture Filter SAPs and ETYPEs dialog box, you will see that the Hexadecimal values are indicated under the Values header. For instance, IP has an ETYPE of x800.

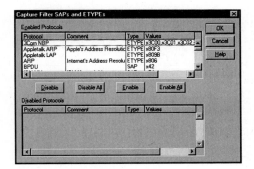

Figure 22.9
SAP/ETYPE filtering.

To disable a protocol, highlight the desired protocol and click on the Disable button. You can also choose to disable all protocols by clicking the Disable All button.

Address Filters

Address filters capture frames from specified computers on your network. Specify one or more address pairs in a capture filter. You can monitor up to four specific address pairs simultaneously.

Address pairs are comprised of

■ The unique hexadecimal addresses of the two computers between which network traffic monitoring will occur.

■ A direction arrow (<->, ->, or <-), which indicates the direction(s) of traffic to be monitored.

■ The INCLUDE and EXCLUDE keywords, which indicate how Network Monitor will respond to a frame that meets a filter's specifications.

No matter how the statement sequence appears in the Capture Filter dialog box, EXCLUDE statements are evaluated first. Because of this, when filters that have both an EXCLUDE and INCLUDE statement and the frame meets the criteria specified by the EXCLUDE statement, that frame is discarded.

Address pairs are created and edited by using the Address Expression dialog box (see fig. 22.10).

Figure 22.10

Assigning Address Pair filtering.

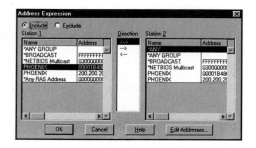

To edit or create address pairs conduct the following applicable step:

■ **Edit address pairs.** Highlight the line under (Address Pairs) in the Capture Filter dialog box and click on the Line button in the Edit section.

■ **Create address pairs.** Choose any available line in the (Address Pairs) section in the Filter dialog box and click on the Address button in the Add section.

As an example, to capture all the traffic from KEYSTONE1 and KEYSTONE2, and ignore all traffic between KEYSTONE1 and KEYSTONE3 you would utilize the following filter:

INCLUDE KEYSTONE1<-> KEYSTONE2

EXCLUDE KEYSTONE1 <-> KEYSTONE3

Data Pattern Filtering

In unique situations, you may have the need to filter frames by a specific inclusion or exclusion of a series of bytes. Specifying a pattern match in a capture filter provides the following:

■ Specify a pattern mask to capture only those frames containing a specified pattern of ASCII or hexadecimal data.

■ Indicate an offset of how many bytes into the packet that the mask match must occur.

When filtering based on a pattern match, you have to indicate where you want the pattern to occur in the frame by indicating the number of bytes from the beginning of the frame. If your network medium has a variable size in the media access control (MAC) protocol, such as Ethernet and Token Ring, choose the From End of Topology Header option.

To add a pattern filter, choose the (Pattern Matches) line from the Capture Filter dialog box and click the Pattern button in the Add section. The Pattern Match dialog box appears, as shown in figure 22.11.

Figure 22.11

The Pattern match filter dialog box.

Using Capture Triggers

As you might suspect, a capture trigger captures an action that occurs when a set of conditions are met. As an example, prior to utilizing the Network Monitor Tool to capture frame data, you may decide to set up a trigger to stop the capture. You can specify conditions under which triggers will happen.

The Network Monitor Tool provides the following trigger-types to specify the conditions that cause a trigger to occur:

- **Nothing.** Default setting, no triggers.

- **Pattern Match.** Causes a trigger when a pattern mask is located within a captured frame.

- **Buffer Space.** Causes a trigger to occur should the buffer space reach a specified setting of 25, 50, 75, or 100 percent.

- **Pattern Match then Buffer Space.** Causes a trigger to occur when both the Pattern Match and Buffer Space settings are true in that order.

- **Buffer Space then Pattern Match.** Causes a trigger to occur when both the Buffer Space and Pattern Match are true in that order.

Once the conditions are correct to cause a trigger to occur, there are three events that can take place, which are specified in the Trigger Action section of the Capture Trigger dialog box (see fig. 22.12). These three actions are:

- **No Action.** Nothing occurs after a trigger.

- **Stop Capture.** Halts the capturing process.

- **Execute Command Line.** Execute the command indicated by the path and executable file.

Figure 22.12

Configuring a capture trigger with the Capture Trigger dialog box.

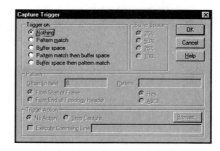

Analyzing Captured Data

The Network Monitor Tool provides you with the ability to investigate minute parts of the individual data frames. There are two methods by which you can examine captured frames, both of which are reflected in figure 22.13:

■ To analyze frames while capturing is active, either click the Stop and View Capture button on the toolbar, choose the Stop and View option from the Capture menu, or press the Shift+F11 key combination.

■ To analyze frames that have been captured, choose the Display Captured Data option from the Capture menu or press F12.

Figure 22.13

Frames currently held in the capture buffer.

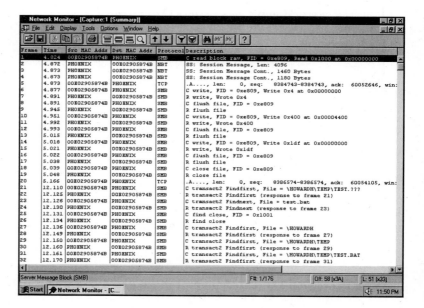

After the frames are displayed, you can analyze a specific frame of data, by simply double-clicking it (see fig. 22.14).

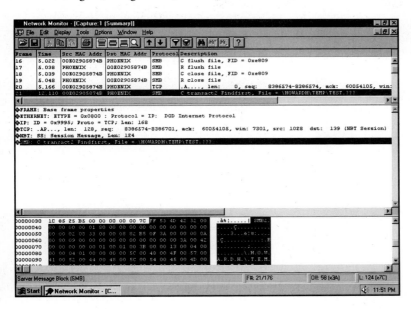

Figure 22.14

Analyzing a single frame of data.

When examining a single frame, you are presented with three panes including:

- **Summary Pane.** A simple single line summary of each frame in the capture buffer. The summary pane contains the following information:

    - The Frame field contains an incremental value assigned to the individual data frames.

    - The Time field contains a time stamp at which the data frame was captured.

    - The source and destination computers are indicated by the Src MAC Addr and Dst Mac Addr address fields. If the name database is established, NetBIOS names will be displayed, otherwise, hexadecimal physical address values will be displayed.

    - The Protocol field specifies the protocol type associated with the frame.

    - The Description filed contains details pertaining to the protocols being examined.

- **Detail Pane.** Frame contents are displayed, arranged by protocol layer.

- **Hex Pane.** Displays data in hexadecimal and ASCII characters, which is associated with the protocol that is currently selected in the Detail Pane.

Creating a Display Filter

When designing a display filter (see fig. 22.15), you have to supply decision statements in the Display Filter dialog box. The information presented by the Display Filter dialog box is in a decision tree format, presenting the filter's logic in a graphic representation. When any changes are made to display filter settings, the GUI decision tree displays the changes.

Figure 22.15

The display filters decision tree.

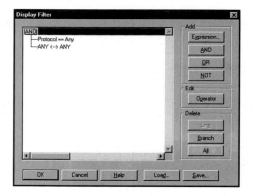

The following three display filter options are available:

- **Protocol.** Use protocol lines to specify the desired protocols or protocol properties.

- **Address Filter.** Use address filter lines to specify the computer addresses on which you want to capture data.

- **Property.** Use this to specify property instances that match your display criterion.

You can only add a single decision statement at a time. You have to click the OK button to save the added decision statement before attempting to add another statement or it will be lost.

Monitoring Network Bandwidth and Capacity

When the Network Monitor tool is launched, it displays four individual panes. The upper-left horizontal bar graph and upper-right Session statistics panes provide real-time network information. These statistics can be of assistance when investigating bandwidth or other network issues. The following list highlights some of these abilities:

- **Frames Per Second status bar.** Aides in determining bandwidth issues.

- **Bytes Per Second status bar.** Also aides in determining bandwidth issues.

- **% Network Utilization status bar.** Aides you in determining how much network capacity is being utilized.

- **# Frames Dropped field.** Specifies how many frames are not processed due to network adapter buffer overflow.

Conclusion

In this chapter, you were given an overview of Microsoft's Windows NT Server Network Monitor tool. This powerful tool provides you with the means to capture and analyze network packets. The chapter covered Network Monitor specifics including security, capturing, filtering, and using data frames.

This chapter also brought to your attention that the Network Monitor Tool packaged with Windows NT Server 4 is a limited variant of that which is included with Microsoft's BackOffice SMS product.

Migration from Windows NT 3.5x

igrating from Windows NT 3.5x to 4 is surprisingly simple. True to Microsoft's reputation, the installation program is intuitive, organized, and provides few opportunities for error. The new installer borrows many interface features and installation steps from its cousin, Windows 95—users who know how to install Windows 95 should feel right at home.

This chapter discusses important issues concerning the Windows NT migration and several new features of the OS, and takes the reader through a step-by-step Windows NT upgrade.

Important Issues before You Begin

This section discusses pertinent issues related to preparing for the Windows NT 4 upgrade. Read through these carefully; one overlooked caveat may turn a smooth upgrade into a problem-filled experience.

Although the opportunity for error is quite small, unforeseen problems can still occur. To prevent the possibility of permanent damage, you must back up all data before you begin. The few short minutes spent backing up your system are well spent.

In addition, do not forget to read the Microsoft NT 4 release notes before you begin. These notes provide the latest, most up-to-date issues about NT 4 (again, a good investment of time).

Pre-Installation Requirements

You need to meet the following requirements before the Windows NT 4 Setup program can begin. If you haven't met these prerequisites, the Windows NT installer alerts you of the shortcoming and quits:

- A local hard disk must be present.

- The destination volume must not be part of a stripe, mirror, or volume set.

- The destination or temporary volume(s) must not be formatted using HPFS. Windows NT 4 no longer supports HPFS formatted volumes.

- The destination volume must have at least 104 MB of disk space available.

After you meet these criteria, the Windows NT 4 Setup program can begin; it guides you through the installation. If space restrictions prevent Setup from beginning, examine the possibilities of performing a *floppyless* installation and using the /T switch to assign an alternative temporary volume. By default, Windows NT 4 Setup uses the destination volume also as the temporary volume; defining a different temporary volume may solve the disk space availability problem. Refer to the section called "A Bit about WINNT32," later in this chapter, for additional information.

HPFS Support Issues

Beginning with Windows NT 4's release, Microsoft has stopped supporting the HPFS file system. HPFS (High Performance File System) is the native file system found in the IBM OS/2 product.

If HPFS volumes are present, and Windows NT 4 must access data on those volumes, you can use a conversion utility (named Convert.exe) to change HPFS to NTFS. You can find the Convert.exe program on the *Windows NT 3.51* installation media (CD-ROM or floppy).

> **Note** The Convert.exe program included in the Windows NT 4 distribution doesn't support conversion of HPFS volumes.

Note also that the Convert.exe application works only on HPFS version 1.*x* volumes smaller than 4 GB in size. You cannot use Convert.exe to convert HPFS version 2.*x* volumes or version 1.*x* volumes larger than 4 GB. If a version 2.*x* volume or a version 1.*x* volume larger than 4 GB exists, you must use an alternative method.

> **Warning** Don't try to convert any volume to which any OS/2 user or application must have access; after conversion, OS/2 cannot access the volume—it will be NTFS format.

If the system meets the previous criteria, forcing you to use an alternative conversion method, the most straightforward solution consists of backing up all data present on the volume and using the following syntax to reformat it:

```
format <drive letter> /fs:ntfs
```

> **Note** Formatting destroys all data present on the volume. Make sure that all data has been safely archived.

New Shell Update

The shell technology preview that Microsoft released in 1995 gave many Windows NT 3.51 users a chance to sample the Windows 95 interface while running Windows NT. The shell preview addition contains nuances and incompatibilities with certain applications—Windows NT 4 included. You must remove the shell technology preview before you upgrade to Windows NT 4.

To remove the new shell technology preview, run the application Shupdate.cmd /u from the directory that corresponds to your hardware platform (MIPS, Alpha, or X86). For X86 platforms, for example, you would use this command:

```
\newshell\I386\shupdate.cmd /u
```

After you successfully complete the Windows NT 4 upgrade, you can restore the desktop and Start menu settings present during the new shell technology preview. Doing so gives you the same custom settings that existed before the upgrade.

At a command prompt, type the following commands:

```
xcopy "%systemroot%\Start Menu" "%USERPROFILE%\Start Menu" /ec
xcopy "%systemroot%\Desktop" "%USERPROFILE%\Desktop" /ec
xcopy "%systemroot%\Recent" "%USERPROFILE%\Recent" /ec
```

Uninterruptible Power Supplies

Most UPS devices communicate with servers via a serial port connection. This enables the server to sense when the UPS is experiencing a power-related problem. It also provides the server the opportunity to intervene and avoid the potential data that a power failure can cause. The Windows NT 4 installer automatically attempts to detect devices connected to a system's serial ports (modems and printers, for example). Consequently, all UPS devices must be powered down and disconnected before beginning the Windows NT 4 upgrade. Failing to remove a UPS device can cause problems with the device and/or the Windows NT 4 installation process.

Windows NT Driver Location Changes

Beginning with Windows NT 4, certain mass storage device drivers have been moved from the installation directory (\I386, \MIPS, or \Alpha, depending on the hardware type) to the Windows NT driver library directory (\DRVLIB). This change might or might not affect your upgrade to Windows NT 4.

Before performing the Windows NT upgrade, record the name of all SCSI adapters currently loaded under Windows NT 3.5*x* (an important step). To obtain this list, perform the following steps:

1. Open the Windows NT Setup application found in the Main program group.

2. Choose **O**ptions, Add Remove **S**CSI Adapters, as shown in figure 23.1.

Figure 23.1

The Windows NT Setup Options menu.

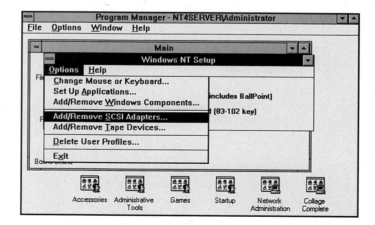

3. Record the list of installed SCSI adapters (see fig. 23.2), and keep it handy for reference during the upgrade.

The effects of this change depend on the mass storage devices currently installed on your system. During the Windows NT 3.5*x* Setup, a set of device drivers automatically load and are used to detect whether the particular driver is needed. This, in effect, enables Windows NT 3.5*x* to automatically detect the mass storage devices resident in your system. In Windows NT 4 Setup, the removal of certain drivers that were part of the Windows NT 3.5*x* installation process becomes an issue only if one of the moved drivers is necessary to run a device in the current system. If you don't currently use the devices in the following list when running Windows NT 3.5*x*, you probably won't need them in NT 4; this section should not apply. If one of the following devices is installed, however, please read the following paragraphs carefully.

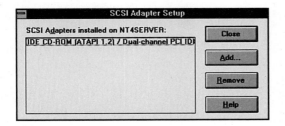

Figure 23.2
Choosing the Add/Remove SCSI Adapters option opens a dialog box that contains a list of installed SCSI adapters.

Devices whose drivers are no longer part of Windows NT Setup:

- Always IN-2000 (always.sys)

- Data Technology Corp. 3290 (dtc329x.sys)

- Maynard 16-bit SCSI Adapter (wd33c93.sys)

- Media Vision Pro Audio Spectrum (tmv1.sys)

- Trantor T-128 (t128.sys)

- Trantor T-130B (t13b.sys)

- Ultrastor 124f EISA Disk Array Controller (ultra124.sys)

If the current system contains an adapter that appears in the preceding list, a driver disk must be created prior to initiating the Windows NT 4 upgrade. You can then use this driver disk to install the necessary driver during the Windows NT 4 installation, or afterwards by adding the driver manually.

Retired Drivers Disk Creation

The procedure to create a driver disk is quite simple:

1. Prepare a blank, formatted 3½-inch disk.

2. Copy all files from \drvlib\storage\retired\<*processor*>, where <*processor*> corresponds to the type of CPU used in the server you're upgrading (MIPS, I386, or Alpha).

If you don't need the mass storage device that appears in the bulleted list of device drivers here to install Windows NT, the easiest method may be to completely skip adding the driver during installation—just add it manually after the installation, reducing the chance for error during the installation.

Windows NT Setup also might detect the mass storage device in the system, but not load the necessary driver because it has been moved to the retired directory. This is the trickiest scenario, and the next section addresses it.

Driver Installation Methods during Windows NT 4 Setup

The following three scenarios provide the means for you to install the relocated driver. Select the method that best suits your system's configuration.

Installing a Driver for a Mass Storage Device That Was Not Detected during Windows NT 4 Setup

Use this method if Windows NT 4 Setup does not detect the necessary mass storage device. You need the driver disk at this point.

1. During Setup, at the point at which NT Setup states, `Setup has recognized the following mass storage devices in your computer`, press **S** to specify additional adapters.

2. Select Other from the bottom of the list.

3. Insert the driver disk when prompted to do so, and select your host adapter from the resulting list.

Windows NT Setup now can recognize all devices connected to the adapter.

Installing a Driver When Setup Recognizes One of the Drivers without Making It Available for Use

Should you encounter the situation described in the section heading, you need to interrupt Windows NT 4 Setup to prevent it from making an initial mass storage device query. Therefore, you must restart Windows NT 4 Setup. Perform the following steps to initiate this process:

1. Restart Windows NT 4 Setup.

2. When prompted `Setup is inspecting your computer's hardware configuration`, press the F6 key.

3. When Setup prompts `Setup could not determine the type of one or more mass storage devices installed in your system, or you have chosen to manually specify an adapter`, type **S** to display a list of supported mass storage adapters.

4. Select Other from the bottom of the list.

5. Insert the previously created driver disk as prompted, then select the appropriate driver from the resulting list.

Windows NT Setup now recognizes all devices connected to this adapter.

Installing the Drivers after Performing the NT 4 Upgrade

If your mass storage device is not necessary to complete the NT 4 upgrade, you may delay installation until after the system upgrade completes.

1. After NT 4 is successfully up and running, open the Control Panel from the Start Menu.

2. In the Control Panel, open the SCSI Adapters applet (see fig. 23.3).

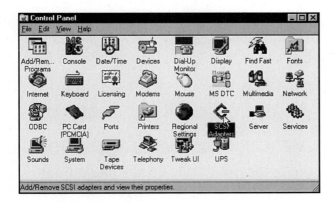

Figure 23.3
The SCSI Adapters icon in the Control Panel.

3. In the SCSI Adapters applet, select the Drivers tab (see fig 23.4), which displays a list of currently installed drivers.

4. Click on the **A**dd button. A list of mass storage device drivers appears (see fig. 23.5).

5. Choose the **H**ave Disk button, which opens the Install From Disk dialog box (see fig. 23.6).

6. Insert the driver disk in drive A, and then click on OK.

7. A list of drivers should appear (see fig. 23.7). Select the appropriate driver and click on OK.

Figure 23.4
*The SCSI Adapters
Drivers tab.*

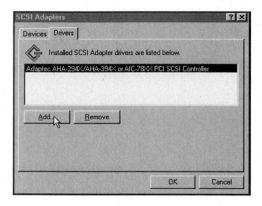

Figure 23.5
*The Install Driver dialog
box, listing mass storage
device drivers.*

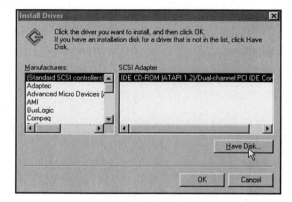

Figure 23.6
*The Install From Disk
dialog box.*

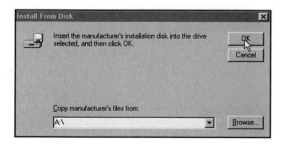

The appropriate driver loads, and Windows NT 4 should recognize the mass storage device.

Other Issues Involving Mass Storage Devices

Several other matters concerning mass storage devices warrant discussion, including IDE controllers, multiple CD-ROMs, ATDISK driver failure, and compressed volumes. The following sections attend to these issues.

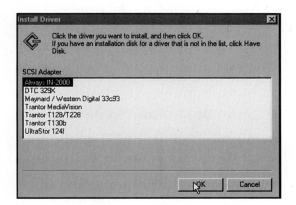

Figure 23.7

Choose the driver you want to install, then click on OK.

IDE Controllers

Computers that utilize a PCI bus-based IDE controller may display inappropriate devices in the Windows NT 4 SCSI Adapters applet found in the Control Panel. The applet displays either some or all of the IDE devices located in the computer. This behavior does not adversely affect the performance or reliability of the system.

Multiple CD-ROMs

If the computer you're upgrading contains multiple CD-ROM drives, Microsoft recommends placing the Windows NT 4 CD-ROM in the CD-ROM drive with the highest priority on the computer.

ATDISK Driver Failure

After completing the Windows NT 4 upgrade, some users of IDE-based mass storage devices may encounter the infamous `At least one service or driver failed during system startup` warning box (see fig. 23.8) when restarting Windows NT 4. The warning also suggests to use the Event Viewer to check the event log for further information.

ATDISK driver failure is a common occurrence, but you can easily eliminate it by performing the following procedure (essentially, you disable the device that causes the error).

Note Anytime you alter the Windows NT 4 setup, you should exercise extreme caution. Incorrectly modifying Windows NT 4 Setup can cause severe problems. Make absolutely certain that ATDISK really is the device that failed before you start tinkering.

1. Check the Event Viewer (see figs. 23.9 and 23.10) to determine that the ATDISK driver actually is the driver that failed. If it isn't the responsible driver or service, troubleshoot as necessary. If the ATDISK driver did fail, proceed to step two.

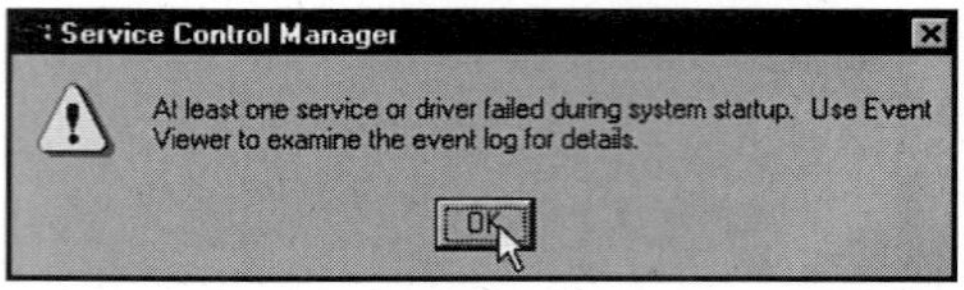

Figure 23.8

The warning box informing users of service or driver failure during startup.

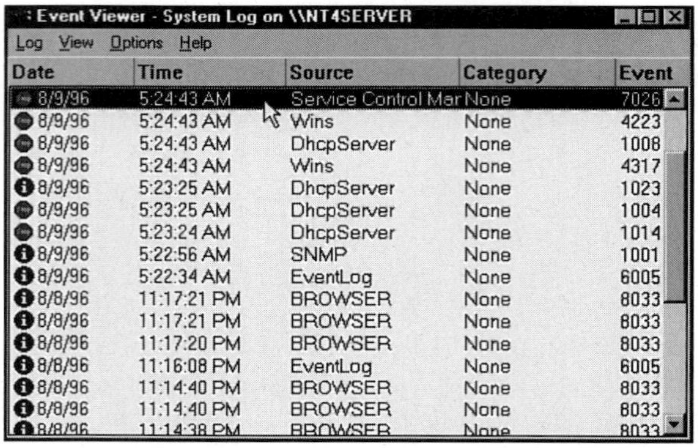

Figure 23.9

The Event Viewer, opening screen.

Figure 23.10

Using the Event Viewer enables you to check the event log for an ATDISK driver failure.

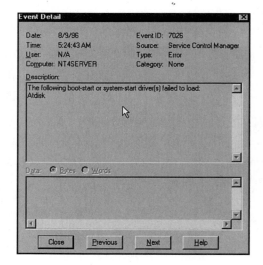

2. In the Control Panel, choose the Devices applet. Scroll to the ATDISK Driver and click on the Startup button.

3. The dialog box that appears furnishes a list of startup options. Choose the **D**isabled button and then click on OK.

4. Click on OK to confirm the action being performed.

5. Restart Windows NT.

The next time Windows NT initializes, the error should not occur because you have disabled the offending device.

Compressed Volumes

If a volume on the system is compressed and the volume must be used as the installation volume or as the temporary volume, you need to decompress it before you install Windows NT 4. The Windows NT 4 Setup program is incompatible with compressed volumes. To alleviate this problem, decompress the volume in question before the installation phase (while operating Windows NT 3.5*x*). After the Windows NT 4 installation completes, you can safely recompress the volume.

Note Windows NT native data compression is available only on NTFS partitions. Windows NT cannot access volumes that are compressed using Windows 95's Drivespace utility. If Windows NT 4 users or resources need to access a "Drivespaced" volume, it must be decompressed before initiating the Windows NT 4 upgrade.

Special Issues for RISC-Based Systems

Before you upgrade a Digital Equipment Corporation Alpha system to Windows NT 4, ensure the presence of the minimum required firmware revision. Use the following simple evaluation to make this determination.

If Windows NT 3.51 is currently installed, the firmware revision supports Windows NT 4. If the system is currently running Windows NT 3.5*x*, you might need to update to the most recent firmware revision.

Tip You still should upgrade to the latest firmware revision to take advantage of any improvements Digital Equipment Corporation has made. Doing so is relatively easy and could well provide significant benefits.

WINS, DHCP, and RPL Database Issues

Windows NT 4 implements a faster and more robust database format to store WINS, DHCP, and RPL information. This new self-compacting format performs better than its predecessor. If the system currently employs the WINS, DHCP, or RPL services, you need to convert the databases storing information for these services before Windows NT 4 can use them. Fortunately, the necessary conversion takes place automatically during the Windows NT 4 upgrade, but important preliminary issues should be addressed to guard against any possible problems.

1. Ensure the availability of the necessary free disk space to complete the conversion. The conversion process requires approximately the same amount of disk space as the existing database(s) and log files currently use.

> **Tip**
>
> If the amount of required free disk space only *almost* equals the amount of currently available free disk space, take the following advice to heart: Make room!
>
> Several *normal* system operations could use up the remaining free disk space and bring your system to a grinding halt. A pagefile increase, DHCP database or log file increase, or a variety of other system actions, could cause significant problems. Pay heed to these computer age-old words of wisdom: It is always better to err and have more room than you need, than to not have enough.

2. Before you initiate the upgrade, ensure that the existing database(s) have been brought to a consistent state. Stop the services by using the Control Panel Services applet or the NET STOP *<service>* command.

More about the Conversion

As mentioned before, Windows NT 4 initiates the conversion process automatically after a successful system upgrade (during the next initialization). The database modification can take anywhere from one minute to one hour depending on the size of the existing database(s). After the database(s) have been converted to the new jet 500 format, it cannot be converted back; the converted database(s) will not be compatible with Windows NT 3.51 or earlier versions. The new database(s) uses log files that have the prefix J50.

Figure 23.11 shows the message box you get the first time you start Windows NT 4 after the upgrade.

Figure 23.11
Let the DHCP terminate for clean conversion purposes.

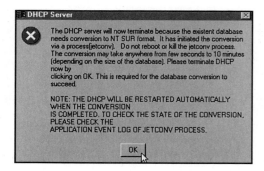

Check the conversion process's progress by using the Event Viewer, which contains a notification in the system event log of whether the database conversion was a success or failure (see fig. 23.12).

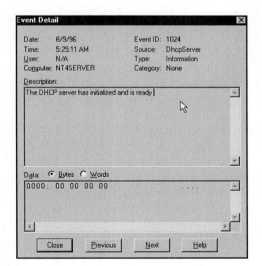

Figure 23.12
*The Event Viewer lets you
check on the success or
failure of the database
conversion.*

Manual Database Conversion

If the conversion fails for some reason, you can convert the database(s) manually. You can find the manual conversion utility, Upg351db.exe, in the <winntdir>\system32\ directory.

The conversion process stores a copy of the original database(s) and log files in the subdirectory named 351db, which you can find in the same directory as you find the other database files. You use the following syntax to execute Upg351db.exe:

```
upg351db [<db>] /e<Type> [/d<dll>] [/y<sysdb>] [/l<LogPath>] [options]
```

The following describes the available parameters and options for Upg351db.exe.

Parameters

- **<db>.** Name of database to convert

- **<Type>.** 1 = Dhcp, 2 = Wins, 3 = RPL

- **<dll>.** Pathed name of 200-series DLL

- **<sysdb>.** Pathed name of 200-series system database

- **<LogPath>.** Path of the old log files

Options

- ■ **/b<db>.** Path of the backup database; use if the main database is not in consistent state

- ■ **/i.** Dump conversion stats to UPGDINFO.TXT

- ■ **/p<dir>.** Preserve the database files in this directory

- ■ **/r.** Remove the backup database at the end of conversion

Examples

To perform a conversion of the WINS database by using default parameters:

```
upg351 <db> /e2
```

To perform a conversion of the DHCP database by using default parameters:

```
upg351 <db> /e1
```

Upgrade the RPL database (locations included in example):

```
upg351db c:\winnt35\system32\dhcp\dhcp.mdb /e1 /dc:\winnt35\system32\jet.dll /
➥yc:\winnt35\system32\dhcp\system.mdb /lc:\winnt35\system32\dhcp\ /pc:\temp
```

Microsoft Mail Client Replacement

The Microsoft Exchange Client replaces the Mail Client Application that comes bundled with Windows NT 3.5*x*. After the NT upgrade, the Mail Client 3.5*x* no longer functions, but Microsoft Exchange is available for sending and receiving mail.

Introducing the NDS-Aware/Gateway Service for NetWare

The new Gateway Service for NetWare included in Windows NT 4 now supports NetWare 4.*x* servers that run NetWare Directory Services (NDS). By using NDS, shared NetWare resources organize in a hierarchical tree fashion.

If the Windows NT 3.5*x* server you're upgrading currently has the Gateway Service installed, Gateway automatically installs the NDS-Aware version during the upgrade to Windows NT 4. After the upgrade completes, you have an opportunity to change your existing non-NDS preferred server connection, or select a new tree and context.

Tip	Before performing the upgrade, be certain to remove any third-party network service or client software.

Windows NT 4 Installation Procedure

If you prepare properly, upgrading to Windows NT 4 is easy. Several ways enable you to initiate Windows NT 4 Setup, both from a non-Windows NT operating system or directly from Windows NT 3.5*x*. Because this chapter discusses upgrading from a previous version of Windows NT, it sticks to the most likely and preferred procedures.

This chapter provides an explanation of two types of available upgrade methods: the traditional method utilizing the three floppy disks that come bundled with Windows NT 4, and the streamlined *floppyless* installation method. Regardless of installation method, the upgrade completes in a matter of minutes.

A Bit about WINNT32

WINNT32.EXE is the application utilized by Windows NT during the floppyless installation process. You can locate this application on the Windows NT 4 CD-ROM, in the directory that corresponds to the type of CPU present in the system being upgraded (MIPS, PPC, Alpha, or I386). This application provides the Administrator with flexibility in the way Windows NT 4 can be installed; the available options in WINNT32 are as follows:

```
WINNT32 [/S[:]sourcepath] [/I[:]inffile] [/T[:]driveletter] [/X] [/B] [/O[X}}
```

- **/S[:]sourcepath.** Specifies the source location of Windows NT files. The default is the current directory.

- **/I[:]inffile.** Specifies the file name (no path) of the setup information file. The default is DOSNET.INF.

- **/T[:]driveletter.** Forces Setup to place temporary files on a given drive.

- **/X.** Requires you to already have Setup boot floppies (from an Administrator, for example).

- **/B.** Floppyless operation.

- **/O.** Creates boot floppies only.

- **/OX.** Creates boot floppies for CD-ROM or floppy-based installation.

The method preferred by the author does not utilize the three installation disks provided with the Windows NT 4 CD-ROM, but utilizes a feature of the WINNT32 application that facilitates a floppyless installation (WINNT32 /B). This method should be attempted only if the administrator installing Windows NT is certain that hardware issues will not impede the installation. Many mass storage devices are not automatically recognized during Windows NT Setup, and could cause an installation failure during a floppyless upgrade.

Installing Windows NT 4 Using the Floppyless Method

The following sections detail a floppyless upgrade of Windows NT 4. Each section serves as a sequential step in the process. Be sure to consider all hardware compatibility issues before proceeding from this point.

Starting Windows NT 4 Setup

In Windows NT 3.5*x*, insert the Windows NT 4 CD-ROM into a local CD-ROM drive. In the Windows NT 3.5*x* Program Manager, choose **F**ile, **R**un and type the following in the **C**ommand Line field (see fig. 23.13):

<CDROM_Letter>:\<cpu>\WINNT32.EXE /B

Replace <CDROM_Letter> with the drive letter where the Windows NT 4 CD-ROM is located and <cpu> with the directory that corresponds to the type of processor present in the system being upgraded.

Figure 23.13
The Run dialog box.

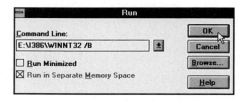

If all installation prechecks check out, the dialog box shown in figure 22.14 appears.

Figure 23.14
The Upgrade/Installation dialog box.

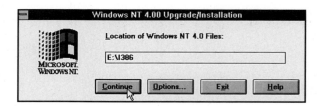

Click on the **C**ontinue button and Setup begins copying the Windows NT 4 upgrade files to the temporary directory, as shown in figure 23.15.

After Setup finishes copying files, you need to make one final check to ensure all pre-upgrade considerations have been taken. Next, click on the **R**estart Computer button (see fig. 23.16) to restart Windows NT and continue the upgrade.

Figure 23.15
The Setup program copying a file to your hard disk.

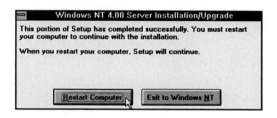

Figure 23.16
Click on the Restart Computer button to continue the upgrade.

Welcome to Setup

After the computer restarts, Windows NT Setup automatically continues the installation. The process continues with a non-GUI blue Welcome to Setup screen. Here, you can select one of four available options:

- **F1.** Learn more about NT Setup

- **Enter.** Set up Windows NT now

- **R.** Repair a damaged NT 4 installation

- **F3.** Quit Setup without installing the upgrade

Barring unforeseen errors, you should now press Enter to continue the installation.

Detecting Mass Storage Devices

This screen enables the user to select the method in which mass storage devices are detected and installed during Windows NT 4 Setup. Two methods are available: auto detection or manual specification. Most people prefer auto detection.

This screen gives you the opportunity to preempt the auto detection of mass storage devices during Windows NT 4 Setup. If the system being upgraded contains a mass storage device whose driver has been retired in Windows NT 4, then you may need to have auto detection preempted. Otherwise, auto detection is the recommended option. The following options are available:

■ **Enter.** Autodetect mass storage devices

■ **S.** Specify mass storage devices installed manually

Pressing Enter initiates auto detection, and typing S brings up a list of common mass storage devices. Refer to the section "Windows NT Driver Location Changes," earlier in this chapter for additional information.

After you make the selection, Windows NT 4 Setup prompts Setup Disk 3. Insert the disk and press Enter.

Detecting Existing Windows NT Installations

Detection of any current Windows NT installations occurs during this step. The options provide an opportunity to upgrade any currently installed versions of Windows NT, or to install a fresh copy of Windows NT 4 in a separate directory.

■ **Enter.** Perform a system upgrade on the Windows NT installation displayed on-screen.

■ **N.** Initiate a fresh installation; the user receives a prompt to enter the destination directory.

Examining Hard Disks for Corruption

By default, Windows NT Setup performs a basic examination of the drives on your computer. In this step, Windows NT 4 Setup provides the option to perform a more thorough examination of the drives.

■ **Enter.** Performs a thorough examination

■ **Esc.** Skips the thorough exam

Building a File List and Copying Files

In this stage, NT builds a list of files that need to be copied for installation. Setup copies a portion of the necessary files to the temporary installation directory. This stage does not require any user intervention.

After copying completes, Windows NT displays a message stating that this portion of Setup completed successfully. Remove any floppy disks present in the floppy disk drive, and press Enter to restart the system and initiate the GUI-based portion of NT 4 Setup.

When the computer restarts, the Windows 95-like portion of NT Setup initiates.

Reviewing the License Agreement

The first step in the Windows NT 4 Setup involves reviewing the Windows NT license agreement. Please read through the license agreement carefully, and then choose Yes or No. Choosing No closes down Windows NT Setup; choosing Yes continues Setup.

Introducing the Windows NT Server Installation Wizard

This wizard guides you through the rest of Setup. Just click on **N**ext to continue.

Specifying Creation of the Emergency Repair Disk

This step enables you to specify creation of an emergency repair disk. Choose Yes or No, then click on the **N**ext button. Microsoft recommends that you do create an emergency repair disk.

Selecting the Desired Windows NT Components

During this step, you have the opportunity to choose the components you want to install in Windows NT 4. Again, you have just two options. One option automatically installs the most common components; the second enables you to customize the components you want to install. Users who have installed Windows 95 will find the component selection screen quite familiar. After the option appears, and if you go with the Custom option and choose your preferred components, choose **N**ext.

Upgrading Windows NT Network Services

Windows NT 4 Setup automatically updates all standard network related services. This section of NT Setup is extremely automated. It requires a simple intervention only: choose **N**ext after the update completes.

Upgrading Networking Components

During this step, Setup automatically updates the network components installed in the server. Again, it requires a simple intervention only: click on the **N**ext button to continue.

Finishing Setup

This final step requires you to click on the Finish button, after which Setup installs the remaining necessary files in Windows NT 4. Windows NT 4 Setup then saves the system configuration.

Creating the Emergency Repair Disk

Finally, Windows NT 4 Setup prompts you to create an Emergency Repair Disk. At this point, place a blank, formatted, 3½-inch disk into drive A, and then click on the OK button. After the disk is created, a final dialog box appears, prompting you to restart Windows NT.

Upgrading Windows NT Using the Three Setup Disks

The following steps detail a Windows NT 4 upgrade utilizing the three Setup disks supplied with the Windows NT 4 CD-ROM. Use this method if you don't know whether the hardware located in the Windows NT 3.5*x* system will cause problems during a floppyless installation. Be sure to back up all data before beginning.

Starting Windows NT 4 Setup

Insert the Setup Boot Disk into a bootable floppy drive and power up the system. Setup automatically runs and begins preparing for the Windows NT 4 installation. A prompt requests Setup Disk Two. Place this disk into the floppy drive and press Enter. Setup continues copying files, and initiates the Welcome to Setup screen.

Domain Name Service

This chapter teaches you how to configure an NT Server as a DNS server, and how to manage DNS after it is running. The instructions include creating name servers and delegating subdomains. It teaches you how to integrate DNS and WINS, as well as troubleshoot name services. It also touches on some security issues. The graphical DNS Manager serves as your main tool for setting up and configuring your DNS Server, although you can use BIND-style text files if you prefer.

One new feature in Windows NT Server 4 is the capability to configure the NT Server as a Domain Name Service (DNS) server. The NT DNS name server is unique in two respects:

■ You can integrate it with WINS, which enables the IP name database to be updated dynamically as NetBIOS names are registered.

■ It comes with a DNS Manager utility, a simple Windows-based front-end for graphically managing all aspects of DNS.

What Is DNS?

DNS is a distributed database designed to provide mappings between host names and IP addresses (and a few other things discussed later in the chapter). Given a computer name, a DNS server returns that computer's IP address or some other requested information. The distributed structure of the DNS database results from different name servers having authority over different parts of the name tree.

This distributed structure of the DNS database is critical to the success of the Internet. Distributing the Internet's name services reduces the work load on any one server, while introducing a naming hierarchy that gives administrators flexibility in choosing their host names. This means that administrators no longer have to worry about whether someone outside of their domain may have already claimed a particular host name.

Relying on a single person or organization to maintain an authoritative hosts file could not scale as quickly as the Internet was growing. The file itself did not provide for any naming hierarchy, which created a problem with name collisions. The hosts file was growing quickly, and had too much information for computers to process efficiently. Perhaps worst of all, because the hosts file on a computer was static, copies were always out of date. People constantly wanted to download the latest hosts file, but all the updates being sent for addition to the master copy were creating such an administrative burden that even the master copy was out of date.

The Internet community solved this problem by creating the Domain Naming System (DNS).

Do You Need DNS?

Before configuring a DNS server, you need to decide whether it is a good idea for you to maintain one. Often, Internet service providers maintain DNS services for a small fee. Utilizing their services is especially appropriate if you have a small network. You may want to maintain your own DNS server if any of the following circumstances apply:

■ You have your own Internet domain name, and would like to create and delegate subdomains within it.

■ You need DNS services under local control for increased flexibility.

■ You are running a firewall that hides at least some of your organization's internal names from the outside.

Preliminary Tasks

To configure a DNS server, several things are necessary. You need to decide where in the domain hierarchy you want to fall so you can register with your parent domains. One domain is used for the name to IP address mapping, and the other domain (IN-ADDR.ARPA) is used for IP address to name mapping. Your Internet service provider will usually supply you with this information. If for some reason they don't, contact the InterNIC, the Internet Network Information Center, at `http://www.internic.net/`. (See Chapter 13, "Introduction to TCP/IP Protocol Architecture," for more details on DNS naming conventions and how DNS works.)

Except for its interaction with WINS, DNS is not a dynamic service and must be configured manually. Plan your DNS name space carefully; a good design saves you a lot of trouble later. To keep administrative overhead down, you want to make as few changes as possible over time. Owing to DNS's hierarchical database structure, the upper levels of your domain name space are particularly important, and you want to keep them as fixed as possible—if your organization reorganizes frequently, for example, consider staying away from using organizational names for your subdomains and instead use regional names.

If you have more than a few hundred hosts, you want to distribute them relatively evenly throughout your network so that they lie in different zones and subdomains. This helps prevent the zones from becoming too large. A network design that includes large zones and little distribution is likely to have congestion problems from zone transfers (when the secondary name servers obtain the updated information from the primaries).

It is important that a DNS server be running at all times to maintain Internet connectivity. It is recommended, therefore, that you set up at least one secondary server in addition to your primary DNS server. In some cases, you may need many more DNS servers, although it is not considered good practice to advertise more than seven of them as authoritative. The secondary server(s) will obtain updates from the primary server periodically. You may want to have a DNS server for each network or subnet in your organization so that if a router fails you can still resolve names of local systems. Often an Internet Service Provider will be able to secondary for you, which helps to minimize network traffic on your network—all outside queries are resolved outside your network.

Installing DNS Services on a Windows NT Server

Installing DNS Services for Windows NT Server is simple. There are two special cases: upgrading from NT 3.51, and migrating from a different DNS name server.

Configuring the Server

After you have installed NT 4, and decided to use it as a DNS name server, you can add the DNS server option from the Control Panel. You must have the TCP/IP protocol installed if you plan to set up DNS. Follow these steps:

1. Log on as an Administrator or equivalent user and make sure that your installation CD is in the CD-ROM drive.

2. Open the Control Panel.

3. From the Control Panel, double-click on the Network icon.

4. Select the Services tab, and click on the **A**dd button (see fig. 24.1).

5. Select Microsoft DNS Server from the **N**etwork Services list (as shown in figure 24.1), then click on OK.

6. Enter the full path for the NT distribution files, then click on Continue. The necessary files copy to your hard disk.

Figure 24.1

The Network dialog box.

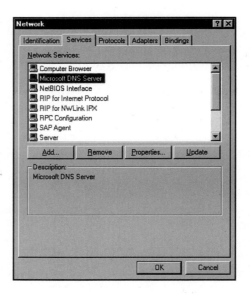

7. Close the Network Services tab. NT reviews the bindings and prompts you to restart the system so the changes can take effect.

Before you use the DNS Manager Program for the first time, you need to do an initial edit on the boot file. Retrieve the boot file from the DNS directory into a text editor such as WordPad. The relevant sections of the file resemble the portion that follows here.

```
;
;   DNS BOOT FILE
;
;   Master configuration for DNS service
;
;   Directives in this file instruct the DNS service when it is starting.
;   Anything on a line following a semicolon ';' is a comment, and is ignored.
```

```
;
;     This file and all files listed in this file must be in
;     %SystemRoot%\system32\dns directory.


;
;     Interoperation with UNIX DNS servers running BIND
;
;     Most BIND versions do not accept properly formatted zone transfers
;     unless they contain only a single resource record in each message
;     of the zone transfer.  This transfer method is grossly inefficient
;     both in terms of speed and bandwidth.  New BIND versions may not
;     have this bug.
;
;     The Microsoft DNS server will accept (receive) any properly formatted
;     zone transfer message, and is configured to send in either fashion.
;     Hence this issue ONLY relates to BIND receiving zone transfers --
;     i.e. BIND server as a secondary.
;
;     YOU SHOULD CHANGE:
;          - uncomment BindSecondaries, if have BIND secondaries for
;               some of your zones
;          - uncomment NoBindSecondaries, if have ONLY Microsoft or
;               other non-BIND DNS servers as your secondaries or if
;               you do not have secondaries for any of these zones
;

;BindSecondaries

;NoBindSecondaries

;
;     CACHE FILE
;
;     The "cache" file contains information necessary to contact the ROOT
;     domain name servers.
;
;     The syntax of this command is:
;
;          cache    .         <filename>
;
;     YOU SHOULD CHANGE:
;
;     =>  Nothing - do NOT change this line, if you are NOT a root domain
;          server.
;          (Note:  if you are not connected to the Internet, be sure and edit
;          the cache file to point at the root servers for your intranet.)
;
;          OR
;
;     =>  Comment out this line, if this DNS server is the ROOT domain
;          server for a private intranet.
;

cache    .         cache
```

You need to edit two lines. First, if you're going to have secondary servers, remove the comment out mark (;) from the BindSecondaries line. Otherwise, remove the ; from the NoBindSecondaries line. Second, if you're going to connect to the Internet, leave the cache line unchanged. The cache file points to the root name servers. If you aren't going to connect to the Internet and want to assign your own root name servers, comment out the cache line by adding a semicolon (;) in front of it. You can't resolve names outside of your network if you don't have a cache file. You need to restart the DNS server after you edit and save the Boot file. Shut down and reboot the computer or use the Control Panel Services icon: Select DNS Server from the list and click on the Stop button. After it notifies you that the DNS service was stopped, click on the Start button. The DNS server restarts with the new Boot file.

Upgrading from NT 3.51

If you currently are running NT server version 3.51 with the DNS Server from Microsoft's 3.51 Resource Kit and you want to upgrade to version 4 with its included DNS Server, use REGEDIT32.EXE to delete all the DNS-related registry entries before beginning the upgrade process.

After your upgrade to Windows NT Server 4 completes, follow the steps listed in the section "Configuring the Server."

Migrating from a BIND-Based DNS Server

BIND still is the most widely used name server program; it is part of most Unix distributions. If you currently run a BIND DNS server on another platform and want to transfer those duties over to NT, you can do so by copying the BIND database files into the directory %Systemroot%\system32\DNS after installing (but before starting) DNS. To use WINS and NBSTAT for integrated NetBIOS name resolution, you need to edit the in-addr.arpa file in the %Systemroot%\system32\DNS directory to include these options. The in-addr.arpa file contains the reverse lookup information mapping IP addresses to host names for DNS. Retrieve the in-addr.arpa file from the DNS directory into a text-editor such as WordPad. The relevant sections of the file resemble the portion below.

```
;
;    arpa-192.rev
;
;    Reverse lookup file for 29.5.192.in-addr.arpa. domain.
;
;    This file provides address to name matching (reverse lookup)
;    for addresses 192.5.29.?.
;
;
;    Note that all domain names given in this file, which are not
;    terminated by a "." and hence fully qualified domain names (FQDN),
;    are implicitly appended with "29.5.192.in-addr.arpa."
;
```

```
;    Examples:
;        "6"  =>  6.29.5.192.in-addr.arpa.
;
;    If a name outside of "29.5.192.in-addr.arpa." is required, then it
;    must be explicitly terminated with a dot, to indicate that it is a
;    FQDN.
;
;    Example:
;        "7.30.5.192.in-addr.arpa."  =>  7.30.5.192.in-addr.arpa.
;
;
;
;    NBSTAT Record
;
;    The NBSTAT RR is specific to Windows NT and may be attached ONLY
;    to the zone root of a reverse lookup domain.
;
;    Presence of a NBSTAT record at the zone root instructs the name server
;    to use a NetBIOS node status request for any reverse lookup
;    requests for IP addresses which are NOT given in PTR records below.
;
;    Examples:
;
;    1) A query for 135.29.5.192.in-addr.arpa. (192.5.29.135)
;        192.5.29.135 has a PTR record below, so DNS server responds
;        with the PTR record without NBSTAT lookup.
;
;    2) A query for 206.29.5.192.in-addr.arpa. (192.5.29.206)
;        192.5.29.206 is within the 29.5.192.in-addr.arpa zone, but
;        there is no PTR record for it in this zone file.
;        DNS will issue an NBSTAT query to 192.5.29.206.
;        If a response is received, the host name in the response will be
;        appended to the result domain in the NBSTAT record and used
;        as the host name corresponding to 192.5.29.206.  The PTR
;        record will be cached and a response sent to the client.
;        If a response is NOT received, the DNS server responds to
;        the client with a name error.
;
;    3) A query for 29.5.192.in-addr.arpa. (192.5.29)
;        192.5.29 is within the 29.5.192.in-addr.arpa zone, but is NOT
;        an IP address.  Hence no NBSTAT lookup is done, and the server
;        responds with a name error.
;
;
;    NBSTAT and zone transfer:
;
;    The MS DNS server will configure NBSTAT information as a resource
;    record to allow it to be transferred to MS DNS secondary servers.
;
;    If you have MS DNS secondaries, and want them to use exactly the
;    same NBSTAT info as the primary server, then omit the LOCAL flag
;    in the NBSTAT record.
;
```

```
;     If you have UNIX secondaries, or MS secondaries using different
;     NBSTAT information, then use the "LOCAL" flag after the "NBSTAT"
;     flag and the NBSTAT information will NOT be considered part of the
;     zone's resource records and will NOT be sent in the zone transfer.
;
;
;     YOU SHOULD CHANGE:
;          - Change the resulting domain that should be appended to
;            names found with NBSTAT lookup.
;          - Uncomment the line with LOCAL flag, if NBSTAT information should
;              not be transferred as part of the zone data.
;          - Uncomment the line without the LOCAL flag, if NBSTAT information
;              should be transferred to MS DNS secondaries.
;              OR
;          - Leave this line commented out, if NBSTAT lookup not desired.

;@   IN   NBSTAT           place.com.
;@   IN   NBSTAT   LOCAL   place.com.
```

To enable NBSTAT, uncomment the NBSTAT line by removing the semicolon (;) in front of it. If you want to use WINS, make certain that you list your WINS servers in the PTR section.

Managing DNS

You can manage the Microsoft DNS Server's database directly by using any text editor to edit the files. Doing so may come naturally to you if you have worked with Unix's BIND before, but most people prefer the graphical environment of Microsoft's DNS Manager.

Database files that contain the server's resource records need to be in the %SystemRoot%\system32\DNS directory. Sample database files are in the %SystemRoot%\system32\DNS\Samples subdirectory; you can use those as a guide. You can use any text editor to edit the DNS database files. Using the graphical management tool provided with NT Server, however, is simpler. The Microsoft DNS Manager operates like the WINS Manager or the DHCP Manager programs. DNS Manager stores the DNS BOOT file information in the Windows NT Registry.

The DNS database files in the %SystemRoot%\System32\DNS folder are read only when the Microsoft DNS Server initializes. If you use a text editor to make changes to those files, you have to stop and restart the DNS Server before your changes can take effect. If you use the DNS Manager to maintain your DNS databases, it automatically communicates changes to the DNS Server without requiring it to shut down and restart.

If you remove and reinstall the DNS Server, it will not replace your existing BOOT, CACHE, or other database files. If you want new copies of these files, rename or move your old ones before you reinstall DNS Server.

The DNS Manager program is in the Administrative Tools folder. To open it, choose Programs from the Start menu. Select Administrative Tools. Click on the DNS Manager icon to start the DNS Manager.

As you make changes with the DNS Manager, those changes write to the appropriate DNS database files periodically. At any point, you can force the DNS Manager to update the files on the DNS server. Choose **D**NS, **U**pdate Server Data Files. All the files are immediately updated. The files update at regular intervals as well as when the DNS Server or the DNS Manager is shut down.

You can use the DNS Manager program to create and manage the following:

- Servers

- Zones

- Records

- Domains

- WINS integration

- Special options

Servers

The following sections deal with various procedures you can perform involving servers, including adding and removing servers in a DNS Manager list and viewing server statistics.

Adding and Removing Servers in the DNS Manager List

You need to add each DNS server you are running to the DNS Manager list, including secondary servers.

1. Click on the Server List icon, indicated by the globe.

2. Choose **D**NS, **N**ew Server, or click on the Server List icon.

3. Type the name or IP address of the server you want to add (see fig. 24.2).

4. Click on the OK button.

Under the Server List, the Microsoft DNS Manager displays a server icon for each configured DNS server. The status of each server is indicated graphically on each server's icon. A green light indicates that the server is running and that the DNS Manager can connect to it. If a red X superimposes the icon, the DNS Manager cannot connect to the DNS service on that server.

Figure 24.2

Adding a server to the DNS Manager Server List.

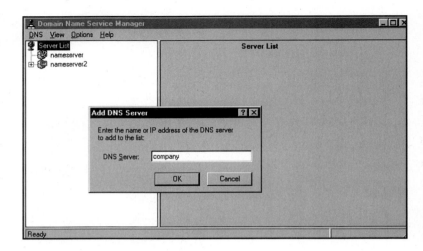

In that case, an error message displays in the bottom right-hand corner of the DNS Manager box. A superimposed yellow question mark indicates that the Manager is trying to connect to the server's DNS service, and will continue to do so at the designated Refresh rate. You can change the refresh rate from the **O**ptions menu. Choose **P**references, then type in the interval of time you prefer; the default is five seconds. To remove a server, click on the server icon and choose **D**NS, **D**elete, or click on the server icon and choose **D**elete from the menu.

As part of its internal setup, the NT DNS Server automatically adds three reverse lookup zones for mapping IP addresses to DNS host names. These zones are as follows:

- 0.in-addr.arpa

- 127.in-addr.arpa

- 255.in-addr.arpa

The 127.in-addr.arpa serves for the standard loopback interface. The reverse lookup zones are part of the in-addr.arpa domain and are added for each DNS server in the Server List. These reverse lookup zones serve performance purposes and you shouldn't edit or delete them. Figure 24.3 shows the Server List with the arpa domains added.

Viewing Server Statistics

The server statistics keep track of various activities, such as the number of UDP queries and responses, TCP client connections, reverse lookups, and WINS lookups (see fig. 24.4). To view the statistics, click on the icon of the server in which you're interested. The statistics show to the right side of the screen. To change the proportions of the right panel versus left panel, choose **V**iew, **S**plit and move the center divider with your mouse. You can have the DNS Manager update its display by choosing **V**iew, **R**efresh. Table 24.1 rounds up the statistics listed in the Server Statistics panel and tells what they measure.

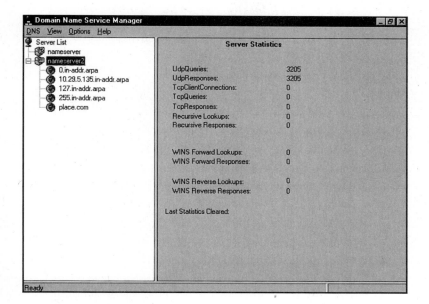

Figure 24.3
The Server List with added arpa domains.

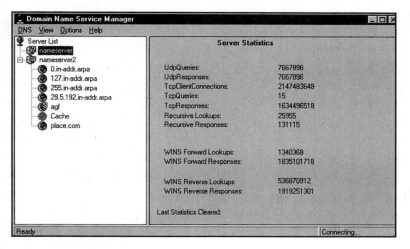

Figure 24.4
The DNS Server Statistics screen.

Table 24.1
Server Statistics

Statistic	What It Measures
UdpQueries	Increments each time the DNS server receives a DNS name resolution request over UDP

continues

Table 24.1, Continued
Server Statistics

Statistic	What It Measures
UdpResponses	Increments each time the DNS server sends a reply using UDP
TcpConnections	Increments each time another system opens a TCP connection to the DNS port on the server
TcpQueries	Increments each time the DNS server receives a DNS name resolution request over TCP
TcpResponses	Increments each time the DNS server sends a reply using TCP
Recursive Lookups	Increments each time the DNS server needs to query other servers to satisfy a client's request for recursion
Recursive Responses	Increments each time the DNS server replies to a client's recursive request
WINS Forward Lookups	Increments each time a WINS name to IP address mapping is requested
WINS Forward Responses	Increments each time a WINS name to IP address mapping request receives a reply
WINS Reverse Lookups	Increments each time an IP address to WINS name mapping is requested
WINS Reverse Responses	Increments each time a WINS name to IP address mapping receives a reply
Last Statistics Cleared	Reports the most recent time and date the DNS statistics were cleared

Zones

A zone is authoritative for all the DNS information within that zone. Any given zone may contain one or several domains. A zone also may contain subdomains. If a subdomain is delegated, the DNS servers to which it is delegated hold the authoritative zone for that subdomain.

The two types of zones are as follows:

- Primary (also known as a zone root domain)

- Secondary

A primary zone is represented by the world icon in the DNS Manager Server List, and has its own SOA resource record. Primary zones depend directly on the information configured in the DNS database files.

A secondary zone has an *S* superimposed on the world icon. Secondary zone name servers rely on information they get from another name server, generally a primary name server. The secondary zone name server gets its information from a *zone transfer.*

Double yellow lines through a zone icon indicate that the zone has been paused. You can pause a zone at any point by highlighting the zone and choosing **D**NS, P**a**use Zone. Pausing a zone takes it offline. To put the zone back online, choose P**a**use Zone again.

Creating a Primary Zone

Follow these steps to create a primary zone.

1. Click on the server icon that represents the name server for the new zone.

2. Choose New **Z**one.

3. In the New Zone dialog box, choose **P**rimary.

4. Click on the **N**ext button.

5. Enter the zone name and choose the zone file type, or use the default zone file name for the database.

6. Click on the **N**ext button.

7. Click on the **F**inish button.

The new zone, represented by a world icon, is added to your server with an SOA record and an A record.

You can see information for a particular zone in the right panel of the DNS Manager by clicking on that zone's icon.

Creating a Secondary Zone

A *secondary zone* is a read-only copy of an existing zone. Its main role is to serve as a backup for the primary zone. A secondary zone can help load share as well as help minimize network traffic if it bypasses the need to use a router to access the primary zone. Select a different server for the secondary zone from the name server for the primary zone. A given server can be the name server for a primary zone, however, and a different secondary zone at the same time.

1. Click on the server icon.

2. Choose New **Z**one.

3. In the New Zone dialog box, choose **S**econdary and type the zone name and server.

4. Click on the **N**ext button.

5. Type the zone name and file name (or use the default file name).

6. Click on the **N**ext button.

7. Type the IP address of the IP Master and click on the **A**dd button.

8. Click on the **N**ext button, and then click on the **F**inish button.

Note   The *IP master* is a name server from which this secondary can get its zone information and updates. You can configure several IP masters if necessary.

Creating a Primary Zone in the in-addr.arpa Domain

The in-addr.arpa domain is a special domain used in the exact opposite way of other domains. Rather than look up a name and return an IP address, it looks up an IP address and returns a host name. This zone must be coordinated with the authoritative zone for the computer names in your domain name space. If your regular name domain and your in-addr.arpa domain are out of sync, many servers on the Internet will deny you access.

1. In the Server List, click on the server icon.

2. Choose New **Z**one, click on **P**rimary, and then click on **N**ext.

3. In the space for the zone name, type the network (or subnetwork, if it was given to you as a class B- or C-sized subnet) portion of your IP address in reverse order followed by in-addr.arpa.

4. Type the zone file name or accept the default.

5. Click on the **N**ext button, and then click on the **F**inish button.

Computers outside of your network will need to reach this zone to verify that you are who you say you are by doing reverse lookups. To enable this, you need to register it with its parent domain, in-addr.arpa. Normally, the organization from which you received your network number(s), either an IS department or an ISP, handles setting up this delegation if you request it. Unless you have your own network number and at least two name servers, you will not be delegated an in-addr.arpa domain. If you have had your numbers for a good long while and never registered them, you may need to contact the InterNIC directly. The DNS Resources Directory on the World Wide Web has registration information along with a great deal of other useful information:

`http://www.dns.net/dnsrd/`

Adding a New Host to a Primary Zone

Follow these steps to add a new host to a primary zone.

1. Click on the Zone icon.

2. Choose New **H**ost.

3. Type the host name and its IP address.

4. If you want the DNS Manager to automatically create the PTR record for reverse lookups, enable the Create Associated PTR Record check box (see fig. 24.5).

Figure 24.5
The New Host dialog box.

5. Click on the **A**dd Host button.

You can add as many hosts as you want at this point. Every host that is reachable from the Internet should have at least an A record and a PTR record. After you finish, click on the **D**one button. The new host and its IP address appear in the zone information window as an address record.

DNS Resource Records

Each set of information stored in the DNS database is referred to as a *resource record*. The essential ones are as follows:

- Name Server (NS)

- Address (A)

- Start of Authority (SOA)

■ Pointer (PTR)

■ Mail Exchange (MX)

Many other record types exist, only a few of which are you likely to ever have reason to use (like the CNAME record). Some of the other record types are experimental; others just aren't widely used. Table 24.2 summarizes the various resource records and the information they contain. Resource records are covered in more detail later in this chapter.

Table 24.2
Most widely used DNS Resource Records

Record name	Description
A (Address)	Maps a host computer or another network device name to an IP address in a DNS zone
CNAME (Canonical name)	Creates an alias for the specified host name
MX (Mail exchange)	Identifies a mail exchange server for a host computer
NS (Name server)	Identifies the DNS name server(s) for the DNS domain
PTR (Pointer)	Maps an IP address to a host name in a DNS reverse zone
SOA (Start of authority)	Indicates that this DNS name server is the best source of information for the data within this DNS domain

Adding a New Record

1. In server list, click on the icon of the server, zone, or domain to which you want to add the record.

2. Choose New Record, which opens the New Resource Record dialog box (see fig. 24.6).

3. From the Record Type list, select a type of resource record, such as MX.

4. Type the required information and click on the OK button.

Many of the resource records are experimental, and not essential for DNS services. Several records are highly important: the address record, the pointer record, the mail exchange record, the canonical name record, and the start of authority record. DNS domain names aren't case-sensitive. Here is a description of the records and the role of each.

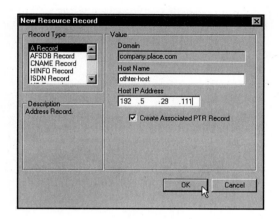

Figure 24.6

Adding a new resource record.

Address Record

The A Record (refer to figure 24.6), which maps a host computer or another network device name to an IP address in a DNS domain, contains three fields:

- **Domain.** Enter the name of the domain that contains the host.

- **Host Name.** Enter the name of a computer or network device.

- **Host IP Address.** Enter the address of the host.

The host name combined with the domain name comprise a fully qualified domain name (FQDN). The DNS Manager automatically generates the A Record when you add a new server, host, or domain.

AFS Database Record

The AFSDB Record (originally from Andrew File System) provides the location of an AFS cell database server or a DCE (Distributed Computing Environment) cell's authenticated name server. In addition to the domain name and the optional host name, you need to provide the Server DNS Name—which is the DNS name for the AFS cell database server or the DCE name server—and then select the type of server. Choose AFS Cell Database Server or choose DCE Name Server. Relatively few networks have these.

Canonical Name Record

The CNAME Record (see fig. 24.7) creates an alias for the particular host name. You can use CNAME records to hide the implementation details of your network from the clients that connect to it. For alias names, you can use shortened forms of the host names. The host name public1.business.com, for example, might have an alias of www.business.com. The three fields required in the DNS database for this type of record are as follows:

■ **Alias Domain.** Enter the domain in which the alias host exists.

■ **Alias Name.** Enter the canonical name.

■ **For Host Name.** Enter the host name (as specified in the Address record) it represents.

Figure 24.7
The CNAME Record.

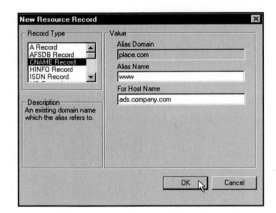

Hardware Information Record

The HINFO Record identifies a host's hardware type and operating system. The Internet standard abbreviations for identifying the operating system of a host are published in the Assigned Numbers RFC (RFC 1700 at the time of this writing) under the System Names List. Abbreviations for the hardware type of hosts also are defined in the Assigned Numbers RFC. The CPU Type identification number is in the Machine Names List. For a small sample of the types specified in the Assigned Numbers RFC, see the following tables. The names are up to 40 characters long and contain uppercase letters and digits, including a hyphen (-) and a slash (/). The name must begin with a letter and end with a letter or digit. Some people choose not to provide this on publicly accessible DNS servers because it reveals information about a computer system that might make it easier for someone to break into a system, perhaps by attacking known security flaws for a particular system type. If you do use HINFO records, be sure to keep up with CERT security advisories for your systems.

RFC 1700 Standard Codes for Common Operating Systems

APOLLO	OPENVMS	TANDEM
AIX/370	OS/2	UNIX
DOMAIN	PCDOS	UNIX-BSD
DOS	SCO-OPEN-DESKTOP-2.0	UNIX-PC
INTERLISP	SCO-OPEN-DESKTOP-3.0	UNKNOWN
ITS	SCO-UNIX-3.2V4.0	VM
LISP	SCO-UNIX-3.2V4.1	VM/370
MSDOS	SCO-UNIX-3.2V4.2	VMS
MULTICS	SUN	WANG
MVS	SUN-OS-3.5	WIN32
NONSTOP	SUN-OS-4.0	X11R3

RFC 1700 Standard Codes for Common CPU Types

APOLLO	IBM-RS/6000	SUN-4/200
APPLE-MACINTOSH	INTEL-386	SUN-4/390
APPLE-POWERBOOK	M68000	SYMBOLICS-3600
CRAY-2	MAC-II	UNKNOWN
DECSTATION	MAC-POWERBOOK	VAX
DEC-VAX	MACINTOSH	VAX-11/725
DEC-VAXCLUSTER	MICROVAX	VAXCLUSTER
DEC-VAXSTATION	PDP-11	VAXSTATION
IBM-PC/AT	SILICON-GRAPHICS	
IBM-PC/XT	SUN	

Integrated Services Digital Network Record

The ISDN Record maps the host name to an ISDN address. The ISDN phone number also can include the Direct Dial In (DDI) number. An ISDN subaddress is optional. ISDN records have several possible uses. The ISDN resource records can provide simple documentation of the correct addresses to use in static configurations of ISDN dial up applications. In the future, they also may be used automatically by Internet routers.

Mailbox Record

The MB Record identifies a mailbox for the indicated host. You must provide the Mailbox name and the FQDN of the host that contains the mailbox. This record type is considered experimental and should not be used unless you are part of the Internet experiment.

Mailgroup Record

The MG Record identifies a mailbox that is a member of the group mailing list in the given DNS domain name. You must type the mailbox name as a FQDN. This record type is considered experimental and should not be used unless you are part of the Internet experiment.

Mail Information Record

The MINFO Record provides information about a mailing list or mailbox. It has two fields: the Responsible Mailbox DNS field, which contains the fully qualified domain name (FQDN) of the mailbox that is responsible for the mailing list identified in the resource record; and the Error Mailbox DNS field, which contains the FQDN of the mailbox that is to receive error messages related to the mailing list. Although you can associate these records with a simple mailbox, they usually are used with a mailing list that uses different mailing addresses for administrative matters, such as subscriptions (usually the responsible mailbox), and for error messages, like `mail not deliverable` (the error mailbox).

Mail Rename Record

The MR Record renames a given mailbox. Type the FQDN of the new mailbox name in the Replacement Mailbox DNS Name field. You can use an alias name if a mailbox is moved from one host to another. This record type is considered experimental and should not be used unless you're part of the Internet experiment.

Mail Exchange Record

An MX Record indicates the host name of a server that will process or forward mail for a given domain or host. The host name of the mail exchanger must be a FQDN. The MX record format consists of the following fields (see fig. 24.8).

- ■ **For Domain.** Enter the host or domain name for which the mail exchanger will process mail.

- ■ **Mail Exchange Server DNS Name.** Enter the FDQN of the mail exchange server.

- ■ **Preference Number.** Enter the preference number of that particular mail exchanger.

The Preference Number is a number from 0 to 65,535 that indicates the mail exchange server's priority with respect to the other mail exchange servers for that destination. Lower preference numbers have higher priority, the highest priority being a preference number of 0. The absolute value of the preference is not significant except in relation to other mail exchangers for the same destination. A mailer attempts delivery to the mail exchange server with the lowest preference number first. If delivery fails, the mail exchange server with the next highest preference number is tried next. If two or more mail exchange servers share the same preference number, the mailer must decide which one to try first. All mail exchange servers with a given preference number are tried before the mailer moves up to the next highest preference number, however. One normally uses a preference of 10 for the *best* mail server, with less preferred mail exchangers identified at 20, and then 30, or some similar scheme. Doing so enables you to insert a new mail exchanger between or before your existing mailers if needed.

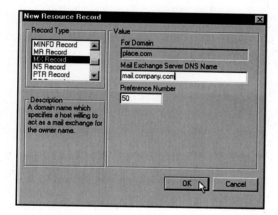

Figure 24.8
The MX Record.

Mail Exchange lookups are not recursive. After an MX record identifies the best destination for mail to a host, the only other lookup performed is for the A record of the mail exchanger. MX records for the mail exchanger itself are ignored unless the mail is addressed directly to that particular mail exchanger.

Name Server Record

The NS Record identifies an authoritative DNS server for the DNS domain. You should always have at least two of these for any domain, but having more than seven generally isn't a good idea. An NS record has two fields (see fig. 24.9):

- **For Domain.** Enter the domain name.

- **Name Server DNS Name.** Enter the authoritative server name (which should refer to an A record).

Pointer Record

Pointer records map an IP address to a host name in the DNS reverse lookup domain (in-addr.arpa), as shown in figure 24.10. You use the IP Address and Host DNS Name fields. You can have the DNS Manager automatically create the associated PTR records for the hosts for which you create address records by enabling the Create Associate PTR Record option when you enter the A record (refer to figure 24.6). Use the FQDN for the host name if you create these records manually. If you use the DNS Manager to create these records, just type the IP address of the host; DNS Manager automatically appends in-addr.arpa to the IP address for you. Many Internet sites deny access to computers that do not have matching Address and Pointer Records as a security measure, so be sure to keep your PTR records synchronized with your A records.

Figure 24.9

The NS Record.

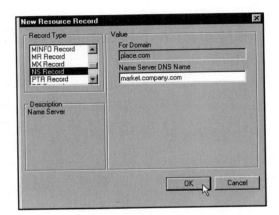

Figure 24.10

The PTR Record.

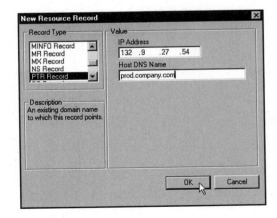

Responsible Person Record

The RP Record indicates who is responsible for the device identified by the specified DNS name. Although the SOA Record indicates who is responsible for a zone and gives the best point of contact for DNS-related issues, different people usually are in charge of various hosts within a domain. The RP Record enables you to indicate who should be contacted if a problem arises associated with something that has a DNS name. Typical problems might be that an important server has become unavailable or that another site is noticing suspicious activity from a host.

An RP Record requires an e-mail address and the FQDN to check for text records with more information. The e-mail address is in standard DNS domain name format, with a period for the *at* symbol (@) used in most e-mail addresses. The DNS text reference is a DNS domain name that acts as a pointer to a TXT resource record. You can use the Text resource record to which the RP record points to provide free-format information about the contact, such as full name and phone or pager number.

Route Through Record

The RT Record identifies an intermediate host that routes packets to a destination host that does not have direct connectivity itself. The Intermediate Host DNS Name must be a fully-qualified domain name (FQDN) of an intermediate host that will accept packets for the destination. An intermediate host functions like a mail exchange server, in that there can only be one level of indirection, which means that the path to an intermediate host cannot be through another intermediate host.

Start of Authority Record

An SOA Record indicates that this DNS name server is the best source of information for the data within this DNS domain. SOA Records serve to identify the e-mail contact for the zone, to identify that changes have been made to a zone's database file, and to set timers on how often other servers update their copies of the zone information.

You can access the SOA Record for each primary zone by clicking on the zone and choosing **P**roperties. Select the SOA Record tab (see fig. 24.11). The Primary Name Server DNS Name field contains the name of the server host that acts as the original or primary source of data for this DNS zone.

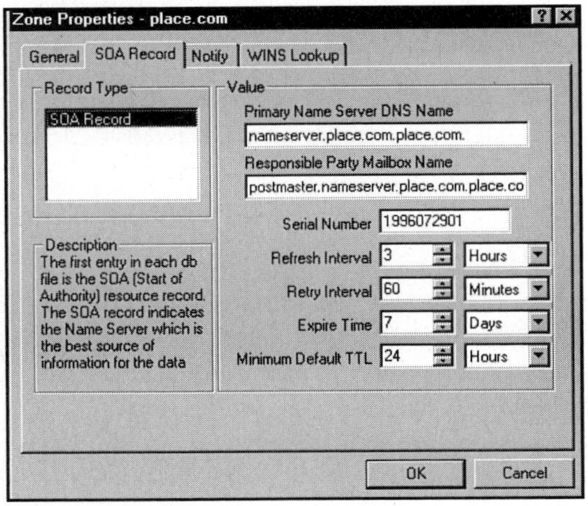

Figure 24.11

The Zone Properties SOA Record tab.

The Serial Number field contains the serial number, which controls DNS zone transfers between primary and secondary DNS name servers. The secondary name server contacts a primary name server periodically and requests the serial number of the primary's zone data. If the primary zone's serial number is larger than the secondary's, the secondary's zone data is out of date and the secondary transfers a new copy of the zone data from the primary. The Microsoft DNS Server attempts to notify secondaries when changes occur, but older versions of BIND may not accept such invitations to refresh their data.

The number in the Refresh Interval field specifies how often the secondary DNS name servers check the zone data of the primary. The default refresh interval is three hours; if your secondaries accept notification of changes, you can safely increase it to a long value (a day or more) to reduce the polling. This is particularly valuable over slow or on-demand lines.

The Retry Interval field determines how often a secondary server should try to reconnect after a failed connection. The Retry Interval usually is shorter than the Refresh Interval. The default value is 60 minutes.

The Expire Time field refers to the amount of time the secondary server's data is good. If a secondary DNS name server fails to contact the primary DNS name server, the secondary's data may be invalid. The secondary server stops responding to queries about the data after the expire time uses up. The default value is three days, and it must exceed both the minimum and retry values.

The Minimum Default TTL (time-to-live) has the greatest effect on DNS traffic. It controls how long a receiving server can cache the data. Each query response is sent with a TTL value. The default value is 24 hours. If you anticipate making major changes to your DNS zone, you should temporarily set this to a short interval, like one hour, and then wait the previous minimum value before making your changes. After you verify the correctness of your changes, you should increase the TTL back up to its previous value. Following this procedure enables your changes to propagate through the Internet much more efficiently and reduces the time during which stale DNS data may lurk in other servers' caches.

Text Record

The TXT Record contains information in straight text form, often a name and phone number of a contact or other relevant information. The text string must be less than 256 characters in length.

Well Known Service Record

The WKS Record describes the services provided by a particular protocol on a particular interface, identified by the IP address. The services include Telnet and FTP. The Access Protocol indicates the protocol for the available service. This record generally isn't used and should be avoided (RFC 1123).

X25 Record

The X25 Record is similar to the A Resource Record, but maps the host name to an X.121 address rather than an IP address. *X.121 addresses* are the standard form of addresses for X.25 networks. The PSDN (Public Switched Data Network) address begins with the four-digit DNIC (Data Network Identification Code) specified in X.121—guidelines established by the International Telephone and Telegraph Consultative Committee. Do not use the national prefixes as part of the address. The X25 resource record is designed for usage in conjunction with the RT (route through) resource record.

Domains

This section focuses on activities related to domains, such as creating a domain within a primary zone.

Creating a Domain within a Primary Zone

1. Click on the zone icon in the Server List.

2. Choose New **D**omain (see fig. 24.12).

3. Type the name of the new domain and click on the OK button.

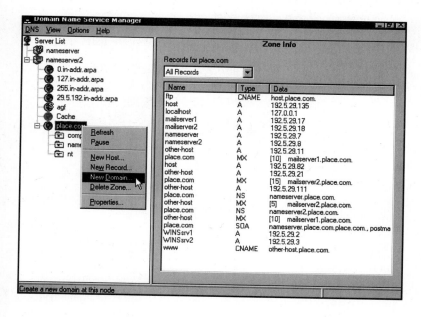

Figure 24.12
The New Domain option.

Creating and Delegating Subdomains

If you create but do not delegate a subdomain, WINS cannot resolve names in that subdomain. You should, therefore, always delegate subdomains when trying to achieve integration between DNS and WINS. For more information on resolving WINS names, see the next section, "WINS Integration."

1. From the DNS Manager Server List, select the server that will be authoritative for the new subdomain. It can be the same server you are delegating from or a different server.

2. Create the subdomain as a new primary zone on the authoritative server.

3. Add the appropriate resource records, such as A, CNAME, and MX, to the new zone. See the previous section on resource records for details on creating the different types of resource records.

4. If you want to use WINS Lookup, click on the zone and choose **P**roperties.

5. Select the WINS Lookup tab and enable the **U**se WINS Resolution check box.

6. Type the IP addresses of the WINS Servers, and then click on the OK button.

7. In the Server List, double-click on the zone icon of the parent domain.

8. Delete all records that now belong to the new subdomain.

9. Click on the zone icon of the parent domain, and then click on New **D**omain.

10. Type the name of the new subdomain that you just created (see fig. 24.13).

Figure 24.13

The New Domain dialog box.

11. Click on the newly created subdomain icon (the one under the parent's primary zone icon), and then click on Ne**w** Record.

12. In the Record Type list, click on NS Record, type the name of the server for the new subdomain in the Name Server DNS Name box, and then click on OK.

13. In the Record Type list, select A Record, type the name of the server for the new subdomain (the same name that you used in the previous step) in the Host Name field, and type its corresponding IP address in the Host IP Address field, and then click on OK.

14. Choose **D**NS, **U**pdate Server Data Files.

WINS Integration

WINS is a dynamic name resolution system that relies on each workstation to register its own name and IP address. This is an automatic service in workstations that run Windows 95 or Windows NT. If you disable this function or turn off the computer, DNS cannot use WINS to resolve that computer's name. Note that WINS only resolves names that are direct children of the primary, or *zone root*, domain. In other words, host names in subdomains cannot be resolved by DNS unless those subdomains are delegated, in which case they are in their own primary domain. Consequently, putting the WINS hosts in one zone if possible is easiest.

Your DNS server also can act as a WINS server, or it can point to a different WINS server. Only Windows NT DNS servers can query a WINS database to resolve dynamically learned names at this time. The differences between WINS and DNS are shown in table 24.3.

You can configure non-NetBIOS hosts to query the Windows NT DNS server for all names in the zone that use WINS for lookups. If the dynamic portion of the network exists in several zones, you can set up one Windows NT DNS server as the primary master name server for each of those zones, or you can give each of those zones its own Windows NT DNS server.

Table 24.3
Comparing WINS and DNS

DNS	WINS
Resolves host names to IP names to addresses	Resolves NetBIOS IP addresses
Hierarchical and static structure	Flat and dynamic structure
Supports TCP/IP applications that require more information than the host name and IP address	Supports DHCP

Enabling WINS Lookup in a Zone Root Domain

Follow these steps to enable WINS lookup in the zone root domain.

1. In the Server List, click on the primary zone icon and choose **P**roperties.

2. Select the WINS Lookup tab (see fig. 24.14).

3. Enable the **U**se WINS Resolution check box.

4. Under **W**INS Servers, add one or more IP addresses for the WINS Servers on your network.

Figure 24.14

The Zone Properties WINS Lookup tab.

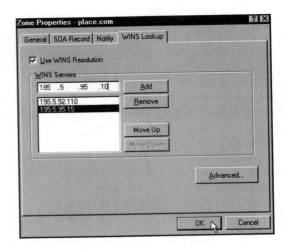

You can click on the **A**dvanced button if you want to change the settings, such as if your network uses a NetBIOS Scope or if you need to alter the default timeout values.

Enabling WINS Reverse Lookup in an in-addr.arpa Zone Root Domain

This is a new feature of the Microsoft DNS Server that became necessary so that WINS-learned names could access resources that performed reverse lookups.

1. In the Server List, click on the in-addr.arpa primary zone icon, then choose **P**roperties.

2. Select the WINS Reverse Lookup tab (see fig. 24.15).

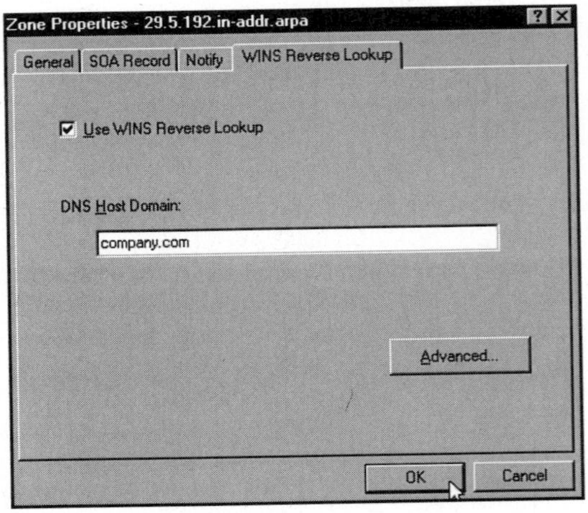

Figure 24.15

Adding WINS reverse lookup to an in-addr.arpa domain.

3. Enable the **U**se WINS Reverse Lookup check box.

4. In the DNS **H**ost Domain text box, type the default domain name to append to responses that WINS returns.

5. If you need to alter the default timeout values, click on the **A**dvanced button.

Special Options

This section takes a look at some less easily categorized areas, such as selectively enabling DNS on a multihomed server, or specifying a boot method for a DNS server.

Selectively Enabling DNS on a Multihomed Server

Note that DNS can operate on all the network adapters of a multihomed server if you don't specify any particular IP addresses. This normally is a primary reason to install multiple network interfaces in a DNS server, but sometimes you may want to specify which interfaces will accept DNS queries. If that's what you need to do, follow these steps:

1. In the Server List, click on the server icon.

2. Choose **P**roperties.

3. In the **D**NS Server IP Addresses section (see fig. 24.16), type the IP addresses for each network adapter that you want to enable for DNS traffic.

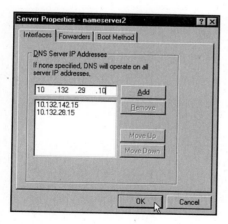

Figure 24.16
The Server Properties Interfaces tab.

Specifying a Boot Method for a DNS Server

1. In the Server List, click on the server icon.

2. Choose **P**roperties.

3. Select the Boot Method tab (see fig. 24.17).

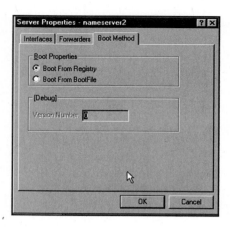

Figure 24.17

*Choosing a boot method
for a DNS server.*

4. In the **B**oot Properties area of the Boot Method tab, enable the Boot From Registry radio option or the Boot From BootFile radio option.

If you boot from the Registry, the Microsoft DNS Server doesn't consult its BOOT file for configuration information, but rather, uses the information in the Registry. If you make changes to the BOOT file that you want to use, you need to be sure to set the Boot Method to "Boot from BootFile."

Setting the Primary Zones to Notify the Secondaries of Changes

Follow these steps if you want to have the primary zones notify the secondaries of changes.

1. In the Server List, click on the primary zone icon.

2. Choose **P**roperties.

3. In the Notify List, type the IP addresses of the secondaries.

You would want to make this arrangement if your secondaries are running the Microsoft DNS Server, version 4.9.3 or newer of BIND, or some other implementation that supports notification of secondaries after changes are made to the primary.

Modifying the Cache

The Cache contains a list of root name servers for the Internet. If you're not connected to the Internet, and so have commented out the cache line in the Boot file, you do not have a cache icon in the DNS Manager server list.

You only have to modify the cache when the root name servers change, which is infrequently. You should plan to check the InterNIC for an updated list about once a year.

1. From the DNS Manager Server List, click on the Cache icon (see fig. 24.18).

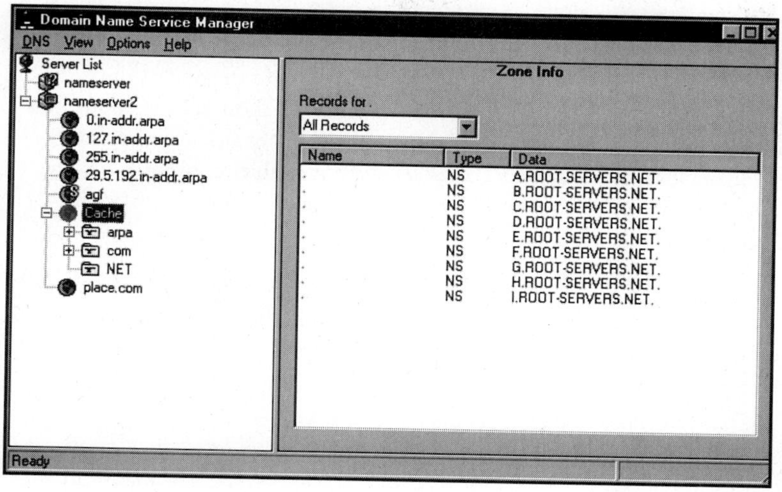

Figure 24.18

Modifying the cache.

2. Click on the record that you need to change, and then choose **P**roperties.

3. For an NS record, type the new name. For an A record, type the new IP address.

The only valid resource records for the cache are the Name Server (NS) and Address (A) Records.

Security Issues

As convenient as you might find being able to access the Internet and other places outside your network, you may not want to let just anyone into your own network. The most common security measures implemented to this end are packet filters on routers and proxy servers for specific applications, such as Telnet, FTP, and Web browsers.

You can take several precautions with DNS to minimize your network's exposure. Some of the most common include configuring your publicly accessible servers to perform reverse lookups to keep out computers that are lying about their identity and restricting zone transfers to authorized secondaries only.

Using reverse lookups is something that you generally must configure for each individual service (FTP, Telnet, for example), but the rationale is fairly obvious—if an unauthorized system is configured to use the same name as a trusted system's, but the name derived from a DNS reverse lookup using in-addr.arpa does not match, the system may be an impostor and should be denied access. If you provide a public and anonymous service, this matter isn't particularly relevant, but if you need to restrict access based on the host name, it's definitely worthwhile.

If you decide to hide some of your internal hosts behind a firewall, you may decide to implement a *split-brain* approach to DNS (a DNS configuration that involves having primary servers that have different information on both sides of a firewall). The one on the outside has limited information about the network on the inside—it typically knows about only a few internal hosts that are permitted through the firewall but has full connectivity to the rest of the Internet. The DNS server on the inside has access to full information about all the computers within the firewall, but is configured to ask the DNS server on the other side of the firewall about anything outside of the local name space. This arrangement enables computers inside the firewall to perform DNS lookups on the entire Internet, but keeps anyone outside the firewall from learning about what is inside.

To implement a split-brain configuration, set both the DNS servers as primary masters, have the one inside the firewall use Forwarders to contact the one outside the firewall as needed, and implement some form of restricted access between them (like a specific-host-to-specific-host router filter that allows only DNS traffic).

Setting a DNS Server to Use Forwarders

Use the following steps to give a DNS server the capability to use forwarders.

1. In the Server List, click on the server icon.

2. Choose **P**roperties.

3. Select the Forwarders tab (see fig. 24.19).

Figure 24.19

The Forwarders tab for a caching-only server.

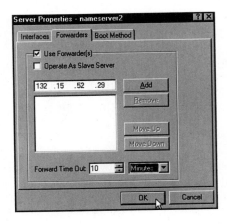

4. Enable the Use Forwarder(s) check box.

5. If you want this DNS Server to use forwarders only, enable the Operate As Slave Server check box.

This makes it a caching-only server now, and you wouldn't use it in the split-brain configuration described earlier.

6. Add IP addresses for the destinations to which you want the server to forward its queries.

You also can change the Forward Time Out value by typing a specific time limitation in the Time Out counter box. The default time out is five seconds (figure 24.19 shows 10 Minutes, however). If a the specific amount of time expires and the server has multiple destinations for forwarding, it retransmits its query to another server on its list.

Controlling Which Secondaries Have Access to the Primary

Restricting zone transfers to authorized secondaries only is useful because it hides the details of your internal network from outsiders. Enabling people to easily learn about all of a network's hosts can divulge enough information to prospective computer crooks that let them know breaking in might prove sporting, interesting, or downright profitable.

1. Click on the primary zone icon.

2. Choose **P**roperties.

3. In the Notify list, add the IP addresses of the secondaries that have permission to access the primary.

4. Click on Only Allow access from Secondaries included on notify list.

After you make any changes in the DNS Manager, you need to update the server data files by choosing Update Server Data Files from the DNS Manager menu. Otherwise, the DNS Database can't write the current information to its configuration files immediately, and the information can end up lost if the system crashes before the next regularly scheduled update.

DNS Troubleshooting

If the DNS Manager will not run, seems to have incorrect data, or indicates an unreachable server, you may need to diagnose the problem. The two best troubleshooting tools for this purpose are NsLookup and the Event Log.

NsLookup

NsLookup serves as the main diagnostic tool for DNS. As with DNS, you must have TCP/IP installed before you can use it. NsLookup is to DNS as PING is to general IP connectivity—the first tool you turn to for testing. It queries DNS name servers and shows you the results it receives, optionally with excruciating detail. The query length must be less than 256 characters. You can interrupt it at any point by pressing Ctrl+C. To leave NsLookup, type exit. All unrecognized commands are interpreted as computer names, and it sends queries to its default server to try to look them up as domain names. NsLookup has two modes, interactive or non-interactive mode. Use the interactive mode when troubleshooting problems, so you can easily perform multiple queries.

Here is a list of NsLookup commands in interactive mode:

- help

- exit

- finger

- ls

- lserver

- root

- server

- set

- view

To use NsLookup for a command-line query, type the nslookup command at the command prompt as follows:

1. Type the name or IP address of the computer you are looking up. (If the computer isn't in the same domain as the name server, type a period after the computer name.)

2. If you want to specify a DNS name server, type its name or IP address. If you leave it blank, NsLookup uses the default name server.

The following sections look at each of the NsLookup interactive mode commands in turn. Consider it a kind of reference section. Each section summarizes the command and furnishes a syntax line.

help

Help displays a brief summary of NsLookup commands. The question mark (?) is a synonym for the help command.

```
help ¦ ?
```

exit

Type **exit** to exit NsLookup.

```
exit
```

finger

Connects with the finger server on the current computer. The current computer is defined when a previous lookup for a computer was successful and returned address information (see the set querytype=A command).

```
finger [username] [> filename] ¦ [>> filename]
```

ls

Use the ls command to list information for a DNS domain. The default information consists of computer names and their IP addresses. You can direct the output to a file. Hash marks separate every 50 records. Table 24.4 lists and describes various options you can use with the ls command.

```
ls [option] dnsdomain [> filename] ¦ [>> filename]
```

Table 24.4
Table of ls Options

Option	Description
-t	Lists all records of the specified type (see the set querytype command that follows)
-a	Lists aliases of computers in the DNS domain (same as -t CNAME)
-d	Lists all records for the DNS domain (same as -t ANY)
-h	Lists CPU and operating system information for the DNS domain (same as -t HINFO)
-s	Lists well-known services of computers in the DNS domain (same as -t WKS)

Specify the DNS domain for which you want information after the option and the file name in which to save the output. You can use the > and >> characters to redirect the output in the usual manner.

Here is a sample ls request and its response:

```
> ls hq.mycompany.com
res_mkquery(0, hq.mycompany.com, 1, 252)
[nameserver1.hq.mycompany.com]
 hq.mycompany.com.                    server = mailer.hq.mycompany.com
 mailer.hq.mycompany.com.             10.132.13.2
 hq.mycompany.com.                    server = nameserver1.hq.mycompany.com
 nameserver1.hq.mycompany.com.        10.132.40.80
 hq.mycompany.com.                    server = sal.hq.mycompany.com
 sal.hq.mycompany.com.                10.132.13.25
 hq.mycompany.com.                    10.132.13.2
 bill.hq.mycompany.com.               10.132.70.3
 database.hq.mycompany.com.           10.132.13.248
 mary.hq.mycompany.com.               10.132.29.4
```

lserver

lserver uses the local DNS server to look up the information about the specified DNS server, and then changes the default server to the one specified as its argument. This command is useful if you have changed your default server to one that no longer responds, and you only know the DNS name of others that may still be working.

```
>lserver <name>
```

root

The current default server for the root of the DNS domain name space is ns.nic.ddn.mil. You can change the default server for the root by using the set root command. The lserver ns.nic.ddn.mil command accomplishes the same thing.

```
>root
```

server

The server command uses the current default server to look up the information about the specified DNS server, and changes to the specified server as the new default server.

```
>server <name>
```

view

You can use the view command to sort and list the output file of previous ls command(s).

```
>view <filename>
```

set

The set command has many subcommands. It changes settings that affect how lookups function. Here is a list of the possibilities:

- set all
- set cl[ass]
- set [no]deb[ug]
- set [no]d2
- set [no]def[name]
- set do[main]
- set [no]ig[nore]
- set po[rt]
- set q[uerytype]
- set [no]rec[urse]
- set ret[ry]
- set ro[ot]
- set [no]sea[rch]
- set srchl[ist]
- set ti[meout]
- set ty[pe]
- set [no]v[c]

set all

Use the set all command to get the current NsLookup configuration settings, such as information about the default server and type of queries being performed.

Here is a sample:

```
> set all
Default Server:  nameserver1.hq.mycompany.com
Address:  10.132.40.254
```

```
Set options:
  nodebug        defname        search         recurse
  nod2           novc           noignoretc     port=53
  querytype=A    class=IN       timeout=6      retry=4
  root=ns.nic.ddn.mil.
  domain=hq.mycompany.com
  srchlist=hq.mycompany.com
```

set cl[ass]

You can change the protocol to the following types:

- **IN.** Internet class

- **CHAOS.** Chaos class

- **HESIOD.** MIT Athena Hesiod class

- **ANY.** Any of the above

The default is the Internet class, and you aren't likely to need any of the other classes; they're not widely used.

```
set class=value
```

set [no]deb[ug]

You can turn debugging on or off. With debugging on, more information is printed about the packet sent to the server and the resulting answer. The default is nodebug.

```
set nodebug
```

Here is part of a sample:

```
- - - - - - - - - - -
Name:     nameserver2.hq.mycompany.com
Address:  10.132.13.251

> set debug
> nameserver2
Server:  nameserver1.hq.mycompany.com
Address:  10.132.40.80

res_mkquery(0, nameserver2.hq.mycompany.com, 1, 1)
- - - - - - - - - - -
SendRequest(), len 40
    HEADER:
        opcode = QUERY, id = 5, rcode = NOERROR
        header flags:  query, want recursion
        questions = 1,  answers = 0,  authority records = 0,  additional = 0
```

```
        QUESTIONS:
                nameserver2.hq.mycompany.com, type = A, class = IN

- - - - - - - - - - - -
- - - - - - - - - - - -
Got answer (56 bytes):
        HEADER:
                opcode = QUERY, id = 5, rcode = NOERROR
                header flags:  response, auth. answer, want recursion, recursion avail.
                questions = 1,  answers = 1,  authority records = 0,  additional = 0

        QUESTIONS:
                nameserver2.hq.mycompany.com, type = A, class = IN
        ANSWERS:
        ->  nameserver2.hq.mycompany.com
                type = A, class = IN, dlen = 4
                internet address = 10.132.13.239
                ttl = 3600 (1 hour)

- - - - - - - - - - - -
Name:      nameserver2.hq.mycompany.com
Address:   10.132.13.239
```

set [no]d2

This command controls the exhaustive debugging mode. Nod2 turns the mode off. When on, the fields of every packet are printed. The default is nod2.

```
set [no]d2
```

set [no]def[name]

Setting the defname appends the default DNS domain name to a single-component lookup request, one that contains no periods. The default is defname.

```
set defname
```

set do[main]

You can change the default DNS domain to the name specified. Some search options append the default DNS domain name to a lookup request. The default is from the host name.

```
set domain=name
```

set [no]ig[nore]

If you set ignore, NsLookup ignores packet truncation errors. The default is noignore.

```
set noignore
```

set po[rt]

To change the DNS name server port from the default TCP/UDP port 53, set port must specify a different port number. For more information on port number values see table 13.5.

```
set port=number
```

set [no]rec[urse]

If the DNS server doesn't have the information requested, the recurse setting tells the DNS name server to query other servers. The default is to set recurse.

```
set recurse
```

set ret[ry]

If a reply is not received in a certain amount of time, the request is resent. By changing the retry value, you change the number of times a request is resent before giving up. The default is four.

```
set ret[ry]=number
```

set ro[ot]

You can change the name of the root server by specifying a different computer name. The default setting is = ns.nic.ddn.mil.

```
set root=<server>
```

set [no]sea[rch]

When search is set and the request contains at least one period but does not end with a trailing period, NsLookup appends the DNS domain names in the DNS domain search list to the request until an answer is received. The default is search.

```
set search
```

set srchl[ist]

You can use a searchlist in a different domain by changing from the default searchlist. You can list up to six names, which you must separate using slashes. This command overrides the set domain command. To display the list, use the set all command. The default searchlist is based on the host name.

```
set srchlist=name1/name2/...
```

For example, the following command sets the DNS domain to mfg.widgets.com and the searchlist to the three specified domain names:

```
set  srchlist=mfg.widgets.com/mrp2.widgets.com/widgets.com
```

set ti[meout]

The timeout governs the waiting time (in seconds) for a reply. If the reply doesn't come within the specified time, the request is sent again with a wait period double the initial timeout value. The default is five seconds.

```
set timeout=number
```

set [no]v[c]

This command sets a virtual circuit when sending requests to the server. The default is [no]v[c].

```
set novc
```

set q[uerytype] or set type

This command changes the type of query. RFC 1035 has more information about different information types. The default query is for address information, A. Table 24.5 summarizes the values used with the set q[uerytype] command.

```
set querytype=value
```

Table 24.5
Value Parameters for Query Type

Value	Description
A	Computer's IP address
ANY	All types of data
CNAME	Canonical name for an alias
GID	Group identifier of a group name
HINFO	Computer's CPU and operating system type
MB	Mailbox domain name
MG	Mail group member
MINFO	Mailbox or mail list information
MR	Mail rename domain name
MX	Mail exchanger
NS	DNS name server for the named zone

continues

Table 24.5, Continued
Value Parameters for Query Type

Value	Description
PTR	Computer name if the query is an IP address, otherwise the pointer to other information
SOA	DNS domain's start-of-authority record
TXT	Text information
UID	User ID
UINFO	User information
WKS	Well-known service description

If NsLookup doesn't display the information you requested, it usually prints an error message. The following section lists common error messages, explaining their meaning and suggesting some possible solutions.

Error Messages

Message: Timed out

Description: Server failed to respond in a certain amount of time.

Suggestions: Ping the server to make certain that it's alive. Look for general network connectivity problems, such as misconfigured default gateways or subnet masks. If the server responds to pings but doesn't answer DNS queries, make certain that its DNS Service is configured correctly. Check the NT Server Event log for messages related to DNS Server problems.

Message: No response from server

Description: DNS is not running on the server. The server responded with an ICMP port unreachable message to inform you that it isn't providing DNS services.

Suggestions: Check the services list in Control Panel to verify that it isn't running. Check the NT Server Event log for messages related to DNS Server problems. Either configure and start the DNS service, or select a different server for your queries.

Message: No records

Description: The DNS server doesn't have the records of the requested type.

Suggestions: Use the DNS Manager to view the DNS database to see what records are available. Use a text editor to check that the DNS database files in %SystemRoot%\System32\DNS have the records that you seek. Check the Event Log to see if DNS found errors while loading of the files.

Message: Format error

Description: The request packet isn't in the proper format.

Suggestions: The error could indicate that you're querying an old version of a DNS server, or it might indicate packet corruption in the network.

Message: Server failure

Description: Internal inconsistency in the DNS database.

Suggestions: Check for typographical errors in the DNS database files, especially in the IP addresses.

Message: Connection refused (or) Network is unreachable

Description: Connection to the server could not be made.

Suggestions: Make certain that the link between you and the server is viable by using ping and tracert.

Message: Refused

Description: DNS name server refused to service the request.

Suggestions: Make certain that your query went to an interface accepting DNS queries. Check whether the server is configured to use only certain interfaces.

Other Diagnostic Utilities

Another very helpful diagnostic tool is the Event Log. It can help identify many different kinds of startup problems. Open the Event Viewer by clicking on the Event Viewer icon in the Administrative Tools directory.

You can configure the Event Log with several different options. Make certain that the System is checked in the Log menu. The following sections enumerate possible problems that the Event Log can identify.

Network Adapter Not Responding

Check that it is seated well with a network cable plugged in. Check that it is configured correctly, particularly for correct IRQ, memory, and I/O address. Make certain that it is using the correct driver.

DNS Failed To Start

Check that there is a Boot and Cache file in the DNS directory, or appropriate entries in the NT Registry under the DNS hive. Check that TCP/IP is installed. Check that the server has enough system resources with the Performance Meter.

Incorrect Data in Boot or Cache File

Check for a typographical error in the Boot or Cache file. Make certain that all necessary trailing periods are present.

COM and DCOM

Component software is a hot topic in the computer industry. It offers great opportunities for several different computer industry communities. Application users, Internet content providers, application vendors, and software developers all are excited about the impact that component software has on their respective activities. Specifically, this chapter looks at component software from both the developer and the application-user perspectives, in terms of the COM model and the DCOM configuration tool.

The COM Model

The first section introduces you to the COM model on which ActiveX is based. It is difficult to do effective ActiveX programming without a basic understanding of the COM model. This section also will help demystify the vast array of acronyms and terminology that has come to be associated with ActiveX.

The Component Object Model should not be confused with another technology by a similar name: Common Object Model (COM). Common Object Model is a technology being jointly developed by Microsoft and Digital.

COM consists of two elements: object bus and object services (see Figure 25.1). The object bus is the infrastructure that is used by objects to communicate with each other. The object services are services such as object storage, automation and scripting, uniform data transfer, and compound document management that are used by objects that are written to the COM model.

Figure 25.1
The Component Object Model.

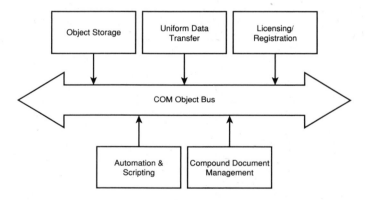

The problem that COM attempts to solve is how an object interacts with another object on the system, even though the objects are written in different languages. Among other things, COM attempts to define how an object can invoke the methods of another object that may be running in the same process or a different process on the system.

COM Objects and Interfaces

Object provides a set of methods and data access to the users of the object. In COM, the methods are modeled by an interface that represents the contract between the object and the users of the object (object clients). The objects may be written in Java or another programming language. When the object is to be encapsulated as a COM object, it is described in terms of its interface (see Figure 25.2). The COM interface can be thought of as representing a COM object.

While the real object behind the COM interface may exhibit state properties (such as the alteration of the object's data), the COM object represented by the COM interface does not have state. Therefore, a COM object is not a true object in the object oriented sense.

The COM interface is a set of related functions (methods in Java). In order to use the COM object, its clients call the functions in the COM interface via pointers. This pointer provides access to the interface method and is not related to the state information of the real object.

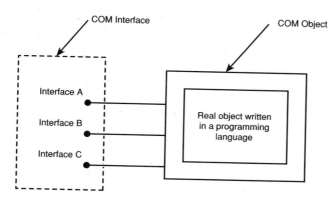

Figure 25.2

COM objects and interfaces.

The COM model is limited to objects within a single computer. The interaction between objects across a network is handled by another model (also by Microsoft), called DCOM (Distributed Component Object Model).

A COM client can access the interface of another COM object (COM server) that is in the same process as the COM client, or in a different process, as long as the COM client and COM object are on the same computer. DCOM permits COM clients and COM objects to be on separate computers.

The binding to the interface of a COM object is a low-level binary API that uses a table of pointers. COM clients use a pointer to this table of pointers that point to the actual methods implemented by the COM object. COM does not use a high-level language binding such as that used in C/C++ and SmallTalk languages that you can use to call the methods of another COM object. You must use this table of pointers approach.

Note   If you are using Microsoft C++, the virtual table (vtab) associated with class instances has the same layout as expected by COM. Another vendor's C++ compiler may not use this layout so you will have to build the method table by some other means. This indirectly implies that the C++ code for COM method invocation is not portable.

In the COM model, the convention is to give interfaces names beginning with a capital "I," such as the IUnknown interface that is used to query COM objects about the COM object. Interface names are used by COM programming tools. When the actual binary code is generated, the interface names disappear. At runtime the interfaces are known by a unique interface identifier. This unique identifier is generated by COM and is called the Globally Unique Identifier (GUID). GUIDs are 128-bit values that are generated by calling the COM API function CoCreateGuid.

> **Note** GUIDs are 128-bit values that are generated by using the current date and time, the network card address, and a high-frequency counter.

The IUnknown interface is implemented by all COM objects. One of the functions that is available through the IUnknown interface is the QueryInterface function. COM objects can use this to query the IUnknown interface of any COM object in order to find out details about that object.

Just as COM Interface is identified by a GUID, the COM class itself is identified by a unique 128-bit identifier called the *Class Identifier (CLSID)*. The COM object is a runtime instance of this COM class.

Multiple COM Interfaces

A COM class can support multiple interfaces. When the COM class is instantiated to produce a COM object, the COM object will provide implementations of the functions for all the COM class's interfaces. All COM objects have at least the IUnknown interface; if they support another interface, they are examples of COM classes with multiple interfaces.

The IUnknown interface is used by COM objects for interface negotiations. For example, a COM object may use the IUnknown interface to query another object about which interfaces are supported and then obtain pointers to them. Clients always access other COM objects through these pointers, and never directly access another COM object.

The Structure of a COM Server

The COM object that responds to a request by another COM object is called a COM server. The COM server is usually in an .EXE or .DLL file. There are one or more COM classes identified by their unique CLSID inside a COM server. The COM server is the serving agent that handles requests for services provided by the classes that it contains.

When a COM server receives a request for a specific CLSID, it loads the COM server code (.EXE or .DLL file). The COM then asks the COM server to create an instance of the requested class. The COM server creates instances by using special class factory interfaces. There are two types of class factory interfaces: IClassFactory or IClassFactory2. These interfaces provide functions to create instances of the server object. The IClassFactory2 additionally provides licensing functions that will allow an object to be created only when the licensing key or licensing file is specified. Figure 25.3 shows the general architecture of a COM server.

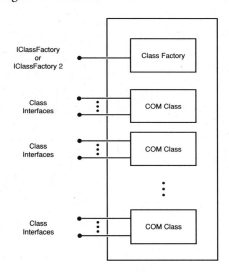

Figure 25.3
The COM server.

Besides implementing the class factories for creating the COM objects, the COM server must provide facilities for registering the class it supports, initialize the COM library (OLE32.DLL) by using the `CoInitialize` API, verify that the library is a compatible version by calling the `CoBuildVersion` API, uninitialize the COM library when it is not in use by calling the `CoUninitialize` API, and provide an unloading mechanism so that the server can unload itself when there is no one using its objects.

Note All COM APIs have a "Co" prefix. You can see this in the examples of the CoInitialize, CoBuildVersion, CoUninitialize APIs mentioned in this section.

Types of COM Servers

COM defines three types of COM servers:

- In-Process servers

- Local servers

- Remote servers

In-Process COM servers are implemented in a single process. The client and the server COM objects are in the same process. There is no need to cross a process boundary (see Figure 25.4). This is typically implemented as a Windows Dynamic Link Library (DLL).

Figure 25.4

In-Process COM servers.

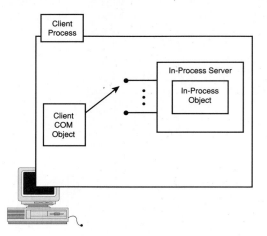

Local Servers are implemented in separate processes on the same computer. The client and the server COM objects are in different processes. There is a need to cross a process boundary (see Figure 25.5). This is typically implemented as an executable file (.EXE extension). The Lightweight Remote Procedure Call (LRPC) is used for interprocess communication on the local server.

Figure 25.5

Local Process COM servers.

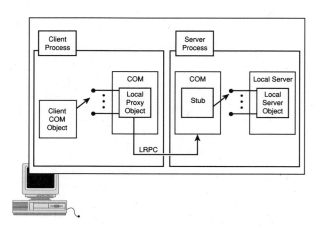

Remote Servers are implemented in separate processes on different computers on a network. The client and the server COM objects are in different processes and different computers. There is a need to cross a process and a network boundary (see Figure 25.6). A DCE (Distributed Computing Environment) based Remote Procedure Call (RPC) is used for interprocess communication to the remote server. Remote server implementation is part of DCOM.

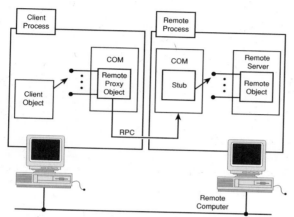

Figure 25.6

Remote Process COM servers.

In In-Process COM servers, the method invocation reaches the COM server through the interface pointer table, without using any system-specific interprocess communication mechanism since the client and server are in the same process.

In both the Local Server and Remote Server, the call has to cross a process boundary. These are both examples of out-of-process servers. A proxy within the client's process intercepts the call and issues an LRPC or RPC to the server process. The LRPC or RPC is received by a stub that performs the parameter marshaling (process of converting between arguments passed from the client object to the server object) and forwards the call to the server object.

For out-of-process servers, the server is located by a COM element called Service Control Manager (SCM).

Negotiating between COM Objects and COM Servers

Negotiations between the COM object and COM server are performed through the server object's IUnknown interface. The IUnknown interface implements three functions:

- QueryInterface

- AddRef

- Release

Clients use the QueryInterface function to find out the rest of the interfaces supported by the object. They are able to do this at runtime, and can determine whether a particular object supports the interface. After the interface pointer is obtained, the client invokes the members of the remote object through the interface pointer. The client must check a failure code returned by the QueryInterface before it proceeds with any calls.

> **Note**   While new interfaces can be added to a COM object and discovered by the QueryInterface, the interface itself cannot be changed without affecting existing code.

When a COM server object is instantiated through the class factory interface, it is kept around until it is no longer in use. There has to be a mechanism to determine when an object is no longer in use. COM implements this by using at least a 31-bit reference count. An interface's AddRef function is called when a client requests a pointer to the interface or passes a reference to it—this increments the reference count. An interface's Release function is called when the client no longer uses that interface—this decreases the reference count.

The reference count is used to determine when an object is no longer in use. Objects delete themselves when they are no longer in use.

Encapsulating Objects in COM

COM does not support multiple inheritance. Instead, it supports multiple interfaces. In COM, components can encapsulate each other and control the set of interfaces that are visible to the client. This is done by providing two methods of encapsulation:

- Containment/delegation

- Aggregation

The containment/delegation encapsulation approach is shown in Figure 25.7. This figure shows that an object X encapsulates an object Y. The object X has interfaces IA and IB, and the object Y has interfaces IC and ID. The interfaces IA and IB are available to users of object X. The interfaces of the inner object IC and ID are made available through the IUnknown interface for object X. When a client calls interfaces IC or ID for object Y, the outer object X calls the inner object and receives these calls and delegates them to the interface methods for the inner object Y.

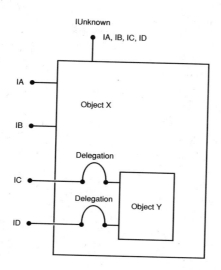

Figure 25.7
*Encapsulation
by using containment/
delegation.*

The aggregation encapsulation approach is shown in Figure 25.8. This figure shows that an object X encapsulates an object Y. The object X has interfaces IA and IB, and the object Y has interfaces IC and ID—available to users of object, as well as the interfaces of the inner object Y, IC, and ID. The outer object makes the inner interfaces directly available, as if they belonged to the outer object. When a client calls interfaces IC or ID, they are handled by object X. The client ends up using these interfaces without the involvement of the outer object.

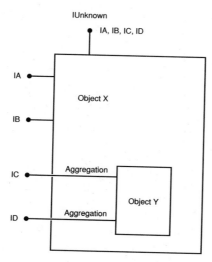

Figure 25.8
*Encapsulation
by using aggregation.*

Figure 25.9 shows how the aggregation approach can be used to give the appearance of pseudo-multiple inheritance. In this figure, objects Y and Z are aggregated in object X. The interfaces for Y and Z are directly available through object X. So object X is seen to inherit interfaces from two sources: object X and object Y. This approach is not true of multiple inheritance because you do not inherit the states of the parent objects. Figure 25.10 shows multiple inheritance where the state as well as the interfaces of the parent objects are inherited.

Figure 25.9

Pseudo-multiple inheritance by using aggregation.

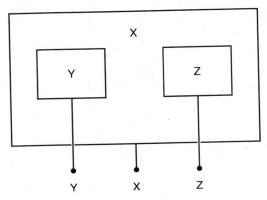

Interface Y and Z are inherited.

Figure 25.10

Classic multiple inheritance.

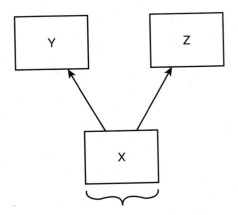

Interface Y, Z and their state are inherited.

Understanding Type Libraries and Monikers

As part of understanding how COM and Java are integrated in Visual J++, there are two additional concepts that are important to understand:

■ Type Libraries

■ Monikers

Type Libraries contain meta-data about an object's interface functions that can be queried at runtime to discover how to invoke these functions. Monikers are persistent objects that are used to assign a persistent name to an individual object instantiation.

Understanding Type Libraries

There are a number of situations where the client needs to learn the services a COM object provides dynamically and at runtime. An example of this is the situation when an automation controller acts as a client to use the services of an automation server (see Figure 25.11).

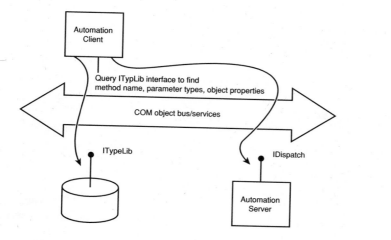

Figure 25.11

Automation server/ client.

The information about the method and properties that an automation server exposes to a client is defined in a *Type Library*. The Type Library contains data about the services that a COM object provides and which the client can obtain dynamically. The Type

Libraries contain information that describe an object's methods and the readable and writeable properties that the services for the object expose. This information is used by ActiveX controls.

After the Type Library is interrogated, the IDispatch interface of the automation server is called. The IDispatch interface provides functions such as GetIDsOfNames, GetTypeInfoCount, and GetTypeInfo to retrieve information about the object's methods and properties. The remaining function, Invoke, is used to call an object's method based on the value of an identifier called the *dispID*, that is passed to the Invoke function. Figure 25.12 illustrates the IDispatch interface. The IDispatch interface provides a runtime "late binding" mechanism for exposing a COM object's functions and properties. The late bound interfaces are called dispatch interfaces or *dispinterfaces*.

Figure 25.12

IDispatch interface.

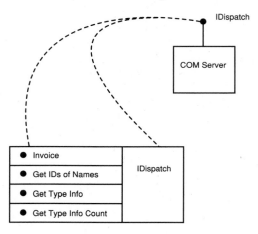

The type of services that a COM object provides is described in the Object Description Language (ODL). The ODL for an object is written as a text file. You can enter this information manually, or use a language tool (such as Microsoft Visual C++) to generate the ODL text file. The text information file is then compiled by a tool such as MKTYPLIB to create the Type Library file (.TLB extension).

Currently, Microsoft uses two description languages: Interface Definition Language (IDL) and Object Description Language (ODL). Microsoft's IDL is a proprietary superset of the DCE IDL and is used to describe an object's interface. The IDL description of the interface is compiled by using the Microsoft Interface Definition Language (MIDL) compiler that converts the text description of an interface to language code for proxies and stubs.

The ODL introduces new extensions to describe both static and dynamic data and the overall structure of a COM class. ODL and IDL have a similar syntax, but they use different keywords and may describe different data. ODL describes in greater detail the structure of COM servers, whereas IDL describes in greater detail the information needed by DCE RPCs.

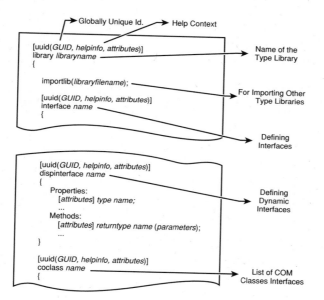

Figure 25.13
ODL Syntax.

The structure of a Type Library is shown in Figure 25.13. The structural elements are explained next.

The *libraryname* is the name of the body of the ODL. Every statement in the top level block ({}) is part of the library. Every library has a name, a GUID, help information, and attributes. This information has the following syntax:

```
[uuid(GUID, helpinfo, attributes]
library libraryname
{

    ...

}
```

The *attributes* for the library include the following: *lcid*, which is the locale id that defines the national language conventions; *hidden*, which means the library is hidden from browsing tools; *restricted*, which means that the library functions are not available for calling; and *version*, which describes the version control.

The import library statement has the following syntax:

```
importlib(libraryfilename);
```

This statement is used to import definitions from another type library. If you need to import automation types, you must import the standard OLE type library, `stdole.tlb`:

```
importlib(stdole.tlb);
```

```
The interface definition has the following syntax:
    [uuid(GUID, helpinfo, attributes]
    interface name
    {
        [attributes] returntype [callingconvention]
            functionname (parameters);


        ...
    }
```

The interface defines the member functions that will make up the interface for the COM object. It has a GUID, help information, and attributes. The *attributes* of the interface include the following: *hidden*, which means the member functions are hidden from browsing tools; *restricted*, which means that the member functions are not available for calling; *dual*, which means that the interface is both static and dynamic; and *ODL*, which is used to indicate that this is an ODL definition and different from an IDL definition.

The interface function definition must specify a return type, a function name, and parameters. The attributes of the functions in the interface include the following: *propget* and *propput*, which indicates a get/put property function; *vararg*, which indicates that the function takes a variable number of arguments; and *id(n)*, which assigns a dispID to a member. Hidden functions are indicated by preceding their function name with an underscore (_).

The parameters list can be void, or consist of a number of entries separated by a comma, that are of the following type:

```
[attributes] type name
```

The attributes of the parameters include the following: *in*, to indicate that the parameter is an input parameter; *out*, to indicate that the parameter is an output parameter; and *optional*, to indicate that the parameter may be omitted.

The dispinterface can have two formats. The first format is the following:

```
[uuid(GUID, helpinfo, attributes]
dispinterface name
{
      interface name;

}
```

In this format, only the interface names are listed. The listed interfaces must have been previously defined, using the syntax for defining interfaces that was discussed earlier in this section. The function names inside the listed interfaces are part of the named dispinterface.

A dispinterface has a GUID, help information, and attributes. The second format of the dispinterface is listed next:

```
[uuid(GUID, helpinfo, attributes]
dispinterface name
{
      Properties:
         [attributes] type name;
      ...
      Methods:
         [attributes] returntype name (parameters);
      ...
}
```

This format explicitly lists the properties and methods that make up the disp-interface. The attributes include the *id(n)*, which is the dispID for the member of the dispinterface.

The coclass lists the incoming and outgoing interfaces for the COM class. The class is identified by a GUID; it can also have the *hidden* and *version* attribute. Other attributes for the coclass include: *appobject*, which identifies the class as an application object; *control*, which identifies the class as an OLE control; and *licensed*, which indicates that the class must be instantiated by using the `IClassFactory2` interface.

A *source* attribute for an interface or dispinterface in a coclass makes the interface an outgoing interface. An incoming interface is the interface on which calls are made to the object. An outgoing interface is typically used to specify events generated by the COM object (see Figure 25.14). These events can be special COM interfaces called *sinks*, which absorb these events and act in a desired manner. Sink components consist of event handlers to handle the events generated by an outgoing interface. COM objects that have outgoing interfaces are called *source objects* or *connectable objects*.

Figure 25.14
*Incoming and
Outgoing interfaces.*

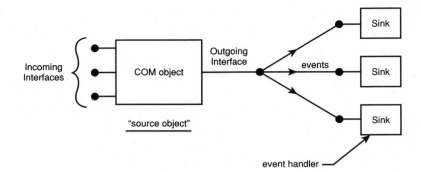

A default interface makes that interface more important than others. You typically have one default incoming and one default outgoing interface.

Figure 25.15 shows the process of creating a Type Library by using the MKTYPLIB tool. The information on which interfaces are defined in the Type Library can be obtained by using the ITypLib interface. The ITypInfo interface for each interface defines a number of functions that you can query to discover information about the COM object's member functions such as names, dispIDs, GUIDs, attributes, and so on.

Figure 25.15
*Using the MKTYPLIB
tool.*

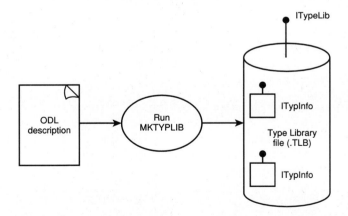

Understanding Monikers

Monikers are persistent objects that implement the IMoniker interface. A persistent COM object is one that can read or write itself from storage. Many objects in a program exist for the duration of execution of the program. When the program terminates and memory for it is released, the objects are destroyed. These types of objects are transient or temporary objects. A persistent object, on the other hand, can write itself into storage (such as disk file) before a program terminates. When the program is restarted, it can read itself from storage into memory.

The IMoniker interface is used to assign a persistent name to a COM persistent object. Moniker classes define the functions that are required for locating an object. The IMoniker interface only defines the interface that each moniker object must support. A moniker class with a unique class ID (CLSID) must implement the functions specified by the IMoniker interface. When the moniker class is instantiated, a moniker object is created. This moniker object maintains persistent information of its name and other data.

DCOMCNFG: DCOM Configuration Tool

Windows NT 4 has a DCOM configuration tool called DCOMCNFG. DCOMCNFG is the first tool Microsoft distributed to configure and administer the DCOM protocol. Consequently, you should consider its functionality preliminary and subject to change.

The intent of the DCOMCNFG utility is to enable administrators to set various application properties for component server applications that exist on the Windows NT 4 computer. Administrators can set properties for specific DCOM component server applications or properties that apply to all components accessed via distributed COM.

DCOM is such a new technology that it's hard to say what types of tasks administrators will have to perform. This chapter, therefore, provides an exhaustive discussion of the DCOMCNFG configuration utility, introducing and discussing each configuration option.

To run DCOMCNFG from the Start menu, click on **R**un, and then enter **DCOMCNFG**. The DCOMCNFG utility is a tabbed dialog box. Each tab contains related information and administrative settings. You bring a tab to the forefront (open a tab, basically) by clicking on it.

DCOMCNFG: Applications Tab

The Applications tab contains a list of the component servers available on the Windows NT 4 system. These applications can be accessed via the DCOM protocol. To view or set the application properties that apply to a specific application, select the application and click on the **P**roperties button.

Remember that these properties and settings apply to the specific component server application you select. The title bar identifies which component server application properties you are administering. Settings that apply to all applications are discussed later.

Note Double-clicking on the desired application has the same effect as choosing the **P**roperties button.

Application General Properties

The General tab displays general information about the component object server application. Specifically, it displays the application type and local path. The two possibilities for the application type are *local* and *remote*. An application can be local, remote, or both. The following section, "Application Location Properties," discusses this issue.

If the application type is local, the Local Path lists the path to the location of the component server application executable file on the Windows NT 4 system. If the application type is remote, you see a Remote Computer field, filled with a computer name. This identifies the computer on which the component server application resides.

The General tab provides information only. You can't alter any properties or settings on this tab. The Location tab, discussed next, however, enables administrators to alter the properties that affect the information displayed here.

Application Location Properties

The following settings are available in the Location tab:

- **Run application on the computer where the data is located.** Indicates that the component server application should run on the computer that contains the component data.

  Example: You might have a database query component available via DCOM to any computer on your network. Although the component may be accessed from other computers, it must run on the computer on which the database exists. Select this setting to make that the case.

- **Run application on this computer.** Indicates that DCOM should execute the component server application on the local computer.

  Example: A user of this machine requests to perform a spell check on a document, and the local computer has a spell check component installed and configured to run on the local computer. The spell check application then runs on the user's local computer.

■ **Run application on the following computer.** Indicates that DCOM executes the component server application on a different (specified) machine. Selecting this setting enables the edit box where administrators must enter the computer name. The computer name may be entered in UNC (\\server1) or DNS (www.microsoft.com) format.

Example: A user may need to put a graph into a document. If the user doesn't have the graph component server installed, the user must access it on a different computer. As a DCOM administrator, you would use this setting to accomplish that end.

Note Any or all the settings may be selected. If more than one of the settings is checked, DCOM uses the first applicable setting.

Application Security Properties

As one feature, DCOM provides a *secure* method for components to communicate over the network. Administrators can set access and launch permissions for individual component server applications via the Security tab. This tab, in conjunction with the DCOM Default Security (discussed later), gives Administrators full control over who uses components on the Windows NT 4 computer.

For each component server application, administrators can set custom access and launch permissions or use default permissions that apply to all DCOM applications. To set custom access permissions, choose the Use custom access permissions button, and then choose the **E**dit button. The resulting dialog box enables you to add or remove users or user groups. For each user or user group, you may specify whether they have (Allow Access) or don't have (Deny Access) access to the component application.

Set custom launch permissions in an identical way to setting the access permissions. Each user or user group has (Allow Launch) or doesn't have (Deny Launch) permission to launch the component server application.

These settings come into play when users try to access the component server application via DCOM. If USER1 tries to use a spell checking component on a Windows NT 4 system, for example, DCOM ascertains whether USER1 has access permissions for the application in question. If not, USER1 is denied use of the spell checking component.

Application Identity Properties

The Identity tab enables Administrators to specify which user account is used to run the component server application.

A list of the available options, with an explanation of each, follows:

- **The interactive user.** Indicates that the account of the currently logged on user be utilized to run the component server application. If the current user does not have permission to access the application, access is denied. Essentially, this means that the component is not available unless the current user has permission to access the component. If no users are logged on to the system, all requests for the component are denied.

- **The launching user.** If selected, the account of the user requesting the server application is used to run the application. If the launching user does not have a suitable account, access is denied.

- **This user.** Enables the Administrator to specify a user whose account is to be used to run the component server application. If selected, you must specify the desired user as well as the appropriate password.

- **The System Account (services only).** Indicates that a built-in system account beutilized to run the component server application. This option is available only on component servers that run as Windows NT 4 services.

The application Identity properties are the final component-server, application-specific properties. The remaining configuration parameters apply to all DCOM component applications on Windows NT 4 computers.

DCOMCNFG: Default Properties Tab

The Default Properties tab is used to set DCOM parameters that affect every DCOM server application installed on the Windows NT 4 computer. Enable or disable DCOM by toggling the Enable Distributed COM on this computer check box. Additionally, Administrators use this tab to set DCOM communication properties.

The Default Authentication Level presents the first communication property with which Administrators must deal. Authentication refers to the process of assuring that potential users of an object (component server application) are who they say they are. This setting establishes whether, how, and when applications using DCOM perform authentication on the connection and use of components. This is a default setting that the applications themselves can modify or override. A list of the available authentication levels, with a definition of each, follows:

Note   In the following list, the term client refers to the application requesting use of the component object.

- ■ **None.** No authentication is enabled by default.

- ■ **Call.** Authentication takes place each time the client application makes a call to the component server application.

- ■ **Connect.** The client application is authenticated only when the initial connection from the client to the component server application is established. Subsequent network traffic between the client and server is not authenticated.

- ■ **Packet.** Every packet used for communication from the client to the component server application is authenticated to ensure it is from the same client.

- ■ **Packet Integrity.** Each packet sent between the client and the component server is authenticated as being from the same client, and is also checksummed to ensure that none of the contents have been modified. This guarantees no tampering, but does not guarantee protection from snooping.

- ■ **Packet Privacy.** Same as packet integrity (above), with the addition of encryption to prevent snooping on the contents of messages between the client and the component server application.

The Default Impersonation Level presents as the second communication property available to Administrators. *Impersonation* refers to the capability of the component application server to act on behalf of the caller. Consider a spell checking component that utilizes a series of personal (access-protected) dictionaries, for example, and is available for use via DCOM. If USER1 logs on to a workstation and uses the spell checking component via DCOM, the component probably wants to limit the dictionaries applied for the spell check operation to those USER1 has access to. To do this, the spell checking component needs to be able to identify who the client is and possibly *impersonate* the client to govern the use of personal dictionaries. A list of the possible impersonation levels, with a definition of each follows:

- ■ **Anonymous.** No identification is used. The server cannot identify callers.

- ■ **Identify.** This is the default impersonation level, and it enables the component application server to identify who the callers are. It does not, however, enable the server to act as the callers, except to *authorize* them against an access control list of some sort (such as access and launch permissions).

- ■ **Impersonate.** The component server can identify the callers and act as them to perform local operations (such as local data base queries). If the server calls another server for some reason, the second server cannot act as the original caller.

- ■ **Delegate.** Identical to Impersonate (preceding item) with the removal of the local designation. That is, subsequent servers called by the original server may act as the original caller.

The final communication property available to Administrators is the Provide additional security for reference tracking option. Checking this results in even deeper security checks on the management of connections between the client and component server application. This option is not typically required.

DCOMCNFG: Default Security Tab

The Default Security tab enables administrators to modify the default security parameters that apply to all DCOM component application servers that do not provide their own security settings (discussed previously under application properties).

Administrators can set the default access and launch permissions by choosing the Edit Default option. The Standard User Permissions dialog box enables administrators to allow or deny access and launch capabilities for the component server application.

Testing the DCOM Configuration

Currently, not many applications are written to take advantage of DCOM. Microsoft has released a DCOM sample on its World Wide Web site in the OLE Development section:

```
http://www.microsoft.com/oledev
```

This application was used to test the techniques discussed in this chapter.

The sample application consists of a DCOM server application (component) and a client application (component). After installing the server application on Windows NT 4, it appears as the Simple Object Server application in the DCOMCNFG configuration utility. Selecting to view its properties enables administrators to play around with the various DCOM settings. Subsequent execution of the client portion utilizes the current DCOM settings and enables administrators to examine and learn from the results.

Conclusion

This chapter introduced you to the COM model that is used to implement ActiveX controls. ActiveX is the new name for OLE or OCX controls. It is difficult to do effective ActiveX programming without a basic understanding of the COM model.

In this chapter you also learned about the basics of COM style interfaces and how they differ from classic object-oriented objects. COM style interfaces do not capture state information. You learned about the different types of COM servers: In-Process, local server, remote server, and how the IClassFactory interface is used to create COM server objects to handle client requests. Other topics covered in this chapter include automation servers, aggregation, type libraries, and monikers.

For a more complete description of the COM model and how it compares with the other industry standard model, CORBA (Common Object Request Broker), an excellent treatment of these topics is the book *The Essential Distributed Objects Survival Guide* by Robert Orfali, Dan Harkey, and Jeri Edwards, published by John Wiley. I am indebted to the authors for providing a clearer understanding of how the COM model compares with the state of the art in object-oriented computing.

This chapter also mentioned how you can apply DCOM to solve a logistical problem with component software—namely, the process required to upgrade software components. This application of the DCOM protocol is useful, and users can readily see that distributed components make their lives easier. What users won't see may be of greater importance to the DCOM technology.

Currently Win95 and WinNT 4 utilize software components to browse their respective namespaces (*namespace* is a term used to reference *everything* on a computer). Documents, folders, applications, and printers comprise a few of the things that can exist in a computer's namespace. The Windows NT Explorer and Find utility, for example, both use software components to determine what's on your computer. In this context, DCOM offers the opportunity to expand these applications to look at any number of computers. Users will be able to find information on networks using the same techniques they use to find information on their own computer. For that reason (among other reasons), Microsoft is investing in DCOM.

The next major version of the Windows operating system is expected to exploit the DCOM technology. Given an ever-increasing dependence on DCOM, you can expect DCOM configuration and administration to evolve accordingly.

Internet Information Server 4.0

Microsoft's Internet Information Server 4.0 builds on the performance and programmability of IIS 3.0 and adds several new servers and tools for developing enterprise-wide transactional web applications. Coupled with Microsoft Transaction Server, IIS 4.0 supports a highly scalable architecture for distributed applications. The added security, communications capabilities, and site analysis tools provide a complete solution for Internet or intranet development.

This chapter outlines the advanced features and benefits of IIS 4.0, the Internet and development standards used, and the basic transaction-based web-programming model utilized by IIS and Transaction Server. This chapter does not discuss setup, hands-on usage, or administration; it is instead a more technical overview of features and development principles.

Internet Information Server 4.0 Servers and Components

Presently, IIS 4.0 comes complete with the following Internet servers and tools:

- **Web Server.** The HTTP server that supports HTTP 1.0 and 1.1, and Microsoft's Active Server Pages.

- **Microsoft Transaction Server 1.0 (MTS).** Microsoft's transaction processing server that provides the infrastructure for distributed applications, including transactional Active Server Page scripts.

- **FTP Server.** The File Transfer Protocol (FTP) server.

- **SMTP Mail Server.** Standards-based mail server for use with web-based applications requiring e-mail functionality.

- **NNTP News Server.** A standards-based news server that enables site developers to host interactive information exchange, newsgroups, and forums.

- **Certificate Server.** A public-key cryptographic security tool for issuing digital certificates for enhanced site security. Certificate Server supports industry standards, as well as custom-developed extensions.

- **Site Analyst.** Provides complex reporting and site analysis, featuring built-in report templates and complete graphical site mapping.

- **Usage Analyst.** Analyzes site usage, including how pages are accessed, how individual content is viewed, and information on who has viewed what content.

- **Posting Acceptor.** This IIS 4.0 add-on enables HTTP 1.1 "PUT"-compliant web browsers to upload files directly to the web server, making updating content much easier and more convenient than using FTP.

IIS 4.0 has evolved into a complete suite of Internet server components. The following sections detail the IIS 4.0 features that are of high concern to network engineers, site administrators, and content developers:

- **Comprehensive List of New Features.** A list and explanation of the new features of IIS 4.0 and their importance.

- **Distributed Web Applications.** Includes Active Server Pages, ActiveX, Transaction Server, and how the Active Platform model uses these technologies to build distributed applications including web applications.

- **Performance Monitor Counters.** IIS 4.0 supports the NT Performance Monitor tool with several new performance monitoring objects. This list includes the performance objects for the IIS server, as well as individual servers and an explanation of their usage.

The latter part of the chapter covers each server component in the IIS 4.0 suite, their features, and any standards compliance that might be important to network engineers.

Comprehensive List of New Features

Many of the new features and capabilities of IIS 4.0 pertain to the new distributed software development model using Active Server Pages and Microsoft Transaction Server.

There have also been major changes in the way IIS performs and how it handles resources for both server activity and programmability, as indicated in the following.

- **Crash Protection and Recovery.** IIS-based applications can run in a separate memory space from the server and from other applications. A failed application cannot endanger the server process or other applications, providing for more robust and reliable content development.

  In the event of an application crash, IIS automatically restarts the application the next time it is referenced.

- **Integrated Security.** IIS 4.0 includes Microsoft Certificate Server, which allows sites to set up their own digital certificate authorities instead of relying on a third-party certificate and limited enterprise security, as in IIS 3.0.

- **Clients Mapped to Digital Certificate.** Clients can be mapped to a Windows NT user account based on their digital certificate. This provides integrated one-stop authentication for the entire network. Wild-card certificate authentication means the server can authenticate users based on their third-party certificates.

- **COM Object Support.** IIS 4.0 and its components support Microsoft's Component Object Model development standards, exposing programming functionality of each server for use with custom application development. Active Server Pages and other development platforms (such as Visual C++ or Visual Basic) can take advantage of a server's COM interfaces in order to create custom software and web content.

- **Content Rating.** IIS 4.0 supports the PIC rating system for web site content.

- **Content Expiration.** Content expiration controls the amount of time a page is cached in the client's browser, forcing updating either at certain intervals or immediately.

- **Document Footers.** Footer information can be instantly added to the bottom of each web page on a site; no actual altering of the HTML files is necessary.

- **Custom Errors.** Custom web pages and applications can be assigned to specific HTTP errors a client might see.

- **Content Replication.** Replication of entire directory trees can be quickly and easily performed between two or more servers.

- **Powerful Indexing and Document Search.** Using Index Server, either simple or custom index searches can be performed for content on the server. Searches are not limited to text documents. Index Server performs searches on all Microsoft Office documents including Word and Excel files.

- **Script Debugging.** The Microsoft Script Debugger can be used to test and debug Active Server Page scripts and detect errors while the application runs.

- **Powerful Logging Capabilities.** IIS 4.0 supports several industry-standard logging formats, as well as custom logging. Logging also takes advantage of the Windows NT Event Viewer for security and application events. Supported standards include ODBC logging, text file, common log format, and W3C extended logging. Log file analysis can be performed with the included Microsoft Site Server Express.

- **Software Development Support.** IIS 4.0 supports Active Server Pages and transactional scripting, which means support for DCOM (Distributed Component Object Model), Microsoft's "Network OLE" programming model. IIS 4.0 also supports ISAPI (Internet Server API) and both CGI and WinCGI. All of these options make porting existing web applications to IIS 4.0 much easier.

- **Microsoft Management Console (MMC).** The MMC is now the preferred administration tool for managing all aspects of Windows NT. IIS 4.0 is administered through snap-ins for MMC. This means that the entire server can be managed from one application.

- **Exposed Administrative Objects.** COM developers can take advantage of IIS 4.0's exposed administrative objects. This feature opens up the entire functionality of server administration, enabling the development of custom administration applications, such as ASP web pages, ActiveX controls, or quick Visual Basic front-ends.

Distributed Web Applications

Internet Information Server 4.0 has evolved into a powerful web application server, supporting the most popular Microsoft and third-party development and scripting languages. IIS 4.0 and Transaction Server 1.0 integrate to provide totally distributed component software systems. This integration enables the developer to concentrate on solving business problems rather than networking, communications, and Internet protocol problems.

Distributed component software provides the ability to place ActiveX components (controls, objects, scripts, resources, and so forth) throughout an organization's network. These components can work together as one highly scalable and reliable application, regardless of the location of each component.

For instance, a business application for entering data in a database might be comprised of several components: the actual database access and filtering components might exist on high-speed servers, with multiple copies on separate servers in case of offline time. The business rules and interface might exist in ActiveX controls that could either be accessed via a web browser or included as standalone front-end applications on each desktop. Security could be employed by restricting certain groups from viewing or changing critical information.

The problems inherent in developing distributed applications for a large organization lie in creating an infrastructure that allows all of these components to communicate over existing networks and protocols, remain secure, and provide transaction processing. Application developers, as well as web content developers, cannot afford to spend months or years coming up with a suitable method of doing this when all they want to do is create applications to solve business problems.

Transaction Server handles these problems, along with managing *transaction-based processing*, which means that each operation performed must work completely or all operations in that particular transaction will be rolled back to their original states. This fail-safe means that tasks are either completed properly or not at all.

By distributing components (such as ActiveX controls, transactional Active Server Page scripts, and so on), developers can create scalable multi-user applications for the entire enterprise. The phrase "enterprise-wide Internet and intranet applications" refers to this type of distributed programming model in which Internet protocols and technologies are used to bring business applications to the desktop. What IIS 4.0 does to extend this model is integrate the Internet/intranet server (including web, mail, news, and security support) with the underlying transaction processing runtime environment.

Transaction Server makes distributing scalable applications much easier, but at first glance it is not a simple piece of software. This section does not delve into the mechanics of Transaction Server, but it does outline its basic functionality and how Transaction Server works with IIS 4.0.

Transaction Server Components

Transaction Server hosts a runtime environment for transaction processing and communication with distributed components such as ActiveX controls. Transaction Server is composed of

- **The MTS Runtime Environment.** Controls transactions, security, manages system resources, creates, and deletes components as necessary. The MTS runtime environment is where components are executed and managed.

- **Resource Dispensers.** Services that manage process resources and allow other objects to share these resources. An obvious and useful example of a resource dispenser is the ODBC resource dispenser for managing ODBC database connections.

- **Resource Managers.** Resource managers handle the data store that MTS objects and client applications manipulate. Resource managers must be transactional and work with the transaction processing service of MTS. The example resource manager data store used in this chapter is Microsoft's SQL Server 6.5.

- **MTS Package.** A group of components that perform similar application functions. An MTS package is used to distribute sets of components and enforce security checks when accessed.

Microsoft Transaction Server integrates with Windows NT and Internet Information Server 4.0 to provide distributed transactional applications with the ability to roll back their state in the event that a transaction could not be completed. This rollback insures that data is either correctly and completely updated or not updated at all.

Transaction Server allows MTS Packages to distribute components across the network. These components can securely access stored data in Resource Managers (such as SQL Server 6.5) via Resource Dispensers (such as ODBC 3.0 drivers). De-coupling all of the components and using the Transaction Server runtime environment to handle security and communications means that developers only have to concentrate on solving business problems and increasing productivity.

Performance Counters

IIS 4.0 uses Windows NT Performance Monitor performance counters for monitoring various performance indicators of bandwidth and usage. Most of the server components in IIS 4.0 support performance counters, and along with the global counters shown in the following list (those that apply to the IIS Internet server as a whole), the performance counters for the web and FTP servers are included in later sections of this chapter.

- **Cache Flushes** is the number of times a portion of the memory cache has been expired due to file or directory changes in an Internet Information Services directory tree.

- **Cache Hits** is the total number of times a file open, directory listing, or service-specific object request was found in the cache.

- **Cache Hits %** is the ratio of cache hits to all cache requests.

- **Cache Misses** is the total number of times a file open, directory listing, or service-specific object request was not found in the cache.

- **Cache Size** is the configured maximum size of the shared HTTP and FTP memory cache.

- **Cache Used** is the total number of bytes currently containing cached data in the shared memory cache. This includes directory listings, file handle tracking, and service-specific objects.

- **Cached File Handles** is the number of open file handles cached by all of the Internet Information Services.

- **Current Blocked Async I/O Requests** is the number of current requests temporarily blocked due to bandwidth throttling settings.

- **Directory Listings** is the number of cached directory listings cached by all of the Internet Information Services.

- **Measured Async I/O Bandwidth Usage** is the measured bandwidth of asynchronous I/O averaged over a minute.

- **Objects** is the number of cached objects cached by all of the Internet Information Services. The objects include file handle tracking objects, directory listing objects, and service-specific objects.

- **Total Allowed Async I/O Requests** is the number of total requests allowed by bandwidth throttling settings (counted since service startup).

- **Total Blocked Async I/O Requests** is the number of total requests temporarily blocked due to bandwidth throttling settings (counted since service startup).

- **Total Rejected Async I/O Requests** is the number of total requests rejected due to bandwidth throttling settings (counted since service startup).

The Internet Information Server 4.0 Suite

IIS 4.0's full installation includes all the servers and tools needed for creating powerful Internet and intranet sites with integrated security, communication, and collaboration, as well as precise administrative control over each component. This section covers the major enhancements, standards, and administrative features of each server in the IIS 4.0 suite.

Web Server

IIS 4.0's Hypertext Transport Protocol (HTTP) web server exceeds the boundaries of traditional web servers by supporting Active Server Page content, transactional scripting, and customizable security. The IIS 4.0 web server's role in distributed enterprise computing is discussed earlier in this chapter.

IIS 4.0 supports HTTP 1.1 functionality built into the HTTP protocol, which now allows for the following:

- **Persistent Connections.** Typically, a web server creates a client connection for every file downloaded. A connection must be established and disconnected for every file (HTML, image, script, and so on) contained on a web page. Managing and supporting all of these connections can be a bandwidth and processor burden on the web server. Persistent connections solve this problem by requiring only one connection to view the requested content.

- **Pipelining.** Web servers normally only accept one request from a client at a time, in sequence, meaning a client cannot send another request until the server has acknowledged the first. Pipelining speeds up the process by allowing multiple requests to be sent before receiving a response, thus speeding up client response time.

- **HTTP "PUT" and "DELETE."** Using an HTTP 1.1–compliant web browser, authorized users can upload files to the web server, and likewise delete them. By supporting web-based interfaces for upload, download, and deletion, users can manage files without using (or learning) FTP clients, and content managers can quickly upload changes to online information.

Several new features based on industry standards and protocols and user demand have been integrated into the new web server, as follows.

■ Multiple web site hosting with multiple domains.

■ Bandwidth throttling to reduce the number of Kbytes per second of content files that the web server will deliver. Networks with more limited bandwidth will find this useful.

■ Web Site Operators can be designated for each individual web site on the IIS server. These operators' accounts are selected Windows NT user accounts and are granted limited administrative control over each site.

■ Custom error messages can be set for each HTTP error, giving more administrative control over errors and page redirection.

■ Content expiration forces cached web pages to be refreshed after a designated period of time—or not to be cached at all. This insures that sensitive information isn't cached and real-time information is always up to date.

■ Custom HTTP headers created and installed to work on specific web sites.

The following information is specific to the web site properties configurable with the Microsoft Management Console (MMC) with IIS 4.0 snap-in. The key features described previously are all configured using the MMC. Each subsection corresponds to a tab on the Properties dialog box for any web site in IIS 4.0.

Web Site

The Web Site tab provides most of the at-a-glance functionality that IIS 3.0's administrative tools provided, including IP and port addressing, connection limitations, and logging formats (see fig. 26.1).

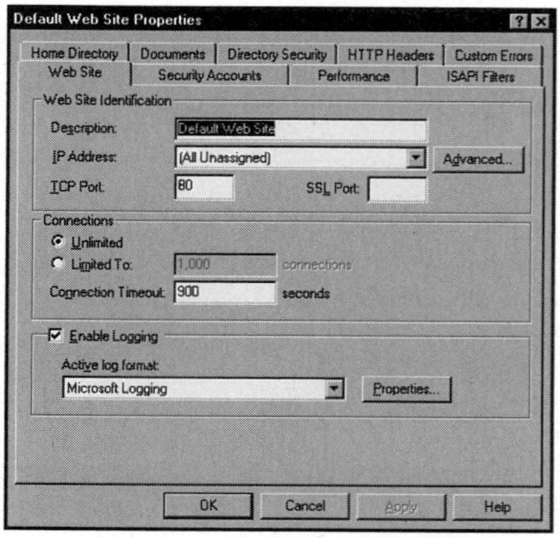

Figure 26.1

The Web Site tab.

The Web Site tab fields are explained here:

- **Description.** The descriptive name given to the individual web site. This is not the host and domain name applied to the site.

- **IP Address.** The IP address of the web site, which can be chosen from the drop-down box of available IP's on the server or further configured using the A**d**vanced button.

- **TCP Port.** Typically an HTTP server listens on port 80, but this can be easily changed using this field.

- **SSL Port.** For specifying the port used for Secure Socket Layer (SSL) protocol communications.

- **Connections.** Web site connections can be set either to unlimited or to a specific number based on whatever is appropriate for the site. Connection timeouts can also be specified, with the default of 900 seconds.

- **Logging.** IIS supports four types of industry standard logging, as mentioned earlier: Extended Logging, Microsoft Logging, NCSA Logging, and ODBC Logging to an ODBC data source. The **P**roperties button enables customization of the fields logged to the specified file.

Security Accounts

Account security can be maintained on both the generic anonymous user account and, new to IIS version 4.0, the Web Site Operators list. See figure 26.2 for an illustration of the Security Accounts tab.

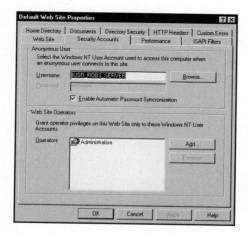

Figure 26.2

The Security Accounts tab.

■ **Anonymous User.** IIS 4.0 uses a Windows NT user account for use with anonymous access. The default user account, IUSR_*servername,* can be changed to a pre-established one if desired.

■ **Web Site Operators.** Each web site can have several designated administrative operators. Operators have the ability to administer and configure attributes of their assigned web site, but not the IIS server. The default operators are users in the Administrators group, but any others can be assigned.

Performance

Basic performance tuning can be administered through the Performance tab (see fig 26.3); while this offers a simplified approach, the Performance Monitor counters can be used to supply in-depth performance information for decision-making and planning.

Figure 26.3
The Performance tab.

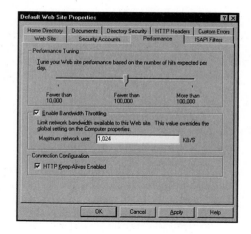

■ **Performance Tuning.** This is done rather simply with a choice between three states of web server performance hits:

  ■ Fewer than 10,000 hits per day

  ■ Fewer than 100,000 hits per day

  ■ More than 100,000 hits per day

■ **Enable Bandwidth Throttling.** The number of Kbytes per second can be set, insuring bandwidth is regulated if it is a concern on the network. The default is set to 1,024 KB/S, or 1MB/S.

■ **HTTP Keep-Alives Enabled.** HTTP keep-alives insure that HTTP connections are kept active ("alive") by the Internet server sending packets to the client repeatedly. Keep-alives can impact performance by increasing bandwidth and utilizing more system resources.

ISAPI Filters

Internet Information Server uses Internet Server Application Programming Interface (ISAPI) filters to extend the functionality of the web server. *Filters* are custom-developed pieces of software that are used to manipulate requests to the web server before they are intercepted. Filters can be used to force authentication, modify and extend logging functionality, parse strings of text, and any type of filtering actions the developer requires.

Multiple ISAPI filters can be installed on each web site and are accessed in sequential order. The order of the filters can be changed, and new ones can be added at any time. The ISAPI Filters tab is shown in figure 26.4.

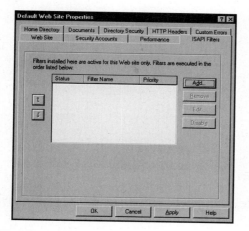

Figure 26.4
The ISAPI Filters tab.

Home Directory

The Home Directory tab enables advanced configuration of the default main directory on each web site. The options include setting permissions for directory access and application usage. Application settings for ISAPI and ASP can be fine-tuned, and the directory can be configured to support other Microsoft technologies such as Index Server and FrontPage. The Home Directory tab is shown in figure 26.5.

- **Home Directory.** The home directory can be set to a directory located on the local computer, a shared directory on another computer, or redirected a different URL.

- **Access Permissions.** **R**ead permission is typically the only one granted to a web content directory. **W**rite permission can be checked if the site will enable content posting using the Posting Acceptor.

- **Content Control.** There are four options for this:

    - **Log access** must be checked to allow IIS logging of access to the site.

    - **Directory browsing allowed** should remain unchecked unless it is acceptable for users to browse the listings of files in a directory that does not have a default document (such as index.asp).

    - **Index this directory** allows Microsoft Index Server to index files on the site for returning index information for user queries.

    - **FrontPage Web** allows Microsoft's FrontPage web development software to access the web site for remote web development. This also supports Microsoft's Visual InterDev development system, which relies on the FrontPage Extensions for IIS.

- **Application Settings.** Web applications can be set to run in separate memory spaces from each other and the sever, meaning more robust and reliable apps that do not run the risk of crashing the server process. Permissions can also be set to allow either no execution of applications, only scripts, or both executable programs *and* scripts.

Documents

The Documents tab (see fig. 26.6) simply enables administrators to set the support file names for default documents that are referenced from a URL that does not include the document name. For example: `http://www.mycompany.com/info/`.

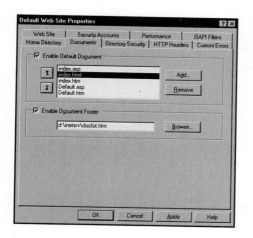

Figure 26.6

The Documents tab.

■ **Enable Default Document.** Default documents are automatically referenced when a directory is accessed on the web site. In IIS 4.0, multiple default document types can be specified in case some directories (particularly content from previous installations of IIS, other web directories, and so forth) have different default HTML documents from others. This is helpful in insuring that every directory, whether its default document is default.htm, index.asp, index.html, and so on, is accessed properly.

■ **Enable Document Footer.** A document footer can automatically be added to every web page on the web site. Document footers can contain advertising or copyright information, or anything else relevant that should appear at the bottom of each page.

Directory Security

Directory security can be tailored for each individual directory, providing very fine-tuned control over content and private information. The Directory Security tab (see fig. 26.7) provides a one-stop location for configuring password security, protocol security, and TCP/IP access restrictions.

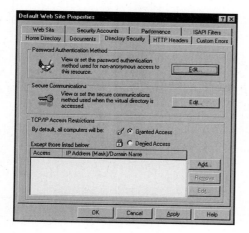

Figure 26.7

The Directory Security tab.

- **Password Authentication Method.** IIS supports the following authentication methods for non-anonymous access:

    - **Basic Authentication (password is sent in clear text).** Passwords and other authentication information is sent via clear text. Although this is supported by all web browsers, it offers no security.

    - **Windows NT Challenge Response.** Offers tighter security with encrypted logon, but is only supported by Microsoft's Internet Explorer 3.0 and above.

- **Enable SSL Client Authentication.** For use with digital certificates for either SSL client authentication or mapping certificates to an NT user account. SSL offers highly secure cryptographic transmission of passwords and credentials and is supported by most web browsers.

HTTP Headers

The HTTP Headers tab enables administrators to control header policies such as cache expiration, content ratings systems, and the MIME types sent via HTTP headers to a web browser to tell it what type of application should be used to view a specific file type. IIS 4 also supports custom HTTP headers (see fig. 26.8), which can be added or removed with this tab.

Figure 26.8
The HTTP Headers tab.

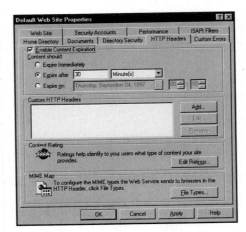

- **Enable Content Expiration.** To enforce updating and restrict caching of content, expiration times can be established. The three options for this are

    - **Expire Immediately.** This forces the content not to be cached by the client's web browser, meaning it must be updated immediately.

    - **Expire after: *<time>*.** Expiration can be set by minutes, hours, or days relative to the time of initial viewing.

    - **Expire on: *<date>*.** Expiration can be set to a specific date.

■ **Custom HTTP Headers.** Custom headers can easily be added, edited, and removed.

■ **Content Rating.** Site operators can enable a ratings system on the web site and configure ratings for the site based on criteria such as language, violence, obscenity, and so on.

■ **MIME Map.** The web server sends MIME types to the web browser, indicating the proper file types for each type of content. These file types can be changed and edited for each specific site.

Custom Errors

With IIS 4.0, HTTP errors can be specially configured to return custom content instead of the default error messages. With the Custom Errors tab, administrators can select every individual error and choose either a file or application to send when the error is encountered on a client browser. Useful applications of this are creating a default search page for `404 File not found` errors, or custom ASP applications to send administrative alerts when unauthorized users attempt multiple access of forbidden directories (see fig. 26.9).

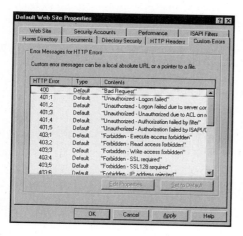

Figure 26.9

The Custom Errors tab.

Web Server Performance Counters

IIS 4.0's Web Server includes Windows NT Performance Monitor counters for measuring the performance of bandwidth usage, connections, and how applications are run. Following is a list of the Web Server performance counters and the descriptions of each given by the Windows NT Performance Monitor.

■ **Anonymous Users/sec** is the rate users are making anonymous connections using the Web Server.

■ **Bytes Received/sec** is the rate data bytes are received by the Web Server.

■ **Bytes Sent/sec** is the rate data bytes are sent by the Web Server.

- **Bytes Total/sec** is the sum of Bytes Sent/sec and Bytes Received/sec. This is the total rate of bytes transferred by the Web Server.

- **CGI Requests/sec** is the rate of CGI requests that are simultaneously being processed by the Web Server.

- **Connection Attempts/sec** is the rate at which connections using the Web Server are being attempted.

- **Current Anonymous Users** is the number of users who currently have an anonymous connection using the Web Server.

- **Current Blocked Async I/O Requests** is the current number of requests temporarily blocked due to bandwidth throttling settings.

- **Current CAL count for authenticated users** is the current count of licenses used simultaneously by the Web Server for authenticated connections.

- **Current CAL count for SSL connections** is the current count of licenses used simultaneously by the Web Server for SSL connections.

- **Current CGI Requests** is the current number of CGI requests that are simultaneously being processed by the Web Server.

- **Current Connections** is the current number of connections established with the Web Server.

- **Current ISAPI Extension Requests** is the current number of Extension requests that are simultaneously being processed by the Web Server.

- **Current NonAnonymous Users** is the number of users who currently have a non-anonymous connection using the Web Server.

- **Delete Requests/sec** is the rate HTTP requests using the DELETE method are made. Delete requests are generally used for file removals.

- **Files Received/sec** is the rate files are received by the Web Server.

- **Files Sent/sec** is the rate files are sent by the Web Server.

- **Files/sec** is the rate files are transferred—that is, sent and received by the Web Server.

- **Get Requests/sec** is the rate at which HTTP requests using the GET method are made. Get requests are generally used for basic file retrievals or image maps, although they can be used with forms.

- **Head Requests/sec** is the rate at which HTTP requests using the HEAD method are made. Head requests generally indicate that a client is querying the state of a document they already have to see whether it needs to be refreshed.

■ **ISAPI Extension Requests/sec** is the rate of ISAPI Extension requests that are simultaneously being processed by the Web Server.

■ **Logon Attempts/sec** is the rate that logons using the Web Server are being attempted.

■ **Maximum Anonymous Users** is the maximum number of users who established concurrent anonymous connections using the Web Server (counted since service startup).

■ **Maximum CAL count for authenticated users** is the maximum count of licenses used simultaneously by the Web Server for authenticated connections.

■ **Maximum CAL count for SSL connections** is the maximum count of licenses used simultaneously by the Web Server for SSL connections.

■ **Maximum CGI Requests** is the maximum number of CGI requests simultaneously processed by the Web Server.

■ **Maximum Connections** is the maximum number of simultaneous connections established with the Web Server.

■ **Maximum ISAPI Extension Requests** is the maximum number of extension requests simultaneously processed by the Web Server.

■ **Maximum NonAnonymous Users** is the maximum number of users who established concurrent non-anonymous connections using the Web Server (counted since service startup).

■ **Measured Async I/O Bandwidth Usage** is the measured bandwidth of asynchronous I/O averaged over a minute.

■ **NonAnonymous Users/sec** is the rate users are making non-anonymous connections using the Web Server.

■ **Not Found Errors/sec** is the rate of errors due to requests that couldn't be satisfied by the server because the requested document could not be found. These are generally reported as an HTTP 404 error code to the client.

■ **Other Request Methods/sec** is the rate HTTP requests are made that do not use the GET, POST, PUT, DELETE, TRACE, or HEAD methods. These may include LINK or other methods supported by gateway applications.

■ **Post Request/sec** is the rate HTTP requests using the POST method are made. Post requests are generally used for forms or gateway requests.

■ **Put Requests/sec** is the rate HTTP requests using the PUT method are made.

■ **Total Allowed Async I/O Requests** is the total number of requests allowed by bandwidth throttling settings (counted since service startup).

- **Total Anonymous Users** is the total number of users who established an anonymous connection with the Web Server (counted since service startup).

- **Total Blocked Async I/O Requests** is the total number of requests temporarily blocked due to bandwidth throttling settings (counted since service startup).

- **Total Common Gateway Interface (CGI) requests** are custom gateway executables (.exe) the administrator can install to add forms processing or other dynamic data sources. CGI requests spawn a process on the server that can be a large drain on server resources. The count is the total since service startup.

- **Total Connection Attempts** is the number of connections that have been attempted using the Web Server (counted since service startup).

- **Total count of failed CAL request for authenticated users** is the number of HTTP requests that failed due to a license being unavailable for an authenticated user. The count is the total since service startup.

- **Total count of failed CAL requests for SSL connections** is the total count of HTTP requests that failed due to a license being unavailable for SSL connections.

- **Total Delete Requests** is the number of HTTP requests using the DELETE method (counted since service startup). Delete requests are generally used for file removals.

- **Total Files Received** is the total number of files received by the Web Server (counted since service startup).

- **Total Files Sent** is the total number of files sent by the Web Server (counted since service startup).

- **Total Files Transferred** is the sum of Files Sent and Files Received. This is the total number of files transferred by the Web Server (counted since service startup).

- **Total Get Requests** is the number of HTTP requests using the GET method (counted since service startup). Get requests are generally used for basic file retrievals or image maps, although they can be used with forms.

- **Total Head Requests** is the number of HTTP requests using the HEAD method (counted since service startup). Head requests generally indicate that a client is querying the state of a document they already have to see whether it needs to be refreshed.

- **Total ISAPI Extension Requests** are custom gateway Dynamic Link Libraries (.dll) that the administrator can install to add forms processing or other dynamic data sources. Unlike CGI requests, ISAPI requests are simple calls to a DLL library routine; thus, they are better suited to high-performance gateway applications. The count is the total since service startup.

- **Total Logon Attempts** is the number of logons that have been attempted using the Web Server (counted since service startup).

- **Total Method Requests** is the number of HTTP GET, POST, PUT, DELETE, TRACE, HEAD and other method requests (counted since service startup).

- **Total Method Requests/Sec** is the rate HTTP requests using GET, POST, PUT, DELETE, TRACE, or HEAD methods are made.

- **Total NonAnonymous Users** is the total number of users who established a non-anonymous connection with the Web Server (counted since service startup).

- **Total Not Found Errors** is the number of requests that couldn't be satisfied by the server because the requested document could not be found. These are generally reported as an HTTP 404 error code to the client. The count is the total since service startup.

- **Total Other Request Methods** is the number of HTTP requests that are not GET, POST, PUT, DELETE, TRACE, or HEAD methods (counted since service startup). These may include LINK or other methods supported by gateway applications.

- **Total Post Requests** is the number of HTTP requests using the POST method (counted since service startup). Post requests are generally used for forms or gateway requests.

- **Total Put Requests** is the number of HTTP requests using the PUT method (counted since service startup).

- **Total Rejected Async I/O Requests** is the total number of requests rejected due to bandwidth throttling settings (counted since service startup).

- **Total Trace Requests** is the number of HTTP requests using the TRACE method (counted since service startup). Trace requests enable the client to see what is being received at the end of the request chain and to use the information for diagnostic purposes.

FTP Server

Although web-based file transfer is becoming more popular and convenient, File Transfer Protocol (FTP) is still a mainstay in providing simple, universally supported file access to the Internet. Microsoft's FTP server is administered through the Microsoft Management Console, supports the same logging standards as other IIS 4.0 servers, and is easily configured in only a few minutes. The following sections cover the configuration choices for the FTP Server.

To configure FTP Server, right-click its directory in the MMC and choose Properties. The Properties tabbed dialog box appears with the following options.

FTP Site

The FTP Site tab, much like the Web Site tab, provides basic information configuration for the selected FTP site. Naming and IP addressing, connection limitations, and logging are all configured here (see fig. 26.10).

Figure 26.10

The FTP Site tab.

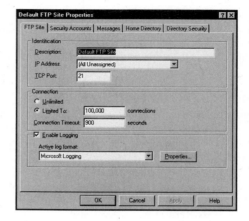

- **Description.** A descriptive name for the FTP site, not the host or domain name.

- **IP Address.** The IP Address of the FTP Server, which can be chosen from available server IP's from the drop-down list.

- **TCP Port.** The TCP port on which the FTP server listens; the default is port 21.

- **Connection.** The number of ftp connections to the server can be set to either Unlimited or to a specific number. Connection timeout, useful in maintaining only active connections to a busy or limited connection site, can be changed. The default is 900 seconds.

- **Enable Logging.** Like the Web Server, the FTP Server supports the four standard log types discussed earlier in this chapter: Extended Logging, Microsoft Logging, NCSA Logging, and ODBC Logging.

Security Accounts

The Security Accounts tab for the FTP server is similar to the one used for configuring the WWW site security accounts. The anonymous user account can be configured here (note that it can be different from the one used for the WWW site), as well as how anonymous connections are handled (see fig. 26.11).

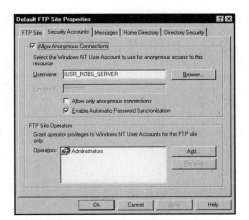

Figure 26.11
The Security Accounts tab.

■ **All_ow Anonymous Connections.** Anonymous FTP permission is decided here. Most ftp sites allow anonymous access to public information via a generic account with low security access. The IUSR_*servername* account is the default anonymous user account.

■ **All_ow only anonymous connections.** For a completely anonymous site that rejects all individual Windows NT user accounts. If this is an appropriate solution for your particular FTP site, it enhances security by denying hackers the opportunity to try to crack user passwords via ftp.

■ **FTP Site Operators.** FTP Operators can be specified from existing NT user accounts to manage and administer specific FTP sites. This works identically to the Web Site Operator role for the Web Server.

Messages

The standard messages a user sees when accessing the FTP server can be set easily, as shown in figure 26.12.

Figure 26.12
The Messages tab.

- **Welcome.** The welcome message the user sees upon connection to the FTP server.

- **Exit.** The message the user sees when logging off the FTP server.

- **Maximum Connections.** When the FTP server reaches its maximum number of connections, it refuses further logins until connections are freed. This is the message displayed when maximum connections have been reached and more connections are denied.

Home Directory

The home directory is the main directory from which FTP files are accessed (see fig 26.13).

Figure 26.13

The Home Directory tab.

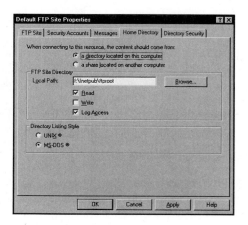

This directory can be either local to the server computer or a shared directory on another computer. Note that the proper permissions to access the share must be configured when the shared directory is selected.

- **FTP Site Directory.** After choosing the directory on either the local machine or another machine, FTP permissions should be applied to the root directory. These permissions are

  - **Read.** Read access to the file; allows viewing and download.

  - **Write.** Ability to upload, change files, and delete files. Also includes the capability to create and delete directories.

  - **Log Access.** This must be enabled before logging of directory access can be utilized.

- **Directory Listing Style.** Both Unix and MS-DOS directory listing styles are supported by the FTP Server. The Unix directory style is much more convenient to Internet users who are familiar with FTP sites, whereas the MS-DOS format is more familiar to users who are less experienced with the Internet or Unix and more comfortable with DOS.

Directory Security

Directory security for the FTP site involves setting access restrictions based on IP or DNS address information. Permissions can be set to be either inclusive or exclusive as described in the following list (see fig.26.14).

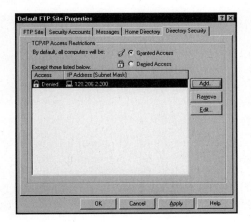

Figure 26.14

The Directory Security tab.

- ■ **TCP/IP Access Restrictions.** This is an effective way of setting restrictions on the FTP server based on the IP address or domain of the users. Access can be restricted in two ways:

  - ■ **Granted Access.** By default, all connections are granted access with the exception of those added to the IP Address box. This maintains an open site, but enables the administrator to restrict individual IPs, groups of IP addresses using a network ID and subnet mask, or domains from accessing the server. Note that using domain names for restricting access requires the server to perform a reverse DNS lookup, which uses more time and resources compared to restricting by numeric IP addresses.

  - ■ **Denied Access.** This virtually closes the FTP site to the outside world, allowing only the specified IPs to establish connections. This is a much more restrictive security measure and is typically used for sites that contain privileged information.

FTP Server Performance Counters

IIS 4.0's FTP Server includes Windows NT Performance Monitor counters for measuring the performance of bandwidth usage, connections, and how files are being transferred. Following is a list of the FTP Server performance counters and the descriptions of each given by the Windows NT Performance Monitor.

- ■ **Bytes Received/sec** is the rate that data bytes are received by the FTP Server.

- ■ **Bytes Sent/sec** is the rate that data bytes are sent by the FTP Server.

- **Bytes Total/sec** is the sum of Bytes Sent/sec and Bytes Received/sec. This is the total rate of bytes transferred by the FTP Server.

- **Current Anonymous Users** is the number of users who currently have an anonymous connection using the FTP Server.

- **Current Blocked Async I/O Requests** is the number current requests that are temporarily blocked due to bandwidth throttling settings.

- **Current Connections** is the current number of connections established with the FTP Server.

- **Current NonAnonymous Users** is the number of users who currently have a non-anonymous connection using the FTP Server.

- **Maximum Anonymous Users** is the maximum number of users who established concurrent anonymous connections using the FTP Server (since service startup).

- **Maximum Connections** is the maximum number of simultaneous connections established with the FTP Server.

- **Maximum NonAnonymous Users** is the maximum number of users who established concurrent non-anonymous connections using the FTP Server (since service startup).

- **Maximum Async I/O Bandwidth Usage** is the measured bandwidth of asynchronous I/O averaged over a minute.

- **Total Allowed Async I/O Requests** is the total number of requests allowed by bandwidth throttling settings (counted since service startup).

- **Total Anonymous Users** is the total number of users who established an anonymous connection with the FTP Server (since service startup).

- **Total Blocked Async I/O Requests** is the total number of requests temporarily blocked due to bandwidth throttling settings (counted since service startup).

- **Total Connection Attempts** is the number of connections that have been attempted using the FTP Server (since service startup).

- **Total Files Received** is the total number of files received by the FTP Server.

- **Total Files Sent** is the total number of files sent by the FTP Server since service startup.

- **Total Files Transferred** is the sum of Files Sent and Files Received. This is the total number of files transferred by the FTP Server since service startup.

- **Total Logon Attempts** is the number of logons that have been attempted using the FTP Server (since service startup).

- **Total NonAnonymous Users** is the total number of users who have established a non-anonymous connection with the FTP Server (since service startup).

- **Total Rejected Async I/O Requests** is the total number of requests rejected due to bandwidth throttling settings (counted since service startup).

News Server

The News Server is a standards-based NNTP news server that provides easy setup and administration, and integration with Windows NT security, event logging, and performance monitoring. News Server uses the NNTP protocol for communication between clients and servers for discussion group reading and posting.

IIS 4.0's news server is designed for hosting corporate intranet-based discussion groups throughout the enterprise, but can also be used as a more limited Internet news server.

Two services that the IIS 4.0 News Server does *not* provide, are

- Newsfeeds from other news servers.

- Replication of newsgroups to other news servers.

Note The Microsoft solution to full-featured, robust Internet News Server support with newsfeed capability and content replication is Microsoft Exchange Server 5.0, which also includes a full-featured Internet e-mail server.

News Server can host enterprise-wide discussion groups and technical support, as well as expand to the Internet to provide the outside world with interaction with company or technical support representatives. Any standard newsreader client (such as Microsoft's Outlook Express newsreader, which ships free with Internet Explorer 4.0) can be used to access newsgroups.

Although NNTP news servers have existed on the Internet for years and basically perform the same operations, IIS 4.0's News Server provides for very easy-to-configure and manage news services without compromising performance and functionality. The following list discusses some of News Server's features.

- Use of the Microsoft Management Console (MMC) for easy administration and customizable administrative screens.

- Support for all IIS 4.0-supported logging formats, including ODBC and W3C extended.

- Web administration ASP tools for graphical administration over any web browser (ASP pages execute on the server and return standard HTML; therefore, they are not web browser–dependent).

- Built-in Windows NT Performance Monitor counter objects for performance monitoring and analysis.

- Use of Secure Socket Layer (SSL) security along with standard NNTP supported clear text transmission.

- Support for SNMP monitoring.

- Integration with Windows NT security for permission control on individual newsgroups.

Mail Server

Much like the News Server, IIS 4.0's Mail Server contains a subset of standards-based e-mail server capabilities in order to bring Internet e-mail functionality to the web. Microsoft's IIS 4.0 Mail Server is intended to enable content developers to use e-mail in their Active Server Page content. Mail Server supports the Simple Mail Transport Protocol (SMTP) for delivering e-mail, and acts as a POP3 mail server from which clients can receive and store mail. (Microsoft recommends Microsoft Exchange Server 5.0 for Internet and enterprise-wide SMTP and POP3 e-mail server functionality.)

Mail Server delivers both local and remote messages, both within an organization or out across the Internet. Although Mail Server is not designed to be a heavy-duty mail server for managing and receiving e-mail (such as a POP server), it offers useful integration with IIS 4.0's web server. Some common examples of using a Mail Server object in Active Server Pages are

- Sending verification information back to a user who has specified his e-mail address.

- Automatically reporting errors and specific log information to the administrator via e-mail.

Mail Server, like all IIS 4.0 server components, supports the following:

- Microsoft Management Console administration

- Multiple logging formats

- SSL Security

- Windows NT Performance Monitor objects and counters

- Integrated NT security

- SNMP monitoring

Mail Server, like IIS 4.0's News Server, is designed to extend the power and functionality of web content. Mail Server's exposed COM interfaces make calls to many of the same functions inherent in Microsoft Exchange Server 5.0 and Microsoft's Commercial Internet System Mail

Server. This means that if an organization decided to upgrade to a full-featured e-mail solution from Microsoft, existing ASP content could easily take advantage of either of these server products with little or no alteration.

IIS 4.0 Tools and Enhancements

Aside from the suite of servers that help make IIS 4.0 a total intranet package and powerful Internet server, there are a few other included tools that deserve mentioning.

Microsoft Site Server Express

One of the most attractive features of IIS 4.0 is the powerful set of server analysis tools in Microsoft Site Server Express: Usage Analyst and Site Analyst. Both tools perform extensive analysis of server information such as log files and site content. These two tools are specially tailored for IIS 4.0 and are based on the commercial Microsoft Site Server product.

Usage Analyst

Microsoft Usage Analyst provides powerful analysis and reporting capabilities for arranging user interaction information on the web server. Trend analysis and content access information can be tracked by using Usage Analyst's report capabilities. Usage analyst translates log file data pertaining to user access into readable and customizable information that administrators can use to learn who is accessing what content and how.

Site Analyst

Microsoft Site Analyst analyzes an entire web site, its content, links, applications, and other important information. After the site analysis is completed, a WebMap is created. WebMaps are Site Analyst's graphical overviews of the entire site; they can be moved around and manipulated and clicked on to provide detailed information.

Site Analyst can detect broken links both locally and on other Internet sites, as well as "Not found" errors from referenced pages that do not exist. Site Analyst can also report on the state of ActiveX components, Java applications, and CGI programs on your web server, including the number of times each has been accessed in a specified time period. Site Analyst comes with several pre-made report templates for generating comprehensive site analysis reports for better decision-making.

Posting Acceptor

Posting Acceptor allows the uploading of web pages and files to an IIS web site by using the Microsoft Web Publishing Wizard or supported clients. ActiveX controls and Netscape plug-ins exist that currently support this type of posting. Web posting makes uploading content easier for the novice and convenient for the developer or experienced user.

Conclusion

Internet Information Server 4.0 is positioned to handle large-volume Internet and intranet traffic and to support the true application development standards needed for creating robust distributed software. With discussion group and mail-enabled web sites, IIS can help create rich content and enhanced communications throughout the organization. Integrated security using digital certificates and certificate authorities are a step toward the distributed security integration promised in Windows NT 5.0. IIS 4.0's compliance with industry standards and simultaneous integration with Windows NT security and administrative tools make it an easy to administer but powerful total server package.

Appendixes

Windows NT Server Protocols

*K*nowledge of protocols, which represent the mechanisms that enable the systems on a network to talk to each other, is important for configuring, troubleshooting networks, and obtaining a better understanding of the network. Protocol knowledge also is very useful in understanding the reasons why networking software from different vendors (and sometimes the same vendor!) do not interoperate.

Before you can understand networking protocols, you must understand the terminology used to define and understand them. The preeminent model for comparing protocols is the Open Systems Interconnection (OSI) reference model. Today, all vendors compare their proprietary, industry-standard, or international standard protocol implementations against the OSI reference model.

The OSI Model

The OSI reference model was developed in 1978 by the *International Organization of Standards* (ISO) to specify a standard that could be used for the development of open systems and as a yardstick to compare different communications systems. Network systems designed according to OSI framework and specifications speak the same language; that is, they use similar or compatible methods of communication. This type of network system enables systems from different vendors to interoperate.

In the early days of computer networks (prior to the OSI model), the proprietary computer network architecture reigned supreme. In those days, an organization that was interested in installing a computer network examined the choices available, including IBM, DEC, HP, Honeywell, and Sperry and Burroughs (now Unisys). Each of those choices had its own proprietary architecture; the capability to interconnect networks from different vendors was almost nonexistent.

Once committed to buying equipment from a specific vendor, the organization was virtually "locked in." Updates or modifications to the system were provided by the vendor, and because the vendor had a closed proprietary architecture, no one could compete with that vendor in supplying equivalent services. Prices were determined based on what the customer could bear without complaining too much!

Today's users probably realize that in many areas of the computer industry, this picture has not changed much. Proprietary architecture history is still around, but the good news is that OSI can change the way it works. In fact, the big debate in computer circles today centers on the amount of time it will take to have the ISO-recommended protocols for the OSI layers become the dominant standard in the networking industry.

For now, the OSI model can, at the very least, provide you with a clearer picture of how the different components of a network relate to each other.

The OSI model has seven layers, as shown in figure A.1. The layers, working from the bottom up, follow:

Physical

Data Link

Network

Transport

Session

Presentation

Application

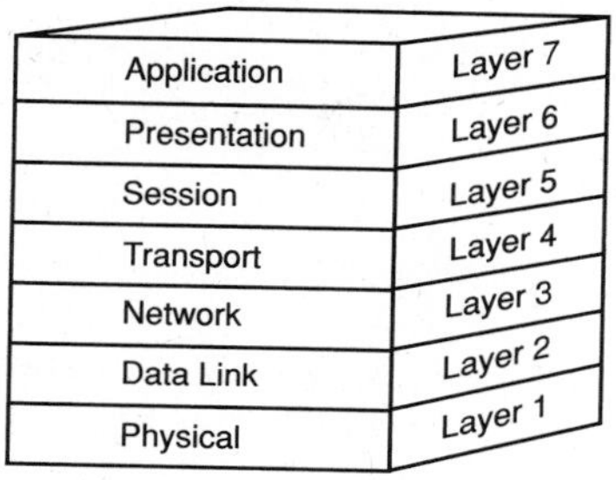

Figure A.1

The OSI reference model.

The ISO applied the following five principles when arriving at the layers:

1. A layer should be created only when a different level of abstraction is needed.

2. Each layer should provide a well-defined function.

3. The function of each layer should define internationally standardized protocols.

4. The layer boundaries should minimize the information flow across layer interfaces.

5. Distinct functions should be defined in separate layers, but the number of layers should be small enough that the architecture does not become unwieldy.

The following sections summarize the functions of the seven layers.

Physical Layer

The *physical layer* transmits bits over a communication channel. The bits can represent database records or file transfers; the physical layer is oblivious to what those bits represent. The bits can be encoded as digital 1s and 0s or in analog form. The physical layer deals with the mechanical, electrical, and procedural interfaces over the physical medium.

Data Link Layer

The *data link layer* builds on the transmission capability of the physical layer. The bits transmitted or received are grouped in a logical unit called a *frame*. In the context of LANs, a frame can be a Token Ring or Ethernet.

The bits in a frame have special meanings. The beginning and ending of a frame are marked by special bit patterns. Additionally, the bits in a frame are divided into an address field, control field, data field, and error control field. Figure A.2 shows a typical data link frame. You see more specific examples of the data link frame in the discussion of Ethernet and Token Ring LANs.

Address Field(s)	Control Field	Data Field	Error Control Field

Figure A.2

A typical data link layer frame.

The *address* field(s) contains the sending and receiving node address. The *control* field indicates the different types of data link frames, which include data frames and frames used for managing the data link channel. The *data* field contains the actual data being transmitted by the frame. The *error control* field usually detects errors in the data link frame. The *data link* layer also is the first layer in which you see error control concerns. The error control field is usually a hardware-generated *checksum* used to detect errors in the data link frame.

Network Layer

The *network layer* builds on the node-to-node connection provided by the data link layer. The node-to-node data link services are extended across a network by this layer. An additional service provided by the network layer is how to route *packets* (units of information at the network layer) between nodes connected through an arbitrarily complex network.

Besides routing, the network layer helps eliminate congestion as well as regulate the flow of data. The network layer also makes it possible for two networks to be interconnected by implementing a uniform addressing mechanism. Token Ring or Ethernet LANs, for example, have different types of data link addresses. To interconnect these two networks, you need a uniform addressing mechanism that can be understood by both Token Ring and Ethernet. For Windows NT-based networks, this capability is provided by the *Internet Packet Exchange* (IPX)—a network layer protocol originated by Novell—and the *Internet Protocol* (IP)—originated by the DoD (Department of Defense).

Transport Layer

The *transport layer* provides enhancements to the services of the network layer. This layer helps ensure reliable data delivery and end-to-end data integrity. To ensure reliable delivery, the transport layer builds on the error-control mechanisms provided by the lower layers. If the lower layers do not do a good enough job, the transport layer has to work harder. This layer is the last chance for error recovery. In fact, when it comes to providing error-free delivery, you could say "The buck stops here" at the transport layer.

The transport layer also may be responsible for creating several logical connections over the same network connection—a process called *multiplexing*. Multiplexing (or time sharing) occurs when a number of transport connections share the same network connection.

The transport layer is the middle layer of the OSI model. The three lower layers constitute the *subnet* (portion of the network model), and the three upper layers usually are implemented by networking software on the node. The transport layer usually is implemented on the node also; its job is to convert an unreliable subnet into a more reliable network.

Because of multiplexing, several software elements (OSI terminology uses the term *protocol entity*) share the same network layer address. To uniquely identify the software elements within the transport layer, a more general form of addressing is necessary. These addresses, called *transport addresses,* usually are a combination of the network layer address and a transport *Service Access Point* (SAP) number. Sometimes the names *sockets* and *port numbers* are used to identify transport addresses.

Examples of transport protocols used by Windows NT server are Sequenced Exchange Protocol (SPX) when the IPX protocol is enabled, and the Transmission Control Protocol (TCP) when the TCP/IP protocol is enabled.

Session Layer

The *session layer* uses the transport layer to provide enhanced session services. Examples of a session include a user being logged into a host across a network or a session being established to transfer files.

The session layer can provide some of the following enhancements:

Dialog control

Token management

Activity management

A session, in general, allows two-way communications (*full duplex*) across a connection. Some applications may require alternate one-way communications (*half duplex*). The session layer has the option of providing two-way or one-way communications; this option is called *dialog control.*

For some protocols, it is essential that only one side attempt a critical operation at a time. To prevent both sides from attempting the same operation, a control mechanism, such as the use of *tokens,* must be implemented. When using the token method, only the side holding a token is permitted to perform the operation. Determining which side has the token and the way in which it is transferred between the two sides is known as *token management.*

The use of the word *token* here should not be confused with Token Ring operation. Token management is a much higher level concept at layer five of the OSI model. IBM's Token Ring operation belongs to layers two and one of the OSI model.

If you are performing a one-hour file transfer between two machines and network crashes occur approximately every 30 minutes, you may never be able to complete the file transfer. After each transfer aborts, you have to start all over again. To avoid this problem, you can treat the entire file transfer as a single activity with checkpoints inserted into the datastream. That way, if a crash occurs, the session layer can synchronize to a previous checkpoint. This operation of managing an entire activity is called *activity management.*

The Windows NT server can be configured to use NetBIOS (Network Basic Input/Output System) over the native NetBEUI (Network BIOS Extended User Interface) protocols or over the TCP/IP protocols. NetBIOS often is described as an example of a session layer protocol.

Presentation Layer

The *presentation layer* manages the way data is represented. Many ways of representing data exist, such as ASCII and EBCDIC for text files, and 1s or 2s for numbers. If the two sides involved in communications use different data representations, they cannot understand each other. The presentation layer represents data with a common syntax and semantics. If all the nodes use and understand this common language, misunderstanding in data representation is eliminated. An example of this common language is *Abstract Syntax Representation, Rev 1* (ASN.1), an OSI recommendation.

The Windows NT server supports the SNMP protocol. The SNMP protocol data units (PDUs—also called application-level packets) are encoded using a subset of the ASN.1 protocol.

Application Layer

The *application layer* contains the protocols and functions needed by user applications to perform communications tasks. Examples of common functions follow:

- Protocols for providing remote file services, such as open, close, read, write, and shared access to files

- File-transfer services and remote database access

- Message-handling services for e-mail applications

- Global directory services to locate resources on a network

- A uniform way of handling a variety of system monitors and devices

- Remote job execution

Many of these services are called *Application Programming Interfaces* (APIs). APIs are programming libraries that an application writer can use to write network applications.

In Windows NT Server, the Server Message Block (SMB) protocol is an example of an application layer protocol. Windows NT Server can be configured to use NetWare client software, in which case the client portion of the NetWare Control Protocol (NCP) is used to make connections to a NetWare server. Third-party support software from Beam & Whiteside and Microsoft's File and Print Services for NetWare (FPSNW) can provide NCP server services on a Windows NT Server—in other words, Windows NT Server can appear as a NetWare server to NetWare clients. The NCP, however, provides bindery emulation services only, and not NetWare 4.*x* NCP server services.

Data Link Layer Interfaces and the OSI Model

Windows NT Server supports two types of interfaces to the OSI's data link layer: the Network Driver Interface Specification (NDIS) and the Open Data link Interface (ODI). The ODI can be supported on top of the NDIS in Windows NT. The NDIS interface was originated by 3COM and Microsoft, and the ODI interface was originated by Apple Computers and Novell. Windows NT Server supports both driver interfaces. Protocol software from Microsoft uses the NDIS interface, and protocol software from Novell for Windows NT Server uses the ODI interface.

The following sections describe both types of driver interface specifications.

Understanding the NDIS Interface

Protocol stacks implemented by Microsoft use the *Network Driver Interface Specification* (NDIS) data link layer interface mechanism. The NDIS protocol layering provides a mechanism for systematically using the protocol components to build the protocol stack.

Strictly speaking, the NDIS mechanism, the native Microsoft protocols, and the protocols from most vendors are not in complete compliance with the OSI reference model. The only protocols that comply closely with the OSI reference model are the ISO recommendations for each of the OSI layers.

ODI Architecture

The NDIS specification allows a large number of network adapters to support different protocol stacks concurrently, such as TCP/IP, OSI, SPX/IPX, and AppleTalk. Prior to NDIS and similar mechanisms (ODI and packet drivers now called *Crynwr drivers*), a separate driver had to be written for each protocol stack. It also was difficult to get these separate drivers to coexist on a workstation, making it difficult to support more than one protocol stack.

The key components of NDIS layers are the NDIS driver and the Protocol Manager, as shown in figure A.3.

In figure A.3, the Ethernet and Token Ring networking technologies correspond to the first and second layers of the OSI model. The NDIS drivers correspond to a portion of the data link layer. The drivers are written to interface with the link support layer (LSL). The LSL, which does not map well onto the OSI model, represents the boundary between the data link and the network layers. Because the LSL provides the interface between MLID drivers and the upper-layer protocols, you can think of the LSL as covering a portion of the data link layer and the lower portion of the network layer of the OSI model.

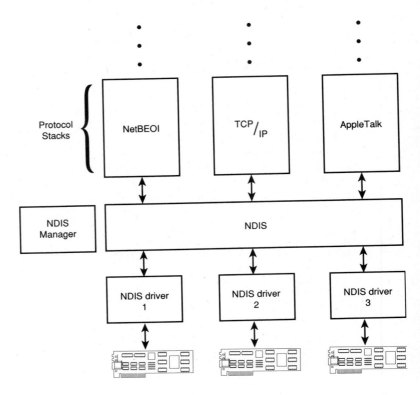

Figure A.3

*NDIS components versus
the OSI model.*

The link support layer is a key element in the ODI specification. It *virtualizes* the network adapter by providing a logical view of the network adapter. The network layer software does not have to be rewritten in order to understand the low-level mechanics and operational details of a new network adapter. The network layer software "sees" a well-defined virtual interface to any network adapter. The well-defined virtual interface means that protocol stacks can be written to interface with the network adapter in a standard way.

The practical significance of this is that the network layer protocol needs to be written just once to this virtual interface. When a new type of network adapter is built, the manufacturer writes an MLID driver for it that can hook into the LSL layer. The LSL provides the same virtual interface to this board, and the protocol software does not need to be rewritten for the new network adapter.

The same MLID driver can support new types of protocol software, as long as the protocols are written to the virtual interface provided by LSL. The MLID driver is able to handle packets from different protocol stacks delivered to it by the LSL.

After receiving the different protocol packets from the network, MLID forwards the packet to the LSL without interpreting the packet contents. The LSL is responsible for sending the packets to the correct protocol stack.

The LSL acts as a software switch through which multiple protocol packet types travel and are delivered to the correct MLID or the correct protocol stack. To provide this routing, the LSL contains information about the MLIDs and the protocol stacks it supports. When MLID drivers or protocol stacks are loaded, they register information about themselves with the LSL. The LSL keeps track of this information in a *data segment* (OSdata). This segment includes items such as network adapter information, protocol stack information, and binding information.

When the MLID loads, the LSL assigns a logical number to each network adapter. When a protocol stack loads and registers with the LSL, it also is assigned a logical protocol stack number. Up to 16 such protocol stacks can be supported.

The LSL also keeps information on the send-and-receive *event control blocks* (ECBs). Event control blocks are data structures used for transmitting and receiving packets; these blocks contain packet ID information. LSL uses the packet ID information in ECBs, and information on network adapters and protocol stacks registered with it, to route packets.

The LSL has a set of routines for the LAN adapters below it and the protocol stacks above it. The LSL calls these routines to move data packets (see fig. A.4). Each network adapter registers a send routine and a control routine, for example. Also associated with each network adapter is a *packet buffer area*. The packet buffer area makes it possible for multiple adapters of the same type to have only one MLID that is loaded reentrantly. In this case, even though the adapters have the same send and control routines, those adapters have a different data area. The protocol stacks above the LSL also register a similar set of support routines with the LSL.

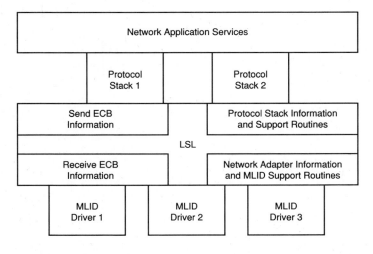

Figure A.4
Information stored in the LSL.

The LSL module is specific to an operating system platform. That means that the actual LSL module cannot be interchanged between operating systems even though LSL is available for DOS, OS/2, NetWare 3.*x*, and NetWare external routers. In DOS, for example, LSL is loaded as a TSR, and in OS/2 it is loaded as a device driver called LSL.SYS.

Every packet on a network has a *Media Access Control* (MAC) frame that encapsulates the communications protocol packet (IPX, AppleTalk, TCP/IP). The MAC is the lower sublayer of the data link layer. For LANs, it represents the mechanisms by which a node on the LAN acquires access to the physical LAN. Within the ODI-based node, a *protocol ID* (PID) consisting of one to six bytes is pre-pended to the frame. This PID identifies the MAC frame and the communications protocol contained in the MAC frame. A code of 8137 (hexadecimal), for example, is used to indicate an Ethernet II MAC frame that has IPX data inside it. The LSL uses the PID value to route the packet to the appropriate protocol stack.

Streams Interface and ODI

In the Windows NT server, the *Streams* interface can be used to encapsulate the communications protocols and to provide a uniform transport interface. Streams, an interface developed by AT&T in Unix System V and originally proposed by Dennis Ritchie (creator of the popular C language), defines a stream head that can be used as a common interface by applications, and a stream tail that interfaces with the drivers. Because the preferred driver in NetWare is ODI-based, the stream tail interfaces with the LSL. Between the stream head and the stream tail, a number of protocol modules can be *pushed* (see fig. A.5).

Figure A.5
Streams and ODI.

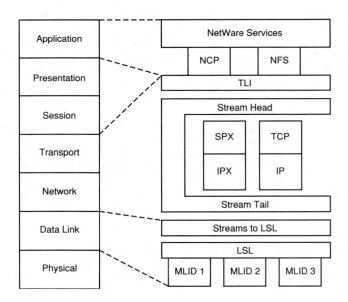

Think of the streams interface as providing a common *software wrapper* around the transport modules. This simplifies the writing of applications. Because Streams is a very low-level interface, an alternate *Transport Layer Interface* (TLI) that makes use of Streams often is used.

Windows NT Native Protocols

When you install Windows NT Server, it gives you a choice of enabling three types of protocols. These choices are the following:

- TCP/IP Protocol

- NWLink IPX/SPX Compatible Transport

- NetBEUI

You can choose **S**elect from list to obtain additional choices:

- NWLink NetBIOS

- DLC Protocol

- Point-to-Point Tunneling Protocol (PPTP)

- Streams Environment

You must select at least one of these protocols. If you select NWLink IPX/SPX Compatible Transport, no additional configuration is required. If you select TCP/IP, you must properly configure the network interface with TCP/IP-related parameters. The NWLink IPX protocol is supported because Windows NT Servers are expected to be deployed in NetWare-based networks. The NetBEUI Protocol is used when NetBEUI compatibility with existing systems is required.

The NetWare native protocols are NCP/SPX/IPX. Of these, SPX/IPX are based on Xerox's XNS protocol suite. The Sequenced Packet Exchange (SPX) protocol is based on the Sequenced Packet Protocol (XNS SPP). The Internet Packet Exchange (IPX) protocol is based on the Internet Datagram Protocol (XNS IDP). IPX corresponds to layer three of the OSI model and is a connectionless datagram protocol. SPX, a connections-oriented protocol, corresponds to the fourth layer of the OSI model.

The NetWare Core Protocol (NCP) was developed by Novell to support NetWare services. The Service Advertising Protocol (SAP) is used by NetWare to advertise NetWare services on a NetWare-based network.

In addition, Novell uses a modified form of XNS RIP as its routing protocol.

The Point-to-Point Tunneling Protocol (PPTP) supports multiprotocol virtual private networks, enabling remote users to access corporate networks securely across the Internet.

The DLC Protocol supports printing to HP printers that are connected directly to the network.

Internet Packet Exchange (IPX)

The IPX protocol is a network layer protocol that provides connectionless datagram services on top of the data link protocols such as Ethernet, Token Ring, ARCnet, and PPP (Point-to-Point) protocols. The IPX protocol can be made to work on virtually all existing data link protocols. The use of the term *connectionless* implies that prior to data transmission, no control packets are sent to establish a connection. Therefore, after the data is transmitted, no teardown or breakdown of the connection is required.

Messages are sent by breaking them into packets and sending complete source address and destination information per packet. No guarantees are made about the successful arrival of the packet (called a *datagram* when it is a packet for a connectionless protocol). If guarantees are to be made, an upper-layer protocol such as SPX or NCP must provide this capability. The datagram-oriented nature of IPX makes it easier to implement the underlying network technology. Datagrams work well with network services that require a broadcast capability.

A unique network address also is available from the IPX layer, per NetWare node. The IPX network address consists of a 32-bit network number and a 48-bit node address pair, making a total of 10 bytes of network address. When configuring NetWare servers, the 32-bit network number must be supplied by the installer and kept unique per physical network. If you are interested in obtaining a unique network number, contact Novell for registering your number.

Because of IPX's origin in the XNS IDP protocol, a 48-bit node address is used (IDP originally ran on Ethernet, which has a 48-bit address). A NetWare node can have several software processes running, such as NCP, SAP, and RIP services. To uniquely identify packets to each of these processes, a *socket number* is used. The socket number is a 16-bit number assigned to each process that wants to communicate using IPX services. Internally, the socket number is used to access data structures used to communicate with the IPX protocol. A few of the well-known socket numbers are 451 hex for NCP, 452 hex for SAP, 453 hex for RIP, 455 hex for NetBIOS, and 456 hex for diagnostics. A complete address description of a process on a NetWare node consists of the following 3-tuple:

> <network number, node address, socket number>

Figure A.6 shows the IPX packet structure. The *Checksum field* usually is set to FFFF hex to indicate that checksums are disabled. IPX expects the data link layer to inform it about packet errors because the data link protocols, such as Ethernet and Token Ring, have a hardware *Cyclic Redundancy Checksum* (CRC).

The *Length field* is the length of the IPX packet in bytes. This includes the IPX header length of 30 bytes plus the data field. IPX originally inherited a 576-byte limit from the XNS IDP packet structure. New IPX drivers can handle larger size packets, even though most of Novell's documentation still refers to the 576-byte limit.

2 bytes	2 bytes	1 byte	1 byte	4 bytes	6 bytes	2 bytes	4 bytes	6 bytes	2 bytes	
Checksum	Length	Transport Control (hops)	Packet Type	Destination Network	Destination Node	Destination Socket	Source Network	Source Node	Source Socket	Data

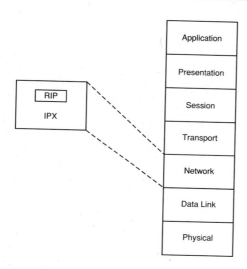

Figure A.6

The IPX packet structure.

The *Transport Control field* is used as a hop count field to count the number of routers traveled by the IPX packet. This field is used by IPX routers and is incremented each time the IPX packet goes through a router. When the hop count reaches 16, the IPX packet is dropped. The 16 hop count limit is inherited from XNS RIP, which was used as the basis for Novell's RIP.

The *Packet Type field* is used for protocol multiplexing and de-multiplexing between the IPX layer and upper-layer protocols. The Packet Type identifies which upper-layer protocol must receive the data portion of the IPX packet. Some of the packet type codes are 4 for *Packet Exchange Protocol* (PXP), 5 for SPX, and 17 for NCP. A packet type code of 0 is reserved for an unknown packet type.

The *Destination Network, Destination Node,* and *Destination Socket fields* uniquely identify processes in the destination node; and the *Source Network, Source Node,* and *Source Socket fields* identify processes in the source node.

The destination network number of an IPX packet is used to decide whether an IPX packet should be sent locally on an IPX network or to a local router. All nodes on the same physical network must have the same network number. A node discovers its IPX network number from an IPX router on that network. Typically, the IPX router also is the NetWare file server, because all NetWare file servers contain an IPX router software module.

If the destination network number is the same as the local network number, the IPX packet is sent directly to the node on the local network. If the destination network number is different from the local network number, and this is the first time an IPX packet is being sent to the destination network, a *route request packet* is sent via the *Routing Information Protocol* (RIP) to determine the fastest route.

The reply contains the address of a local router capable of forwarding the packet. The IPX packet then is forwarded to this router. IPX routers hold *routing tables*, which contain routing information on all networks reachable by that router. These routing tables are kept updated by sending routing information using the RIP protocol every 60 seconds.

Sequenced Packet Exchange (SPX)

The SPX protocol is a transport layer protocol that provides connection-oriented services on top of the connectionless IPX protocol. SPX is used when a reliable virtual-circuit connection is needed between two stations. The SPX protocol takes care of flow control and sequencing issues to ensure that packets arrive in the right order. SPX also ensures that destination node buffers are not overrun with data that arrives too rapidly.

Prior to data transmission, SPX control packets are sent to establish a connection, and a connection ID is associated for that virtual circuit. This connection ID is used in all data transmissions. At the end of data transmission, an explicit control packet is sent to break down the connection. SPX uses an acknowledgment scheme to make sure that messages arrive at the destination. Lost packets are re-sent, and sequencing is used to keep track of packets so that they arrive in the proper order and are not duplicated.

SPX uses a time-out algorithm to decide when a packet needs to be retransmitted. The time-out is dynamically adjusted based on the delay experienced in packet transmission. If a packet times out too early, its value is increased by 50 percent. This process can continue until a maximum time-out value is reached or the time-out value stabilizes. To verify that a session still is active when there is no data activity, SPX sends probe packets to verify the connection. The frequency of these probe packets can be controlled by settings in the NET.CFG file.

An interesting aspect of SPX is that many SPX connections can use the same IPX socket (see fig. A.7). This allows multiple connection IDs to be multiplexed and de-multiplexed across the same IPX socket.

Figure A.8 shows the SPX packet structure. The *Connection Control field* is used for regulating the flow of data across the connection. The bit sequence 0001000, for example, is used as an end-of-message signal, and the bit sequence 01000000 indicates that an acknowledgment is requested.

The *Data Stream Type* indicates the nature of the data contained in the SPX data field. It identifies the upper layer protocol to which the SPX data must be delivered. It serves a role similar to the Packet Type field in the IPX packet.

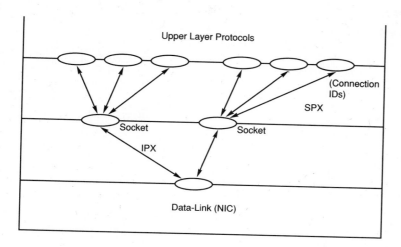

Figure A.7
SPX connection IDs and sockets.

1 byte	1 byte	2 bytes	2 bytes	2 bytes	2 bytes	2 bytes	
Connection Control	Data Stream Type	Source Connection ID	Destination Connection ID	Sequence Number	Acknowl- edgement Number	Allocation Number	Data

Figure A.8
The SPX packet structure.

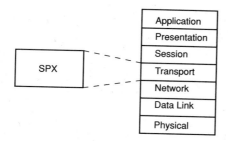

The *Source Connection ID* and *Destination Connection ID fields* are the virtual circuit numbers used to identify a session. These IDs are used to de-multiplex separate virtual circuits on a single socket.

The *Sequence Number field* numbers every packet sent. This is used by SPX to detect lost and out-of-sequence packets.

The *Acknowledgment Number field* indicates the next packet the receiver expects. It means that all packets prior to the Acknowledgment value have been received correctly.

The *Allocation Number field* indicates how many free buffers the receiver has available on a connection. This value is used by the sender to pace the sending of data. The use of the Allocation Number helps avoid overwhelming the receiver with packets that do not have a corresponding buffer available to hold them.

The Packet Exchange Protocol

The PXP (Packet eXchange Protocol) is derived from the XNS PEP (Packet Exchange Protocol) and is a transport layer protocol. PXP provides a lower reliability of service than SPX, but is more reliable than IPX. It is used to transmit a request and to receive a response. The request/response sequence is called a *transaction*. PXP does not keep track of duplicate requests and therefore is suitable for *idempotent transactions*, or upper-layer protocols that can handle duplicate requests. An idempotent transaction causes no undue side effects, even if the transaction is duplicated by mistake. An example of this is the reading of a data block from a file. If this request is mistakenly duplicated, no harm is done.

An example of an application that makes use of PXP is the NetBIOS emulation software, which can run on NetWare workstations.

Figure A.9 illustrates the structure of the PXP packet. The *ID field* is a 32-bit field that identifies the requesting packet. This field serves as a transaction ID that is used to match the PXP packet request and its reply.

The *Client Type field* identifies the user of the PXP protocol. The user of the PXP protocol is called the *Client Protocol*.

Figure A.9

PXP packet structure.

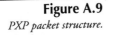

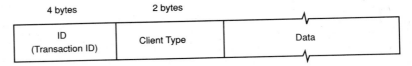

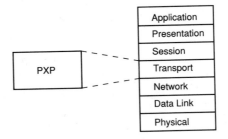

NetWare Core Protocol

The *NetWare Core Protocol* (NCP) implements NetWare's file services, print services, name-management services, file locking, synchronization, and bindery operations. A *bindery* refers to the internal database of network objects kept on the NetWare server. Currently, the Windows NT server's NCP implementation provides access to bindery-based servers such as NetWare 3.*x* and NetWare 4.*x* running in the bindery-emulation mode. NCP support containing NDS (NetWare Directory Service) extensions needed for accessing NetWare 4.*x* servers are available in the NetWare Client for Windows NT product.

NCP is implemented at the workstation and the NetWare server. On the workstation side, NCP is implemented in the Windows NT client software and is limited to making requests for services to an NCP server. The NetWare server (NCP server) contains a full implementation of NCP that can execute or process requests for NCP services. NCP provides transparent remote file and print services to a NetWare client. These remote services have the appearance of being local to the client.

NCP directly uses the IPX protocol, avoiding the use of SPX or PXP. This enables NCP to be more efficient because it avoids the protocol overhead of the SPX and PXP protocols. NCP provides its own mechanism for session control, error detection, and retransmission. Figure A.10 shows an NCP packet structure.

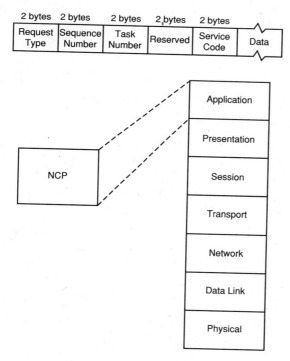

Figure A.10

An NCP packet structure.

In figure A.10, the *Request Type field* indicates the type of NCP request. Examples of NCP request types are Create Service Connection, Negotiate Buffer Size, Logout, Get Server Date and Time, Get Station Number, and End of Job. The *Sequence Number field* is used as a transaction ID field and identifies an NCP request and its corresponding response. The *Service Code field* further identifies the service requested by the workstation.

Packet Burst Mode

The NCP protocol numbers each request and reply packet with a *sequence number*. This sequence number is used as a transaction ID field to identify an NCP request and its corresponding response for a particular session. The session is identified by the connection number and is placed in every NCP transaction.

The NCP transaction models the client/server interaction between a workstation and a NetWare server quite well. This transaction, however, introduces a new set of problems when NetWare servers are used in wide area networks. Typically, WAN link capacities today are in the range of tens of kilobits per second. This is quite slow compared with the megabits-per-second speed used in LANs; WANs therefore run at slower speeds than LANs. In addition, WANs have longer delays because they span longer distances. Using a single request and single response model, as shown in figure A.11, means that the effective throughput of the transaction follows:

$$E = (Q + N*Pn)/(N*Td) \qquad\qquad (1)$$

E = effective throughput of the NCP transaction

Q = size of the request packet

N = number of reply packets

Pn = size of the Nth single reply packet

Td = round-trip delay

As figure A.11 shows, if the reply is larger than a single packet, it has to be sent in a series of successive transactions, each of which takes additional time equal to the round-trip delay. Many earlier NetWare routers have a limit of 512 bytes per packet, which means that if a 64 KB file had to be transferred, 128 of the 512 bytes would have to be sent.

To get an idea of what the throughputs are like, substitute numerical values in the preceding equation. Assume that the size of the NCP request packet is 128 bytes, and the reply is a 1,000-byte packet. Also assume that the round-trip delay on the link is one second, and the reply consists of four packets. Plugging these values into the equation, you get the following:

$$E = (128 + 4*1,000)/(4*1) = 1032 \text{ bytes/sec} = 8,256 \text{ bits/sec}$$

In Packet Burst mode, a single read reply can be sent as a series of successive packets that do not have to wait for an NCP acknowledgment of every message sent. Also, an NCP request can consist of a series of requests that do not have to wait to be acknowledged by a reply. Figure A.12 shows a request and a four-packet reply using packet burst. The effective throughput is now computed by this equation:

$$Ep = (Q + N*Pn)/Td \qquad\qquad (2)$$

Ep = effective throughput of the NCP transaction using packet burst

Q = size of the request packet

Pn = size of the Nth single reply packet

Td = round-trip delay

N = number of reply packets

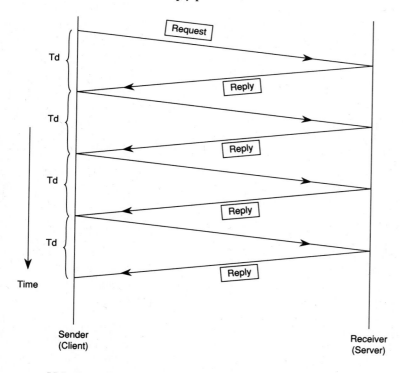

Figure A.11

Single request/reply transactions.

Using equation 2, you can calculate the effective throughput using packet burst:

Ep = (128 + 4*1000)/1 = 4128 bytes/sec = 33,024 bits/sec

You can see that the effective throughput for packet burst, in this example, is four times that of the normal throughput. This is not surprising, because dividing equation 2 by equation 1 reveals the following:

Ep/E = N   (3)

or

Ep = N*E   (4)

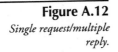

Figure A.12
Single request/multiple reply.

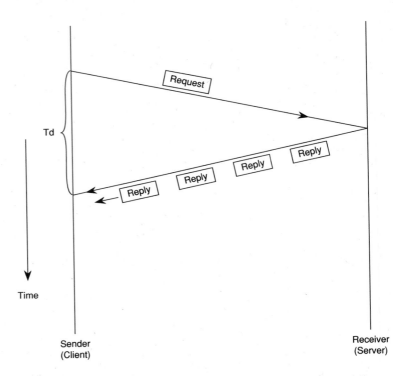

Effective throughput of packet burst, therefore, is N times that of a normal NCP. Tests done by Novell reveal that performance improvements of up to 300 percent can be achieved on a WAN. Packet burst also can improve performance on a LAN by up to 50 percent. Burst mode also can be used in situations in which a transaction consists of a multiple request/single reply sequence (see fig. A.13).

Burst mode implements a dynamic window size algorithm and dynamic time-out mechanism. The dynamic window size allows burst mode to adjust the number of frames that can be sent in burst mode. The *dynamic time-out* (also called *transmission metering*) adjusts itself to line quality, line bandwidth, and line delay.

Understanding the TCP/IP Protocol

One of the strengths of Windows NT Server is that it includes built-in support for TCP/IP. Today, most people agree that the Transmission Control Protocol and the Internet Protocol (TCP/IP) is the *de facto* mechanism by which interoperability can be achieved. When people talk about TCP/IP, they usually refer to a variety of communications protocols such as TCP, IP, ICMP, ARP, FTP, TELNET, and NFS. The list is quite long and impressive, and new protocols and services are added continually.

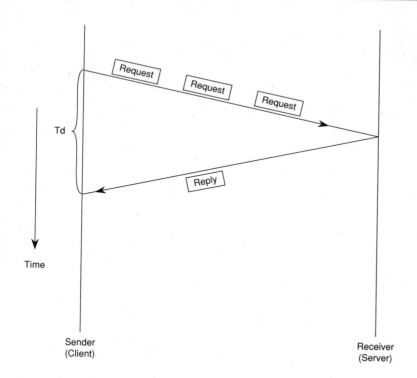

Figure A.13
Multiple request/single reply.

The TCP/IP protocols evolved from the former ARPANET and from the Internet. The *Internet* is the largest network in the world, connecting thousands of nodes. TCP/IP is used as the primary transport and network protocol on the Internet.

The initial Internet protocols were developed at Stanford University and *Bolt, Beranek, and Newman* (BBN) in the 1970s. The impetus for this development came from DoD (Department of Defense) Advanced Research Project Agency (DARPA). DARPA funded the development of the *Advanced Research Project Agency NETwork* (ARPANET). ARPANET was one of the earliest packet-switched networks.

The TCP/IP protocol was integrated in the kernel of a very popular and seminal version of Unix called the *Berkeley Software Distribution* (BSD) Unix. BSD Unix was a very popular version of Unix used in many university computer science departments. Many of the commercial versions of Unix based their TCP/IP implementation on BSD Unix. In the mid 1980s, vendor interest in TCP/IP became very high, and it became the *de facto* standard for interoperability.

TCP/IP is important for the Windows NT server system manager, because Windows NT Server comes with a TCP/IP stack that allows the Windows NT server to function as an FTP server. If you want TCP/IP application services such as *Network File System* (NFS), you can use third-party products such as NFSware and Chameleon NFS for Windows NT. The relationship of TCP/IP to the OSI model is shown in figure A.14.

Figure A.14
*TCP/IP and the OSI
model.*

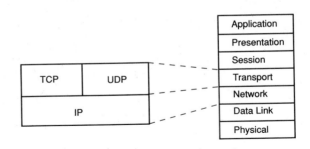

TCP = Transmission Control Protocol

UDP = User Datagram Protocol

IP = Internet Protocol

Transmission Control Protocol (TCP) is a transport layer protocol, and *Internet Protocol* (IP) is a network layer protocol. Figure A.15 shows a partial list of the TCP/IP protocols. As you can see from this list, TCP/IP protocols are numerous, and a detailed discussion of these is beyond the scope of this book. Only a few of these protocols, such as IP and TCP, are discussed.

The IP Protocol

The IP protocol is a network layer protocol that provides connectionless datagram services on top of many data link protocols (see fig. A.15).

Figure A.15
A few TCP/IP protocols.

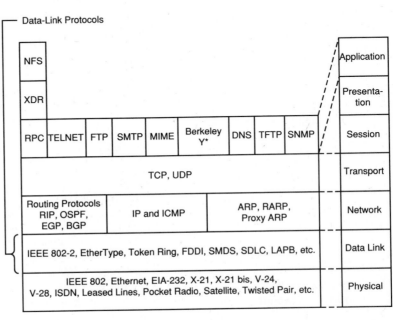

IP does not guarantee delivery of datagrams; it makes the best effort it can to deliver data. Upper layer protocols, such as TCP, can be used to build guaranteed delivery services on top of IP. IP provides a number of interesting services that have become the basis of design for other protocols.

IP provides the notion of a *logical network address* independent of the underlying network. It makes use of an *Address Resolution Protocol* (ARP) to provide the binding between this logical address (called the *IP address*) and the physical node address of a node.

IP datagrams can be fragmented into smaller units to accommodate the *Maximum Transmission Unit* (MTU) of the underlying network. If fragmentation takes place, the fragments are created with sufficient information so that they can be reassembled. Reassembly of fragments to make up the original datagram is done at the destination node. Problems with IP, such as unreachable destinations and reassembly time-outs, are reported to the sender by the *Internet Control Message Protocol* (ICMP).

IP addresses are represented by a 32-bit number. Each network interface in a node that supports an IP stack must have an IP address assigned to it. The IP address is a two-part address consisting of a network ID and a host ID, as shown in figure A.16. The most significant bits are used to determine how many bits are used for the netid and the hostid. Five address classes currently are defined: Class A, B, C, D, and E. Of these, class A, B, and C addresses are assignable. Class D is reserved for multicasting and is used by special protocols to transmit messages to a select group of nodes. Class E is reserved for future use.

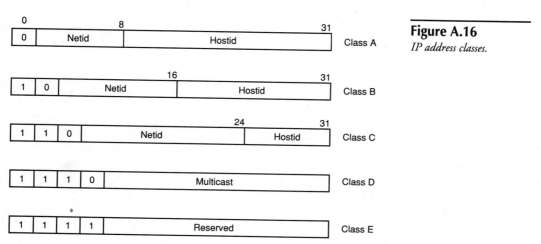

Figure A.16
IP address classes.

The netid portion of the IP address is similar to the network number used in IPX protocols. It identifies the network uniquely. Interconnected networks must have unique netids. If your network is going to be connected to other networks, such as the Internet, you must apply to a central authority to obtain a unique netid (network number) not in use by anyone else. You can contact the central *Internet Address Network Authority* (IANA) at the following address:

DDN Network Information Center

14200 Park Meadow Drive, Suite 200

Chantilly, VA 22021, USA

voice mail: 800-365-3642

electronic mail address: HOSTMASTER@NIC.DDN.MIL

WWW URL: www.internic.com

Older reference works on TCP/IP might list the *Stanford Research Institute* (SRI) as the *Network Information Center* (NIC). This no longer is true, but you can still obtain *Request For Comments* (RFCs) from SRI. RFCs are documents that define the Internet protocol standards and other information pertaining to the Internet. The standards that define IP and TCP protocols are RFC 791 and RFC 793, for example. RFC documents are in the public domain, and their distribution is unlimited.

The different types of IP address classes are defined to address the needs of networks of different sizes. Table A.1 shows the number of networks and nodes possible with each address class.

Table A.1
Reasons for Using Specific Address Class

Address Class	Number of Networks	Number of Nodes
A	127	16,777,214
B	16,383	65,534
C	2,097,151	254

A class A network is suited for very large networks, but because its netid field (refer to figure A.16) is only 7 bits, there can be only 127 such networks. The original ARPANET is an example of a class A network. Class B networks are medium-size networks and are suited for medium to large organizations. Class C networks are suited for small organizations, in which each network can have no more than 254 nodes.

The 32-bit number is represented for convenience as four decimal numbers corresponding to the decimal value of the four bytes that make up the 32-bit IP address. The decimal numbers are separated by periods (.). This shorthand notation for IP addresses is called *dotted decimal notation*. Figure A.18 shows the format of an IP packet. The following shows an IP address in its binary form and also as a dotted decimal notation:

IP Address = 10010000 0001011 01001010 1001010

IP Address = 144.19.74.202

In figure A.17, the version number field is four bits long and indicates the format of the IP header. This allows future IP packet structures to be defined. The current version number is four. Table A.2 shows the other possible values of the version number field. IP version seven may be the next possible IP format that allows for longer IP addresses; however, this is still the subject of considerable debate.

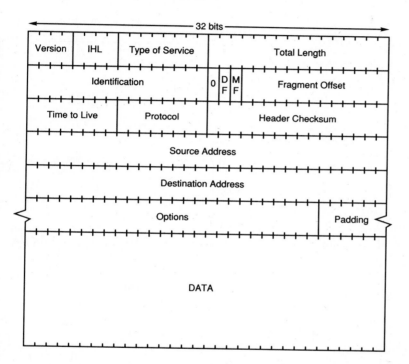

Figure A.17

IP Packet structure.

Table A.2
IP Version Number Values

IP Version	Meaning
0	Reserved
1-3	Unassigned
4	IP
5	Stream IP (Experimental IP)
6-14	Unassigned
15	Reserved

The *Internet Header Length* (IHL) is the length of the header in 32-bit words. This field is required because the IP header contains a variable-length option field.

The *Type Of Service* (TOS) field informs the networks of the *Quality Of Service* (QOS) desired, such as precedence, delay, throughput, and reliability. Figure A.18 shows the meaning of this eight-bit field.

Figure A.18
Type of Service field for IP packets.

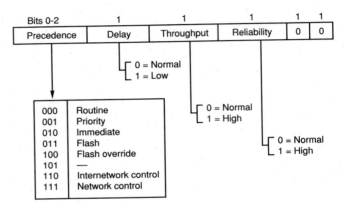

The *Precedence* field reflects the military origin of IP networks. The following are the meanings of some of the precedence values:

- Flash: ASAP (As Soon As Possible); maximum priority on all circuits

- Immediate: Within four hours

- Priority: Same day

- Routine: Within one day

Most IP implementations and routing protocols (RIP, HELLO, and so on) ignore the Type of Service field.

The Precedence field is intended for Department of Defense applications of the Internet protocols. The use of nonzero values in this field is outside the scope of the IP standard specification. Vendors should consult the *Defense Information Systems Agency* (DISA) for guidance on the IP Precedence field and its implications for other protocol layers.

Vendors should note that the use of precedence most likely requires that its value be passed between protocol layers in much the same way as the TOS field is passed. The IP layer must provide a means for the transport layer to set the TOS field of every datagram sent; the default is all zero bits. The IP layer should pass received TOS values up to the transport layer.

Although little used in the past, the TOS field is expected to play an increasing role in the near future with routing protocols such as OSPF that could use the TOS field. The TOS field is expected to be used to control two aspects of router operations: routing and queuing algorithms. The TOS field also can be mapped into the data link layer for effective sharing of serial lines by different classes of TCP traffic.

The *Total Length* field contains the length of the IP header and data in bytes. The maximum size of the datagram is 65,535 bytes. All IP nodes must be prepared to receive a minimum size of 576 bytes (512 bytes of data plus 64 bytes of protocol overhead).

The *Identification* field is set uniquely for each datagram, and is the datagram number. It is used with the fragment flags *DF* (Don't Fragment), *MF* (More Fragments), and Fragment Offset fields to reassemble the datagram. If the DF flag is set to 1, the datagram should not be fragmented. An MF flag set to 1 indicates to the receiver that more fragments are to come. An MF set to 0 indicates the last fragment.

The *Fragment Offset* field indicates the position of the fragment's data relative to the start of the original datagram. This is a 13-bit field and is measured in 8-byte groups. This means that the Fragment Offset value must be multiplied by 8 to get the byte offset.

The *Time To Live* (TTL) is measured in seconds and represents the maximum time an IP datagram can live on the network. It should be decremented at each router by the amount of time taken to process the packet. The intent is that TTL expiration causes a datagram to be discarded by a router, but not by the destination host. Hosts that act as routers by forwarding datagrams (such as NetWare 3.*x*) must follow the router rules for TTL. The TTL field has two functions: limiting the lifetime of TCP segments and terminating Internet routing loops. Although TTL is time in seconds, it also has some attributes of a hop count because each gateway is required to reduce the TTL field by at least one. This is why some implementers mistakenly set it to 16, because 16 is infinity for RIP. But TTL is independent of RIP metrics.

Other considerations for TTL fields follow:

■ A host must not send a datagram with a TTL value of zero, and a host must not discard a datagram just because it is received with TTL less than two.

■ An upper layer protocol may want to set the TTL to implement an expanding scope search for some Internet resource. This is used by some diagnostic tools and is expected to be useful for locating the "nearest" server of a given class using IP multicasting, for example. A particular transport protocol also may want to specify its own TTL boundary on maximum datagram lifetime.

■ A fixed value must be at least big enough for the Internet *diameter*—the longest possible path. A reasonable value is about twice the diameter, which allows for continued Internet growth.

■ The IP layer must provide a means for the transport layer to set the TTL field of every datagram sent. When a fixed TTL value is used, that value must be configurable. Unfortunately, most implementations do not allow the initial TTL value to be set. A default value of 32 or 64 is very common.

The *Protocol* field indicates the upper layer protocol that is to receive the IP data. It is similar in function to the Packet Type field for IPX packets. The "assigned numbers" RFC 1060 contain the defined values for this field; for example, TCP has a protocol field value of 6; UDP has a value of 17; and ICMP has a value of 1.

The *header checksum* is used for the IP header only. The 1's complement of each 16-bit value making up the header is added (excluding the Header Checksum field). Then the 1's complement of the sum is taken. This field is recomputed at each router because the TTL field is decremented, and the header is modified.

The *source address* and *destination address* are the 32-bit IP addresses of the source and destination nodes.

The IP options are security, loose source routing, strict source routing, record route, and Internet timestamp.

The TCP Protocol

TCP is the primary transport protocol used to provide reliable, full-duplex, virtual-circuit connections. The connections are made between port numbers of the sender and the receiver nodes. TCP has an octet-stream orientation. An *octet* is a group of eight bits. Therefore, an *octet stream* is an 8-bit stream. There is no inherent notion of a block of data. TCP can be used to provide multiple virtual-circuit connections between two TCP hosts.

Figure A.19 shows the TCP packet structure. The *source port* and *destination port* numbers identify the end-point processes in the TCP virtual circuit. Some port numbers are well-known, whereas others are assigned dynamically. RFC 1066 contains a description of some of the well-known port numbers. A few of these are shown in table A.3.

Figure A.19

TCP packet structure.

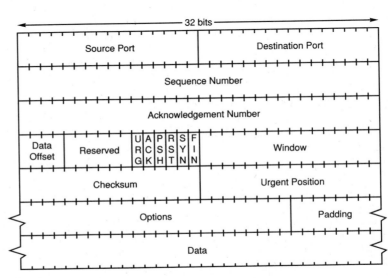

Table A.3
Some Well-Known TCP Port Numbers

Port Number	Description
0	Reserved
5	Remote Job Entry
7	Echo
9	Discard
11	Systat
13	Daytime
15	Netstat
17	Quotd (quote of the day)
20	ftp_data
21	ftp (Control)
23	telnet
25	smtp
37	time
53	name server
102	ISO-TSAP
103	X.400
104	X.400 sending service
111	Sun RPC
139	NetBIOS session source
160-223	Reserved

The 32-bit *sequence number* is the number of the first byte of data in the current message. If the SYN flag is set to 1, this field defines the initial sequence number to be used for that session. A 32-bit value is used to avoid using old sequence numbers that already may be assigned to data in transit on the network.

The *acknowledgment number* indicates the sequence number of the next byte expected by the receiver. TCP acknowledgments are cumulative—that is, a single acknowledgment can be used to acknowledge a number of prior TCP message segments.

The *Data Offset* field is the number of 32-bit words in the TCP header. This field is needed because the TCP options field can be variable in length.

The flags that follow have the following meanings:

- **URG.** This flag is used to send out-of-band data without waiting for the receiver to process octets already in the stream. When the URG flag is set, the Urgent Pointer field is valid. RFC 1122 states that the urgent pointer points to the sequence number of the LAST octet (not LAST + 1) in a sequence of urgent data, and that RFC 793 describes it incorrectly as LAST + 1. A TCP implementation must support a sequence of urgent data of any length. A TCP layer must inform the application layer asynchronously whenever the TCP layer receives an Urgent pointer with no previous pending urgent data, or whenever the Urgent pointer advances in the data stream.

  There must be a way for the application to learn how much urgent data remains to be read from the connection, or at least to determine whether more urgent data remains to be read. Although the Urgent mechanism can be used for any application, it normally is used to send interrupt-type commands to a Telnet program. The asynchronous, or *out-of-band*, notification allows the application to go into urgent mode, reading data from the TCP connection. This allows control commands to be sent to an application whose normal input buffers are full of unprocessed data.

- **ACK.** The ACK flag indicates that the Acknowledgment Number field is valid.

- **PSH.** This flag tells TCP to immediately deliver data for this message to the upper-layer process. When an application issues a series of send calls without setting the PSH flag, the TCP may aggregate the data internally without sending it. Similarly, when a series of segments is received without the PSH bit, a TCP may queue the data internally without passing it to the receiving application.

  The PSH bit is not a record marker and is independent of segment boundaries. Some implementations incorrectly think of the PSH as a record marker, however. The transmitter should collapse successive PSH bits when it packetizes data to send the largest possible segment.

  A TCP can implement PSH flags on send calls. If PSH flags are not implemented, then the sending TCP must not buffer data indefinitely and must set the PSH bit in the last buffered segment (for example, when no more queued data is to be sent).

  RFC-793 erroneously implies that a received PSH flag must be passed to the application layer. Passing a received PSH flag to the application layer now is optional.

An application program is logically required to set the PSH flag in a send call whenever it needs to force delivery of the data to avoid a communication deadlock. A TCP should send a maximum-size segment whenever possible to improve performance, however. This means that on the sender side, a PSH may not result in the segment being immediately transmitted.

When the PSH flag is not implemented on send TCP calls (or when the application/TCP interface uses a pure streaming model), responsibility for aggregating any tiny data fragments to form reasonable-size segments is partially borne by the application layer. Generally, an interactive application protocol must set the PSH flag at least in the last send call in each command or response sequence. A bulk transfer protocol like FTP should set the PSH flag on the last segment of a file, or when necessary to prevent buffer deadlock.

At the receiver, the PSH bit forces buffered data to be delivered to the application (even if less than a full buffer is received). Conversely, the lack of a PSH can be used to avoid unnecessary wake-up calls to the application process; this can be an important performance optimization for large time-sharing hosts.

■ **RST.** The RST bit resets the virtual circuit due to unrecoverable errors. The reason could be a host crash or delayed duplicate SYN packets.

■ **SYN.** This flag indicates the opening of a virtual-circuit connection. TCP connections are opened using the *three-way-handshake* procedure. The SYN and the ACK flags are used to indicate the following packets:

SYN = 1 and ACK = 0   Open connection packet

SYN = 1 and ACK = 1   Open connection acknowledgment

SYN = 0 and ACK = 1   Data packet or ACK packet

■ **FIN.** The FIN flag terminates the connection. Connection termination in TCP is accomplished by using a graceful close mechanism. Both sides must agree to terminate by sending a FIN = 1 flag before connection termination can occur; doing this ensures that data is not unexpectedly lost by either side by an abrupt connection termination.

The *Window* field implements flow control and is used by the receiver to advertise the number of additional bytes of data it is willing to accept.

The *Checksum* field is 1's complement of the sum of all the 16-bit words in the TCP packet. A 96-bit pseudoheader (see fig. A.20) is pre-pended to the TCP header for checksum computation. The pseudoheader identifies whether the packet has arrived at the right destination. The pseudoheader has the protocol ID (6 for TCP), source, and destination IP address. Because the TCP header contains the source and destination port number, this describes the connection between the endpoints.

Figure A.20
*Pseudoheader in TCP
checksum.*

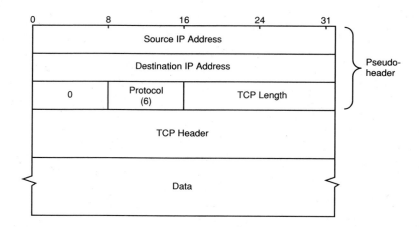

The *Options* field currently defines only the *Maximum Segment Size* (MSS) option, which is negotiated during connection establishment.

Windows NT Server supports applications such as FTP and NFS, which directly use the TCP/IP stack. It also supports the use of NetBIOS over the TCP/IP protocols. Using NetBIOS over TCP/IP is discussed later in this book.

Point-to-Point Tunneling Protocol (PPTP)

The *Point-to-Point Tunneling Protocol* (PPTP) is a new protocol proposed in March, 1996, by Microsoft and several other communications products vendors, including Ascend Communications Inc., ECI Telematics Inc., 3Com Corp., and U.S. Robotics, Inc.

PPTP is an extension of PPP, (that is, Point-to-Point Protocol). PPP is supported by Windows 3.*x*, Windows 95, Windows NT, Unix, NetWare, and mainframes. PPP provides dial-up Internet Protocol support for modems, allowing for excellent cross-platform support.

PPTP is under review until November, 1996, by the Internet Engineering Task Force (IETF).

A draft working paper was posted to the Internet in June, 1996. You can access additonal information on this new protocol from Microsoft:

`http://www.microsoft.com/workshop/prog/prog-gen/pptp.htm`   (This link is subject to change.)

Note The preceding link contains information geared more to developers, rather than end users or integrators.

Although the aforementioned vendors have already begun their own implementation of PPTP, the IETF is considering the addition of several options to this protocol. (Microsoft generally updates protocols and operating system features via Service Pack Updates.)

Virtual Private Networks

The goal of PPTP is to provide a secure communications channel between client and server on both corporate and public networks. PPTP does this by *tunneling*, or encapsulation of normal data in an *encrypted envelope*.

Until the emergence of PPTP, a WAN or LAN connection could be established through dial-up lines or leased lines.

Using PPTP, a corporate client can gain access to corporate servers in distant locations by using a local Internet Service Provider (ISP), and open a secure channel over the public Internet to the corporate servers that also are tied into the Internet. Local ISPs do not need to support PPTP, just PPP.

Thus, a Virtual Private Network can be created using the Internet, eliminating the need for costly leased lines from point to point.

A *Virtual Private Network* (VPN) simply is a network created by *virtual*, or logical, connections that "appear" the same as physical connections. PPTP enables you to create your own VPNs.

Pros and Cons of PPTP

PPTP will enable remote access to Windows NT-based networks with a single dial-up PPP connection.

PPTP can save you considerable cost versus traditional high-speed links.

You need to realize that a logical network is not necessarily going to take the shortest route as a correctly configured leased line network will.

The logical connections may in reality traverse many more pieces of telecommunications gear, traveling through many more cities and connections than it would using specific leased lines. You cannot guarantee or predict bee-line routes with VPNs.

The biggest risks from using a public network are security and reliability of data. The Internet's reliability and security have been the biggest show stoppers to most corporations wanting to use the Internet for commercial and business applications.

Security through technologies such as PPTP and firewalling are enabling a safe path for data. The Internet's reliability also continues to improve as the large common carriers have replaced aging and under-capacity equipment.

Even with PPTP, you may experience additional latency, and even virtual circuit outages, by using the Internet as a transport medium for you data. The considerable costsavings for dial-up connections make PPTP highly worthwhile to implement.

Installation

You need to have previously installed the TCP/IP protocol and must have modem on an active serial port before you can install PPTP. Use the following steps to install PPTP:

1. In the Control Panel, click on the Network icon and select Protocols in the Network dialog box.

2. Select Point-to-Point Tunneling Protocol and click on the **A**dd button.

3. Enter the path to the NT 4.0 distribution files and choose OK. Setup begins to copy and install the appropriate files.

4. Enter the number of Virtual Private Networks you want.

5. RAS Setup wants to start and add PPTP to RAS. Choose OK.

6. Select the appropriate port on your system that for RAS to use, then click on OK.

    You may need to add a modem at this point. If so, select a modem, then click on Continue.

7. Setup takes you back to the Network Protocols tab and should show Point-to-Point Tunneling Protocol as an installed protocol.

8. Choose OK. Setup finishes by automatically updating the protocol bindings in the system.

9. You then are prompted for a system restart, which you need to do to finish PPTP setup.

Services for Macintosh

AppleTalk is a set of proprietary protocols used by Apple Computers to network its Macintosh desktop computers. AppleTalk protocols are important to Windows NT users and Administrators, because the Macintosh computer can be found in many organizations, and Macintosh users and other NetWare users often need to share information. You learned that Windows NT supports Macintosh users in Windows NT–based networks by running the AppleTalk protocols directly on the Windows NT server, enabling the Windows NT server to emulate an AppleShare server to Macintosh clients.

Macintosh users can use their familiar graphical user interface to access the Windows NT/AppleShare server. The AppleShare emulation solution also is used to connect Macintosh users to other network architectures, such as DEC VAX computers, Unix computers, and NetWare servers. This section helps you understand the background and protocol architecture of AppleTalk.

Development of AppleTalk protocols began in 1983 and became available in 1984. What is unusual about Apple's approach is that the AppleTalk protocols were implemented in the Macintosh OS; it was not a separate piece of client networking software that had to be loaded onto the Macintosh OS.

Also, no additional networking hardware had to be added to provide the equivalent of a Network Adapter interface. The networking hardware was built into the Macintosh system board in the form of the LocalTalk interface. LocalTalk is RS-449/RS-422 based at the physical layer and can operate at up to 230.4 Kbps. Whereas this speed is much less than that of Ethernet and Token Ring, it is adequate for small networks and applications that do not have high network bandwidth requirements.

The first set of AppleTalk protocols had a limitation of 254 nodes per physical network and ran on LocalTalk hardware. This was called AppleTalk Phase I. In 1989, Apple released an updated set of protocols called AppleTalk Phase II. AppleTalk Phase II overcomes the 254 node/network limit by allowing a range of network numbers to be associated with a physical network. A node is identified by a pair of numbers: the network number and the node number. When a specific network number is used up to form the network number/node number pair, another network number from the network range can be used.

AppleTalk Phase II, besides providing support for LocalTalk, also supports other data link access protocols such as Ethernet, IEEE 802.3, and the IEEE 802.5 Token Ring. These hardware technologies are discussed in greater detail in Appendix B. The Ethernet and Token-Ring network boards used in Macintosh networks are called *EtherTalk* and *TokenTalk*, respectively. Figure A.21 shows the link access technologies used in AppleTalk in relationship with the OSI model.

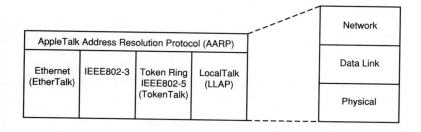

LLAP = LocalTalk Link Access Procedure

Figure A.21
AppleTalk link access technologies.

AppleTalk Data Link Layer

The *AppleTalk Address Resolution Protocol* (AARP) is modeled after TCP/IP's ARP protocol and provides a binding between upper-layer network addresses and data link layer addresses. AARP makes it possible to run AppleTalk protocols on different data link layer technologies with the data link layer address of a destination node being determined dynamically.

Figure A.22 shows examples of how AARP can be used. AARP can be used in a situation in which a sender station knows the destination's upper-layer protocol address, but does not know the data link layer address. The data link layer address is needed by the AppleTalk drivers to send the AppleTalk frame over the physical link. In this case, an AARP broadcast request is sent that contains the destination's upper protocol address.

Figure A.22

AppleTalk AARP examples.

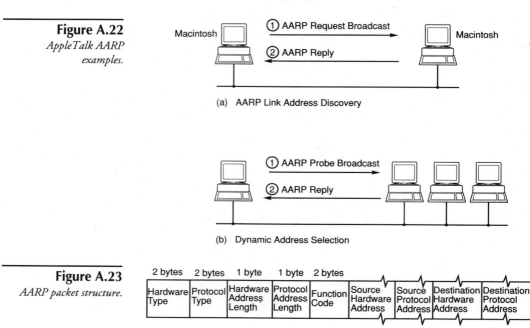

(a) AARP Link Address Discovery

(b) Dynamic Address Selection

Figure A.23

AARP packet structure.

All nodes receive the broadcast, but only the node that has the same upper protocol address as in the AARP request packet responds with its data link address. The protocol address and data link address mappings are kept in a local cache in memory and are called the *Address Mapping Table* (AMT). Before sending a data transmission, the AMT is consulted to discover the data link address of the destination. If no entry is in the AMT, AARP is used to discover the mapping. Old AMT entries automatically are timed-out and purged from the AMT table.

Another situation in which AARP can be used is in *dynamic address selection.* When a Macintosh computer is booted on a network, it picks a node address randomly and sends an AARP request broadcast with the same node address. If a reply is received, it implies that the node address is in use. In this case, the station must pick another address and repeat the process until a unique node address is determined. Figure A.23 shows the AARP packet structure.

The meanings of the fields in figure A.23 follow:

■ **Hardware Type and Protocol Type.** These fields together define the data link and protocol address type used by AARP. The hardware type could be EtherTalk, TokenTalk, or LocalTalk; and the protocol type is AppleTalk.

- **Hardware Address Length and Protocol Address Lengths.** These fields are needed because AARP was designed to provide mappings between a number of different hardware and protocol technologies. Because the length of the hardware address (data link address) and protocol address could be different, their length values are placed in the AARP packet.

- **Function Code.** This field determines the type of AARP packet. Currently, three codes are defined for the three AARP packets. Function Code 1 indicates an AARP request; Function Code 2 indicates an AARP reply; and Function Code 3 indicates an AARP probe used for dynamic address selection.

- **Source Hardware Address, Source Protocol Address, Destination Hardware Address, and Destination Protocol Address.** These fields have lengths specified by the Hardware Address Length and Protocol Address Length fields. These fields contain the hardware address and protocol address of the nodes involved in the AARP exchange.

AppleTalk Network Layer

Figure A.24 shows the network layer used in AppleTalk that is related to the OSI model. The *Datagram Delivery Protocol* (DDP) is the major protocol used by the network layer. Other protocols such as *Routing Table Maintenance Protocol* (RTMP), *Zone Information Protocol* (ZIP), and *Name Binding Protocol* (NBP) also help support the operation of the network layer.

The DDP is a connectionless protocol between two processes running on separate nodes on the network. Because it is connectionless, DDP by itself cannot be used to guarantee delivery of the datagram. Upper-layer protocols at the transport layer must be used to guarantee delivery.

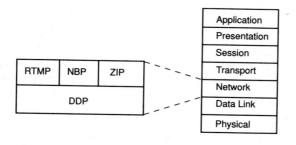

Figure A.24

AppleTalk network layer.

The DDP processes by which it delivers data must attach to sockets. *Sockets* define the boundary points between DDP and the upper layers through which data exchange takes place. DDP sockets are similar in concept to IPX sockets and TCP/IP port numbers discussed earlier. The sockets are described by numbers ranging from 1 to 255. Numbers 1 to 127 have well-defined meanings and are *Statically Assigned Sockets* (SASs). Socket numbers from 128 to 254 are assigned dynamically on demand and are called *Dynamically Assigned Sockets* (DASs).

DDP contains a provision for assigning unique network addresses for each node by using a combination of a 16-bit network number and an 8-bit node number. To further distinguish *Upper Layer Processes* (ULPs) running on a node, the socket number can be used. Thus a complete process address consists of the following 3-tuple:

<network number, node number, socket number>

Older networks such as LocalTalk are limited to a single network number and 8-bit node number associated with that network number. Each node number of these *nonextended networks* is unique. In AppleTalk Phase II, data link layer technologies can support more nodes than the 8-bit value of Phase I. To support these networks the concept of extended networks was introduced. Extended networks can have a range of network numbers assigned to them. This allows for more nodes than can be accommodated by an 8-bit value.

Figure A.25 shows an example of a short header DDP packet structure. The short header DDP packet is designed for nonextended networks. The extended header packets have additional fields for the network number, node numbers, hop count, and checksum. The network numbers are used by routers to distinguish between the different networks. The hop count also is used by routers to determine the distance a packet has to traverse.

Figure A.25
Short header DDP packet structure.

6 bits	10 bits	8 bits	8 bits	8 bits	≤ 586 bytes
0 0 0 0 0 0	Length	Destination Socket	Source Socket	Type	Data

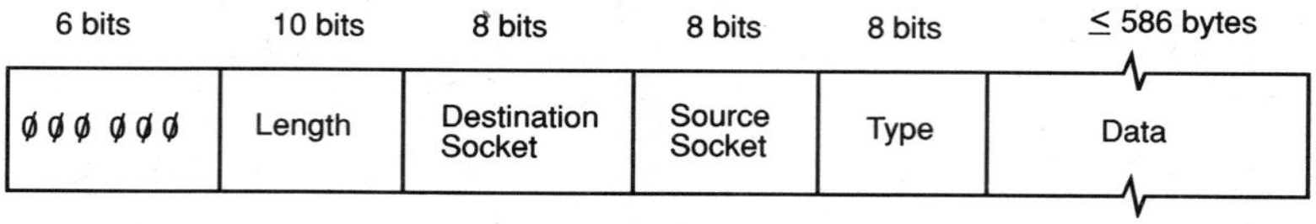

The first six bits are unused and set to zero. The next 10 bits represent the length of the datagram, which cannot exceed 586 bytes. The destination and source socket numbers follow next and identify the processes on the nodes. The Type field is used to indicate to which Upper Layer Process the DDP packet data should be sent.

In an AppleTalk Internet, several physical AppleTalk networks are connected by routers. The routers are responsible for directing the packet to the correct destination network. The source node must determine whether the packet is to be sent to a router or the local network. It does this by examining the destination network number. If this number is in the range assigned to the local network, the destination node is in the local network.

If the number is not in the range assigned for the local network, it is sent to one of the AppleTalk routers. The routers exchange information using the RTMP protocol. The RTMP protocol was derived from the XNS RIP protocol and is an example of a Distance-Vector routing protocol. These classes of protocols are discussed in Appendix B, "Bridging and Routing."

The Name Binding Protocol (NBP) provides a logical association between AppleTalk names and network addresses. It is similar in concept to the *Domain Name System* (DNS) protocol used in TCP/IP networks. AppleTalk names are symbolic names used to designate services on the network and therefore are easier for users to deal with than network addresses, which are numeric quantities. AppleTalk services are called *Network Visible Entities* (NVEs). Examples of NVEs are sockets and mailboxes. NVEs have names called *entity names* and attributes that specify the characteristics of the NVE. NBP is used to build an association (called *name binding*) between the NVE name and its network address. The name and address associations are kept in name tables.

All the name tables on the AppleTalk Internet make up the *name directory*. When an application wants to use a name, it consults its local name table. If it cannot find the name, it issues an NBP lookup packet to find the name's address. The address is returned by NBP. Because DDP does not perform Internet broadcasts, NBP lookups across the entire Internet are not possible. To make it possible to look up names on an Internet, the concept of a zone was created. NBP lookups can be done on a zone basis.

A *zone* represents a group of logically related AppleTalk nodes. They are a means of categorizing how nodes typically are used on the internetwork. They can span multiple networks. A zone can include a few nodes from one network, some nodes from another network, and so on. Or, a zone can include all the nodes in one physical network or only few of the nodes on that network. When a node is powered up, the zone it belongs to is selected from a list of zones for that network. All nodes in a nonextended network must belong to the same zone.

A zone-wide NBP lookup is sent to the local router responsible for broadcasting the NBP lookup request to all networks in the specified zone. Only nodes in the selected zone can reply to the NBP lookup packet.

When the concept of zone was created to solve the NBP broadcast problem, a mechanism was needed to maintain the mapping between network numbers and zones. The *Zone Information Protocol* (ZIP) was created to maintain this mapping. This mapping is maintained in tables called *Zone Information Tables* (ZITs). ZITs are maintained in AppleTalk routers. When a node starts up, it uses a ZIP request packet to discover the zone it belongs to. When a router discovers new networks by way of the RTMP protocol, that router sends a ZIP request for obtaining the zone list for the new network.

AppleTalk Transport Layer

Figure A.26 shows the transport layer used in AppleTalk that is related to the OSI model. AppleTalk uses two transport protocols: *AppleTalk Transaction Protocol* (ATP) and *AppleTalk Data Stream Protocol* (ADSP).

The ATP protocol is based on the concept of completing a transaction reliably. A *transaction* is defined as a request/response sequence between a client and a server. Each transaction is numbered by a transaction ID, which enables the client to associate a transaction response with the correct transaction request. Because either a transaction request or response can get lost in transmission, it is important for the client to know which transactions must be *executed once* (XO) only, and which must be done *at least once* (ALO).

The ALO transactions can be repeated without any harm; an example of this is a read request for a block of data in a file. ALO transactions also are called *idempotent transactions*. The XO transactions must not be repeated because they could have undesirable consequences. An example of an XO transaction is a request by a client to append a data block to the end of a file. If this command is repeated, an additional data block is added to the end of the file. XO transactions also are called *non-idempotent transactions*.

Figure A.26

AppleTalk transport layer.

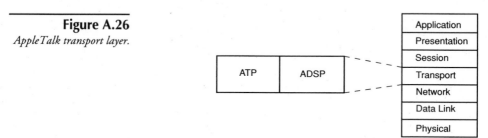

If the data to be transmitted is larger than can be transmitted by the underlying network, ATP can fragment and reassemble data with the limitation that the original message must be limited to eight fragments. Because of varying delays and errors in transmission, a packet could get out of sequence or become lost. A bitmap/sequence number field is used in the ATP header to keep track of packets. For a transaction request, this field represents a bitmap; for a transaction reply, it represents a sequence number. The *bitmap* refers to the number of responses expected by the client. The client allocates a buffer to hold each response.

Figure A.27 shows an initial transaction request with a bitmap of 00000111. Each bit position that is a 1 corresponds to an expected response. The responses contain sequence numbers. In the example in the figure, responses 0 and 2 are received correctly, but response 1 is lost. The client makes a request with a bitmap of 00000010, which indicates to the server that packet 1 is outstanding and needs to be sent again. If the number of responses is less than the expected number, an end-of-message packet is sent.

The *Control Information* field in an ATP packet indicates the type of ATP packet such as request, response, XO, or ALO (see fig. A.28). The *Bitmap/Sequence Number* field indicates the expected response and the sequence number of the response packet. The *Transaction ID* field matches a response with a request.

Another AppleTalk transport layer protocol is the ADSP. The ADSP protocol provides full duplex virtual circuit capability between two sockets. The data flow is stream-oriented in a manner similar to TCP. Each byte in the stream has a sequence number. Flow control is achieved by a sliding-window mechanism. The window size is adjusted based on the amount of data the other side is willing to accept and has a maximum size of 64 KB.

Two types of ADSP packets are defined: *control* and *data packets*. ADSP control packets are defined so that they can be used for virtual circuit operation, such as creation and teardown. The ADSP protocol, unlike ATP, does not have any inherent client/server orientation. Any side can initiate the virtual circuit connection.

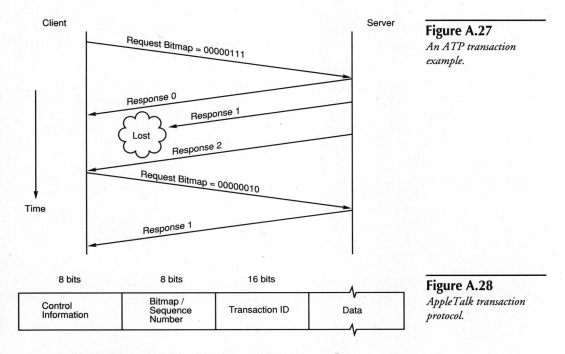

Figure A.27

An ATP transaction example.

Figure A.28

AppleTalk transaction protocol.

AppleTalk Session Layer Protocol

Figure A.29 shows the session layer used in AppleTalk in relationship with the OSI model. AppleTalk uses two session protocols: *AppleTalk Session Protocol* (ASP) and *Printer Access Protocol* (PAP).

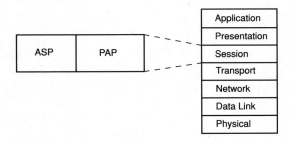

Figure A.29

AppleTalk session layer.

ASP is used to create, maintain, and destroy sessions that use the underlying transport mechanism provided by the ATP layer. ASP builds on the concept of the transaction to provide a *session* consisting of series of transactions. The ASP user, such as a workstation, does not have to deal in terms of transactions; the workstation can open an ASP session with the server, over which it can send commands and not have to worry about commands being sent out of order, lost, or duplicated.

ASP can be used by a client to obtain status information on the server. The server also can send an ASP attention command to workstations informing them of a change in server status.

The PAP session protocol is used to create, maintain, and destroy connections to remote printer services. Although designed to be used with printers, PAP is quite general and can be used to provide connections to other services as well. PAP uses the NBP protocol to obtain the address of the server and establishes a connection by building on the services provided by ATP. All transactions are sent using the XO mode of ATP. PAP can be used to read data from the server or write data to it.

AppleTalk Application Layer

AppleTalk does not have an explicit presentation layer. Its most common application layer protocols are the *Apple Filing Protocol* (AFP) and *AppleTalk Print Services* (APS) (see fig. A.30). The APS is used to provide remote printer services to a client; it uses the PAP protocol to provide printer services.

The AFP protocol uses ASP to provide remote file services. It is similar in concept to NetWare's NCP and the NFS protocols used in TCP/IP networks.

Figure A.30
AppleTalk application layer.

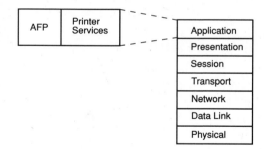

File access requests from application programs are processed by AFP to determine whether they are for local or remote file access (see fig. A.31). AFP sends local file requests to the local file system. If the file request is remote, AFP uses the *AppleTalk Filing Interface* (AFI) to transmit the file request across the network. The AFI uses the AppleTalk protocols (ASP, ATP, DDP) to send the request to the server. The request is processed by the AppleTalk protocols on the server and communicated to the file server control program.

AFP includes security mechanisms through a user/password authentication mechanism, volume passwords, and directory access control. Directory access control consists of Search, Read, and Write privileges.

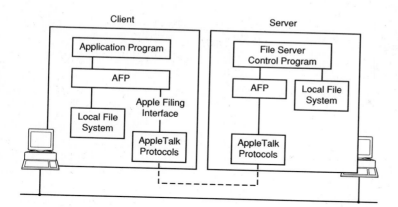

Figure A.31
AppleTalk filing protocol.

Conclusion

This appendix laid the foundation for a better understanding of network protocols. The OSI reference model was discussed as a means to compare different protocol architectures. The NDIS and ODI protocol architectures were compared with respect to the OSI reference model.

The protocol structure of some of the major protocols such as NCP/SPX/IPX, TCP/IP, PPTP, and Services for Macintosh was discussed. These protocols commonly are found in a Windows NT Server environment.

Bridging and Routing

If the network manager must go beyond the capabilities of a single LAN and access network or computing resources on other networks, he must determine which devices to use to extend the range of a LAN. Bridges, repeaters, and routers are often the choices to extend the range of a single LAN or to combine a number of LANs in a single internetwork.

In this appendix, you learn to connect several Windows NT networks. This appendix first lays the foundation for understanding bridges, repeaters, and routers. The latter part of this chapter examines Windows NT routing problems. You also learn about performance issues for software- and hardware-based routers.

Understanding Repeaters, Bridges, and Routers

Repeaters, bridges, and routers are devices that extend the range of a LAN. Most LANs such as Ethernet, ARCnet, and Token Ring have distance limitations. The maximum span of an Ethernet LAN, for example, is 2,500 meters using multiple segments and repeaters. Although you can use repeaters to go beyond a single coaxial segment, you cannot use more than four repeaters. If you use bridges and routers, you can go beyond the 2,500-meter Ethernet limitation. Each Ethernet LAN still has the 2,500-meter and four repeater rule, but after a packet crosses a bridge it is on another logical LAN and subject to the restrictions of that LAN only. You also can use an interconnecting device such as a repeater, bridge, or router to go beyond the limit of the maximum number of nodes that can be placed on a physical LAN segment or network. In 10BASE5 Ethernet, for example, you can have a maximum of 100 station attachments per Ethernet cable segment. If you want to place more than 100 stations on an Ethernet LAN, you can use a repeater to connect another segment and place the additional nodes on this new segment. Similarly, if you want to go beyond the 1,024 station attachment limit for an Ethernet LAN, you can use a bridge or a router to connect to another Ethernet LAN and place the additional nodes on the new Ethernet LAN.

Bridges and routers do more than extend the range of a LAN. You can use them to connect dissimilar LANs and to alleviate traffic bottleneck problems. The IBM 8209 bridge, for example, can be used to connect an Ethernet and a Token Ring LAN. Conceptually, these devices *bridge* the gap between dissimilar LANs. They also can connect to LANs of the same type, such as two Ethernet LANs.

Although bridges and routers are described as devices, you may wonder exactly what that means. They consist of a computer that runs algorithms to perform bridging or routing functions. If high performance is desired, these devices are special dedicated computers that can perform bridging and routing functions efficiently. For bridges, the algorithms usually are encoded in EPROM (firmware) for rapid execution. Routers, as you learn shortly, are more complicated than bridges and may require frequent fixes by the vendor to correct problems. It is easier to implement the routing algorithms in software so that they can be changed more easily.

Many vendors allow incremental expanding of their bridges and routers. Hardware modules that consist of one or more network boards can be used to connect to different types of networks. These hardware modules fit into a slot in the bridge or router and connect to a high-speed backplane bus used for data transfer between the modules.

Vendors who make routers and bridges include Cisco, DEC, Vitalink, Wellfleet, NewBridge, 3COM, Timeplex, BBN, Novell, and many others. Microsoft does not make a specialized router product like the other vendors. You can buy routers from third-party vendors. If you are embedding your Windows NT server in a NetWare LAN, and if you have configured your Windows NT server to use IPX, you can use the NetWare server as an IPX router. Up to four network boards can be added to a server or a workstation in a NetWare LAN so that it can perform routing among the network boards.

Repeaters

A *repeater* operates at the physical layer of the OSI model. It takes a signal from one LAN, reconditions and retimes it, and sends it to another LAN. The reconditioning usually amplifies and boosts the power level of the signal. The repeater has no knowledge of the meaning of the individual bits in the packet. A repeater cannot be addressed individually; no address field exists in the packet for a repeater.

The repeater's job is simple. Detect the signal, amplify and retime it, and send it through all the ports except the one on which the signal was seen. In the case of Ethernet, the signals transmitted include data packets and even collisions. The segments of the LAN that are connected participate in the media access mechanism such as CSMA/CD or Token Access. For Token Ring LANs, each station performs the repeater function so that usually no separate repeater device is needed. Some fiber-optic media extensions to the Token Ring may use special repeater devices to boost the signal over long distances.

Bridges

Bridges connect two separate networks to form a logical network. Figure B.1 shows an example of a bridge between an IEEE 802.3 and IEEE 802.5 LAN. This bridge has two network cards: a Token Ring card and an Ethernet card. The Token Ring card is used to connect the bridge to the Token Ring LAN, and the Ethernet card connects to the Ethernet LAN.

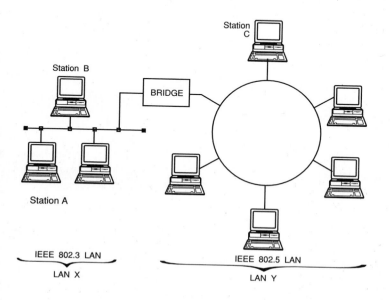

Figure B.1

A bridge between IEEE 802.3 and IEEE 802.5 LAN.

One way of looking at this concept is that a bridge has a split personality. It behaves as a Token Ring station and also as an Ethernet station, and herein lies the key to understanding its function. In figure B.1, a packet sent from station A to station B does not cross the bridge in its normal mode of operation. The bridge detects that stations A and B are on the same LAN, and a bridging function is not required.

If, however, station A sends a packet to station C, the bridge realizes that station C is on another LAN (Token Ring) and places the packet on the Token Ring LAN. It cannot place the Ethernet packet directly on the Token Ring LAN because the Ethernet frame cannot be understood by the Token Ring LAN. The bridge must remove the Ethernet header and replace it with a Token-Ring header containing C's address. The bridge also must wait for a free token before placing the packet on the Token Ring LAN. As it waits, other packets can be sent to it for transmission to the Token Ring LAN. These packets must be queued for processing. A bridge, therefore, must have storage capacity to store frames and acts as a store-and-forward device.

In figure B.1, most of the stations on LAN X communicate among themselves. Occasionally, stations in LAN X may need to communicate with stations in LAN Y. Another way of saying this is that most of the traffic is intra-LAN (within a LAN), and a small fraction is inter-LAN (between two LANs). A good rule of thumb is the 80/20 rule. About 80 percent or more of traffic should be intra-LAN traffic, and 20 percent or less should be inter-LAN traffic.

If the 80/20 rule is violated frequently, the stations generating excessive inter-LAN traffic should be detected and relocated to another LAN so that they do not cause excessive inter-LAN traffic. Stations generating excessive traffic can be detected by using protocol analyzers, such as LANalyzer, or SNMP (Simple Network Management Protocol) managers, such as SunNet Manager and OpenView manager.

A bridge operates at the data link layer of the OSI model. A bridge performs most of its work at layer 2. Bridges examine the *Media Access Control* (MAC) header of a data packet. The MAC address corresponds to the layer 2 address and represents the physical station address or the hardware address of the network board. MAC addresses are unique for every station. Bridges rely on MAC addresses for their operation.

Unlike a repeater, a bridge actually sees the data packet. Bridge ports have unique MAC addresses. A bridge has an understanding of the data packet up to the data link layer and can decode it up to this level. Bridges isolate the media access mechanisms of the LANs to which they are connected. Thus, collisions in a CSMA/CD LAN do not propagate across a bridge. In the case of Token Ring LANs joined by a bridge, the token does not cross a bridge. Because bridges are selective about which data packets can be transferred, they help solve traffic bottleneck problems.

Bridges are effective for a small number of LANs, but as the number of LANs grow, the number of possible paths between the sender and receiving station become very large. Not all the possible paths are optimal—some paths involve roundabout ways of getting to the destination, and this can create unnecessary traffic. If a bridge is to be effective for large LANs, it must have knowledge about the optimal path. A bridge only operates at the data link layer, however, and the routing information is part of layer 3 (network layer) operation. Most bridges cannot make decisions about routes through the network because information on routes is encoded in the network address. And the network address is accessible only by the network layer.

Although a bridge can seem limited, it is a simple and inexpensive way to interconnect two LANs. To perform intelligent routing decisions, you need a router.

Routers

A *router* operates at the network layer of the OSI model. A router performs most of its work at layer 3. Bridges are limited to examining the MAC address of a data packet, but routers can examine the network address. Because the network address usually has routing information encoded in it, routers can use this capability to make intelligent decisions. Thus, a *route* in a network consists of network addresses and paths. Routers are aware of many possible paths to get to a destination and also are aware of which path is the most optimal. The optimum path can be determined by various cost metrics. A *cost metric* is a formula that can be based on the following parameters:

- Is the destination reachable?

- How many hops does it take to reach the destination? The link between two store-and-forward devices is one hop.

- What is the time delay to reach the destination?

- What is the cost of transmission for the paths along the route?

- What is the data transfer capacity (bandwidth) of various paths?

- What is the status of links along the path?

The cost metric for determining the best route can become complex. Routers can be distinguished on the basis of the criteria they use to determine the optimal path.

Because routers have a lot more information to work with, they can do more things with a packet than a bridge, and they also are more complex. Because they are more difficult and costly to develop, routers cost more. They do more processing of the packets than a bridge; therefore, they tend to be slower than bridges.

Routers are the devices of choice to use to interconnect large LANs. You also can use routers to connect LANs over long distances. In figure B.2, a gateway device is shown operating at layer 7. In general, a *gateway* is a device that can operate at any layer of the OSI model and provides translation between two incompatible protocols. A gateway operating at layer 7 is an application layer gateway. Examples of this concept are X.400 gateways. Devices that connect to IBM's SNA networks usually are called gateways because SNA (Systems Network Architecture) protocols are proprietary, and wholesale translation must be done to connect to IBM's SNA networks.

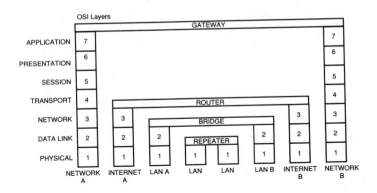

Figure B.2

The OSI model for repeaters, bridges, and routers.

Repeaters, Bridges, Routers, and the OSI Model

The best way to understand the difference between repeaters, bridges, and routers is in reference to the OSI model. If you are not familiar with the OSI model, you might want to review the discussion in Appendix A, "Windows NT Server Protocols."

Figure B.2 shows a model for several interconnection devices in relationship to the OSI model. The model shown in figure B.2 is for a repeater, bridge, and router.

Local versus Remote Connections

Bridges and routers also can be classified on the basis of whether they are local or remote (wide area network). The difference depends on their network interfaces or ports.

Local bridges and routers have ports that connect them to local transmission media over relatively short distances. An example of this setup is the transceiver cable used in Ethernet LANs. You can choose from a variety of choices such as coaxial, twisted-pair, and fiber-optic media to connect local devices to a network. The actual media choice often is dictated by the LAN being connected.

Remote bridges and routers require ports that can connect them to long-haul transmission media. You have fewer interface choices for long transmission media. Some popular choices include RS-232 ports and V.35 ports. Many remote devices have two or more remote connections and at least one local connection. LANs separated by large distances, therefore, can be connected by two remote devices as shown in figure B.3. Router A has two local ports and one remote port. Router B has one remote port and one local port. The remote ports are connected by a point-to-point link. You can run a number of protocols on these point-to-point links. Some of the choices include X.25, Frame Relay, T1, SONET, and SMDS (see Appendix C, "WANs and MANs").

Besides point-to-point links, you also can use *cloud* technologies to connect LANs. *Point-to-point* links are telephone circuits, or T1 circuits, that you can lease from telephone companies or other vendors. Because these lines are dedicated for the communications from the sender point to a destination point, they are named point-to-point. *Cloud* technologies, such as the type shown in figure B.4, are based on switching systems. The router, acting as the *Customer Premise Equipment* (CPE) is used to connect to the cloud. The details of the cloud are not known to the LAN. It may use an X.25/X.75 protocol, Frame Relay, SMDS switches, or a proprietary technology. The cloud or *wide area network* (WAN) is managed by the organization that provides the long-haul service.

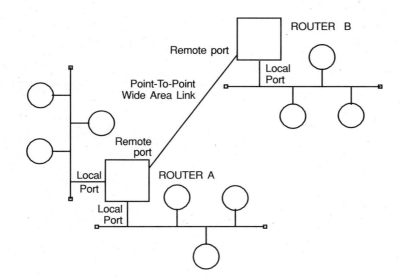

Figure B.3

Remote routers.

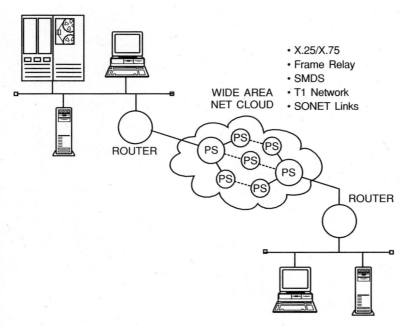

• X.25/X.75
• Frame Relay
• SMDS
• T1 Network
• SONET Links

Figure B.4

Routers connected by means of WAN cloud technologies.

A difference between local and remote bridges and routers is the cost of the connection. Because local connections are managed entirely by the organization that owns the LAN, no additional cost is incurred. For remote connections, you must pay for the services provided by the long-haul vendor. Typical costs of such services are $2,000 per month or higher. This amount is beyond the budget of small organizations. With advances in technology, it is hoped that these costs will come down.

Transparent Bridges versus Source-Routing Bridges

The two predominant methods of bridging are the *Transparent Bridge* (TB) and the *Source-Routing* (SR) bridge. In transparent bridging (also called *spanning tree bridges*), the decision to relay packets is performed by the bridge and is transparent to workstations.

Figure B.5 shows a transparent bridge network. Each bridge maintains a table that keeps track of station addresses. Transparent bridges examine the source address of every packet they see and record this source address in the bridge table along with the number of the port on which the packet was seen. Transparent bridges also maintain a time-out field for each table entry so that old entries can be purged periodically.

Figure B.5

Transparent bridge network.

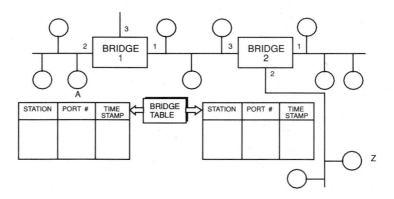

Consider what happens if station A transmits a packet to station Z. Bridge 1 sees the packet and consults its table to see whether it has an entry for station Z. If it does not, it forwards the packet through all its out ports, excluding the port on which the packet was observed. Bridge 1 also checks the source address field of the packet and records it in its table that station A can be reached at its port 2. When Bridge 2 sees the packet, it repeats the algorithm just described. If no entry exists for station Z, it forwards the packet through all its outgoing ports (flooding). It also records the fact that station A can be reached through its port 3. When station Z acknowledges the message from A, it sends a packet with source address Z and destination address A. After Bridge 2 consults its table, it notes that A can be reached through port 3 and forwards the packet only through port 3. It also records that station Z can be reached through its port 2.

To prevent endless circulation of packets, transparent bridge networks cannot have loops. The transmission path forms a spanning tree that covers all the stations on the network. If there are bridges that could form a loop, as shown in figure B.6, these bridges must remain inactive. The inactive bridges act like redundant bridges. Redundant bridges are activated after the spanning tree topology changes. Topology changes are transmitted by *Bridge Protocol Data Units* (BPDUs). This special protocol is used to maintain the overall spanning tree topology. The process of arriving at the spanning tree is called the *spanning tree algorithm.* One bridge in the spanning tree becomes the *root*, and all other bridges transmit frames in the direction of the root by using a least-cost metric.

The spanning tree bridge is the preferred method for Ethernet and IEEE 802.3 networks and is supported by vendors that manufacture bridges for these LANs.

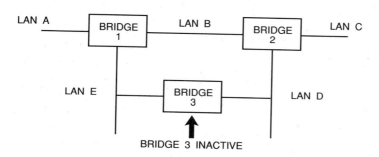

Figure B.6

Avoiding loops on transparent bridge networks.

Source routing, a different method sponsored by IBM, connects bridges to its Token Ring networks. In Source Routing, the source (sender) must determine the best path to get to a destination. After this path is discovered, the source station maintains this path in its routing table and includes this path in the *Routing Information* (RI) field for every packet sent. Figure B.7 shows the RI field along with its relationship to the Token Ring packet. The RI field is present whenever the I/G bit of the source address is set to 1. This I/G bit also is referred to as the *Routing Information Indicator* (RII) bit. The *Routing Designator* (RD) fields contain the path the packet must follow to arrive at the destination. RD fields consist of a ring number and a bridge number pair. SR bridges simply follow the directions in the routing information field. A total of 14 RD fields are possible, which limits the largest transmission path to 13 bridges or hops. IBM's implementation currently limits total RD fields to eight, which corresponds to seven bridges or hops.

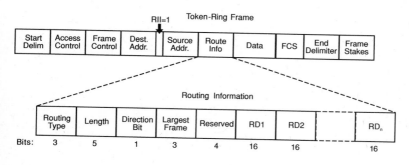

Figure B.7

The routing information field.

Figure B.8 shows the path from station A to Z using source routing. The details of the routing field also are shown.

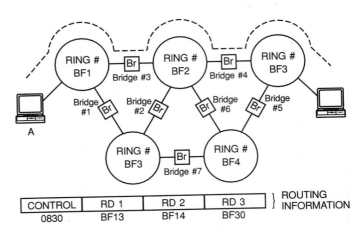

The key to the operation of source routing is discovering the initial route. This is done by sending a *discovery frame* sent by the source node when it wants to discover the best path to a destination. The discovery frame circulates on the network and arrives at the destination with a record of the path taken. The discovery frames are returned to the sender, who then selects the best possible path.

IEEE 802.5 networks prefer the source-routing method. To connect IEEE 802.3 networks that use transparent bridges with IEEE 802.5 networks that use source routing, you can use several methods. One method is to have a bridge, such as the IBM 8209 bridge, that provides translation of routing information between the two separate bridge mechanisms. Another method is to use a bridge that is a combination of source-routing and transparent bridges. These bridges are called *Source-Routing Transparent* (SRT) bridges. In SRT, transparent bridging is used when no RI field exists; otherwise, source routing is used. Figure B.9 shows the model for SRT bridges. The MAC layer entity consists of SR and TB algorithms. These algorithms are invoked depending on the setting of the RII bit.

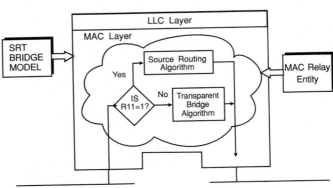

Adapted from IEEE

How Does Routing Work?

An internetwork based on routers consists of many distinct logical networks (see fig. B.10). A logical network is characterized by having its own unique network address. This network address is common to all the nodes in the logical network. The individual nodes in a logical network are distinguished by their own unique addresses. For LANs, this is the MAC layer or physical address, such as an Ethernet address or Token Ring address. Therefore, to address a node on a different logical network, the sending station must know the network address and the node address of the destination node. This information then is encoded in the packet sent. Routers that connect these two networks rely on the network address information in the packet to forward the packet to its correct destination.

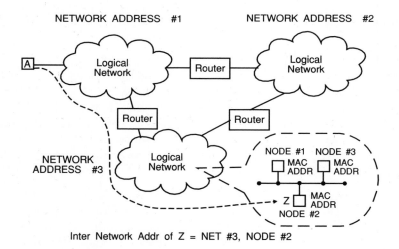

Figure B.10

Internetworking addressing.

The logical networks in the internetwork can be managed by potentially independent organizations and can be viewed as separate administrative domains. These separate administrative domains make their own decisions about which kind of networking software to run. Because different networking software uses different protocols, the internetwork runs a variety of protocols. Any router used to connect the logical networks must understand all these different protocols. Most routers made today, therefore, are multiprotocol routers. Some of the common protocols supported by multiprotocol routers follow:

- IPX/SPX

- XNS Protocols

- TCP/IP

- SLIP (Serial Line Internet Protocol)

- PPP (Point-to-Point Protocol)

- SNAP (Sub-Net Access Protocol)

- DECnet

- SNA (Systems Network Architecture)

- X.25

- CLNP (Connectionless Network Protocol)

- IS-IS (Intermediate System to Intermediate System)

- ES-IS (End System to Intermediate System)

Windows NT networks can use IPX or IP. The IPX protocol is preferred if you are using the Windows NT server in a NetWare network. Otherwise, you should use the IP protocol because it is a nonvendor-specific protocol. Both IPX and IP can be routed across multiple networks. If you use the NetBEUI protocol, you cannot route it because the NetBEUI protocol does not have an explicit network layer.

Routers depend on the network layer for their operation. The network layer is needed to route a protocol. Protocols that do not have a network layer are unroutable. Unroutable protocols must be bridged. You can use the NetBEUI protocol if you have a small Windows NT LAN and there are no requirements for connecting it to other networks using a router. Even though the NetBEUI protocol cannot be routed, it can be bridged. Other examples of nonroutable protocols are *Local Area Transport* (LAT) from DEC and LU 6.2. These protocols also do not have an explicit network layer.

Routers examine the network layer source and destination address in the packet to determine where a packet came from and where it needs to be delivered. The packets may not tell the router how it should accomplish this task. Routers are expected to figure out the best possible path. A number of criteria, such as cost and distance, help determine the best possible path. The information related to determining the best possible path is kept in an internal database called the *routing table*. A fundamental requirement of a router is to initialize and maintain its routing table. Based on the routing table information, a router should determine the next hop in the journey of the packet.

Routing tables can be global or local. Global routing tables have a table entry for every node on the network and therefore can use global optimization techniques to determine the best possible path. For large networks, the cost of maintaining a very large routing table with the most recent information can become prohibitive. Most modern routing protocols use local routing information, by which routers know information about the "local" portion of the internetwork to which they connect. The routing tables for such routing protocols tend to be smaller and more manageable.

Another distinction between routers is the manner in which the information in routing tables is updated. Two approaches are static and dynamic. In *static routing*, the Administrators must manually set each entry in the routing table. Although this approach may be advantageous for total security and control, it also is inflexible and does not automatically adapt to network changes. In *dynamic routing*, the routing tables are set automatically by each router. Special packets that contain routing information are exchanged by routers. These packets contain updates on path information and are used by routers to update their routing tables. The manner in which these special packets exchange information constitutes a routing protocol. Many types of routing protocols exist. The *Routing Information Protocol* (RIP) used in NetWare routers is based on Xerox's XNS protocols. Dynamic routing always involves the use of some routing protocol and is more flexible than static routing. Dynamic routing is the preferred approach in most modern routers.

To make the most current information available to the network, a router broadcasts information whenever it detects a change in the network. If a certain link goes down or a new link is available to form an additional path, the information concerning it is broadcast by using a routing protocol. The amount of information sent can vary from an incremental update to an entire routing table. The number of routers to which this information is sent and the actual amount of information sent depends on the routing protocol used.

After a router sees a packet, it examines its routing table for the destination address to send the packet along the best possible path. The determination of the best possible path depends on these factors:

- The routing metric

- The routing algorithm

- Available information in the routing table

- The topology of the network and the locations of the routers in the network

If the routing metric is based on distance, the best possible path is the shortest path. Most routers use a simplifying metric, which is called the *hop metric*, to measure distances. A *hop* is a path between two store-and-forward devices, such as a router or a station. The number of hops, therefore, is a measure of the number of times a packet has to be processed by a router.

The shortest path can turn out to be the most expensive path. A metric is needed that can factor other variables, such as economic cost, line speed, and transmission delay. The routing algorithms that use these metrics can be classified into two broad categories: *Distance Vector Algorithms* (DVAs) and *Link State Algorithms* (LSAs).

A knowledge of these classifications is important. LSA-based networks, for example, adapt more quickly to network changes and are more robust than their DVA counterparts. Because of their quick response time, LSA-based networks make better use of communications facilities and have better performance figures.

The major distinction between DVA and LSA is the manner in which they compute the cost for each path. In DVA, the model of the network is computed by each router telling its neighboring routers information about the rest of the network. This process is much like the party game in which a message is whispered to one individual who whispers it to another and so on, until everyone has heard the information. The last person to hear the information often hears an entirely different message. Although routers tend to transmit information more reliably than people, this example points out the weakness of the DVA algorithm. As information is propagated from router to router, not all routers have the same view of the network. Also, it takes a while for the information to propagate. During this period of time, the routing tables will be inconsistent with the network topology, and this may lead to transient anomalies such as packets being lost or delivered by inefficient routes. NetWare routers handle this problem by providing a RESET ROUTER command that can cause routing tables to be updated immediately.

LSAs compute the model of the network based on each router telling the rest of the network about its connections. Because each router knows exactly who its neighbors are and the type of connections it has, other nodes on the network have a more complete picture. LSA-based routers contribute to more router traffic on the network and more work for the router. An advantage of LSA is that the topological map of the network can be more easily constructed from LSA information. Topological maps are a great help in routing hierarchical networks.

Hierarchical networks are useful in the construction of large networks (see fig. B.11). To make routing more manageable, the network is divided into regions or areas. Each area has its own routers. The routers within an area only perform routing for nodes in that area. These intra-area routers are called level 1 routers. Areas are joined by inter-area routers called level 2 routers. The level 2 routers form a logical router backbone, which is used for transmitting inter-area traffic. An example of a hierarchical network is DECnet or the DoD Internet.

Figure B.11

Hierarchical networks.

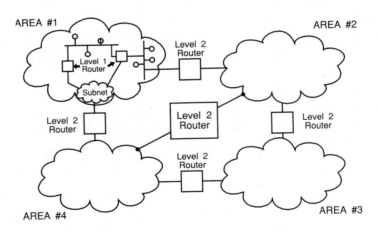

The other type of network is a *flat network*, which consists of only one level. This network contains no hierarchy of areas and routers. All routers are on the same logical level with no distinction between parts of the network. Flat area networks are suited for small networks. Examples of flat networks are Windows NT LANs connected by IPX or IP routers.

Both DVA- and LSA-routing algorithms can be used for either flat or hierarchical networks. LSA works better, however, with hierarchical networks because the network topology can be derived more easily from it.

Until recently, most routing protocols have been DVA-based and implemented on flat networks. The XNS routing protocol from which the IPX routing protocol, *Routing Information Protocol* (RIP) is derived, is DVA-based. The XNS routing protocol also is called the *Routing Information Protocol* (RIP). Do not confuse it with the protocol of the same name, RIP, that is used for TCP/IP-based networks. The TCP/IP RIP and XNS RIP are different. TCP/IP RIP also is DVA-based.

Newer protocols, such as *Open Shortest Path First* (OSPF) for TCP/IP networks and *Intermediate System to Intermediate System* (IS-IS) for OSI-based networks use LSA techniques.

DVA- and LSA-based routing techniques have been used for flat and hierarchical networks. The LSA algorithm, because it deals with topological maps of the network, can be used more easily to partition networks into areas. This is exactly what is required for hierarchical networks divided into special areas. Therefore, LSA techniques adapt better to hierarchical networks.

As networks grow in size, DVA-based routers do not perform very efficiently. They transmit their entire routing tables, which can get very large as networks grow. Networks that use LSA-based routers scale much better as networks grow.

Initially, most of the networks started using DVA-based routers. The problems with DVA did not surface until the networks began growing in size. A classic example of this is the TCP/IP-based Internet, in which networks that connect to the backbone still use DVA-based RIP. Many of the DVA-based protocols were derived from XNS routing protocol, also called RIP, which also stands for Routing Information Protocol. This includes the TCP/IP RIP and IPX RIP. All three RIPs (XNS, TCP/IP, and IPX RIP) are different, and unfortunately, they all use the same acronym. If you are dealing with a multi-vendor network, you are likely to see all three on the Internet, and this can cause some confusion.

The two LVA-based routing protocols that you should be aware of are OSPF for TCP/IP networks and IS-IS for OSI-based networks. Both protocols use LSA techniques. As networks evolve to more open standards, vendors may be forced to adopt these routing protocols.

Bridges versus Routers

Bridges and routers can both be used to consolidate networks. They provide a wide range of functionality and features that can be helpful in simplifying the task of network administration. Bridges and routers have their own unique advantages and disadvantages. Table B.1 summarizes the pros and cons of bridges, and table B.2 examines the advantages and disadvantages of routers.

Table B.1
Bridging: Pros and Cons

Pros	Cons
Simple to install, load, and configure	Cannot perform effective balancing
Perform automatic reconfiguration	Can cause traffic overload problems
Can be used with protocols that cannot be routed	Ineffective in preventing broadcast storms
Can be moved easily with bridge networks	Certain applications may not run on bridge networks
Have good cost/performance ratio	

Table B.2
Routing: Pros and Cons

Pros	Cons
More flexible than bridges	More difficult to set up
Can perform load balancing/sharing	Moving stations can be difficult
Are effective in controlling broadcast storms	Routers based on static routing can cause problems
More effective for large networks with arbitrary topologies	Some protocols cannot be routed
Can accommodate growth more easily	

Bridges do not require complex configurations. You can power them on and connect them to networks without any problem. This makes them easy to install. Some of the more advanced bridges may require some configuration if you want to manually enter routing information in the bridges' tables, but the interface is easy to use.

Because bridges do not have a network address (they operate below the network layer), the networking software on the nodes does not need to be configured to recognize newly installed bridges. In other words, under typical circumstances, bridges are transparent to the network software. The only time you may have to do any configuring at the nodes is if you are dealing with IBM bridges that use source routing.

Because bridges operate below the network layer of the OSI model, they need to know about protocol details of upper layers. Numerous upper-layer protocols exist, and the complexity of dealing with them is hidden from bridges. A consequence of this is that bridges do not have to be configured for upper-layer protocols as long as they can understand the data link protocols, such as Ethernet, Token Ring, and so on. Certain upper-layer protocols, such as NetBEUI (PC networks), LU6.2 (IBM SNA networks), and LAT (DECnet), cannot be routed effectively, but they can be used with bridges because bridges do not need to know the details of upper-layer protocols.

Bridges form a single logical network that has the same network address. The stations and bridge ports in a bridge internetwork have their own unique node address, but because they share the same network address, they can be moved around in the same logical network without having to configure them for new network addresses.

Bridges provide very rapid packet transfer at relatively low cost. In many situations, a negligible penalty is paid (one to five percent drop in data rate) when transferring data between two networks.

Because bridges are not aware of redundant paths on the network, they cannot perform load sharing across these paths. A single path can get heavily congested by Internet traffic even though alternative paths can be used to reduce the congestion.

Bridges can flood the network unexpectedly. This results in very slow networks.

Large networks connected by bridges may experience *broadcast storms*. As the name suggests, a sudden rise in the number of broadcast packets occurs. Broadcast packets are used by the upper-layer protocols (layers 3 and above) to communicate general information about themselves to the rest of the network. An example of this is the RIP protocols used for route advertisement. Bridges use BPDUs that are broadcast to all other bridges. All this extra traffic can cause significant network load. Most of these broadcast protocols use a 60-second (or a multiple) interval, and if they get synchronized, very high-peak loads can occur at 60-second intervals.

Bridges can prevent certain types of applications from running on the networks. Some applications need unique network names based on the network address. Because one network address exists for a bridged network, multiple copies of the application cannot run on the same network.

Routers have more options for partitioning networks in different ways. They can perform load sharing if alternate paths of equal cost are available, for example. They can associate a cost metric called the *Route Path Cost* (RPC) for each route and select the optimum route. The route-path cost can be determined as a function of economic cost, data rate, path delays, security cost, and priorities.

Routers can be configured to prevent broadcast storms. They can be used to selectively filter out certain types of traffic for networks. For example, it does not make sense to broadcast IP RIP packets to an interconnected AppleTalk network if no IP routers are on that network. Routers can be used to contain broadcast traffic within a single network because they have knowledge of the broadcast protocols.

Routers are more effective than bridges for maintaining and configuring large networks. They can support arbitrary topologies and can more easily accommodate network growth.

Setting up routers may require specialized training. Many router vendors offer week-long training classes. Each individual protocol that will be routed needs to be set up independently. The information on protocols in this book will help you understand a router's configuration parameters.

Moving end systems (ES-OSI terminology for user stations) between network segments is more difficult because their network addresses have to be changed to the network address of the relocated end system.

Some routers use static routing. This means that routing information has to be entered manually into the router's table by the network manager. This can be a very laborious and tedious process. Also, manual entry always is prone to errors and easily can become outdated when network changes are made. Many networking problems on large networks can be traced to incorrect entries in static routing tables.

Some protocols, such as NetBEUI, LU6.2, and LAT, cannot be routed. Many of these protocols do not follow the OSI model in terms of having an explicit network layer. The router needs an explicit network header from which a network address can be extracted. If the protocol cannot provide a router with this information, it cannot perform routing. For this reason, some vendors provide a product that is a combination of a bridge and a router (*Brouter* = Bridge + Router). A brouter tries to route a protocol. If it cannot do so, it tries to bridge it.

Examining IPX Routers Used with Windows NT Networks

This section discusses IPX routers. IPX routers are discussed because IPX is one of the routable protocols supported by the Windows NT server. The actual routing mechanism used is discussed, followed by a discussion about the IPX and RIP mechanisms essential to routing. This section also discusses limitations of IPX routers and how to manage the network number assignment for routers.

Understanding IPX Routing

IPX routers can be hardware-based routers from vendors such as Cisco, Wellfleet, and so on. You also can configure ordinary PC workstations to act as routers. Because servers perform the dual role of router and server, such configurations are called *internal routers*. If a PC workstation is set up to perform DOS and routing functions, it also is a *nondedicated router*; if it is set up to perform routing functions only, it is called a *dedicated router*. Because the routing is done on a separate external device, such routers are called *external routers*.

Figure B.12 shows the routing processes running on an IPX router. This routing process is an integral part of a NetWare server and IPX hardware-based routers. If you have access to NetWare software, you can generate and configure software for external routers by using Novell's ROUTEGEN utility.

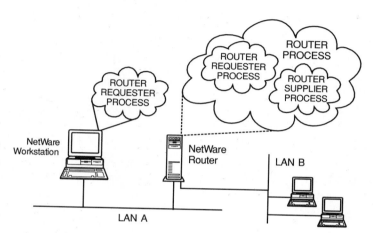

Figure B.12

IPX router processes.

All stations on an IPX LAN are somewhat aware of routing. They all have a *router requester process* used for requesting routing information from other routers. NetWare routers additionally have a *router supplier process* used to supply routing information to the router requester process. In short, all stations, including routers, have a router requester process. Only IPX routers have the router supplier process (refer to figure B.12). The request for routing information and the reply to it are transmitted by using the routing information protocol.

When a packet is sent to a router (see fig. B.13), the NIC card in the router observes the packet and reports it to the network driver by using the hardware interrupt mechanism. The network driver performs data link layer processing (layer 2 of OSI model) on the packet. This process strips the data link layer header and passes the data to the next higher layer, which is the network layer. The network layer in NetWare routers implements the IPX protocol. If the destination network address of the IPX packet differs from the network address of the network on which the IPX packet was seen, the IPX packet is sent to the routing process. The routing process determines which of its NIC ports should be used to forward the packet.

Figure B.14 shows two LANs connected by an IPX router. Each network to which the router connects has a unique logical network address. In a pure IPX-based network, stations on the same cabling plant or logical network have the same unique network address (also called the network number). If stations have the same network address, no routing is necessary to transfer packets between them. Destinations on the same logical network are reached using the broadcast mechanism inherent in LANs. If the destination has a different network address, a router is needed to route the packet to the appropriate destination LAN. If a packet is sent from station A to station B, no routing is necessary because both stations are on the same LAN and have the same network number. If a packet is sent from station A to station C, routing is necessary because station C has a different network number from station A.

Figure B.13

Router packet processing.

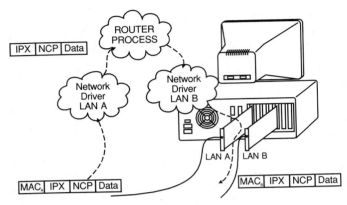

Figure B.14

IPX routing model.

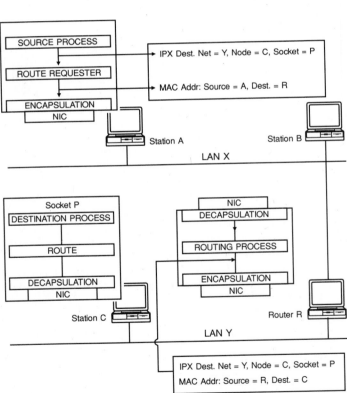

The full destination address of a packet is encoded in the IPX header and consists of the network number, the node address, and the socket number. The node address is the data link layer address of a station and is the address of the NIC card in a station. This address is fixed (burned in ROM on NIC) or set by switch settings on the NIC. The socket number uniquely identifies the software process running on the station.

Figure B.14 shows the Internet IPX address of a packet sent from station A to station C. The routing requester process at station A realizes that the network destination is different from LAN X. Station A knows of router R on the network. During data link encapsulation, the destination data link address is set to that of the router. The router receives the packet addressed to it and decapsulates the data link header. This process recovers the original IPX packet sent from station A. The IPX packet's destination address is examined by the routing process in the router. The routing process consults its routing table and determines that the destination network is connected to one of its ports. It then sends the packet to the appropriate NIC port for encapsulation and transmission. Finally, destination C receives the packet and decapsulates it. On further examination of the IPX destination address, station C determines that it is indeed the correct recipient of the packet.

If the router had determined after examining its routing table that the destination LAN was not directly attached to one of its ports, then the router would forward the packet on one of its ports. The decision on which port to send the packet would be based on the hops and delays it would take to reach the destination.

In general, there are three possibilities for forwarding a packet:

■ If the router is an internal router and the destination is the internal router, the packet is passed directly to the *File Service Process* (FSP).

■ If the destination number of the IPX packet is the same as that of the network number to which the router is directly connected, the router forwards the packet to the directly connected network. Before sending this packet, it properly encapsulates it by using the MAC header (data link layer header). This situation is essentially the same as that shown in figure B.14.

■ If the destination number of the IPX packet is different from that of the directly connected networks, the router must determine the next router responsible for transmission of the packet. This determination is based on the entry for the destination network in its routing table, which contains the fastest path to get to the destination network.

As the packet passes through the routers, the IPX source and destination addresses do not change. Only the MAC header changes by the encapsulation and decapsulation process. The MAC header contains the immediate source and immediate destination address to forward the packet on its next hop. The IPX header essentially remains the same so that all routers can follow the same algorithm to reach the destination. The only modification is that the transport control field (discussed in the next section) is incremented to count the number of routers the packet has passed through.

Internet Packet Exchange (IPX)

To understand IPX routing, you should understand the manner in which stations are addressed in a Windows NT LAN configured to use IPX. This address is encoded in the IPX packet and is used by routers. RIP and the algorithms associated with it are based on the semantics of the

IPX packet structure. This section introduces the fundamentals of IPX semantics. Some of the information in this section may seem a little too detailed, but if as a LAN manager, you are involved in managing your LAN with a protocol analyzer, this information is invaluable.

An IPX packet encapsulated by an Ethernet packet. The IPX packet encapsulates upper-layer protocols. Table B.3 summarizes the meaning of the fields in the IPX packet. The diagram is shown for descriptive purposes.

The *checksum* field is a 1s complement add-and-left-cycle (rotate) of all the 16-bit words in the IPX packet. The checksum does not include the checksum word itself and is designed to be easily computable. Another characteristic of the checksum is that it can be incrementally computed if only a few words change, such as a change in the network address fields. The checksum is inherited from the XNS *Internet Datagram Packet* (IDP) from which IPX is derived. It is in addition to any hardware-generated checksums used at the data link layer of the OSI model.

Table B.3
IPX Packet Structure

Field	Meaning
Checksum	Optional 1s complement checksum
Length	Byte length of IPX packet
Transport Control	Used by routers as a "hop count" field
Packet Type	Identifies type of data encoded in the data portion of IPX packet
Destination Network	Uniquely identifies destination network from a number of interconnected networks
Destination Number Node Address	Uniquely identifies the node address of the destination station
Destination Socket	Software address in destination node
Source Network	Uniquely identifies source network from a Number number of interconnected networks
Source Node Address	Uniquely identifies the source node of the sending station
Source Socket	Software address in sending node

At the time XNS was designed, hardware and memory systems were not very reliable. One of the functions of this checksum is to verify the data path between the NIC and memory in the station. IPX ignores the checksum field and places all 1s (FFFF hex) in this field to indicate that the field is not used. NetWare-based networks rely on the data link control and other upper-layer mechanisms for error control. This avoids the processing overhead of computing the checksum.

The *length* field contains the complete maximum length of the IPX packet measured in bytes. This figure includes the IPX header length of 30 bytes plus the data. If the packet contains an odd number of bytes in the data portion of the packet, an extra "garbage" byte is added to make the packet an integral number of 16-bit words. The garbage byte is not included in the length field. Originally, IPX packets had a nominal maximum length of 576 bytes. Allowing for 30 bytes of IPX header, this allowed a maximum of 576 – 30 = 546 bytes of data. This maximum length was inherited from the specification of the XNS IDP packets. Many LANs can accommodate larger packet sizes (1,514 bytes for Ethernet), and the 576-byte maximum length restriction has been removed by Novell. IPX packets that use a longer packet length than 576 bytes do not interoperate with pure XNS routers that use smaller packet sizes. Because there are few installed examples of the original XNS routers, this is not a serious problem.

The *transport control* field is used for transporting Internet packets across routers. This field is used only by routers. Workstations set this field to zero when sending a packet. The transport control field is an eight-bit field, but only four bits are used:

Transport	Control						
Bit:	7	6	5	4	3	2	1	0
	X	X	X	X	H	H	H	H

Bits marked X X X X are unused and set to zero. Bits marked H H H H represent the hop count field. The hop count field is increased by one each time it is processed by a router. A router can determine the number of routers encountered by the packet. The four-bit hop count field limits the maximum number of routers in any path. A maximum of 15 routers is permissible on any transmission path. After the hop count field reaches a value of 16 (that is, when it reaches the sixteenth router), it is discarded. The XNS Error protocol is used to transmit this fact to the source. But because a datagram protocol (IPX) is used for this, there is no guarantee that the message will be seen by the source. Applications that need greater reliability must use the SPX protocol or some other internal mechanism.

The maximum hop count field ensures that IPX packets are not routed indefinitely in a loop. With a maximum value of 15 for the hop count field, you can have a maximum of 16 networks in any transmission path.

The *packet type* field is used to identify the data contents of the data portion of the IPX packet. This field is used for protocol multiplexing. It allows a number of client protocols to reside on top of IPX and allows the IPX module to determine which of the client protocols—SPX, PXP, NCP, Echo, Error, Serial (copy protection), Watch Dog, RIP, or SAP—to send the packet to (see fig. B.15). Table B.4 shows some of the more common packet types. Developers interested in a new packet type assignment must contact Xerox.

Figure B.15
IPX clients.

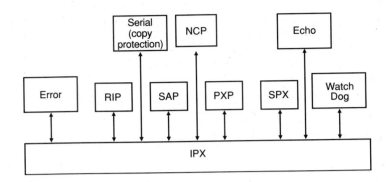

Table B.4
Common Packet Type Assignments for IPX

Packet Type	Protocol
1	Routing Information Protocol (RIP)
2	Echo
3	Error
4	Packet Exchange Protocol (PXP)
5	Sequenced Packet Exchange (SPX)
20-37	Experimental

Network numbers uniquely identify the logical network to which a station is attached. Network numbers primarily are used for routing. The router routes the packet to the LAN that has the same destination number as the destination number in the IPX packet. This network number field in the IPX packet is four bytes. This field therefore can accommodate a network number size of eight hexadecimal digits. If the routing is to work correctly, all logical networks in an internetwork must have a unique network number. The network number must be different from the internal network number for NetWare 3.*x* servers. The network number is assigned at the time of installation for each logical network connected to the router. A value of zero for the destination network number means that the packet is not to be processed by an internetwork router.

From an administrative point of view, you must exercise control in keeping these network numbers unique within an organization. This administrative control is essential if LAN operations within an organization are decentralized. The node address uniquely identifies the station NIC within a logical network. After a packet is routed to the correct destination LAN, it must be sent to the correct station. The node address uniquely identifies the station to receive the packet. The IPX packet has a six-byte field for the node address and can accommodate a 12-digit hexadecimal number. XNS networks originally were designed for Ethernet, which has a six-byte address field. Fortunately, the six-byte address field is the same size used for IEEE LANs and FDDI. For LANs that use a smaller address size for stations, such as ARCnet or Proteon-10, the address field can be padded with zeros in the most significant digits. A node address of all 1s (hexadecimal FF FF FF FF FF FF) indicates a broadcast packet.

The *socket number* identifies the software or client process running at a station. A station can have a number of client processes running (see fig. B.16). Because they run on the same station, they each have the same network number and node address. If a packet is to be sent to a specific client process, a means should exist to identify it uniquely. The socket number is used to identify the client process uniquely. Socket numbers are analogous to mailboxes. A client process is notified when a packet is delivered to its mailbox. Sockets are implemented as data structures that can be used to send and receive packets at a unique software address within a station. They are inherently bidirectional in their nature.

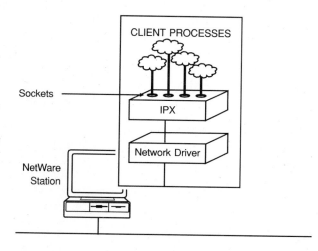

Figure B.16
IPX socket numbers.

Certain protocols use a standard socket number. These standard socket numbers are called *well-known socket numbers*. Table B.5 lists some well-known socket numbers. You can obtain well-known socket numbers by contacting Xerox or Novell. Socket numbers above 8000 (hex) are assigned by Novell.

Table B.5
Well-Known
Socket Numbers for IPX

Socket Number (hex)	Meaning
1	XNS Routing Information Protocol (RIP)
2	Echo Protocol Packet

continues

Table B.5, Continued
Well-Known Socket Numbers for IPX

Socket Number (hex)	Meaning
3	Error Handler Packet
20 _ 03F	Experimental
1 _ BB8	Registered with Xerox
BB9 _	Dynamically Assignable
451	NetWare File Service Packet
452	NetWare Service Advertising Packet (SAP)
453	NetWare Routing Information Protocol (RIP)
455	NetBIOS Packet
456	NetWare Diagnostic Packet
4001	NetWare Watchdog Packet
4003	NetWare Shell Socket
8000 _	Well-Known Socket Numbers Assigned by Novell

Using RIP and SAP

Routers use the RIP protocol to maintain a cache containing routing information (routing table). The routing algorithms used by routers serve the following purposes:

- Quickly initializes the routing table after the router starts

- Ensures that the routing table adapts quickly to changes in network topologies

- Ensures that if routers come up or go down, other routers learn about this change as quickly as possible

Every routing table contains at least the following information for every network that can be reached by the router:

- Timing delay to reach the network

- Number of hops to network

- A list of networks directly connected to the router

- Node address of a router on the directly connected network by which packets will reach the specified network for the amount of time delay and hops in the table entry

■ A timer used for routing table maintenance to age out old entries

Figure B.17 illustrates the routing table in a router.

During initialization, the router initializes the routing table to contain network numbers for directly connected networks. In figure B.17, the directly connected networks LAN A, LAN B, LAN C, and LAN D have network numbers 1001, 1002, 1003, and 1004. This information is

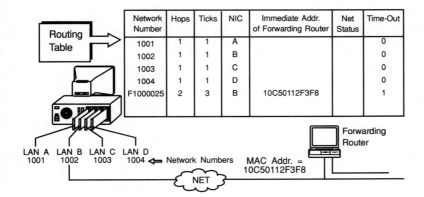

Figure B.17

A routing table in a IPX router.

Network Number	Hops	Ticks	NIC	Immediate Addr. of Forwarding Router	Net Status	Time-Out
1001	1	1	A			0
1002	1	1	B			0
1003	1	1	C			0
1004	1	1	D			0
F1000025	2	3	B	10C50112F3F8		1

built into the router during installation time, and the routing process simply reads this information and initializes its routing table.

Requests for routing information and their corresponding replies are encoded in a RIP packet. Because transmission on the LAN is through a broadcast mechanism, routers see all RIP responses. Some responses answer RIP requests originated by the router and others are gratuitous information in reply to RIP requests from other routers. The router updates its tables if any of the following conditions is true:

■ The RIP reply originated from an internetwork router connected to the directly connected network

■ The existing entry in the routing table has not been updated for 90 seconds

■ A better route was discovered to the specified network

Every time the router entry is updated, its time-out value is reset to 90 seconds. If a table entry has not been updated for three minutes (twice 90 seconds), it is assumed to be suspect. The number of hop fields is set to infinity (actually set to 16) to indicate that the network no longer is reachable. These entries are kept for another 60 seconds before being purged so that other routers know that the network cannot be reached.

Routers also broadcast a copy of their routing table in the RIP packet to other routers on all the networks to which it is connected. This response packet is sent at intervals of 60 seconds. In addition, whenever a router modifies its routing table entry, the change is broadcast to all routers on its directly connected networks. As the recipients of this information modify their routing table entries, they too send RIP response packets to routers on their directly connected networks. This ripple effect quickly transmits the changes throughout the network.

When routers broadcast information, they follow the "best information algorithm." The first rule is that the router does not broadcast routing information about networks to a directly connected network that was obtained from the same directly connected network. In figure B.18, when router ROUTER_BC sends information on segment B, it should not include any information that it received from ROUTER_AB about segment A. If it did, a user might think that segment A could be reached directly through ROUTER_AB and ROUTER_BC. The second rule is similar to the first rule. It states that a router should not include information about a directly connected network to which it is sending routing information broadcasts. In the example in figure B.18, ROUTER_BC cannot broadcast information about segment B on segment B. It can broadcast only on segment B information on segments C and D.

Figure B.18

Multiple LAN segments joined by IPX routers.

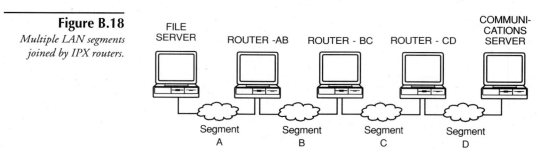

Figures B.19 through B.22 illustrate the router operations. When the router ROUTER_BC is first brought up, it initializes its routing tables with information on its directly connected networks. Next, the router sends an initial RIP response (see fig. B.19) to inform routers on its directly connected segments (ROUTER_AB and ROUTER_CD) of the segments it now makes available (segments B and C).

Figure B.19

Initial router broadcast.

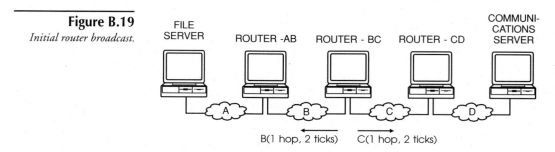

Next, the router broadcasts a general RIP request on its directly connected networks for information on all network segments that exist on the internetwork (see fig. B.20). All routers on its directly connected segment (ROUTER_AB and ROUTER_CD) send a RIP response to this request by using the best information algorithm. The router then initializes its routing table with this information. At periodic intervals, the router is the recipient of routing information from other routers (see fig. B.21).

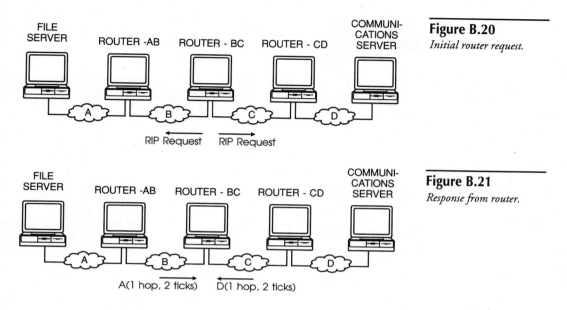

Figure B.20

Initial router request.

Figure B.21

Response from router.

After the router is up, it broadcasts its routing information in a RIP response packet at 60-second intervals (see fig. B.22).

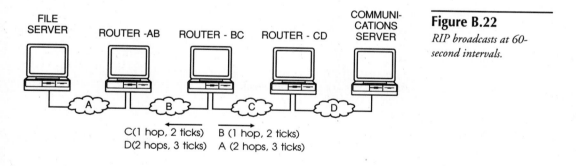

Figure B.22

RIP broadcasts at 60-second intervals.

When routers are shut down gracefully by using the DOWN command (the power plug is not pulled suddenly), they broadcast a RIP response packet, which sets the delay for all networks it can reach to infinity. This response packet informs other routers that the router has been shut down and cannot be used.

This mechanism is illustrated in figure B.23. When ROUTER_BC is shut down, it sends a RIP response to other routers, such as ROUTER_AB and ROUTER_CD, that it is no longer available. These routers then update their tables.

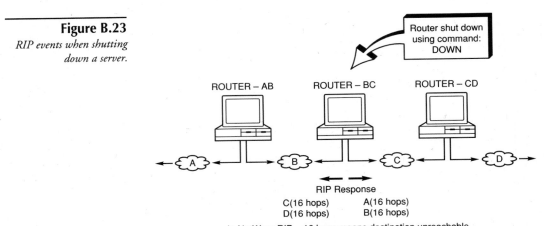

Figure B.23

RIP events when shutting down a server.

If you do not use the DOWN command to shut down a router gracefully or you have an unexpected power failure or hardware glitch, the neighboring routers are not immediately aware that a change has occurred. Unexpected shutdown can cause transient routing problems until the time-out mechanism for routing table entries goes into effect. It takes a delay of three minutes before other routers remove the entries in their routing table for the failed router.

When a router receives a request for information, it supplies the information in a RIP response packet. If it does not have the information, it returns a delay of infinity for the requested network to indicate that the network cannot be reached.

The RIP protocol is crucial so that routers can keep their routing tables up to date. Figure B.24 shows the structure of the RIP packet, and figure B.25 shows a RIP packet captured and decoded through the LANalyzer protocol analyzer. Figure B.26 shows the RIP packet structure defined by Xerox. The only difference between the IPX RIP and the Xerox RIP is the addition of the Time Delay measured in ticks, with each tick being approximately 1/18 second. (18.21 ticks occur per second.) This change improves a NetWare router's capability to select the fastest route to a destination. It also prohibits a straight integration between IPX RIP and pure XNS implementations.

The *operation* field of the RIP packet indicates whether the packet is a request or response. The following codes are used for the operation field:

Operation	Description
1	Request
2	Response

IPX Packet Structure

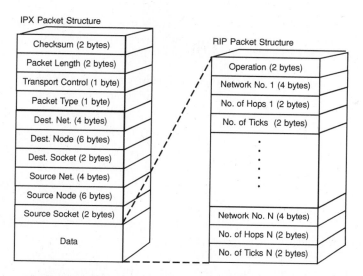

RIP Packet Structure

Figure B.24
Novell RIP packet structure.

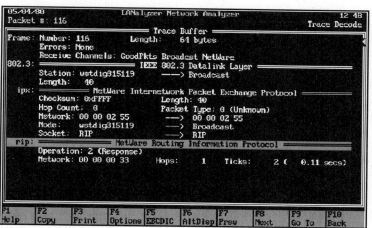

Figure B.25
RIP packet captured and decoded by LANalyzer.

XNS RIP Packet Structure

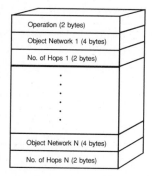

Figure B.26
XNS RIP.

After the operations field comes the contents field, which describes one or more sets, or *tuples,* of routing information. Each tuple describes an object network's network number and the number of hops and time ticks it takes to get to that network number.

A hop is counted every time a packet goes through a router. The maximum number of permissible hops is 15. A value of 16 is synonymous to infinity and means that the destination is unreachable.

The time delay field measures (in clock ticks) how much time it takes to get to the network number. Novell added the time field to better determine the fastest path. The time delay also permits better integration with IBM SNA or T1 networks that are more time-sensitive.

If the operation specified in the RIP packet is a request (1), then each tuple represents the object network for which the requester wants routing information. If the requester wants information on all object networks, only one tuple is included whose network number field is set to all 1s. If the operation specified in the RIP packet is a response (2), then each tuple represents routing information for the object network in the form of number of hops and clock ticks to reach the network number. If the number of hops field is set to infinity (16), it indicates that the destination is unreachable.

If you are integrating Windows NT with NetWare servers, you can use the NetWare server as IPX routers. You should be aware that you might have to deal with other broadcast packets generated by NetWare servers. NetWare servers act as repositories of other information besides RIP. They contain a database of services provided by servers on the network. They obtain this information through *Service Advertising Protocol* (SAP). The SAP follows the spirit of the Xerox Clearinghouse Protocol, but differs from it in detail and implementation.

The Service Advertising Protocol permits servers such as file servers, print servers, and gateway servers to advertise their services and addresses. These services are recorded dutifully by NetWare IPX routers in a table called the *Server Information Table* (SIT). The Server Address field includes the full internetwork address, the network number, node address, and socket number of the server. The Server Type holds the type of service being performed. Table B.6 lists examples of some server type designations.

Table B.6
Server Type Designations

Type of Service (Server Type)	Object Type Code (Hex)
File Server	4
Job Server	5
Gateway	6
Print Server	7
Administration	B

Type of Service (Server Type)	Object Type Code (Hex)
NAS SNA Gateway	21
Remote Bridge Server	24
Bridge Server	26
TCP/IP Gateway	27
Time Synchronization Server	2D
Advertising Print Server	47
TES - NetWare for VMS	7A
NetWare Access Server	98
Portable NetWare	9E
NNS Domain	133

The Time Since Changed or Time-Out field is used to age and retire entries for servers that unexpectedly go down. Currently, the SIT information is not organized for quick database-type queries. To rapidly access SIT information, this information is copied to the file server's bindery, which is an internal database used to keep track of certain resources on the server. SAP agents in the file server periodically update the file server's bindery so that any client attached to a server can obtain information on other services on the internetwork. If a client needs to determine which services are available on the network, it can query a nearby router or server.

The SAP packet uses the IPX packet for its transport. Figure B.27 details the SAP packet.

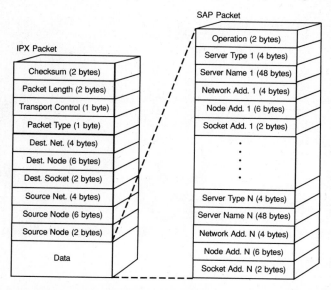

Figure B.27

Service Advertising Protocol (SAP).

The Operation field in the SAP packet defines the type of operation being performed. The four possible values for this operation code follow:

- A request by a client for the name and address of a server of a certain type (such as file server, print server, and communications server). If the client loads the NetWare shell, it issues this SAP request.

- A response to the nearest server query.

- A general request for information on all servers of a certain type.

- A response to the general request.

Figures B.28 through B.30 illustrate these SAP packets obtained by using LANalyzer.

Figure B.28

SAP request packet.

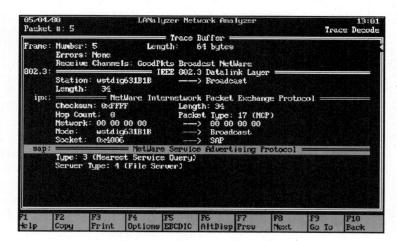

Figure B.29

SAP response packet.

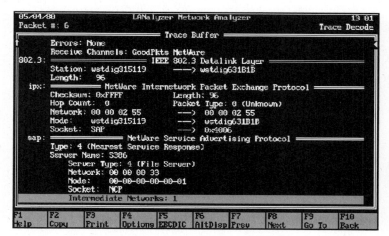

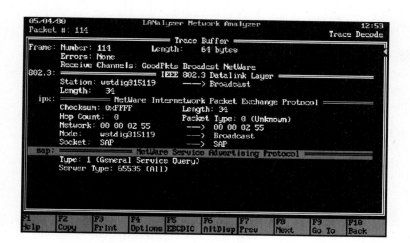

Figure B.30

SAP general request packet.

The Server Information Table in a router is updated in a manner similar to the RIP table, except that the request/response packets are SAP packets. SAP request/responses also follow the best information algorithm for RIP packets. After a server is brought up for the first time, it broadcasts information about itself to all routers. At every 60-second interval, the router process broadcasts SAP packets that contain information about all servers of which they are aware. After a server is shut down, it broadcasts a SAP packet to indicate that its services no longer are available.

Tracking Network Numbers

You must keep network numbers unique within an organization. If you do not keep network numbers unique, you encounter problems. The IPX router detects duplicate routing number assignments.

When network numbers are not kept unique, the NetWare IPX router detects a conflict in the routing number assignment. You see the following displayed:

```
1/11/93 7:18am: 1.1.112 Router configuration error detected
Router at node C0DC3F19 claims network 00000333 should be 00000255
1/11/93 7:18am: 1.1.112 Router configuration error detected
Router at node C0DC3F19 claims network 00000333 should be 00000255
1/11/93 7:18am: 1.1.112 Router configuration error detected
Router at node C0DC3F19 claims network 00000333 should be 00000255
1/11/93 7:18am: 1.1.112 Router configuration error detected
Router at node C0DC3F19 claims network 00000333 should be 00000255
```

The router error message is saying that another node claims the network number is incorrect. In this case, network number 00000333 should be 00000255 because the other node (router) has this number in its configuration. Set the same network number in the configuration for both routers to solve this problem.

In many large organizations, LAN operations are decentralized. As a result, different installers may select the same network numbers, with the default network number of 1 being the most common. When it is time to internetwork the separate departmental LANs, the network number conflicts become painfully apparent. You can avoid these conflicts by using a universal network number assignment scheme. This scheme is not something mandated by Novell; it is a recommendation to simplify network administration.

The network number field in IPX packets is four bytes long, which means that the network number can be eight hexadecimal digits. These eight hexadecimal digits can be assigned the meanings shown in table B.7.

Table B.7
Meanings Assigned to Hexadecimal Digits

Byte 3 I D	Byte 2 D N	Byte 1 N N	Byte 0 N N
I =	1-digit hexadecimal code for network number or internal network number (NetWare 3.*x*). A value of 0 (hex) indicates a network number. A value of F (hex) indicates an internal network number.		
D D =	2-digit hexadecimal number for department code.		
N N N N N =	5-digit hexadecimal number for each logical network or internal network number.		

Consider the example of an organization with the following departments: Corporate, Engineering, Manufacturing, Marketing, Accounting, and Field Services. Each of these departments has its own LAN. Department codes can be assigned as indicated in table B.8. This table also illustrates examples of some network numbers and internal assignments.

Table B.8
Network Number Assignments

Department	Code (D D) Hex
Corporate	10
Engineering	11
Manufacturing	12
Marketing	13

Department	Code (D D) Hex
Accounting	14
Field Services	15

Network Number or Internal Number	Comments
0 1 0 0 0 0 0 1	Network number (0) for department Corporate (10) and logical network 00001
F 1 0 0 0 0 0 2	Internal network number (F) for department Corporate (10) and NetWare 3.x server 00002 (second file server)
0 1 5 0 0 0 0 7	Network number (0) for department Field Services (15) and logical network 00007
F 1 3 0 0 0 0 9	Internal network number (F) for department Marketing (13) and NetWare 3.x server 00009 (ninth file server)

You can tell at a glance whether the network number assignment is for a cable segment or IPX internal number by examining the first hexadecimal digit. The next two digits tell you the department responsible for administering the network number. Each department can keep track of its network number assignments. Using this scheme greatly simplifies the problem of network number assignments.

Installing and Managing External IPX Routers

This section discusses installation procedures for IPX routers. You learn to configure IPX routers through a guided tour. You can configure external IPX routers in several ways: dedicated/nondedicated and protected/real mode. You learn about the differences between these configurations in the following sections.

Dedicated and Nondedicated Mode Routers

A *dedicated router* is a computer that performs only routing functions. It cannot be used as a DOS workstation. Because all the computer resources are set aside for routing functions, dedicated routers have better performance. Another advantage of the dedicated router approach is greater reliability and security. No applications are running on the computer that could cause it to hang, and because users cannot use it as a workstation, it also is more secure from inadvertent reboot of the router computer.

A *nondedicated router* is a computer that performs both routing and workstation functions. It can be used as a DOS workstation to run applications while the routing function is performed in the background. Because computer resources are shared between routing functions and applications running on the router, nondedicated routers have poorer performance. The advantage of the nondedicated router approach is that it saves the cost of an extra workstation. Because nondedicated routers are exposed to applications and users, they are less reliable and secure compared to dedicated routers.

Dedicated router configuration should be selected if possible because of potential problems with the nondedicated approach. Choose the nondedicated router approach only if severe budgetary constraints do not permit the purchase of an additional computer.

The dedicated mode router can be set up in the protected mode or real mode depending on the microprocessor inside the workstation. If an Intel 8086 microprocessor is being used, the router can operate only in real mode. Real-mode routers can use memory up to 1 MB (see fig. B.31). If the workstation has an Intel 80286, 80386, or higher microprocessor, and if it has sufficient extended memory, it can run in protected mode (see fig. B.32).

Figure B.31

Real-mode router.

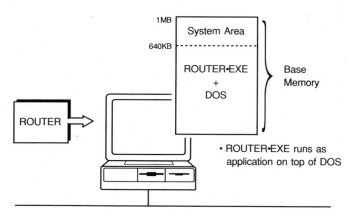

Figure B.32

Protected-mode router.

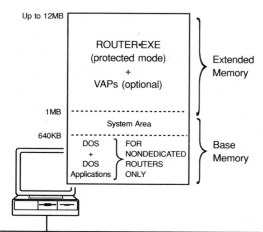

Router Hardware and Software Requirements

Each PC that must act as a router must be installed with two or more NICs. The limit is four NICs for external routers. The NICs should have no hardware conflicts with each other or with other hardware inside the PC. Hardware parameters such as interrupt request line, DMA channels, I/O ports, and base memory addresses must be set uniquely. If a protected-mode router is to be configured, you must allow at least 500 KB of extended memory for the router process. You can have up to 12 MB of RAM in the protected-mode router. Extra memory can be used for router buffers to improve the performance.

The software requirements follow:

- ROUTEGEN disk

- Network driver disks such as LAN_DRV_XXX

- DOSUTIL-1 disk containing CONSOLE.COM if nondedicated router is to be set up

Installing a NetWare-Based IPX Router

Figure B.33 shows the process of generating the routing software. The utility to generate the routing software is ROUTEGEN, which can be found in the ROUTEGEN disk that comes with NetWare (2.x and 3.x). The ROUTEGEN utility is the same for NetWare 2.x and NetWare 3.x.

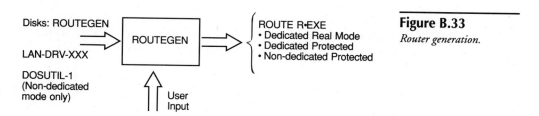

Figure B.33

Router generation.

The result of the ROUTEGEN.EXE is a ROUTER.EXE program that implements the router. This ROUTER.EXE program file must be copied to the router boot disk. The router then must be configured to boot correctly. The boot process is slightly different between dedicated and nondedicated routers and is discussed after a guided tour of the router installation.

Router Generation

To install a router, follow these steps:

1. Install the NICs into the workstation to be used as a router. You can install up to four NICs. Base address must not conflict with any other hardware in the router. Only two IBM Token Ring network boards can be used in a router.

2. Boot the workstation to be used as a router with DOS 3.*x* or higher.

3. Insert the ROUTEGEN disk into drive A and enter **ROUTEGEN**. After a `Please Wait` message, a screen appears.

4. Press Enter to continue. The Router Generation screen appears with the following fields:

   - **Operating system mode.** You have a choice between two modes of configuration: dedicated and nondedicated. If you select nondedicated mode, you must assign a process address.

   - **Nondedicated process address.** This address is a unique hexadecimal number. It identifies the workstation DOS environment to the router process.

   - **Number of communication buffers.** Communication buffers are temporary areas in the router's RAM to hold incoming/outgoing packets. The default number is 150, which is adequate for most router configurations. If you anticipate heavy router traffic, the number of communication buffers should be increased. The maximum number of communication buffers is 1,000.

   - **Network board.** This field shows information on the router's NICs. The first NIC is called Network board A, the second Network board B, and so on.

   - **Driver.** For a given network board, the driver to be used is shown. To deselect a driver, press Del. To see a list of available drivers, press Enter. If the driver you want is not listed, press Ins and follow the instructions to select another driver.

   - **Configuration option.** A driver can have a number of combinations of its parameter settings. You must select the setting that corresponds to the NIC's settings. Some NICs and drivers are software-configurable.

   - **Network address.** Every cabling segment attached to the Network boards A, B, C, and D must have a unique address. This address is expressed as an eight-digit hexadecimal number and is used by the IPX packets to uniquely identify the different networks. It is part of the internetwork address, which consists of network address, node address, and socket number.

5. Select either the dedicated or nondedicated router operating mode.

6. Increase the number of communication buffers to 200.

7. Highlight the Driver field under Network board A and press Enter.

   A list of drivers for network board A is displayed. If the driver you want is not listed, you must press Ins and follow the instructions to add it to the list.

   ROUTEGEN contains a bug; therefore, if you are adding a driver to the list and it does not work, copy the drivers to the ROUTEGEN disk and repeat the preceding steps.

8. After you select the driver, highlight Configuration option and press Enter. A list of configuration options appears.

9. Highlight the configuration option that matches the NIC's setting and press Enter.

10. Assign a unique network address for the LAN connected to the NIC. This address is an eight-digit hexadecimal number. You do not need to enter leading zeros.

11. Repeat steps 7 to 10 for as many NICs as are in the router. These steps must be done for network boards B, C, and D.

12. Review the information. Make any corrections. If satisfied, press F10 to continue. A series of messages appears to inform you that the router is being linked.

Creating the Router Boot Disk

The ROUTER.EXE file created in the preceding section must be copied to the router boot disk. The router can be booted from either the hard disk or a floppy disk.

Both of these disks must be DOS-bootable and run DOS 3.*x* or higher. To make the DOS disk bootable, use the FORMAT command with the /S parameter.

Installing a Dedicated Router

After you create the DOS boot disk, perform the following steps:

1. Copy the ROUTER.EXE file from the ROUTEGEN disk to a DOS bootable disk.

2. Create an AUTOEXEC.BAT file with the ROUTER command.

3. Boot the router machine. ROUTER.EXE loads and activates the router.

Understanding TCP/IP-Based Networks

Before you can understand how TCP/IP and Windows NT server integration works, you must understand TCP/IP. TCP/IP is two protocols: TCP and IP. *TCP* is a transport protocol that fits into layer four of the OSI model. *IP* is a network protocol that fits into layer three of the OSI model. Figure B.34 illustrates the relationship between TCP/IP and the OSI model. The *User Datagram Protocol* (UDP) is a cousin of TCP, but is simpler and not as reliable as TCP.

Note that the OSI model commonly is used as a means of describing the functionality of a protocol such as TCP/IP; it is not meant to imply that TCP/IP is an International Organization of Standards recommendation. The transport layer's job is to ensure end-system to end-system data integrity.

Figure B.34

TCP/IP comparison with the OSI model.

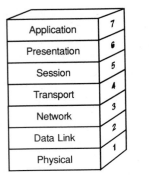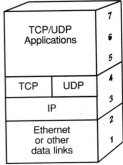

Over the years, TCP has acquired a reputation for robustness and reliability. TCP has had its trial by fire and has had to undergo changes to fix problems dealing with data-transmission integrity. In addition to reliability, TCP allows software processes within a node to be referred to by unique addresses. This address is called the *TCP port number*. This port number is similar in concept to the IPX/SPX sockets discussed earlier.

Whereas the TCP protocol runs on an end-system, such as a user system or a host/server, the IP protocol can run on intermediate systems used to connect the end-system together (see fig. B.35). Examples of these intermediate systems are IP routers. The job of the IP layer is to prepare the messages from the TCP layer. The IP layer must know the address of the destination IP layer. This address is a 32-bit address called the *IP address* (or the *Internet address*). In general, the destination node can be on a different network, so a portion of this IP address is used to refer to the network number of the destination network. The remaining portion is used to refer to the host number within that network.

Figure B.35

IP router connecting end-systems.

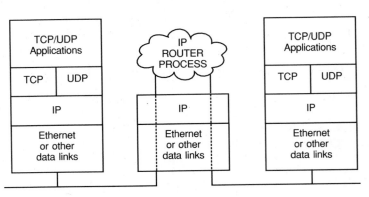

The IP layer must send the message by the best route it can. If the message is too large, it can be broken down into smaller pieces (fragmented or segmented) by the sender or at any point along the path to the destination. At the destination, the fragments must be put back together in the correct order. The IP layer adds enough information to each piece of message to accomplish this task.

The IP layer provides a means of connecting a large number of networks. An IP packet can go across 255 routers. IPX LANs are limited to 15 routers along a transmission path. One benefit of integration with IP networks is that an IPX packet can be routed across larger networks using the more flexible IP mechanism.

Hardware-Based Routers

Although internal routers based on PCs can be used for most networks, they are not designed to handle heavy traffic loads. For handling heavy traffic loads, special computers designed for routing functions are used. Besides handling heavy loads, these computers can be used for routing almost any industry-standard protocol. These hardware-based routers are made by a number of companies such as Cisco, Wellfleet, Proteon, Digital, Timeplex, and Advanced Computer Communications.

The hardware-based routers use a multiprocess architecture and proprietary high-speed buses to facilitate high-speed routing. Figure B.36 shows a diagram that models the general architecture for most hardware-based routers.

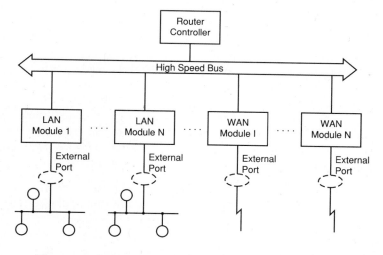

Figure B.36

Model for high-speed routers.

The router architecture is modular and allows for network hardware modules to be installed in bus slots. Addition of each of these modules gives the router the capability to connect to a specific type of network. These network modules can be designed for LANs and WANs. Each network module is designed for a specific type of network. To connect to an Ethernet network, for example, an Ethernet network module needs to be installed. To connect the Ethernet network to an FDDI network, an Ethernet and an FDDI module need to be installed. The router controller in figure B.36 usually is implemented on the router's motherboard.

Routers can be purchased with standard network module configurations. Popular choices are Ethernet and Token Ring for LAN modules, and T1, leased-line, or dial-up lines for WAN modules. These routers permit multiple links to a network. The secondary links can be used as a backup and, in some routers, also can be used for *load balancing*—when traffic is diverted equally among the links to achieve a higher sustained throughput. This feature is valuable particularly for point-to-point wide-area links, as shown in figure B.37.

Figure B.37

Load balancing on wide-area links.

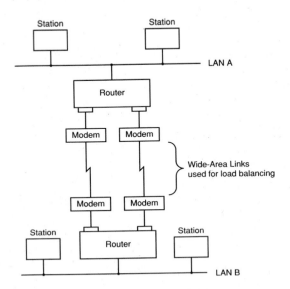

Some hardware-based routers can be booted from a special floppy disk that contains the routing software. The advantage of this is that the routing logic can easily be updated when bug fixes and new features need to be released. An example of this kind of router is ACS 4200 from Advanced Computer Communications. Many of the routers available today also can be configured to act as bridges. As mentioned earlier in this chapter, these routers are called brouters. The bridge operation is particularly useful for protocols such as *NetBIOS Extended User Interface* (NetBEUI) and LAT that are not routable because they do not have a network layer.

Routers can be configured through a local terminal attached to an RS-232 port on the router box. If a dumb terminal is not available, a computer running terminal emulation software such as PROCOMM or SmartCom can be used. Some of the high-end routers also provide TELNET server services. This means that any computer running TELNET client services can log in remotely to the router and configure the router. Figure B.38 shows the variety of configuration options.

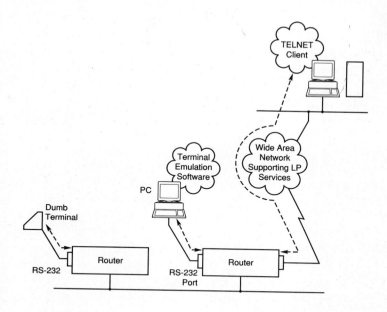

Figure B.38
Router configuration options.

The router configuration typically is done through a command-line or menu-driven interface. The TimeLan 100 router, for example, has a menu-driven interface. Many of the Wellfleet and ACC routers have a command-line interface.

The router must be configured for each protocol it needs to route. An example of the configuration commands needed for the IP network routing in figure B.39 is shown next. The example commands are shown for the ACS 4200 router connecting two LANs over a wide-area link. Other routers have similar commands. The syntax details are different, but the semantics are very similar.

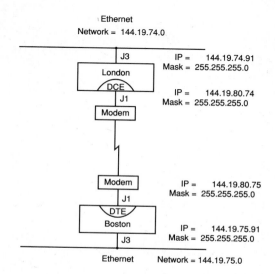

Figure B.39
A simple IP routing example.

The configuration for the London router follows:

```
login netman            # Login to the router
set prompt to london    # For descriptive purpose only
add ip network entry 144.19.74.91 255.255.255.0 j3
add ip network entry 144.19.80.74 255.255.255.0 j1
# The above commands assign IP address and subnet masks
# to the router's J3 and J1 ports.

set rip protocol on
# This activates the IP RIP protocol. Other choices
# are OSPF etc.

delete ip route entry 144.19.75.0
# This command deletes any routing table entry for the
# network 14.19.75.0

add ip route entry 144.19.75.0 255.255.255.0 144.19.80.75 1
# This command adds an entry to the routing table that
# says that network 144.19.75.0 can be reached by sending
# IP traffic to port 144.19.80.75. The network is 1 hop
# away.

reset                   # This makes the change permanent
```

The configuration for the Boston router follows:

```
login netman            # Login to the router
set prompt to london    # For descriptive purpose only
add ip network entry 144.19.75.91 255.255.255.0 j3
add ip network entry 144.19.80.75 255.255.255.0 j1
# The above commands assign IP address and subnet masks
# to the router's J3 and J1 ports.

set rip protocol on
# This activates the IP RIP protocol. Other choices
# are OSPF etc.

delete ip route entry 144.19.74.0
# This command deletes any routing table entry for the
# network 14.19.74.0

add ip route entry 144.19.74.0 255.255.255.0 144.19.80.74 1
# This command adds an entry to the routing table that
# says that network 144.19.74.0 can be reached by sending
# IP traffic to port 144.19.80.74. The network is 1 hop
# away.

reset                   # This makes the change permanent
```

Conclusion

In this appendix, you learned the differences between bridges and routers and the advantages and disadvantages of using them. The operation of two types of bridges—the spanning tree and source routing—were examined.

The operation of routers was discussed in some detail. You learned how IPX routers can be used. This is useful particularly when Windows NT servers are being integrated with existing NetWare-based networks.

WANs and MANs

As networks expand, you must connect islands of LANs to provide an integrated network computing platform. This appendix discusses the technologies you use to create large LANs.

You might want to interconnect LANs for the following reasons:

- Integrating existing LANs

- Extending the capabilities of existing LANs

- Increasing performance by providing access to faster networks or networks with more powerful servers and hosts

- Improving network availability by providing redundant network links, hosts, and servers

Exploring Wide Area Networks

Local area network (LAN) technologies offer high performance, but they are suited for use only in limited geographic areas, usually within a building or campus setting. If you need to connect LANs for longer distances, you must use other technologies. Networks that span long distances frequently are referred to as *wide area networks* (WANs). This section introduces the methods you can use to interconnect LANs over large geographic areas. Each method has advantages and disadvantages based on cost, availability, and performance.

FDDI

Fiber Distributed Data Interface (FDDI) is regarded by many as a high-speed LAN (100 Mbps). Because it can span a distance of 100 kilometers, however, it can be used as a WAN to interconnect LANs or serve as a backbone to LANs. FDDI spans layers 1 and 2 of the OSI model and can be used to provide IEEE 802.2 or LLC services to upper layers (see fig. C.1). FDDI can be used to run client/server applications that rely on IEEE 802.2 services, including NetWare, which provides IEEE 802.2 encapsulation. The FDDI physical station address follows the IEEE 48-bit (6 octet) addressing convention.

A full FDDI configuration consists of two fiber rings. The primary ring is used for data transfer, and the secondary ring serves as a backup ring in case the primary ring fails. If the primary ring fails, an auto-sense mechanism causes a ring wrap so that traffic is diverted to the secondary ring (see fig. C.2). Only stations that have a *dual-attachment* (connected to primary and secondary rings) tolerate this failure.

Figure C.1

FDDI spans layers 1 and 2 of the OSI model.

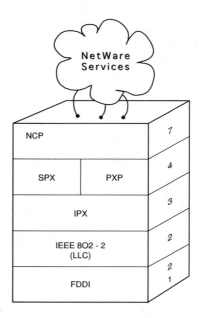

FDDI is based on the Token Ring access method that runs at 100 Mbps. A token is used to control access to the ring, but the details of token management are different from IEEE 802.5 LANs. The maximum length of FDDI is 200 kilometers (100 kilometers for dual rings), and the distance between two nodes on a FDDI LAN cannot exceed two kilometers. Distance parameters are based on a maximum latency (delay) of 1.617 milliseconds. Maximum FDDI frame size is 4,500 bytes. This size makes it suited for high-speed file transfers, such as graphics, image, and other data files. Because the frame size is larger, more data can be packed into the frame and fewer packets are needed to send the file. The total number of connections to an FDDI ring cannot exceed 2,000 (1,000 for dual-attached stations).

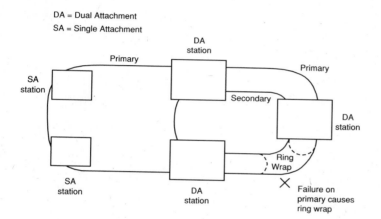

Figure C.2

FDDI ring with dual- and single-attachments.

The FDDI networks expect that PC workstations will not be attached directly to them, but attached by means of an FDDI concentrator or router (see fig. C.3). PC workstations are turned on and off often in normal usage. If workstations are connected directly to the FDDI ring, their powering on and off causes frequent ring reconfigurations that may become costly in a large FDDI network. PC workstations connected directly to FDDI networks also may not keep up with the high data rates in FDDI. The newer AT computers, based on Intel 80386, 80486, or 80586 chips, may keep pace with the FDDI data rates, but they are hampered by slow I/O buses.

The FDDI concentrators, or *Multi Access Station Units* (MAUs), also serve as a fan-out box so that multiple stations can be connected. Several FDDI concentrators can be cascaded to increase the fan-out. Although the FDDI concentrator has a dual-attachment, the stations attached to the concentrator have a single attachment to save on FDDI NIC costs. FDDI concentrators should be powered on all the time to reduce ring reconfigurations.

FDDI token management enables several FDDI frames to be resident on the ring at a time, which better utilizes the data bandwidth on the ring.

Figure C.3

FDDI network with router.

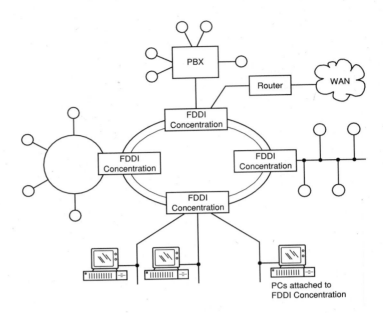

PCs attached to
FDDI Concentration

The FDDI ring operates in two modes: synchronous and asynchronous. In *synchronous mode*, stations are guaranteed a percentage of total bandwidth available on the ring. This bandwidth allocation is calculated in terms of percentage of *Target Token Rotation Time* (TTRT). The TTRT is the expected token rotation time for the expected traffic on the network and is negotiated during ring initialization. A station with synchronous bandwidth allocation can transmit data for a period of time not to exceed the percentage of TTRT allocated to it. Any remaining time left after all stations finish synchronous transmission is allocated to the remaining nodes. Thus, if the actual *Token Rotation Time* (TRT) is less than TTRT, the leftover time (TTRT_TRT) is used for asynchronous transfer.

In *asynchronous mode*, transfer can take place in two modes: restricted and nonrestricted. A station can perform an extended transfer in restricted asynchronous mode. The *Station Management* (SMT) negotiates a maximum restricted time. Stations running in restricted asynchronous mode should not take up the entire ring for a period of time greater than TTRT.

In *nonrestricted mode*, leftover time is divided between any node that wants to send data. This mode of operation is the default. The division of time can be based on priority schemes in which stations have a threshold TRT. Stations with lower threshold TRT are cut off earlier.

FDDI uses multi-mode fiber. Extensions to FDDI that use single-mode fiber currently are in development. Although multi-mode can use a mix of light frequencies, a single-mode fiber uses laser and a smaller-core diameter fiber. Single-mode fiber has less signal attenuation and can be used over longer distances. With these FDDI extensions, two stations can be up to 60 kilometers apart. FDDI-II permits circuit switching in the synchronous mode with up to 16 synchronous channels of 6.144 Mbps each.

Many vendors are interested in running the FDDI protocols over a copper medium. Some vendors propose *Unshielded Twisted-Pair* (UTP) wire, whereas other vendors favor *Shielded Twisted-Pair* (STP) wire. ANSI's goal is to have one unifying protocol, rather than separate protocols for STP and UTP wiring. Using copper-based FDDI wiring is cheaper than using the fiber-based products. One problem of using twisted-pair wiring is compliance with FCC regulations and signal attenuation that limits the distance between a workstation and the FDDI concentrator. It is the goal of copper-based FDDI to have at least distances of 100 meters between workstations and FDDI concentrators.

Some vendors, such as Crescendo Communications, Inc., of Sunnyvale, California, have copper-based FDDI products. Crescendo Communications' *Copper Distributed Data Interface* (CDDI) runs on UTP wiring. Crescendo currently offers an eight-station MAU (1,000 Workgroup Concentrator) that connects workstations at distances of 50 meters. An SBus CDDI adapter can be used as the FDDI interface for the Sun Microsystems, Inc., SPARC station. IBM offers a version of FDDI on STP wiring.

Defining HIPPI

The *High Performance Parallel Interface* (HIPPI) is a LAN standard that the ANSI X3T9.3 committees currently are investigating to provide data rates between 800 Mbps to 1,600 Mbps.

HIPPI transfers 32 bits of data in parallel across distances of about 25 meters. The parallel transmission runs over a 50-pair twisted-pair wire cable—32 pairs are used for data lines, and the remaining lines are used for control.

HIPPI evolved from the proprietary HSX I/O bus that CRAY supercomputers use. Graphic workstations require high I/O data rates to perform real-time modeling and display.

Figure C.4 shows how you can adapt HIPPI for LAN usage. The HIPPI standard proposes a HIPPI framing protocol layer that allows IEEE 802.2 protocol to run on top of it. Any protocol stack that uses IEEE 802.2, such as NetWare, can use HIPPI.

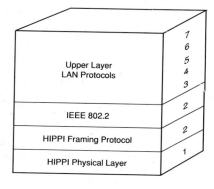

Figure C.4
Adapting HIPPI for LAN usage.

Because of distance limitations and cabling costs, the current HIPPI probably will not be used for the backbone or WAN connectivity. Nevertheless, it represents an interesting development for those applications that require very high-speed LANs.

Metropolitan Area Network

Metropolitan Area Networks (MANs) are an interesting development in computer network standards. The MAN standard originally was intended for local area networking, but its size and scope mandate that it be managed by a central body, such as the telephone company or other commercial organizations. In this regard, it is similar to WANs.

You can implement city-wide MANs that can carry data rates as high as 155 Mbps. The IEEE 802.6 committee is trying to standardize MANs. The MAN standard has a checkered past. MAN structure originally was based on coaxial technology with a slotted ring approach, but that standard was superseded by growth in fiber-optic technology.

The following list summarizes the differences between LANs and MANs:

- City and suburban areas employ MANs, whereas areas that cover smaller geographical distances employ LANs.

- Public operation of MANs through a telephone company raises issues of security, reliability, cost, and central billing that do not arise in LAN setups.

- MANs can serve as high-speed backbones faster than FDDI.

- MANs can carry a mix of voice, video, and data traffic more effectively than LANs.

- MANs cross public rights-of-way. Service utilities such as telephone companies have these permissions; LAN owners typically do not.

MANs can transmit a mix of voice and data traffic. Another possible use of MAN technology is to provide LAN connectivity. The media access technology used by MAN, *Dual Queue Dual Bus* (DQDB), unlike FDDI, scales very well across longer distances and higher data rates than the current MAN specification. For this reason, perhaps, Bell Communications Research (Bellcore) is interested in using DQDB as one of the techniques for its *Switched Multi-Megabit Data System* (SMDS) services.

MAN services can be supplied city-wide by phone companies or by commercial organizations. You can use routers with a MAN connection to interconnect LANs at data speeds up to 100 Mbps; or the MAN can be used as a backbone for LANs.

MAN networks are of two types: private and public. These types are similar to private and public X.25 networks. For organizations that have stringent security or large data transfer requirements, a private MAN, such as that depicted in figure C.5, can be used. Private MANs use dedicated cables; because only the organization's data is on the MAN, this simplifies security and billing issues. This type of MAN is like a very large LAN. Not all organizations, however, can justify the expense of a private MAN. Most organizations use shared cables that have traffic from a variety of sources, including city and state governments and private organizations.

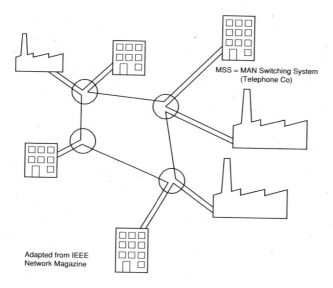

MSS = MAN Switching System
(Telephone Co)

Adapted from IEEE
Network Magazine

Figure C.5

A MAN configuration.

DQDB is the media access protocol used in MAN and is based on a proposal by Telecom Australia and its subsidiary QPSX. Originally, this protocol was known as the *Queued Packet and Synchronous Exchange* (QPSX) protocol, but later was changed to DQDB to avoid confusion with the QPSX company. It consists of two loops of fiber in the form of a bus (see fig. C.6). DQDB is arranged in the form of a ring so that a central station can provide clocking and synchronization information for transmission of frames. Data frames are sent on both buses but in opposite directions. Fault isolation mechanisms can bypass malfunctioning nodes or breaks in the cable. The dual bus architecture permits the use of a clever MAC protocol that enables requests for transmission from stations to be placed in a distributed queue. This distributed queue mechanism provides access characteristics independent of network size and speeds.

The MAN data frame is shown in figures C.6 and C.7. Each slot contains two control bits: BUSY and REQ. A BUSY bit indicates that a slot is busy, and REQ is used by a station to request an empty slot. A station that wants to send data on a bus makes its request on the reverse bus by setting the REQ bit flag. The REQ bit informs the upstream neighbors that a station downstream wants access to a slot. Each node keeps track of requests downstream from it by counting the REQ bits as they pass on the reverse bus (see fig. C.7). The REQ counter is incremented for requests on the reverse bus. The REQ counter contents are transferred to the *Count Down* (CD) counter (see fig. C.8). The CD counter is decremented for each free slot on the forward bus because a free slot will be used by a station downstream that previously made its request through the REQ bit. A station can use the first free slot after its CD counter reaches zero. Using these counters, a first-in-first-out queue is formed. The queue position is indicated by the value of CD in each station. It is truly a distributed queue that is 100 percent fair.

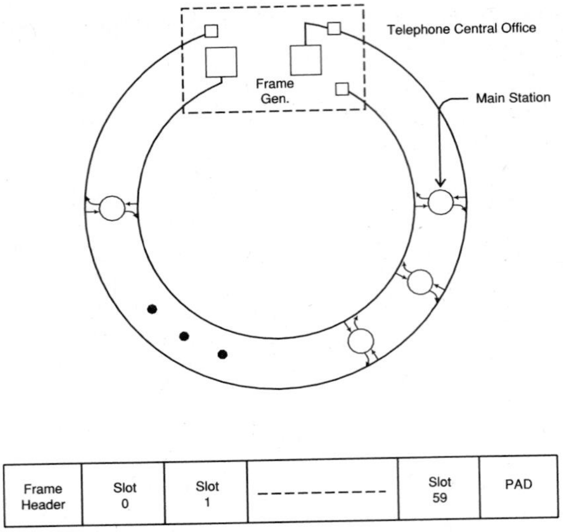

Figure C.6

DQDB architecture and frame format for MANs.

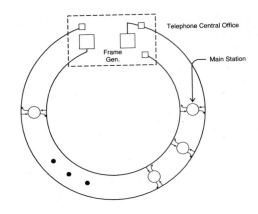

Figure C.7

Distributed Queue formation on a bus for MAN.

Figure C.8

DQDB operation used in MAN.

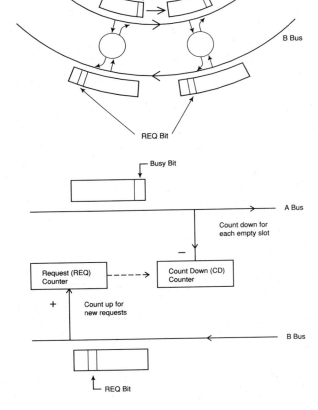

X.25

Figure C.9 shows the elements of an X.25 network, and figure C.10 shows how these elements can be used to connect LANs. An X.25 network contains a number of packet switches that switch and route packets transmitted between two nodes, such as a terminal and host machine. Although data transfer takes place using packets, the appearance to higher layers of software is that a single continuous logical channel (or virtual circuit) exists between two nodes. Typical packet sizes of X.25 networks are 128 bytes, although other sizes are possible and can be negotiated at connection time.

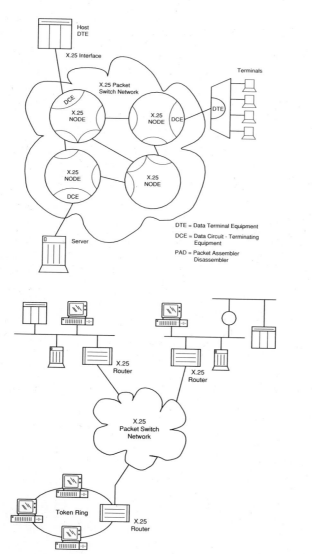

Figure C.9

Elements of an X.25 network.

Figure C.10

Connecting LANs through the X.25 network.

Although terminals are attached to the X.25 network through a *Packet Assembler Disassembler* (PAD), host machines can be attached directly or through synchronous modems. The X.25 network uses the X.25 protocols, which actually are three protocols. These protocols include the X.21 or X.21bis at the physical level, *Link Access Procedure Balanced* (LAPB) at the data link level, and X.25 *Packet Level Protocol* (PLP) at the network level. Figure C.11 shows this relationship.

The X.25 protocol enables a maximum of 4,095 virtual circuits to be time-multiplexed across a physical link between the node and an X.25 network. In actual practice, fewer virtual circuits are used because most physical links cannot support the aggregate data rate for 4,095 virtual circuits.

Figure C.11
X.25 protocols.

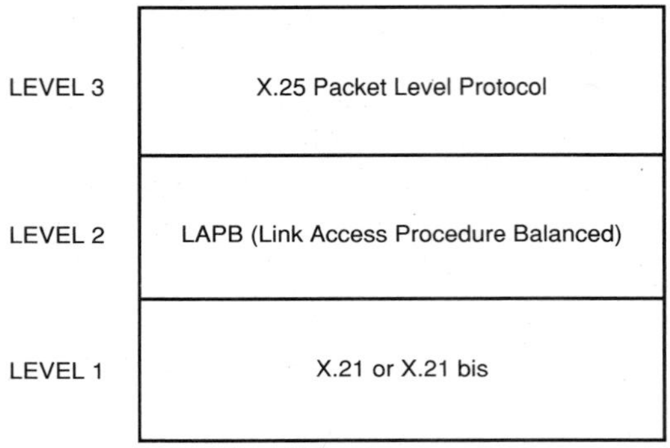

LEVEL 3	X.25 Packet Level Protocol
LEVEL 2	LAPB (Link Access Procedure Balanced)
LEVEL 1	X.21 or X.21 bis

Typical transmission speeds of X.25 networks are 64 Kbps, but higher speeds are available. If two LANs are connected through an X.25 network, data transfer between the LANs is limited to this speed. This setup limits the kind of applications you can run across X.25 networks. Many LAN applications require data-transfer rates of at least 1 Mbps to run efficiently. File transfers and terminal emulation applications run efficiently across an X.25 network, but workstation applications run slowly.

Frame Relay

Frame Relay technology was developed for *Broadband Integrated Services Digital Network* (B-ISDN). It can provide higher transfer-data rates by eliminating much of the overhead inherent in an X.25 network. Multiplexing and switching are provided at the lower data link layer rather than the network layer. The flow control and error control that exist between packet switch nodes for X.25 do not exist in Frame Relay. Frame Relay relies on higher-level software mechanisms to provide this service if necessary. Frame Relay assumes that the media used for data transmission is inherently reliable. It does error checking, but does not perform error recovery, leaving this to higher layers.

Interest in Frame Relay is rising. Frame Relay overcomes the limitations of X.25 networks by enabling you to connect LANs at speeds up to 2 Mbps. These speeds, which rival LAN speeds, allow workstation applications to run well. As the need for LAN interconnectivity over wide area networks increases, so will the interest in Frame Relay technology.

T1

The *T1 circuit* is a point-to-point full-duplex digital circuit originally intended for carrying digitized voice. You can connect several point-to-point circuits to form a T1 network. The T1 circuit can use a variety of media besides copper, such as coaxial cables, fiber optics, infrared, 18- and 23-GHz microwave radio, or satellite links.

T1 networks provide a physical level connection with a data rate of 1.544 Mbps. This rate is in the range that can run workstation applications efficiently across T1 networks. The basis for T1 networks is the T1 circuit. Figure C.12 shows two LANs connected by a T1 circuit.

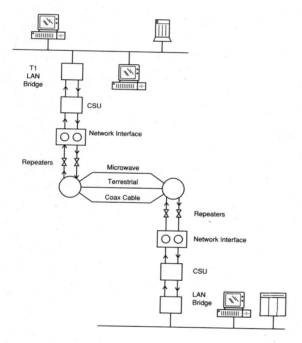

Figure C.12

LANs connected by means of T1 circuit.

Broadband ISDN

X.25, Frame Relay, and T1 networks can be used to interconnect LANs at 2 Mbps or less. One technology under development to interconnect LANs at higher data rates is based on B-ISDN. B-ISDN was developed to respond to the need to improve the basic and primary rates provided by ISDN (Narrowband ISDN). Voice, video, data, image, and multimedia are examples of applications that require high bandwidth.

Initial B-ISDN interfaces provide data-rate transmission of 51 Mbps, 155 Mbps, or 622 Mbps over fiber-optic media. Figure C.13 shows that the physical layer support for B-ISDN is provided by SONET and ATM, which are described in the following sections. With appropriate adaptation layers, SONET and ATM can be used for LAN interconnectivity. A client layer in figure C.13 can be frame relay, SMDS, or IEEE 802.2, for example.

Figure C.13

B-ISDN support infrastructure.

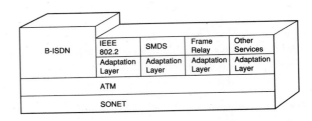

SONET

The *Synchronous Optical Network* (SONET) first was proposed as a standard by Bellcore for a family of interfaces to be used in optical networks. The lack of standards for high-speed digital transport to be used for single-mode fiber led to a number of proprietary standards. SONET is now an international standard accepted by ANSI.

The SONET standard provides a point-to-point link over fiber-optic media. It provides the physical layer connection for B-ISDN and is defined in terms of a hierarchy of data rates. This hierarchy is defined in terms of the *Optical Carrier* (OC) speeds and the corresponding electrical signals (*Synchronous Transport Signals*) used to interface with electrical components. Table C.1 shows this hierarchy.

Table C.1
SONET Data Rates

OC Hierarchy	STS Hierarchy	Data Rate
OC-1	STS-1	51.84
OC-3	STS-3	155.52
OC-9	STS-9	466.56
OC-12	STS-12	622.08
OC-18	STS-18	933.12
OC-24	STS-24	1244.16
OC-36	STS-36	1866.24
OC-48	STS-48	2488.32

The OC and STS rates are multiples of 51.84 Mbps. The basic building block is the 51.84 Mbps line rate. Thus OC-48 is 48 × 51.84 Mbps = 2488.32 Mbps. The standard defines up to OC-240; that is, 240 × 51.48 = 12.4416 Gbps rate. STS-1 rates are roughly equivalent to the T3 (45 Mbps) data rates available today.

Design goals of SONET included providing a way to accommodate T3 data rates and resolving the incompatibility between the North American and European digital hierarchies, as expressed in the T1, T2, and T3 signals. The North American standard is based on a T1 rate of 1.544 Mbps, whereas the European standard is based on 2.048 Mbps. As a result of this incompatibility, T1-based routers for NetWare LANs operate differently in North America than they do in Europe.

STS data streams can be combined to yield higher STS rates. Three STS-1 rates multiplexed together, therefore, can yield a data rate of STS-3.

The STS-1 frame is 810 bytes and is made up of a 90 column-by-9-row matrix with each cell of this matrix being one byte long. This data matrix is transmitted in one STS-1 frame, as shown in figure C.14. The first three bytes of each row contain overhead information. The first three rows contain nine bytes of section overhead, and the remaining six rows contain 18 bytes of line overhead. The combined section and line overhead of each frame is 27 bytes. The remaining 87 columns contain the payload or data. This frame payload is called the *synchronous payload envelope* (SPE) and works out to be 783 bytes (9 × 87). Not all the SPE contains data; the first nine bytes contain path information.

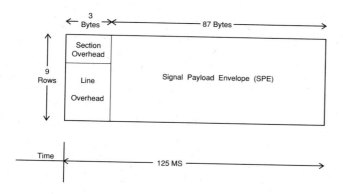

Figure C.14

STS-1 frame in SONET.

The STS-1 frame is sent once every 125 microseconds or at the rate of 8,000 frames every second. Because each byte in the frame is eight bits, the data for each byte of data in a frame corresponds to an 8,000 × 8 = 64,000 bps channel. You can use this data rate to transport digitized speech or data.

Of the 783 bytes that make up the SPE, nine bytes are used for transport overhead for every row. This transport overhead contains a pointer to the location in the SPE that the actual data begins, thus allowing data to float.

Detailed consideration of section, line, and path overhead is beyond the scope of this book. A table of their definitions is included, however, to show the reader the rich functionality and robustness of SONET, as well as the reasoning for an interest in it for WAN/LAN communications.

Understanding Asynchronous Transfer Mode (ATM)

Asynchronous Transfer Mode (ATM) has its origins in the evolving Broadband ISDN (B-ISDN) networks and provides high-bandwidth, low-delay switching technology that multiplexes data over cells of a fixed size. Although ATM's origins are in the B-ISDN public wide area networks, vendors are very interested in ATM as a technology for LANs that need high bandwidths. Examples of LAN applications that can benefit from the high bandwidth of ATM are desk-to-desk video conferencing, desk-to-desk multimedia conferencing for local and remote users, medical imaging, CAD/CAM, distance learning, scientific visualization, data fusion, animation, video libraries, multimedia e-mail, supercomputer access, and communications.

Consider a desk-to-desk video conferencing that requires 1.544 Mbps. If 30 users on a LAN perform desk-to-desk video conferencing, the aggregate bandwidth requirement would be the following:

$$1.544 \times 30 = 46.32 \text{ Mps}$$

Moreover, video conferencing applications need a sustained bandwidth and low delays. Current LAN access methods such as CSMA/CD and Token Access require modification to be capable of sustaining such high data rates and low delays. ATM, on the other hand, because it uses B-ISDN technology, easily can meet these requirements.

In figure C.13, ATM is used above SONET to provide services for ISDN signaling or Frame Relay applications.

ATM is one of a general class of packet-switching services that relays and routes information based on the address contained in the packet. Unlike other packet-switching technologies such as X.25 or Frame Relay, however, ATM uses fixed-length packets called *cells*.

The fixed-length ATM cells are made available on demand to applications and provide a flexible and fast packet-switching service. The packets are 53 bytes in size. The 53-byte cell size includes five bytes of header information. Therefore, the actual cell size in terms of data transmitted is 48 bytes. The cells are the fundamental unit for data transport. Data traffic from multiple channels are multiplexed at the cell level. The fixed-packet size of ATM is in contrast to the variable length information field in other packet-switching technologies. For example, frame relay, which relays frames of data, can have packet sizes from 64 bytes to 1,500 bytes.

Synchronous Transfer Mode versus Asynchronous Transfer Mode

Packet-switching technologies such as ATM exploit communication channels more efficiently than *Synchronous Transfer Mode* (STM) technologies. A classic example of an STM technology is the T1 carrier. In T1, a period of time called the *frame* is divided into 24 time slots. Each time slot is assigned to a separate voice channel, making it possible to *time multiplex* 24 voice channels in a single frame. The time slots are combined with a frame bit from the T1 signal. Each time slot is synchronized with respect to the frame bit—hence the name Synchronous Transfer Mode. In STM, the data for a particular voice channel is identified by its position in the frame. This type of technique uses *position multiplexing*. In ATM, the data is identified by a label (address information) in the five-byte header of the ATM cell. For this reason, ATM sometimes is referred to as a *label multiplexing* technique. Both STM and ATM use time-multiplexing techniques. One of the fundamental differences between the two is the method used to identify a data slot: STM uses position multiplexing, and ATM uses label multiplexing.

In STM, because a time slot is assigned per voice channel, each voice channel is guaranteed a certain bandwidth. If a voice channel is not used, the bandwidth goes unused. Even if the voice signals obtain additional unused time slots, the voice communications do not improve significantly. If, however, unused time slots become available for data traffic, data-transfer rates improve dramatically. In ATM, access can be given to data traffic or voice traffic on command. In general, data traffic tends to occur at random interval and for random lengths of time. ATM is well-suited for transporting this type of traffic because additional data cells can be generated on command. Voice, video, and other real-time traffic that is time sensitive and needs immediate access to data cells, never has to wait for more than one 53-byte cell. For a 155 Mbps physical transport, this works out to be:

$$53 \text{ Bytes}/155 \text{ Mbps} = 53 \text{ bytes} \times 8 \text{ bits/byte}/155000000 = 2.7 \text{ microseconds}$$

By keeping the cells short, real-time traffic is guaranteed quick access. For data traffic, however, the longer the packet size, the greater is the efficiency of transfer. Because of this, the size of the ATM cell is the subject of much controversy. Originally, the voice people wanted small cell sizes of 32 bytes. This increases the likelihood of cells being available when they are needed on short notice. The data people felt that small cells introduce greater overhead in packet splitting and recombination because data packet sizes in LAN applications tend to be large. They were willing to settle for a cell size of 64 bytes. A compromise of 48 data bytes per cell was adopted. Together with an additional header of five bytes, the ATM cell size became 53 bytes. Breaking a large data packet into small cells introduces a certain inefficiency for data traffic, but enables the cells to be used for voice services and multimedia applications. Cells from different traffic types are multiplexed into a common path called the *virtual path*. The cell multiplexing in ATM provides a better bandwidth utilization. Cells are allocated on demand. This is well-suited for LAN applications, which typically have *bursty* traffic. When no traffic exists, no new data cells are generated. The term *asynchronous* in ATM refers to the fact that the recurrence of cells containing information from individual users does not occur periodically. That is, the cells for individual users occur asynchronously.

Each user on an ATM network is assured that, although the ATM network contains cells from other users and other communication sessions, the user's data can be transmitted in a manner consistent with the subscribed *Quality of Service* (QOS). To provide the desired QOS, the user's data is sent on a *virtual channel* (VC). The virtual channel is unidirectional and is identified by the *Virtual Channel Identifier* (VCI). To provide bidirectional communications, two virtual channels are needed. The bandwidth for the return virtual channel can be assigned symmetrically (same as the sending channel), asymmetrically (different from the sending channel), or can be zero (unidirectional session).

ATM Interfaces

Figure C.15 shows an ATM interface between two desktop computers. In this example, the desktop computers obtain a physical link of a certain capacity, such as 155 Mbps. Other data rates also are possible. The initial path created is called a virtual path and is identified by the *Virtual Path Identifier* (VPI). The VPI can represent a high-speed trunk line between the desktop computers or a LAN connection using ATM devices. Within the virtual path, a number of separate virtual circuits are possible. Virtual circuits within the VPI are identified by a VCI. These virtual circuits can be used by data, voice, or multimedia applications being shared by the two desktop computers. The VPI and VCI values have a local significance only, and a new VPI/VCI value can be assigned at the receiving end.

Figure C.15

ATM interface between two computers.

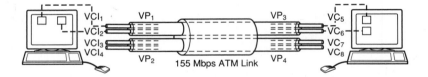

The VPI/VCI addressing mechanism can be viewed as a hierarchical addressing scheme. Figure C.16 shows the frame structure of an ATM cell. The VPI is a one-byte field, followed by a two-byte VCI field. ATM switching equipment can route the ATM cell on the basis of the first byte. When the cell reaches the destination, the VCI can be used to further determine the exact location in which to send the cell. The VPI/VCI together make a three-byte field, which allow a maximum of 16 million circuits to be used over a single interface. From a practical point of view, fewer virtual circuits are used. Many vendors of ATM equipment provide a maximum of 4,096 virtual circuits per user interface. The virtual circuit capacity in the ATM switches used in an ATM network have to be much higher. The ATM switches use the VPI/VCI label information in the header of the ATM cell to uniquely identify the virtual circuit to which the cell belongs.

The VPI/VCI have a local significance only and undergo a mapping based on the routing tables kept at each ATM switch. When a virtual path is created, each ATM switch in the virtual path is assigned a set of lookup tables. The lookup tables identify an incoming cell by its header address and the port to which the ATM cell should be routed. They also contain information to overwrite the incoming VPI/VCI address with a new address recognizable by the next ATM switch as an entry in its local routing table. The cell is passed from ATM switch to ATM switch over the prescribed route set during the call establishment phase. The path used is *virtual* in the sense that the physical communications facility is dedicated to the cell only when the cell *traverses* it. At other times, the physical communications facility may be used by other cells belonging to other virtual circuits. By sharing the physical communications facility among several virtual circuits, the communications efficiency for ATM can be much higher than for STM. It is possible to push the communications efficiency and the network utilization as high as the user is willing to push. Public ATM networks' tariff parameters can be used to assign different grades of service. Users have the option of paying higher rates for guaranteed service or lower rates for "best-efforts" service.

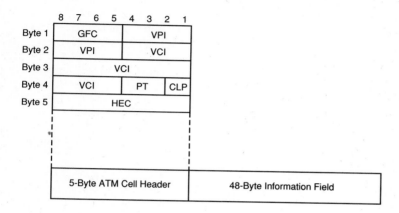

Figure C.16
ATM cell structure.

Legend

GFC = Generic Flow Control
VPI = Virtual Path Identifier
VCI = Virtual Channel Identifier
PT = Payload Type
CLP = Cell Loss Priority
HEC = Header Error Control

The transfer capacity on the virtual circuit is determined on a per-call basis and is influenced by the Quality of Service parameters requested during the call-establishment phase, network capacity, and other factors. The other fields in figure C.16 deal with flow control (*Generic Flow Control*—GFC), type of data being sent (*Payload Type*—PT) and header integrity (*Header Error Control*—HEC). The *Cell Loss Priority* (CLP) field, if set to one, indicates that the cell is subject to discarding on the network. When set to zero, the CLP indicates that the cell has a high priority and should not be discarded.

ATM Protocol Stack

Figure C.17 shows a typical protocol stack used with ATM communications. The physical layer for ATM consists of two sublayers: the *Physical Media Dependent* (PMD) layer and the *Transmission Convergence* (TC) layer. The PMD layer deals with physical functions such as bit transmission, bit alignment, encoding, and electrical conversion. ATM can support diverse media types such as twisted-pair wiring, fiber optic, and coaxial. If fiber-optic cables are used, the PMD layer performs the electrical conversion between light and electrical signals. The TC layer provides a conversion between the ATM cells used by upper layers and bits used by the

PMD layer. It also performs transmission frame generation and recovery, transmission frame adaptation, cell delineation, header error control sequence generation and verification, and cell rate decoupling.

The *transmission frame adaptation* is used for formatting the data in the cells to the transmission frame structure to be used for transmission. In the United States, SONET is used as one of the transmission frame options for ATM. This means that data in the cells must be extracted and placed in the DS3 envelope format used by SONET. When data is received in a DS3 payload format, it must be extracted and placed in the ATM cell format.

The *transmission frame generation and recovery* is responsible for the physical generation and reception of the transmission frame (such as SONET).

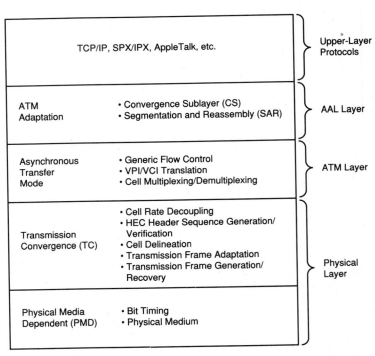

Figure C.17
ATM communications protocol stack.

The *cell delineation* prepares the flow of cells so that the cell boundaries can be recovered by the receiver. The ATM cells are scrambled and placed in the cell stream to protect against malicious users. Either a polynomial-based, self-synchronizing scrambler or a modulo addition of a pseudo-random sequence can be used. At the receiver, the cell boundaries must be identified by reversing the scrambling process and the cells recovered.

The *header error control sequence generation and verification* is used to compute the header checksum at the transmitter. The header checksum also is computed at the receiver to detect errors in the ATM cell header. The checksum can be used to perform single-bit error correction or multiple-bit error detection.

The *cell rate decoupling* is used to insert or suppress idle cells so that the rate of valid cells matches the payload capacity of the physical transmission system used.

The ATM layer (refer to figure C.17) provides cell multiplexing and demultiplexing, VPI and VCI translation, and cell header generation and extraction.

The *cell multiplexing and demultiplexing* function of the ATM layer performs cell multiplexing functions in the transmit direction and cell demultiplexing function in the receive direction. In the transmit direction, cells from a individual virtual paths and virtual channels are placed in a cell flow. In the receive direction, the cells are sent to the appropriate VP or VC.

The *VPI and VCI translation* occur within ATM switches. The values of the VPI and VCI fields in the incoming ATM cells are mapped to a new VPI and VCI value based on the lookup tables within the ATM switch.

The *cell header generation and extraction* are performed at the end-points of the ATM connection, such as desktops and servers that need to send the ATM cells for processing to a higher layer. At the transmitting ATM station, the cell header generation function receives the data from an upper layer and generates an ATM cell header except for the *Header Error Control* (HEC) field, which is computed by the ATM physical layer. At the receiving station, the ATM cell header information is stripped, and the resulting 48-byte cell is sent to the upper layer.

ATM Services

The services used over the AAL are grouped into five classes based on the following service parameters:

- **Time relation between source and destination.** This service can be required or not required. Certain applications such as sending 64 Kbps Pulse Code Modulated (PCM) voice signals require a timing relation between source and destination for the voice sample values to be decoded at the receiver. Most traffic from computer applications does not require a timing relationship between source and destination.

- **Bit Rate.** Some services require a Constant Bit Rate (CBR), whereas other services do not. Services that do not require a constant bit rate are called Variable Bit Rate (VBR) services.

- **Connection Mode.** Applications may need connection-oriented service or connectionless service.

Based on the preceding service parameter descriptions, the following five classes of AAL services are defined as the following:

- **Class A.** Timing Required, Constant Bit Rate, Connection-oriented

- **Class B.** Timing Required, Variable Bit Rate, Connection-oriented

- ■ **Class C.** Timing Not Required, Variable Bit Rate, Connection-oriented

- ■ **Class D.** Timing Not Required, Variable Bit Rate, Connectionless

- ■ **Class X.** Unrestricted, Variable Bit Rate, Connectionless or Connection-oriented

In addition to the preceding classifications, another recommendation by CCITT has resulted in four types of AAL protocols. These are Type AAL 1, Type AAL 2, Type AAL 3/4, and Type AAL 5. The ATM Forum that consists of computer communication vendors has specified that they will use AAL Type 5 (AAL 5) for computer communications.

One of the most active areas of ATM applications is the use of ATM for LANs. This approach uses ATM to provide the media access control mechanism traditionally used by LANs. LANs traditionally use datagram services at the MAC layer in which reliable delivery is not guaranteed. Reliable services are provided by upper layer mechanisms, such as the transport layer. In some applications, such as real-time modeling, it is sensible to provide a guaranteed service between a supercomputer and a graphic workstation to perform image transfers at high rates, at the lower OSI layers.

ATM supports a broad spectrum of traffic types including LAN traffic. In the case of LAN traffic, the longer packet sizes are broken down to small cells by LAN Terminal Adapters that implement the adaptation layer. As figure C.13 shows, the packet switch services provided by ATM also can be used by other transport services such as Frame Relay.

Traditional LAN applications such as Ethernet, Token Ring, and FDDI depend on sharing of the media to provide low-cost media access. Media sharing was important in the early days of LANs when Thick Ethernet networks were prevalent. In Thick Ethernet network, the cost of the coaxial cable was higher, and therefore it was important to share the expensive media between the LAN stations. Because the media is shared in traditional LANs, arbitration techniques—such as CSMA/CD for Ethernet, Token Access for Token Ring, and FDDI— have been devised that select a single station for accessing the media for a certain duration of time. These techniques avoid conflicts when multiple stations need access to the media at the same time. The disadvantage of shared media access LANs is that stations can access the media only one at a time, and because packet sizes on LANs can be large, other stations can access the media only one at a time, and because packet sizes on LANs can be large, other stations have to wait for longer times for the media to become "free." This is a drawback for real-time applications that need more immediate access to the transmissions facility. The other disadvantage of traditional LANs is that all stations run at the same data rate regardless of their data throughput requirements. The only exception to this is ARCnet PLUS LANs that can run a mix of stations at 2.5 Mbps and 20 Mps. It is interesting to note that to overcome some of the limitations of the shared media access technique of Ethernet, vendors have developed Ethernet switches that dedicate the 10 Mbps communications facility to a single workstation. Appendix B, "Bridging and Routing," covers Ethernet switches.

Local ATM

ATM-based LANs, often called *Local ATM* (LATM), replace the shared media of traditional LANs with a dedicated communications facility between the station and an ATM switch. The control of the network resides in the ATM switch, which routes messages and controls access in case of congestion. This is in contrast to traditional LANs in which control is distributed in each LAN interface. Figure C.18 shows an example of an ATM LAN that uses ATM switches and ATM interfaces at the workstation. Each workstation communicates through a dedicated link to the ATM switch. A message sent from a workstation is routed by the ATM switch to the appropriate destination. Because each link is dedicated, its full bandwidth can be assigned to the workstation and there is no contention or wait delay for the media. Unlike conventional LANs, users do not have to communicate at the same data rate. For example, a few of the ports in the ATM switch can be 155 Mbps fiber-optic ports, and others can be lower cost 1.544 Mbps, 10 Mbps, or 45 Mbps over twisted pair. This flexibility makes it possible to customize the network for different needs without paying for excess capacity upfront.

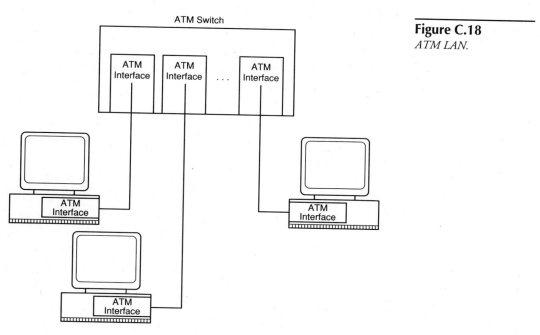

Figure C.18
ATM LAN.

Conventional LANs use a set of physical layer protocols different from WANs. Consequently, conventional LANs need a separate device, such as a bridge or router, to convert LAN protocols, data rates, and signals to the protocols used for WANs (see fig. C.19). The ATM protocol, on the other hand, can be used for both WANs and LANs. This makes it possible to build a LAN/WAN network comprising of ATM switches only. To connect an LATM to a wide area network, you can use a single port in the LATM switch to connect to a network of

ATM switches. Figure C.20 shows an ATM LAN/WAN network. If you compare figure C.20 with the router-based solution in figure C.19, you can see that a router for a LAN can require multiple port connections to connect to different sites. As the number of WAN ports on a router increases, so does the wide-area communication cost. The connections for these ports typically are leased lines, T1 carrier, and so on, and typically are paid on a monthly basis regardless of the actual usage. Using ATM, it is possible to perform billing on a per-cell basis (or giga-cell basis because many cells are used by users), and this results in more accurate billing of actual usage.

The switches that make up the ATM WAN can be part of a public network or private to an enterprise. In the former case, the switches are owned by the public carrier, and network management of these switches is performed by the public carrier. In the latter case, the ATM switches are owned by a private enterprise that also is responsible for maintaining the switches.

Figure C.19
Router based LAN/WAN.

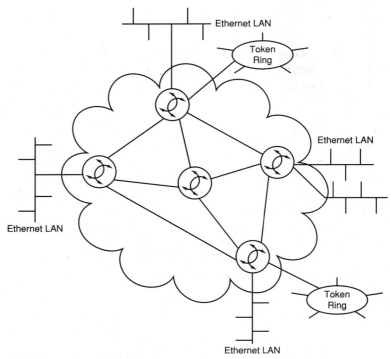

Other possible uses of ATM in LANs follow:

- ■ Simple point-to-point links

- ■ ATM ports on routers

- ■ Private ATM switch connecting conventional LANs

- ■ Public ATM switch network connecting conventional LANs

Figure C.21 shows a point-to-point ATM link connecting two ATM-configured devices. Such a configuration is used in special dedicated applications or for initial testing of ATM technology.

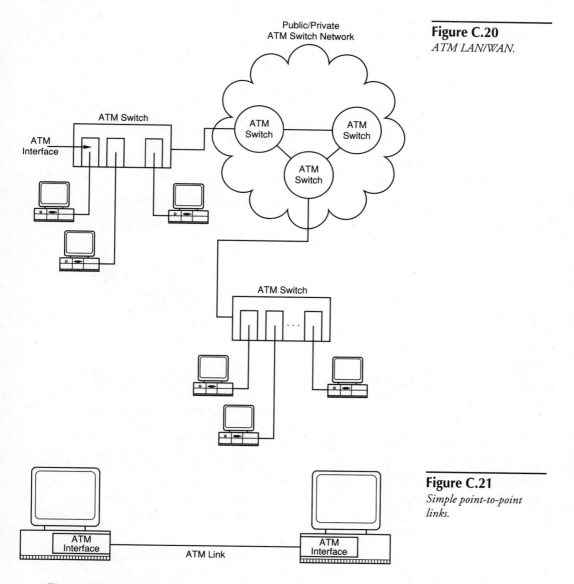

Figure C.20
ATM LAN/WAN.

Figure C.21
Simple point-to-point links.

Figure C.22 shows two conventional LANs using routers to communicate between themselves. The routers have an ATM port, and therefore can use ATM communications for transferring messages. This allows networks to use existing LAN technology and still use ATM communications for evaluation purposes and lower costs. (A cost analysis should be done to see whether the ATM link provides the desired service at a reduced cost.)

Figure C.22

ATM ports on routers.

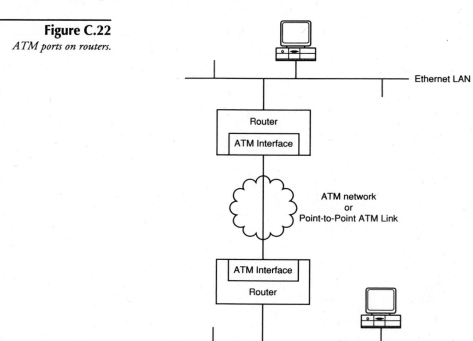

Figure C.23 shows a private ATM switch connecting several conventional LANs. Each LAN has a router with an ATM port. A link from the router's ATM port connects to the ATM switch. LAN traffic from the router is forwarded to the private ATM switch, which routes the LAN traffic to the appropriate router on another LAN. The advantage of this solution is that if *N* sites need to be connected, *N* links are needed to the private ATM switch. If *N* sites are connected to each other using router-based technology, $N(N-1)/2$ links are needed. As the number of sites grows, the number of such links and their cost grows exponentially.

Figure C.24 shows an ATM switch network connecting several conventional LANs. The ATM switches are provided by a public network, which relieves the network manager from having to acquire, maintain, and manage this network.

Figures C.22 to C.24 show ATM-based solutions that can be used with conventional LAN-based technology. The ATM switch is used to provide the WAN communications for the network.

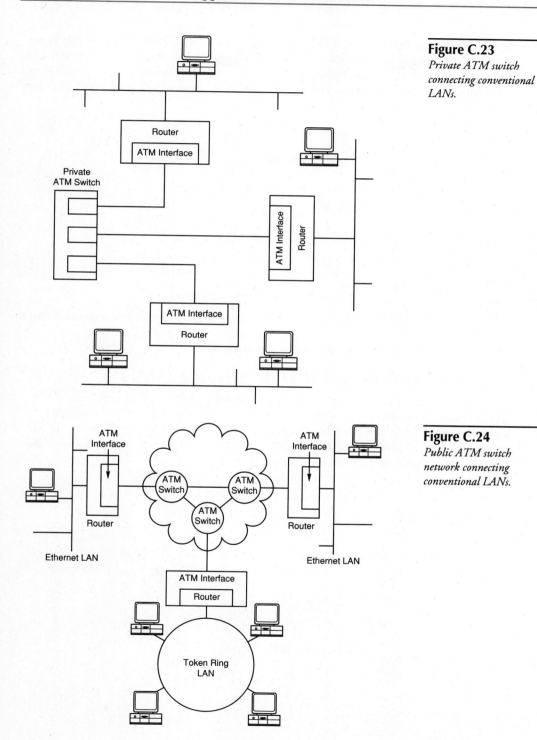

Figure C.23
Private ATM switch connecting conventional LANs.

Figure C.24
Public ATM switch network connecting conventional LANs.

Another interesting aspect is that ATM is a scaleable technology. The ATM technology is not tied to any specific media or particular bandwidth. Figure C.25 shows that the physical media dependent layer can use coaxial, twisted pair, or fiber-optic. Data rates can vary from 64 Kbps, 1.544 Mbps, 45 Mbps, 155 Mbps, and higher. Users send bursts of cells for as much data they need to send.

Figure C.25

ATM scaleable technology.

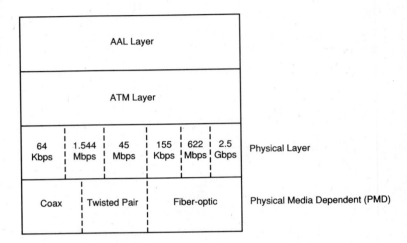

Switched Multi-Megabit Data Service (SMDS)

Switched Multi-Megabit Data Service (SMDS), developed by Bellcore, interfaces with WAN/ LAN by using a three-layer approach (see fig. C.26). The top layer, the SMDS Interface Protocol level 3 (SIP 3), provides a datagram service of up to 9,188 bytes. At level 2 (SIP 2), this datagram is broken down to 53-byte ATM cells. The ATM cells are transported over the MAN network, discussed earlier in this chapter.

Figure C.26

SMDS protocol stack.

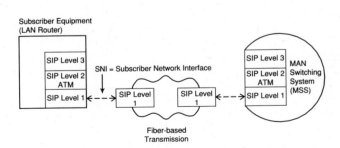

Adapted from IEEE Network Magazine

SMDS is compatible with B-ISDN in its use of ATM. ATM cells in turn use the MAN standard, which is the subject of standardization by IEEE (IEEE 802.6). Figure C.27 shows an SMDS network based on MAN. The router to the 10BASE5 LAN serves the role of *Customer Premise Equipment* (CPE) and *Channel Service Unit* (CSU). The OSI stack shown next to this router provides translation between Ethernet protocols and SMDS protocols. Because SMDS in its current version uses MAN, the router uses the DQDB to communicate with the *Metropolitan Switching System* (MSS). This link is the *Subscriber Network Interface* (SNI) used to connect the LAN subscriber to the MSS. The MSS switches are provided to the subscriber by the telephone company or other commercial organization.

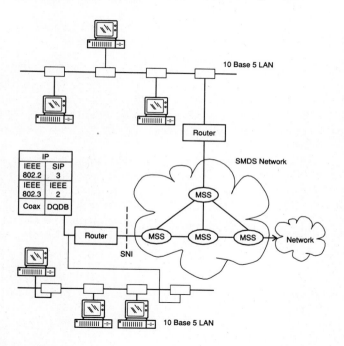

Figure C.27
SMDS network used to interconnect LANs.

Conclusion

In this appendix, you learned some of the reasons why you need to expand the range of a LAN to include WANs. Technologies discussed included X.25, Frame Relay, MANs, SONET, SMDS, and FDDI. You learned the principles behind MANs, SONET, SMDS, and FDDI.

Command Line Reference

APPEND

Description: This works similar to the PATH statement, but is for data files, not programs. Where PATH will seek all directories contained in the PATH statement for programs to run, APPEND searches directories contained within it for data files to open. This is part of the MS-DOS subsystem.

Syntax:
```
APPEND [;] [[drive:]path[;...]] [/x:{on ¦off}]
[/path:{on ¦ off}] [/e]
```

Arguments:

[;] If used by itself, cancels appended directories.

[drive:]path The drive and directory to append. This can have multiple entries, each separated by a semicolon.

/x:{on | off} Indicates if MS-DOS subsystem will search appended directories when executing programs. This is a fast way to lengthen the PATH statement beyond 127 characters, but it will take additional memory. */x* or */x:on* must be specified the first time each session APPEND is run, but it may be turned off and on later.

/path:{on | off}	If */path:on* (the default) is used, APPEND will function even if a directory path is specified. If */path:off* is used, APPEND will only function if a file name does not have a directory specified. For example:
	/path:on edit *c:\winnt\system32\autoexec.nt*. Edit will open AUTOEXEC.NT even if it is not in the directory specified. Also, *edit autoexec.nt* will open the file if it is found on the APPEND path.
	/path:off edit c:\winnt\system32\autoexec.nt. Edit will only open AUTOEXEC.NT if it is in the directory specified, but *edit autoexec.nt* will open the file if it is found on the APPEND path.
/e	Creates an environment variable named APPEND and adds the appended directories to the variable. If */e* is used, you may view the list of appended directories using SET (See SET). If you wish to use */e*, it *must* be used the *first time* you use APPEND after starting Windows NT.

ARP

Description:	Displays the current mapping of MAC (physical adapter) addresses to IP addresses. This is terrific to detect whether or not your IP protocol stack is properly bound to your adapter, and whether you can view other devices on your network. Will not display an entry for the current adapter; you must use *IPCONFIG -all* to view the MAC address of your current adapter.
Syntax:	`ARP -a [inet_addr] [-N [if_addr]]`
	`ARP -d -g in_addr [if_addr]`
	`ARP -s in_addr ether_addr [if_addr]`
Arguments:	
-a	Displays current entries in the ARP cache. By default, all IP addresses other than the current adapter are displayed. If an *inet_addr* value is provided after *-a*, the entry for that adapter only is displayed.
-g	Same as -a.
inet_addr	Specify an IP address here, in the familiar *xxx.xxx.xxx.xxx* notation, where *xxx* can be any value from 0 to 255.
-N	Displays the ARP entries for the network interface specified by if_addr.

if_addr	Short for interface address. This is used if you have multiple adapters in your system, and you need to view or modify the ARP cache for a particular adapter. If this is left blank, the first available interface will be used, or the only available interface will be used.
-d	Deletes the specified entry.
-s	Adds an entry in the ARP cache to associate the IP address inet_addr with the MAC address ether_addr.
ether_addr.	The MAC address. The physical address is entered as HH-HH-HH-HH-HH-HH, where H is a hexadecimal value from 0 to F. Each network adapter will have a burned-in address from the factory (the UAA or Universally Administered Address) that can be overridden in the Control Panel with an address of your choosing (LAA, or Locally Administered Address).

This can be the address of a token-ring network adapter. The parameter *ether_addr* was probably used for historical reasons, as Ethernet technology and IP technology have a closely linked history.

IPCONFIG will list the MAC addresses for all physical adapters on your system, including the modem if you are connected to an IP network. Moreover, PINGing an IP address on your LAN will automatically add it to the ARP cache of your default adapter.

ASSOC

Description:	Lists and modifies file extension associations. Use this with the definitions created or modified with FTYPE.
Syntax:	`ASSOC [.ext[=[filetype]]]`
Arguments:	
.ext	You *must* use the . with the file extension. Extensions can be more than three characters. Try *ASSOC .java*, for example.
filetype	This value corresponds to the definition name listed in FTYPE.

AT

Description:	AT is used to schedule programs to run automatically, and it requires the schedule service to be running. (The schedule service can be started from the command prompt by entering **net start schedule**.) AT can schedule commands to run on one or more computers. AT with no parameters lists the current entries.

Syntax:	`AT [\\computername] [[id] [/delete [/yes]]`
	`AT [\\computername] time [/interactive]` `[/every:date[,...] ¦ /next:date[,...]] "command"`

Arguments:

\\computername	Specifies a specific computer. You may ignore this parameter if the task is to be run on the local computer.
id	This number uniquely identifies the task. If no value is specified, the next available number is used.
/d or /delete [id]	Deletes the specified AT entry. Be careful! If *id* is not specified, all AT commands will be deleted!
/yes	This forces a confirmation prompt before deleting AT entries.
Time (hh:mm)	Time when the command is to run. Time is entered as hours:minutes in 24-hour notation (00:00 through 23:59).
/interactive	Allows the job to interact with the desktop.
/every:date[,...]	Schedules a recurring event. Values are M,T,W,Th,F,S,Su, or 1 through 31. If you need to add non-consecutive dates, separate them with commas. For example: */every:T, Th* will run the event every Tuesday and every Thursday. You may also simply use */every:* with no value and the current day of the month will be used. This can be a real time saver.
/next:date[,...]	The logic behind this parameter is the same as */every:*, but this creates non-recurring events. The events will be run on the day or dates specified, and will be deleted from the AT list.

ATTRIB

Description:	Displays, sets, or removes file and directory attributes. Valid attributes are read-only, archive, system, and hidden. Many hidden files also have the system attribute set, but this is not a requirement. Files with the hidden attribute set will not appear in a DIR listing, but can be executed.
Syntax:	`attrib [+r¦-r] [+a¦-a] [+s¦-s] [+h¦-h][[drive:]` `[path] filename][/s]`

Arguments:

[[drive:][path] filename]	Indicates the location and name of the directory, file, or set of files you want to process.
+r, -r	Sets or removes the read-only attribute.
+a, -a	Sets or removes the archive attribute.
+s, -s	Sets or removes the system attribute.
+h, -h	Sets or removes the hidden attribute.
/s	Changes the attributes of files in the current directory and all subdirectories.

BACKUP

Description:	NT 4 contains a graphical backup utility that supports tape drives. If at all possible, the graphical utility should be used. However, the older command-prompt backup utility still exists. It is most useful backing up files from one type of floppy disk to another, but can be used to back up hard drives to multiple floppy disks. If you would like to back up your 1.6 GB data drive to 1.44 MB floppies, you will need over one thousand floppy disks.
Syntax:	`backup source destination-drive: [/s] [/m] [/a]` `[/f[:size]] [/d:date [/t:time]][/l[:[drive:]]` `[path]logfile]]`

Arguments:

source	The disk or files to be backed up. This can be a drive, a file, a directory, or a combination.
destination-drive:	The target drive for the backup. The files will not be accessible until the RESTORE command is used. The backup process will destroy all information on the destination drive.
/s	Includes all subdirectories in the backup.
/m	Backs up only those files with the archive attribute set, and removes the archive attribute.
/a	Appends the current backup set. If this is not used, all data in the current backup set is deleted. This parameter will not function if the existing backup set was created using the BACKUP program from MS-DOS version 3.2 or earlier.

/f[:size]	Formats the target disk with the default size for that disk type. If the disk is not already formatted, BACKUP automatically formats the disk. FORMAT must be in the path or current directory. See FORMAT for valid sizes.
/d:date	Only backs up files with a date-stamp on or after the specified date.
/t:time	Only backs up files with a time-stamp the same or later than the specified time. This can be used alone or together with the */d:date* parameter.
/l[:[drive:][path]logfile]	Creates a log file. If the log file already exists, it will append to the log file. If you use the */l* parameter alone, BACKUP will create a log called BACKUP.LOG in the root directory of the source drive.

BATCH PROGRAMS

Description:	BATCH PROGRAMS (also called batch files) allow you to simplify routine or repetitive tasks. Batch files are simply text files that contain commands, program names, or simple logic statements. FOR, GOTO, and IF are the logic operators, and sophisticated arrays can be built using these operators. Under Windows NT, batch files can have either a BAT or CMD extension; under MS-DOS, batch files may only have a BAT extension.
Syntax:	Simply type the name of the batch file from a command prompt to execute it.
Arguments:	Batch files may or may not take arguments, depending on the internal logic. If a parameter is passed to the batch file, it can be used by the batch file as %n, with *n* being the parameter passed to the batch file. For example, consider:

```
batch.bat over under sideways down
```

BATCH.BAT is the batch file, and *over under sideways down* are the parameters passed to it. Internally, the batch file would process *over* as %1, *under* as %2, and so on. If the batch file contained the statement:

echo %1

The line in the batch file would be processed as *echo over*, and the output would be:

over

If the batch file contained the statement:

echo %4 %3 %2 %1

The statement would be interpreted as *echo down sideways under over*, and the output would be:

down sideways under over

In this way, parameters can be passed to the batch file to control its execution.

BREAK

Description:	This is present for compatibility with DOS systems. It has no effect under Windows NT. It is used for running DOS mode debuggers, and should not be used on an NT server. Consult your MS-DOS documentation for advanced help on this command.

BUFFERS

Description:	Neither Windows NT nor the MS-DOS subsystem use this command. It is included for compatibility with programs that attempt to set the number of buffers.

CACLS

Description:	This is used to modify file-level security access. This can only be used on volumes that support file-level access security. Currently, only NTFS supports file-level access security.
Syntax:	`CACLS filename [/t] [/e] [/c] [/g user:perm]` `[/r user [...]] [/p user:perm [...]] [/d user ]`
Arguments:	
filename	Displays ACLs for specified files. Wildcards are acceptable.
/t	Changes ACLs of specified files in the current directory and all subdirectories. This has the same effect of *s* in other commands.

/e	Edits ACL instead of replacing it.
/c	Forces changing of ACLs, regardless of errors.
/g user:perm	Grants a specified user access rights. perm can be:

	r	Read
	c	Change (write)
	f	Full control

/r user:perm	Deletes a specified user's rights; this can only be used with /e.
/p user:perm	Replaces specified user's access rights. perm can be:

	n	None
	r	Read
	c	Change (write)
	f	Full control

/d user	Denies specified user access.

CALL

Description:	Used in a batch file to execute another batch file. If this is not used, the first batch file will not continue after the second batch file is run. With CALL, control passes back to the first batch file after the second batch file has completed.
Syntax:	`CALL [drive:][path] filename [parameters]`
Arguments:	
[drive:][path] filename	Name and location of the additional batch file.
parameters	These parameters will be passed to the additional batch file and processed by it.

CHCP

Description:	Displays or changes the current code page. Code pages are used to define how the character-based display handles extended characters. Usually the code page used is 437 (U.S. default) or 850 (multinational). Changing the active code page from 437 to 850 will have

no noticeable effect on standard characters, but will affect how extended characters, such as Portuguese or Cyrillic, are displayed.

Syntax:	CHCP [nnn]

Arguments:

nnn

Which code page to use. If no code page is specified, the current code page is displayed.

437	United States
850	Multilingual (Latin I)
852	Slavic (Latin II)
855	Cyrillic (Russian)
857	Turkish
860	Portuguese
861	Icelandic
863	Canadian-French
865	Nordic
866	Russian
869	Modern Greek

CHDIR (CD)

Description:

Displays or changes the current directory.

Syntax:

CHDIR (or CD) [/d] [drive:][path] [..] or [/d]
[drive:][path] [..]

Arguments:

[/d]

You may change the current directory on a different drive without changing to that drive. For example, if you are on drive C: and you enter:

CD A:\BIN

The default directory on drive A: will be set to BIN, but you will still be logged to drive C:. If, however, you use the */d* parameter, you will be in BIN on drive A:.

[drive:][path]	Specifies the drive (if other than the current drive) and directory that you want to change.
[..]	Moves back up the directory tree by one step.
[\]	Changes to the root directory on the current drive.
[\][dir]	Calculates the directory from the root rather than the current directory.

CHKDSK

Description:	Checks a drive for errors, and will display a report showing the statistics of the drive. CHKDSK will issue a detailed report whether or not you use the /f parameter. To run CHKDSK on a hard drive, you must be a member of the Administrators group. CHKDSK will fix errors if you use the /f parameter. If CHKDSK cannot fix errors because the drive is locked for use by the system, CHKDSK will ask if you would like to check the disk the next time the system boots. Lost allocation units will be placed in a folder called FOUND.000 in the root directory of the NT system drive. If CHKDSK runs during the boot process, it will display a message while CHKDSK is analyzing the drive, and while the system boots.
Syntax:	`CHKDSK [drive:][[path] filename] [/f] [/v] [/r]`
Arguments:	
drive:	Which drive CHKDSK should check. If no disk is specified, CHKDSK will check the current drive.
[path] filename	If you specify a file name or file names, CHKDSK will display a fragmentation report on each file. This can be useful to compare the relative fragmentation of different disk format types.
/f	If this parameter is used, CHKDSK will fix the errors it finds. Lost file allocation units are saved in a folder called FOUND.000 in the root directory of the NT system drive. If the disk being check is in use and the /f parameter is used, CHKDSK will offer to check the drive the next time the system boots. It is best to run CHKDSK without the /f parameter once. If CHKDSK reports truncated allocation entries and cross-linked files, you should copy all the affected files to a different disk before using the /f parameter.

/v
Lists each file as the disk is checked.

/r
This parameter finds bad sectors, marks them as bad, and attempts to recover data in the bad sectors and move the data to undamaged areas of the disk.

CLS

Description:	Clears the screen.
Syntax:	CLS
Arguments:	Not applicable.

CMD

Description:	Runs a new copy of the NT command interpreter, CMD.EXE. This is *not* a DOS window, which runs the NT version of COMMAND.COM, but is a fully functioning copy of the NT interpreter. You can enter this from the Start menu's Run box, or use it as part of an automated process. Using CMD is very similar to invoking a new copy of the DOS command interpreter under MS-DOS.
Syntax:	CMD [/x ¦ /y] [/a ¦ /u] [/q] [/t:fg] [[/c ¦ /k] string]

Arguments:

/c
Executes the command *string* and terminates.

/k
Executes the command *string* and stays resident. This is useful for CMD files that initialize the environment.

/q
Sets ECHO OFF.

/a
Uses ANSI-capable output, including colors and ANSI characters.

/u
Uses UNICODE-capable (16-bit) output.

/t:fg
Sets the screen colors. Replace *f* with a hexadecimal value between 0 and F to set the foreground color, and replace *g* with a hexadecimal value between 0 and F to set the background color. For more information, see COLOR.

/x	Enables the NT command-shell extensions. Available extension commands are DEL, COLOR, CD, MD, PROMPT, PUSHD, POPD, SET, SETLOCAL, ENDLOCAL, IF, FOR, CALL, SHIFT, GOTO, START, ASSOC and FTYPE. This is the default setting.
/y	Disables extensions to CMD.EXE. Use this only if your program will not work with the extensions enabled.
string	A command, batch file, or program.

CODEPAGE

Description:	If your OS/2 version 1.3 program requires a specific code page (check its documentation), set it in the OS/2 C:\CONFIG.SYS file. Programs written for OS/2 versions later than 1.3 or OS/2 programs written for Presentation Manager will not run under NT.
Syntax:	`CODEPAGE=xxx[,yyy]`
Arguments:	
xxx	Specifies the first code page. This must be a three-digit number from this list:

437	United States
850	Multilingual (Latin I)
852	Slavic (Latin II)
855	Cyrillic (Russian)
857	Turkish
860	Portuguese
861	Icelandic
863	Canadian-French
865	Nordic
866	Russian
869	Modern Greek

yyy	This parameter is not used by the OS/2 subsystem. However, NT will still process the C:\CONFIG.SYS file if it has this parameter in the CODEPAGE line. In this way, NT is compatible with OS/2 1.3 CONFIG.SYS files.

COLOR

Description:	Sets the foreground and background colors. If no color is specified, the colors present when CMD was started are restored. If the foreground and background values are the same, COLOR will not reset the screen colors, and returns ERRORLEVEL 1.
Syntax:	`COLOR bf`
Arguments:	
bf	Background and foreground colors. Each is a hexadecimal digit, 0 through F.

0	Black
1	Blue
2	Green
3	Aqua
4	Red
5	Purple
6	Yellow
7	White
8	Gray
9	Light blue
A	Light green
B	Light aqua
C	Light red
D	Light purple
E	Light yellow
F	Bright white

Note that on some adapters, BRIGHT or LIGHT color values may appear as blinking text in full-screen mode.

COMP

Description:	Compares the contents of two files at the byte level. If the files are different sizes, COMP may terminate comparing the files unless you use the /n=n parameter. Or, simply use FC. (See FC).
Syntax:	COMP [data1] [data2] [/d] [/a] [/l] [/n=number] [/c]
Arguments:	
data1	The first file or files to be compared. Wildcards are acceptable.
data2	The second file or files to be compared. Wildcards are acceptable. For example, you could compare the root directories on the current drive and another drive by:
	COMP *.* d:*.* /n=1000
/d	If /d is used, the differences will be displayed as decimal (0–9). The default method is to display values in hexadecimal (0–F).
/a	Displays differences as characters (bytes).
/l	Displays line numbers containing the differences rather than the differences themselves.
/n=number	Compares *number* lines, even if the file sizes differ.
/c	This is a case-insensitive text comparison.

COMPACT

Description:	Displays and sets compression for files on NTFS volumes. Use COMPACT with no parameters to display compression information. NTFS compression does not work on the same principles as STACKER or DOUBLESPACE, but is built into the file system.
Syntax:	COMPACT [/c] [/u] [/s] [/i] [/f] [/l] filename
Arguments:	
/c	You can use this to compress a single file, a group of files, an entire directory, or a whole drive.
/u	This uncompresses files, directories, or drives.
/s:directory	Specifies that the requested action should be applied to all subdirectories. If no value is provided but the /s parameter is still used, the current directory and all subdirectories will be compressed.

/i	Ignores errors.
/f	Forces compression or uncompression. If compression was started and the system crashed before the compression could be completed, COMPACT may not compress the specified target. In such cases, you can force compression to be performed again.
filename	File or directory. Multiple file names and wildcards are allowed.

CONVERT

Description:	Converts FAT volumes to NTFS. You cannot convert the current drive or any other drive locked for use by the system. CONVERT will offer to convert the volume on reboot if the drive is locked by the system.
	Because it is not practical to reboot a production server during business hours, do not try to convert the current drive. Instead, try to close all processes accessing the drive to be converted. If the drive is still locked by the system, allow CONVERT to execute at the next system boot. Before you attempt a conversion, please consult the section of the book dedicated to converting drives. In addition, be sure to check the disk for errors before converting any drive.
Syntax:	`CONVERT [drive:] /fs:ntfs [/v] [/nametable:filename`
Arguments:	
drive	Specifies the drive to be converted.
/fs:ntfs	Specifies the file system the drive is to be converted to. Currently, the only available file type to convert to is NTFS.
/v	Verbose mode. Errors and other conversion messages will be displayed. By default, most messages are suppressed.
/nametable:filename	Some conversions may fail due to unusual file names. If the conversion fails during a reboot, the errors will appear in the Event Viewer. If the cause of the problem was related to file names, run CONVERT again using this parameter. The file *FILENAME* is created during the initial phases of the conversion and consulted during the actual conversion process.

COPY

Description:	Copies or combines files. If more than one file is copied, each file will be listed during the copy. See also XCOPY.
Syntax:	COPY [/a¦/b] source [/a¦/b] [+ source [/a¦/b] [+ ...]] [/z] [destination [/a¦/b]] [/v] [/n]
Arguments:	

source	Drive, directory, and file name to be copied. If no drive or directory is specified, the current drive and directory is used. If you list a different drive or directory, COPY will use all files in that directory as the source.
+	Use + to indicate multiple single files or multiple wildcard specifications to be combined into a new file. Separate each file or wildcard with a +.
=	This works just like +, but you can specify a single wildcard as the source (such as *.*) and precede the destination file name with =. All the files matching the wildcard will be combined into the destination file name.
destination	Specifies the target. If *destination* is a file name only, the destination will be in the current directory with the supplied file name. If *destination* is a directory but no file name is specified, the files will be copied to the target directory with their current file names.
/a	Indicates an ASCII text file. You may mix the */a* parameter and the */b* (BINARY) parameter. In such cases, the files appearing after */a* will be treated as ASCII until the */b* parameter is encountered. When */a* is used, the copy is terminated when a CTRL-Z character (end-of-file marker) is reached. This is the default mode when combining files.
/b	Indicates a binary file. This is the default mode for COPY except when combining files using + or =. When */b* is used, the copy is terminated based on byte count, rather than a an end-of-file marker.
/v	Verifies the copy after it is written.
/n	This will convert a nonstandard NT as the associated DOS-compatible 8.3 file name, if available.
/z	This helps minimize network write errors. Immediately precedes the destination drive and/or directory.

COUNTRY

Description:	Sets the country settings for the MS-DOS subsystem.
Syntax:	(in CONFIG.NT) `COUNTRY=xxx[,[yyy][,[drive:]` `[path] filename]]`

Each parameter must be separated by commas, and if a parameter is omitted, you must still include the comma. For example:

country=001,,c:\winnt\system32\country.sys

is valid, omitting the code page, but

country=001,c:\winnt\system32\country.sys

is not valid because there is no comma separating the omitted code page and the country code. The most explicit entry would be

country=001,047,c:\winnt\system32\country.sys

listing both the country code and code page.

Arguments:

xxx	Specifies the country code.
yyy	Specifies the code page for the country.
[drive:][path] filename	The location and file name containing information about the country specified in *xxx*.

DATE

Description:	Displays or changes the system date.
Syntax:	`DATE [mm-dd-yy]`
Arguments:	
mm-dd-yy	Sets the date. Day, month, and year can be separated by . - or /.

mm can be 1–12.

dd can be 1–31.

yy can be 80–99 or 1980–2099.

DEBUG

Description:	Starts DEBUG, a program that allows you to test and debug MS-DOS executable files. DEBUG is an advanced programming tool that should only be used by qualified programmers and not as an NT system administration tool. Do not attempt to run DEBUG on your server without consulting a DEBUG manual or the DEBUG section of your MS-DOS manual explaining the intricacies of DEBUG.
Syntax:	`DEBUG [[drive:][path] filename [testfile-parameters]]`
Arguments:	
[drive:][path] filename	Specifies the location and name of the executable file to debug.
testfile-parameters	Specifies any command-line information required by the program to test.
?	Once debug starts, you can type ? to display a list of valid DEBUG commands.

DEL (See ERASE)

DEVICE

Description:	Loads the specified device driver into the MS-DOS subsystem. This command is used in the %systemroot%\ SYSTEM32\CONFIG.NT file, or the file specified in the program's shortcut. CONFIG.NT is processed whenever a new MS-DOS or 16-bit Windows application is started in a separate memory space, or started for the first time.
Syntax:	`DEVICE=[drive:][path] filename [parameters]`
Arguments:	
[drive:][path] filename	The location and name of the device driver.
[dd-parameters]	Specifies any parameters required by the driver.

ECHO

Description:	Toggles the ECHO state, or displays the message following the ECHO command.
Syntax:	`ECHO [on ¦ off] [message]`
Arguments:	
on | off	Turns ECHO on or off. If ECHO is on, commands executed by a batch file will appear on the screen. If ECHO is off, the commands will be suppressed. This is why most batch files begin with the statement *@echo off.* (@ suppresses the echo for a single line in a batch file.)
message	The desired text to be displayed.

ECHOCONFIG

Description:	When a DOS virtual machine is started, NT processes CONFIG.NT and AUTOEXEC.NT. This happens any time a DOS or 16-bit Windows program is started. By default, NT does not display messages during the processing of these files. If you place ECHOCONFIG in CONFIG.NT, messages will be displayed.
Syntax:	`ECHOCONFIG`
Arguments:	Not applicable.

EDIT

Description:	Starts the familiar MS-DOS full screen text editor. Note that the NT version of the DOS editor is not the Windows 95 version, which allows you to edit multiple text files simultaneously, but is the DOS 6.x version which limits you to editing one file at a time. The DOS editor requires QBASIC.EXE, which should be on your path or in the current directory, but does not need to be in the same directory as EDIT.COM.
Syntax:	`EDIT [[drive:][path] filename] [/b] [/g] [/h] [/nohi]`
Arguments:	
[drive:][path]	Use this if the file you want to edit is not in your current directory, and you need to specify the drive and directory.

filename	If you specify a file, EDIT will load with that file ready for editing. If you do not specify a file name, EDIT will instead display a help screen, which you must close before opening a file to edit.
/b	Starts EDIT in black and white, for resolutions below EGA.
/g	Utilizes appropriate screen updates for a CGA system.
/h	Expands EDIT for use with screens that display more than 25 lines. For fun, open an NT command window, set it for 35 lines (under Properties, Layout), and then start EDIT. Exit the editor, and then start EDIT using the /h option and observe the difference. (Okay, maybe it wasn't that fun.)
/nohi	Does not use the BRIGHT attribute for text. Use this if the shortcuts appear as blinking text rather than bold. This limits EDIT to the 8-color text palette, rather than the 16-color text palette.

EDLIN

Description:	Starts EDLIN, the line-by-line text editor that predates EDIT. EDLIN was last included with DOS version 4, but still exists as part of NT. EDLIN may be useful in situations where EDIT (and QBASIC) won't fit on a floppy, as it is a much smaller file. Unfortunately, because EDLIN only allows you to replace lines of a text file, one line at a time, it is difficult and cumbersome to use. It is probably retained only for compatibility purposes.
Syntax:	`edlin [drive:][path] filename [/b]`
Arguments:	
[drive:][path] filename	*You must specify a file name.* You may specify the drive and directory if the file is not in the default directory. For example, to edit AUTOEXEC.BAT, simply enter **edlin autoexec.bat**. If your default directory is currently C:\ and you want to edit SYSTEM.INI in the C:\WINDOWS directory, simply enter **edlin c:\windows\system.ini**.
/b	Use this parameter if your text file has an end-of-file character (CTRL-Z) that you want to ignore when you edit your text file.

ENDLOCAL

Description:	Stops variable localization started with SETLOCAL. This is usually done in a batch or *.cmd file, but works from the command prompt as well. When you use SETLOCAL, all environment variables set (using *set variable=value*) will disappear when ENDLOCAL is used. This is most valuable when setting and using variables in a logon script, but is also quite useful when setting temporary variables from the command line or resetting system variables. Simply use ENDLOCAL, and all your original variables will be restored.
Syntax:	ENDLOCAL
Arguments:	Not applicable.

ERASE (DEL)

Description:	Deletes one or more files.
Syntax:	DEL [drive:][path] filename [; ...] [/p] [/f] [/s] [/q] [/a[:attributes]]
	ERASE [drive:][path] filename [; ...] [/p] [/f] [/s] [/q] [/a[:attributes]]

Arguments:

[drive:][path]

You can delete files not in the current directory by specifying another drive and directory here.

filename

This parameter can be a single file name or a wildcard specification using the * and ? characters. For example, *erase autoexec.bat* will delete only AUTOEXEC.BAT, but by using wildcards you can delete multiple files. The ? is used to replace a single character, while the * character is used to replace multiple characters. Because the ? is used to replace only a single character, it is used in situations where you need greater control. The following table should help explain how wildcards are used:

Wildcard	Files.
.	All.
*.bat	All files with the BAT extension.
au*.*	All files starting with the two characters AU.

au?.*   Files with AU as the first characters and any character as the third character. Files with four characters in the prefix will not be deleted.

Here's a tip: Because DIR and DEL have the same number of letters and because DIR will accept the same wildcards as DEL, you can use DIR to verify which files you'll delete. Suppose you want to delete all backup copies of AUTOEXEC.BAT. You can enter *dir autoexec.0**, which might list AUTOEXEC.001 through AUTOEXEC.020. Then simply press the up arrow key followed by the Home key, and replace DIR with DEL, and then press the Enter key. Because the NT command interpreter caches your recently used command-lines, you will be assured that you will delete only those files listed after your DIR command.

/p   This stands for PROMPT, which will ask you to confirm deleting each file.

/f   This stands for FORCE, and forces the deletion of read-only files.

/s   Like DIR, the NT version of DEL will act on subdirectories! Beware! With NT, it is possible to delete your entire hard drive in one motion.

/q   Ordinarily, DEL will prompt you to confirm erasing files on a global delete (*.*). This parameter suppresses the confirmation prompt.

/a   This parameter further qualifies the wildcards mentioned above, or the file name if specified. Therefore, the command *del *.* /as* would only delete files with the system attribute set, rather than all files. The command *del *.doc /aa* would delete all files ending in DOC with the archive attribute set. Appropriate values are as follows:

/ar   Read-only

/ah   Hidden

/as   System

/aa   Archive

-            Prefix meaning "not," used as follows:

/a-r   Not Read-only

/a-h   Not Hidden

/a-s   Not System

/a-a   Not Archive

EXE2BIN

Description:	Transforms EXE files into BIN files for use with DEBUG. This program will not convert the command-line DOS and NT utilities.
Syntax:	`exe2bin [drive1:][path1]input-file` `[[drive2:][path2]output-file]`
Arguments:	
[drive1:][path1]input-file	Indicates the site and file name of the input file.
[drive2:][path2]output-file	Indicates the site and file name of the output file.

EXIT

Description:	Closes the current command shell. You may close CMD.EXE by using the CLOSE button, but COMMAND.COM and other command shells must be closed by EXIT. If the command shell was run in full-screen mode, this returns you to the Explorer or Program Manager.
Syntax:	`EXIT`
Arguments:	Not applicable.

EXPAND

Description:	Enlarges and retrieves files compressed with the Microsoft distribution format. These files are easily recognized as the last character of the uncompressed file and are replaced by an underscore. For example, the compressed version of CONTROL.EXE would be CONTROL.EX_. The Windows 3.x version does not support wildcards (*.*), but the Windows NT version does. If you prefer, you may simply specify a set of files and a target directory.
Syntax:	`EXPAND [-r] source [destination]`
Arguments:	
-r	This is used to override the default name. You can specify a new name and avoid overwriting files.
source	You must specify the source files to be expanded. Unlike the Windows 3.x version of EXPAND, wildcards are allowed.

destination

By default, EXPAND will place your new files in the current directory. You may specify a different directory if you want, but the directory must already exist. EXPAND will not create directories.

FASTOPEN

Description:

FASTOPEN is included only for compatibility with MS-DOS programs that require it. If your program directs you to add FASTOPEN to AUTOEXEC.BAT, add it to AUTOEXEC.NT.

Syntax:

FASTOPEN

Arguments:

Not applicable.

FC

Description:

Compares the internal contents of a file and indicates differences. If you specify BINARY mode, FC will list all the differences, whereas ASCII mode will attempt to re-sync the comparison to locate areas of text common to both files. This can be useful to help determine if the NT and 95 versions of a program are similar. Try comparing the Windows 95 and Windows NT 4 versions and 3.0 of Internet Explorer.

Syntax:

FC [/a] [/b] [/c] [/l] [/lbn] [/n] [/t] [/u] [/w]
[/nnnn] [drive1:][path1]filename1
[drive2:][path2]filename2

Arguments:

/a

Shortens the ASCII output to list only the first and last lines of each different area. This can be helpful in locating areas of text to be edited.

/b

Binary mode, for comparing programs, DLLs, or other compiled files. FC compares both files on a byte-by-byte basis, and does not re-sync the comparison to locate similar areas of the files. EXE, COM, SYS, OBJ, LIB, and BIN files are compared in binary mode by default.

/c

Ignores whether the characters are in upper- or lowercase.

/l	Compares files in ASCII mode. FC compares the two files, and unlike BINARY mode, attempts to resynchronize them after mismatches. This is invaluable for identifying differences in program source files, for example, or text files, but not compiled files where the location of data within a file is important. ASCII mode is the default mode for all files *except* EXE, COM, SYS, OBJ, LIB, and BIN files.
/lbn	Replace *n* with an integer, to set the internal line buffer to *n* lines. The internal line buffer holds the number of consecutive differing lines, and if the line buffer is exceeded, FC will cancel the operation. The default size of the buffer is 100 lines.
/n	If used with an ASCII comparison, this will list the line numbers.
/t	Because the tab character is a valid ASCII code, it may be treated as a tab or as spaces. By default, FC converts tabs to 8 spaces. If this causes false differences to be detected, use this parameter to treat tabs as tabs, and not to convert them to spaces.
/u	Compares files as Unicode text files (16-bit text rather than 8-bit text).
/w	This is another switch used to overcome the differences between the tab character and space character. This parameter compresses all consecutive tabs and spaces together into a single space during the comparison. Also, multiple tabs and spaces at the beginning and end of the file are ignored.
/nnnn	When attempting to resynchronize ASCII files comparison, this parameter specifies the number of lines that must match before FC considers an area to be identical. By default, two lines must match before FC considers an area to be resynchronized.
[drive1:][path1]filename1	The location and file name of the first file to compare.
[drive2:][path2]filename2	The location and file name of the second file to compare.

FCBS

Description:	This is used to set the number of file control blocks (FCBs) that the MS-DOS subsystem can have open at the same time. A file control block is a data structure that stores information about a file. If you need to change this from the default, simply add the following line to CONFIG.NT.
Syntax:	`fcbs=x`
Arguments:	
x	Replace x with the number of File Control Blocks you require the DOS subsystem to have. The default is 4; you may specify 1 to 255.

FILES

Description:	Sets the number of file handles available to the DOS subsystem. If a DOS or 16-bit Windows program requires you to have more than the default 8 file handles, use FILES.
Syntax:	`FILES=x`
Arguments:	
x	Replace x with any value from 1 to 255.

FILTER COMMANDS

Description:	Filter commands help you sort, view, and select parts of the output of a command.
Syntax:	`primary_command ¦ filter, or primary_command > filter`
Arguments:	With filter commands, the filter itself becomes the parameter for the primary command, separated by a redirector such as <, >, or ¦. For example, DIR ¦ SORT would sort the output of DIR in alphabetic order, while DIR ¦ MORE would pause after each screen of information. This is useful for programs that do not support the built in "/p" parameter. Be careful! If you enter DIR ¦ MORE ¦ SORT ¦ MORE your program will wait until you press Enter before displaying information.

more   Specifies that each screen of information should pause and wait
                            for a keystroke.

sort   Sorts the screen output in alphabetic order. Try entering *type
                            autoexec.bat | sort* at a command prompt, and you will see the
                            lines of AUTOEXEC.BAT re-sorted.

find   Parses the input file for the string specified. For example, *find
                            "Macintosh" < readme.txt* searches "readme.txt" for the string
                            "Macintosh," which will be displayed on the screen. As with any
                            screen output, the output redirector > (opposite of the input
                            redirector <) can be used to send the output to a file or the
                            printer.

                            Examples:

                            |Pipe redirector. The filter command receives its input from the
                            command preceding the pipe.

                            <Input redirector. The filter goes on the left; the file to be
                            filtered through goes on the right. In the above example, this
                            would be `sort < autoexec.bat` rather than `type autoexec.bat`
                            `¦ sort`.

                            >Output redirector. Instead of displaying items on-screen, this
                            sends output to a file or print device. > `file.txt` or
                            > `prn` sends output to the specified destination, while >>
                            `file.txt` appends output to "file.txt."

FIND

Description: Searches inside files for a given text string. The string may
                          contain spaces, and must be contained in double-quotes. After
                          searching the specified files, FIND displays any lines of text that
                          contain the specified string.

Syntax: `FIND [/v] [/c] [/n] [/i] "string"`
                          `[[drive:][path]filename`

Arguments:

"string"   This is the case-sensitive string for which to search. The string
                          must be enclosed in double quotes.

filename   In order for FIND to operate properly, you must specify a file
                          name, although wildcards are acceptable. If you do not specify a

file name, FIND will not immediately report an error, but your specified text string will also not be found. For example:

FIND *.* "blaster" will list all the files that contains the string "blaster."

FIND autoexec.bat "blaster" will list AUTOEXEC.BAT if it contains the string "blaster."

FIND "blaster" will not report an error, but will not locate any files, either. It will appear to be finding files, but if you wait for it to finish, you will be waiting for a long, long time.

[drive:][path]	If the file or files you want to search are not in the current directory, you may specify the directory here.
/v	Displays each line in the specified file that does not contain the specified string.
/c	Lists the file and the number of lines that contain the specified string.
/n	When a file's contents are listed, this precedes each line with a line number.
/i	By default, FIND searches are case-sensitive. If you specify this parameter, uppercase and lowercase characters will be considered to be the same.

FINDSTR

Description:	Operates similar to FIND, but searches for literal text strings (such as *"x - y - 2 (note)"* including the double quotes) or combinations of multiple words or parts of words.
Syntax:	`FINDSTR [/b] [/e] [/l] [/c:string] [/r] [/s] [/i] [/x] [/v]` `[/n] [/m] [/o] [/g:file] [/f:file] strings`
Arguments:	
strings	Text or string to be searched for. Double quotes are not required unless your search string contains spaces. If the string contains spaces and you fail to use double quotes, all strings after the first space will be treated as files to be searched rather than strings to be searched for.
files	Which files you wish to search. Wildcards are allowed.
String operators	Within the specified string, you may use search operators to help customize the search. Some of the more common operators:

(Wildcard). Replace with any single character. For example, *Micro.* would search for all six-letter words beginning with the string "Micro".

* (Repeat). Zero or more occurrences of the previous character or character class. To modify the previous example, the string *Micro.** would find all words, of any length, beginning with the string "Micro".

^ (Beginning of line). This is very useful when searching program source code for specific functions, or for searching text files for text that appears at the beginning of a paragraph. For example, the string *^it* would find only those occurrences of "it" at the beginning of a line or immediately following a CR-LF (carriage return - line feed).

$ (End of line). In this case, the required string would be at the end of a line. If you wanted to find all lines ending in "it," you would use the string *it$*.

\x. If you need to search for one of the characters reserved as a search operator, such as $ or *, precede it with the slash. For example, the string \ . would search for the "." character rather than use it as a wildcard.

\ <*string*. Searches for a string appearing only at the beginning of a word.

string \ >. Searches for a string appearing only at the end of a word.

There are additional operators, such as [class], [^class], and [range], that help search for character classes, exclude character classes, and search based on the range of characters within a character set. For help on these topics, you can search the Windows NT online help documentation, the Microsoft Knowledge Base at http://www.microsoft.com/kb, or the Microsoft TechNet CD.

/b	Indicates a match only if the search string is at the beginning of a line.
/e	Indicates a match only if the search string is at the end of a line.
/c	By default, FINDSTR searches for each text element in the specified string separately. For example:

FINDSTR "Microsoft Word" *.* searches all files for Microsoft or Word, but not necessarily for "Microsoft Word."

FINDSTR /c:"Microsoft Word" *.* searches all files for the exact string "Microsoft Word."

However, the use of /c still permits the use of search operators. For example:

FINDSTR /c: "Micro.* Word" will search for all words beginning with the string "Micro" such as "Microsoft" or "MicroMan" followed by the word "Word."

/l	If this parameter is used, the search operators will be treated as actual characters to be searched for.
/r	This parameter is the default setting for FINDSTR, which treats strings as search expressions using the search operators.
/s	Searches files in the current directory and all subdirectories.
/i	Case-insensitive search, so that *Micro* and *miCRO* will be treated as the same string.
/x	Prints only those lines that match exactly. This requires the use of /c: or /l, or no lines will be considered to match exactly. Curiously, search wildcards will be treated as an exact match.
/v	Prints all lines that do not contain a match.
/n	Prints the line number for every line that contains a match.
/m	This suppresses the printing of lines that contain a match, but prints the file name only. This is very useful if you are searching for text files that contain a specific string.
/o	This stands for *offset.* If your string is 90 characters into a file, the line would be proceeded by *90:* when printed.
/g:*file*	Rather than type your search strings directly from the command line, you may place them in a file.
/f:*file*	Similarly, you may place all the files to be searched in a file, and avoid typing them in from the command line.

The two preceding parameters, /g and /f, can be used with sophisticated batch files to automatically search for files whose search criteria and file name may change as a result of system time and date or user information.

FINGER

Description:	This is a common Internet utility, which can be used to display information about a particular user on a system or default information about that system. This requires TCP/IP and a connection to the Internet or a connection to the network running the desired Finger server. In addition, a Finger server must be running on the system you use FINGER on.
Syntax:	`FINGER [-l] [user]@computer [...]`
Arguments:	
-l	Appends information to include long list information, which may or may not include additional information depending on the Finger server you are querying.
user	FINGER can be used to find out about all users on a system, or just one particular user. If you specify a computer name only, leaving off the user name, you *must* use the "@" sign. If not, FINGER may assume you are querying about a user on the current system. So, to query about all users at the domain *winternet.com*, try:
	`finger @winternet.com`
@computer	This is the server name or domain. If you leave this off, FINGER may assume you are querying the current system. Most often, the user@computer corresponds to the person's e-mail address, but you may need the person's POP3 server name, rather than just the e-mail address (for example, solar@pop03.ca.us.ibm.net rather than solar@ibm.net).

FOR

Description:	Runs a specified command for each file in a file set. Can be used from the command prompt directly, or invoked from batch files.
Syntax:	To use FOR from the command prompt, use the following syntax:
	`for %variable in (set) do command [command-parameters]`
	To use FOR in a batch program, use the following syntax:
	`FOR %%variable in (set) do command [command-parameters]`
	In other words, simply use the extra variable indicator (%) when invoking FOR from a batch file.

Arguments:

%%variable or %variable   This *must* be a single character! Represents a replaceable variable. FOR replaces %%variable (or %variable) with each text string in the specified set. If your variable contains multiple text strings or if you specify a wildcard, the command is repeated once for each entry.

(set)   Specifies one or more files or text strings that you want to process with the specified command. The parentheses are required.

command   Specifies the command that you want to carry out on each file included in the specified set.

command-parameters   Specifies any parameters or switches that you want to use with the specified command (if the specified command uses any parameters or switches).

Example:

`FOR %s in (*.txt) do type %s` types the contents of each TXT file in the current directory. If you specify (*.doc *.txt), the command will be repeated for all DOC and TXT files.

FOR can be combined with FIND. `FOR %f in (*.bat) do find "PROMPT" %f` searches all BAT files in the current directory for the string "PROMPT."

FORCEDOS

Description: Starts the specified program in the MS-DOS subsystem, rather than CMD.EXE. Use this if NT does not recognize your program as an MS-DOS program, or if it does not function from the NT command prompt.

Syntax: `FORCEDOS [/d directory] filename [parameters]`

Arguments:

/d directory   You may specify a directory for the program to start in. This is useful for programs that have configuration files in their home directory.

filename   This is the program you want to start. If not in the current directory or Windows NT path, you must provide a fully qualified path, such as c:\programs\wp51\wp.exe.

parameters   These will be the actual program parameters, not parameters passed to FORCEDOS.

FORMAT

Description:	Formats the specified floppy disk or hard drive. Windows NT security requires you to be a member of the Administrators group to format hard drives. This may be used instead of Disk Administrator.
Syntax:	`FORMAT drive: [/fs:file-system] [/v[:label]] [/a:unitsize]` `[/q] [/f:size] [/t:tracks/n:sectors] [/1] [/4] [/8]`

Arguments:

drive:	The current drive letter to be formatted. If the disk has just been partitioned and has no drive letter, you must format it from Disk Administrator. FORMAT will determine the default settings for the drive type, chosen from the following list.
/fs:file-system	Formats the disk as either NTFS or FAT. NTFS is not available for floppy disks.
/v[:label]	Specifies the volume label, which is used for informational purposes, and is not necessary. If you have specified a volume label, FORMAT and FDISK will require you to correctly enter it before the command will be carried out. If you omit the /v switch, you will be prompted for a volume label after the disk format is complete. If you use /v: with no label, you can avoid the label prompt. See also LABEL, DIR.
/a:unitsize	Specifies the allocation unit size to use on NTFS disks. Use 512 to 32768 for unitsize, which indicates the bytes per cluster. The larger the cluster size, the larger the disk partition may be, but the more space may be wasted on files smaller than the allocation unit. 512 bytes per cluster is the default for disks smaller than 512 MB; 1024 bytes is the default for disks 512 MB to 1 GB; 2048 bytes is the default cluster size for disks 1 GB to 2 GB; 4096 bytes per cluster is the default for disks over 2 GB. If you specify 32768, you may waste significant amounts of space on small files, but the formatted partition may be quite large.
/q	Quick format. Nulls the file table and the root directory of a previously formatted disk, but does not scan the disk for bad areas.
/f:size	Specifies the size of the floppy disk to format. When possible, use this switch instead of the /t and /n switches. The most common values are 360 or 1.2 (for 5.25-inch disks) and 720 or 1.44 (for 3.5-inch disks), but other valid values are 160, 180, and 320 (for 5.25-inch disks), 2880 or 2.88 (for 3.5-inch disks), and 20.8 (for 3.5-inch floptical disks).
/t:tracks	Specifies the number of tracks on the disk. This is an alternative to /f (the two may not be used together).

/n:sectors	Specifies the number of sectors per track. This is used with /t:, and cannot be used with /f.
/1	Formats a single side of a floppy disk.
/4	Formats a 5.25-inch, 360 KB, double-sided, double-density floppy disk on a 1.2-MB disk drive.
	Some 360 KB drives cannot reliably read disks formatted with this switch. When used with the /1 switch, this switch formats a 5.25-inch, 180 KB, single-sided floppy disk.
/8	Formats a 5.25-inch disk with 8 sectors per track. This switch formats a floppy disk to be compatible with MS-DOS versions prior to 2.0.

FTP

Description:	Invokes the command-line FTP client. When started with no parameters, changes your command prompt to an ftp> prompt from which you can issue FTP commands. See "FTP COMMANDS" for a description of available FTP commands. This command is available only if the TCP/IP protocol has been installed. If parameters are specified, FTP will behave as follows.
Syntax:	FTP [-v] [-d] [-i] [-n] [-g] [-s:filename] [-a] [-w:windowsize] [computer]
Arguments:	
-v	Suppresses display of remote server responses.
-n	Suppresses auto-logon upon initial connection.
-i	If you are executing multiple file transfers, this turns prompting off, for unattended downloads or uploads.
-d	DEBUG mode. This displays all messages sent between the client and server, including messages usually suppressed. In addition, you can view which commands are acknowledged by the server.
-g	Allows use of wildcard characters in local file and path names. (See the GLOB command.)
-s:filename	Specifies a text file containing FTP commands; the commands will automatically run after FTP starts. No spaces are allowed in this parameter. Use this switch instead of redirection (>).
-a	This is used to help connections, which uses any available interface to bind the data connection.

-w:windowsize	The default transfer window size is 4096, but you can specify a different value here.
computer	If you use this parameter, FTP will connect to the specified host. This is the same as specifying an OPEN command when interactively using FTP. If you use this parameter, it *must* be the last parameter on the line.

FTP COMMANDS

Description:	If you start FTP with no parameters, you will be seated at an FTP prompt. The following commands may be entered at any FTP prompt.
ascii	Sets transfer mode to ASCII. This should be set for text file transfers, to preserve CR-LF end-of-line markers.
binary	Sets transfer mode to BINARY, which is necessary for transferring programs or other binary data.
!	Escapes to the command shell. "EXIT" brings you back to FTP.
?	Help on FTP commands. For help on GLOB, type **? glob**. **?** may be interchanged with HELP.
append	Initiates download, but appends to a file if it exists, rather than overwriting the file.
bell	Toggles BELL, which beeps upon completion of each command.
close	Terminates current FTP session without exiting program.
debug	Toggles debug mode on or off. Same as specifying -d on startup.
delete, mdelete	Deletes remote files. DELETE is for a single file; MDELETE can delete multiple files.
disconnect	Terminates a connection to a remote machine.
get	See recv.
glob	Turns globbing on or off. If globbing is off, you may use wildcards in local file names.
hash	Turns HASH on or off. If HASH is on, a # character will be printed when a buffer is transferred. This is useful when transferring large files because there is no other status indicator to show transfer progress.
help	Same as ?. For fun, try HELP ? and ? HELP.
lcd	Changes local directory. For example, **lcd c:\windows** or **lcd windows.**

ls	Gives an abbreviated list of the remote directory, ignoring file size, attributes, and security tags. You can specify a remote directory and a local file name, and the output will be stored in the local file rather than displayed on the screen. *Ls -l* lists all the directory information, rather than an abbreviated list.
mdir, mkdir, rmdir	Creates and removes directories on a remote machine. RMDIR is the command used to remove directories.
open	Starts connection to a remote machine. **Open winternet.com**, for example, would initiate a connection to the FTP server at winternet.com on port 20.
put, mput.	Copies a file from your local machine to the remote host. **Put command.com**, for example, copies COMMAND.COM to the remote machine. MPUT puts multiple files.
pwd	Prints a working directory on a remote machine. The output is the same as DIR, which lists the current directory on the remote machine.
prompt	Toggles PROMPT mode, which forces interactive prompts for multiple commands, such as MGET, MPUT, and MDELETE.
quit	Exits FTP; terminates session. Same as using Ctrl+C.
recv, get, mget	Downloads a file from remote machine. MGET downloads multiple files.
remotehelp	Help from remote server. (? and HELP are local, handled by the FTP program itself.)
status	Displays status. This includes your current settings (hash on or off, glob on or off), if you are connected to a remote host, and the name of the remote host if connected.
trace	Similar to the Unix utility TRACEROUTE. Helps trace the IP route of a file transfer.
type	Toggles between BINARY and ASCII transfer modes as an alternative to specifying.
user	If you are connected but not logged on to a remote machine, USER starts the logon procedure. USER can also be used to change users while maintaining a connection.
verbose	Toggles verbose mode on and off.

FTYPE

Description:	Manages NT file types used with file extension associations. This is not a table of the file extension associations, but is a file type name with the definition of that file type. When a file extension is defined as a file type, the file type definition is managed with FTYPE. For example:

FTYPE *.doc is not valid, but

FTYPE Word.Document.6 displays the current definition of the file type, and the program used to start it.

Syntax:	`FTYPE [filetype[=[command]]]`
Arguments:	
filetype	The file type that you want to display or change. If you do not specify a file type, FTYPE will display all the currently defined file types in the system. Use FTYPE	MORE to pause after each screen of information.
command	Specifies the program or command to use when launching files of this type. If you use the = without a program or command, the information for that file type is deleted. If you do not use the =, the definition is displayed.

GOTO

Description:	Controls execution in a batch file. GOTO causes the batch file to immediately change to the label.
Syntax:	`GOTO label`
Arguments:	
label	Specifies the line in a batch program to which Windows NT should go. Labels are listed as *:label*, and GOTO can be used with IF... statements. For example, the line IF %OS% == Windows_NT GOTO NT checks the OS variable. If it is equal to *Windows_NT*, the file jumps to the :NT line. If the OS variable does not equal *Windows_NT*, the file continues processing normally.

GRAFTABL

Description:	Enables Windows NT to display the extended characters of a specified code page in full-screen mode. This allows extended characters, such as Portuguese or Cyrillic characters, to be displayed in character-mode programs. Extended characters will not display in window mode. If you are not sure which code page your system is using, simply type **CHCP** from a command prompt. Extended characters will not be displayed in windowed mode.

Syntax: `GRAFTABL [xxx] [/status]`

Arguments:

xxx   Specifies which code page to use. The most commonly used code pages
                           in the U.S.A are 437 (US) and 850 (Multilingual).

                           437   United States

                           850   Multilingual (Latin I)

                           852   Slavic (Latin II)

                           855   Cyrillic (Russian)

                           857   Turkish

                           860   Portuguese

                           861   Icelandic

                           863   Canadian-French

                           865   Nordic

                           866   Russian

                           869   Modern Greek

GRAPHICS

Description: Allows you to print the screen contents to a printer.
                           GRAPHICS.COM loads into memory, and is primarily for
                           DOS applications that need to use the PrintScrn key to send
                           output to a printer, but cannot because they are not text-
                           mode applications (they run in color or graphics mode).

Syntax: `GRAPHICS [type] [[drive:][path] filename] [/r] [/b]`
                           `[/lcd] [/printbox:std ¦ /printbox:lcd]`

Arguments:

[drive:][path][filename]   This indicates the name and location of the printer profiles. If
                           this is not specified, NT will look for a file called
                           GRAPHICS.PRO, for example, in the same directory as
                           GRAPHICS.COM. To print, you need to use Shift+Print
                           Screen, as Print Screen will simply copy the current screen to
                           the Clipboard. Some printers will simply load the informa-
                           tion in the print buffer, and won't print out until you take
                           the printer offline and press FORM FEED. This varies
                           depending on make and model of your printer.

/r

Prints the image as it appears on the screen. The default is black characters on a white page, which conserves ink. If you specify this parameter, the background will appear dark, which could use significant printer resources.

/b

Prints the background in color only on COLOR4 or COLOR8 printers.

/lcd

Adjusts the aspect ratio for a typical early laptop LCD screen, which is only necessary for older LCD-style laptops, not the current VGA laptops, even though they use LCD technology.

/printbox:std, or printbox:lcd

Toggles the print mode. /printbox:lcd is the same as using the /lcd parameter.

/type

Specifies the type of printer. Valid types are the following:

color1	IBM Personal Computer Color Printer with black ribbon
color4	IBM PC Color Printer with RGB ribbon
color8	IBM PC Color Printer with CYMK ribbon
hpdefault	Any HP PCL printer
deskjet	Any HP deskjet printer
graphics	IBM Personal Graphics printer, Personal printer, ProPrinter, or QuietWriter printer
graphicswide	IBM Personal Graphics printer with 11-inch cartridge
laserjet	HP LaserJet printer
laserjetii	HP LaserJet II printer
quietjet	HP QuietJet printer
quietjetplu	HP QuietJet Plus printer
ruggedwriter	HP RuggedWriter printer
ruggedwriter wide	HP RuggedWriterwide printer
thermal	IBM PC-convertible thermal printer
thinkjet	IBM ThinkJet printer

HELP

Description:	On-screen information about command-line utilities. This is the same as typing a command followed by /?. For example, help xcopy and xcopy /? both provide help for the XCOPY command. Because HELP invokes the command and then initiates the program's help index, the second method, xcopy /? yields faster results.
Syntax:	`HELP [command]`
Arguments:	
command	Specifies the name of the command about which you want information. If you do not specify a command name, the HELP command lists and briefly describes every Windows NT system command.

HOSTNAME

Description:	Displays the computer name (host). This command is available only if the TCP/IP protocol has been installed.
Syntax:	`hostname`
Arguments:	Not applicable.

IF

Description:	IF is used in batch files to control execution of the file. IF can be used with environment variables and error levels to create sophisticated program arrays using batch files. If the condition being tested by the IF statement is true, NT carries out the command specified. If not, the command is ignored. Note there is no THEN component, unlike other programming languages. Each IF statement is basically an encapsulated IF...THEN test, with the THEN alternative simply being "continue."
Syntax:	`IF [not] errorlevel number command`
	`IF [not] string1==string2 command`
	`IF [not] exist filename command`
Arguments:	
not	Reverses the outcome of the IF test. If the condition is true, the command is skipped; if the condition is false, the command is executed.

errorlevel number	Certain programs return an error level value when run. In DOS, an example is NETX.EXE, which returns an error level of 1. IF can check the error level after the program is run, and perform an action based on the error level. The condition is true if the error level is equal to or greater than *number*. For example:
	IF errorlevel == 1 goto YIPES
	would cause execution of the batch file to jump to the label :YIPES if the error level generated by the command immediately preceding the IF statement was greater than or equal to 1. Advanced error level checking arrays can be very useful but difficult to set up. If you are using a sophisticated batch file for an NT logon script, you should consider an advanced MS-DOS batch programming manual.
command	Specifies the command that Windows NT should carry out if the preceding condition is met. This can be a program, an internal NT command, or a GOTO statement.
string1==string2	Specifies a true condition only if string1 and string2 are the same. These values can be literal strings or batch variables (%1, for example). Variables need to be encapsulated in the % sign, as *%variable%*.
exist filename	Specifies a true condition if a file exists. This is useful for testing whether or not a person is logged in to the network, whether a certain program is running, or perhaps whether a certain program is installed.

INSTALL

Description:	Loads a memory-resident program into memory in CONFIG.NT. This works the same way INSTALL works in CONFIG.SYS under MS-DOS. This is not a command that can be executed from the NT command prompt.
Syntax:	INSTALL=[drive:][path] filename [command-parameters]
Arguments:	
[drive:][path] filename	Specifies the location and name of the memory-resident program you want to run.
command-parameters	Specifies parameters for the program you specify for filename.

IPCONFIG

Description:	Displays TCP/IP values for LAN adapters, including the modem if RAS is connected to a TCP/IP network, including the Internet. This is useful in a variety of situations in which you need to determine your IP address quickly, and will display information for all adapters currently installed. This can be very useful in a DHCP environment (where IP addresses change frequently) and across a WAN, where an IP address may be allocated dynamically to dial-in clients. Moreover, IPCONFIG can be used to determine your Internet address. The command lists the IP address, netmask, and default gateway for each adapter.

Syntax:

```
IPCONFIG [/all ¦ /renew [adapter] ¦ /release [adapter]]
```

Arguments:

/all	Produces a full display. Without this switch, IPCONFIG displays only the IP address, subnet mask, and default gateway values for each network card.
/renew [adapter]	Using RENEW forces the DHCP client to request new address information from the DHCP server. If your addresses are allocated differently, or if your system does not use DHCP, this option will not function. You may renew a particular adapter by specifying the adapter name. To list the adapter names, use IPCONFIG with no parameters.
/release [adapter]	Using RELEASE forces the DHCP client to clear all IP information for that adapter, disabling TCP/IP for the specified adapter, or for all adapters if no adapter is specified.

IPXROUTE

Description:	Displays and modifies IPX default and source routing tables.

Syntax:

```
IPXROUTE servers [/type=x]

IPXROUTE stats [/show] [/clear]

IPXROUTE table

IPXROUTE [config] board=n [clear] [def] [gbr] [mbr]
[remove=xxxxx]
```

Arguments:

General IPX options:

servers [/type=x]

Displays the SAP table for the specified server type. Replace *x* with the valid server type. For example, /type=4 displays all file servers. To list all servers, do not specify a type. For valid *x* values, consult your IPX/SPX documentation.

stats [/show] [/clear]

/show is the default. */clear* deletes the current table of statistics.

table

Shows the IPX routing table, sorted by network number.

Source Routing Options:

config

Shows information for current IPX bindings.

board=n

Specifies the network adapter card.

clear

This will obliterate the current source routing table.

remove=xxxxx

Deletes the specified node address from the source routing table, without disturbing the other entries.

def

If an adapter address is not found in the source routing table, this instructs IPX to send packets destined for that adapter to the ALL ROUTES broadcast. The default is to send such packets to the SINGLE ROUTES broadcast.

gbr

If a packet is sent to the broadcast address,(address FFFFFFFFFFFF), it will be routed to the ALL ROUTES broadcast. The default is to send broadcast address packets to the SINGLE ROUTES broadcast instead, which may not reach all routes.

mbr

If a packet is sent to the multicast address, (C000xxxxxxxx), send packets to the ALL ROUTES broadcast. The default is to send multicast address packets to the SINGLE ROUTES broadcast.

KEYB

Description:	Used to reconfigure the keyboard for another language.
Syntax:	`keyb [xx[,[yyy][,[drive:][path] filename]]] [/e] [/id:nnn]`

If a CONFIG.NT file is used along with the DOS program being run, use this syntax:

```
install=[[drive:]path]keyb.com
[xx[,[yyy][,[drive:][path] filename]]] [/e] [/id:nnn]
```

Arguments:

xx	Specifies a keyboard code. See the table at the end of this section for a list of valid values.
yyy	This parameter is used for compatibility with MS-DOS files and programs only.
[drive:][path] filename	This parameter is used for compatibility with MS-DOS files and programs only.
[drive:]path	This parameter is used only for compatibility with MS-DOS files and programs; not for use with the NT MS-DOS subsystem.
/e	This parameter is used for compatibility with MS-DOS files and programs; not for use with the NT MS-DOS subsystem.
/id:nnn	This parameter is used for compatibility with MS-DOS files and programs only; not for use with the NT MS-DOS subsystem.
Values for xx	The following table shows the valid values for xx for each country or language:

Country or Keyboard Language Code
(xx = value):

Country	Code
Belgium	be
Brazil	br
Canadian-French	cf
Czech	cz
Slovak	sl
Denmark	dk
Finland	su
France	fr
Germany	gr
Hungary	hu
Italy	it
Latin America	la
Netherlands	nl
Norway	no
Poland	pl

Portugal	po
Spain	sp
Sweden	sv
Switzerland (French)	sf
Switzerland (German)	sg
United Kingdom	uk
United States	us
Serbo-Croatian	yu

LABEL

Description:	Used to create, change, or delete the volume label of a disk.
Syntax:	`label [drive:][label]`
Arguments:	
none	Type LABEL without any arguments to change or delete the current volume label.
drive:	The drive letter of the disk you want to name.
label	The new volume label. There must be a colon between the drive and label.

LASTDRIVE

Description:	Drives are always set to Z:. Used for compatibility with MS-DOS files and programs only; not used by the NT MS-DOS subsystem.
Syntax:	Not applicable.
Arguments:	Not applicable.

LIBPATH

Description:	Edit the OS/2 CONFIG.SYS file to specify directories the OS/2 subsystem uses to search for dynamic link libraries.

Syntax:	`libpath=[drive:]path[;[drive:]path][...]`
Arguments:	
drive:	If a drive letter is not specified, the OS/2 subsystem searches the current drive.
path	You can specify more than one directory to search for dynamic link libraries, separating each subdirectory with semicolons.

LOADFIX

Description:	Used to ensure that a DOS program is loaded above the first 64 KB of conventional memory, and then runs the specified program.
Syntax:	`loadfix [drive:][path] filename` `[program-parameters]`
Arguments:	
[drive:][path]	Specifies the drive and directory of the DOS program to be loaded.
filename	Specifies the name of the DOS program.
program-parameters	Specifies any of the DOS program's parameters to be used.

LOADHIGH (LH)

Description:	Used to load a DOS program into upper memory.
Syntax:	`loadhigh [drive:][path] filename [parameters]` `lh [drive:][path] filename [parameters]`
Arguments:	
[drive:][path] filename	Specifies the path and name of the DOS program to load.
parameters	Specifies command-line information the DOS program requires.

LPQ

Description:	A diagnostic utility used to obtain the status of a print queue on an NT server computer running the LPD server service. The command is only available if the TCP/IP printing utilities are loaded.
Syntax:	`lpq -SServer -PPrinter [-l]`

Arguments:

-SServer	Specifies the name of the NT server that is running the LPD service. The command is case sensitive.
-PSrinter	Specifies the name of the printer to print to. The command is case sensitive.
-l	Specifies that a detailed status of the print queue be displayed.

LPR

Description:	Used to print a file to a computer running an LPD server. The command is only available if the TCP/IP printing utilities are loaded.
Syntax:	`lpr -SServer -PPrinter [-CClass] [-JJobname]` `[-O option] filename`

Arguments:

-SServer	Specifies the name or IP address of the computer that is running the LPD server service. The command is case sensitive.
-PPrinter	Specifies the name of the printer to print to. The command is case sensitive.
-CClass	Specifies the content of the banner page. The command is case sensitive.
-JJobname	Specifies the name of the print job. The command is case sensitive.
-O option	Indicates the type of file; text files are the default value. Binary files are indicated by -Ol (lowercase "l"). The command is case sensitive.
filename	The file to be printed.

MEM

Description:	Used to display information about allocated memory, free memory, and programs currently loaded into memory in the NT MS-DOS subsystem.
Syntax:	`mem [/program¦/debug¦/classify]`
Arguments:	
none	Type **mem** without any arguments to display the status of the NT MS-DOS subsystem's used and free memory.
/program or /p	Displays the status of programs currently loaded into memory. The /program switch cannot be used with the /debug switch or /classify switch.
/debug or /d	Displays the status of currently loaded programs and internal drivers. You cannot use the /debug switch with the /program switch or the /classify switch.
/classify or /c	Displays the status of programs loaded into conventional and upper memory in decimal and hexadecimal notation, provides a summary of memory use, and lists the largest memory blocks available. You cannot use the /classify switch with the /program switch or the /debug switch.

MKDIR (MD)

Description:	Used to create a directory or subdirectory.
Syntax:	`mkdir [drive:]path`
	`md [drive:]path`
Arguments:	
drive:	Specifies the drive where you want the new directory created.
path	Specifies the path and name of the new directory.

MODE

Description:	Used to configure system devices, including port configuration and system settings. The MODE command can also be used to display system status.

Because the MODE command performs many different tasks, the necessary syntax to carry out each task is different. The following is a list of tasks that can be performed by the MODE command:

Configuring a printer attached to a parallel port (PRN, LPT1, LPT2, or LPT3) for printing at 80 or 132 characters per line, 6 or 8 lines per inch.

Configuring the baud rate, parity, and number of data bits and stop bits of a serial communications port (COM1, COM2, COM3, and COM4) for use with a specific printer, modem, or other serial device.

Displaying the current status of a single device, or of multiple devices.

Redirecting printer output from a parallel port to a serial port.

Changing the size of the command prompt window.

Setting a keyboard's typematic rate.

Syntax:	Not applicable.
Arguments:	Not applicable.

MORE

Description:	Used to prevent long files from scrolling when viewed on-screen so that one page of screen output is displayed at a time. Enable additional features using switches to control the display.
Syntax:	`command name ¦ more [/e] [/c] [/p] [/s] [/tn] [+n]`
	`more [/e] [/c] [/p] [/s] [/tn] [+n] < [drive:] [path] filename`
	`more [/e] [/c] [/p] [/s] [/tn] [+n] files`
Arguments:	
[drive:] [path] filename	Specifies the file to display.
command name	Specifies the command whose output is displayed.
/e	Enables extended features.
/c	Clears the screen before displaying a page.
/p	Expands form-feed characters.

/s	Converts multiple blank lines to one blank line.
/t*n*	Changes the current tab setting to *n* spaces.
+n	Displays the first file beginning at the line specified by n.
files	List of files to display, separating each file with a space.

If the extended features are enabled, the following commands are accepted at the --More--prompt:

Key	Action
space	Display next page
Enter	Display next line
F	Display next file
Q	Quit
?	Show available commands
=	Show line number
P n	Display next *n* lines
S n	Skip next *n* lines

MOVE

Description:	Used to move files from one directory to another directory.
Syntax:	`move [source] [target]`
Arguments:	
source	Specifies the path and name of files to move.
target	Specifies the path and name where the files are to be moved.

NBTSTAT

Description:	Displays TCP/IP statistics and current connections using NetBIOS over TCP/IP, if TCP/IP has been installed.
Syntax:	`NBTSTAT [-a remotename] [-A IP address] [-c] [-n] [-R] [-r]` `[-S] [-s] [interval]`
Arguments:	
-a remotename	Displays a remote computer's name table by name.
-A IP address	Displays a remote computer's name table by IP address.

-c	Displays the contents and IP addresses of the local computer's NetBIOS name cache.
-n	Displays the local NetBIOS names.
-R	Reloads the LMHOSTS file after deleting the names from the NetBIOS name cache.
-r	Displays the name resolution statistics for Windows networking name resolution. On an NT system configured to use WINS, this argument lists the number of NetBIOS names resolved and registered by broadcast or by WINS.
-S	Displays all client and server sessions, with remote systems listed by their IP addresses.
-s	Displays all client and server sessions. Using the local HOSTS file, attempts to convert the remote system's IP address to a host name.
interval	Redisplays some statistics, stopping for a couple of seconds between each display. To stop, press Ctrl+C. If interval is omitted, NBTSTAT lists the configuration information one time.

NET

Description:	Several Windows NT networking commands begin with NET, followed by an additional command and arguments. NET commands have similar characteristics:
	By entering **NET /?**, a listing of all the NET commands is displayed.
	By entering **NET HELP** followed by a specific NET command, such as NET HELP USE, you get help on the command's particular syntax.
	For NET commands that accept the /yes and /no arguments, /yes can be abbreviated /y and /no can be abbreviated /n.
Syntax:	Not applicable.
Arguments:	Not applicable.

NET ACCOUNTS

Description:	Used to modify user account logon options for all users in the entire NT user account database. The Net Logon Service must be running in order for this command to work.
	Entering NET ACCOUNTS without any arguments lists the current account settings.

Syntax:	`NET ACCOUNTS [/domain] [/forcelogoff:{minutes ¦ no}]`
	`[/minpwlen:length] [/maxpwage:{days ¦ unlimited}]`
	`[/minpwage:days] [/sync][/uniquepw:number]`

Arguments:

/domain
When using this command from an NT Workstation that is part of a domain, the command will affect the NT Workstation's local accounts database by default. To change a domain accounts database instead, use the /domain argument to specify the name of the domain to change. This argument is only used from NT Workstations that belong to a domain.

/forcelogoff:
{minutes | no}
If you have limited hourly access to users, this option allows you to set the time (in minutes) between when the user's time expires and the actual time the user is disconnected. By default, this option is set to no, which means that the user is not forced to log off when the user's account time expires. If this option is set, the users receive a warning that their accounts will expire, allowing them time to finish up their work.

/minpwlen:length
Lets you set the minimum number of characters the password length must be. The default is 6, and the range is 0–14.

/maxpwage:
{days | unlimited}
Specifies the number of days that a password is good. The password expires after this time. The default is 90 days, and the range is 1–49,710 days, or unlimited.

/minpwage:days
Specifies the minimum number of days before a user can change his password. The default is 0 days, and the range is 0–49,710 days.

/sync
When used from a primary domain controller (PDC), it synchronizes all backup domain controllers (BDCs) with the PDC. When used from a BDC, it will only synchronize that BDC with the PDC.

/uniquepw:number
Specifies the number of unique passwords a user must cycle through before reusing one. The default is 5, and the range is 0–8.

NET COMPUTER

Description:
Used to add or delete NT servers and workstations from a domain. This command only works on NT Server computers and for the default domain.

Syntax:
`NET COMPUTER \\computername {/add ¦ /del}`

Arguments:

\\computername   The name of the computer to be added or deleted from the domain.

/add   Adds the computer to the domain.

/del   Deletes the computer from the domain.

NET CONFIG

Description: Used to display and configure configurable services. Typing the NET CONFIG command without any parameters displays all configurable services.

Syntax: `NET CONFIG [service [options]]`

Arguments:

service   The name of the service to be configured (either Server or Workstation).

[options]   See the NET CONFIG SERVER or NET CONFIG WORKSTATION commands that follow for specific options.

NET CONFIG SERVER

Description: Used to display or change the Server service's configuration while the service is active. To display the current Server service settings, type **NET CONFIG SERVER**.

Syntax: `NET CONFIG SERVER [/autodisconnect:time] [/srvcomment:"text"] [/hidden:{yes ¦ no}]`

Arguments:

/autodisconnect: time   Sets the number of minutes a user's session on that computer can be inactive before it is disconnected. The default (-1) is to never disconnect. The range is -1–65535 (no commas allowed).

/srvcomment:"text"   Adds a comment for a server that can be displayed in browse lists and by using the NET VIEW command. Enter the comment, using a maximum of 48 characters, with surrounding quote marks.

/hidden:{yes | no}   Allows you to prevent a server from being displayed in browser lists. The default is no. Although a server is hidden from view, it is still accessible.

NET CONFIG WORKSTATION

Description:	Used to display or change the Workstation service's configuration while the service is active. To display the current Server service settings, type **NET CONFIG WORKSTATION**.
Syntax:	`NET CONFIG WORKSTATION [/charcount:bytes] [/chartime:msec] [/charwait:sec]`

Arguments:

/charcount:bytes	The amount of data collected before sending it to a communications device. The default is 16. The range is 0–65535 (no commas). If /chartime:msec is also set, NT acts on whichever condition is met first.
/chartime:msec	The amount of time (in milliseconds) that the computer collects data for transmittal before sending it to a communications device. The default is 250. The range is 0–65535000 (no commas). If /charcount: bytes is also set, NT acts on whichever condition is met first.
/charwait:sec	The number of seconds that NT waits until a communications device becomes available. The default is 3600. The range is 0–65535 (no commas).

NET CONTINUE

Description:	Resumes a suspended service.
Syntax:	`NET CONTINUE service`

Arguments:

service	Services that can be suspended and then resumed include: Services for Macintosh, FTP service, LPDSVC, Net Logon, Network DDE, Network DDE DSDM, NT LM Security Support Provider, Remoteboot, Remote Access Server, Schedule, Server, Simple TCP/IP services, and Workstation.

NET FILE

Description:	Lists and closes open files on the computer. The NET FILE command, without arguments, displays a complete listing of open files, including file locks (if any) and the user name of the open file's user.
Syntax:	`NET FILE [id [/close]]`

Arguments:

id $\qquad$ The open file's identification number.

/close $\qquad$ Closes an open file and releases locked records (if any).

NET GROUP

Description: $\qquad$ Displays, adds, or modifies global groups in NT Server domains. Type **NET GROUP** to display a list of all global groups.

Syntax: $\qquad$ `NET GROUP [groupname [/comment:"text"]]`

`NET GROUP groupname {/add [/comment:"text"] ¦ /delete}`

`NET GROUP groupname username[...] {/add ¦ /delete}`

Arguments:

/add $\qquad$ Adds a global group, or adds a user name to a preexisting global group. A user account must already be created to add it to a global group.

/comment:"text" $\qquad$ Adds an optional description to a new or existing global group. The comment can have up to 48 characters and must be enclosed in quotes.

/delete $\qquad$ Deletes a global group, or a user name from a global group.

groupname $\qquad$ The name of the global group to be added, deleted, or modified. Use the command NET GROUP GROUPNAME to view a list of all users of a global group.

username[...] $\qquad$ The user name to add or to remove from a global group. Separate more than one user name with a space.

NET HELP

Description: $\qquad$ Displays a list of the NET commands that have help information available, or displays help about a specific NET command. Type **NET HELP** to display a list of the NET commands with available help.

Syntax: $\qquad$ `NET HELP [command] net command {/help ¦ /?}`

Arguments:

/help $\qquad$ Displays the help text differently.

/? $\qquad$ Displays the proper syntax for the NET command.

NET HELPMSG

Description: Displays help about NT error messages.

Syntax: `NET HELPMSG message#`

Arguments:

message#   The four-digit number of the NT message you want more information about.

NET LOCALGROUP

Description: Displays, adds, or modifies local groups in user account databases. Type **NET LOCALGROUP** to display a list of all local groups.

Syntax: `NET LOCALGROUP [groupname [/comment:"text"]] [/domain]`

`NET LOCALGROUP groupname {/add [/comment:"text"] ¦ /delete} [/domain]`

`NET LOCALGROUP groupname name[...] {/add ¦ /delete} [/domain]`

Arguments:

/add   Adds a local group, a user name from the local domain (or from other domains), or a global group to a preexisting local group. These accounts must be already created to add them to a local group.

/comment:"text"   Adds an optional description to a new or existing local group. The comment can have up to 48 characters and must be enclosed in quotes.

/delete   Deletes a local group, a user name from the local domain (or from other domains), or a global group from a local group.

/domain   For use on NT Workstations that are members of a domain. By default, if this command is executed on an NT Workstation, the change affects the local computer's user account database only. By specifying a domain, the command affects the user account database on the Primary Domain Controller (PDC) instead.

groupname   The name of the local group to be added, deleted, or modified. Use the command NET LOCALGROUP GROUPNAME to view a list of all users of a local group.

name[...]   The user name (from this domain or other domains) or global group name to add or remove from a local group. Separate more than one name with a space.

NET NAME

Description:	When the messenger service is running, add or delete a messaging name (an alias) for a workstation. Type **NET NAME** to display a list of messaging names for a workstation.
Syntax:	`NET NAME [name [/add ¦ /delete]]`
Arguments:	
name	The messaging name designated to receive messages. Fifteen characters maximum.
/add	Adds a messaging name to the computer. Typing **NET NAME name** also works.
/delete	Deletes a messaging name from a computer.

NET PAUSE

Description:	Temporarily halts a running service.
Syntax:	`NET PAUSE service`
Arguments:	
service	Services that can be paused include: Services for Macintosh, FTP service, LPDSVC, Net Logon, Network DDE, Network DDE DSDM, NT LM Security Support Provider, Remoteboot, Remote Access Server, Schedule, Server, Simple TCP/IP services, and Workstation.

NET PRINT

Description:	Controls or displays information about print jobs and print queues.
Syntax:	`NET PRINT \\computername\sharename`
	`NET PRINT [\\computername] job# [/hold ¦ /release ¦ /delete]`
Arguments:	
\\computername	The name of the computer with the shared printer.
sharename	The share name of the computer's shared printer queue.
job#	The number assigned to the print job in a print queue.

/hold	Pauses the print job specified by the job#.
/release	Releases a print job that has been paused.
/delete	Deletes a print job from a print queue.

NET SEND

Description: If the messaging service is running, sends messages to users, computers, or messaging names on the network.

Syntax: `NET SEND {name ¦ * ¦ /domain[:name] ¦ /users} message`

Arguments:

name	The user name, computer name, or messaging name to send a message to. If a computer name contains blank characters, enclose the computer name in quotation marks.
*	Sends a message to all users in your domain.
/domain[:name]	If only /domain is used, the message is sent to everyone in the same domain. If the optional name argument is used, you can specify the name of the domain or workgroup to receive the message.
/users	Sends the message to all users connected to the same server.
message	The actual message. Quotes are not required.

NET SESSION

Description: Used to display or disconnect sessions between a server and the workstations connected to it. Type **NET SESSION** without any arguments to list all the workstations currently connected to a server.

Syntax: `NET SESSION [\\computername] [/delete]`

Arguments:

| \\computername | The name of the computer to display additional session information or to disconnect. |
| /delete | Used to disconnect a session between a workstation and a server. If \\computername is not used, then all sessions to the server are disconnected. |

NET SHARE

Description:	Used to create, delete, or display shared resources on a server. Type **NET SHARE** without arguments for information about all resources being shared.
Syntax:	`NET SHARE sharename`
	`NET SHARE sharename=drive:path [/users:number ¦ /unlimited] [/remark:"text"]`
	`NET SHARE sharename [/users:number ¦ unlimited] [/remark:"text"]`
	`NET SHARE {sharename ¦ drive:path} /delete`

Arguments:

sharename	The share name of the network resource being shared. Type **NET SHARE** with a share name to display information about one particular share.
drive:path	The complete path of the directory to be shared.
/users:number	Specifies the maximum number of concurrent users who can access the shared resource.
/unlimited	Specifies that an unlimited number of users can concurrently access the shared resource.
/remark:"text"	Adds an optional descriptive comment about the resource. Enclose the comment in quotation marks.
/delete	Stops sharing the specified resource.

NET START

Description:	Starts network services, or lists network services that are running. Enclose service names of two or more words in quotation marks. Type **NET START** without any arguments to display a list of network services that are running.
Syntax:	`NET START [service]`

Arguments:

service
Services that can be started with this command include: Alerter, Client Service for NetWare, Clipbook Server, Computer Browser, DHCP Client, Directory Replicator, Eventlog, FTP Publishing Service, LPDSVC, Messenger, Net Logon, Network DDE, Network DDE DSDM, Network Monitor Agent, NT LM Security Support Provider, OLE, Remote Access Connection Manager, Remote Access ISNSAP Service, Remote Access Server, Remote Procedure Call (RPC) Locator, Remote Procedure Call (RPC) Service, Schedule, Server, Simple TCP/IP Services, SNMP, Spooler, TCP/IP NetBIOS Helper, UPS, and Workstation.

These services are available only on Windows NT Server: File Server for Macintosh, Gateway Service for NetWare, Microsoft DHCP Server, Print Server for Macintosh, Remoteboot, and Windows Internet Name Service.

NET START ALERTER

Description: Starts the Alerter service, which sends messages about the network to users.

Syntax: `NET START ALERTER`

Arguments: Not applicable.

NET START CLIENT SERVICE FOR NETWARE

Description: Starts the Client Service for NetWare. Allows NT computers to access NetWare file and print resources on a NetWare server. The Client Service for NetWare must be installed on an NT Workstation client.

Syntax: `NET START "client service for netware"`

Arguments: Not applicable.

NET START CLIPBOOK SERVER

Description: Starts the ClipBook Server service. Creates a temporary or permanent storage place for text and graphics for cutting and pasting.

Syntax: `NET START "clipbook server"`

Arguments: Not applicable.

NET START COMPUTER BROWSER

Description: Starts the Computer Browser service. Used to maintain a browse list of network resources.

Syntax: `NET START "computer browser"`

Arguments: Not applicable.

NET START DHCP CLIENT

Description: Starts the DHCP Client service if the TCP/IP protocol has been installed.

Syntax: `NET START "dhcp client"`

Arguments: Not applicable.

NET START DIRECTORY REPLICATOR

Description: Starts the Directory Replicator service, which replicates designated directories and files from export servers to import servers.

Syntax: `NET START "directory replicator"`

Arguments: Not applicable.

NET START EVENTLOG

Description: Starts the event logging service.

Syntax: `NET START eventlog`

Arguments: Not applicable.

NET START FILE SERVER FOR MACINTOSH

Description: Starts the File Server for Macintosh service on an NT Server, which allows Macintosh computers to access NT file resources.

Syntax: `NET START "file server for macintosh"`

Arguments: Not applicable.

NET START FTP PUBLISHING SERVICE

Description: Starts the FTP publishing service when the Internet Information
                           Server is present.

Syntax: `NET START "ftp publishing service"`

Arguments: Not applicable.

NET START GATEWAY SERVICE FOR NETWARE

Description: Starts the Gateway Service for NetWare, which allows Microsoft clients
                           to access NetWare resources without a NetWare redirector. This
                           command is available if the Gateway Service for NetWare has been
                           installed.

Syntax: `NET START "gateway service for netware"`

Arguments: Not applicable.

NET START LPDSVC

Description: Starts the LPDSVC service, which allows Unix hosts to print to NT
                           print resources. This command is available only if the TCP/IP
                           protocol and LPDSRV service has been loaded.

Syntax: `NET START lpdsvc`

Arguments: Not applicable.

NET START MESSENGER

Description: Starts the Messenger service, enabling a computer to receive messages.

Syntax: `NET START messenger`

Arguments: Not applicable.

NET START MICROSOFT DHCP SERVER

Description: Starts the Microsoft DHCP Server service, which dynamically allocates
                           TCP/IP addresses to DHCP clients. Available on NT Server computers
                           when the TCP/IP protocol and DHCP server service have been
                           installed.

Syntax:	NET START "microsoft dhcp server"
Arguments:	Not applicable.

NET START NET LOGON

Description:	Starts the Net Logon service, which handles user authentication and domain accounts database replication.
Syntax:	NET START "net logon"
	NET START netlogon
Arguments:	Not applicable.

NET START NETWORK DDE

Description:	Starts the Network DDE service, which provides an interprocess control (IPC) medium for some network programs.
Syntax:	NET START "network dde"
Arguments:	Not applicable.

NET START NETWORK DDE DSDM

Description:	Starts the Network DDE share database manager service, which works with the Network DDE service to manage DDE conversations.
Syntax:	NET START "network dde dsdm"
Arguments:	Not applicable.

NET START NETWORK MONITOR AGENT

Description:	Starts the Network Monitor Agent service, which is used to track network statistics by the Network Manager tool. This command is available only if the Network Monitor Agent has been installed.
Syntax:	NET START "network monitor agent"
Arguments:	Not applicable.

NET START NT LM SECURITY SUPPORT PROVIDER

Description: Starts the NT LM Security Support Provider service, which is used to provide NT security to RPC applications that use transports other than named pipes. This command is available only if the NT LM Security Support Provider has been installed.

Syntax: `NET START "nt lm security support provider"`

Arguments: Not applicable.

NET START PRINT SERVER FOR MACINTOSH

Description: Starts the Print Server for Macintosh service, which allows Macintosh computers to access print resources on NT Servers. This command is available only on computers running NT Server and which have the Macintosh Services loaded.

Syntax: `NET START "print server for macintosh"`

Arguments: Not applicable.

NET START REMOTE ACCESS CONNECTION MANAGER

Description: Starts the Remote Access Connection Manager service when the Remote Access Service has been installed.

Syntax: `NET START "remote access connection manager"`

Arguments: Not applicable.

NET START REMOTE ACCESS ISNSAP SERVICE

Description: Starts the Remote Access ISNSAP service when the Remote Access Service has been installed.

Syntax: `NET START "remote access isnsap service"`

Arguments: Not applicable.

NET START REMOTE ACCESS SERVER

Description: Starts the Remote Access Server service, if installed.

Syntax: `NET START "remote access server"`

Arguments: Not applicable.

NET START REMOTE PROCEDURE CALL (RPC) LOCATOR

Description:	Starts the Remote Procedure Call (RPC) Locator service, which allows distributed applications to use the RPC-provided pointer by directing the applications toward those pointers.
Syntax:	`NET START "remote procedure call (rpc) locator"`
Arguments:	Not applicable.

NET START REMOTE PROCEDURE CALL (RPC) SERVICE

Description:	Starts the Remote Procedure Call (RPC) Service, which is used by programmers to develop distributed applications by providing pointers to direct the applications.
Syntax:	`NET START "remote procedure call (rpc) service"`
Arguments:	Not applicable.

NET START REMOTEBOOT

Description:	Starts the Remoteboot service, which permits NT Workstation clients to load their operating system from the server.
Syntax:	`NET START remoteboot`
Arguments:	Not applicable.

NET START SCHEDULE

Description:	Starts the Schedule service, enabling the computer to run a program or batch file at a predetermined time.
Syntax:	`NET START schedule`
Arguments:	Not applicable.

NET START SERVER

Description:	Starts the Server service, which allows a computer to share resources on the network.
Syntax:	`NET START server`
Arguments:	Not applicable.

NET START SIMPLE TCP/IP SERVICES

Description: Starts the Simple TCP/IP Services. This command is available only if both TCP/IP and the Simple TCP/IP Services have been installed.

Syntax: NET START "simple tcp/ip services"

Arguments: Not applicable.

NET START SNMP

Description: Starts the SNMP service, which allows the server to communicate with an SNMP management console. This command is available only if TCP/IP and SNMP have been installed.

Syntax: NET START snmp

Arguments: Not applicable.

NET START SPOOLER

Description: Starts the Spooler service, which allows a printer to spool print jobs.

Syntax: NET START spooler

Arguments: Not applicable.

NET START TCP/IP NETBIOS HELPER

Description: Starts the NetBIOS over TCP service, which allows NetBIOS commands to be used with the TCP/IP protocol. This command is available only if TCP/IP has been installed.

Syntax: NET START "tcp/ip netbios helper"

Arguments: Not applicable.

NET START UPS

Description: Starts the Uninterruptible Power Supply service, which monitors a UPS via a serial cable.

Syntax: NET START ups

Arguments: Not applicable.

NET START WINDOWS INTERNET NAME SERVICE

Description: Starts the Windows Internet Name Service (WINS) when both TCP/
                          IP and WINS have been installed.

Syntax: NET START "windows internet name service"

Arguments: Not applicable.

NET START WORKSTATION

Description: Starts the Workstation service, or redirector, which allows a worksta-
                          tion to access shared network resources.

Syntax: NET START workstation

Arguments: Not applicable.

NET STATISTICS

Description: Used to display network statistics for local Workstation or Server
                          services. Type **NET STATISTICS** without any arguments to list the
                          services for which statistics are currently available.

Syntax: NET STATISTICS [workstation ¦ server]

Arguments:

workstation   Displays Workstation service network statistics.

server   Displays Server service network statistics.

NET STOP

Description: Stops a running NT network service.

Syntax: NET STOP service

Arguments:

service   Services that can be stopped with this command include: Alerter,
                          Client Service for NetWare, Clipbook Server, Computer Browser,
                          DHCP Client, Directory Replicator, Eventlog, FTP Publishing Service,
                          LPDSVC, Messenger, Net Logon, Network DDE, Network DDE
                          DSDM, Network Monitor Agent, NT LM Security Support Provider,
                          OLE, Remote Access Connection Manager, Remote Access ISNSAP
                          Service, Remote Access Server, Remote Procedure Call (RPC)

Locator, Remote Procedure Call (RPC) Service, Schedule, Server, Simple TCP/IP Services, SNMP, Spooler, TCP/IP NetBIOS Helper, UPS, and Workstation.

These services are available only on Windows NT Server: File Server for Macintosh, Gateway Service for NetWare, Microsoft DHCP Server, Print Server for Macintosh, Remoteboot, Windows Internet Name Service.

NET TIME

Description:	If run from a server, it displays the current time. If run from a workstation, you can synchronize its clock with that of a server.
Syntax:	`NET TIME [\\computername ¦ /domain[:name]] [/set]`
Arguments:	
\\computername	The name of a server you want to check for time, or synchronize a workstation with.
/domain[:name]	Specifies a domain, rather than a computer, with which to synchronize time.
/set	Synchronizes the workstation's clock with the time on the specified server or domain.

NET USE

Description:	Used to connect a workstation to or disconnect a workstation from a shared resource, or display information about network connections. Type **NET USE** without any arguments to display a list of network connections.

Syntax:	`NET USE [devicename ¦ *]`
	`[\\computername\sharename[\volume]] [password ¦ *]]`
	`[/user:[domainname\]username] [[/delete] ¦`
	`[/persistent:{yes ¦ no}]]`
	
	`NET USE devicename [/home[password ¦ *]]`
	`[/delete:{yes ¦ no}]`
	
	`NET USE [/persistent:{yes ¦ no}]`

Arguments:	
devicename	Assigns a device to connect to or disconnect from. A device name is either a disk drive or a printer. Type an asterisk instead of a device name to assign the next available device name.

\\computername\ sharename	The UNC name of the server and share to be connected to. If the computer name contains blank characters, enclose the double backslash (\\) and the computer name in quotation marks.
\volume	Specifies a NetWare volume name if connecting to a NetWare server. Client Services for NetWare or Gateway Services for NetWare must be in use.
password	The password needed to access the shared resource, if applicable.
*	Prompts for a required password.
/user	Specifies a different user name to make the network connection instead of using the user name of the currently logged on user.
domainname	Specifies another domain other than the current domain.
username	Specifies the user name with which to log on, assuming you are not currently logged on.
/home	Connects a user to his home directory specified in his user information.
/delete	Disconnects the specified network connection. If the connection is specified with an asterisk, all network connections are disconnected.
/persistent	Determines whether the connection is persistent. The default is the last setting used.
yes	Makes a connection persistent.
no	Does not make a connection persistent.

NET USER

Description:	Used to add, delete, modify, or display user account information. Type **NET USER** without any arguments to display the user accounts on the computer.
Syntax:	NET USER [username [password ¦ *] [options]] [/domain]
	NET USER username {password ¦ *} /add [options] [/domain]
	NET USER username [/delete] [/domain]
Arguments:	
username	The name of the user account to manipulate.

password	Assigns or changes a password for a user account.
*	Prompts for a password to be entered.
/domain	Applies only to NT Workstation computers that are members of an NT Server domain. Specifies that the operation occur on the domain's accounts database on the primary domain controller (PDC) of the computer's domain, instead of the local computer's local accounts database.
/add	Adds a user account.
/delete	Deletes a user account.
[options]	Substitute any of the following actions for [options] in the above syntax:
active:{no | yes}	Enables or disables a user account. If an account is not active, the user cannot log on. The default is yes.
/comment:"text"	A comment of up to 48 characters can be added to describe the user account. Enclose the text in quotation marks.
/countrycode:nnn	Specifies the operating-system country code. A value of 0 is the default.
/expires:{date | never}	Determines whether or not the user account expires. The default is never. Expiration dates can be in mm/dd/yy, dd/mm/yy, or mmm,dd,yy format, depending on the /countrycode.
/fullname:"name"	Allows the full name of the user account to be entered. Enclose between quotation marks.
/homedir:path	Sets the path of the user's home directory. The path must preexist.
/homedirreq:{yes | no}	Determines whether a home directory is required for a user account.
/passwordchg:{yes | no}	Determines whether users can change their own password. The default is yes.
/passwordreq:{yes | no}	Determines whether a user account must have a password. The default is yes.

/profilepath:[path]

Specifies the path for the location of the user's profile.

/scriptpath:path

Specifies the name of a user's logon script.

/times:{times | all}

Specifies the hours and days a user is allowed to log on. The times value is expressed as day [-day][,day[-day]], time[-time][,time[-time]], limited to 1-hour time increments. Days can be spelled out or abbreviated (M,T,W,Th,F,Sa,Su). Hours can be 12- or 24-hour notation. For 12-hour notation, use AM, PM, or A.M., P.M. The value all means a user can always log on. A null value (blank) means a user can never log on. Separate day and time with commas, and units of day and time with semicolons (for example, M,4AM-5PM;T,1PM-3PM). Do not use spaces when specifying times.

/usercomment:"text"

Allows a user comment to be added or changed. Enclose the comment in quotation marks.

/workstations:{computername[,...] | *}

Lists as many as eight workstations from which a user can log on. Separate multiple entries in the list with commas. If /workstations has no list, or if the list is *, the user can log on from any computer.

NET VIEW

Description:

Used to display a list of domains, computers, or resources available. Type **NET VIEW** without any arguments to display a list of local computers in the current domain.

Syntax:

```
NET VIEW [\\computername ¦
/domain[:domainname]]

NET VIEW /network:nw [\\computername]
```

Arguments:

\\computername

Specifies the computer name for which to view shared resources.

/domain[:domainname]	Specifies the domain for which you want to view the computers that have resources available. If domainname is omitted, all domains on the network are listed.
/network:nw	Displays all the servers on a NetWare network. If specified by computername, only the resources available on that computer are displayed.

NETSTAT

Description:	Used to display the current TCP/IP network connections and protocol statistics.
Syntax:	NETSTAT [-a] [-e] [-n] [-s] [-p protocol] [-r] [interval]
Arguments:	
-a	Displays connections and listening ports.
-e	Displays Ethernet statistics. May be combined with the -s option for more options.
-n	Displays addresses and port numbers.
-s	Displays per protocol statistics. Used in conjunction with the -p option, you can ask for a subset of the default (TCP, UDP, ICMP, and IP).
-p	Displays connections for the protocol specified (tcp or udp). If the -s option is used in conjunction with this parameter, proto may be tcp, udp, icmp, or ip.
-r	Displays the contents of the routing table.
interval	Redisplays selected statistics, pausing between each display. In order to stop the redisplay, press Ctrl+C. If this interval is omitted, information is only displayed once.

NLSFUNC

Description:	NLSFUNC is only for compatibility with MS-DOS files and programs.

Syntax:	Not applicable.
Arguments:	Not applicable.

NSLOOKUP

Description:

Shows the status of Domain Name System (DNS) name servers. To use this command, you must have the TCP/IP network protocol installed on your system.

You can run NSLOOKUP in either "interactive" or "non-interactive" modes. Use interactive mode when you're trying to browse through DNS information or when you need to see more than one piece of information. Use non-interactive mode when you know exactly what you're trying to look up.

To run NSLOOKUP in interactive mode, type a dash by itself in place of the -option argument. Typing NSLOOKUP with no arguments runs NSLOOKUP in interactive mode against the default server.

Syntax:

`NSLOOKUP [-option] [computer ¦ - [server]]`

Arguments:

-option

Run NSLOOKUP with one or more NSLOOKUP commands. (See NSLOOKUP Commands.) Options are in the form -command=value. For example, to change the default query type to host (computer) information, type:

NSLOOKUP -querytype=hinfo

Not every command takes a value. In cases where the command takes no value, the equal sign is omitted. Command lines can be no longer than 256 characters.

computer

Looks up information for a particular computer. This lookup will use the default server unless you specify a different server using the server argument. If computer is an IP address and the type of query is A or PTR, the command will return the name of the computer. If computer is a name that ends with a period, the default DNS domain name is added to the end of the name, depending on how the options domains, srchlist, defname, and search have been set. You can look at a computer outside of the current DNS domain by adding a period to its name. Typing a dash (-) by itself instead of the computer argument runs NSLOOKUP in interactive mode.

server	The DNS name server to use. If you don't specify which server, NSLOOKUP will use the default name server.

NTBOOKS

Description:	Runs the Windows NT online manuals. NTBOOKS will attempt to load the manuals from the drive and path where it last found them; if they exist on CD, you'll be prompted to insert it into the drive.
Syntax:	`NTBOOKS [/s] [/w] [/n:path]`
Arguments:	
/s	Permits you to access Windows NT Server manuals from a Windows NT workstation.
/w	Permits you to access Windows NT Workstation manuals from a Windows NT server.
/n	Tells NTBOOKS where to find the online manuals. This option is not usually necessary because NTBOOKS remembers the location of the files.

NTCMDPROMPT

Description:	Launches the Windows NT command interpreter. Use this command to tell the system to launch the command interpreter CMD.EXE, rather than COMMAND.COM, when running terminate-stay-resident programs or MS-DOS applications.
Syntax:	`NTCMDPROMPT`
Arguments:	Not applicable.

OS/2 CONFIGURATION COMMANDS

Description:	OS/2 configuration commands are comprised of the following: CODEPAGE, DEVINFO, LIBPATH, and PROTSHELL. These commands are used in the configuration file CONFIG.SYS to configure the OS/2 subsystem.
Syntax:	`CODEPAGE=xxx[,yyy]`
	`DEVINFO=devtype,subtype,[drive:][path]` `filename[,ROM=[[(]xxx[,yyy)]][,...]]`
	`LIBPATH=[drive:]path[;[drive:]path][...]`
	`PROTSHELL=[drive:][path]`

Arguments:

xxx	Indicates the first code page, which must be one of the three-digit numbers from this following list:

437	United States
850	Multilingual (Latin I)
852	Slavic (Latin II)
855	Cyrillic (Russian)
857	Turkish
860	Portuguese
861	Icelandic
863	Canadian-French
865	Nordic
866	Russian
869	Modern Greek

yyy	This parameter is not utilized by NT's OS/2 subsystem. It is only used for backward compatibility for files from Microsoft OS/2 version 1.3 or earlier.
devtype	Indicates a specific type of device including: keyboard, monitor, and parallel printer.
subtype	Indicates a specific model of the device.
filename	Indicates a specific file that stores information regarding code pages for the specific device.
ROM=	Not utilized by NT's OS/2 subsystem. It is only used for backward compatibility for files from Microsoft OS/2 version 1.3 or earlier.
xxx	Not utilized by NT's OS/2 subsystem. It is only used for backward compatibility for files from Microsoft OS/2 version 1.3 or earlier.
yyy	Not utilized by NT's OS/2 subsystem. It is only used for backward compatibility for files from Microsoft OS/2 version 1.3 or earlier.

drive:	Indicates which drive the dynamic-link libraries are located on (the current drive is default).
path	Indicates which directory to search for dynamic-link libraries. You can search more than one directory by separating directory names with a semicolon (;).
PROTSHELL	Not utilized by NT's OS/2 subsystem. It is only used for backward compatibility for files from Microsoft OS/2 version 1.3 or earlier.

PATH

Description: Establishes a set of subdirectories, known as a "search path," in which the operating system searches for executable files. Normally when you execute a program, the system will only look for the file in the current directory. Establishing a path tells the system to look in a number of different directories for the file you want to run.

If you type PATH with no arguments, Windows NT displays the current search path.

Syntax: `PATH [[drive:]path[;...]] [%path%]`

Arguments:

[drive:]path	Denotes a drive and directory or subdirectory in which to search.
;	Used as a separator between multiple drives and paths. When used as a parameter by itself, clears the previously set PATH settings.
%path%	Adds the PATH setting to the existing PATH setting.

PAUSE

Description: Causes a batch program to pause processing. When a batch program encounters a PAUSE command, the user is instructed to press a key to continue.

Syntax: `PAUSE`

Arguments: Not applicable.

PAX

Description: Launches the Portable Archive Interchange utility.

Because PAX is a POSIX utility, you must use POSIX-style

arguments with it. For example, instead of specifying the Windows-style path c:\users\default as an argument, you must instead use the POSIX-style syntax //c:/users/default.

You can instruct PAX to read, write, and list the contents of an archive, or move files to a different directory by using the -r and -w arguments.

Syntax:

PAX [-cimopuvy] [-f archive] [-s replstr] [-t device]
[pattern...]

PAX -r [-cimnopuvy] [-f archive] [-s replstr] [-t device]
[pattern...]

PAX -w [-adimuvy] [-b blocking] [-f archive] [-s replstr]
[-t device] [-x format] [pathname...]

PAX -rw [-ilmopuvy] [-s replstr] [pathname...] directory

Arguments:

-r

Reads an archive file from standard input. PAX selects only files specified in the pattern argument. Output files are created, if necessary, and copied to the destination directory, unless other options, described later, are invoked. Ownership of the files is the same as that of the invoking process; permissions are the same as those in the archive file. PAX automatically detects the format of the archive (cpio or ustar) when it reads the archive file. The output archive format is ustar, unless the cpio format is selected (via the -x option, described later).

-w

Writes files specified in pathname to standard output; includes pathname and status information dictated by the archive format. If pathname is missing, PAX uses standard input to get a list of file names to copy (one file name per line).

-rw

Reads files and directories specified in pathname and copies them to the destination directory. If pathname is missing, PAX uses standard input to get a list of file names to copy (one file name per line). The target directory must exist and be writable.

-a

Appends files in pathname to the target archive.

-b blocking

Block the output at blocking bytes per write to the archive file. A k suffix multiplies blocking by 1024, a b suffix multiplies it by 512, and an m suffix multiplies blocking by 1,048,576 (one megabyte).

-c

Complements the match sense of pattern.

-d

Don't create directories unless they are explicitly listed in the archive. This option is ignored unless the -r option is also specified.

-f archive

The path name of the input or output archive. This option overrides the default of standard input (for -r) or standard output (for -w).

-i

Prompts the user to rename files. Substitutions specified by -s options (described below) are performed before requesting the new file name from the user. A file is skipped if an empty line is entered. PAX exits with an exit status of 0 if EOF is encountered.

-l

Links files instead of copying them.

-m

Discards file modification times.

-n

When -r is specified but -w is not, treat `pattern` as a list of ordinary file names. Only the first occurrence of each of these files in the input archive is read. PAX exits after reading all the files in the list. If any files in the list are not found, PAX writes an error for each of the files and exits with a non-zero exit status. The file names are compared before any of the -i, -s, or -y options are applied.

-o

Restores file ownership as specified in the archive. The invoking process must have appropriate privileges to accomplish this.

-p

Preserves the original access time of the input files after they have been copied.

-s replstr

Modifies file names according to the substitution expression using the syntax of ed(1) as shown:

-s /old/new/[gp]

Any non-null character may be used as a delimiter (a / is used here as an example). You can specify more than one -s expression; PAX applies the expressions in the order specified, ending with the first successful substitution. Adding a p to the expression causes successful mappings to be sent to standard error. Adding a g to the expression replaces the old expression each time it occurs in the source string. Files that substitute to an empty string are ignored.

-t device

Names the input or output archive device, overriding the default of standard input for -r and standard output for -w.

-u

Copies each file only if it is newer than an existing file with the same name. This option implies -a.

-v	Lists file names as they are processed. Sends a table of contents listing to standard output when both -r and -w are omitted. Without this option, file names are printed to standard error as they are encountered in the archive.
-x format	The output archive format. The input format, which must be one of the following, is automatically determined when the -r option is used. The supported formats are:

    ustar   The extended TAR interchange format, specified in Extended TAR Format in IEEE Std. 1003.1-1988. This is the default archive.

    cpio   The extended CPIO interchange format specified in Extended CPIO Format in IEEE Std. 1003.1-1988.

-y	Prompts for the disposition of each file. Substitutions specified by -s options (described earlier) are performed before prompting the user for disposition. EOF or an input line starting with the character q causes PAX to exit. Otherwise, an input line starting with anything other than y causes the file to be ignored. You can't use this option with the -i option.
directory	The destination directory path name for copies when both the -r and -w options are specified. The directory must exist and be writable before the copy or an error results.
pathname	A file whose contents are used instead of the files named on the standard input. When `pathname` is a directory, all of its files and subdirectories are copied as well.
pattern	A pattern of files, using wildcards. The default is all files.

PENTNT

Description:	Detects the floating-point division error in Pentium processors. Turns floating-point emulation on or off.
Syntax:	PENTNT [-c] [-f] [-o] [-? ¦ -h]
Arguments:	
-c	Conditional emulation. If the system detects the Pentium error at start time, it will emulate the functions of floating-point processing in software. You must restart the computer for this option to take effect.
-f	Emulates the functions of floating-point processing in software, bypassing the Pentium floating-point division error. You must restart the computer for this option to take effect.

-o   Disables floating-point emulation and re-enables floating point
                            hardware. You must restart the computer for this option to take
                            effect.

-? | -h   Displays help information for this command.

PING

Description: Sends data to a computer in order to determine if a network
                            connection to the computer exists. You need to install the
                            TCP/IP network protocol to use this command.

Syntax:
```
PING [-t] [-a] [-n count] [-l length] [-f] [-I ttl]
[-v tos] [-r count] [-s count] [[-j computer-list] ¦
[-k computer-list]] [-w timeout] destination-list
```

Arguments:

-t   Pings repeatedly until interrupted.

-a   Displays the name of the computer, given the IP address, when
                            pinging.

-n count   The number of times to ping the computer; the default is 4.

-l length   The number of bytes to send to the computer being pinged.
                            The default is 64 bytes; the maximum is 8192 bytes.

-f   Instructs gateways on the way to the computer not to fragment
                            the data packet.

-I ttl   Sets the Time To Live field to the value `ttl`.

-v tos   Sets the Type Of Service field to the value `tos`.

-r count   Displays the route taken by the ping data. Count can be
                            between 1 and 9 computers.

-s count   The timestamp for the number of hops specified by count.

-j computer-list   Utilizes the *computer-list* to specify packet routes. Successive
                            computers can be separated by transitional gateways.

-k computer-list   Utilizes the *computer-list* to specify packet routes. Successive
                            computers cannot be separated by transitional gateways.

-w timeout   A timeout interval specified in milliseconds.

destination-list   A list of computers to ping.

POPD

Description:	Changes to the directory stored by the PUSHD command. You can only use POPD once; the buffer is cleared after you use it.
Syntax:	POPD
Arguments:	Not applicable.

PORTUAS

Description:	Merges a user accounts database from a LAN Manager 2.x system into a Windows NT user accounts database.
Syntax:	PORTUAS -f filename [-u username] [-v] [/codepage codepage] [/log filename]

Arguments:

-f filename	The LAN Manager 2.x NET.ACC file to merge.
-u username	The user or group to restore.
-v	Verbose mode; displays all messages.
/codepage codepage	The OEM codepage in which the LAN Manager 2.x NET.ACC resides.
/log filename	The name of a file to log results of the merge operation.

PRINT

Description:	Prints a file in the background. Displays the contents of the print queue.
Syntax:	PRINT [/d:device] [drive:][path] filename[...]

Arguments:

/d:device	The name of the device to print to; can be parallel ports LPT1, LPT2, LPT3, or serial ports COM1, COM2, COM3, or COM4.
[drive:][path] filename	The file or files you want to print. (Multiple files on the same command line can be specified by separating each file with a space.)

PROMPT

Description:	Alters the appearance of the Windows NT command prompt.
Syntax:	`PROMPT [text]`
Arguments:	
text	The text, including special codes, to include in your command prompt. You can choose from the following special codes:

$q	Equal sign
$$	Dollar sign
$t	The current time
$d	The current date
$p	The current drive and path
$v	Windows NT version number
$n	The current drive
$g	Greater-than sign (>)
$l	Less-than sign (<)
&b	Pipe symbol (|)
$_	Linefeed
$e	ANSI escape code (27)
$h	Backspace
$a	Ampersand
$c	Left parenthesis
$f	Right parenthesis
$s	Space

PROTSHELL

Description:	This command is not used in Windows NT; it is included only for compatibility with Microsoft OS/2 1.3 and earlier.

PUSHD

Description:	For use with the POPD command; stores the current directory, and then changes to the specified directory.
Syntax:	PUSHD [path ¦ ...]
Arguments:	
path	The directory to make the current directory.

QBASIC

Description:	Launches the Qbasic interpreter.
Syntax:	QBASIC [/b] [/editor] [/g] [/h] [/mbf] [/nohi] [[/run][drive:][path] filename]
Arguments:	
[drive:][path] filename	The Basic source file to load when Qbasic is launched.
/b	Runs Qbasic in black and white mode, even if you have a color graphics card.
/editor	Runs the MS-DOS editor (without Qbasic).
/g	Refreshes graphics quickly on CGA monitors.
/h	Displays the maximum number of lines of text possible, depending on the capabilities of your video card.
/mbf	Converts the internal functions MKS$, MKD$, CVS, and CVD to MKSMBF$, MKDMBF$, CVSMBF, and CVDMBF.
/nohi	Allows you to use a monitor that does not support a high-intensity picture.
/run	Runs the program specified by [drive:][path] filename.

RCP

Description:	Command run by Windows NT to copy files to a Unix system running the remote shell daemon (rshd).
Syntax:	RCP [-a ¦ -b] [-h] [-r] source1 source2 ... sourceN destination

Arguments:

-a
Uses ASCII file transfer mode (default). This mode translates end-of-line characters to carriage-return-linefeeds for Windows or carriage returns for Unix.

-b
Uses binary file transfer mode.

-h
Transfers hidden files.

-r
The contents of all subdirectories are copied from the source to the destination recursively. For this option to be valid, `destination` must be a directory.

source/destination
The syntax of `source` is expressed as `computer.user:filename`. You can specify the local computer by simply referring to the file name. Omitting `user` specifies the current Windows NT user. If you specify a computer, you must specify a user. On a Unix file system, file and directory names are separated with forward slashes (/). In Windows NT, file and directory names are separated with backslashes (\). If no directory name is specified, the default logon directory is used.

RECOVER

Description:
Recovers data from a defective disk.

Syntax:
`RECOVER [drive:][path] filename`

Arguments:

[drive:][path] filename
Indicates the disk, path, and file to be recovered.

REDIRECTION

Description:
Designates the destination of standard input or output. Normally, the Windows NT command prompt accepts input from the keyboard (also known as "standard input") and sends output to the screen (also known as the terminal, or "standard output"). You have the ability to redirect the input or output of certain commands using redirection symbols.

Use the greater-than sign (>) to redirect output to a file or other location.

Use the less-than sign (<) to redirect input from a file.

Use the double greater-than sign (>>) to append (rather than overwrite) output to a file.

For example, the DIR command lists files in the current directory to the standard output. To redirect the output of the DIR command to a file called mydir.txt instead, use the command:

DIR > mydir.txt

To append the directory listing to an existing file called mydir.txt, use the double greater-than sign (>>):

DIR >> mydir.txt

Note that not all commands can be redirected.

You can use the input redirection symbol (<) to designate that a program's input should come from a file instead of the keyboard. For example, the SORT command normally takes a list of text strings from standard input, sorts the list, and then outputs the list. But instead of typing the list, you can designate that the items to be sorted should be taken from the file mylist.txt by using the command:

sort < mylist.txt

This command will sort the items in mylist.txt and output the result to standard output (the screen).

REM

Description:	Indicates a comment in a batch program or a configuration file. Lines that begin with the REM command will not be interpreted.
Syntax:	`REM [comment]`
Arguments:	
comment	Text you choose to include as a comment.

RENAME (REN)

Description:	Changes the name of a file.
Syntax:	`RENAME [drive:][path] filename1 filename2`
	`REN [drive:][path] filename1 filename2`

Arguments:

[drive:][path] filename1	The file to rename.
filename2	The new name of the file.

REPLACE

Description:	Replaces files in one directory with files from another directory.
Syntax:	REPLACE [drive1:][path1] filename [drive2:][path2] [/a] [/p] [/r] [/w]
	REPLACE [drive1:][path1] filename [drive2:][path2] [/p] [/r] [/s] [/w] [/u]

Arguments:

[drive1:][path1] filename	The source file name(s).
[drive2:][path2]	The destination file name.
/a	Adds new files to the destination directory. This option can't be used with the /s or /u options.
/p	Prompts for confirmation during the process of adding or replacing files.
/r	Includes read-only and unprotected files.
/s	Replaces files in all subdirectories of the destination directory. Can't be used with the /a switch.
/w	Waits for the user to insert a disk before proceeding with the replace. If you don't specify this option, replacing begins immediately after you enter the command.
/u	Updates only those files in the destination directory that are older than the files in the source directory. You can't use the /a switch with this option.

RESTORE

Description:	Restores files backed up with the MS-DOS BACKUP command.
Syntax:	RESTORE drive1: drive2:[path[filename]] [/s] [/p] [/b:date] [/a:date] [/e:time] [/l:time] [/m] [/n] [/d]

Arguments:

drive1:	The source drive where the backed up files are stored.
drive2:[path[filename]]	The destination drive (and, optionally, the path and file name) to which the backed up file(s) will be restored.
/s	Restores all subdirectories under path.
/p	Prompts the user before restoring files that are read-only or files changed since the last backup.
/b:date	Restores only those files that have changed on or before date.
/a:date	Restores only those files that have changed on or after date.
/e:time	Restores only those files that have changed at or earlier than time.
/l:time	Restores only those files that have changed at or earlier than time.
/m	Restores only the files that have changed since the last backup.
/n	Restores only those files that don't exist on the destination disk drive2.
/d	Displays a list of files on the backup disk without restoring any files. (With this option, you must specify disk2, even though no files are restored.)

REXEC

Description:	Executes commands on computers running the REXEC service. You can only execute this command if your computer has the TCP/IP network protocol installed.
Syntax:	`REXEC computer [-l username] [-n] command`
Arguments:	
computer	The remote computer on which to run a command.
-l username	The user name on the remote computer. REXEC will prompt you for a password before running the remote command.

-n	Redirects the output of the command to NULL.
command	The command to run on the remote computer.

RMDIR (RD)

Description:	Removes a directory.
Syntax:	`RMDIR [drive:]path [/s]`
Arguments:	
[drive:]path	The location and name of the directory you want to delete.
/s	Removes subdirectories and files under the target directory in addition to the target directory itself.

ROUTE

Description:	Manages network routing tables. You can only execute this command if your computer has the TCP/IP network protocol installed.
Syntax:	`ROUTE [-f] [-p] [command [destination] [mask subnetmask] [gateway] [metric costmetric]`
Arguments:	
-f	Clears the routing table of gateway entries. If you use this option prior to running a command, the tables are cleared before the command is executed.
-p	When used with the ADD command, makes a route persistent so it continues to exist when the system is restarted. When used with the PRINT command, prints a list of persistent routes.
command	Use one of the following commands:

	print	Prints a route
	add	Adds a route
	delete	Deletes a route
	change	Modifies a route

destination	A computer to send the command.
mask subnetmask	A subnet mask to associate with the route entry. Default is 255.255.255.255.

gateway — The gateway. Symbolic names for the `destination` or `gateway` are retrieved from the network database file NETWORKS and computer name database file HOSTS. For the PRINT or DELETE commands, wildcards may be used for `destination` and `gateway`; `gateway` may also be omitted.

metric costmetric — Assigns a numeric cost metric from 1 to 9999 used in calculating the most economical routes.

RSH

Description: Executes commands on remote computers running the RSH service. You can only execute this command if your computer has the TCP/IP network protocol installed.

Syntax: `RSH computer [-l username] [-n] command`

Arguments:

computer — The computer on which to run a command.

-l username — The user name to be used on the computer.

-n — Redirects the output of the command to NULL.

command — The command to execute.

SET

Description: Lists or modifies Windows NT environment variables. Environment variables are used to alter the behavior of some programs and to control some aspects of how the operating system works. SET is used most commonly in AUTOEXEC.NT.

Syntax: `SET [variable=[string]]`

Arguments:

variable — The variable you want to set or modify. Leaving both `variable` and `string` blank lists the current environment variables.

string — The string you want to associate with variable.

SETLOCAL

Description: Creates a temporary set of environment variables specific to a batch file. Environment variables set in a batch file can be rolled back to their original values by executing an ENDLOCAL command.

Syntax:	`SETLOCAL`
Arguments:	Not applicable.

SETVER

Description:	Sets the MS-DOS version number reported to a program.
Syntax:	`SETVER [drive:path] [filename n.nn]`
	`SETVER [drive:path] [filename [/delete [/quiet]]`

Arguments:

[drive:path]	The location of SETVER.EXE. To display the current version table, use this option only.
filename	The name of the executable file to add to the version table.
n.nn	The MS-DOS version (for example, 3.3 or 4.01) that the MS-DOS subsystem reports to `filename` when it is run.
/delete	Deletes the version table entry for `filename`. (Can be abbreviated /d.)
/quiet	Suppresses the display of the message usually displayed when an entry is deleted from the version table.

SHARE

Description:	This command is not used in Windows NT. It exists primarily for compatibility with batch programs and other applications written in MS-DOS and Windows.

SHELL

Description:	Designates an alternate command interpreter for the MS-DOS subsystem.
Syntax:	`SHELL=[[drive:]path] filename [parameters]`

Arguments:

[[drive:]path] filename	The location and name of the command interpreter you want Windows NT to use.
parameters	Command-line parameters required by the alternate command interpreter.

SHIFT

Description:	Rearranges the order of parameters in a batch program.
Syntax:	SHIFT
Arguments:	Not applicable.

SORT

Definition:

Sorts data.

Syntax:

SORT [/r] [+n] [<] [drive1:][path1] filename1
[> [drive2:][path2] filename2]

[command ¦] SORT [/r] [/+n] [> [drive2:]
[path2] filename2]

Arguments:

[drive1:][path1] filename1

The file whose data you want to sort. If you do not specify a file name, SORT takes data from standard input (i.e., the keyboard).

[drive2:][path2] filename2

The output file into which sorted data is stored. If you do not specify a file name, SORT sends sorted data to standard output (i.e., the screen).

command

A command whose output you want to sort.

/r

Sorts in reverse order (Z to A and 9 to 0).

/+n

Sorts according to the character in column n of the input file. If you do not specify this option, SORT will sort the file according to the character in column 1 of the input file.

STACKS

Description:	Specifies dynamic data stacks to handle hardware interrupts.
Syntax:	STACKS=n,s
Arguments:	

n

The number of stacks. You can specify zero stacks, or a number between 8 and 64.

s   The size (in bytes) of each stack. You can specify zero bytes, or a
                           number between 32 and 512.

START

Description:	Runs a command or application in a separate window.

Syntax:	``` START ["title"] [/d path] [/I] [/min] [/max] [/separate]```
	 ``` [/low] [/normal] [/high] [/realtime] [/wait] [/b] [filename]```
	 ``` [parameters]```

Arguments

"title"	The text to display in the new window's title bar.
/d path	The default directory for the new window.
/i	Passes CMD.EXE's startup environment variables to the new window.
/min	Minimizes the new window.
/max	Maximizes the new window.
/separate	Launches 16-bit Windows programs in a separate memory space.
/low	Gives the command or application low processor priority.
/normal	Gives the command or application normal processor priority.
/high	Gives the command or application high processor priority.
/realtime	Gives the command or application realtime processor priority.
/wait	Waits for the application to terminate.
/b	Starts the command or application without creating a new window. If you need to halt an application started in this way, you must use Ctrl+Break, unless the application supports Ctrl+C.
filename	The application or command to launch.
parameters	Parameters to pass to the application or command.

SUBST

Description:	Maps a directory path to a drive letter, thereby creating a "virtual drive." With no arguments, SUBST displays the names of virtual drives that exist on your system.

Syntax:	SUBST [drive1: [drive2:]path]
	SUBST drive1: /d
Arguments:	
drive1:	The letter of a virtual drive you want to create.
drive2:path	The physical drive and directory path that will be aliased as a virtual drive.
/d	Deletes a virtual drive.

SWITCHES

Description:	Causes an enhanced keyboard to operate like a conventional keyboard. This command should be placed in your CONFIG.NT file.
Syntax:	SWITCHES=/k (The "k" is used in conjunction with ANSI.SYS)

TFTP

Description:	Uploads and downloads files from a remote computer running the TFTP service. To use this command, you must have the TCP/IP network protocol installed on your system.
Syntax:	TFTP [-i] computer [get ¦ put] source [destination]
Arguments:	
-i	Transfers files in binary mode. If you omit this option, TFTP transfers files in ASCII text mode. In ASCII mode, end-of-line characters are translated into a carriage return (for Unix systems) and carriage return-linefeed (for DOS and Windows systems).
computer	The computer from which to upload or download.
put	Indicates that you want to send, or upload, files to computer.
get	Indicates that you want to receive, or download, files from computer.
source	The file you want to transfer. To send data from standard input (i.e., the keyboard) when PUTting, type a dash (-) in place of source.
destination	The location where the files are to be transferred. To print the file to standard output (i.e., the screen) when GETting, type a dash (-) in place of destination.

TIME

Description:	Displays or sets the current system time.
Syntax:	`TIME [hours:[minutes[:seconds[.hundredths]]][A¦P]]`
Arguments:	
hours	The hour, in the range 0 through 23.
minutes	Minutes, in the range 0 through 59.
hundredths	Hundredths of a second, in the range 0 through 99.
A|P	A.M. or P.M. The default is A.M.

TITLE

Description:	Sets the text that appears in the title bar of the command prompt window.
Syntax:	`TITLE [string]`
Arguments:	
string	The text to display in the title bar.

TRACERT

Description:	A utility that displays the path between the local computer and a remote computer over a network. The TRACERT command works by sending Internet Control Message Protocol (IMCP) echo packets to the destination. It displays the number of network "hops" between the local computer and a remote computer in addition to the number of milliseconds the data packet took to travel between each hop. Be aware that some routers can be configured to drop packets sent by command such as TRACERT; such hops will not appear in TRACERT's output.
Syntax:	`TRACERT [-d] [-h maximum_hops] [-j computer-list]` `[-w timeout] target_name`
Arguments:	
-d	Does not convert the IP addresses of computers between the local computer and `target_name` into computer names.
-h maximum_hops	The maximum number of hops between the local computer and `target_name`.

-j computer-list	Specifies loose source route along `computer-list`.
-w timeout	Waits the specified number of milliseconds before timing out.
target_name	The remote computer to locate.

TREE

Description:	Displays the directory structure of a disk or directory in a graphical format.
Syntax:	`TREE [drive:][path] [/f] [/a]`
Arguments:	
drive:path	The disk drive and directory path you want to display.
/f	Lists files in addition to directories.
/a	Uses text characters instead of graphic characters to graphically display relationships between directories and subdirectories.

TYPE

Description:	Outputs the contents of a text file to the screen. You can use the TYPE command to view the contents of a file, such as a text file, without making changes to it.
Syntax:	`TYPE [drive:][path] filename [...]`
Arguments:	
[drive:][path] filename	The location and name of the file you want to view. You can indicate multiple file names by separating each file name with a space. If the file is on a disk that supports embedded spaces in file names, such as an NTFS volume, enclose the file name in quotation marks (" ").

VER

Description:	Displays the Windows NT version number.
Syntax:	`VER`
Arguments:	Not applicable.

VERIFY

Description: This command is not used by Windows NT. It exists only for compatibility with MS-DOS batch programs and other applications.

VOL

Description: Displays a disk's volume label.

Syntax: VOL [drive:]

Arguments:

drive: The drive that contains the disk whose volume label you want to view. For disks formatted under MS-DOS 4.0 and later, VOL also displays a serial number.

WINNT

Description: Performs an installation or upgrade of Windows NT.

Syntax: WINNT [/s:sourcepath] [/i:inf_file] [/t:drive_letter] [/x] [/b] [/f] [/c] [/ox] [/u[:script]

Arguments:

/s:sourcepath The location of the Windows NT files.

/i:inf_file The file name (not the path) of the setup information file. The default is DOSNET.INF.

/t:drive_letter Tells Setup to place temporary installation files on the drive you specify.

/x Tells Setup not to create Setup boot floppies. Use this option in situations where you already have a set of boot floppies.

/b Loads boot files onto the computer's hard drive instead of floppy disks. This prevents the user from having to load or remove floppy disks during Setup.

/f Does not verify files as they are copied to the setup boot disk.

/c Skips the free-space check on the setup boot disks.

/ox Tells Setup to create boot floppies for CD-ROM.

/u Upgrades Windows NT in unattended mode, taking user settings from your previous installation of Windows NT.

/u:script — Upgrades in unattended mode, using a script file instead of settings from your previous Windows NT installation.

/r:directory — Creates a new directory where Windows NT files are stored. To install multiple directories, use multiple /r switches.

WINNT32

Description:	Performs an installation or upgrade of Windows NT on a computer already running Windows NT.
Syntax:	`WINNT32 [/s:sourcepath] [/i:inf_file] [/t:drive_letter] [/x]` `[/b] [/ox] [/u[:script] [/r:directory] [/e:command]`

Arguments:

/s:sourcepath — The location of the Windows NT files.

/i:inf_file — The file name (not the path) of the setup information file. The default is DOSNET.INF.

/t:drive_letter — Tells Setup to place temporary installation files on the drive you specify.

/x — Tells Setup not to create Setup boot floppies. Use this option in situations where you already have a set of boot floppies.

/b — Loads boot files onto the computer's hard drive instead of floppy disks. This prevents the user from having to load or remove floppy disks during Setup.

/ox — Tells Setup to create boot floppies for CD-ROM.

/u — Upgrades Windows NT in unattended mode, taking user settings from your previous installation of Windows NT.

/u:script — Upgrades in unattended mode, using a script file instead of settings from your previous Windows NT installation.

/r:directory — Creates a new directory where Windows NT files are stored. To install multiple directories, use multiple /r switches.

/e:command — Tells Setup to execute a command after it runs.

XCOPY

Description:	Copies files, directories, and subdirectories.

Syntax:	`XCOPY source [destination] [/w] [/p] [/c] [/v] [/q] [/f] [/l]`
	`[/d[:date]] [/u] [/i] [/s [/e]] [/t] [/k] [/r] [/h] [/a¦/m]`
	`[/n] [/exclude:filename] [/z]`

Arguments:

source	The file or files you want to copy. Source must include a drive or path.
destination	The destination of the files to copy. Destination can be a drive letter and colon, a directory name, and/or a file name.
/w	Prompts the user to press a key before copying files.
/p	Prompts the user to confirm whether to create each file on destination.
/c	Continues to copy files even if errors occur.
/v	Verifies copy. This switch is ignored in Windows NT because verification is inherent to the operating system; it is provided for compatibility with MS-DOS and previous versions of windows.
/q	Quiet mode; does not display file names while copying.
/f	Displays both source and destination file names while copying.
/l	Lists files to be copied instead of actually copying them.
/d[:date]	Copies only those files that have been modified on or after date. If you include this option but omit date, XCOPY will copy all files from source that are newer than existing files on destination. When specifying a date, use the format mm-dd-yy instead of mm/dd/yy, since the "/" might be interpreted as another command-line option.
/u	Updates by copying only those files from source that already exist on destination.
/i	Tells XCOPY to create directories or subdirectories on destination if they don't already exist. Normally, XCOPY will ask you if destination is a file or a directory.
/s	Copies files and subdirectories under source. XCOPY will not copy empty directories unless you also specify the /e switch.
/e	Copies files and subdirectories under source, even if the subdirectories are empty. Used with the /s and /t switches.
/t	Copies the subdirectory tree, but not the files in those directories. To copy empty directories, you must also include the /e switch.
/k	Keeps the read-only attribute of files. Without this option, the read-only attribute is removed from files copies by XCOPY.

/r   Overwrites read-only files on `destination`.

/h   Copies files with hidden and system attributes set. Without this
                          option, XCOPY ignores such files.

/a   Copies only those files that have their archive file attribute set;
                          that is, files that have been modified since the last backup. (For
                          more information on file attributes, see ATTRIB.)

/m   Identical to the /a switch, except that this option turns off ~~Mark~~ them
                          archive file attributes for the files in `source`. This tells the   *as having*
                          operating system that these files have been backed up.   *been archived.*

/n   Copies files using short file names. You must use this option
                          when copying files from disk that support long file names to a
                          FAT disk, since FAT disks don't support long file names.

/exclude:filename   Instructs XCOPY to exclude a list of files stored in `filename`
                          containing one file name per line, but without wildcard
                          characters.

/z   Copies files over a network in restartable mode.

N.B. Does NOT preserve/creation (original) dates on directories.

INDEX

Symbols

B

D

G

X-Y-Z